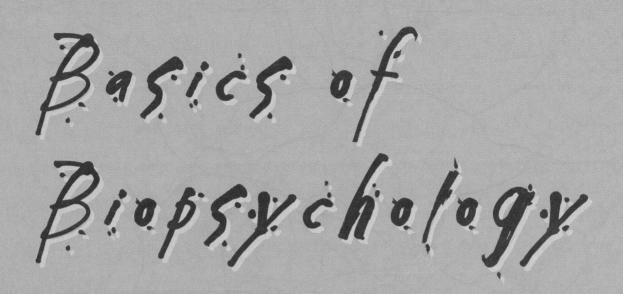

Basics of Biopsychology

John P. J. Pinel

University of British Columbia

PEARSON

Boston • New York • San Francisco
Mexico City • Montreal • Toronto • London • Madrid • Munich • Paris
Hong Kong • Singapore • Tokyo • Cape Town • Sydney

Editor-in-Chief: Susan Hartman
Series Editorial Assistant: Therese Felser
Executive Marketing Manager: Pamela Laskey
Development Editor: Erin K. Liedel
Production Editor: Claudine Bellanton
Editorial Production Service: Jane Hoover/Lifland et al., Bookmakers
Composition Buyer: Linda Cox
Manufacturing Manager: Megan Cochran
Electronic Composition: Modern Graphics, Inc.
Interior Design: Carol Somberg
Electronic Composition (Visual Summaries): Gina Hagen
Photo Researcher: Sarah Evertson
Cover Administrator/Designer: Kristina Mose-Libon
Illustration Design and Art Direction: Maggie Edwards, Gnosis Consulting
Illustrations: Frank Forney, William C. Ober and Claire W. Garrison, Mark
Leftowitz, Adrienne Lehmann, Leo Harrington, Gale Mueller

For related titles and support materials, visit our online catalog at
www.ablongman.com.

Between the time website information is gathered and then published, it is not
unusual for some sites to have closed. Also, the transcription of URLs can result in
typographical errors. The publisher would appreciate notification where these
errors occur so that they may be corrected in subsequent editions.

Library of Congress Cataloging-in-Publication Data

Pinel, John P. J.
    Basics of biopsychology / John P. J. Pinel.
        p. cm.
    Includes bibliographical references and index.
    ISBN 0-205-46108-5
      1. Psychobiology. I. Title.

  QP360.P4628 2007
  612.8--dc22

                                                    2006042851

Printed in the United States of America
10 9 8 7 6 5 4 3 2 1 Q-WC-V 10 09 08 07 06

To my talented partner, Maggie Edwards,
for making the visual aspects of this book
as engaging and edifying as I have tried
to make my words

Brief Contents

Contents

Part 2 Sensory and Motor Systems   98

chapter 4

The Visual System
How We See   **100**

The Case of Mrs. Richards: Fortification Illusions and the Astronomer   101

4.1 Light Enters the Eye and Reaches the Retina   102

Mechanisms of Perception: Hearing, Touch, Smell, Taste, and Attention

chapter 5

How You Know the World **140**

The Sensorimotor System
How You Do What You Do 170

chapter 9

Learning, Memory, and Amnesia
How Your Brain Stores Information   **264**

Part 4 Biopsychology of Motivation 298

chapter 10 Hunger, Eating, and Health
Why Do Many People Eat Too Much? 300

The Case of the Man Who Forgot Not to Eat 301

Hormones and Sex
What's Wrong with the Mamawawa?   332

Part 5 Biopsychology of Health 402

chapter 13

Health Psychology: Addiction, Emotion, and Stress
Impact of Psychological Factors on Health 404

Lateralization, Language, and the Split Brain
The Left Brain and the Right Brain of Language   442

chapter 15

Behavioral Neuroscience of Psychiatric Disorders
The Brain Unhinged   480

Welcome to *Basics of Biopsychology*! I wrote *Basics of Biopsychology* as a clear, engaging introduction to current biopsychological theory and research. It is intended for use as a primary text in one-semester courses in biopsychology—variously titled Biopsychology, Physiological Psychology, Brain and Behavior, Psychobiology, Behavioral Neuroscience, or Behavioral Neurobiology.

The defining feature of *Basics of Biopsychology* is its unique combination of biopsychological science and personal, reader-oriented discourse. It is a textbook that is "untextbooklike." Rather than introducing biopsychology in the usual textbook fashion, it interweaves the fundamentals of the field with clinical case studies, social issues, personal implications, and humorous anecdotes. It is a friendly mentor that speaks directly to the reader, enthusiastically relating recent advances in biopsychological science.

The friendly persona of *Basics of Biopsychology* is more than just window dressing. Readers find that this text's engaging pedagogical approach facilitates the acquisition and retention of information—they learn more biopsychology with less effort and with more enjoyment.

What Makes *Basics of Biopsychology* Unique?

The following features make this biopsychology textbook unlike any other.

An Emphasis on Behavior. In some biopsychological textbooks, the coverage of neurophysiology, neurochemistry, and neuroanatomy overshadows the coverage of behavioral research. *Basics of Biopsychology* gives top billing to behavior: It stresses that neuroscience is a team effort and that biopsychologists' unique contribution to this effort is their behavioral expertise.

A Broad Definition of Biopsychology. Biopsychology is the study of the biology of behavior. *Basics of Biopsychology* focuses on the neural mechanisms of behavior but also emphasizes its evolution, genetics, and adaptiveness.

A Focus on the Scientific Method. *Basics of Biopsychology* emphasizes important—but frequently misunderstood—points about the scientific method, including these three: (1) The scientific method is a means of answering questions that is as applicable in daily life as it is in the laboratory or clinic. (2) The scientific method is fun—it is basically the same method used by detectives and treasure hunters. (3) Scientific theories are current best estimates, not statements of absolute fact.

An Integrated Approach. *Basics of Biopsychology*'s approach is integrative. The text creates a strong fabric of research and ideas by weaving together related subject areas and research findings into 15 chapters of intermediate length. The chapters are grouped into five, three-chapter parts.

Emphasis on the Human and Clinical Elements of Biopsychology. *Basics of Biopsychology* features many case studies, which are highlighted in the text. These provocative true stories stimulate interest and allow students to learn how biopsychological principles apply to the real world.

Emphasis on Personal and Social Relevance. Several chapters of *Basics of Biopsychology*—namely those on eating, sleeping, sex, and drug addiction—carry strong personal and social messages. In these chapters, students are encouraged to consider the relevance of biopsychological research to their lives outside the classroom.

Emphasis on Themes. The emphasis in *Basics of Biopsychology* is on broad themes rather than on details. In order to emphasize "the big picture," four themes—Cognitive Neuroscience, Clinical Implications, The Evolutionary Perspective, and Thinking Clearly—have been selected for special prominence, and they are highlighted by distinctive tags. A Themes Revisited section at the end of each chapter briefly summarizes how the themes were developed in that chapter. The four themes provide excellent topics for essay assignments and exam questions.

Wit and Enthusiasm. Most people who work in biopsychology laboratories are not only dedicated but also full of enthusiasm and good humor. *Basics of Biopsychology* communicates these important aspects of the "biopsychological life."

Remarkable Illustrations and Design. The illustrations in *Basics of Biopsychology* are special. This is because each illustration was conceptualized and meticulously designed by a scientist–artist team uniquely qualified to clarify and illustrate the text. That team: Pinel and his wife, artist/designer Maggie Edwards. The design of this text is bold, colorful, and unlike anything you might have seen before.

Coverage of the Most Up-to-Date and Cutting-Edge Research

Biopsychology remains one of the most rapidly progressing scientific fields. *Basics of Biopsychology* has kept abreast of recent developments; it contains citations to much recent research. Some of the text's coverage of recent research findings is as follows:

- Subsection entitled "Human Genome Project: What's Next?"
- Subsection entitled "Glial Cells: The Forgotten Majority"
- Discovery that action potentials are not generated on the axon hillock but on the adjacent part of the axon
- The new brain-image archives
- Functional brain-imaging studies of facial recognition and the fusiform facial area
- New understanding of the layout of human auditory cortex
- Recent discovery that Penfield incorrectly inverted the face of the somatosensory homunculus
- Recent discovery of another area of secondary somatosensory cortex
- The new one-olfactory-receptor-one-neuron rule
- Description of the topographic organization of olfactory receptors
- Clarification of the difference between egocentric and object-based contralateral neglect
- The role of the posterior parietal lobes in initiating movement
- Recent changes in knowledge about areas of secondary motor cortex
- Case study of the mind control of a robot by Belle, an owl monkey
- Discussion of radial and tangential neural migration

- Comparison of somal translocation and glia-mediated migration of neurons
- Systematic discussion of guidance molecules
- New findings about the role of glial cells in synaptogenesis
- The issue of "promiscuity" in synaptogenesis
- Discussion of the heterogeneity of autism
- Sex differences in multiple sclerosis
- Recent attempts to develop treatments for Alzheimer's disease
- Possible contributions of adult neurogenesis to recovery of function after brain damage
- Results of the first double-blind placebo-control study of the treatment of Parkinson's disease with tissue transplants
- Recent findings on the treatment of spinal damage with stem cells
- Discussion of the concept of reconsolidation
- A subsection on the variability of LTP
- Systematic coverage of hunger and satiety peptides
- Systematic coverage of sex differences in brain structure
- Recent evidence that sex chromosomes have effects on brain development that are not mediated by sex hormones
- Discovery that sex differences in brain size result from higher apoptotic cell loss in females
- The suicide of "John," the patient who experienced infantile sex re-assignment
- Discussion of the neuroprotective effects of estradiol
- Discussion of transsexualism and sexual reassignment
- Independence of sexual orientation and sexual identity
- Default theory of REM sleep
- Newly discovered circadian photoreceptors in the retinal ganglion cell layer
- Recent discovery that all cells of the body contain circadian timing mechanisms
- Role of orexin in narcolepsy and sleep
- Recent finding that healthy people who sleep 8 hours or more per night tend to have a shorter life expectancy than those who sleep between 5 and 7 hours per night
- Discussion of recent reports that marijuana causes brain damage and memory problems
- Recent correlational studies linking MDMA and brain damage
- Description of the current view of the involvement of dopamine in addiction
- Hand preference and the asymmetry of the hand area of the motor homunculus
- Right-handedness of apes
- The paradox involving right-hemisphere activity during language use and the failure of right-hemisphere lesions to disrupt language use
- How stress affects immune function—the surprising results of a recent meta-analysis
- Why decreases in immune function do not necessarily translate into increases in disease
- How D_2 receptors are not the entire story of schizophrenia
- The relationship between schizophrenia and brain damage
- Discussion of atypical neuroleptics
- Comparison of the effectiveness of various drugs in the treatment of affective disorders
- The relationship between brain pathology and affective disorders
- Concept of orphan drugs

Pedagogical Features

Basics of Biopsychology has several features that are expressly designed to help students learn and remember the material:

- **Visual summaries** located at the end of all the chapters encourage students to review each chapter by presenting an attractive and carefully integrated combination of illustrations from the chapter and accessible summarizing text. This two-page spread also includes **Themes Revisited,** a section that summarizes the ways the book's four major themes relate to the chapter's material, and **Think about It,** a set of discussion questions that challenge students to think critically about the chapter's information. The visual summaries offer everything in one easy place for maximum studying benefit!

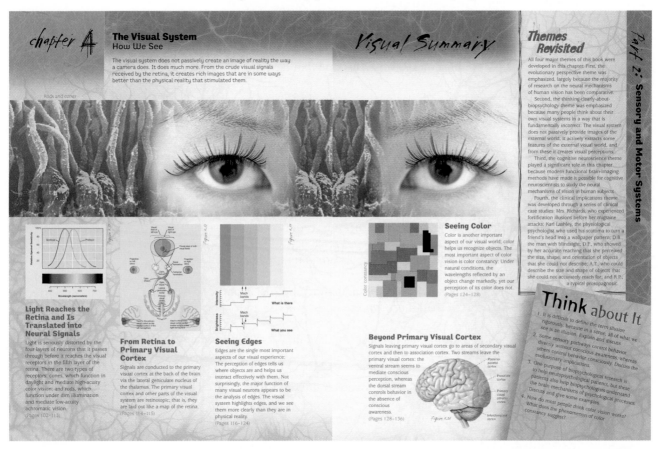

- **Scan Your Brain** features present study exercises that occur at key transition points in the chapters, where students can review preceding material before continuing.

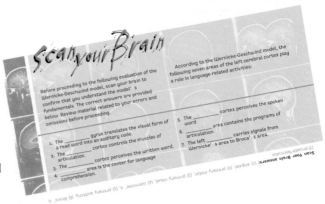

- **Check It Out** demonstrations emphasize application of concepts with activities for students to try in or out of the classroom.

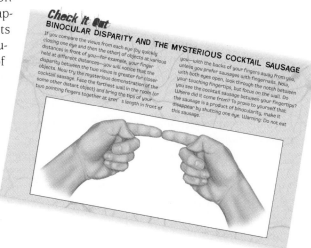

- **Tagged themes** emphasize the four broad considerations of biopsychology—Cognitive Neuroscience, Clinical Implications, The Evolutionary Perspective, and Thinking Clearly—which are highlighted where they appear.

- **Boldfaced key terms** appear throughout every chapter and are listed at the end of each chapter, sorted by main section. Additional terms of lesser importance appear in the text in italics.
- **Appendixes** serve as convenient sources of important information that is supplemental to the text material.

Ancillary Materials Available with *Basics of Biopsychology*

For Instructors. The following ancillaries are available to qualified adopters of the text.

- **Instructor's Manual.** Skillfully prepared by Nancy J. Woolf, University of California, Los Angeles, the Instructor's Manual contains helpful teaching tools, including at-a-glance grids, activities and demonstrations for the classroom, handouts, lecture notes, chapter outlines, and other valuable course organization material for both new and experienced instructors.
- **Test Bank.** The Test Bank for *Basics of Biopsychology* written by John Pinel, comprises more than 1,000 questions in multiple-choice, fill-in-the-blank, and essay formats. The difficulty of each question is rated to assist instructors with their test construction. Each item is also labeled with a topic and page reference so that instructors can easily select questions to customize their own tests. Textbook authors rarely create their own test banks; the fact that Pinel insists on preparing his own attests to its quality—and to his commitment to helping students learn.
- **Computerized Test Bank.** The computerized version of the Test Bank is available with Tamarack's easy-to-use TestGen software, which lets instructors

prepare tests for printing as well as for network and online testing. This computerized test bank is fully editable in both Windows and Macintosh platforms.

- **PowerPoint Presentation.** Michelle L. Pilati, Rio Hondo College, has created a PowerPoint package with detailed outlines of key points for each chapter supported by charts, graphs, diagrams, and other visuals from the textbook. Go to www.ablongman.com/catalog to download this instructor supplement for *Basics of Biopsychology*.

- **Physiological Psychology Transparency Set.** This set of 145 full-color acetate transparencies is available from your local Allyn & Bacon sales representative upon adoption of the text. The transparency package includes images from Allyn & Bacon's major physiological psychology texts.

- **Allyn & Bacon Digital Media Archive CD-ROM for Physiological Psychology.** This instructor's resource, available on CD-ROM from your Allyn & Bacon sales representative, provides more than 400 full-color images from the text and from other sources. A booklet listing the images by chapter accompanies the CD-ROM for easy reference.

- **VideoWorkshop for Physiological Psychology CD-ROM.** This CD-ROM for students and instructors contains over 50 minutes of content relevant to the physiological psychology course.

- **VideoWorkshop for Physiological Psychology Instructor Teaching Guide with CD-ROM.** The Instructor Teaching Guide offers a multitude of ideas for integrating VideoWorkshop into your course, including summaries for each video clip, classroom activities, writing activities, discussion starters, correlation grids, learning objectives, and an answer key for the Student Learning Guide. The content of the CD-ROM and Student Learning Guide is also printed at the end of the Teaching Guide, giving you the complete program in one easy reference!

- **Biopsychology Video.** Instructors who adopt *Basics of Biopsychology* can obtain a 60-minute biopsychology videotape. Based on the *Films for the Humanities* series, this video provides students with glimpses of important biopsychological phenomena, such as sleep recording, axon growth, memory testing in monkeys, the formation of synapses, gender differences in brain structure, human amnesic patients, rewarding brain stimulation, and brain scans.

For Students

- **The *Beyond the Brain & Behavior* CD-ROM.** Packaged free with every new textbook, the CD-ROM contains many activities and demonstrations designed to increase students' interest and encourage them to relate to biopsychology in an active way. Some of the key elements featured on *Beyond the Brain & Behavior* include:

  Animations and other demonstrations. Media demonstrations specially designed for this CD allow students to experience important text concepts for themselves. New animations focus on the receptive fields of visual neurons, Sperry's classic eye rotation experiments, and the anatomy of neurons.

  Neural modules. Animated neural modules from the acclaimed A.D.A.M. Interactive Physiology CD-ROM (Benjamin/Cummings) help students understand fundamental physiological principles. Through audio explanations and visual demonstrations, each module brings a complex aspect of biopsychology to life on students' own computer monitors.

  Video clips. In some video clips, Pinel speaks personally to students and communicates his enthusiasm for biopsychology. Most of these clips were filmed in Pinel's home. In other video clips, students see research laboratories in action and hear from the well-known biopsychologists who run them.

Practice tests. On the CD, students will find 15 multiple-choice questions per chapter, written by Pinel himself. These self-scoring tests will help students prepare for exams.

Electronic flash cards. Students can review key terms and their definitions for each chapter using convenient electronic flash cards.

■ **Grade Aid.** This robust study guide, written by Michael J. Mana of Western Washington University, provides students with comprehensive learning resources and offers a rich and highly structured guide through *Basics of Biopsychology*'s most important concepts. Each chapter of the study guide includes the following sections:

"Before You Read," containing a brief chapter summary and learning objectives

"As You Read," offering a collection of demonstrations, bidirectional study questions, activities, and exercises

"After You Read," consisting of three short practice quizzes and one comprehensive practice test

"When You Have Finished," presenting Web links for further information and a crossword puzzle using key terms from the text

■ **Study Card for Physiological Psychology.** Colorful, affordable, and packed with useful information, Allyn & Bacon/Longman's Study Cards make studying easier, more efficient, and more enjoyable. Course information is distilled down to the basics, helping students quickly master the fundamentals, review a subject for better understanding, or prepare for an exam.

■ **A Colorful Introduction to the Anatomy of the Human Brain.** This coloring book provides an easy and enjoyable means of learning or reviewing the fundamentals of human neuroanatomy through the acclaimed directed-coloring method.

■ **VideoWorkshop for Physiological Psychology Student Learning Guide with CD-ROM.** The Student Learning Guide contains many in-depth learning questions—organized into the categories "Observation," "Multiple-Choice," "The Next Step," and "Connecting to the Web"—to help students connect what they see to what they've learned in class.

Acknowledgments

I wrote *Basics of Biopsychology*, but Maggie Edwards took the responsibility for all other aspects of the manuscript and CD preparation. Maggie is a talented artist and designer, and my partner in life. I am grateful for her encouragement and support and for her many contributions to this book. I also thank her on behalf of the many students who will benefit from her efforts.

Allyn & Bacon did a remarkable job of producing this book. They shared my dream of a textbook that meets the highest standards of pedagogy but is also personal, attractive, and enjoyable. Thank you to Bill Barke, Susan Hartman, and other executives at Allyn & Bacon for having faith in *Basics of Biopsychology* and providing the financial and personal support necessary for it to take its place at the forefront of its field. A special thank you goes to Erin Liedel for her development assistance, her moral support, and her willingness to put up with our eccentricities. Another special thank you goes to Claudine Bellanton, Michael Granger, and Jane Hoover for coordinating the production—an excruciatingly difficult and often thankless job. Jane was also the copyeditor, making many improvements in the text and art, which were greatly appreciated. And thank you to Jennifer Trebby, the supplements editor, and to Cristina Vasuta, for assistance in compiling the references and test bank.

I thank the following instructors for providing me with reviews of various drafts of *Basics of Biopsychology*. Their comments have contributed substantially to its evolution and to the evolution of its CD-ROM.

John Dale Alden, III, Lipscomb University
Michael Babcock, Montana State University
Ronald Baenninger, Temple University
Christopher M. Bloom, University of Southern Indiana
Veda E. Brown, Prairie View A&M University
Stanley N. Bursten, Santa Barbara City College
Juan M. Dominguez, Florida State University
Douglas Engwall, Central Connecticut State University
Perry Fuchs, University of Texas at Arlington
Leonard W. Hamilton, Rutgers University
Michael R. Hoane, Southern Illinois University
David A. Holtzman, University of Rochester
Brian M. Kelley, Bridgewater College
Jack B. Kelly, Carleton University
R. Michelle Lewellen, Cerritos College
Charles J. Long, The University of Memphis
Michael J. Mana, Western Washington University
Mary McNaughton-Cassill, University of Texas at San Antonio
Michelle L. Pilati, Rio Hondo College
Joseph H. Porter, Virginia Commonwealth University
Andrea Rashtian, California State University, Northridge
Margaret G. Ruddy, The College of New Jersey
Susan L. Scharoun, Le Moyne College
Dale R. Sengelaub, Indiana University
Soni Verma, Sierra College
Linda L. Walsh, University of Northern Iowa
Stephen P. Weinert, Grossmont-Cuyamaca Community College District
Scott Wersinger, University at Buffalo, The State University of New York
Shawanda Williams-Anderson, Prairie View A&M University
Nancy J. Woolf, University of California, Los Angeles
Tommy L. Woods, Texas Southern University

In the 1960s, I was, in the parlance of the times, "turned on" by an undergraduate course in biopsychology. I could not imagine anything more interesting than a field of science dedicated to studying the relation between psychological processes and the brain. My initial fascination led to a long career as a student, researcher, and teacher of biopsychological science. *Basics of Biopsychology* is my attempt to share this fascination with you.

I have tried to make *Basics of Biopsychology* a different kind of textbook, a textbook that includes clear, concise, and well-organized explanations of the key points but is still interesting to read—a book from which you might suggest a suitable chapter to an interested friend or relative. To accomplish this goal, I thought about what kind of textbook I would have liked when I was a student and concluded that I would have to avoid the stern formality and ponderous style of conventional textbook writing.

I wanted *Basics of Biopsychology* to have a relaxed and personal style. In order to accomplish this, I imagined that you and I were chatting as I wrote, and that I was telling you—usually over a glass of something—about the interesting things that go on in the field of biopsychology. Imagining these chats kept my writing from drifting back into conventional "textbookese," and it never let me forget that I was writing this book for you, the student.

I am particularly excited about the visual aspects of this book. If you have looked through it, you will already be aware that it is stunning—it has been purposely designed to attract and engage student interest. For example, check out the Visual Summaries at the ends of the chapters. Students often pay little attention to important chapter-concluding material because it tends to be as dull as dishwater: Dullness will not be a problem for you with this book.

You will not fully appreciate the most important visual feature of *Basics of Biopsychology* until you start to work with it. You will discover that every illustration perfectly complements the written words; every illustration is a friendly teaching assistant that clarifies and reinforces what you are reading. The words and images are one.

Some of the reviewers of this book have marveled at its engaging design and the educational value of its illustrations, and they have wondered how I accomplished what so many other authors have not been able to do. The answer is Maggie, my partner in life. Maggie is a professional artist and designer who shares my interest in biopsychology and my belief that the most effective teaching involves a synergistic combination of words and images. We have spent thousands of hours working, bickering, and laughing together to create this book for you.

I hope that you learn much of value from *Basics of Biopsychology*—and that reading it generates in you the same personal feeling that writing it did in me. If you are so inclined, I welcome your comments and suggestions. You can contact me at the Department of Psychology, University of British Columbia, Vancouver, BC, Canada, V6T 1Z4, or at the following e-mail address: jpinel@psych.ubc.ca. Maggie can be reached at maggie.edwards@telus.net.

John Pinel, the author of *Basics of Biopsychology*, obtained his PhD from McGill University in Montreal. He worked briefly at the Massachusetts Institute of Technology before taking up his current position at the University of British Columbia in Vancouver. Professor Pinel is an award-winning teacher and the author of over 200 scientific papers; however, he feels that his biopsychology textbooks are his major career-related accomplishments. "They tie together everything that I love about my job: students, teaching, writing, and research."

When we asked him about his personal interests, Professor Pinel spoke glowingly of his wife Maggie Edwards, who is a professional artist and designer. "I love working with Maggie; she continually astounds me with her ability and creativity. I think that we draw the best work from each other, and students are the beneficiaries."

Pinel's enthusiasm for research, teaching, and writing belies the fact that he is a professional West African drummer. "For a truly inspirational experience, improvising Kpanlogo rhythms with my friend, Nigerian master drummer Kwasi Iruoje, is hard to beat." (Be sure to view "The Beat Goes On" video clip on the *Beyond the Brain & Behavior* CD-ROM—free with the purchase of a new text.) "Most of my relaxation comes from cuddling our cats, Sambala, Rastaman, and Squeak."

Basics of Biopsychology

Part 1

Biopsychology and Its Foundations

Welcome to *Basics of Biopsychology!* Before we begin Part 1 of this book, let me give you a bit of background. As a student, I took a course in biopsychology, and it excited me. I could not imagine anything more interesting than a field of science dedicated to studying the relation between psychological processes and the brain. My fascination led to a long career as a researcher and teacher of biopsychological science. *Basics of Biopsychology* is my attempt to share this fascination with you.

I have tried to make *Basics of Biopsychology* a different kind of textbook, one that includes clear, concise, and well-organized explanations of the key points but that is still interesting to read—a book from which you might suggest a suitable chapter to an interested friend or relative. To accomplish this goal, I thought about what kind of textbook I would have liked when I was a student, and I decided immediately to avoid the stern formality and ponderous style of conventional textbook writing. I wanted *Basics of Biopsychology* to have a relaxed and personal style. In order to accomplish this, I imagined as I wrote that you and I were chatting and that I was telling you—usually over a glass of something—about the interesting things that go on in the field of biopsychology. Imagining these chats kept my writing from drifting back into conventional "textbookese" and kept in my mind that I was writing this book for you, the student. I hope that *Basics of Biopsychology* teaches you much, and that reading it generates in you the same personal feeling that writing it did in me. I welcome your comments and suggestions. You can contact me at the Department of Psychology, University of British Columbia, Vancouver, BC, Canada, V6T 1Z4, or at jpinel@psych.ubc.ca.

Part 1 of *Basics of Biopsychology* focuses on the foundations of biopsychology, rather than on biopsychology itself. Its three chapters provide you with background information that you will need in the rest of the book. Chapter 1 introduces you to the field of biopsychology, and Chapters 2 and 3 cover, respectively, the anatomy and the physiology of the brain. Part 1 is the key that will open the door to the wonders of biopsychology, which lie ahead.

chapter 1

Introduction to Biopsychology
How Biopsychologists Think
about Behavior

chapter 2

The Anatomy of the Brain
The Systems, Structures, and Cells
That Make Up Your Nervous System

chapter 3

**Neural Activity and How
to Study It**
How Neurons Work

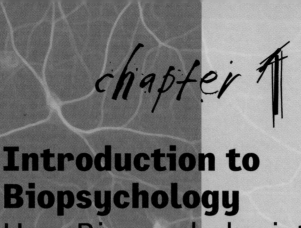

Introduction to Biopsychology
How Biopsychologists Think about Behavior

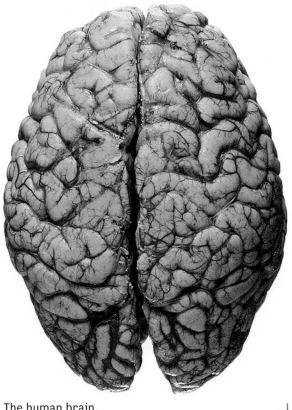

The human brain.

Figure 1.1 ―――――

The appearance of the human brain is far from impressive (see Figure 1.1). The human brain is a squishy, wrinkled, walnut-shaped hunk of tissue weighing about 1.3 kilograms. It looks more like something that you might find washed up on a beach than like one of the wonders of the world—which it surely is. Despite its disagreeable external appearance, the human brain is an amazingly intricate network of **neurons** (cells that receive and transmit electrochemical signals). Contemplate for a moment the complexity of your own brain's neural circuits. Consider the 100 billion neurons in complex array, the estimated 100 trillion connections among them, and the almost infinite number of paths that neural signals can follow through this morass.

ON THE CD

Visit the *Greetings from the Author* module. Pinel welcomes you personally and explains an often overlooked aspect of biopsychology he has included in this text.

The complexity of the human brain is hardly surprising, considering what it can do. An organ capable of creating a *Mona Lisa*, an artificial limb, and a supersonic aircraft; of traveling to the moon and to the depths of the sea; and of experiencing the wonders of an alpine sunset, a newborn infant, and a reverse slam dunk *must* be complex. Paradoxically, **neuroscience** (the scientific study of the nervous system) may prove to be the brain's ultimate challenge: Does the brain have the capacity to understand something as complex as itself?

Neuroscience comprises several related disciplines. The primary purpose of this chapter is to introduce you to one of them: *biopsychology* (or *behavioral neuroscience*).

Before you proceed to the body of this chapter, I would like to tell you about two things: (1) the case of Jimmie G., which will give you a taste of the interesting things that lie ahead, and (2) the major themes of this book.

The Case of Jimmie G., the Man Frozen in Time

Jimmie G. was a good-looking, friendly 49-year-old. He liked to talk about his school days and his experiences in the navy, which he was able to describe in detail. Jimmie was an intelligent man with superior abilities in math and science. In fact, it was not readily apparent why he was a resident of a neurological ward.

When Jimmie talked about his past, there was a hint of his problem. When he talked about his school days, he used the past tense; when he recounted his early experiences in the navy, however, he switched to the present tense. More worrisome was that he never talked about anything that happened to him after his time in the navy.

Jimmie G. was tested by eminent neurologist Oliver Sacks, and a few simple questions revealed a curious fact: The 49-year-old patient believed that he was 19. When he was asked to describe what he saw in a mirror, Jimmie

Clinical Implications

became so frantic and confused that Dr. Sacks immediately took the mirror out of the room.

Returning a few minutes later, Dr. Sacks was greeted by a once-again cheerful Jimmie, who acted as if he had never seen Sacks before. Indeed, even when Sacks suggested that they had met recently, Jimmie was certain that they had not.

Then Dr. Sacks asked where Jimmie thought he was. Jimmie replied that all the beds and patients made him think that the place was a hospital. But he couldn't understand why he would be in a hospital. He was afraid that he might have been admitted because he was sick, but didn't know it.

Further testing confirmed what Dr. Sacks feared. Although Jimmie had good sensory, motor, and cognitive abilities, he had one terrible problem: He forgot everything that was said or shown to him within a few seconds. Basically, Jimmie could not remember anything that happened to him since his early 20s, and he was not going to remember anything that happened to him for the rest of his life. Sacks was stunned by the implications of Jimmie's condition.

Jimmie G.'s situation was heart-wrenching. Unable to form new lasting memories, he was, in effect, a man frozen in time, a man without a recent past and no prospects for a future, stuck in a continuous present, lacking any context or meaning (Sacks, 1985).

Four Major Themes of This Book

You will learn many new facts in this book—new findings, concepts, brain structures, and the like. But more importantly, many years from now, long after you have forgotten most of those facts, you will still be carrying with you productive new ways of thinking. I have selected four new ideas for special emphasis: They are the major themes of this book.

To help you give these themes the special attention they deserve and to help you follow their development as you progress though the book, I have marked relevant passages with tags. The following are the four major themes and their related tags.

Thinking Clearly about Biopsychology.   Because many biopsychological topics are so interesting (as you have already seen in the case of Jimmie G.) and often relevant to everyday life, we are fed a steady diet of biopsychological information and opinion—by television, newspapers, the Internet, friends, relatives, books, teachers, etc. One major purpose of this book is to help you make the transition from being a passive consumer of biopsychological claims to being an effective, critical thinker, a person who takes nothing at face value, judges the reasonableness of various claims, and assesses their relevance to her or his own social views and lifestyle. To help you achieve this goal, I have marked each directly relevant passage in this book with a thinking clearly tag.

Clinical Implications.   Clinical (pertaining to illness or treatment) considerations are woven through the fabric of biopsychology. Much of what biopsychologists learn about the functioning of the normal brain comes from studying the diseased or damaged brain; and, conversely, much of what biopsychologists discover has relevance for the treatment of brain disorders. This book focuses on the interplay between brain dysfunction and biopsychology, and each major example of that interplay is highlighted by a clinical implications tag.

The Evolutionary Perspective.   Although the events that led to the evolution of the human species can never be determined with certainty, thinking of the environmental pressures that likely led to the evolution of our brains and behavior often

leads to important biopsychological insights. This approach is called the **evolutionary perspective**. An important aspect of the evolutionary perspective is the *comparative approach* (trying to understand biological phenomena by comparing them in different species). You will learn throughout the text that we humans have learned much about ourselves by studying species that are related to us through evolution. The evolutionary/comparative approach has proven to be one of the cornerstones of modern biopsychological inquiry. Each discussion that relates to this approach is marked by an evolutionary perspective tag.

Cognitive Neuroscience. The advances in any field of science are driven to a large degree by technological innovation: The development of an effective new research instrument is often followed by a series of discoveries. There is no better example of this than **cognitive neuroscience**, a relatively new field of biopsychology that has been fueled by the development of methods for creating images of the activity of the living human brain. Using these functional brain-imaging methods, cognitive neuroscientists study the areas of the human brain that become active while subjects engage in particular *cognitive* (pertaining to thinking) processes, such as memory, attention, and perception. Each discussion involving this type of research is highlighted by a cognitive neuroscience tag.

Cognitive Neuroscience

What Is Biopsychology?

Biopsychology is the scientific study of the biology of behavior—see Dewsbury (1991). Some refer to this field as *behavioral neuroscience*, *behavioral biology*, or *psychobiology*, but I prefer the term *biopsychology* because it denotes a biological approach to the study of psychology rather than a psychological approach to the study of biology: Psychology commands center stage in this text. *Psychology* is the scientific study of behavior—the scientific study of all overt activities of an organism as well as all the internal processes that are presumed to underlie them (e.g., learning, memory, motivation, perception, and emotion).

The study of the biology of behavior has a long history, but biopsychology did not develop into a major neuroscientific discipline until the 20th century. Although it is not possible to specify the exact date of biopsychology's birth, the publication of *The Organization of Behavior* in 1949 by D. O. Hebb played a key role in its emergence (see Brown & Milner, 2003; Milner, 1993; Milner & White, 1987). In his book, Hebb developed the first comprehensive theory of how complex psychological phenomena, such as perceptions, emotions, thoughts, and memories, might be produced by brain activity. Hebb's theory did much to discredit the view that psychological functioning is too complex to have its roots in the physiology and chemistry of the brain. Hebb based his theory on experiments involving both humans and laboratory animals, on clinical case studies, and on logical arguments developed from his own insightful observations of daily life. This eclectic approach has become a hallmark of biopsychological inquiry.

In comparison to physics, chemistry, and biology, biopsychology is an infant—a healthy, rapidly growing infant, but an infant nonetheless. In this book, you will reap the benefits of biopsychology's youth. Because biopsychology does not have a long and complex history, you will be able to move directly to the excitement of current research.

Neuroscience is a team effort, and biopsychologists are important members of the team (see Albright, Kandel, & Posner, 2000; Kandel & Squire, 2000). Biopsychologists are neuroscientists who bring to their research a knowledge of behavior and of

Table 1.1

Other Disciplines of Neuroscience That Are Particularly Relevant to Biopsychology	
Neuroanatomy	The study of the structure of the nervous system (see Chapter 2)
Neurochemistry	The study of the chemical bases of neural activity (see Chapter 3)
Neuroendocrinology	The study of interactions between the nervous system and the endocrine system (see Chapters 11 and 13)
Neuropathology	The study of nervous system disorders (see Chapters 7 and 8)
Neuropharmacology	The study of the effects of drugs on neural activity (see Chapters 3, 13, and 15)
Neurophysiology	The study of the functions and activities of the nervous system (see Chapter 3)

the methods of behavioral research. It is their behavioral orientation and expertise that make their contribution to neuroscience unique. You will be able to better appreciate the importance of this contribution if you consider that the ultimate purpose of the nervous system is to produce and control behavior (see Doupe & Heisenberg, 2000; Grillner & Dickinson, 2002).

Biopsychology is an integrative discipline. Biopsychologists draw together knowledge from the other neuroscientific disciplines and apply it to the study of behavior. Table 1.1 lists and defines a few of the disciplines of neuroscience that are particularly relevant to biopsychology.

Perhaps the most important aspect of biopsychology from your perspective is the way biopsychologists tend to think about the brain and behavior. The main purpose of this book is to convince you of the value of this way of thinking, both in the biopsychology laboratory and in your personal life. The biopsychological perspective on the brain and behavior is illustrated in Figure 1.2. Please examine it carefully; it is the focus of this chapter.

Thinking Clearly

Like other powerful theoretical frameworks, the biopsychological way of thinking is simple and logical. The model boils down to the principle that all behavior is the product of interactions among three factors: (1) the organism's genetic endowment, which is a product of its evolution; (2) the organism's experience; and (3) the organism's perception of the current situation. The brain, of course, is the major site of interaction among these three factors.

Let me illustrate this model by describing how some biopsychologists have approached the study of physical attractiveness. Have you ever seen a stranger—perhaps at a party or other social gathering—and immediately felt a powerful attraction to her or him? Some biopsychologists have identified facial features that almost everybody finds attractive (e.g., markers of health, such as facial symmetry, and secondary sex characteristics, such as a strong jawline in males), and they have speculated about the evolution of these universal preferences. Other biopsychologists have focused on exceptions to the usual pattern of attraction—for example, they have focused on individuals who are attracted primarily by members of their own sex—and have tried to identify the brain and hormonal differences that underlie these exceptions. And still other biopsychologists have focused on how the experiences of individuals within their cultural contexts can influence their standards of attractiveness.

What comes next is largely dictated by the model of the brain and behavior that you have just examined. In the next two sections, you will learn the fundamentals of human evolution and of genetics, respectively. Then, in this chapter's fourth and final section, you will see biopsychological thinking in action: how biopsychologists approach three important controversial issues.

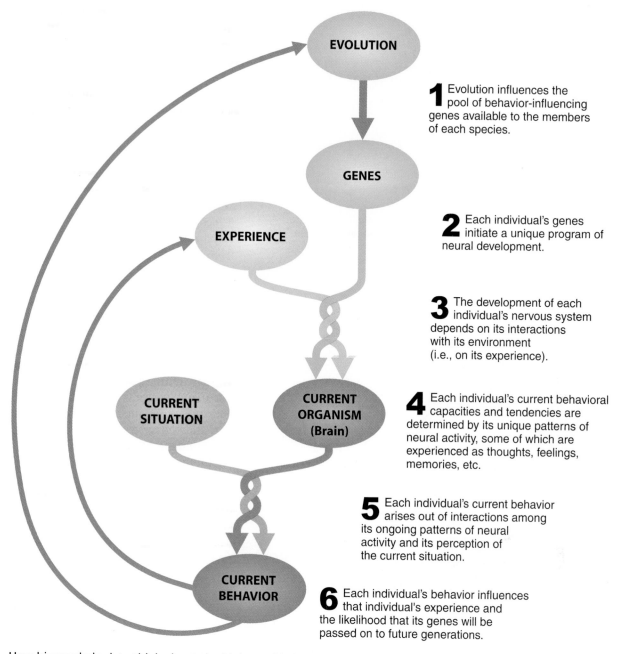

1 Evolution influences the pool of behavior-influencing genes available to the members of each species.

2 Each individual's genes initiate a unique program of neural development.

3 The development of each individual's nervous system depends on its interactions with its environment (i.e., on its experience).

4 Each individual's current behavioral capacities and tendencies are determined by its unique patterns of neural activity, some of which are experienced as thoughts, feelings, memories, etc.

5 Each individual's current behavior arises out of interactions among its ongoing patterns of neural activity and its perception of the current situation.

6 Each individual's behavior influences that individual's experience and the likelihood that its genes will be passed on to future generations.

How biopsychologists think about the biology of behavior.

Figure 1.2

1.2

Human Evolution

Modern biology began in 1859 with the publication of Charles Darwin's *On the Origin of Species*. In this monumental work, Darwin described his theory of evolution—the single most influential theory in the biological sciences. Darwin was not the first to suggest that species **evolve** (undergo gradual orderly change) from preexisting species, but he was the first to amass a large body of supporting evidence and the first to suggest how evolution occurs.

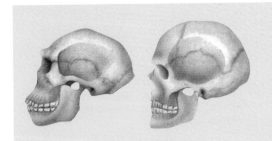

Fossil records change systematically through geological layers. Illustrated here is the evolution of the hominid skull.

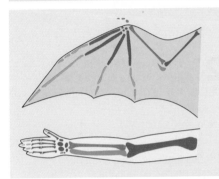

There are striking structural similarities among diverse living species (e.g., between a human arm and a bat's wing).

Major changes have been created in domestic plants and animals by programs of selective breeding.

Evolution has been observed in progress. For example, an 18-month drought on one of the Galápagos Islands left only large, difficult-to-eat seeds and increased the beak size in one species of finch.

Four kinds of evidence supporting the theory that species evolve.

Darwin presented three kinds of evidence to support his assertion that species evolve: (1) He documented the evolution of fossil records through progressively more recent geological layers. (2) He described striking structural similarities among living species (e.g., a human's hand, a bird's wing, and a cat's paw), which suggested that they had evolved from common ancestors. (3) He pointed to the major changes that had been brought about in domestic plants and animals by programs of selective breeding. However, the most convincing evidence of evolution comes from direct observations of evolution in progress. For example, Grant (1991) observed evolution of the finches of the Galápagos Islands—a population studied by Darwin himself—after only a single season of drought. Figure 1.3 illustrates these four kinds of evidence.

Darwin argued that evolution occurs through **natural selection**. He pointed out that the members of each species vary greatly in their structure, physiology, and behavior, and that the heritable traits that are associated with high rates of survival and reproduction are the most likely ones to be passed on to future generations. He argued that natural selection, when repeated for generation after generation, leads to the evolution of species that are better adapted to surviving and reproducing in their particular environmental niche. Darwin called this process *natural selection* to emphasize its similarity to the artificial selective breeding practices employed by breeders of domestic animals. Just as horse breeders create faster horses by selectively breeding the fastest of their existing stock, nature creates fitter animals by selectively breeding the fittest.

Fitness, in the Darwinian sense, is the ability of an organism to survive and contribute its genes to the next generation.

The theory of evolution was at odds with the various dogmatic views that were embedded in 19th-century thinking, so it met with initial resistance. Although traces of this resistance still exist, virtually none comes from people who understand the evidence (see Mayr, 2000):

Evolution by natural selection meets no significant opposition within biological science. The principle of natural selection has a logical necessity to it; indeed . . . development of biology in major new areas like genetics and biochemistry has only reinforced Darwin's conclusion that the facts make a belief in the theory of evolution by natural selection "inescapable." (Daly & Wilson, 1983, p. 7)

Evolution and Behavior

Some behaviors play an obvious role in evolution. For example, the ability to find food, avoid predation, or defend one's young obviously increases an animal's ability to pass on its genes to future generations. Other behaviors play roles that are less obvious but no less important (e.g., Bergman et al., 2003; Dunbar, 2003; Silk, Alberts, & Altmann, 2003). Two examples are social dominance and courtship display.

Social Dominance. The males of many species establish a stable *hierarchy of social dominance* through combative encounters with other males. In some species, these encounters often involve physical damage; in others, they involve mainly posturing and threatening until one of the two combatants backs down. The dominant male usually wins encounters with all other males of the group; the number 2 male usually wins encounters with all males except the dominant male; and so on down the line. Once a hierarchy is established, hostilities diminish because the low-ranking males learn to avoid or quickly submit to the dominant males. Because most of the fighting goes on between males competing for positions high in the social hierarchy, low-ranking males fight little; thus, the lower levels of the hierarchy tend to be only vaguely recognizable.

Why is social dominance an important factor in evolution? One reason is that in some species dominant males copulate more than nondominant males and thus are more effective in passing on their characteristics to future generations. McCann (1981) studied the effect of social dominance on the rate of copulation in 10 bull elephant seals that cohabited the same breeding beach. Figure 1.4 illustrates how these massive animals challenge each other by raising themselves to full height and pushing chest to chest. Usually, the smaller of the two backs down; if it does not, a vicious neck-biting battle ensues. McCann found that the dominant male accounted for about 37% of the copulations during the study, whereas poor number 10 accounted for only about 1% (see Figure 1.4).

Courtship Display. An intricate series of courtship displays precedes copulation in many species. The male approaches the female and signals his interest. His signal (which may be olfactory, visual, auditory, or tactual) may elicit a signal in the female, which may elicit another response in the male, and so on until copulation ensues. But copulation is unlikely to occur if one of the pair fails to react appropriately to the signals of the other.

Courtship displays are thought to promote the evolution of new species. Let me explain. A **species** is a group of organisms that is reproductively isolated from other organisms; that is, the members of one species can produce fertile offspring only by mating with members of the same species. A new species begins to branch off from an existing species when some barrier discourages breeding between a subpopulation of the existing species and the remainder of the species (Peterson,

Two massive bull elephant seals challenge one another. Dominant bull elephant seals copulate more frequently than those that are lower in the dominance hierarchy.

(Adapted from McCann, 1981.)

Figure 1.4

Soberón, & Sánchez-Cordero, 1999). Once such a reproductive barrier forms, the subpopulation evolves independently of the remainder of the species until cross-fertilization becomes impossible.

The reproductive barrier may be geographic; for example, a few birds may fly together to an isolated island, where many generations of their offspring breed among themselves and evolve into a separate species. Alternatively—to get back to the main point—the reproductive barrier may be behavioral. A few members of a species may develop different courtship displays, and these may form a reproductive barrier between themselves and the rest of their **conspecifics** (members of the same species).

Course of Human Evolution

By studying fossil records and comparing current species, we humans have looked back in time and pieced together the evolutionary history of our species—and although some of the details are still controversial, the principles are not. Human evolution, as it is currently understood, is summarized in this section. Remember as you read this section that you are a product of the very evolutionary changes that you are reading about.

Evolution of Vertebrates. Complex multicellular water-dwelling organisms first appeared on earth about 600 million years ago (Vermeij, 1996). About 150 million years later, the first chordates evolved. **Chordates** (pronounced "KOR-dates") are animals with dorsal nerve cords (large nerves that run along the center of the back, or *dorsum*); they are 1 of the 20 or so large categories, or *phyla* (pronounced "FY-la"), into which zoologists group animal species. The first chordates with spinal bones to protect their dorsal nerve cords evolved about 25 million years later. The spinal bones are called *vertebrae* (pronounced "VERT-eh-bray"), and the chordates that possess them are called **vertebrates**. The first vertebrates were primitive bony fishes. Today, there are seven classes of vertebrates: three classes of fishes, plus amphibians, reptiles, birds, and mammals.

Evolution of Amphibians. About 410 million years ago, the first bony fishes ventured out of the water. Fishes that could survive on land for brief periods of time had two great advantages: They could escape from stagnant pools to nearby fresh water, and they could take advantage of terrestrial food sources. The advantages of life on land were so great that natural selection transformed the fins and gills of bony fishes to legs and lungs, respectively—and so it was that the first **amphibians** evolved about 400 million years ago. Amphibians (e.g., frogs, toads, and salamanders) in their larval form must live in the water; only adult amphibians can survive on land.

Evolution of Reptiles. About 300 million years ago, reptiles (e.g., lizards, snakes, and turtles) evolved from amphibians. Reptiles were the first vertebrates to lay shell-covered eggs and to be covered by dry scales. Both of these adaptations reduced the reliance of reptiles on watery habitats. A reptile does not have to spend the first stage of its life in the watery environment of a pond or lake; instead, it spends the first stage of its life in the watery environment of a shell-covered egg. And once hatched, a reptile can live far from water, because its dry scales greatly reduce water loss through its water-permeable skin.

Evolution of Mammals. About 180 million years ago, during the height of the age of dinosaurs, a new class of vertebrates evolved from one line of small reptiles. The females of this new class fed their young with secretions from special glands called *mammary glands*, and the members of the class are called **mammals** after these glands. Eventually, mammals stopped laying eggs; instead, the females nurtured their young in the watery environment of their bodies until the young were mature enough to be born. The duck-billed platypus is one of only two surviving mammalian species that lay eggs.

Spending the first stage of life inside one's mother proved to have considerable survival value; it provided the long-term security and environmental stability necessary for complex programs of development to unfold. Today, there are 14 different orders of mammals. The one to which we belong is the order **primates**. We humans—in our usual humble way—named our order after the Latin *primus*, which means "first" or "foremost." There are five families of primates: prosimians, New-World monkeys, Old-World monkeys, apes, and hominids. Examples of the five primate families appear in Figure 1.5.

APE
Silver-Backed Lowland Gorilla

HOMINID
Human

OLD-WORLD MONKEY
Hussar Monkey

NEW-WORLD MONKEY
Squirrel Monkey

PROSIMIAN
Tarsus Monkey

Examples of the five different families of primates.

Figure 1.5

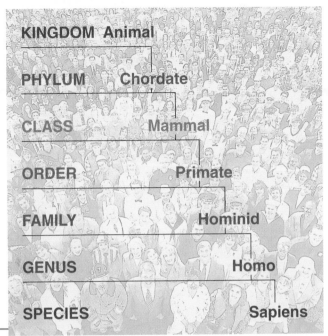

The taxonomy of the human species. One of my colleagues uses the following mnemonic to remember this classification system: King Philip Came Over For Green Salad.

Figure 1.6

KINGDOM	**Animal**
PHYLUM	**Chordate**
CLASS	**Mammal**
ORDER	**Primate**
FAMILY	**Hominid**
GENUS	**Homo**
SPECIES	**Sapiens**

Apes (gibbons, orangutans, gorillas, and chimpanzees) are thought to have evolved from a line of Old-World monkeys. Like Old-World monkeys, apes have long arms and grasping hind feet that are specialized for arboreal travel, and they have opposable thumbs that are not long enough to be of much use for precise manipulation. Unlike Old-World monkeys, though, apes have no tails and can walk upright for short distances. Chimpanzees are the closest living relatives of humans; approximately 99% of the genetic material in the two species is identical (see O'Neill, Murphy, & Gallager, 1994).

Emergence of Humankind. The family of primates that includes humans is the **hominids**. According to one simple view, this family is composed of two genera (the plural of genus): *Australopithecus* and *Homo* (*Homo erectus* and *Homo sapiens*). However, humans (*Homo sapiens*) are the only surviving hominid species. The *taxonomy* (classification) of the human species is illustrated in Figure 1.6.

It is believed that the Australopithecines evolved about 6 million years ago in Africa from a line of apes (*australo* means "southern," and *pithecus* means "ape"). Several species of *Australopithecus* are thought to have roamed the African plains for about 5 million years before becoming extinct (see Tattersall & Matternes, 2000). Australopithecines were only about 1.3 meters (4 feet) tall, and they had small brains; but analysis of their pelvis and leg bones indicates that their posture was as upright as yours or mine. Any doubts about their upright posture were erased by the discovery of the fossilized footprints pictured in Figure 1.7 (Agnew & Demas, 1998).

Fossilized footprints of Australopithecine hominids who strode across African volcanic ash about 3.6 million years ago. They left a 70-meter trail. There were two adults and a child; the child often walked in the footsteps of the adults.

Figure 1.7

The first *Homo* species is thought to have evolved from a species of *Australopithecus* about 2 million years ago (Wood & Collard, 1999). The most distinctive feature of the early *Homo* species was their large brain cavity (about 850 cubic centimeters), larger than that of *Australopithecus* (about 500 cubic centimeters) but smaller than that of modern humans (about 1,330 cubic centimeters). The early *Homo* species used fire and tools (see Ambrose, 2001), coexisted in Africa with various species of *Australopithecus* for about a half-million years until *Australopithecus* died out, and began to move out of Africa into Europe and Asia in large numbers about 1.7 million years ago (see Vekua et al., 2002).

About 200,000 years ago (Pääbo, 1995), the early *Homo* species were gradually replaced in the fossil record by modern humans (*Homo sapiens*). Paradoxically, although the big three human attributes—large brain, upright posture, and free hands with an opposable thumb—have been evident for hundreds of thousands of years, most human accomplishments are of comparatively recent origin. Artistic products (e.g., wall paintings and carvings) did not appear until about 40,000 years ago, ranching and farming were not established until about 10,000 years ago (e.g., Denham et al., 2003), and writing was not invented until about 3,500 years ago.

Thinking about Human Evolution

Figure 1.8 on page 16 illustrates the main branches of vertebrate evolution. You can follow the path of human evolution from left to right.

You should be feeling pleased with yourself: You have just learned about the major events in the evolution of your own species. However, more important than knowing the events of your evolutionary history is the ability to think clearly about evolution and its implications for biopsychology and your own life.

Thinking Clearly

Many people think of evolution as a ladder progressing linearly toward perfection, with humans at the very top. There are three serious problems with this way of thinking. First, metaphorically speaking, evolution is more like a bush than a ladder, with many dead branches at the core—it is important to realize that only about 1 % of known species still exist today. Second, we humans have little reason to claim evolutionary supremacy; we may be one of the most complex organisms, but we are the last surviving species of a family that has existed for only a blip of evolutionary time. Third, evolution does not proceed toward some perfect design. Adaptations occur through changes to existing programs, and thus organisms are never perfectly designed. For example, the fact that mammalian sperm do not develop efficiently at body temperature led to the evolution of the scrotum—hardly a perfect solution to any design problem.

People often make two related assumptions about the adaptiveness of current traits. First, they assume that all existing traits must serve some adaptive function. Second, they assume that the current function of a trait indicates why the trait evolved in the first place. Neither assumption is always true. Evolution occurs through changes in genetic programs of development that usually influence the development of several traits, only some of which may be adaptive. Also, traits that were once adaptive may become nonadaptive, or even maladaptive, if the environment changes. Furthermore, some traits that evolved to perform one function may later be co-opted to perform another; for example, forelimbs evolved in amphibians and reptiles for the purpose of walking, but subsequently they were used for flying by birds and some now-extinct reptiles.

Finally, people tend to assume that similarities between existing species indicate a common evolutionary origin, but this assumption is not always correct. It depends on the nature of the similarity. Similar traits in species that have a common evolutionary ancestor are called **homologous**; similar traits in species that do not have a common ancestor are called **analogous**. The evolution of similarities in unrelated species because they live under similar environmental demands is called **convergent evolution**. Whether a similarity is homologous or analogous is usually revealed by a careful analysis of the similarity. For example, a human's arm and a

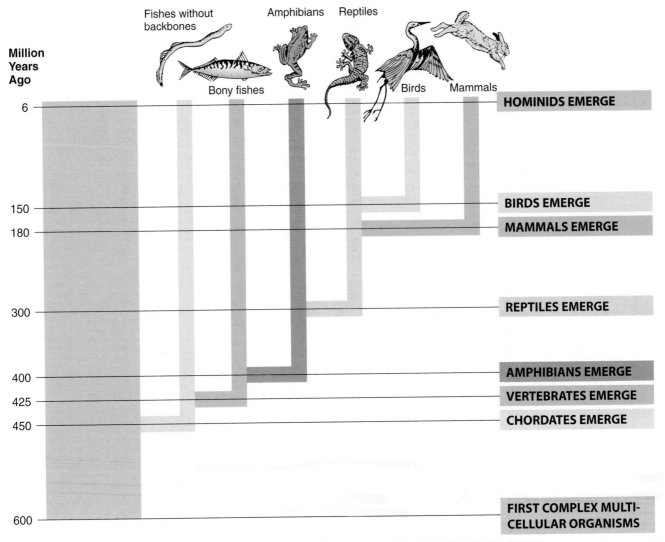

Million Years Ago

6	HOMINIDS EMERGE
150	BIRDS EMERGE
180	MAMMALS EMERGE
300	REPTILES EMERGE
400	AMPHIBIANS EMERGE
425	VERTEBRATES EMERGE
450	CHORDATES EMERGE
600	FIRST COMPLEX MULTI-CELLULAR ORGANISMS

Fishes without backbones · Bony fishes · Amphibians · Reptiles · Birds · Mammals

Vertebrate evolution. Note that many evolutionary biologists consider birds to be specialized reptiles, not an independent class, as shown here.

Figure 1.8

bird's wing have the same fundamental skeletal structure, suggesting that they are homologous; whereas a bird's wing and a bee's wing accomplish flight in entirely different ways, suggesting that they are analogous.

Evolution of the Human Brain

The Evolutionary Perspective

Early research on the evolution of the human brain focused on size. This research was stimulated by the assumption that brain size and intellectual capacity are closely related—an assumption that quickly ran into two problems. First, it was shown that modern humans, who believe themselves to be the most intelligent of all creatures, do not have the biggest brains. With brains weighing about 1,350 grams, humans rank far behind whales and elephants, whose brains weigh between 5,000 and 8,000 grams (Harvey & Krebs, 1990). Second, the sizes of the

The brains of animals of different evolutionary age.
Cerebrums are shown in yellow; brain stems are shown
in purple.

Figure 1.9

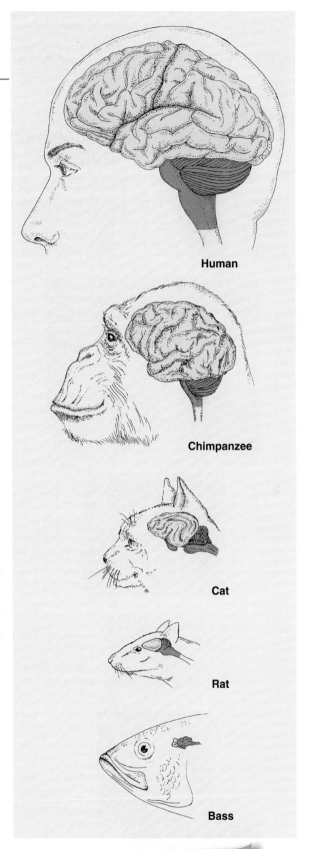

Human

Chimpanzee

Cat

Rat

Bass

The Evolutionary Perspective

brains of acclaimed intellectuals (e.g., Einstein) were found to be unremarkable, certainly no match for their gigantic intellects. It is now clear that, although healthy adult human brains vary greatly in size—between about 1,000 and 2,000 grams—there is no clear relationship between brain size and intelligence.

One obvious problem in relating brain size to intelligence is the fact that larger animals tend to have larger brains, presumably because larger bodies require more brain tissue to control and regulate them. Thus, the facts that large men tend to have larger brains than small men, that men tend to have larger brains than women, and that elephants have larger brains than humans do not suggest anything about the relative intelligence of these populations. This problem led to the proposal that brain weight expressed as a percentage of total body weight might be a better measure of intellectual capacity. This measure allows humans (2.33%) to take their rightful place ahead of elephants (0.20%), but it also allows both humans and elephants to be surpassed by that intellectual giant of the animal kingdom, the shrew (3.33%).

A more reasonable approach to the study of brain evolution has been to compare the evolution of different brain regions (Finlay & Darlington, 1995; Killacky, 1995). For example, it has been informative to consider the evolution of the **brain stem** separately from the evolution of the **cerebrum** (cerebral hemispheres). In general, the brain stem regulates reflex activities that are critical for survival (e.g., heart rate, respiration, and blood glucose level), whereas the cerebrum is involved in more complex adaptive processes such as learning, perception, and motivation.

Figure 1.9 is a schematic representation of the relative size of the brain stems and cerebrums of several species that are living descendants of species from which humans evolved. This figure makes three important points about the evolution of the human brain: The first is that it has increased in size during evolution; the second is that most of the increase in size has occurred in the cerebrum; and the third is that there has been an increase in the number of **convolutions**—folds on the cerebral surface—that has greatly increased the volume of the cerebral cortex (the outermost layer of cerebral tissue).

More significant than the differences among the brains of various related species are the similarities. All brains are constructed of neurons, and the neural structures that compose the brains of one species can almost always be found in the brains of related species. For example, the brains of humans, monkeys, rats, and mice contain the same gross (major) structures connected in the same way. Moreover, similar structures tend to perform similar functions. For example, neurons that respond to the number of objects in a display, independent of the identity of the objects, have been found in the *parietal cortex* of humans, monkeys, and cats (see Dehaene, 2002; Nieder, Freedman, & Miller, 2002).

Biopsychological Research Involves Both Human and Nonhuman Subjects

Because of the evolutionary continuity of the brain, both human and nonhuman animals are the subject of biopsychological research. Of the nonhumans, rats, mice, and nonhuman primates are among the most widely studied.

Humans have several advantages over other animals as experimental subjects of biopsychological research: They can follow instructions, they can report their subjective experiences, and their cages are easier to clean. Obviously, I am joking about the cages, but the joke does draw attention to one advantage that humans have over other species as experimental subjects: Humans are often cheaper. Because only the highest standards of animal care are acceptable, the cost of maintaining an animal laboratory can be prohibitive for all but the most well-funded researchers.

Of course, the greatest advantage that humans have as experimental subjects for researchers focused on understanding the intricacies of human brain function is that they have human brains. In fact, you might wonder why biopsychologists would bother studying nonhuman subjects at all. The answer lies in the evolutionary continuity of the brain. The brains of humans differ from the brains of their mammalian relatives primarily in their overall size and the extent of their cortical development. In other words, the differences between the brains of humans and those of related species are more quantitative than qualitative, and thus many of the principles of human brain function can be derived from the study of nonhumans (e.g., Nakahara et al., 2002).

Conversely, nonhuman animals have three advantages over humans as subjects in biopsychological research. The first is that the brains and behavior of nonhuman subjects are simpler than those of human subjects. Hence, the study of nonhuman species is more likely to reveal fundamental brain–behavior interactions. The second advantage is that insights frequently arise from the **comparative approach**, the study of biological processes by comparing different species. For example, comparing the behavior of species that do not have a cerebral cortex with the behavior of species that do can provide valuable clues about cortical function. The third advantage of nonhuman animals as subjects is that it is possible to conduct laboratory research on animals that, for ethical reasons, is not possible with human subjects. This is not to say that the study of nonhuman animals is not governed by a strict code of ethics (see Institute of Laboratory Animal Resources, 1996)—it is. However, there are fewer ethical constraints on the study of laboratory species than on the study of humans.

In my experience, most biopsychologists display considerable concern for their subjects, whether they are of their own species or not; however, ethical issues are not left to the discretion of the individual researcher. All biopsychological research, whether it involves human subjects or nonhuman ones, is regulated by independent committees according to strict ethical guidelines: "Researchers cannot escape the logic that if the animals we observe are reasonable models of our own most intricate actions, then they must be respected as we would respect our own sensibilities" (Ulrich, 1991, p. 197).

If you are concerned about the ethics of biopsychological research on human and nonhuman species, be sure to look at the Check It Out feature.

Thinking Clearly

1.3

Fundamental Genetics

Darwin did not understand two of the key facts on which his theory of evolution was based. He did not understand why conspecifics differ from one another, and he did not understand how anatomical, physiological, and behavioral characteristics are passed from parent to offspring. While Darwin puzzled over these questions, there was an unread manuscript in his files that contained the answers. It had been sent to him by an unknown Augustinian monk, Gregor Mendel. Unfortunately for Darwin (1809–1882) and for Mendel (1822–1884), the significance of Mendel's research was not recognized until the early part of the 20th century, well after both their deaths.

Mendelian Genetics

Mendel studied inheritance in pea plants. In designing his experiments, he made two wise decisions. He decided to study dichotomous traits, and he decided to begin his experiments by crossing the offspring of true-breeding lines. **Dichotomous traits** are traits that occur in one form or the other, not normally in combination. For example, seed color is a dichotomous pea plant trait: Every pea plant has either brown seeds or white seeds. **True-breeding lines** are breeding lines in which inter-bred members always produce offspring with the same trait (e.g., brown seeds), generation after generation.

In one of his early experiments, Mendel studied the inheritance of seed color: brown or white. He began by cross breeding the offspring of a line of pea plants that had bred true for brown seeds with the offspring of a line of pea plants that had bred true for white seeds. The offspring of this cross all had brown seeds. Then, Mendel bred these first-generation offspring with one another, and he found that about three-quarters of the resulting second-generation offspring had brown seeds and about one-quarter had white seeds. Mendel repeated this experiment many times with various pairs of dichotomous pea plant traits, and each time the result was the same. One trait, which Mendel called the **dominant trait**, appeared in all of the first-generation offspring; the other trait, which he called the **recessive trait**, appeared in about one-quarter of the second-generation offspring. Mendel would have obtained a similar result if he had conducted an experiment with true-breeding lines of brown-eyed (dominant) and blue-eyed (recessive) humans.

The results of Mendel's experiment challenged the central premise upon which all previous ideas about inheritance had rested: that offspring inherit the traits of their parents. Somehow, the recessive trait (white seeds) was passed on to one-

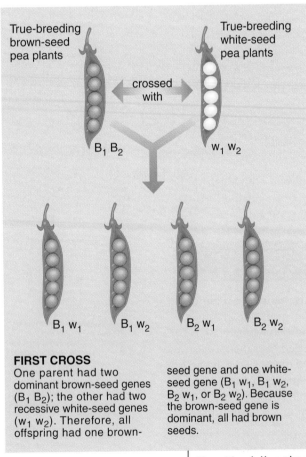

FIRST CROSS
One parent had two dominant brown-seed genes ($B_1 B_2$); the other had two recessive white-seed genes ($w_1 w_2$). Therefore, all offspring had one brown-seed gene and one white-seed gene ($B_1 w_1$, $B_1 w_2$, $B_2 w_1$, or $B_2 w_2$). Because the brown-seed gene is dominant, all had brown seeds.

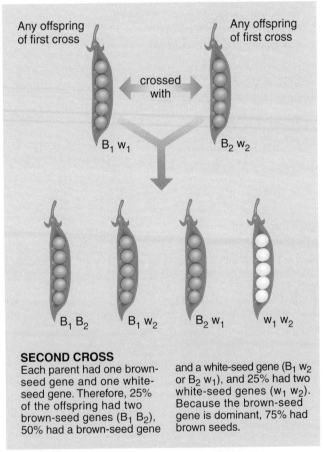

SECOND CROSS
Each parent had one brown-seed gene and one white-seed gene. Therefore, 25% of the offspring had two brown-seed genes ($B_1 B_2$), 50% had a brown-seed gene and a white-seed gene ($B_1 w_2$ or $B_2 w_1$), and 25% had two white-seed genes ($w_1 w_2$). Because the brown-seed gene is dominant, 75% had brown seeds.

How Mendel's theory accounts for the results of his experiment on the inheritance of seed color in pea plants.

Figure 1.10

quarter of the second-generation pea plants by first-generation pea plants that did not themselves possess it. An organism's observable traits are referred to as its **phenotype**; the traits that it can pass on to its offspring through its genetic material are referred to as its **genotype**.

Mendel devised a theory to explain his results. It comprised four ideas. First, Mendel proposed that there are two kinds of inherited factors for each dichotomous trait—for example, that a brown-seed factor and a white-seed factor control seed color. Today, we call each inherited factor a **gene**. Second, Mendel proposed that each organism possesses two genes for each of its dichotomous traits; for example, each pea plant possesses either two brown-seed genes, two white-seed genes, or one of each. The two genes that control the same trait are called **alleles** (pronounced "a-LEELZ"). Organisms that possess two identical genes for a trait are said to be **homozygous** for that trait; those that possess two different genes for a trait are said to be **heterozygous** for that trait. Third, Mendel proposed that one of the two kinds of genes for each dichotomous trait dominates the other in heterozygous organisms. For example, pea plants with a brown-seed gene and a white-seed gene always have brown seeds because the brown-seed gene always dominates the white-seed gene. And fourth, Mendel proposed that for each trait each organism randomly inherits one of its "father's" two factors and one of its "mother's" two factors. Figure 1.10 illustrates how Mendel's theory accounts for the result of his experiment on the inheritance of seed color in pea plants.

Chromosomes and Reproduction

It was not until the early 20th century that genes were found to be located on **chromosomes**—threadlike structures in the *nucleus* of each cell. Chromosomes occur in matched pairs, and each species has a characteristic number of pairs in each of its body cells; humans have 23 pairs. The two genes (alleles) that control each trait are situated at the same locus, one on each chromosome of a particular pair.

The process of cell division that produces **gametes** (egg cells and sperm cells) is called **meiosis** (pronounced "my-OH-sis")—see Sluder and McCollum (2000). In meiosis, the chromosomes divide, and one chromosome of each pair goes to each of the two gametes that result from the division. As a result, each gamete has only half the usual number of chromosomes (23 in humans); and when a sperm cell and an egg cell combine during fertilization (see Figure 1.11), a **zygote** (a fertilized egg cell) with the full complement of chromosomes is produced. All other cell division in the body occurs by **mitosis** (pronounced "my-TOE-sis"). Just prior to mitotic division, the number of chromosomes doubles so that, when the division occurs, both daughter cells end up with the full complement of chromosomes. Figure 1.12 on page 22 illustrates meiosis, fertilization, and mitosis.

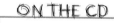

ON THE CD

Visit the *Mitosis* module to see how this type of cell division works.

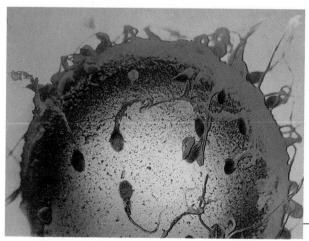

During fertilization, sperm cells attach themselves to the surface of an egg cell; only one will enter the egg cell and fertilize it.

Figure 1.11

**Sperm Cells Are Created
by Meiotic Division**

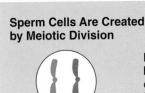

Each of the father's body cells has 23 pairs of chromosomes; 1 pair is shown here.

The cell divides to create two sperm cells, each with 23 chromosomes.

**Egg Cells Are Created
by Meiotic Division**

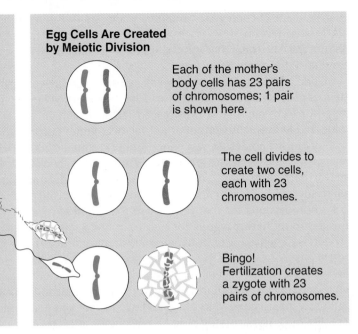

Each of the mother's body cells has 23 pairs of chromosomes; 1 pair is shown here.

The cell divides to create two cells, each with 23 chromosomes.

Bingo! Fertilization creates a zygote with 23 pairs of chromosomes.

Meiotic cell division, fertilization, and mitotic cell division.

Figure 1.12

**The Zygote Grows
by Mitotic Division**

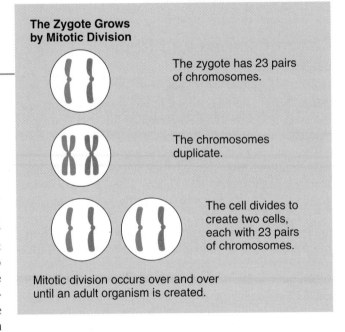

The zygote has 23 pairs of chromosomes.

The chromosomes duplicate.

The cell divides to create two cells, each with 23 pairs of chromosomes.

Mitotic division occurs over and over until an adult organism is created.

Meiosis accounts for much of the genetic diversity within each species. In humans, for example, each meiotic division produces two gametes; each gamete contains one chromosome from each of the 23 pairs contained in each body cell. Because each of the 23 pairs is randomly sorted into the two gametes, each human can produce gametes with 2^{23} (8,388,608) different combinations of chromosomes.

Sex Chromosomes and Sex-Linked Traits

There is one exception to the rule that chromosomes always come in matched pairs. That exception is the **sex chromosomes**—the pair of chromosomes that determines an individual's sex. There are two types of sex chromosomes, X and Y, and the two look different and carry different genes. Female mammals have two X chromosomes, and male mammals have an X and a Y. Traits that are influenced by genes on the sex chromosomes are referred to as **sex-linked traits**. Virtually all sex-linked traits are controlled by genes on the X chromosome because the Y chromosome is small and carries few genes (see Jegalian & Lahn, 2001).

Traits that are controlled by genes on the X chromosome occur more frequently in one sex than the other. If the trait is dominant, it occurs more frequently in females. Females have twice the chance of inheriting the dominant gene because they have twice the number of X chromosomes. In contrast, recessive sex-linked traits occur more frequently in males. The reason is that recessive sex-linked traits are manifested only in females who possess two of the recessive genes—one on each of their X chromosomes—whereas the traits are manifested in all males who possess the gene because they have only one X chromosome. The classic example of a recessive sex-linked trait is color blindness. Because the color-blindness gene is quite rare, females almost never inherit two of them and thus almost never develop the disorder; in contrast, every male who possesses one color-blindness gene is color blind.

Chromosome Structure and Replication

Each chromosome is a double-stranded molecule of **deoxyribonucleic acid (DNA)**. Each strand is a sequence of **nucleotide bases** attached to a chain of *phosphate* and *deoxyribose*; there are four nucleotide bases: *adenine, thymine, guanine*, and *cytosine*. It is the sequence of these bases on each chromosome that constitutes the genetic code—just as the sequence of letters constitutes the code of our language.

The two strands that compose each chromosome are coiled around each other and bonded together by the attraction of adenine for thymine and guanine for cytosine. This specific bonding pattern has an important consequence: The two strands that compose each chromosome are exact complements of each other. For example, the sequence of adenine, guanine, thymine, cytosine, and guanine on one strand is always attached to the complementary sequence of thymine, cytosine, adenine, guanine, and cytosine on the other. Figure 1.13 illustrates the structure of DNA.

Replication is a critical process of the DNA molecule. Without it, mitotic cell division would not be possible. Figure 1.14 on page 24 illustrates how DNA replication is thought to work (see Losick & Shapiro, 1998). The two strands of DNA start to unwind. Then the exposed nucleotide bases on each of the two strands attract loose complementary bases from the fluid of the nucleus. Thus, when the unwinding is complete, two double-stranded DNA molecules, both of which are identical to the original, have been created.

Chromosome replication does not always go according to plan; there may be errors. Sometimes, these errors are gross errors. For example, in *Down syndrome*, which you will learn about in Chapter 8, there is an extra chromosome in each cell. But more commonly, errors in duplication take the form of **mutations**—accidental alterations in individual genes. In most cases, mutations disappear from the genetic pool within a few generations because the organisms that inherit them are less fit. However, in rare instances, mutations increase fitness and in so doing contribute to rapid evolution.

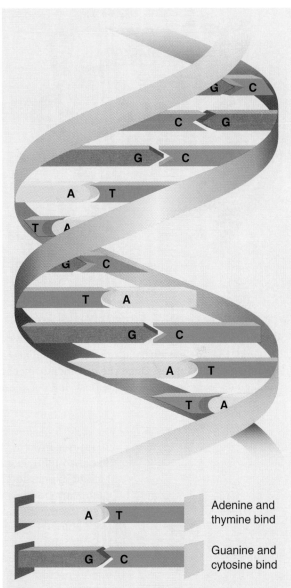

Adenine and thymine bind

Guanine and cytosine bind

A schematic illustration of the structure of a DNA molecule. Notice the complementary binding of nucleotide bases: thymine to adenine, and guanine to cytosine.

Figure 1.13

The Genetic Code and Gene Expression

There are several different kinds of genes. The most well understood are the **structural genes**—genes that contain the information necessary for the synthesis of a single protein. **Proteins** are long chains of **amino acids**; they control the physiological activities of cells and are important components of cellular structure. All the cells in the body (e.g., brain cells, hair cells, and bone cells) contain exactly the same structural genes. How then do different kinds of cells develop? The answer lies in a complex category of genes, often called the **operator genes**.

Each operator gene controls a structural gene or a group of related structural genes. The function of an operator gene is to determine whether or not each of its structural genes initiates the synthesis of a protein (i.e., whether or not the structural gene will be *expressed*) and at what rate.

The control of **gene expression** by operator genes is an important process because it determines how a cell will develop and how it will function once it reaches maturity. Operator genes are like switches; and, like switches, they can be regulated in two ways. Some operator genes are normally off, and they are regulated by **DNA-binding proteins** that turn them on; others are normally on, and they are regulated by DNA-binding proteins that turn them up, down, or off. Many of the DNA-binding proteins that control operator genes are influenced by signals received by the cell from its environment (see Darnell, 1997). This, then—if it has not already occurred to you—is the major mechanism by which experience interacts with genes to influence development.

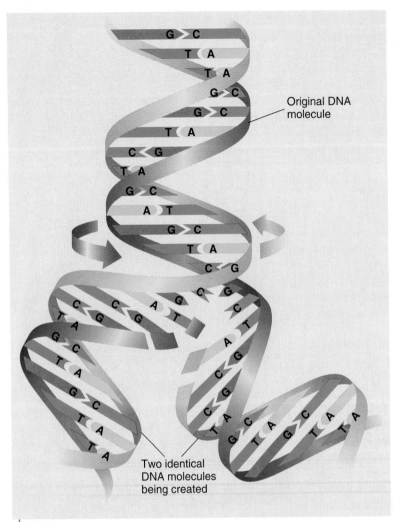

DNA replication. As the two strands of the original DNA molecule unwind, the nucleotide bases on each strand attract loose complementary bases. Once the unwinding is complete, two DNA molecules, each identical to the first, will have been created.

Figure 1.14

The expression of a structural gene is illustrated in Figure 1.15. The process of gene expression occurs in two phases: the **transcription** of the DNA base-sequence code to an RNA base-sequence code and the **translation** of the RNA base-sequence code into a sequence of amino acids.

First, the small section of the chromosome that contains the structural gene unravels, and the unraveled section of one of the DNA strands serves as a template for the transcription of a short strand of **ribonucleic acid (RNA)**. RNA is like DNA except that it contains the nucleotide base uracil instead of thymine and has a phosphate and ribose backbone instead of a phosphate and deoxyribose backbone. The strand of transcribed RNA is called **messenger RNA** because it carries the genetic code from the nucleus of the cell. Once it has left the nucleus, the messenger RNA attaches itself to one of the many **ribosomes** in the cell's *cytoplasm* (the clear fluid within the cell). The ribosome then moves along the strand of messenger RNA, translating the genetic code as it proceeds.

Each group of three consecutive nucleotide bases along the messenger RNA strand is called a **codon**. Each codon instructs the ribosome to add 1 of the 20 dif-

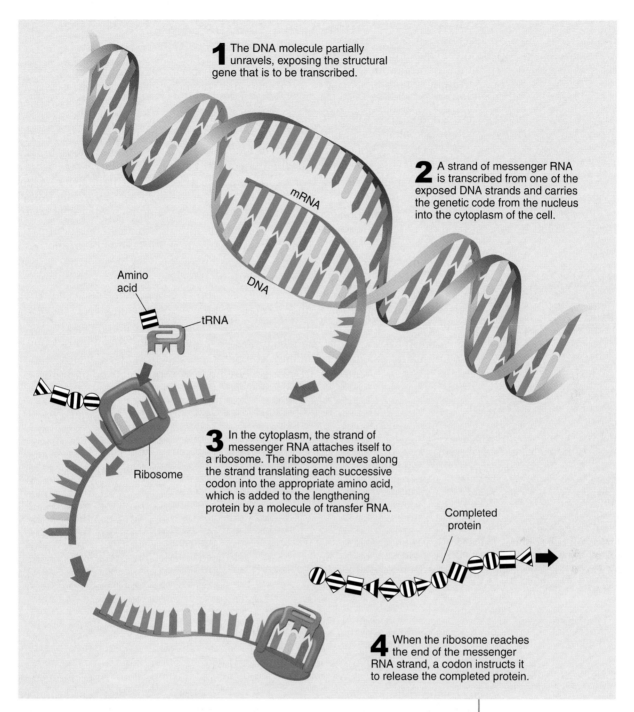

1 The DNA molecule partially unravels, exposing the structural gene that is to be transcribed.

2 A strand of messenger RNA is transcribed from one of the exposed DNA strands and carries the genetic code from the nucleus into the cytoplasm of the cell.

mRNA

DNA

Amino acid

tRNA

Ribosome

3 In the cytoplasm, the strand of messenger RNA attaches itself to a ribosome. The ribosome moves along the strand translating each successive codon into the appropriate amino acid, which is added to the lengthening protein by a molecule of transfer RNA.

Completed protein

4 When the ribosome reaches the end of the messenger RNA strand, a codon instructs it to release the completed protein.

Gene expression. Transcription of a section of DNA into a complementary strand of messenger RNA is followed by the translation of the messenger RNA strand into a protein.

Figure 1.15

ferent kinds of amino acids to the protein that it is constructing; for example, the sequence guanine-guanine-adenine instructs the ribosome to add the amino acid glycine. Each kind of amino acid is carried to the ribosome by molecules of **transfer RNA**; as the ribosome reads a codon, it attracts a transfer RNA molecule that is attached to the appropriate amino acid. The ribosome reads codon after codon and adds amino acid after amino acid until it reaches a codon that tells it the protein is complete; at that point, the completed protein is released into the cytoplasm.

Human Genome Project: What's Next?

Arguably, the most ambitious scientific project of all time began in 1990. Known as the **human genome project**, it was a loosely knit collaboration of major research institutions and individual research teams in several countries. The purpose of this collaboration was to compile a map of the human genome, that is, of all 3 billion bases that compose our chromosomes. This ambitious task was completed in 2001 with the simultaneous publication of the first draft of the human genome in *Nature* and *Science*, two of the most respected scientific journals.

Perhaps the most surprising attribute of the human genome is the relatively small number of genes it includes—only a fraction of the bases in the human genome are components of classic protein-coding genes. Current estimates of the total number of these classic structural genes tend to range around 34,000, only about half again as many as in the mouse genome and only three times as many as in the fruit fly genome. The function of the many bases that are not involved in protein synthesis remains a mystery.

Thinking Clearly

The relatively small number of human structural genes suggests that human complexity is the product of a relatively small number of genetic changes and that biological complexity evolves more through refinements in gene expression than through increases in gene number (Claverie, 2001).

Many people overestimate the degree to which deciphering the human genome will contribute to the understanding of human development. It is a major step, but it still leaves us a great distance from the ultimate goal: understanding how each gene interacts with other genes and experience to determine human behavior (see Figure 1.2).

Scan your Brain

This is a good place for you to pause to scan your brain to see if you are ready to proceed to the rest of this chapter. Fill in the following blanks with the most appropriate terms from the first three sections of the chapter. The correct answers are provided below. Before proceeding, review material related to your errors and omissions.

1. Using functional brain imaging, _____ study the areas of the brain involved in cognition.

2. _____ is the study of the functions and activities of the nervous system.

3. In the Darwinian sense, _____ refers to the ability of an organism to survive and produce large numbers of fertile offspring.

4. A _____ is a group of reproductively isolated organisms.

5. Mammals are thought to have evolved from _____ about 180 million years ago.

6. There are five different families of primates: prosimians, New-World monkeys, Old-World monkeys, _____, and _____.

7. _____ are the closest living relatives of humans; they have about 99% of the same genetic material.

8. The first hominids were _____.

9. An organism's observable traits are its _____; the traits that it can pass to its offspring through its genetic material are its _____.

10. The process of cell division that produces _____ is meiosis.

11. Each structural gene contains the information for the production of a single _____.

12. Structural genes can be turned off or on by _____ genes.

13. Gene expression occurs in two stages: transcription and _____.

14. The massive international research effort to physically map human chromosomes was the _____ project.

Scan Your Brain answers: (1) cognitive neuroscientists, (2) Neurophysiology, (3) fitness, (4) species, (5) reptiles, (6) apes, hominins, (7) Chimpanzees, (8) Australopithecines, (9) phenotype, genotype, (10) gametes, (11) protein, (12) operator, (13) translation, (14) human genome

Thinking about the Biology of Behavior: Mind–Brain and Nature–Nurture Issues

his, the final section of the chapter, completes your introduction to biopsychological thinking. It focuses on three important biopsychological issues—important for a variety of reasons, not the least of which is that they are all relevant to life outside the classroom. How you think about each of these issues is related to how you think about yourself and others. The three issues, which you will learn about in the next three subsections, are (1) the mind–brain issue, (2) the nature–nurture issue, and (3) the question about the extent to which individual differences are inborn.

Thinking Clearly

The Mind–Brain Issue

The *mind–brain issue* (the debate over the existence of a mind independent of the brain) has a long history, but the argument was brought to a head in the 17th century by the conflict between science and the Roman Church. During the dark ages of Western civilization, truth was whatever the Church decreed to be true. Then, in about 1400, things started to change. The famines, plagues, and marauding armies that had repeatedly swept Europe during the Middle Ages subsided, and interest turned to art, commerce, and scholarship. This was the period of the *Renaissance*, or rebirth (1400 to 1700). Some Renaissance scholars were not content to follow the dictates of the Church; instead, they started to study things directly by observing them—and so it was that modern science was born.

Much of the scientific knowledge that accumulated during the Renaissance was at odds with Church dictates. However, the conflict was resolved by the prominent French philosopher René Descartes (pronounced "day-CART"). Descartes (1596–1650) proposed a philosophy that, in a sense, gave one part of the universe to science and the other part to the Church. He argued that the universe is composed of two elements: (1) physical matter, which behaves according to the laws of nature and is thus a suitable object of scientific investigation; and (2) the human mind (soul, self, or spirit), which lacks physical substance, controls human behavior, obeys no natural laws, and is thus the appropriate purview of the Church. The human body, including the brain, was assumed to be entirely physical, and so were nonhuman animals.

Cartesian dualism, as Descartes's philosophy became known, was sanctioned by the Roman Church. As a result, the idea that the human brain and the mind are separate entities became widely accepted. Although it had some opponents, the belief in the dichotomy of mind and brain became the dominant view and remained so for centuries.

Most scholarly efforts to support the idea of a mind–brain dichotomy boiled down to that fact that it did not seem possible for the brain to produce conscious experience in all its richness and complexity. It seemed that there *must* be some portion of human experience that cannot be attributable to that squishy, wrinkled, 1.3-kilogram organ described on the first page of this chapter.

Centuries have passed since the mind–brain dichotomy became the dominant way of thinking about the brain, and much information about the functions of the brain has accumulated in the interim. As a result, most people now appreciate that most human behavior and experience are a product of brain activity, but they still cling to the dualistic assumption that there is a category of human activity that somehow transcends the human brain (Searle, 2000). What does the evidence suggest?

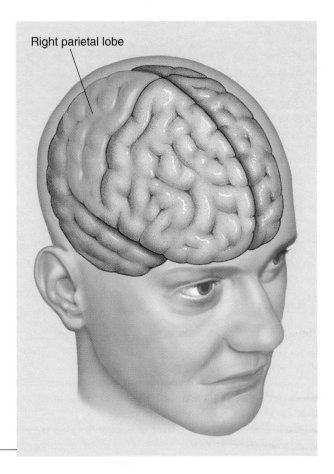

Right parietal lobe

Asomatognosia typically involves damage to the right parietal lobe.

Figure 1.16

As you progress through this book, you will encounter many studies in which changes in brain functioning induce extremely complex changes in psychological experience. For example, the following case study concerns a man who suffered damage to an area in the right parietal cortex (see Figure 1.16), which resulted in **asomatognosia**, a deficiency in the awareness of parts of one's own body—and self-awareness has long been considered to be one of the most complex *cognitive* (pertaining to thinking) abilities and the defining feature of human experience.

The Case of the Man Who Fell Out of Bed

Clinical Implications

When he awoke, Dr. Sacks' s patient felt fine—that is, until he touched the thing in bed next to him. It was a severed human leg, all hairy and still warm!

At first, the patient was confused. Then, he figured it out. One of the nurses must have taken it from the autopsy department and put it in his bed as a joke. Some joke; it was disgusting. So, he threw the leg out of the bed, but somehow he landed on the floor with it attached to him.

The patient became agitated and desperate, and Dr. Sacks tried to comfort him and help him back into the bed. Making one last effort to reduce the patient' s confusion, Sacks asked him where his left leg was, if the one attached to him wasn' t it. Turning pale and looking like he was about to pass out, the patient replied that he had no idea where his own leg was—it had disappeared (Sacks, 1985).

Let me remind you why you just read this case study. Its purpose was to illustrate a fact that will become more apparent to you as you advance through the following chapters: that manipulations of the brain (whether through accidental damage, surgery, drug treatment, or other means) can have incredibly complex psychological effects. Indeed, as evidence has accumulated, it has become clear that there is no need to postulate the existence of anything other than the brain to account for particularly complicated psychological experiences. The brain can do it all. And therein lies the real mystery of human existence, a realization that may have brought many of you to this book.

Thinking Clearly

Some scholars still use the term *mind*, but many are not using it in the traditional way, as if it were an entity different from the brain: Most view the mind as a product of neural activity, a philosophy that is termed *monism*.

The Nature–Nurture Issue

For centuries, scholars have debated whether humans and other animals inherit their behavioral capacities or whether they acquire them through learning. This debate is commonly referred to as the **nature–nurture issue**.

Most of the early North American experimental psychologists were totally committed to the nurture (learning) side of the nature–nurture issue (de Waal, 1999). The degree of this commitment is illustrated by the oft-cited words of John B. Watson, the father of *behaviorism*:

> We have no real evidence of the inheritance of [behavioral] traits. I would feel perfectly confident in the ultimately favorable outcome of careful upbringing of a healthy, well-formed baby born of a long line of crooks, murderers and thieves, and prostitutes. Who has any evidence to the contrary?
>
> . . . Give me a dozen healthy infants, well-formed, and my own specified world to bring them up in and I'll guarantee to take any one at random and train him to become any type of specialist I might select—doctor, lawyer, artist, merchant-chief and, yes even beggar-man and thief. (Watson, 1930, pp. 103–104)

At the same time that experimental psychology was taking root in North America, **ethology** (the study of animal behavior in the wild) was becoming the dominant approach to the study of behavior in Europe. European ethology, in contrast to North American experimental psychology, focused on the study of **instinctive behaviors** (behaviors that occur in all like members of a species, even when there seems to have been no opportunity for them to have been learned), and it emphasized the role of nature, or inherited factors, in behavioral development. Because instinctive behaviors do not seem to be learned, the early ethologists assumed that they are entirely inherited. They were wrong, but then so were the early experimental psychologists.

As biopsychological research accumulated, it supported neither the nature side nor the nurture side of the debate. The evidence strongly supported a third view: that the nature–nurture issue cannot be resolved because it is based on flawed thinking.

The nature–nurture issue went through several revisions before eventually being abandoned. The first revision of the nature–nurture issue was necessitated by the discovery that factors other than genetics and learning were shown to influence behavioral development; factors such as the fetal environment, nutrition, stress, and sensory stimulation also proved to be influential. This led to a broadening of the concept of nurture to include a variety of experiential factors in addition to learning. In effect, it changed the nature-or-nurture dichotomy from "genetic factors or learning" to "genetic factors or experience."

Next, it was argued convincingly that behavior always develops under the combined control of both nature and nurture (see Johnston, 1987; Rutter, 1997), not under the control of one or the other. Faced with this new information, many people merely substituted one kind of nature-or-nurture thinking for another. They stopped asking, "Is it genetic, or is it the result of experience?" and started asking, "How much of it is genetic, and how much of it is the result of experience?"

Like earlier versions of the nature-or-nurture question, the how-much-of-it-is-genetic-and-how-much-of-it-is-the-result-of-experience version is fundamentally flawed. The problem is that it is based on the premise that genetic factors and experiential factors combine in an additive fashion—that a behavioral capacity, such as intelligence, is created through the combination or mixture of so many parts of genetics and so many parts of experience, rather than through the interaction of genetics and experience. Once you learn more about how genetic factors and experience interact, you will better appreciate the folly of this assumption. For the time being, however, let me illustrate its weakness with a metaphor embedded in an anecdote.

The Case of the Thinking Student

One of my students told me that she had read that intelligence was one-third genetic and two-thirds experience, and she wondered whether this was true. She must have been puzzled when I began my response by describing an alpine experience. "I was lazily wandering up a summit ridge when I heard an unexpected sound. Ahead, with his back to me, was a young man sitting on the edge of a precipice, blowing into a peculiar musical instrument. I sat down behind him on a large sun-soaked rock, ate my lunch, and shared his experience with him. Then, I got up and wandered back down the ridge, leaving him undisturbed."

I put the following question to my student: "If I wanted to get a better understanding of this music, would it be reasonable for me to begin by asking how much of it came from the musician and how much of it came from the instrument?"

"That would be dumb," she said. "The music comes from both; it makes no sense to ask how much comes from the musician and how much comes from the instrument. Somehow the music results from the interaction of the two together. You would have to ask about the interaction."

"That's exactly right," I said. "Now, do you see why . . . "

"Don't say any more," she interrupted. "I see what you're getting at. Intelligence is the product of the interaction of genes and experience, and it is dumb to try to find how much comes from genes and how much comes from experience."

"And the same is true of any other behavioral trait," I added.

Several days later, the student strode into my office, reached into her pack, and pulled out a familiar object. "I believe that this is your mystery musical instrument," she said. "It's a Peruvian panpipe." She was right . . . again.

The point of this metaphor, in case you have forgotten, is to illustrate why it is nonsensical to try to understand interactions between two factors by asking how much each factor contributes. We would not ask how much the musician and how much the panpipe contributes to panpipe music; we would not ask how much the water and how much the temperature contributes to evaporation; and we would not ask how much the male and how much the female contributes to copulation. Similarly, we shouldn't ask how much genetic and experiential factors contribute to behavioral development. In each case, the answers lie in understanding the nature of the interactions (see Lederhendler & Schulkin, 2000; Newcombe, 2002; Rutter & Silberg, 2002).

The Heritability of Individual Differences

People differ from one another in complex psychological ways: Some are intelligent, some are nurturing, some are timid, and so on. What kind of person are you? This final subsection of this chapter discusses the degree to which psychological differences are the result of genetic, as opposed to experiential, differences.

Please pause and consider what I just said. Don't you have a problem with it? You just learned in the last subsection that a century of research on the nature–

nurture issue has revealed that that debate was misguided—that all developmental change is a product of the *interaction* of nature and nurture, not the sum of so much of one and so much of the other. Why then did I just tell you that this subsection is going to focus on the relative contributions of genes and experience to individual differences?

There does appear to be a contradiction here, but there isn't. You see, there are two productive ways of thinking about the contributions of nature and nurture to development. One way of thinking is useful when considering the development of individuals, and one way is useful for considering the development of differences among individuals. So far, you have learned that individual development is always the result of the interaction of nature and nurture. Now, you are going to learn about the influences of nature and nurture on individual differences. Let's return to the musician–panpipe metaphor for some help in understanding the two ways of thinking about the contributions of nature and nurture.

The music of an individual panpipe player is the product of the interaction of the musician and the panpipe, and it is nonsensical to ask what proportion of the music is produced by the musician and what proportion by the panpipe. However, if we measured the panpipe playing of a large sample of subjects, we could statistically estimate the degree to which the differences among them in the quality of their music resulted from differences in the subjects themselves as opposed to differences in their instruments. For example, if we selected 100 Peruvians at random and gave each a test on a professional-quality panpipe, we would likely find that most of the variation in the quality of the music resulted from differences in the subjects, some being experienced players and some never having played before. In the same way, researchers can select a group of subjects and ask what proportion of the variation among them in some attribute (e.g., intelligence) results from genetic differences as opposed to experiential differences. What do you think such studies have found?

To assess the relative contributions of genes and experience to the development of differences in psychological attributes, behavioral geneticists study individuals of known genetic similarity. For example, they often compare **identical twins** (monozygotic twins), who developed from the same zygote and thus are genetically identical, with **fraternal twins** (dizygotic twins), who developed from two zygotes and thus are no more similar than any pair of siblings. Studies of pairs of identical and fraternal twins who have been separated at infancy by adoption are particularly informative about the relative contributions of genetics and experience to differences in human psychological development. The most extensive of such studies is the Minnesota Study of Twins Reared Apart (see Bouchard & Pedersen, 1998).

The Minnesota Study of Twins Reared Apart involved 59 pairs of identical twins and 47 pairs of fraternal twins who had been reared apart, as well as many pairs of identical and fraternal twins who had been reared together. Their ages ranged from 19 to 68 years. Each twin was brought to the University of Minnesota for approximately 50 hours of testing, which focused on the assessment of intelligence and personality. Would the adult identical twins reared apart prove to be similar because they were genetically identical, or would they prove to be different because they had been brought up in different family environments?

The results of the Minnesota Study of Twins Reared Apart proved to be remarkably consistent—both internally, between the various cognitive and personality dimensions that were studied, and externally, with the findings of other, similar studies. In general, adult identical twins were substantially more similar to one another on every single psychological dimension than were adult fraternal twins, whether or not both twins of a pair were raised in the same family environment (see Turkheimer, 2000). General intelligence (as measured by the Wechsler Adult Intelligence Scale) has been the most widely studied psychological attribute of twins; Figure 1.17 on page 32 illustrates the general pattern of findings (see Bouchard, 1998).

Thinking Clearly

ON THE CD

Visit the *Twin Studies* module to learn about twin research.

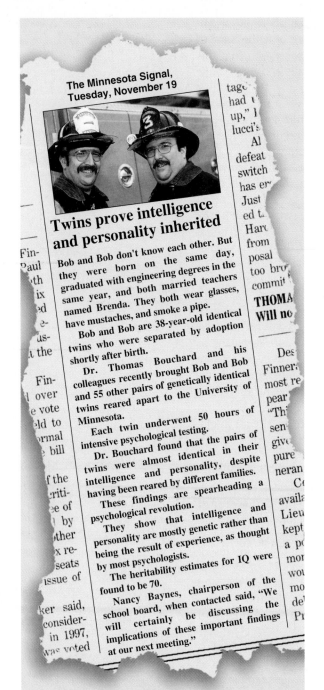

The Minnesota Signal,
Tuesday, November 19

Twins prove intelligence and personality inherited

Bob and Bob don't know each other. But they were born on the same day, graduated with engineering degrees in the same year, and both married teachers named Brenda. They both wear glasses, have mustaches, and smoke a pipe.

Bob and Bob are 38-year-old identical twins who were separated by adoption shortly after birth.

Dr. Thomas Bouchard and his colleagues recently brought Bob and Bob and 55 other pairs of genetically identical twins reared apart to the University of Minnesota.

Each twin underwent 50 hours of intensive psychological testing.

Dr. Bouchard found that the pairs of twins were almost identical in their intelligence and personality, despite having been reared by different families.

These findings are spearheading a psychological revolution.

They show that intelligence and personality are mostly genetic rather than being the result of experience, as thought by most psychologists.

The heritability estimates for IQ were found to be 70.

Nancy Baynes, chairperson of the school board, when contacted said, "We will certainly be discussing the implications of these important findings at our next meeting."

Thinking Clearly

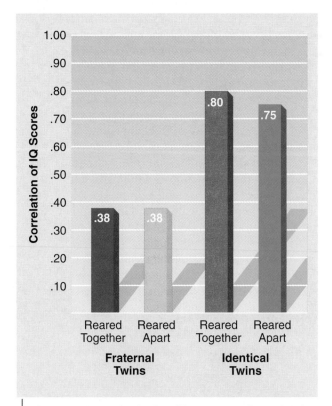

The correlation is the intelligence quotients (IQs) of identical and fraternal twins, reared together or apart.

Figure 1.17

The results of the Minnesota study have been widely disseminated by the popular press. Unfortunately, the meaning of the results has often been distorted. Sometimes, the misrepresentation of science by the popular press does not matter—at least not much. This is not one of those times. People's misbeliefs about the origins of human intelligence and personality are often translated into inappropriate and discriminatory social attitudes and practices. The adjacent newspaper story illustrates how the results of the Minnesota study have been misrepresented to the public.

The story is misleading in four ways. You should have no difficulty spotting the first: It oozes nature-or-nurture thinking and all of the misconceptions associated with it. Second, by focusing on the similarities between Bob and Bob, the story creates the impression that Bob and Bob (and the other monozygotic pairs of twins reared apart) are cognitively identical. They are not. It is easy to come up with a long list of similarities between any two people if one asks them enough questions and ignores the dissimilarities. Third, the story creates the impression that the results of the Minnesota study are revolutionary. On the contrary, the importance of the Minnesota study lies mainly in the fact that it constitutes a particularly thorough confirmation of the results of previous adoption studies. Fourth, and most important and relevant to our discussion, the story creates the false impression that the results of the Minnesota study make some general point about the relative contributions of genes and experience to the development of intelligence and personality in individuals. They do not, and neither do the results of any other adoption study. True, Bouchard and his colleagues estimated the heritability of IQ to be .70, but they did not conclude that IQ is 70% genetic. A **heritability estimate** is not about individual development; it is a numerical estimate of the proportion of variability that occurred in a particular trait in a particular study as a result of the genetic variation in that study (see Plomin & DeFries, 1998). Thus, heritability estimates tell us about the contribution of genetic differences to phenotypic differences among subjects; they have nothing to say about the relative contributions of genes and experience to the development of individuals.

Occasionally, students ask me to quantify the roles of nature and nurture in individual development. I always begin by explaining that their question tells me that they are a bit confused: The key point about individual development is that the contributions of nature and nurture are not additive (i.e., their influence cannot be reduced to so many parts nature and so many parts nurture). However, if students remain insistent that numbers will help them, I tell them to think of individual development as the product of 100% nature and 100% nurture.

The magnitude of a study's heritability estimate depends on the amount of genetic and environmental variation from which it was calculated, and it cannot be applied to other kinds of situations. For example, in the Minnesota study, there was relatively little environmental variation. All subjects were raised in industrialized countries (e.g., Great Britain, Canada, and the United States) by parents who could meet the standards required for adoption. Accordingly, most of the variation in the subjects' intelligence and personality is likely to have resulted from genetic variation. If the twins had instead been separately adopted into random families from a worldwide range of cultures and the entire spectrum of socioeconomic conditions, the resulting heritability estimates for IQ and personality would likely have been much lower.

Key Terms

ON THE CD

Studying for an exam? Get some help from the electronic flash cards of the key terms and the practice tests for this chapter.

chapter 1

Introduction to Biopsychology
How Biologists Think about Behavior

This chapter introduced you to the field of biopsychology and provided critical background information about evolution, about genetics, and about how biopsychologists think about the brain's role in psychological processes.

What Is Biopsychology?

Biopsychology is the scientific study of the biology of behavior. It is an important subdiscipline of neuroscience. Particularly important in this chapter was the explanation of how contemporary biopsychologists tend to think about behavior—see Figure 1.2. Biopsychologists often consider the environmental pressures that led to the evolution of certain behaviors and the genetic factors that contribute to their development. Thus, this chapter went on to focus on evolution and genetics.
(Pages 7–9)

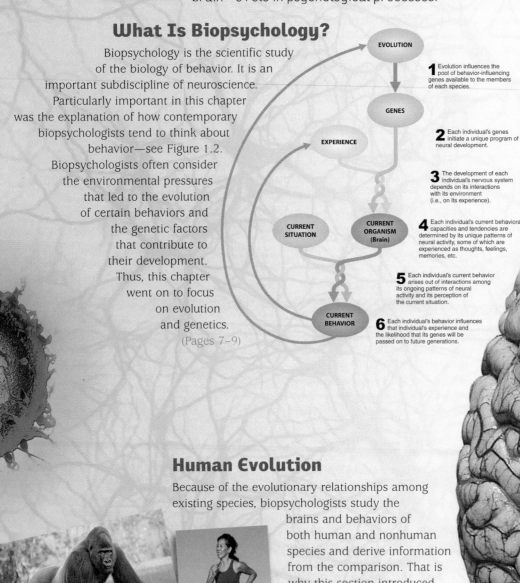

figure 1.2

1 Evolution influences the pool of behavior-influencing genes available to the members of each species.

2 Each individual's genes initiate a unique program of neural development.

3 The development of each individual's nervous system depends on its interactions with its environment (i.e., on its experience).

4 Each individual's current behavioral capacities and tendencies are determined by its unique patterns of neural activity, some of which are experienced as thoughts, feelings, memories, etc.

5 Each individual's current behavior arises out of interactions among its ongoing patterns of neural activity and its perception of the current situation.

6 Each individual's behavior influences that individual's experience and the likelihood that its genes will be passed on to future generations.

EVOLUTION

GENES

EXPERIENCE

CURRENT SITUATION

CURRENT ORGANISM (Brain)

CURRENT BEHAVIOR

Human Evolution

Because of the evolutionary relationships among existing species, biopsychologists study the brains and behaviors of both human and nonhuman species and derive information from the comparison. That is why this section introduced the fundamentals of evolution, emphasizing evolution of the human brain. Four common misconceptions about evolution were discussed: (1) that evolution is a ladder with humans at the top, (2) that current traits must be adaptive, (3) that the current function of a trait always indicates why it evolved, and (4) that similarities among species always indicate a common evolutionary origin. The evolution of the human brain was also discussed.
(Pages 9–19)

Primates

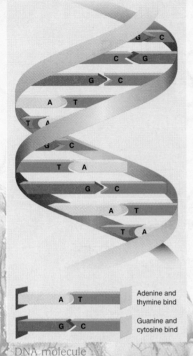

DNA molecule

Fundamental Genetics

After describing fundamental genetics, this section outlined the means by which the genetic code is transcribed onto sections of messenger RNA, which are then translated into proteins in the cytoplasm of cells. The section ended with a discussion of the human genome project and where it is going. Although we now have complete maps of the location of each human gene, we are still a long way from understanding how the genes interact with one another and with experience to influence human psychological traits.
(Pages 19–26)

Thinking about the Biology of Behavior: Mind–Brain and Nature–Nurture Issues

Heritability estimates

This section covered three important biopsychological issues. First was the mind–brain issue, and you learned that current evidence suggests that mental experience is the product of brain activity. Second was the nature–nurture issue (the question of the relative contributions of genetics and experience to individual development), and you learned that all individual development is the product of the interaction of genetics and experience—not the sum of so much of one and so much of the other. Finally, you learned that it is possible to calculate the degree to which genes and experience contribute to the differences in some trait (e.g., I.Q.) among a sample of individuals—and that the contribution of genes to the individual differences in some trait is called a heritability estimate.
(Pages 27–33)

Themes Revisited

Because the focus of this chapter was on how biopsychologists tend to think about key questions, it is not surprising that, of this book's four major themes, the thinking-clearly-about-biopsychology theme received the most attention. This chapter singled out several biopsychological issues about which there tends to be a lot of fuzzy thinking and tried to convince you that there are better ways to think about them. Thinking clearly tags encouraged you to sharpen up your thinking about human evolution, the implications of the human genome project, the mind–brain issue, the nature–nurture issue, and the role of genetics in the development of human psychological differences.

Two of this book's other themes were also marked by appropriate tags. The evolutionary perspective naturally received much attention in the section on human evolution. The clinical implications theme was illustrated by the cases of the man frozen in time and the man who fell out of bed.

The fourth theme, the cognitive neuroscience theme, becomes prominent in later chapters.

Think about It

1. Nature-or-nurture thinking about intelligence is sometimes used as an excuse for racial discrimination. How can the interactionist approach, which is championed in this chapter, be used as a basis for arguing against discriminatory practices?

2. Imagine that you are a biopsychology instructor. One of your students asks you whether depression is physiological or psychological. What would you say?

3. Embryos can now be screened for some genetic diseases. But what constitutes a disease? Should genetic testing be used to select a child's characteristics? If so, what characteristics?

4. In the year 2030, a major company demands that all executives take a genetic test. As a result, some lose their jobs, and others fail to qualify for health insurance. Discuss.

chapter 2

The Anatomy of the Brain
The Systems, Structures, and Cells That Make Up Your Nervous System

In order to understand what the brain does, it is first necessary to understand what it is—to know the names and locations of its major parts. This chapter introduces you to these fundamentals of brain *anatomy* (structure).

Before you begin this chapter, I want to apologize for the lack of foresight displayed by early neuroanatomists when they chose names for neuroanatomical structures—but, then, how could they have anticipated that Latin and Greek, universal languages of the educated in their day, would not be compulsory university fare in our time? To help you, I have provided the literal English meanings of many of the neuroanatomical terms, and I have kept this chapter as brief and to the point as possible by covering only the most important structures. Still, there is no denying that learning their names and locations will require considerable effort. I hope you find that the effort is worth it. When you have completed this chapter, you will have a better understanding of an organ that is the seat of your being, and you will have the knowledge of brain anatomy needed to begin to delve into modern behavioral neuroscience.

2.1 General Layout of the Nervous System

Divisions of the Nervous System

The vertebrate nervous system is composed of two divisions: the central nervous system and the peripheral nervous system (see Figure 2.1). Roughly speaking, the **central nervous system (CNS)** is the division of the nervous system that is located within the skull and spine; the **peripheral nervous system (PNS)** is the division that is located outside the skull and spine.

The central nervous system is composed of two divisions: the brain and the spinal cord. The *brain* is the part of the CNS that is located in the skull; the *spinal cord* is the part that is located in the spine.

The peripheral nervous system is also composed of two divisions: the somatic nervous system and the autonomic nervous system. The **somatic nervous system (SNS)** is the part of the PNS that interacts with the external environment. It is composed of **afferent nerves** that carry sensory signals from the skin, skeletal muscles, joints, eyes, ears, and so on, to the central nervous system, and **efferent nerves** that carry motor signals from the central nervous system to the skeletal muscles. The **autonomic nervous system (ANS)** is the part of the peripheral nervous system that regulates the body's internal environment. It is composed of afferent nerves that carry sensory signals from internal organs to the CNS and efferent nerves that carry motor signals from the CNS to internal organs. You will not confuse the terms *afferent* and *efferent* if you remember that many words that involve the idea of going toward something—in this case, going toward the CNS—begin with an *a* (e.g., *advance*, *approach*, *arrive*) and that many words that involve the idea of going away from something begin with an *e* (e.g., *exit*, *embark*, *escape*).

The autonomic nervous system has two kinds of efferent nerves: sympathetic nerves and parasympathetic

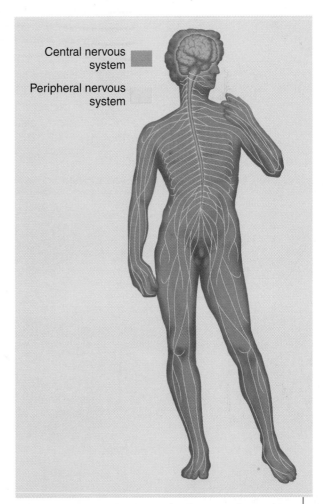

Central nervous system

Peripheral nervous system

The human central nervous system (CNS) and peripheral nervous system (PNS). The CNS is represented in red; the PNS in yellow. Notice that even those portions of nerves that are within the spinal cord are considered to be part of the PNS.

Figure 2.1

⊙N THE CD

You can review the differences between the efferent branches of the somatic and autonomic divisions of the PNS in the module titled *The Nervous System*. In particular, note the different transmitters used by the two divisions.

nerves. The **sympathetic nerves** are those autonomic motor nerves that project from the CNS in the *lumbar* (small of the back) and *thoracic* (chest area) regions of the spinal cord. The **parasympathetic nerves** are those autonomic motor nerves that project from the brain and *sacral* (lower back) region of the spinal cord. See Appendix I. (Ask your instructor to specify the degree to which you are responsible for material in the appendices.) All sympathetic and parasympathetic nerves are two-stage neural paths: The sympathetic and parasympathetic neurons project from the CNS and go only part of the way to the target organs before they *synapse* on other neurons (second-stage neurons) that carry the signals the rest of the way. However, the sympathetic and parasympathetic systems differ in that the sympathetic neurons that project from the CNS synapse on second-stage neurons at a substantial distance from their target organs, whereas the parasympathetic neurons that project from the CNS terminate near their target organs on very short second-stage neurons (see Appendix I).

The conventional view of the respective functions of the sympathetic and parasympathetic systems stresses three important principles: (1) that sympathetic nerves stimulate, organize, and mobilize energy resources in threatening situations, whereas parasympathetic nerves act to conserve energy; (2) that each autonomic target organ receives opposing sympathetic and parasympathetic input, and its activity is thus controlled by relative levels of sympathetic and parasympathetic activity; and (3) that sympathetic changes are indicative of psychological arousal, whereas parasympathetic changes are indicative of psychological relaxation. Although these principles are generally correct, there are significant exceptions to each of them (see Blessing, 1997; Hugdahl, 1996)—see Appendix II.

Most of the nerves of the peripheral nervous system project from the spinal cord, but there are 12 pairs of exceptions: the 12 pairs of **cranial nerves**, which project from the brain. They are numbered in sequence from front to back. The cranial

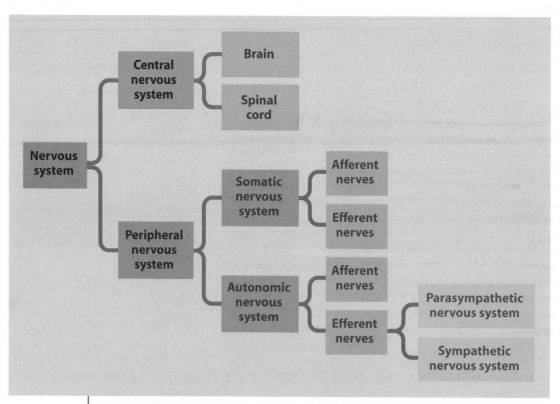

The major divisions of the nervous system. The 12 cranial nerves are part of the peripheral nervous system.

Figure 2.2

nerves include purely sensory nerves such as the olfactory nerves (I) and the optic nerves (II), but most contain both sensory and motor fibers. The longest cranial nerves are the vagus nerves (X), which contain motor and sensory fibers traveling to and from the gut. The 12 pairs of cranial nerves and their targets are illustrated in Appendix III; the functions of these nerves are listed in Appendix IV. The autonomic motor components of the cranial nerves are parasympathetic.

The functions of the various cranial nerves are commonly assessed by neurologists as a basis for diagnosis. Because the functions and locations of the cranial nerves are specific, disruptions of particular cranial nerve functions provide excellent clues about the location and extent of tumors and other kinds of brain pathology.

Clinical Implications

Figure 2.2 summarizes the major divisions of the nervous system. Notice that the nervous system is a "system of twos."

Meninges, Ventricles, and Cerebrospinal Fluid

The brain and spinal cord (the CNS) are the most protected organs in the body. They are encased in bone and covered by three protective membranes, the three **meninges** (pronounced "men-IN-gees"; the singular form of the word is *meninx*). See Figure 2.3.

Also protecting the CNS is the **cerebrospinal fluid (CSF)**, which fills the subarachnoid space, the central canal of the spinal cord, and the cerebral ventricles of the brain. The **central canal** is a small central channel that runs the length of the spinal cord; the **cerebral ventricles** are the four large internal chambers of the brain: the two lateral ventricles, the third ventricle, and the fourth ventricle (see Figure 2.4 on page 40). The subarachnoid space, central canal, and cerebral ventricles are interconnected by a series of openings and thus form a single reservoir.

The cerebrospinal fluid supports and cushions the brain. These functions are all too apparent to patients who have had some of their cerebrospinal fluid drained away; they suffer raging headaches and experience stabbing pain each time they jerk their heads.

Clinical Implications

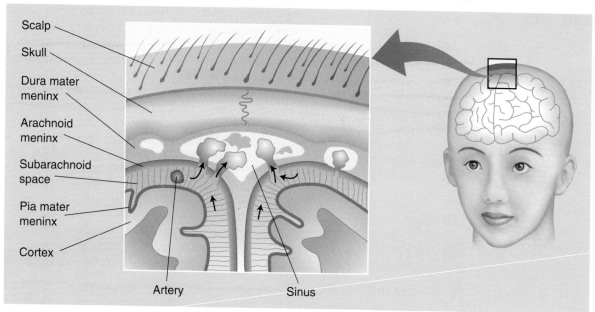

The absorption of cerebrospinal fluid from the subarachnoid space (blue) into a major sinus. Note the three meninges. (Note also that the singular of *meninges* is *meninx*.)

Figure 2.3

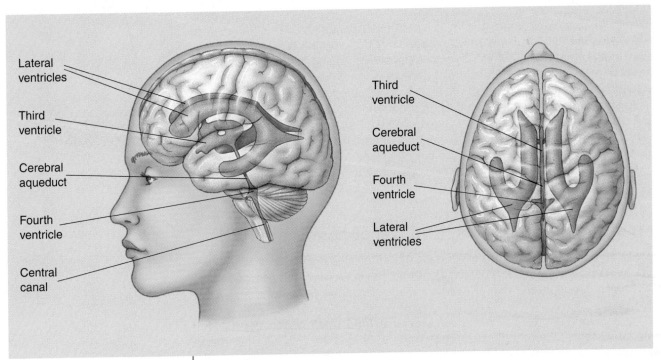

The cerebral ventricles.

Figure 2.4

Blood–Brain Barrier

The brain is a finely tuned electrochemical organ whose function can be severely disturbed by the introduction of certain kinds of chemicals. Fortunately, there is a mechanism that impedes the passage of many toxic substances from the blood into the brain: the **blood–brain barrier**. This barrier is a consequence of the special structure of cerebral blood vessels. In the rest of the body, the cells that compose the walls of blood vessels are loosely packed; as a result, most molecules pass readily through them into surrounding tissue. In the brain, however, the cells of the blood vessel walls are tightly packed, thus forming a barrier to the passage of many molecules—particularly proteins and other large molecules.

The blood–brain barrier does not impede the passage of all large molecules. Some large molecules that are critical for normal brain function (e.g., glucose) are actively transported through cerebral blood vessel walls. Also, the blood–brain barrier is not the same in all parts of the brain. For example, sex hormones, which have difficulty permeating some parts of the brain, readily enter those parts involved in sexual behavior.

2.2
Cells of the Nervous System

Most of the cells of the nervous system are of two fundamentally different types: neurons and glial cells. Their anatomy is discussed in this section.

Anatomy of Neurons

Neurons are cells that are specialized for the reception, conduction, and transmission of electrochemical signals. They come in an incredible variety of shapes and sizes (see

Maccaferri & Lacaille, 2003; Mott & Dingledine, 2003; Silberberg, Gupta, & Markram, 2002); however, many are similar to the one illustrated in Figures 2.5 and 2.6.

External Anatomy of Neurons. Figure 2.5 is an illustration of the major external features of one type of neuron. For your convenience, the definition of each feature is included in the illustration.

Internal Anatomy of Neurons. Figure 2.6 on page 42 is an illustration of the major internal features of one type of neuron. Again, the definition of each feature is included in the illustration.

ON THE CD

Want some help with the anatomy of neurons? Visit the *Learning the External Parts of a Neuron* module.

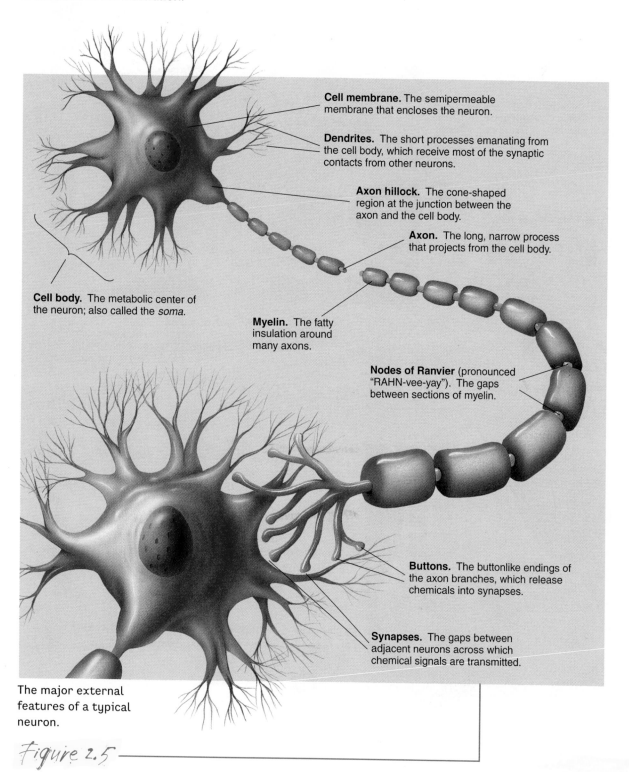

Cell membrane. The semipermeable membrane that encloses the neuron.

Dendrites. The short processes emanating from the cell body, which receive most of the synaptic contacts from other neurons.

Axon hillock. The cone-shaped region at the junction between the axon and the cell body.

Axon. The long, narrow process that projects from the cell body.

Cell body. The metabolic center of the neuron; also called the *soma*.

Myelin. The fatty insulation around many axons.

Nodes of Ranvier (pronounced "RAHN-vee-yay"). The gaps between sections of myelin.

Buttons. The buttonlike endings of the axon branches, which release chemicals into synapses.

Synapses. The gaps between adjacent neurons across which chemical signals are transmitted.

The major external features of a typical neuron.

Figure 2.5

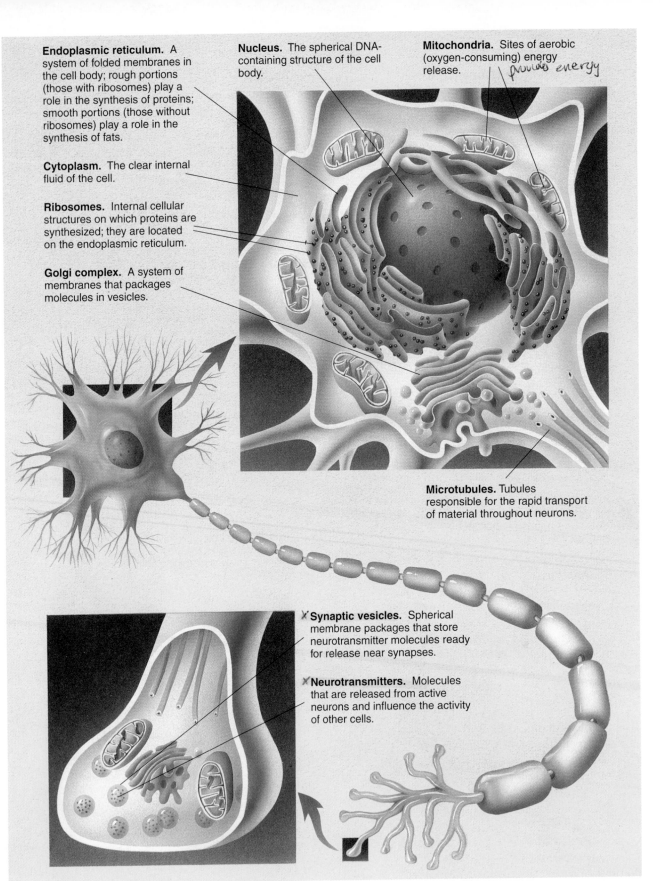

Endoplasmic reticulum. A system of folded membranes in the cell body; rough portions (those with ribosomes) play a role in the synthesis of proteins; smooth portions (those without ribosomes) play a role in the synthesis of fats.

Cytoplasm. The clear internal fluid of the cell.

Ribosomes. Internal cellular structures on which proteins are synthesized; they are located on the endoplasmic reticulum.

Golgi complex. A system of membranes that packages molecules in vesicles.

Nucleus. The spherical DNA-containing structure of the cell body.

Mitochondria. Sites of aerobic (oxygen-consuming) energy release. *provides energy*

Microtubules. Tubules responsible for the rapid transport of material throughout neurons.

Synaptic vesicles. Spherical membrane packages that store neurotransmitter molecules ready for release near synapses.

Neurotransmitters. Molecules that are released from active neurons and influence the activity of other cells.

The major internal features of a typical neuron.

Figure 2.6

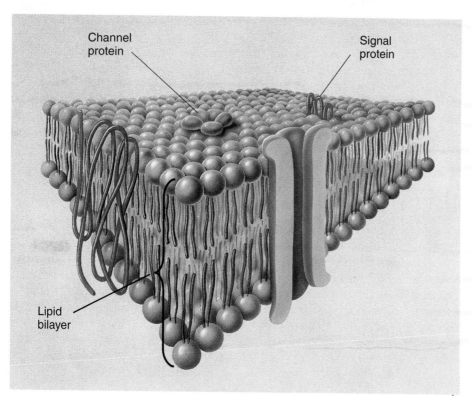

Channel protein

Signal protein

Lipid bilayer

The cell membrane is a lipid bilayer with signal proteins and channel proteins embedded in it.

Figure 2.7

Neuron Cell Membrane. The cell membrane of a neuron is composed of a *lipid bilayer*—two layers of fat molecules (see Figure 2.7). Embedded in the lipid bilayer are numerous protein molecules that are the basis of many of the cell membrane's functional properties. Some membrane proteins are *channel proteins*, through which certain molecules can pass; others are *signal proteins*, which transfer a signal to the inside of the neuron when particular molecules bind to them on the outside of the membrane.

Classes of Neurons. Figure 2.8 illustrates a way of classifying neurons that is based on the number of processes (i.e., projections) emanating from their cell bodies. A neuron with more than two processes extending from its cell body is classified as a **multipolar neuron**; most neurons are multipolar. A neuron with one process extending from its cell body is classified as a **unipolar neuron**, and a neuron with two processes extending from its cell body is classified as a **bipolar neuron**. Neurons with short axons or no axon at all are called **interneurons**; their

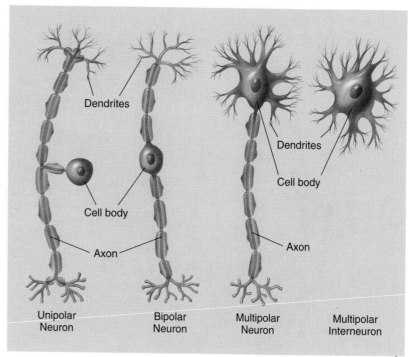

Dendrites

Cell body

Axon

Dendrites

Cell body

Axon

Unipolar Neuron

Bipolar Neuron

Multipolar Neuron

Multipolar Interneuron

A unipolar neuron, a bipolar neuron, a multipolar neuron, and an interneuron.

Figure 2.8

function is to integrate the neural activity within a single brain structure, not to conduct signals from one structure to another.

In general, there are two kinds of gross neural structures in the nervous system: those composed primarily of cell bodies and those composed primarily of axons. In the central nervous system, clusters of cell bodies are called **nuclei** (singular *nucleus*); in the peripheral nervous system, they are called **ganglia** (singular *ganglion*). (Note that the word *nucleus* has two different neuroanatomical meanings: It is a structure in the neuron cell body and a cluster of cell bodies in the CNS.) In the central nervous system, bundles of axons are called **tracts**; in the peripheral nervous system, they are called **nerves**.

Glial Cells: The Forgotten Majority

Neurons are not the only cells in the nervous system; the others are called **glial cells**. Glial cells outnumber neurons by 10 to 1.

There are four kinds of glial cells (Fields & Stevens-Graham, 2002). **Oligodendrocytes** are one class of glial cells; they send out extensions that wrap around the axons of some neurons of the central nervous system. These extensions are rich in *myelin*, a fatty insulating substance, and the myelin sheaths that they form increase the speed and efficiency of axonal conduction. A similar function is performed in the peripheral nervous system by **Schwann cells**, a second class of glial cells. Oligodendrocytes and Schwann cells are illustrated in Figure 2.9. Notice that each

Myelination in the Central Nervous System

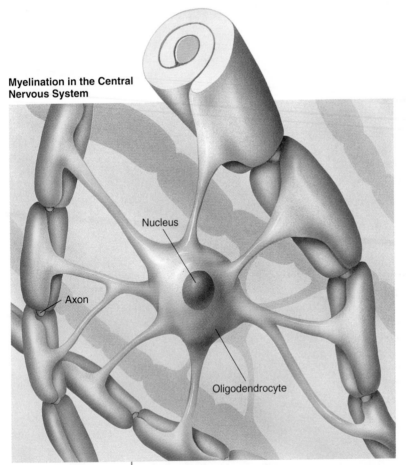

Nucleus

Axon

Oligodendrocyte

Myelination in the Peripheral Nervous System

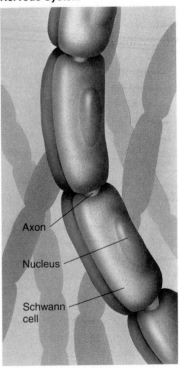

Axon

Nucleus

Schwann cell

The myelination of CNS axons by an oligodendrocyte and the myelination of PNS axons by Schwann cells.

Figure 2.9

Schwann cell constitutes one myelin segment, whereas each oligodendrocyte provides several myelin segments, often on more than one axon. Another important difference between Schwann cells and oligodendrocytes is that only Schwann cells can guide axonal *regeneration* (regrowth) after damage. That is why effective axonal regeneration in the mammalian nervous system is restricted to the PNS.

Astrocytes are a third class of glial cells. They are the largest glial cells, and they are so named because they are star-shaped (*astron* means "star"). The armlike extensions of some astrocytes cover the outer surfaces of blood vessels that course through the brain; they also make contact with neuron cell bodies (see Figure 2.10). These particular astrocytes play a role in the passage of chemicals from the blood into CNS neurons (i.e., they are part of the blood–brain barrier), but other astrocytes perform a variety of different functions.

Microglia are a fourth class of glial cells and the smallest of these cells. They respond to injury or disease by multiplying, engulfing cellular debris, and triggering inflammatory responses.

For decades, it was assumed that the function of glial cells was merely to provide support for neurons—providing them with nutrition, clearing waste, and forming a physical matrix to hold neural circuits together (*glia* means "glue"). But this limited view of the role of glial cells is rapidly disappearing. In the last few years, glial cells have been shown to participate in the transmission of signals by sending signals to neurons and receiving signals from them; they have been shown to control the establishment and maintenance of synapses between neurons; and they have been shown to participate in glial circuits (Haydon, 2001). Now that this wave of discoveries has focused neuroscientific attention on glial cells, appreciation of their role in nervous system function should increase quickly. These underappreciated supporting players are moving closer to center stage.

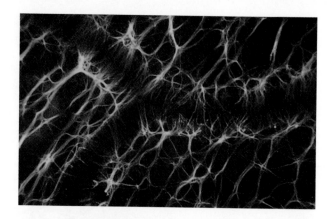

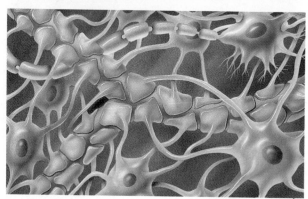

Astrocytes have an affinity for blood vessels, and they form a supportive matrix for neurons. The photograph on the top is of a slice of brain tissue stained with a glial stain; the unstained channels are blood vessels. The illustration on the bottom is a three-dimensional representation of the top image showing how the feet of astrocytes cover blood vessels and contact neurons. Compare the two images. (Photograph courtesy of T. Chan-Ling.)

Figure 2.10

2.3

Neuroanatomical Techniques and Directions

This section of the chapter introduces a few of the most common neuroanatomical techniques. Then, it explains the system of directions that neuroanatomists use to describe the location of structures in vertebrate nervous systems.

Some Neuroanatomical Techniques

The major problem in visualizing neurons is not their minuteness. The major problem is that neurons are so tightly packed and their axons and dendrites so intricately intertwined that looking through a microscope at unprepared neural tissue reveals almost nothing about them. The key to the study of neuroanatomy lies in preparing neural tissue in a variety of ways, each of which permits a clear view of a different aspect of neuronal structure, and then combining the knowledge obtained from each of the preparations. Researchers use the following neuroanatomical techniques.

Golgi Stain. The greatest blessing to befall neuroscience in its early years was the accidental discovery of the **Golgi stain** by Camillo Golgi (pronounced "GOLE-jee"), an Italian physician, in the early 1870s. Golgi was trying to stain the meninges, by exposing a block of neural tissue to potassium dichromate and silver nitrate, when he noticed an amazing thing. For some unknown reason, the silver chromate created by the chemical reaction of the two substances Golgi was using invaded only a few neurons in each slice of tissue and stained each invaded neuron entirely black. This selective staining made it possible to see individual neurons for the first time, although only in silhouette. (Stains that totally dye all neurons on a slide reveal nothing of their structure because the neurons are so tightly packed.) Golgi-stained neurons are presented in Figure 2.11. As you examine this figure and those that follow, remember that the neurons were once part of a living brain.

Nissl Stain. Although the Golgi stain permits an excellent view of the silhouettes of the few neurons that take up the stain, it provides no indication of the number of neu-

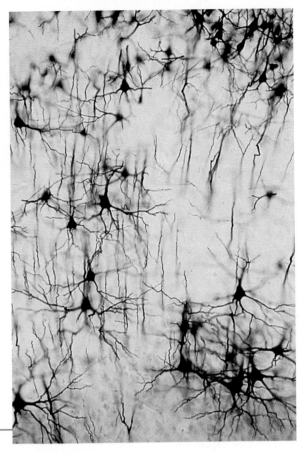

Neural tissue that has been stained by the Golgi method. Because only a few neurons take up the stain, their silhouettes are revealed in great detail, but their internal details are invisible. Usually, only part of a neuron is captured in a single slice.
(Ed Reschke © Peter Arnold, Inc.)

Figure 2.11

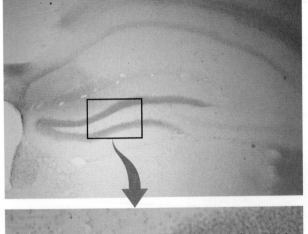

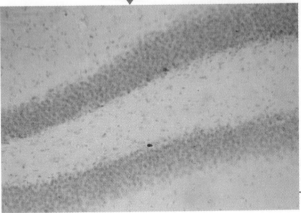

The Nissl stain. Presented here is a Nissl-stained coronal section through the rat hippocampus, at two levels of magnification to illustrate two uses of Nissl stains. Under low magnification (top panel), Nissl stains provide a gross indication of brain structure by selectively staining groups of neural cell bodies—in this case, the layers of the hippocampus. Under higher magnification (bottom panel), one can distinguish individual neural cell bodies and thus count the number of neurons in various areas.
(Courtesy of my good friends Carl Ernst and Brian Christie, Department of Psychology, University of British Columbia.)

Figure 2.12

rons in an area or the nature of their inner structure. The first neural staining procedure to overcome these shortcomings was the **Nissl stain**, which was developed by Franz Nissl, a German psychiatrist, in the 1880s. The most common dye used in the Nissl method is cresyl violet. Cresyl violet and other Nissl dyes penetrate all cells on a slide, but they bind effectively only to structures in neuron cell bodies. Thus, one can estimate the number of cell bodies in an area by counting the number of Nissl-stained dots. Figure 2.12 is a photograph of a slice of brain tissue stained with cresyl violet. Notice that only the layers composed mainly of neuron cell bodies are densely stained.

Electron Microscopy. A neuroanatomical technique that provides information about the details of neuronal structure is **electron microscopy** (pronounced "my-CROSS-cuh-pee"). Because of the nature of light, the limit of magnification in light microscopy is about 1,500 times, a level of magnification that is insufficient to reveal the fine anatomical details of neurons. Greater detail can be obtained by first coating thin slices of neural tissue with an electron-absorbing substance that is taken up by different parts of neurons to different degrees, then passing a beam of electrons through the tissue onto a photographic film. The result is an *electron micrograph*, which captures neuronal structure in exquisite detail (see Figure 3.8 on page 76). A *scanning electron microscope* provides spectacular electron micrographs in three dimensions (see Figure 2.13) but is not capable of as much magnification as a conventional electron microscope.

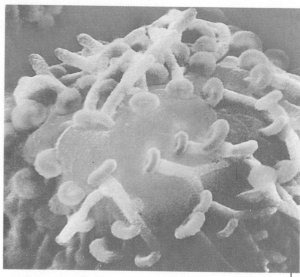

A color-enhanced scanning electron micrograph of a neuron cell body (green) studded with terminal buttons (orange). Each neuron receives numerous synaptic contacts.

(Courtesy of Jerold J. M. Chun, M.D., Ph.D.)

Figure 2.13

Directions in the Vertebrate Nervous System

It would be difficult for you to develop an understanding of the layout of an unfamiliar city without a system of directional coordinates: north–south, east–west. The same goes for the nervous system. Thus, before introducing you to the locations of major nervous system structures, I will describe the three-dimensional system of directional coordinates used by neuroanatomists.

Directions in the vertebrate nervous system are described in relation to the orientation of the spinal cord. This system is straightforward for most vertebrates, as Figure 2.14 indicates. The vertebrate nervous system has three axes:

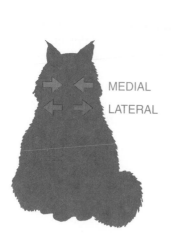

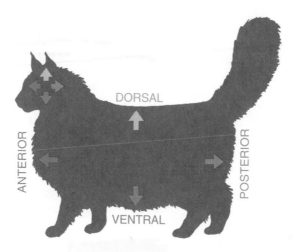

Anatomical directions in representative vertebrates, my cats Sambala and Rastaman.

Figure 2.14

Chapter 2 Anatomy of the Brain

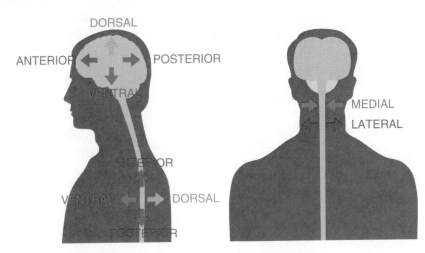

DORSAL

ANTERIOR ←→ POSTERIOR

VENTRAL

ANTERIOR

VENTRAL ←→ DORSAL

POSTERIOR

MEDIAL

LATERAL

Anatomical directions in a human. Notice that the directions in the cerebral hemispheres are rotated by 90° in comparison to those in the spinal cord and brain stem because of the unusual upright posture of humans.

Figure 2.15

anterior–posterior, dorsal–ventral, and medial–lateral. First, **anterior** means toward the nose end (the anterior end), and **posterior** means toward the tail end (the posterior end); these same directions are sometimes referred to as *rostral* and *caudal*, respectively. Second, **dorsal** means toward the surface of the back or the top of the head (the dorsal surface), and **ventral** means toward the surface of the chest or the bottom of the head (the ventral surface). Third, **medial** means toward the midline of the body, and **lateral** means away from the midline toward the body's lateral surfaces.

We humans complicate this simple three-axis (anterior–posterior, ventral–dorsal, medial–lateral) system of neuroanatomical directions by insisting on walking around on our hind legs. This changes the orientation of our cerebral hemispheres in relation to our spines and brain stems.

You can save yourself a lot of confusion if you remember that the system of vertebrate neuroanatomical directions was adapted for use in humans in such a way that the terms used to describe the positions of various body surfaces are the same in humans as they are in more typical, non-upright vertebrates. Specifically, notice that the top of the human head and the back of the human body are both referred to as *dorsal* even though they are in different directions, and the bottom of the human head and the front of the human body are both referred to as *ventral* even though they are in different directions (see Figure 2.15). To circumvent this complication, the terms **superior** and **inferior** are often used to refer to the top and bottom of the primate head, respectively.

Proximal and distal are two other common directional terms. In general, *proximal* means "close," and *distal* means "far." Specifically, with regard to the peripheral nervous system, *proximal* means closer to the CNS, and *distal* means farther from the CNS—for example, the nerve terminals of the shoulders are proximal to those of the fingers.

In the next few pages, you will be seeing drawings of sections (slices) of the brain cut in one of three different planes: **horizontal sections**, **frontal** (also termed *coronal*) **sections**, and **sagittal sections**. These three planes are illustrated in Figure 2.16. A section cut down the center of the brain, between the two hemispheres, is called a *midsagittal section*. A section cut at a right angle to any long, narrow structure, such as the spinal cord or a nerve, is called a **cross section**.

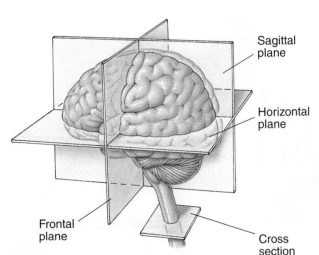

Sagittal plane

Horizontal plane

Frontal plane

Cross section

Horizontal, frontal (coronal), and sagittal planes in the human brain and a cross section of the human spinal cord.

Figure 2.16

Scan your Brain

This is a good place for you to pause to scan your brain. Are you ready to proceed to the structures of the brain and spinal cord? Test your grasp of the preceding sections of this chapter by drawing a line between each term in the left column and the appropriate phrase in the right column. The correct answers are provided below. Before proceeding, review material related to your incorrect answers.

1. Autonomic nervous system
2. Cerebral aqueduct
3. Axon hillock
4. Dorsal
5. Cell membrane
6. Cranial nerves
7. Superior or dorsal
8. Cell body
9. Synaptic vesicles
10. Oligodendrocytes
11. Nissl
12. Meninges
13. Midsagittal section
14. Golgi

a. Packets of neurotransmitter molecules
b. PNS minus the somatic nervous system
c. Connects the third and fourth ventricles
d. Stains cell bodies
e. Top of a vertebrate's head
f. Protective membranes
g. Between cell body and axon
h. Contains the nucleus of a neuron
i. Olfactory, optic, and vagus
j. Myelinate CNS axons
k. A slice down the center of the brain
l. Top of the primate head
m. Silhouette
n. Lipid bilayer

Scan Your Brain answers: (1) b, (2) c, (3) g, (4) e, (5) n, (6) i, (7) l, (8) h, (9) a, (10) j, (11) d, (12) f, (13) k, (14) m

2.4

The Spinal Cord

In the first three sections of this chapter, you learned about the divisions of the nervous system, the cells that compose it, and some of the neuroanatomical techniques that are used to study it. This section begins your ascent of the human CNS by focusing on the spinal cord. The final two sections of the chapter focus on the brain.

In cross section, it is apparent that the spinal cord comprises two different areas (see Figure 2.17): an inner H-shaped core of gray matter and a surrounding area of white matter. *Gray matter* is composed largely of cell bodies and unmyelinated interneurons, whereas *white matter* is composed largely of myelinated axons. (It is the myelin that gives the white matter its glossy white sheen.) The two dorsal arms of the spinal gray matter are called the **dorsal horns**, and the two ventral arms are called the **ventral horns**.

Pairs of *spinal nerves* are attached to the spinal cord—one on the left and one on the right—at 31 different levels of the spine. Each of these 62 spinal nerves divides as it

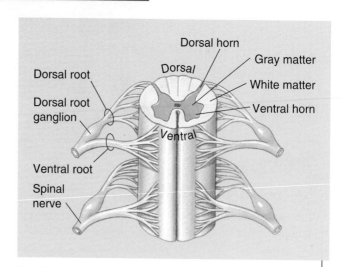

The dorsal and ventral roots of the spinal cord.

Figure 2.17

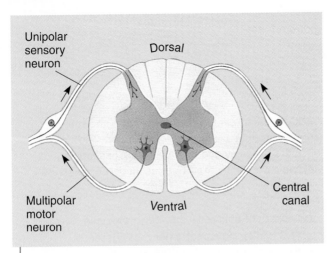

A schematic cross section of the spinal cord.

Figure 2.18

nears the cord (see Figure 2.17), and its axons are joined to the cord via one of two roots: the *dorsal root* or the *ventral root*.

All dorsal root axons, whether somatic or autonomic, are sensory (afferent) unipolar neurons with their cell bodies grouped together just outside the cord to form the *dorsal root ganglia*. Many of their synaptic terminals are in the dorsal horns of the spinal gray matter (see Figure 2.18). In contrast, the neurons of the ventral root are motor (efferent) multipolar neurons with their cell bodies in the ventral horns. Those that are part of the somatic nervous system project to skeletal muscles; those that are part of the autonomic nervous system project to ganglia (i.e., to clusters of neuron cell bodies in the PNS), where they synapse on neurons that in turn project to internal organs (heart, stomach, liver, etc.). See Appendix I.

2.5
The Five Divisions of the Brain

As you read earlier, learning your way around the brain is like learning your way around an unfamiliar city. In both cases, you need a system of directional coordinates, and you have just learned the coordinates used to identify locations in the brain. Also, in both cases, you need to learn the name of the major neighborhoods or divisions. Those who possess this information can easily communicate the general location of any destination in the city. This section of the chapter introduces you to the five "neighborhoods," or divisions, of the brain—for much the same reason.

To understand why the brain is considered to have five divisions, it is necessary to understand its early development (see Swanson, 2000). In the vertebrate embryo, the tissue that eventually develops into the CNS is recognizable as a fluid-filled tube (see Figure 2.19). The first indications of the developing brain are three swellings that occur at the anterior end of this tube. These three swellings eventually develop into the adult *forebrain, midbrain*, and *hindbrain*.

Before birth, the initial three swellings in the neural tube become five (see Figure 2.19). This occurs because the forebrain swelling grows into two different swellings, and so does the hindbrain swelling. From anterior to posterior, the five swellings that compose the developing brain at birth are the *telencephalon*, the *diencephalon*, the *mesencephalon* (or midbrain), the *metencephalon*, and the *myelencephalon* (*encephalon* means "within the head"). These swellings ulti-

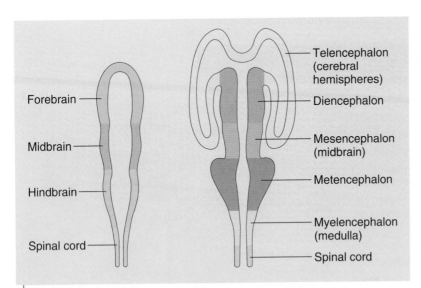

The early development of the mammalian brain illustrated in schematic horizontal sections. Compare with the adult human brain in Figure 2.20.

Figure 2.19

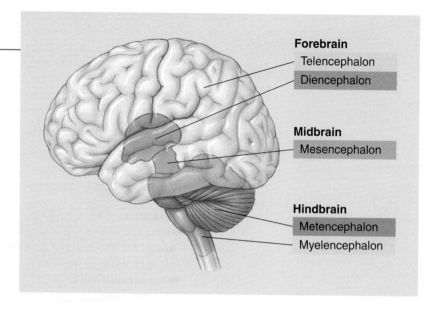

Forebrain
Telencephalon
Diencephalon

Midbrain
Mesencephalon

Hindbrain
Metencephalon
Myelencephalon

mately develop into the five divisions of the adult brain. As a student, I memorized their order by remembering that the *tel*encephalon is on the *top* and the other four divisions are arrayed below it in alphabetical order.

Figure 2.20 illustrates the locations of the telencephalon, diencephalon, mesencephalon, metencephalon, and myelencephalon in the adult human brain. Notice that in humans, as in other higher vertebrates, the telencephalon (the left and right *cerebral hemispheres*) undergoes the greatest growth during development. The other four divisions of the brain are often referred to collectively as the **brain stem**—the stem on which the cerebral hemispheres sit. The myelencephalon is often referred to as the *medulla*.

2.6

NOT on First exam

Major Structures of the Brain

Now that you have learned the five major divisions of the brain, it is time to introduce you to their major structures. This section of the chapter begins its survey of brain structures in the myelencephalon, then ascends through the other divisions to the telencephalon. The brain structures boldfaced and defined in this section are not only included in the Key Terms list at the end of the chapter but are also arranged according to their locations in the brain in Figure 2.29 on page 58.

Here is a reminder before you delve into the anatomy of the brain: The directional coordinates are the same for the brain stem as for the spinal cord, but they are rotated by 90° for the forebrain.

Myelencephalon

Not surprisingly, the **myelencephalon** (or **medulla**), the most posterior division of the brain, is composed largely of tracts carrying signals between the rest of the brain and the body. An interesting part of the myelencephalon from a psychological perspective is the **reticular formation** (see Figure 2.21). It is a complex network of

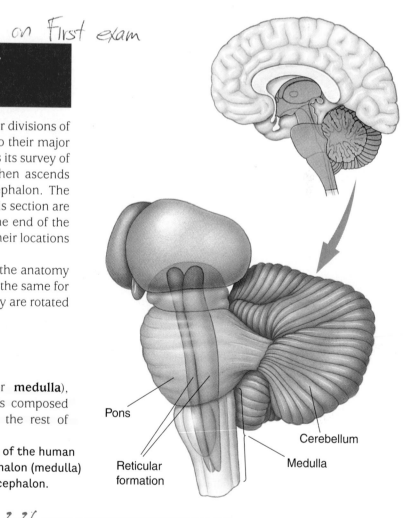

Structures of the human myelencephalon (medulla) and metencephalon.

Figure 2.21

Pons

Reticular formation

Cerebellum

Medulla

about 100 tiny nuclei that occupies the central core of the brain stem from the posterior boundary of the myelencephalon to the anterior boundary of the midbrain. It is so named because of its netlike appearance (*reticulum* means "little net"). Sometimes, the reticular formation is referred to as the *reticular activating system* because parts of it seem to play a role in arousal. However, the various nuclei of the reticular formation are involved in a variety of functions—including sleep, attention, movement, the maintenance of muscle tone, and various cardiac, circulatory, and respiratory reflexes. Indeed, damage to this part of the myelencephalon is often life-threatening.

Metencephalon

The **metencephalon**, like the myelencephalon, houses many ascending and descending tracts and part of the reticular formation. These structures create a bulge, called the **pons**, on the brain stem's ventral surface. The pons is one major division of the metencephalon; the other is the cerebellum (little brain)—see Figure 2.21. The **cerebellum** is the large, convoluted structure on the brain stem's dorsal surface. It is an important sensorimotor structure; cerebellar damage elim-

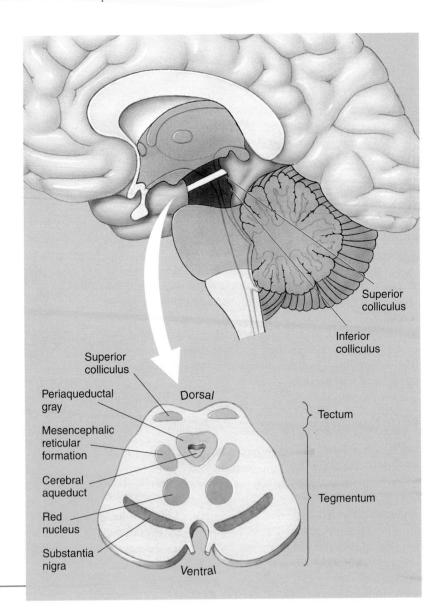

The human mesencephalon (midbrain).

Figure 2.22

inates the ability to precisely control one's movements and to adapt them to changing conditions.

Mesencephalon

The **mesencephalon**, like the metencephalon, has two divisions. The two divisions of the mesencephalon are the tectum and the tegmentum (see Figure 2.22). The **tectum** (roof) is the dorsal surface of the midbrain. In mammals, the tectum is composed of two pairs of bumps, the *colliculi* (little hills). The posterior pair, called the **inferior colliculi**, have an auditory function; the anterior pair, called the **superior colliculi**, have a visual function.

The **tegmentum** is the division of the mesencephalon ventral to the tectum. In addition to the reticular formation and tracts of passage, the tegmentum contains three colorful structures that are of particular interest to biopsychologists: the periaqueductal gray, the substantia nigra, and the red nucleus (see Figure 2.22). The **periaqueductal gray** is the gray matter situated around the **cerebral aqueduct**, the duct connecting the third and fourth ventricles; it is of special interest because of its role in mediating the analgesic (pain-reducing) effects of opiate drugs (e.g., morphine and heroin). The **substantia nigra** (black substance) and the **red nucleus** are both important components of the sensorimotor system.

Diencephalon

The **diencephalon** is composed of two structures: the thalamus and the hypothalamus (see Figure 2.23). The **thalamus** is the large, two-lobed structure that constitutes the top of the brain stem. One lobe sits on each side of the third ventricle, and the two lobes are joined by the **massa intermedia**, which runs through the ventricle.

The thalamus comprises many different pairs of nuclei, most of which project to the cortex. Several are *sensory relay nuclei*—nuclei that receive signals from sensory receptors, process the signals, and then transmit them to the appropriate areas of sensory cortex. For example, the **lateral geniculate nuclei** are visual sensory relay nuclei. The organization of the thalamus is illustrated in Appendix V.

The **hypothalamus** is located just below the anterior thalamus (*hypo* means "below")—see Figure 2.24 on page 54. It plays an important role in the regulation of several motivated behaviors. It exerts its

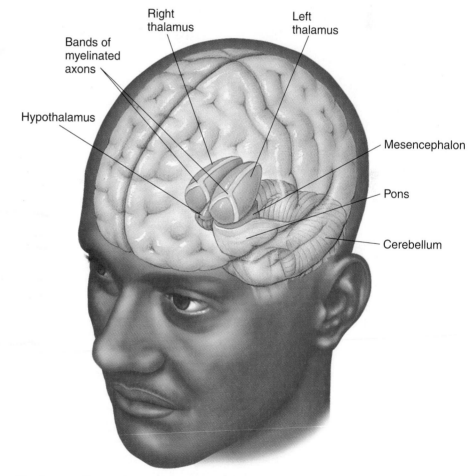

The human diencephalon comprises the thalamus and the hypothalamus.

Figure 2.23

effects in part by regulating the release of hormones from the **pituitary gland**, which dangles from it on the ventral surface of the brain. The literal meaning of *pituitary gland* is "snot gland"; it was discovered in a gelatinous state behind the nose of an unembalmed cadaver and was incorrectly assumed to be the main source of nasal mucus.

In addition to the pituitary gland, two other structures are obvious on the inferior surface of the hypothalamus: the optic chiasm and the mammillary bodies (see Figure 2.24). The **optic chiasm** is the point at which the *optic nerves* from each eye come together. The X shape is created because some of the axons of the optic nerve **decussate** (cross over to the other side of the brain) via the optic chiasm. The decussating fibers are said to be **contralateral** (projecting from one side of the body to the other), and the nondecussating fibers are said to be **ipsilateral** (staying on the same side of the body). The **mammillary bodies**, which are often considered to be part of the hypothalamus, are a pair of spherical nuclei located on the inferior surface of the hypothalamus, just behind the pituitary. The locations of the mammillary bodies and the other nuclei of the hypothalamus are illustrated in Appendix VI.

Telencephalon

The **telencephalon**, the largest division of the human brain, mediates the brain's most complex functions. It initiates voluntary movement, interprets sensory input, and mediates complex cognitive processes such as learning, speaking, and problem solving.

Cerebral Cortex. The cerebral hemispheres are covered by a layer of tissue called the **cerebral cortex** (cerebral bark). In humans, the cerebral cortex is deeply *convoluted* (furrowed)—see Figure 2.25. The *convolutions* have the effect of increasing the amount of cerebral cortex without increasing the overall volume of the brain. Not all mammals have convoluted cortexes; most mammals are *lissencephalic* (smooth-brained). It was once believed that the number and size of cortical convolutions determined a species' intellectual capacities; however, the number and size of cortical convolutions appear to be related more to body size. Every large mammal has an extremely convoluted cortex.

The large furrows in a convoluted cortex are called **fissures**, and the small ones are called *sulci* (singular *sulcus*). The ridges between fissures and sulci are called **gyri** (singular *gyrus*). It is apparent in Figure 2.25 that the cerebral hemispheres are al-

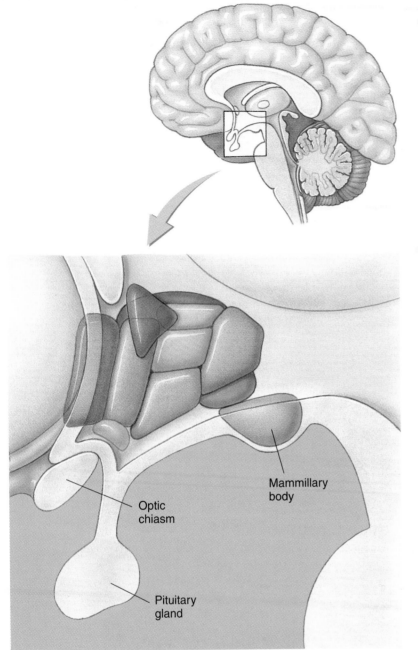

The human hypothalamus in relation to the optic chiasm and the pituitary gland. Each color represents a different nucleus of the hypothalamus.

Figure 2.24

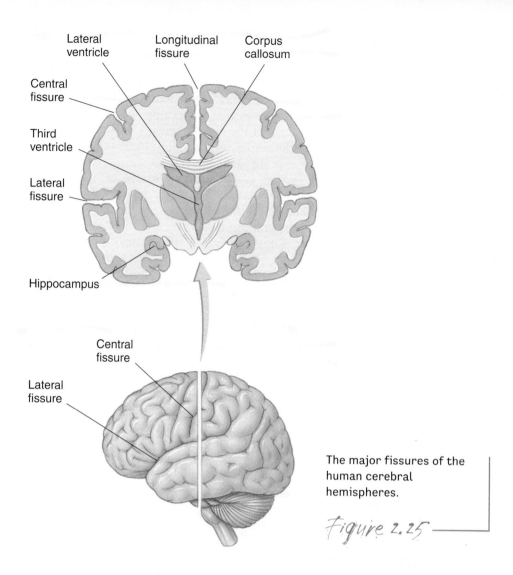

Lateral ventricle
Longitudinal fissure
Corpus callosum
Central fissure
Third ventricle
Lateral fissure
Hippocampus

Central fissure
Lateral fissure

The major fissures of the human cerebral hemispheres.

Figure 2.25

most completely separated by the largest of the fissures: the **longitudinal fissure**. The cerebral hemispheres are directly connected by only a few tracts spanning the longitudinal fissure; these hemisphere-connecting tracts are called **cerebral commissures**. The largest cerebral commissure, the **corpus callosum**, is clearly visible in Figure 2.25.

As Figure 2.26 on page 56 indicates, the two major landmarks on the lateral surface of each hemisphere are the **central fissure** and the **lateral fissure**. These fissures partially divide each hemisphere into four lobes: the **frontal lobe**, the **parietal lobe** (pronounced "pa-RYE-e-tal"), the **temporal lobe**, and the **occipital lobe** (pronounced "ok-SIP-i-tal"). Among the largest gyri are the **precentral gyri**, which contain motor cortex; the **postcentral gyri**, which contain somatosensory (body-sensation) cortex; and the **superior temporal gyri**, which contain auditory cortex. The function of occipital cortex is entirely visual.

About 90% of human cerebral cortex is **neocortex** (new cortex); that is, it is six-layered cortex of relatively recent evolution (Northcutt & Kaas, 1995). By convention, the layers of neocortex are numbered I through VI, starting at the surface. There are two fundamentally different kinds of neurons in the neocortex: pyramidal (pyramid-shaped) cells and stellate (star-shaped) cells. **Pyramidal cells** are large multipolar neurons with pyramid-shaped cell bodies, a large dendrite called an *apical dendrite* that extends from the apex of the pyramid straight toward the cortex surface, and a very long axon (see Figure 2.30 on page 59). In contrast, *stellate cells* are small star-shaped interneurons (neurons with short axons or no axon).

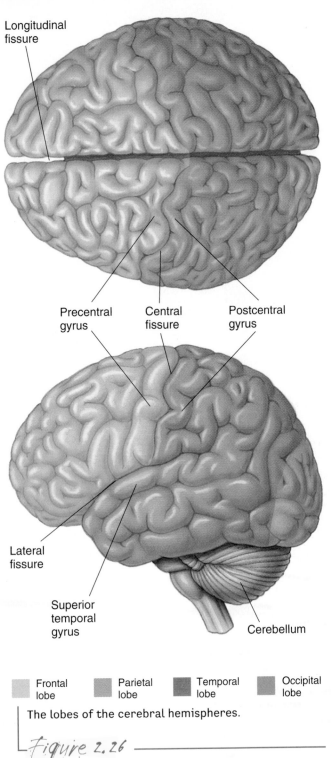

Longitudinal
fissure

Precentral
gyrus

Central
fissure

Postcentral
gyrus

Lateral
fissure

Superior
temporal
gyrus

Cerebellum

■ Frontal
lobe

■ Parietal
lobe

■ Temporal
lobe

■ Occipital
lobe

The lobes of the cerebral hemispheres.

Figure 2.26

The 10% of the cerebral cortex that is not neocortex has fewer than six layers and is thought to be of more primitive evolutionary origin. One area of primitive cortex that has been the focus of much research is the **hippocampus**, which is thought to play a major role in memory. The hippocampus is located at the medial edge of the cerebral cortex as it folds back on itself in the medial temporal lobe (refer to Figure 2.25). Notice that this folding produces a shape that is, in cross section, somewhat reminiscent of a sea horse: *Hippocampus* means "sea horse." Another area of primitive cortex is the cingulate cortex. Both the hippocampus and the cingulate cortex are considered to be part of the limbic system.

Limbic System. The **limbic system** is a circuit of midline brain structures that circle the thalamus (*limbic* means "ring"). The limbic system is involved in the regulation of motivated behaviors—including the four *F*s of motivation: fleeing, feeding, fighting, and sexual behavior. (This joke is as old as biopsychology itself, but it is a good one.) In addition to the two cortical structures about which you have just read (hippocampus and cingulate cortex), the limbic system includes the following subcortical structures: the mammillary bodies, the amygdala, the fornix, and the septum.

Let's begin tracing the limbic circuit (see Figure 2.27) at the **amygdala**—the almond-shaped nucleus in the anterior temporal lobe (*amygdala*, pronounced "a-MIG-dah-lah," means "almond")—see Swanson and Petrovich (1998). Posterior to the amygdala is the hippocampus, which runs beneath the thalamus in the medial temporal lobe. Next in the ring are the cingulate cortex and the fornix. The **cingulate cortex** is the large area of neocortex in the **cingulate gyrus** on the medial surface of the cerebral hemispheres, just superior to the corpus callosum; it encircles the dorsal thalamus (*cingulate* means "encircling"). The **fornix**, the major tract of the limbic system, also encircles the dorsal thalamus; it leaves the dorsal end of the hippocampus and sweeps forward in an arc coursing along the superior surface of the third ventricle and terminating in the septum and mammillary bodies (*fornix* means "arc"). The **septum** is a midline nucleus that is located at the anterior tip of the cingulate cortex. Several tracts connect the septum and mammillary bodies with the amygdala and hippocampus, thereby completing the limbic ring.

Basal Ganglia. The **basal ganglia** are a group of subcortical structures that play an important role in voluntary movement. They are illustrated in Figure 2.28. As we did with the limbic system, let's begin our examination of the basal ganglia with the amygdala, which is considered to be part of both systems. Sweeping out of each amygdala, first in a posterior direction and then in an anterior direction, is the long tail-like **caudate** (*caudate* means "tail-like"). Each caudate forms an almost complete circle; in its center, connected to it by a series of fiber bridges, is the **putamen** (pronounced "pew-TAY-men"). Together, the caudate and the putamen, which both have a striped appearance, are known as the **striatum** (striped structure). The remaining structure of the basal ganglia is the pale circular structure known as the **globus pallidus** (pale globe). The globus pallidus is located medial to the putamen, between the putamen and the thalamus.

Because the basal ganglia are involved in the regulation of movement, damage to these subcortical structures is associated with motor disorders. Of particular interest in this context is a pathway that projects to the striatum from the substantia nigra of the midbrain. *Parkinson's disease*, a disorder that is characterized by rigidity, tremors, and poverty of voluntary movement, is associated with the deterioration of this pathway.

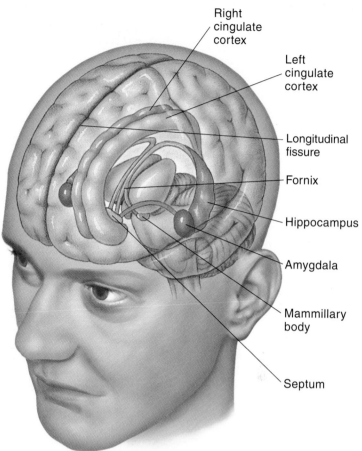

The major structures of the limbic system: amygdala, hippocampus, cingulate cortex, fornix, septum, and mammillary body.

Figure 2.27

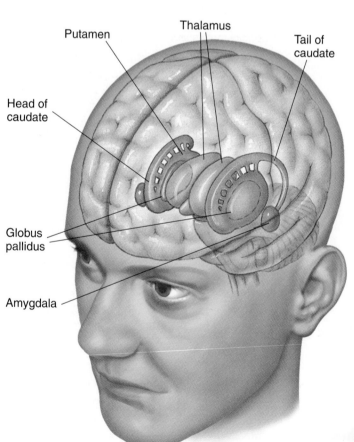

The basal ganglia: amygdala, striatum (caudate plus putamen), and globus pallidus. Notice that, in this view, the right globus pallidus is largely hidden behind the right thalamus, and the left globus pallidus is totally hidden behind the left putamen.

Figure 2.28

The major brain divisions and structures are summarized in Figure 2.29, which organizes all the terms that have appeared in boldface in this section. These are structures that you will repeatedly encounter throughout this text: Learn them.

Telencephalon	Cerebral cortex	Neocortex Hippocampus
	Major fissures	Central fissure Lateral fissure Longitudinal fissure
	Major gyri	Precentral gyrus Postcentral gyrus Superior temporal gyrus Cingulate gyrus
	Four lobes	Frontal lobe Temporal lobe Parietal lobe Occipital lobe
	Limbic system	Amygdala Hippocampus Fornix Cingulate cortex Septum Mammillary bodies
	Basal ganglia	Amygdala Caudate } Putamen } Striatum Globus pallidus
	Cerebral commissures	Corpus callosum
Diencephalon	Thalamus	Massa intermedia Lateral geniculate nuclei
	Hypothalamus	Mammillary bodies
	Optic chiasm	
	Pituitary gland	
Mesencephalon	Tectum	Superior colliculi Inferior colliculi
	Tegmentum	Reticular formation Cerebral aqueduct Periaqueductal gray Substantia nigra Red nucleus
Metencephalon	Reticular formation Pons Cerebellum	
Myelencephalon or Medulla	Reticular formation	

Summary of major brain structures. This display contains all the brain anatomy terms that appear in boldface in Section 2.6.

Figure 2.29

I end this chapter with Figure 2.30, for reasons that too often get lost in the shuffle of neuroanatomical terms and technology. I have included this image here to illustrate the beauty of the brain and the art of those who study its structure. I hope you are inspired by it. I wonder what thoughts these neural circuits once produced.

The art of neuroanatomical staining. This slide was stained with both a Golgi stain and a Nissl stain. Clearly visible on the Golgi-stained pyramidal neurons are the pyramid-shaped cell bodies, the large apical dendrites, and numerous dendritic spines. Each pyramidal cell has a long, narrow axon, which projects off the bottom of the slide.

(Courtesy of Miles Herkenham, Unit of Functional Neuroanatomy, National Institute of Mental Health, Bethesda, MD.)

Figure 2.30

Scan your Brain

If you have not previously studied the gross anatomy of the brain, your own brain is probably straining under the burden of new terms. To determine whether you are ready to proceed to the next chapter, scan your brain by labeling the following midsagittal view of a real human brain. (It will be challenging to switch from color-coded diagrams to a photograph.)

The correct answers are provided below. Before proceeding, review material related to your errors and omissions. Remember that Figure 2.29 includes all the brain anatomy terms that have appeared in bold type in this section and thus is an excellent review tool.

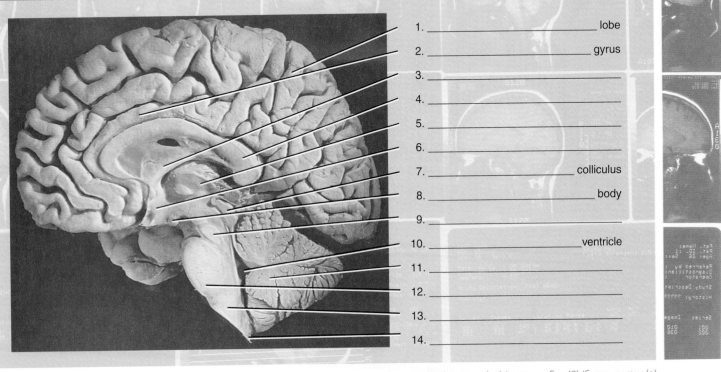

1. _____ lobe
2. _____ gyrus
3. _____
4. _____
5. _____
6. _____
7. _____ colliculus
8. _____ body
9. _____
10. _____ ventricle
11. _____
12. _____
13. _____
14. _____

Scan Your Brain answers: (1) parietal, (2) cingulate, (3) fornix, (4) corpus callosum, (5) thalamus, (6) hypothalamus, (7) superior, (8) mammillary, (9) tegmentum, (10) fourth, (11) cerebellum, (12) pons, (13) medulla, or myelencephalon, (14) spinal cord

Key Terms

2.1 General Layout of the Nervous System

Afferent nerves (p. 37)
Autonomic nervous system (ANS) (p. 37)
Blood–brain barrier (p. 40)
Central canal (p. 39)
Central nervous system (CNS) (p. 37)
Cerebral ventricles (p. 39)
Cerebrospinal fluid (CSF) (p. 39)
Cranial nerves (p. 38)
Efferent nerves (p. 37)
Meninges (p. 39)
Parasympathetic nerves (p. 38)

Peripheral nervous system (PNS) (p. 37)
Somatic nervous system (SNS) (p. 37)
Sympathetic nerves (p. 38)

2.2 Cells of the Nervous System

Astrocytes (p. 45)
Bipolar neuron (p. 43)
Ganglia (p. 44)
Glial cells (p. 44)
Interneurons (p. 43)
Microglia (p. 45)
Multipolar neuron (p. 43)

Nerves (p. 44)
Nuclei (p. 44)
Oligodendrocytes (p. 44)
Schwann cells (p. 44)
Tracts (p. 44)
Unipolar neuron (p. 43)

2.3 Neuroanatomical Techniques and Directions

Anterior (p. 48)
Cross section (p. 48)
Dorsal (p. 48)
Electron microscopy (p. 47)

ON THE CD

Studying for an exam? Get some help from the electronic flash cards of the key terms and the practice tests for this chapter.

chapter 2

Anatomy of the Brain
The Systems, Structures, and Cells That Make Up Your Nervous System

This chapter introduced you to the structure of the human brain. Why? Because before you can begin to consider how the human brain works, you need a general idea of its parts. And you need to know the names of the parts before you can discuss them.

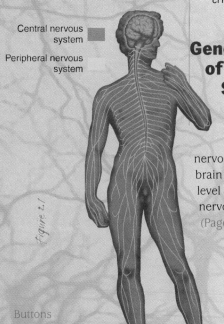

Central nervous system

Peripheral nervous system

figure 2.1

Buttons

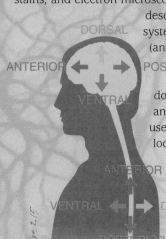

General Layout of the Nervous System

The nervous system is composed of the central and peripheral nervous systems. The brain is the highest level of the central nervous system.
(Pages 37–40)

Neuroanatomical Techniques and Directions

This section introduced you to some of the techniques that are commonly used to study brain anatomy (Golgi stains, Nissl stains, and electron microscopy). Also described was the system of directions (anterior–posterior, dorsal–ventral, and medial–lateral) used to specify locations in the brain.
(Pages 45–49)

DORSAL

ANTERIOR ← → POSTERIOR

VENTRAL

ANTERIOR

VENTRAL ← → DORSAL

POSTERIOR

figure 2.15

Cells of the Nervous System

The nervous system is composed of many different kinds of cells. Most are either neurons, which conduct neural signals, or glial cells, which support and influence neural function in various ways.
(Pages 40–45)

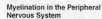

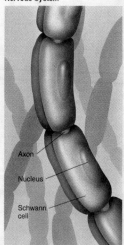

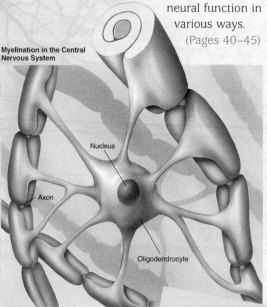

Myelination in the Central Nervous System

Nucleus

Axon

Oligodendrocyte

Myelination

Myelination in the Peripheral Nervous System

Axon

Nucleus

Schwann cell

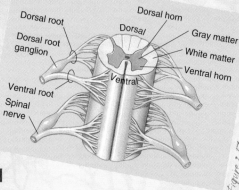

Dorsal root

Dorsal root ganglion

Ventral root

Spinal nerve

Dorsal horn

Dorsal

Ventral

Gray matter

White matter

Ventral horn

figure 2.17

The Spinal Cord

The central nervous system has two components: the brain and the spinal cord. This section introduced you to the anatomy of the spinal cord. Dorsal nerves carry signals into the spinal cord; ventral nerves carry signals out of the spinal cord.
(Pages 49–50)

Visual Summary

Themes Revisited

This chapter contributed relatively little to the development of the book's major themes; that development was temporarily slowed while you were being introduced to the anatomy of the human brain. However, the clinical implications theme did arise several times: You learned that neurologists tend to base their diagnoses on disruptions of cranial nerve function, that the loss of cerebrospinal fluid leads to severe headaches, that the blood–brain barrier protects the brain from toxins, that Schwann cells mediate the regeneration of damaged PNS neurons, that cerebellar damage produces motor problems, that the periaqueductal gray mediates the effects of analgesic drugs, and that damage to nigrostriatal pathways is associated with Parkinson's disease.

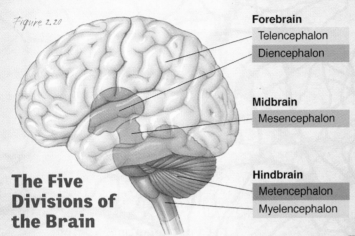

Figure 2.20

Forebrain
- Telencephalon
- Diencephalon

Midbrain
- Mesencephalon

Hindbrain
- Metencephalon
- Myelencephalon

The Five Divisions of the Brain

There are five major divisions of the brain: telencephalon, diencephalon, mesencephalon, metencephalon, and myelencephalon. The telencephalon and the diencephalon together compose the forebrain.
(Pages 50–51)

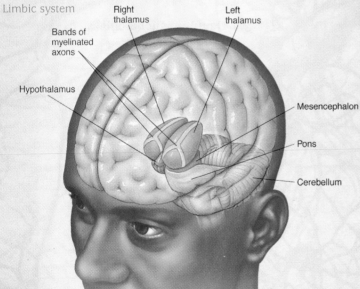

Limbic system
Right thalamus
Left thalamus
Bands of myelinated axons
Hypothalamus
Mesencephalon
Pons
Cerebellum

Major Structures of the Brain

The major structures that compose each division of the brain were introduced in the final section. Particularly important for understanding complex human abilities are the cerebral hemispheres (telencephalon) and the neocortex, which covers them. Many of the subcortical structures of the telencephalon are organized into two systems: the limbic system and the basal ganglia.
(Pages 51–60)

Think about It

1. Which of the following do you think is closer to the truth? (a) All psychologists should understand the structure of the human brain. (b) Neuroanatomy is a subfield of biology and has nothing to do with psychology. Explain.
2. A rat will press a lever at a high rate if every press produces a brief electrical stimulation to its own brain through an implanted electrode. What procedures could be used to identify the neural circuits involved in the rewarding effects of the stimulation?
3. When it comes to neural stains, seeing less is seeing more. Explain.
4. Why have glial cells been referred to as "the forgotten majority"?
5. The mammalian nervous system is a "system of twos." Explain.

chapter 3

Neural Activity and How to Study It
How Neurons Work

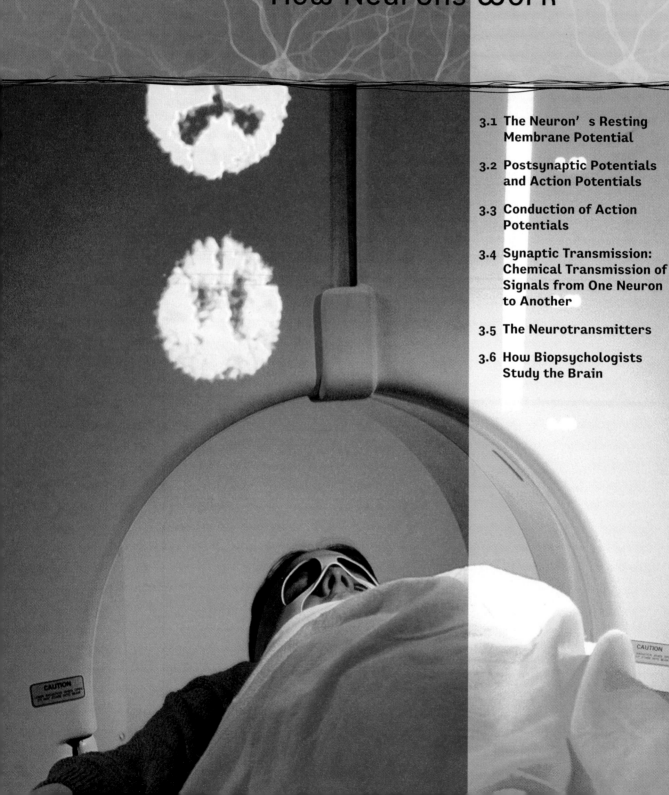

Chapter 2 introduced you to the anatomy of the nervous system. This chapter is about how neurons conduct and transmit electrochemical signals. It begins with a description of how signals are generated in resting neurons; then, it follows the signals as they are conducted through neurons and transmitted across synapses to other neurons.

"The Lizard," a case study of a patient with Parkinson's disease, Roberto Garcia d'Orta, will help you appreciate why a knowledge of neural conduction and synaptic transmission is an integral part of biopsychology.

The Lizard, a Case of Parkinson's Disease

"I have become a lizard," he began. "A great lizard frozen in a dark, cold, strange world."

His name was Roberto Garcia d' Orta. He was a tall thin man in his sixties, but like most patients with Parkinson' s disease, he appeared to be much older than his actual age. Not many years before, he had been an active, vigorous businessman. Then it happened—not all at once, not suddenly, but slowly, subtly, insidiously. Now he turned like a piece of granite, walked in slow shuffling steps, and spoke in a monotonous whisper.

What had been his first symptom?

A tremor.

Had his tremor been disabling?

"No," he said. "My hands shake worse when they are doing nothing at all"—a symptom called *tremor-at-rest*.

The other symptoms of Parkinson' s disease are not quite so benign. They can change a vigorous man into a lizard. These include rigid muscles, a marked poverty of spontaneous movements, difficulty in starting to move, and slowness in executing voluntary movements once they have been initiated.

The term "reptilian stare" is often used to describe the characteristic lack of blinking and the widely opened eyes gazing out of a motionless face, a set of features that seems more reptilian than human. Truly a lizard in the eyes of the world.

What was happening in Mr. d' Orta' s brain? A small group of nerve cells called the *substantia nigra* (black substance) were unaccountably dying. These neurons make a particular chemical neurotransmitter called dopamine, which they deliver to another part of the brain, known as the striatum. As the cells of the substantia nigra die, the amount of dopamine they can deliver goes down. The striatum helps control movement, and to do that normally, it needs dopamine.

(Paraphrased from *Newton' s Madness: Further Tales of Clinical Neurology* by Harold L. Klawans, pp. 53–57. New York: Harper & Row, © Harold Klawans, 1990.)

Dopamine is not an effective treatment for Parkinson's disease because it does not readily penetrate the blood–brain barrier. However, knowledge of dopaminergic transmission has led to the development of an alternative treatment: L-dopa, the chemical precursor of dopamine, which readily penetrates the blood–brain barrier and is converted to dopamine once inside the brain.

Mr. d'Orta's neurologist prescribed L-dopa, and it worked. He still had a bit of tremor; but his voice became stronger, his feet no longer shuffled, his reptilian stare faded away, and he was once again able to perform with ease many of the activities of daily life (e.g., eating, bathing, writing, speaking, and even making love with his wife). Mr. d'Orta had been destined to spend the rest of his life trapped inside a body that was becoming increasingly difficult to control, but his life sentence was repealed.

Mr. d'Orta's story does not end here. You will encounter him in a later chapter as he desperately seeks a cure for his Parkinson's disease—L-dopa produces a temporary improvement, but it does not cause damaged neurons to regenerate or stop the progression of the disorder.

Keep Mr. d'Orta in mind as you read the remainder of this chapter. His case will remind you that normal neural activity is necessary for normal psychological function. A knowledge of neural conduction and synaptic transmission is a major asset for any psychologist; it is a must for any biopsychologist.

3.1
The Neuron's Resting Membrane Potential

The Evolutionary Perspective

Most of what we know about neurons comes from the study of nonhumans. Fortunately, human neurons do not differ from those of other species.

One key to understanding neural function is the **membrane potential**, the difference in electrical charge between the inside and the outside of a cell. To record a neuron's membrane potential, it is necessary to position the tip of one electrode inside the neuron and the tip of another electrode outside the neuron in the extracellular fluid. Although the size of the extracellular electrode is not critical, it is paramount that the tip of the intracellular electrode be fine enough to pierce the neural membrane without severely damaging it. The intracellular electrodes are called **microelectrodes**; their tips are less than one-thousandth of a millimeter in diameter—much too small to be seen by the naked eye.

What Is the Resting Potential?

When both electrode tips are in the extracellular fluid, the voltage difference between them is zero. However, when the tip of the intracellular electrode is inserted into a neuron, a steady potential of about −70 millivolts (mV) is recorded. This indicates that the potential inside the resting neuron is about 70 mV less than that outside the neuron. This steady membrane potential of about −70 mV is called the neuron's **resting potential**. In its resting state, with the −70 mV charge built up across its membrane, a neuron is said to be *polarized*.

The Ionic Basis of the Resting Potential

Why are resting neurons polarized? Like all salts in solution, the salts in neural tissue separate into positively and negatively charged particles called **ions**—mainly *sodium, potassium*, and *chloride ions* in this context. The resting potential results from the fact that the ratio of negative to positive charges is greater inside the neuron than outside.

ON THE CD

The *Ion Channels* module illustrates the locations and functions of different types of ion channels.

Why is there a greater negative charge inside neurons than outside? Two properties of the neural membrane contribute to the difference. The first property of the neural membrane that contributes to the resting potential is its *differential permeability* (a property that allows some substances to pass through but not others). Ions pass through the neural membrane at specialized pores called **ion channels**, each type of which is specialized for the passage of particular ions. When the neuron is at rest, only some of the ion channels are open.

The second property of the neural membrane that contributes to the resting potential is the presence of **sodium–potassium pumps**. These pumping mechanisms transfer many positively charged sodium ions out of the neuron and many fewer positively charged potassium ions into it.

These two properties of the neural membrane together contribute to the resting potential. Many sodium ions are pumped out of the neuron, and they have difficulty getting back in, because the ion channels through which they can enter are closed. Because sodium ions are positively charged, the congregation of sodium ions outside the neuron is a major contributor to the resting potential.

The most important thing to understand about the resting potential is that there is a great pressure on sodium ions to enter resting neurons. This pressure comes from two sources: The first is the −70 mV internal charge—sodium ions outside the neuron are driven in by the external positive charge and attracted in by the internal negative charge. The second source of pressure on sodium ions to enter resting neurons comes from the fact that ions are always in *random motion*, and because there are many more sodium ions outside than inside resting neurons, random motion produces more movement of sodium ions into neurons than out.

Figure 3.1 illustrates the forces on the sodium ions during the resting potential. I like to think of a resting neuron as if it were the venue for a rock concert. In the moments before the doors open to allow the audience to enter, people are milling about, attracted by the promise of the concert and pushed toward the doors by the crowd that has accumulated behind them.

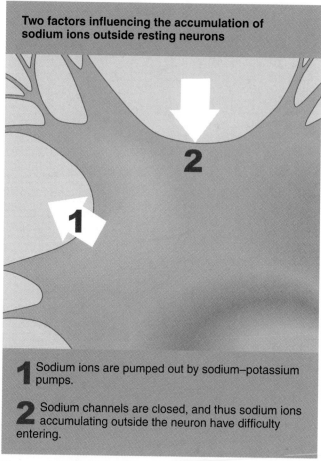

Two factors influencing the accumulation of sodium ions outside resting neurons

1 Sodium ions are pumped out by sodium–potassium pumps.

2 Sodium channels are closed, and thus sodium ions accumulating outside the neuron have difficulty entering.

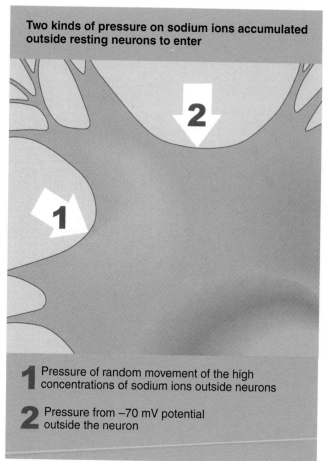

Two kinds of pressure on sodium ions accumulated outside resting neurons to enter

1 Pressure of random movement of the high concentrations of sodium ions outside neurons

2 Pressure from −70 mV potential outside the neuron

The resting potential of neurons and the pressure on sodium ions to enter resting neurons.

Figure 3.1

3.2

Postsynaptic Potentials and Action Potentials

When neurons fire, they release from their terminal buttons chemicals called *neurotransmitters*, which diffuse across the synaptic clefts and interact with specialized receptor molecules on the receptive membranes of the next neurons in the circuit. When neurotransmitter molecules bind to postsynaptic receptors, they typically have one of two effects, depending on the structure of both the neurotransmitter and the receptor in question. They may **depolarize** the receptive membrane (reduce the negative membrane potential, from −70 to −67 mV, for example), or they may **hyperpolarize** it (increase the negative membrane potential, from −70 to −72 mV, for example). Postsynaptic depolarizations are called **excitatory postsynaptic potentials (EPSPs)** because, as you will soon learn, they increase the likelihood that the neuron will fire. Postsynaptic hyperpolarizations are called **inhibitory postsynaptic potentials (IPSPs)** because they decrease the likelihood that the neuron will fire. Both EPSPs and IPSPs are **graded responses**. This means that the amplitudes of EPSPs and IPSPs are proportional to the intensity of the signals that elicit them: Weak signals elicit small postsynaptic potentials, and strong signals elicit large ones.

EPSPs and IPSPs travel passively from their sites of generation at synapses, usually on the dendrites or cell body, in much the same way that electrical signals travel through a cable. Accordingly, the transmission of postsynaptic potentials has two important characteristics. First, it is rapid—so rapid that it can be assumed to be instantaneous for most purposes. It is important not to confuse the duration of EPSPs and IPSPs with their rate of transmission; although the duration of EPSPs and IPSPs varies considerably, all

ON THE CD

To visualize the interactions between inputs from inhibitory neurons and those from excitatory neurons, visit the *Interactions between EPSPs and IPSPs* module.

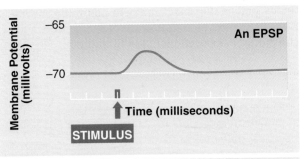

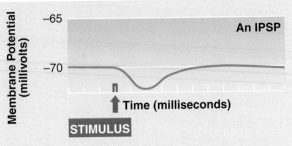

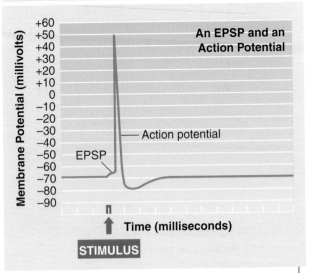

An EPSP, an IPSP, and an EPSP followed by an AP.

Figure 3.2

postsynaptic potentials, whether brief or enduring, are transmitted at great speed. Second, the transmission of EPSPs and IPSPs is *decremental*: EPSPs and IPSPs decrease in amplitude as they travel through the neuron, just as a sound wave grows fainter as it travels through air.

The postsynaptic potentials created at a single synapse typically have little effect on the firing of the postsynaptic neuron. The receptive areas of most neurons are covered with thousands of synapses, and whether or not a neuron fires is determined by the net effect of their activity. More specifically, whether or not a neuron fires depends on the balance between the excitatory and inhibitory signals reaching its axon. Until recently, it was believed that each *action potential* (neuronal firing) begins at the **axon hillock** (the conical structure at the junction between the cell body and the axon), but it actually begins in the adjacent, first section of the axon.

The graded EPSPs and IPSPs created by the action of neurotransmitters at particular receptive sites on a neuron's membrane are conducted instantly and decrementally to the axon hillock. If the sum of the depolarizations and hyperpolarizations reaching the section of the axon adjacent to the axon hillock at any time is sufficient to depolarize the membrane to a level referred to as its **threshold of excitation**—usually about −65 mV—an action potential is generated near the axon hillock. The **action potential (AP)** is a massive, momentary—lasting for 1 millisecond—reversal of the membrane potential from about −70 to about +50 mV. Unlike postsynaptic potentials, action potentials are not graded responses; their magnitude is not related in any way to the intensity of the stimuli that elicit them. To the contrary, they are **all-or-none responses**; that is, they either occur to their full extent or do not occur at all. See Figure 3.2 for an illustration of an EPSP, an IPSP, and an AP.

In effect, each multipolar neuron adds together all the graded excitatory and inhibitory postsynaptic potentials reaching its axon and decides to fire or not to fire on the basis of their sum. Neurons sum up incoming signals in two ways: over space and over time.

Figure 3.3 illustrates the three possible combinations of **spatial summation**. It shows how local EPSPs that are produced simultaneously on different parts of the receptive membrane sum to form a greater EPSP, how simultaneous IPSPs sum to form a greater IPSP, and how simultaneous EPSPs and IPSPs sum to cancel each other out.

Figure 3.4 on page 70 illustrates **temporal summation**. It shows how postsynaptic potentials produced in rapid succession at the same synapse sum to form a greater signal. The reason that stimulations of a neuron can add

ON THE CD

Visit the *Summation of EPSPs* module for an illustration of how temporal summation or spatial summation of EPSPs can elicit an action potential.

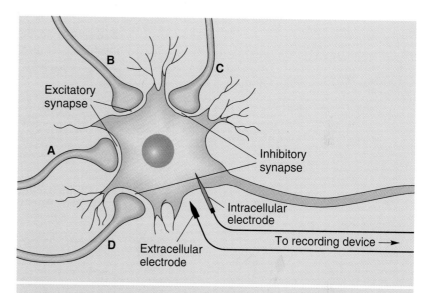

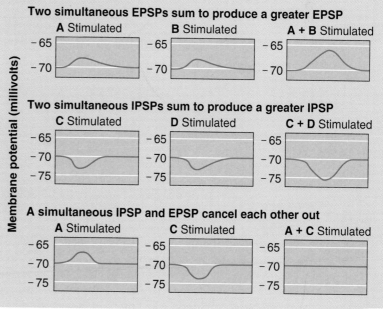

The three possible combinations of spatial summation.

Figure 3.3

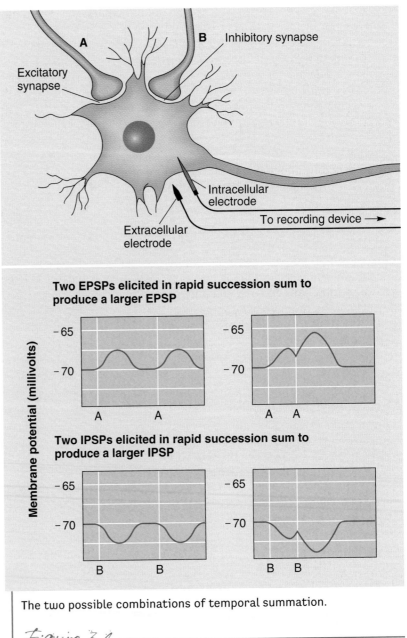

Two EPSPs elicited in rapid succession sum to produce a larger EPSP

Two IPSPs elicited in rapid succession sum to produce a larger IPSP

The two possible combinations of temporal summation.

Figure 3.4

ON THE CD

For more about how the interactions between EPSPs and IPSPs determine whether a neuron will fire, take a look at the *Integration of Postsynaptic Potentials* module.

together over time is that the postsynaptic potentials they produce often outlast them. Thus, if a particular synapse is activated and then activated again before the original postsynaptic potential has completely dissipated, the effect of the second stimulus will be superimposed on the lingering postsynaptic potential produced by the first. Accordingly, it is possible for a brief subthreshold excitatory stimulus to fire a neuron if it is administered twice in rapid succession. In the same way, an inhibitory synapse activated twice in rapid succession can produce a greater IPSP than that produced by a single stimulation.

Each neuron continuously adds together signals over both time and space as it is continually bombarded with stimuli through the thousands of synapses covering its dendrites and cell body. Remember that, although schematic diagrams of neural circuitry rarely show neurons with more than a few representative synaptic contacts, most neurons have thousands of such contacts.

In some ways, the firing of a neuron is like the firing of a gun. Both are all-or-none reactions triggered by graded responses. As a trigger is squeezed, it gradually moves back until it causes the gun to fire; as a neuron is stimulated, it becomes less polarized until the threshold of excitation is reached and firing occurs. Furthermore, just as squeezing a trigger harder does not make the bullet travel faster or farther, stimulating a neuron more intensely does not increase the speed or amplitude of the resulting action potential.

Thinking Clearly

3·3
Conduction of Action Potentials

Sodium Ions and Action Potentials

How are action potentials produced, and how are they conducted along the axon? The answer to both questions is basically the same: through the action of **voltage-activated ion channels**—ion channels that open or close in response to changes in the level of the membrane potential (see McCormick, 1999).

The membrane potential of a neuron at rest is relatively constant despite the high pressure acting to drive sodium ions into the cell. This is because the resting membrane is relatively impermeable to sodium ions and because those few that do pass in are pumped out. But things suddenly change when the membrane potential of the axon is reduced to the threshold of excitation. The voltage-activated sodium channels in the axon membrane open wide, and sodium ions rush in, suddenly driving the membrane potential from about −70 mV to about +50 mV.

Once the action potential is initiated, many changes occur rapidly in the neuron. One key event is the closing of the sodium ion channels, which occurs when the action potential reaches its peak (see Figure 3.5). Once these channels have closed, the resting potential can be re-established so that the neuron can fire again.

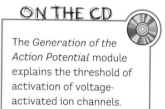

ON THE CD

The *Generation of the Action Potential* module explains the threshold of activation of voltage-activated ion channels.

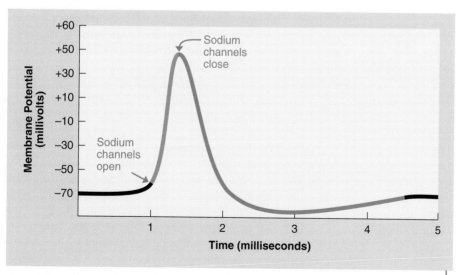

Timing of the opening and closing of sodium ion channels during an action potential.

Figure 3.5

Refractory Periods

There is a brief period of about 1 to 2 milliseconds after the initiation of an action potential during which it is impossible to elicit a second one. This period is called the **absolute refractory period**. The absolute refractory period is followed by the **relative refractory period**—the period during which it is possible to fire the neuron again, but only by applying higher-than-normal levels of stimulation. The end of the relative refractory period is the point at which the amount of stimulation necessary to fire a neuron returns to baseline.

The refractory period is responsible for two important characteristics of neural activity. First, it is responsible for the fact that action potentials normally travel along axons in only one direction. Because the portions of an axon over which an action potential has just traveled are left momentarily refractory, an action potential cannot reverse direction. Second, the refractory period is responsible for the fact that the rate of neural firing is related to the intensity of the stimulation. If a neuron is subjected to a high level of continual stimulation, it fires and then fires again as soon as its absolute refractory period is over—a maximum of about 1,000 times per second. However, if the level of stimulation is of an intensity just sufficient to fire the neuron when it is at rest, the neuron does not fire again until both the absolute and the relative refractory periods have run their course. Intermediate levels of stimulation produce intermediate rates of neural firing.

Axonal Conduction of Action Potentials

The conduction of action potentials along an axon differs from the conduction of EPSPs and IPSPs in two important ways. First, the conduction of action potentials along an axon is *nondecremental*; action potentials do not grow weaker as they travel along the axonal membrane. Second, action potentials are conducted more slowly than postsynaptic potentials.

The reason for these two differences is that the conduction of EPSPs and IPSPs is entirely passive, whereas the axonal conduction of action potentials is largely active. Once an action potential has been generated, it travels passively along the axonal membrane to the adjacent voltage-activated sodium channels, which have yet to open. The arrival of the electrical signal opens these channels, thereby allowing sodium ions to rush into the neuron and generate a full-blown action potential on this portion of the membrane. This signal is then conducted passively to the next sodium channels, where another action potential is actively triggered. These events are repeated again and again until a full-blown action potential is triggered in all the terminal buttons (Huguenard, 2000). However, because there are so many ion channels on the axonal membrane and they are so close together, it is usual to think of axonal conduction as a single wave of excitation spreading actively at a constant speed along the axon, rather than as a series of discrete events.

The wave of excitation triggered by the generation of an action potential near the axon hillock also spreads passively back through the cell body and dendrites of the neuron. Although little is yet known about the functions of these backward action potentials, they are currently the subject of intensive investigation.

The following analogy may help you appreciate the major characteristics of axonal conduction. Consider a row of mousetraps on a wobbly shelf, all of them set and ready to be triggered. Each trap stores energy by holding back its striker against the pressure of the spring, in the same way that each sodium channel stores energy by holding back sodium ions, which are under pressure to move down their concentration and electrostatic gradients into the neuron. When the first trap in the row is triggered, the vibration is transmitted passively through the shelf, and the next trap is sprung—and so on down the line.

The nondecremental nature of action potential conduction is readily apparent from this analogy; the last trap on the shelf strikes with no less intensity than did the first. This analogy also illustrates the refractory period: A trap cannot respond again until it has been reset, just as a section of axon cannot fire again until it has been repolarized.

Conduction in Myelinated Axons

In Chapter 2, you learned that the axons of many neurons are insulated from the extracellular fluid by segments of fatty tissue called *myelin*. In myelinated axons, ions can pass through the axonal membrane only at the **nodes of Ranvier**—the gaps between adjacent myelin segments. Indeed, in myelinated axons, sodium channels are concentrated at the nodes of Ranvier (Salzer, 2002). How, then, are action potentials transmitted in myelinated axons?

When an action potential is generated in a myelinated axon, the signal is conducted passively—that is, instantly and decrementally—along the first segment of myelin to the next node of Ranvier. Although the signal is somewhat diminished by the time it reaches that node, it is still strong enough to open the voltage-activated sodium channels at the node and to generate another full-blown action potential. This action potential is then conducted passively along the axon to the next node, where another full-blown action potential is elicited, and so on.

Myelination increases the speed of axonal conduction. Because conduction along the myelinated segments of the axon is passive, it occurs instantly, and the signal thus "jumps" along the axon from node to node. There is, of course, a slight delay at each node of Ranvier while the action potential is actively generated, but conduction is still much faster in myelinated axons than in unmyelinated axons, in which passive conduction plays a less prominent role. The transmission of action potentials in myelinated axons is called **saltatory conduction** (*saltare* means "to skip or jump").

The Velocity of Axonal Conduction

At what speed are action potentials conducted along an axon? The answer to this question depends on two properties of the axon. Conduction is faster in large-diameter axons, and—as you have just learned—it is faster in those that are myelinated. Mammalian *motor neurons* (neurons that synapse on skeletal muscles) are large and myelinated; thus, some can conduct at speeds up to 100 meters per second (about 224 miles per hour). In contrast, small, unmyelinated axons conduct action potentials at about 1 meter per second.

Conduction in Neurons without Axons

Action potentials are the means by which axons conduct all-or-none signals nondecrementally over relatively long distances. Thus, to keep what you have just learned about action potentials in perspective, it is important for you to remember that many neurons in mammalian brains do not have axons and thus do not display action potentials. Neural conduction in these *interneurons* is typically by graded, decrementally conducted potentials (Juusola et al., 1996).

3·4
Synaptic Transmission: Chemical Transmission of Signals from One Neuron to Another

So far, you have learned how postsynaptic potentials are generated on the receptive membrane of a resting neuron, how these graded potentials are conducted passively to the axon, how the sum of these graded potentials can trigger action potentials, and how these all-or-none potentials are actively conducted down

the axon to the terminal buttons. You will now learn how action potentials arriving at terminal buttons trigger the release of neurotransmitters into synapses and how neurotransmitters carry signals to other cells. This section provides an introduction to five aspects of synaptic transmission: (1) the structure of synapses; (2) the synthesis and transport of neurotransmitter molecules; (3) the release of neurotransmitter molecules; (4) the activation of receptors by neurotransmitter molecules; and (5) the termination of neurotransmitter effects.

Structure of Synapses

Most communication among neurons occurs across synapses such as the one illustrated in Figure 3.6. Neurotransmitter molecules are released from buttons into synaptic clefts, where they induce EPSPs or IPSPs in other neurons by binding to receptors on their postsynaptic membranes. The synapses featured in Figure 3.6 are *axodendritic synapses*—synapses of axon terminal buttons on dendrites. Many excitatory synapses terminate on **dendritic spines** (nodules that occur on many dendrites—see Figure 2.30). Also common are *axosomatic synapses*—synapses of axon terminal buttons on *somas* (cell bodies). Although axodendritic and axosomatic synapses are the most prevalent synaptic arrangements in the mammalian nervous system, there are others (Shepherd & Erulkar, 1997). For example, there are many *dendrodendritic* and *axoaxonic synapses*.

The synapses depicted in Figure 3.6 are **directed synapses**—synapses at which the site of neurotransmitter release and the site of neurotransmitter reception are in close proximity. This is a common arrangement, but there are also many nondirected synapses in the mammalian nervous system. **Nondirected synapses** are synapses at which the site of release and the site of reception of neurotransmitters are some distance apart. One type of nondirected synapse is depicted in Figures 3.7 and 3.11 (on page 80). In this type of arrangement, neurotransmitter molecules are released from a series of bead-like structures along the axon and its branches, and thus the neurotransmitters are widely dispersed to surrounding targets. Because of their appearance, these synapses are often referred to as *string-of-beads synapses*.

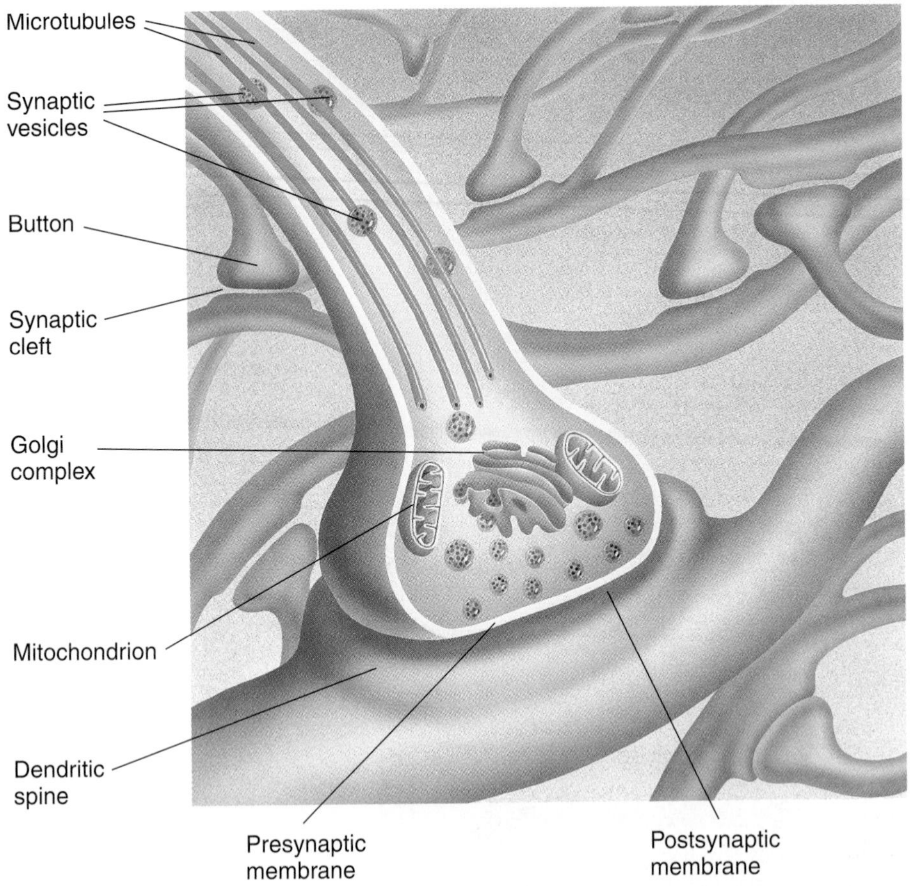

Synthesis and Transport of Neurotransmitter Molecules

There are two basic categories of neurotransmitter molecules: small and large. There are several types of small neurotransmitters, but large neuro-

Microtubules

Synaptic vesicles

Button

Synaptic cleft

Golgi complex

Mitochondrion

Dendritic spine

Presynaptic membrane

Postsynaptic membrane

The anatomy of a typical synapse.

Figure 3.6

transmitters come in only one variety: peptides. **Peptides** are amino acid chains that are composed of 10 or fewer amino acids; in effect, peptides are short proteins.

Small-molecule neurotransmitters are typically synthesized in the cytoplasm of the terminal button and packaged there in **synaptic vesicles**. Once filled with neurotransmitter, the vesicles are stored in clusters next to the presynaptic membrane. In contrast, peptide neurotransmitters, like other proteins, are assembled in the cytoplasm of the cell body on *ribosomes*; they are then packaged in vesicles by the **Golgi complex** and transported by *microtubules* to the terminal buttons, at a rate of about 40 centimeters per day. The vesicles that contain large-molecule neurotransmitters tend to be larger than those that contain small-molecule neurotransmitters, and their clusters are not as close to the presynaptic membrane.

It may have escaped your notice that the button illustrated in Figure 3.6 contains synaptic vesicles of two sizes. This means that it contains two neuro-

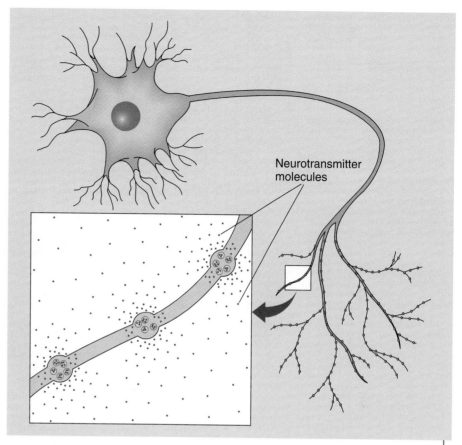

Nondirected neurotransmitter release. Some neurons release neurotransmitter molecules diffusely from beadlike structures along the axon and its branches.

transmitters: a large-molecule (peptide) neurotransmitter in the larger vesicles and a small-molecule neurotransmitter in the smaller vesicles. It was once believed that each neuron synthesizes and releases only one neurotransmitter, but it is now clear that many neurons contain both a small-molecule and a large-molecule neurotransmitter—a situation that is referred to as **coexistence**.

Release of Neurotransmitter Molecules

Exocytosis—the process of neurotransmitter release—is illustrated in Figure 3.8 (on page 76) (see Zucker, Kullman, & Bennett, 1999). When a neuron is at rest, synaptic vesicles that contain small-molecule neurotransmitters congregate next to sections of the presynaptic membrane that are particularly rich in *voltage-activated calcium channels*. When stimulated by action potentials, these channels open, and calcium ions enter the button. The entry of the calcium ions causes the synaptic vesicles to fuse with the presynaptic membrane and empty their contents into the synaptic cleft (see Rettig & Neher, 2002).

The exocytosis of small-molecule neurotransmitters differs from the exocytosis of peptide neurotransmitters in one important respect. Small-molecule neurotransmitters are typically released in a pulse each time an action potential triggers a momentary influx of calcium ions through the presynaptic membrane. In contrast, peptide neurotransmitters are typically released gradually in response to general increases in the level of intracellular calcium ions, such as might occur during a general increase in the rate of neuron firing.

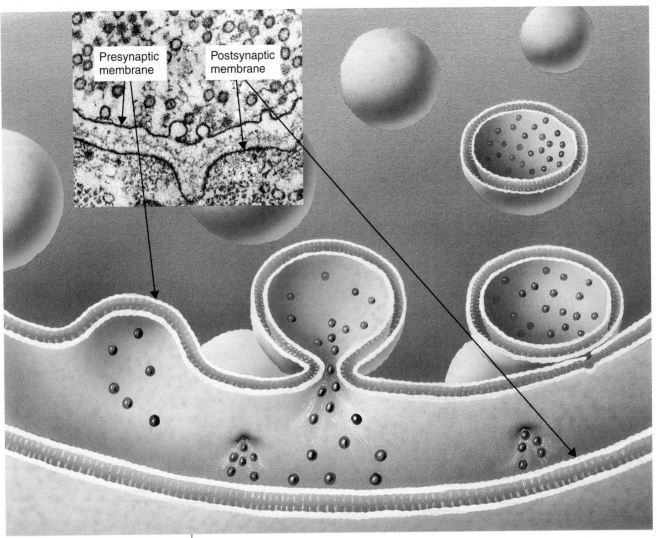

Presynaptic membrane

Postsynaptic membrane

Schematic and photographic illustrations of exocytosis.
(The photomicrograph was reproduced from J. E. Heuser et al., *Journal of Cell Biology*, 1979, 81, 275–300, by copyright permission of The Rockefeller University Press.)

Figure 3.8

Activation of Receptors by Neurotransmitter Molecules

Once released, neurotransmitter molecules produce signals in postsynaptic neurons by binding to **receptors** in the postsynaptic membrane. Each receptor is a protein that contains binding sites for only particular neurotransmitters; thus, a neurotransmitter can influence only those cells that have receptors for it. Any molecule that binds to another is referred to as its **ligand**, and a neurotransmitter is thus said to be a ligand of its receptor.

It was initially assumed that there is only one type of receptor for each neurotransmitter, but this has not proved to be the case. As more receptors have been identified, it has become clear that most neurotransmitters bind to several different types of receptors. The different types of receptors to which a particular neurotransmitter can bind are called the **receptor subtypes** for that neurotransmitter. The various receptor subtypes for a neurotransmitter are typically located in different brain areas, and they typically respond to the neurotransmitter in different ways (see Darlison & Richter, 1999). Thus, one advantage of receptor subtypes is that they enable a neurotransmitter to transmit different kinds of messages to different parts of the brain.

The binding of a neurotransmitter to one of its receptor subtypes can influence a postsynaptic neuron in one of two fundamentally different ways, depending on whether the receptor is ionotropic or metabotropic (Heuss & Gerber, 2000; Waxham, 1999). **Ionotropic receptors** are those receptors that are associated with ligand-activated ion channels; **metabotropic receptors** are those receptors that are associated with signal proteins and *G proteins (guanosine-triphosphate–sensitive proteins)*—see Figure 3.9.

When a neurotransmitter molecule binds to an ionotropic receptor, the associated ion channel usually opens or closes immediately, thereby inducing an immediate postsynaptic potential. For example, in some neurons, EPSPs (depolarizations) occur because the neurotransmitter opens sodium channels, thereby increasing the flow of sodium ions into the neuron.

Metabotropic receptors are more prevalent than ionotropic receptors, and their effects are slower to develop, longer-lasting, more diffuse, and more varied. There are many different kinds of metabotropic receptors, but each is attached to a signal protein that winds its way back and forth through the cell membrane seven times. The metabotropic receptor is attached to a portion of the signal protein outside the neuron; the G protein is attached to a portion of the signal protein inside the neuron.

When a neurotransmitter binds to a metabotropic receptor, a subunit of the associated G protein breaks away. Then, one of two things happens, depending on the particular G protein: The subunit may move along the inside surface of the membrane and bind to a nearby ion channel, thereby inducing an EPSP or IPSP; or it may trigger the synthesis of a chemical called a **second messenger** (neurotransmitters are considered to be the *first messengers*). Once created, a second messenger diffuses through the cytoplasm and may influence the activities of the neuron in a variety of ways (Neves, Ram, & Iyengar, 2002)—for example, it may enter the nucleus and bind to the DNA, thereby influencing genetic expression (see Noselli & Perrimon, 2000). You can see why activating metabotropic receptors can have radical, long-lasting effects on neural activity.

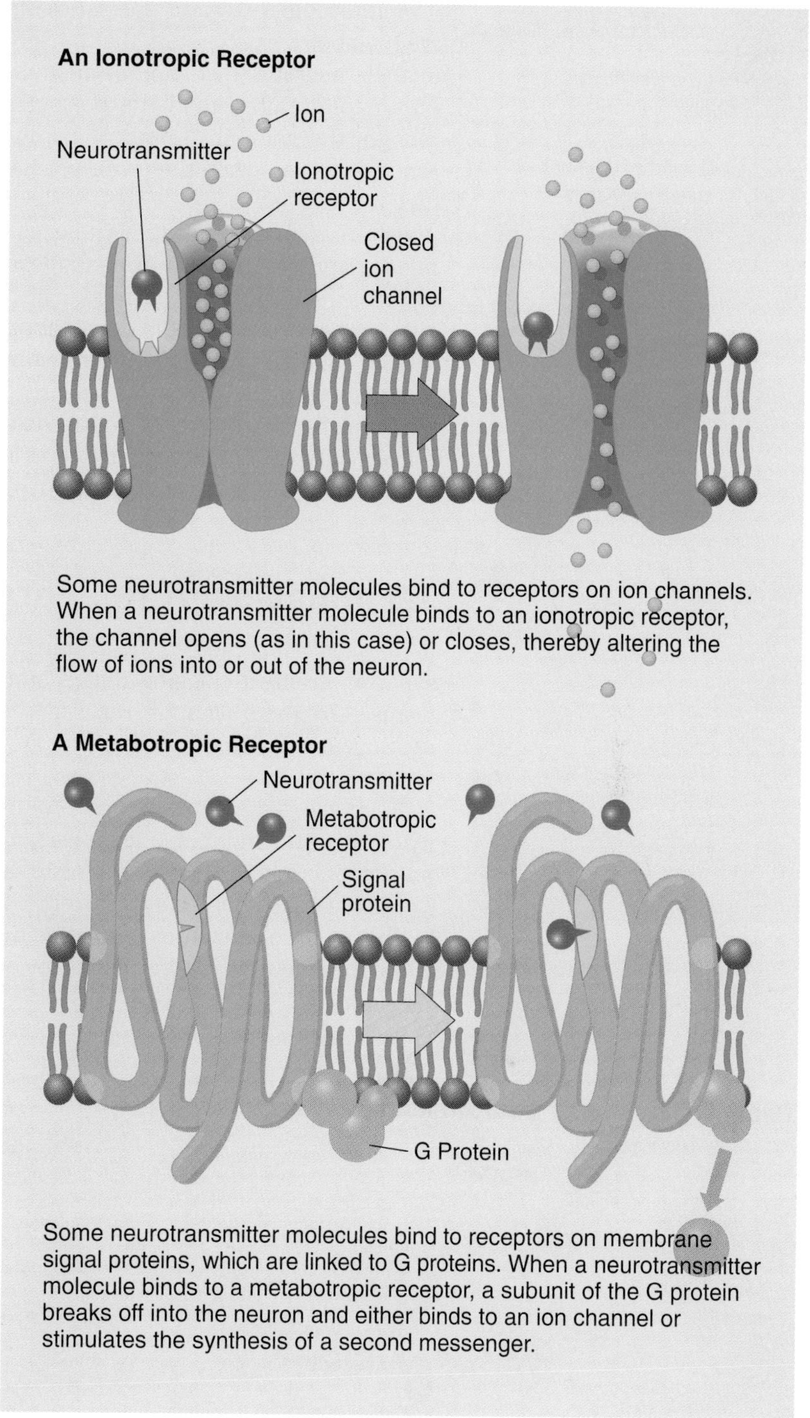

An Ionotropic Receptor

Some neurotransmitter molecules bind to receptors on ion channels. When a neurotransmitter molecule binds to an ionotropic receptor, the channel opens (as in this case) or closes, thereby altering the flow of ions into or out of the neuron.

A Metabotropic Receptor

Some neurotransmitter molecules bind to receptors on membrane signal proteins, which are linked to G proteins. When a neurotransmitter molecule binds to a metabotropic receptor, a subunit of the G protein breaks off into the neuron and either binds to an ion channel or stimulates the synthesis of a second messenger.

Ionotropic and metabotropic receptors.

Figure 3.9

ON THE CD

The *Review of Synaptic Transmission* module takes an in-depth look at the different stages of synaptic transmission.

Autoreceptors warrant special mention (see Parnas et al., 2000). **Autoreceptors** are metabotropic receptors that have two unconventional characteristics: They bind to their neuron's own neurotransmitter molecules; and they are located on the presynaptic, rather than the postsynaptic, membrane. Their usual function is to monitor the number of neurotransmitter molecules in the synapse, to reduce subsequent release when the levels are high, and to increase subsequent release when they are low.

Differences between small-molecule and peptide neurotransmitters in patterns of release and receptor binding suggest that they serve different functions. Small-molecule neurotransmitters tend to be released into directed synapses and to activate either ionotropic receptors or metabotropic receptors that act directly on ion channels. In contrast, peptide neurotransmitters tend to be released diffusely and to bind to metabotropic receptors that act through second messengers. Consequently, the function of small-molecule neurotransmitters appears to be the transmission of rapid, brief excitatory or inhibitory signals to adjacent cells; and the function of peptide neurotransmitters appears to be the transmission of slow, diffuse, long-lasting signals.

Termination of Neurotransmitter Effects

If nothing intervened, a neurotransmitter molecule would remain active in the synapse, in effect clogging that channel of communication. However, two mechanisms terminate synaptic messages and keep that from happening. These two message-terminating mechanisms are **reuptake** and **enzymatic degradation** (see Figure 3.10).

Reuptake is the more common of the two deactivating mechanisms. The majority of neurotransmitters, once released, are almost immediately drawn back into the presynaptic buttons (see Clements et al., 1992).

In contrast, other neurotransmitters are degraded (broken apart) in the synapse by the action of **enzymes**—proteins that stimulate or inhibit biochemical reactions without being affected by them. For example, *acetylcholine*, one of the few neuro-

Two Mechanisms of Neurotransmitter Deactivation

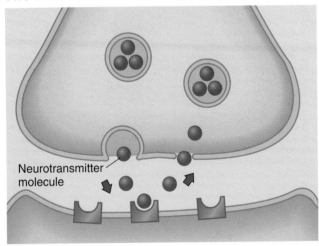

Reuptake

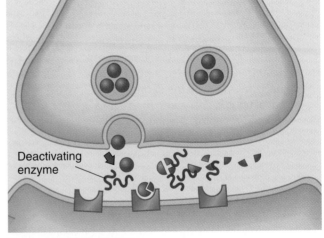

Enzymatic Degradation

The two mechanisms for terminating neurotransmitter action in the synapse: reuptake and enzymatic degradation.

Figure 3.10

transmitters for which enzymatic degradation is the main mechanism of synaptic deactivation, is broken down by the enzyme **acetylcholinesterase**.

Terminal buttons are models of efficiency. Neurotransmitter molecules that have been released into the synapse or their breakdown products are drawn back into the button and recycled, regardless of the mechanism of their deactivation. Even the vesicles are recycled from the presynaptic membrane (Harata et al., 2001).

3·5
The Neurotransmitters

Now that you understand the basics of neurotransmitter function, let's take a look at some of the neurotransmitter molecules (see Deutch & Roth, 1999). There are four types of small-molecule neurotransmitters: the *amino acids*, the *monoamines*, the *soluble gases*, and *acetylcholine*. In contrast, as you have already learned, large-molecule neurotransmitters come in only one variety: peptides. Peptide neurotransmitters are often called **neuropeptides**.

The most important functional property of each neurotransmitter is whether it is excitatory or inhibitory—most neurotransmitters produce either excitation or inhibition, not both. Thus, neurotransmitters are often categorized as excitatory or inhibitory. It is important to realize, however, that a few cases have been documented in which the same neurotransmitter produces activation when it binds to one subtype of a receptor and inhibition when it binds to another subtype.

All of the neurotransmitter classes and individual neurotransmitters that appear in this section in boldface type will be summarized in Figure 3.13 on page 81.

Amino Acid Neurotransmitters

The neurotransmitters in the vast majority of fast-acting, directed synapses in the central nervous system are **amino acids**—the molecular building blocks of proteins. The four most widely acknowledged amino acid neurotransmitters are **glutamate, aspartate, glycine**, and **gamma-aminobutyric acid (GABA)**. The first three are common in the proteins we consume, whereas GABA is synthesized by a simple modification of the structure of glutamate. Glutamate is the most prevalent excitatory neurotransmitter in the mammalian central nervous system; GABA is the most prevalent inhibitory neurotransmitter.

> ### ON THE CD
> The *Amino Acid Synapses* module summarizes the effects of three amino acid neurotransmitters—glutamate, GABA, and glycine.

Monoamine Neurotransmitters

Monoamines are another class of small-molecule neurotransmitters. Each is synthesized from a single amino acid—hence the name *monoamine* (one amine). Monoamine neurotransmitters are slightly larger than amino acid neurotransmitters, and their effects tend to be more diffuse (see Bunin & Wightman, 1999). The monoamines are present in small groups of neurons whose cell bodies are, for the most part, located in the brain stem. These neurons often have highly branched axons with many varicosities (string-of-beads synapses), from which monoamine neurotransmitters are diffusely released into the extracellular fluid (see Figures 3.7 and 3.11).

There are four monoamine neurotransmitters: **dopamine, epinephrine, norepinephrine**, and **serotonin**. They are subdivided into two groups, **catecholamines** and **indolamines**, on the basis of their structures. Dopamine, norepinephrine, and epinephrine are catecholamines. Each is synthesized from the amino acid *tyrosine*.

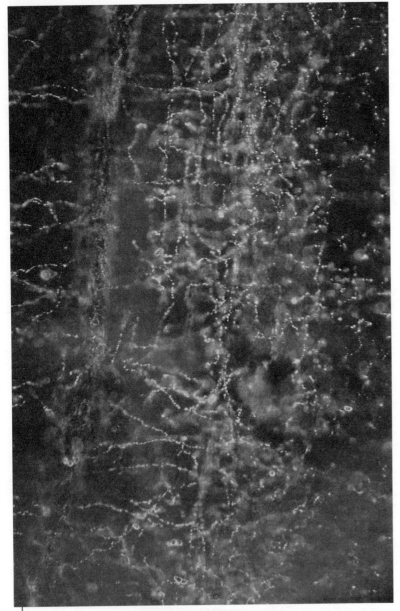

String-of-beads noradrenergic nerve fibers in rat cerebellar cortex. The bright beaded structures represent sites in these multiply branched axons where the monoamine neurotransmitter norepinephrine is stored in high concentration and released into the surrounding extracellular fluid.

(Courtesy of Floyd E. Bloom, M.D., The Scripps Research Institute, La Jolla, California.)

Figure 3.11

Tyrosine is converted to *L-dopa*, the substance that was given to Roberto Garcia d'Orta, and L-dopa in turn is converted to dopamine. Neurons that release norepinephrine have an extra enzyme (one that is not present in dopaminergic neurons), which converts the dopamine in them to norepinephrine. Similarly, neurons that release epinephrine have all the enzymes present in neurons that release norepinephrine, along with an extra enzyme that converts norepinephrine to epinephrine (see Figure 3.12). In contrast to the other monoamines, serotonin (also called *5-hydroxytryptamine*, or *5-HT*) is synthesized from the amino acid *tryptophan* and is classified as an indolamine.

Neurons that release norepinephrine are called *noradrenergic*; those that release epinephrine are called *adrenergic*. There are two reasons for this naming. One is that epinephrine and norepinephrine used to be called *adrenaline* and *noradrenaline*, respectively, by many scientists, until a drug company registered *Adrenalin* as a brand name. The other reason will become apparent to you if you try to say *norepinephrinergic*.

Soluble-Gas Neurotransmitters

Another class of small-molecule neurotransmitters, the **soluble gases**, includes **nitric oxide** and *carbon monoxide*. The soluble gases do not act like the other neurotransmitters (Boehning & Snyder, 2003). They are produced in the neural cytoplasm; and once produced, they immediately diffuse through the cell membrane into the extracellular fluid and then into nearby cells. They easily pass through cell membranes because they are soluble in lipids.

Soluble-gas neurotransmitters have been shown to be involved in *retrograde transmission*. At some synapses, they transmit feedback signals from the postsynaptic neuron back to the presynaptic neuron. The function of retrograde transmission seems to be to reduce the activity of presynaptic neurons (Ludwig & Pittman, 2003). Retrograde transmission by other neurotransmitters has been documented but seems to be less prevalent (Blakely, 2001; Falkenburger, Barstow, & Mintz, 2001).

Acetylcholine

Acetylcholine (abbreviated Ach) is a small-molecule neurotransmitter that is in one major respect like a professor who is late for a lecture: It is in a class by it-

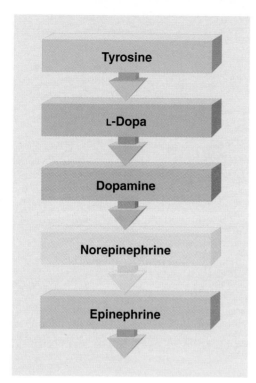

The steps in the synthesis of catecholamines from tyrosine.

Figure 3.12

self. It is created by adding an *acetyl group* to a *choline molecule*. Acetylcholine is the neurotransmitter at neuromuscular junctions, at many of the synapses in the autonomic nervous system, and at synapses in several parts of the central nervous system. As you learned in the last section, acetylcholine is broken down in the synapse by the enzyme *acetylcholinesterase*. Neurons that release acetylcholine are said to be *cholinergic*.

Neuropeptides

Close to 100 neuropeptides have been identified (Greengard, 2001). Among the most interesting of this class of neurotransmitters are the **endorphins** (see Stefano et al., 2000); endorphins are endogenous opiates (opiumlike chemicals that are produced within the body). The existence of endorphins was first suggested by the discovery that opiate drugs (e.g., opium, morphine, and heroin) bind to receptors in the brain; presumably, there would not be receptors in the brain for substances that are not themselves produced by the body. This suggestion was subsequently confirmed by the discovery of several different endorphins and several subtypes of the endorphin receptor. Both opiate drugs and endorphins activate neural systems that produce *analgesia* (pain suppression) and neural systems that mediate the experience of pleasure. These effects are presumably why opiate drugs are so addictive.

Figure 3.13 summarizes the neurotransmitters that were introduced in this section.

Amino acids		Glutamate Aspartate Glycine GABA
Monoamines	Catecholamines	Dopamine Epinephrine Norepinephrine
	Indolamines	Serotonin
Soluble gases		Nitric oxide
Acetylcholine		Acetylcholine
Neuropeptides	Endorphins	
	Other neuropeptides	

Classes of neurotransmitters and the particular neurotransmitters that have been introduced, and appear in boldface, in this section.

Figure 3.13

Clinical Implications

Scan your Brain

This is a good place for you to pause to scan your brain to see if you are ready to proceed. Are you familiar with the neurotransmitters to which you have just been introduced? Find out by filling in the blanks. The correct answers are provided below. Before proceeding, review material related to your errors and omissions.

1. Amino acids are the neurotransmitters in the vast majority of _____-acting, directed synapses.

2. The four amino acids widely recognized as neurotransmitters are _____, _____, _____, _____.

3. The _____ are small-molecule neurotransmitters that belong to one of two categories: _____ or indolamines.

4. There are three catecholamine neurotransmitters: epinephrine, _____ and _____.

5. There is only one indolamine neurotransmitter: _____.

6. Neuropeptide neurotransmitters are short chains of _____.

7. At neuromuscular junctions, the neurotransmitter is _____.

8. Nitric oxide is a _____ neurotransmitter.

Scan Your Brain answers: (1) fast, (2) glutamate, aspartate, glycine, and GABA, in any order, (3) monoamines, catecholamines, (4) norepinephrine and dopamine, in either order, (5) serotonin, (6) amino acids, (7) acetylcholine, (8) soluble-gas.

3.6

How Biopsychologists Study the Brain

This final section of the chapter continues to focus on neural activity, but it does so from an entirely different perspective. It introduces some of the main methods that are now being used to record and manipulate brain activity in biopsychological research. These research methods are grouped under the following five headings: (1) stereotaxic surgery; (2) conventional lesion, stimulation, and recording methods; (3) pharmacological methods; (4) brain imaging; and (5) genetic engineering.

Notice that some biopsychological research methods are *invasive* (meaning that they involve penetrating the brain) and therefore can be used to study human brains only in special cases—for example, when the method serves some diagnostic or therapeutic function. Because invasive methods involve direct contact with the brain, they tend to be more informative than noninvasive methods; however, their use is often limited to nonhuman species.

Clinical Implications

Because virtually all biopsychological research involves the manipulation or measurement of brain activity and behavior, it almost always raises difficult ethical issues—whether the subjects are human or nonhuman. This would be a good point for you to reconsider the Check It Out on page 19 in Chapter 1, concerning the ethics of biopsychological research.

Stereotaxic Surgery

The first step in many biopsychological experiments is **stereotaxic surgery**, which is the means by which experimental devices are precisely positioned in the depths of the brain. Two things are required in stereotaxic surgery: an atlas to provide directions to the target site and an instrument for getting there.

A *stereotaxic atlas* is used to locate brain structures in much the same way that a geographic atlas is used to locate geographic landmarks. There is, however, one important difference. In contrast to the surface of the earth, which has only two dimensions, the brain has three. Accordingly, the brain is represented in a stereotaxic atlas by a series of individual maps, each representing the structure of a single, two-dimensional frontal brain slice. In stereotaxic atlases, all distances are given in millimeters from a designated reference point. In some rat atlases, the reference point is **bregma**—the point on the top of the skull where two of the major *sutures* (seams in the skull) intersect.

A **stereotaxic instrument** has two parts: a *head holder*, which firmly holds the subject's brain in the prescribed position and orientation; and an *electrode holder*, which holds the device to be inserted. A system of precision gears allows the electrode holder to be moved along three dimensions: anterior–posterior, dorsal–ventral, and lateral–medial.

The implantation by stereotaxic surgery of an electrode in the amygdala of a rat is illustrated in Figure 3.14. A similar stereotaxic procedure is used in brain surgery on humans.

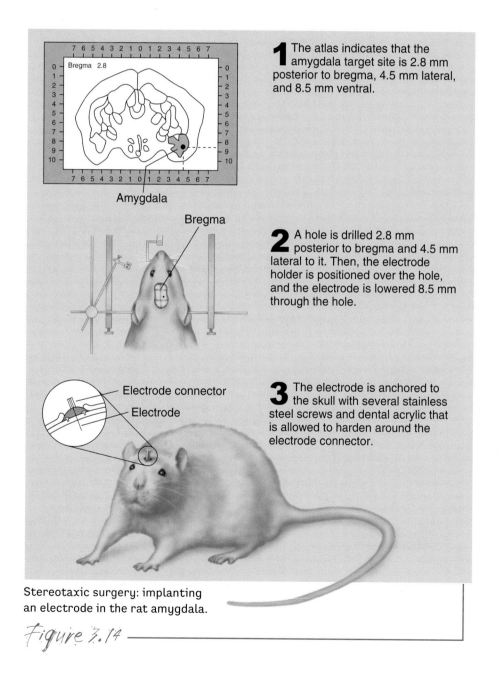

1 The atlas indicates that the amygdala target site is 2.8 mm posterior to bregma, 4.5 mm lateral, and 8.5 mm ventral.

Amygdala

Bregma

2 A hole is drilled 2.8 mm posterior to bregma and 4.5 mm lateral to it. Then, the electrode holder is positioned over the hole, and the electrode is lowered 8.5 mm through the hole.

Electrode connector

Electrode

3 The electrode is anchored to the skull with several stainless steel screws and dental acrylic that is allowed to harden around the electrode connector.

Stereotaxic surgery: implanting an electrode in the rat amygdala.

Figure 3.14

Conventional Lesion, Stimulation, and Recording Methods

The three fundamental methods of studying brain function are the lesion, stimulation, and recording methods. Conventional lesion, stimulation, and recording methods have been based largely on surgical and electrophysiological technology.

Lesion Methods.   Those of you with an unrelenting drive to dismantle objects to see how they work will appreciate **lesion methods** of biopsychological brain re-

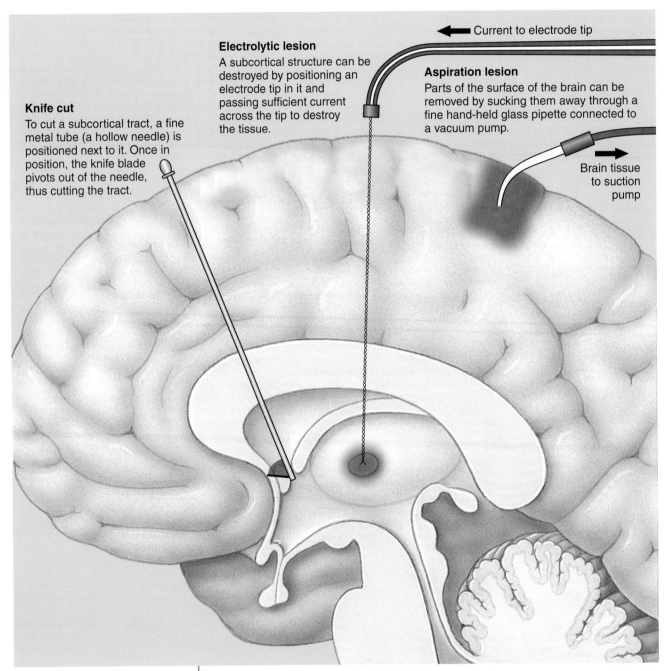

Knife cut
To cut a subcortical tract, a fine metal tube (a hollow needle) is positioned next to it. Once in position, the knife blade pivots out of the needle, thus cutting the tract.

Electrolytic lesion
A subcortical structure can be destroyed by positioning an electrode tip in it and passing sufficient current across the tip to destroy the tissue.

Current to electrode tip

Aspiration lesion
Parts of the surface of the brain can be removed by sucking them away through a fine hand-held glass pipette connected to a vacuum pump.

Brain tissue to suction pump

Three common methods for making brain lesions.

Figure 3.15

search. Often the first step in determining the behavioral function of a brain struc-ture is to *lesion* (or destroy) the structure and then, once the subject recovers, assess the effects of the damage on behavior. *Brain lesions* (areas of brain damage) are often made electrically; that is, the tip of an electrode is lowered into the target structure, and the area at the tip of the electrode is lesioned by passing a strong elec-tric current across the tip of the electrode—the greater the intensity and duration of the current, the larger the **electrolytic lesion**.

Two other brain lesion methods are commonly used. First, structures, such as the cortex, that are visible on the surface of the brain are often lesioned by *aspiration* (suction). To make an **aspiration lesion**, the surgeon deftly draws away the target tissue through the fine tip of a glass pipette attached to a vacuum pump. Second, long, narrow structures, such as tracts, are often destroyed with a tiny, accurately placed knife cut.

The electrolytic, aspiration, and knife cut methods of making brain lesions are il-lustrated in Figure 3.15. Brain lesion studies are always conducted in nonhuman species, unless they are used as a treatment for human patients.

Stimulation Methods. Conventional **stimulation methods** involve passing tiny currents across the tip of a permanently implanted electrode to activate neurons near the tip, and then assessing the effects of the stimulation on behavior. The ef-fects of brain stimulation on behavior are clues to the function of the stimulated structure. Stimulation of a brain structure often has effects on behavior opposite to those produced by a lesion to the same structure.

Conventional brain stimulation methods are rarely used in human subjects be-cause they involve probing the brain. There are, however, a few interesting excep-tions, some of which you will encounter in later chapters.

Recording Methods. Patterns of brain activity—especially those associated with particular experiences or behaviors—produce some of the best evidence about the functions of various brain structures. There are two quite different approaches to recording electrical activity of the brain. The first is **unit recording**: recording the activity of individual neurons. One variation of unit recording is multiple-unit recording. In *multiple-unit recording*, the overall firing rate of many neurons in the area around the electrode tip is recorded and combined, to provide a general meas-ure of the neural activity in the area.

The second approach to recording the electrical activity of the brain is **EEG recording** (electroencephalographic recording): recording the moment-to-moment variations in the differences in electrical potential between two large electrodes. The major advantage of EEG recording is that EEG signals can be recorded from electrodes placed on the scalp. This means that EEG recording can be noninva-sive and thus that it can be used with human subjects; unit recording, in con-trast, is seldom possible in human subjects because it involves penetrating the brain. The main disadvantage of EEG recording is that the large EEG electrodes pick up so many electrical signals that the overall shapes of the signals provide little information about neural activity. Methods of electrophysiological recording are compared in Figure 3.16 on page 86.

Pharmacological Methods

Pharmacological (involving drugs) methods are widely used in the investigation of the brain and behavior, both in human and nonhuman subjects. The most com-monly used pharmacological research methods entail the administration of agonists and antagonists. **Agonists** of a particular neurotransmitter are drugs that increase the neurotransmitter's effects; **antagonists** of a particular neurotransmitter are drugs that reduce the neurotransmitter's effects.

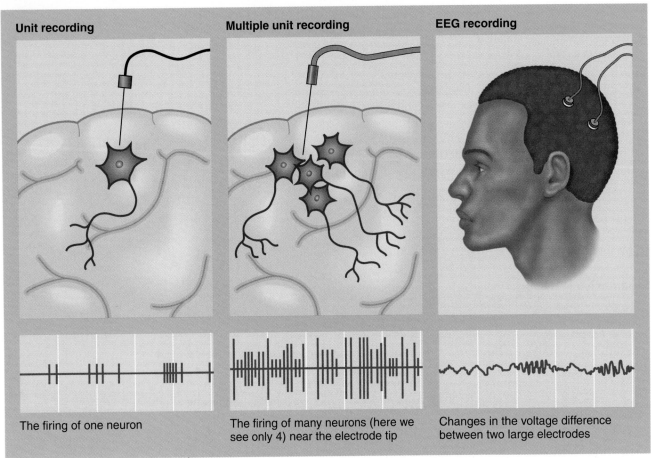

Unit recording

The firing of one neuron

Multiple unit recording

The firing of many neurons (here we see only 4) near the electrode tip

EEG recording

Changes in the voltage difference between two large electrodes

Common methods of recording the electrical activity of the brain in behavioral studies.

Figure 3.16

The mechanisms of agonistic and antagonistic drug effects are illustrated in Figures 3.17 and 3.18. First, Figure 3.17 illustrates seven steps in neurotransmitter action. The steps in neurotransmitter action vary somewhat from one neurotransmitter to another, but these seven are common to most: (1) synthesis of the neurotransmitter, (2) storage in vesicles, (3) breakdown in the cytoplasm of any neurotransmitter that leaks from the vesicles, (4) exocytosis (release of the neurotransmitter to the synapse), (5) inhibitory feedback via autoreceptors, (6) activation of postsynaptic receptors, and (7) deactivation. Figure 3.18 on page 88 illustrates various ways in which drugs can exert agonistic and antagonist effects through involvement in these seven steps.

Examples of Agonists and Antagonists.   Following are one example of a drug that has an agonistic effect and two examples of drugs that have antagonistic effects. You will encounter many more examples of agonists and antagonists in subsequent chapters.

Cocaine   Cocaine is a potent catecholamine agonist that is highly addictive. It increases the activity of both dopamine and norepinephrine by blocking their reuptake from the synapse into the presynaptic button. Accordingly, when there are high levels of cocaine in the brain, molecules of dopamine and norepinephrine

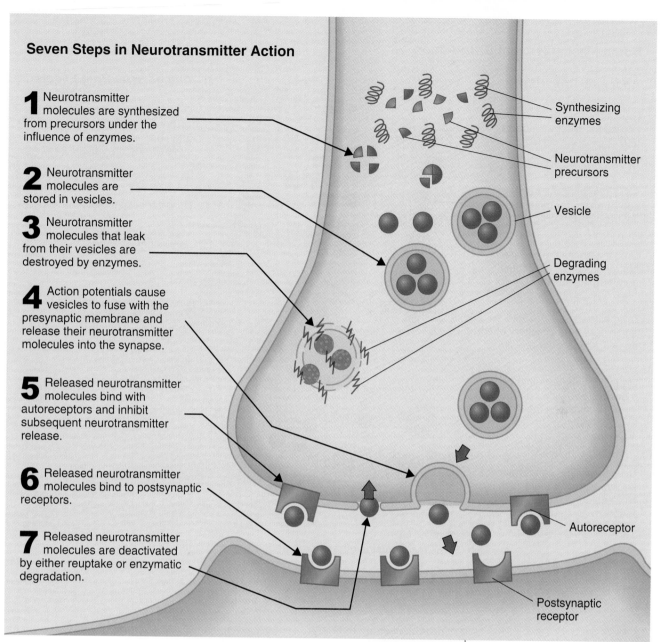

Seven Steps in Neurotransmitter Action

1 Neurotransmitter molecules are synthesized from precursors under the influence of enzymes.

2 Neurotransmitter molecules are stored in vesicles.

3 Neurotransmitter molecules that leak from their vesicles are destroyed by enzymes.

4 Action potentials cause vesicles to fuse with the presynaptic membrane and release their neurotransmitter molecules into the synapse.

5 Released neurotransmitter molecules bind with autoreceptors and inhibit subsequent neurotransmitter release.

6 Released neurotransmitter molecules bind to postsynaptic receptors.

7 Released neurotransmitter molecules are deactivated by either reuptake or enzymatic degradation.

Synthesizing enzymes

Neurotransmitter precursors

Vesicle

Degrading enzymes

Autoreceptor

Postsynaptic receptor

Seven steps in neurotransmitter action: (1) synthesis, (2) storage in vesicles, (3) breakdown of any neurotransmitter leaking from the vesicles, (4) exocytosis, (5) inhibitory feedback via autoreceptors, (6) activation of postsynaptic receptors, and (7) deactivation.

Figure 3.17

that have been released into the synapse continue to activate postsynaptic receptors, because their primary method of deactivation has been blocked. This continued activation produces a variety of psychological effects, including euphoria, loss of appetite, and insomnia.

Curare   South American Indians have long used **curare**—an extract of a certain class of woody vines—to kill game and occasionally their enemies. Curare is a

Some Mechanisms of Drug Action

Agonistic Drug Effects

Drug increases the synthesis of neurotransmitter molecules (e.g., by increasing the amount of precursor).

Drug increases the number of neurotransmitter molecules by destroying degrading enzymes.

Drug increases the release of neurotransmitter molecules from terminal buttons.

Drug binds to autoreceptors and blocks their inhibitory effect on neurotransmitter release.

Drug binds to postsynaptic receptors and either activates them or increases the effect on them of neurotransmitter molecules.

Drug blocks the deactivation of neurotransmitter molecules by blocking degradation or reuptake.

Antagonistic Drug Effects

Drug blocks the synthesis of neurotransmitter molecules (e.g., by destroying synthesizing enzymes).

Drug causes the neurotransmitter molecules to leak from the vesicles and be destroyed by degrading enzymes.

Drug blocks the release of the neurotransmitter molecules from terminal buttons.

Drug activates autoreceptors and inhibits neurotransmitter release.

Drug is a receptor blocker; it binds to the postsynaptic receptors and blocks the effect of the neurotransmitter.

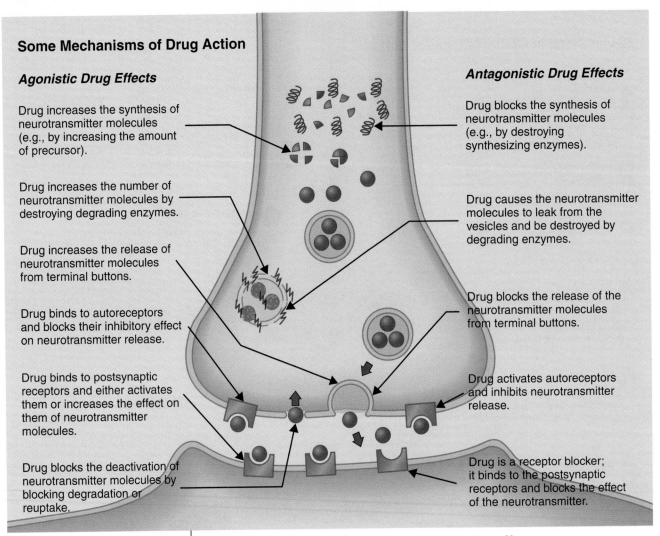

Some mechanisms of agonistic and antagonistic drug effects.

Figure 3.18

receptor blocker at cholinergic synapses that acts at one subtype of acetylcholine receptors: *nicotinic acetylcholine receptors*. By binding to these nicotinic receptors, curare blocks transmission at **neuromuscular junctions**, thus paralyzing its recipients and killing them by blocking their respiration.

The active ingredient of curare is sometimes administered to human patients during surgery to ensure that their muscles do not contract during an incision. When curare is used for this purpose, the patient's breathing must be artificially maintained by a respirator.

Botox Botox (short for *Botulinium toxin*), a neurotoxin released by a bacterium often found in spoiled food, is also a nicotinic antagonist: It blocks the release of acetylcholine at neuromuscular junctions and is thus a deadly poison. However, injected in minute doses at specific sites, it has applications in medicine (e.g., reduction of tremors) and cosmetics (e.g., reduction of wrinkles).

Selective Chemical Lesions

Although the main use of drugs in behavioral neuroscience research is as agonists or antagonists to specific neurotransmitters or receptors, drugs can also be used to make brain lesions. The main advantage of chemical lesions is that they can be very selective. The effects of surgical and electrolytic lesions are frequently difficult to interpret because the lesions affect all neurons in the target area. In some cases, it is possible to make more selective lesions by injecting **neurotoxins** (neural poisons) that have an affinity for certain components of the nervous system. There are many selective neurotoxins. For example, when *kainic acid* is administered by microinjection, it is preferentially taken up by cell bodies at the tip of the *cannula* (a fine metal tube through which chemicals can be delivered to specific sites in the brain) and destroys those neurons, while leaving neurons whose axons pass through the area largely unscathed.

Another widely used selective neurotoxin is *6-hydroxydopamine (6-OHDA)*. It is taken up by only those neurons that release the neurotransmitter *norepinephrine* or *dopamine*, and it leaves other neurons at the injection site undamaged.

Brain Imaging

Prior to the early 1970s, biopsychological research was impeded by the inability to obtain images of the organ of primary interest: the living human brain. Conventional X-ray photography is next to useless for this purpose. When an X-ray photograph is taken, an X-ray beam is passed through an object and then onto a photographic plate. Each of the molecules through which the beam passes absorbs some of the radiation; thus, only the unabsorbed portions of the beam reach the photographic plate. X-ray photography is therefore effective in characterizing internal structures that differ substantially from their surroundings in the degree to which they absorb X-rays—for example, a revolver in a suitcase full of clothes or a bone in flesh. However, by the time an X-ray beam has passed through the numerous overlapping structures of the brain, which differ only slightly from one another in their ability to absorb X-rays, it carries little information about the shape of the individual structures through which it has passed.

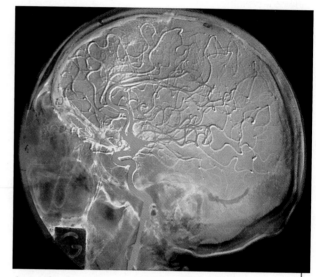

A cerebral angiogram of a healthy subject.

Figure 3.19

Contrast X-Rays. Although conventional X-ray photography is not useful for visualizing the brain, contrast X-ray techniques are. **Contrast X-ray techniques** involve injecting into one compartment of the body a substance that absorbs X-rays either less than or more than the surrounding tissue. The injected substance then heightens the contrast between the compartment and the surrounding tissue during X-ray photography.

One contrast X-ray technique, **cerebral angiography**, uses the infusion of a radio-opaque dye into a cerebral artery to visualize the cerebral circulatory system during X-ray photography (see Figure 3.19). Cerebral angiograms are most useful for localizing vascular damage, but the displacement of blood vessels from their normal position can sometimes indicate the location of a tumor.

Clinical Implications

X-Ray Computed Tomography. In the early 1970s, the study of the living human brain was revolutionized by the introduction of computed tomography. **Computed tomography (CT)** is a computer-assisted X-ray procedure that can be used to visualize the brain and other internal structures of the living body. During cerebral computed tomography, the neurological patient lies with his or her head positioned in the center of a large cylinder, as depicted in Figure 3.20 on page 90. On one side of the cylinder is an X-ray tube that projects an X-ray beam through the head to an X-ray detector mounted on the other side. The X-ray tube and detector automatically rotate around the head of the patient at one level of the brain, taking many individual X-ray

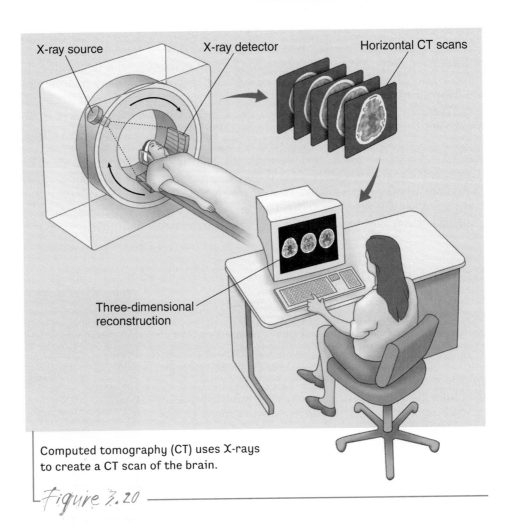

X-ray source   X-ray detector   Horizontal CT scans

Three-dimensional
reconstruction

Computed tomography (CT) uses X-rays
to create a CT scan of the brain.

Figure 3.20

photographs as they rotate. The meager information in each X-ray photograph is combined by a computer to generate a CT scan of one horizontal section of the brain. Then, the X-ray tube and detector are moved along the axis of the patient's body to another level of the brain, and the process is repeated. Scans of eight or nine horizontal brain sections are typically obtained from a patient; combined, they provide a three-dimensional representation of the brain. CT scans are used to study brain structure and to identify certain kinds of brain pathology.

Clinical Implications

Magnetic Resonance Imaging. The success of computed tomography stimulated the development of other techniques for obtaining images of the inside of the living body. Among these techniques is **magnetic resonance imaging (MRI)**— a procedure in which high-resolution images are constructed from the measurement of waves that hydrogen atoms emit when they are activated by radio-frequency waves in a magnetic field. MRI provides clearer images of the brain than does CT. A color-enhanced two-dimensional MRI scan of the midsagittal brain is presented in Figure 3.21.

In addition to providing relatively high *spatial resolution* (the ability to detect differences in spatial location), MRI can produce images in three dimensions. Accordingly, MRI is much better than CT for identifying many kinds of brain pathology. Figure 3.22 is a three-dimensional MRI scan.

Clinical Implications

Cognitive Neuroscience

Positron Emission Tomography. Positron emission tomography (PET) is a brain-imaging technique that has been widely used in biopsychological research because it provides images of brain activity rather than brain structure. In one

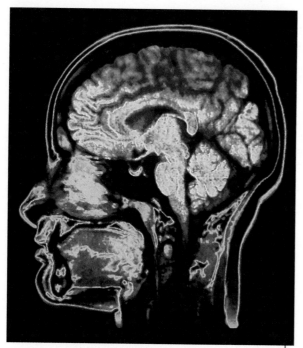

A color-enhanced midsagittal MRI scan.

Figure 3.21 ————————

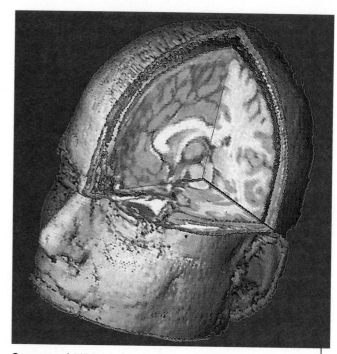

Structural MRI can be used to provide three-dimensional images of the entire brain. (Courtesy of Bruce Foster and Robert Hare, University of British Columbia.)

Figure 3.22 ————————

common version of PET, radioactive **2-deoxyglucose (2-DG)** is injected into the patient's *carotid artery* (an artery of the neck that feeds the ipsilateral cerebral hemisphere). Because of its similarity to glucose, the primary metabolic fuel of the brain, 2-deoxyglucose is rapidly taken up by active (energy-consuming) neurons. However, unlike glucose, 2-deoxyglucose cannot be metabolized; it therefore accumulates in active neurons until it is gradually broken down. Each PET scan is an image of the levels of radioactivity (indicated by color coding) in various parts of one horizontal level of the brain. Thus, if a PET scan is taken of a patient who engages in an activity such as reading for about 30 seconds after the 2-DG injection, the resulting scan will indicate the areas at that brain level that were most active during the 30 seconds of activity (see Figure 3.23 on page 92). Usually, several different levels of the brain are scanned so that the extent of brain activity can be better assessed.

Notice from Figure 3.23 that PET scans are not, strictly speaking, images of the brain. Each PET scan is merely a colored map of the amount of radioactivity in each of the tiny cubic voxels (volume pixels) that compose the scan. One can only estimate how each voxel maps onto a particular brain structure.

Functional MRI. MRI technology has been applied with great success to the measurement of brain activity (see Cabeza & Nyberg, 2000). Conventional techniques of **functional MRI (fMRI)** produce images of the increase in oxygen flow in the blood to active areas of the brain.

Cognitive Neuroscience

Functional MRI has four advantages over PET: (1) Nothing has to be injected into the subject; (2) it provides both structural and functional information in the same image; (3) its spatial resolution is better; and (4) it can be used to produce three-dimensional images of activity over the brain. Functional MRIs are shown in Figure 3.24 on page 92.

Functional MRI is currently the predominant brain-recording technique of cognitive neuroscience; like all other research methods, however, it has its

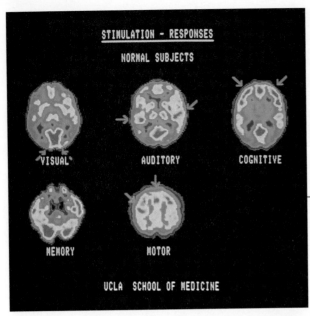

A series of PET scans. Each scan is a horizontal section recorded during a different psychological activity. Areas of high activity are indicated by reds and yellows. For example, notice the high level of activity in the visual cortex of the occipital lobe when the subject scanned a visual display.

(From "Positron Tomography: Human Brain Function and Biochemistry" by Michael E. Phelps and John C. Mazziotta, *Science*, 228 [9701], May 17, 1985, p. 804. Copyright 1985 by the AAAS. Reprinted by permission. Courtesy of Drs. Michael E. Phelps and John Mazziotta, UCLA School of Medicine.)

Figure 3.23

weaknesses. Here are three major ones: First, in order to create an fMRI image, brain activity from many subjects must typically be added together: Because there are major differences among people in the locations in their brains of the circuits that control various cognitive activities, images of activity averaged over many subjects are unlikely to be indicative of what is happening in individual brains. Second, although the spatial resolution of fMRI is better than that of PET, it still has difficulty detecting small areas of brain activity. Third, fMRI does not detect neural activity directly; that activity is inferred from changes in oxygen flow.

Genetic Engineering

Genetics is a science that has made amazing progress in the last decade, and biopsychologists are reaping the benefits. Modern genetic methods are now widely used in biopsychological research. Gene knockout and gene replacement techniques are two of these methods.

Gene knockout techniques are procedures for creating organisms that lack a particular gene under investigation. Once these subjects have been created, efforts are made to identify and then investigate any observable neural or behavioral anomalies they might possess. Mice (the favored mammalian subjects of genetic research) that are the products of gene knockout techniques are referred to as *knockout mice*. This term often makes me smile, as images of little mice with boxing gloves flit through my mind.

There has been much enthusiasm for gene knockout technology, and many gene knockout studies are in progress. However, behavioral studies of knockout mice may be more difficult to interpret than first anticipated (e.g., Cook et al., 2002; Phillips & Belknap, 2002). At least three warnings have been issued. First, most behavioral traits are influenced by the activities of many interacting genes; consequently, the elimination of a behavioral trait by knockout of a gene can at best identify only one small genetic contribution to the behavior. Second, elimination of a gene often influences the expression of other genes; as a result, any observed change in the behavior of knockout mice may be only indirectly related to the knocked-out gene, or, conversely, the effects of a knocked-out gene can be masked by compensatory changes to other genes (Mogil, Yu, & Basbaum, 2000). And, third, the expression of genes can be influenced by experience; thus, gene knockouts are likely to interact in complex ways with the mice's experiences (Crabbe, Wahlsten, & Dudek, 1999).

It is now possible to replace one gene with another in mice (Tsien, 2000). **Gene replacement techniques** are creating some interesting possibilities for develop-

Right hemisphere lateral surface

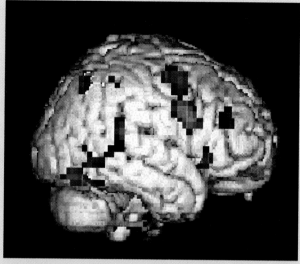

Left hemisphere lateral surface

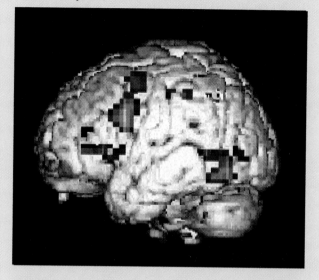

Left hemisphere medial surface

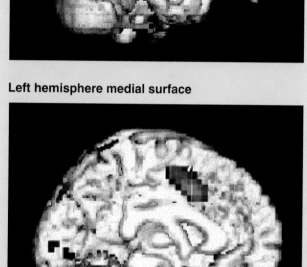

Right hemisphere medial surface

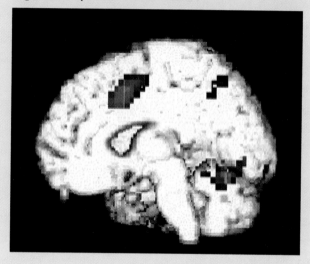

Functional magnetic resonance images (fMRIs). These images illustrate the areas of cortex that became more active when the subjects observed strings of letters and were asked to specify which strings were words; in the control condition, subjects viewed strings of asterisks (Kiehl et al., 1999). These fMRIs illustrate surface activity, but images of sections through the brain can also be displayed.

(Courtesy of Kent Kiehl and Peter Liddle, Department of Psychiatry, University of British Columbia.)

Figure 3.24

mental research and therapy. For example, scientists have removed pathological genes from human cells and inserted them in mice (mice that contain the genetic material of another species are called **transgenic mice**). It is also possible to replace a gene with one that is identical except for the addition of a few bases that can act as a switch, turning the gene off or on in response to particular chemicals. These chemicals can be used to activate or suppress a gene at a particular point in development or in a particular brain structure (see Gingrich & Roder, 1998).

Gene knockout and gene replacement technologies are now the focus of intensive investigation. How much they will teach us about the neural basis of behavior and how useful they will be in the treatment of brain disorders remain to be determined.

Clinical Implications

Scan your Brain

This self-test illustrates a psychological disorder suffered by many scientists. I call this condition "unabbreviaphobia"—the fear of leaving any term unabbreviated. To help determine whether you have mastered the material in this chapter, supply the full term for each of the following abbreviations. The correct answers are provided below. Review material related to your incorrect answers and omissions.

1. EPSP: _____
2. IPSP: _____
3. AP: _____
4. G protein: _____
5. GABA: _____
6. EEG: _____

7. CT: _____
8. MRI: _____
9. PET: _____
10. 2-DG: _____
11. fMRI: _____

Scan Your Brain answers: (1) excitatory postsynaptic potential, (2) inhibitory postsynaptic potential, (3) action potential, (4) guanosine-triphosphate–sensitive protein, (5) gamma-aminobutyric acid, (6) electroencephalograph, (7) computed tomography, (8) magnetic resonance imaging, (9) positron emission tomography, (10) 2-deoxyglucose, (11) functional magnetic resonance imaging

Key Terms

3.1 The Neuron's Resting Membrane Potential

Ion channels (p. 66)
Ions (p. 66)
Membrane potential (p. 66)
Microelectrodes (p. 66)
Resting potential (p. 66)
Sodium–potassium pumps (p. 66)

3.2 Postsynaptic Potentials and Action Potentials

Action potential (AP) (p. 69)
All-or-none responses (p. 69)
Axon hillock (p. 69)
Depolarize (p. 68)
Excitatory postsynaptic potentials (EPSPs) (p. 68)
Graded responses (p. 68)
Hyperpolarize (p. 68)
Inhibitory postsynaptic potentials (IPSPs) (p. 68)
Spatial summation (p. 69)

Temporal summation (p. 69)
Threshold of excitation (p. 69)

3.3 Conduction of Action Potentials

Absolute refractory period (p. 72)
Nodes of Ranvier (p. 73)
Relative refractory period (p. 72)
Saltatory conduction (p. 73)
Voltage-activated ion channels (p. 71)

3.4 Synaptic Transmission: Chemical Transmission of Signals from One Neuron to Another

Acetylcholinesterase (p. 79)
Autoreceptors (p. 78)
Coexistence (p. 75)
Dendritic spines (p. 74)
Directed synapses (p. 74)
Enzymatic degradation (p. 78)

Enzymes (p. 78)
Exocytosis (p. 75)
Golgi complex (p. 75)
Ionotropic receptors (p. 77)
Ligand (p. 76)
Metabotropic receptors (p. 77)
Nondirected synapses (p. 74)
Peptides (p. 75)
Receptor subtypes (p. 76)
Receptors (p. 76)
Reuptake (p. 78)
Second messenger (p. 77)
Synaptic vesicles (p. 75)

3.5 The Neurotransmitters

Acetylcholine (p. 80)
Amino acids (p. 79)
Aspartate (p. 79)
Catecholamines (p. 79)
Dopamine (p. 79)
Endorphins (p. 81)
Epinephrine (p. 79)

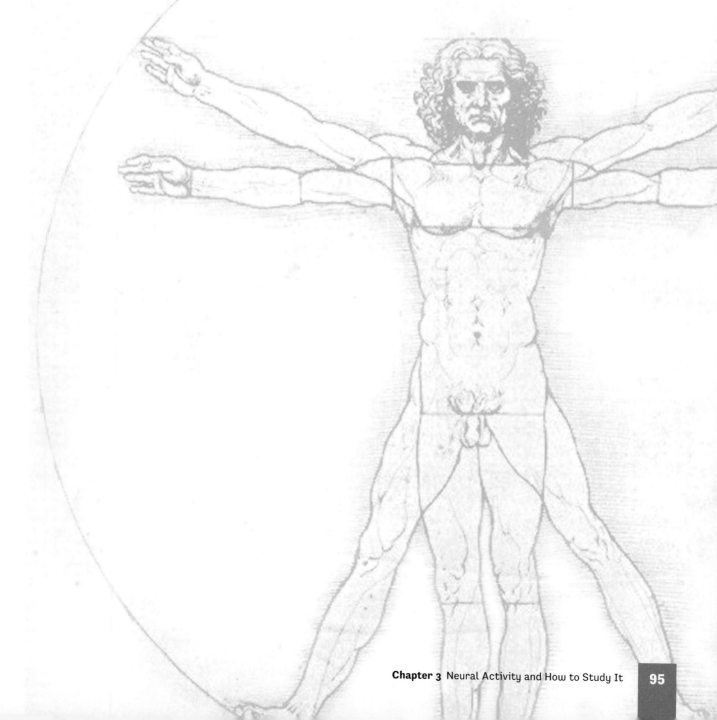

ON THE CD

Studying for an exam?
Get some help from the
electronic flash cards of
the key terms and the
practice tests for this
chapter.

chapter 3

Neural Activity and How to Study It
How Neurons Work

The previous chapter focused on the structure of the brain; in contrast, this chapter focused on how the brain works. Specifically, this chapter discussed neural conduction, synaptic transmission, neurotransmitters, and how biopsychologists study neural activity.

Figure 3.1

Two factors influencing the accumulation of sodium ions outside resting neurons

2

1

1 Sodium ions are pumped out by sodium–potassium pumps.

2 Sodium channels are closed, and thus sodium ions accumulating outside the neuron have difficulty entering.

Two kinds of pressure on sodium ions accumulated outside resting neurons to enter

2

1

1 Pressure of random movement of the high concentrations of sodium ions outside neurons

2 Pressure from –70 mV potential outside the neuron

The Neuron's Resting Membrane Potential

The resting potential characterizes the state of inactive neurons, which are said to be polarized. Many neurons have a resting membrane potential of about –70 millivolts.
(Pages 66–67)

Postsynaptic Potentials and Action Potentials

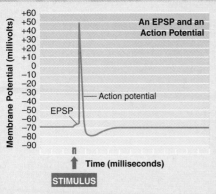

An EPSP and an Action Potential

Action potential

EPSP

STIMULUS

Time (milliseconds)

Membrane Potential (millivolts)

Figure 3.2

When a neuron receives synaptic stimulation, tiny brief signals called postsynaptic potentials are generated. Normally, most neurons receive many excitatory and inhibitory signals at any given time, and these are continuously added together. When the sum of the signals becomes sufficiently positive to exceed the threshold of excitation, a large action potential is generated in an all-or-none manner.
(Pages 68–71)

Conduction of Action Potentials

Action potentials are the means by which neurons conduct signals down their axons. Conduction of action potentials is nondecremental; that is, action potentials do not lose strength as they travel along axons, even if the axons are very long.
(Pages 71–73)

An action potential

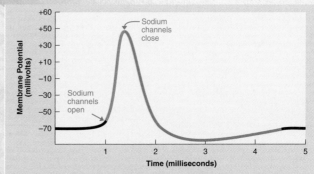

Sodium channels close

Sodium channels open

Time (milliseconds)

Membrane Potential (millivolts)

Visual Summary

Synaptic Transmission and the Neurotransmitters

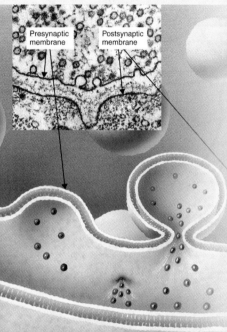

Once action potentials reach the terminal buttons of axons, they trigger the release of molecules called neurotransmitters into the synapses. Neurotransmitters activate receptors in the postsynaptic membrane; this activation triggers an excitatory or inhibitory response in the postsynaptic neuron. There are many different neurotransmitter molecules; each neuron releases only one or two of them. The four major categories of small-molecule neurotransmitters are amino acids, monoamines, soluble gases, and acetylcholine. Large-molecule neurotransmitters are peptides, or neuropeptides.
(Pages 73–82)

Exocytosis

How Biopsychologists Study the Brain

Midsagittal structural MRI

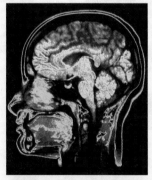

Biopsychologists use a variety of methods to study how the brain controls behavior and other psychological processes, including conventional brain lesioning, brain stimulation, and recording techniques. Two methods that have become more prominent in biopsychological research in recent years are brain imaging and genetic engineering.
(Pages 82–94)

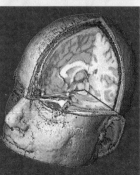

3-D structural MRI

Themes Revisited

This chapter developed all four of the book's major themes. The clinical implications theme was illustrated by the opening case of Roberto Garcia d'Orta, whose symptoms resulted from a disruption of dopaminergic transmission. Also, the chapter discussed the therapeutic use of opiate drugs, brain lesions, curare, and Botox, as well the use of brain imaging in medical diagnosis.

The evolutionary perspective theme was implicit throughout the chapter, because almost all neurophysiological research is conducted on the synapses of nonhuman subjects, and the results are applied to human brains.

The thinking-clearly-about-biopsychology theme arose during the discussion of three metaphors: the rock concert metaphor of the forces acting on sodium ions in the resting neuron, the firing-gun metaphor of action potentials, and the mouse-traps-on-a-wobbly-shelf metaphor of axonal conduction. Scientists find metaphors useful for thinking about the phenomena they study and for generating hypotheses.

Finally, this chapter touched on the cognitive neuroscience theme. The field of cognitive neuroscience is based largely on methods of functional brain imaging (e.g., PET and fMRI), which were introduced in the final section.

Think about It

1. Just as computers operate on binary (yes–no or on–off) signals, the all-or-none action potential is the basis of neural conduction. The human brain is thus nothing more than a particularly complex computer. Discuss.

2. How have the findings described in this chapter changed your understanding of brain function?

3. Why is it important for biopsychologists to understand neural conduction and synaptic transmission? Is it important for all psychologists to have such knowledge? Discuss.

4. Which do you think is the most useful method for studying brain activity that biopsychologists have at their disposal? Why is it the best?

Part 2

Sensory and Motor Systems

Congratulations, you have completed Part 1 of *Basics of Biopsychology*. The strength of biopsychology is its diversity: Biopsychologists use information and methods from relevant fields of biology and neuroscience (e.g., evolution, genetics, neuroanatomy, and neurophysiology) and apply them to the study of psychological processes. Unfortunately, this diversity can create a barrier for beginning students, who must learn about this foundation material before delving into biopsychology itself. But you have now surmounted that barrier and are ready to proceed.

I hope that you feel good about your efforts in completing Part 1—for two reasons. First, your efforts will allow you to proceed to learn about the real subject matter of biopsychology, which I think—in my not-particularly-impartial view as a biopsychologist—you will find well worth the effort. Second, and more importantly, as a result of your efforts, you are much more knowledgeable about a topic that should be particularly important to you: yourself. You now have a fundamental knowledge of the genetics, evolution, anatomy, and activity of your own brain.

Part 2, "Sensory and Motor Systems," focuses on the flow of information into the brain and the flow of behavior from it. Chapters 4 and 5 focus on five sensory systems: vision, hearing, touch, smell, and taste. Chapter 6 deals with the neural systems that control behavior (movement).

To be honest, as a student, I did not enjoy studying the sensory and motor systems; but scientists know much more about these systems now than they did when I was a student, and much of this new knowledge is pretty darned interesting. For example, you will learn in Part 2 that there are systems in the brain that can perceive objects without any conscious awareness of the perception. Similarly, there are systems in the brain that can unconsciously perform an act that cannot be performed under conscious direction. This is exciting stuff, and I have highlighted these sorts of new findings in Part 2.

chapter 4

The Visual System
How We See

This chapter is about the visual system. Most people think that their visual system has evolved to respond as accurately as possible to the patterns of light that enter their eyes. They recognize the obvious limitations in their visual system's accuracy, of course; and they appreciate those curious instances, termed *visual illusions*, in which it is "tricked" into seeing things the way they aren't. But such shortcomings are generally regarded as minor imperfections in a system that responds as faithfully as possible to the external world.

Despite its intuitive appeal, this way of thinking about the visual system is wrong. The visual system does not produce an accurate internal copy of the external world. It does much more. From the tiny, distorted, upside-down, two-dimensional retinal images projected on the visual receptors that line the backs of the eyes, the visual system creates an accurate, richly detailed, three-dimensional perception that is— and this is the really important part—in some respects even better than the external reality from which it was created.

Regardless of what you may have heard to the contrary, what you see is not necessarily what you get. One of my primary goals in this chapter is to help you recognize and appreciate the inherent creativity of your own visual system.

This chapter is composed of six sections. The first three sections take you on a journey from the external visual world to the visual receptors of the retina and from there over the major visual pathway to the primary visual cortex. The next two sections describe how the neurons of this pathway mediate the perception of two particularly important features of the visual world: edges and color. The final section deals with the flow of visual signals from the primary visual cortex to other, more complex parts of cortex that participate in vision.

You will learn in this chapter that understanding the visual system requires the integration of two types of research: (1) research that probes the visual system with sophisticated neuroanatomical, neurochemical, and neurophysiological techniques; and (2) research that focuses on the assessment of what we see. Both types of research receive substantial coverage in this chapter, but it is the second type that provides you with a unique educational opportunity: the opportunity to participate in the very research you are studying. Throughout this chapter, you will be encouraged to participate in a series of Check It Out demonstrations designed to give you a taste of the excitement of scientific discovery and to illustrate the relevance of what you are learning in this text to life outside its pages.

Before you begin the first section of the chapter, I'd like you to consider an interesting clinical case. Have you ever wondered whether one person's subjective experiences are like those of others? This case provides evidence that at least some of them are. It was reported by Whitman Richards (1971), and his subject was Mrs. Richards. Mrs. Richards suffered from migraine headaches, and like 20% of migraine sufferers, she often experienced visual displays, called *fortification illusions*, prior to her attacks (see Pietrobon & Striessnig, 2003).

Thinking Clearly

The Case of Mrs. Richards: Fortification Illusions and the Astronomer

€ach fortification illusion began with a gray area of blindness near the center of her visual field—see Figure 4.1. During the next few minutes, the gray area would begin to expand into a horseshoe shape, with a zig-zag pattern of flickering lines at its advancing edge. It normally took about 20 minutes for the lines and the trailing area of blindness to reach the periphery of her visual field. At this point, her headache would usually begin.

Because the illusion expanded so slowly, Mrs. Richards was able to stare at a point on the center of a blank sheet of paper and periodically trace on the sheet the details of her illusion. This method made it apparent that the lines became thicker and the expansion of the area of blindness occurred faster as the illusion spread into the periphery.

The features of fortification illusions are quite interesting, but they are not the most intriguing aspect of this case. Dr. Richards discovered that a

Clinical Implications

1 An attack begins, often when reading, as a gray area of blindness near the center of the visual field.

2 Over the next 20 minutes, the gray area assumes a horseshoe shape and expands into the periphery, at which point the headache begins.

The fortification illusions associated with migraine headaches.

Figure 4.1

similar set of drawings was published in 1870 by the famous British astronomer George Biddell Airy, and they were virtually identical to those done by Mrs. Richards. (By the way, the illusions got their name because their advancing edges reminded people of the plans for a fortification.)

We will return to fortification illusions after we have learned a bit about the visual system. At that point, you will be able to appreciate the significance of their features.

4.1

Light Enters the Eye and Reaches the Retina

Everybody knows that cats, owls, and other nocturnal animals can see in the dark. Right? Wrong! Some animals have special adaptations that allow them to see under very dim illumination, but no animal can see in complete darkness. The light reflected into your eyes from the objects around you is the basis for your ability to see them; if there is no light, there is no vision.

You may recall from high-school physics that light can be thought of in two different ways: as discrete particles of energy, called *photons*, traveling through space at about 300,000 kilometers (186,000 miles) per second, or as waves of energy. Both theories are useful; in some ways light behaves like a particle, and in others it behaves like a wave. Physicists have learned to live with this nagging inconsistency, and we must do the same.

Light is sometimes defined as waves of electromagnetic energy that are between 380 and 760 nanometers (billionths of a meter) in length (see Figure 4.2). There is nothing special about these wavelengths except that the human visual system responds to them. In fact, some animals can see wavelengths that we cannot (see Fernald, 2000). For example, rattlesnakes can see *infrared waves*, which are too long for humans to see; as a result, they can see warm-blooded prey in what for us would be complete darkness. Accordingly, if I were writing this book for rattlesnakes, I would be forced to provide another, equally arbitrary, definition of light.

Wavelength and intensity are two properties of light that are of particular interest—wavelength because it plays an important role in the perception of color, and intensity because it plays an important role in the perception of brightness. The concepts of *wavelength* and *color* are typically regarded as interchangeable, and so are *intensity* and *brightness*. For example, we commonly refer to an intense light with a wavelength of 700 nanometers as being a bright red light (see Figure 4.2), when in fact it is our perception of the light, not the light itself, that is bright and red. I know that these distinctions may seem trivial to you now, but by the end of the chapter you will appreciate their importance.

The amount of light reaching the retinas is regulated by the donut-shaped bands of contractile tissue, the *irises*, which give our eyes their characteristic color (see Figure 4.3). Light enters the eye through the *pupil*, the hole in the iris. The adjustment of pupil size in response to changes in illumination represents a compromise between **sensitivity** (the ability to detect the presence of dimly lit objects) and **acuity** (the ability to see the details of objects). When the level of illumination is high and sensitivity is thus not important, the visual system takes

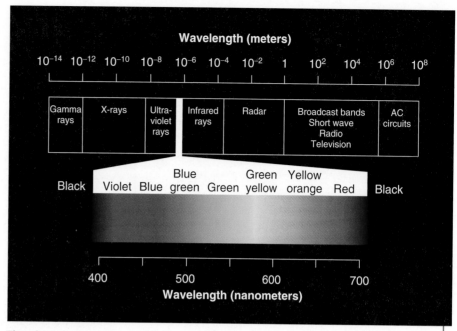

The electromagnetic spectrum and the colors associated with the wavelengths that are visible to humans.

Figure 4.2

The Evolutionary Perspective

The human eye. Light enters the eye through the pupil, whose size is regulated by the iris. The iris gives the eye its characteristic color—blue, brown, or other.

Figure 4.3

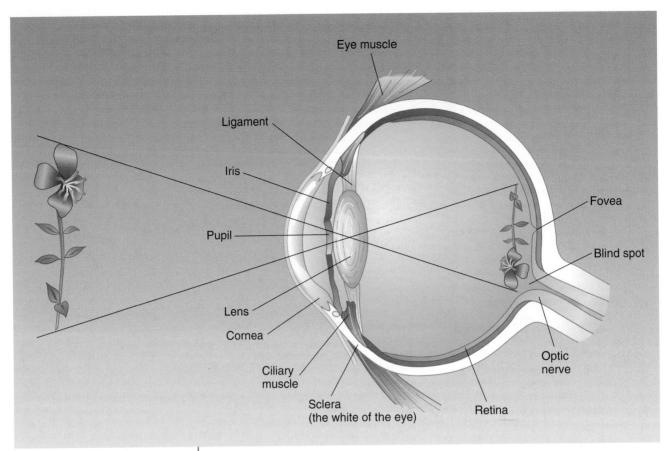

A diagram of the human eye.

Figure 4.4

advantage of the situation by constricting the pupils. When the pupils are constricted, the image falling on each retina is sharper and there is a greater *depth of focus*; that is, a greater range of depths are simultaneously kept in focus on the retinas. However, when the level of illumination is too low to adequately activate the receptors, the pupils dilate to let in more light, thereby sacrificing acuity and depth of focus.

Behind each pupil is a *lens*, which focuses incoming light on the retina (see Figure 4.4). When we direct our gaze at something near, the tension on the ligaments holding each lens in place is adjusted by the **ciliary muscles**, and the lens assumes its natural cylindrical shape. This increases the ability of the lens to *refract* (bend) light and thus brings close objects into sharp focus. When we focus on a distant object, the lens is flattened. The process of adjusting the configuration of the lenses to bring images into focus on the retina is called **accommodation**.

No description of the eyes of vertebrates would be complete without a discussion of their most obvious feature: the fact that they come in pairs. One reason vertebrates have two eyes is that vertebrates have two sides: left and right. By having one eye on each side, which is by far the most common arrangement, vertebrates can see in almost every direction without moving their heads. But then why do some vertebrates, including humans, have their eyes mounted side by side on the front of their heads? This arrangement sacrifices the ability to see

Here you see three animals whose eyes are on the front of their heads (a human, an owl, and a lion) and three whose eyes are on the sides of their heads (an antelope, a canary, and a squirrel). Why do a few vertebrate species have their eyes side by side on the front of the head while most species have one eye on each side?

In general, predators tend to have front-facing eyes because this enables them to accurately perceive how far away prey animals are; prey animals tend to have side-facing eyes because this gives them a larger field of vision and the ability to see predators approaching from most directions.

behind so that what is in front can be viewed through both eyes simultaneously—an arrangement that is an important basis for our visual system's ability to create three-dimensional perceptions (to see depth) from two-dimensional retinal images. Why do you think the two-eyes-on-the-front arrangement has evolved in some species but not in others? (The above Check It Out demonstration will help you answer this question.)

The Evolutionary Perspective

The movements of your eyes are coordinated so that each point in your visual world is projected to corresponding points on your two retinas. To accomplish this, your eyes must *converge* (turn slightly inward); convergence is greatest when you are inspecting things that are close. But the positions of the retinal images on your two eyes can never correspond exactly because your two eyes do not view the world from exactly the same position. **Binocular disparity**—the difference in the position of the same image on the two retinas—is greater for close objects than for distant objects; therefore, your visual system can use the degree of binocular disparity to construct one three-dimensional perception from two two-dimensional retinal images. (Look at the next Check It Out demonstration.)

Check It Out

BINOCULAR DISPARITY AND THE MYSTERIOUS COCKTAIL SAUSAGE

If you compare the views from each eye (by quickly closing one eye and then the other) of objects at various distances in front of you—for example, your finger held at different distances—you will notice that the disparity between the two views is greater for closer objects. Now try the mysterious demonstration of the cocktail sausage. Face the farthest wall in the room (or some other distant object) and bring the tips of your two pointing fingers together at arm's length in front of you—with the backs of your fingers away from you, unless you prefer sausages with fingernails. Now, with both eyes open, look through the notch between your touching fingertips, but focus on the wall. Do you see the cocktail sausage between your fingertips? Where did it come from? To prove to yourself that the sausage is a product of binocularity, make it disappear by shutting one eye. Warning: Do not eat this sausage.

4.2

The Retina and Translation of Light into Neural Signals

Figure 4.5 illustrates the fundamental cellular structure of the retina. The retina is composed of five layers of different types of neurons: **receptors, horizontal cells, bipolar cells, amacrine cells,** and **retinal ganglion cells.** Each of these five types of retinal neurons comes in a variety of subtypes: About 55 different kinds of retinal neurons have been identified (Masland, 2001). Notice that the amacrine cells and the horizontal cells are specialized for *lateral communication* (communication across the major channels of sensory input).

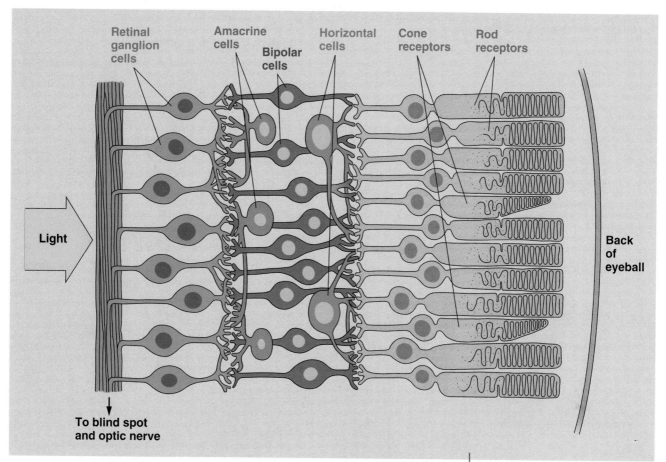

The cellular structure of the mammalian retina.

Figure 4.5

Also notice in Figure 4.5 that the retina is in a sense inside-out: Light reaches the receptor layer only after passing through the other four layers. Then, once the receptors have been activated, the neural message is transmitted back out through the retinal layers to the retinal ganglion cells, whose axons project across the inside of the retina before gathering together in a bundle and exiting the eyeball. This inside-out arrangement creates two visual problems. One is that the incoming light is distorted by the retinal tissue through which it must pass before reaching the receptors. The other is that for the bundle of retinal ganglion cell axons to leave the eye, there must be a gap in the receptor layer; this gap is called the **blind spot**.

The first of these two problems is minimized by the fovea (see Figure 4.6 on page 108). The **fovea** is an indentation, about 0.33 centimeter in diameter, at the center of the retina; it is the area of the retina that is specialized for high-acuity vision (for seeing fine details). The thinning of the retinal ganglion cell layer at the fovea reduces the distortion of incoming light. The blind spot, the second of the two visual problems created by the inside-out structure of the retina, requires a more creative solution—which is illustrated in the Check It Out demonstration on page 109.

In this demonstration, you will experience **completion**. The visual system uses information provided by the receptors around the blind spot to fill in the gaps in your retinal images. When the visual system detects a straight bar going into one side of the blind spot and another straight bar leaving the other side, it fills in the missing bit for you; and what you see is a continuous straight bar, regardless of what is actually there. The completion phenomenon is one of the most compelling

ON THE CD

Visit the *Surface Interpolation* module. The Cornsweet Illusion demonstrates that your visual system creates much of what you see.

Thinking Clearly

demonstrations that the visual system does much more than create a faithful copy of the external world.

It is a mistake to think that completion is merely a response to blind spots (see Ramachandran, 1992; Spillman & Werner, 1996). Indeed, completion is a fundamental visual system function. When you look at an object, your visual system does not conduct an image of that object from your retina to your cortex. Instead, it extracts key information about the object—primarily information about its edges and their location—and conducts that information to the cortex, where a perception of the entire object is created from that partial information. For example, the color and brightness of large unpatterned surfaces are not directly perceived but are filled in (completed) by a completion process, in this case called *surface interpolation*.

Cone and Rod Vision

You likely noticed in Figure 4.5 that there are two different types of receptors in the human retina: cone-shaped receptors called **cones**, and rod-shaped receptors called **rods** (see Figure 4.7). The existence of these two types of receptors puzzled researchers until 1866, when it was first noticed that species active only in the day tend to have cone-only retinas and that species active only at night tend to have rod-only retinas.

From this observation emerged the **duplexity theory** of vision—the theory that cones and rods mediate different kinds of vision. Cone-mediated vision (**photopic vision**) predominates in good lighting and provides high-acuity (finely detailed) colored perceptions of the world. In dim illumination, there is not enough light to reliably excite the cones, and the more sensitive rod-mediated vision (**scotopic vision**) predominates. However, the sensitivity of scotopic vi-

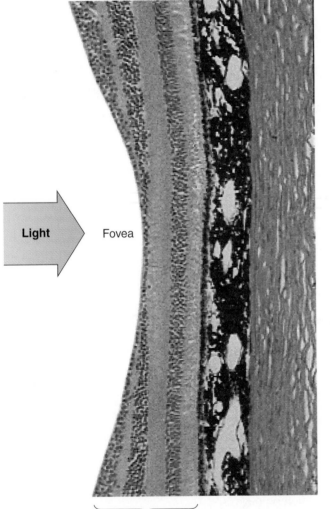

Axons of retinal ganglion cells | Cell bodies of retinal ganglion cells | Receptors | Back of eyeball

Light

Fovea

Retina

A section of the retina. The fovea is the indentation at the center of the retina; it is specialized for high-acuity vision.

Figure 4.6

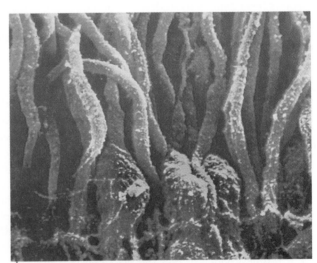

Cones and rods. The smaller, conical cells are cones; the larger, cylindrical cells are rods.

Figure 4.7

YOUR BLIND SPOT AND COMPLETION

First, prove to yourself that you do have areas of blindness that correspond to your retinal blind spots. Close your left eye and stare directly at the A below, trying as hard as you can to not shift your gaze. While keeping the gaze of your right eye fixed on the A, hold the book at different distances from you until the black dot to the right of the A becomes focused on your blind spot and disappears at about 20 centimeters (8 inches).

If each eye has a blind spot, why is there not a black hole in your perception of the world when you look at it with one eye? You will discover the answer by focusing on B with your right eye while holding the book at the same distance as before. Suddenly, the broken line to the right of B will become whole. Now focus on C at the same distance with your right eye. What do you see?

sion is not achieved without cost: Scotopic vision lacks both the detail and the color of photopic vision.

The differences between photopic (cone) and scotopic (rod) vision result in part from a difference in the way the two systems are "wired." As Figure 4.8 illustrates, there is a large difference in *convergence* between the two systems. The output of several hundred rods may ultimately converge on a single retinal ganglion cell, whereas it is not uncommon for a retinal ganglion cell to receive input from only a few cones. As a result, the

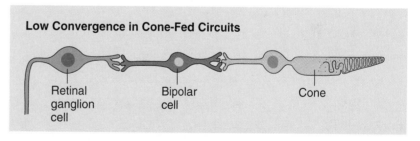

A schematic representation of the convergence of cones and rods on retinal ganglion cells. There is a low degree of convergence in cone-fed pathways and a high degree of convergence in rod-fed pathways.

Figure 4.8

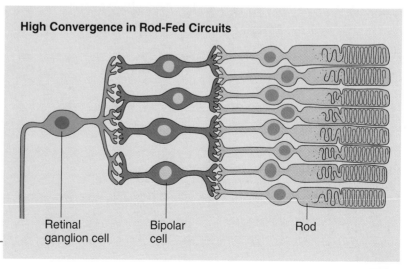

effects of dim light simultaneously stimulating many rods can summate (add) to influence the firing of a retinal ganglion cell onto which the output of the stimulated rods converges, whereas the effects of the same dim light applied to a sheet of cones cannot summate to the same degree, and the retinal ganglion cells may not respond to the light.

The convergent scotopic system pays for its high degree of sensitivity with a low level of acuity. When a retinal ganglion cell that receives input from hundreds of rods changes its firing, the brain has no way of knowing which portion of the rods contributed to the change. Although a more intense light is required to change the firing of a retinal ganglion cell that receives signals from cones, when such a retinal ganglion cell does react, there is less ambiguity about the location of the stimulus that triggered the reaction.

Cones and rods differ in their distribution on the retina. As Figure 4.9 illustrates, there are no rods at all in the fovea, only cones. At the boundaries of the foveal indentation, the proportion of cones declines markedly, and there is an increase in the number of rods. The density of rods reaches a maximum at 20° from the center of the fovea. Notice that there are many more rods in the **nasal hemiretina** (the half of each retina next to the nose) than in the **temporal hemiretina** (the half next to the temples).

Generally speaking, more intense lights appear brighter. However, wavelength also has a substantial effect on the perception of brightness. Because our visual systems are not equally sensitive to all wavelengths in the visible spectrum, lights of the same intensity but of different wavelengths can differ markedly in brightness. A graph of the relative brightness of lights of the same intensity presented at different wavelengths is called a *spectral sensitivity curve*.

By far the most important thing to remember about spectral sensitivity curves is that humans and other animals with both cones and rods have two of them: a **photopic spectral sensitivity curve** and a **scotopic spectral sensitivity curve**. The photopic spectral sensitivity of humans can be determined by having subjects judge the relative brightness of different wavelengths of light shone on the fovea. Their scotopic spectral sensitivity can be determined by asking subjects to judge the relative brightness of different wavelengths of light shone on the periphery of the retina at an intensity too low to activate the few peripheral cones that are located there.

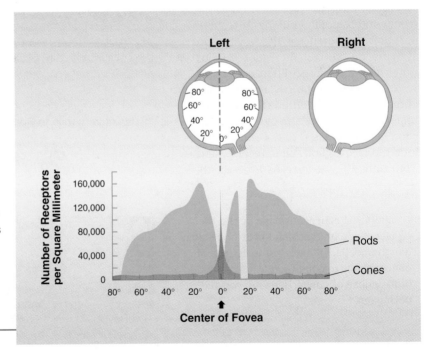

The distribution of cones and rods over the human retina. The figure illustrates the number of cones and rods per square millimeter as a function of distance from the center of the fovea.
(Adapted from Lindsay & Norman, 1977.)

figure 4.9

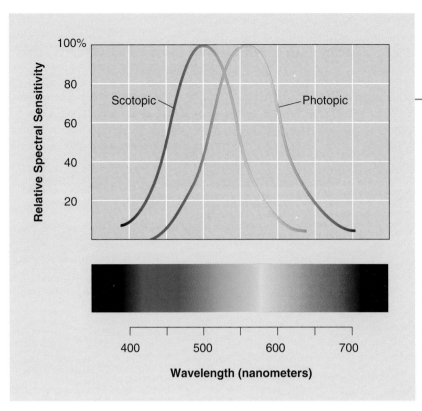

Human photopic (cone) and scotopic (rod) spectral sensitivity curves. The peak of each curve has been arbitrarily set at 100%.

—Figure 4.10—

The photopic and scotopic spectral sensitivity curves of human subjects are plotted in Figure 4.10. Notice that under photopic conditions, the visual system is maximally sensitive to wavelengths of about 560 nanometers; thus, under photopic conditions, a light at 500 nanometers would have to be much more intense than one at 560 nanometers to be seen as equally bright. In contrast, under scotopic conditions, the visual system is maximally sensitive to wavelengths of about 500 nanometers; thus, under scotopic conditions, a light of 560 nanometers would have to be much more intense than one at 500 nanometers to be seen as equally bright.

Because of the difference in photopic and scotopic spectral sensitivity, an interesting visual effect can be observed during the transition from photopic to scotopic vision. In 1825, Jan Purkinje described the following occurrence, which has become known as the **Purkinje effect** (pronounced "pur-KIN-jee"). One evening, just before dusk, while Purkinje was walking in his garden, he noticed how bright most of his yellow and red flowers appeared in relation to his blue ones. What amazed him was that just a few minutes later the relative brightness of his flowers had somehow been reversed; the entire scene, when viewed at night, appeared completely in shades of gray, but most of the blue flowers appeared as brighter grays than did the yellow and red ones. Can you explain this shift in relative brightness by referring to the photopic and scotopic spectral sensitivity curves in Figure 4.10?

Eye Movement

If cones are in fact responsible for mediating high-acuity color vision under photopic conditions, how can they accomplish their task when most of them are crammed into the fovea? Look around you. What you see is not a few colored details at the center of a grayish scene. You seem to see an expansive, richly detailed, lavishly colored visual world. How can such a perception be the product of a photopic system that, for the most part, is restricted to a few degrees in the center of your *visual field* (the entire area that you can see at a particular moment)? The following Check It Out demonstration provides a clue.

PERIPHERY OF YOUR RETINA DOES NOT MEDIATE THE PERCEPTION OF DETAIL OR COLOR

Close your left eye, and with your right eye stare at the fixation point (✛) at a distance of about 12 centimeters (4.75 inches) from the page. Be very careful that your gaze does not shift. You will notice when your gaze is totally fixed that it is difficult to see detail and color at 20° or more from the fixation point because there are so few cones there. Now look at the page again with your right eye, but this time without fixing your gaze. Notice the difference that eye movement makes to your vision.

W	F	D	M	E	A	✛
50°	40°	30°	20°	10°	5°	0°

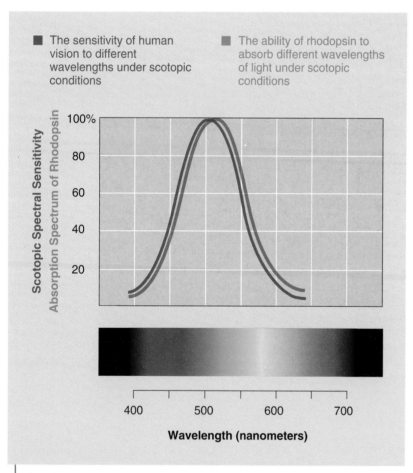

■ The sensitivity of human vision to different wavelengths under scotopic conditions

■ The ability of rhodopsin to absorb different wavelengths of light under scotopic conditions

The absorption spectrum of rhodopsin compared with the human scotopic spectral sensitivity curve.

Figure 4.11

What this demonstration shows is that what we see is determined not just by what is projected on the retina at that instant. Although we are not aware of it, the eyes continually scan the visual field by making a series of brief fixations. About three fixations occur every second, and they are connected by very quick eye movements called **saccades** (pronounced "sah-KAHDS"). The visual system *integrates* (adds together) some of the information from the fixations to produce a wide-angled, high-acuity, richly colored perception (see Irwin, 1996). It is because of this *temporal integration* that the world does not vanish momentarily each time we blink.

Visual Transduction: The Conversion of Light to Neural Signals

Transduction is the conversion of one form of energy to another. *Visual transduction* is the conversion of light to neural signals by the visual receptors. A breakthrough in the study of visual transduction came in 1876, when a red *pigment* (a pigment is any substance that absorbs light) was extracted from the retina of the frog, in which rods predominate. This pigment had a curious property. When the pigment (which became known as **rhodopsin**), was exposed to continuous intense light, it was *bleached* (lost its color), and it lost its ability to absorb light; but when it was returned to the dark, it regained both its redness and its light-absorbing capacity.

It is now clear that rhodopsin's absorption of light (and the accompanying bleaching) is the first step in rod-mediated vision. Evidence comes from demonstrations that the degree to which rhodopsin absorbs light in various situations predicts how humans see under the very same conditions. For example, it has been shown that the degree to which rhodopsin absorbs lights of different wavelengths is related to the ability of humans and other animals with rods to detect the presence of different wavelengths of light under scotopic conditions. Figure 4.11 illustrates the relationship between the **absorption spectrum** of rhodopsin and the human scotopic spectral sensitivity curve. The goodness of the fit leaves little doubt that, in dim light, our sensitivity to various wavelengths is a direct consequence of rhodopsin's ability to absorb them.

Rhodopsin is a G-protein–linked receptor that responds to light rather than to neurotransmitter molecules (see Koutalos & Yau, 1993; Molday & Hsu, 1995). Rhodopsin receptors, like other G-protein–linked receptors, initiate a cascade of intracellular chemical events when they are activated (see Figure 4.12). When rods are in darkness, their sodium channels are partially open, thus keeping the rods slightly depolarized and allowing a steady flow of excitatory glutamate neurotransmitter molecules to emanate from them. However, when rhodopsin receptors are

In the DARK

cyclic GMP

1 Rhodopsin molecules are inactive.

2 Sodium channels are kept open.

3 Sodium ions flow into the rods, partially depolarizing them.

4 Rods continuously release glutamate.

In the LIGHT

1 Light bleaches rhodopsin molecules.

2 As a result, sodium channels close.

3 Sodium ions cannot enter rods, and, as a result, the rods become hyperpolarized.

4 Glutamate release is reduced.

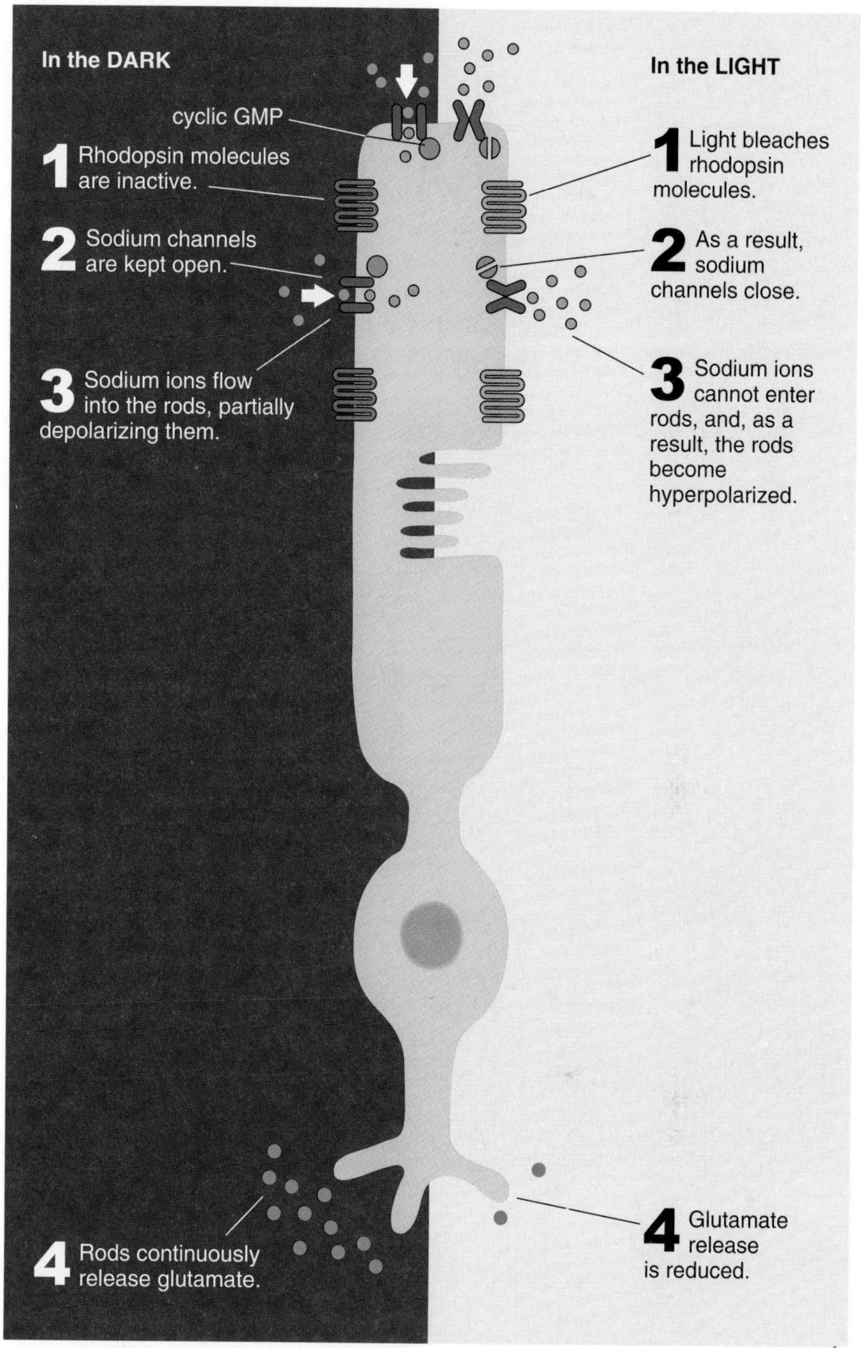

The inhibitory response of rods to light. When light bleaches rhodopsin molecules, the rods' sodium channels close; as a result, the rods become hyperpolarized and release less glutamate.

Figure 4.12

bleached by light, the resulting cascade of intracellular chemical events closes the sodium channels, hyperpolarizes the rods, and reduces the release of glutamate. The transduction of light by rods exemplifies an important point: Signals are often transmitted through neural systems by inhibition.

Less is known about the cone photopigments than about rhodopsin. However, their structure and function appear to be similar to those of rhodopsin.

Many pathways in the brain carry visual information. By far the largest and most thoroughly studied visual pathways are the **retina-geniculate-striate pathways**, which conduct signals from each retina to the **primary visual cortex**, or *striate cortex*, via the **lateral geniculate nuclei** of the thalamus.

About 90 % of axons of retinal ganglion cells become part of the retina-geniculate-striate pathways (see Tong, 2003). No other sensory system has such a predominant pair (left and right) of pathways to the cortex. The organization of these visual pathways is illustrated in Figure 4.13. Examine it carefully.

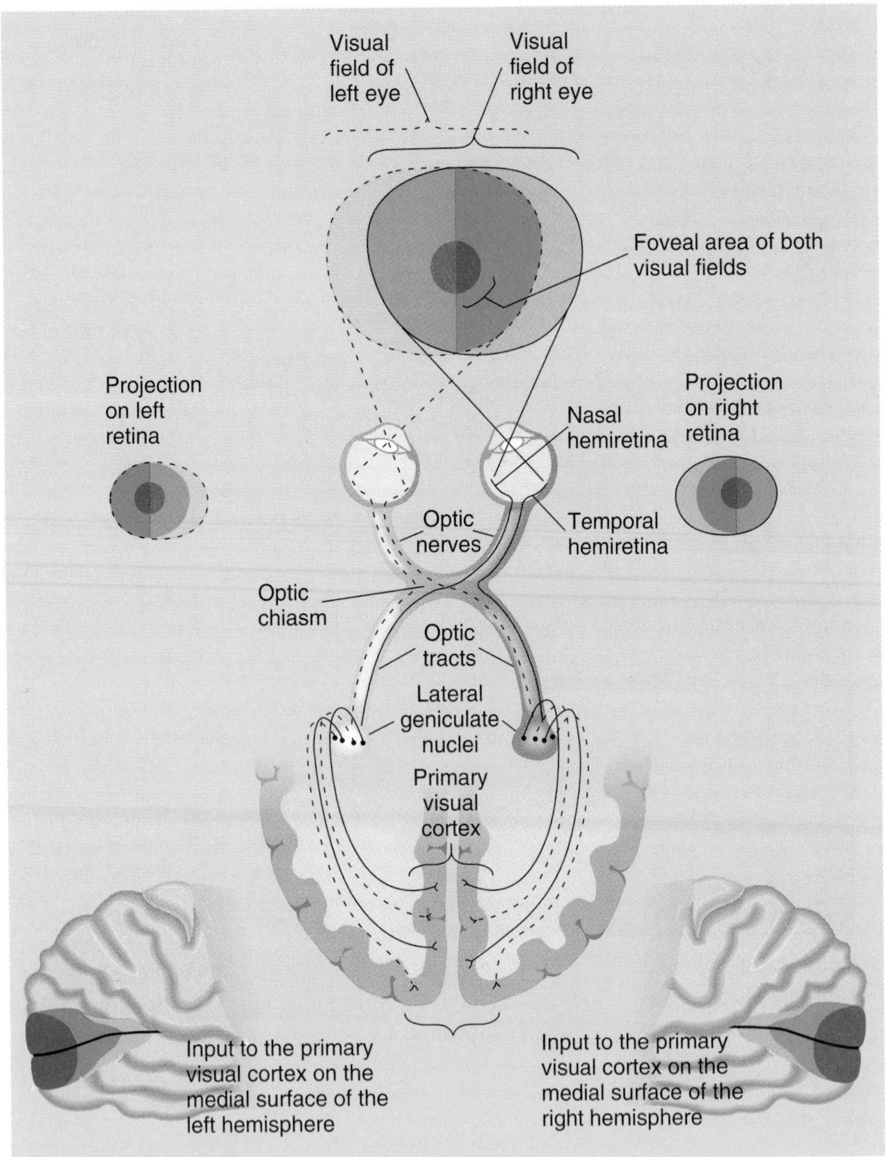

The main thing to notice from Figure 4.13 is that all signals from the left visual field reach the right primary visual cortex, either ipsilaterally from the *temporal hemiretina* of the right eye or contralaterally (via the *optic chiasm*) from the *nasal hemiretina* of the left eye—and that the opposite is true of all signals from the right visual field. Each lateral geniculate nucleus has six layers, and each layer of each nucleus receives input from all parts of the contralateral visual field of one eye. In other words, each lateral geniculate nucleus receives visual input only from the contralateral visual field; three layers receive input from one eye, and three from the other. Most of the lateral geniculate neurons that project to the primary visual cortex terminate in the lower part of cortical layer IV (see Figure 4.22), producing a characteristic stripe, or striation, when viewed in cross section—hence the name *striate cortex*.

The retina-geniculate-striate system: The neural projections from the retinas through the lateral geniculate nuclei to the left and right primary visual cortex (striate cortex). The colors indicate the flow of information from various parts of the receptive fields of each eye to various parts of the visual system. (Adapted from Netter, 1962.)

Figure 4.13

Retinotopic Organization

The retina-geniculate-striate system is **retinotopic**; each level of the system is organized like a map of the retina. This means that two stimuli presented to adjacent areas of the retina excite adjacent neurons at all levels of the system. The retinotopic layout of the primary visual cortex has a disproportionate representation of the fovea; although the fovea is only a small part of the retina, a relatively large proportion of the primary visual cortex (about 25%) is dedicated to the analysis of its input.

A dramatic demonstration of the retinotopic organization of the primary visual cortex was provided by Dobelle, Mladejovsky, and Girvin (1974). They implanted an array of electrodes in the primary visual cortex of patients who were blind because of damage to their eyes. If electrical current was administered simultaneously through an array of electrodes forming a shape, such as a cross, on the surface of a patient's cortex, the patient reported "seeing" a glowing image of that shape.

Clinical
Implications

The M and P Channels

Not apparent in Figure 4.13 is the fact that at least two independent channels of communication flow through each lateral geniculate nucleus (see Hendry & Calkins, 1998). One channel runs through the top four layers. These layers are called the **parvocellular layers** (or *P layers*) because they are composed of neurons with small cell bodies (*parvo* means "small"). The other channel runs through the bottom two layers, which are called the **magnocellular layers** (or *M layers*) because they are composed of neurons with large cell bodies (*magno* means "large").

The parvocellular neurons are particularly responsive to color, to fine pattern details, and to stationary or slowly moving objects. In contrast, the magnocellular neurons are particularly responsive to movement. Cones provide the majority of the input to the P layers, whereas rods provide the majority of the input to the M layers.

The parvocellular and magnocellular neurons project to slightly different sites in the lower part of layer IV of the striate cortex. In turn, these M and P portions of lower layer IV project to different parts of visual cortex (Levitt, 2001; Yabuta, Sawatari, & Callaway, 2001).

This is a good place to pause to scan your brain. Are you ready to proceed to the next two sections of the chapter, which describe how the visual system mediates the perception of edges and color? Find out by filling in the following blanks. The correct answers are provided below. Before proceeding, review material related to your errors and omissions.

1. Neural signals are carried from the retina to the lateral geniculate nuclei by the axons of _____ cells.
2. The axons of retinal ganglion cells leave the eyeball at the _____.
3. The area of the retina that mediates high-acuity vision is the _____.
4. Cones are the receptors of the _____ system, which functions only in good lighting.
5. The retinal ganglion cells from the nasal hemiretinas decussate (cross over to the other side of the brain) via the _____.
6. The photopigment of rods is _____.
7. The most important organizational principle of the retina-geniculate-striate system is that it is laid out _____.
8. Evidence that rhodopsin is the scotopic photopigment is provided by the fit between the _____ spectrum of rhodopsin and the scotopic spectral sensitivity curve.
9. The high degree of _____ characteristic of the scotopic system increases its sensitivity but decreases its acuity.

Scan Your Brain answers: (1) retinal ganglion, (2) blind spot, (3) fovea, (4) photopic, (5) optic chiasm, (6) rhodopsin, (7) retinotopically, (8) absorption, (9) convergence

Edge perception (seeing edges) does not sound like a particularly important topic, but it is. Edges are the most informative features of any visual display because they define the extent and position of the various objects in it. Given the importance of perceiving visual edges and the unrelenting pressure of natural selection, it is not surprising that the visual systems of many species are particularly good at edge perception.

Before considering the visual mechanisms underlying edge perception, it is important to appreciate exactly what a visual edge is. In a sense, a visual edge is nothing: It is merely the place where two different areas of a visual image meet. Accordingly, the perception of an edge is really the perception of a *contrast* between two adjacent areas of the visual field. This section of the chapter reviews the perception of edges (the perception of contrast) between areas that differ from one another in brightness (i.e., show brightness contrast).

Lateral Inhibition and Contrast Enhancement

Carefully examine the stripes in Figure 4.14. The intensity graph in the figure indicates what is there—a series of homogeneous stripes of different intensity. But this is not exactly what you see, is it? What you see is indicated in the brightness graph. Adjacent to each edge, the brighter stripe looks brighter than it really is and the darker stripe looks darker than it really is. The nonexistent stripes of brightness and darkness running adjacent to the edges are called *Mach bands*; they enhance the contrast at each edge and make the edge easier to see.

It is important to appreciate that **contrast enhancement** is not something that occurs just in books. Although we are normally unaware of it, every edge we look at is highlighted for us by the contrast-enhancing mechanisms of our nervous systems. In effect, our perception of edges is better than the real thing.

The classic studies of the physiological basis of contrast enhancement were conducted on the eyes of an unlikely subject: the *horseshoe crab* (e.g., Ratliff, 1972). The *lateral eyes* of the horseshoe crab are ideal for certain types of neurophysiological research. Unlike mammalian eyes, they are composed of very large receptors, called **ommatidia**, each with its own large axon. The axons of the ommatidia are interconnected by a lateral neural network.

In order to understand the physiological basis of contrast enhancement in the horseshoe

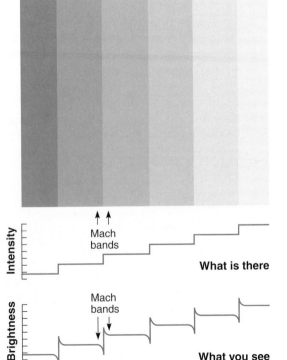

The illusory bands visible in this figure are often called Mach bands, although Ernst Mach used a different figure to generate them in his studies (see Eagleman, 2001).

Figure 4.14

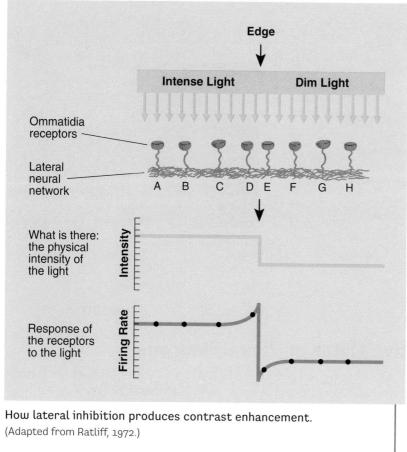

How lateral inhibition produces contrast enhancement.
(Adapted from Ratliff, 1972.)

Figure 4.15

crab, you must know two things. The first is that if a single ommatidium is illuminated, it fires at a rate that is proportional to the intensity of the light striking it; more intense lights produce more firing. The second is that when a receptor fires, it inhibits its neighbors via the lateral neural network; this inhibition is called **lateral inhibition** because it spreads laterally across the array of receptors. The amount of lateral inhibition produced by a receptor is greatest when the receptor is most intensely illuminated, and the inhibition has its greatest effect on the receptor's immediate neighbors.

The neural basis of contrast enhancement can be understood in terms of the firing rates of the receptors on each side of an edge, as indicated in Figure 4.15. Notice that the receptor adjacent to the edge on the more intense side (receptor D) fires more than the other intensely illuminated receptors (A, B, C), while the receptor adjacent to the edge on the less well-illuminated side (receptor E) fires less than the other receptors on that side (F, G, H). Lateral inhibition accounts for these differences. Receptors A, B, and C all fire at the same rate, because they are all receiving the same high level of stimulation and the same high degree of lateral inhibition from all their highly stimulated neighbors. Receptor D fires more than A, B, and C, because it receives as much stimulation as they do but less inhibition from its neighbors, many of which are on the dimmer side of the edge. Now consider the receptors on the dimmer side. Receptors F, G, and H fire at the same rate, because they are all being stimulated by the same low level of light and receiving the same low level of inhibition from their neighbors. However, receptor E fires even less, because it is receiving the same excitation but more inhibition from its neighbors, many of which are on the more intense side of the edge. Now that you understand the neural basis of contrast enhancement, take another look at Figure 4.14. Also, if you are still having a hard time believing that Mach bands are created by your own visual system, look at the following Check It Out demonstration.

Receptive Fields of Visual Neurons

The Evolutionary Perspective

The Nobel Prize–winning research of David Hubel and Torsten Wiesel is the fitting climax to this discussion of brightness contrast. Their research has revealed much about the neural mechanisms of vision, and their methods have been adopted by a generation of sensory neurophysiologists. Hubel and Wiesel's subjects are single neurons in the visual systems of cats and monkeys; because it is invasive, their technique cannot be employed on human subjects.

First, the tip of a microelectrode is positioned near a single neuron in the visual area of interest. During testing, eye movements are blocked by paralyzing the eye muscles, and the images on a screen in front of the subject are focused sharply on the retina by an experimenter using an adjustable lens. The next step in the procedure is to identify the receptive field of the neuron. The **receptive field** of a visual neuron is the area of the visual field within which it is possible for a visual stimulus to influence the firing of that neuron. Visual system neurons tend to be continually active; thus, effective stimuli are those that either increase or decrease the rate of firing. The final step in the method is to record the responses of the neuron to various stimuli within its receptive field in order to characterize the types of stimuli that most influence its activity. Then, the electrode is advanced slightly, and the entire process of identifying and characterizing the receptive field properties is repeated for another neuron, and then for another, and another, and so on. The general strategy is to begin by studying neurons near the receptors and gradually working up through "higher" and "higher" levels of the system in an effort to understand the increasing complexity of the neural responses at each level.

ON THE CD

The *How the Receptive Fields of Visual Systems Neurons Are Studied* module is definitely worth a visit.

Receptive Fields: Neurons of the Retina-Geniculate-Striate System

Hubel and Wiesel (e.g., 1979) began their studies of visual system neurons by recording from the three levels of the retina-geniculate-striate system: first from retinal ganglion cells, then from lateral geniculate neurons, and finally from the striate neurons of lower layer IV, the terminus of the system. They found little change in the receptive fields as they worked their way along the left and right pathways.

When Hubel and Wiesel compared the receptive fields recorded from retinal ganglion cells, lateral geniculate nuclei, and lower layer IV neurons, four commonalties were readily apparent:

- At each level, the receptive fields in the foveal area of the retina were smaller than those at the periphery; this is consistent with the fact that the fovea mediates fine-grained (high-acuity) vision.
- All the neurons (retinal ganglion cells, lateral geniculate neurons, *and* lower layer IV neurons) had receptive fields that were circular.
- All the neurons were **monocular**; that is, each neuron had a receptive field in one eye but not the other.
- Many neurons at each of the three levels of the retina-geniculate-striate system had receptive fields that comprised an excitatory area and an inhibitory area separated by a circular boundary.

It is this last discovery that is most important. Let me explain.

When Hubel and Wiesel shone a spot of white light onto the various parts of the receptive fields of neurons in the retina-geniculate-striate pathway, they discovered two different responses. The neuron responded with either "on" firing or "off" firing, depending on the location of the spot of light in the receptive field. That is, the neuron either displayed a burst of firing when the light was turned on (*"on" firing*), or it displayed an inhibition of firing when the light was turned on and a burst of firing when it was turned off (*"off" firing*).

For most of the neurons in the retina-geniculate-striate system, the reaction —"on" firing or "off" firing—to a light in a particular part of the receptive field was quite predictable. It depended on whether they were on-center cells or off-center cells, as illustrated in Figure 4.16.

On-center cells respond to lights shone in the central region of their receptive fields with "on" firing and to lights shone in the periphery of their receptive fields with inhibition, followed by "off" firing when the light is turned off. **Off-center cells** display the opposite pattern: They respond with inhibition and "off" firing in response to lights in the center of their receptive fields and with "on" firing to lights in the periphery of their receptive fields.

In effect, on-center and off-center cells respond best to contrast. Figure 4.17 on page 120 illustrates this point. The most effective way to influence the firing rate of an on-center or off-center cell is to maximize the contrast between the center and the periphery of its receptive field by illuminating either the entire center or the entire surround

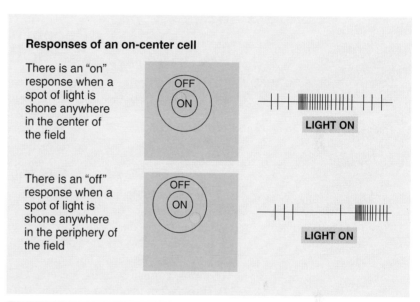

Responses of an on-center cell

There is an "on" response when a spot of light is shone anywhere in the center of the field

There is an "off" response when a spot of light is shone anywhere in the periphery of the field

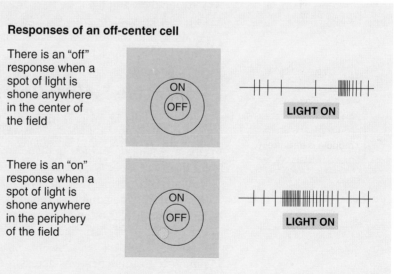

Responses of an off-center cell

There is an "off" response when a spot of light is shone anywhere in the center of the field

There is an "on" response when a spot of light is shone anywhere in the periphery of the field

The receptive fields of an on-center cell and an off-center cell.

Figure 4.16

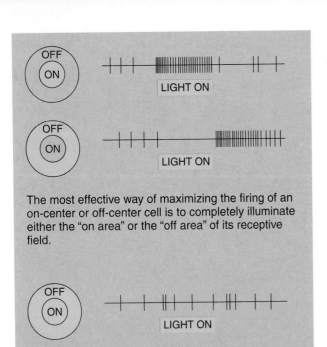

The most effective way of maximizing the firing of an on-center or off-center cell is to completely illuminate either the "on area" or the "off area" of its receptive field.

If both areas of a cell's receptive field are illuminated together, there is little reaction from the cell.

The responses of an on-center cell to contrast.

Figure 4.17 ——————————————

(periphery), while leaving the other region completely dark. Diffusely illuminating the entire receptive field has little effect on firing. Hubel and Wiesel thus concluded that one function of many of the neurons in the retina-geniculate-striate system is to respond to the degree of brightness contrast between the two areas of their receptive fields (see Livingstone & Hubel, 1988).

Before leaving Figures 4.16 and 4.17, notice one important thing about visual system neurons: Most are continually active, even when there is no visual input (Tsodyks et al., 1999). Indeed, spontaneous activity is a characteristic of most cerebral neurons. Arieli and his colleagues (1996) have shown that the level of activity of visual cortical neurons at the time that a visual stimulus is presented influences how the cells respond to the stimulus—this may be the means by which cognition influences perception.

Receptive Fields: Simple Cortical Cells

The striate cortex neurons that you just read about—that is, the neurons of lower layer IV—are exceptions. Their receptive fields are unlike those of the vast majority of striate neurons. The receptive fields of most primary visual cortex neurons fall into one of two classes: simple or complex. Neither of these classes includes the neurons of lower layer IV.

Simple cells, like lower layer IV neurons, have receptive fields that can be divided into antagonistic "on" and "off" regions and are thus unresponsive to diffuse light. And like lower layer IV neurons, they are all monocular. The main difference is that the borders between the "on" and "off" regions of the cortical receptive fields of simple cells are straight lines rather than circles. Several examples of receptive fields of simple cortical cells are presented in Figure 4.18. Notice that simple cells respond best to bars of light in a dark field, dark bars in a light field, or single straight edges between dark and light areas; that each simple cell responds maximally only when its preferred straight-edge stimulus is in a particular position and in a particular orientation; and that the receptive fields of simple cortical cells are rectangular rather than circular.

Receptive Fields: Complex Cortical Cells

Complex cells are more numerous than simple cells. Like simple cells, complex cells have rectangular receptive fields, respond best to straight-line stimuli in a specific orientation, and are unresponsive to diffuse light. However, complex cells differ from simple cells in three important ways. First, they have larger receptive fields. Second, it is not possible to divide the receptive fields of complex cells into static "on" and "off" regions: A complex cell responds to a particular straight-edge stimulus of a particular orientation regardless of its position within the receptive field of that cell. Thus, if a stimulus (e.g., a 45° bar of light) that produces "on" firing in a particular complex cell is swept across its receptive field, the cell will respond continuously to it as it moves across the field. Many complex cells respond more robustly to the movement of a straight line across their receptive fields in a particular direction. Third, unlike simple cortical cells, which are all monocular (respond to stimulation of only one of the eyes), many complex cells are **binocular** (respond to stimulation of either eye). Indeed, in monkeys, over half the complex cortical cells are binocular.

If the receptive field of a binocular complex cell is measured through one eye and then through the other, the receptive fields in each eye turn out to have almost exactly the same position in the visual field, as well as the same orientation preference. In other words, what you learn about the cell by stimulating one eye is confirmed by stimulating the other. What is more, if the appropriate stimulation is applied through both eyes simultaneously, a binocular cell usually fires more robustly than if only one eye is stimulated.

Most of the binocular cells in the primary visual cortex of monkeys display some degree of *ocular dominance*; that is, they respond more robustly to stimulation of one eye than they do to the same stimulation of the other. In addition, some binocular cells fire best when the preferred stimulus is presented to both eyes at the same time but in slightly different positions on the two retinas (e.g., Ohzawa, 1998). In other words, these cells respond best to *retinal disparity* and thus are likely to play a role in depth perception (e.g., Livingstone & Tsao, 1999).

Columnar Organization of Primary Visual Cortex

The study of the receptive fields of primary visual cortex neurons has led to two important conclusions. The first conclusion is that the characteristics of the receptive fields of visual cortex neurons are attributable to the flow of signals from neurons with simpler receptive fields to those with more complex fields (see Reid & Alonso, 1996). Specifically, it seems that signals flow from on-center and off-center cells in lower layer IV to simple cells and from simple cells to complex cells.

The second conclusion is that primary visual cortex neurons are grouped in functional vertical columns (in this context, *vertical* means at right angles to the cortical layers). Much of the evidence for this conclusion comes from studies of the receptive fields of neurons along various vertical and horizontal electrode tracks (see Figure 4.19 on page 122). If an electrode is advanced vertically through the layers of the visual cortex, with stops to plot the receptive fields of many neurons along the way, the results show that each cell in the column has a receptive field in the same area of the visual field. In addition, all the cells in a column respond best to straight lines in the very same orientation, and those neurons in a column that are either monocular or binocular with ocular dominance are all most sensitive to light in the same eye, left or right.

In contrast, if an electrode is advanced horizontally through the tissue of the primary visual cortex, each successive cell encountered is likely to have a receptive field in a slightly different location and to be maximally responsive to straight lines of a slightly different orientation. And during a horizontal electrode pass, the tip passes alternately through areas of left-eye dominance and right-eye dominance—commonly referred to as *ocular dominance columns*.

All of the functional columns in the primary visual cortex that analyze input from one area of the retina are clustered together. Half of a cluster receives input primarily from the left eye, and half receives input primarily from the right eye. Indeed, input from the eyes has been found to enter layer IV in alternating patches. The best kind of evidence of this alternating arrangement first came from a study (LeVay,

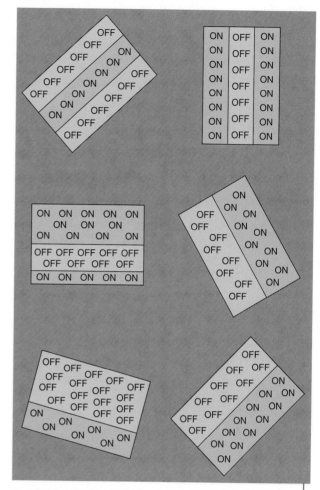

Examples of visual fields of simple cortical cells.

Figure 4.18

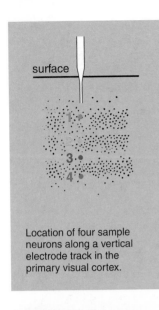

Location of four sample neurons along a vertical electrode track in the primary visual cortex.

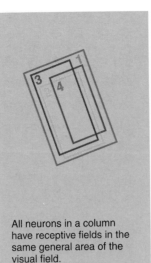

All neurons in a column have receptive fields in the same general area of the visual field.

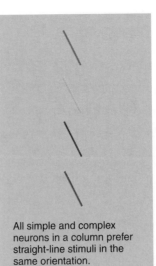

All simple and complex neurons in a column prefer straight-line stimuli in the same orientation.

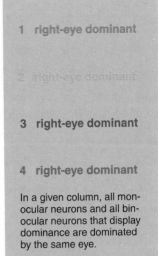

1 right-eye dominant

2 right-eye dominant

3 right-eye dominant

4 right-eye dominant

In a given column, all monocular neurons and all binocular neurons that display dominance are dominated by the same eye.

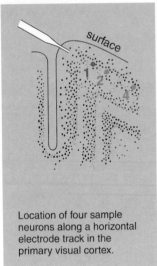

Location of four sample neurons along a horizontal electrode track in the primary visual cortex.

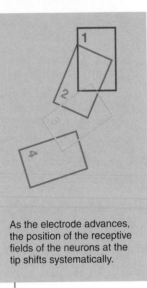

As the electrode advances, the position of the receptive fields of the neurons at the tip shifts systematically.

As the electrode advances, the preferred orientation of the neurons at the tip shifts systematically.

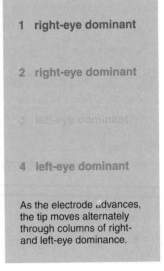

1 right-eye dominant

2 right-eye dominant

3 left-eye dominant

4 left-eye dominant

As the electrode advances, the tip moves alternately through columns of right- and left-eye dominance.

The organization of the primary visual cortex: The receptive-field properties of cells encountered along typical vertical and horizontal electrode tracks in the primary visual cortex.

Figure 4.19

Hubel, & Wiesel, 1975) in which a radioactive amino acid was injected into one eye in sufficient quantities to cross the synapses of the retina-geniculate-striate system and show up in lower layer IV of the primary visual cortex, and to a lesser degree in the layers just above and below it. The alternating patches of radioactivity and nonradioactivity in the autoradiograph in Figure 4.20 mark the alternating patches of input from the two eyes.

All of the clusters of functional columns that analyze input from one area of the retina are thought to include neurons with preferences for straight-line stimuli of various orientations. The columns of orientation specificity were visualized in a study (Hubel, Wiesel, & Stryker, 1977) in which radioactive 2-DG was injected into monkeys that then spent 45 minutes viewing a pattern of vertical stripes moving back and forth. As you know from Chapter 3, radioactive 2-DG is taken up by active neurons and accumulates in them, thus identifying the loca-

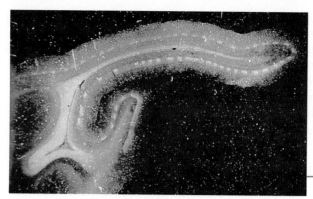

The alternation of input into lower layer IV of the primary visual cortex from the left and right eyes. Radioactive amino acids that were injected into one eye were subsequently revealed on autoradiographs of the visual cortex as patches of radioactivity alternating with patches of nonradioactivity.

(From D. H. Hubel and T. N. Wiesel, "Brain Mechanisms of Vision," *Scientific American*, vol. 241, p. 151. Copyright © 1979 by Scientific American. Used by permission.)

Figure 4.20

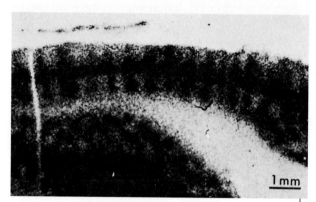

The columns of orientation specificity in the primary visual cortex of a monkey as revealed by 2-DG autoradiography.

(From D. H. Hubel, T. N. Wiesel, and M. P. Stryker, "Orientation Columns in Macaque Monkey Visual Cortex Demonstrated by the 2-Deoxyglucose Autoradiographic Technique," *Nature*, vol. 269, p. 329. Copyright © 1977 by Nature Publishing Group. Reprinted with permission of Nature Publishing Group in the format textbook via Copyright Clearance Center.)

Figure 4.21

tion of neurons that are particularly active during the test period. The autoradiograph in Figure 4.21 reveals the columns of cells in the primary visual cortex that were activated by exposure to the moving vertical stripes. Notice that the neurons in lower layer IV show no orientation specificity—because they do not respond to straight-line stimuli.

Figure 4.22 summarizes Hubel and Wiesel's theory of how the vertical columns of the primary visual cortex are organized (see Martinez & Alonso, 2003).

A block of tissue such as this is assumed to analyze visual signals from one area of the visual field.

Left Eye Dominant
Right Eye Dominant
Lower Layer IV

Half the block of tissue is presumed to be dominated by right-eye input and half by left-eye input.

Each slice of the block of tissue is presumed to specialize in the analysis of straight lines in a particular orientation.

Hubel and Wiesel's model of the organization of functional columns in the primary visual cortex.

Figure 4.22

The Case of Mrs. Richards, Revisited

There was obviously a disturbance in Mrs. Richards's visual system: But where? And what kind of disturbance? And why the straight lines? A simple test located the disturbance. Mrs. Richards was asked to shut one eye and then the other and to report what happened to her illusion. The answer was, "Nothing." This suggested that the disturbance was cortical, because the visual cortex is the first part of the retina-geniculate-striate system that contains neurons that receive input from both eyes.

Clinical Implications

This hypothesis was confirmed by a few simple calculations: The gradual acceleration of the illusion as it spread out to the periphery is consistent with a wave of disturbance expanding from the "foveal area" of the primary visual cortex to its boundaries at a constant rate of about 3 millimeters per minute—the illusion accelerated because proportionally less visual cortex is dedicated to receiving signals from the periphery of the visual field.

And why the lines? Would you expect anything else from an area of the cortex whose elements appear to be specialized for coding straight-line stimuli?

4·5
Seeing Color

Color is one of the most obvious qualities of human visual experience. So far in this chapter, we have largely limited our discussion of vision to black, white, and gray. Black is experienced when there is an absence of light, the perception of white is produced by an intense mixture of a wide range of wavelengths in roughly equal proportion, and the perception of gray is produced by the same mixture at lower intensities. In this section, we deal with the perception of colors such as blue, green, and yellow. The correct term for colors is *hues*, but in everyday language they are referred to as colors; and for the sake of simplicity, I will do the same.

What is there about a visual stimulus that determines the color we perceive? To a large degree, the perception of an object's color depends on the wavelengths of light that it reflects into the eye. Figure 4.2 on page 103 is an illustration of the colors associated with individual wavelengths; however, outside the laboratory, one never encounters objects that reflect single wavelengths. Sunlight and most sources of artificial light contain complex mixtures of most visible wavelengths. Most objects absorb the different wavelengths of light that strike them to varying degrees and reflect the rest. The mixture of wavelengths that objects reflect influences our perception of their color, but it is not the entire story—as you are about to learn.

Component and Opponent Processing

The **component theory** (trichromatic theory) of color vision was proposed by Thomas Young in 1802 and refined by Hermann von Helmholtz in 1852. According to this theory, there are three different kinds of color receptors (cones), each with a different spectral sensitivity, and the color of a particular stimulus is presumed to be encoded by the ratio of activity in the three kinds of receptors. Young and Helmholtz derived their theory from the observation that any color of the visible spectrum can be matched by a mixing together of three different wavelengths of light in different proportions. This can be accomplished with any three wavelengths, provided that the color of any one of them cannot be matched by a mixing of the other two. The fact that three is normally the minimum number of different wavelengths necessary to match every color suggested that there were three types of receptors.

Another theory of color vision, the **opponent-process theory** of color vision, was proposed by Ewald Hering in 1878. He suggested that there are two different classes of cells in the visual system for encoding color and another class for encoding brightness. Hering hypothesized that each of the three classes of cells encoded two complementary color perceptions. One class of color-coding cells signaled red by changing its activity in one direction (e.g., hyperpolarization) and signaled red's complementary color, green, by changing its activity in the other direction (e.g., hypopolarization). Another class of color-coding cells was hypothesized to signal blue and its complement, yellow, in the same opponent fashion; and a class of brightness-coding cells was hypothesized to similarly signal both black and white. **Complementary colors** are pairs of colors that produce white or gray when combined in equal measure (e.g., green light and red light).

Hering based his opponent-process theory of color vision on several behavioral observations. One was that complementary colors cannot exist together: There is no such thing as bluish yellow or reddish green. Another was that the afterimage produced by staring at red is green and vice versa, and the afterimage produced by staring at yellow is blue and vice versa (see the accompanying Check It Out demonstration).

A somewhat misguided debate raged for many years between supporters of the component (trichromatic) and opponent theories of color vision. I say "misguided" because it was fueled more by the adversarial predisposition of scientists than by the incompatibility of the two theories. In fact, research subsequently proved that both color-coding mechanisms coexist in our visual systems (see DeValois et al., 2000).

It was the development in the early 1960s of a technique for measuring the absorption spectrum of the photopigment contained in a single cone that allowed researchers (e.g., Wald, 1964) to confirm the conclusion that Young had reached over a century and a half before. They found that there are indeed three different kinds of cones in the retinas of those vertebrates with good color vision, and they found that each of the three has a different photopigment with its own characteristic absorption spectrum. As Figure 4.23 illustrates, some cones are most sensitive to short wavelengths, some are most sensitive to medium wavelengths, and some are most sensitive to long wavelengths.

Although the coding of color by cones seems to operate on a purely component basis (see Jameson, Highnote, & Wasserman, 2001), there is evidence of opponent processing of color at all subsequent levels of the retina-geniculate-striate system. That is, at all subsequent levels, there are cells that respond in one direction (e.g., increased firing) to one color and in the opposite direction (e.g., decreased firing) to its complementary color (see Chatterjee & Callaway, 2003; Gegenfurtner & Kiper, 2003).

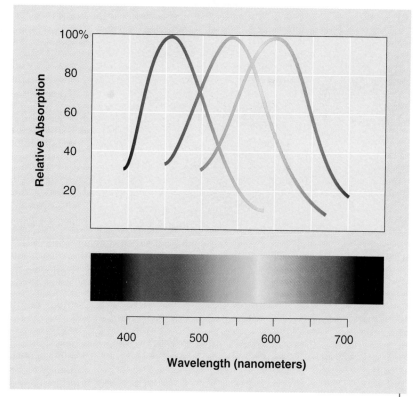

The absorption spectra of the three classes of cones.

Figure 4.23

Color Constancy and the Retinex Theory

Neither component nor opponent processing can account for the single most important characteristic of color vision: color constancy. **Color constancy** refers to the fact that the perceived color of an object is not a simple function of the wavelengths reflected by it.

As I write this at 7:15 on a December morning, it is dark outside, and I am working in my office by the light of a tiny incandescent desk lamp. Later in the morning, when students start to arrive, I turn on my nasty fluorescent office lights; and then, in the afternoon, when the sun has shifted to my side of the building, I turn off the lights and work by natural light. The point is that because these light sources differ markedly in the wavelengths they contain, the wavelengths reflected by various objects in my office—my blue shirt, for example—change substantially during the course of the day. However, although the wavelengths reflected by my shirt change markedly, its color does not. My shirt will be just as blue in midmorning and in late afternoon as it is now. Color constancy is the tendency for an object to stay the same color despite major changes in the wavelengths of light that it reflects.

Although the phenomenon of color constancy is counterintuitive, its advantage is obvious. Color constancy improves our ability to tell objects apart in a memorable way so that we can respond appropriately to them; our ability to recognize objects would be greatly lessened if their color changed every time there was a change in illumination. In essence, if it were not for color constancy, color vision would have little survival value.

Although color constancy is an important feature of our vision, we are normally unaware of it. Under everyday conditions, we have no way of appreciating just how much the wavelengths reflected by an object can change without the object changing its color. It is only in the controlled environment of the laboratory that one can fully appreciate that color constancy is more than an important factor in color vision: It is the essence of color vision.

Edwin Land (1977), the inventor of the Polaroid camera, developed several dramatic laboratory demonstrations of color constancy. In these demonstrations, Land used three adjustable projectors. Each projector emitted only one wavelength of light: one a short-wavelength light, one a medium-wavelength light, and one a long-wavelength light. Thus, it was clear that only three wavelengths of light were involved in the demonstrations. Land shone the three projectors on a test display like the one in Figure 4.24. (These displays are called *Mondrians* because they resemble the paintings of the Dutch master painter Piet Mondrian.)

Land found that adjusting the amount of light emitted from each projector—and thus the amount of light of each wavelength being reflected by the Mondrian—had no effect at all on the perception of its colors. For

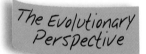

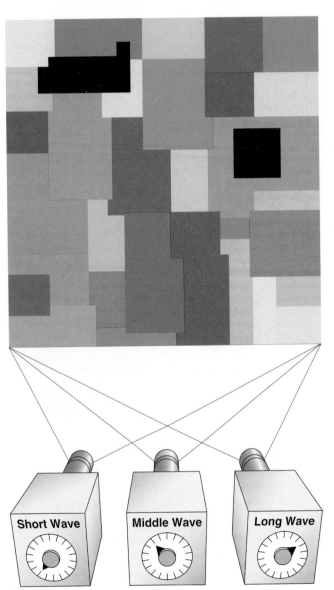

Land's (1977) color-vision experiments. Subjects viewed Mondrians that were illuminated by light made up of various proportions of three different wavelengths: a short wavelength, a medium wavelength, and a long wavelength.

Figure 4.24

example, in one demonstration Land used a photometer to measure the amounts of the three wavelengths being reflected by a rectangle judged to be pure blue by his subjects. He then adjusted the emittance of the projectors, and he measured the wavelengths reflected by a red rectangle on a different Mondrian, until the wavelengths were exactly the same as those that had been reflected by the blue rectangle on the original. When he showed this new Mondrian to his subjects, the red rectangle looked—you guessed it—red, even though it reflected exactly the same wavelengths as had the blue rectangle on the original Mondrian.

The point of Land's demonstration is that blue objects stay blue, green objects stay green, and so forth, regardless of the wavelengths they reflect. This color constancy occurs as long as the object is illuminated with light that contains some short, medium, and long wavelengths (such as daylight, firelight, and virtually all manufactured lighting) and as long as the object is viewed as part of a scene, not in isolation.

According to Land's **retinex theory** of color vision, the color of an object is determined by its *reflectance*—the proportion of light of different wavelengths that a surface reflects. Although the wavelengths of light reflected by a surface change dramatically with changes in illumination, the efficiency with which a surface absorbs each wavelength and reflects the unabsorbed portion does not change. According to the retinex theory, the visual system calculates the reflectance of surfaces, and thus perceives their colors, by comparing the light reflected by adjacent surfaces in at least three different wavelength bands (short, medium, and long)—see Hurlbert and Wolf (2004).

Why is Land's research so critical for neuroscientists trying to discover the neural mechanisms of color vision? It is important because it suggests one type of cortical neuron that is likely to be involved in color vision (see Shapely & Hawken, 2002). If the perception of color depends on the analysis of contrast between adjacent areas of the visual field, then the critical neurons should be responsive to color contrast (see Hurlbert, 2003). And they are. For example, **dual-opponent color cells** in the monkey visual cortex respond with vigorous "on" firing when the center of their circular receptive field is illuminated with one wavelength, such as green, and the surround (periphery) is simultaneously illuminated with another wavelength, such as red. And the same cells display vigorous "off" firing when the pattern of illumination is reversed—for example, red in the center and green in the surround. In essence, dual-opponent color cells respond to the contrast between wavelengths reflected by adjacent areas of their receptive field.

A major breakthrough in the understanding of the organization of the primary visual cortex came with the discovery that dual-opponent color cells are not distributed evenly throughout the primary visual cortex of monkeys (see Zeki, 1993a). Livingstone and Hubel (1984) found that these neurons are concentrated in the primary visual cortex in peglike columns that penetrate the layers of the monkey primary visual cortex, with the exception of lower layer IV. Many neurons in these peglike columns are particularly rich in the mitochondrial enzyme **cytochrome oxidase**; thus, their distribution in the primary visual cortex can be visualized if one stains slices of tissue with stains that have an affinity for this enzyme.

When a section of monkey striate tissue is cut parallel to the cortical layers and stained in this way, the pegs are seen as "blobs" of stain scattered over the cortex (unless the section is cut from lower layer IV). To the relief of instructors and students alike, the term **blobs** has become the accepted scientific label for peglike, cytochrome oxidase–rich, dual-opponent color columns. The blobs were found to be located in the middle of ocular dominance columns (compare Figure 4.25 with

The Evolutionary Perspective

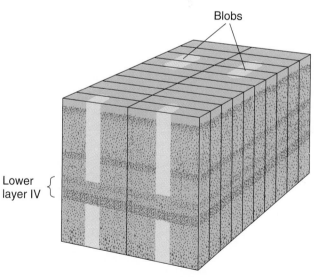

Hubel and Livingstone's model of primary visual cortex organization. The blobs are peglike columns that contain dual-opponent color cells.

Figure 4.25

Figure 4.22). Functional MRI studies have provided evidence of dual-opponent color cells in the human visual cortex (Engel, 1999).

4.6

Cortical Mechanisms of Vision: Beyond Primary Visual Cortex

So far, you have followed the major visual pathways from the eyes to the primary visual cortex, but there is much more to the human visual system—we are visual animals. The entire occipital cortex as well as large areas of temporal cortex and parietal cortex are involved in vision (see Figure 4.26).

Visual cortex is often considered to be of three different types. *Primary visual cortex*, as you have learned, is that area of cortex that receives most of its input from the visual relay nuclei of the thalamus (i.e., from the lateral geniculate nuclei). The areas of **secondary visual cortex** are those that receive most of their input from the primary visual cortex, and areas of **visual association cortex** are those that receive input from areas of secondary visual cortex as well as from the secondary areas of other sensory systems.

The primary visual cortex is located in the posterior region of the occipital lobes, much of it hidden from view in the longitudinal fissure. The areas of secondary visual cortex are located in two general regions: in the prestriate cortex and in the inferotemporal cortex. The **prestriate cortex** is the band of tissue in the occipital lobe that surrounds the primary visual cortex. The **inferotemporal cortex** is the cortex of the inferior temporal lobe. Areas of association cortex that receive visual input are located in several parts of the cerebral cortex, but the largest single area is in the **posterior parietal cortex**.

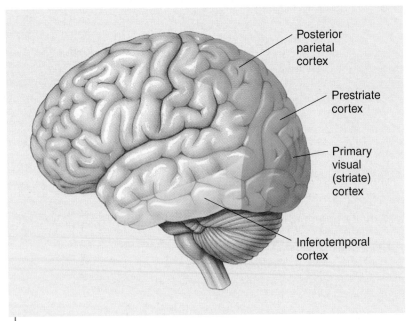

Posterior parietal cortex

Prestriate cortex

Primary visual (striate) cortex

Inferotemporal cortex

The visual areas of the human cerebral cortex.

Figure 4.26

The major flow of visual information in the cortex is from the primary visual cortex to the various areas of secondary visual cortex to the areas of association cortex. As one moves up this visual hierarchy, the neurons have larger receptive fields and the stimuli to which the neurons respond are more specific and more complex (see Zeki, 1993b).

Scotomas: Completion

Clinical Implications

Damage to an area of the primary visual cortex produces a **scotoma**—an area of blindness—in the corresponding area of the contralateral visual field of both eyes (see Figure 4.13). Neurological patients with suspected damage to the primary visual cortex are usually given a **perimetry test**. While the patient's head is held motionless on a chin rest, the patient stares with one eye at a fixation point on a screen. A small dot of light is then flashed on various parts of the screen, and the patient presses a button to record when the dot is seen. Then, the entire process is

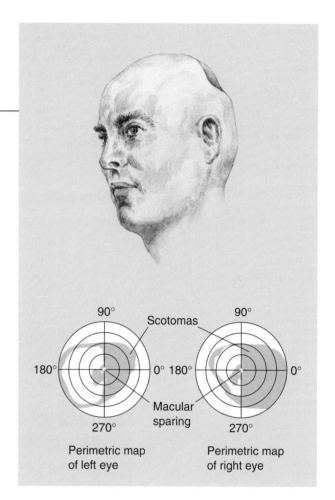

The perimetric maps of a subject with a bullet wound in his left primary visual cortex. The scotomas (areas of blindness) are indicated in gray.

(Adapted from Teuber, Battersby, & Bender, 1960.)

Figure 4.27

repeated for the other eye. The result is a map of the visual field of each eye, which indicates any areas of blindness. Figure 4.27 illustrates the perimetric maps of the visual fields of a man with a bullet wound in his left primary visual cortex. Notice the massive scotoma in the right visual field of each eye.

Many patients with extensive scotomas are unaware of their deficits. One of the factors that contributes to this lack of awareness is *completion*. A patient with a scotoma who looks at a complex figure, part of which lies in the scotoma, often reports seeing a complete image (Zur & Ullman, 2003). In some cases, this completion may depend on residual visual capacities in the scotoma; however, completion also occurs in cases in which this explanation can be ruled out. For example, patients who are **hemianopsic** (having a scotoma covering half of the visual field) may see an entire face when they focus on a person's nose, even when the side of the face in the scotoma has been covered by a blank card.

Consider the completion phenomenon experienced by the esteemed physiological psychologist Karl Lashley (1941). He often developed a large scotoma next to his fovea during a migraine attack (see Figure 4.28).

Lashley's scotoma

What Lashley saw

The completion of a migraine-induced scotoma as described by Karl Lashley (1941).

Figure 4.28

The Case of the Physiological Psychologist Who Made Faces Disappear

> Talking with a friend I glanced just to the right of his face wherein his head disappeared. His shoulders and necktie were still visible but the vertical stripes on the wallpaper behind him seemed to extend down to the necktie. It was impossible to see this as a blank area when projected on the striped wallpaper of uniformly patterned surface although any intervening object failed to be seen. (Lashley, 1941, p. 338)

Scotomas: Blindsight

Blindsight is another phenomenon displayed by patients with scotomas resulting from damage to primary visual cortex. **Blindsight** is the ability of such patients to respond to visual stimuli in their scotomas even though they have no conscious awareness of the stimuli (Weiskrantz, 2004). Of all visual abilities, perception of motion is most likely to survive damage to primary visual cortex (Intriligator, Xie, & Barton, 2002). For example, a subject might reach out and grab a moving object in her scotoma, all the while claiming not to see it.

If blindsight confuses you, imagine how it confuses people who experience it. Consider, for example, the reactions to blindsight of D.B., a patient who was blind in his left visual field following surgical removal of his right occipital lobe (Weiskrantz, 2002; Weiskrantz et al., 1974).

The Case of D.B., the Man Confused by His Own Blindsight

> Even though the patient had no awareness of "seeing" in his blind [left] field, evidence was obtained that (a) he could reach for visual stimuli [in his left field] with considerable accuracy; (b) could differentiate the orientation of a vertical line from a horizontal or diagonal line; (c) could differentiate the letters "X" and "O."
>
> Needless to say, he was questioned repeatedly about his vision in his left half-field, and his most common response was that he saw nothing at all. . . . When he was shown his results [through his good, right-half field] he expressed surprise and insisted several times that he thought he was just "guessing." When he was shown a video film of his reaching and judging orientation of lines, he was openly astonished. (Weiskrantz et al., 1974, pp. 721, 726)

Two neurological interpretations of blindsight have been proposed. One is that the striate cortex is not completely destroyed and the remaining islands of functional cells are capable of mediating some visual abilities in the absence of conscious awareness (see Wüst, Kasten, & Sabel, 2002). The other is that those visual pathways that ascend directly to the secondary visual cortex from subcortical visual structures without passing through the primary visual cortex are capable of maintaining some visual abilities in the absence of cognitive awareness (see Kentridge, Heywood, & Weiskrantz, 1997). There is some support for both theories, but the evidence is not conclusive for either (see Gross, Moore, & Rodman, 2004; Rosa, Tweedale, & Elston, 2000; Schärli, Harman, & Hogben, 1999a, 1999b). Indeed, it is possible that both mechanisms contribute to the phenomenon.

Functional Areas of Secondary and Association Visual Cortex

Secondary visual cortex and the portions of association cortex that are involved in visual analysis are both composed of different areas, each specialized for a particular type of visual analysis. For example, in the macaque monkey, whose visual cortex has been thoroughly mapped, there are more than 30 different functional areas of visual cortex; in addition to primary visual cortex, 24 areas of secondary visual cortex and 7 areas of association visual cortex have been identified. The neurons in each functional area respond most vigorously to different aspects of visual stimuli (e.g., to their color, movement, or shape); selective lesions to the different areas produce different visual losses; and there are anatomical differences among the areas.

The various functional areas of secondary and association visual cortex in the macaque are prodigiously interconnected. Anterograde and retrograde tracing studies have identified over 300 interconnecting pathways (Van Essen, Anderson, & Felleman, 1992). Although connections between areas are virtually always reciprocal, the major flow of information is from more simple to more complex areas.

PET (positron emission tomography) and fMRI have been used to identify various areas of visual cortex in humans. The activity of the subjects' brains has been monitored while they inspect various types of visual stimuli (e.g., Grossman et al., 2000; Kourtzi & Kanwisher, 2000). By identifying the areas of activation associated with various visual properties (e.g., movement or color), researchers have so far delineated about a dozen different functional areas of human visual cortex. A map of these areas is shown in Figure 4.29. Most are similar in terms of location, anatomical characteristics, and function to areas in the macaque (Courtney & Ungerleider, 1997).

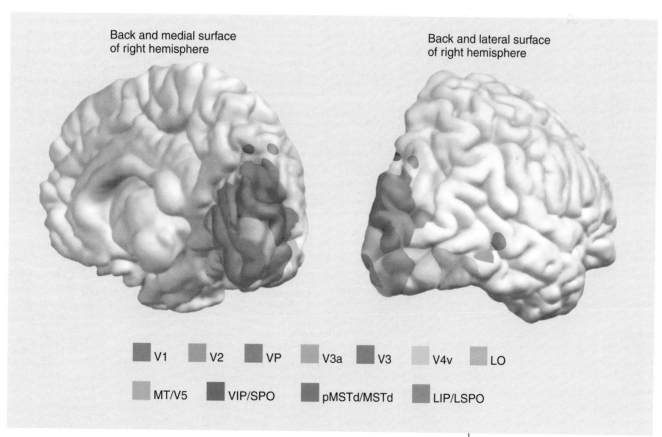

Areas of visual cortex so far discovered in humans. Their names are based on similarities to areas of visual cortex in the more thoroughly studied macaque monkey.

(Based on Tootell et al., 1996.)

Figure 4.29 ————

Dorsal and Ventral Streams

As you have already learned, most visual information enters the primary visual cortex via the lateral geniculate nuclei. The information from the two lateral geniculate nuclei is received in the primary visual cortex, combined, and then segregated into multiple pathways that project separately to the various functional areas of secondary, and then association, visual cortex (see Cabeza & Nyberg, 1997; Logothetis, 1998).

Many pathways that conduct information from the primary visual cortex through various specialized areas of secondary and association cortex are parts of two major streams: the dorsal stream and the ventral stream (Courtney & Ungerleider, 1997; Ungerleider & Mishkin, 1982). The **dorsal stream** flows from the primary visual cortex to the dorsal prestriate cortex to the posterior parietal cortex, and the **ventral stream** flows from the primary visual cortex to the ventral prestriate cortex to the inferotemporal cortex—see Figure 4.30.

Ungerleider and Mishkin (1982) proposed that the dorsal and ventral visual streams perform different visual functions. They suggested that the dorsal stream is involved in the perception of "where" objects are and the ventral stream is involved in the perception of "what" objects are.

The major implication of the **"where" versus "what" theory** and other parallel-processing theories of vision is that damage to some areas of cortex may abolish certain aspects of vision while leaving others unaffected. Indeed, the most convincing support for the influential "where" versus "what" theory has come from the comparison of the specific effects of damage to the dorsal and ventral streams (see Ungerleider & Haxby, 1994). Patients with damage to the posterior parietal cortex often have difficulty reaching accurately for objects that they have no difficulty describing; conversely, patients with damage to the inferotemporal cortex often have no difficulty reaching accurately for objects that they have difficulty describing.

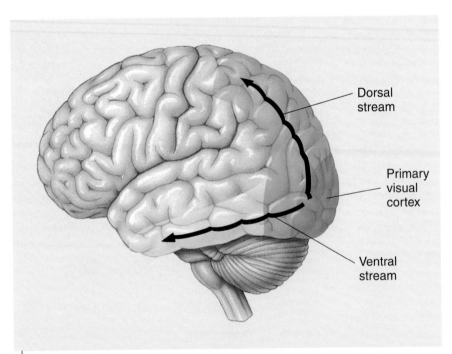

Information about particular aspects of a visual display flow out of the primary visual cortex over many pathways. The pathways can be grouped into two general streams: dorsal and ventral.

Figure 4.30

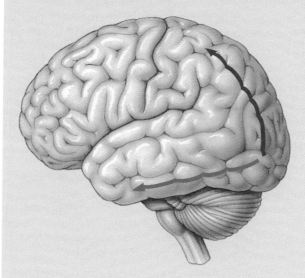

Dorsal and Ventral Streams: Two Theories and What They Predict

"Where" vs. "What" Theory

Dorsal stream specializes in visual spatial perception
Ventral stream specializes in visual pattern recognition

Predicts
- Damage to **dorsal stream** disrupts visual spatial perception
- Damage to **ventral stream** disrupts visual pattern recognition

"Control of Behavior" vs. "Conscious Perception" Theory

Dorsal stream specializes in visually guided behavior
Ventral stream specializes in conscious visual perception

Predicts
- Damage to **dorsal stream** disrupts visually guided behavior but not conscious visual perception
- Damage to **ventral stream** disrupts conscious visual perception but not visually guided behavior

The "where" versus "what" and the "control of behavior" versus "conscious perception" theories make different predictions.

 Figure 4.31 _____

Although the "where" versus "what" theory has many advocates, there is an alternative interpretation for the same evidence (Goodale, 1993; Milner & Goodale, 1993). Goodale and Milner argued that the key difference between the dorsal and ventral streams is not the kinds of information they carry but the use to which that information is put. They suggested that the function of the dorsal stream is to direct behavioral interactions with objects, whereas the function of the ventral stream is to mediate the conscious perception of objects; this is the **"control of behavior" versus "conscious perception" theory** (see Logothetis & Sheinberg, 1996).

The "control of behavior" versus "conscious perception" theory can readily explain the two major neuropsychological findings that are the foundation of the "where" versus "what" theory. Namely, the "control of behavior" versus "conscious perception" theory suggests that patients with dorsal stream damage may do poorly on tests of location and movement because most tests of location and movement involve performance measures, and that patients with ventral stream damage may do poorly on tests of visual recognition because most tests of visual recognition involve verbal, and thus conscious, report.

The major support for the "control of behavior" versus "conscious perception" theory is the confirmation of its two primary assertions: (1) that some patients with bilateral lesions to the ventral stream have no conscious experience of seeing and yet are able to interact with objects under visual guidance, and (2) that some patients with bilateral lesions to the dorsal stream can consciously see objects but cannot interact with them under visual guidance (see Figure 4.31). Following are two such cases.

 Clinical Implications

The Case of D.F., the Woman Who Could Grasp Objects She Did Not Consciously See

D.F. has bilateral damage to her ventral prestriate cortex, thus interrupting the flow of the ventral stream (Goodale et al., 1991). Amazingly, she can respond accurately to visual stimuli that she does not consciously see. Goodale and Milner (1992) describe her thusly:

Despite her profound inability to recognize the size, shape and orientation of visual objects, D.F. showed strikingly accurate guidance of hand and finger movements directed at the very same objects. Thus, when she was presented with a pair of rectangular blocks of the same or different dimensions, she was unable to distinguish between them. When she was asked to indicate the width of a single block by means of her index finger and thumb, her matches bore no relationship to the dimensions of the object and showed considerable trial to trial variability. However, when she was asked simply to reach out and pick up the block, the aperture between her index finger and thumb changed systematically with the width of the object, just as in normal subjects. In other words, D.F. scaled her grip to the dimensions of the objects she was about to pick up, even though she appeared to be unable to [consciously] "perceive" those dimensions.

A similar dissociation was seen in her responses to the orientation of stimuli. Thus, when presented with a large slot that could be placed in one of a number of different orientations, she showed great difficulty in indicating the orientation either verbally or manually (i.e., by rotating her hand or a hand-held card). Nevertheless, she was as good as normal subjects at reaching out and placing her hand or the card into the slot, turning her hand appropriately from the very onset of the movement. (p. 22)

The Case of A.T., the Woman Who Could Not Accurately Grasp Unfamiliar Objects That She Saw

The case of A.T. is in major respects complementary to that of D.F. The patient A.T. is a woman with a lesion of the occipitoparietal region, which likely interrupts her dorsal route.

A.T. was able to recognize objects, and was also able to demonstrate their size with her fingers. By contrast, pre-shape of the hand during object-directed movements was incorrect. Correlation between object size and maximum grip size was lacking, with the consequence that objects could not be grasped between the fingertips; instead, the patient made awkward palmar grasps. The schema framework offers a compelling explanation for this deficit. Because the grasp schemas were destroyed by the lesion, or disconnected from visual input, the grip aperture did not stop at the required size, grip closure was delayed and the transport was prolonged in order to remain co-ordinated with the grasp.

A.T. cannot preshape her hand for neutral objects like plastic cylinders, yet, when faced with a familiar object whose size is a semantic property, like a lipstick, she can grasp it with reasonable accuracy. This interaction reflects the role of the abundant anatomical interconnections between the two cortical systems. (Jeannerod et al., 1995, p. 320)

Prosopagnosia

Prosopagnosia is an interesting and, as you will learn, controversial neuropsychological disorder of visual recognition. Its investigation has provided further support for the "control of behavior" versus "conscious perception" theory.

What is prosopagnosia? **Prosopagnosia**, briefly put, is visual agnosia for faces. Let me explain. **Agnosia** is a failure of recognition (*gnosis* means "to know") that is not attributable to a sensory deficit or to verbal or intellectual impairment; **visual agnosia** is a specific agnosia for visual stimuli. Visual agnosics can see visual stimuli, but they don't know what they are.

Visual agnosias themselves are often specific to a particular aspect of visual input and are named accordingly; for example, *movement agnosia, object agnosia,* and *color agnosia* are difficulties in recognizing movement, objects, and color, respectively. It is presumed that each specific visual agnosia results from damage to an area of secondary visual cortex that mediates the recognition of that particular attribute. Prosopagnosics are visual agnosics with a specific difficulty in recognizing faces.

Prosopagnosics can usually recognize a face as a face, but they have problems recognizing whose face it is. They often report seeing a jumble of individual facial parts (e.g., eyes, nose, chin, cheeks) that for some reason are never fused, or bound, into an easy-to-recognize whole. In extreme cases, prosopagnosics cannot recognize themselves: Imagine what it would be like to stare in the mirror every morning and not recognize the face that is looking back.

The belief that prosopagnosia is a deficit specific to the recognition of faces has been challenged. To understand this challenge, you need to know that the diagnosis of prosopagnosia is typically applied to neuropsychological patients who have difficulty recognizing particular faces, but can readily identify other test objects (e.g., a chair, a dog, or a tree). Surely, this is powerful evidence that prosopagnosics have recognition difficulties specific to faces. Not so. Pause for a moment, and think about this evidence: It is seriously flawed.

Because prosopagnosics have no difficulty recognizing faces as faces, the fact that they can recognize chairs as chairs, pencils as pencils, and doors as doors is not relevant. The critical question is whether they can recognize which chair, which pencil, and which door. Careful testing of many prosopagnosics has revealed that their recognition deficits are not restricted to faces: A farmer lost his ability to recognize particular cows when he became prosopagnosic, and a bird-watcher lost his ability to distinguish species of birds. These cases suggest that many prosopagnosics have a general problem recognizing specific objects that belong to complex classes of objects (e.g., particular automobiles or particular houses), not a specific problem recognizing faces (see Dixon, Bub, & Arguin, 1998; Gauthier, Behrmann, & Tarr, 1999). Although it is now well established that the recognition deficits of most prosopagnosics are not restricted to faces, there are a few cases of prosopagnosia in which thorough testing has failed to detect recognition deficits unrelated to faces (De Renzi, 1997; Farah, 1990).

Thinking Clearly

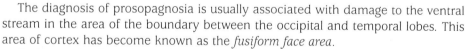

R.P., a Typical Case of Prosopagnosia

R.P. is a typical prosopagnosic. With routine testing, he displayed a severe deficit in recognizing faces and in identifying facial expressions (Laeng & Caviness, 2001) but no other recognition problems. If testing had stopped there, it would have been concluded that R.P. is an agnosic with recognition problems specific to human faces. However, more thorough testing suggested that R.P. is deficient in recognizing all objects with complex curved surfaces (e.g., amoeboid shapes), not just faces.

The diagnosis of prosopagnosia is usually associated with damage to the ventral stream in the area of the boundary between the occipital and temporal lobes. This area of cortex has become known as the *fusiform face area*.

An interesting hypothesis about prosopagnosia can be derived from the "control of behavior" versus "conscious perception" theory. (Remember that I told you that the study of prosopagnosia has lent support to this theory.) The fact that prosopagnosia results from bilateral damage to the ventral stream suggests that dorsal-stream function may be intact. In other words, it suggests that prosopagnosics may be able to unconsciously recognize faces that they cannot recognize consciously. Remarkably, this is, indeed, the case.

Tranel and Damasio (1985) were the first to demonstrate unconscious facial recognition in prosopagnosics. They presented a series of photographs to each

Thinking Clearly

patient, some familiar to the patient, some not. The subjects claimed not to recognize any of the faces. However, when familiar, but not unfamiliar, faces were presented, the subjects displayed a large skin conductance response, thus indicating that the faces were being unconsciously recognized by undamaged portions of the brain.

Conclusion

A key goal of this chapter was to help you understand that vision is a creative process. The visual system does not transmit intact visual images to the cortex. It carries information about a few critical features of the visual field—for example, information about location, movement, brightness contrast, and color contrast—and from these bits of information, it creates a perception that is better than the retinal image in all respects and better than the external reality in some.

The Check It Out demonstrations in this chapter offered you many opportunities to experience firsthand important aspects of the visual process. I hope that you did take the time to check them out and that your experience made you more aware of the amazing abilities of your own visual system and the relevance of what you have learned in this chapter to your everyday life.

Key Terms

4.1 Light Enters the Eye and Reaches the Retina

Accommodation (p. 104)
Acuity (p. 103)
Binocular disparity (p. 105)
Ciliary muscles (p. 104)
Sensitivity (p. 103)

4.2 The Retina and Translation of Light into Neural Signals

Absorption spectrum (p. 113)
Amacrine cells (p. 106)
Bipolar cells (p. 106)
Blind spot (p. 107)
Completion (p. 107)
Cones (p. 108)
Duplexity theory (p. 108)
Fovea (p. 107)
Horizontal cells (p. 106)
Nasal hemiretina (p. 110)
Photopic spectral sensitivity curve (p. 110)
Photopic vision (p. 108)

Purkinje effect (p. 111)
Receptors (p. 106)
Retinal ganglion cells (p. 106)
Rhodopsin (p. 113)
Rods (p. 108)
Saccades (p. 112)
Scotopic spectral sensitivity curve (p. 110)
Scotopic vision (p. 108)
Temporal hemiretina (p. 110)
Transduction (p. 112)

4.3 From Retina to Primary Visual Cortex

Lateral geniculate nuclei (p. 114)
Magnocellular layers (p. 115)
Parvocellular layers (p. 115)
Primary visual cortex (p. 114)
Retina-geniculate-striate pathway (p. 114)
Retinotopic (p. 114)

4.4 Seeing Edges

Binocular (p. 120)
Complex cells (p. 120)
Contrast enhancement (p. 116)
Lateral inhibition (p. 117)
Monocular (p. 119)
Off-center cells (p. 119)
Ommatidia (p. 116)
On-center cells (p. 119)
Receptive field (p. 118)
Simple cells (p. 120)

4.5 Seeing Color

Blobs (p. 127)
Color constancy (p. 126)
Complementary colors (p. 125)
Component theory (p. 124)
Cytochrome oxidase (p. 127)
Dual-opponent color cells (p. 127)
Opponent-process theory (p. 124)
Retinex theory (p. 127)

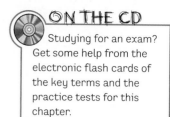

ON THE CD

Studying for an exam? Get some help from the electronic flash cards of the key terms and the practice tests for this chapter.

chapter 4

The Visual System
How We See

The visual system does not passively create an image of reality the way a camera does. It does much more. From the crude visual signals received by the retina, it creates rich images that are in some ways better than the physical reality that stimulated them.

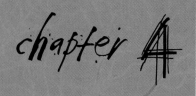

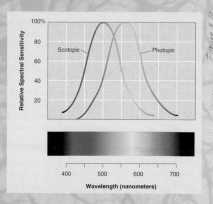

Figure 4.10

Light Reaches the Retina and Is Translated into Neural Signals

Light is seriously distorted by the four layers of neurons that it passes through before it reaches the visual receptors in the fifth layer of the retina. There are two types of receptors: cones, which function in daylight and mediate high-acuity color vision; and rods, which function under dim illumination and mediate low-acuity achromatic vision.

(Pages 102–113)

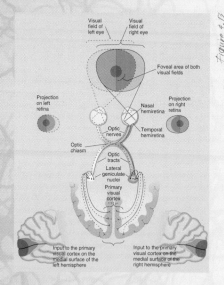

Figure 4.13

From Retina to Primary Visual Cortex

Signals are conducted to the primary visual cortex at the back of the brain via the lateral geniculate nucleus of the thalamus. The primary visual cortex and other parts of the visual system are retinotopic; that is, they are laid out like a map of the retina.

(Pages 114–115)

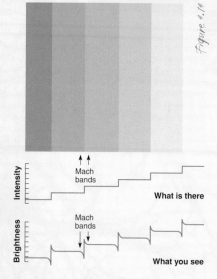

Figure 4.14

Seeing Edges

Edges are the single most important aspects of our visual experience: The perception of edges tells us where objects are and helps us interact effectively with them. Not surprisingly, the major function of many visual neurons appears to be the analysis of edges. The visual system highlights edges, and we see them more clearly than they are in physical reality.

(Pages 116–124)

Visual Summary

Themes Revisited

All four major themes of this book were developed in this chapter. First, the evolutionary perspective theme was emphasized, largely because the majority of research on the neural mechanisms of human vision has been comparative.

Second, the thinking-clearly-about-biopsychology theme was emphasized because many people think about their own visual systems in a way that is fundamentally incorrect: The visual system does not passively provide images of the external world; it actively extracts some features of the external visual world, and from these it creates visual perceptions.

Third, the cognitive neuroscience theme played a significant role in this chapter because modern functional brain-imaging methods have made it possible for cognitive neuroscientists to study the neural mechanisms of vision in human subjects.

Fourth, the clinical implications theme was developed through a series of clinical case studies: Mrs. Richards, who experienced fortification illusions before her migraine attacks; Karl Lashley, the physiological psychologist who used his scotoma to turn a friend's head into a wallpaper pattern; D.B., the man with blindsight; D.F., who showed by her accurate reaching that she perceived the size, shape, and orientation of objects that she could not describe; A.T., who could describe the size and shape of objects that she could not accurately reach for; and R.P., a typical prosopagnosic.

Seeing Color

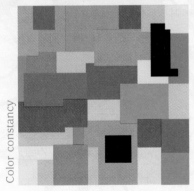

Color constancy

Color is another important aspect of our visual world; color helps us recognize objects. The most important aspect of color vision is color constancy: Under natural conditions, the wavelengths reflected by an object change markedly, yet our perception of its color does not. (Pages 124–128)

Beyond Primary Visual Cortex

Signals leaving primary visual cortex go to areas of secondary visual cortex and then to association cortex. Two streams leave the primary visual cortex: the ventral stream seems to mediate conscious perception, whereas the dorsal stream controls behavior in the absence of conscious awareness. (Pages 128–136)

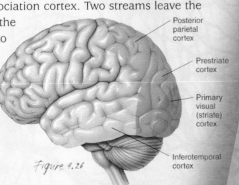

Posterior parietal cortex

Prestriate cortex

Primary visual (striate) cortex

Inferotemporal cortex

Figure 4.26

Think about It

1. It is difficult to define the term *illusion* rigorously, because in a sense, all of what we see is an illusion. Explain and discuss.
2. Some sensory pathways control behavior directly without conscious awareness, whereas others control behavior consciously. Discuss the evolutionary implications.
3. One purpose of biopsychological research is to help neuropsychological patients, but these patients also help biopsychologists understand the brain mechanisms of psychological processes. Discuss and give some examples.
4. How do most people think color vision works? What does the phenomenon of color constancy suggest?

chapter 5

Mechanisms of Perception: Hearing, Touch, Smell, Taste, and Attention

How You Know the World

Two chapters in this text focus primarily on sensory systems. Chapter 4 was the first, and this is the second. Chapter 4 introduced the visual system; this chapter focuses on the *auditory* (hearing), *somatosensory* (touch), *olfactory* (smell), and *gustatory* (taste) systems. In addition, it deals with the mechanisms of attention: how our brains manage to attend to a small number of sensory stimuli despite being continually bombarded by thousands of them.

Before you begin the first section of this chapter, consider the following case (Williams, 1970). By the time you have reached the final section of this chapter, you will be prepared to diagnose the patient and interpret the case.

The Case of the Man Who Could See Only One Thing at a Time

A 68-year-old patient was referred because he had difficulty finding his way around—even around his own home. The patient attributed his problems to his "inability to see properly."

It was found that if two objects (e.g., two pencils) were held in front of him at the same time, he could see only one of them, whether they were held side by side, one above the other, or even one partially behind the other. Pictures of single objects or faces could be identified, even when quite complex; but if a picture included two objects, only one object could be identified at one time, though that one would sometimes fade, whereupon the other would enter the patient's perception. If a sentence were presented in a line, only the rightmost word could be read, but if one word were presented spread over the entire area covered by the previous sentence, the word could be read in its entirety. If the patient was shown overlapping drawings (i.e., one drawn on top of another), he would see one but deny the existence of the other.

Clinical Implications

As you read this chapter, think about this patient. Think about the nature of his deficit and the likely location of his brain damage.

5.1 Principles of Sensory System Organization

The visual system is by far the most thoroughly studied sensory system and, as a result, the most well understood. As more has been discovered about the other sensory systems, it has become increasingly clear that they are organized in a way similar to the visual system. The following are the general principles of sensory system organization.

Three Types of Sensory Cortex

The sensory areas of the cortex are of three fundamentally different types: primary, secondary, and association. The **primary sensory cortex** of a system is the area of sensory cortex that receives most of its input directly from the thalamic relay nuclei of that system. For example, as you learned in Chapter 4, the primary visual cortex is the area of the cerebral cortex that receives most of its input from the lateral geniculate nucleus of the thalamus. The **secondary sensory cortex** of a system comprises the areas of the sensory cortex that receive most of their input from the primary sensory cortex of that system or from other areas of the secondary sensory cortex of the same system. **Association cortex** is any area of cortex that receives input from more than one sensory system. Most input to areas of association cortex comes via areas of secondary sensory cortex.

The interactions among these three types of sensory cortex are characterized by three major principles: hierarchical organization, functional segregation, and parallel processing.

Hierarchical Organization

Sensory systems are characterized by **hierarchical organization**. A *hierarchy* is a system whose members can be assigned to specific levels or ranks in relation to one another. For example, the army is a hierarchical system because all soldiers are ranked with respect to their authority. In the same way, sensory structures are organized in a hierarchy on the basis of the specificity and complexity of their function (see Figure 5.1). As one moves through a sensory system from receptors, to thalamic nuclei, to primary sensory cortex, to secondary sensory cortex, to association cortex, one finds neurons that respond optimally to stimuli of greater and greater specificity and complexity. Each level of a sensory hierarchy receives its input from lower levels and adds another layer of analysis before passing it on up the hierarchy (see Rees, Kreiman, & Koch, 2002).

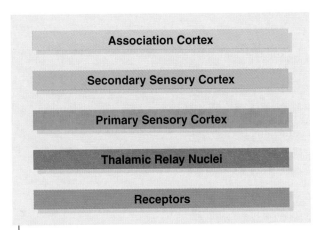

| Association Cortex |
| Secondary Sensory Cortex |
| Primary Sensory Cortex |
| Thalamic Relay Nuclei |
| Receptors |

The hierarchical organization of the sensory systems. The receptors perform the simplest and most general analyses, and the association cortex performs the most complex and specific analyses.

Figure 5.1

The hierarchical organization of sensory systems is apparent from a comparison of the effects of damage to various levels: The higher the level of damage, the more specific and complex the deficit. For example, destruction of a sensory system's receptors produces a complete loss of ability to perceive in that sensory modality (e.g., total blindness or deafness); in contrast, destruction of an area of association or secondary sensory cortex typically produces complex and specific sensory deficits, while leaving fundamental sensory abilities intact. Dr. P., the man who mistook his wife for a hat (Sacks, 1985), displayed such a pattern of deficits.

The Case of the Man Who Mistook His Wife for a Hat

Clinical Implications

Dr. P. was a highly respected musician and teacher—a charming and intelligent man. He had been referred to eminent neurologist Oliver Sacks for help with a vision problem. At least, as Dr. P explained to the neurologist, other people seemed to think that he had a vision problem, and he did admit that he sometimes made odd errors.

Dr. Sacks tested Dr. P.'s vision and found his visual acuity to be excellent—Dr. P. could easily spot a pin on the floor. The first sign of a problem appeared when Dr. P. needed to put his shoe back on following a standard reflex test. Gazing at his foot, he asked Sacks if it was his shoe.

Continuing the examination, Dr. Sacks showed Dr. P. a glove and asked him what it was. Taking the glove and puzzling over it, Dr. P could only guess that it was a container divided into five compartments for some reason. Even when Sacks asked whether the glove might fit on some part of the body, Dr. P. displayed no signs of recognition.

At that point, Dr. P. seemed to conclude that the examination was over and, from the expression on his face, that he had done rather well. Preparing to leave, he turned and grasped his wife's head and tried to put it on his own. Apparently, he thought it was his hat.

Mrs. P. showed little surprise. That kind of thing happened a lot (Sacks, 1985).

In recognition of the hierarchical organization of sensory systems, psychologists sometimes divide the general process of perceiving into two general phases: sensation and perception. **Sensation** is the process of detecting the presence of stimuli, and **perception** is the higher-order process of integrating, recognizing, and interpreting complete patterns of sensations. Dr. P.'s problem was clearly one of visual perception, not visual sensation.

Functional Segregation

It was once assumed that the primary, secondary, and association areas of a sensory system were each *functionally homogeneous*. That is, it was assumed that all areas of cortex at any given level of a sensory hierarchy acted together to perform the same function. However, research has shown that **functional segregation**, rather than functional homogeneity, characterizes the organization of sensory systems. It is now clear that each of the three levels of cerebral cortex—primary, secondary, and association—in each sensory system contains functionally distinct areas that specialize in different kinds of analysis.

Parallel Processing

It was once believed that the different levels of a sensory hierarchy were connected in a serial fashion. A *serial system* is a system in which information flows among the components over just one pathway, like a string through a strand of beads. However, there is now evidence that sensory systems are *parallel systems*—systems in which information flows through the components over multiple pathways. Parallel systems feature **parallel processing**—the simultaneous analysis of a signal in different ways by the multiple parallel pathways of a neural network.

There appear to be two fundamentally different kinds of parallel streams of analysis in our sensory systems: one that is capable of influencing our behavior without our conscious awareness and one that influences our behavior by engaging our conscious awareness.

The Current Model of Sensory System Organization

Figure 5.2 on page 144 summarizes the information in this section of the chapter by illustrating how thinking about the organization of sensory systems has changed. In the 1960s, sensory systems were believed to be hierarchical, functionally homogeneous, and serial. However, subsequent research has established that sensory systems are hierarchical, functionally segregated, and parallel (see Tong, 2003).

Sensory systems are characterized by a division of labor: Multiple specialized areas, at multiple levels, are interconnected by multiple parallel pathways. For example, each area of the visual system is specialized for perceiving specific aspects of visual scenes (e.g., shape, color, movement). Yet, complex stimuli are normally perceived as integrated wholes, not as combinations of independent attributes. How does the brain combine individual sensory attributes to produce integrated perceptions? This is called the *binding problem* (see Bernstein & Robertson, 1998; de Gelder, 2000; Friedman-Hill, Robertson, & Treisman, 1995).

One possible solution to the binding problem is that there is a single area of the cortex at the top of the sensory hierarchy that receives signals from all other areas of the sensory system and puts them together to form perceptions; however, there are no areas of cortex to which all areas of a single sensory system report. It seems, then, that perceptions must be a product of the combined activity of the many interconnected cortical areas.

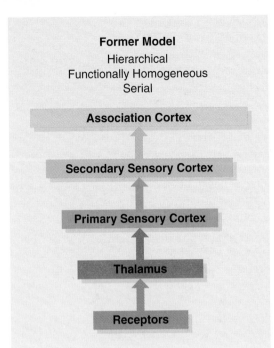

Former Model
Hierarchical
Functionally Homogeneous
Serial

Association Cortex

Secondary Sensory Cortex

Primary Sensory Cortex

Thalamus

Receptors

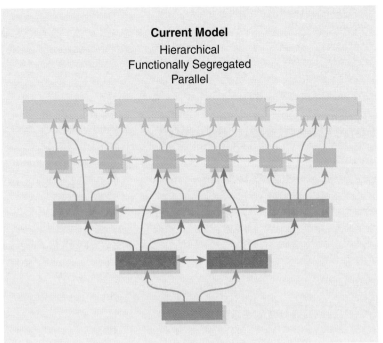

Current Model
Hierarchical
Functionally Segregated
Parallel

Two models of sensory system organization: The former model was hierarchical, functionally homogeneous, and serial; the current model, which is more consistent with the evidence, is hierarchical, functionally segregated, and parallel. Not shown in the current model are descending pathways that enable higher levels to influence lower levels.

Figure 5.2

Not shown in Figure 5.2 are the many neurons that descend through the sensory hierarchies. Although most sensory neurons carry information from lower to higher levels of their respective sensory hierarchies, some conduct in the opposite direction (from higher to lower levels). These are said to carry *top-down signals* (see Engel, Fries, & Singer, 2001; Gao & Suga, 2000).

Now that you have an understanding of the general principles of sensory system organization, let's take a look at the auditory system, the somatosensory system, and the chemical sensory systems (smell and taste).

5.2
Auditory System

The function of the auditory system is the perception of sound—or, more accurately, the perception of objects and events through the sounds that they make. Sounds are vibrations of air molecules that stimulate the auditory system; humans hear only those molecular vibrations between about 20 and 20,000 hertz (cycles per second). Figure 5.3 illustrates how sounds are commonly recorded in the form of waves and the relation between the physical dimensions of sound vibrations and our perceptions of them. The *amplitude, frequency,* and *complexity* of the molecular vibrations are perceived as *loudness, pitch,* and *timbre,* respectively.

Pure tones (sine wave vibrations) exist only in laboratories and sound recording studios; in real life, sound is always associated with complex patterns of vibrations. For example, Figure 5.4 illustrates the complex sound wave associated with one note

The relation between the physical and perceptual dimensions of sound.

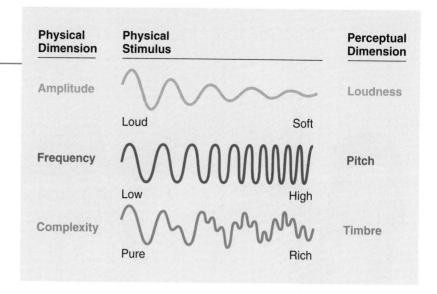

Physical Dimension	Physical Stimulus	Perceptual Dimension
Amplitude	Loud ⟶ Soft	Loudness
Frequency	Low ⟶ High	Pitch
Complexity	Pure ⟶ Rich	Timbre

of a clarinet. The figure also illustrates that any complex sound wave can be broken down mathematically into a series of sine waves of various frequencies and amplitudes; these component sine waves produce the original sound when they are added together. *Fourier analysis* is the mathematical procedure for breaking down complex waves into their component sine waves. One theory of audition is that the auditory system performs a Fourier-like analysis of complex sounds in terms of their component sine waves.

The Ear

The ear is illustrated in Figure 5.5 on page 146. Sound waves travel down the *auditory canal* and cause the **tympanic membrane** (the eardrum) to vibrate. These vibrations are then transferred to the three **ossicles**—the small bones of the middle ear: the *malleus* (the hammer), the *incus* (the anvil), and the *stapes* (the stirrup). The vibrations of the stapes trigger vibrations of the membrane called the **oval window**, which in turn transfers the vibrations to the fluid of the snail-shaped **cochlea** (*kokhlos* means "land snail"). The cochlea is a long, coiled tube with an internal membrane running almost to its tip. This internal membrane is the auditory receptor organ, the **organ of Corti**.

Each pressure change at the oval window travels along the organ of Corti as a wave. The organ of Corti is composed of two membranes: the basilar membrane and the tectorial membrane. The auditory receptors, the **hair cells**, are mounted in the **basilar membrane**, and the **tectorial membrane** rests on the hair cells. Accordingly, a deflection of the organ of Corti at any point along its length produces a shearing force on the hair cells at the same point (Corwin & Warchol, 1991). This force stimulates the hair cells and thereby triggers action potentials in axons of the **auditory nerve**—a branch of cranial nerve VIII (the *auditory-vestibular nerve*). The vibrations of the cochlear fluid are ultimately dissipated by the *round window*, an elastic membrane in the cochlea wall.

The major principle of cochlear coding is that different frequencies produce maximal stimulation of hair cells at different points along the basilar membrane—with higher frequencies producing greater activation closer to the windows. Thus, the many component frequencies that compose each complex sound activate hair cells

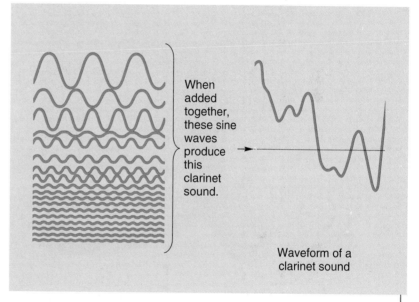

When added together, these sine waves produce this clarinet sound.

Waveform of a clarinet sound

The breaking down of a sound—in this case, the sound of a clarinet—into its component sine waves by Fourier analysis. When added together, the sine waves produce the complex sound wave.

Figure 5.4

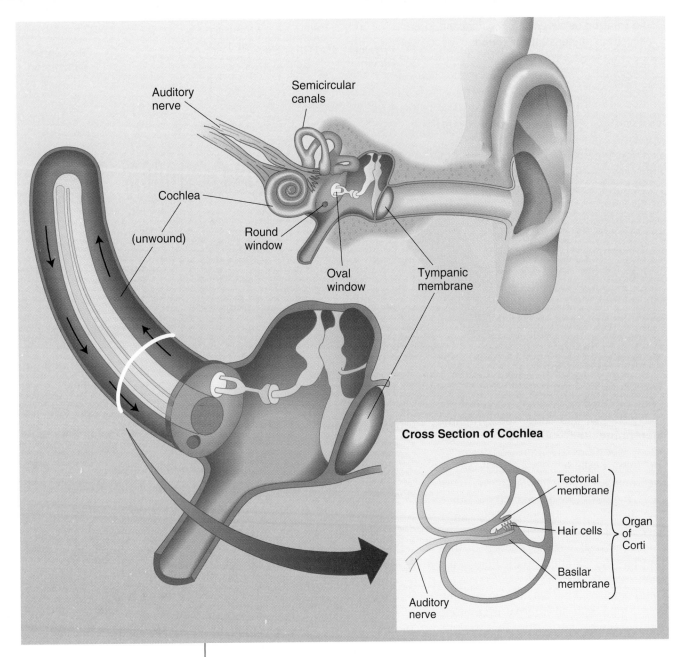

Anatomy of the ear.

Figure 5.5

at many different points along the basilar membrane, and the many signals created by a single complex sound are carried out of the ear by many different auditory neurons. Like the cochlea, most other structures of the auditory system are arrayed according to frequency. Thus, in the same way that the organization of the visual system is primarily **retinotopic**, the organization of the auditory system is primarily **tonotopic**.

This brings us to the major unsolved mystery of auditory processing. Imagine yourself in a complex acoustic environment such as a party. The music is playing; people are dancing, eating, and drinking; and numerous conversations are going on around you. Because the component frequencies in each individual sound activate many sites along your basilar membrane, the number of sites simultaneously activated at any one time by the party noises is enormous. But somehow your auditory system manages to sort these individual frequency messages into separate categories and combine them so that you hear each source of complex sounds independently (see Feng & Ratnam, 2000). For example, you hear the speech of the person standing next to you as a separate sequence of sounds, despite the fact that it contains many of the same component frequencies coming from other sources.

Figure 5.5 also shows the **semicircular canals**—the receptive organs of the vestibular system. The **vestibular system** carries information about the direction and intensity of head movements, which helps us maintain our balance.

From the Ear to the Primary Auditory Cortex

There is no major auditory pathway to the cortex comparable to the visual system's retina-geniculate-striate pathway. Instead, there is a network of auditory pathways (see Masterton, 1992), some of which are illustrated in Figure 5.6. The axons of each *auditory nerve* synapse in the ipsilateral *cochlear nuclei*, from which many projections lead to the **superior olives** at the same level. The axons of the olivary neurons project via the *lateral lemniscus* to the **inferior colliculi**, where they synapse on neurons that project to the **medial geniculate nuclei** of the thalamus, which in turn project to the *primary auditory cortex*. Notice that signals from each ear are transmitted to both ipsilateral and contralateral auditory cortex.

Primary Auditory Cortex

In humans, the primary auditory cortex is located in the temporal lobe, hidden from view within the *lateral fissure* (see Figure 5.7 on page 148). Adjacent to the primary auditory cortex are two bands of secondary auditory cortex. There are thought to be two or three areas of primary auditory cortex and about seven areas of secondary auditory cortex (see Semple & Scott, 2003).

Two important principles of organization of the primary auditory cortex have been identified. First, like the primary visual cortex, the primary auditory cortex is organized in functional columns (see Schreiner, 1992): All of the neurons encountered during a vertical microelectrode penetration of primary auditory cortex (i.e., a penetration at right angles to the cortical layers) respond optimally to sounds in the same frequency range. Second, like the cochlea, primary

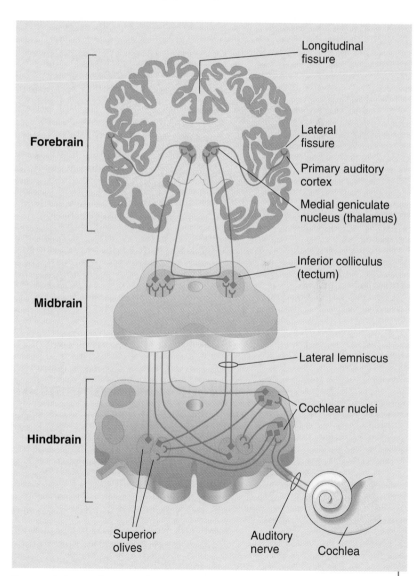

Some of the pathways of the auditory system that lead from one ear to the cortex.

Figure 5.6

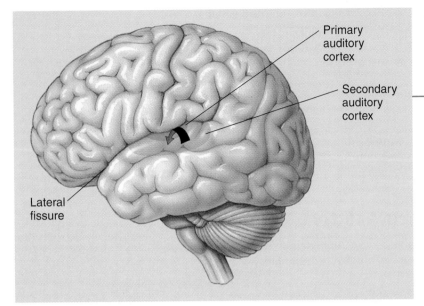

Primary
auditory
cortex

Secondary
auditory
cortex

Lateral
fissure

Location of the primary and secondary auditory cortex in the temporal cortex. Most of the auditory cortex is hidden in the lateral fissure.

Figure 5.7

The Evolutionary
Perspective

auditory cortex is organized tonotopically (see Schreiner, Read, & Sutter, 2000): Posterior regions are more sensitive to higher frequencies.

Little is known about the neurons in primate secondary auditory cortex because they respond weakly and inconsistently to the pure tones typically used by researchers. Rauschecker, Tian, and Hauser (1995) reasoned on the basis of what was known about the neurons of secondary visual cortex that they might have more success in studying the neurons of secondary auditory cortex if they used more complex stimuli—secondary visual cortex neurons respond to complex visual stimuli but show little response to dots of light. These researchers found that pure tones are more effective in activating neurons in monkeys' primary auditory cortex, but monkey calls are more effective in activating neurons in their secondary auditory cortex. A similar pattern of preferential activation of human primary and secondary auditory cortex by pure and complex sounds, respectively, has been documented using fMRI (Wessinger et al., 2001). This suggests that auditory cortex is organized hierarchically in humans and other primates (Semple & Scott, 2003).

You learned in the last chapter how many of the secrets of visual cortex organization were unlocked once it became obvious that visual cortex neurons respond to edges. You learned in the preceding paragraph that we still do not understand which aspects of sound effectively activate auditory neurons, and thus we know relatively little about the organization of the auditory cortex. The same holds for other auditory brain structures.

The following are three major areas of research on the auditory system: neural mechanisms of sound localization, effects of auditory cortex damage, and causes of deafness. These three topics are discussed in the next three subsections.

Neural Mechanisms of Sound Localization

Localization of sounds in space is mediated by the lateral and medial superior olives, but in different ways. When a sound originates to a person's left, it reaches the left ear first, and it is louder at the left ear. Some neurons in the *medial superior olives* respond to slight differences in the time of arrival of signals from the two ears, whereas some neurons in the *lateral superior olives* respond to slight differences in the amplitude of sounds from the two ears (see Heffner & Masterton, 1990).

The medial and lateral superior olives project to the *superior colliculus* (not shown in Figure 5.6), as well as to the inferior colliculus. In contrast to the general tonotopic organization of the auditory system, the deep layers of the superior colliculi, which receive auditory input, are laid out according to a map of auditory space (King, Schnupp, & Thompson, 1998). The superficial layers of the superior colliculi, which receive visual input, are organized retinotopically. Thus, it appears that the general function of the superior colliculi is locating sources of sensory input in space.

Many researchers interested in sound localization have studied barn owls because these owls can locate sources of sounds better than any other animal whose hearing has been tested (see Konishi, 2003). They are nocturnal hunters and must be able to locate field mice solely by the rustling sounds the mice make in the dark. Not surprisingly, the auditory neurons of the barn owl's superior colliculus region are very finely tuned; that is, each neuron responds only to sounds from a particular location near the owl (see Cohen & Knudsen, 1999).

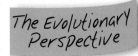
The Evolutionary Perspective

Effects of Auditory Cortex Damage

Efforts to characterize the effects of damage to the auditory cortex have been complicated by the fact that most human auditory cortex is deep in the lateral fissure. Consequently, it is rarely destroyed in its entirety; and if it is, there is inevitably extensive damage to surrounding tissue. As a result of this problem, efforts to understand the effects of auditory cortex damage have relied largely on the study of nonhumans.

The Evolutionary Perspective

Surprisingly, complete bilateral lesions of the primary auditory cortex in laboratory mammals produce no permanent deficits in their ability to detect the presence of sounds (e.g., Kavanagh & Kelly, 1988), even when the lesions include substantial secondary auditory cortex. However, such lesions do disrupt the abilities to localize brief sounds and to recognize rapid complex sequences of sound.

Causes of Deafness

You have just learned that damage to auditory cortex does not produce total deafness or anything resembling it; indeed, total deafness does not result from damage to any single structure or area of the brain's auditory system, even when the damage is bilateral. As a result, total deafness is rare, occurring in only 1 % of all hearing-impaired individuals. This resistance to brain-damage–produced deafness is one advantage of the diffuse, parallel network of auditory pathways: If one auditory brain structure is destroyed, there remain several alternative pathways over which auditory information can flow.

Clinical Implications

Because of the parallel organization of the auditory system, total deafness typically results only from damage to receptors or to the nerves leading from them. Accordingly, there are two common classes of hearing impairment: those associated with damage to the ossicles (*conductive deafness*) and those associated with damage to the cochlea or auditory nerve (*nerve deafness*).

If only part of the cochlea is damaged, individuals may have nerve deafness for some frequencies but not others. This is how age-related hearing loss works. Your experience with elderly relatives may have already taught you that some hearing loss is an inevitable part of aging. Fortunately, age-related hearing loss rarely progresses to total deafness.

The first age-related hearing loss to develop is usually a specific deficit in perceiving high frequencies. That is why elderly people often have difficulty distinguishing "s," "f," and "t" sounds: They can hear people speaking to them but often have difficulty understanding what people are saying. Often, they do not even realize that they have a hearing problem.

5·3
Somatosensory System: Touch and Pain

You have undoubtedly experienced a wide variety of sensations emanating from your body. These are generally referred to as *somatosensations*. The system that mediates these bodily sensations—the *somatosensory system*—is, in fact, three separate but interacting systems: (1) an *exteroceptive system*, which senses external stimuli that are applied to the skin; (2) a *proprioceptive system*, which monitors information about the position of the body that comes from receptors in the muscles, joints, and organs of balance; and (3) an *interoceptive system* (see Craig, 2002), which provides general information about conditions within the body (e.g., temperature and blood pressure). This discussion deals almost exclusively with the exteroceptive system, which itself comprises three somewhat distinct divisions: a division for perceiving *mechanical stimuli* (touch), one for *thermal stimuli* (temperature), and one for *nociceptive stimuli* (pain).

Cutaneous Receptors

There are several different kinds of receptors in the skin (see Johnson, 2001). Figure 5.8 illustrates four. The simplest cutaneous receptors are the **free nerve endings** (neuron endings with no specialized structures on them), which are particularly sensitive to temperature change and pain. The largest and deepest cutaneous receptors are the onionlike **Pacinian corpuscles**; because they adapt rapidly, they respond immediately to sudden displacements of the skin. In contrast, *Merkel's disks* and *Ruffini endings* both adapt slowly and respond best to gradual skin indentation and gradual skin stretch, respectively.

To appreciate the functional significance of fast and slow receptor adaptation, consider what happens when a constant pressure is applied to the skin. The pressure evokes a burst of firing in all receptors, which corresponds to the sensation of being touched; however, after a few hundred milliseconds, only the slowly adapting receptors remain active, and the quality of the sensation changes. In fact, you are often totally unaware of constant skin pressure; for example, you are usually unaware of the feeling of your clothes against your body until you focus attention on it. As a consequence, when you try to identify objects by touch, you manipulate them in your hands so that the pattern of stimulation continually changes. The identification of objects by touch is called **stereognosis**.

Each type of somatosensory receptor serves a different function and works in a different way. The most well understood type is the Pacinian corpuscle—because it is large and responds quickly. Inside its onionlike outer structure (see Figure 5.8) is a dendrite. When pressure on the onionlike shell deflects the membrane of the core dendrite (this requires sudden skin displacement), resistance to the inflow of sodium ions is decreased; sodium ions then enter the dendrite, generating a neural signal.

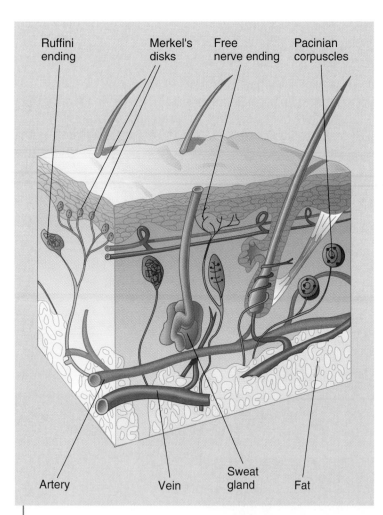

Ruffini ending   **Merkel's disks**   **Free nerve ending**   **Pacinian corpuscles**

Artery   Vein   Sweat gland   Fat

Four cutaneous receptors that occur in human skin.

Figure 5.8

Dermatomes

The neural fibers that carry information from cutaneous receptors and other somatosensory receptors gather together in nerves and enter the spinal cord via the *dorsal roots*. The area of the body that is innervated by the left and right dorsal roots of a given segment of the spinal cord is called a **dermatome**. Figure 5.9 is a dermatomal map of the human body. Because there is considerable overlap between adjacent dermatomes, destruction of a single dorsal root typically produces little somatosensory loss.

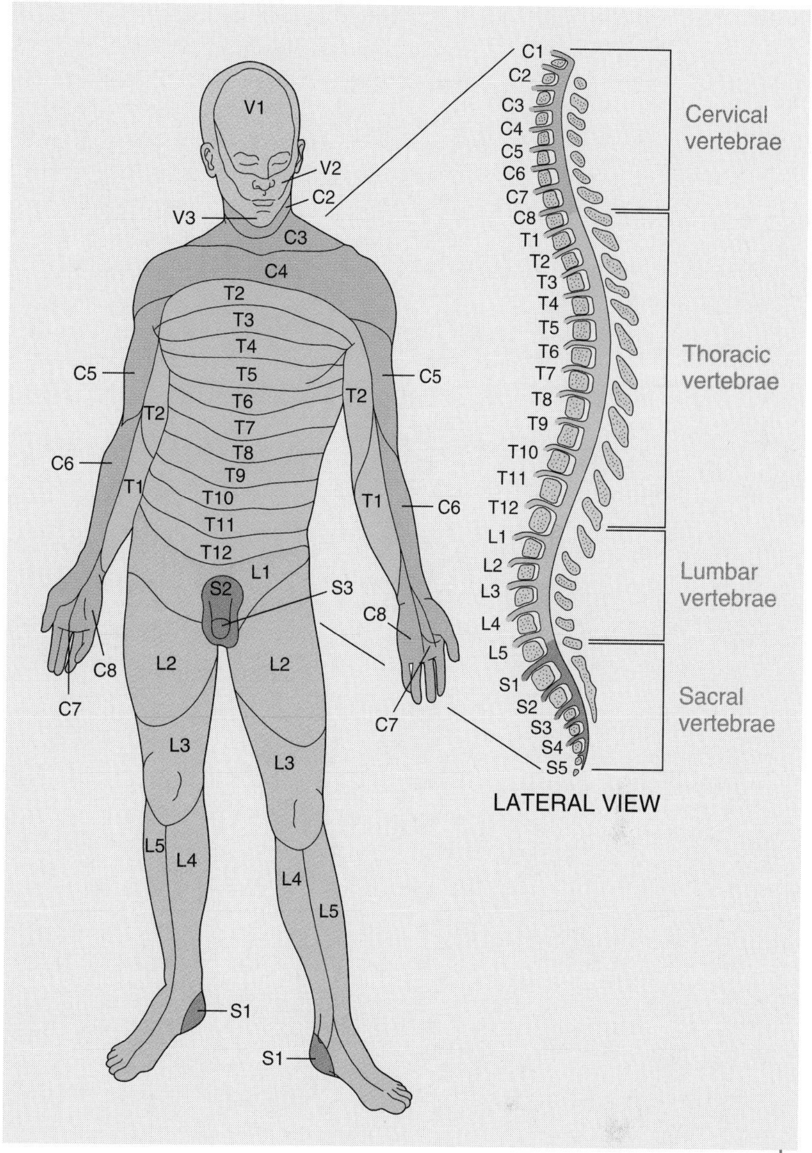

The Two Major Somatosensory Pathways

Somatosensory information ascends from each side of the body to the human cortex over two major pathways: the dorsal-column medial-lemniscus system and the anterolateral system. The **dorsal-column medial-lemniscus system** carries information about touch and proprioception. The **anterolateral system** carries information about pain and temperature.

The dorsal-column medial-lemniscus system is illustrated in Figure 5.10 on page 152. The sensory neurons of this system enter the spinal cord via a dorsal root, ascend ipsilaterally in the **dorsal columns**, and synapse in the *dorsal column nuclei* of the medulla. The axons of dorsal column nuclei neurons *decussate* (cross over to the other side of the brain) and then ascend in the **medial lemniscus** to the contralateral **ventral posterior nucleus** of the thalamus. The ventral posterior nuclei also receive input via the three branches of the *trigeminal nerve*, which carry somatosensory information from the contralateral areas of the face. Most neurons of the ventral posterior nucleus project to the *primary somatosensory cortex (SI)*; others project to the

The dermatomes of the human body. S, L, T, and C refer respectively to the *sacral, lumbar, thoracic*, and *cervical* regions of the spinal cord. V1, V2, and V3 stand for the three branches of the trigeminal nerve.

Figure 5.9

secondary somatosensory cortex (SII) or the posterior parietal cortex. Neuroscience trivia buffs will almost certainly want to add to their collection the fact that the dorsal column neurons that originate in the toes are the longest neurons in the human body.

The anterolateral system is illustrated in Figure 5.11 on page 153. Most dorsal root neurons of the anterolateral system synapse as soon as they enter the spinal cord. The axons of most of the second-order neurons decussate but then ascend to the brain in the contralateral anterolateral portion of the spinal cord; however, some do not decussate but ascend ipsilaterally. The anterolateral system comprises three different tracts: the *spinothalamic tract*, which projects to the *ventral posterior nucleus* of the thalamus (as does the dorsal-column medial-lemniscus system); the *spinoreticular tract*, which projects to the *reticular formation* (and then to the *parafascicular nuclei* and *intralaminar nuclei* of the thalamus); and the *spinotectal tract*, which projects to the *tectum* (colliculi). The three branches of the trigeminal

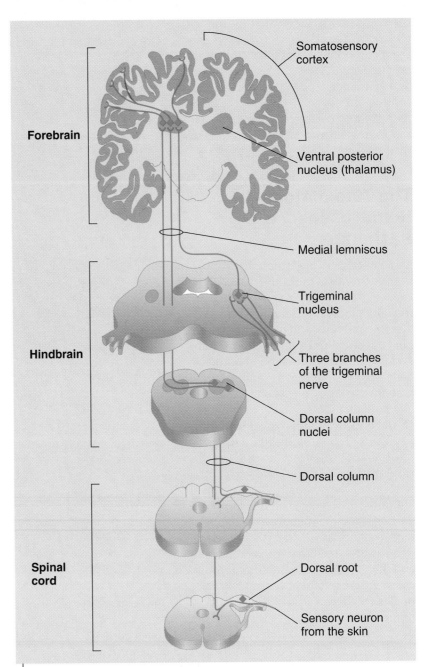

Somatosensory
cortex

Forebrain

Ventral posterior
nucleus (thalamus)

Medial lemniscus

Hindbrain

Trigeminal
nucleus

Three branches
of the trigeminal
nerve

Dorsal column
nuclei

Dorsal column

**Spinal
cord**

Dorsal root

Sensory neuron
from the skin

The dorsal-column medial-lemniscus system. The pathways from only
one side of the body are shown.

Figure 5.10

nerve carry pain and temperature information from the face to the same thalamic sites. The pain and temperature information that reaches the thalamus is then distributed to SI, SII, posterior parietal cortex, and other parts of the brain.

If both ascending somatosensory paths are completely transected by a spinal injury, the patient can feel no body sensation from below the level of the break. Clearly, when it comes to spinal injuries, lower is better.

Mark, Ervin, and Yakolev (1962) assessed the effects of lesions to the thalamus on the chronic pain of patients in the advanced stages of cancer. Lesions to the ventral posterior nuclei, which receive input from both the spinothalamic tract and the dorsal-column medial-lemniscus system, produced some loss of cutaneous sensitivity to touch, to temperature change, and to sharp pain; but the lesions had no effect on deep, chronic pain. In contrast, lesions of the parafascicular and intralaminar nu-

Clinical
Implications

Clinical
Implications

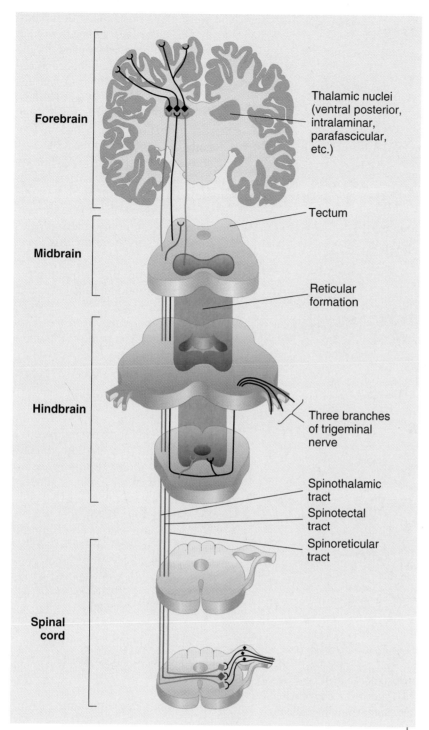

The anterolateral system. The pathways from only one side of the body are shown.

Figure 5.11

clei, both of which receive input from the spinoreticular tract, reduced deep chronic pain without disrupting cutaneous sensitivity.

Cortical Areas of Somatosensation

In 1937, Penfield and his colleagues mapped the primary somatosensory cortex of patients during neurosurgery (see Figure 5.12 on page 154). Penfield applied electrical stimulation to various sites on the cortical surface, and the patients,

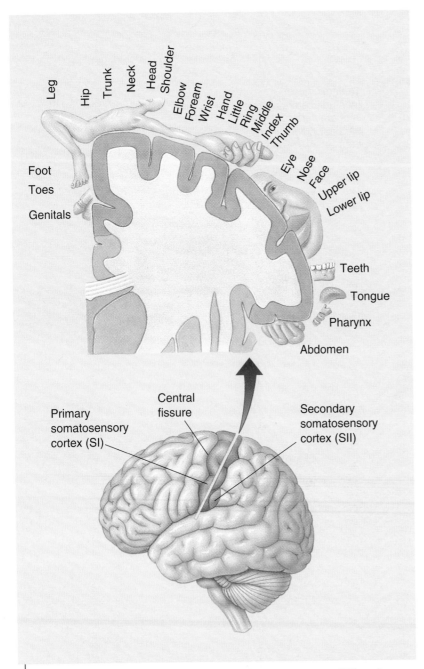

The locations of human primary somatosensory cortex (SI) and one area of secondary somatosensory cortex (SII) with the conventional portrayal of the somatosensory homunculus. Something has always confused me about this portrayal of the somatosensory homunculus: The body is upside-down, while the head is right side up. It now appears that this conventional portrayal is wrong. The results of an fMRI study suggest that the face representation is also inverted (Servos et al., 1999).

Figure 5.12

who were fully conscious under a local anesthetic, described what they felt. When stimulation was applied to the *postcentral gyrus*, the patients reported somatosensory sensations in various parts of their bodies. When Penfield mapped the relation between each site of stimulation and the part of the body in which the sensation was felt, he discovered that the human primary somatosensory cortex (SI) is **somatotopic**—organized according to a map of the body surface. This somatotopic map is commonly referred to as the **somatosensory homunculus** (*homunculus* means "little man").

Notice in Figure 5.12 that the somatosensory homunculus is distorted; the greatest proportion of SI is dedicated to receiving input from the parts of the body that are capable of the finest tactile discriminations (e.g., hands, lips, and tongue).

A second somatotopically organized area, SII, lies just ventral to SI in the postcentral gyrus, and much of it extends into the lateral fissure. SII receives most of its input from SI and is thus regarded as secondary somatosensory cortex. In contrast to SI, whose input is largely contralateral, SII receives substantial input from both sides of the body. Much of the output of SI and SII goes to the association cortex of the *posterior parietal lobe*.

There are several other areas of secondary somatosensory cortex in humans (see Kaas & Collins, 2001). For example, there are two narrow bands, one on either side of SI, and there is another adjacent to SII. Each is somatotopically organized, but the function of each is unclear.

Kaas and others (1981) found that the primary somatosensory cortex is composed of four functional strips, each with a similar, but separate, somatotopic organization. Each strip of primary somatosensory cortex is most sensitive to a different kind of somatosensory input (e.g., to light touch or temperature). Thus, if one were to record from neurons in a horizontal line across the four strips, one would find neurons that "preferred" four different kinds of tactile stimulation, all to the same part of the body. Also, one would find that as one moved from anterior to posterior, the preferences of the neurons would tend to become more complex and specific (see Caselli, 1997), suggesting an anterior-to-posterior hierarchical scheme (Iwamura, 1998).

The receptive fields of many neurons in the primary somatosensory cortex, like those of visual system neurons, can be divided into antagonistic excitatory and inhibitory areas (Di-Carlo & Johnson, 2000; DiCarlo, Johnson, & Hsaio, 1998). Figure 5.13 illustrates the receptive field of a neuron of the primary somatosensory cortex that is responsive to light touch (Mountcastle & Powell, 1959).

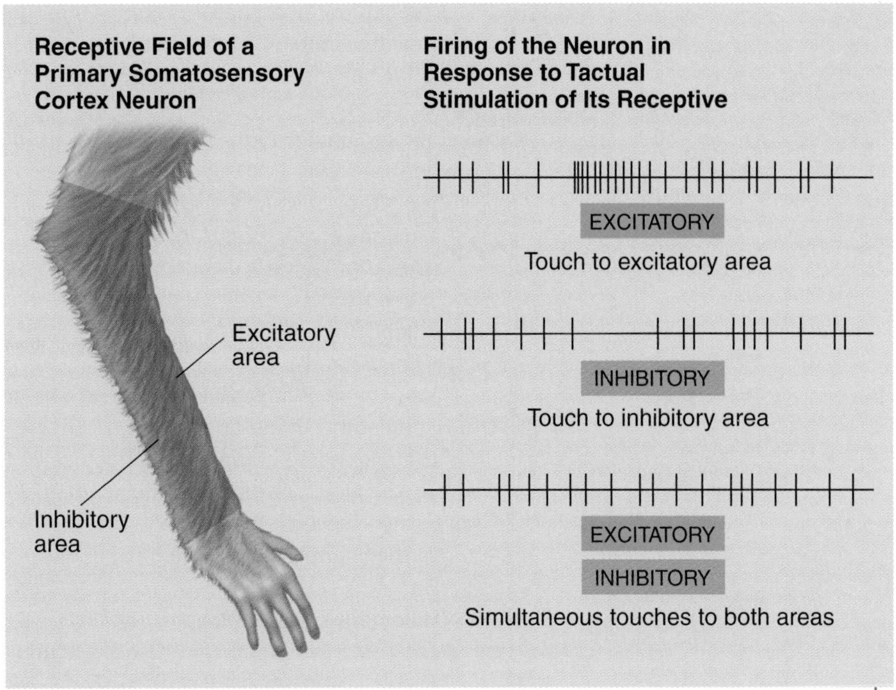

Effects of Damage to the Primary Somatosensory Cortex

Like the effects of damage to the primary auditory cortex, the effects of damage to the primary somatosensory cortex are often remarkably mild—presumably because both auditory and somatosensory systems feature numerous parallel pathways.

Receptive Field of a Primary Somatosensory Cortex Neuron

Excitatory area

Inhibitory area

Firing of the Neuron in Response to Tactual Stimulation of Its Receptive

EXCITATORY
Touch to excitatory area

INHIBITORY
Touch to inhibitory area

EXCITATORY
INHIBITORY
Simultaneous touches to both areas

The receptive field of a neuron of the primary somatosensory cortex. Notice the antagonistic excitatory and inhibitory areas.

Figure 5.13

Corkin, Milner, and Rasmussen (1970) assessed the somatosensory abilities of epileptic patients both before and after a unilateral excision that included SI. Following surgery, the patients displayed two minor contralateral deficits: a reduced ability to detect light touch and a reduced ability to identify objects by touch (i.e., a deficit in stereognosis). These deficits were bilateral only in those cases in which the unilateral lesion encroached on SII.

Somatosensory Agnosias

There are two major types of somatosensory agnosia. One is **astereognosia**—the inability to recognize objects by touch. Cases of pure astereognosia—those that occur in the absence of simple sensory deficits—are rare (Corkin, Milner, & Rasmussen, 1970). The other type of somatosensory agnosia is **asomatognosia**—the failure to recognize parts of one's own body. Asomatognosia is usually unilateral, affecting only the left side of the body; and it is usually associated with extensive damage to the right posterior parietal lobe. The case of Aunt Betty is an example.

The Case of Aunt Betty, Who Lost Half of Her Body

It was time to see Aunt Betty—she wasn't really my aunt, but I grew up thinking that she was. She was my mother's best friend. She had had a stroke in her right hemisphere.

As we walked to her room, one of the medical students described the case. "Left hemiplegia [left-side paralysis]," I was told.

Aunt Betty was lying on her back with her head and eyes turned to the right. "Betty," I called out. Not Aunt Betty, but Betty. I was 37; I'd dropped the "Aunt" long ago—at least 2 years earlier.

I approached her bed from the left, but Aunt Betty did not turn her head or even her eyes to look towards me.

"Hal," she called out. "Where are you?"

I turned her head gently toward me. We talked. It was clear that she had no speech problems, no memory loss, and no confusion. She was as bright as ever. But her eyes still looked to the right as if the left side of her world did not exist.

I picked up her right hand and held it in front of her eyes. "What's this?" I asked.

"My hand, of course," she said with an intonation that suggested what she thought of my question.

"Well then, what's this?" I said, as I held up her limp left hand where she could see it.

"A hand."

"Whose hand?"

"Your hand, I guess," she replied. She seemed genuinely puzzled. I carefully placed her hand on the bed.

"Why have you come to this hospital?" I asked.

"To see you," she replied hesitantly. I could tell that she didn't really know the answer.

"Is there anything wrong with you?"

"No."

"How about your left hand and leg?"

"They're fine," she said. "How are yours?"

"They're fine too," I replied. There was nothing else to do. Aunt Betty was in trouble.

(Paraphrased from pp. 12–14 of *Newton's Madness: Further Tales of Clinical Neurology* by Harold L. Klawans. New York: Harper & Row, 1990.)

As in the case of Aunt Betty, asomatognosia is often accompanied by **anosognosia**—the failure of neuropsychological patients to recognize their own symptoms. Asomatognosia may also be accompanied by **contralateral neglect**—the tendency not to respond to stimuli that are contralateral to a right-hemisphere injury. (You will learn more about contralateral neglect in Chapter 6).

The Paradoxes of Pain

A paradox is a logical contradiction. The perception of pain is paradoxical in three important respects, which are explained in the following three subsections.

Adaptiveness of Pain.   One paradox of pain is that an experience that seems in every respect to be so bad is in fact extremely important for our survival. There is no special stimulus for pain; it is a response to excessive (potentially harmful) stimulation of any type (see Craig, 2003). The value of pain is best illustrated by the case of a person who did not experience it.

The Case of Miss C., the Woman Who Felt No Pain

Clinical Implications

The best documented of all cases of congenital insensitivity to pain is Miss C., a young Canadian girl who was a student at McGill University in Montreal. . . . The young lady was highly intelligent and seemed normal in every way except that she had never felt pain. As a child, she had bitten off the tip of her tongue while chewing food, and had suffered third-degree burns after kneeling on a radiator to look out of the window. . . . She felt no pain when parts of her body were subjected to strong electric shock, to hot water at temperatures that usually produce reports of burning pain, or to a prolonged ice-bath. Equally astonishing was the fact that she showed no changes in blood pressure, heart rate, or respiration when these stimuli were presented. Furthermore, she could not remember ever sneezing or coughing, the gag reflex could be elicited only with great difficulty, and corneal reflexes (to protect the eyes) were absent. A variety of other stimuli, such as inserting a stick up through the nostrils, pinching tendons, or injections of histamine under the skin—which are normally considered as forms of torture—also failed to produce pain.

Miss C. had severe medical problems. She exhibited pathological changes in her knees, hip, and spine, and underwent several orthopaedic operations. The surgeon attributed these changes to the lack of protection to joints usually given by pain sensation. She apparently failed to shift her weight when standing, to turn over in her sleep, or to avoid certain postures, which normally prevent inflammation of joints. . . .

Miss C. died at the age of twenty-nine of massive infections . . . and extensive skin and bone trauma.

(From *The Challenge of Pain*, pp. 16–17, by Ronald Melzack and Patrick D. Wall, 1982, London: Penguin Books Ltd. Copyright © Ronald Melzack and Patrick D. Wall, 1982.)

Lack of Clear Cortical Representation of Pain.   The second paradox of pain is that it has no obvious cortical representation (Rainville, 2002). Painful stimuli often activate areas of cortex, but the areas of activation have varied greatly from study to study (Apkarian, 1995).

Painful stimuli usually elicit responses in SI and SII. However, removal of SI and SII in humans is not associated with any change in the threshold for pain. Indeed, *hemispherectomized patients* (those with one cerebral hemisphere removed) can still perceive pain from both sides of their bodies.

The cortical area that has been most frequently linked to the experience of pain is the **anterior cingulate cortex** (the cortex of the anterior cingulate gyrus; see Figure 5.14). For example, using PET, Craig and colleagues (1996) demonstrated increases in anterior cingulate cortex activity when subjects placed a hand on painfully cold bars, painfully hot bars, or even on a series of alternating cool and warm bars, which produce an illusion of painful stimulation.

Evidence suggests that the anterior cingulate cortex is involved in the emotional reaction to pain rather than to the perception of pain itself (Panksepp, 2003; Price, 2000). For example, *prefrontal lobotomy*, which damages the anterior cingulate cortex and its connections, typically reduces the emotional reaction to pain without changing the threshold for pain.

Descending Pain Control.   The third paradox of pain is that this most compelling of all sensory experiences can be so effectively suppressed by cognitive and emotional factors. For example, men participating in a certain religious ceremony suspend objects from hooks embedded in their backs with little evidence of pain (see Figure 5.15 on page 158); severe wounds suffered by soldiers in battle are often associated with little pain; and people injured in life-threatening situations frequently feel no pain until the threat is over.

Melzack and Wall (1965) proposed the **gate-control theory** to account for the ability of cognitive and emotional factors to block pain. They theorized that signals descending from the brain can activate neural gating circuits in the spinal cord to block incoming pain signals.

Three discoveries led to the identification of a descending pain-control circuit. First was the discovery that electrical stimulation of the **periaqueductal gray (PAG)** has analgesic (pain-blocking) effects: Reynolds

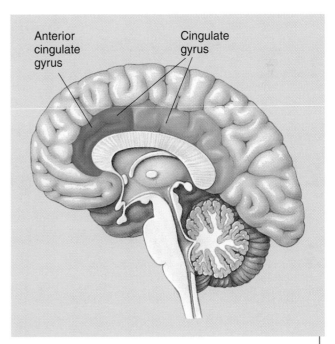

Location of anterior cingulate cortex in the cingulate gyrus.

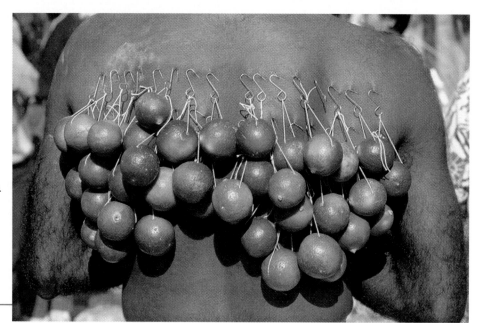

When experienced as part of a religious rite, normally excruciating conditions often produce little pain. Limes are used here because of the caustic effects of lime juice.

Figure 5.15

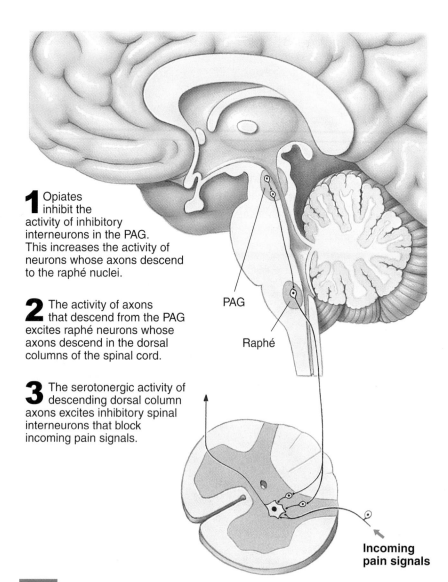

1 Opiates inhibit the activity of inhibitory interneurons in the PAG. This increases the activity of neurons whose axons descend to the raphé nuclei.

2 The activity of axons that descend from the PAG excites raphé neurons whose axons descend in the dorsal columns of the spinal cord.

3 The serotonergic activity of descending dorsal column axons excites inhibitory spinal interneurons that block incoming pain signals.

PAG

Raphé

Incoming pain signals

(1969) was able to perform surgery on rats with no analgesia other than that provided by PAG stimulation. Second was the discovery that the PAG and other areas of the brain contain specialized receptors for opiate analgesic drugs such as morphine. And third was the isolation of several endogenous (internally produced) opiate analgesics, the **endorphins**, which you learned about in Chapter 3. These three findings together suggested that analgesic drugs and psychological factors might block pain through an endorphin-sensitive circuit that descends from the PAG.

Figure 5.16 illustrates the descending analgesia circuit first hypothesized by Basbaum and Fields (1978). They proposed that the output of the PAG excites the serotonergic neurons of

Basbaum and Fields' s (1978) model of the descending analgesia circuit.

Figure 5.16

the *raphé nuclei* (a cluster of serotonergic nuclei in the core of the medulla), which in turn project down the dorsal columns of the spinal cord and excite interneurons that block incoming pain signals in the dorsal horn.

Descending analgesia pathways have been the subject of intensive investigation since the first model was proposed by Basbaum and Fields in 1978. In order to incorporate the mass of accumulated data, models of the descending analgesia circuits have grown much more complex (see Borszcz, 1999; McNally, 1999). Still, a descending component involving opiate activity in the PAG and serotonergic activity in the raphé nuclei remains a key part of most of these models.

5·4
The Chemical Senses: Smell and Taste

lfaction (smell) and *gustation* (taste) are referred to as the chemical senses because their function is to monitor the chemical content of the environment. Smell is the response of the olfactory system to airborne chemicals that are drawn by inhalation over receptors in the nasal passages, and taste is the response of the gustatory system to chemicals in solution in the oral cavity.

When we are eating, smell and taste act in concert. Molecules of food excite both smell and taste receptors and produce an integrated sensory impression termed **flavor**. The contribution of olfaction to flavor is often underestimated, but you won't make this mistake if you remember that people with no sense of smell have difficulty distinguishing the flavors of apples and onions.

In humans, the main adaptive role of the chemical senses is flavor recognition. However, in many other species, the chemical senses also play a significant role in regulating social interactions (e.g., DeCatanzaro et al., 2000; Luo, Fee, & Katz, 2003). The members of many species release **pheromones**—chemicals that influence the physiology and behavior of *conspecifics* (others of the same species). For example, Murphy and Schneider (1970) showed that the sexual and aggressive behavior of hamsters is under pheromonal control. Normal male hamsters attack and kill unfamiliar males that are placed in their colonies, whereas they mount and impregnate unfamiliar sexually receptive females. However, male hamsters that are unable to smell the intruders engage in neither aggressive nor sexual behavior. Murphy and Schneider confirmed the olfactory basis of hamsters' aggressive and sexual behavior in a particularly devious fashion. They swabbed a male intruder with the vaginal secretions of a sexually receptive female before placing it in an unfamiliar colony; in so doing, they converted it from an object of hamster assassination to an object of hamster lust.

The possibility that humans may release sexual pheromones has received considerable attention because of its financial and recreational potential. There have been many suggestive findings. For example, (1) the olfactory sensitivity of women is greatest when they are ovulating or pregnant; (2) the menstrual cycles of women living together tend to become synchronized; (3) humans—particularly women—can tell the sex of a person from the breath or the underarm odor; and (4) men can judge the stage of a woman's menstrual cycle on the basis of her vaginal odor. However, there is still no direct evidence that human odors can serve as sex attractants. Most subjects do not find the aforementioned body odors to be particularly attractive.

Another feature of the chemical senses that has attracted attention is that they are involved in some interesting forms of learning. Animals, including humans, that suffer from gastrointestinal upset after consuming a particular food develop a *conditioned aversion* to that taste. Conversely, it has been shown that rats develop preferences for flavors they encounter in their mother's milk or on the breath of conspecifics (Galef, 1989). And adult male rats that were nursed as pups by lemon-scented mothers copulate more effectively with females that smell of

The Evolutionary Perspective

lemons (Fillion & Blass, 1986)—a phenomenon that has been aptly referred to as the *I-want-a-girl-just-like-the-girl-who-married-dear-old-dad phenomenon* (Diamond, 1986).

The Olfactory System

ON THE CD

Visit *Investigating Olfaction: The Nose Knows*. This module will provide you with everything you ever wanted to know about olfaction and the olfactory system.

The olfactory system is illustrated in Figure 5.17. The olfactory receptors are located in the upper part of the nose, embedded in a layer of mucus-covered tissue called the **olfactory mucosa**. Their dendrites are located in the nasal passages, and they have axons, which pass through a porous portion of the skull (the *cribriform plate*) and enter the **olfactory bulbs**, where they synapse on neurons that project via the *olfactory tracts* to the brain.

For decades, it was widely assumed that there were only a few different kinds of olfactory receptors. Different profiles of activity in a relatively small number of receptor types were thought to lead to the perception of various smells—in the same way that the profiles of activity in three different cones lead to the perception of all possible colors.

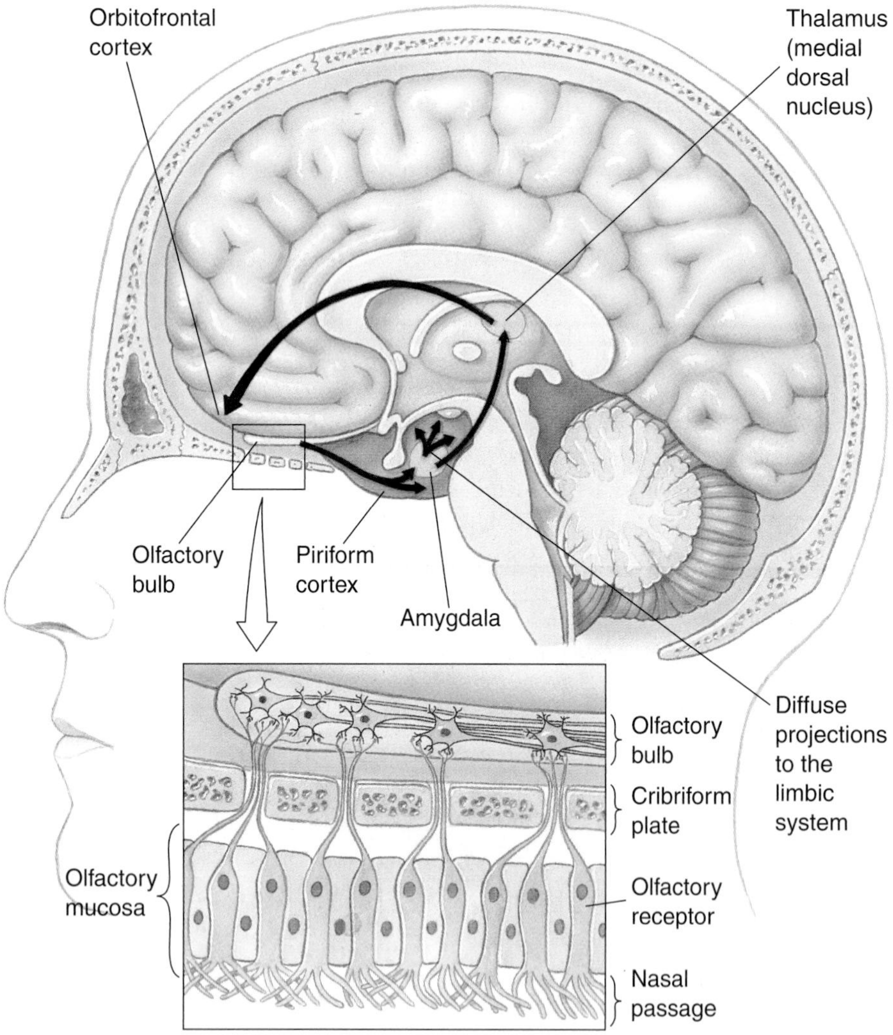

The human olfactory system.

Figure 5.17

Estimates of the number of olfactory receptor types changed markedly with the discovery at the turn of the 21st century that rats and mice have about one thousand different kinds of receptor proteins and that humans likely have several hundred kinds (Gibson & Garbers, 2000).

In mammals, each olfactory receptor cell contains only one type of receptor protein molecule (Serizawa et al., 2003). This is called the *one-olfactory-receptor-one-neuron rule* (Lewcock & Reed, 2003). Olfactory receptor proteins are in the membranes of the dendrites of the olfactory receptor cells, where they can be stimulated by circulating airborne chemicals in the nasal passages. Researchers have attempted to discover the functional principle by which the various receptors are distributed through the olfactory mucosa. If there is such a principle, it has not yet been discovered: All of the types of receptor appear to be scattered throughout the mucosa, providing no clue about the organization of the system.

Despite the fact that olfactory receptors of each kind seem to be scattered throughout the olfactory mucosa, somehow all the olfactory receptors with the same receptor protein project to the same general location in the olfactory bulb (see Lewcock & Reed, 2003). Accordingly, different odors produce different spatial patterns of activity on the olfactory bulbs, patterns that can be detected with the 2-deoxyglucose technique (Leon & Johnson, 2003). Because each type of receptor responds in varying degrees to a wide variety of odors, each odor seems to be encoded by component processing—that is, by the pattern of activity across many receptor types (Doty, 2001).

The olfactory receptor cells differ from the receptor cells of other sensory systems in one important way. New olfactory receptor cells are created throughout each individual's life, to replace those that have deteriorated (Doty, 2001). Once created, the new receptor cells develop axons, which grow until they reach appropriate sites in the olfactory bulb. Each new olfactory receptor cell survives only a few weeks before being replaced.

Each olfactory tract projects to several structures of the medial temporal lobes, including the amygdala and the **piriform cortex**—an area of medial temporal cortex adjacent to the amygdala. The piriform cortex is considered to be primary olfactory cortex. The olfactory system is the only sensory system whose major sensory pathway reaches the cerebral cortex without first passing through the thalamus.

Two major olfactory pathways leave the amygdala-piriform area. One projects diffusely to the limbic system, and the other projects via the **medial dorsal nuclei** of the thalamus to the **orbitofrontal cortex**—the area of cortex on the inferior surface of the frontal lobes, next to the *orbits* (eye sockets). The limbic projection is thought to mediate the emotional response to odors; the thalamic-orbitofrontal projection is thought to mediate the conscious perception of odors. Little is known about how neurons receptive to different odors are organized in the cortex (see Savic, 2002).

The Gustatory System

Taste receptors are found on the tongue and in parts of the oral cavity; they typically occur in clusters of about 50, called **taste buds**. On the tongue, taste buds are often located around small protuberances called *papillae* (singular *papilla*). The relation between taste receptors, taste buds, and papillae is illustrated in Figure 5.18 (see Gilbertson, Damak, & Margolskee, 2000). Unlike olfactory receptors, taste receptors do not

Surface of Tongue

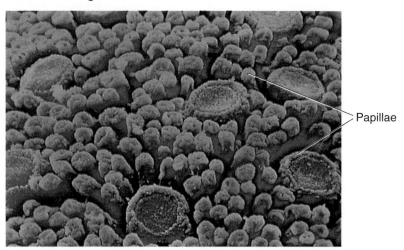

Papillae

Cross Section of a Papilla

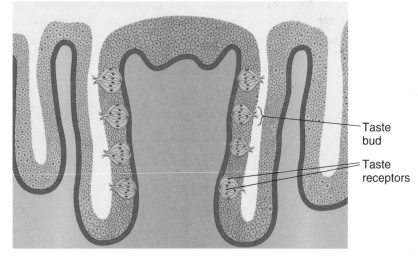

Taste bud

Taste receptors

Taste receptors, taste buds, and papillae on the surface of the tongue. Two sizes of papillae are visible in the photograph; only the larger papillae contain taste buds and receptors.

Figure 5.18

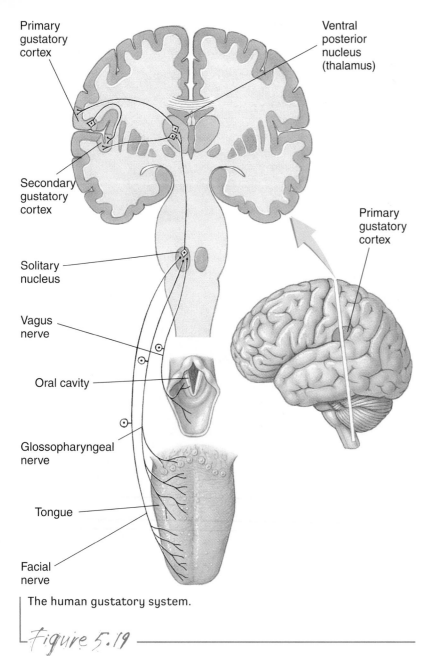

The human gustatory system.

Figure 5.19

have their own axons; each neuron that carries impulses away from a taste bud receives input from many receptors.

It was once believed that there are four primary tastes—sweet, sour, bitter, and salty—and four kinds of taste receptors, one for each primary taste. The perception of any taste was assumed to be a product of the relative amounts of activity produced in these four kinds of receptors.

This simple component-processing theory of taste has several major problems (see Smith & Margolskee, 2001). One is that it is now clear that there are at least five primary tastes; *unami* (meaty or savory) is the fifth. Another problem is that many tastes cannot be created by combinations of the primary tastes (Schiffman & Erickson, 1980). Yet another is that some tastes (salty and sour) seem to have no receptors specific to them; instead, they have been shown to influence the activity of some taste receptors by acting directly on their ion channels (see Montmayeur & Matsunami, 2002).

The major pathways over which gustatory signals are conducted to the cortex are illustrated in Figure 5.19. Gustatory afferent neurons leave the mouth as part of the *facial* (VII), *glossopharyngeal* (IX), and *vagus* (X) *cranial nerves*, which carry information from the front of the tongue, back of the tongue, and back of the oral cavity, respectively. These fibers all terminate in the **solitary nucleus** of the medulla, where they synapse on neurons that project to the *ventral posterior nucleus* of the thalamus. The gustatory axons of the ventral posterior nucleus project to the *primary gustatory cortex*, which is near the face area of the somatosensory homunculus on the superior lip of the lateral fissure, and to the *secondary gustatory cortex*, which is hidden from view in the lateral fissure (Sewards & Sewards, 2001). Unlike the projections of other sensory systems, the projections of the gustatory system are primarily ipsilateral. Thus, particular tastes seem to be encoded in the brain by profiles of activity in groups of neurons (e.g., high activity in some and low in others).

Brain Damage and the Chemical Senses

The inability to smell is called **anosmia**; the inability to taste is called **ageusia**. The most common neurological cause of anosmia is a blow to the head that causes a displacement of the brain within the skull and shears the olfactory nerves where they pass through the cribriform plate. Less complete deficits in olfaction have been linked to a wide variety of neurological disorders including Alzheimer's disease, Down syndrome, epilepsy, multiple sclerosis, Korsakoff's syndrome, and Parkinson's disease (see Doty, 2001).

Ageusia is rare, presumably because sensory signals from the mouth are carried via three separate pathways. However, partial ageusia, limited to the anterior two-thirds of the tongue on one side, is sometimes observed after damage to the ear on the same side of the body. This is because the branch of the facial nerve (VII) that carries gustatory information from the anterior two-thirds of the tongue passes through the middle ear.

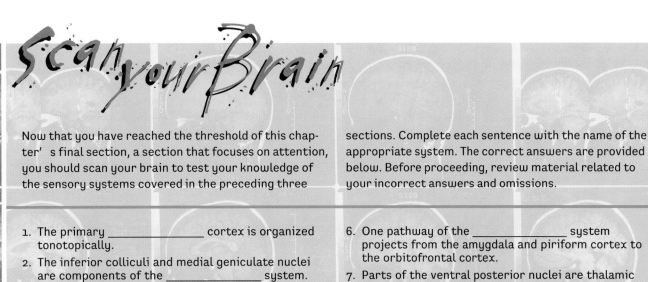

Scan your Brain

Now that you have reached the threshold of this chapter's final section, a section that focuses on attention, you should scan your brain to test your knowledge of the sensory systems covered in the preceding three sections. Complete each sentence with the name of the appropriate system. The correct answers are provided below. Before proceeding, review material related to your incorrect answers and omissions.

1. The primary _____ cortex is organized tonotopically.
2. The inferior colliculi and medial geniculate nuclei are components of the _____ system.
3. The dorsal-column medial-lemniscus system and the anterolateral system are pathways of the _____ system.
4. The ventral posterior nuclei, the intralaminar nuclei, and the parafascicular nuclei are all thalamic nuclei of the _____ system.
5. The periaqueductal gray and the raphé nuclei are involved in blocking the perception of _____.
6. One pathway of the _____ system projects from the amygdala and piriform cortex to the orbitofrontal cortex.
7. Parts of the ventral posterior nuclei are thalamic relay nuclei of both the somatosensory system and the _____ system.
8. Unlike the neuronal projections of all other sensory systems, those of the _____ system are primarily ipsilateral.
9. Ageusia is caused by damage to the _____ system.

Scan Your Brain answers: (1) auditory, (2) auditory, (3) somatosensory, (4) somatosensory, (5) pain, (6) olfactory, (7) gustatory, (8) gustatory, (9) gustatory

Selective Attention

We consciously perceive only a small subset of the many stimuli that excite our sensory organs at any one time and largely ignore the rest. The process by which this occurs is **selective attention**.

There are two features of selective attention: It improves the perception of the stimuli that are its focus, and it interferes with the perception of the stimuli that are not its focus. For example, if you focus your attention on a potentially important announcement in a noisy airport, your chances of understanding it increase; but your chances of understanding a simultaneous comment from a traveling companion decrease.

Attention can be focused in two different ways: by internal cognitive processes (*endogenous attention*) or by external events (*exogenous attention*)—see Treue (2003). For example, your attention can be focused on a table top because you are searching for your keys (endogenous attention), or it can be drawn there because your cat tipped over a lamp (exogenous attention). Endogenous attention is thought to be mediated by *top-down* (from higher to lower levels) neural mechanisms, whereas exogenous attention is thought to be mediated by *bottom-up* (from lower to higher levels) neural mechanisms.

Attention is an extremely important aspect of perception. There is no better illustration of its importance than the phenomenon of **change blindness** (Rensink, 2002). To study change blindness, a subject is shown a photographic image on a computer screen and is asked to report any change in the image as soon as it is noticed. In fact, the image is composed of two images that alternate with a delay of less than 0.1 second between. The two photographic images are identical except for one gross feature. For example, the two images in Figure 5.20 are identical except that the picture in the center of the wall is missing from one. You might think that any subject would immediately notice the picture disappearing and reappearing. But this is not what happens—most subjects spend many seconds staring at the image—searching, as instructed, for some change—before they notice the disappearing and reappearing picture. When this finally happens, they wonder in amazement why it took them so long.

Why does change blindness occur? It occurs because, contrary to our impression, when we view a scene, we have absolutely no memory for parts of the scene that are not the focus of our attention. When viewing the scene in Figure 5.20, most subjects attend to the two people and do not notice when the picture disappears from the wall between them. Because they have no memory of the parts of the image to which they did not attend, they are not aware when those parts change.

The change blindness phenomenon does not occur without the brief (i.e., less than 0.1 second) intervals between images, although they barely produce a flicker. Without the intervals, no memory is required and the changes are immediately perceived.

<0.1 second

The change blindness phenomenon. These two illustrations were continually alternated, with a brief (less than 0.1 second) interval between each presentation, and the subjects were asked to report any changes they noticed. Amazingly, it took most of them many seconds to notice the disappearing and reappearing picture in the center of the wall.

(Photographs prepared by James Enns, Department of Psychology, University of British Columbia.)

Figure 5.20

Moran and Desimone (1985) were the first to demonstrate the effects of attention on neural activity in the visual system. They trained monkeys to stare at a fixation point on the screen while they recorded the activity of neurons in a prestriate area that was part of the ventral stream and particularly sensitive to color. In one experiment, they recorded from individual neurons that responded to either red or green bars of light in their receptive fields. When the monkey was trained to perform a task that required attention to the red cue, the response to the red cue was increased, and the response to the green cue was reduced. The opposite happened when the monkey attended to green.

Experiments paralleling those in monkeys have been conducted in humans using functional brain-imaging techniques. For example, Corbetta and colleagues (1990) presented a collection of moving, colored stimuli of various shapes and asked their subjects to discriminate among the stimuli based on their movement, color, *or* shape. Attention to shape or color produced increased activity in areas of the ventral stream; attention to movement produced increased activity in an area of the dorsal stream (see Chapter 4).

In another study of attention in human subjects, Ungerleider and Haxby (1994) showed subjects a series of faces. The subjects were asked whether the faces belonged to the same person or whether they were located in the same position relative to the frame. When the subjects were attending to identity, regions of the ventral stream were more active; when the subjects were attending to position, regions of the dorsal stream were more active.

How do the mechanisms of selective attention work? According to current theories, neural representations of various aspects of a visual display compete with one another. Selective attention is thought to work by strengthening the representations of the attended-to aspects and by weakening the others (Chun & Marois, 2002). In general, anticipation of a stimulus increases neural activity in the same circuits affected by the stimulus itself (Carlsson et al., 2000).

A cognitive neuroscience experiment by Kastner and colleagues (1998) illustrates the type of evidence on which these theories are based. The researchers used fMRI to measure activity in various areas of visual cortex during the visual presentation of one and then four objects. First, they showed that the activity produced by the presence of the single object declined markedly when the other three objects were presented along with it. Second, they showed that the magnitude of this decline was less if subjects were instructed to attend to the first object.

Eye movements often play an important role in visual attention, but it is important to realize that visual attention can be shifted without shifting the direction of visual focus (Rees et al., 1999). To prove this to yourself, look at the following Check It Out demonstration.

One last important characteristic of selective attention is the cocktail-party phenomenon (see Feng & Ratnam, 2000). The **cocktail-party phenomenon** is the fact that even when you are focusing so intently on one conversation that you are totally unaware of the content of other conversations going on around you, the mention of your name in one of the other conversations will immediately gain access to your consciousness. This phenomenon suggests that your brain can block from conscious awareness all stimuli except those of a particular kind while still unconsciously monitoring the blocked-out stimuli just in case something comes up that requires attention.

No, I have not forgotten that I asked you to think about the patient whose case opened this chapter. He could identify objects in any part of his visual field if they were presented individually; thus, he was not suffering from blindness or other visual field defects. His was a disorder of visual attention. He suffered from visual **simultanagnosia**, a difficulty in attending to more than one visual object at a time. Because the dorsal stream is responsible for visually localizing objects in space, you may have hypothesized that the patient's problem was associated with damage to this area. If you did, you were correct. The damage associated with simultagnosia is typically bilateral.

Cognitive Neuroscience

Cognitive Neuroscience

Clinical Implications

SHIFTING VISUAL ATTENTION WITHOUT SHIFTING VISUAL FOCUS

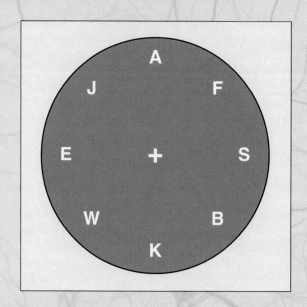

Fix your gaze on the +, concentrate on it. Next, shift your attention to one of the letters without shifting your gaze from +. Now, shift your attention to other letters, again without shifting your gaze from the +. You have experienced *covert attention*—a shift of visual attention without corresponding eye movement. A change in visual attention that involves a shift in gaze is called *overt attention*.

Key Terms

Chapter 5 Mechanisms of Perception: Hearing, Touch, Smell, Taste, and Attention

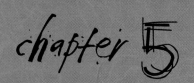

Mechanisms of Perception: Hearing, Touch, Smell, Taste, and Attention
How You Know the World

In this chapter, you learned about the sensory systems that mediate hearing, touch, smell, and taste, with an emphasis on cortical function. The chapter culminated with a discussion of selective attention and its mechanisms; attentional mechanisms modulate everything that we perceive.

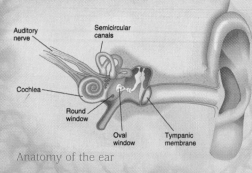

Current Model
Hierarchical
Functionally Segregated
Parallel

Principles of Sensory System Organization

All sensory systems are similarly organized. They were once assumed to be hierarchical, functionally homogeneous, and serial. However, it is now clear that they are, as indicated in the adjacent diagram, hierarchical, functionally segregated, and parallel.
(Pages 141–144)

Auditory System

The primary auditory cortex is located in the lateral fissure. It, like most other parts of the auditory system, is tonotopically organized. Surprisingly, total bilateral destruction of primary auditory cortex has only selective effects on hearing.
(Pages 144–149)

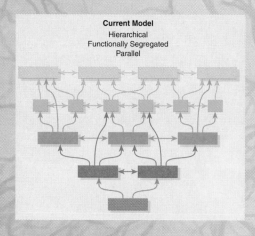

Auditory nerve
Semicircular canals
Cochlea
Round window
Oval window
Tympanic membrane

Anatomy of the ear

Somatosensory System: Touch and Pain

Primary somatosensory cortex is located in the postcentral gyrus and is somatotopically organized. Although the primary somatosensory cortex is the destination of two ascending pathways on each side of the spinal cord, damage to it has only selective effects on touch—thus confirming the parallel organization of the somatosensory system. No particular area of the cortex seems to be dedicated to the perception of pain.
(Pages 149–159)

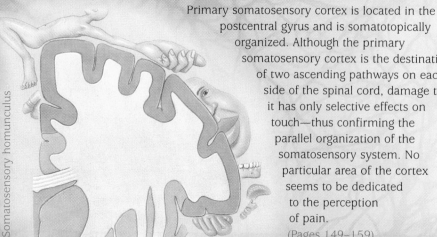

Somatosensory homunculus

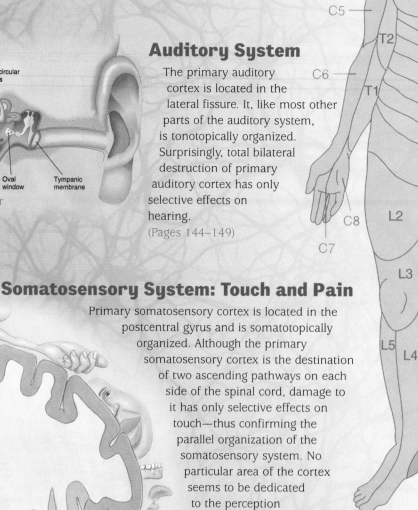

V1
V2
V3
C2
C3
Dermatomes
C4
T2
T3
T4
T5
T6
T7
T8
T9
T10
T11
T12
C5
C5
T2
T2
C6
T1
T1
C6
S2
L1
S3
C8
L2
L2
C8
C7
C7
L3
L3
L5
L4
L4
L5
S1
S1

Visual Summary

The Chemical Senses: Smell and Taste

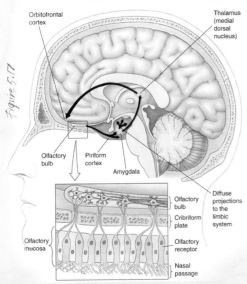

Figure 5.17

Olfaction (smell) and gustation (taste) are the senses responsive to the chemical composition of the environment. Our sense of flavor depends on both taste and smell. Primary olfactory cortex is in an area of medial temporal cortex (i.e., the piriform cortex), and primary gustatory cortex is on the superior lip of the lateral fissure. Anosmia is the inability to smell, and ageusia is the inability to taste. (Pages 159–163)

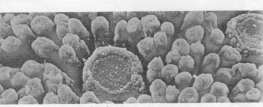

Taste buds

Change blindness

<0.1 second

Selective Attention

At any moment, numerous stimuli excite our sensory systems, yet we are consciously aware of only a few of them. The mechanism that focuses our perception on a few stimuli and filters out the rest is selective attention. Change blindness and the cocktail-party phenomenon are two widely studied examples of selective attention. (Pages 163–166)

Themes Revisited

The clinical implications theme was prominent in this chapter, but you saw it in a different light. Previous chapters focused on how biopsychological research is leading to the development of new treatments; this chapter focused on what particular clinical cases reveal about the organization of healthy sensory systems. The following cases played a key role in this chapter: the patient with visual simultanagnosia; Dr. P., the visual agnostic who mistook his wife for a hat; Aunt Betty, the asomatognosic who lost the left side of her body; and Miss C., the student who felt no pain and died as a result.

Two of the other major themes were also developed in this chapter. You learned how the study of the neural organization of the sensory systems has been extended to healthy human subjects by using the functional brain-imaging techniques of cognitive neuroscience. And you learned that the comparative study of some species has been particularly informative because of their evolutionary specializations (e.g., the auditory localization abilities of the barn owl and the tendency of the secondary auditory cortex of monkeys to respond to monkey calls).

Think about It

1. How has this chapter changed your concept of perception?

2. Why are most people amazed by the change blindness phenomenon? Why does change blindness occur and what does it indicate about attentional mechanisms?

3. Which sensory system would you study if you were a biopsychologist who studies sensory systems? Why?

4. Bob went through a stop sign and hit a car near a busy school crossing. If you were his lawyer, how could you use the change blindness phenomenon to plead for leniency?

5. Discuss the paradoxes of pain.

6. Design an experiment to demonstrate that flavor is the product of both taste and smell. Try it on yourself.

7. Damage to areas of primary sensory cortex has surprisingly little impact on perception. Discuss with respect to parallel pathways.

chapter **6**

The Sensorimotor System
How You Do What You Do

The evening before I started to write this chapter, I was standing in a checkout line at the local market. As I waited, I furtively scanned the headlines on the prominently displayed magazines—WOMAN GIVES BIRTH TO CAT; FLYING SAUCER LANDS IN CLEVELAND SHOPPING MALL; HOW TO LOSE 20 POUNDS IN 2 DAYS. Then, my mind began to wander, and I started to think about beginning to write this chapter. That is when I began to watch Rhonda's movements and to wonder about the neural system that controlled them. Rhonda is a cashier—the best in the place.

The Case of Rhonda, the Dexterous Cashier

I was struck by the complexity of even Rhonda's simplest movements. As she deftly transferred a bag of tomatoes to the scale, there was a coordinated adjustment in almost every part of her body. In addition to her obvious finger, hand, arm, and shoulder movements, coordinated movements of her head and eyes tracked her hand to the tomatoes; and there were adjustments in the muscles of her feet, legs, trunk, and other arm, which kept her from lurching forward. The accuracy of these responses suggested that they were guided in part by the patterns of visual, somatosensory, and vestibular changes they produced. The term *sensorimotor* in the title of this chapter formally recognizes the critical contribution of sensory input to guiding motor output.

As my purchases flowed through her left hand, Rhonda registered the prices with her right hand and bantered with Rick, the bagger. I was intrigued by how little of what Rhonda was doing appeared to be under her conscious control. She made general decisions about which items to pick up and where to put them, but she seemed to give no thought to the exact means by which these decisions were carried out. Each of her responses could have been made with an infinite number of different combinations of finger, wrist, elbow, shoulder, and body adjustments; but somehow she unconsciously picked one. The higher parts of her sensorimotor system—perhaps her cortex—seemed to issue conscious general commands to other parts of the system, which unconsciously produced a specific pattern of muscular responses that carried them out.

The automaticity of Rhonda's performance was a far cry from the slow, effortful responses that had characterized her first days at the market. Somehow, experience had integrated her individual movements into smooth sequences, and it seemed to have transferred the movements' control from a mode that involved conscious effort to one that did not.

I was suddenly jarred from my contemplations by a voice. "Sir, excuse me, sir, that will be $18.65," Rhonda said, with just a hint of delight at catching me in mid-daydream. I hastily paid my bill, muttered "thank you," and scurried out of the market.

As I write this, I am smiling both at my own embarrassment and at the thought that Rhonda has unknowingly introduced you to three principles of sensorimotor control that are the foundations of this chapter: (1) The sensorimotor system is hierarchically organized. (2) Motor output is guided by sensory input. (3) Learning can change the nature and the locus of sensorimotor control.

6.1
Three Principles of Sensorimotor Function

Before getting into the details of the sensorimotor system, let's take a closer look at the three principles of sensorimotor function introduced by Rhonda. You will better appreciate these principles if you recognize that they are the very same principles that govern the operation of a large, efficient company—perhaps because both are systems of controlling output that have evolved in a competitive environment.

The Sensorimotor System Is Hierarchically Organized

The operation of both the sensorimotor system and a large, efficient company is directed by commands that cascade down through the levels of a hierarchy (see Koechlin, Ody, & Kouneiher, 2003)—from the association cortex or the company president (the highest levels) to the muscles or the workers (the lowest levels). Like the orders that are issued from the office of a company president, the commands that emerge from the association cortex specify general goals rather than specific plans of action. Neither the association cortex nor the company president routinely gets involved in the details. The main advantage of this *hierarchical organization* is that the higher levels of the hierarchy are left free to perform more complex functions.

Both the sensorimotor system and a large, efficient company are parallel hierarchical systems; that is, they are hierarchical systems in which signals flow between levels over multiple paths (see Darian-Smith, Burman, & Darian-Smith, 1999). This parallel structure enables the association cortex or company president to exert control over the lower levels of the hierarchy in more than one way. For example, the association cortex may directly inhibit an eyeblink reflex to allow the insertion of a contact lens, and a company president may personally organize a delivery to an important customer.

The sensorimotor and company hierarchies are also characterized by *functional segregation*. That is, each level of the sensorimotor and company hierarchies tends to be composed of different units (neural structures or departments), each of which performs a different function.

In summary, the sensorimotor system—like the sensory systems you read about in Chapters 4 and 5—is a parallel, functionally segregated, hierarchical system. The main difference between the sensory systems and the sensorimotor system is the primary direction of information flow. In sensory systems, information mainly flows up through the hierarchy; in the sensorimotor system, information mainly flows down.

Motor Output Is Guided by Sensory Input

Efficient companies continuously monitor the effects of their own activities, and they use this information to fine-tune those activities. The sensorimotor system does the same (Dietz, 2002b). The eyes, the organs of balance, and the receptors in skin, muscles, and joints all monitor the body's responses; and they feed their information back into sensorimotor circuits. In most instances, this **sensory feedback** plays an important role in directing the continuation of the responses that produced it. The only responses that are not normally influenced by sensory feedback are *ballistic movements*—brief, all-or-none, high-speed movements, such as swatting a fly.

Behavior in the absence of just one kind of sensory feedback—the feedback that is carried by the somatosensory nerves of the arms—was studied in G.O., a former darts champion.

The Case of G.O., the Man with Too Little Feedback

An infection had selectively destroyed the somatosensory nerves of G.O.'s arms. He had great difficulty performing intricate behaviors such as doing up his buttons or picking up coins, even under visual guidance. Other difficulties resulted from his inability to adjust his motor output in the light of unanticipated external disturbances; for example, he could not keep from spilling a cup of coffee if somebody brushed against him. However, G.O.' s greatest problem was his inability to maintain a constant level of muscle contraction:

> The result of this deficit was that even in the simplest of tasks requiring a constant motor output to the hand, G.O. would have to keep a visual check on his progress. For example, when carrying a suitcase, he would frequently glance at it to reassure himself that he had not dropped it some paces back. However, even visual feedback was of little use to him in many tasks. These tended to be those requiring a constant force output such as grasping a pen while writing or holding a cup. Here, visual information was insufficient for him to be able to correct any errors that were developing in the output since, after a period, he had no indication of the pressure that he was exerting on an object; all he saw was either the pen or cup slipping from his grasp. (Rothwell et al., 1982, p. 539)

Clinical Implications

Many adjustments in motor output that occur in response to sensory feedback are controlled unconsciously by the lower levels of the sensorimotor hierarchy without the involvement of the higher levels (see Poppele & Bosco, 2003). In the same way, large companies run more efficiently if the clerks do not have to check with the company president each time they encounter a minor problem.

Learning Changes the Nature and Locus of Sensorimotor Control

When a company is just starting up, each individual decision is made by the company president after careful consideration. However, as the company develops, many individual actions are coordinated into sequences of prescribed procedures that are routinely carried out by personnel at lower levels of the hierarchy.

Similar changes occur during sensorimotor learning (see Willingham, 1999). During the initial stages of motor learning, each individual response is performed under conscious control; then, after much practice, individual responses become organized into continuous integrated sequences of action that flow smoothly and are adjusted by sensory feedback without conscious regulation. If you think for a moment about the sensorimotor skills you have acquired (e.g., typing, swimming, knitting, playing basketball, dancing, playing piano), you will appreciate that the organization of individual responses into continuous motor programs and the transfer of their control to lower levels of the nervous system characterizes most sensorimotor learning.

ON THE CD

Visit *The Beat Goes On*. In this module, Pinel demonstrates an important feature of the sensorimotor system.

A General Model of Sensorimotor System Function

Figure 6.1 on page 174 is a model that illustrates several principles of sensorimotor system organization; it is the framework of this chapter. Notice its hierarchical structure, the functional segregation of the levels (e.g., of secondary motor cortex), the parallel connections between levels, and the numerous feedback pathways.

This chapter focuses on the neural structures that play important roles in the control of voluntary behavior (e.g., picking up an apple). It begins at the level of association cortex and traces major motor signals as they descend the sensorimotor hierarchy to the skeletal muscles that ultimately perform the movements.

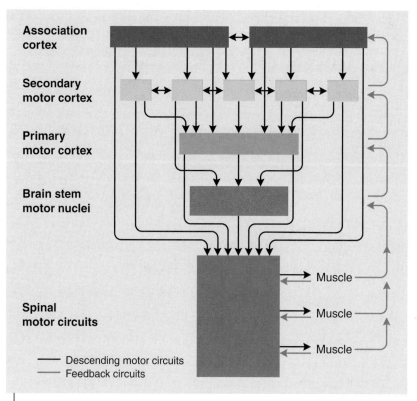

A general model of the sensorimotor system. Notice its hierarchical structure, its functional segregation, its parallel descending pathways, and its feedback circuits.

Figure 6.1

6.2

Sensorimotor Association Cortex

Association cortex is at the top of your sensorimotor hierarchy. There are two major areas of sensorimotor association cortex: the posterior parietal association cortex and the dorsolateral prefrontal association cortex (see Barash, 2003; Szameitat et al., 2002). Experts agree that the posterior parietal cortex and the dorsolateral prefrontal cortex are each composed of several different areas, each of which has a different function (see Culham & Kanwisher, 2001; Fuster, 2000); however, they do not yet agree on how best to divide them up (see Rushworth, 2000).

Posterior Parietal Association Cortex

Before an effective movement can be initiated, certain information is required. The nervous system must know the original positions of the parts of the body that are to be moved, and it must know the positions of any external objects with which the body is going to interact. The **posterior parietal association cortex** plays an important role in integrating these two kinds of information and in directing attention (see Andersen & Buneo, 2003; Assad, 2003; Cohen & Andersen, 2002).

The major cortical input and output pathways of the posterior parietal association cortex. Shown are the lateral surface of the left hemisphere and the medial surface of the right hemisphere.

Figure 6.2

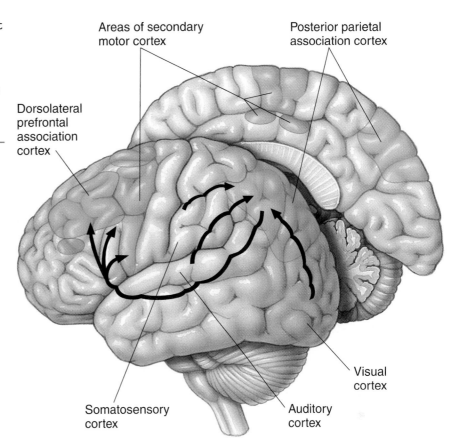

Areas of secondary motor cortex

Posterior parietal association cortex

Dorsolateral prefrontal association cortex

Visual cortex

Somatosensory cortex

Auditory cortex

You learned in Chapter 4 that the posterior parietal cortex is classified as *association cortex* because it receives input from more than one sensory system. It receives information from the three sensory systems that play roles in the localization of the body and external objects in space: the visual system, the auditory system, and the somatosensory system (see Andersen & Buneo, 2003; Macaluso, Driver, & Frith, 2003). In turn, much of the output of the posterior parietal cortex goes to areas of motor cortex, which are located in the frontal cortex: to the *dorsolateral prefrontal association cortex*, to the various areas of *secondary motor cortex*, and to the primary motor cortex (see Figure 6.2).

Damage to the posterior parietal cortex can produce a variety of sensorimotor deficits, including deficits in the perception and memory of spatial relationships, in accurate reaching and grasping, in the control of eye movement, and in attention (Freund, 2003). However, apraxia and contralateral neglect are the two most striking consequences of posterior parietal cortex damage.

Apraxia is a disorder of voluntary movement that is not attributable to a simple motor deficit (e.g., not to paralysis or weakness) or to any deficit in comprehension or motivation (see Heilman, Watson, & Rothi, 1997). Remarkably, apraxic patients have difficulty making specific movements when they are requested to do so, particularly when the movements are out of context; however, they can often readily perform the very same movements under natural conditions, when they are not thinking about doing so. For example, an apraxic carpenter who has no difficulty at all hammering a nail during the course of her work might not be able to demonstrate hammering movements when requested to make them, particularly in the absence of a hammer. Although its symptoms are bilateral, apraxia is often caused by unilateral damage to the left posterior parietal lobe or its connections.

Contralateral neglect is a disturbance of a patient's ability to respond to stimuli on the side of the body opposite (contralateral) to the side of a brain lesion, in the absence of simple sensory or motor deficits (see Heilman, Watson, & Valenstein, 1997). The disturbance is often associated with large lesions of the right posterior parietal lobe (see Mort et al., 2003). For example, Mrs. S. suffered from contralateral neglect after a massive stroke to the posterior portions of her right hemisphere. Like many other neuropsychological patients, she developed ways of dealing with her deficiency.

Clinical Implications

The Case of Mrs. S., the Woman Who Turned in Circles

Mrs. S.'s stroke had left her unable to recognize or respond to things to the left—including external objects as well as parts of her own body. For example, Mrs. S. often put makeup on the right side of her face but ignored the left.

Mrs. S.'s left-side contralateral neglect created many problems for her, but a particularly bothersome one was that she had difficulty getting enough to eat. When a plate of food was put in front of her, she could see only the food on the right half of the plate and thus ate only that much, even if she was very hungry.

After asking for and receiving a wheelchair capable of turning in place, Mrs. S. developed an effective way of getting more food if she was still hungry after completing a meal. She turns her wheelchair around to the right in a full circle until she sees the remaining half of her meal. Then, she eats that food, or more precisely, she eats the right half of that food. If she is still hungry after that, she turns once again to the right until she discovers the remaining quarter of her meal and eats half of that . . . and so on (Sacks, 1985).

Most patients with contralateral neglect have difficulty responding to things to the left. But to the left of what? In particular, what happens when patients tilt their heads? Does the boundary between left and right tilt accordingly, or does it stay vertical, defined by gravity and external objects? This question is currently the subject of intensive investigation (see Bartholmeo & Chokron, 2002; Kerkoff, 2001; Palovskaya et al., 2002). For most patients with contralateral neglect, the deficits in responding occur for stimuli to the left of their own bodies, a direction referred to as *egocentric left*. Egocentric left is partially defined by gravitational coordinates: When patients tilt their heads, their field of neglect is not normally tilted with it (see the top panel of Figure 6.3).

In addition to failing to respond to objects on their egocentric left, many patients tend not to respond to the left sides of objects, regardless of where the objects are in their visual fields. Neurons that have egocentric receptive fields and others with object-based receptive fields have been found in primate parietal cortex (Olson, 2003; Pouget & Driver, 2000).

Object-based contralateral neglect is illustrated in the lower panel of Figure 6.3. Patients with contralateral neglect had deficits in responding to the right hand of an experimenter who was facing them, regardless of its specific location in the patients' visual field.

A somatosensory study of contralateral neglect also demonstrated that it is not a straightforward matter to define the field of neglect. Patients were found to be more responsive to touches on their neglected left hand if their arms were crossed (Aglioti, Smania, & Peru, 1999).

Patients with contralateral neglect often fail to report visual stimuli presented to the left of their bodies. However, as you have already learned, the failure to consciously perceive an object does not necessarily mean that the object was not perceived. Indeed, two types of evidence suggest that information about objects that are not noticed by patients with contralateral neglect is, in fact, perceived unconsciously. First, when objects were repeatedly presented at the same spot to the left of patients with contralateral neglect, they tended to look to the same spot on future trials although they were unaware of the objects (Geng & Behrmann, 2002). Second, patients could more readily identify fragmented (partial) drawings viewed to their right if complete versions of the drawings had previously been presented to the left, where they were not consciously perceived (Vuilleumier et al., 2002).

Dorsolateral Prefrontal Association Cortex

The other large area of association cortex that has important sensorimotor functions is the **dorsolateral prefrontal association cortex**. It receives projections

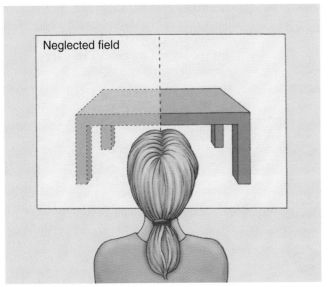
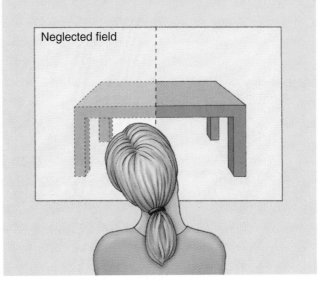

Patient is unresponsive to things to the left, even if the head is tilted.

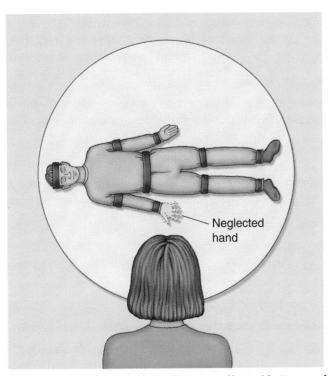
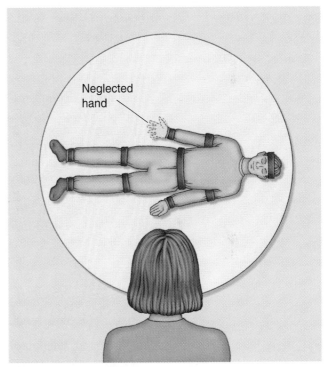

Contralateral neglect is sometimes manifested in terms of object-based coordinates.

Contralateral neglect is sometimes manifested in terms of gravitational coordinates, sometimes in terms of object-based coordinates.

Figure 6.3

from the posterior parietal cortex, and it sends projections to areas of *secondary motor cortex* and to the *primary motor cortex*. These projections are shown in Figure 6.4 on page 178. Not shown are the major projections back from dorsolateral prefrontal cortex to posterior parietal cortex.

Dorsolateral prefrontal cortex seems to play a role in the evaluation of external stimuli and the initiation of voluntary reactions to them (Christoff & Gabrieli, 2000; Ohbayashi, Ohki, & Miyashita, 2003). This view is supported by the response characteristics of neurons in this area of association cortex. Several

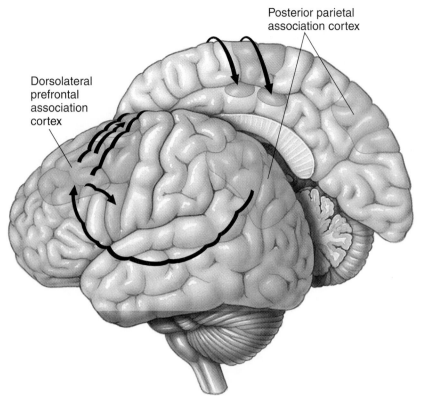

Dorsolateral prefrontal association cortex

Posterior parietal association cortex

The major cortical input and output pathways of the dorsolateral prefrontal association cortex. Shown are the lateral surface of the left hemisphere and the medial surface of the right hemisphere.

Figure 6.4

studies have characterized the activity of monkey dorsolateral prefrontal neurons as the monkeys identify and respond to objects (e.g., Rao, Rainer, & Miller, 1997). The activity of some neurons depends on the characteristics of objects; the activity of others depends on the locations of objects; and the activity of still others depends on a combination of both. The activity of other dorsolateral prefrontal neurons is related to the response, rather than to the object. These neurons typically begin to fire before the response and continue to fire until the response is complete. There are neurons in all cortical motor areas that begin to fire in anticipation of a motor activity, but those in the dorsolateral prefrontal association cortex fire first.

The response properties of dorsolateral prefrontal neurons and the pattern of connections between this area and other areas of sensorimotor cortex suggest that decisions to initiate voluntary movements may be made in this area of cortex (Rowe et al., 2000; Tanji & Hoshi, 2001). However, it is more likely that such decisions arise from the interaction of dorsolateral prefrontal cortex and posterior parietal cortex (Connolly, Andersen, & Goodale, 2003; Jeannerod & Farne, 2003; Rushworth et al., 2003).

6.3
Secondary Motor Cortex

Areas of **secondary motor cortex** are those that receive much of their input from association cortex and send much of their output to primary motor cortex (see Figure 6.5). For many years, only two areas of secondary motor cortex were known: the supplementary motor area and the premotor cortex. Both of these large areas are clearly visible on the lateral surface of the frontal lobe, just anterior to the *primary motor cortex*. The **supplementary motor area** wraps over the top of the frontal lobe and extends down its medial surface into the longitudinal fissure, and the **premotor cortex** runs in a strip from the supplementary motor area to the lateral fissure.

In the past few years, this simple two-area conception of secondary motor cortex has become more complex. Neuroanatomical and neurophysiological research with monkeys has made a case for at least seven different areas in each hemisphere: two different supplementary motor areas (SMA and preSMA), two premotor areas (dorsal and ventral), and three small areas—the **cingulate motor areas**—in the cortex of the cingulate gyrus.

Recent functional brain-imaging studies have suggested that human secondary motor cortex is similar to that of other primates (see Rizzolatti, Fogassi, & Gallese, 2002). There is evidence of at least two cingulate motor areas in humans, and a

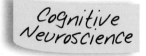

Cognitive Neuroscience

Four areas of secondary motor cortex—the supplementary motor area, the premotor cortex, and two cingulate motor areas—and their output to the primary motor cortex. Shown are the lateral surface of the left hemisphere and the medial surface of the right hemisphere.

Figure 6.5

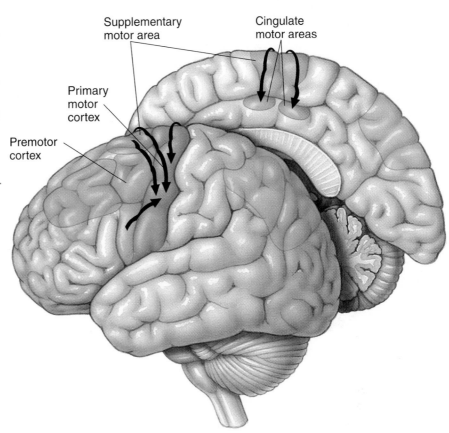

Supplementary motor area

Cingulate motor areas

Primary motor cortex

Premotor cortex

strong case can be made for subdividing both the supplementary motor area and the premotor cortex. However, there is still no general consensus about the exact boundaries of these newly identified areas or even whether they are better classified as secondary motor cortex or association cortex (see Kollias et al., 2001; Picard & Strick, 2001).

The various unresolved issues regarding secondary motor cortex are currently the focus of a major research effort. To qualify as secondary motor cortex, an area must be appropriately connected with other sensorimotor areas (see Figure 6.5). From a functional perspective, electrical stimulation of an area of secondary motor cortex typically elicits complex movements, often involving both sides of the body; and neurons in an area of secondary motor cortex often become more active just prior to the initiation of a voluntary movement and continue to be active throughout the movement.

In general, areas of secondary motor cortex are thought to be involved in the programming of specific patterns of movements after taking general instructions from dorsolateral prefrontal cortex. Evidence of such a function comes from brain-imaging studies in which the patterns of activity in the brain have been measured while the subject is either imagining or planning the performance of a particular series of movements (see Kosslyn, Ganis, & Thompson, 2001; Sirigu & Duhamel, 2001). For example, Parsons and colleagues (1995) found that there was increased PET activity in the supplementary motor area, premotor cortex, and cingulate motor areas while subjects imagined grasping and picking up an object.

Despite evidence of similarities among areas of secondary motor cortex, substantial effort has been put into discovering their differences. Until recently, this research has focused on differences between the supplementary motor area and the premotor cortex as originally defined. Although several theories have been proposed to explain functional differences between these areas, none has received consistent support. One important clue is that most of the input that comes into the premotor cortex directly from sensory areas is visual, whereas most of the direct sensory input into the supplementary motor area is somatosensory. Once the number and location of the various areas of human secondary motor cortex have been established, it should prove easier to determine the function of each area.

One interesting line of research on premotor cortex neurons has focused on how they encode spatial relations (Graziano & Gross, 1998). Many premotor neurons respond to touch, and each of these has a somatosensory receptive field on a particular part of the body. Many of these neurons also respond to visual input and are thus referred to as *bimodal neurons* (neurons that can be affected by stimuli in two

Cognitive Neuroscience

different stimulus modalities). The visual receptive field of a bimodal neuron is always adjacent to its somatosensory receptive field. For example, if a bimodal neuron has its somatosensory receptive field on the left hand, its visual receptive field is usually in the space adjacent to the left hand. Remarkably, the visual receptive field remains next to the left hand regardless of where the left hand is or where the eyes are focused. Such neurons seem to be dedicated to the programming of movements of the left hand.

6.4
Primary Motor Cortex

he **primary motor cortex** is located in the *precentral gyrus* of the frontal lobe (see Figures 6.5 and 6.6). It is the major point of convergence of cortical sensorimotor signals, and it is the major point of departure of sensorimotor signals from the cerebral cortex.

In 1937, Penfield and Boldrey mapped the primary motor cortex of conscious human patients during neurosurgery by applying electrical stimulation to various points on the cortical surface and noting which part of the body moved in response to each stimulation. They found that the primary motor cortex is somatotopically organized. The **somatotopic** (organized according to a map of the body) layout of the human primary motor cortex is commonly referred to as the **motor homunculus** (see Figure 6.6). Notice that most of the primary motor cortex is dedicated to controlling parts of the body that are capable of intricate movements, such as the hands and mouth.

More recent research has necessitated an important revision to the original motor homunculus proposed by Penfield and Boldrey, with respect to the hand areas. Recordings from individual primary motor cortex neurons in monkeys while they performed individual finger movements revealed that the control of any individual finger movement depended on the activity of a network of

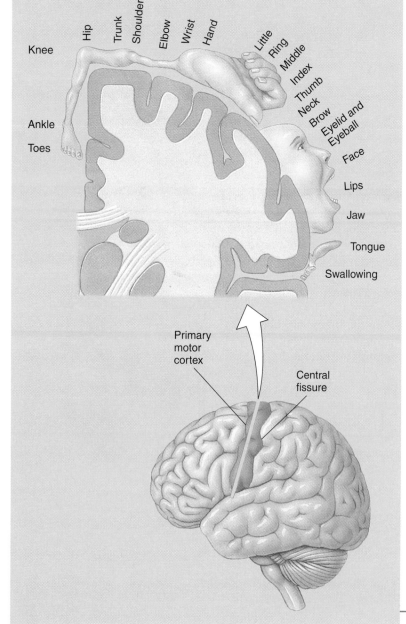

The motor homunculus: the somatotopic map of the human primary motor cortex. Stimulation of sites in the primary motor cortex elicits simple movements in the indicated parts of the body.

(Adapted from Penfield & Rasmussen, 1950.)

— *Figure 6.6* —

neurons that was widely distributed throughout the primary motor cortex hand area rather than being located in one somatotopically segregated finger area (Schieber & Hibbard, 1993). A similar pattern in the hand area of the human primary motor cortex has also been documented using fMRI (Sanes et al., 1995). Furthermore, small lesions in the hand area of the primary motor cortex of humans (Schieber, 1999) and monkeys (Schieber & Poliakov, 1998) never selectively disrupt the activity of a single finger. It is now clear that the area of primary motor cortex that controls any particular finger is large and overlaps areas controlling other fingers.

Each general area in the primary motor cortex controls the movements of particular groups of muscles, and each receives somatosensory feedback, via somatosensory cortex, from receptors in these muscles and in the joints that they influence. One interesting exception to this general pattern of feedback has been described in monkeys: Monkeys have two different hand areas in the primary motor cortex of each hemisphere, and one receives input from receptors in the skin rather than from receptors in the muscles and joints. Presumably, this adaptation facilitates **stereognosis**—the process of identifying objects by touch. Close your eyes and explore an object with your hands; notice how stereognosis depends on a complex interplay between motor responses and the somatosensory stimulation produced by them.

Neurons in the arm area of the primary motor cortex fire maximally when the arm reaches in a particular direction; each neuron has a different preferred direction. Georgopoulos (1995) dissociated the direction of force and the direction of movement by applying external forces to monkeys' arms while the arms reached in various directions. The firing of primary motor cortex neurons was correlated with the direction of the resulting movement rather than with the direction of the force that was generated to produce the movement. Each neuron fired most during and just before movements in a preferred direction but also fired to movements in other directions; the closer to the preferred direction, the more it fired.

Belle: The Monkey That Controlled a Robot with Her Mind

The neurons of the primary motor cortex play a major role in initiating body movements and controlling their direction. With an appropriate interface, could they control the movements of a machine (see Craelius, 2002; König & Verschure, 2002; Taylor, Tillery, & Schwartz, 2002)? Belle says, "yes."

In the laboratory of Miguel Nicolesis and John Chapin (2002), a tiny owl monkey called Belle watched a series of lights on a control panel. Belle had learned that if she moved the joystick in her right hand in the direction of a light, she would be rewarded with a drop of fruit juice. On this particular day, Nicolesis and Chapin demonstrated an amazing feat. As a light flashed on the panel, 100 microelectrodes recorded extracellular unit activity from neurons in Belle's primary motor cortex. This activity moved Belle's arm toward the light, but at the same time, the signals were analyzed by a computer, which fed the output to a laboratory several hundred kilometers away, at the Massachusetts Institute of Technology. At MIT, the signals from Belle's brain entered the circuits of a robotic arm. On each trial, the activity of Belle's primary motor cortex moved her arm toward the test light, and it moved the robotic arm in the same direction. Belle's neural signals were directing the activity of a robot.

This truly remarkable feat raises a possibility. Perhaps one day injured people will be able to control wheelchairs, prosthetic limbs, or even their own paralyzed limbs through the power of their own thoughts.

Extensive damage to the human primary motor cortex has less effect than you might expect, given that this cortex is the major point of departure of motor fibers from the cerebral cortex. Large lesions to the primary motor cortex may disrupt a

Clinical Implications

patient's ability to move one body part (e.g., one finger) independently of others, may produce **astereognosia** (deficits in stereognosis), and may reduce the speed, accuracy, and force of a patient's movements. They do not, however, eliminate voluntary movement, presumably because there are pathways that descend directly from secondary motor areas to subcortical motor circuits without passing through primary motor cortex.

6.5 Cerebellum and Basal Ganglia

The cerebellum and the basal ganglia (see Figures 2.21 on page 51 and 2.28 on page 57) are both important sensorimotor structures, but neither is a major part of the pathway by which signals descend through the sensorimotor hierarchy; instead, both the cerebellum and the basal ganglia interact with different levels of the sensorimotor hierarchy, and in so doing, they coordinate and modulate its activities. The interconnections between sensory and motor areas via the cerebellum and basal ganglia are thought to be what ensures that damage to cortical connections between visual cortex and frontal motor areas does not abolish visually guided responses (Glickstein, 2000).

Cerebellum

The complexity of the cerebellum is suggested by its structure. Although it constitutes only 10% of the mass of the brain, it contains more than half of its neurons (see Goldowitz & Hamre, 1998; Voogd & Glickstein, 1998). The cerebellum receives information from primary and secondary motor cortex, information about descending motor signals from brain stem motor nuclei, and feedback from motor responses via the somatosensory and vestibular systems. The cerebellum is thought to compare these three sources of input and correct ongoing movements that deviate from their intended course (see Garwicz, 2002; Ohyama et al., 2003). By performing this function, it is believed to play a major role in motor learning, particularly in the learning of sequences of movements in which timing is a critical factor (Medina et al., 2000; Spencer et al., 2003).

The consequences of diffuse cerebellar damage for motor function are devastating. The patient loses the ability to control precisely the direction, force, velocity, and amplitude of movements and the ability to adapt patterns of motor output to changing conditions. It is difficult to maintain steady postures (e.g., standing), and attempts to do so frequently lead to tremor. There are also severe disturbances in balance, gait, speech, and the control of eye movement. Learning new motor sequences is very difficult (Shin & Ivry, 2003; Thach & Bastian, 2004).

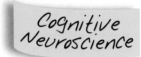

The traditional view that the function of the cerebellum is limited to the fine-tuning and learning of motor responses has been challenged. The basis for this challenge has come from the observation by functional brain imaging of activity in the cerebellum during the performance of a variety of nonmotor cognitive tasks by healthy human subjects (e.g., Lotze et al., 1999) and from the documentation of cognitive deficits in patients with cerebellar damage (e.g., Fabbro et al., 2004; Townsend et al., 1999). Various alternative theories have been proposed, but the most promising of them tend to argue that the cerebellum functions in the fine-tuning and learning of cognitive responses in the same way that it functions in the fine-tuning and learning of motor responses (e.g., Doya, 2000).

Basal Ganglia

The basal ganglia do not contain as many neurons as the cerebellum, but in one sense they are more complex. Unlike the cerebellum, which is organized systematically in lobes, columns, and layers, the basal ganglia are a complex heterogeneous collection of interconnected nuclei.

The anatomy of the basal ganglia suggests that, like the cerebellum, they perform a modulatory function. They contribute no fibers to descending motor pathways; instead, they are part of neural loops that receive cortical input from various cortical areas and transmit it back via the thalamus to the various areas of motor cortex (see Bar-Gad & Bergman, 2001; Groenewegen, 2003).

Theories of basal ganglia function have evolved—in much the same way that theories of cerebellar function have changed. The traditional view of the basal ganglia was that they, like the cerebellum, play a role in the modulation of motor output. Now, the basal ganglia are thought to be involved in a variety of cognitive functions in addition to their role in the modulation of motor output (see Perkel & Farries, 2000). This expanded view of the function of the basal ganglia is consistent with the fact that they project to cortical areas known to have cognitive functions (e.g., the prefrontal lobes).

In experiments on rats, the basal ganglia have been shown to participate in learning to respond correctly to learned associations, a type of response learning which characteristically progresses gradually, trial by trial (e.g., McDonald & White, 1993). However, the basal ganglia's cognitive functions do not appear to be limited to this form of response learning (e.g., Ravizza & Ivry, 2001).

Scan your Brain

Are you ready to continue your descent into the sensorimotor circuits of the spinal cord? This is a good place for you to pause to scan your brain to evaluate your knowledge of the sensorimotor circuits of the cortex, cerebellum, and basal ganglia by completing the following statements. The correct answers are provided below. Before proceeding, review material related to your incorrect answers and omissions.

1. Visual, auditory, and somatosensory input converges on the _____ association cortex.

2. Contralateral neglect is often associated with large lesions of the right _____ lobe.

3. The _____ prefrontal cortex seems to play an important role in initiating complex voluntary responses.

4. The secondary motor area that is just dorsal to the premotor cortex and is largely hidden from view on the medial surface of each hemisphere is the _____.

5. Most of the direct sensory input to the supplementary motor area comes from the _____ system.

6. Most of the direct sensory input to the premotor cortex comes from the _____ system.

7. The _____ cortex is the main point of departure of motor signals from the cerebral cortex to lower levels of the sensorimotor hierarchy.

8. The foot area of the motor homunculus is in the _____ fissure.

9. Although the _____ constitutes only 10% of the mass of the brain, it contains more than half of its neurons.

10. The _____ are part of neural loops that receive input from various cortical areas and transmit it back to various areas of motor cortex via the thalamus.

11. Although both are considered to be motor structures, damage to the _____ or the _____ produces cognitive deficits.

Scan Your Brain answers: (1) posterior parietal, (2) parietal, (3) dorsolateral, (4) supplementary motor area, (5) somatosensory, (6) visual, (7) primary motor, (8) longitudinal, (9) cerebellum, (10) basal ganglia, (11) cerebellum; basal ganglia

Descending Motor Pathways

Neural signals are conducted from the primary motor cortex in each hemisphere to the motor neurons of the spinal cord over four different pathways. Two pathways descend in the *dorsolateral* region of the spinal cord, and two descend in the *ventromedial* region of the spinal cord. These pathways act together in the control of voluntary movement (see Iwaniuk & Whishaw, 2000).

Dorsolateral Corticospinal Tract and Dorsolateral Corticorubrospinal Tract

One group of axons that descends from the primary motor cortex descends through the *medullary pyramids*—two bulges on the ventral surface of the medulla—then decussates and continues to descend in the contralateral dorsolateral spinal white matter. This group of axons constitutes the **dorsolateral corticospinal tract**. Most notable among its neurons are the **Betz cells**—extremely large pyramidal neurons of the primary motor cortex. Their axons terminate in the lower regions of the spinal cord on motor neurons that project to the muscles of the legs. They are thought to be the means by which we exert rapid and powerful voluntary control over our legs.

Most axons of the dorsolateral corticospinal tract synapse on small interneurons of the spinal gray matter, which synapse on the motor neurons of distal muscles of the wrist, hands, fingers, and toes. Primates and the few other mammals that are capable of moving their digits independently (e.g., hamsters and raccoons) have dorsolateral corticospinal tract neurons that synapse directly on digit motor neurons (see Porter & Lemon, 1993).

A second group of axons that descends from the primary motor cortex synapses in the *red nucleus* of the midbrain. The axons of neurons in the red nucleus then decussate and descend through the medulla, where some of them terminate in the nuclei of the cranial nerves that control the muscles of the face. The rest continue to descend in the dorsolateral portion of the spinal cord. This pathway is called the **dorsolateral corticorubrospinal tract** (*rubro* refers to the red nucleus). The axons of the dorsolateral corticorubrospinal tract synapse on interneurons that in turn synapse on motor neurons that project to the distal muscles of the arms and legs.

The two divisions of the dorsolateral motor pathway—the direct dorsolateral corticospinal tract and the indirect dorsolateral corticorubrospinal tract—are illustrated schematically in Figure 6.7.

Ventromedial Corticospinal Tract and Ventromedial Cortico-Brainstem-Spinal Tract

Just as there are two major divisions of the dorsolateral motor pathway, one direct (the corticospinal tract) and one indirect (the corticorubrospinal tract), there are two major divisions of the ventromedial motor pathway, one direct and one indirect. The direct ventromedial pathway is the **ventromedial corticospinal tract**, and the indirect one—as you might infer from its cumbersome but descriptive name—is the **ventromedial cortico-brainstem-spinal tract**.

The long axons of the ventromedial corticospinal tract descend ipsilaterally from the primary motor cortex directly into the ventromedial areas of the spinal white matter. As each axon of the ventromedial corticospinal tract descends, it branches diffusely and innervates the interneuron circuits in several different spinal segments on both sides of the spinal gray matter.

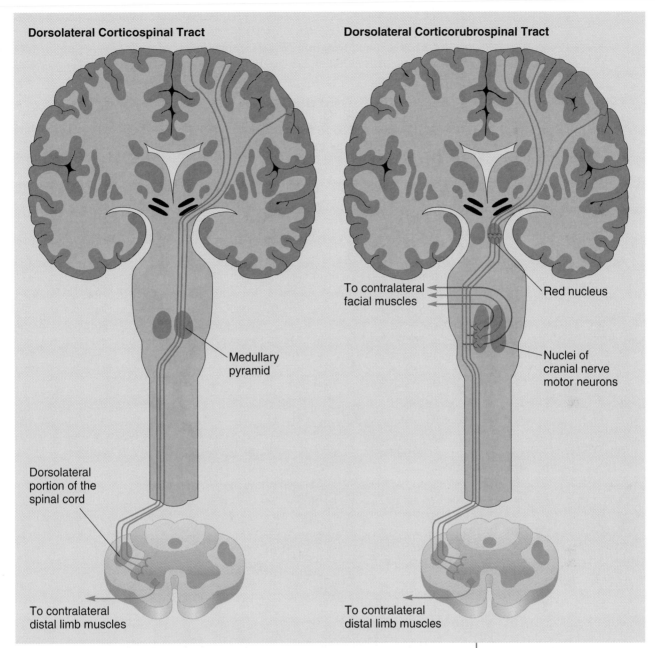

Dorsolateral Corticospinal Tract

Dorsolateral Corticorubrospinal Tract

Red nucleus

To contralateral facial muscles

Medullary pyramid

Nuclei of cranial nerve motor neurons

Dorsolateral portion of the spinal cord

To contralateral distal limb muscles

To contralateral distal limb muscles

The two divisions of the dorsolateral motor pathway: the dorsolateral corticospinal tract and the dorsolateral corticorubrospinal tract. The projections from only one hemisphere are shown.

Figure 6.7

The ventromedial cortico-brainstem-spinal tract comprises motor cortex axons that feed into a complex network of brain stem structures. The axons of some of the neurons in this complex brain stem motor network then descend bilaterally in the ventromedial portion of the spinal cord. Each side carries signals from both hemispheres, and each neuron synapses on the interneurons of several different spinal cord segments that control the proximal muscles of the trunk and limbs.

Which brain stem structures interact with the ventromedial cortico-brainstem-spinal tract? There are four major ones: (1) the **tectum**, which receives auditory and visual information about spatial location; (2) the **vestibular nucleus**, which receives information about balance from receptors in the semicircular canals of the inner ear; (3) the **reticular formation**, which, among other things, contains motor programs that regulate complex species-typical movements such as walking, swimming, and jumping; and (4) the motor nuclei of the cranial nerves that control the muscles of the face.

The two divisions of the descending ventromedial pathway—the direct ventromedial corticospinal tract and the indirect ventromedial cortico-brainstem-spinal tract—are illustrated in Figure 6.8.

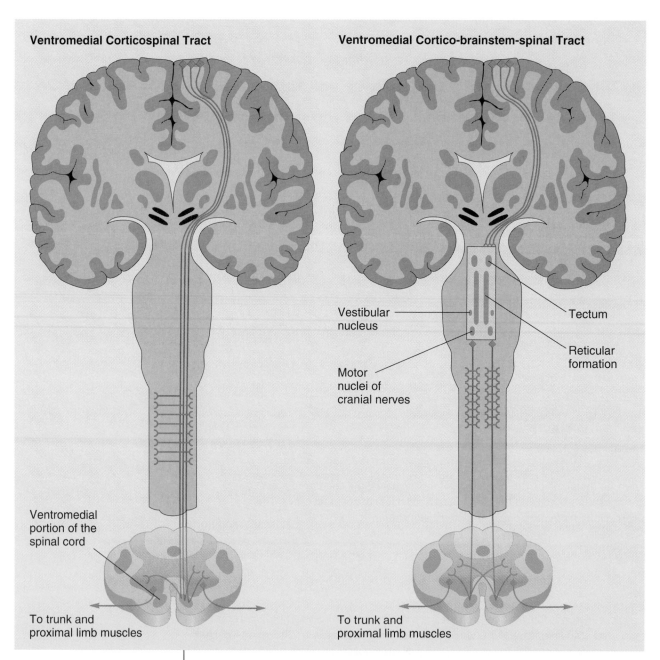

Ventromedial Corticospinal Tract

Ventromedial Cortico-brainstem-spinal Tract

Vestibular nucleus

Tectum

Motor nuclei of cranial nerves

Reticular formation

Ventromedial portion of the spinal cord

To trunk and proximal limb muscles

To trunk and proximal limb muscles

The two divisions of the ventromedial motor pathway: the ventromedial corticospinal tract and the ventromedial cortico-brainstem-spinal tract. The projections from only one hemisphere are shown.

Figure 6.8

Comparison of the Two Dorsolateral Motor Pathways and the Two Ventromedial Motor Pathways

The descending dorsolateral and ventromedial pathways are similar in that each is composed of two major tracts, one whose axons descend directly to the spinal cord and another whose axons synapse in the brain stem on neurons that in turn descend to the spinal cord. However, the two dorsolateral tracts differ from the two ventromedial tracts in two major respects:

1. The two ventromedial tracts are much more diffuse. Many of their axons innervate interneurons on both sides of the spinal gray matter and in several different segments, whereas the axons of the two dorsolateral tracts terminate in the contralateral half of one spinal cord segment, sometimes directly on a motor neuron.
2. The motor neurons that are activated by the two ventromedial tracts project to proximal muscles of the trunk and limbs (e.g., shoulder muscles), whereas the motor neurons that are activated by the two dorsolateral tracts project to distal muscles (e.g., finger muscles).

Because all four of the descending motor tracts originate in the cerebral cortex, all are presumed to mediate voluntary movement; however, major differences in their routes and destinations suggest that they have different functions. This difference was first demonstrated in two experiments that were reported by Lawrence and Kuypers in 1968.

The Evolutionary Perspective

In their first experiment, Lawrence and Kuypers (1968a) *transected* (cut through) the left and right dorsolateral corticospinal tracts of their monkey subjects in the medullary pyramids, just above the decussation of the tracts. Following surgery, these monkeys could stand, walk, and climb quite normally; however, their ability to use their limbs for other activities was impaired. For example, their reaching movements were weak and poorly directed, particularly in the first few days following the surgery. Although there was substantial improvement in the monkeys' reaching ability over the ensuing weeks, two other deficits remained unabated. First, the monkeys never regained the ability to move their fingers independently of one another; when they picked up pieces of food, they did so by using all of their fingers as a unit, as if they were glued together. And second, they never regained the ability to release objects from their grasp; as a result, once they picked up a piece of food, they often had to root for it in their hand like a pig rooting for truffles in the ground. In view of this latter problem, it is remarkable that they had no difficulty releasing their grasp on the bars of their cage when they were climbing. This point is important because it shows that the same response performed in different contexts can be controlled by different parts of the central nervous system.

In their second experiment, Lawrence and Kuypers (1968b) made additional transections in the monkeys whose dorsolateral corticospinal tracts had already been transected in the first experiment. The dorsolateral corticorubrospinal tract was transected in one group of these monkeys. The monkeys could stand, walk, and climb after this second transection; but when they were sitting, their arms hung limply by their sides (remember that monkeys normally use their arms for standing and walking). In those few instances in which the monkeys did use an arm for reaching, they used it like a rubber-handled rake—throwing it out from the shoulder and using it to draw small objects of interest back along the floor.

The other group of monkeys in the second experiment had both of their ventromedial tracts transected. In contrast to the first group, these subjects had severe postural abnormalities: They had great difficulty walking or sitting. If they did manage to sit or stand without clinging to the bars of their cages, the slightest disturbance, such as a loud noise, frequently made them fall. Although they had some use of their arms, the additional transection of the two ventromedial tracts eliminated their ability to control their shoulders. When they fed, they did so with elbow and whole-hand movements while their upper arms hung limply by their sides.

What do these experiments tell us about the roles of the various descending sensorimotor tracts in the control of movement? They suggest that the two ventromedial tracts are involved in the control of posture and whole-body movements (e.g., walking and climbing) and that they can exert control over the limb movements involved in such activities. In contrast, both dorsolateral tracts—the corticospinal tract and the corticorubrospinal tract—control the movements of the limbs. This redundancy was presumably the basis for the good recovery of limb movement after the initial lesions of the corticospinal dorsolateral tract. However, only the corticospinal division of the dorsolateral system is capable of mediating independent movements of the digits.

6.7
Sensorimotor Spinal Circuits

Muscles

Motor units are the smallest units of motor activity. Each motor unit comprises a single motor neuron and all of the individual skeletal muscle fibers that it innervates (see Figure 6.9). When the motor neuron fires, all the muscle fibers of its unit contract together. Motor units differ appreciably in the number of muscle fibers they contain; the units with the fewest fibers—those of the fingers and face—permit the highest degree of selective motor control.

A skeletal muscle comprises hundreds of thousands of threadlike muscle fibers bound together in a tough membrane and attached to a bone by a *tendon. Acetylcholine*, which is released by motor neurons at *neuromuscular junctions*, activates the **motor end-plate** on each muscle fiber and causes the fiber to contract. All of the motor neurons that innervate the fibers of a single muscle are called its **motor pool**.

Skeletal muscle fibers are often considered to be of two basic types: fast and slow. *Fast muscle fibers*, as you might guess, are those that contract and relax quickly. Although they are capable of generating great force, they fatigue quickly because they are poorly *vascularized* (not well supplied with blood vessels, which gives them a pale color). In contrast, *slow muscle fibers*, although slower and weaker, are capable of more sustained contraction because they are more richly vascularized (and hence much redder). Depending on their function, muscles have different proportions of fast and slow fibers.

Many skeletal muscles belong unambiguously to one of two categories: flexors or extensors. **Flexors** act to bend or flex a joint, and **extensors** act to straighten or extend it. Figure 6.10 illustrates the *biceps* and *triceps*—the flexor and extensor, respectively, of the elbow joint. Any two muscles whose contraction produces the same movement, be it flexion or extension, are said to be **synergistic muscles**; those that act in opposition, like the biceps and the triceps, are said to be **antagonistic muscles**.

To understand how muscles work, it is important to realize that muscles have elastic, rather than inflexible, cable-

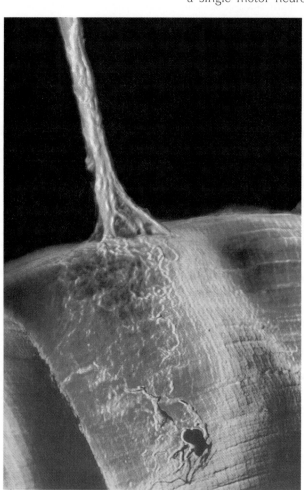

An electron micrograph of a motor unit: a motor neuron (pink) and the muscle fibers that it innervates.

Figure 6.9 ————————

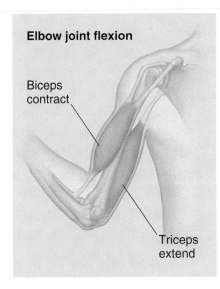

Elbow joint flexion

Biceps contract

Triceps extend

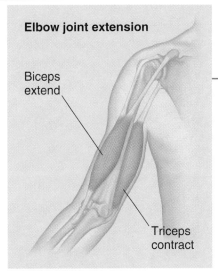

Elbow joint extension

Biceps extend

Triceps contract

The biceps and triceps, which are the flexor and extensor, respectively, of the elbow joint.

Figure 6.10

like, properties. If you think of an increase in muscle tension as being analogous to an increase in the tension of an elastic band joining two bones, you will appreciate that muscle contraction can be of two types. Activation of a muscle can increase the tension that it exerts on two bones without shortening and pulling them together; this is termed **isometric contraction**. Or it can shorten and pull them together; this is termed **dynamic contraction**. The tension in a muscle can be increased by increasing the number of neurons in its motor pool that are firing, by increasing the firing rates of those that are already firing, or more commonly by a combination of the two.

Thinking Clearly

Receptor Organs of Tendons and Muscles

The activity of skeletal muscles is monitored by two kinds of receptors: Golgi tendon organs and muscle spindles. **Golgi tendon organs** are embedded in the *tendons*, which connect each skeletal muscle to bone; **muscle spindles** are embedded in the muscle tissue itself. Because of their different locations, Golgi tendon organs and muscle spindles respond to different aspects of muscle contraction. Golgi tendon organs respond to increases in muscle tension (i.e., to the pull of the muscle on the tendon), but they are completely insensitive to changes in muscle length. In contrast, muscle spindles respond to changes in muscle length, but they do not respond to changes in muscle tension.

Under normal conditions, the function of Golgi tendon organs is to provide the central nervous system with information about muscle tension, but they also serve a protective function. When the contraction of a muscle is so extreme that there is a risk of damage, the Golgi tendon organs excite inhibitory interneurons in the spinal cord that cause the muscle to relax.

Figure 6.11 on page 190 is a schematic diagram of the *muscle-spindle feedback circuit*. Examine it carefully. Notice that each muscle spindle (shown here much enlarged) has its own threadlike **intrafusal muscle**, which is innervated by its own **intrafusal motor neuron**. Why would a receptor have its own muscle and motor neuron? The reason becomes apparent when you consider what would happen to a muscle spindle without them. Without its intrafusal motor input, a muscle spindle would fall slack each time its **skeletal muscle (extrafusal muscle)** contracted. In this slack state, the muscle spindle could not do its job, which is to respond to slight changes in extrafusal muscle length. As Figure 6.12 on page 191 illustrates, the intrafusal motor neuron solves this problem by shortening the intrafusal muscle each time the extrafusal muscle becomes shorter, thus keeping enough tension on the

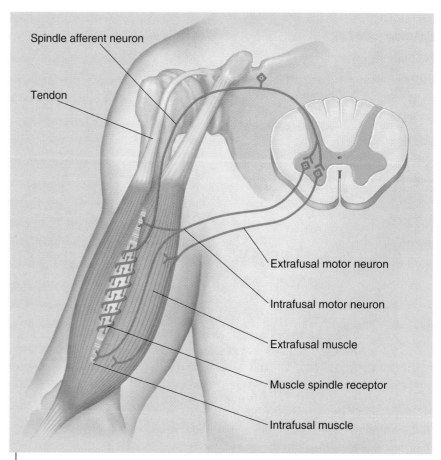

Spindle afferent neuron

Tendon

Extrafusal motor neuron

Intrafusal motor neuron

Extrafusal muscle

Muscle spindle receptor

Intrafusal muscle

The muscle-spindle feedback circuit. There are many tiny muscle spindles in each muscle; for clarity, only one much-enlarged muscle spindle is illustrated here.

Figure 6.11

middle, stretch-sensitive portion of the muscle spindle to keep it responsive to slight changes in the length of the extrafusal muscle.

Stretch Reflex

When the word *reflex* is mentioned, many people think of themselves sitting on the edge of their doctor's examination table having their knees rapped with a little rubber-headed hammer. The response in this case is a **stretch reflex**—a reflex that is elicited by a sudden external stretching force on a muscle.

When your doctor strikes the tendon of your knee, the extensor muscle running along your thigh is stretched. This initiates the chain of events that is depicted in Figure 6.13. The sudden stretch of the thigh muscle stretches its muscle-spindle stretch receptors, which in turn initiates a volley of action potentials that is carried from the stretch receptors into the spinal cord by **spindle afferent neurons** via the *dorsal root*. This volley of action potentials excites motor neurons in the *ventral horn* of the spinal cord, which respond by sending action potentials back to the muscle whose stretch originally excited them (see Illert & Kümmel, 1999). The arrival of these impulses back at the starting point results in a compensatory muscle contraction and a sudden leg extension.

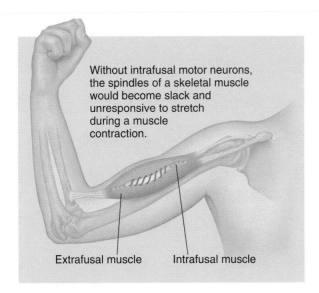

Without intrafusal motor neurons, the spindles of a skeletal muscle would become slack and unresponsive to stretch during a muscle contraction.

Extrafusal muscle   Intrafusal muscle

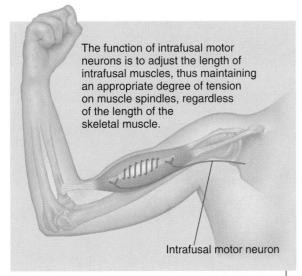

The function of intrafusal motor neurons is to adjust the length of intrafusal muscles, thus maintaining an appropriate degree of tension on muscle spindles, regardless of the length of the skeletal muscle.

Intrafusal motor neuron

The function of intrafusal motor neurons.

Figure 6.12 ————

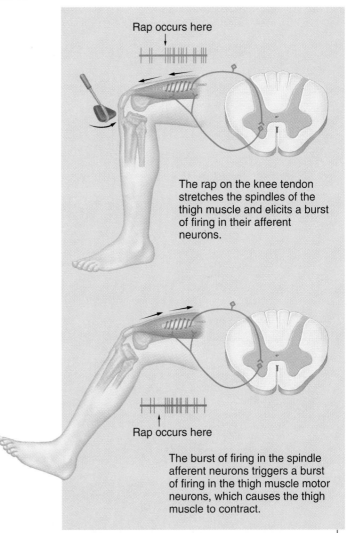

Rap occurs here

The rap on the knee tendon stretches the spindles of the thigh muscle and elicits a burst of firing in their afferent neurons.

Rap occurs here

The burst of firing in the spindle afferent neurons triggers a burst of firing in the thigh muscle motor neurons, which causes the thigh muscle to contract.

The elicitation of a stretch reflex. All of the muscle spindles in a muscle are activated during a stretch reflex, but only a single muscle spindle is depicted here.

Figure 6.13 ————

The method by which the *knee jerk* (patellar tendon) reflex is typically elicited in a doctor's office—that is, by a sharp blow to the tendon of a completely relaxed muscle—is designed to make the reflex readily observable. However, it does little to communicate its functional significance. In real-life situations, the function of the stretch reflex is to keep external forces from altering the intended position of the body. When an external force, such as a push on your arm while you are holding a cup of coffee, causes an unanticipated extrafusal muscle stretch, the muscle-spindle feedback circuit produces an immediate compensatory contraction of the muscle that counteracts the force and keeps you from spilling the coffee—unless, of course, you are wearing your best clothes.

The mechanism by which the stretch reflex maintains limb stability is illustrated in Figure 6.14 on page 192. Examine it carefully because it illustrates two of the principles of sensorimotor system function that are the focus of this chapter: the important role played by sensory feedback in the regulation of motor output and the ability of lower circuits in the motor hierarchy to take care of "business details" without the involvement of higher levels.

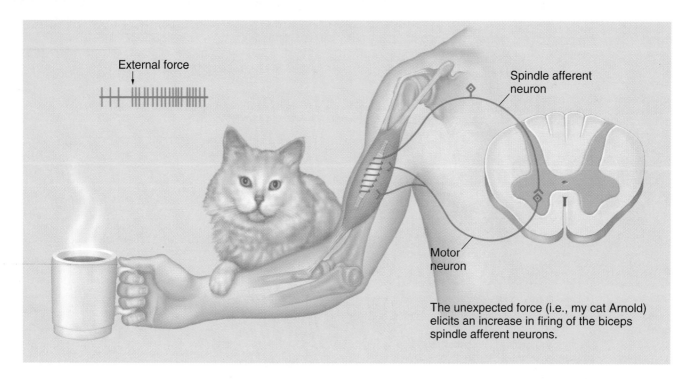

External force

Spindle afferent neuron

Motor neuron

The unexpected force (i.e., my cat Arnold) elicits an increase in firing of the biceps spindle afferent neurons.

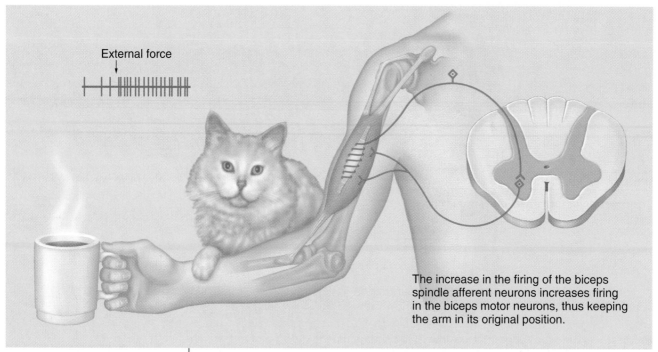

External force

The increase in the firing of the biceps spindle afferent neurons increases firing in the biceps motor neurons, thus keeping the arm in its original position.

The automatic maintenance of limb position by the muscle-spindle feedback system.

Figure 6.14

Withdrawal Reflex

I am sure that, at one time or another, you have touched something painful—a hot pot, for example—and suddenly pulled back your hand. This is a **withdrawal reflex**. Unlike the stretch reflex, the withdrawal reflex is *not monosynaptic*. When a painful

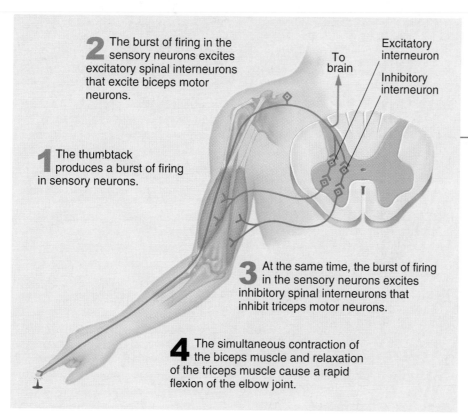

2 The burst of firing in the sensory neurons excites excitatory spinal interneurons that excite biceps motor neurons.

To brain

Excitatory interneuron

Inhibitory interneuron

1 The thumbtack produces a burst of firing in sensory neurons.

3 At the same time, the burst of firing in the sensory neurons excites inhibitory spinal interneurons that inhibit triceps motor neurons.

4 The simultaneous contraction of the biceps muscle and relaxation of the triceps muscle cause a rapid flexion of the elbow joint.

The reciprocal innervation of antagonistic muscles in the arm. During a withdrawal reflex, elbow flexors are excited, and elbow extensors are inhibited.

—Figure 6.15—

stimulus is applied to the hand, the first responses are recorded in the motor neurons of the arm flexor muscles about 1.6 milliseconds later, about the time it takes a neural signal to cross two synapses. Thus, the shortest route in the withdrawal-reflex circuit involves one interneuron. Other responses are recorded in the motor neurons of the arm flexor muscles after the initial volley; these responses are triggered by signals that have traveled over multisynaptic pathways—some involving the cortex. See Figure 6.15.

Reciprocal Innervation

Reciprocal innervation is an important principle of spinal cord circuitry. It refers to the fact that antagonistic muscles are innervated in a way that permits a smooth, unimpeded motor response: When one is contracted, the other relaxes. Figure 6.15 illustrates the role of reciprocal innervation in the withdrawal reflex. "Bad news" of a sudden painful event in the hand arrives in the dorsal horn of the spinal cord and has two effects: The signals excite both excitatory and inhibitory interneurons. The excitatory interneurons excite the motor neurons of the elbow flexor; the inhibitory interneurons inhibit the motor neurons of the elbow extensor. Thus, a single sensory input produces a coordinated pattern of motor output; the activities of synergists and antagonists are automatically coordinated by the internal circuitry of the spinal cord.

Movements are quickest when there is simultaneous excitation of all synergists and complete inhibition of all antagonists; however, this is not the way voluntary movement is normally produced. Most muscles are always contracted to some degree, and movements are produced by adjustment in the level of relative contraction between antagonists. Movements that are produced by **cocontraction** are smooth, and they can be stopped with precision by a slight increase in the contraction of the antagonistic muscles. Moreover, cocontraction insulates us from the effects of unexpected external forces.

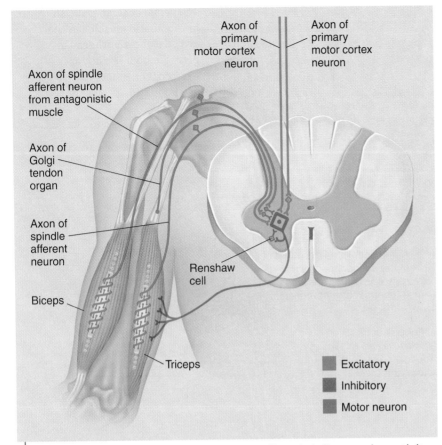

Axon of primary motor cortex neuron

Axon of primary motor cortex neuron

Axon of spindle afferent neuron from antagonistic muscle

Axon of Golgi tendon organ

Axon of spindle afferent neuron

Biceps

Triceps

Renshaw cell

Excitatory
Inhibitory
Motor neuron

The excitatory and inhibitory signals that directly influence the activity of a motor neuron.

Figure 6.16

Recurrent Collateral Inhibition

Like most workers, muscle fibers and the motor neurons that innervate them need an occasional break, and there are inhibitory neurons in the spinal cord that make sure they get it. Each motor neuron branches just before it leaves the spinal cord, and the branch synapses on a small inhibitory interneuron, which inhibits the very motor neuron from which it receives its input (see Illert & Kümmel, 1999). The inhibition produced by these local feedback circuits is called **recurrent collateral inhibition**, and the small inhibitory interneurons that mediate recurrent collateral inhibition are called *Renshaw cells*. As a consequence of recurrent collateral inhibition, each time a motor neuron fires, it momentarily inhibits itself and shifts the responsibility for the contraction of a particular muscle to other members of the muscle's motor pool.

Figure 6.16 provides a summary; it illustrates recurrent collateral inhibition and other factors that directly excite or inhibit motor neurons.

Walking: A Complex Sensorimotor Reflex

Most reflexes are much more complex than withdrawal and stretch reflexes. Think for a moment about the complexity of the program of reflexes that is needed to control an activity such as walking (see Capaday, 2002; Dietz, 2002a; Nielsen, 2002). Such a program must integrate visual information from the eyes; somatosensory information from the feet, knees, hips, arms, and so on; and information about balance from the semicircular canals of the inner ears. And it must produce, on the basis of this information, an integrated series of movements that involves the muscles of the trunk, legs, feet, and upper arms. This program of reflexes must also be incredibly flexible; it must be able to adjust its output immediately to changes in the slope of the terrain, to instructions from the brain, or to external forces such as a bag of groceries. Nobody has yet managed to build a robot that can come close to duplicating these feats.

Grillner (1985) showed that walking can be controlled by circuits in the spinal cord. Grillner's subjects were cats whose spinal cords had been separated from their brains by transection. He suspended the cats in a sling over a treadmill; amazingly, when the treadmill was started so that the cats received sensory feedback of the sort that normally accompanies walking, they began to walk. Similar effects have been observed in other species, but in humans the descending motor pathways play a greater role in walking (see Drew, Jiang, & Widajewicz, 2002).

The Evolutionary Perspective

Central Sensorimotor Programs

In this chapter, you have learned that the sensorimotor system is like the hierarchy of a large efficient company. You have learned how the executives—the dorsolateral prefrontal cortex, the supplementary motor area, and the premotor cortex—issue commands based on information supplied to them by the posterior parietal cortex. And you have learned how these commands are forwarded to the director of operations (the primary motor cortex) for distribution over four main channels of communication (the two dorsolateral and the two ventromedial spinal motor pathways) to the metaphoric office managers of the sensorimotor hierarchy (the spinal sensorimotor circuits). Finally, you have learned how spinal sensorimotor circuits direct the activities of the workers (the muscles).

One theory of sensorimotor function is that the sensorimotor system comprises a hierarchy of **central sensorimotor programs** (see Brooks, 1986; Georgopoulos, 1991). The central sensorimotor program theory suggests that all but the highest levels of the sensorimotor system have certain patterns of activity programmed into them and that complex movements are produced by activating the appropriate combinations of these programs (see Swinnen, 2002; Tresch et al., 2002). Accordingly, if your association cortex decides that you might like to look at a magazine, it activates high-level cortical programs that in turn activate lower-level programs—perhaps in your brain stem—for walking, bending over, picking up, and thumbing through. These programs in turn activate specific spinal programs that control the various elements of the sequences and cause your muscles to complete the objective.

Once activated, each level of the sensorimotor system is capable of operating on the basis of current sensory feedback, without the direct control of higher levels. Thus, although the highest levels of your sensorimotor system retain the option of directly controlling your activities, most of the individual responses that you make are performed without direct cortical involvement, and you are barely aware of them.

In much the same way, a company president who wishes to open a new branch office simply issues the command to one of the executives, and the executive responds in the usual fashion by issuing a series of commands to the appropriate people lower in the hierarchy, who in turn do the same. Each of the executives and workers of the company knows how to complete many different tasks and executes them in the light of current conditions when instructed to do so. Good companies have mechanisms for ensuring that the programs of action at different levels of the hierarchy are well coordinated and effective. In the sensorimotor system, these mechanisms seem to be the responsibility of the cerebellum and basal ganglia.

Thinking Clearly

Central Sensorimotor Programs Are Capable of Motor Equivalence

Like a large, efficient company, the sensorimotor system does not always accomplish a particular task in exactly the same way. The fact that the same basic movement can be carried out in different ways involving different muscles is called **motor equivalence**. For example, you have learned to sign your name with stereotypical finger and hand movements, yet if you signed your name with your toe on a sandy beach, your signature would still retain many of its typical characteristics. This example of motor equivalence suggests that the central sensorimotor programs for signing your name are not stored in the neural circuits that directly control your preferred hand, but higher in your sensorimotor hierarchy. Where?

In an fMRI study, Rijntjes and others (1999) showed that the central sensorimotor programs for signing one's name seem to be stored in areas of secondary motor cortex that control the preferred hand. Remarkably, these same hand areas were also activated when the signature was made with a toe.

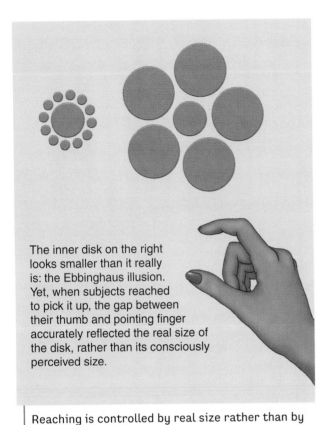

The inner disk on the right looks smaller than it really is: the Ebbinghaus illusion. Yet, when subjects reached to pick it up, the gap between their thumb and pointing finger accurately reflected the real size of the disk, rather than its consciously perceived size.

Reaching is controlled by real size rather than by consciously perceived size (Haffenden & Goodale, 1998).

Figure 6.17

Sensory Information That Controls Central Sensorimotor Programs Is Not Necessarily Conscious

In Chapter 4, you learned that the neural mechanisms of conscious visual perception (ventral stream) are not necessarily the same as those that mediate the visual control of behavior (dorsal stream). Initial evidence for this theory came from neuropsychological patients who could respond to visual stimuli of which they had no conscious awareness and from others who could not effectively interact with objects that they consciously perceived.

Is there evidence for the separation of conscious perception and sensory control of behavior in intact subjects? Haffenden and Goodale (1998) supplied such evidence. They showed healthy subjects a three-dimensional version of the Ebbinghaus illusion presented in Figure 6.17—notice that the two central disks appear to be different sizes, even though they are identical. Remarkably, when subjects were asked to indicate the size of each central disk with their right thumb and pointing finger, they judged the disk on the left to be bigger than the one on the right; however, when they were asked to reach out and pick up the disks with the same two digits, the preparatory gap between the digits was a function of the actual size of each disk rather than its perceived size. These results show that the circuits in the brain that produce conscious experience are not always the same as those that control behavior.

Central Sensorimotor Programs Can Develop without Practice

What type of experience is necessary for the normal development of central sensorimotor programs? In particular, is it necessary to practice a particular behavior for its central sensorimotor program to develop?

Although central sensorimotor programs for some behaviors can be established by practicing the behaviors, the central sensorimotor programs for many species-typical behaviors are established without explicit practice of the behaviors. This point was made clear by the classic study by Fentress (1973). Fentress showed that adult mice raised from birth without forelimbs still made the patterns of shoulder movements typical of grooming in their species—and that these movements were well coordinated with normal tongue, head, and eye movements. For example, the mice blinked each time they made the shoulder movements that would have swept their forepaws across their eyes. Fentress's study also demonstrated the importance of sensory feedback in the operation of central sensorimotor programs. The forelimbless mice, deprived of normal tongue–forepaw contact during face grooming, would often interrupt ostensible grooming sequences to lick a cage-mate or even the floor.

Practice Can Create Central Sensorimotor Programs

Although central sensorimotor programs for many species-typical behaviors develop without practice, practice is a certain way to generate or modify such programs. Theories of sensorimotor learning emphasize two kinds of processes that influence the learning of central sensorimotor programs: response chunking and shifting control to lower levels of the sensorimotor system.

Response Chunking. According to the **response-chunking hypothesis**, practice combines the central sensorimotor programs that control individual responses into programs that control sequences (chunks) of behavior. In a novice typist, each response necessary to type a word is individually triggered and controlled; in a skilled typist, sequences of letters are activated as a unit, with a marked increase in speed and continuity.

An important principle of chunking is that chunks can themselves be combined into higher-order chunks. For example, the responses needed to type the individual letters and digits of one's address may be chunked into longer sequences necessary to produce the individual words and numbers, and these chunks may in turn be combined so that the entire address can be typed as a unit.

Shifting Control to Lower Levels. In the process of learning a central sensorimotor program, control is shifted from higher levels of the sensorimotor hierarchy to lower levels (see Ramnani & Passingham, 2001; Sanes, 2003). Shifting the level of control to lower levels of the sensorimotor system during training (see Seitz et al., 1990) has two advantages. One is that it frees up the higher levels of the system to deal with more esoteric aspects of performance. For example, skilled pianists can concentrate on interpreting a piece of music because they do not have to consciously focus on pressing the right keys. The other advantage of shifting the level of control is that it permits great speed because different circuits at the lower levels of the hierarchy can act simultaneously, without interfering with one another. It is possible to type 120 words per minute only because the circuits responsible for activating each individual key press can become active before the preceding response has been completed.

Functional Brain Imaging of Sensorimotor Learning

Functional brain-imaging techniques have provided opportunities for studying the neural correlates of sensorimotor learning. By recording the brain activity of human subjects as they learn to perform new motor sequences, researchers can develop hypotheses about the roles of various structures in sensorimotor learning. A good example of this approach is the PET study by Jenkins and colleagues (1994). These researchers made PET recordings of the brain activity of human subjects as they performed two different sequences of key presses. There were four different keys, and each sequence was four presses long. The presses were performed with the right hand, one every 3 seconds, and tones indicated when to press and whether or not a press was correct. There were three conditions: a rest control condition, a condition in which the subjects performed a newly learned sequence, and a condition in which the subjects performed a well-practiced sequence.

Cognitive Neuroscience

The following are six major findings of this study (see Figure 6.18 on page 198). They recapitulate important points that have already been made in this chapter.

> **Finding 1**: Posterior parietal cortex was activated during the performance of both the newly learned sequence and the well-practiced sequence, but it was more active during the newly learned sequence. This finding is consistent

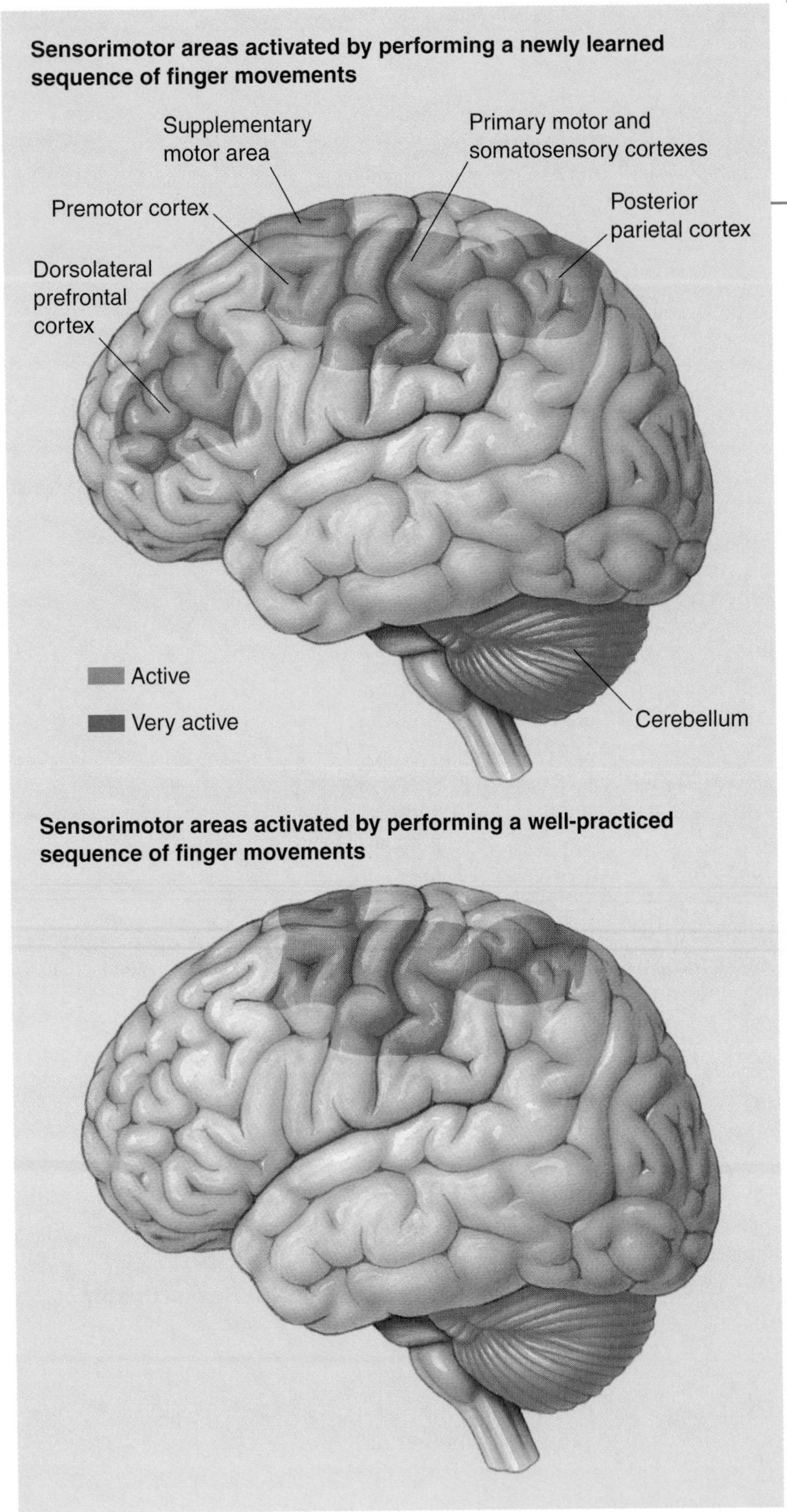

Sensorimotor areas activated by performing a newly learned sequence of finger movements

Supplementary motor area

Primary motor and somatosensory cortexes

Premotor cortex

Posterior parietal cortex

Dorsolateral prefrontal cortex

Active

Very active

Cerebellum

Sensorimotor areas activated by performing a well-practiced sequence of finger movements

The activity recorded by PET scans during the performance of newly learned and well-practiced sequences of finger movements.
(Adapted from Jenkins et al., 1994.)

Figure 6.18

with the hypothesis that the posterior parietal cortex integrates sensory stimuli (in this case, the tones) that are used to guide motor sequences, and it is consistent with the finding that the posterior parietal cortex is more active when subjects are attending more to the stimuli, as is often the case during the early stages of motor learning.

Finding 2: Dorsolateral prefrontal cortex was activated during the performance of the newly learned sequence but not the well-practiced sequence. This suggests that the dorsolateral prefrontal cortex plays a particularly important role when motor sequences are being performed largely under conscious control, as is often the case during the early stages of motor learning.

Finding 3: The areas of secondary motor cortex responded differently. The contralateral premotor cortex was more active during the performance of the newly learned sequence, whereas the supplementary motor area was more active bilaterally during the well-practiced sequence. This finding is consistent with the hypothesis that the premotor cortex plays a more prominent role when performance is being guided largely by sensory stimuli, as is often the case in the early stages of motor learning, and that the supplementary motor area plays a more prominent role when performance is largely independent of sensory stimuli, as is often the case for well-practiced motor sequences, which can be run off automatically with little sensory feedback.

Finding 4: Contralateral primary motor and somatosensory cortexes were equally activated during the performance of both the newly learned and the well-practiced motor sequences. This finding is consistent with the fact that the motor elements were the same during both sequences.

Finding 5: The contralateral basal ganglia were equally activated during the performance of the newly learned sequence and the well-practiced sequence.

Jenkins and colleagues speculated that different subpopulations of basal ganglia neurons may have been active during the two conditions, but this could not be detected because of the poor spatial resolution of PET.

Finding 6: The cerebellum was activated bilaterally during the performance of both the newly learned and the well-practiced sequences, but it was more active during the newly learned sequence. This is consistent with the idea that the cerebellum plays a prominent role in motor learning.

The Case of Rhonda, Revisited

A few days after I finished writing this chapter, I stopped off to pick up a few fresh vegetables and some fish for dinner, and I once again found myself waiting in Rhonda's line. It was the longest line, but I am a creature of habit. This time, I felt rather smug as I watched her. All of the reading and thinking that had gone into the preparation of this chapter had provided me with some new insights into what she was doing and how she was doing it. I wondered whether she appreciated her own finely tuned sensorimotor system as much as I did. Then I hatched my plot—a little test of Rhonda's muscle-spindle feedback system. How would Rhonda's finely tuned sensorimotor system react to a bag that looked heavy but was in fact extremely light? Next time, I would get one of those paper bags at the mushroom counter, blow it up, drop one mushroom in it, and then fold the top so it looked completely full. I smiled at the thought. But I wasn't the only one smiling. My daydreaming ended abruptly, and the smile melted from my face, as I noticed Rhonda's extended hand and her amused grin. Will I never learn?

Key Terms

6.1 Three Principles of Sensorimotor Function

Sensory feedback (p. 172)

6.2 Sensorimotor Association Cortex

Apraxia (p. 175)
Contralateral neglect (p. 175)
Dorsolateral prefrontal association cortex (p. 176)
Posterior parietal association cortex (p. 174)

6.3 Secondary Motor Cortex

Cingulate motor areas (p. 178)
Premotor cortex (p. 178)
Secondary motor cortex (p. 178)
Supplementary motor area (p. 178)

6.4 Primary Motor Cortex

Astereognosia (p. 182)
Motor homunculus (p. 180)
Primary motor cortex (p. 180)
Somatotopic (p. 180)
Stereognosis (p. 181)

6.6 Descending Motor Pathways

Betz cells (p. 184)
Dorsolateral corticorubrospinal tract (p. 184)
Dorsolateral corticospinal tract (p. 184)
Reticular formation (p. 186)
Tectum (p. 185)
Ventromedial cortico-brainstem-spinal tract (p. 184)
Ventromedial corticospinal tract (p. 184)
Vestibular nucleus (p. 186)

6.7 Sensorimotor Spinal Circuits

Antagonistic muscles (p. 188)
Cocontraction (p. 193)
Dynamic contraction (p. 189)
Extensors (p. 188)
Flexors (p. 188)
Golgi tendon organs (p. 189)
Intrafusal motor neuron (p. 189)
Intrafusal muscle (p. 189)
Isometric contraction (p. 189)
Motor end-plate (p. 188)
Motor pool (p. 188)

Motor units (p. 188)
Muscle spindles (p. 189)
Reciprocal innervation (p. 193)
Recurrent collateral inhibition (p. 194)
Skeletal muscle (extrafusal muscle) (p. 189)
Spindle afferent neurons (p. 190)
Stretch reflex (p. 190)
Synergistic muscles (p. 188)
Withdrawal reflex (p. 192)

6.8 Central Sensorimotor Programs

Central sensorimotor programs (p. 195)
Motor equivalence (p. 195)
Response-chunking hypothesis (p. 197)

ON THE CD

Studying for an exam? Get some help from the electronic flash cards of the key terms and the practice tests for this chapter.

The Sensorimotor System
How You Do What You Do

The sensorimotor system controls the movements of the body: It controls what you do. Remarkably, much of the control exerted by your sensorimotor system occurs without your conscious awareness.

Three Principles of Sensorimotor Function

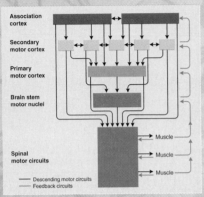

Current model

- The sensorimotor system is hierarchically organized.
- Motor output is guided by sensory feedback.
- Learning changes the nature and locus of sensorimotor control.

(Pages 171–174)

Muscle-spindle system

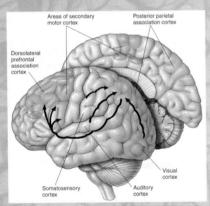

Figure 6.2

The Three Levels of Sensorimotor Cortex: Association, Secondary, and Primary

Two areas of sensorimotor association cortex are the posterior parietal cortex and the dorsolateral prefrontal cortex, which are thought to provide information about the location of the body relative to external objects and to make decisions to initiate movement, respectively. Several areas of secondary motor cortex that are found in the frontal lobe are thought to be involved in programming patterns of voluntary movement. The primary motor cortex lies in the precentral gyrus, and it is thought to activate the motor circuits of the spinal cord.

(Pages 174–183)

Descending Motor Pathways, the Cerebellum, and Basal Ganglia

Two pathways descend from the primary motor cortex in each hemisphere. One descends in dorsolateral portions of the spinal cord and controls the muscles of the extremities; the other descends in the ventromedial portions of the spinal cord and controls the muscles of the trunk. The cerebellum and basal ganglia are important subcortical sensorimotor structures, but they are not components of the descending motor pathways. Instead, they interact with various levels of the sensorimotor system to adjust motor output to correct deviations from the intended outcome and to participate in sensorimotor learning.

(Pages 184–188)

Dorsolateral motor pathways

Visual Summary

Stretch reflex

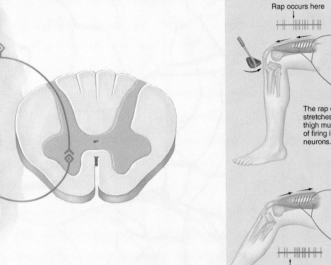

Rap occurs here

The rap on the knee tendon stretches the spindles of the thigh muscle and elicits a burst of firing in their afferent neurons.

Rap occurs here

The burst of firing in the spindle afferent neurons triggers a burst of firing in the thigh muscle motor neurons, which causes the thigh muscle to contract.

Sensorimotor Spinal Circuits

Motor neurons project from the spinal cord to muscles, and sensory neurons carry information from receptors in muscles back to the spinal cord. The motor and sensory neurons are part of spinal circuits that automatically coordinate many complex behaviors (e.g., walking).

(Pages 188–194)

Central Sensorimotor Programs

Most aspects of behavior occur without the need for our awareness; they are controlled instead by automatic sensorimotor programs. Practice can create new sensorimotor programs, and it can chunk individual responses into sequences of behavior.

(Pages 195–199)

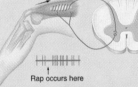

Sensorimotor areas activated by performing a newly learned sequence of finger movements

Supplementary motor area

Premotor cortex

Dorsolateral prefrontal cortex

Primary motor and somatosensory cortexes

Posterior parietal cortex

Active

Very active

Cerebellum

Figure 6.15

Themes Revisited

All four of this book's major themes were addressed in this chapter. Most prominent were the clinical implications and cognitive neuroscience themes: You learned how research on neuropsychological patients with sensorimotor deficits (G.O. and Mrs. S.) and studies of functional brain images of human subjects engaging in sensorimotor activities have contributed to current theories of sensorimotor functioning.

The evolutionary perspective theme was evident in the discussion of several comparative experiments on the sensorimotor system, largely in nonhuman primates. An important point to keep in mind is that although the sensorimotor functions of nonhuman primates are similar to those of humans, they are not identical (e.g., monkeys walk with their hands).

Finally, you learned how metaphors can be used productively to think about science—in particular, how a large, efficient company can serve as a useful metaphor for the sensorimotor system.

Think about It

1. Sensorimotor systems and large businesses are both complex systems trying to survive in a competitive milieu. It is no accident that they function in similar ways. Discuss.

2. We humans tend to view cortical mechanisms as preeminent, presumably because we are the species with the largest cortexes. However, one might argue from several perspectives that sensorimotor functions are more important. Discuss.

3. Some neural circuits perform their function under conscious awareness, and others perform the same function in the absence of consciousness. Discuss this form of parallel processing.

4. Belle, the owl monkey, controlled a robotic arm with her brain. How might the technology that allowed her to do this be used to improve the lives of paralyzed patients?

5. Discuss the importance of sensory feedback in guiding motored output. Provide evidence to support your discussion.

Part 3

Plasticity of the Brain

In Part 2, you learned about the input and output systems of the brain: about the sensory and motor systems, respectively. Two ideas dominated that part of this book: (1) Your sensory and motor mechanisms are far more complex, and thus far more interesting, than you likely expected; and (2) much can be accomplished by your brain in the absence of any conscious awareness.

Part 3 focuses on a topic that has become one of the hottest areas of neuroscientific research: neuroplasticity. Many people view their brains as static organs—very complex, but basically unchanging. We now know that the brain never stops changing—even in mature adults, new neurons, synapses, and circuits are continually developing. In this part of the book, you will learn about the neuroplastic processes that mediated the original growth of your brain (Chapter 7); about the role of neuroplastic responses in the prevention of, treatment of, and recovery from brain damage (Chapter 8); and about the changes in your brain that are thought to store memories (Chapter 9). Chapter 9 emphasizes the memory problems experienced by people with brain damage—and I think that you will be astounded to learn that many of these amnesics can remember experiences of which they have no conscious awareness.

There is a good reason why the coverage of neuroplasticity follows the material on the sensory and motor systems. As you are about to learn, much of the research on neuroplasticity has focused on the sensory and motor systems because their organization (e.g., retinotopic or somatotopic) is so systematic and well understood. Efforts to change the organization of the brain have focused on these systems because changes in them are relatively easy to detect.

chapter 7

Development of the Nervous System
From Fertilized Egg to You

chapter 8

Brain Damage and Neuroplasticity
Can the Brain Recover from Damage?

chapter 9

Learning, Memory, and Amnesia
How Your Brain Stores Information

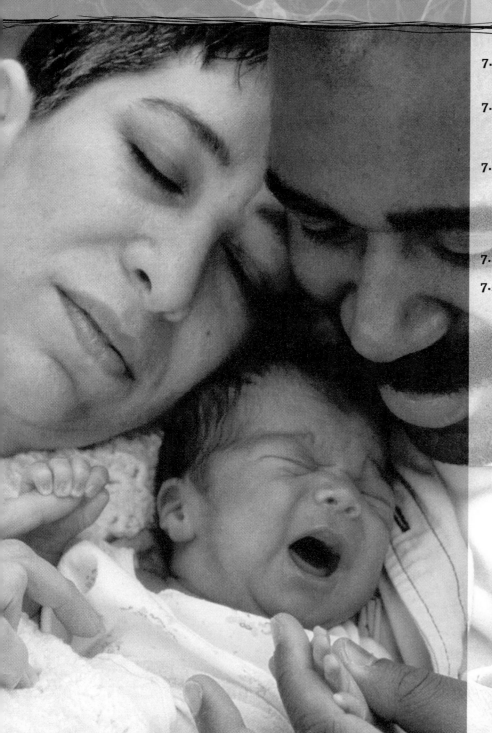

chapter 7

Development of the Nervous System
From Fertilized Egg to You

Most of us tend to think of the nervous system as a three-dimensional array of neural elements "wired" together in a massive network of circuits. The sheer magnitude and complexity of such a wiring diagram would be staggering, but the analogy sells the nervous system short by failing to capture one of its most important features. The nervous system is not a static network of interconnected elements, as is implied by the wiring-diagram model; rather, it is a *plastic* (changeable), living organ that grows and changes continuously in response to its genetic programs and its interactions with its environment.

This chapter focuses on the amazing process of *neurodevelopment* (neural development), which begins with a single fertilized egg cell (see Figure 1.11 on page 21) and ends with a functional adult brain. The goal of this chapter is to impress upon you three key points: (1) the complexity and wonder of neurodevelopment, (2) the important role experience plays in neurodevelopment, and (3) the dire consequences when neurodevelopment goes wrong. The chapter progresses through these three points, culminating in a discussion of two devastating disorders of human neurodevelopment: autism and Williams syndrome.

But first is the sad case of Genie. People tend to underestimate the role of experience in human neural and psychological development. One of the reasons is that most of us are reared in similar environments. Because there is so little variation in most people's early experience, the critical role of experience in human cerebral and psychological development is not obvious. This misconception can be corrected by considering cases of children who have been reared in grossly abnormal environments. Genie is such a case (Curtiss, 1977; Rymer, 1993).

Thinking Clearly

The Case of Genie

Clinical Implications

> When Genie was admitted to the hospital at the age of 13, she was only 1.35 meters (4 feet, 5 inches) tall and weighed only 28.1 kilograms (62 pounds). She could not stand erect, chew solid food, or control her bladder or bowels. Since the age of 20 months, Genie had spent most days tied to a potty in a small, dark, closed room. Her only clothing was a cloth harness, which kept her from moving anything other than her feet and hands. In the evening, Genie was transferred to a covered crib and a straitjacket. Her father was intolerant of noise, and he beat Genie if she made any sound whatsoever. According to her mother, who was almost totally blind, Genie's father and brother rarely spoke to Genie, although they sometimes barked at her like dogs. The mother was permitted only a few minutes with Genie each day, during which time she fed Genie cereal or baby food—Genie was allowed no solid food. Genie's severe childhood deprivation left her seriously scarred. When she was admitted to hospital, she made almost no sounds and was totally incapable of speech.
>
> After Genie's discovery, a major effort was made to get her development back on track and to document her problems and improvements; however, after a few years, Genie "disappeared" in a series of legal proceedings, foster homes, and institutions. (Rymer, 1993)

Although Genie did show some improvement in the years after her rescue, during which time she was receiving special care, it was readily apparent that she would never achieve anything approximating normal psychological development. The following were a few of her continuing problems: She did not react to extremes of warmth and cold; she tended to have silent tantrums during which she would flail, spit, scratch, urinate, and rub her own snot all over herself; she was easily terrified (e.g., of dogs and men wearing khaki); she could not chew; she could speak only short, poorly pronounced utterances. Genie is currently living in a home for retarded adults. Clearly, experience plays a major role in the processes of neurodevelopment, processes to which you are about to be introduced.

Phases of Neurodevelopment

n the beginning, there is a *zygote*, a single cell formed by the amalgamation of an *ovum* and a *sperm*. The zygote divides to form two daughter cells. These two divide to form four, the four divide to form eight, and so on, until a mature organism is produced. Of course, there must be more to development than this; if there were not, each of us would have ended up like a bowl of rice pudding: an amorphous mass of homogeneous cells.

To save us from this fate, three things other than cell multiplication must occur. First, cells must *differentiate*; some must become muscle cells, some must become multipolar neurons, some must become glial cells, and so on. Second, cells must make their way to appropriate sites and align themselves with the cells around them to form particular structures. And third, cells must establish appropriate functional relations with other cells (see Kozloski, Hamzei-Sichani, & Yuste, 2001). This section describes how developing neurons accomplish these things in five phases: (1) induction of the neural plate, (2) neural proliferation, (3) migration and aggregation, (4) axon growth and synapse formation, and (5) neuron death and synapse rearrangement.

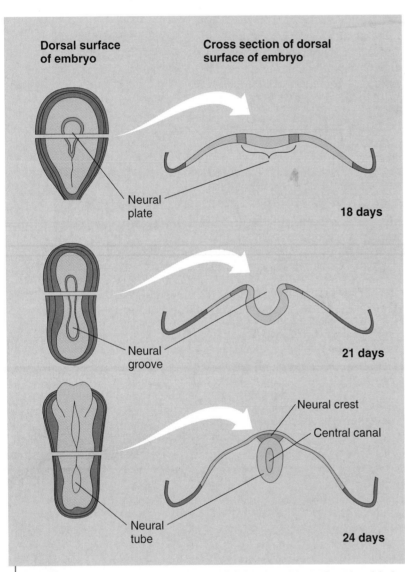

Dorsal surface of embryo

Cross section of dorsal surface of embryo

Neural plate — 18 days

Neural groove — 21 days

Neural crest

Central canal

Neural tube — 24 days

How the neural plate develops into the neural tube during the third and fourth weeks of human embryological development.
(Adapted from Cowan, 1979.)

Figure 7.1

Induction of the Neural Plate

About 2.5 weeks after conception, the tissue that is destined to develop into the human nervous system becomes recognizable as the **neural plate**—a small patch of tissue on the dorsal surface of the developing embryo. An important change occurs to the cells of the developing nervous system at about the time that the neural plate becomes visible. The earliest cells of the human embryo are **totipotent**—that is, they have the ability to develop into any type of cell in the body if transplanted to the appropriate site. However, as the embryo develops, the destiny of various cells becomes more *specified*. With the development of the neural plate, its cells lose much of their potential to become different kinds of cells. Each cell of the neural plate still has the potential to develop into any type of mature nervous system cell, but it cannot normally develop into other kinds of cells. Cells like these are said to be **multipotent**, rather than totipotent.

The cells of the neural plate are often referred to as embryonic **stem cells**.

Stem cells are cells that meet two specific criteria (see Brivanlou et al., 2003; Seaberg & van der Kooy, 2003): (1) They have a seemingly unlimited capacity for self-renewal, and (2) they have the ability to develop into different types of mature cells. The cells of the neural plate meet both of these criteria: If maintained in an appropriate cell culture, they will continue to multiply, and, as you have just learned, they have the capacity to develop into any type of cell in the adult nervous system. However, as the neural tube develops, some of its cells become specified as future glial cells of various types, and others become specified as future neurons of various types. Because these cells still have the capacity for self-renewal and are still multipotent, these cells are termed *glial stem cells* and *neural stem cells*, respectively.

Because of the ability of embryonic stem cells to develop into different types of mature cells, their therapeutic potential is currently under intensive investigation. Will embryonic stem cells injected into a damaged part of a mature brain develop into the appropriate brain structure and improve function? You will learn about the potential of stem-cell therapy in Chapter 8.

As Figure 7.1 illustrates, the neural plate folds to form the *neural groove*, and then the lips of the neural groove fuse to form the **neural tube**. The inside of the neural tube eventually becomes the *cerebral ventricles* and *spinal canal*. By 40 days after conception, three swellings are visible at the anterior end of the human neural tube; these swellings ultimately develop into the *forebrain, midbrain*, and *hindbrain* (see Figure 2.19 on page 50).

Neural Proliferation

Once the lips of the neural groove have fused to create the neural tube, the cells of the tube begin to *proliferate* (increase greatly in number). This **neural proliferation** does not occur simultaneously or equally in all parts of the tube. In each species, the cells in different parts of the neural tube proliferate in a characteristic sequence that is responsible for the pattern of swelling and folding that gives the brain its species-characteristic shape. Most cell division in the neural tube occurs in the **ventricular zone**—the region adjacent to the *ventricle* (the fluid-filled center of the tube).

Migration and Aggregation

Migration. Once cells have been created through cell division in the ventricular zone of the neural tube, they migrate to the appropriate target location. During this period of **migration**, the cells are still in an immature form, lacking the processes (i.e., axons and dendrites) that characterize mature neurons.

Cell migration in the developing neural tube is considered to be of two kinds (see Figure 7.2): **Radial migration** proceeds from the ventricular zone in a straight line outward toward the outer wall of the tube; **tangential migration** occurs at a right angle to radial migration—that is, parallel to the tube's walls. Most cells engage in both radial and tangential migration to get from their point of origin in the ventricular zone to their target destination (see Hatten, 2002).

There are two methods by which developing cells migrate (see Figure 7.3 on page 208). One is somal translocation. In **somal translocation**, a process, or an extension, grows from the developing cell in the general direction of the migration; the extension seems to explore the immediate environment for cues as it grows. The process grows toward attractive cues and away from repulsive cues. Then,

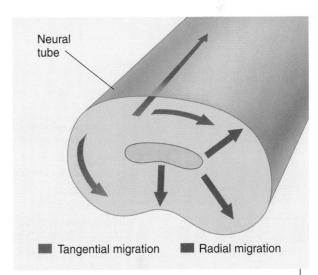

Two types of neural migration: radial migration and tangential migration.

Figure 7.2

Somal Translocation (Radial or Tangential)

Glia-Mediated Migration (Radial Only)

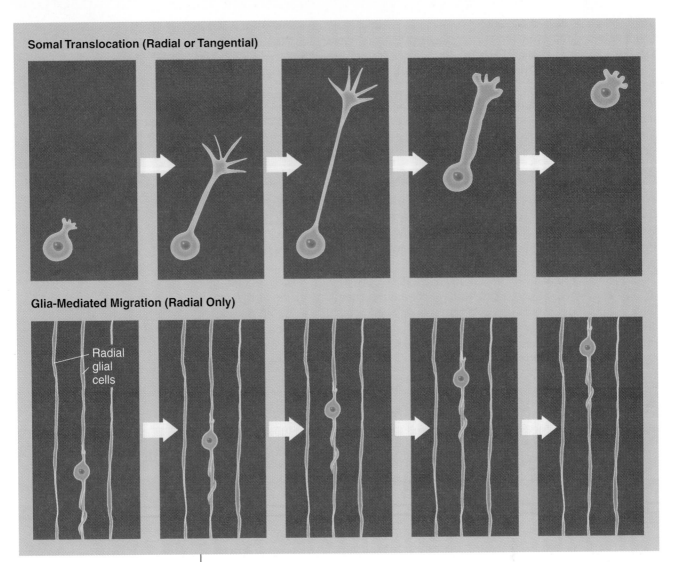

Radial
glial
cells

Two methods by which cells migrate in the developing neural tube: somal translocation and glia-mediated migration.

Figure 7.3

the cell body itself moves into and along the extending process, and trailing processes are retracted (see Nadarajah & Parnavelas, 2002; Ridley et al., 2003).

The second method of migration is **glia-mediated migration** (see Figure 7.3). Once the period of neural proliferation is well underway and the walls of the neural tube are thickening, a temporary network of glial cells, called **radial glial cells**, appears in the developing neural tube (Campbell & Gotz, 2002). At this point, most cells engaging in radial migration do so by moving along the radial glial network (see Nadarajah & Parnavelas, 2002).

Most research on migration in the developing neural tube has focused on the cortex (see Marin & Rubenstein, 2001; Qi, Stapp, & Qiu, 2002). This line of research makes an important point about migration: Timing is everything. The neurons of each of the six layers of the cortex are created and migrate at six different times, and then they develop layer-specific anatomical and functional characteristics (Hanashima et al., 2004; Levitt, 2004).

Most studies of the migration of cortical neurons have focused on radial patterns. These studies have revealed orderly waves of migrating cells, progressing from deeper to more superficial layers. Because each wave of cortical cells migrates through the already formed lower layers of cortex before stopping, this radial pattern of cortical development is referred to as an **inside-out pattern**. However, it is clear that cortical migration patterns are much more complex than first thought; many cortical cells engage in lengthy tangential migration to reach their final destinations. Developing interneurons and glial cells are the most likely to take long tangential journeys.

Numerous chemicals that guide migrating neurons by either attracting or repelling them have been discovered (Marin & Rubenstein, 2003). Some of these **chemoattractants** and **chemorepellants** are released by glial cells (see Auld, 2001; Marin et al., 2001).

Aggregation. Once developing neurons have migrated, they must align themselves with other developing neurons that have migrated to the same area to form the structures of the nervous system. This process is called **aggregation**.

Both migration and aggregation are thought to be mediated by various kinds of **cell-adhesion molecules (CAMs)**, which are located on the surfaces of neurons and other cells. Cell-adhesion molecules have the ability to recognize molecules on other cells and adhere to them.

Axon Growth and Synapse Formation

Axon Growth. Once neurons have migrated to their appropriate positions and aggregated into neural structures, axons and dendrites begin to grow from them. For the nervous system to function, these projections must grow to appropriate targets. At each growing tip of an axon or dendrite is an amoebalike structure called a **growth cone**, which extends and retracts fingerlike cytoplasmic extensions (see Figure 7.4), as if searching for the correct route.

Remarkably, most growth cones reach their correct targets, even when they must travel a considerable distance. A series of studies of neural regeneration by Roger Sperry in the early 1940s first demonstrated that axons are capable of precise growth and suggested how the precise growth occurs.

In one study, Sperry cut the optic nerves of frogs, rotated their eyeballs 180° in the plane of the face, and waited for the axons of the **retinal ganglion cells**, which compose the optic nerve, to *regenerate* (grow again). (Frogs, unlike mammals, have retinal ganglion cells that regenerate.) Once regeneration was complete, Sperry used a convenient behavioral test to assess the frogs' visual capacities (see Figure 7.5 on page 210). When he dangled a lure behind the frogs, they struck forward, thus indicating that their visual world, like their eyes, had been rotated 180°. Frogs whose eyes had been rotated, but whose optic nerves had not been cut, responded in exactly the same way. This was strong behavioral evidence that each retinal ganglion cell had grown back to the same point of the **optic tectum** (called the superior colliculus in mammals) to which it had originally been connected. Neuroanatomical investigations have confirmed that this is exactly what happens (see Guo & Udin, 2000).

ON THE CD

The module *Roger Sperry' s Classic Study of Axonal Regeneration* provides a vivid look at this remarkable study.

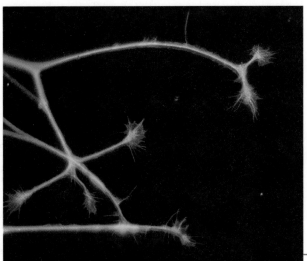

Growth cones. The cytoplasmic fingers of growth cones seem to grope for the correct route.

(Courtesy of Naweed I. Syed, Ph.D., Departments of Anatomy and Medical Physiology, the University of Calgary.)

Figure 7.4

On the basis of his studies of regeneration, Sperry proposed the **chemoaffinity hypothesis** of axonal development (see Sperry, 1963). He hypothesized that each postsynaptic surface in the nervous system releases a specific chemical label and that each growing axon is attracted by the label to its postsynaptic target during both neural development and regeneration. Indeed, it is difficult to imagine another mechanism by which an axon growing out from a rotated eyeball could find its precise target on the optic tectum.

Although the chemoaffinity hypothesis was a major first step toward understanding the mechanisms of accurate axonal growth in the developing nervous system, it fails to account for one of the major features of such growth. The chemoaffinity hypothesis does not account for the fact that some axons follow exactly the same circuitous route to reach their target in every member of a species, rather than growing directly to it (see Araújo & Tear, 2003).

Since Sperry's groundbreaking research, much has been learned about the processes of accurate axonal growth. Key to advances in our understanding of these processes is the fact that the mechanisms that guide growing axons in simple invertebrates (e.g., worms and flies) have been found to perform the same functions in vertebrates (see Jessell & Sanes, 2000). A revised notion of how growing axons reach their specific targets is emerging from this comparative research. This new notion is an elaboration of Sperry's original chemoaffinity hypothesis.

According to the new hypothesis, a growing neuron is not attracted to its target by a single specific attractant released by the target, as Sperry thought. Instead, axonal growth seems to be influenced by a series of chemical signals along the route. Some of these *guidance molecules* (chemoattractants) attract the growing axons, whereas others (chemorepellants) repel them (see Guan & Rao, 2003). Several families of guidance molecules have been identified (see Holmberg & Frisén, 2002; Inatani et al., 2003; Markus, Patel, & Snider, 2002; Owens & Kriegstein, 2002). It is noteworthy that several guidance molecules are released by glia (Lemke, 2001).

Guidance molecules are not the only signals that guide growing axons to their targets. Other signals come from adjacent growing axons. **Pioneer growth cones**—the first growth cones to travel along a particular route in a developing nervous system—are presumed to follow the correct trail by interacting with guidance molecules along the route. Then, subsequent growth cones embarking on the same journey follow the routes blazed by the pioneers. The tendency of developing axons to grow along the paths established by preceding axons is called **fasciculation**. When pioneer axons in the fish spinal cord were destroyed with a laser, subsequent axons of the same nerves did not reach their usual destinations.

The Evolutionary Perspective

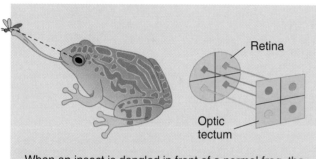

When an insect is dangled in front of a normal frog, the frog strikes at it accurately with its tongue.

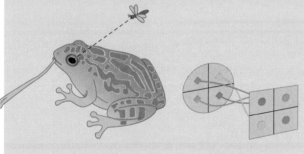

When the eye is rotated 180° without cutting the optic nerve, the frog misdirects its strikes by 180°.

When the optic nerve is cut and the eye is rotated by 180°, at first the frog is blind; but once the optic nerve has regenerated, the frog misdirects its strikes by 180°. This is because the axons of the optic nerve, although rotated, grow back to their original synaptic sites.

Sperry's classic study of eye rotation and regeneration.

Figure 7.5

Much of the axonal development in complex nervous systems involves growth from one topographic array of neurons to another. The neurons on one array project to another, maintaining the same topographic relation they had on the first; for example, the topographic map of the retina is maintained on the optic tectum.

At first, it was assumed that the integrity of topographical relations in the developing nervous system was maintained by a point-to-point chemoaffinity, with each retinal ganglion cell, for example, growing toward a specific chemical label. However, evidence indicates that the mechanism must be more complex. In most species, the synaptic connections between retina and optic tectum are established long before either reaches full size. Then, as the retinas and the optic tectum grow at different rates, the initial synaptic connections shift to other tectal neurons so that the retina is always faithfully mapped onto the tectum, regardless of their relative sizes.

Studies of the regeneration (rather than the development) of retinal-tectum projections tell a similar story. In one informative series of studies, the optic nerves of mature frogs or fish were cut and their pattern of regeneration was assessed after parts of either the retina or the optic tectum had been destroyed. In both cases, the

The Evolutionary Perspective

axons did not grow out to their original points of connection (as the chemoaffinity hypothesis predicted they would); instead, they grew out to fill the available space in an orderly fashion. Axons growing from the remaining portion of a lesioned retina "spread out" in an orderly fashion to fill all of the space on an intact tectum. Conversely, axons growing from an intact retina "squeeze in" in an orderly fashion to fill the remaining space on a lesioned tectum. These results are illustrated schematically in Figure 7.6.

The **topographic gradient hypothesis** has been proposed to explain accurate axonal growth involving topographic mapping in the developing brain (see Debski & Cline, 2002; Grove & Fukuchi-Shimogori, 2003; McLaughlin, Hindges, & O'Leary, 2003). According to this hypothesis, axons growing from one topographic surface (e.g., the retina) to another (e.g., the optic tectum) are guided to specific targets that are arranged on the terminal surface in the same way as the axons' cell bodies are arranged on the original surface. The key part of this hypothesis is that the growing axons are guided to their destinations by two intersecting chemical gradients on the original surface.

Synapse Formation. Once axons have reached their intended sites, they must establish an appropriate pattern of synapses. A single neuron can grow an axon on its own, but it takes coordinated activity in at least two neurons to create a synapse between them (see

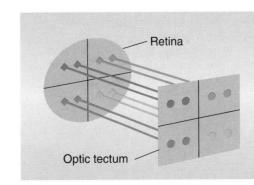

Retina

Optic tectum

Axons normally grow from the frog retina and terminate on the optic tectum in an orderly fashion. The assumption that this orderliness results from point-to-point chemoaffinity is challenged by the following two observations.

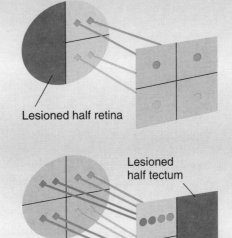

Lesioned half retina

1 When half the retina was destroyed and the optic nerve cut, the retinal ganglion cells from the remaining half retina projected systematically over the entire tectum.

Lesioned half tectum

2 When half the optic tectum was destroyed and the optic nerve cut, the retinal ganglion cells from the retina projected systematically over the remaining half retina.

The regeneration of the optic nerve of the frog after portions of either the retina or the optic tectum have been destroyed. These phenomena support the topographic gradient hypothesis.

Figure 7.6

Yuste & Bonhoeffer, 2004). This is one reason why our understanding of how axons connect to their targets has lagged behind our understanding of how they reach them (see Benson, Colman, & Huntley, 2001; Lee & Sheng, 2000). Still, some exciting breakthroughs have been made.

Perhaps the most exciting recent discovery about **synaptogenesis** (the formation of new synapses) is that it depends on the presence of glial cells, particularly astrocytes (see Barres & Smith, 2001; Fields, 2004; Slezak & Pfrieger, 2003). Retinal ganglion cells maintained in culture formed seven times more synapses when astrocytes were present. Moreover, synapses formed in the presence of astrocytes were quickly lost when those cells were removed.

Most current research on synaptogenesis is focusing on elucidating the chemical signals that must be exchanged between presynaptic and postsynaptic neurons for a synapse to be created (see Scheiffele, 2003). One complication this research faces is the promiscuity that developing neurons display when it comes to synaptogenesis. On one hand, it seems that, in order to function, the brain must be wired-up according to a specific plan; however, in a tissue culture, any type of neuron will form synapses with any other type. This suggests that any given synapse is not created under the control of a single set of chemical signals. Rather, a more hierarchical process, in which each presynaptic and postsynaptic neuron weighs a variety of synapse-promoting and synapse-inhibiting signals before forming synapses with the best available cells, must be operating. This will not be an easy problem to solve.

Neuron Death and Synapse Rearrangement

Neuron Death. Neuron death is a normal and important part of neurodevelopment. Such development seems to operate on the principle of survival of the fittest: Many more neurons—about 50% more—are produced than are required, and only the fittest survive. Large-scale death is not a time-limited stage of development; it occurs in waves in various parts of the brain throughout development.

Three findings suggest that developing neurons die because of their failure to compete successfully for life-preserving chemicals that are supplied to them by their targets. First, the implantation of extra target sites decreases neuron death. For example, grafting an extra limb on one side of a chick embryo reduces motor neuron death on that side. Second, destroying some of the neurons growing into an area before the period of cell death increases the survival rate of the remaining neurons. Third, increasing the number of axons that initially innervate a target decreases the proportion that survive.

Several life-preserving chemicals that are supplied to developing neurons by their targets have been identified. The most prominent class of these chemicals is the **neurotrophins. Nerve growth factor (NGF)** was the first neurotrophin to be isolated (see Levi-Montalcini, 1952, 1975), but since then three others have been identified in mammals—and many more in other species. The neurotrophins perform a variety of functions: For example, they promote the growth and survival of neurons, function as axon guidance molecules, and stimulate synaptogenesis (see Huang & Reichardt, 2001; Vicario-Abejón et al., 2002).

Neuron death during development was initially assumed to be a passive process. It was assumed that the appropriate neurotrophins are needed for the survival of neurons and that without them neurons passively degenerate and die. However, it is now clear that cell death during development is usually an active process: The absence of the appropriate neurotrophins can trigger a genetic program inside neurons that causes them to actively commit suicide. Passive cell death is called **necrosis** (ne-KROE-sis); active cell death is called **apoptosis** (A-poe-TOE-sis).

Apoptosis is safer than necrosis. Necrotic cells break apart and spill their contents into extracellular fluid, and the consequence is potentially harmful inflammation. In contrast, in apoptotic cell death, DNA and other internal structures are cleaved apart and packaged in membranes before the cell breaks apart. These membranes contain molecules that attract scavenger cells and other cells that prevent inflammation (Li et al., 2003; Savill, Gregory, & Haslett, 2003; Wang et al., 2003).

During the phase of neuron death, apoptosis removes excess neurons—for example, neurons that do not obtain enough neurotrophins—in a safe, neat, and orderly way. But apoptosis has a dark side as well. If genetic programs for apoptotic cell death are inhibited, the consequence can be cancer; if the programs are inappropriately activated, the consequence can be neurodegenerative disease.

Synapse Rearrangement.   During the period of cell death, neurons that have established incorrect connections are particularly likely to die. As they die, the space they vacate on postsynaptic membranes is filled by the sprouting axon terminals of surviving neurons. Thus, cell death results in a massive rearrangement of synaptic connections.

Clinical Implications

Scan your Brain

Are you ready to focus on neurodevelopment in the human brain after birth? To find out, scan your brain by filling in the blanks in the following chronological list of stages of neurodevelopment. The correct answers are provided below. Before proceeding, review material related to your errors and omissions.

1. Induction of the neural _____
2. Formation of the _____ tube
3. Neural _____
4. Neural _____
5. _____ aggregation

6. Growth of neural _____
7. Formation of _____
8. Neuron _____ and synapse _____

Scan Your Brain answers: (1) plate, (2) neural, (3) proliferation, (4) migration, (5) Neural, (6) processes (axons and dendrites), (7) synapses (8) death; rearrangement

Postnatal Cerebral Development in Human Infants

Most of our knowledge of neurodevelopment comes from the study of nonhuman species. This fact emphasizes the value of the comparative approach and the evolutionary perspective. There is, however, one way in which the development of the human brain is unique: The human brain develops far more slowly than that of other species, not achieving full maturity until late adolescence (Spear, 2000).

The Evolutionary Perspective

This section deals with that part of the development of the human brain that occurs after birth. It focuses on the development of the prefrontal cortex (see Figure 7.7 on page 214). The **prefrontal cortex** (the portion of the frontal cortex in front of the motor cortex) is the last part of the brain to reach maturity, and it is thought to mediate many higher cognitive abilities.

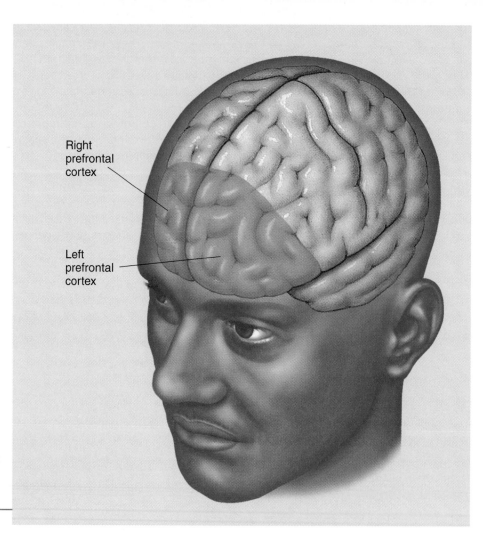

Right
prefrontal
cortex

Left
prefrontal
cortex

The prefrontal cortex, the portions of the frontal cortex in front of the motor cortex.

Figure 7.7

Postnatal Growth of the Human Brain

The human brain grows substantially after birth: Its volume quadruples between birth and adulthood (see Johnson, 2001). This increase in size does not, however, result from the development of additional neurons. With the exception of a few structures (e.g., the olfactory bulb and the hippocampus) in which many new neurons continue to be created during the adult years, all of the neurons that will compose the adult human brain have developed and migrated to their appropriate locations by the seventh month of prenatal development. The postnatal growth of the human brain seems to result from three other kinds of growth: *synaptogenesis*, myelination of many axons, and increased branching of dendrites.

There has been particular interest in the postnatal formation of synapses because the number of connections between neurons in a particular region of the brain is assumed to be an indicator of the analytic ability of that region. There seems to be an increase in the rate of formation of synapses throughout the human cortex shortly after birth, but there are differences among the cortical regions in the course of this development (Huttenlocher, 1994). For example, in the primary visual and auditory cortexes, there is a major burst of synaptogenesis in the fourth postnatal month, and maximum synapse density (150% of adult levels) is achieved in the seventh or eighth month; whereas synaptogenesis in the prefrontal cortex occurs at a relatively steady rate, reaching maximum synapse density in the second year.

Myelination increases the speed of axonal conduction, and the myelination of various areas of the human brain during development roughly parallels their functional development. Myelination of sensory areas occurs in the first few months after birth, and myelination of the motor areas follows soon after that, whereas myelination of prefrontal cortex continues into adolescence.

In general, the pattern of dendritic branching duplicates the original pattern of neural migration. Just as the cells of the deeper layers are first to migrate into position, and the cells of progressively more superficial layers migrate through them to assume their positions, dendritic branching progresses from deeper to more superficial layers. For example, the growth of dendritic trees in layer V always seems to precede that in layers II and III, regardless of the cortical area.

Postnatal human brain development is not a one-way street; there are regressive changes as well as growth (Huttenlocher, 1994). For example, once maximum synaptic density has been achieved, there are periods of synaptic loss. Like periods of synaptogenesis, periods of synaptic loss occur at different times in different parts of the brain. For example, synaptic density in primary visual cortex declines to adult levels by about 3 years of age, whereas synaptic density in the prefrontal cortex does not decline to adult levels until adolescence. It has been suggested that the overproduction of synapses may underlie the greater plasticity of the young brain.

Development of the Prefrontal Cortex

As you have just learned, the prefrontal cortex displays the most prolonged period of development of any brain region. Its development is believed to be largely responsible for the course of human cognitive development, which occurs over the same period.

Given the size, complexity, and heterogeneity of the prefrontal cortex, it is hardly surprising that there is no single widely accepted theory explaining its function. Nevertheless, three types of cognitive functions have consistently been linked to this area in studies of adults with prefrontal damage. The prefrontal cortex seems to play a role in (1) *working memory*, that is, keeping relevant information accessible for short periods of time while a task is being completed; (2) planning and carrying out sequences of actions; and (3) inhibiting responses that are inappropriate in the current context but not in others (see Hauser, 1999).

One interesting line of research on prefrontal cortex development is based on Piaget's classic studies of psychological development in human babies. In his studies of 7-month-old children, Piaget noticed an intriguing error. A small toy was shown to an infant; then it was placed, as the child watched, behind one of two screens, left or right. After a brief delay period, the infant was allowed to reach for the toy. Piaget found that almost all 7-month-old infants reached for the screen behind which they had seen the toy being placed. However, if, after being placed behind the same screen on several consecutive trials, the toy was placed behind the other screen (as the infant watched), most of the 7-month-old infants kept reaching for the previously correct screen, rather than the screen that currently hid the toy (see Figure 7.8 on page 216). Children tend to make this *perseverative error* between about 7 and 12 months, but not thereafter (Diamond, 1985). **Perseveration** is the tendency to continue making a formerly correct response when it is currently incorrect.

Diamond (1991) hypothesized that this perseverative error occurred in infants between 7 and 12 months old because the neural circuitry of the prefrontal cortex is not yet fully developed during that period. Synaptogenesis in the prefrontal cortex is not maximal until early in the second year, and correct performance of the task involved two of the major functions of this brain area: holding information in working memory and suppressing previously correct, but currently incorrect, responses.

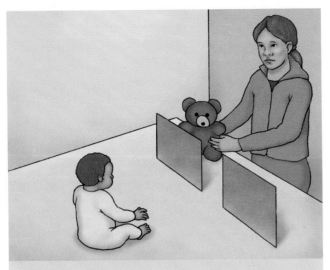

1 To test for a perseverative reaching error in infants, they are first shown a toy being placed behind one of two screens.

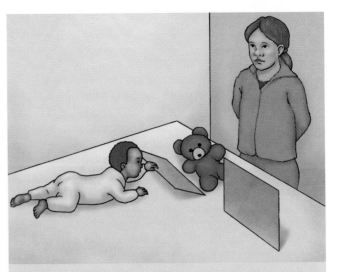

2 Infants older than 7 months usually look behind the correct screen. To conduct a perseveration test, this trial is repeated several times, each time with the toy behind the same screen.

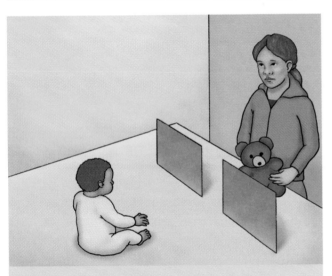

3 Then, on the test trial, the infant is shown the toy being placed behind the other screen.

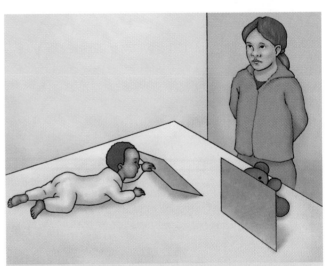

4 Infants between 7 and 12 months tend to reach for the incorrect screen, which had been correct on previous trials.

The perseverative error typically made by children between the ages of 7 and 12 months.

Figure 7.8

The Evolutionary Perspective

To test her hypothesis, Diamond conducted a series of comparative experiments. First, she showed that infant, but not adult, monkeys make the same perseverative error as 7-to-12-month-old human infants on Piaget's test. Then, she tested adult monkeys with bilateral lesions to their dorsolateral prefrontal cortex (see Figure 6.2 on page 175 for the location of this area of cortex), and she found that the lesioned adult monkeys made perseverative errors similar to those made by the infant monkeys. Control monkeys with lesions in the hippocampus or posterior parietal cortex did not make such errors.

Effects of Experience on the Early Development, Maintenance, and Reorganization of Neural Circuits

Genetic programs of neurodevelopment do not act in a vacuum. Neurodevelopment unfolds through interactions between neurons and their environment. You learned in the first section of this chapter how factors (e.g., neurotrophins and CAMs) in neurons' immediate environment can influence their migration, aggregation, and growth. This section focuses on how the experiences of the developing organism influence the development, maintenance, and reorganization of neural circuits. The main principle that governs the effects of early experience on neural circuits is simple: Neurons and synapses that are not activated by experience do not usually survive (see Hockfield & Kalb, 1993; Kalil, 1989). That is, use it or lose it.

You have just learned that humans are uniquely slow in their neural development. One advantage of this slowness may be that it offers many opportunities for experience to fine-tune developing systems (Johnson, 2001).

The Evolutionary Perspective

Early Studies of Experience and Neurodevelopment

Many of the first demonstrations of the impact of early experience on neurodevelopment came from two lines of research: the study of the effects of early visual deprivation and the study of early exposure to enriched environments. For example, rats reared from birth in the dark were found to have fewer synapses and fewer dendritic spines in their primary visual cortexes, and they were found to have deficits in depth and pattern vision as adults. Conversely, rats that were raised in enriched group cages (cages that offered many opportunities for play and sensory stimulation) rather than by themselves in barren cages were found to have thicker cortexes with more dendritic spines and more synapses per neuron.

Competitive Nature of Experience and Neurodevelopment

Experience promotes the development of active neural circuits and the maintenance or reorganization of existing ones, but there seems to be a competitive aspect to this. This competitive aspect is clearly illustrated by the disruptive effects of early monocular deprivation.

Depriving one eye of input for a few days early in life has a lasting adverse effect on vision in the deprived eye, but this does not happen if the other eye is also blindfolded. When only one eye is blindfolded, the ability of that eye to activate the visual cortex is reduced, whereas the ability of the other eye is increased. Both these effects occur because early monocular deprivation changes the pattern of synaptic input into layer IV of the primary visual cortex.

In many species, ocular dominance columns (see Figure 4.22 on page 123) in layer IV of the primary visual cortex are almost fully developed at birth (see Katz & Crowley, 2002). However, if just one eye is deprived of light for several days at some point during the first few months of life, the system is reorganized: The width of the columns of input from the deprived eye is decreased, and the width of the columns of input from the nondeprived eye is increased (Hata & Stryker, 1994; Hubel, Wiesel, & LeVay, 1977). The exact timing of the *sensitive period* for this effect is specific to each species.

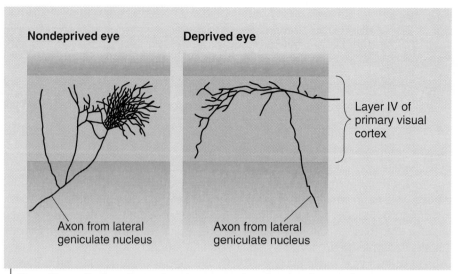

Nondeprived eye	Deprived eye

Layer IV of primary visual cortex

Axon from lateral geniculate nucleus

Axon from lateral geniculate nucleus

The effect of a few days of early monocular deprivation on the structure of axons projecting from the lateral geniculate nucleus into layer IV of the primary visual cortex. Axons carrying information from the deprived eye displayed substantially less branching.

(Adapted from Antonini & Stryker, 1993.)

Figure 7.9

Because the adverse effects of early monocular deprivation manifest themselves so quickly (i.e., in a few days), it was believed that they could not be mediated by structural changes. However, Antonini and Stryker (1993) found that a few days of monocular deprivation produce a massive decrease in the axonal branching of the lateral geniculate nucleus neurons that normally carry signals from the deprived eye to layer IV of the primary visual cortex (see Figure 7.9).

The competitive nature of the effects of neural activity on synapse rearrangement has also been demonstrated in experiments on motor neurons and muscle cells. In *neonates* (newborns), each muscle cell is normally innervated by several motor neurons, and then all but one are eliminated during the course of development. Lo and Poo (1991) studied an in vitro preparation in which one developing muscle cell was innervated by two developing motor neurons. Applying pulses of electrical stimulation to one of these neurons caused a rapid degradation in the synaptic contacts of the other. Apparently, motor neurons compete with one another for synaptic contacts on muscle cells, and active synapses take precedence.

Effects of Experience on Topographic Sensory Cortex Maps

Some of the most remarkable demonstrations of the effects of experience on the organization of the nervous system come from studies of cortical topographic maps of the sensory systems. The following are four such studies.

First, Roe and colleagues (1990) surgically altered the course of developing axons of ferrets' retinal ganglion cells so that the axons synapsed in the medial geniculate nucleus of the auditory system instead of in the lateral geniculate nucleus of the visual system. Remarkably, the experience of visual input caused the auditory cortex of the ferrets to become organized retinotopically (laid out like a map of the retina). See Pallas (2001) for a review of *cross-modal* (involving at least two different sensory systems) rewiring experiments.

Second, Knudsen and Brainard (1991) raised barn owls with vision-displacing prisms over their eyes. This led to a corresponding change in the auditory spatial map in the tectum. For example, an owl that was raised wearing prisms that shifted its visual world 23° to the right had an auditory map that was also shifted 23° to the right, so that objects were heard to be where they were seen to be (see Gutfreund, Zheng, & Knudsen, 2002; Miller & Knudsen, 1999).

Third, Weliky and Katz (1997) periodically disturbed the spontaneous optic nerve activity of neonatal ferrets that had yet to open their eyes. This disrupted the orientation and direction selectivity of the ferrets' primary visual cortex neurons. Thus, it appears that patterns of spontaneous neural activity emanating from fetal eyes prior to the onset of vision play a role in the development or maintenance of the visual cortex (see Katz & Shatz, 1996).

Fourth, several studies have shown that early music training influences the organization of human auditory cortex (see Münte, Altenmüller, & Jänke, 2002). In particular, fMRI studies have shown that early musical training tends to expand the area of auditory cortex that responds to complex musical tones, and behavioral studies have shown that early musical training leads to the development of *absolute pitch* (the ability to identify the pitch of any tone).

The Evolutionary Perspective

Cognitive Neuroscience

7·4
Neuroplasticity in Adults

If this book were a road trip that you and I were taking together, at this point, the following highway sign would appear: SLOW, IMPORTANT VIEWPOINT AHEAD. You see, you are about to encounter an idea that is currently one of the most influential in all of neuroscience, one that is changing how neuroscientists are thinking about the human brain.

Until the early 1990s, neuroplasticity was thought to be restricted to the brain's developmental period. Mature brains were considered to be set in their ways, incapable of substantial reorganization. Now, it is apparent that mature brains are also plastic. It has become clear that the mature brain is not a static organ but is continually changing and adapting. Discovering the nature of these changes is currently a top priority of neuroscientific research (see Kolb, Gibb, & Robinson, 2003). Many lines of research are contributing to neuroscientists' excitement about adult neuroplasticity. For now, consider the following two. You will encounter more in the next two chapters.

Neurogenesis in Adult Mammals

When I was a student, I learned two important principles of brain development. The first I learned through experience: The human brain starts to function in the womb and never stops working until one stands up to speak in public. The second I learned in a course on brain development: **Neurogenesis** (the growth of new neurons) does not occur in adults. The first principle appears to be fundamentally correct, at least when applied to me, but the second has been proved to be wrong (see Kempermann & Gage, 1999; Ormerod & Galea, 2001a).

Prior to the early 1980s, all neurons were thought to be created during early stages of development. Accordingly, subsequent brain development was seen as a downhill slope: Neurons continually die throughout a person's life, and it was assumed that the lost cells are never replaced by new ones. Although researchers began to chip away at this misconception in the early 1980s, it persisted until recently as one of the central principles of neurodevelopment.

The first serious challenge to the assumption that neurogenesis is restricted to early stages of development came in the early 1980s, with the discovery of the

growth of new neurons in the brains of adult birds. Nottebohm and colleagues (e.g., Goldman & Nottebohm, 1983) found that brain structures involved in singing begin to grow in songbirds just before each mating season and that this growth results from an increase in the number of neurons. This finding stimulated the re-examination of earlier unconfirmed claims that new neurons are created in the adult rat hippocampus.

Then, in the 1990s, researchers, armed with newly developed immunohisto-chemical markers that had a selective affinity for recently created cells, convincingly showed that neurogenesis does indeed occur in the hippocampus of the adult rat (Cameron et al., 1993)—see Figure 7.10. And shortly thereafter, it was discovered that new neurons are also continually added to adult rat olfactory bulbs (Gould et al., 1999; Kornack & Rakic, 2001).

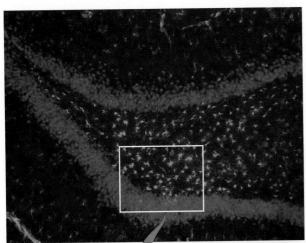

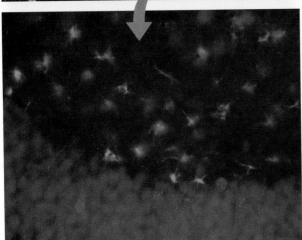

Adult neurogenesis. The top panel shows new cells in the dentate gyrus of the hippocampus—the cell bodies of neurons are stained blue, mature glial cells are stained green, and new cells are stained red. The bottom panel shows the new cells from the top panel under higher magnification, which makes it apparent that the new cells have taken up both blue and red stain and are thus new neurons.

(Courtesy of my friends Carl Ernst and Brian Christie, Department of Psychology, University of British Columbia.)

Figure 7.10

At first, reports of adult neurogenesis were not embraced by a generation of neuroscientists who had been trained to think of the adult brain as fixed, but acceptance grew as confirmatory findings accumulated. Particularly influential were the findings that new neurons are added to the hip-pocampi (plural of *hippocampus*) of primates (e.g., Kornack & Rakic, 1999), including humans (Erikkson et al., 1998), and that the number of new neurons added to the adult hip-pocampus is substantial, an estimated 2,000 per hour (West, Slomianka, & Gunderson, 1991).

Where do the neurons created in adult neurogenesis come from? *Adult neural stem cells* are created in certain parts of the neural layer adjacent to the lining of the lateral ventricles (Momma, Johansson, & Frisén, 2000; Morshead & van der Kooy, 2001); from there, they migrate to the ol-factory bulbs. In contrast, new hippocampal cells appear to be created near their final location.

Substantial adult neurogenesis occurs in mammalian hippocampi and olfactory bulbs, but what about other brain structures? This question is currently under inten-sive investigation, but it is still too early to tell what the evidence is going to show. There has been one report of adult neurogenesis in the neocortex of monkeys (Gould et al., 1999), but two other research teams failed to repli-cate those results (Koketsu et al., 2003; Kornack & Rakic, 2001), suggesting that the original claim may have been an error. On the other hand, there have been recent reports of neurogenesis in the neocortex (Dayer et al., 2005) and underlying white matter (Takemura, 2005) of adult rats.

Many lines of research are focused on adult neurogen-esis, and you will learn about some of these in later chap-ters. One particularly promising line began with a study of the effects on adult rodents of living in enriched environ-ments. It turned out that adult rats living in enriched en-vironments (environments that include toys, running wheels, and other rats) produced 60% more new hip-pocampal neurons than did adult rats living in nonenriched environments (Kempermann & Gage, 1999). However, be-fore you start enriching your apartment or dorm room, you should be aware that the observed positive effect on neurogenesis in the adult rat hippocampus is not a direct consequence of the enriched environments. The effect de-pends largely, if not entirely, on the increases in exercise that typically occur in enriched environments (Farmer et al., 2004; Van Praag et al., 1999). This finding has a provocative implication: In view of the fact that the hippocampus is involved in some kinds of memory (see Duffy et al., 2001; Rhodes et al., 2002), perhaps exercise can be used as a treatment for human memory problems (Cottman & Berchtold, 2002).

Effects of Experience on the Reorganization of the Adult Cortex

I said that we would consider two current lines of research on adult neuroplasticity. You have just learned about the research on adult neurogenesis; the second line of research focuses on the effects of experience on the reorganization of adult cortex (see Elbert & Rockstroh, 2004).

Surprisingly, experience in adulthood can lead to reorganization of sensory and motor cortical maps (e.g., Jones, 2000; Sanes & Donoghue, 2000). For example, Mühlnickel and colleagues (1998) found that *tinnitus* (ringing in the ears) produces a major reorganization of primary auditory cortex, and Elbert and colleagues (1995) showed that adult musicians who play stringed instruments that are fingered with the left hand (e.g., violin) have an enlarged hand-representation area in their right somatosensory cortex. Evidence suggests that it is skill training rather than strength or endurance training that leads to reorganization of the motor cortex (Remple et al., 2001).

In a more controlled demonstration of the ability of experience to reorganize the adult human brain, healthy human volunteers received 1 hour of tactile experience on each of 20 days (Braun et al., 2000). For the 20 hours, the subjects experienced patterns of touch simultaneously delivered to the tips of their left thumb and left little finger. There were two conditions: In one, the subjects sat passively while the stimuli were delivered; in the other, the subjects were required to identify the patterns. The areas of the right somatosensory cortex activated by stimulation of the tip of either the left thumb or the left little finger were measured by high-resolution EEG evoked potentials. The results differed with the experimental condition. In the passive condition, the areas of somatosensory cortex responding to touches of the thumb and little finger moved closer together as the experiment progressed. In the active identification condition, the areas of somatosensory cortex responding to touches of the thumb and little finger moved farther apart. Remember that both these changes occurred in just 20 hours.

The discovery of adult neuroplasticity is changing the way that we humans think about ourselves. More importantly for those with brain disorders, it has suggested some promising new treatment options. You will learn about these in the next chapter.

7·5
Disorders of Neurodevelopment: Autism and Williams Syndrome

I have tried to keep this chapter focused on fundamentals rather than on details. Still, I hope you have managed to get a sense of the incredible complexity of neurodevelopment. Like all complex processes, neurodevelopment is easily thrown off track; and, unfortunately, one tiny screw-up can have far-reaching and tragic consequences because it can disrupt all subsequent stages. This fact will become apparent to you in this, the final, section of the chapter, which focuses on two disorders of neurodevelopment: autism and Williams syndrome.

Autism

Autism is a complex neurodevelopmental disorder that typically occurs in about 6 of every 1,000 individuals. It usually becomes apparent before the age of 3 and changes little thereafter (Happé & Frith, 1996). The diagnosis of autism is based on the presence of three core symptoms: (1) a reduced ability to interpret the emotions and intentions of others (see Adolphs, Sears, & Piven, 2001); (2) a reduced capacity for social interaction and communication; and (3) a preoccupation with a single subject or activity (Pierce & Courchesne, 2001). Although this triad of symptoms defines the disorder, other signs are commonly, but not universally, associated with it. For example, about 75% of those with autism are male, about 75% suffer from mental retardation, and about 35% suffer from epilepsy. Most people with autism have difficulty mimicking the gestures of others (Williams et al., 2001).

Autism is a difficult disorder to treat. Intensive behavioral therapy can improve the lives of some individuals, but it is rarely possible for a person with autism to live independently, even if he or she represents one of those few cases in which intelligence is reasonably normal. How is a person who has very little appreciation for the feelings and motivations of others, who has difficulty communicating, who compulsively bangs his head against the wall, and who is obsessed by bus schedules going to function in society?

Autism Is a Heterogeneous Disorder.   Although many scientists who study autism do so in an effort to help those who have the disorder, many are interested in it because of one of its major features—its heterogeneity (Happé & Frith, 1996). In autism, some functions are severely impaired, whereas others are normal or even superior. It is these "spotty" patterns of neuropsychological deficits that have the most potential to teach us about the neural bases of psychological functions.

Unfortunately, not all autistic patients display the same pattern of deficits and spared abilities, which greatly complicates the study of this disorder. This suggests that autism has no single cause and that it is best regarded as a group of related disorders (Eigsti & Shapiro, 2004; Trottier, Srivastava, & Walker, 1999).

Despite the heterogeneity of autism, there are some common patterns. For example, most autistic individuals—even those who are severely retarded—display the following preserved abilities: rote memory, the ability to complete jigsaw puzzles, musical ability, and artistic ability.

Even within the single category of speech disability, there is often a heterogeneous pattern of deficits. Many autistic individuals have sizable vocabularies, are good spellers, and can read aloud even text that they do not understand. However, the same individuals are often unable to use intonation to communicate emotion, to coordinate eye gaze and facial expression with speech, and to speak metaphorically. About a quarter of autistic individuals have little or no language ability.

Autistic Savants.   Perhaps the single most remarkable aspect of autism is the tendency for autistic individuals to be savants. **Savants** are intellectually handicapped individuals who nevertheless display amazing and specific cognitive or artistic abilities. About 1 in 10 autistic individuals display savant abilities. Savant abilities can take many forms, but common among these rare individuals are feats of memory, naming the day of the week for any future or past date, identifying prime numbers (any number divisible only by itself and 1), drawing, and playing musical instruments (see Bonnel et al., 2003).

Savant abilities may be the most puzzling phenomena in all of neuroscience. Consider the following cases (Ramachandran & Blakeslee, 1998; Sacks, 1985).

Some Examples of Amazing Savant Abilities

Nadia suffered from severe autism; her IQ was between 60 and 70. She could barely put two words together. Yet, by the time she reached the age of 6, she could draw gallery-quality pictures of people, animals, and other complex subjects.

One savant could tell the time of day to the exact second without ever referring to his watch. Even when he was asleep, he would mumble the correct time.

Another savant could specify the width of objects. For example, she was asked the width of a rock that lay on the ground about 20 feet away. "Exactly two feet, eleven and three-quarter inches," she replied. She was right; indeed, she was always right.

Tom was a blind, autistic 13-year-old who could not tie his own shoes. He had never had any musical training, but he could play the most difficult piano piece after hearing it just once, even if he was playing with his back to the piano. Once, he played one song with one hand and a second with the other, while singing a third.

One pair of autistic twins had difficulty doing simple addition and subtraction and could not even comprehend multiplication and division. Yet, if given any date in the last or next 40,000 years, they could specify the day of the week that it would fall on. Their short-term memory for digits was amazing: They were able to correctly repeat a list of 300 digits after hearing it only once. A box of matches fell on the floor: "One hundred and eleven," they immediately cried out together. There were 111.

These and many other well-documented savant cases remain a mystery. Savant abilities do not develop through rote learning or practice; they seem to emerge spontaneously. People with savant abilities seem naturally to recognize implicit patterns and relations that escape others. We can only regard these cases with wonder and speculate that somehow damage to certain parts of their brains has led to compensatory overdevelopment in other parts. For example, it has been suggested that savant abilities are created when damage to the left hemisphere triggers compensatory functional improvement in the right hemisphere (Treffert & Wallace, 2002).

Neural Basis of Autism. Two lines of research show that genetic factors influence the development of autism (see Rodier, 2000). First, autism has been found to run in families; various studies have shown that siblings of people with autism have about a 5% chance of being diagnosed with the disorder. This is well above the rate in the general population, but well below the 50% chance that would be expected if autism were caused solely by a single dominant gene or the 25% chance that would be expected if autism were caused solely by a single recessive gene. Second, several studies have shown that the development of autism is highly related in monozygotic twins; if one twin is diagnosed as autistic, the other has a 60% chance of receiving the same diagnosis. Although this high correlation shows that autism has a genetic basis, it also shows that it is not entirely genetic. If it were, the concordance rate would be 100% in individuals with identical genes. Together, these two lines of research suggest that autism is triggered by several genes interacting with the environment (see Zoghbi, 2003).

Given the patient-to-patient variability of both the symptoms and the genetics of autism, it is not surprising that the brain damage associated with the disorder is also variable. Damage has been most commonly observed in the cerebellum and related parts of the brain, but it generally tends to be widespread throughout the brain (see Machado et al., 2003; Müller et al., 2001; Müller et al., 2003).

Given the diffuse and variable pattern of autism-related brain damage, it is clear that any line of research focusing on one area of the brain will not provide ultimate answers about the disorder. Nevertheless, the following line of experiments was a promising beginning. Strömland and colleagues (1994) discovered that a pregnant woman's taking *thalidomide*, the morning-sickness pill that caused an epidemic of birth defects in the 1960s, greatly increased the probability that the child would be born with autism. Because a prescription for thalidomide was restricted to the early weeks of pregnancy, this relationship suggests that autism is created by a neurodevelopmental error occurring at this time.

A boy with autism shows the typical anomalies of ear structure.

Figure 7.11

Knowing when something happens provides *embryologists* (scientists who study embryos) with important clues. Knowing that thalidomide-induced autism develops in the first few weeks of embryological development has focused attention on the motor neurons of the cranial nerves that control the face, mouth, and eyes, because few neurons other than these are formed by the fourth week. Indeed, it was shown that both thalidomide-induced and typical autism are associated with various deficits in face, mouth, and eye control (e.g., Strömland et al., 1994).

Another clue came from analysis of the physical appearance of individuals with autism—whether or not the disorder was thalidomide-induced. Their appearance is typically normal; however, there are a few minor anomalies of ear structure—square shape, tops flopped over—and placement—positioned too low on the head, rotated slightly backward (see Figure 7.11). This evidence suggested that autism is triggered by an abnormal event occurring between 20 and 24 days after conception, when the ears are developing. Remarkably, most of the cases of thalidomide-induced autism did not display the stunted and misshapen limbs typical of most cases of thalidomide-induced birth defects; they did, however, display anomalies of external ear structure.

Rodier (2000) had the opportunity to conduct an autopsy examination of the brain of an autistic woman, and influenced by the research on thalidomide-induced autism, she focused her examination on the brain stem. She made a remarkable finding: The woman's brain stem was shortened, as if a slice had failed to develop. Nuclei in the slice were either underdeveloped (facial nucleus) or totally missing (superior olive) (see Figure 7.12).

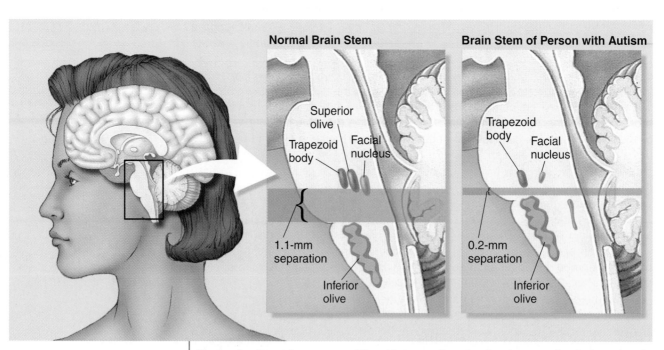

The brain stem of a woman with autism was found to be shortened, missing a band of tissue at the junction of the pons and the medulla. (Adapted from Rodier, 2000.)

Figure 7.12

As Rodier examined the shortened brain stem of the autistic woman, she experienced a "powerful shock of recognition." She had seen this pattern before. From the stacks of papers on her office floor, she retrieved an article about the brains of knockout mice, engineered to lack the expression of a gene known as *Hoxa 1*. These mice exhibited shortening of the brain stem, an underdeveloped facial nucleus, and no superior olive. Moreover, the mice had ear malformations and abnormal eye movements. Rodier (2000) subsequently discovered that some people have a variant form of Hoxa 1, which is located on chromosome 7, and that the variant form is prevalent in people with autism—it is found in 40% of autistic persons, compared with 20% of the general population.

Let's put these findings in perspective. First, it is unlikely that the developmental distortions in the midbrain are responsible for all, or even most, of the symptoms of autism. Second, the Hoxa 1 gene has been implicated in only some cases of autism.

The Evolutionary Perspective

Thinking Clearly

Williams Syndrome

Williams syndrome, like autism, is a neurodevelopmental disorder associated with mental retardation and a strikingly uneven pattern of abilities and disabilities. Williams syndrome occurs in approximately 1 of every 20,000 births (see Rourke et al., 2002).

In contrast to the withdrawn, emotionally insensitive, uncommunicative person with autism, people with Williams syndrome are sociable, empathetic, and talkative. It is their language abilities that have attracted the most attention. Although they display a delay in language development and language deficits in adulthood (Bishop, 1999; Paterson et al., 1999), their language skills are remarkable considering their characteristically poor IQs—which average around 60. For example, when asked about his infantile scribble on a piece of paper, one severely retarded Williams teenager, with an IQ of 49, identified it as an elephant and offered the following verbal commentary (Bellugi et al., 1999):

Clinical Implications

> And what an elephant is it is one of the animals. And what the elephant does, it lives in the jungle. It can also live in the zoo. And what it has, it has long gray ears, fan ears, ears that can blow in the wind. It has a long trunk that can pick grass, or pick up hay . . . if they're in a bad mood it can be terrible. . . . If the elephant gets mad it could stomp; it could charge. Sometimes elephants can charge. They have long tusks. You don't want an elephant as a pet. You want a cat or a dog or a bird. . . . (p. 199)

The remarkable language skills of Williams children have also been demonstrated by objective tests (Bellugi et al., 1999). For example, in one test, Williams children were asked to name as many animals as they could in 60 seconds. Answers included koala, yak, ibex, condor, chihuahua, brontosaurus, and hippopotamus. When asked to look at a picture and tell a story about it, Williams children often produced an animated narrative. As they told the story, the children altered the pitch, volume, rhythm, and vocabulary of their speech to engage the audience. Sadly, the verbal and social skills of these children often lead teachers to overestimate their cognitive abilities, and thus they do not always receive the extra academic support they need.

Williams people have other cognitive strengths, several of which involve music (Lennoff et al., 1997). Although most cannot learn to read music, some have perfect or near-perfect pitch and an uncanny sense of rhythm. Many retain melodies for years, and some are professional musicians. As a group, Williams people show more interest in, and emotional reaction to, music than does the general population. One Williams child said, "Music is my favorite way of thinking." Yet another cognitive strength of Williams people is their remarkable ability to recognize faces.

Like any group of individuals with an average IQ of 60, Williams people display many severe cognitive deficits. Against this background, their strengths tend to stand out. However, there is one class of cognitive problems that is noteworthy because it is even more severe in them than it is in other people with similar IQs: They have a profound impairment in spatial cognition. For example, they have great difficulty remembering the location of a few blocks placed on a test board, their space-related speech is poor, and their ability to draw objects is almost nonexistent (Jordan et al., 2002).

Williams syndrome is also associated with a variety of health problems, including several involving the heart. Ironically, the study of one of these disorders in people who did not have the syndrome led to the identification of a major genetic factor in the syndrome. This heart disorder was found to result from a mutation in a gene on chromosome 7 that controls the synthesis of *elastin*, a protein that imparts elasticity to many organs and tissues. Aware that the same cardiac problem is prevalent in Williams people, investigators assessed the status of this gene in that group. Remarkably, they found that the gene on one of the two copies of chromosome 7 was absent in 95% of Williams people. Other genes were missing as well; through an accident of reproduction, an entire region of chromosome 7 had been deleted. Once the other genes in this region have been identified and their functions determined, there will be a much fuller understanding of the etiology of Williams syndrome.

In general, Williams people display gross underdevelopment of occipital and parietal cortex, which could account for their poor spatial abilities; normal frontal and temporal cortex, which could account for their preserved speech; and abnormalities in the limbic system, which could account for their heightened friendliness (see Bellugi et al., 1999).

You may have unknowingly encountered stories of Williams people. Many cultures feature tales involving magical little people: pixies, elves, leprechauns, etc. Remarkably, descriptions and drawings of these creatures portray them as virtually identical to Williams people, who are often described as elfin in appearance. Williams people tend to be short, and they have small upturned noses, oval ears, broad mouths with full lips, puffy eyes, and small chins (see Figure 7.13). Accordingly, many believe that folk tales about elves may have originally been based on Williams people. Even the typical behavioral characteristics of elves—engaging storytellers, talented musicians, loving, trusting, and sensitive to the feelings of others—match those of Williams people.

Williams people are characterized by their elfin appearance.

Figure 7.13

7.1 Phases of Neurodevelopment

Aggregation (p. 209)
Apoptosis (p. 212)
Cell-adhesion molecules (CAMs) (p. 209)
Chemoaffinity hypothesis (p. 210)
Chemoattractants (p. 209)
Chemorepellants (p. 209)
Fasciculation (p. 210)
Glia-mediated migration (p. 208)
Growth cone (p. 209)
Inside-out pattern (p. 209)
Migration (p. 207)
Multipotent (p. 206)
Necrosis (p. 212)
Nerve growth factor (NGF) (p. 212)
Neural plate (p. 206)
Neural proliferation (p. 207)
Neural tube (p. 207)
Neurotrophins (p. 212)
Optic tectum (p. 209)
Pioneer growth cones (p. 210)

Radial glial cells (p. 208)
Radial migration (p. 207)
Retinal ganglion cells (p. 209)
Somal translocation (p. 207)
Stem cells (p. 206)
Synaptogenesis (p. 212)
Tangential migration (p. 207)
Topographic gradient hypothesis (p. 211)
Totipotent (p. 206)
Ventricular zone (p. 207)

7.2 Postnatal Cerebral Development in Human Infants

Perseveration (p. 215)
Prefrontal cortex (p. 213)

7.4 Neuroplasticity in Adults

Neurogenesis (p. 219)

7.5 Disorders of Neurodevelopment: Autism and Williams Syndrome

Autism (p. 222)
Savants (p. 222)
Williams syndrome (p. 225)

ON THE CD

Studying for an exam? Get some help from the electronic flash cards of the key terms and the practice tests for this chapter.

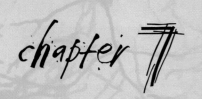

Development of the Nervous System
From Fertilized Egg to You

This chapter traced the development of the nervous system from fertilized egg to adulthood. It also examined what can happen when programs of neurodevelopment go wrong.

Phases of Neurodevelopment

The development of the nervous system begins with the appearance of the neural plate on the dorsal surface of the embryo. Once the neural plate appears, neurons begin to proliferate, migrate to their correct locations, aggregate into various neural structures, grow axons and dendrites, and establish synaptic connections. Paradoxically, the final stage of neurodevelopment is a period of neuron death, during which many neurons die and synapses are rearranged. (Pages 206–213)

Figure 7.3

Somal Translocation (Radial or Tangential)

Glia-Mediated Migration (Radial Only)

(Radial glial cells)

Postnatal Cerebral Development in Human Infants

The human brain continues to go through major developmental changes after birth. For example, the human brain continues to increase in size until after puberty, as a consequence of synaptogenesis, myelination, and increased dendritic branching. The prefrontal cortex is the last part of the human brain, to develop along with the abilities controlled by it. (Pages 213–216)

Figure 7.8

1 To test for a perseverative reaching error in infants, they are first shown a toy being placed behind one of two screens.

2 Infants older than 7 months usually look behind the correct screen. To conduct a perseveration test, this trial is repeated several times, each time with the toy behind the same screen.

3 Then, on the test trial, the infant is shown the toy being placed behind the other screen.

4 Infants between 7 and 12 months tend to reach for the incorrect screen, which had been correct on previous trials.

Effects of Experience on the Early Development, Maintenance, and Reorganization of Neural Circuits

The development of the brain is greatly influenced by experience. Many studies have shown that early experience during the sensitive period can influence the formation of topographic cortical sensory maps. A more dramatic demonstration of the role of experience in fostering normal development is the case of Genie. (Pages 217–219)

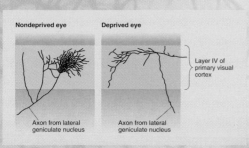

Figure 7.9

Nondeprived eye

Deprived eye

Layer IV of primary visual cortex

Axon from lateral geniculate nucleus

Axon from lateral geniculate nucleus

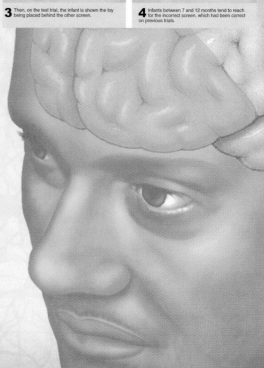

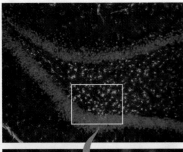

Neuroplasticity in Adults

Neuroplasticity was once believed to be limited to early stages of development. It is now clear, however, that the brain continues to develop and change throughout life. Most noteworthy is the discovery that many new neurons are added each day to the hippocampi and olfactory bulbs of adult mammals. The function of these new neurons is still unknown.
(Pages 219–221)

Disorders of Neurodevelopment: Autism and Williams Syndrome

Some neurological disorders happen when programs of neurodevelopment go wrong. Two such disorders are autism and Williams syndrome. In contrast to the

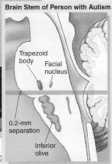

Figure 7.17

Brain Stem of Person with Autism

Trapezoid body
Facial nucleus

0.2-mm separation

Inferior olive

withdrawn and uncommunicative people who have autism, people with Williams syndrome are sociable and talkative. However, they suffer from severe cognitive deficits, which tend to be spotty—that is, some abilities tend to be severely disrupted, but others are not.
(Pages 221–226)

Themes Revisited

The clinical implications and evolutionary perspective themes were heavily emphasized in this chapter. One of the best ways to understand the principles of normal neurodevelopment is to consider what happens when it goes wrong: The clinical theme was emphasized in the tragic case of Genie and in the discussions of autism and Williams syndrome. The evolutionary perspective theme was frequently emphasized because much of the information that we have about normal human neurodevelopment and human neurodevelopmental disorders has come from studying other species.

The thinking-clearly-about-biopsychology tag appeared infrequently in this chapter, because the theme was pervasive. This tag highlighted discussions that made two general points. First, neurodevelopment always proceeds from gene–experience interactions rather than from a sum of so much genetics and so much experience. Second, it is important not to overreact to the impressive recent advances in the study of neurodevelopment: Important steps have been taken, but we are still a long way from a complete understanding of how the nervous system develops.

The cognitive neuroscience theme came up infrequently in this chapter. Only recently has the power of brain-imaging techniques been brought to bear on the study of neurodevelopment and neurodevelopmental disorders

Think about It

1. What does the case of Genie teach us about normal development?
2. Neuron death is a necessary stage in neurodevelopment. Discuss.
3. Even the adult brain displays plasticity. What do you think is the evolutionary significance of this ability?
4. Discuss the evolutionary significance of the slow development of the human brain.
5. Autism and Williams syndrome are opposites in several ways; thus, they can be fruitfully studied together. Discuss.

chapter 8

Brain Damage and Neuroplasticity
Can the Brain Recover from Damage?

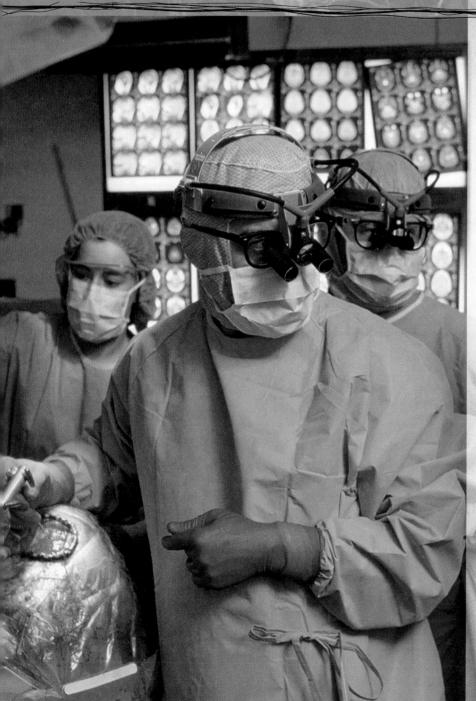

The study of human brain damage serves two purposes: It increases our understanding of the healthy brain, and it serves as a basis for the development of new treatments. The first three sections of this chapter focus on brain damage itself. The last two sections continue the neuroplasticity theme that was introduced in Chapter 7: The fourth section focuses on the recovery and reorganization of the brain after damage, and the fifth discusses exciting new neuroplasticity-promoting treatments. But first, the ironic case of Professor P. relates the personal tragedy of brain damage.

The Ironic Case of Professor P.

One night Professor P. sat at his desk staring at a drawing of the cranial nerves, much like the one in Appendix III of this book. As he mulled over the location and function of each cranial nerve (see Appendix IV), the painful truth became impossible for him to deny. The irony of the situation was that Professor P. was a neuroscientist, all too familiar with what he was experiencing.

His symptoms started subtly, with slight deficits in balance. He probably wouldn't have even noticed them except that his experience as a mountaineer had taught him to pay attention to such things. Professor P. chalked these occasional lurches up to aging—after all, he thought to himself, he was past his prime, and things like this happen. Similarly, his doctor didn't seem to think that it was a problem worth looking into, but Professor P. monitored his symptoms carefully nevertheless. Three years later, his balance problems still unabated, Professor P. really started to worry. He was trying to talk with a colleague on the phone but was not having much success because of what he thought was a bad connection. Then, he changed the phone to his other ear, and all of a sudden, the faint voice on the other end became louder. He tried this switch several times over the ensuing days, and the conclusion became inescapable: Professor P. was going deaf in his right ear.

Professor P. immediately made an appointment with his doctor, who referred him to a specialist. After a cursory and poorly controlled hearing test, the specialist gave him good news. "You're fine, Professor P.; lots of people experience hearing loss when they reach middle age, and your problems are not serious enough to worry about." To this day, Professor P. regrets that he did not insist on a second opinion; his problem would have been so much easier to deal with at that stage.

It was about a year later that Professor P. sat staring at the illustration of the cranial nerves. By then he had begun to experience numbness on the right side of his mouth; he was having minor problems swallowing; and his right tear ducts were not releasing enough tears. There he sat staring at the point where the auditory and vestibular nerves come together to form cranial nerve VIII (the auditory-vestibular nerve). He knew it was there, and he knew that it was large enough to be affecting cranial nerves V through X as well, but he didn't know what it was: a tumor, a stroke, an angioma, an infection? Was he going to die? Was his death going to be terrible and lingering as his brain and intellect gradually deteriorated?

He didn't make an appointment with his doctor right away. A friend of his was conducting a brain MRI study, and Professor P. volunteered to be a control subject, knowing that his problem would show up on the scan. It did: a large tumor sitting, as predicted, on the right cranial nerve VIII.

Then, MRI in hand, Professor P. went back to his doctor, who referred him to a neurologist, who in turn referred him to a neurosurgeon. Several stressful weeks later, Professor P. found himself on life support in the intensive care unit of his local hospital, hands tied to the bed and tubes emanating seemingly from every part of his body. You see, the tumor was so convoluted that it took 6 hours to remove; and during the 6 hours that

Clinical Implications

ON THE CD

Visit the module *My Tumor and Welcome To It*. Pinel, relaxing in his own garden, describes his struggle with a brain tumor.

Professor P.' s brain was exposed, air entered his circulatory system, and he developed pneumonia. Near death and hallucinating from the morphine, Professor P. thought he heard his wife, Maggie, calling for help and tried to go to her assistance: That is why he was tied down. One gentle morphine-steeped professor was no match for five burly nurses intent on saving his life.

Professor P.' s auditory-vestibular nerve was transected during his surgery, which has left him permanently deaf and without vestibular function on the right side. He was also left with partial hemifacial paralysis, including serious blinking and tearing problems, but these facial symptoms have largely cleared up.

Professor P. has now returned to his students, his research, and his writing, hoping that the tumor was completely removed and that he will not have to endure another surgery. Indeed, at the very moment that I am writing these words, Professor P. is working on Chapter 8 of his new textbook. . . . If it has not yet occurred to you, I am Professor P.

8.1 Causes of Brain Damage

Clinical Implications

This section provides an introduction to six causes of brain damage: brain tumors, cerebrovascular disorders, closed-head injuries, infections of the brain, neurotoxins, and genetic factors. It concludes with a discussion of programmed cell death, which mediates many forms of brain damage.

Brain Tumors

A **tumor**, or **neoplasm** (literally, "new growth"), is a mass of cells that grows independently of the rest of the body (see Wechsler-Reya & Scott, 2001). In other words, it is a cancer.

About 20% of tumors found in the human brain are **meningiomas** (see Figure 8.1)—tumors that grow between the *meninges*, the three membranes that cover the central nervous system. All meningiomas are **encapsulated tumors**—tumors that grow within their own membrane. As a result, they are particularly easy to identify on a CT scan, they can influence the function of the brain only by the pressure they exert on surrounding tissue, and they are almost always **benign tumors**—tumors that are surgically removable with little risk of further growth in the body (see Grimson et al., 1999). However, even benign tumors can leave behind residual damage once removed.

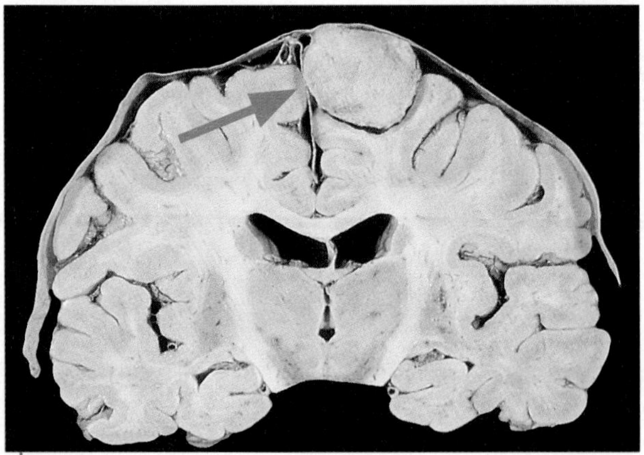

A meningioma.

(Courtesy of Kenneth Berry, Head of Neuropathology, Vancouver General Hospital.)

Figure 8.1

Unfortunately, encapsulation is the exception rather than the rule when it comes to brain tumors. Aside from meningiomas, most brain tumors are infiltrating. **Infiltrating tumors** are those that grow diffusely through surrounding tissue. As a result, they are usually **malignant tumors**; it is difficult to remove or destroy them completely, and any cancerous tissue that remains after surgery continues to grow.

About 10% of brain tumors do not originate in the brain. They grow from infiltrating tumor fragments carried to the brain by the bloodstream from some other part of the body. (The brain is a particularly fertile ground for tumor growth.) These tumors are called **metastatic tumors**; *metastasis* refers to the transmission of disease from one organ to another. Most metastatic brain tumors originate as cancers

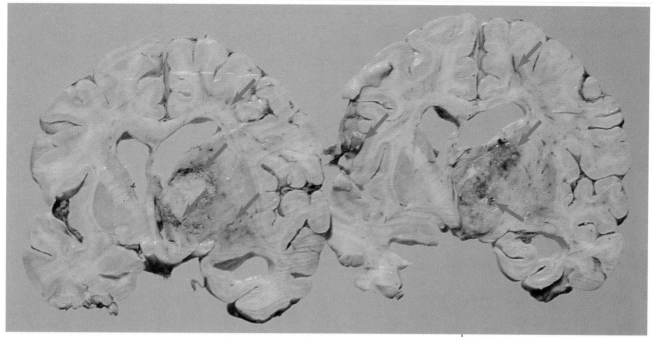

Multiple metastatic brain tumors. The arrows indicate some of the more advanced areas of metastatic tumor development.

Figure 8.2

of the lungs. Obviously, the chance of recovering from a cancer that has already attacked two or more separate sites is slim at best. Figure 8.2 illustrates the ravages of metastasis.

Fortunately, my tumor was encapsulated. Figure 8.3 is an MRI scan of my *acoustic neuroma* (an encapsulated tumor located on the 8th cranial nerve at the point where it enters the brain), the very same scan that I took to my doctor.

Cerebrovascular Disorders

Strokes are sudden-onset cerebrovascular disorders that cause brain damage. There are two major types of strokes: those resulting from cerebral hemorrhage and those resulting from cerebral ischemia (pronounced "iss-KEEM-ee-a"). In the United States, stroke is the third leading cause of death and the most common cause of adult disability (Janardhan & Qureshi, 2004). Common consequences of stroke are amnesia, aphasia (language difficulties), paralysis, and coma.

Cerebral Hemorrhage. **Cerebral hemorrhage** (bleeding in the brain) occurs when a cerebral blood vessel ruptures and blood seeps into the surrounding neural tissue and damages it. Bursting aneurysms are a common cause of intracerebral hemorrhage. An **aneurysm** is a pathological balloonlike dilation that forms in the wall of a blood vessel at a point where the elasticity of the vessel wall is defective. Aneurysms can be **congenital** (present at birth) or can result from exposure to vascular poisons or infection (see Kalaria, 2001). Individuals who have aneurysms should make every effort to avoid high blood pressure.

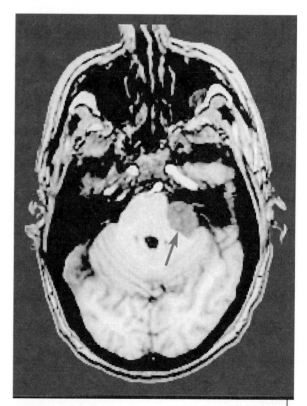

An MRI of Professor P.' s brain tumor. The arrow indicates the tumor.

Figure 8.3

Cerebral Ischemia. Cerebral ischemia is a disruption of the blood supply to an area of the brain. The three main causes of cerebral ischemia are thrombosis, embolism, and arteriosclerosis. In **thrombosis**, a plug called a *thrombus* is formed and blocks blood flow at the site of its formation. A thrombus may be composed of a blood clot, fat, oil, an air bubble, tumor cells, or any combination thereof. **Embolism** is similar except that the plug, called an *embolus* in this case, is carried by the blood from a larger vessel, where it was formed, to a smaller one, where it becomes lodged; in essence, an embolus is just a thrombus that has taken a trip. In **arteriosclerosis**, the walls of blood vessels thicken and the channels narrow, usually as the result of fat deposits; this narrowing can eventually lead to complete blockage of the blood vessels (Libby, 2002). The *angiogram* in Figure 8.4 illustrates partial blockage of one carotid artery.

Paradoxically, some of the brain's own neurotransmitters play a key role in the development of the damage produced by cerebral ischemia (Wahlgren & Ahmed, 2004). Much of the brain damage associated with stroke is a consequence of excessive release of excitatory amino acid neurotransmitters, in particular **glutamate**, the brain's most prevalent excitatory neurotransmitter.

Here is how this mechanism is thought to work (see Dirnagl, Iadecola, & Moskowitz, 1999). After a blood vessel becomes blocked, many of the blood-deprived neurons become overactive and release excessive quantities of glutamate. The glutamate in turn overactivates glutamate receptors in the membranes of postsynaptic neurons; the glutamate receptors that are most involved in this reaction are the **NMDA (N-methyl-D-aspartate) receptors**. As a result, large numbers of sodium and calcium ions enter the postsynaptic neurons.

The excessive internal concentrations of sodium and calcium ions affect the postsynaptic neurons in two ways: They trigger the release of excessive amounts of glutamate from them, thus spreading the toxic cascade to yet other neurons; and they trigger a sequence of internal reactions that ultimately kill the postsynaptic neurons. (See Figure 8.5.)

Ischemia-induced brain damage has three important properties (Krieglstein, 1997). First, it takes a while to develop. Soon after a temporary cerebral ischemic episode, say, one that is 10 minutes in duration, there usually is little or no evidence of brain damage; however, substantial neuron loss can often be detected a day or two later. Second, ischemia-induced brain damage does not occur equally in all parts of the brain; particularly susceptible are neurons in certain areas of the hippocampus (Ohtaki et al., 2003). Third, the mechanisms of ischemia-induced damage vary somewhat from structure to structure within the brain.

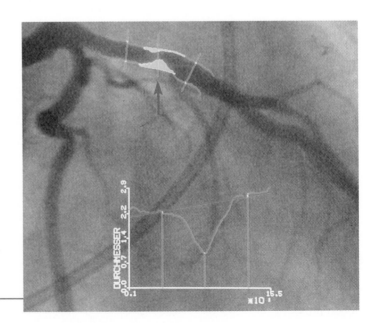

An angiogram that illustrates narrowing of the carotid artery (see arrow), the main pathway of blood to the brain. Compare this angiogram with the normal angiogram in Figure 3.19 on page 89.

Figure 8.4

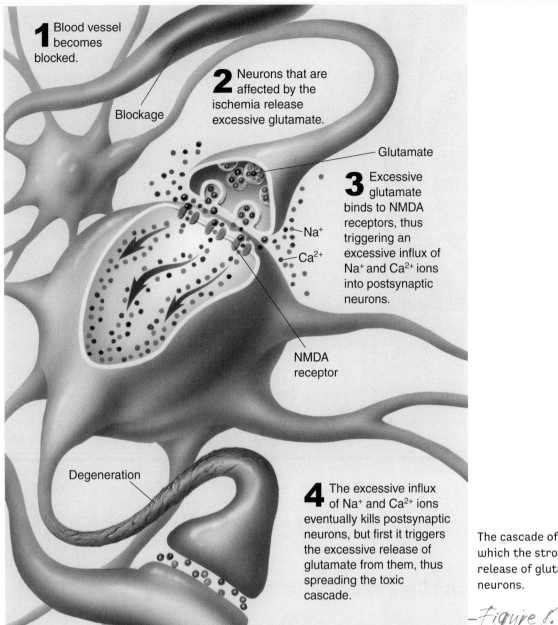

1 Blood vessel becomes blocked.

Blockage

2 Neurons that are affected by the ischemia release excessive glutamate.

Glutamate

3 Excessive glutamate binds to NMDA receptors, thus triggering an excessive influx of Na⁺ and Ca²⁺ ions into postsynaptic neurons.

Na^+

Ca^{2+}

NMDA receptor

Degeneration

4 The excessive influx of Na⁺ and Ca²⁺ ions eventually kills postsynaptic neurons, but first it triggers the excessive release of glutamate from them, thus spreading the toxic cascade.

The cascade of events by which the stroke-induced release of glutamate kills neurons.

Figure 8.5

An exciting implication of the discovery that excessive glutamate release causes much of the brain damage associated with stroke is the possibility of preventing stroke-related brain damage by blocking the glutaminergic cascade. The search is on for a glutamate antagonist that is effective and safe for use in human stroke victims (Leker & Shohami, 2002; Lo, Dalkara, & Moskowitz, 2003). Several have proved to be effective in laboratory animals, but so far none has been shown to limit brain damage from strokes in humans. Wahlgren and Ahmed (2004) have argued that if such treatments are to be effective, they need to be initiated in the ambulance, not hours later in the hospital.

Closed-Head Injuries

It is not necessary for the skull to be penetrated for the brain to be seriously damaged. In fact, any blow to the head should be treated with extreme caution, particularly when confusion, sensorimotor disturbances, or loss of consciousness ensues. Brain injuries produced by blows that do not penetrate the skull are called *closed-head injuries*.

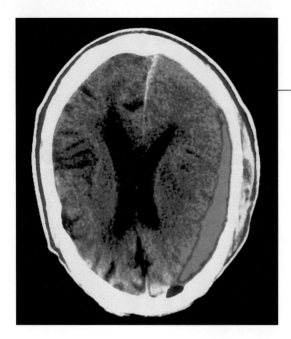

A CT scan of a subdural hematoma. Notice that the subdural hematoma (the red area on the left side of the brain) has displaced the left lateral ventricle.

Figure 8.6

Contusions are closed-head injuries that involve damage to the cerebral circulatory system. Such damage produces internal hemorrhaging, which results in a hematoma. A **hematoma** is a localized collection of clotted blood in an organ or tissue—in other words, a bruise.

It is paradoxical that the very hardness of the skull, which protects the brain from penetrating injuries, is the major factor in the development of contusions. Contusions from closed-head injuries occur when the brain slams against the inside of the skull. As Figure 8.6 illustrates, blood from such injuries can accumulate in the *subdural space*—the space between the dura mater and arachnoid membrane—and severely distort the surrounding neural tissue.

It may surprise you to learn that contusions frequently occur on the side of the brain opposite the side struck by a blow. The reason for such so-called **contrecoup injuries** is that the blow causes the brain to strike the inside of the skull on the other side of the head.

When there is a disturbance of consciousness following a blow to the head and there is no evidence of a contusion or other structural damage, the diagnosis is **concussion**. It is sometimes assumed that concussions entail a temporary disruption of normal cerebral function with no long-term damage. However, the punch-drunk syndrome suggests otherwise. The **punch-drunk syndrome** is the **dementia** (general intellectual deterioration) and cerebral scarring that is observed in boxers and other individuals who experience repeated concussions. If there were no damage associated with a single concussion, the effects of many concussions could not add up to produce severe damage (McCrory & Berkovic, 1998).

One of the most dangerous aspects of concussion is the complacency with which it is regarded. Flippant references to it, such as "having one's bell rung," do little to communicate its hazards.

Thinking Clearly

Clinical Implications

The Case of Jerry Quarry, Ex-Boxer

Jerry Quarry [see Figure 8.7] thumps his hard belly with both fists. Smiles at the sound. Like a stone against a tree.

"Feel it," he says proudly, punching himself again and again.

He pounds big, gnarled fists into meaty palms. Cocks his head. Stares. Vacant blue eyes. Punch-drunk at 50. Medical name: *Dementia pugilistic* [punch-drunk syndrome]. Cause: Thousands of punches to the head.

A top heavyweight contender in the 1960s and ' 70s, Quarry now needs help shaving, showering, putting on shoes and socks. Soon, probably, diapers. His older brother, James, cuts meat into little pieces so he won' t choke. Jerry smiles like a kid. Shuffles like an old man.

Slow, slurred speech. Random thoughts snagged on branches in a dying brain. Memories twisted. Voices no one else hears. (Steve Wiltstein, Associated Press, 1995)

Figure 8.7

Jerry Quarry absorbed many blows to his head during his boxing career. The result: punch-drunk syndrome.

Infections of the Brain

An invasion of the brain by microorganisms is a *brain infection*, and the resulting inflammation is **encephalitis**. There are two common types of brain infections: bacterial infections and viral infections.

Bacterial Infections. When bacteria infect the brain, they often lead to the formation of *cerebral abscesses*—pockets of pus in the brain. They also often attack and inflame the meninges, creating a disorder known as **meningitis**, which is fatal in 25% of adults (Nau & Brück, 2002). Penicillin and other antibiotics sometimes eliminate the infection, but they cannot reverse brain damage that has already been produced.

Syphilis is one bacterial brain infection you have likely heard about. Syphilis bacteria are passed from infected to noninfected individuals through contact with genital sores. The infecting bacteria then go into a dormant stage for several years before they become virulent and attack many parts of the body, including the brain. The syndrome of insanity and dementia that results from a syphilitic infection is called **general paresis**.

Syphilis has a particularly interesting history (see Klawans, 1990). The first Europeans to visit America stripped the natives of their gold and left smallpox in return. But the deal was not totally one-sided; the booty carried back to Europe by Columbus's sailors and the adventurers who followed included a cargo of syphilis bacteria. Until then, syphilis had been restricted to the Americas, but it quickly spread to the rest of the world.

Viral Infections. There are two types of viral infections of the nervous system: those that have a particular affinity for neural tissue and those that attack neural tissue but have no greater affinity for it than for other tissues.

Rabies, which is usually transmitted through the bite of a rabid animal, is a well-known example of a viral infection that has a particular affinity for the nervous system. The fits of rage caused by the virus's effects on the brain increase the probability that rabid animals that normally attack by biting (e.g., dogs, cats, raccoons, bats, and mice) will spread the disorder. Although the effects of the rabies virus on the brain are ultimately lethal, the virus does have one redeeming feature: It does not usually attack the brain for at least a month after it has been contracted, thus allowing time for a preventive vaccination.

The *mumps* and *herpes* viruses are common examples of viruses that can attack the nervous system but have no special affinity for it. Although these viruses sometimes spread into the brain, they typically attack other tissues of the body.

Viruses may play a far greater role in neuropsychological disorders than is currently thought. Their involvement in the *etiology* (cause) of disorders is often difficult to recognize because they may lie dormant for many years before producing symptoms.

Neurotoxins

The nervous system can be damaged by exposure to any one of a variety of toxic chemicals, which can enter general circulation from the gastrointestinal tract, from the lungs, or through the skin. For example, heavy metals such as mercury and lead can accumulate in the brain and permanently damage it, producing a **toxic psychosis** (chronic insanity produced by a neurotoxin). Have you ever wondered why Alice in Wonderland's Mad Hatter was a mad hatter and not a mad something else? In 18th- and 19th-century England, hatmakers were commonly driven mad by the mercury employed in the preparation of the felt used to make hats. In a similar vein, the word *crackpot* originally referred to the toxic psychosis observed in some people in England—primarily the poor—who steeped their tea in cracked ceramic pots with lead cores.

There are many kinds of neurotoxins, but three kinds are noteworthy in this context. First, sometimes the very drugs used to treat neurological disorders prove to have neurotoxic side effects. For example, some of the antipsychotic drugs introduced in the early 1950s often produced a serious motor disorder after several years of use (this disorder is called *tardive dyskinesia*). Second, some neurotoxins are *endogenous* (produced by the patient's own body). For example, the body can for unknown reasons produce antibodies that attack particular components of the nervous system (see Newsom-Davis & Vincent, 1991). And third, some drugs that are addictive because of their pleasurable effects (e.g., alcohol, solvents) also have neurotoxic effects.

Do you remember the case of Jimmie G. from Chapter 1? Jimmie G. suffered from **Korsakoff's syndrome**. The primary symptom of Korsakoff's syndrome is severe memory loss, which is made all the more heartbreaking—as you have seen in Jimmie G.'s case—by the fact that its sufferers are often otherwise quite capable. Because Korsakoff's syndrome commonly occurs in alcoholics, it was initially believed to be a direct consequence of the toxic effects of alcohol on the brain. However, subsequent research showed that Korsakoff's syndrome is largely caused by the brain damage associated with *thiamine* (vitamin B_1) deficiency (see Heap et al., 2002; Thomson, 2000).

The first support for the thiamine-deficiency interpretation of Korsakoff's syndrome came from the discovery of the syndrome in malnourished persons who consumed little or no alcohol. Additional support came from experiments in which thiamine-deficient rats were compared with otherwise identical groups of control rats. The thiamine-deficient rats displayed memory deficits and patterns of brain damage similar to those observed in human alcoholics (see Mumby, Cameli, & Glenn, 1999). Alcoholics often develop Korsakoff's syndrome because most of their caloric intake comes in the form of alcohol, which lacks vitamins, and because alcohol interferes with the metabolism of what little thiamine they do consume. However, alcohol has been shown to accelerate the development of brain damage in thiamine-deficient rats, so it may have a direct toxic effect on the brain as well (Zimitat et al., 1990). Alcoholics are often treated with massive doses of thiamine. The thiamine reduces the development of further brain damage and often leads to a slight improvement in the patient's condition; but, unfortunately, brain damage, once produced, is largely permanent.

Genetic Factors

Normal human cells have 23 pairs of chromosomes; however, sometimes accidents of cell division occur, and the fertilized egg ends up with an abnormal chromosome or with an abnormal number of normal chromosomes. Then, as the fertilized egg divides and redivides, these chromosomal anomalies are duplicated in every cell of the body.

Most neuropsychological diseases of genetic origin are caused by abnormal recessive genes that are passed from parent to offspring. Inherited neuropsychological disorders are rarely associated with dominant genes because dominant genes that disturb neuropsychological function tend to be eliminated from the gene pool—every individual who carries one is at a major survival and reproductive disadvantage. In contrast, individuals who inherit one abnormal recessive gene do not develop the disorder, and the gene is passed on to future generations.

There are, however, two possible situations in which neurological disorders can be associated with dominant genes. One is the case in which an abnormal dominant gene manifests itself only in rare environmental circumstances. The other is the case in which an abnormal dominant gene is not expressed until the individual is well past puberty.

Down syndrome is a genetic disorder that is caused not by a faulty gene, but by a genetic accident, which occurs in 0.15% of births. The usual cause is an accident that happens during ovulation. During ovulation an extra chromosome 21 is created in the egg; thus, when the egg is fertilized, there are three rather than two in the zygote. The superfluous chromosome 21 has several effects. In addition to characteristic disfigurement—flattened skull and nose, folds of skin over the inner corners of the eyes, and short fingers (see Figure 8.8)—intellectual development is retarded, and there are often serious medical complications. The probability of giving birth to a child with Down syndrome increases with advancing maternal age (Carothers et al., 2001).

Rapid progress is being made in locating and characterizing the faulty genes that are associated with some neuropsychological disorders. Achievement of this goal will open up a variety of new treatment and prevention strategies, such as splicing in healthy genes to replace faulty ones and developing specific DNA-binding proteins that can enter neurons and block the expression of faulty genes.

Programmed Cell Death

You learned in Chapter 7 that neurons and other cells have genetic programs for suicide, that the process by which cells destroy themselves is called **apoptosis** (pronounced "A-poe-TOE-sis"), and that apoptosis plays a critical role in early development

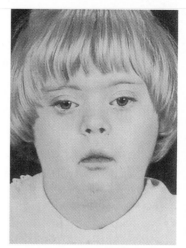
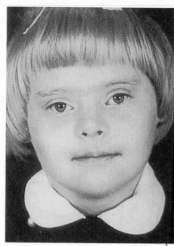

A child with Down syndrome, before and after plastic surgery. The purpose of these photographs is not to promote cosmetic surgery but to challenge our culture's reaction to individuals with Down syndrome. The little girl on the left and the little girl on the right are the same girl; they deserve the same respect and consideration.

(Courtesy of Kenneth E. Salyer, Director, International Craniofacial Institute.)

Figure 8.8

by eliminating some of the excessive neurons that are initially created. Apoptosis also plays a role in brain damage. Indeed, each of the six causes of brain damage that have already been discussed in this chapter (tumors, cerebrovascular disorders, closed-head injuries, infections, toxins, and genetic factors) appears to produce its effect, in part, by activating apoptotic programs of self-destruction (Allsop & Fazakerley, 2000; Dirnagl, Simon, & Hallenbeck, 2003; Nijhawan, Honarpour, & Wang, 2000).

It was once assumed that the death of neurons following brain damage was totally necrotic—*necrosis* is passive cell death resulting from injury. It now seems that if cells are not damaged too severely, they will attempt to marshal enough resources to commit suicide.

It is easy to understand why apoptotic mechanisms have evolved: Apoptosis is clearly more adaptive than necrosis. In necrosis, the damaged neuron swells and breaks apart, beginning in the axons and dendrites and ending in the cell body. This fragmentation leads to inflammation, which can damage other cells in the vicinity. Necrotic cell death is quick, it is typically complete in a few hours. In contrast, apoptotic cell death is slow, typically requiring a day or two. Apoptosis of a neuron proceeds gradually, starting with shrinkage of the cell body. Then, as parts of the neuron die, the resulting debris is packaged in vesicles. As a result, there is no inflammation, and damage to nearby cells is kept to a minimum.

8.2

Neuropsychological Diseases

The preceding section focused on the causes of human brain damage. This section considers five neuropsychological disorders that are associated with brain damage: epilepsy, Parkinson's disease, Huntington's disease, multiple sclerosis, and Alzheimer's disease.

Clinical Implications

Epilepsy

The primary symptom of **epilepsy** is the epileptic seizure, but not all persons who suffer seizures are considered to have epilepsy. It is not uncommon for an otherwise healthy person to have a seizure during temporary illness or following exposure to a convulsive agent. The label *epilepsy* is applied to only those patients whose seizures appear to be generated by their own chronic brain dysfunction. About 1 % of the population are diagnosed as epileptic at some point in their lives.

In view of the fact that epilepsy is characterized by epileptic seizures—or, more accurately, by spontaneously recurring epileptic seizures—you might think that the task of diagnosing this disorder would be an easy one. But you would be wrong. The task is made difficult by the diversity and complexity of epileptic seizures. You are probably familiar with seizures that take the form of **convulsions** (motor seizures); these often involve tremors (*clonus*), rigidity (*tonus*), and loss of both balance and consciousness. But many seizures do not take this form; instead, they involve subtle changes of thought, mood, or behavior that are not easily distinguishable from normal ongoing activity.

There are many causes of epilepsy. Indeed, all of the causes of brain damage that have been described in this chapter—including viruses, neurotoxins, tumors, and blows to the head—can cause epilepsy, and over 70 different faulty genes have been linked to it (Noebels, 2003). Many cases of epilepsy appear to be associated with faults at inhibitory synapses that cause large numbers of neurons to fire in synchronous bursts (Köhling, 2002).

The diagnosis of epilepsy rests heavily on evidence from electroencephalography (EEG). The value of scalp electroencephalography in confirming suspected cases of epilepsy stems from the fact that epileptic seizures are associated with bursts of high-amplitude EEG spikes, which are often apparent in the scalp EEG during an attack (see Figure 8.9), and from the fact that individual spikes often punctuate the scalp EEGs of epileptics between attacks (Cohen et al., 2002). Although the observation of spontaneous epileptic discharges is incontrovertible evidence of epilepsy, the failure to observe them does not always mean that the patient is not epileptic. It could mean that the patient is epileptic but did not happen to experience epileptic discharges during the test or that epileptic discharges did occur during the test but were not recorded through the scalp electrodes.

Some epileptics experience peculiar psychological changes just before a convulsion. These changes, called **epileptic auras**, may take many different forms—for example, a bad smell, a specific thought, a vague feeling of familiarity, a hallucination, or a tightness of the chest. Epileptic auras are important for two reasons. First, the nature of the auras provides clues concerning the location of the epileptic focus. Second, because the epileptic auras experienced by a particular patient are often similar from attack to attack, they warn the patient of an impending convulsion.

Once an individual has been diagnosed as epileptic, it is usual to assign the epilepsy to one of two general categories—*partial epilepsy* or *generalized epilepsy*—and then to one of their respective subcategories. The various seizure types are so different from one another that epilepsy is best viewed not as a single disease but as a number of different, but related, diseases.

Partial Seizures A **partial seizure** is a seizure that does not involve the entire brain. The epileptic neurons at a focus begin to discharge together in bursts, and it is this synchronous discharging of neurons (see Figure 8.10) that pro-

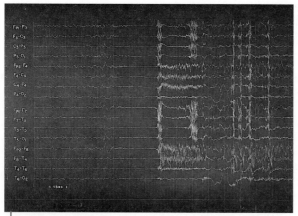

Cortical electroencephalogram (EEG) record from various locations on the scalp during the beginning of a complex partial seizure. The letters and numbers to the left of each trace indicate the conventional locations of the electrodes over the frontal (F), temporal (T), parietal (P), and occipital (O) lobes.

Figure 8.9

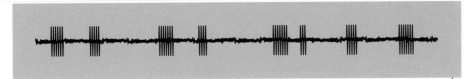

Bursts of discharges from an epileptic neuron, recorded by extracellular unit recording.

Figure 8.10

duces epileptic spiking in the EEG. The synchronous activity may stay restricted to the focus until the seizure is over, or it may spread to other areas of the brain—but, in the case of partial seizures, not to the entire brain. The specific behavioral symptoms of a partial epileptic seizure depend on where the disruptive discharges begin and into what structures they spread. Because partial seizures do not involve the entire brain, they are not usually accompanied by a total loss of consciousness or equilibrium.

There are two major categories of partial seizures: simple and complex. **Simple partial seizures** are partial seizures whose symptoms are primarily sensory or motor or both; they are sometimes called *Jacksonian seizures* after the famous 19th-century neurologist Hughlings Jackson, who first characterized them. As the epileptic discharges spread through the sensory or motor areas of the brain, the symptoms spread systematically through the body.

In contrast, **complex partial seizures** are often restricted to the temporal lobes, and those who experience them are often said to have *temporal lobe epilepsy*. During a complex partial seizure, the patient engages in compulsive, repetitive, simple behaviors commonly referred to as *automatisms* (e.g., doing and undoing a button) and in more complex behaviors that appear almost normal. The diversity of complex partial seizures is illustrated by the following four cases.

The Subtlety of Complex Partial Seizures: Four Cases

A war veteran subject to many automatisms read in the newspaper about a man who had embraced a woman in a park, followed her into a women' s toilet, and then boarded a bus. From the description given, he realized he was the man.

One morning a doctor left home to answer an emergency call from the hospital and returned several hours later, a trifle confused, feeling as though he had experienced a bad dream. At the hospital he had performed a difficult . . . [operation] with his usual competence, but later had done and said things deemed inappropriate.

A young man, a music teacher, when listening to a concert, walked down the aisle and onto the platform, circled the piano, jumped to the floor, did a hop, skip, and jump up the aisle, and regained his senses when partway home. He often found himself on a trolley [bus] far from his destination.

A man in an attack went to his employer and said, "I have to have more money or [I] quit." Later, to his surprise, he found that his salary had been raised. (Lennox, 1960, pp. 237–238)

Clinical Implications

Although patients appear to be conscious throughout their complex partial seizures, they usually have little or no subsequent recollection of them. About half of all cases of epilepsy are of the complex partial variety—the temporal lobes are particularly susceptible to epileptic discharges.

Generalized Seizures. **Generalized seizures** involve the entire brain. Some begin as focal discharges that gradually spread through the entire brain. In other

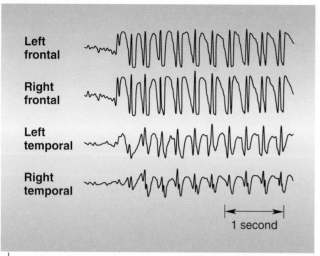

The bilaterally symmetrical, 3-per-second spike-and-wave EEG discharge that is associated with petit mal epileptic seizures.

Figure 8.11

cases, the discharges seem to begin almost simultaneously in all parts of the brain. Such sudden-onset generalized seizures may result from diffuse pathology or may begin focally in a structure, such as the thalamus, that projects to many parts of the brain.

Like partial seizures, generalized seizures occur in many forms. One is the **grand mal** (literally, "big trouble") **seizure**. The primary symptoms of a grand mal seizure are loss of consciousness, loss of equilibrium, and a violent *tonic-clonic convulsion*—a convulsion involving both tonus and clonus. Tongue biting, urinary incontinence, and *cyanosis* (turning blue as a result of excessive extraction of oxygen from the blood during the convulsion) are common manifestations of grand mal convulsions. The **hypoxia** (shortage of oxygen supply to tissue, for example, to the brain) that accompanies a grand mal seizure can itself cause brain damage, some of which develops slowly after the attack and is mediated by the excessive release of excitatory amino acid neurotransmitters.

A second major category of generalized seizure is the **petit mal** (literally, "small trouble") **seizure** (see Crunelli & Leresche, 2002). Petit mal seizures are not associated with convulsions; their primary behavioral symptom is the *petit mal absence*—a disruption of consciousness that is associated with a cessation of ongoing behavior, a vacant look, and sometimes fluttering eyelids. The EEG of a petit mal seizure is different from that of other seizures; it is a bilaterally symmetrical **3-per-second spike-and-wave discharge** (see Figure 8.11). Petit mal seizures are most common in children, and they frequently cease at puberty. They often go undiagnosed; thus, children with petit mal epilepsy are sometimes considered to be "daydreamers" by their parents and teachers.

Although there is no cure for epilepsy, the frequency and severity of seizures can often be reduced by anticonvulsant medication. Brain surgery is sometimes prescribed in life-threatening situations.

Parkinson's Disease

Parkinson's disease is a movement disorder of middle and old age that affects about 0.5% of the population (see Strickland & Bertoni, 2004). It is about 2.5 times more prevalent in males than in females (see Sawada & Shimohama, 2000; Wooten et al., 2004).

The initial symptoms of Parkinson's disease are mild—perhaps no more than a slight stiffness or tremor of the fingers—but they inevitably increase in severity with advancing years. The most common symptoms of the full-blown disorder are a tremor that is pronounced during inactivity but not during voluntary movement or sleep, muscular rigidity, difficulty initiating movement, slowness of movement, and a masklike face. Pain and depression often develop before the motor symptoms become severe.

Although Parkinson's patients often display some cognitive deficits, dementia is not typically associated with the disorder. In essence, Parkinson's disease victims are thinking people trapped inside bodies they cannot control. Do you remember from Chapter 3 the case of "The Lizard"—Roberto Garcia d'Orta?

Like epilepsy, Parkinson's disease seems to have no single cause; faulty genes, brain infections, strokes, tumors, traumatic brain injury, and neurotoxins have all been implicated in specific cases (see Greenamyre & Hastings, 2004). However, in the majority of cases, no cause is obvious, and there is no family history of the disorder (see Calne et al., 1987).

Parkinson's disease is associated with degeneration of the **substantia nigra**—the midbrain nucleus whose neurons project via the **nigrostriatal pathway** to the **striatum** of the basal ganglia. Although *dopamine* is normally the major neurotransmitter released by most neurons of the substantia nigra, there is little dopamine in the substantia nigra and striatum of long-term Parkinson's patients.

As you saw in the case of Mr. d'Orta, the symptoms of Parkinson's disease can be alleviated by injections of **L-dopa**—the chemical from which dopamine is synthesized. However, L-dopa is rarely a permanent solution; it typically becomes less and less effective with continued use, until its side effects (e.g., involuntary movements; see Bezard, Brotchie, & Gross, 2001) outweigh its benefits. This is exactly what happened to d'Orta. L-Dopa therapy gave him a 3-year respite from his disease, but ultimately it became totally ineffective. His prescription was then changed to another dopamine agonist, and again his condition improved—but again the improvement was only temporary. We will return to d'Orta's roller-coaster case later in this chapter.

About 10 different gene mutations have been linked to Parkinson's disease (see Dawson & Dawson, 2003; Le & Appel, 2004). These findings have led many people to believe that a cure is just around the corner. However, it is important to realize that each of these gene mutations has been discovered in a different family, each of which had members suffering from a rare form of early-onset Parkinson's disease that runs in families. Thus, these mutations are unlikely to be factors in typical forms of the disease. Still, the study of the effects of these gene mutations may eventually lead to a better understanding of the physiological changes that underlie the symptoms of the disorder (see Vila, Wu, & Przed-borski, 2001).

Thinking Clearly

Huntington' s Disease

Like Parkinson's disease, **Huntington's disease** is a progressive motor disorder of middle and old age; but, unlike Parkinson's disease, it is rare, it has a strong genetic basis, and it is associated with severe dementia.

The first motor signs of Huntington's disease are often increased fidgetiness; as the disorder develops, rapid, complex, jerky movements of entire limbs (rather than individual muscles) begin to predominate. Eventually the motor and intellectual deterioration become so severe that sufferers are incapable of feeding themselves, controlling their bowels, or recognizing their own children. There is no cure; death typically occurs about 15 years after the appearance of the first symptoms.

Huntington's disease is passed from generation to generation by a single dominant gene; thus, all of the individuals carrying the gene develop the disorder, as do about half their offspring. The Huntington's gene is readily passed from parent to child because the first symptoms of the disease do not appear until the parent is well past the peak reproductive years (at about age 40).

The abnormal dominant gene that causes Huntington's disease was identified and characterized in 1993. The abnormal protein produced by the Huntington's gene has also been isolated and characterized. However, the precise effect of this protein, which has been named *huntingtin*, has not yet been determined (see Mc-Murray, 2001). Curiously, huntingtin is produced in all parts of the brains of Huntington's sufferers, yet brain damage is largely restricted to the striatum and cerebral cortex (see DiFiglia et al., 1997; Jakel & Maragos, 2000).

If one of your parents were to develop Huntington's disease, the chance would be 50/50 that you too would develop it. If you were in such a situation, would you want to know whether you would suffer the same fate? Medical geneticists have developed a test that can tell relatives of Huntington's patients whether they are carrying the gene (Gilliam, Gusella, & Lehrach, 1987; Martin, 1987). Some choose to take the test, and some do not. One advantage of the test is that it permits the relatives of Huntington's patients who have not inherited the gene to

Clinical Implications

Dear Dr. Pinel:

I am worried about my children and their future. In fact, I am worried sick. After reading your book, I feel that you are my friend and I have nowhere else to turn.

My wife came down with Huntington's disease 7 years ago, and today she can't walk or take care of herself. I have three young children. Where can I take them to see if they have inherited my wife's infected cells? I am presently incarcerated, which adds to my psychological pain. I look to be released soon, and could take my wife and kids just about anywheres to find help and get answers.

Any kind of advice that you could give us would be greatly appreciated by me and my family. I wish to thank you for any assistance that you can give. I remain with warmest personal regards.

Very truly yours,
Walter S. Miller

THE UNIVERSITY OF BRITISH COLUMBIA

Department of Psychology
2136 West Mall
Vancouver, BC, Canada V6T 1Z4

Dear Mr. Miller:

I was saddened to learn of your unhappy situation. I am pleased to tell you what I can. I hope that you understand that I am not a physician.

If your wife does have Huntington's disease and not some other neurological disorder, each of your children has a 50/50 chance of developing Huntington's disease. There is no cure.

Please seek the advice of a neurologist, who can explain your options to you and provide you with the support that you surely need. You must decide whether or not to have your children tested for the Huntington's gene. One option would be to let your children decide for themselves when they mature. Some people whose parents develop Huntington's disease decide to take the test; others decide not to. In either case, it is extremely important for them not to risk passing on the gene to future generations.

I am sorry that I cannot provide you with a more optimistic assessment, but your children's situation is too serious for me to be less than totally frank. But do not lose hope. There is a chance (1/8) that none of your children is carrying the Huntington's gene.

I wish you, your wife, and your children good fortune.

Cordially,

John P. J. Pinel
Professor

An exchange of letters between Walter Miller, whose wife had been diagnosed with Huntington's disease, and John Pinel.

Figure 8.12

have children without the fear of passing on the disorder. Figure 8.12 presents a letter that speaks for itself. I received it from a man who read one of my textbooks. I altered the letter slightly to protect the identity of its author and his family. I never heard from him again.

Multiple Sclerosis

Multiple sclerosis (MS) is a progressive disease that attacks the myelin of axons in the CNS. It is particularly disturbing because it typically attacks young people just as they are beginning their adult life. First, there are microscopic areas of degeneration on myelin sheaths; but eventually there is a breakdown of both the myelin and the associated axons, along with the development of many areas of hard scar tissue (*sclerosis* means "hardening"). Figure 8.13 illustrates degeneration in the white matter of a patient with multiple sclerosis.

Diagnosing multiple sclerosis is difficult because the nature and severity of the disorder depend on the number, size, and position of the sclerotic lesions. Furthermore, in some cases, there are lengthy periods of remission (up to 2 years), during which the patient seems almost normal; however, these are usually just oases in the progression of the disorder. Common symptoms of advanced multiple sclerosis are visual disturbances, muscular weakness, numbness, tremor, and **ataxia** (loss of motor coordination).

Epidemiological studies of multiple sclerosis have provided evidence of the environmental and genetic factors that influence its development. **Epidemiology** is the study of the various factors, such as diet, geographic location, age, sex, and race, that influence the distribution of a disease in the general population.

Evidence that environmental factors influence the development of multiple sclerosis comes from the finding that the incidence of multiple sclerosis is far greater in people who spent their childhood in a cool climate, even if they subsequently moved to a warm climate. In contrast, evidence of genetic involvement comes from the finding that multiple sclerosis is rare among certain groups, such as Africans and Asians, even when they live in environments in which the incidence of the disease is high in other groups. The disorder occurs in 0.15% of Caucasians and is about twice as common in females (Steinman et al., 2002). Research indicates that there is a strong genetic predisposition to multiple sclerosis, with involvement of a large number of different genes, each making a small contribution (Hemmer, Archelos, & Hartung, 2002).

Multiple sclerosis is an *autoimmune disorder*—a disorder in which the body's immune system attacks part of the body, as if it were a foreign substance. In multiple sclerosis, myelin is the focus of the faulty immune reaction. Indeed, an animal model of multiple sclerosis can be induced by injecting laboratory animals with myelin and a preparation that stimulates the immune system.

There are a number of drugs that retard the progression of multiple sclerosis or block some of its symptoms. However, there is no cure.

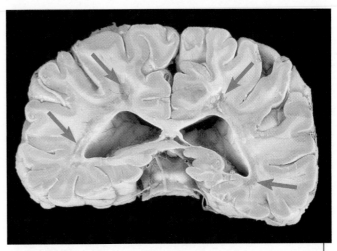

Areas of sclerosis (see arrows) in the white matter of a patient with MS.

Figure 8.13

Alzheimer's Disease

Alzheimer's disease is the most common cause of *dementia*. It sometimes appears in individuals as young as 40, but the likelihood of its development becomes greater with advancing years. About 10% of the general population over the age of 65 suffer from the disease, and the proportion is about 35% in those over 85 (St. George-Hyslop, 2000).

Alzheimer's disease is progressive. Its early stages are often characterized by a selective decline in memory; its intermediate stages are marked by confusion, irritability, anxiety, and deterioration of speech; and in its advanced stages, the patient deteriorates to the point that even simple responses such as swallowing

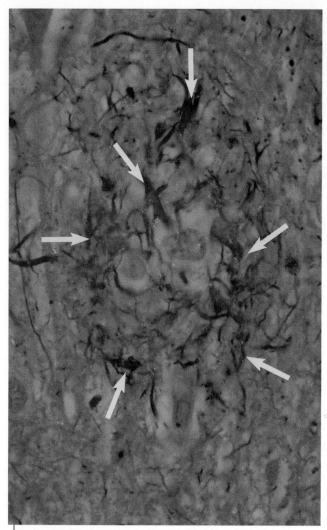

Amyloid plaques (see arrows) in the brain of a patient with Alzheimer's disease.

Figure 8.14

and controlling the bladder are difficult. Alzheimer's disease is terminal.

Because Alzheimer's disease is not the only cause of dementia, it cannot be diagnosed with certainty on the basis of its behavioral symptoms—definitive diagnosis of Alzheimer's disease must await autopsy. The two defining characteristics of the disease are neurofibrillary tangles and amyloid plaques. *Neurofibrillary tangles* are threadlike tangles of protein in the neural cytoplasm, and *amyloid plaques* are clumps of scar tissue composed of degenerating neurons and a protein called **amyloid**, which is present in normal brains in only very small amounts. In addition, there is substantial neuron loss. The presence of amyloid plaques in the brain of a patient who died of Alzheimer's disease is illustrated in Figure 8.14.

Although neurofibrillary tangles, amyloid plaques, and neuron loss tend to occur throughout the brains of Alzheimer's patients, they are more prevalent in some areas than in others. For example, they are particularly prevalent in medial temporal lobe structures such as the *entorhinal cortex, amygdala,* and *hippocampus*—all structures that are involved in various aspects of memory (see Collie & Maruff, 2000; Selkoe, 2002). They are also prevalent in the inferior temporal cortex, posterior parietal cortex, and prefrontal cortex—all areas that mediate complex cognitive functions. (See Figure 8.15.)

Studying the genetics of Alzheimer's disease is hindered by the fact that its carriers often die of natural causes before their Alzheimer's symptoms can be manifested. Nevertheless, it is clear that Alzheimer's disease has a major genetic component. People with an Alzheimer's victim in their immediate family have a 50% chance of being stricken by the disease if they survive into their 80s (Breitner, 1990).

Much of the research on the genetics of Alzheimer's disease has focused on rare early-onset *familial* forms of the disease. Several gene mutations have been found to be associated with early-onset Alzheimer's disease, and all of them have been implicated in the synthesis of amyloid or *tau*, a protein found in neurofibrillary tangles (see St. George-Hyslop, 2000).

One factor complicating the search for a treatment or cure for Alzheimer's disease is that it is still not clear which symptom is primary (see Lee, 2001; Mudher & Lovestone, 2002). This is a key issue because

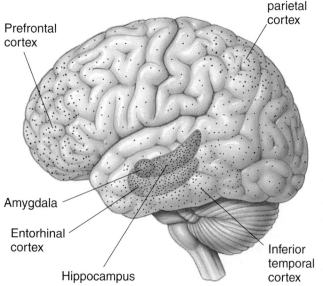

The typical distribution of neurofibrillary tangles and amyloid plaques in the brains of patients with advanced Alzheimer's disease.

(Based on Goedert, 1993, and Selkoe, 1991.)

Figure 8.15

an effective treatment is most likely to be developed only by research focusing on the primary symptom. The most popular candidate is the amyloid plaques; the *amyloid hypothesis* holds that the development of these plaques is the primary symptom of the disorder, which causes all other symptoms (see Hardy & Selkoe, 2002). However, others believe that the development of tau and neurofibrillary tangles is the primary symptom.

Scan your Brain

This is a good place for you to pause to scan your brain. Are you ready to progress to the following section, which discusses animal models of some of the disorders that you have just learned about? Fill in the following blanks. The correct answers are provided below. Before proceeding, review material related to your errors and omissions.

1. The two major categories of epileptic seizures are _____ and _____.

2. _____ are simple repetitive responses that occur during complex partial seizures.

3. The disorder characterized by tremor at rest is _____ disease.

4. Parkinson's disease is associated with degeneration in the _____ dopamine pathway.

5. _____ disease is passed from generation to generation by a single dominant gene.

6. Genetic studies of Parkinson's disease and Alzheimer's disease have focused on early-onset _____ forms of the disorder.

7. Multiple sclerosis attacks _____ in the CNS.

8. Multiple sclerosis is considered to be a(n) _____ disease.

9. The most common cause of dementia is _____ disease.

10. Two major neuropathological symptoms of Alzheimer's disease are _____ tangles and _____ plaques.

Scan Your Brain answers: (1) partial and generalized, in either order, (2) Automatisms, (3) Parkinson's, (4) nigrostriatal, (5) Huntington's, (6) familial, (7) myelin, (8) autoimmune, (9) Alzheimer's, (10) neurofibrillary; amyloid

8.3

Animal Models of Human Neuropsychological Diseases

The first two sections of this chapter focused on neuropsychological diseases and their causes, but they also provided some glimpses into the ways in which researchers have attempted to solve the many puzzles of neurological dysfunction. This section focuses on one of these ways: the experimental investigation of animal models. Because the experimentation necessary to identify the neuropathological basis of human neuropsychological diseases is seldom possible on the patients themselves, animal models of the diseases play an important role in such investigations (see Cenci, Whishaw, & Schallert, 2002).

What Is an Animal Model?

An **animal model** is a condition that occurs or is induced in a nonhuman animal and is similar in some respects to a human disease. By studying an animal model, researchers hope to discover information about the cause, mechanisms, and/or treatment of the human neuropsychological disease that it somewhat resembles.

It is important to appreciate that even the best animal models of human neuropsychological diseases display only some of the features of those diseases (see Maries et al., 2003). Consequently, animal models must be employed with caution. Studying an animal model is like exploring a section of an unknown maze. One enters an unfamiliar section with little more than a hope that its exploration will prove fruitful, and only after the entire section has been carefully explored can one know whether the decision to enter it was wise. In the same way, it is not possible to evaluate the currently available animal models of any neuropsychological disease until each model has been thoroughly explored. Surely, only a few animal models will lead toward the goals of understanding and prevention, but only time and effort can tell which ones these are.

There are animal models of all five of the disorders that you have just read about. The remainder of this section focuses on the MPTP model of Parkinson's disease.

MPTP Model of Parkinson's Disease

The preeminent animal model of Parkinson's disease grew out of an unfortunate accident, which resulted in the following anomalous cases of Parkinson's disease.

The Case of the Frozen Addicts

Parkinson's disease . . . rarely occurs before the age of 50. It was somewhat of a surprise then to see a group of young drug addicts at our hospital in 1982 who had developed symptoms of severe and what proved to be irreversible parkinsonism. The only link between these patients was the recent use of a new "synthetic heroin." They exhibited virtually all of the typical motor features of Parkinson's disease, including the classic triad of bradykinesia (slowness of movement), tremor and rigidity of their muscles. Even the subtle features, such as seborrhea (oiliness of the skin) and micrographia (small handwriting), that are typical of Parkinson's disease were present. After tracking down samples of this substance, the offending agent was tentatively identified as 1-methyl-4-phenyl-1,2,3,6-tetrahydropyridine or **MPTP**. . . . There has been no sign of remission, and most are becoming increasingly severe management problems. (Langston, 1985, p. 79)

Researchers immediately turned the misfortune of these few to the advantage of many by developing a much-needed animal model of Parkinson's disease (Langston, 1986). It was quickly established that non-human primates respond in the same way humans do to MPTP exposure. The brains of primates exposed to

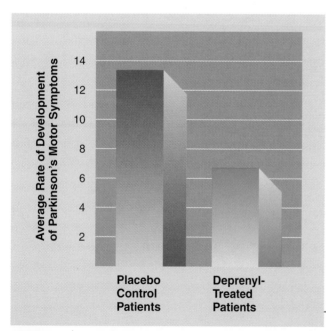

Average rate of motor symptom development in early Parkinson's patients treated with deprenyl (a monoamine oxidase inhibitor) or with a placebo. Deprenyl slowed the progression of the disease by 50%. (Based on Tetrud and Langston, 1989.)

Figure 8.16

MPTP and its metabolites have cell loss in the substantia nigra similar to that observed in the brains of Parkinson's patients. Considering that the substantia nigra is the major source of the brain's dopamine, it is not surprising that the level of dopamine is greatly reduced in both the MPTP model and in the naturally occurring disorder. However, it is curious that in a few monkeys MPTP produces a major depletion of dopamine without producing any gross motor symptoms (Taylor et al., 1990).

The MPTP animal model has already benefited patients with Parkinson's disease. For example, it was discovered that **deprenyl**, a monoamine agonist, blocks the effects of MPTP in an animal model, and it was subsequently shown that deprenyl administered to early Parkinson's patients retards the progression of the disease (Tetrud & Langston, 1989)—see Figure 8.16.

8.4

Neuroplastic Responses to Nervous System Damage: Degeneration, Regeneration, Reorganization, and Recovery

Damage to the nervous system may trigger four neuroplastic responses: degeneration, regeneration, reorganization, and recovery of function. Each of these four responses is discussed in this section.

Neural Degeneration

A widely used method for the controlled study of the responses of neurons to damage is to cut their axons (to perform *axotomy*). Two kinds of neural *degeneration* (deterioration) ensue: anterograde degeneration and retrograde degeneration (see Coleman & Perry, 2002; Raff, Whitmore, & Finn, 2002). **Anterograde degeneration** is the degeneration of the **distal segment**—the segment of a cut axon between the cut and the synaptic terminals. **Retrograde degeneration** is the degeneration of the **proximal segment**—the segment of a cut axon between the cut and the cell body.

Anterograde degeneration occurs quickly following axotomy, because the cut separates the distal segment of the axon from the cell body, which is the metabolic center of the neuron. The entire distal segment becomes badly swollen within a few hours, and it breaks into fragments within a few days.

The course of retrograde degeneration is different; it progresses gradually back from the cut to the cell body. In about 2 or 3 days, major changes become apparent in the cell bodies of most axotomized neurons. These early cell body changes are either degenerative or regenerative in nature. Early degenerative changes to the cell body (e.g., a decrease in size) suggest that the neuron will ultimately die. Early regenerative changes (e.g., an increase in size) indicate that the cell body is involved in a massive synthesis of the proteins that will be used to replace the degenerated axon. But early regenerative changes in the cell body do not guarantee the long-term survival of the neuron; if the regenerating axon does not manage to make synaptic contact with an appropriate target, the neuron eventually dies.

Sometimes, degeneration spreads from damaged neurons to neurons that are linked to them by synapses; this is called **transneuronal degeneration**. Neural and transneuronal degeneration are illustrated in Figure 8.17 on page 250.

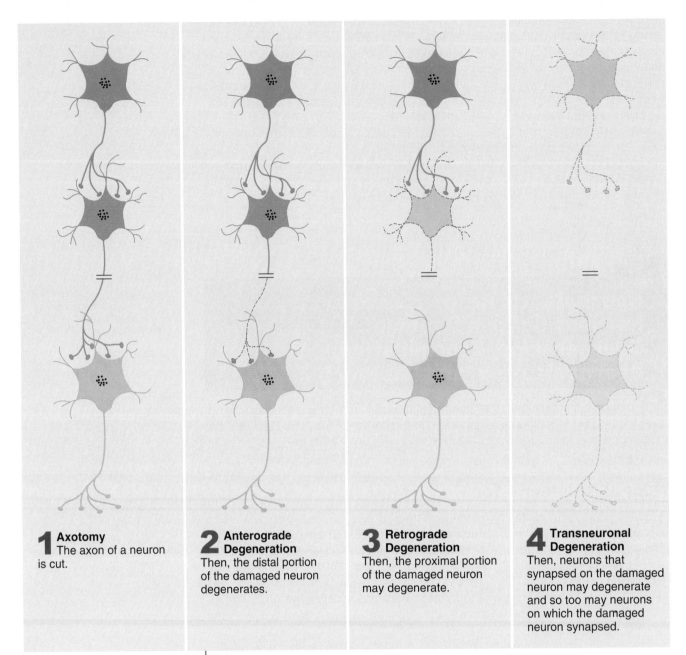

1 Axotomy
The axon of a neuron is cut.

2 Anterograde Degeneration
Then, the distal portion of the damaged neuron degenerates.

3 Retrograde Degeneration
Then, the proximal portion of the damaged neuron may degenerate.

4 Transneuronal Degeneration
Then, neurons that synapsed on the damaged neuron may degenerate and so too may neurons on which the damaged neuron synapsed.

Neuronal and transneuronal degeneration following axotomy.

Figure 8.17

Neural Regeneration

Neural regeneration—the regrowth of damaged neurons—does not proceed as successfully in mammals and other higher vertebrates as it does in most invertebrates and lower vertebrates. The capacity for accurate axonal growth, which is possessed by higher vertebrates during their original development, is lost once they reach maturity. Regeneration is virtually nonexistent in the CNS of adult mammals, and is at best a hit-or-miss affair in the PNS.

In the mammalian PNS, regrowth from the proximal stump of a damaged nerve usually begins 2 or 3 days after axonal damage. What happens next depends on the nature of the injury (see Tonge & Golding, 1993); there are three possibilities. First,

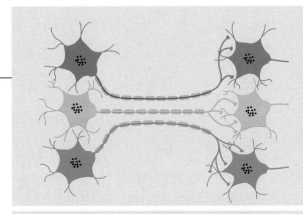

When a nerve is damaged without severing the Schwann cell sheaths (e.g., by crushing), individual axons regenerate to their correct targets.

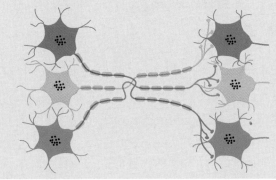

When a nerve is damaged and the severed ends of the Schwann cell sheaths are slightly separated, individual axons often regenerate up incorrect sheaths and reach incorrect targets.

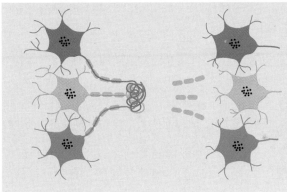

When a nerve is damaged and the severed ends of the Schwann cell sheaths are widely separated, there is typically no functional regeneration.

if the original Schwann cell myelin sheaths remain intact, the regenerating peripheral axons grow through them to their original targets at a rate of a few millimeters per day. Second, if the peripheral nerve is severed and the cut ends become separated by a few millimeters, regenerating axon tips often grow into incorrect sheaths and are guided by them to incorrect destinations; that is why it is often difficult to regain the coordinated use of a limb affected by nerve damage even if there has been substantial regeneration. And third, if the cut ends of a severed mammalian peripheral nerve become widely separated or if a lengthy section of the nerve is damaged, there may be no meaningful regeneration at all; regenerating axon tips grow in a tangled mass around the proximal stump, and the neurons ultimately die. These three patterns of mammalian peripheral nerve regeneration are illustrated in Figure 8.18.

Why do mammalian PNS neurons regenerate, and mammalian CNS neurons do not? The obvious answer is that PNS neurons are inherently capable of regeneration while CNS neurons are not, but this answer has proved to be incorrect. CNS neurons are capable of regeneration if they are transplanted to the PNS, whereas PNS neurons are not capable of regeneration if they are transplanted to the CNS. Clearly, there is something about the environment of the PNS that promotes regeneration and something about the environment of the CNS that does not (Goldberg & Barres, 2000). Schwann cells are the key.

Schwann cells, which myelinate PNS axons, promote regeneration in the mammalian PNS by producing both neurotrophic (survival-promoting) factors and cell-adhesion molecules (CAMs). The neurotrophic factors released by Schwann cells stimulate the growth of new axons, and the cell-adhesion molecules on the cell membranes of Schwann cells provide the paths along which regenerating PNS axons grow. In contrast, **oligodendroglia**, which myelinate CNS axons, do not stimulate or guide regeneration; indeed, they release factors that actively block regeneration (Filbin, 2003; Fournier & Strittmatter, 2001).

In contrast to neural regeneration in mammals, that in lower vertebrates is extremely accurate. It is accurate in both the CNS and the PNS, and it is accurate even when the regenerating axons do not grow into remnant Schwann cell myelin sheaths. The accuracy of regeneration in lower vertebrates offers hope of a medical breakthrough: If the factors that promote accurate regeneration in lower

The Evolutionary Perspective

Chapter 8 Brain Damage and Neuroplasticity

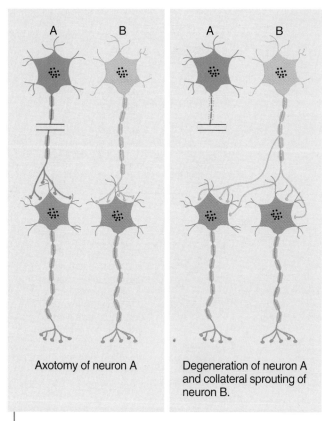

Axotomy of neuron A

Degeneration of neuron A and collateral sprouting of neuron B.

Collateral sprouting after neural degeneration.

Figure 8.19

vertebrates can be identified and applied to the human brain, it might be possible to cure currently untreatable brain injuries.

When an axon degenerates, axon branches grow out from adjacent healthy axons and synapse at the sites vacated by the degenerating axon; this is called **collateral sprouting**. Collateral sprouts may grow out from the axon terminal branches or the nodes of Ranvier on adjacent neurons. Collateral sprouting is illustrated in Figure 8.19.

Neural Reorganization

It has long been assumed that major changes in mammalian nervous systems were possible only during the period of early development: Adult mammalian nervous systems were thought to be limited to the subtle functional changes that mediate learning and memory. However, as you learned in Chapter 7, it was recently discovered that adult mammalian brains retain the ability to reorganize themselves in response to experience. They also retain the ability to reorganize themselves in response to damage.

Examples of Cortical Reorganization Following Nervous System Damage. Most studies of neural reorganization following damage have focused on adult sensory and motor systems (see Donoghue, 1995; Wall, Xu, & Wang, 2002). Sensory and motor systems are ideally suited to the study of neural reorganization because of their topographic layout. The damage-induced reorganization of the primary sensory and motor systems has been studied in two fundamentally different conditions: following damage to peripheral nerves and following damage to the primary cortical areas (Buonomano & Merzenich, 1998). Let's consider some studies that illustrate these two approaches.

Kaas and colleagues (1990) assessed the effect of making a small lesion in one retina and removing the other. Several months after the retinal lesions were made, primary visual cortex neurons that originally had receptive fields in the lesioned area of the retina were found to have receptive fields in the area of the retina next to the lesion; remarkably, this change began within minutes of the lesion (Gilbert & Wiesel, 1992).

Pons and colleagues (1991) mapped the primary somatosensory cortex of monkeys whose contralateral arm sensory neurons had been cut 10 years before. They found that the cortical face representation had systematically expanded into the original arm area. This study created a stir because the scale of the reorganization was far greater than had been assumed to be possible: The primary somatosensory cortex face area had expanded its border by well over a centimeter, likely as a consequence of the particularly long (10-year) interval between surgery and testing.

Sanes, Suner, and Donoghue (1990) assessed the reorganization of primary motor cortex following transection of the motor neurons that control movement of rats' *vibrissae* (whiskers). A few weeks after the transection, stimulation of the area of motor cortex that had previously elicited vibrissae movement now activated other muscles of the face. This result is illustrated in Figure 8.20.

Mechanisms of Neural Reorganization. Two kinds of mechanisms have been proposed to account for the reorganization of neural circuits: (1) the strengthening of existing connections, possibly through release from inhibition, and (2) the establish-

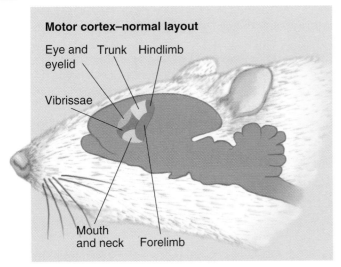

Motor cortex–normal layout

Eye and eyelid
Trunk
Hindlimb
Vibrissae
Mouth and neck
Forelimb

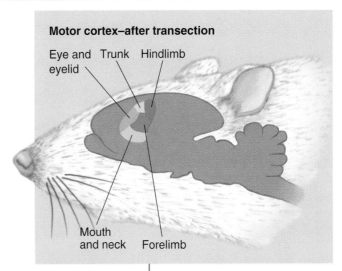

Motor cortex–after transection

Eye and eyelid
Trunk
Hindlimb
Mouth and neck
Forelimb

Reorganization of the rat motor cortex following transection of the motor neurons that control movements of the vibrissae. The motor cortex was mapped by brain stimulation before transection and then again a few weeks after. (Adapted from Sanes, Suner, & Donoghue, 1990.)

Figure 8.20

ment of new connections by collateral sprouting (see O'Leary, Ruff, & Dyck, 1994). Support for the first mechanism comes from two observations: Reorganization often occurs too quickly to be explained by neural growth, and rapid reorganization never involves changes of more than 2 millimeters of cortical surface. Support for the second mechanism comes from the observation that the magnitude of long-term reorganization can be too great to be explained by changes in existing connections. Figure 8.21 on page 254 shows how these two mechanisms might account for the reorganization that occurs after damage to a peripheral somatosensory nerve.

Recovery of Function after Brain Damage

Understanding the mechanisms that underlie the recovery of function after nervous system damage is a high priority for neuroscientists. If these mechanisms were understood, steps could be taken to promote recovery. However, recovery of function after nervous system damage is a poorly understood phenomenon.

Little is known about recovery of function after nervous system damage for two reasons. The first is that it is difficult to conduct controlled experiments on populations of brain-damaged patients. The second is that nervous system damage may result in a variety of compensatory changes that can easily be confused with true recovery of function. For example, any improvement in the week or two after damage could reflect a decline in *cerebral edema* (brain swelling) rather than a recovery from the neural damage itself, and any gradual improvement in the months after damage could reflect the learning of new cognitive and behavioral strategies (i.e., substitution of functions) rather than the return of lost functions (see Wilson, 1998). Recovery of function is most likely when the patient is young (see Figure 8.22 on page 255) and the lesions are small (see Payne & Lomber, 2001).

Cognitive reserve (roughly equivalent to education and intelligence) is thought to play an important role in the apparent recovery of cognitive function after brain damage. Kapur (1997) conducted a biographical study of doctors and neuroscientists with brain damage, and he observed a great deal of cognitive recovery. He concluded that the observed improvement did not represent the actual recovery of lost cognitive function; rather, the patients' cognitive reserve allowed them to accomplish cognitive tasks in alternative ways.

Thinking Clearly

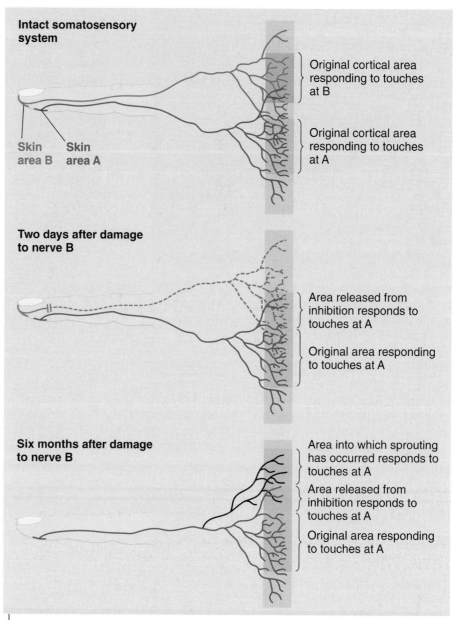

Intact somatosensory system

Original cortical area responding to touches at B

Original cortical area responding to touches at A

Skin area B   Skin area A

Two days after damage to nerve B

Area released from inhibition responds to touches at A

Original area responding to touches at A

Six months after damage to nerve B

Area into which sprouting has occurred responds to touches at A

Area released from inhibition responds to touches at A

Original area responding to touches at A

The two-stage model of neural reorganization: (1) strengthening of existing connections through release from inhibition and (2) establishment of new connections by collateral sprouting.

Figure 8.21

The mechanisms of recovery of function after brain damage remain unknown. It seems likely that neural reorganization contributes to such recovery, but so far most of the evidence for this hypothesis has been indirect (see Hallett, 2001). The strongest evidence comes from a study in which the degree of motor recovery in stroke patients was found to be correlated with the degree of motor cortex reorganization (Lipert et al., 2000).

For years, neural reorganization seemed to be the only explanation for recovery from brain damage. However, the discovery of adult neurogenesis raised another possibility: Perhaps the growth of new neurons plays a role in such recovery, par-

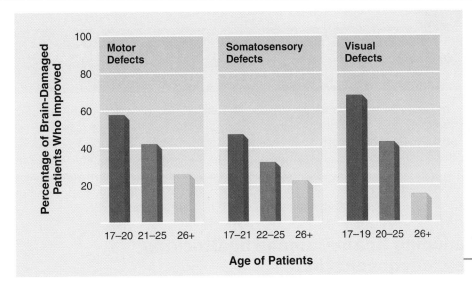

ticularly when the damage affects the hippocampus. It has recently been shown (see Kokaia & Lindvall, 2003) that damage to the hippocampus can increase adult neurogenesis in that structure—see Figure 8.23.

It is thus possible that an increase in adult neurogenesis contributes to recovery from stroke, but there is currently no direct evidence for this attractive hypothesis. However, if this hypothesis is proven, exercise—which has been shown to increase adult neurogenesis (Holmes et al., 2004; Van Praag et al., 2002)—could prove to be therapeutic for patients with hippocampal damage.

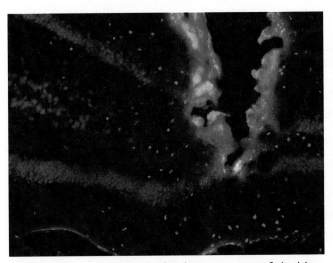 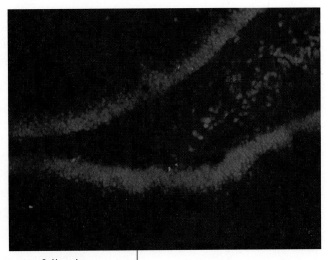

Increased neurogenesis in the dentate gyrus of the hippocampus following damage. The left panel shows (1) an electrolytic lesion in the dentate gyrus of the hippocampus (damaged neurons are stained turquoise) and (2) the resulting increase in the formation of new cells (stained red), many of which develop into mature neurons (stained dark blue). The right panel displays the comparable control area in the unlesioned hemisphere, showing the normal number of new cells (stained red). (These beautiful images are courtesy of my good friends Carl Ernst and Brian Christie, Department of Psychology, University of British Columbia.)

Figure 8.23

8.5

Neuroplasticity and the Treatment of Nervous System Damage

The study of neuroplasticity is currently one of the most active and exciting areas of research in neuroscience. This section reveals the major reason for all the excitement: the dream that recent discoveries about neuroplasticity—with which you are now familiar—can be applied to the treatment of brain damage in human patients. The following four subsections describe research on some major new treatment approaches. Most of this research has focused on animal models, but some of it has progressed to clinical trials with human patients.

Reducing Brain Damage by Blocking Neurodegeneration

Several studies have shown that it may be possible to reduce brain damage by blocking neural degeneration in human patients. For example, in one study, Xu and colleagues (1999) induced cerebral ischemia in rats by limiting blood flow to the brain. This had two major effects: It produced damage in the hippocampus, a structure that is particularly susceptible to ischemic damage, and it produced deficits in the rats' performance in a maze. The hippocampuses of rats in the experimental group were treated with viruses genetically engineered to release *apoptosis inhibitor protein*. Amazingly, the apoptosis inhibitor protein prevented both the loss of hippocampal neurons and the deficits in maze performance.

In addition to apoptosis inhibitor protein, several other neurochemicals have been shown to block the degeneration of damaged neurons. The most widely studied of these is *nerve growth factor* (see Sofroniew, Howe, & Mobley, 2001). You may be surprised to learn that estrogens have a similar effect (see Behl, 2002; Sawada & Shimohama, 2000; Stein, 2001; Wise et al., 2001). **Estrogens** are a class of steroid hormones that are released in large amounts by the *ovaries* (the female gonads). These hormones have several important effects on the maturation of the female body, which you will learn about in Chapter 11, but they also have some protective influences on the brain. The neuroprotective effects of estrogens may explain why several brain disorders (e.g., Parkinson's disease) are more prevalent in males than in females. Although there is considerable interest in the potential of estrogens as neuroprotective agents, the report that estrogen treatments slightly increase susceptibility to Alzheimer's disease (Webber et al., 2005) suggests that these hormones do not act against all forms of brain pathology.

Promoting Recovery from CNS Damage by Promoting Regeneration

Although regeneration does not normally occur in the mammalian CNS, several studies have shown that it can be induced. The following three studies are particularly promising because they have shown that such regeneration can be associated with functional recovery.

Eitan and colleagues (1994) transected the left optic nerves of rats. In the control rats, the retinal ganglion cells, which compose the left optic nerve, permanently degenerated. The experimental rats received injections of an agent that is toxic to oligodendrocytes, thus eliminating these cells' ability to block regeneration. In these experimental subjects, the optic nerves regenerated, and 6 weeks after the injury, the researchers were able to record responses from the optic nerve when light flashes were presented to the left eye.

Cheng, Cao, and Olson (1996) transected the spinal cords of rats, thus rendering them *paraplegic* (paralyzed in the posterior portion of their bodies). The researchers

The Evolutionary Perspective

Clinical Implications

Clinical Implications

then transplanted sections of myelinated peripheral nerve across the transection. As a result, spinal cord neurons regenerated through the implanted Schwann cell myelin sheaths, and the regeneration allowed the rats to regain use of their hindquarters.

A similar study involved transplanting *olfactory ensheathing cells* rather than Schwann cells. Olfactory ensheathing cells, which are similar to Schwann cells, were selected because the olfactory system is unique in its ability to support continual growth of axons from new PNS neurons into the CNS (i.e., into the olfactory bulbs). Li, Field, and Raisman (1998) made lesions in the corticospinal tract of rats and then implanted bridges of olfactory ensheathing cells across the lesion. Axons grew through the lesion, and the motor function of the affected paw was partially restored.

Promoting Recovery from CNS Damage by Neurotransplantation

A few years ago, the idea of brain transplantation was little more than science fiction. Today, the treatment of brain damage by transplanting neural tissue is approaching reality. Efforts to treat CNS damage by neurotransplantation have taken two different approaches (see Björklund & Lindvall, 2000). The first is to transplant fetal tissue; the second is to transplant stem cells.

Clinical Implications

Transplanting Fetal Tissue. The first approach to neurotransplantation was to replace a damaged structure with fetal tissue that would develop into the same structure. Could the *donor* tissue develop and become integrated into the *host* brain, and in so doing alleviate the symptoms? This approach focused on Parkinson's disease. Parkinson's patients lack the dopamine-releasing cells of the nigrostriatal pathway: Could they be cured by transplanting the appropriate fetal tissue into the site?

Early signs were positive. Bilateral transplantation of fetal substantia nigra cells was successful in treating the MPTP monkey model of Parkinson's disease (Bankiewicz et al., 1990; Sladek et al., 1987). Fetal substantia nigra transplants survived in the MPTP-treated monkeys; they innervated adjacent striatal tissue, released dopamine, and, most importantly, alleviated the severe poverty of movement, tremor, and rigidity produced by the MPTP.

Soon after the favorable effects of neurotransplants in the MPTP monkey model were reported, neurotransplantation was offered as a treatment for Parkinson's disease at major research hospitals. The results of the first case studies were promising. The fetal substantia nigra implants survived, and they released dopamine into the host striatum (see Sawle & Myers, 1993). More importantly, some of the patients improved.

The results of these case studies triggered a large-scale double-blind evaluation study of patients suffering from advanced Parkinson's disease. The study was extremely thorough; it even included placebo controls—patients who received surgery but no implants. The initial results were encouraging: Although control patients showed no improvement, the implants survived in the experimental patients, and some displayed a modest improvement. Unfortunately, however, about 15% of these patients started to display a variety of uncontrollable writhing and chewing movements about a year after the surgery (Greene et al., 1999).

The results of this first double-blind placebo-controlled clinical trial of the effectiveness of fetal tissue transplants created widespread debate (see Dunnett, Björklund, & Lindvall, 2001). The incidence of adverse motor side effects is likely to stifle future attempts to develop neurotransplantation as a treatment for Parkinson's disease. However, many still believe that this is an extremely promising therapeutic approach, but that the large-scale clinical trial was premature. Researchers do not yet know how to maximize the survival and growth of neurotransplants and how to minimize their side effects. It is important to achieve a balance between the pressure to develop new treatments quickly and the need to base treatments on a carefully constructed foundation of scientific understanding (see Döbrössy & Dunnett, 2001).

In Chapter 3, you were introduced to Roberto Garcia d'Orta—the Lizard. D'Orta, who suffered from Parkinson's disease, initially responded to L-dopa therapy; but, after 3 years of therapy, his condition worsened. Then he responded to treatment with a dopamine agonist, but again the improvement was only temporary. D'Orta was in a desperate state when he heard about *adrenal medulla autotransplantation* (transplanting a patient's own adrenal medulla cells into her or his striatum, usually for the treatment of Parkinson's disease). Adrenal medulla cells release small amounts of dopamine, and there were some early indications that adrenal medulla autotransplantation might alleviate the symptoms of Parkinson's disease.

D'Orta demanded adrenal medulla autotransplantation from his doctor. When his doctor refused, on the grounds that the effectiveness of the treatment was still in doubt, d'Orta found himself another doctor—a neurosurgeon who was not nearly so cautious.

The Case of Roberto Garcia d'Orta: The Lizard Gets an Autotransplant

Roberto flew to Juarez. The neurosurgeon there greeted him with open arms. As long as Roberto could afford the cost, he'd be happy to do an adrenal implant on him. . . .

Were there any dangers?

The neurosurgeon seemed insulted by the question. If Señor d'Orta didn't trust him, he could go elsewhere. . . .

Roberto underwent the procedure.

He flew back home two weeks later. He was no better. He was told that it took time for the cells to grow and make the needed chemicals. . . .

Then I received an unexpected call from Roberto's wife. Roberto was dead. . . .

He'd died of a stroke. . . Had the stroke been a complication of his surgery? It was more than a mere possibility. (Klawans, 1990, pp. 63–64)

Transplanting Stem Cells. In Chapter 7, you learned about *embryonic neural stem cells*, which are *multipotent* (having the capacity to develop into many types of mature neurons). Investigators are trying to develop procedures for repairing brain damage by injecting embryonic neural stem cells into the damaged site. Once injected, the stem cells could develop and replace the damaged cells, under guidance from surrounding tissue. This line of research received a major boost from the development of renewable cultures of stem cells (see Wakayama et al., 2001), which can serve as a source for transplantation and research (Gage, 2000). The study by McDonald and colleagues (1999) illustrates the potential of this method.

McDonald and colleagues injected embryonic neural stem cells into an area of spinal damage. Their subjects were rats that had been rendered paraplegic by a spinal injury. The stem cells migrated to different areas around the damaged area, where they developed into mature neurons. Remarkably, the rats receiving the implants became capable of supporting their weight with their hindlimbs and walking, albeit awkwardly.

Promoting Recovery from CNS Damage by Rehabilitative Training

Clinical Implications

Several demonstrations of the important role of experience in the organization of the developing and adult brain kindled a renewed interest in the use of rehabilitative training to promote recovery from CNS damage; see Figure 8.24. The following innovative rehabilitative training programs were derived from such findings.

Strokes. Small strokes produce a core of brain damage, which is often followed by a gradually expanding loss of neural function around this core. Nudo, Jenkins, and Merzenich (1996) produced small *ischemic lesions* (lesions produced by an interruption of blood supply) in the hand area of the motor cortex of monkeys. Then,

5 days later, a program of hand training and practice was initiated. During the ensuing 3 or 4 weeks, the monkeys plucked hundreds of tiny food pellets from food wells of different sizes. This practice substantially reduced the expansion of cortical damage. The monkeys that received the rehabilitative training also showed greater recovery in the use of their affected hand.

One of the principles that has emerged from the study of neurodevelopment is that neurons seem to be in a competitive situation: They compete with other neurons for synaptic sites and neurotrophins, and the losers die. Weiller and Rijntjes (1999) designed a rehabilitative program based on this principle, tested it on monkeys, and then tested it on unilateral stroke patients who had difficulty using one arm. Their procedure, called *constraint-induced therapy* (Taub, Uswatte, & Elbert, 2002), was to tie down the functioning arm for 2 weeks while the affected arm received intensive training. Performance with the affected arm improved markedly over the 2 weeks, and there was an increase in the area of motor cortex controlling that arm.

A patient with CNS damage receiving rehabilitative training.

Spinal Injury. In one approach to treating patients with spinal injuries (see Rossignol, 2000; Wolpaw & Tennissen, 2001), patients incapable of walking were supported by a harness over a moving treadmill. With most of their weight supported and the treadmill providing appropriate feedback, the patients gradually learned to make walking movements. Then, as they improved, the amount of support was gradually reduced. In one study using this technique, over 90% of the trained patients eventually became independent walkers, compared with only 50% of those receiving conventional physiotherapy.

Phantom Limbs. Most amputees have the sense that they still possess limbs that have in fact been amputated—a condition referred to as **phantom limb**. The most striking feature of phantom limbs is how real they feel. The sensation of the limb is so compelling that a patient may try to jump out of bed onto a nonexistent leg or to lift a cup with a nonexistent hand. In most cases, the amputated limb behaves like a normal limb; for example, as an amputee walks, he or she feels a phantom arm swinging back and forth in perfect coordination with the intact arm. However, sometimes an amputee feels that the amputated limb is stuck in a peculiar position. For example, one amputee felt that his phantom arm extended straight out from the shoulder, and as a result, he turned sideways whenever he passed through doorways (Melzack, 1992).

About 50% of amputees experience chronic severe pain in their phantom limbs. A typical complaint is that an amputated hand is clenched so tightly that the fingernails are digging into the palm of the hand. Occasionally, phantom limb pain can be treated by having the amputee concentrate on opening the amputated hand. However, when this does not work, the pain can become so intense that desperate measures are attempted.

Based on the premise that phantom limb pain results from irritation at the stump, many efforts to control it involved cutting off the stump or surgical destruction of various parts of the neural pathway between the stump and the cortex. Unfortunately, none of these surgical interventions provided patients with relief from the pain or eliminated the phantom limb (see Melzack, 1992). Still, the idea that phantom limbs and phantom limb pain result from irritation of nerves in the stump persisted. There seemed to be no other possibility.

This chapter ends with the stories of two patients suffering from phantom limb pain and their exceptional doctor. The patients were Tom and Philip, and their physician was the neuropsychologist V. S. Ramachandran. In the process of treating Tom and Philip, Dr. Ramachandran solved a long-standing neuropsychological puzzle and developed a new treatment to boot.

The Cases of Tom and Philip: Phantom Limbs and Ramachandran

Clinical Implications

Thinking Clearly

Dr. Ramachandran read an article about a study you have already encountered in this chapter, the study by Pons and colleagues (1991). In this study, severing the sensory neurons in the arms of monkeys led to a reorganization of somatosensory cortex: The area of the somatosensory cortex that originally received input from the damaged arm now received input from areas of the body normally mapped onto adjacent areas of somatosensory cortex. Ramachandran was struck by a sudden insight: Perhaps phantom limbs were not in the stump at all, but in the brain; perhaps the perception of a phantom arm originated from parts of the body that now innervated the original arm area of the somatosensory cortex (see Ramachandran & Blakeslee, 1998).

Excited by his hypothesis, Dr. Ramachandran asked one of his patients, Tom, if he would participate in a simple test. He touched various parts of Tom's body and asked Tom what he felt. Remarkably, when he touched the side of Tom's face on the same side as his amputated arm, Tom felt sensations from various parts of his phantom hand as well as his face. Indeed, when some warm water was dropped on his face, he felt it running down his phantom hand. A second map of his hand was found on his shoulder (see Figure 8.25).

Philip, another patient of Dr. Ramachandran, suffered from severe chronic pain in his phantom arm. For a decade, Philip had been unable to move the joints of the phantom arm: It was frozen in an awkward position (Ramachandran & Rogers-Ramachandran, 2000), and Philip suffered great pain in all of its joints, particularly the elbow.

Dr. Ramachandran applied a bit of biopsychological ingenuity to the problem. Could he relieve Philip's pain by teaching him to move his phantom arm? Knowing how important feedback is in movement (see Chapter 6), Dr. Ramachandran constructed a special feedback apparatus for Philip. This was a box divided in two by a vertical mirror. Philip was instructed to put his good right hand into the box through a hole in the front and view it through a hole in the top. When he looked at his hand, he could see it and its mirror image. He was instructed to put his phantom limb in the box and try to position it, as best he could, so that it corresponded to the mirror image of his good hand. Then, he was instructed to make synchronous, bilaterally symmetrical movements of his arms—his actual right arm and his phantom left arm—while viewing his good arm and its mirror image (see Figure 8.26).

> "Oh my God! Oh my God, doctor! This is unbelievable. It's mind-boggling." He was jumping up and down like a kid. "My left arm is plugged in again. It's as if I'm in the past. . . . I can move my arm again. I can feel my elbow moving, my wrist moving. It's all moving again. (Ramachandran & Blakeslee, 1998, pp. 47–48)

But when Philip shut his eyes or removed his arms from the apparatus, his phantom limb was frozen once again . . . and the pain was as bad as ever. So, Ramachandran sent Philip home with the box and instructions to use it. Three weeks later, Philip phoned.

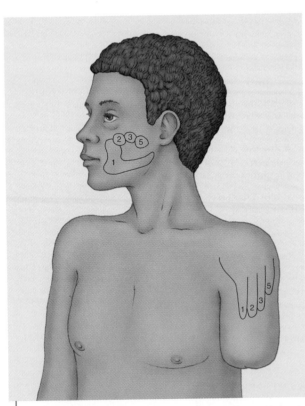

The places on Tom's body where touches elicited sensations in his phantom hand.

(Adapted from Ramachandran & Blakeslee, 1998.)

Figure 8.25

"Doctor," he exclaimed, "it's gone!"

"What's gone?" (I thought maybe he had lost the mirror box.)

"My phantom is gone."

"What are you talking about?"

"You know, my phantom arm, which I had for 10 years. It doesn't exist anymore. All I have is my phantom fingers and palm dangling from my shoulder."

. . . "Philip—does this bother you?"

"No, no, no. . . . On the contrary. You know the excruciating pain that I always had in my elbow? . . . Well, now I don't have an elbow and I don't have that pain anymore." (Ramachandran & Blakeslee, 1998, p. 49)

I hope that I have managed to communicate to you some of the excitement that is being generated by the discovery that the adult human brain is plastic and by the possibility of applying neuroplastic processes to repair brain damage. Effective new treatments have not yet been developed; there is still a lot of work to be done to translate the successes with animal models into safe and effective treatments for human patients. Still, I am optimistic that there will soon be a breakthrough because, as you have just learned, progress is being made on so many different fronts.

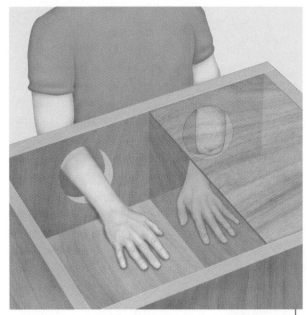

The apparatus used by Ramachandran to treat Philip's phantom limb pain.

Figure 8.26

Key Terms

8.1 Causes of Brain Damage

Aneurysm (p. 233)
Apoptosis (p. 239)
Arteriosclerosis (p. 234)
Benign tumors (p. 232)
Cerebral hemorrhage (p. 233)
Cerebral ischemia (p. 234)
Concussion (p. 236)
Congenital (p. 233)
Contrecoup injuries (p. 236)
Contusions (p. 239)
Dementia (p. 236)
Down syndrome (p. 238)
Embolism (p. 234)
Encapsulated tumors (p. 232)
Encephalitis (p. 237)
General paresis (p. 237)
Glutamate (p. 234)
Hematoma (p. 236)
Infiltrating tumors (p. 232)
Korsakoff's syndrome (p. 238)
Malignant tumors (p. 232)
Meningiomas (p. 232)
Meningitis (p. 237)
Metastatic tumors (p. 232)
NMDA (N-methyl-D-aspartate)
  receptors (p. 234)
Punch-drunk
  syndrome (p. 236)
Strokes (p. 233)
Thrombosis (p. 234)
Toxic psychosis (p. 237)
Tumor (neoplasm) (p. 232)

8.2 Neuropsychological Diseases

Alzheimer's disease (p. 245)
Amyloid (p. 246)
Ataxia (p. 245)
Complex partial seizures (p. 241)
Convulsions (p. 240)
L-Dopa (p. 243)
Epidemiology (p. 245)
Epilepsy (p. 240)
Epileptic auras (p. 240)
Generalized seizures (p. 241)
Grand mal seizure (p. 242)
Huntington's disease (p. 243)
Hypoxia (p. 242)
Multiple sclerosis (MS) (p. 244)
Nigrostriatal pathway (p. 243)
Parkinson's disease (p. 242)
Partial seizure (p. 240)
Petit mal seizure (p. 242)
Simple partial seizures (p. 241)
Striatum (p. 243)
Substantia nigra (p. 243)
3-per-second spike-and-wave
  discharge (p. 242)

8.3 Animal Models of Human Neuropsychological Diseases

Animal model (p. 247)
Deprenyl (p. 249)
MPTP (p. 248)

8.4 Neuroplastic Responses to Nervous System Damage

Anterograde degeneration (p. 249)
Collateral sprouting (p. 252)
Distal segment (p. 249)
Neural regeneration (p. 250)
Oligodendroglia (p. 251)
Proximal segment (p. 249)
Retrograde degeneration (p. 249)
Schwann cells (p. 251)
Transneuronal degeneration (p. 249)

8.5 Neuroplasticity and the Treatment of Nervous System Damage

Estrogens (p. 256)
Phantom limb (p. 259)

ON THE CD

Studying for an exam? Get some help from the electronic flash cards of the key terms and the practice tests for this chapter.

 **chapter 8**

Brain Damage and Neuroplasticity
Can the Brain Recover from Damage?

This chapter focused on brain damage: its causes, its symptoms, its treatment, and recovery from it. Noteworthy was the chapter-opening case of Professor P.

Causes of Brain Damage

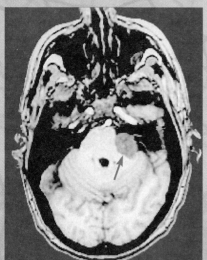

Pinel's tumor

There are many causes of brain damage, including brain tumors, cerebrovascular disorders, injury to the head, infections, neurotoxins, and faulty genes. Some of these causes are thought to exert their effects by altering normal programs of cell death (i.e., of apoptosis).
(Pages 232–239)

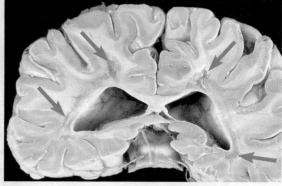

Multiple sclerosis

Neuropsychological Diseases

Five major brain disorders are epilepsy, Parkinson's disease, Huntington's disease, multiple sclerosis, and Alzheimer's disease. Huntington's disease is caused by a single dominant gene mutation, but the others seem to result from the interaction of a variety of genetic and environmental factors, which are not necessarily the same in each case.
(Pages 239–247)

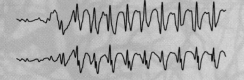

Animal Models of Human Neuropsychological Diseases

For a variety of ethical and technical reasons, it is often difficult to conduct experimental studies of neuropsychological disorders in human subjects. Thus, the existence of a good animal model of a disorder can greatly facilitate its study. One such model is the MPTP model of Parkinson's disease, which was discovered when several heroin addicts were exposed to the MPTP in a bad batch of synthetic heroin and developed the symptoms of Parkinson's disease. MPTP is now used to induce the Parkinson's model in laboratory animals.
(Pages 247–249)

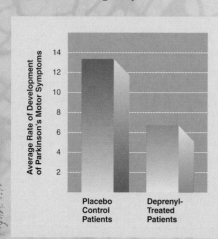

Figure 8.18

Average Rate of Development of Parkinson's Motor Symptoms

14
12
10
8
6
4
2

Placebo Control Patients | Deprenyl-Treated Patients

Visual Summary

Neuroplastic Responses to Nervous System Damage: Degeneration, Regeneration, Reorganization, and Recovery

After damage to the brain, neurons degenerate, and compensatory neural sprouting and reorganization of affected circuits often

Damage-induced neurogenesis

follow. Although accurate neural regeneration occurs in the CNSs of many species, there is no meaningful regeneration of damaged structures in the human brain. Recovery of function after brain damage in humans is poorly understood; it appears to be less common than generally assumed and largely limited to young subjects with small areas of damage.
(Pages 249–255)

Neuroplasticity and the Treatment of Nervous System Damage

Recent progress in the study of neuroplasticity is leading to the development of exciting new treatments for patients with brain

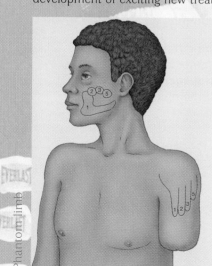

Phantom limb

damage. These treatments include various procedures for blocking neural degeneration, for promoting neural regeneration and neurotransplantation, and for rehabilitative training.
(Pages 256–261)

Themes Revisited

Because this entire chapter dealt with clinical issues, the clinical implications tag made numerous appearances: the ironic case of Professor P.; Jerry Quarry, the punch-drunk ex-boxer; cases of complex partial epilepsy; Walter S. Miller, whose wife had Huntington's disease; cases of MPTP poisoning; and amputees with phantom limbs.

The chapter stressed the theme of thinking clearly about biopsychology in several places. Stressed also was the importance of thinking clearly about the cumulative effects of concussions, about genes and Parkinson's disease, about the primary symptom of Alzheimer's disease, about animal models of neuropsychological diseases, and about recovery of function after brain damage. Particularly interesting were the insightful approaches taken by Ramachandran in treating phantom limb pain.

The evolutionary perspective was also highlighted. You learned about animal models, which are based on the comparative approach; and you learned about how they have been used to study neural regeneration and reorganization following brain damage. Finally, you learned that research into the mechanisms of mammalian neural regeneration has been stimulated by the accurate regeneration that occurs in some species.

Think about It

1. An epileptic is brought to trial for assault. The lawyer argues that her client is not a criminal and that the assaults in question were psychomotor attacks. The prosecution lawyer argues that the defendant has a long history of violent assault. What do you think the judge should do?

2. The more that is known about a disease, the easier it is to diagnose; and the more accurately it can be diagnosed, the easier it is to find things out about it. Explain and discuss.

3. Total dementia often creates less suffering than partial dementia. Discuss.

4. In order to be useful, animal models do not have to have all the features of the disorder they are modeling. Discuss.

5. What do you think should be the next step in the study of neurotransplantation as a treatment for Parkinson's disease? Explain.

chapter 9

Learning, Memory, and Amnesia
How Your Brain Stores Information

Learning and memory are, in a sense, two aspects of the same thing: Both involve the ability of the brain to change its functioning in response to experience. **Learning** occurs when experience changes the brain, and **memory** is the means by which these changes are stored and subsequently reactivated. In essence, learning and memory both result when neuroplastic changes are induced by experience. If our brains could not change in response to experience, we could not learn or remember, and we would experience every moment as if waking from a lifelong sleep— each person would be a stranger, each act a new challenge, and each word incomprehensible.

The chapter focuses on the roles played by various brain structures in the processes of learning and memory. Knowledge about these roles is largely based on studies of amnesic patients with brain damage and on animal models of brain-damage–produced amnesia.

9.1
Amnesic Effects of Bilateral Medial Temporal Lobectomy

Ironically, the person who has contributed more than any other to our understanding of the neuropsychology of memory is not a neuropsychologist. In fact, although he has collaborated on dozens of studies of memory, he has no formal research training and not a single degree to his name. He is H.M., a man who in 1953, at the age of 27, had the medial portions of his temporal lobes removed for the treatment of a severe case of epilepsy. Just as the Rosetta Stone provided archaeologists with important clues to the meaning of Egyptian hieroglyphics, H.M.'s memory deficits have been instrumental in the achievement of our current understanding of the neural bases of memory (see Corkin, 2002).

The Case of H.M., the Man Who Changed the Study of Memory

During the 11 years preceding his surgery, H.M. suffered an average of one generalized convulsion each week and many partial convulsions each day, despite massive doses of anticonvulsant medication. Electroencephalography suggested that H.M.'s convulsions arose from foci in the medial portions of both his left and right temporal lobes. Because the removal of one medial temporal lobe had proved to be an effective treatment for patients with a unilateral temporal lobe focus, the decision was made to perform a **bilateral medial temporal lobectomy**—the removal of the medial portions of both temporal lobes, including most of the **hippocampus, amygdala**, and adjacent cortex (see Figure 9.1). (A **lobectomy** is an operation in which a lobe, or a major part of one, is removed from the brain; a **lobotomy** is an operation in which a lobe, or a major part of one, is separated from the rest of the brain by a large cut but is not removed.)

In several respects, H.M.'s bilateral medial temporal lobectomy was an unqualified success. His generalized convulsions were all but eliminated, and the incidence of his minor seizures was reduced to one or two per day, even though the level of his anticonvulsant medication was substantially reduced. Furthermore, H.M. entered surgery a reasonably well-adjusted individual with normal perceptual and motor abilities and above-average intelligence, and he left it in the same condition. Indeed, H.M.'s IQ increased from 104 to 118 as a result of his surgery, presumably because of the decline in the incidence of his seizures. Be that as it may, H.M. was the last patient to receive a bilateral medial temporal lobectomy—because of its devastating amnesic effects.

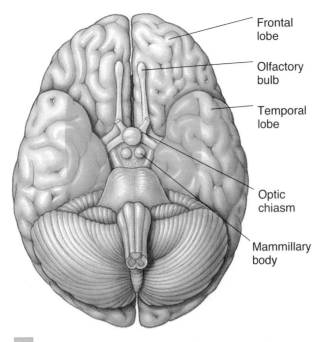

Tissue typically excised in medial temporal lobectomy

Medial temporal lobectomy. The portions of the medial temporal lobes that were removed from H.M.'s brain are illustrated in a view of the inferior surface of the brain.

Figure 9.1

Frontal lobe

Olfactory bulb

Temporal lobe

Optic chiasm

Mammillary body

In assessing the amnesic effects of brain surgery, it is usual to administer tests of the patient's ability to remember things learned before the surgery and tests of the patient's ability to remember things learned after the surgery. Deficits on the former tests lead to a diagnosis of **retrograde** (backward-acting) **amnesia**; those on the latter tests lead to a diagnosis of **anterograde** (forward-acting) **amnesia**.

Like his intellectual abilities, H.M.'s memory for events predating his surgery remains largely intact. Although he seems to have a mild retrograde amnesia for events that occurred in the 2 years before his surgery, his memory for more remote events (e.g., for the events of his childhood) is reasonably normal.

In contrast, H.M. suffers from a severe anterograde amnesia. Memories are often considered to be of two major types: **short-term memories** (memories that are fleeting, lasting only for as long as one thinks about them) and **long-term memories** (lasting memories that persist even after we stop thinking about them). H.M. has a normal short-term memory; the classic measure of short-term memory is the **digit span** (the average number of random digits that can be correctly repeated immediately after hearing the sequence just once), and H.M. has a digit span of 6 digits, which is within the normal range (Wickelgren, 1968). H.M. has extreme difficulty in forming new long-term memories; once he stops thinking about a new experience, it is usually lost forever. In effect, H.M. became suspended in time on that day in 1953 when he regained his health but lost his future:

> As far as we can tell, this man has retained little if anything of events subsequent to the operation. . . . Ten months before I examined him, his family had moved from their old house to a new one a few blocks away on the same street. He still had not learned the new address (though remembering the old one perfectly), nor could he be trusted to find his way home alone. He did not know where objects in constant use were kept, and his mother stated that he would read the same magazines over and over again without finding their contents familiar. . . . [F]orgetting occurred the instant the patient's focus of attention shifted. (Milner, 1965, pp. 104–105)

> During three of the nights at the Clinical Research Center, the patient rang for the night nurse, asking her, with many apologies, if she would tell him where he was and how he came to be there. He clearly realized that he was in a hospital but seemed unable to reconstruct any of the events of the previous day. On another occasion he remarked "Every day is alone in itself, whatever enjoyment I've had, and whatever sorrow I've had." Our own impression is that . . . events fade for him long before the day is over. He often volunteers stereotyped descriptions of his own state, by saying that it is "like waking from a dream." His experience seems to be that of a person who is just becoming aware of his surroundings without fully comprehending the situation, because he does not remember what went before.

> He still fails to recognize people who are close neighbours or family friends but who got to know him only after the operation. When questioned, he tries to use accent as a clue to a person's place of origin and weather as a clue to the time of year. Although he gives his date of birth unhesitatingly and accurately, he always underestimates his own age and can only make wild guesses as to the date. (Milner, Corkin, & Teuber, 1968, pp. 216–217)

H.M. has lived in a nursing home for many years. He spends much of each day doing crossword puzzles; his progress on a crossword puzzle is never lost because it is written down.

Discovery of an Important Feature of H.M.' s Amnesia

Many tests confirmed H.M.'s inability to form new long-term memories. The results of the following four tests revealed an unanticipated feature of H.M.'s anterograde amnesia.

Mirror-Drawing Test. The first indication that H.M.'s anterograde amnesia does not involve all long-term memories came from the results of a *mirror-drawing test* (Milner, 1965). H.M.'s task was to draw a line within the boundaries of a star-shaped target by watching his hand in a mirror. H.M. was asked to trace the star 10 times on each of 3 consecutive days, and the number of times he went outside the boundaries on each trial was recorded. As Figure 9.2 shows, H.M.'s performance improved over the 3 days, which indicates retention of the task. However, despite his improved performance, H.M. could not recall ever having seen the task before.

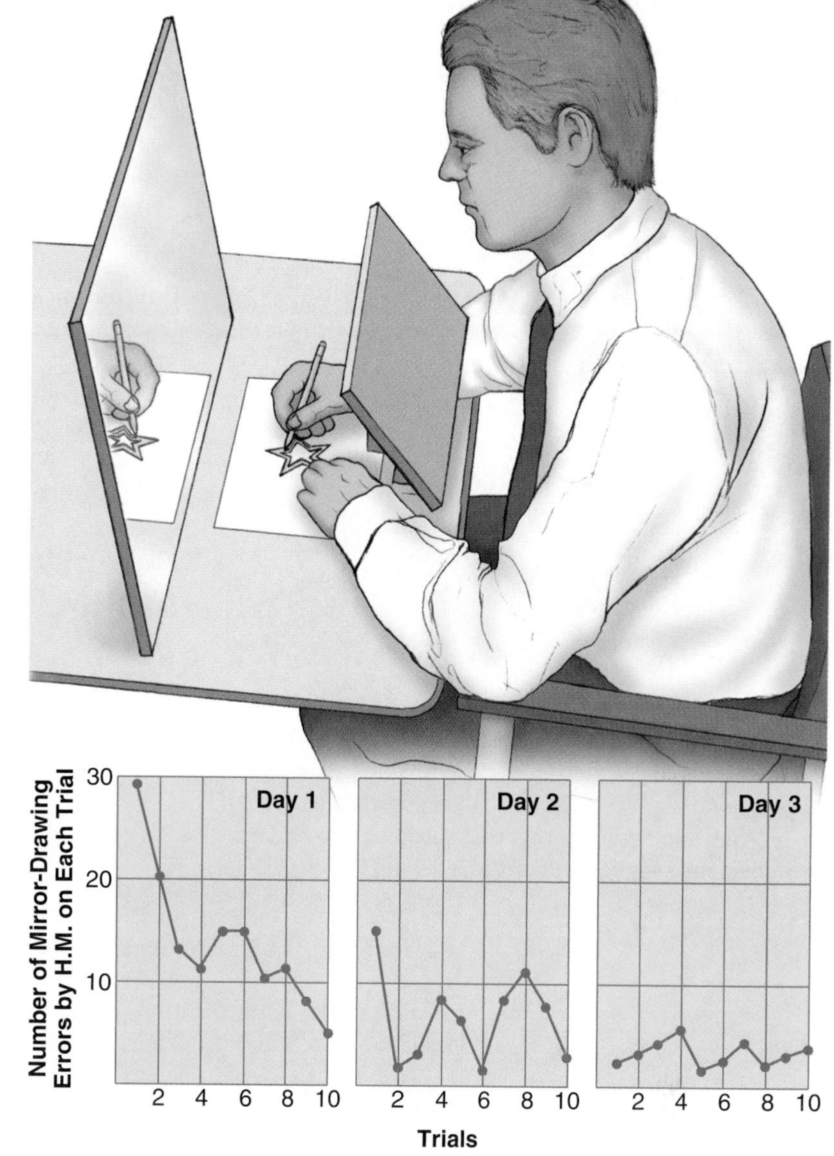

The learning and retention of the mirror-drawing task by H.M. Despite his good retention of the task, H.M. had no conscious recollection of having performed it before.
(Adapted from Milner, 1965.)

Figure 9.2

Rotary-Pursuit Test. In the *rotary-pursuit test* (see Figure 9.3 on page 268), the subject tries to keep the tip of a stylus in contact with a target that rotates on a revolving turntable. Corkin (1968) found that H.M.'s performance on the rotary-pursuit test improved significantly over 9 daily practice sessions, despite the fact that H.M. claimed each day that he had never seen the pursuit rotor before. His improved performance was retained over a 7-day retention interval.

Incomplete-Pictures Test. The discovery that H.M. is capable of forming long-term memories for mirror drawing and rotary pursuit suggested that sensorimotor tasks were the one exception to his inability to form long-term memories. However, this view was challenged by the demonstration that H.M. could also form new long-term memories for the **incomplete-pictures test** (Gollin, 1960)—a nonsensorimotor test of memory that employs five sets of fragmented drawings. Each set contains drawings of the same 20 objects, but they differ in their degree of sketchiness:

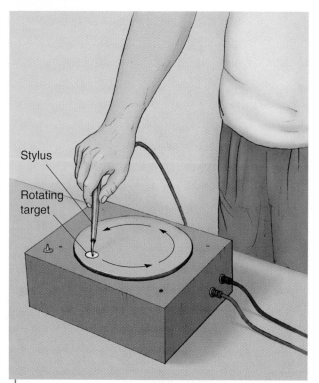

Stylus

Rotating
target

The rotary-pursuit task. The subject tries to keep the stylus in contact with the rotating target, and time-on-target is automatically recorded. H.M. learned and retained this task, although he had no conscious recollection of the learning trials.

Figure 9.3

Set 1 contains the most fragmented drawings, and set 5 contains the complete drawings. The subject is asked to identify the 20 objects from the sketchiest set (set 1); then, those objects that go unrecognized are presented in their set 2 versions, and so on, until all 20 items have been identified. Figure 9.4 illustrates H.M.'s performance on this test and his improved performance 1 hour later (Milner, Corkin, & Teuber, 1968). Despite his improved performance, H.M. could not recall previously performing the task.

Pavlovian Conditioning. H.M. learned an eye-blink Pavlovian conditioning task, albeit at a slower-than-normal rate (Woodruff-Pak, 1993). A tone was sounded just before a puff of air was administered to his eye, until the tone alone elicited an eyeblink. Two years later, H.M. retained this conditioned response almost perfectly, although he had no conscious recollection of the training.

Scientific Contributions of H.M.'s Case

H.M.'s case is a story of personal tragedy, but his contributions to the study of the neural basis of memory have been immense. By showing that the medial temporal lobes play an especially important role in memory, H.M.'s case challenged the then-prevalent view that memory functions are diffusely and equivalently distributed throughout the forebrain—a view championed by the prominent physiological psychologist Karl Lashley (1950). In so doing, H.M.'s case renewed efforts to relate individual brain structures to specific *mnemonic* (memory-related) processes. Particularly, his case spawned a massive research effort aimed at clarifying the mnemonic functions of the hippocampus and other medial temporal lobe structures.

The discovery that bilateral medial temporal lobectomy abolished H.M.'s ability to form certain kinds of new long-term memories without disrupting his ability to form new short-term memories supported the theory that there are different modes of storage for the two types of memory. According to this theory, all memories are stored initially as patterns of unstable, transient neurophysiological changes. However, the storage of some of these short-term memories (e.g., those that have been the subject of thought) is gradually converted to more stable, enduring physiological changes—and in the process, these short-term memories become long-term memories. H.M.'s specific problem appears to be a difficulty in **memory consolidation**, in transferring memories from short-term to long-term modes of storage.

Finally, H.M.'s case was the first to reveal that an amnesic patient might claim no recollection of a previous experience, while demonstrating memory for it by improved performance. Conscious memories are called **explicit memories**, whereas memories that are expressed by improved test performance without conscious awareness are called **implicit memories**.

Medial Temporal Lobe Amnesia

Clinical Implications

Neuropsychological patients with a profile of mnemonic deficits similar to those of H.M., with preserved intellectual functioning, and with evidence of medial temporal lobe damage are said to suffer from **medial temporal lobe amnesia**.

Research on medial temporal lobe amnesia has shown that H.M.'s difficulty in forming explicit long-term memories while retaining the ability to form implicit long-term memories of the same experiences is not unique to him (see Eichen-

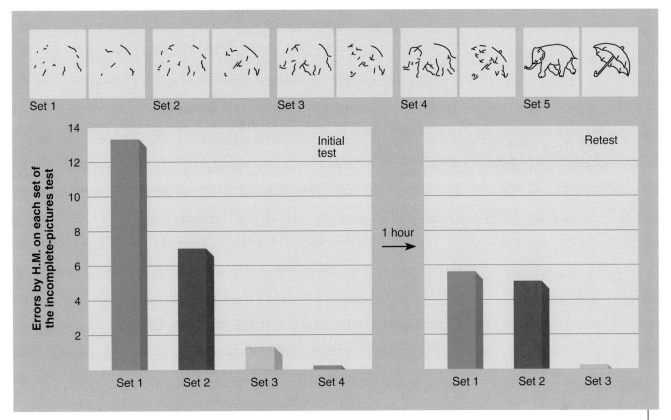

Two items from the incomplete-pictures test. H.M.'s memory for the 20 items on the test was indicated by his ability to recognize the more fragmented versions of them when he was retested. Nevertheless, he had no conscious awareness of having previously seen the items.

Figure 9.4

baum, 1999). This problem has proved to be a symptom of medial temporal lobe amnesia, as well as many other amnesic disorders. As a result, the assessment of implicit long-term memories has played an important role in the study of human amnesia.

Tests that have been developed to assess implicit memory are called **repetition priming tests**. The incomplete-pictures test is an example, but repetition priming tests that involve memory for words are more common. First, the subjects are asked to examine a list of words; they are not asked to learn or remember anything. Later, they are shown a series of fragments (e.g., __ O B __ T E __) of words from the original list, and they are simply asked to complete them. Control subjects who have seen the original words perform well. Surprisingly, amnesic subjects often perform equally well, even though they have no explicit memory of seeing the original list.

Most medial temporal lobe amnesics have difficulty forming explicit long-term memories, but, unlike H.M., they do not completely lose this ability. Consequently, medial temporal lobe amnesics have been studied to determine whether particular kinds of explicit long-term memories are more susceptible to disruption by medial temporal lobe damage. Indeed, research on medial temporal lobe amnesics has shown that not all of their explicit long-term memories are equally effected. The semantic memories of medial temporal lobe amnesics are often quite normal, but their episodic memories are largely absent (see Baddeley, Vargha-Khadem, & Mishkin, 2002; Tulving, 2002). **Semantic memories** are explicit memories for general facts or information, whereas **episodic memories** are explicit memories for the particular events or experiences of one's life. For example, Vargha-Khadem and colleagues (1997) identified three individuals who had experienced bilateral medial temporal lobe damage early in life and then assessed the memory problems experienced by these amnesics as they matured. Remarkably, despite the fact that they remembered few of the experiences that they had during their daily lives (episodic memory), they progressed through mainstream schools and acquired reasonable levels of language ability and factual knowledge (semantic memory).

The Evolutionary Perspective

The symptoms of medial temporal lobe amnesia raise an important question: Why do we have two parallel memory systems, one conscious (explicit) and one unconscious (implicit)? Presumably, the implicit system was the first to evolve, so the question is actually this: What advantage is there in having a second, conscious system?

Two experiments, one in amnesic patients (Reber, Knowlton, & Squire, 1996) and one in amnesic monkeys with medial temporal lobe lesions (Buckley & Gaffan, 1998), suggest that the answer is "flexibility." In both experiments, the amnesic subjects learned an implicit learning task as well as control subjects did; however, if they were asked to use their implicit knowledge in a different way or in a different context, they failed miserably. Presumably, the evolution of explicit memory systems provided for the flexible use of information.

Effects of Cerebral Ischemia on the Hippocampus and Memory

Patients who have experienced **cerebral ischemia**—that is, have experienced an interruption of blood supply to their brains—often suffer from medial temporal lobe amnesia. R.B. is one such individual (Zola-Morgan, Squire, & Amaral, 1986).

The Case of R.B., the Product of a Bungled Operation

Clinical Implications

At the age of 52, R.B. underwent cardiac bypass surgery. The surgery was bungled, and, as a consequence, R.B. suffered brain damage. The pump that was circulating R.B.'s blood to his body while his heart was disconnected broke down, and it was several minutes before a replacement arrived from another part of the hospital. R.B. lived, but the resulting ischemic brain damage left him amnesic.

Although R.B.'s amnesia was not as severe as H.M.'s, it was comparable in many aspects. R.B. died in 1983 of a heart attack, and a detailed postmortem examination of his brain was carried out with the permission of his family. Obvious brain damage was restricted largely to the **pyramidal cell layer** of just one part of the hippocampus—the **CA1 subfield** (see Figure 9.5). The axons of the pyramidal cells of the CA1 subfield compose the largest tract carrying signals out of the hippocampus.

R.B.'s case and others like it suggested that hippocampal damage by itself can produce amnesia; however, this conclusion has been challenged—as you will learn later in this chapter.

9.2 Amnesia of Korsakoff's Syndrome

Clinical Implications

Korsakoff's syndrome is a disorder of memory that is most common in people who have consumed large amounts of alcohol. However, nondrinkers who have diets deficient in *thiamine* (vitamin B₁) display a similar disorder, and there is good evidence that Korsakoff's syndrome in alcoholics is mediated in part by an alcohol-produced disruption of the body's ability to use thiamine. In its advanced stages, Korsakoff's syndrome is characterized by a variety of sensory and motor problems, extreme confusion, personality changes, and a risk of death from liver, gastrointestinal, or heart disorders. Postmortem examination typically reveals lesions to the *medial diencephalon* (the medial thalamus and the medial hypothalamus) and diffuse damage to several other brain structures, most notably the neocortex, hippocampus, and cerebellum (e.g., Sullivan & Marsh, 2003).

The amnesia of Korsakoff's syndrome is similar to medial temporal lobe amnesia in some respects. For example, during the early stages of the disorder, anterograde amnesia for explicit episodic memories is the most prominent symptom. However, as the disorder progresses, severe retrograde amnesia, which can extend back into childhood, also develops.

The gradual, insidious onset and progressive development of Korsakoff's syndrome complicate the study of the resulting retrograde amnesia. It is never entirely clear to what extent Korsakoff amnesia for recent events reflects the retrograde disruption of existing memories or the gradually increasing anterograde blockage of the formation of new ones.

Because the brain damage associated with Korsakoff's syndrome is diffuse, it has not been easy to identify the portion of this damage that is specifically responsible for the amnesia. The first hypothesis, which was based on several small postmortem studies, was that damage to the *mammillary bodies* of the hypothalamus was responsible for the memory deficits of Korsakoff patients; however, subsequent studies revealed cases of Korsakoff amnesia with no mammillary body damage. But in all of these exceptional cases, there was damage to another pair of medial diencephalic nuclei: the **mediodorsal nuclei** of the thalamus. The occurrence of **medial diencephalic amnesia** (amnesia, such as Korsakoff amnesia and similar memory disorders, associated with damage to the medial diencephalon) in stroke patients with small ischemic lesions to the mediodorsal nuclei provides additional evidence of the importance of these structures to mnemonic function (e.g., Graff-Radford et al., 1985; Winocur et al., 1984). However, it is unlikely that the memory deficits of Korsakoff patients are attributable to the damage of any single diencephalic structure (see Vann & Aggleton, 2004).

Thinking Clearly

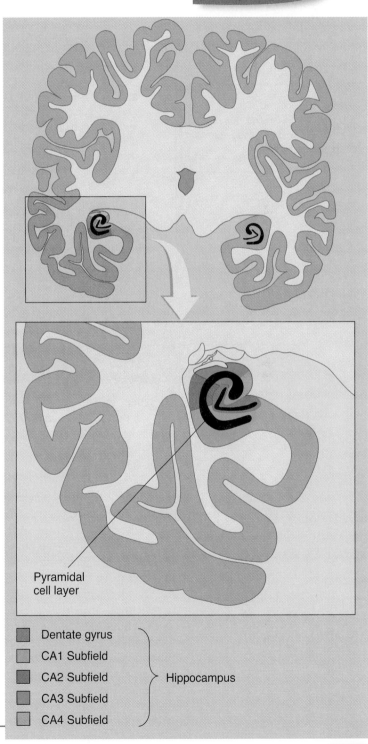

The major components of the hippocampus: CA1, CA2, CA3, and CA4 subfields and the dentate gyrus. R.B.' s brain damage appeared to be restricted largely to the pyramidal cell layer of the CA1 subfield. (CA stands for *cornu ammonis*, another name for hippocampus.)

Pyramidal cell layer

Dentate gyrus
CA1 Subfield
CA2 Subfield } Hippocampus
CA3 Subfield
CA4 Subfield

Figure 9.5

The Up-Your-Nose Case of N.A.

Clinical Implications

After a year of junior college, N.A. joined the U.S. Air Force; he served as a radar technician until his accident in December of 1960. On that fateful day, N.A.

> was assembling a model airplane in his barracks room. His roommate had removed a miniature fencing foil from the wall and was making thrusts behind N.A.'s chair. N.A. turned suddenly and was stabbed through the right nostril. The foil penetrated the cribriform plate [the thin bone around the base of the frontal lobes], taking an upward course to the left into the forebrain. (Squire, 1987, p. 177)
>
> The examiners . . . noted that at first he seemed to be unable to recall any significant personal, national or international events for the two years preceding the accident, but this extensive retrograde amnesia appeared to shrink. . . . Two-and-a-half years after the accident, the retrograde amnesia was said to involve a span of perhaps two weeks immediately preceding the injury, but the exact extent of this retrograde loss was (and remains) impossible to determine. . . .
>
> During . . . convalescence (for the first six to eight months after the accident), the patient's recall of day-to-day events was described as extremely poor, but "occasionally some items sprang forth uncontrollably; he suddenly recalled something he seemed to have no business recalling." His physicians thus gained the impression that his memory was patchy; he appeared to have difficulty in calling up at will many things that at other times emerged spontaneously. . . .
>
> Since his injury, he has been unable to return to any gainful employment, although his memory has continued to improve, albeit slowly. (Teuber, Milner, & Vaughan, 1968, pp. 268–269)

ON THE CD

Interested in the case of N.A.? Visit the *Memory Deficit* module to see him being tested.

An MRI of N.A.'s brain was taken in the late 1980s (Squire et al., 1989). It revealed extensive medial diencephalic damage, including damage to the mediodorsal nuclei and mammillary bodies.

9·3
Amnesia of Alzheimer's Disease

Clinical Implications

Alzheimer's disease is another major cause of amnesia. The first sign of Alzheimer's disease is often a mild deterioration of memory. However, the disorder is progressive: Eventually, *dementia* develops and becomes so severe that the patient is incapable of even simple activities (e.g., eating, speaking, recognizing a spouse, or bladder control). Alzheimer's disease is terminal.

Efforts to understand the neural basis of Alzheimer's amnesia have focused on *predementia Alzheimer's patients* (Alzheimer's patients who have yet to develop dementia). The memory deficits of these patients are more general than those associated with medial temporal lobe damage, medial diencephalic damage, or Korsakoff's syndrome (see Butters & Delis, 1995). In addition to major anterograde and retrograde deficits in tests of explicit memory, predementia Alzheimer's patients often display deficits in short-term memory and in some types of implicit memory: Implicit memory for verbal and perceptual material is often deficient, whereas implicit memory for sensorimotor learning is not (see Gabrieli et al., 1993; Postle, Corkin, & Growdon, 1996).

The level of acetylcholine is greatly reduced in the brains of Alzheimer's patients. This reduction results from the degeneration of the **basal forebrain** (a midline area located just above the hypothalamus; see Figure 9.17 on page 286), which is the brain's main source of acetylcholine. This finding, coupled with the finding that strokes in the basal forebrain area can cause amnesia (Morris et al., 1992), led to the view that acetylcholine depletion is the cause of Alzheimer's amnesia. However, although acetylcholine depletion resulting from damage to cholinergic neurons of the basal forebrain may contribute to Alzheimer's amnesia, it is unlikely to be the only factor. The brain damage associated with Alzheimer's disease is extremely diffuse (see Figure 8.15 on page 246) and involves areas such as the medial temporal lobe and prefrontal cortex, which play major roles in memory. Furthermore, damage to some structures of the basal forebrain produces attentional deficits, which can easily be mistaken for memory problems (see Baxter & Chiba, 1999; Everitt & Robbins, 1997).

9·4
Amnesia after Concussion: Evidence for Consolidation

Blows to the head that do not penetrate the skull but are severe enough to produce *concussion* (a temporary disturbance of consciousness produced by a nonpenetrating head injury) are the most common causes of amnesia (see Levin, 1989). Amnesia following a nonpenetrating blow to the head is called **posttraumatic amnesia (PTA)**.

Clinical Implications

Posttraumatic Amnesia

The *coma* (pathological state of unconsciousness) following a severe blow to the head usually lasts a few seconds or minutes, but in severe cases it can last weeks. Then, once the patient regains consciousness, there is a period of confusion. Victims of concussion are typically not tested by a neuropsychologist until after the period of confusion—if they are tested at all. Testing usually reveals that the patient has a permanent retrograde amnesia for the events that led up to the blow and a permanent anterograde amnesia for many of the events that occurred during the subsequent period of confusion.

The anterograde memory deficits that follow a nonpenetrating head injury are often quite puzzling to the friends and relatives who have talked to the patient during the period of confusion—for example, during a hospital visit. The patient may seem reasonably lucid at the time, because short-term memory is normal, but later may have no recollection whatsoever of the conversation.

Figure 9.6 summarizes the effects of a closed-head injury on memory. Note that the duration of the period of confusion and anterograde amnesia is typically longer than that of the coma, which is typically longer than the period of retrograde amnesia. More severe blows to the head tend to produce longer comas, longer periods of confusion, and longer periods of amnesia (Levin, Papanicolaou, &

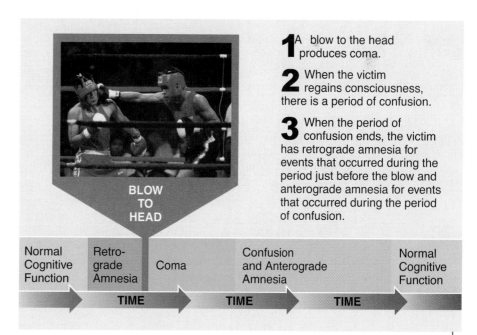

1 A blow to the head produces coma.

2 When the victim regains consciousness, there is a period of confusion.

3 When the period of confusion ends, the victim has retrograde amnesia for events that occurred during the period just before the blow and anterograde amnesia for events that occurred during the period of confusion.

| Normal Cognitive Function | Retro-grade Amnesia | Coma | Confusion and Anterograde Amnesia | Normal Cognitive Function |

BLOW TO HEAD

TIME — TIME — TIME

The retrograde amnesia and anterograde amnesia that are associated with a concussion-producing blow to the head.

Figure 9.6

Eisenberg, 1984). Not illustrated in Figure 9.6 are *islands of memory*—memories that sometimes survive for isolated events that occurred during periods that have otherwise been wiped out.

Gradients of Retrograde Amnesia and Memory Consolidation

Gradients of retrograde amnesia after concussion seem to provide evidence for *memory consolidation* (see Riccio, Millin, & Gisquet-Verrier, 2003). The fact that concussions preferentially disrupt recent memories suggests that the storage of older memories is somehow strengthened (i.e., consolidated).

The most prominent theory of memory consolidation is Hebb's theory. He argued that memories of experiences are stored in the short term by neural activity triggered by the experience and *reverberating* (circulating) in closed neural circuits. These reverberating patterns of neural activity are susceptible to disruption—for example, by a blow to the head—but eventually the reverberating activity induces structural changes in the active synapses, which provide stable long-term storage.

Electroconvulsive shock seemed to provide a controlled method of studying memory consolidation. **Electroconvulsive shock (ECS)** is an intense, brief, diffuse, seizure-inducing current that is administered to the brain through large electrodes attached to the scalp. The rationale for using ECS to study memory consolidation was that by disrupting neural activity, ECS would erase from storage only those memories that had not yet been converted to structural synaptic changes; the length of the period of retrograde amnesia produced by an ECS would thus provide an estimate of the amount of time needed for memory consolidation.

The Evolutionary Perspective

Many studies have employed ECS to study consolidation. Some studies have been conducted on human patients, who receive ECS for the treatment of depression. However, the most well-controlled studies have been conducted with laboratory animals.

In one such study, thirsty rats were placed for 10 minutes on each of 5 consecutive days in a test box that contained a small niche. By the 5th of these habituation sessions, most rats explored the niche only 1 or 2 times per session. On the 6th day, a water spout was placed in the niche, and each rat was allowed to drink for 15 seconds after it discovered the spout. This was the learning trial. Then, 10 seconds, 1 minute, 10 minutes, 1 hour, or 3 hours later, each experimental rat received a single ECS. The next day, the retention of all subjects was assessed on the basis of how many times each explored the niche when the water spout was not present. The control rats that experienced the learning trial but received no ECS explored the empty niche an average of 10 times during the 10-minute test session, thereby indicating that they remembered their discovery of water the previous day. The rats that had received ECS 1 hour or 3 hours after the learning trial also explored the niche about 10 times. In contrast, the rats that received the ECS 10 seconds, 1 minute, or 10 minutes after the learning trial explored the empty niche significantly less on the test day. This result suggested that the consolidation of the memory of the learning trial took between 10 minutes and 1 hour (see Figure 9.7).

Numerous variations of this experiment were conducted in the 1950s and 1960s, with different learning tasks, different species, and different numbers and intensities of electroconvulsive shocks. Initially, there was some consistency in the findings: Most seemed to suggest a rather brief consolidation time of a few minutes or less (e.g., Chorover & Schiller, 1965). But some researchers observed very long gradients of ECS-produced retrograde amnesia. For example, Squire, Slater, and Chace (1975) measured the memory of a group of ECS-treated patients for television shows that had played for only one season in different

Learning trial

During the learning trial, thirsty rats discover water in a previously empty niche in the wall of a familiar test box.

Control test

During the retention test, control rats displayed their retention by exploring the dry niche many times.

Experimental test

During the retention test, rats that received ECS within 10 minutes of the learning trial largely ignored the dry niche.

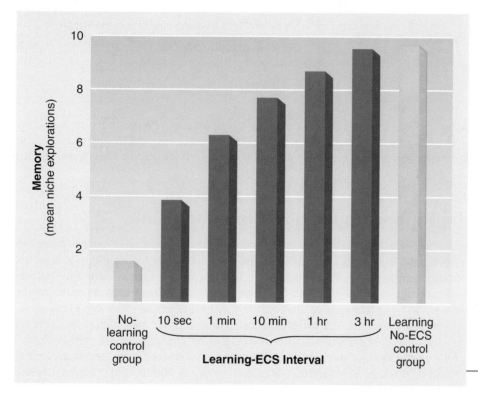

A short gradient of ECS-produced retrograde amnesia. Retention of one-trial learning by a control group of rats and by groups of rats that received ECS at various intervals after the learning trial. Only the rats that received ECS within 10 minutes of the learning trial displayed significant retrograde amnesia for it.
(Adapted from Pinel, 1969.)

Figure 9.7

years prior to their electroconvulsive therapy. They tested each subject twice on different forms of the test: once before they received a series of five electroconvulsive shocks and once after. The difference between the before-and-after scores served as an estimate of memory loss for the events of each year. Figure 9.8 on page 276 illustrates that five electroconvulsive shocks disrupted the retention of television shows that had played in the 3 years prior to treatment but not those that had played earlier.

Long gradients of retrograde amnesia are incompatible with Hebb's theory of consolidation. It is reasonable to think of the neural activity resulting from an experience reverberating through the brain for a few seconds or even a few minutes; but gradients of retrograde amnesia covering days, weeks, or years

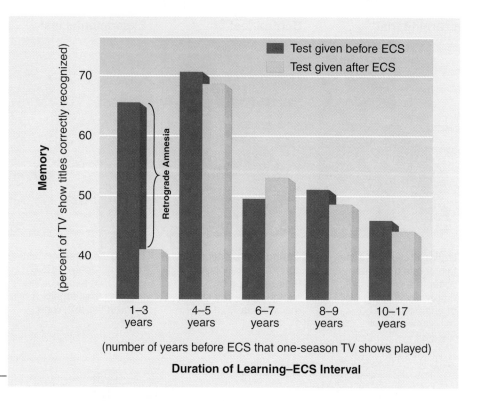

Demonstration of a long gradient of ECS-produced retrograde amnesia. A series of five electroconvulsive shocks produced retrograde amnesia for television shows that played for only one season in the 3 years before the shocks; however, the shocks did not produce amnesia for one-season shows that had played prior to that.
(Adapted from Squire, Slater, & Chace, 1975.)

Figure 9.8

cannot be easily accounted for by the disruption of reverberatory neural activity (e.g., Squire & Spanis, 1984). Long gradients of retrograde amnesia indicate that memory consolidation can continue for a very long time after learning, perhaps indefinitely.

The Hippocampus and Consolidation

The discovery that H.M. seemed to be suffering from a temporally graded retrograde amnesia led Scoville and Milner (1957) to conclude that the hippocampus and related structures play a role in consolidation. To account for the fact that the bilateral medial temporal lobectomy disrupted only those retrograde memories acquired in the period just before H.M.'s surgery, they suggested that memories are temporarily stored in the hippocampus until they can be transferred to a more stable cortical storage system. This theory has been supported by several demonstrations that medial temporal lobe lesions produce temporally graded retrograde amnesia in experimental animals (e.g., Haist, Bowden, & Mao, 2001; Hanson, Bunsey, & Riccio, 2002; Squire, Clark, & Knowlton, 2001).

Several alternative theories of memory consolidation have been proposed (see James & MacKay, 2001). The theory of Nadel and Moscovitch (1997) is particularly compatible with the finding that gradients of retrograde amnesia are often very long. Nadel and Moscovitch proposed that the hippocampus and other structures involved in memory storage store memories for as long as they exist—not just during the period immediately after learning. When a conscious experience occurs, it is rapidly and sparsely encoded in a distributed fashion throughout the hippocampus and other involved structures. According to Nadel and Moscovitch, retained memories become progressively more resistant to disruption by hippocampal damage because each time a similar experience occurs or the original memory is recalled, a new **engram** (a change in the brain that stores a memory) is established and linked to the original engram, making the memory easier to recall and the original engram more difficult to disrupt.

Scan your Brain

This chapter is about to move from discussion of human memory disorders to consideration of animal models of human memory disorders. Are you ready? Scan your brain to assess your knowledge of human memory disorders by filling in the blanks in the following sentences. The correct answers are provided below. Before proceeding, review the material related to your errors and omissions.

1. H.M. had his _____ temporal lobes removed.

2. The mirror-drawing test, the rotary pursuit test, the incomplete-pictures test, and the repetition priming test are all tests of _____ memory.

3. H.M. appears incapable of forming new long-term _____ memories.

4. Support for the view that hippocampal damage can by itself cause amnesia comes from the study or R.B., who suffered _____ damage to the pyramidal cells of his CA1 hippocampal subfield.

5. The current view is that damage to the _____ diencephalon is responsible for most of the memory deficits of people with Korsakoff's disease.

6. The gradual onset of Korsakoff's syndrome complicates the study of the resulting _____ amnesia.

7. The _____ nuclei are the medial diencephalic nuclei that have been most frequently implicated in memory.

8. Alzheimer's disease is associated with degeneration of _____ neurons in the basal forebrain.

9. Posttraumatic amnesia can be induced with _____ shock, which is used in the treatment of depression.

10. The transfer of a memory from short-term storage to long-term storage is termed _____.

11. Because some gradients of retrograde amnesia are extremely long, it is unlikely that memory consolidation is mediated by _____ neural activity, as hypothesized by Hebb.

12. The changes in the brain that store memories are called _____.

Scan Your Brain answers: (1) medial, (2) implicit, (3) explicit, (4) ischemic, (5) medial, (6) retrograde, (7) mediodorsal, (8) cholinergic, (9) electroconvulsive, (10) consolidation, (11) reverberating, (12) engrams

9·5
Neuroanatomy of Object-Recognition Memory

As interesting and informative as the study of amnesic patients can be, it has major limitations. Many important questions about the neural bases of amnesia can be answered only by controlled experiments. For example, in order to identify the particular structures of the brain that participate in various kinds of memory, it is necessary to make precise lesions in various structures and to control what and when the subjects learn, and how and when their retention is tested. Because such experiments are not feasible with human subjects, there has been a major effort to develop animal models of human brain-damage–produced amnesia.

The first reports of H.M.'s case in the 1950s triggered a massive effort to develop an animal model of his disorder so that it could be subjected to experimental analysis. In its early years, this effort was a dismal failure; lesions of medial temporal lobe structures did not produce severe anterograde amnesia in rats, monkeys, or other nonhuman species.

In retrospect, there were two reasons for the initial difficulty in developing an animal model of medial temporal lobe amnesia. First, it was not initially

Thinking Clearly

The Evolutionary Perspective

1 The monkey moves the sample object to obtain food from the well beneath it.

2 A screen is lowered in front of the monkey during the delay period.

3 The monkey is confronted with the sample object and an unfamiliar object.

4 The monkey must remember the sample object and then select the unfamiliar object to obtain the food beneath it.

The correct performance of a delayed nonmatching-to-sample trial.
(Adapted from Mishkin & Appenzeller, 1987.)

Figure 9.9

apparent that H.M.'s anterograde amnesia did not extend to all kinds of long-term memory—that is, that it was specific to explicit long-term memories—and most animal memory tests that were widely used in the 1950s and 1960s were tests of implicit memory (e.g., Pavlovian and operant conditioning). Second, it was incorrectly assumed that the amnesic effects of medial temporal lobe lesions were largely, if not entirely, attributable to hippocampal damage; and most efforts to develop animal models of medial temporal lobe amnesia thus focused on hippocampal lesions.

Monkey Model of Object-Recognition Amnesia: The Delayed Nonmatching-to-Sample Test

Finally, in the mid 1970s, over two decades after the first reports of H.M.'s remarkable case, an animal model of his disorder was developed. It was hailed as a major breakthrough because it opened up the neuroanatomy of medial temporal lobe amnesia to experimental investigation.

In separate laboratories, Gaffan (1974) and Mishkin and Delacour (1975) showed that monkeys with bilateral medial temporal lobectomies have major problems forming long-term memories for objects encountered in the **delayed nonmatching-to-sample test**. In this test, a monkey is presented with a distinctive object (the *sample object*), under which it finds food (e.g., a banana pellet). Then, after a delay, the monkey is presented with two test objects: the sample object and an unfamiliar object. The monkey must remember the sample object so that it can select the unfamiliar object to obtain food concealed beneath it. The correct performance of a trial is illustrated in Figure 9.9.

Intact, well-trained monkeys performed correctly on about 90% of the delayed nonmatching-to-sample trials when the retention intervals were a few minutes or less. In contrast, monkeys with bilateral medial temporal lobe lesions had major object-recognition deficits (see Figure 9.10). These deficits modeled those of H.M. in key respects. For example, the monkeys' performance was normal at delays of a few seconds but fell off to near chance levels at delays of several minutes, and their performance was extremely susceptible to the disruptive effects of distraction (Squire & Zola-Morgan, 1985). In fact, human medial temporal lobe amnesics have been tested on the delayed nonmatching-to-sample test—their rewards were coins rather than banana pellets—and their performance mirrored the performance of monkeys with similar brain damage.

The development of the delayed nonmatching-to-sample test for monkeys provided a means of testing the assumption that the amnesia resulting from medial temporal lobe damage is entirely the consequence of hippocampal damage—Figure 9.11 illustrates the locations in the monkey brain of the three major temporal lobe structures: hippocampus, amygdala, and adjacent **rhinal cortex**. But before we consider this important line of research, we need to look at another important methodological development: the rat version of the delayed nonmatching-to-sample test.

The Delayed Nonmatching-to-Sample Test for Rats

In order to understand why the development of the rat version of the delayed nonmatching-to-sample test played an important role in assessing the specific role of hippocampal damage in medial temporal lobe amnesia, examine Figure 9.12 on page 280, which illustrates the usual methods of making hippocampal lesions in

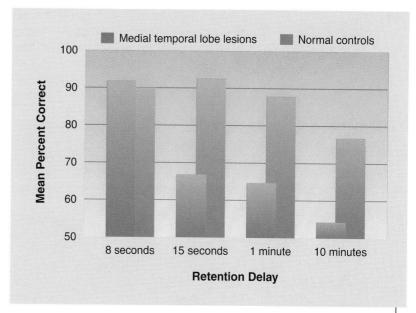

The performance deficits of monkeys with large bilateral medial temporal lobe lesions on the delayed nonmatching-to-sample test. There were significant deficits at all but the shortest retention interval. These deficits parallel the memory deficits of human medial temporal lobe amnesics on the same task.

(Adapted from Squire & Zola-Morgan, 1991.)

Figure 9.10 ——————————

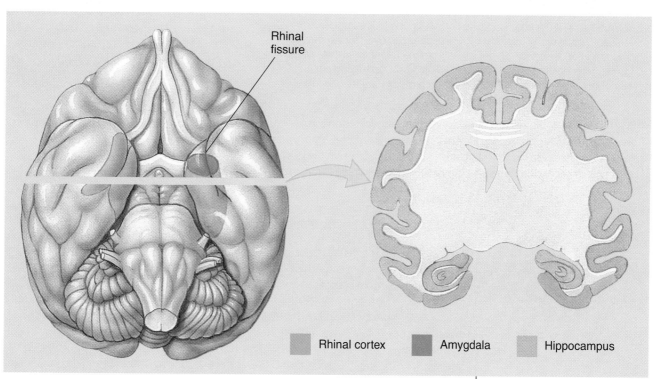

The three major structures of the medial temporal lobe, illustrated in the monkey brain: the hippocampus, the amygdala, and the rhinal cortex.

Figure 9.11 ——————————

monkeys and rats. Because of the size and location of the hippocampus, almost all studies of hippocampal lesions in monkeys have involved *aspiration* (suction) of large portions of the rhinal cortex in addition to the hippocampus. However, in rats the extraneous damage associated with aspiration lesions of the hippocampus is typically limited to a small area of parietal neocortex. Furthermore, the rat hippocampus is small enough that it can readily be lesioned electrolytically or with intracerebral neurotoxin injections; in either case, there is little extraneous damage.

The version of the delayed nonmatching-to-sample test for rats that most closely resembles that for monkeys was developed by David Mumby using an apparatus that has become known as the **Mumby box**. This rat version of the test is illustrated in Figure 9.13.

It was once assumed that rats could not perform a task as complex as that required for the delayed nonmatching-to-sample test; Figure 9.14 on page 282 indicates otherwise. Rats perform almost as well as monkeys with delays of up to 1 minute (Mumby, Pinel, & Wood, 1989).

The validity of the rat version of the delayed nonmatching-to-sample test has been established by studies of the effects of medial temporal lobe lesions. Combined bilateral lesions of rats' hippocampus, amygdala, and rhinal cortex produce major retention deficits at all but the shortest retention intervals (Mumby, Wood, & Pinel, 1992).

The Location of the Hippocampus

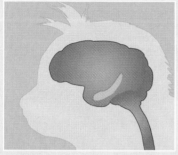

Monkeys

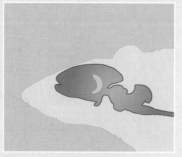

Rats

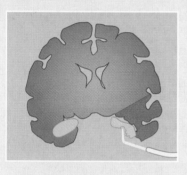

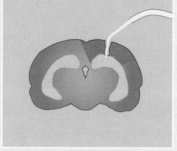

In monkeys, the hippocampus is usually removed by aspiration via the inferior surface of the brain, thus destroying substantial amounts of rhinal cortex.

In rats, the hippocampus is usually removed by aspiration from the superior surface of the brain, thus destroying small amounts of parietal neocortex.

Aspiration lesions of the hippocampus in monkeys and rats. Because of differences in the size and location of the hippocampus in monkeys and in rats, hippocampectomy typically involves the removal of large amounts of rhinal cortex in monkeys, but not in rats.

Figure 9.12

Neuroanatomical Basis of the Object-Recognition Deficits Resulting from Medial Temporal Lobectomy

To what extent are the object-recognition deficits following bilateral medial temporal lobectomy a consequence of hippocampal damage? In the early 1990s, researchers began assessing the relative effects on performance in the delayed nonmatching-to-sample test of lesions to various medial temporal lobe structures in both monkeys and rats. Early challenges to the preeminence of the hippocampus (Meunier et al., 1990; Mumby, Wood, & Pinel, 1992; Zola-Morgan et al., 1989) attracted the interest of other researchers and yielded many relevant findings. Reviewers of this research (Brown & Aggleton, 2001; Duva, Kornecook, & Pinel, 2000; Mumby, 2001; Murray, 1996; Murray & Richmond, 2001) have all reached similar conclusions: Bilateral surgical removal of the rhinal cortex consistently produces severe and permanent deficits in performance on the delayed nonmatching-to-sample test and other tests of object recognition. In contrast, bilateral surgical removal of the hippocampus produces either moderate deficits or none at all, and bilateral destruction of the amygdala has no effect. Figure 9.15 on page 282 compares the effects of rhinal cortex lesions and hippocampus-plus-amygdala lesions on object recognition in rats.

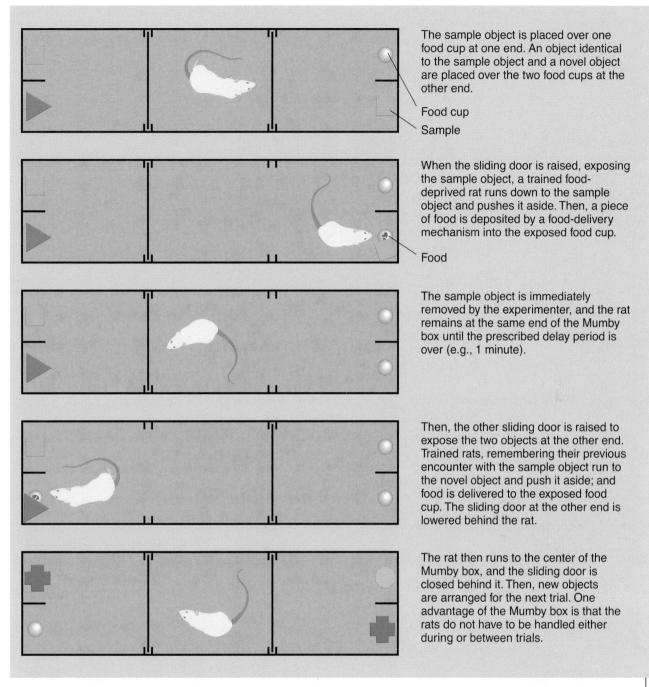

The sample object is placed over one food cup at one end. An object identical to the sample object and a novel object are placed over the two food cups at the other end.

Food cup

Sample

When the sliding door is raised, exposing the sample object, a trained food-deprived rat runs down to the sample object and pushes it aside. Then, a piece of food is deposited by a food-delivery mechanism into the exposed food cup.

Food

The sample object is immediately removed by the experimenter, and the rat remains at the same end of the Mumby box until the prescribed delay period is over (e.g., 1 minute).

Then, the other sliding door is raised to expose the two objects at the other end. Trained rats, remembering their previous encounter with the sample object run to the novel object and push it aside; and food is delivered to the exposed food cup. The sliding door at the other end is lowered behind the rat.

The rat then runs to the center of the Mumby box, and the sliding door is closed behind it. Then, new objects are arranged for the next trial. One advantage of the Mumby box is that the rats do not have to be handled either during or between trials.

The Mumby box and the rat version of the delayed nonmatching-to-sample test.

Figure 9.13

The reports that object-recognition memory is severely disrupted by rhinal cortex lesions but only moderately by hippocampal lesions led to a resurgence of interest in the case of R.B. and others like it. Earlier in this chapter, you learned that R.B. was left amnesic following an ischemic accident that occurred during heart surgery and that subsequent analysis of his brain revealed that obvious cell loss was restricted largely to the pyramidal cell layer of his CA1 hippocampal subfield (see Figure 9.5 on page 271). This result has been replicated in both monkeys and rats. In both monkeys (Zola-Morgan et al., 1992) and rats (Wood et al., 1993), cerebral ischemia leads to a loss of CA1 hippocampal pyramidal cells and severe deficits in the delayed nonmatching-to-sample task.

The relation between ischemia-produced hippocampal damage and object-recognition deficits in humans, monkeys, and rats seems to provide strong support for the theory that the hippocampus plays a key role in object-recognition memory. But there is a gnawing problem with this line of evidence: How can ischemia-

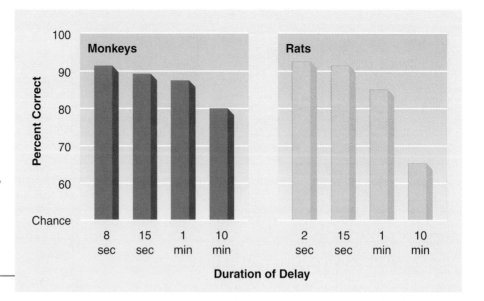

A comparison of the performance of intact monkeys (Zola-Morgan, Squire, & Mishkin, 1982) and intact rats (Mumby, Pinel, & Wood, 1989) on the delayed nonmatching-to-sample test.

Figure 9.14

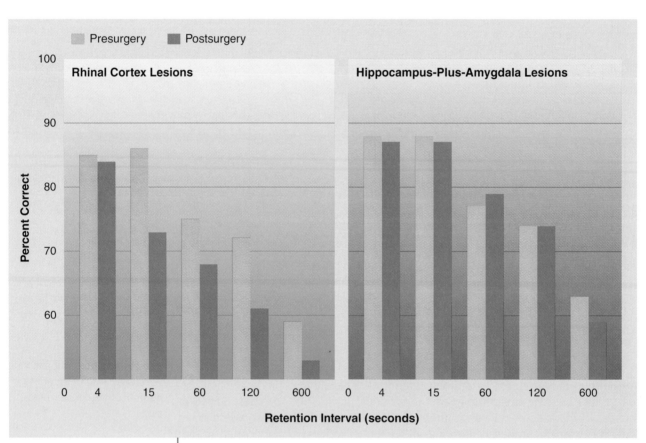

Effects of rhinal cortex lesions and hippocampus-plus-amygdala lesions in rats. Lesions of the rhinal cortex, but not of the hippocampus and amygdala combined, produced severe deficits in performance of the delayed nonmatching-to-sample test in rats.

(Adapted from Mumby & Pinel, 1994; Mumby, Wood, & Pinel, 1992.)

Figure 9.15

produced lesions to one small part of the hippocampus be associated with severe deficits in performance on the delayed nonmatching-to-sample test when the deficits associated with total removal of the hippocampus are only moderate?

Mumby and his colleagues (1996) conducted an experiment that appears to resolve this paradox. They hypothesized the following: (1) that the ischemia-produced hyperactivity of CA1 pyramidal cells damages neurons outside the hippocampus, possibly through the excessive release of excitatory amino acid neurotransmitters; (2) that this extrahippocampal damage is not readily detectable by conventional histological analysis (i.e., it does not involve concentrated cell loss); and (3) that this extrahippocampal damage is largely responsible for the object-recognition deficits that are produced by cerebral ischemia. Mumby and colleagues supported their hypothesis by showing that bilateral hippocampectomy actually blocks the development of ischemia-produced deficits in performance on the delayed nonmatching-to-sample test. First, they produced cerebral ischemia in rats by temporarily tying off their carotid arteries. Then, one group of the ischemic rats received a bilateral hippocampectomy 1 hour later, a second group received a bilateral hippocampectomy 1 week later, and a third group received no bilateral hippocampectomy. Following recovery, the latter two groups of ischemic rats displayed severe object-recognition deficits, whereas the rats whose hippocampus had been removed 1 hour after ischemia did not. Explaining how hippocampectomy can prevent the development of the object-recognition deficits normally produced by cerebral ischemia is a major problem for the theory that the hippocampus plays a critical role in object-recognition memory.

Support for the theory that the object-recognition deficits of ischemic patients result from extrahippocampal disturbances comes from functional brain-imaging studies. Widespread cerebral dysfunction is commonly observed in neuroanatomically intact areas distant from sites of ischemic cell loss (e.g., Baron, 1989; Fazio et al., 1992). Consequently, cases of obvious ischemia-produced amnesia with hippocampal cell loss (cases such as that of R.B.) do not prove that the hippocampus plays the major role in object recognition.

Cognitive Neuroscience

9.6

The Hippocampus and Memory for Spatial Location

The discovery that the rhinal cortex plays a more important role than the hippocampus in object recognition does not mean that the hippocampus plays no significant role in memory. Indeed, the hippocampus plays a key role in memory for spatial location.

Hippocampal Lesions Disrupt Spatial Memory

Bilateral lesions of the hippocampus in laboratory animals often have little or no effect on performance on memory tests. But there is one exception to this general result: Hippocampal lesions consistently disrupt the performance of tasks that involve the memory for spatial location (e.g., Kaut & Bunsey, 2001; McDonald & White, 1993; O'Keefe, 1993). For example, hippocampal lesions disrupt performance on the *Morris water maze test* and the *radial arm maze test* (see Figure 9.16 on page 284).

In the **Morris water maze test**, intact rats placed at various locations in a circular pool of murky water rapidly learn to swim to a stationary platform hidden just below the surface. Rats with hippocampal lesions learn this simple task with great difficulty.

Morris Water Maze

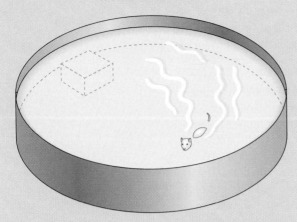

The rat is placed in the milky water, and it swims until it discovers the safety platform, invisible just below the surface of the pool. As the rat learns the location of the platform, the rat's latency to find it decreases on each trial.

Radial Arm Maze

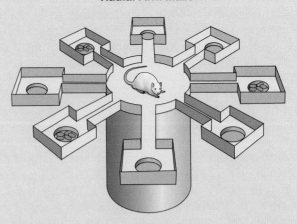

Typically, the same arms are baited on each trial. After they are trained, rats begin each trial by first entering the baited arms (e.g., three), once each. In effect, rats learn two things: (1) which arms are baited and (2) not to visit any arm twice on a given trial.

Two tests of spatial memory: the Morris water maze test and the radial arm maze test.

Figure 9.16

In the **radial arm maze test**, several arms (e.g., eight arms) radiate out from a central starting chamber, and the same few arms are baited with food each day. Intact rats readily learn to visit only those arms that contain food, without visiting the same arm more than once each day. The ability to visit only the baited arms of the radial arm maze is a measure of **reference memory** (memory for the general principles and skills that are required to perform a task), and the ability to refrain from visiting an arm more than once in a given day is a measure of **working memory** (temporary memory that is necessary for the successful performance of a task on which one is currently working). Rats with hippocampal lesions display major deficits on both the reference memory and the working memory measures of radial arm maze performance.

Hippocampal Place Cells

Consistent with the observation that hippocampal lesions disrupt spatial memory is the fact that many hippocampal neurons are **place cells** (Best, White, & Minai, 2001; Brun et al., 2002; Moser & Paulsen, 2001; O'Keefe & Dostrovsky, 1971)—neurons that respond only when a subject is in specific locations (i.e., in the *place fields* of the neurons). For example, when a rat is first placed in an unfamiliar test environment, none of its hippocampal neurons have a place field in that environment; then, as the rat familiarizes itself with the environment, many hippocampal neurons acquire a place field in it—that is, each fires only when the rat is in a particular part of the test environment. Each place cell has a place field in a different part of the environment. The firing of most place cells is also influenced by the direction of the rat's movements in the field.

By placing a rat in an ambiguous situation in a familiar test environment, it is possible to determine where the rat thinks it is from the route that it takes to get to the location in the environment where it has previously been rewarded. Using this strategy, researchers (O'Keefe & Speakman, 1987; Wilson & McNaughton, 1993) have shown that the firing of a rat's place cells indicates where the rat "thinks" it is in the test environment, not necessarily where it actually is.

Comparative Studies of the Hippocampus and Spatial Memory

Although most of the evidence that the hippocampus plays a role in spatial memory comes from research on rats, the hippocampus seems to perform a similar function in many other species (see Colombo & Broadbent, 2000). Most noteworthy has been the research in food-caching birds. Food-caching birds must have remarkable spatial memories, because in order to survive, they must remember the locations of hundreds of food caches scattered around their territories. In one study, Sherry and Vaccarino (1989) found that food-caching species tended to have larger hippocampi than related non–food-caching species. Indeed, Clayton (2001) found that caching and retrieving are required to trigger hippocampal growth and maintain its size in mountain chickadees.

The Evolutionary Perspective

Although research on a variety of species indicates that the hippocampus does play a role in spatial memory, the evidence from primate studies has been less consistent. The hippocampal pyramidal cells of primates do have place fields (Rolls, Robertson, & Georges-François, 1995), but the effects of hippocampal damage on the performance of spatial memory tasks have been mixed (e.g., Henke et al., 1999; Kessels et al., 2001; Maguire et al., 1998). The problem may be that spatial memory in humans and monkeys is typically tested by having subjects remain stationary and make judgments of locations on computer screens, whereas spatial memory in rats, mice, and birds is typically studied as subjects navigate through controlled test environments (see Suzuki & Clayton, 2000). The results of two studies by Maguire and colleagues suggest that this is the case.

Thinking Clearly

First, Maguire and colleagues (1998) used positron emission tomography (PET) to record the brain activity of subjects as they learned to find their way around a virtual-reality town. Activation of the right hippocampus was strongly associated with knowing where places were and navigating accurately to them. Second, Maguire and colleagues (2000) used structural magnetic resonance imaging (MRI) to estimate hippocampal volume in a group of humans who had intensive spatial training—London taxi drivers. They found that London taxi drivers with more than 20 years of experience had significantly more posterior hippocampal gray matter than usual.

Cognitive Neuroscience

Theories of Hippocampal Function

There are many theories of hippocampal function, all of which acknowledge the important role of the hippocampus in spatial memory. Let's take a look at three of these theories.

O'Keefe and Nadel (1978) proposed the **cognitive map theory** of hippocampal function. According to this theory, there are several systems in the brain that specialize in the memory for different kinds of information, and the specific function of the hippocampus is the storage of memories for spatial location. Specifically, O'Keefe and Nadel proposed that the hippocampus constructs and stores allocentric maps of the external world from the sensory input that it receives. *Allocentric* refers to representations of space based on relations among external objects and landmarks; in contrast, *egocentric* refers to representations of space based on relations to one's own position.

Another influential theory of hippocampal function is the *configural association theory* (Rudy & Sutherland, 1992). The configural association theory is based on the premise that spatial memory is one specific manifestation of the hippocampus's more general function. The configural association theory is that the hippocampus plays a role in the retention of the behavioral significance of combinations of stimuli but not of individual stimuli. For example, according to this theory, the hippocampus is involved in remembering that a flashing light in a particular context (i.e., at a particular location or time) signals food but not that a flashing light signals food irrespective of the context. There is substantial support for this theory; however, there have also been some failures to disrupt the performance of nonspatial configural tasks with hippocampal lesions (e.g., Bussey et al., 1998).

Finally, Brown and Aggleton (2001) have proposed a specific theory of the role of the hippocampus in object recognition and its relation to that of the rhinal cortex. They concur with the evidence that the rhinal cortex, not the hippocampus, plays a role in most object-recognition tasks. However, they suggest that the hippocampus plays a role in recognizing spatial arrangements of objects, as in a visual scene, for example (see Wan, Aggleton, & Brown, 1999).

9·7
Where Are Memories Stored?

Evidence suggests that each memory is stored diffusely throughout the structures of the brain that participated in its original experience (see Fries, Fernández, & Jensen, 2003; Nyberg et al., 2000; Wheeler, Petersen, & Buckner, 2000). This chapter has focused on two structures of the medial temporal lobes—the hippocampus and the rhinal cortex—and their roles in spatial location and object recognition, respectively. Attention was also given to the mediodorsal nucleus and the basal forebrain; the mnemonic functions of these structures is less well understood, but they have been implicated in memory by studies of Korsakoff's and Alzheimer's patients, respectively. In this section, we take a brief look at five other areas of the brain that have been implicated in memory storage: inferotemporal cortex, amygdala, prefrontal cortex, cerebellum, and striatum. See Figure 9.17.

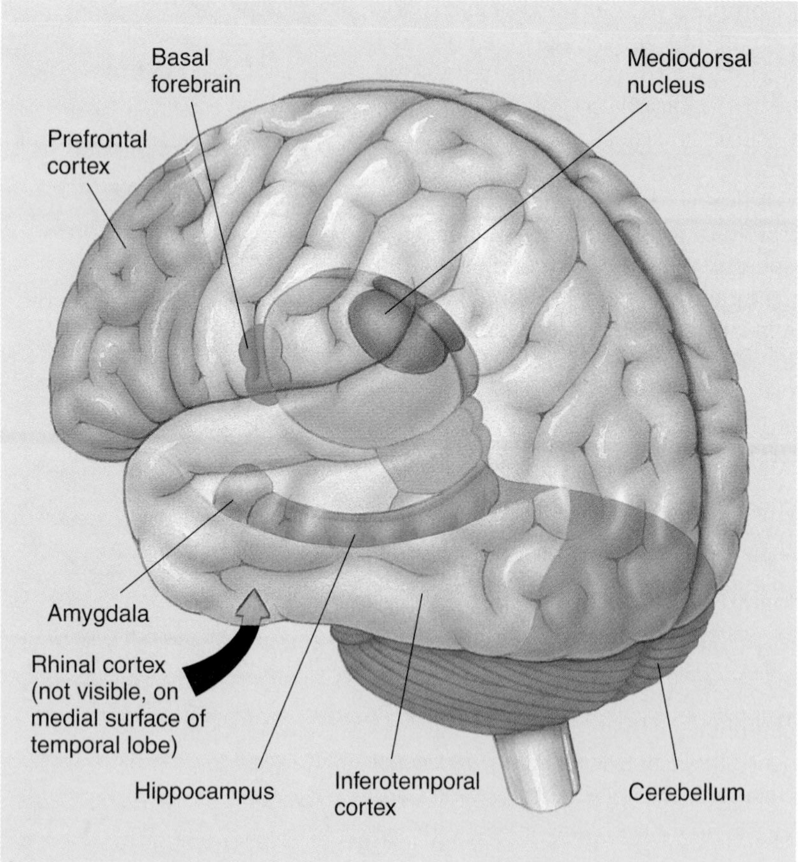

The structures of the brain that have been shown to play a role in memory. Because it would have blocked the view of other structures, the striatum is not included. (See Figure 2.28 on page 57.)

Figure 9.17

Inferotemporal Cortex

Areas of secondary sensory cortex are presumed to play an important role in storing sensory memories. For example, because the **inferotemporal cortex** (the cortex of the inferior temporal lobe) is involved in the visual perception of objects, it is thought to participate in storing memories of visual patterns (see Rossion et al., 2001). In support of this view, Naya, Yoshida, and Miyashita (2001) recorded the responses of neurons in inferotemporal cortex and rhinal cortex while monkeys learned the relation between the two items in pairs of visual images. When a pair was presented, responses were first recorded in inferotemporal neurons and then in rhinal neurons; however, when the monkeys were required to recall the same pair, activity was recorded in rhinal neurons before inferotemporal neurons. Naya and colleagues concluded that this reversed pattern of activity reflected the retrieval of visual memories from inferotemporal cortex.

Amygdala

The amygdala seems to play a role in memory for the emotional significance of experiences. Rats with amygdalar lesions, unlike intact rats, do not respond with fear to a neutral stimulus that has been repeatedly followed by electric foot shocks (see McGaugh, 2002; Medina et al., 2002). Also, Bechara and colleagues (1995) reported the case of a neuropsychological patient with bilateral damage to the amygdala who could not acquire conditioned autonomic startle responses to various visual or auditory stimuli but had good explicit memory for them. You will learn much more about the amygdala's involvement in emotion in Chapter 13.

Prefrontal Cortex

Patients with damage to the *prefrontal cortex* are not grossly amnesic; they often display no deficits at all on conventional tests of memory (see Müller, Machado, & Knight, 2002; Petrides, 1996). They do, however, display deficits in memory for the temporal order of events, even when they can remember the events themselves, as well as deficits in *working memory* (the ability to maintain relevant memories while a task is being completed)—see Kimberg, D'Esposito, and Farah (1998) and Smith (2000). As a result of these two deficits, patients with prefrontal cortex damage have particular difficulty performing tasks that involve a series of responses (see Colvin, Dunbar, & Grafman, 2001).

The Case of the Cook Who Couldn't

The story of one patient with prefrontal cortex damage is very well known because she was the sister of Wilder Penfield, the famous Montreal neurosurgeon. Before her brain damage, she had been an excellent cook; and afterward, she retained all the prerequisite knowledge. She remembered her favorite recipes, and she remembered how to perform each individual cooking technique. However, she was incapable of preparing even simple meals because she could not carry out the various steps in proper sequence (Penfield & Evans, 1935).

Clinical Implications

The prefrontal cortex is a large heterogeneous structure; it is composed of numerous anatomically distinct areas that have different connections and, presumably, different functions. Do different areas of prefrontal cortex mediate different kinds of working memory—spatial, visual, verbal, and so forth? The answer seems to be, "yes and no." Functional brain-imaging studies suggest that some regions of prefrontal cortex perform fundamental cognitive processes (e.g., attention and task management) during all working memory tasks; however, there are other regions of prefrontal cortex that seem to mediate specific kinds of working memory (Collette & Van der Linden, 2002; Petrides, 2000; Rämä et al., 2001).

Cognitive Neuroscience

Cerebellum and Striatum

Just as explicit memories of experiences are presumed to be stored in the circuits of the brain that mediated their original perception, implicit memories of sensorimotor learning are presumed to be stored in sensorimotor circuits (see Ohyama et al., 2003). Most research on the neural mechanisms of memory for sensorimotor tasks have focused on two structures: the *cerebellum* and the *striatum*.

The **cerebellum** is thought to store memories of learned sensorimotor skills. Its role in the Pavlovian conditioning of the eyeblink response of rabbits has been most intensively investigated (see Linden, 2003). In this paradigm, a tone (conditional stimulus) is sounded just before a puff of air (unconditional stimulus) is delivered to the eye. After several trials, the tone comes to elicit an eyeblink. The convergence of evidence from stimulation, recording, and lesion studies suggests that the effects of this conditioning are stored in the form of changes in the way cerebellar neurons respond to the tone (see Koekkoek et al., 2003).

The **striatum** is thought to store memories for consistent relationships between stimuli and responses—the type of memories that develop incrementally over many trials (see White, 1997). Sometimes this striatum-based form of learning is referred to as *habit formation* (Packard & Knowlton, 2002; Schultz, Tremblay, & Hollermar, 2003).

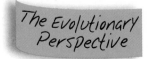

Clinical Implications

One study of striatal function compared Parkinson's patients, who all have striatal damage, with patients suffering from medial temporal lobe damage. Knowlton, Mangels, and Squire (1996) found that the Parkinson's patients could not solve a probabilistic discrimination problem. The problem was a computer "weather forecasting" game, and the task of the subjects was to correctly predict the weather by pressing one of two keys, rain or shine. They based their predictions on stimulus cards presented on the screen—each card had a different probability of leading to sunshine. The Parkinson's patients did not improve over 50 trials, although they displayed normal explicit (conscious) memory for the training episode. In contrast, amnesic patients with medial temporal lobe or medial diencephalic damage displayed marked improvement in performance but had no explicit memory of their training.

9.8
Synaptic Mechanisms of Learning and Memory

So far, this chapter has focused on the particular structures of the human brain that are involved in learning and memory and what happens when these structures are damaged. In this section, the level of analysis changes: The focus shifts to the neuroplastic mechanisms within these structures that are thought to be the fundamental bases of learning and memory.

Most modern thinking about the neural mechanisms of memory began with Hebb (1949). Hebb argued so convincingly that enduring changes in the efficiency of synaptic transmission were the basis of long-term memory that the search for the neural bases of learning and memory has focused almost exclusively on the synapse (see Kandel, 2001; Malenka, 2003).

Long-Term Potentiation

Because Hebb's hypothesis that enduring facilitations of synaptic transmission are the neural basis of learning and memory was so influential, there was great excitement when such an effect was discovered. In 1973, Bliss and Lømø showed that there is a facilitation of synaptic transmission following high-frequency electrical stimulation applied to presynaptic neurons. This phenomenon has been termed **long-term potentiation (LTP)**.

LTP has been demonstrated in many species and in many parts of their brains, but it has been most frequently studied in the rat hippocampus. Figure 9.18 illustrates the three hippocampal synapses at which LTP is commonly studied.

Figure 9.19 is a demonstration of LTP in the granule cell layer (see Figure 9.18) of the rat hippocampal dentate gyrus. First, a single low-intensity pulse of current was delivered to the *perforant path* (the major input to the dentate gyrus), and the

The Evolutionary Perspective

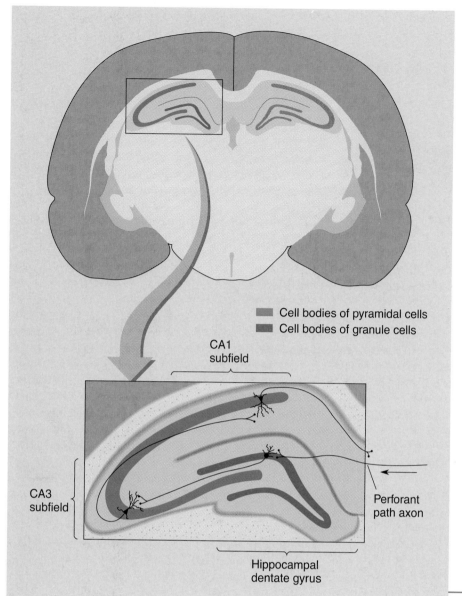

A slice of rat hippocampal tissue that illustrates the three synapses at which LTP is most commonly studied: (1) the dentate granule cell synapse, (2) the CA3 pyramidal cell synapse, and (3) the CA1 pyramidal cell synapse.

Figure 9.18

Cell bodies of pyramidal cells
Cell bodies of granule cells

CA1 subfield

CA3 subfield

Perforant path axon

Hippocampal dentate gyrus

response was recorded through an extracellular multiple-unit electrode in the granule cell layer of the hippocampal dentate gyrus; the purpose of this initial stimulation was to determine the initial response baseline. Second, high-intensity, high-frequency stimulation lasting 10 seconds was delivered to the perforant path to induce the LTP. Third, the granule cells' responses to single pulses of low-intensity current were measured again after various delays. As Figure 9.19 on page 290 illustrates, transmission at the granule cells' synapses was still potentiated 1 week after the high-frequency stimulation.

LTP is among the most widely studied neuroscientific phenomena. Why? The reason goes back to 1949 and Hebb's influential theory of memory. The synaptic changes that Hebb hypothesized to underlie long-term memory seemed to be the same kind of changes that underlie LTP.

LTP has two key properties that Hebb proposed as characteristics of the physiological mechanisms of learning and memory. First, LTP can last for a long time—for many weeks after multiple stimulations. Second, LTP develops only if the firing of the presynaptic neuron is followed by the firing of the postsynaptic neuron; it does not develop when the presynaptic neuron fires and the postsynaptic neuron does not, and it does

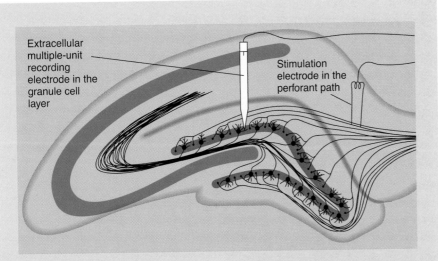

Extracellular multiple-unit recording electrode in the granule cell layer

Stimulation electrode in the perforant path

A single pulse of stimulation was administered to the perforant path, and the baseline response was recorded by an extracellular electrode in the granule cell layer. Then, several trains of intense high-frequency stimulation were applied to the perforant path to induce the LTP.

A single pulse of stimulation was administered 1 day later and again 1 week later to assess the magnitude of and duration of the potentiation. The usual measure of LTP is the increased amplitude of the *population spike*, in this case, the spike created by the firing of a greater number of granule cells.

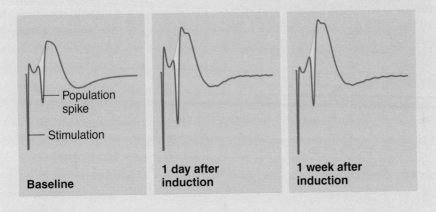

Population spike

Stimulation

Baseline

1 day after induction

1 week after induction

Long-term potentiation in the granule cell layer of the rat hippocampal dentate gyrus.

(Traces courtesy of Michael Corcoran, Department of Psychology, University of Saskatchewan.)

Figure 9.19

not develop when the presynaptic neuron does not fire and the postsynaptic neuron does (see Bi & Poo, 2001). The *co-occurrence* of firing in presynaptic and postsynaptic cells is now recognized as the critical factor in LTP, and the assumption that co-occurrence is a physiological necessity for learning and memory is often referred to as *Hebb's postulate for learning.*

Additional support for the idea that LTP is related to the neural mechanisms of learning and memory has come from several observations (see Lisman, Lichtman, & Sanes, 2003; Lynch, 2004; Morris et al., 2003): (1) LTP can be elicited by low levels of stimulation that mimic normal neural activity; (2) LTP effects are most prominent in structures that have been implicated in learning and memory, such as the hippocampus; (3) behavioral conditioning can produce LTP-like changes in the hippocampus; (4) many drugs that influence learning and memory have parallel effects on LTP; (5) the induction of maximal LTP blocks the learning of a Morris water maze until the LTP has subsided; (6) mutant mice that display little hippocampal LTP have difficulty learning the Morris water maze; and (7) LTP occurs at specific synapses that have been shown to participate in learning and memory in simple invertebrate nervous systems. Still, it is important to keep in mind that all of this evidence is indirect and that LTP as induced in the laboratory by electrical stimulation is at best a caricature of the subtle cellular events that underlie learning and memory (see Cain, 1997; Eichenbaum, 1996).

Conceiving of LTP as a three-part process, many researchers are investigating the mechanisms of *induction, maintenance*, and *expression*—that is, the processes by which high-frequency stimulations induce LTP (learning), the changes responsible for storing LTP (memory), and the changes that allow it to be expressed during the test (recall).

Induction of LTP: Learning

LTP has been studied most extensively at synapses at which the NMDA (N-methyl-D-aspartate) receptor is prominent. The **NMDA receptor** is a receptor for glutamate—the main excitatory neurotransmitter of the brain. The NMDA receptor has a special property. It does not respond maximally unless two events occur simultaneously: Glutamate must bind to it, and the postsynaptic neuron must already be partially depolarized. This dual requirement stems from the fact that the calcium channels that are linked to NMDA receptors allow only small numbers of calcium ions to enter the neuron unless the neuron is already depolarized when glutamate binds to the receptor; it is the influx of calcium ions that triggers action potentials and the cascade of events in the postsynaptic neu-

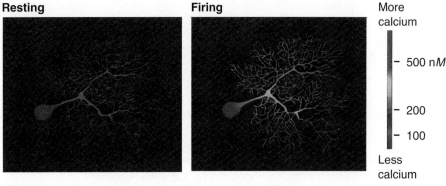

Resting   **Firing**   More calcium

— 500 n*M*

— 200

— 100

Less calcium

The influx of calcium ions into active neurons. This influx can be visualized with microfluorometric techniques. Notice that the greatest influx (measured in nanomolars) occurs in the axon terminal branches.

(Reprinted with permission from David W. Tank et al., "Spatially Resolved Calcium Dynamics of Mammalian Purkinje Cells in Cerebellar Slice," *Science*, vol. 242, pp. 773–777. Copyright © 1988 American Association for the Advancement of Science.)

Figure 9.20

ron that induces LTP. The study of calcium influx has been greatly facilitated by the development of *optical imaging techniques* for visualizing it (see Figure 9.20).

An important characteristic of the induction of LTP at glutaminergic synapses stems from the nature of the NMDA receptor and LTP's requirement for co-occurrence. This characteristic is not obvious under the usual, but unnatural, experimental condition in which LTP is induced by high-intensity, high-frequency stimulation, which always activates the postsynaptic neurons through massive temporal and spatial summation. However, when a more natural, low-intensity stimulation is applied, the postsynaptic neurons do not fire and thus LTP is not induced—unless the postsynaptic neurons are already partially depolarized so that their calcium channels open wide when glutamate binds to their NMDA receptors.

The requirement for the postsynaptic neurons to be partially depolarized when the glutamate binds to them is an extremely important characteristic of LTP because it permits neural networks to learn associations. Let me explain. If one glutaminergic neuron were to fire by itself and release its glutamate neurotransmitter across a synapse onto the NMDA receptors of a postsynaptic neuron, there would be no potentiation of transmission at that synapse because the postsynaptic cell would not fire. However, if the postsynaptic neuron were partially depolarized by input from other neurons when the presynaptic neuron fired, the binding of the glutamate to the NMDA receptors would open wide the calcium channels, calcium ions would flow into the postsynaptic neuron, and transmission across the synapses between the presynaptic and postsynaptic neuron would be potentiated. Accordingly, the requirement for co-occurrence and the dependence of NMDA receptors on simultaneous binding and partial depolarization mean that, under natural conditions, synaptic facilitation records the fact that there has been simultaneous activity in at least two converging inputs to the postsynaptic neuron—as would be produced by the "simultaneous" presentation of a conditional stimulus and an unconditional stimulus.

The exact mechanisms by which calcium influx induces LTP are complex and unclear (see Lisman, 2003); however, there is substantial evidence that calcium exerts some of its effects by activating *protein kinases* (a class of enzymes that influence many chemical reactions of the cell) in the neural cytoplasm (see Kind & Neumann, 2001). A consistent finding has been that protein kinase inhibitors block the induction of LTP (see Bashir & Collingridge, 1992). Figure 9.21 on page 292 summarizes the induction of NMDA-receptor–mediated LTP. Although it is well established that the induction of LTP at synapses with NMDA receptors depends on the influx of calcium ions into the postsynaptic neuron, the next stages of the induction process are not well understood. This is probably because several mechanisms are involved (see Sheng & Kim, 2002).

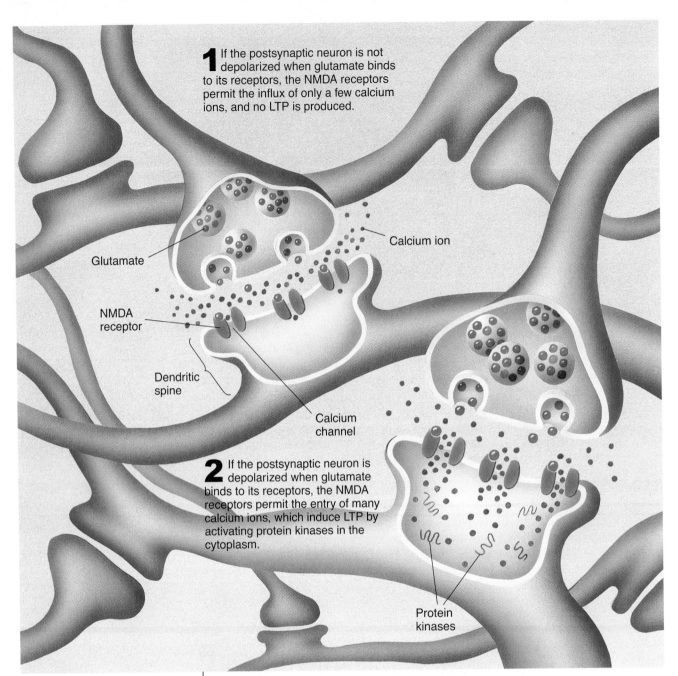

1 If the postsynaptic neuron is not depolarized when glutamate binds to its receptors, the NMDA receptors permit the influx of only a few calcium ions, and no LTP is produced.

Glutamate

Calcium ion

NMDA receptor

Dendritic spine

Calcium channel

2 If the postsynaptic neuron is depolarized when glutamate binds to its receptors, the NMDA receptors permit the entry of many calcium ions, which induce LTP by activating protein kinases in the cytoplasm.

Protein kinases

The induction of NMDA-receptor-mediated LTP.

Figure 9.21

Maintenance and Expression of LTP: Storage and Recall

The search for the mechanisms underlying the maintenance and expression of LTP began with attempts to determine whether these mechanisms occur in presynaptic or postsynaptic neurons. This question has been answered: The maintenance and expression of LTP involve changes in both presynaptic and postsynaptic neurons. This discovery has complicated the identification of the mechanisms of maintenance and expression (see Lisman, 2003). Nevertheless, five particularly important advances have been made.

First, once it became apparent that only those synapses that were depolarized before the high-frequency stimulation were involved in LTP (other synapses on the same postsynaptic neurons were unaffected), it was clear that there must be a mechanism for keeping the events at one set of synapses on a postsynaptic neuron from affecting other synapses on the same neuron. This specificity appears to be due to the **dendritic spines**; the calcium ions that enter one dendritic spine do not readily diffuse out of it, and thus they exert their effects locally (see Harris & Kater, 1994).

Second, it has become apparent that the changes that occur immediately and maintain the experience of the high-frequency stimulation for a time are not the same as those that maintain the experience weeks later. Specifically, the long-term maintenance, because of its permanence, is likely to involve structural changes, which depend on changes in gene expression and the resulting changes in protein synthesis. Protein synthesis cannot be responsible for the short-term maintenance because it does not occur rapidly enough.

Third, there is direct evidence that presynaptic changes are involved in the maintenance and expression of LTP at synapses having NMDA receptors. LTP at these synapses has been shown to be associated with a long-lasting increase in the extracellular levels of glutamate and with an increase in the degree to which extracellular glutamate is increased by subsequent electrical stimulation (Errington, Galley, & Bliss, 2003).

Fourth, given that the induction of LTP begins in the postsynaptic neurons and that its maintenance and expression involve presynaptic changes, there must be some type of signal that passes from the postsynaptic neurons back to the presynaptic neurons. Evidence suggests that at NMDA synapses, this signal takes the form of the soluble-gas neurotransmitter **nitric oxide**. Nitric oxide is synthesized in the postsynaptic neurons in response to calcium influx and then diffuses back into the terminal buttons of the presynaptic neurons (e.g., Harris, 1995).

And fifth, it is now well-established that structural changes occur at NMDA synapses in association with long-lasting LTP. There are changes in gene expression and increases in the number and size of synapses, in the number and size of dendritic spines, and in the number of postsynaptic NMDA receptors (see Harris, Fiala, & Ostroff, 2003; Lüscher & Frerking, 2001; Yuste & Bonhoeffer, 2001).

Variability of LTP

When I first started reading about research on LTP, I was excited at the potential. If LTP were the key to understanding the neural basis of learning and memory, then important discoveries would soon be forthcoming. A generation of neuroscientists has shared my view, and LTP has become the most researched topic in all of neuroscience. With such a massive effort, it seemed that identifying the mechanisms underlying the induction, maintenance, and expression of LTP should be relatively straightforward.

As I read the current literature on LTP, however, it seems that researchers are further from ultimate answers than I naively thought they were about a quarter-century ago. What has happened? Many important discoveries have been made, but rather than leading to ultimate solutions, they have often simply revealed how complex and varied LTP is.

Thinking Clearly

Most of the research on LTP has focused on NMDA-receptor–mediated LTP in the hippocampus. It is now clear that NMDA-receptor–mediated LTP involves a complex array of changes that are difficult to sort out. In addition, LTP has been documented in many other parts of the CNS where it tends to be mediated by different mechanisms (e.g., Gaiarsa, Caillard, & Ben-Ari, 2002; Ikeda et al., 2003). And then there is LTD (long-term depression), the flip side of LTP; LTD occurs in response to prolonged low-frequency stimulation of presynaptic neurons (Bliss & Schoepfer, 2004; Liu et al., 2004). Presumably, a full understanding of LTP will require an understanding of LTD (Christie, Kerr, & Abraham, 1994).

The dream of discovering the neural basis of learning and memory is what has attracted so many neuroscientists to focus on LTP. Although this dream has not yet been fulfilled, the study of LTP has led to many important discoveries about the function and plasticity of neural systems. By this criterion, this massive research effort should be judged as worthwhile.

9.9

Conclusion: Infantile Amnesia and the Biopsychologist Who Remembered H.M.

Thinking Clearly

We tend to think of memory as a unitary ability. Nevertheless, individuals with brain damage often display severe deficits in one memory process but not in others. Because this chapter has so far focused on the amnesic affects of brain damage, you may have been left with the impression that the dissociations among various kinds of memory have little direct relevance to individuals with intact healthy brains. This final section of the chapter emphasizes that such is not the case. It makes the point with one interesting line of experiments and one provocative case study.

We all experience *infantile amnesia*; that is, we remember virtually nothing of the events of our infancy (Howe, 2003). Newcombe and her colleagues (2000) addressed the following question: Do normal children who fail explicitly to recall or recognize things from their early childhood display preserved implicit memory for these things? The results of two experiments indicate that the answer is "yes."

In one study of infantile amnesia (Newcombe & Fox, 1994), children were shown a series of photographs of preschool-aged children, some of whom had been their preschool classmates. The subjects recognized a few of their former preschool classmates. However, whether they explicitly remembered a former classmate or not, they consistently displayed a large skin conductance response to the photographs of those classmates.

In a second study of infantile amnesia, Drummey and Newcombe (1995) used a modern version of the incomplete-pictures test. They showed a series of drawings to 3-year-olds, 5-year-olds, and adults. Three months later, subjects' memory for these drawings was assessed by asking them to identify them and some control drawings as quickly as they could. The drawings were initially badly out of focus, but became progressively sharper. Following this test of implicit memory, the subjects were asked which of the drawings they remembered seeing before. The 5-year-olds and adults showed better explicit memory than the 3-year-olds did; that is, they were more likely to recall seeing drawings from the original series. However, all three groups displayed substantial implicit memory: All subjects were able to identify more quickly the drawings they had seen before, even when they had no conscious recollection of having seen them before.

This chapter began with the case of H.M.; it ends with the case of R.M. The case of R.M. is one of the most ironic that I have encountered, which is why I have saved it for a chapter-ending treat. R.M. is a biopsychologist, and, as you will learn, his vocation played an important role in one of his symptoms.

The Case of R.M., the Biopsychologist Who Remembered H.M.

R.M. fell on his head while skiing; when he regained consciousness, he was suffering from both retrograde and anterograde amnesia. For several hours, he could recall few of the events of his previous life. He could not remember if he was married, where he lived, or where he worked. He had lost most of his episodic memory.

Also, many of the things that happened to him in the hours after his accident were forgotten as soon as his attention was diverted from them. For example, in the car on his way to the hospital, R.M. chatted with the person sitting next to him—a friend of a friend with whom he had skied all day. But each time his attention was drawn elsewhere—for example, by the mountain scenery—he completely forgot this person and their previous conversations, and subsequently reintroduced himself.

This was a classic case of posttraumatic amnesia. Like H.M., R.M. was trapped in the present, with only a cloudy past and seemingly no future. The irony of the situation was that during those few hours, when R.M. could recall few of the events of his own life, his thoughts repeatedly drifted to one semantic memory—his memory of a person he remembered learning about somewhere in his muddled past. Through the haze, he remembered H.M., his fellow prisoner of the present and wondered if the same fate lay in store for him.

R.M. recovered fully and looks back on what he can recall of his experience with relief and a feeling of empathy for H.M. Unlike H.M., R.M. received a reprieve, but his experience left him with a better appreciation for the situation of those amnesics, like H.M., who are serving life sentences.

Key Terms

Learning (p. 265)
Memory (p. 265)

9.1 Amnesic Effects of Bilateral Medial Temporal Lobectomy

Amygdala (p. 265)
Anterograde amnesia (p. 266)
Bilateral medial temporal lobectomy (p. 265)
CA1 subfield (p. 270)
Cerebral ischemia (p. 270)
Digit span (p. 266)
Episodic memories (p. 269)
Explicit memories (p. 268)
Hippocampus (p. 265)
Implicit memories (p. 268)
Incomplete-pictures test (p. 267)
Lobectomy (p. 265)
Lobotomy (p. 265)
Long-term memories (p. 266)
Medial temporal lobe amnesia (p. 268)
Memory consolidation (p. 268)
Pyramidal cell layer (p. 270)
Repetition priming tests (p. 269)
Retrograde amnesia (p. 266)
Semantic memories (p. 269)
Short-term memories (p. 266)

9.2 Amnesia of Korsakoff's Syndrome

Korsakoff's syndrome (p. 270)
Medial diencephalic amnesia (p. 271)
Mediodorsal nuclei (p. 271)

9.3 Amnesia of Alzheimer's Disease

Basal forebrain (p. 272)

9.4 Amnesia after Concussion: Evidence for Consolidation

Electroconvulsive shock (ECS) (p. 274)
Engram (p. 276)
Posttraumatic amnesia (PTA) (p. 273)

9.5 Neuroanatomy of Object-Recognition Memory

Delayed nonmatching-to-sample test (p. 278)
Mumby box (p. 280)
Rhinal cortex (p. 279)

9.6 The Hippocampus and Memory for Spatial Location

Cognitive map theory (p. 285)
Morris water maze test (p. 283)
Place cells (p. 284)
Radial arm maze (p. 284)
Reference memory (p. 284)
Working memory (p. 284)

9.7 Where Are Memories Stored?

Cerebellum (p. 288)
Inferotemporal cortex (p. 286)
Striatum (p. 288)

9.8 Synaptic Mechanisms of Learning and Memory

Dendritic spines (p. 293)
Glutamate (p. 291)
Long-term potentiation (LTP) (p. 288)
Nitric oxide (p. 293)
NMDA receptor (p. 290)

ON THE CD

Studying for an exam? Get some help from the electronic flash cards of the key terms and the practice tests for this chapter.

Learning, Memory, and Amnesia
How Your Brain Stores Information

Experiences change your brain, and these changes underlie your ability to remember the experiences. This chapter emphasized how knowledge about the neural mechanisms of memory has been derived from studying amnesia in brain-damaged patients.

Amnesic Effects of Brain Damage

There are four types of brain-damage-produced amnesia: amnesia associated with medial temporal lobe damage, with Korsakoff's syndrome, with Alzheimer's disease, and with concussion. The case study of H.M., the man who had a bilateral medial temporal lobectomy, has been particularly influential in furthering the understanding of memory. The most important finding to emerge from the study of brain-damage–produced amnesia is that not all memories are equally susceptible to disruption: Episodic explicit memories are particularly susceptible to disruption; semantic implicit memories are less so. With concussion, memories for events that occurred just before the concussion are most likely to be disturbed.
(Pages 265–277)

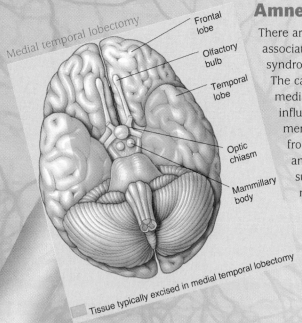

Medial temporal lobectomy

Frontal lobe
Olfactory bulb
Temporal lobe
Optic chiasm
Mammillary body

Tissue typically excised in medial temporal lobectomy

Neuroanatomy of Object-Recognition Memory

The hippocampus is widely believed to be the main memory structure of the brain. The main evidence for this is the fact that bilateral hippocampectomy produces huge object-recognition deficits in humans and monkeys. However, recent evidence shows that most of the disruptive effects of bilateral hippocampectomy on this form of memory result from damage to the adjacent rhinal cortex.
(Pages 277–283)

3 The monkey is confronted with the sample object and an unfamiliar object.

4 The monkey must remember the sample object and then select the unfamiliar object to obtain the food beneath it.

Delayed nonmatching to sample

The Hippocampus and Memory for Spatial Location

Although the hippocampus does not appear to play the central role in object-recognition memory, it is an important memory structure. There is strong evidence that the hippocampus is involved in memory for spatial location. It is currently unclear whether the hippocampus plays a major role in memories other than those for spatial location.
(Pages 283–286)

figure 9.16

Morris Water Maze

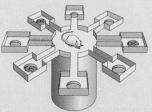

Radial Arm Maze

Visual Summary

Where Are Memories Stored?

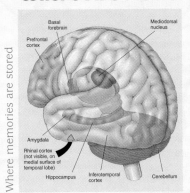

Where memories are stored

Memories for experiences are thought to be stored in the brain structures that participated in the original experience: for example, the hippocampus, rhinal cortex, mediodorsal nucleus, basal forebrain, inferotemporal cortex, amygdala, prefrontal cortex, cerebellum, and striatum.
(Pages 286–288)

Synaptic Mechanisms of Learning and Memory

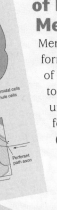

Hippocampus

Memories are presumed to be formed through the facilitation of synaptic transmission. Efforts to understand the mechanisms underlying this facilitation have focused on long-term potentiation (LTP), often in the hippocampus. In LTP experiments, high-frequency electrical stimulation is briefly applied to a tract of presynaptic neurons. This produces a lasting increase in the responsiveness of the postsynaptic neurons to subsequent stimulations of the same tract.
(Pages 288–294)

Conclusion: Infantile Amnesia and the Biopsychologist Who Remembered H.M.

The discussion of infantile amnesia and one case study concluded the chapter. We all experience infantile amnesia; we have no memory for things we experienced during infancy. R.M. is a biopsychologist who could not remember anything about his life following a ski accident, but he remembered H.M.
(Pages 294–295)

Themes Revisited

Because this chapter was based almost entirely on the study of human memory disorders and animal models of them, the clinical implications and evolutionary perspective themes predominated. The clinical study of memory disorders has so far been a one-way street: We have learned much about memory and its neural mechanisms from studying amnesic patients, but we have not yet learned enough to treat their memory problems.

The cognitive neuroscience theme emerged infrequently in this chapter. However, modern functional brain-imaging methods are starting to play a major role in the study of brain-damage–produced memory disorders.

Finally, the thinking-clearly-about-biopsychology tag appeared at several points in the chapter. It alerted you to (1) recognize the limitations of case studies, (2) not think about memory as a unitary process, (3) appreciate the difficulty in distinguishing between anterograde and retrograde effects when disorders have a gradual onset (e.g., Korsakoff's disease), (4) recognize that cases of cerebral ischemia (e.g., that of R.B.) do not provide conclusive evidence of the role of the hippocampus in memory, and (5) appreciate that, although most research has focused on NMDA-receptor–mediated LTP in the hippocampus, LTP is a complex and varied phenomenon.

Think about It

1. The study of the anatomy of memory has come a long way since H.M.'s misfortune. What kind of advances do you think will be made in the next decade?
2. Using examples from your own experience, compare implicit and explicit memory.
3. What are the advantages and shortcomings of animal models of amnesia? Compare the usefulness of monkey and rat models.
4. LTP is one of the most intensely studied of all neuroscientific phenomena. Why? Has the effort been successful?
5. Case studies have played a particularly important role in the study of memory. Discuss.

Part 4

Biopsychology of Motivation

I hope that you now understand, after completing Part 3, why neuroplasticity is currently one of the "hottest" subjects of neuroscientific research. Researchers are making such rapid progress in understanding so many different aspects of neuroplasticity that it seems that major breakthroughs will soon be forthcoming. The potential clinical applications of this research are exciting.

I think you will find Part 4 particularly interesting. The chapters in this part deal with three important areas of motivational research: eating, sexual behavior, and sleeping. At any given moment, you have the ability to engage in many different behaviors. For example, right now you could be eating, sleeping, or having sex, but you are reading these words. (Or perhaps you are doing two things at once?) Motivational processes of the brain determine what you do and how intensely or vigorously you do it—in short, they have a lot to say about the kind of person you are.

If you are like me, you originally decided to take psychology courses to learn more about human behavior, especially your own. Part 4 will provide you with this information, as well as insight into your own behavior and, more importantly, into possibilities for changing it that could have a positive effect on your health and longevity. I guarantee that this is no hollow promise.

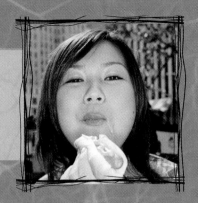

chapter 10

Hunger, Eating, and Health
Why Do Many People Eat Too Much?

Eating is a behavior that is of interest to virtually everyone. We all do it, and most of us derive great pleasure from it. But for many of us, it becomes a source of serious personal and health problems.

Most eating-related health problems are associated with eating too much (see Kopelman, 2000). For example, by one estimate, over half of the adult U.S. population meets the current criteria for clinical obesity, qualifying this problem for epidemic status. The resulting financial and personal costs are huge. Each year in the United States, $45 billion is spent treating obesity-related disorders; missed work costs another $23 billion; and $33 billion is spent on weight-loss products and services. Moreover, each year an estimated 300,000 U.S. citizens die from disorders caused by their excessive eating (e.g., diabetes, hypertension, cardiovascular diseases, and some cancers). Although the United States is the trend-setter when it comes to overeating and obesity, many other countries are not far behind.

Ironically, as overeating and obesity have reached epidemic proportions, there has been a related increase in disorders associated with eating too little (see Polivy & Herman, 2002). For example, about 3% of U.S. adolescents currently suffer from *anorexia nervosa*, which is life-threatening in extreme cases.

The message is clear: At some time in your life, you or somebody you care about will almost certainly suffer from an eating-related disorder.

The massive increases in obesity and other eating-related disorders that have occurred over the last few decades in many countries stand in stark contrast to most people's thinking about hunger and eating. Most people—and I assume you are included—believe that hunger and eating are normally triggered when the body's energy resources fall below a prescribed optimal level, or **set point**: Most people appreciate that many factors influence hunger and eating, but they assume that the hunger and eating system has evolved to supply the body with just the right amount of energy.

The incompatibility of set-point thinking with the current epidemic of eating disorders is the focus of this chapter. If we all have hunger and eating systems whose primary function is to maintain energy resources at optimal levels, then eating disorders should be rare. The fact that they are so prevalent suggests that hunger and eating are regulated in some other way.

The first sections of this chapter examine some of the fundamental characteristics of hunger and eating; this examination will provide the basis for a different way of thinking about hunger, eating, and health. Armed with this new perspective, we will reexamine the clinical problems of obesity and anorexia nervosa in the final sections. This chapter will definitely provide you with new insights of major personal relevance.

Before you move on to the body of the chapter, I would like you to pause to consider a case study. What would a severely amnesic patient do if offered a meal shortly after finishing one? If his hunger and eating were controlled by energy set points, he would refuse the second meal. Did he?

ON THE CD

In the module *Thinking about Hunger*, Pinel welcomes you to this chapter and talks about a common misconception about mealtime hunger.

The Case of the Man Who Forgot Not to Eat

R.H. was a 48-year-old male whose progress in graduate school was interrupted by the development of severe amnesia for long-term explicit memory. His amnesia was similar in pattern and severity to that of H.M., whom you met in Chapter 9, and an MRI examination revealed bilateral damage to the medial temporal lobes.

The meals offered to R.H. were selected on the basis of interviews with him about the foods he liked: veal parmigiana (about 750 calories) plus all the apple juice he wanted. On one occasion, he was offered a second meal about 15 minutes after he had eaten the first, and he ate it. When offered a third meal 15 minutes later, he ate that, too. When offered a fourth meal, he rejected it, claiming that his "stomach was a little tight."

Then, a few minutes later, R.H. announced that he was going out for a good walk and a meal. When asked what he was going to eat, his answer was "veal parmigiana." Clearly, R.H.'s hunger (i.e., motivation to eat) did not result from an energy deficit (Rozin et al., 1998).

Clinical Implications

The primary purpose of eating is to supply the body with the energy it needs to survive and function. This section provides a brief overview of the processes by which food is digested, stored, and converted to energy.

Process of Digestion

The *gastrointestinal tract* and the process of digestion are illustrated in Figure 10.1. **Digestion** is the gastrointestinal process of breaking down food and absorbing its constituents into the body. In order to appreciate the basics of digestion, it is useful

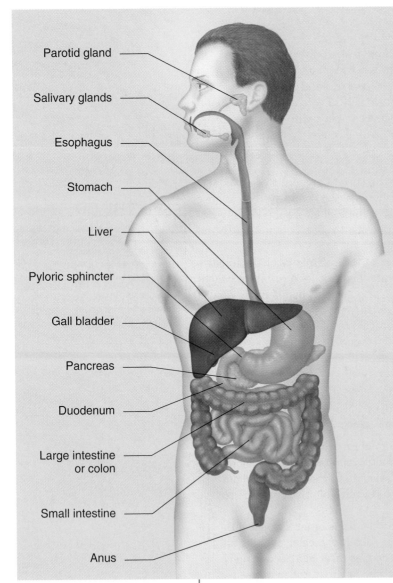

Parotid gland

Salivary glands

Esophagus

Stomach

Liver

Pyloric sphincter

Gall bladder

Pancreas

Duodenum

Large intestine
or colon

Small intestine

Anus

Steps in Digestion

1 Chewing breaks up food and mixes it with saliva.

2 Saliva lubricates food and begins its digestion.

3 Swallowing moves food and drink down the esophagus to the stomach.

4 The primary function of the stomach is to serve as a storage reservoir. The hydrochloric acid in the stomach breaks food down into small particles, and pepsin begins the process of breaking down protein molecules to amino acids.

5 The stomach gradually empties its contents through the pyloric sphincter into the duodenum, the upper portion of the intestine, where most of the absorption takes place.

6 Digestive enzymes in the duodenum, many of them from the gall bladder and pancreas, break down protein molecules to amino acids, and starch and complex sugar molecules to simple sugars. Simple sugars and amino acids readily pass through the duodenum wall into the bloodstream and are carried to the liver.

7 Fats are emulsified (broken into droplets) by bile, which is manufactured in the liver and stored in the gall bladder until it is released into the duodenum. Emulsified fat cannot pass through the duodenum wall and is carried by small ducts in the duodenum wall into the lymphatic system.

8 Most of the remaining water and electrolytes are absorbed from the waste in the large intestine, and the remainder is ejected from the anus.

The gastrointestinal tract and the process of digestion.

Figure 10.1

to consider the body without its protuberances, as a simple living tube with a hole at each end. To supply itself with energy and other nutrients, the tube puts food into one of its two holes—the one with teeth—and passes the food along its internal canal so that it can be broken down and partially absorbed from the canal into the body. The leftovers are jettisoned from the other end. Although this is not a particularly appetizing description of eating, it does serve to illustrate that, strictly speaking, food has not been consumed until it has been digested.

As a consequence of digestion, energy is delivered to the body in three forms: (1) **lipids** (fats), (2) **amino acids** (the breakdown products of proteins), and (3) **glucose** (a simple sugar that is the breakdown product of complex *carbohydrates*, that is, complex starches and sugars).

The body uses energy continuously, but its consumption of fuel (food) is intermittent; therefore, it must store energy for use in the intervals between meals. Energy is stored in three forms: *fats, glycogen*, and *proteins*. Most of the body's energy reserves are stored as fats, relatively little as glycogen and proteins (see Figure 10.2). Thus, changes in the body weights of adult humans are largely a consequence of changes in the amount of body fat.

Three Phases of Energy Metabolism

There are three phases of *energy metabolism* (the chemical changes by which energy is made available for an organism's use): the cephalic phase, the absorptive phase, and the fasting phase. The **cephalic phase** is the preparatory phase; it often begins with the sight, smell, or even just the thought of food, and it ends when the food starts to be absorbed into the bloodstream. The **absorptive phase** is the period during which the energy absorbed into the bloodstream from the meal is meeting the body's immediate energy needs. The **fasting phase** is the period during which all of the unstored energy from the previous meal has been used and the body is withdrawing energy from its reserves to meet its immediate energy requirements; it ends with the beginning of the next cephalic phase. During periods of rapid weight gain, people often go directly from one absorptive phase into the next cephalic phase, without experiencing an intervening fasting phase.

The flow of energy during the three phases of energy metabolism is controlled by two pancreatic hormones: insulin and glucagon. During the cephalic and absorptive phases, the pancreas releases a great deal of insulin into the bloodstream and very little glucagon. The **insulin** does three things: (1) It promotes the use of glucose as the primary source of energy by the body. (2) It promotes the conversion of bloodborne fuels to forms that can be stored: glucose to glycogen and fat, and amino acids to proteins. (3) It promotes the storage of glycogen in liver and muscle, fat in *adipose tissue* (a layer of tissue beneath the skin), and proteins in muscle. In short, the function of insulin during the cephalic phase is to lower the levels of bloodborne fuels, primarily glucose, in anticipation of the impending influx; and its function during the absorptive phase is to minimize the increasing levels of bloodborne fuels by utilizing and storing them.

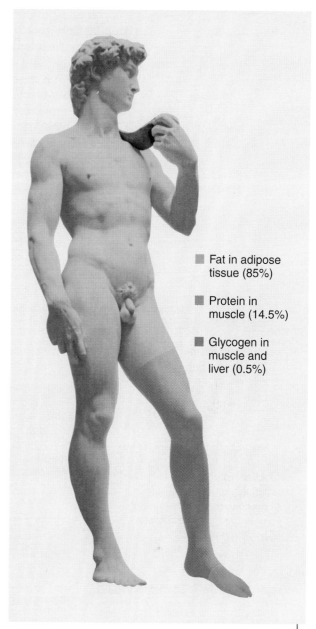

Fat in adipose tissue (85%)

Protein in muscle (14.5%)

Glycogen in muscle and liver (0.5%)

Distribution of stored energy in an average person.

Figure 10.2

In contrast to the cephalic and absorptive phases, the fasting phase is characterized by high blood levels of **glucagon** and low levels of insulin. Without high levels of insulin, glucose has difficulty entering most body cells; thus, glucose stops being the body's primary fuel. In effect, this saves the body's glucose for the brain, because insulin is not required for glucose to enter most brain cells. The low levels of insulin also promote the conversion of glycogen and protein to glucose. (The conversion of protein to glucose is called **gluconeogenesis**.)

On the other hand, the high levels of fasting-phase glucagon promote the release of **free fatty acids** from adipose tissue and their use as the body's primary fuel. The high glucagon levels also stimulate the conversion of free fatty acids to **ketones**, which are used by muscles as a source of energy during the fasting phase. After a prolonged period without food, however, the brain also starts to use ketones, thus further conserving the body's resources of glucose.

Figure 10.3 summarizes the major metabolic events associated with the three phases of energy metabolism.

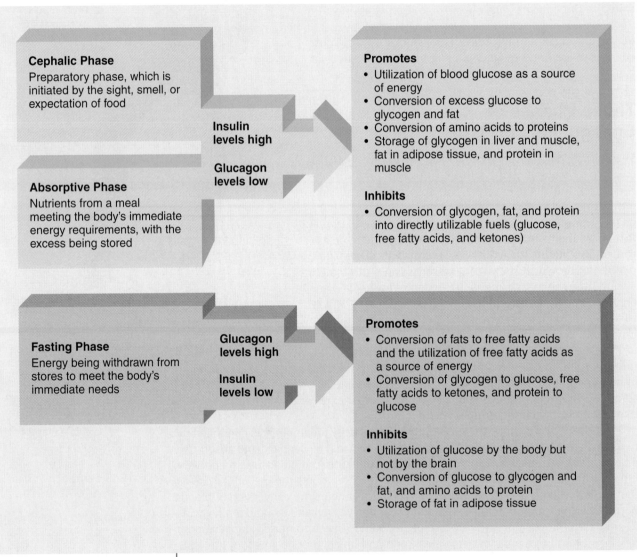

Cephalic Phase
Preparatory phase, which is initiated by the sight, smell, or expectation of food

Absorptive Phase
Nutrients from a meal meeting the body's immediate energy requirements, with the excess being stored

Insulin levels high

Glucagon levels low

Promotes
- Utilization of blood glucose as a source of energy
- Conversion of excess glucose to glycogen and fat
- Conversion of amino acids to proteins
- Storage of glycogen in liver and muscle, fat in adipose tissue, and protein in muscle

Inhibits
- Conversion of glycogen, fat, and protein into directly utilizable fuels (glucose, free fatty acids, and ketones)

Fasting Phase
Energy being withdrawn from stores to meet the body's immediate needs

Glucagon levels high

Insulin levels low

Promotes
- Conversion of fats to free fatty acids and the utilization of free fatty acids as a source of energy
- Conversion of glycogen to glucose, free fatty acids to ketones, and protein to glucose

Inhibits
- Utilization of glucose by the body but not by the brain
- Conversion of glucose to glycogen and fat, and amino acids to protein
- Storage of fat in adipose tissue

The major events associated with the three phases of energy metabolism: the cephalic, absorptive, and fasting phases.

Figure 10.3

One of the main difficulties I have in teaching the fundamentals of hunger, eating, and body weight regulation is the **set-point assumption**. Although it dominates most people's thinking about hunger and eating (Assanand, Pinel, & Lehman, 1998a, 1998b), whether they realize it or not, it is inconsistent with the bulk of the evidence. What exactly is the set-point assumption?

Set-Point Assumption

Most people attribute *hunger* (the motivation to eat) to the presence of an energy deficit, and they view eating as the means by which the energy resources of the body are returned to their optimal level—that is, to the *energy set point*. Figure 10.4 summarizes this set-point assumption. After a *meal* (a bout of eating), a person's energy resources are thought to be near their set point and to decline thereafter as the body uses energy to fuel its physiological processes. When the level of the body's energy resources falls far enough below the set point, a person becomes motivated by hunger to initiate another meal. The meal continues, according to the set-point assumption, until the energy level returns to its set point and the person feels *satiated* (no longer hungry).

The set-point model of hunger and eating works in much the same way as a thermostat-regulated heating system in a cool climate. The heater increases the house temperature until it reaches its set point (the thermostat setting). This turns off the heat, and then the temperature of the house gradually declines until the decline is large enough to turn the heater back on. All set-point systems have three components: a set-point mechanism, a detector mechanism, and an effector mechanism. The *set-point mechanism* defines the set point, the *detector mechanism* detects deviations from the set point, and the *effector mechanism* acts to eliminate the deviations. For example, the set-point, detector, and effector mechanisms of a heating system are the thermostat, the thermometer, and the heater, respectively.

All set-point systems include **negative feedback mechanisms** in which feedback from changes in one direction elicits compensatory effects in the opposite direction. Negative feedback mechanisms are common in mammals because they act to maintain **homeostasis**—a constant internal environment—which is critical for mammals' survival (see Wenning, 1999).

Most people are influenced by the set-point assumption and thus view the relation between meals and energy reserves as represented here. Do you?

Figure 10.4

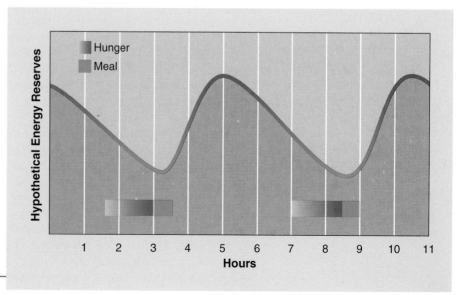

Glucostatic and Lipostatic Set-Point Theories of Hunger and Eating

In the 1940s and 1950s, researchers working under the assumption that eating is regulated by some type of set-point system speculated about the nature of the regulation. Several researchers suggested that eating is regulated by a system that is designed to maintain a blood glucose set point—the idea being that we become hungry when our blood glucose levels drop significantly below their set point and that we become satiated when eating returns our blood glucose levels to their set point. Various versions of this theory are referred to as the **glucostatic theory**. It seemed to make good sense that the main purpose of eating is to defend a blood glucose set point, because glucose is the brain's primary fuel.

The **lipostatic theory** is another set-point theory that was proposed in various forms in the 1940s and 1950s. According to this theory, every person has a set point for body fat, and deviations from this set point produce compensatory adjustments in the level of eating that return levels of body fat to their set point. The most frequently cited support for the theory is the fact that the body weights of adults stay relatively constant.

The glucostatic and lipostatic theories were viewed as complementary, not mutually exclusive. The glucostatic theory was thought to account for meal initiation and termination, whereas the lipostatic theory was thought to account for long-term regulation. Thus, the dominant view in the 1950s was that eating is regulated by the interaction between two set-point systems: a short-term glucostatic system and a long-term lipostatic system. The simplicity of these 1950s theories is appealing. Remarkably, they are still being presented as the latest word in some textbooks; perhaps you have encountered them.

Problems with Set-Point Theories of Hunger and Eating

Set-point theories of hunger and eating have several serious weaknesses (see de Castro & Plunkett, 2002). You have already learned one fact that undermines these theories: the current epidemic of obesity and other eating disorders. Let's look at three more.

The Evolutionary Perspective

First, set-point theories of hunger and eating are inconsistent with basic eating-related evolutionary pressures as we understand them. The major eating-related problem faced by our ancestors was the inconsistency and unpredictability of the food supply. Thus, in order to survive, it was important for them to eat large quantities of good food when it was available so that calories could be banked in the form of body fat. Any ancestor—human or otherwise—that stopped feeling hungry as soon as immediate energy needs were met would not have survived the first hard winter or prolonged drought. For any warm-blooded species to survive under natural conditions, it needs a hunger and eating system that prevents energy deficits, rather than one that merely responds to them once they have developed. From this perspective, it is difficult to imagine how a set-point hunger and feeding system could have evolved in mammals (see Pinel, Assanand, & Lehman, 2000).

Second, major predictions of the set-point theories of hunger and eating have not been confirmed. Early studies seemed to support the set-point theories by showing that large reductions in body fat, produced by starvation, or large reductions in blood glucose, produced by insulin injections, induce increases in eating in laboratory animals. The problem is that reductions of the magnitude needed to reliably induce eating rarely occur naturally. Indeed, as you have already learned in this chapter, over 50% of the U.S. adult population have a significant excess of fat deposits when they begin a meal. Conversely, efforts to reduce meal size by having subjects consume a high-calorie drink before eating have been largely unsuccessful; indeed, beliefs about the caloric content of a premeal drink often influence the size of a subsequent meal more than does its actual caloric content (see Lowe, 1993).

Third, set-point theories of hunger and eating are deficient because they fail to recognize the major influences on hunger and eating of such important factors as taste, learning, and social factors. To convince yourself of the importance of these factors, pause for a minute and imagine the sight, smell, and taste of your favorite food. Perhaps it is a succulent morsel of lobster meat covered with melted garlic butter, a piece of chocolate cheesecake, or a plate of sizzling homemade french fries. Are you starting to feel a bit hungry? If the homemade french fries—my personal weakness—were sitting in front of you right now, wouldn't you reach out and have one, or maybe the whole plateful? Have you not on occasion felt discomfort after a large main course, only to polish off a substantial dessert? Does Figure 10.5 make you feel a bit hungry? The usual positive answers to these questions lead unavoidably to the conclusion that hunger and eating are not rigidly controlled by deviations from energy set points.

Thinking Clearly

Positive-Incentive Perspective

The inability of set-point theories to account for the basic phenomena of eating and hunger has led to the development of an alternative theoretical perspective (see Berridge, 2004). The central assertion of this new theoretical perspective, commonly referred to as **positive-incentive theory**, is that humans and other animals are not normally driven to eat by internal energy deficits but are drawn to eat by the anticipated pleasure of eating—the anticipated pleasure of a behavior is called its **positive-incentive value** (see Bolles, 1980; Booth, 1981; Collier, 1980; Rolls, 1981; Toates, 1981). There are several different positive-incentive theories, and I refer generally to all of them as the *positive-incentive perspective.*

The major tenet of the positive-incentive perspective on eating is that eating is controlled in much the same way as sexual behavior: We engage in sexual behavior not because we have an internal deficit, but because we have evolved to crave it. The evolutionary pressures of unexpected food shortages have shaped us and all other warm-blooded animals, who need a continuous supply of energy to maintain their body temperatures, to take advantage of good food when it is present and eat it. According to the positive-incentive perspective, it is the presence of good food, or the anticipation of it, that normally makes us hungry, not an energy deficit.

According to the positive-incentive perspective, the degree of hunger you feel at any particular time depends on the interaction of all the factors that influence the positive-incentive value of eating. These include the following: the flavor of the food you are likely to consume, what you have learned about the effects of this food either from eating it previously or from other people, the amount of time since you last ate, the type and quantity of food in your gut, whether or not other people are present and eating, whether or not your blood glucose levels are within the normal range. This partial list illustrates one strength of the positive-incentive perspective. Unlike set-point theories, positive-incentive theories do not single out one factor as the major determinant of hunger and ignore the others; they acknowledge that many factors interact to determine a person's hunger at any time, and they suggest that this interaction occurs through the influence of these various factors on the positive-incentive value of eating (see Cabanac, 1971).

The positive-incentive perspective of hunger does not deny that major energy deficits trigger hunger—see Figure 10.6 on page 308. However, the positive-incentive perspective is based in part on the fact that such energy deficits are extremely rare in most modern societies, and thus they cannot be the major factor in making us hungry (i.e., in motivating us to eat).

In this section, you learned that most people think about hunger and eating in terms of energy set points, and you were introduced to an alternative: the

A dessert table. Few of us would refuse a sample—or two—even after completing a large meal.

Figure 10.5

Thinking Clearly

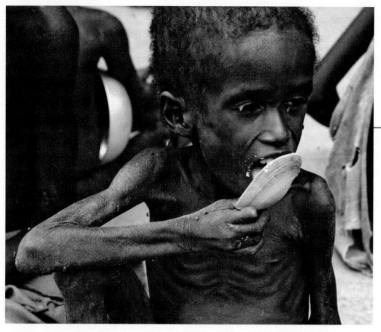

Too many people in this world experience starvation-produced hunger. However, in food-replete societies, few people experience energy deficits at the beginning of meals, and thus energy deficits cannot explain why we normally feel hungry.

Figure 10.6

positive-incentive perspective. Which is correct? If you are like most people, you will have an attachment to familiar ways of thinking and a resistance to new ones. The principles of clear thinking, however, require that you put these tendencies aside and base your views about this important issue entirely on the evidence.

You have already learned about some of the major weaknesses of set-point theories of hunger and eating. In the next section, you will learn some of the things that biopsychological research has taught us about hunger and eating. Notice the superiority of the positive-incentive theories over set-point theories in accounting for these basic facts.

10.3
Factors That Determine What, When, and How Much We Eat

This section describes major factors that commonly determine what we eat, when we eat, and how much we eat. Notice that energy deficits are not included among these factors. Although major energy deficits clearly increase hunger and eating, they are not a common factor in the eating behavior of people like us, who live in food-replete societies. Although you may believe that your body is short of energy just before a meal, it is not. This misconception is one that is addressed in this section. Also, notice that research on nonhumans has played an important role in furthering understanding of eating by our species.

Factors That Determine What We Eat

The Evolutionary Perspective

Certain tastes have a high positive-incentive value for virtually all members of a species. For example, most humans have a special fondness for sweet, fatty, and salty tastes. This species-typical pattern of human taste preferences is adaptive because in nature sweet and fatty tastes are typically characteristic of high-energy foods that are rich in vitamins and minerals, and salty tastes are characteristic of sodium-rich foods. In contrast, bitter tastes, for which most humans have an aversion, are often associated with toxins. Superimposed on our species-typical taste preferences and aversions, each of us has the ability to learn specific taste preferences and aversions (see Rozin & Shulkin, 1990).

Learned Taste Preferences and Aversions. Animals, including humans, learn to prefer tastes that are followed by an infusion of calories, and they learn to avoid tastes that are followed by illness (e.g., Baker & Booth, 1989; Sclafani, 1990). In addition, humans and other animals learn what to eat from their conspecifics. For example, rats learn to prefer flavors that they experience in mother's milk and those that they smell on the breath of other rats (see Galef, 1995, 1996). Similarly, in humans, many food preferences are culturally specific—for example, in some cultures, various nontoxic insects are considered to be a delicacy. Galef and Wright (1995) have shown that rats reared in groups, rather than in isolation, are more likely to learn to eat a healthy diet.

Learning to Eat Vitamins and Minerals.   How do animals select a diet that provides all of the vitamins and minerals they need? To answer this question, researchers have studied how dietary deficiencies influence diet selection. Two patterns of results have emerged: one for sodium and one for the other essential vitamins and minerals. When an animal is deficient in sodium, it develops an immediate and compelling preference for the taste of sodium salt (see Rowland, 1990). In contrast, an animal that is deficient in some vitamin or mineral other than sodium must learn to consume foods that are rich in the missing nutrient by experiencing their positive effects; this is because vitamins and minerals other than sodium normally have no detectable taste in food. For example, rats maintained on a diet deficient in *thiamine* (vitamin B_1) develop an aversion to the taste of that diet; and if they are offered two new diets, one deficient in thiamine and one rich in thiamine, they often develop a preference for the taste of the thiamine-rich diet over the ensuing days.

If we, like rats, are capable of learning to select diets that are rich in the vitamins and minerals we need, why are dietary deficiencies so prevalent in our society (see Willett, 1994)? One reason is that, in order to maximize profits, manufacturers produce foods with the tastes that we prefer but with most of the essential nutrients extracted from them. (Even rats prefer chocolate chip cookies to nutritionally complete rat chow.) The second reason is illustrated by the classic study by Harris and associates (1933). When thiamine-deficient rats were offered two new diets, one with thiamine and one without, almost all of them learned to eat the complete diet and avoid the deficient one. However, when they were offered ten new diets, only one of which contained the badly needed thiamine, few developed a preference for the complete diet. The number of different substances consumed each day by most people in industrialized societies is immense, and this makes it difficult, if not impossible, for their bodies to learn which foods are beneficial and which are not.

There is not much about nutrition in this chapter: Although it is certainly important to eat a nutritious diet, nutrition has little direct effect on our hunger and eating. However, while I am on the topic, I would like to direct you to a good source of information about nutrition. Many popular books on nutrition are of questionable validity, and even governments, inordinately influenced by economic considerations and special-interest groups, often do not provide the best nutritional advice (see Nestle, 2003). For sound research-based advice on nutrition, check out an article by Willett and Stampfer (2003) and the book on which it is based (Willett, Skerrett, & Giovannucci, 2001): *Eat, Drink, and Be Healthy*.

Clinical Implications

Factors That Influence When We Eat

Collier and his colleagues (see Collier, 1986) found that most mammals choose to eat many small meals (snacks) each day if they have ready access to a continuous supply of food. Only when there are physical costs involved in initiating meals—for example, having to travel a considerable distance or making a kill—does an animal opt for a few large meals.

The number of times humans eat each day is influenced by cultural norms, work schedules, family routines, personal preferences, wealth, and a variety of other factors. However, in contrast to the usual mammalian preference, most people, particularly those living in family groups, tend to eat a few large meals each day at regular times. Interestingly, each person's regular mealtimes are the very same times at

The Evolutionary Perspective

which that person is likely to feel most hungry; in fact, many people experience attacks of malaise (headache, nausea, and an inability to concentrate) when they miss a regularly scheduled meal.

Premeal Hunger. I am sure that you have experienced attacks of premeal hunger. Subjectively, they seem to provide compelling support for set-point theories. Your body seems to be crying out: "I need more energy. I cannot function without it. Please feed me." But things are not always the way they seem. Woods has straightened out the confusion (see Woods, 1991; Woods & Ramsay, 2000; Woods & Strubbe, 1994).

According to Woods, the key to understanding hunger is to appreciate that eating meals stresses the body. Before a meal, the body's energy reserves are in reasonable homeostatic balance; then, as a meal is consumed, there is a homeostasis-disturbing influx of fuels into the bloodstream. The body does what it can to defend its homeostasis. At the first indication that a person will soon be eating—for example, when the usual mealtime approaches—the body enters the cephalic phase and takes steps to soften the impact of the impending homeostasis-disturbing influx by releasing insulin into the blood and thus reducing blood glucose. Woods's message is that the strong, unpleasant feelings of hunger that you may experience at mealtimes are not cries from your body for food; they are the sensations of your body's preparations for the expected homeostasis-disturbing meal. Mealtime hunger is caused by the expectation of food, not by an energy deficit.

As a high school student, I ate lunch at exactly 12:05 every day and was overwhelmed by hunger as the time approached. Now, my eating schedule is different, and I never experience noontime hunger pangs; I now get hungry just before the time at which I usually eat. Have you had a similar experience?

Pavlovian Conditioning of Hunger. In a clever series of Pavlovian conditioning experiments on laboratory rats, Weingarten (1983, 1984, 1985) provided strong support for the view that hunger is often caused by the expectation of food, not by an energy deficit. During the conditioning phase of one of his experiments, Weingarten presented rats with six meals per day at irregular intervals, and he signaled the impending delivery of each meal with a buzzer-and-light conditional stimulus. This conditioning procedure was continued for 11 days. Throughout the ensuing test phase of the experiment, the food was continuously available. Despite the fact that the subjects were never deprived during the test phase, the rats started to eat each time the buzzer and light were presented—even if they had recently completed a meal.

Factors That Influence How Much We Eat

The motivational state that causes us to stop eating a meal when there is food remaining is **satiety**. Satiety mechanisms play a major role in determining how much we eat.

Satiety Signals. As you will learn in the next section of the chapter, food in the gut and glucose entering the blood can induce satiety signals, which inhibit subsequent consumption. These signals depend on both the volume and the **nutritive density** (calories per unit volume) of the food.

The effects of nutritive density have been demonstrated in studies in which laboratory rats have been maintained on a single diet. Once a stable baseline of consumption has been established, the nutritive density of the diet is changed. Some rats learn to adjust the volume of food they consume to keep their caloric intake and body weights relatively stable. However, there are limits to this adjustment: Most rats do not increase their intake sufficiently to maintain their body weights if the nutritive density of their conventional laboratory feed is reduced by more than 50%. Moreover, they do not maintain the consistency of their caloric intake, as set-point theories predict they should, if there is a major change in the palatability of their diet.

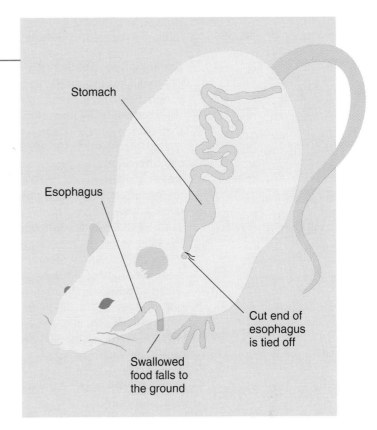

The sham-eating preparation.

Figure 10.7

Sham Eating.

The study of **sham eating** indicates that satiety signals from the gut or blood are not necessary to terminate a meal. In sham-eating experiments, food is chewed and swallowed by the subject; but rather than passing down the subject's esophagus into the stomach, the food passes out of the body through an implanted tube (see Figure 10.7).

Because sham eating adds no energy to the body, set-point theories predict that all sham-eaten meals should be huge. But this is not the case. Weingarten and Kulikovsky (1989) sham fed rats a diet that they had naturally eaten many times before. The first sham meal was the same size as the previously eaten meals; then, on ensuing days the rats began to sham eat more and more (see Figure 10.8). Kulikovsky concluded that the amount we eat is influenced largely by our previous experience with the particular food's postingestive effects, not by the immediate effect of the food on the body.

Appetizer Effect and Satiety.

The next time you attend a dinner party, you may experience a major weakness of the set-point theory of satiety. If appetizers are served, you will experience the fact that small amounts of food consumed before a meal actually increase hunger rather than reduce it. This is the **appetizer effect**. Presumably, it occurs because the consumption of a small amount of food is particularly effective in eliciting cephalic-phase responses.

Thinking Clearly

Social Influences and Satiety.

Feelings of satiety depend on whether we are eating alone or with others. Redd and de Castro (1992) found that their subjects consumed 60% more when eating with others. Laboratory rats also eat substantially more when fed in groups.

In humans, social factors have also been shown to reduce consumption. Many people eat less than they would like in order to achieve their society's ideal of slenderness, and others refrain from eating large amounts in front of others so as not to appear gluttonous.

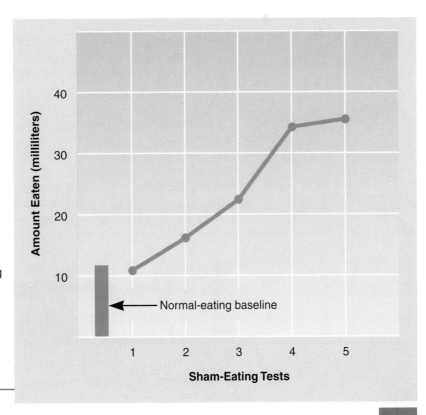

Change in the magnitude of sham eating over repeated sham-eating trials. The rats in one group sham ate the same diet they had eaten before the sham-eating phase.

(Adapted from Weingarten, 1990.)

Figure 10.8

Unfortunately, in our culture, females are greatly influenced by such pressures, and, as you will learn later in the chapter, some develop serious eating disorders as a result.

Sensory-Specific Satiety. The number of different tastes available at each meal has a major effect on meal size. For example, the effect of offering a laboratory rat a varied diet of highly palatable foods—a **cafeteria diet**—is dramatic. Adults rats that were offered bread and chocolate in addition to their usual laboratory diet increased their average intake of calories by 84%, and after 120 days they had increased their average body weights by 49% (Rogers & Blundell, 1980). The spectacular effects of cafeteria diets on consumption and body weight clearly run counter to the idea that satiety is rigidly controlled by internal energy set points.

The effect on meal size of cafeteria diets results from the fact that satiety is to a large degree taste-specific. As you eat one food, the positive-incentive value of all foods declines slightly, but the positive-incentive value of that particular food plummets. As a result, you soon become satiated on that food and stop eating it. However, if another food is offered to you, you will often begin eating again.

In one study of **sensory-specific satiety** (Rolls et al., 1981), human subjects were asked to rate the palatability of eight different foods, and then they ate a meal of one of them. After the meal, they were asked to rate the palatability of the eight foods once again, and it was found that their rating of the food they had just eaten had declined substantially more than had their ratings of the other seven foods. Moreover, when the subjects were offered an unexpected second meal, they consumed most of it unless it was the same as the first.

Booth (1981) asked subjects to rate the momentary pleasure produced by the flavor, the smell, the sight, or just the thought of various foods at different times after consuming a large, high-calorie, high-carbohydrate liquid meal. There was an immediate sensory-specific decrease in the palatability of foods of the same or similar flavor as soon as the liquid meal was consumed. This was followed by a general decrease in the palatability of all substances about 30 minutes later. Thus, it appears that signals from taste receptors produce an immediate decline in the positive-incentive value of similar tastes and that signals associated with the postingestive consequences of eating produce a general decrease in the positive-incentive value of all foods.

Rolls (1990) suggested that sensory-specific satiety has two kinds of effects: relatively brief effects that influence the selection of foods within a single meal and relatively enduring effects that influence the selection of foods from meal to meal. Some foods seem to be relatively immune to long-lasting sensory-specific satiety; foods such as rice, bread, potatoes, sweets, and green salads can be eaten almost every day with only a slight decline in their palatability (Rolls, 1986).

The Evolutionary Perspective

The phenomenon of sensory-specific satiety has two adaptive consequences. First, it encourages the consumption of a varied diet. If there were no sensory-specific satiety, a person would tend to eat her or his preferred food and nothing else, and the result would be malnutrition. Second, sensory-specific satiety encourages animals that have access to a variety of foods to eat a lot; an animal that has eaten its fill of one food will often begin eating again if it encounters a different one (Raynor & Epstein, 2001). This encourages animals to take full advantage of times of abundance, which are all too rare in nature.

10.4
Physiological Research on Hunger and Satiety

Now that you have been introduced to the set-point and positive-incentive perspectives and some basic eating-related facts, this section introduces you to five prominent lines of research on the physiology of hunger and satiety.

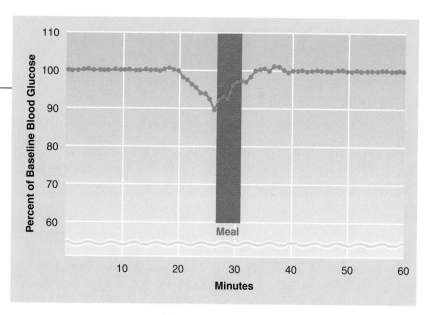

Meal-related changes in blood glucose levels.

(Based on Campfield and Smith, 1990.)

Figure 10.9

Role of Blood Glucose Levels in Hunger and Satiety

As I have already explained, efforts to link blood glucose levels to eating have been largely unsuccessful. Indeed, blood glucose levels rarely fluctuate by more than 2%; they are normally maintained at steady levels by pancreatic hormones (Campfield & Smith, 1990). However, about 10 minutes before a meal, these levels suddenly drop by about 8% (see Figure 10.9).

Does this sudden drop in premeal blood glucose levels lend support to the glucostatic theory of hunger? I think not, for four reasons. First, it is a simple matter to construct a situation in which decreases in blood glucose levels do not precede eating (e.g., Strubbe & Steffens, 1977)—for example, by unexpectedly serving food with a high positive-incentive value. Second, premeal decreases in blood glucose seem to be a response to the intention to start eating, not the other way around. Premeal decreases in blood glucose are preceded by increases in blood insulin levels. This indicates that the premeal decreases do not occur because of a gradual decline in energy reserves, but rather that blood glucose levels are being actively and suddenly reduced by the insulin. Third, if the expected meal is not served, blood glucose levels return to their previous homeostatic level. And fourth, injections of insulin do not reliably induce eating in experimental subjects unless the injections are sufficiently great to reduce blood glucose levels by at least 50% (see Rowland, 1981).

Instead, the drop in blood glucose levels prior to a meal appears to be part of the body's effort to protect itself from the expected homeostasis-disturbing influx of calories (i.e., the meal). As noted earlier, these adaptive premeal reductions in blood glucose presumably contribute to the feelings that are misinterpreted by many people as a need for energy.

Myth of Hypothalamic Hunger and Satiety Centers

In the 1950s, experiments on rats seemed to suggest that eating behavior is controlled by two different regions of the hypothalamus: satiety by the **ventromedial hypothalamus (VMH)** and feeding by the **lateral hypothalamus (LH)**—see Figure 10.10. This theory turned out to be wrong, but it stimulated several important discoveries.

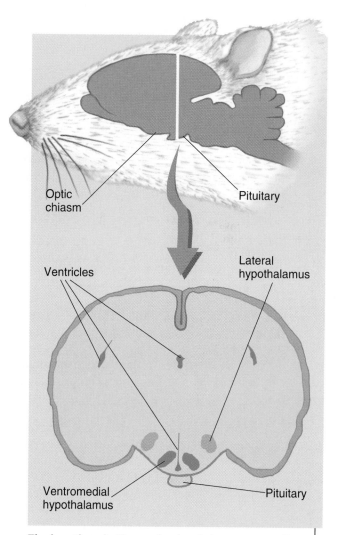

The locations in the rat brain of the ventromedial hypothalamus and the lateral hypothalamus.

Figure 10.10

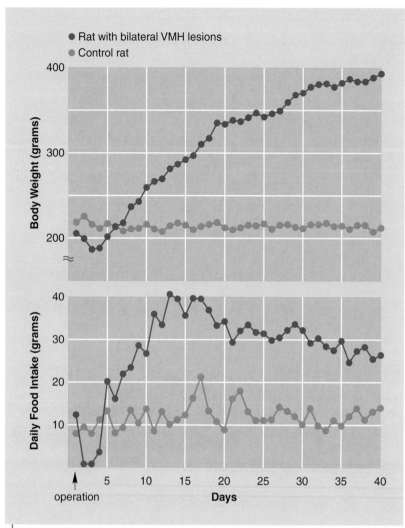

● Rat with bilateral VMH lesions
● Control rat

Postoperative hyperphagia and obesity in a rat with bilateral VMH lesions.

(Adapted from Teitelbaum, 1961.)

Figure 10.11

VMH Satiety Center. In 1940, it was discovered that large bilateral electrolytic lesions to the ventromedial hypothalamus produce **hyperphagia** (excessive eating) and extreme obesity in rats (Hetherington & Ranson, 1940). This *VMH syndrome* has two different phases: dynamic and static. The **dynamic phase**, which begins as soon as the subject regains consciousness after the operation, is characterized by several weeks of grossly excessive eating and rapid weight gain. However, after that, consumption gradually declines to a level that is just sufficient to maintain a stable level of obesity; this marks the beginning of the **static phase**. Figure 10.11 illustrates the weight gain and food intake of an adult rat with bilateral VMH lesions.

LH Feeding Center. In 1951, Anand and Brobeck reported that bilateral electrolytic lesions to the *lateral hypothalamus* produce **aphagia**—a complete cessation of eating. Even rats that were first made hyperphagic by VMH lesions were rendered aphagic by the addition of LH lesions. Anand and Brobeck concluded that the lateral region of the hypothalamus is a feeding center. Teitelbaum and Epstein (1962) subsequently discovered two important features of the *LH syndrome*. First, they found that the aphagia was accompanied by **adipsia**—a complete cessation of drinking. Second, they found that LH-lesioned rats partially recover if they are kept alive by tube feeding. First, they begin to eat wet, palatable foods, such as chocolate chip cookies soaked in milk, and eventually they will eat dry food pellets if water is concurrently available.

Reinterpretation of the Effects of VMH and LH Lesions. The theory of VMH satiety and LH feeding centers became very popular, and it was served up to wave after wave of students as if the evidence for it were unassailable. However, little about it is true.

The theory that the VMH is a satiety center has crumbled in the face of two lines of evidence. One of these lines has shown that the primary role of the hypothalamus is the regulation of energy metabolism, not the regulation of eating. The initial interpretation was that VMH-lesioned animals become obese because they overeat; however, the evidence suggests the converse—that they overeat because they become obese. Bilateral VMH lesions increase blood insulin levels, which increases **lipogenesis** (the production of body fat) and decreases **lipolysis** (the breakdown of body fat to utilizable forms of energy)—see Powley et al. (1980). Both are likely to be the result of the increases in insulin levels that occur following the lesion. Because the calories ingested by VMH-lesioned rats are converted to fat at a high rate, the rats must keep eating to ensure that they have enough calories in their blood to meet their immediate energy requirements (e.g., Hustvedt & Løvø, 1972); they are like misers who run to the bank each time they make a bit of money and deposit it in a savings account from which withdrawals cannot be made.

The second line of evidence that has undermined the theory of a VMH satiety center has shown that many of the effects of VMH lesions are not attributable to VMH damage. A large fiber bundle, the *ventral noradrenergic bundle*, courses past the VMH and is thus inevitably damaged by large electrolytic VMH lesions; in particular, fibers that project from the nearby **paraventricular nuclei** of the hypothalamus are damaged (see Figure 10.12). Bilateral lesions of the noradrenergic bundle (e.g., Gold et al., 1977) or the paraventricular nuclei (Leibowitz, Hammer, & Chang, 1981) produce hyperphagia and obesity similar to those produced by VMH lesions.

Most of the evidence against the notion that the LH is a feeding center has come from a thorough analysis of the effects of bilateral LH lesions. Early research focused exclusively on the aphagia and adipsia that are produced by LH lesions, but subsequent research has shown that LH lesions produce a wide range of severe motor disturbances and a general lack of responsiveness to sensory input (of which food and drink are but two examples). Consequently, the idea that the LH is a center specifically dedicated to feeding no longer warrants serious consideration.

Role of the Gastrointestinal Tract in Satiety

One of the most influential early studies of hunger was published by Cannon and Washburn in 1912. It was a perfect collaboration: Cannon had the ideas, and Washburn had the ability to swallow a balloon. First, Washburn swallowed an empty balloon tied to the end of a thin tube. Then, Cannon pumped some air into the balloon and connected the end of the tube to a water-filled glass U-tube so that Washburn's stomach contractions produced a momentary increase in the level of the water at the other end of the U-tube. Washburn reported a "pang" of hunger each time that a large stomach contraction was recorded (see Figure 10.13 on page 316).

Cannon and Washburn's finding led to the theory that hunger is the feeling of contractions caused by an empty stomach, whereas satiety is the feeling of stomach distention. However, support for this theory and interest in the role of the gastrointestinal tract in hunger and satiety quickly waned with the discovery that human patients whose stomachs had been surgically removed and whose esophaguses had been hooked up directly to their **duodenums** continued to report feelings of hunger and satiety and continued to maintain their normal body weights by eating more meals of smaller size.

In the 1980s, there was a resurgence of interest in the role of the gastrointestinal tract in eating. It was stimulated by a series of experiments that indicated that the gastrointestinal tract is the source of satiety signals. For example, Koopmans (1981) transplanted an extra stomach and length of intestine into rats and then joined the major arteries and veins of the implants to the recipients' circulatory systems (see

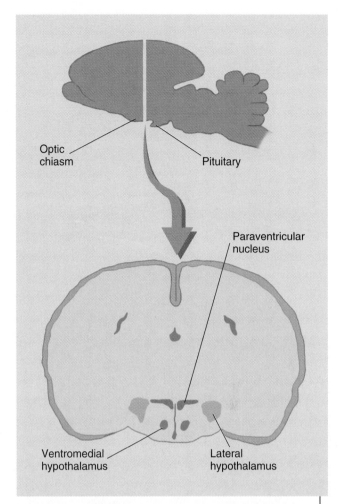

Location of the paraventricular nucleus in the rat hypothalamus. Note that the section through the hypothalamus is slightly different than the one in Figure 10.10.

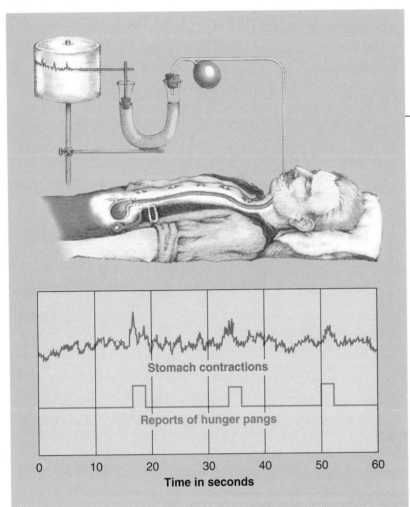

The system developed by Cannon and Washburn in 1912 for measuring stomach contractions. They found that large stomach contractions were related to pangs of hunger.

Figure 10.13

Stomach contractions

Reports of hunger pangs

Time in seconds

Figure 10.14). Koopmans found that food injected into the transplanted stomach and kept there by a noose around the *pyloric sphincter* decreased eating in proportion to both its caloric content and volume. Because the transplanted stomach had no functional nerves, the gastrointestinal satiety signal had to be reaching the brain through the blood. And because nutrients are not absorbed from the stomach, the bloodborne satiety signal could not have been a nutrient. It had to be some chemical or chemicals that were released from the stomach in response to the caloric value and volume of the food—which leads us nicely into the next subsection.

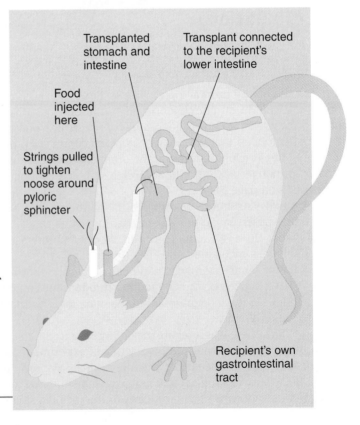

Transplanted stomach and intestine

Transplant connected to the recipient's lower intestine

Food injected here

Strings pulled to tighten noose around pyloric sphincter

Recipient's own gastrointestinal tract

Transplantation of an extra stomach and length of intestine in a rat. Koopmans (1981) implanted an extra stomach and length of intestine in each of his experimental subjects. He then connected the major blood vessels of the implanted stomachs to the circulatory systems of the recipients. Food injected into the extra stomach and kept there by a noose around the pyloric sphincter decreased eating in proportion to its volume and caloric value.

Figure 10.14

Hunger and Satiety Peptides

Soon after the discovery that the stomach and other parts of the gastrointestinal tract release chemicals, evidence began to accumulate that these were *peptides*, short chains of amino acids that function as hormones and neurotransmitters. Ingested food interacts with receptors in the gastrointestinal tract and in so doing causes the tract to release peptides into the bloodstream. In 1973, Gibbs, Young, and Smith injected one of these gut peptides, **cholecystokinin (CCK)**, into hungry rats and found that they ate smaller meals. This led to the hypothesis that circulating gut peptides provide the brain with information about the quantity and nature of food in the gastrointestinal tract and that this information plays a role in satiety.

The Evolutionary Perspective

There has been considerable support for the hypothesis that peptides can function as satiety signals (see Ritter, 2004). Several gut peptides have been shown to bind to receptors in the brain, and a dozen or so have been reported to reduce food intake (see Beck, 2001; Halford & Blundell, 2000a; Strubbe & van Dijk, 2002).

In studying the appetite-reducing effects of peptides, researchers had to rule out the possibility that these effects are not merely the consequence of illness (see Moran, 2004). Indeed, there is evidence that CCK induces illness: CCK administered to rats after they have eaten an unfamiliar substance induces a *conditioned taste aversion* for that substance, and CCK induces nausea in human subjects. However, CCK reduces appetite and eating at doses substantially below those that are required to induce taste aversion in rats, and thus it qualifies as a legitimate *satiety peptide* (a peptide that decreases appetite).

Several *hunger peptides* (peptides that increase appetite) have also been discovered (e.g., Inui, 2001; Rodgers et al., 2001; Williams et al., 2004). These peptides tend to be synthesized in the brain, particularly in the hypothalamus. The most widely studied of these is neuropeptide Y.

The discovery of the hunger and satiety peptides has had two major effects on the search for the neural mechanisms of hunger and satiety. First, the sheer number of these hunger and satiety peptides indicates that the neural system that controls eating likely reacts to many different signals (see Berthoud, 2002; Schwartz & Azzara, 2004), not just to one or two (e.g., not just to glucose and fat). Second, the discovery that many of the hunger and satiety peptides have receptors in the hypothalamus has renewed interest in the role of the hypothalamus in the control of eating (Mercer & Speakman, 2001). The strongest support for this role comes from demonstrations that microinjections of particular gut peptides into certain sites in the hypothalamus have major effects on eating. Still, there is a general acceptance that hypothalamic circuits are only one part of a much larger system.

Serotonin and Satiety

The monoaminergic neurotransmitter serotonin plays a role in satiety. The initial evidence for this role came from a line of research on rats that was initiated in the 1970s. In these studies, serotonin agonists consistently reduced rats' food intake.

The Evolutionary Perspective

In rats, the satiety-inducing effects of serotonin have three major characteristics (see Blundell & Halford, 1998). First, they are powerful: They can even overcome the powerful attraction of highly palatable cafeteria diets. Second, they reduce the amount of food that is consumed during each meal rather than reducing the number of meals (see Clifton, 2000). And third, they are associated with a shift in food preferences away from fatty foods.

In humans, serotonin agonists (e.g., fenfluramine, dexfenfluramine, fluoxetine) have been shown to reduce hunger, eating, and body weight under a variety of conditions (see Blundell & Halford, 1998). Later in this chapter, you will learn about the use of serotonin in the treatment of obesity (see De Vry & Schreiber, 2000).

10.5
Body Weight Regulation: Set Points versus Settling Points

Most people in our culture believe that body weight is regulated by a body-fat set point (Assanand, Pinel, & Lehman, 1998a, 1998b). They believe that when fat deposits are below a person's set point, a person becomes hungrier and eats more, which results in a return of body-fat levels to that person's set point; and, conversely, they believe that when fat deposits are above a person's set point, a person becomes less hungry and eats less, which results in a return of body fat levels to their set point.

Set-Point Assumptions about Body Weight and Eating

You have already learned that set-point theories do a poor job of predicting the major properties of hunger and eating. Do they do a better job of accounting for the facts of body-weight regulation? Let's begin by looking at three lines of evidence that challenge fundamental aspects of many set-point theories of body weight regulation.

Variability of Body Weight. The set-point model was expressly designed to explain why adult body weights remain constant. Indeed, a set-point mechanism should make it virtually impossible for an adult to gain or lose large amounts of weight. Yet, many adults experience large and lasting changes in body weight. Moreover, set-point thinking crumbles in the face of the epidemic of obesity that is currently sweeping fast-food societies.

Set-point theories of body weight regulation suggest that the best method of maintaining a constant body weight is to eat each time there is a motivation to eat—because the main function of these hunger motivations is to defend the set point. However, as I am sure many of you know from personal experience, many people avoid obesity only by resisting their urges to eat.

Set Points and Health. One implication of set-point theories of body weight regulation is that each person's set point is optimal for that person's health—or at least not incompatible with good health. This is why media psychologists commonly advise people to "listen to the wisdom of their bodies" and eat as much as they need to satisfy their hunger. Experimental results indicate that this common prescription for good health could not be further from the truth.

Two kinds of evidence suggest that *ad libitum* (free-feeding) levels of consumption are unhealthy (see Brownell & Rodin, 1994). First are the results of studies of humans who consume fewer calories than others. For example, people living on the Japanese island of Okinawa seemed to eat so few calories that it was of concern to health officials. When they took a closer look, here is what they found (see Kagawa, 1978). Adult Okinawans were found to consume, on average, 20% fewer calories than other adult Japanese, and Okinawan schoolchildren were found to consume 38% fewer calories than recommended by public health officials. It was somewhat surprising then that rates of morbidity and mortality and of all aging-related diseases were found to be substantially lower in Okinawa than in other parts of Japan, a country in which overall levels of caloric intake and obesity are far below Western norms. For example, the death rates from stroke, cancer, and heart disease in Okinawa were only 59%, 69%, and 59%, respectively, of those in the rest of Japan. Indeed, the proportion of Okinawans living to be over 100 years of age was up to 40 times greater than that of inhabitants of various other regions of Japan.

The Okinawan study and the other studies that have reported major health benefits in humans who eat less (e.g., Manson et al., 1995; Walford & Walford, 1994) are not controlled experiments; therefore they must be interpreted with caution. For example, perhaps it is not the consumption of fewer calories per se that leads to the health and longevity; perhaps people who eat less tend to eat healthier diets. Fortunately, calorie-restriction experiments conducted in over a dozen different species, including monkeys, do not have these problems of interpretation.

The effects of calorie restriction are the second kind of evidence that *ad libitum* levels of consumption are unhealthy. In *calorie-restriction experiments*, one group of subjects is allowed to eat as much as they choose, while other groups of subjects have their caloric intake of the same diets substantially reduced (by between 25% and 65% in various studies). Results of such experiments have been remarkably consistent (see Bucci, 1992; Masoro, 1988; Weindruch, 1996; Weindruch & Walford, 1988): In experiment after experiment, substantial reductions in the caloric intake of balanced diets have improved numerous indices of health and increased longevity. For example, in one experiment (Weindruch et al., 1986), groups of mice had their caloric intake of a well-balanced commercial diet reduced by either 25%, 55%, or 65% after weaning. All levels of dietary restriction substantially improved health and increased longevity, but the benefits were greatest in the mice whose intake was reduced the most. Those mice that consumed the least had the lowest incidence of cancer, the best immune responses, and the greatest maximum life span—they lived 67% longer than did mice that ate as much as they liked.

Please stop and think about the implications of these amazing calorie-restriction experiments. How much do you eat?

Regulation of Body Weight by Changes in Efficiency of Energy Utilization.

Implicit in many set-point theories is the premise that body weight is largely a function of how much a person eats. Of course, how much someone eats plays a role in his or her body weight, but it is now clear that the body controls its fat levels, to a large degree, by changing the efficiency with which it uses energy. As a person's level of body fat declines, that person starts to use energy resources more efficiently, which limits further weight loss (see Martin, White, & Hulsey, 1991); conversely, weight gain is limited by a progressive decrease in the efficiency of energy utilization. Rothwell and Stock (1982) created a group of obese rats by maintaining them on a cafeteria diet, and they found that the resting level of energy expenditure in these obese rats was 45% greater than in control rats.

This point is illustrated by the progressively declining effectiveness of weight-loss programs. Initially, low-calorie diets produce substantial weight loss. But the rate of weight loss diminishes with each successive week on the diet, until an equilibrium is achieved and little or no further weight loss occurs. Most dieters are familiar with this disappointing trend. A similar effect occurs with weight-gain programs (see Figure 10.15).

The mechanism by which the body adjusts the efficiency of its energy utilization in response to its levels of body fat has been

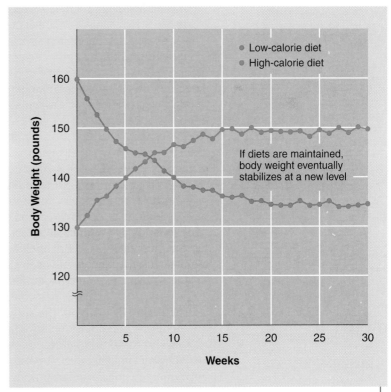

The diminishing effects on body weight of a low-calorie diet and a high-calorie diet.

Figure 10.15

termed **diet-induced thermogenesis**. Increases in the levels of body fat produce increases in body temperature, which require additional energy to maintain them—and decreases in the level of body fat have the opposite effects.

There are major differences among subjects both in their **basal metabolic rate** (the rate at which they utilize energy to maintain bodily processes when resting) and in their ability to adjust their metabolic rate in response to changes in the levels of body fat. We all know people who remain slim even though they eat gluttonously. However, the research on calorie-restricted diets suggests that these people may not eat with impunity: There may be a health cost to pay for overeating even in the absence of obesity.

Set Points and Settling Points in Weight Control

The theory that eating is part of a system designed to defend a body-fat set point has long had its critics (see Booth, Fuller, & Lewis, 1981; Wirtshafter & Davis, 1977); but for many years their arguments were largely ignored and the set-point assumption ruled. This situation is changing: Several recent prominent reviews of research on hunger and weight regulation generally acknowledge that a strict set-point model cannot account for the facts of weight regulation, and they argue for a more flexible model (see Berthoud, 2002; Mercer & Speakman, 2001; Woods et al., 2000). Because body-fat set points still dominate the thinking of many people—presumably including you—I want to review the main advantages of one such flexible regulatory model: the settling-point model.

According to the settling-point model, body weight tends to drift around a natural **settling point**—the level at which the various factors that influence body weight achieve an equilibrium. The idea is that as body-fat levels increase, changes occur that tend to limit further increases until a balance is achieved between all factors that encourage weight gain and all those that discourage it.

The settling-point model provides a loose kind of homeostatic regulation, without a set-point mechanism or mechanisms to return body weight to a set point. According to the settling-point model, body weight remains stable as long as there are no long-term changes in the factors that influence it; and if there are such changes, their impact is limited by negative feedback. In the settling-point model, the feedback merely limits further changes in the same direction, whereas in the set-point model, negative feedback triggers a return to the set point. A neuron's resting potential is a well-known biological settling point—see Chapter 3.

The seductiveness of the set-point mechanism is attributable in no small part to the existence of the thermostat model, which provides a vivid means of thinking about it. Figure 10.16 presents an analogy I like to use to think about the settling-point mechanism. I call it the **leaky-barrel model**: (1) The amount of water entering the hose is analogous to the amount of food available to the subject; (2) the water pressure at the nozzle is analogous to the positive-incentive value of the available food; (3) the amount of water entering the barrel is analogous to the amount of energy consumed; (4) the water level in the barrel is analogous to the level of body fat; (5) the amount of water leaking from the barrel is analogous to the amount of energy being expended; and (6) the weight of the barrel on the hose is analogous to the strength of the satiety signal.

Thinking Clearly

ON THE CD

Visit the *Leaky Barrel* animation. See the leaky-barrel model of settling-point regulation in action.

The main advantage of the settling-point model of body weight regulation over the body-fat set-point model is that it is more consistent with the data. Another advantage is that in those cases in which both models make the same prediction, the settling-point model does so more parsimoniously—that is, with a simpler mechanism that requires fewer assumptions. Let's use the leaky-barrel analogy to see how the two models account for four key facts of weight regulation.

Fact 1: Body weight remains relatively constant in many adult animals. On the basis of this fact, it has been argued that body fat must be regulated around a set point. However, constant body weight does not require, or even imply, a set point. Consider the leaky-barrel model. As water from the tap begins to fill the barrel, the weight of the water in the barrel increases. This increases

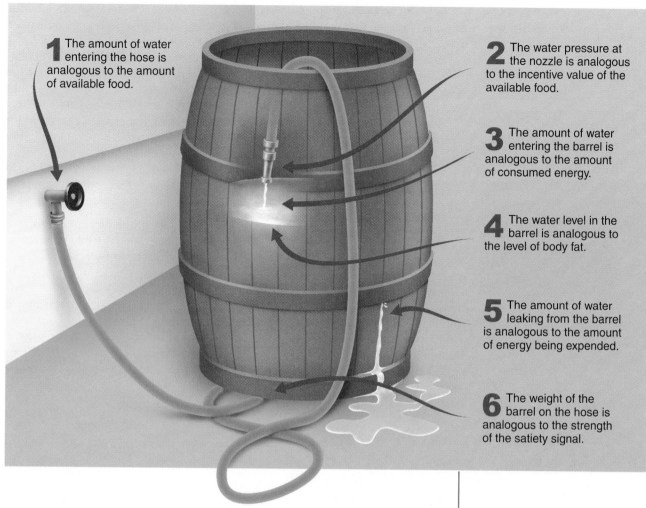

1 The amount of water entering the hose is analogous to the amount of available food.

2 The water pressure at the nozzle is analogous to the incentive value of the available food.

3 The amount of water entering the barrel is analogous to the amount of consumed energy.

4 The water level in the barrel is analogous to the level of body fat.

5 The amount of water leaking from the barrel is analogous to the amount of energy being expended.

6 The weight of the barrel on the hose is analogous to the strength of the satiety signal.

The leaky-barrel model: a settling-point model of eating and body weight homeostasis.

Figure 10.16

the amount of water leaking out of the barrel and decreases the amount of water entering the barrel by increasing the pressure of the barrel on the hose. Eventually, this system settles into an equilibrium where the water level stays constant; but because this level is neither predetermined nor actively defended, it is a settling point, not a set point.

Fact 2: Many adult animals experience enduring changes in body weight. Set-point systems are designed to maintain internal constancy in the face of fluctuations of the external environment. Thus, the fact that many adult animals experience long-term changes in body weight is a strong argument against the set-point model. In contrast, the settling-point model predicts that when there is an enduring change in one of the parameters that affect body weight—for example, a major increase in the positive-incentive value of available food—body weight will drift to a new settling point.

Fact 3: If a subject's intake of food is reduced, metabolic changes that limit the loss of weight occur; the opposite happens when the subject overeats. This fact is often cited as evidence for set-point regulation of body weight; however, because the metabolic changes merely limit further weight changes rather than eliminating those that have occurred, they are more consistent with a settling-point model. For example, when water intake in the leaky-barrel model is reduced, the water level in the barrel begins to drop; but the drop is limited by a decrease in leakage and an increase in inflow attributable to the falling water pressure in the barrel. Eventually, a new settling point is achieved, but the reduction in water level is not as great as one might expect because of the loss-limiting changes.

Fact 4: After an individual has lost a substantial amount of weight (by dieting, exercise, or the surgical removal of fat), there is a tendency for the original weight to be regained once the subject returns to the previous eating- and energy-related lifestyle. Although this finding is often offered as irrefutable evidence of a body-weight set point, the settling-point model readily accounts for it. When the water level in the leaky-barrel model is reduced—by temporarily decreasing input (dieting), by temporarily increasing output (exercising), or by scooping out some of the water (surgical removal of fat)—only a temporary drop in the settling point is produced. When the original conditions are reinstated, the water level inexorably drifts back to the original settling point.

Thinking Clearly

Does it really matter whether we think about body weight regulation in terms of set points or settling points—or is it just splitting hairs? It certainly matters to biopsychologists: Understanding that body weight is regulated by a settling-point system helps them better understand, and more accurately predict, the changes in body weight that are likely to occur in various situations; it also indicates the kinds of physiological mechanisms that are likely to mediate these changes. And it should matter to you. If the set-point model is correct, attempting to change your body weight would be a waste of time; you would inevitably be drawn back to your body-weight set point. On the other hand, the leaky-barrel model suggests that it is possible to permanently change your body weight by permanently changing any of the factors that influence energy intake and output.

Scan your Brain

Are you ready to move on to the final two sections of the chapter, which deal with eating disorders? This is a good place to pause and scan your brain to see if you understand the biopsychological principles of eating and weight regulation. Complete the following sentences by filling in the blanks. The correct answers are provided below. Before proceeding, review material related to your incorrect answers and omissions.

1. The primary function of the _____ is to serve as a storage reservoir for undigested food.

2. Most of the absorption of nutrients into the body takes place through the wall of the _____, or upper intestine.

3. The phase of energy metabolism that is triggered by the expectation of food is the _____ phase.

4. During the absorptive phase, the pancreas releases a great deal of _____ into the bloodstream.

5. During the fasting phase, the primary fuels of the body are _____.

6. During the fasting phase, the primary fuel of the brain is _____.

7. The three components of a set-point system are a set-point mechanism, a detector, and an _____.

8. The theory that hunger and satiety are regulated by a blood glucose set point is the _____ theory.

9. Evidence suggests that hunger is a function of the current _____ value of food.

10. The _____ hypothalamus was once believed to be the satiety center.

11. Evidence suggests that the monoaminergic neurotransmitter _____ plays a role in satiety.

12. Research evidence supports a _____ model of body weight regulation rather than a set-point model.

Scan Your Brain answers: (1) stomach, (2) duodenum, (3) cephalic, (4) insulin, (5) free fatty acids, (6) glucose, (7) effector, (8) glucostatic, (9) positive-incentive, (10) ventromedial, (11) serotonin, (12) settling-point

You have already learned that obesity is currently a major health problem in many parts of the world (see Figure 10.17). What is more distressing is the rate at which the problem is growing; in the United States, for example, its incidence more than doubled during the 20th century (see Kuczmarski, 1992) and continues to rise. This rapid rate of increase indicates that environmental factors play a significant role in obesity.

Genetic factors also contribute to obesity. For example, it was estimated from a sample of U.S. twins that environmental and genetic factors contribute equally to individual differences in body fat in this population (see Price & Gottesman, 1991). However, the current surge in obesity is occurring too rapidly to be a product of genetic changes. Also, set-point theories are of no help in trying to understand the epidemic of obesity; according to that view, permanent weight gain should not occur in healthy adults.

Obesity has become a serious health problem in many parts of the world

Figure 10.17

Why Is There an Epidemic of Obesity?

Let's begin our analysis of obesity by considering the pressures that are likely to have led to the evolution of our eating and weight-regulation systems (see Pinel et al., 2000). During the course of evolution, inconsistent food supplies were one of the main threats to survival. As a result, the fittest individuals were those who preferred high-calorie foods, ate to capacity when food was available, stored as many excess calories as possible in the form of body fat, and used their stores of calories as efficiently as possible. Individuals who did not have these characteristics were unlikely to survive a food shortage, and so these characteristics were passed on to future generations.

The Evolutionary Perspective

Augmenting the effects of evolution has been the development of numerous cultural practices and beliefs that promote consumption. For example, in my culture, it is commonly believed that one should eat three meals per day at regular times, whether one is hungry or not; that food should be the focus of most social gatherings; that meals should be served in courses of progressively increasing palatability; and that salt, sweets (e.g., sugar), and fats (e.g., butter) should be added to foods to improve their flavor, thereby increasing their consumption.

Each of us possesses an eating and weight-regulation system that evolved to deal effectively with periodic food shortages, and many of us live in cultures whose eating-related practices evolved for the same purpose. However, our current food-related environment differs from our "natural" environment in critical ways. We live in an environment in which an endless variety of foods of the highest positive-incentive value are readily and continuously available. The consequence is an appallingly high level of consumption.

Why Do Some People Become Obese While Others Do Not?

Why do some people become obese while others living under the same obesity-promoting conditions do not? At a superficial level, the answer is obvious: Those who are obese are those whose energy intake has grossly exceeded their energy output; those who are slim are those whose energy intake has not grossly exceeded their energy output. Although this answer provides little insight, it does serve to emphasize that two kinds of individual differences play a role in obesity: those that lead to differences in energy input and those that lead to differences in energy output. Let's consider examples of each kind.

There are many factors that lead some people to eat more than others who have comparable access to food. For example, some people consume more energy because they have strong preferences for the taste of high-calorie foods (see Blundell & Finlayson, 2004); some consume more because they were raised in families and/or cultures that promote excessive eating; and some consume more because they have particularly strong cephalic-phase responses to the sight or smell of food (Rodin, 1985).

With respect to energy output, people differ markedly from one another in the degree to which they can dissipate excess consumed energy. The most obvious difference is that people differ substantially in the amount of exercise they get; however, there are others. You have already learned about two of them: differences in *basal metabolic rate* and in the ability to react to fat increases by *diet-induced thermogenesis*. The third factor is called *NEAT*, or *nonexercise activity thermogenesis*, which is generated by activities such as fidgeting and the maintenance of posture and muscle tone (Ravussin & Danforth, 1999). Although the effects of NEAT on body weight have not been investigated systematically, evidence suggests that it plays a significant role in dissipating excess energy (Levine, Eberhardt, & Jensen, 1999).

Why Are Weight-Loss Programs Typically Ineffective?

Figure 10.18 describes the course of the typical dietary weight-loss program. Most weight-loss programs are unsuccessful in the sense that, as predicted by the settling-

Figure 10.18

The five stages of a typical weight-loss program.

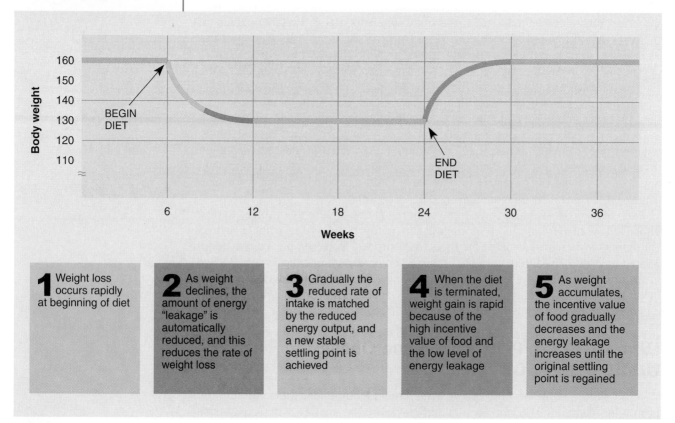

1 Weight loss occurs rapidly at beginning of diet

2 As weight declines, the amount of energy "leakage" is automatically reduced, and this reduces the rate of weight loss

3 Gradually the reduced rate of intake is matched by the reduced energy output, and a new stable settling point is achieved

4 When the diet is terminated, weight gain is rapid because of the high incentive value of food and the low level of energy leakage

5 As weight accumulates, the incentive value of food gradually decreases and the energy leakage increases until the original settling point is regained

point model, most of the lost weight is regained once the program is terminated and the original conditions are reestablished. Clearly, the key to permanent weight loss is a permanent lifestyle change.

People who have difficulty controlling their weight may receive some solace by understanding that the tendency to eat large amounts of food, to accumulate body fat, and to use energy efficiently would all be highly adaptive tendencies in a natural environment. It is our current environment that is "pathological," not the people with weight problems.

Exercise has many health-promoting effects; however, despite the general belief that exercise is the most effective method of losing weight, several studies have shown that it often contributes little to weight loss (e.g., Sweeney et al., 1993). One reason is that physical exercise normally accounts for only a small proportion of total energy expenditure: About 80 % of the energy you expend is used to maintain the resting physiological processes of your body (Calles-Escandon & Horton, 1992). Another reason is that after exercise, many people consume extra drinks and foods that contain more calories than the relatively small number that were expended during the exercise.

Severe cases of obesity are sometimes treated by wiring the jaw shut to limit consumption to liquid diets, stapling part of the stomach together to reduce the size of meals, or cutting out a section of the duodenum to reduce the absorption of nutrients from the gastrointestinal tract. Unfortunately, some patients with wired jaws do not lose weight on a liquid diet, and those who do typically regain it once the wires are removed. Problems with both the two aforementioned methods of gastric surgery include diarrhea, flatulence, and vitamin and mineral deficiencies. Death occurs in approximately 1 case out of 300. Despite these problems, approximately 150,000 gastric operations for the treatment of obesity are performed each year in the United States alone.

An ob/ob mouse and a control mouse.

Figure 10.19

Mutant Obese Mice and Leptin

In 1950, a genetic mutation occurred spontaneously in the mouse colony being maintained in the Jackson Laboratory at Bar Harbor, Maine. It was thought that this fortuitous development might prove to be the key to understanding and treating extreme forms of human obesity. You see, the mice that were *homozygous* for this mutant gene (ob) were grossly obese, weighing up to three times as much as typical mice (see Figure 10.19). These homozygous obese mice are commonly referred to as **ob/ob mice**.

The Evolutionary Perspective

Ob/ob mice eat more and convert calories to fat more efficiently than controls, and they use their fat calories more efficiently. Coleman (1979) hypothesized that ob/ob mice lack a critical hormone that normally inhibits fat production.

In 1994, Friedman and his colleagues characterized and cloned the gene that is mutated in ob/ob mice (Zhang et al., 1994). They found that this gene is *expressed* only in fat cells, and they characterized the protein hormone that it encodes. They named this protein **leptin**.

Research has shown that leptin satisfies three criteria for a negative feedback fat signal (Ahima & Osei, 2004; Seeley & Schwartz, 1997): (1) Levels of leptin in the blood have been found to be positively correlated with fat deposits in humans and other animals (Schwartz et al., 1996a); (2) injections of leptin at doses too low to be aversive have been shown to reduce eating and body fat in ob/ob mice (Campfield et al., 1995); and (3) receptors for leptin have been found in the brain (Schwartz et al., 1996b).

Do obese humans, like ob/ob mice, have a mutation to the ob gene, and do they have low levels of the satiety signal, leptin? The answer to both these questions is "not usually." Genetic mutations are rare in obese humans, and most have high levels of circulating leptin. Moreover, injections of leptin have not reliably reduced the body fat of obese individuals (Heymsfield et al., 1999). Although few obese humans have a genetic mutation to the ob gene, leptin can be a panacea for those few who do. Consider the following case.

The Case of the Child with No Leptin

The patient was of normal weight at birth, but soon it began to increase at an excessive rate. She demanded food continually and was disruptive when denied food. As a result of her extreme obesity, deformities of her legs developed, and surgery was required.

She was 9 when she was referred for treatment. At this point, she weighed 94.4 kilograms (about 210 pounds), and her weight was still increasing at an alarming rate. She was found to be homozygous for the ob gene and had no detectable leptin. Thus, leptin therapy was commenced.

The leptin therapy immediately curtailed the weight gain. She began to eat less, and she lost weight steadily over the 12-month period of the study, a total of 16.5 kilograms (about 36 pounds), almost all in the form of fat. There were no obvious side effects (Farooqi et al., 1999).

Serotonergic Drugs and the Treatment of Obesity

Because—as you have already learned—serotonin agonists have been shown to reduce food consumption in both human and nonhuman subjects, they have considerable potential in the treatment of obesity (Halford & Blundell, 2000a). Serotonin agonists seem to act by a mechanism different from that for leptin and insulin, which produce long-term satiety signals based on fat stores. Serotonin agonists seem to increase short-term satiety signals associated with the consumption of a meal (Halford & Blundell, 2000b).

Serotonin agonists have been found in various studies of obese patients to reduce the following: the urge to eat high-calorie foods, the consumption of fat, the subjective intensity of hunger, the size of meals, the number of between-meal snacks, and bingeing. Because of this extremely positive profile of effects and the severity of the obesity problem, two serotonin agonists (fenfluramine and dexfenfluramine) were rushed into clinical use. However, they were subsequently withdrawn from the market because chronic use was found to be associated with heart disease in a small, but significant, number of users. Currently, the search is on for serotonergic weight-loss medications that do not have dangerous side effects. There is reason for optimism. The variety of different serotonin receptor subtypes means that it may be possible to develop serotonin agonists that selectively promote weight loss.

10.7
Anorexia Nervosa

In contrast to obesity, **anorexia nervosa** is a disorder of underconsumption of food (see Klein & Walsh, 2004). Anorexics eat so little that they experience health-threatening weight loss; and despite their grotesquely emaciated appearance, they often perceive themselves as fat (see Figure 10.20). Common health problems of those with anorexia include cardiovascular problems, kidney damage, liver damage, damage to the digestive tract, bone loss, infertility, and malnutrition; death can result in some cases.

About 50% of anorexics periodically engage in binges of eating, which are usually followed by purging with large doses of laxatives or by self-induced vomiting. Individuals who display the cycles of fasting, bingeing, and purging without the extreme weight loss are said to suffer from **bulimia nervosa**.

The incidence of anorexia nervosa among North American student populations is about 2.5%, with the vast majority of sufferers being female. Unfortunately, there are currently no proven effective treatments. Few sufferers display complete recovery, and those who respond to treatment often relapse.

Anorexics are ambivalent about food. On the one hand, they display a higher than normal cephalic-phase insulin response (Broberg & Bernstein, 1989), and they are often preoccupied with the discussion, purchase, and preparation of food. However, eating food is a different matter; they are often disgusted by sweet and fatty tastes, and they often feel ill after a meal.

Anorexia and Dieting

Although some degree of dietary restraint appears to be essential for the maintenance of optimal health by most people in wealthy, fast-food cultures, the practice of restrained eating is associated with risks. Virtually all patients with eating disorders—at least those in the United States—have a history of strict dieting prior to the onset of the disorder. For example, in one study (Patton, 1988), 21% of teenage girls who were dieting at the time of their initial interview had developed an eating disorder 1 year later, compared with only 3% of nondieters.

Evidence suggests that people—primarily adolescent females—begin dieting in response to great pressure from a cultural emphasis on slenderness, and those who are highly controlled, rigid, and obsessive overcome the attraction of food and develop the disorder (see Wilson, Heffernan, & Black, 1996). However, the new ideas about hunger and eating that you have encountered in this chapter point to another factor that might contribute to some cases of anorexia nervosa. Consider the following hypothesis.

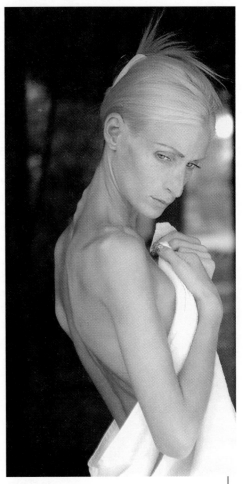

Anorexia nervosa

Figure 10.20

Anorexia and Positive Incentives

The positive-incentive perspective on eating suggests that the decline in eating that defines anorexia nervosa is likely a consequence of a corresponding decline in the positive-incentive value of food. However, the positive-incentive value of food for anorexic patients has received little attention—in part, because anorexic patients often display substantial interest in food. The fact that many anorexic patients are obsessed with food—continually talking about it, thinking about it, and preparing it for others (Crisp, 1983)—seems to suggest that it still holds a high positive-incentive value for them. However, to avoid confusion, it is necessary to keep in mind that the positive-incentive value of interacting with food is not necessarily the same as the positive-incentive value of eating food—and it is the positive-incentive value of eating food that is critical when considering anorexia nervosa.

A few studies have examined the positive-incentive value of various tastes in anorexic patients (see, e.g., Drewnowski et al., 1987; Sunday & Halmi, 1990). In general, these studies have found that the positive-incentive value of various tastes is lower in anorexic patients than in control participants. However, these studies grossly underestimate the importance of reductions in the positive-incentive value of food in the etiology of anorexia nervosa because the anorexic participants and the normal-weight control participants were not matched for weight. Let me explain.

People who have had starvation imposed on them—although difficult to find—are the suitable equal-weight comparison subjects for anorexic participants. Starvation normally triggers a radical increase in the positive-incentive value of food. This has been best documented by the descriptions and behavior of participants voluntarily undergoing experimental semistarvation. When asked how it felt to starve, one participant replied:

> I wait for mealtime. When it comes I eat slowly and make the food last as long as possible. The menu never gets monotonous even if it is the same each day or is of poor quality. It is food and all food tastes good. Even dirty crusts of bread in the street look appetizing. (Keys et al., 1950, p. 852)

The Puzzle of Anorexia

The domination of set-point theories over research into the regulation of hunger and eating has resulted in widespread inattention to one of the major puzzles of anorexia: Why does the adaptive massive increase in the positive-incentive value of eating that occurs in victims of starvation not occur in starving anorexics? The positive-incentive value of eating normally increases to such high levels under conditions of starvation that it is difficult to imagine how anybody who is starving—no matter how controlled, rigid, obsessive, and motivated—could refrain from eating in the presence of palatable food. Why is this protective mechanism not activated in severe anorexics?

I believe that part of the answer lies in the research of Woods and his colleagues on the aversive physiological effects of meals. At the beginning of meals, people are normally in reasonably homeostatic balance, and this homeostasis is disrupted by the sudden infusion of calories. The other part of the answer lies in the finding that the aversive effects of meals are much greater in people who have been eating little (Brooks & Melnik, 1995). Meals, which produce adverse, but tolerable, effects in healthy individuals, may be dangerous for individuals who have undergone food deprivation. Evidence for the extremely noxious effects that eating meals has on starving humans is found in the reactions of World War II concentration camp victims to refeeding—many were rendered ill and some were even killed by the very food given to them by their liberators (Keys et al., 1950; see also Soloman & Kirby, 1990).

So why do severe anorexics not experience a massive increase in the positive-incentive value of eating, similar to the increase experienced by other starving individuals? The answer may be *meals*—meals "forced" on these patients as a result of the misconception of our society that meals are the healthy way to eat. Each meal consumed by anorexics may produce a variety of conditioned taste aversions that reduce their motivation to eat. This hypothesis needs to be addressed because of its implication for treatment: If it is true, anorexic patients—or anybody else who is severely undernourished—should not be encouraged, or even permitted, to eat meals. They should be fed—or infused with—small amounts of food intermittently throughout the day.

I have described the preceding hypothesis to show you the value of the new ideas that you have encountered in this chapter: The major test of a new theory is whether it leads to innovative hypotheses. Recently, as I was perusing an article on global famine and malnutrition, I noticed an intriguing comment: One of the clinical complications that results from feeding meals to famine victims is anorexia (Blackburn, 2001). What do you make of this?

The Case of the Anorexic Student

In a society in which obesity is the main disorder of consumption, anorexics are out of step. People who are struggling to eat less have difficulty understanding those who have to struggle to eat. Still, when you stare anorexia in the face, it is difficult not to be touched by it.

She began by telling me how much she had been enjoying the course and how sorry she was to be dropping out of the university. She was articulate and personable, and her grades were high. Her problem was anorexia; she weighed only 82 pounds, and she was about to be hospitalized.

"But don't you want to eat?" I asked naively. "Don't you see that your plan to go to medical school will go up in smoke if you don't eat?"

"Of course I want to eat. I know I am terribly thin—my friends tell me I am. Believe me, I know this is wrecking my life. I try to eat, but I just can't force myself. In a strange way, I am pleased with my thinness."

She was upset, and I was embarrassed by my insensitivity. "It's too bad you're dropping out of the course before we cover the chapter on eating," I said, groping for safer ground.

"Oh, I've read it already," she responded. "It's the first chapter I looked at. It had quite an effect on me; a lot of things started to make more sense. The bit about positive incentives and learning was really good. I think my problem began when eating started to lose its positive-incentive value for me—in my mind, I kind of associated eating with being fat and all the boyfriend problems I was having. This made it easy to diet, but every once in a while I would get hungry and binge, or my parents would force me to eat a big meal. I would eat so much that I would feel ill. So I would put my finger down my throat and make myself throw up. This kept me from gaining weight, but I think it also taught my body to associate my favorite foods with illness—kind of a conditioned taste aversion. What do you think of my theory?"

Her insightfulness impressed me; it made me feel all the more sorry that she was going to discontinue her studies. How could such a bright, personable young woman knowingly risk her health and everything that she had worked for?

After a lengthy chat, she got up to leave, and I walked her to the door of my office. I wished her luck and made her promise to come back for a visit. I never saw her again. The image of her emaciated body walking down the hallway from my office has stayed with me.

Key Terms

Set point (p. 301)

10.1 Digestion and Energy Flow

Absorptive phase (p. 303)
Amino acids (p. 303)
Cephalic phase (p. 303)
Digestion (p. 302)
Fasting phase (p. 303)
Free fatty acid (p. 304)
Glucagon (p. 304)
Gluconeogenesis (p. 304)
Glucose (p. 303)
Insulin (p. 303)
Ketones (p. 304)
Lipids (p. 303)

10.2 Theories of Hunger and Eating: Set Points versus Positive Incentives

Glucostatic theory (p. 306)
Homeostasis (p. 305)
Lipostatic theory (p. 306)
Negative feedback
    mechanisms (p. 305)
Positive-incentive theory (p. 307)
Positive-incentive value (p. 307)
Set-point assumption (p. 305)

10.3 Factors That Determine What, When, and How Much We Eat

Appetizer effect (p. 311)
Cafeteria diet (p. 312)
Nutritive density (p. 310)
Satiety (p. 310)
Sensory-specific satiety (p. 312)
Sham eating (p. 311)

10.4 Physiological Research on Hunger and Satiety

Adipsia (p. 314)
Aphagia (p. 314)
Cholecystokinin (CCK) (p. 317)
Duodenum (p. 315)
Dynamic phase (p. 314)
Hyperphagia (p. 314)
Lateral hypothalamus (LH) (p. 313)
Lipogenesis (p. 314)
Lipolysis (p. 314)
Paraventricular nuclei (p. 315)
Static phase (p. 314)
Ventromedial hypothalamus
    (VMH) (p. 313)

10.5 Body Weight Regulation: Set Points versus Settling Points

Basal metabolic rate (p. 320)
Diet-induced thermogenesis (p. 320)
Leaky-barrel model (p. 320)
Settling point (p. 320)

10.6 Human Obesity

Leptin (p. 325)
Ob/ob mice (p. 325)

10.7 Anorexia Nervosa

Anorexia nervosa (p. 326)
Bulimia nervosa (p. 327)

ON THE CD

Studying for an exam? Get some help from the electronic flash cards of the key terms and the practice tests for this chapter.

chapter 10

Hunger, Eating, and Health
Why Do Many People Eat Too Much?

This chapter summarized recent research on hunger (i.e., the motivation to eat) and eating, and their relation to health. In particular, it focused on why many people eat too much (i.e., more than is optimal for good health).

Digestion, Energy Flow, and the Set-Point and Positive-Incentive Perspectives

There are two ways of thinking about hunger and eating: the commonly held set-point perspective and the positive-incentive perspective. Are we motivated to eat when our energy reserves fall below an energy set point, or are we motivated to eat by the anticipated pleasure of eating? (Pages 302–308)

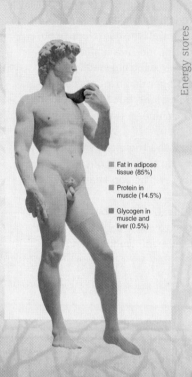

Energy stores

- Fat in adipose tissue (85%)
- Protein in muscle (14.5%)
- Glycogen in muscle and liver (0.5%)

Sham feeding

Stomach

Esophagus

Cut end of esophagus is tied off

Swallowed food falls to the ground

Factors That Determine What, When, and How Much We Eat

From research on factors that influence what, when, and how much we eat, it has become clear that although set points dominate most people's thinking about hunger and eating, many facts are inconsistent with this perspective and more supportive of the positive-incentive view. (Pages 308–312)

Physiological Research on Hunger and Satiety

The dominance of set-point thinking has led to the view that glucose deficits motivate eating; however, in food-replete societies, virtually nobody has a glucose deficit as mealtime approaches. Similarly, the once popular view that eating is regulated by hypothalamic hunger and satiety centers has been discredited. Research on how the gastrointestinal tract communicates with the brain has led to the discovery of many peptides that either increase or decrease eating. (Pages 312–317)

Stomach contractions

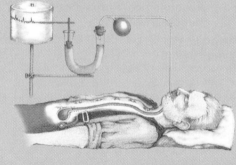

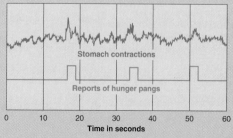

Stomach contractions

Reports of hunger pangs

0   10   20   30   40   50   60
Time in seconds

ob/ob mouse

Visual Summary

Settling-point model

1 The amount of water entering the hose is analogous to the amount of available food.

2 The water pressure at the nozzle is analogous to the incentive value of the available food.

3 The amount of water entering the barrel is analogous to the amount of consumed energy.

4 The water level in the barrel is analogous to the level of body fat.

5 The amount of water leaking from the barrel is analogous to the amount of energy being expended.

6 The weight of the barrel on the hose is analogous to the strength of the satiety signal.

Body Weight Regulation and Human Obesity

Set-point theories of body weight regulation cannot account for the current epidemic of obesity. Humans evolved in an environment in which starvation was a major threat and the availability of food was unpredictable. Therefore, we evolved to eat as much as possible whenever food was plentiful. Now, palatable foods are continuously available to most of us. The result is that many of us suffer from obesity and associated ill health.
(Pages 318–326)

Anorexia and Dieting

Many people need to restrain their eating to keep from getting obese. However, in some, this restraint turns into a serious disorder of undereating: anorexia nervosa. One of the puzzles about this eating disorder is that people who have experienced starvation report that their lives became dominated by hunger. Why does this protective mechanism not function in anorexics?
(Pages 326–329)

Themes Revisited

Three of the book's four themes played prominent roles in this chapter. The thinking clearly theme was predominant: You were repeatedly challenged to critically evaluate your own beliefs and ambiguous research findings, to consider the scientific implications of your own experiences, and to think creatively about the new ideas you encountered. The chapter ended by using these new ideas to develop a potentially important hypothesis about the etiology of anorexia nervosa, one with implications for treatment.

Both aspects of the evolutionary theme were emphasized repeatedly. First, you saw how thinking about hunger and eating from an evolutionary perspective led to important insights. Clearly, for any hunger and eating system to have survival value in natural environments, where food availability is unpredictable, it would have to function to prevent bodily energy deficits rather than to respond to them. Second, you saw how controled research on nonhuman species has contributed to our current understanding of human hunger and eating.

Finally, the clinical implications theme was featured in the chapter-opening case of the man who forgot not to eat and in the final two sections of the chapter on human obesity and anorexia nervosa.

Think about It

1. On the basis of what you have learned in this chapter, design an effective weight-loss program.
2. Most of the eating-related health problems that people in our society face occur because the conditions in which we live are different from those in which our species evolved. Discuss.
3. Develop a feeding program for laboratory rats that would lead to obesity. Compare this program with the eating habits prevalent in those cultures in which obesity is a serious problem.
4. What causes anorexia nervosa? Summarize the evidence that supports your view.
5. In a natural environment (i.e., like the one in which our species evolved), people who tend to put on weight would tend to be the most healthy. Discuss.

chapter 11

Hormones and Sex
What's Wrong with the Mamawawa?

This chapter is about hormones and sex, a topic that fascinates most people. Perhaps it is because we hold our sexuality in such high esteem that we are intrigued by the fact that it is influenced by the secretions of a pair of glands that some regard as unfit topics of conversation. Perhaps it is because we each think of our gender as fundamental and immutable that we are fascinated by the fact that it can be altered with a snip or two and a few hormone injections. Perhaps what fascinates us is the idea that our sex lives might be enhanced by the application of a few hormones. For whatever reason, the topic of hormones and sex is always a hit. Some remarkable things await you in this chapter; let's go directly to them.

The Developmental and Activational Effects of Sex Hormones

Hormones influence sex in two ways: (1) by influencing the development from conception to sexual maturity of the anatomical, physiological, and behavioral characteristics that distinguish one as female or male; and (2) by activating the reproduction-related behavior of sexually mature adults. Both the *developmental* (often referred to as *organizational*) and *activational* effects of sex hormones are discussed in this chapter.

The Men-Are-Men-and-Women-Are-Women Assumption

Almost everybody brings to the topic of hormones and sex a piece of excess baggage: the men-are-men-and-women-are-women assumption—or the "mamawawa." This assumption is seductive; it seems so right that we are continually drawn to it without considering alternative views. Unfortunately, it is fundamentally flawed.

The men-are-men-and-women-are-women assumption is the tendency to think about femaleness and maleness as discrete, mutually exclusive, complementary categories. In thinking about hormones and sex, this general attitude leads one to assume that females have female sex hormones that give them female bodies and make them do female things, and that males have male sex hormones that give them male bodies and make them do opposite male things. Despite the fact that this approach to hormones and sex is totally wrong, its simplicity, symmetry, and comfortable social implications draw us to it. That's why this chapter grapples with it throughout.

11.1

The Neuroendocrine System

This section introduces the general principles of neuroendocrine function. It introduces these principles by focusing on the glands and hormones that are directly involved in sexual development and behavior, the topic of this chapter.

The endocrine glands are illustrated in Figure 11.1 on page 334. By convention, only the organs whose primary function appears to be the release of hormones are referred to as endocrine glands. However, other organs (e.g., the stomach, liver, and intestine) also release hormones into general circulation (see Chapter 10), and they are thus, strictly speaking, also part of the endocrine system.

Glands

There are two types of glands: exocrine glands and endocrine glands. **Exocrine glands** (e.g., sweat glands) release their chemicals into ducts, which carry them to

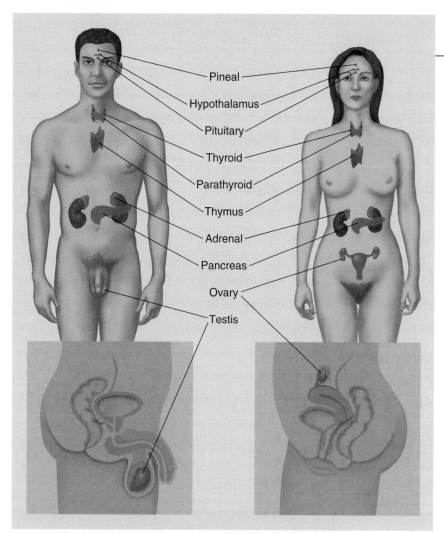

their targets, mostly on the surface of the body. **Endocrine glands** (ductless glands) release their chemicals, which are called **hormones**, directly into the circulatory system. Once released by an endocrine gland, a hormone travels via the circulatory system until it reaches the targets on which it normally exerts its effect (e.g., other endocrine glands or sites in the nervous system).

Gonads

Central to any discussion of hormones and sex are the **gonads**—the male **testes** (pronounced TEST-eez) and the female **ovaries** (see Figure 11.1). The primary function of testes is the production of *sperm cells*, and the primary function of ovaries is the production of *ova* (egg cells). After **copulation** (sexual intercourse), a single sperm cell may combine with an *ovum* to form a cell called a **zygote**, which contains all of the information necessary for the normal growth of a complete adult organism in its natural environment. The amalgamation of sperm and egg cells is called *fertilization* (see Primakoff & Myles, 2002).

With the exception of ova and sperm cells, each cell of the human body has 23 pairs of chromosomes (see Figure 11.2). In contrast, the ova and sperm cells contain only half that number, one member of each of the 23 pairs. Thus, when a sperm cell fertilizes an ovum, the resulting zygote ends up with the full complement of 23 pairs of chromosomes, one of each pair from the father and one of each pair from the mother.

Of particular interest in the context of this chapter is the pair of chromosomes called the **sex chromosomes** (see Figure 11.3), so named because they contain the genetic programs that direct sexual development. The cells of females have two large sex

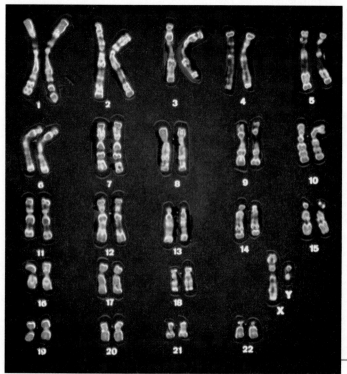

The 23 pairs of human chromosomes.

chromosomes, called *X chromosomes*. In males, one sex chromosome is an X chromosome, and the other is a smaller X-shaped chromosome called a *Y chromosome*. Consequently, the sex chromosome of every ovum is an X chromosome, whereas half the sperm cells have X chromosomes and half have Y chromosomes. Your gender with all its social, economic, and personal ramifications was determined by which of your father's sperm cells managed to fertilize your mother's ovum. If a sperm cell with an X sex chromosome was successful, you are a female; if one with a Y sex chromosome was successful, you are a male.

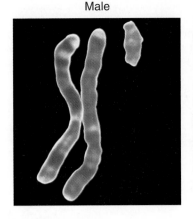

Male   Female

The male (XY) and female (XX) sex chromosomes.

Figure 11.3

Writing this section reminded me of my grade 7 basketball team, the "Nads." The name puzzled our teacher because it was not at all like the names usually favored by pubescent boys—names such as the "Avengers," the "Marauders," and the "Vikings." Her puzzlement ended abruptly at our first game as our fans began to chant their support. You guessed it; "Go Nads, Go! Go Nads, Go!" My 14-year-old spotted-faced teammates and I considered this to be humor of the most mature and sophisticated sort. The teacher didn't.

Sex Steroids

The gonads do more than create sperm and egg cells; they also produce and release hormones. Most people are surprised to learn that the testes and ovaries release the very same hormones. The two main classes of gonadal hormones are **androgens** and **estrogens**—**testosterone** is the most common androgen, and **estradiol** is the most common estrogen. The fact that adult ovaries tend to release more estrogens than they do androgens and that adult testes tend to release more androgens than they do estrogens has led to the common, but misleading, practice of referring to androgens as "the *male* sex hormones" and to estrogens as "the *female* sex hormones." This practice should be avoided because of its men-are-men-and-women-are-women implication that androgens produce maleness and estrogens produce femaleness. They don't.

The ovaries and testes also release a third class of hormones called **progestins**. The most common progestin is **progesterone**, which in females prepares the uterus and the breasts for pregnancy. Its function in males is unclear.

Because the primary function of the **adrenal cortex**—the outer layer of the *adrenal glands* (see Figure 11.1)—is the regulation of glucose and salt levels in the blood, it is not generally thought of as a sex gland. However, it does release small amounts of all of the sex hormones that are released by the gonads.

Gonadal hormones that play a direct role in sexual development and behavior are **steroid hormones**, hormones that are synthesized from *cholesterol*, a type of fat molecule. Steroid molecules can influence cells by binding to receptors in cell membranes; however, because these molecules are small and fat-soluble, they can readily penetrate cell membranes and often affect cells in a second way. Once inside a cell, steroid molecules can bind to receptors in the cell's cytoplasm or nucleus and, by so doing, can directly influence gene expression. Consequently, steroid hormones tend to have diverse and long-lasting effects on cellular function (Brown, 1994).

Steroid hormones are the only class of hormones synthesized from cholesterol; all of the other hormones in the body are synthesized from amino acids. **Amino acid derivative hormones** are hormones that are synthesized in a few simple steps from a single amino acid molecule; an example is *epinephrine*, which is synthesized from the amino acid *tyrosine* and released from the *adrenal medulla*. **Peptide hormones** and **protein hormones** are chains of amino acids—peptide hormones are short chains, and protein hormones are long chains.

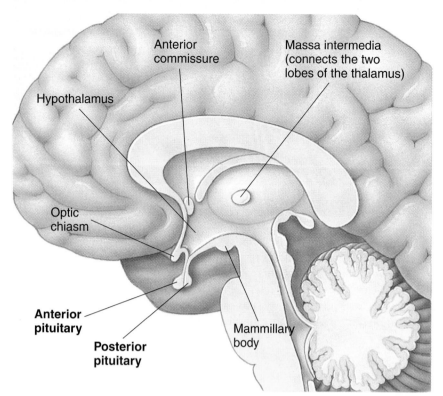

A midline view of the posterior and anterior pituitary and surrounding structures.

Figure 11.4

Labels on figure:
- Anterior commissure
- Massa intermedia (connects the two lobes of the thalamus)
- Hypothalamus
- Optic chiasm
- Anterior pituitary
- Posterior pituitary
- Mammillary body

Hormones of the Pituitary

In contrast to the gonads, the pituitary gland releases peptide and protein hormones. The pituitary is frequently referred to as the *master gland* because most of its hormones are tropic hormones. *Tropic hormones* are hormones whose primary function is to influence the release of hormones from other glands (*tropic* is an adjective used to describe things that stimulate or change other things). For example, **gonadotropin** is a pituitary tropic hormone that travels through the circulatory system to the gonads, where it stimulates the release of gonadal hormones.

The pituitary gland is really two glands, the posterior pituitary and the anterior pituitary, which fuse during the course of embryological development. The **posterior pituitary** develops from a small outgrowth of hypothalamic tissue that eventually comes to dangle from the *hypothalamus* on the end of the **pituitary stalk** (see Figure 11.4). In contrast, the **anterior pituitary** begins as part of the same embryonic tissue that eventually develops into the roof of the mouth; during the course of development, it pinches off and migrates upward to assume its position next to the posterior pituitary. It is the anterior pituitary that releases tropic hormones; thus, it is the anterior pituitary in particular, rather than the pituitary in general, that qualifies as the master gland.

Female Gonadal Hormone Levels Are Cyclic; Male Gonadal Hormone Levels Are Steady

The major difference between the endocrine function of women and men is that in women the levels of gonadal and gonadotropic hormones go through a cycle that repeats itself every 28 days or so (see Appendix VIII). It is these more-or-less regular hormone fluctuations that control the female **menstrual cycle**. In contrast, human males are, from a neuroendocrine perspective, rather dull creatures; the levels of their gonadal and gonadotropic hormones change little from day to day.

Because the anterior pituitary is the master gland, many early scientists assumed that an inherent difference between the male and female anterior pituitary was the basis for the difference in their patterns of gonadotropic and gonadal hormone release. However, this hypothesis was discounted by a series of clever transplant studies conducted by Geoffrey Harris in the 1950s (see Raisman, 1997). In these studies, a cycling pituitary removed from a mature female rat became a steady-state pituitary when transplanted at the appropriate site in a male, and a steady-state pituitary removed from a mature male rat began to cycle once transplanted in a female. What these studies established was that anterior pituitaries are not inherently female (cyclical) or male (steady-state); their patterns of hormone release are controlled by some other part of the body. The master gland seemed to have its own master. Where was it?

Neural Control of the Pituitary

The search for the structure that controlled the anterior pituitary turned, naturally enough, to the *hypothalamus*, the structure from which the pituitary is suspended. Hypothalamic stimulation and lesion experiments quickly established that the hypothalamus is the regulator of the anterior pituitary, but how the hypothalamus carries out this role was not so obvious. You see, the anterior pituitary, unlike the posterior pituitary, receives no neural input whatsoever from the hypothalamus, or from any other neural structure (see Figure 11.5). How, then, does the hypothalamus control the anterior pituitary?

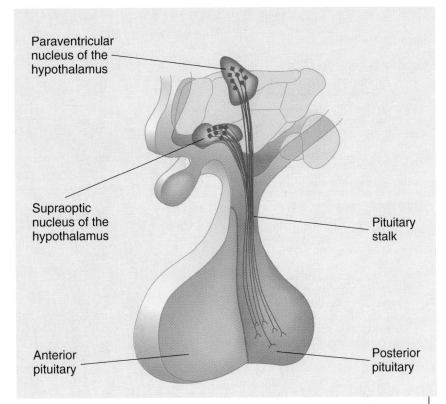

The neural connections between the hypothalamus and the pituitary. All neural input to the pituitary goes to the posterior pituitary; the anterior pituitary has no neural connections.

Control of the Anterior and Posterior Pituitary by the Hypothalamus

There are two different mechanisms by which the hypothalamus controls the pituitary: one for the posterior pituitary and one for the anterior pituitary. The control of the posterior pituitary is reasonably straightforward. The two major hormones of the posterior pituitary, **vasopressin** and **oxytocin**, are hormones that are synthesized in the cell bodies of neurons in the **paraventricular nuclei** and **supraoptic nuclei** of the hypothalamus (see Figure 11.5). They are then transported along the axons of these neurons to their terminals in the posterior pituitary and are stored there until the arrival of action potentials causes them to be released into the bloodstream. Oxytocin stimulates contractions of the uterus during labor and the ejection of milk during suckling. Vasopressin facilitates the reabsorption of water by the kidneys.

The means by which the hypothalamus controls the release of hormones from the neuron-free anterior pituitary was more difficult to explain. Two early findings indicated that the release of hormones from the anterior pituitary was itself regulated by hormones released from the hypothalamus (Harris, 1955). The first was the discovery of a vascular network, the **hypothalamopituitary portal system**, that is well suited to the task of carrying hormones from the hypothalamus to the anterior pituitary. As Figure 11.6 on page 338 illustrates, a network of hypothalamic capillaries feeds a bundle of portal veins that carries blood down the pituitary stalk into another network of capillaries in the anterior pituitary. (A *portal vein* is a vein that connects one capillary network with another.) The second finding was the discovery that cutting the portal veins of the pituitary stalk disrupts the release of anterior pituitary hormones until the damaged veins regenerate.

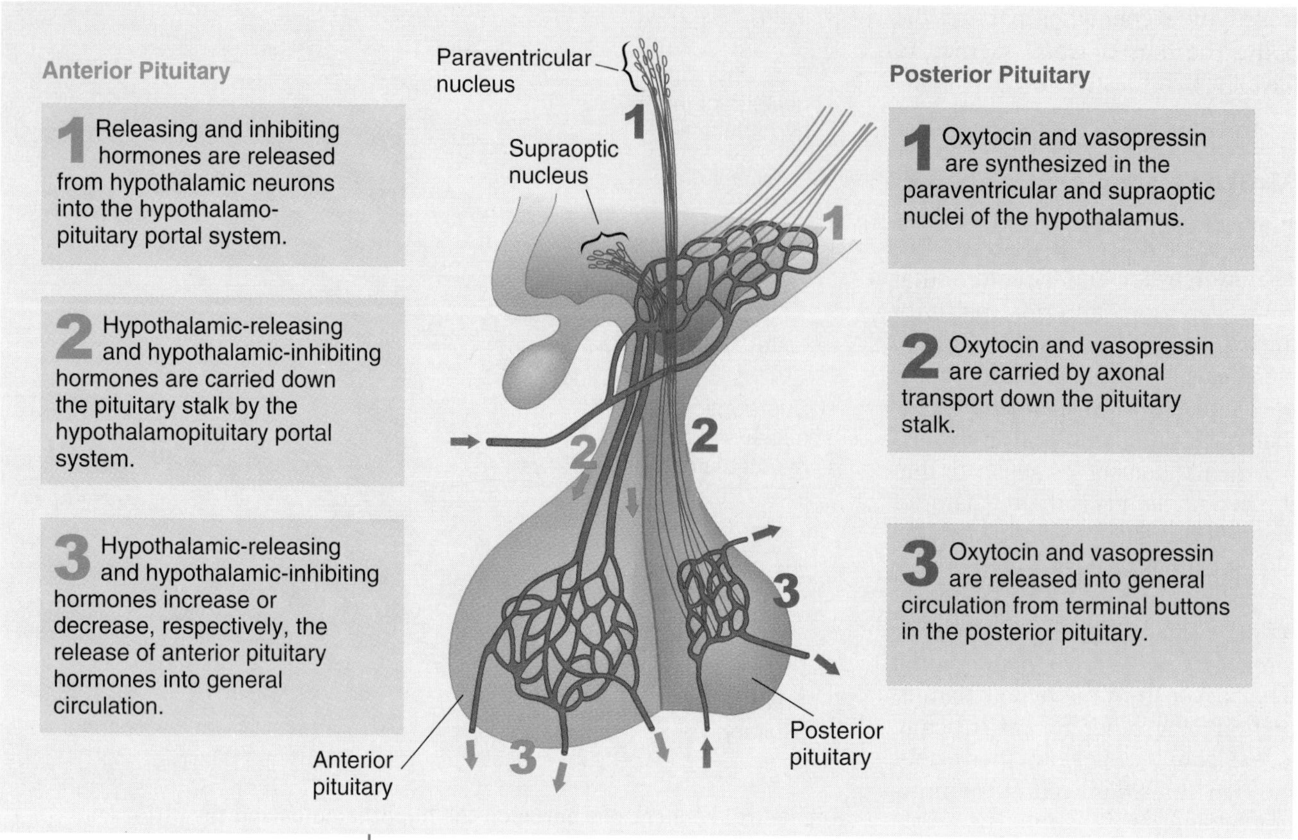

Anterior Pituitary

1 Releasing and inhibiting hormones are released from hypothalamic neurons into the hypothalamo-pituitary portal system.

2 Hypothalamic-releasing and hypothalamic-inhibiting hormones are carried down the pituitary stalk by the hypothalamopituitary portal system.

3 Hypothalamic-releasing and hypothalamic-inhibiting hormones increase or decrease, respectively, the release of anterior pituitary hormones into general circulation.

Posterior Pituitary

1 Oxytocin and vasopressin are synthesized in the paraventricular and supraoptic nuclei of the hypothalamus.

2 Oxytocin and vasopressin are carried by axonal transport down the pituitary stalk.

3 Oxytocin and vasopressin are released into general circulation from terminal buttons in the posterior pituitary.

Paraventricular nucleus

Supraoptic nucleus

Anterior pituitary

Posterior pituitary

Control of the anterior and posterior pituitary by the hypothalamus.

Figure 11.6

Discovery of Hypothalamic Releasing Hormones

The Evolutionary Perspective

We know now that the release of each anterior pituitary hormone is controlled by a different hypothalamic hormone. The hypothalamic hormones that were thought to stimulate the release of an anterior pituitary hormone were referred to as **releasing hormones**.

The first releasing hormone was isolated in the late 1960s. Guillemin and his colleagues isolated **thyrotropin-releasing hormone** from the hypothalami of sheep, and Schally and his colleagues isolated the same hormone from the hypothalami of pigs. Thyrotropin-releasing hormone triggers the release of **thyrotropin** from the anterior pituitary, which in turn stimulates the release of hormones from the *thyroid gland*.

It is difficult to appreciate the effort that went into the initial isolation of thyrotropin-releasing hormone. Releasing hormones exist in such small amounts that a mountain of hypothalamic tissue was required to extract even minute quantities. Schally reported that the work of his group required over 1 million pig hypothalami. And where did Schally get such a quantity of pig hypothalami? From Oscar Mayer & Company—where else?

Why would two research teams dedicate over a decade of their lives to accumulate a pitifully small quantity of thyrotropin-releasing hormone? The reason was that the small sample enabled both Guillemin and Schally to determine the chemical composition of thyrotropin-releasing hormone and then to develop methods of synthesizing larger quantities of the hormone for research and clinical use. For their efforts, Guillemin and Schally were awarded Nobel Prizes in 1977.

Schally's and Guillemin's isolation of thyrotropin-releasing hormone confirmed that hypothalamic releasing hormones control the release of hormones from the anterior pituitary and thus provided the major impetus for the isolation and synthesis of several other releasing hormones. Of direct relevance to the study of sex hormones was the subsequent isolation of **gonadotropin-releasing hormone** by Schally and his group (Schally, Kastin, & Arimura, 1971). This releasing hormone stimulates the release of both of the anterior pituitary's gonadotropins: **follicle-stimulating hormone (FSH)** and **luteinizing hormone (LH)**. All hypothalamic releasing hormones, like all tropic hormones, have proven to be peptides.

Pulsatile Hormone Release

Hormones tend to be released in pulses (Karsch, 1987); they are discharged several times per day in large surges, which typically last no more than a few minutes. Hormone levels in the blood are regulated by changes in the frequency and duration of the hormone pulses (Reame et al., 1984). One consequence of **pulsatile hormone release** is that there are often large minute-to-minute fluctuations in the levels of circulating hormones (e.g., Koolhaas, Schuurman, & Wierpkema, 1980). Accordingly, when the pattern of human male gonadal hormone release is referred to as "steady," it means that there are no major systematic changes in circulating gonadal hormone levels from day to day, not that the levels never vary.

Summary Model of Gonadal Endocrine Regulation

Figure 11.7 is a summary model of the regulation of gonadal hormones. According to this model, the brain controls the release of gonadotropin-releasing hormone from the hypothalamus into the hypothalamopituitary portal system, which carries it to the anterior pituitary. In the anterior pituitary, the gonadotropin-releasing hormone stimulates the release of

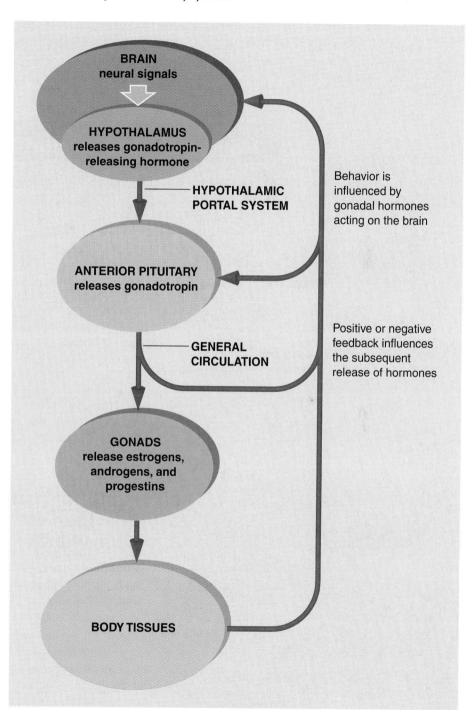

A summary model of the regulation of gonadal hormones.

Figure 11.7

gonadotropin, which is carried by the circulatory system to the gonads. In response to the gonadotropin, the gonads release androgens, estrogens, and progestins, which feed back into the pituitary and hypothalamus to regulate subsequent gonadal hormone release. This feedback is usually negative; that is, high levels of a hormone reduce its release, and low levels increase its release.

The effects of experience on hormone release are usually mediated by signals from the nervous system. It is extremely important to remember that hormone release is regulated by experience. This means that hormonal explanations do not in any way rule out experiential explanations; in fact, they may be different aspects of the same mechanism.

Armed with this general perspective of neuroendocrine function, you are ready to consider how gonadal hormones direct sexual development and activate adult sexual behavior.

11.2
Hormones and Sexual Development

You have undoubtedly noticed that humans are *dimorphic*—that is, they come in two standard models: female and male. This section describes how the development of female and male characteristics is directed by hormones.

Sexual differentiation in mammals begins at fertilization with the production of one of two different kinds of zygotes: either one with an XX (female) pair of sex chromosomes or one with an XY (male) pair. It is the genetic information on the sex chromosomes that normally determines whether development will occur along female or male lines. But be cautious here: Do not fall into the seductive embrace of the men-are-men-and-women-are-women assumption. Do not begin by assuming that there are two parallel but opposite genetic programs for sexual development, one for female development and one for male development. As you are about to learn, sexual development seems to unfold according to an entirely different principle. This principle is that we are all genetically programmed to develop female bodies; genetic males develop male bodies only because their fundamentally female program of development is overruled.

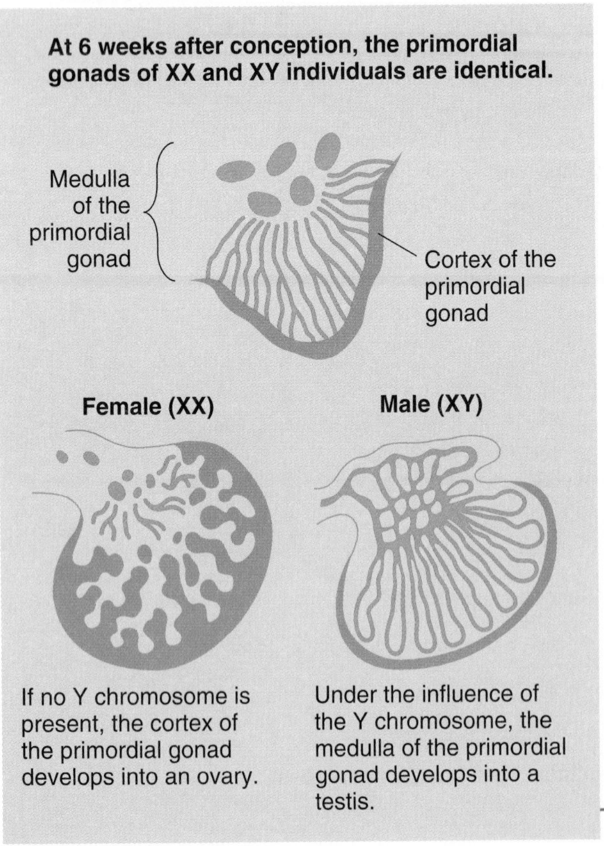

Fetal Hormones and Development of Reproductive Organs

Gonads. Figure 11.8 illustrates the structure of the gonads as they appear 6 weeks after fertilization. Notice that at this stage of development, each fetus, regardless

At 6 weeks after conception, the primordial gonads of XX and XY individuals are identical.

Medulla of the primordial gonad

Cortex of the primordial gonad

Female (XX)

Male (XY)

If no Y chromosome is present, the cortex of the primordial gonad develops into an ovary.

Under the influence of the Y chromosome, the medulla of the primordial gonad develops into a testis.

The development of an ovary and a testis from the cortex and the medulla, respectively, of the primordial gonadal structure that is present 6 weeks after conception.

Figure 11.8

of its genetic sex, has the same pair of gonadal structures, called *primordial gonads* (*primordial* means "existing at the beginning"). Each primordial gonad has an outer covering, or *cortex*, which has the potential to develop into an ovary; and each has an internal core, or *medulla*, which has the potential to develop into a testis (singular of *testes*).

Six weeks after conception, the Y chromosome of the male triggers the synthesis of **H-Y antigen** (see Haqq et al., 1994; Wang et al., 1995), and this protein causes the medulla of each primordial gonad to grow and to develop into a testis. There is no female counterpart of H-Y antigen; in the absence of H-Y antigen, the cortical cells of the primordial gonads automatically develop into ovaries. Accordingly, if H-Y antigen is injected into a genetic female fetus 6 weeks after conception, the result is a genetic female with testes; or if drugs that block the effects of H-Y antigen are injected into a male fetus, the result is a genetic male with ovaries. Such "mixed-gender" individuals expose in a dramatic fashion the weakness of the "mamawawa."

Internal Reproductive Ducts. Six weeks after fertilization, both males and females have two complete sets of reproductive ducts. They have a male **Wolffian system**, which has the capacity to develop into the male reproductive ducts (e.g., the *seminal vesicles*, which hold the fluid in which sperm cells are ejaculated; and the *vas deferens*, through which the sperm cells travel to the seminal vesicles). And they have a female **Müllerian system**, which has the capacity to develop into the female ducts (e.g., the *uterus*; the upper part of the *vagina*; and the *fallopian tubes*, through which ova travel from the ovaries to the uterus, where they can be fertilized).

In the third month of male fetal development, the testes secrete testosterone and **Müllerian-inhibiting substance**. As Figure 11.9 illustrates, the testosterone stimulates the development of the Wolffian system, and the Müllerian-inhibiting substance causes the Müllerian system to degenerate and the testes to descend into the **scrotum**—the sac that holds the testes outside the body cavity. (You may recall from Chapter 1 that the creation of sperm cells progresses most efficiently at temperatures cooler than body temperature, which is why the scrotum evolved.) Because it is testosterone—not the sex chromosomes—that triggers Wolffian development, genetic females who are injected with testosterone during the appropriate fetal period develop male reproductive ducts along with their female ones.

The differentiation of the internal ducts of the female reproductive system (see Figure 11.9) is not under the control of ovarian hormones; the ovaries are almost completely inactive during fetal development. The development of the Müllerian system occurs in any fetus that is not exposed to testicular hormones during the critical fetal period. Accordingly, normal female fetuses, ovariectomized female fetuses, and orchidectomized male fetuses all develop female reproductive ducts (Jost, 1972). **Ovariectomy** is the removal of the ovaries, and **orchidectomy** is the removal of the testes (*orchis* means "testicle"). **Gonadectomy**, or *castration*, is the surgical removal of gonads—either ovaries or testes.

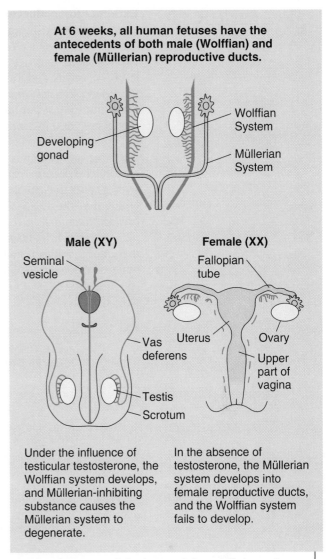

At 6 weeks, all human fetuses have the antecedents of both male (Wolffian) and female (Müllerian) reproductive ducts.

Developing gonad

Wolffian System

Müllerian System

Male (XY)

Seminal vesicle

Vas deferens

Testis

Scrotum

Female (XX)

Fallopian tube

Uterus

Ovary

Upper part of vagina

Under the influence of testicular testosterone, the Wolffian system develops, and Müllerian-inhibiting substance causes the Müllerian system to degenerate.

In the absence of testosterone, the Müllerian system develops into female reproductive ducts, and the Wolffian system fails to develop.

The development of the internal ducts of the male and female reproductive systems from the Wolffian and Müllerian systems, respectively.

Figure 11.9

External Reproductive Organs.   There is a basic difference between the differentiation of the external reproductive organs and the differentiation of the internal reproductive organs (i.e., the gonads and reproductive ducts). As you have just read, every normal fetus develops separate precursors for the male (medulla) and female (cortex) gonads and for the male (Wolffian system) and female (Müllerian system) reproductive ducts; then, only one set, male or female, develops. In contrast, both male and female **genitals**—external reproductive organs—develop from the same precursor. This *bipotential precursor* and its subsequent differentiation are illustrated in Figure 11.10.

In the second month of pregnancy, the bipotential precursor of the external reproductive organs consists of four parts: the glans, the urethral folds, the lateral bodies, and the labioscrotal swellings. Then it begins to differentiate. The *glans* grows into the head of the *penis* in the male or the *clitoris* in the female, the *urethral folds* fuse in the male or enlarge to become the *labia minora* in the female, the *lateral bodies* form the shaft of the penis in the male or the hood of the clitoris in the female, and the *labioscrotal swellings* form the *scrotum* in the male or the *labia majora* in the female.

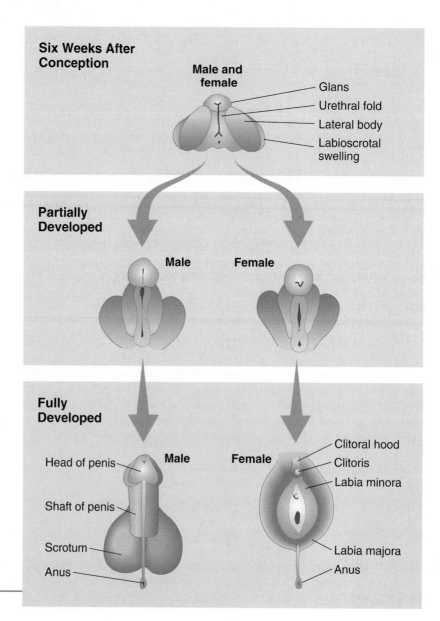

The development of male and female external reproductive organs from the same bipotential precursor.

Figure 11.10

Like the development of the internal reproductive ducts, the development of the external genitals is controlled by the presence or absence of testosterone. If testosterone is present at the appropriate stage of fetal development, male external genitals develop from the bipotential precursor; if testosterone is not present, the development of the external genitals proceeds along female lines.

Sex Differences in the Brain

The brains of men and women may look the same on casual inspection, and it may be politically correct to believe that they are. But they are not. The brains of men tend to be about 15% larger than those of women, and numerous other anatomical differences exist. There are major sex differences in the volumes of various nuclei and fiber tracts, in the numbers and types of neural and glial cells that compose various structures, and in the numbers and types of synapses that connect the cells in various structures. *Sexual dimorphisms* (male–female structural differences) of the brain are typically studied in nonhuman mammals, but many have also been documented in humans (see Simerly, 2002; Stone, 1996; Woodson & Gorski, 2000).

Research on sexual dimorphisms of mammalian brains is in transition. Initially, neuroscientists focused on identifying and describing examples, but now they are trying to understand the causes and functions of these differences. Before I discuss this important area of current research, I need to tell you how the first brain sexual dimorphism was identified and studied. It set the stage for everything that followed.

Discovery of the First Sex Differences in the Mammalian Brain. The first attempts to discover sex differences in the mammalian brain focused on the factors that control the development of the steady and cyclic patterns of gonadotropin release in males and females, respectively. The seminal experiments were conducted by Pfeiffer in 1936. In his experiments, some neonatal rats (males and females) were gonadectomized and some were not, and some received gonad transplants (ovaries or testes) and some did not.

Remarkably, Pfeiffer found that gonadectomizing neonatal rats of either genetic sex caused them to develop into adults with the female cyclic pattern of gonadotropin release. In contrast, transplantation of testes into gonadectomized or intact female neonatal rats caused them to develop into adults with the steady male pattern of gonadotropin release. Transplantation of ovaries had no effect on the pattern of hormone release. Pfeiffer concluded that the female cyclic pattern of gonadotropin release develops unless the preprogrammed female cyclicity is overridden by testosterone during *perinatal* (around the time of birth) development (see Harris & Levine, 1965).

The Evolutionary Perspective

Pfeiffer incorrectly concluded that the presence or absence of testicular hormones in neonatal rats influenced the development of the pituitary because he was not aware of something we know today: that the release of gonadotropins from the anterior pituitary is controlled by the hypothalamus. Once this was discovered, it became apparent that Pfeiffer's experiments had provided the first evidence of the role of perinatal androgens in the sexual differentiation of the hypothalamus.

Aromatization and Sex Differences in the Brain. Soon a complication to the simple androgen theory of hypothalamic differentiation was discovered. You see, all gonadal and adrenal sex hormones are steroid hormones that have similar structures and are readily converted from one to the other. For example, a slight change converts testosterone to estradiol; this process is called **aromatization** (see Balthazart & Ball, 1998). There is good evidence that aromatization is a critical step in the masculinization of the brain by testosterone in some species.

According to this aromatization hypothesis, perinatal testosterone does not directly masculinize the brain; the brain is masculinized by estradiol that has been aromatized from perinatal testosterone. Although the idea that estradiol—the alleged female hormone—masculinizes the brain is counterintuitive, there is strong evidence for it in several mammalian species (e.g., rats).

In humans, aromatization does not appear to be necessary for testosterone to have masculinizing effects on the brain; nevertheless, estradiol is capable of masculinizing effects similar to those of testosterone. How then are female fetuses protected from the masculinizing effects of the mother's estrogens? They are protected by the *placenta* (the membrane through which the developing fetus receives nourishment and oxygen and eliminates waste products). Unfortunately, this barrier is not as effective against some synthetic estrogens (e.g., *diethylstilbestrol*). As a result, the female offspring of mothers who have been exposed to synthetic estrogens while pregnant may display a variety of male characteristics (see McEwen, 1983).

One cellular mechanism of the development of brain dimorphisms is well understood. Volumetric differences between particular structures in male and female brains develop by preferential apoptotic cell loss, not by preferential cell growth. Typically, males and females begin with the same number of neurons in a particular brain structure, and then programs of apoptotic cell death become more active in that structure in one sex (see McCarthy et al., 2002).

Sex Differences in the Brain: What Do They Mean?   It is important to keep in perspective the sex differences in the brain. There are two important points to keep in mind. First, the documentation of so many structural differences between the brains of men and women—and between the brains of males and females of other mammalian species—suggests that many of the behavioral differences between men and women are not entirely attributable to cultural differences. Second, although neuroscientists have been successful in documenting numerous sex differences in brain anatomy, they have not managed to discover the functional significance of even one of these differences. For example, consider the overall size difference—remember that the brains of men tend to be about 15% larger than the brains of women. We have no idea why men tend have larger brains: It does not necessarily mean that they have more neurons; it could mean that men's brains contain more water, fat, or glial cells. Another problem is that larger animals need larger brains to control their larger bodies. When the difference in brain size between women and men is corrected to allow for the average difference in body size, it disappears. Finally, although it is clear that men have larger brains, it is just as clear that they do not have any general cognitive superiority.

Perinatal Hormones and Behavioral Development

In view of the fact that perinatal hormones influence the development of the brain, it should come as no surprise that they also influence the development of behavior. Much of the research on hormones and behavioral development has focused on the role of perinatal hormones in the development of sexually dimorphic copulatory behaviors in laboratory animals.

Phoenix and colleagues (1959) were among the first to demonstrate that the perinatal injection of testosterone **masculinizes** and **defeminizes** a genetic female's adult copulatory behavior. First, they injected pregnant guinea pigs with testosterone. Then, when the litters were born, they ovariectomized the female offspring. Finally, when these ovariectomized female guinea pigs reached maturity, the researcher injected them with testosterone and assessed their copulatory behavior. Phoenix and his colleagues found that the females that had been exposed to perinatal testosterone displayed more malelike mounting behavior in response to testosterone injections in adulthood than did adult females that had not been exposed to perinatal testosterone. And when as adults they were injected with progesterone and estradiol and mounted by males, they displayed less **lordosis**—the arched-back posture that signals female rodent receptivity and facilitates insertion of the penis.

In a study complementary to that of Phoenix and colleagues, Grady, Phoenix, and Young (1965) found that the lack of early exposure of male rats to testosterone both **feminizes** and **demasculinizes** their copulatory behavior as adults. Male rats castrated shortly after birth failed to display the normal male copulatory pattern of mounting, **intromission** (penis insertion), and **ejaculation** (ejection of sperm) when they were treated with testosterone and given access to a sexually receptive female; and when they were injected with estrogen and progesterone as adults, they exhibited more lordosis than did uncastrated controls. The aromatization of perinatal testosterone to estradiol seems to be important for both the defeminization and the masculinization of rodent copulatory behavior (Goy & McEwen, 1980; Shapiro, Levine, & Adler, 1980).

Because much of the research on hormones and behavioral development has focused on the copulatory act itself, we know less about the role of hormones in the development of **proceptive behaviors** (solicitation behaviors) and in the development of gender-related behaviors that are not directly related to reproduction. However, perinatal testosterone has been reported to disrupt the proceptive hopping, darting, and ear wiggling of receptive female rats; to increase the aggressiveness of female mice; to disrupt the maternal behavior of female rats; and to increase rough social play in female monkeys and rats.

In thinking about hormones and behavioral development, it is important to remember two things. First, feminizing and demasculinizing effects do not always go together; nor do defeminizing and masculinizing effects. Hormone treatments can enhance or disrupt female behavior without affecting male behavior, and vice versa (Bloch, Mills, & Gale, 1995). Second, timing is important. The ability of single injections of testosterone to masculinize and defeminize the rat brain seems to be restricted to the first 11 days after birth. However, large multiple doses of testosterone can have masculinizing effects outside this *sensitive period* (Bloch & Mills, 1995).

Thinking Clearly

Puberty: Hormones and Development of Secondary Sex Characteristics

During childhood, levels of circulating gonadal hormones are low, reproductive organs are immature, and males and females differ little in general appearance. This period of developmental quiescence ends abruptly with the onset of *puberty*—the transitional period between childhood and adulthood during which fertility is achieved, the adolescent growth spurt occurs, and the secondary sex characteristics develop. **Secondary sex characteristics** are those features other than the reproductive organs that distinguish sexually mature men and women. The body changes that occur during puberty are illustrated in Figure 11.11 on page 346.

Puberty is associated with an increase in the release of hormones by the anterior pituitary (see Grumbach, 2002). The increase in the release of **growth hormone**— the only anterior pituitary hormone that does not have a gland as its primary target—acts directly on bone and muscle tissue to produce the pubertal growth spurt. Increases in gonadotropic hormone and **adrenocorticotropic hormone** release cause the gonads and adrenal cortex to increase their release of gonadal and adrenal hormones, which in turn initiate the maturation of the genitals and the development of secondary sex characteristics.

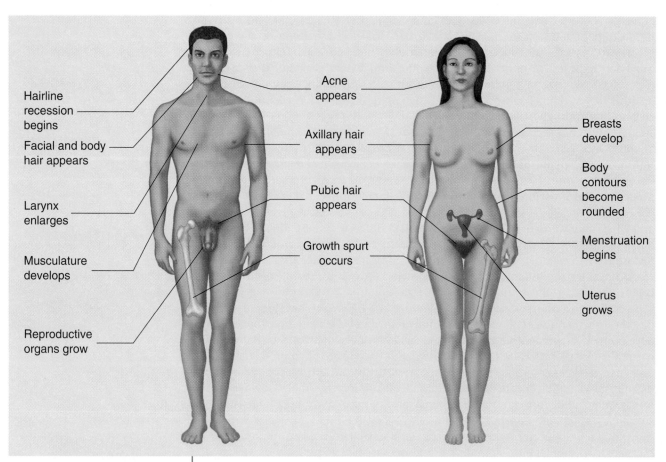

Hairline recession begins	Acne appears	
Facial and body hair appears	Axillary hair appears	Breasts develop
Larynx enlarges	Pubic hair appears	Body contours become rounded
Musculature develops	Growth spurt occurs	Menstruation begins
Reproductive organs grow		Uterus grows

The changes that normally occur in males and females during puberty.

Figure 11.11

The general principle guiding normal pubertal sexual maturation is a simple one: In pubertal males, androgen levels are higher than estrogen levels, and masculinization is the result; in pubertal females, the estrogens predominate, and the result is feminization. Individuals castrated prior to puberty do not become sexually mature unless they receive replacement injections of androgens or estrogens.

But even during puberty, its only major time of relevance, the men-are-men-and-women-are-women assumption stumbles badly. You see, **androstenedione**, an androgen that is released primarily by the adrenal cortex, is normally responsible for the growth of pubic hair and *axillary hair* (underarm hair) in females. It is hard to take seriously the practice of referring to androgens as "male hormones" when one of them is responsible for the development of the female pattern of pubic hair growth. The male pattern is a pyramid, and the female pattern is an inverted pyramid (see Figure 11.11).

Do you remember how old you were when you started to go through puberty? In most North American and European countries, puberty begins at about 10.5 years of age for girls and 11.5 years for boys. I am sure that you would have been unhappy if you had not started puberty until you were 15 or 16, but this was the norm in North America and Europe just a century and a half ago. Presumably, this acceleration of puberty has resulted from changes in dietary, medical, and socioeconomic conditions.

Scan your Brain

Before you proceed to a consideration of three cases of exceptional human sexual development, scan your brain to see whether you understand the basics of normal sexual development by completing the following exercise. The correct answers are provided below. Review material related to your errors and omissions before proceeding.

1. Six weeks after conception, the Y chromosome of the human male triggers the production of _____.

2. In the absence of H-Y antigen, the cortical cells of the primordial gonads develop into _____.

3. In the third month of male fetal development, the testes secrete testosterone and _____ substance.

4. The hormonal factor that triggers the development of the human Müllerian system is the lack of _____ around the third month of fetal development.

5. The scrotum and the _____ develop from the same bipotential precursor.

6. The female pattern of cyclic _____ release from the anterior pituitary develops in adulthood unless androgens are present in the body during the perinatal period.

7. It has been hypothesized that perinatal testosterone must first be changed to estradiol before it can masculinize the male rat brain. This is called the _____ hypothesis.

8. _____ is normally responsible for pubic and axillary hair growth in human females during puberty.

9. Girls usually begin puberty _____ boys do.

Scan Your Brain answers: (1) H-Y antigen, (2) ovaries, (3) Müllerian-inhibiting, (4) androgens (or testosterone), (5) labia majora, (6) gonadotropin, (7) aromatization, (8) Androstenedione, (9) before

11.3

Three Cases of Exceptional Human Sexual Development

This section discusses three cases of exceptional sexual development. I am sure you will be intrigued by these three cases, but that is not the only reason I have included them. My main reason is expressed by a proverb: "The exception proves the rule." Most people think this proverb means that the exception "proves" the rule in the sense that it establishes its truth, but this is nonsense: The truth of a rule is challenged by exceptions, not confirmed by them. The word *proof* comes from the Latin *probare*, which means "to test"—as in *proving ground* or *printer's proof*—and this is the sense in which it is used in the proverb. Hence, the proverb means that the explanation of exceptional cases is a major challenge for any theory.

So far in this chapter, you have learned the "rules" according to which hormones seem to influence normal sexual development. Now, three exceptional cases are offered to prove (to test) these rules.

Thinking Clearly

The Case of Anne S., the Woman Who Wasn't

Anne S., an attractive 26-year-old female, sought treatment for two sex-related disorders: lack of menstruation and pain during sexual intercourse (Jones & Park, 1971). She sought help because she and her husband of

Clinical Implications

Chapter 11 Hormones and Sex **347**

4 years had been trying without success to have children, and she correctly surmised that her lack of a menstrual cycle was part of the problem. A physical examination revealed that Anne was a healthy young woman. Her only readily apparent peculiarity was the sparseness and fineness of her pubic and axillary hair. Examination of her external genitals revealed no abnormalities; however, there were some problems with her internal genitals. Her vagina was only 4 centimeters long, and her uterus was underdeveloped.

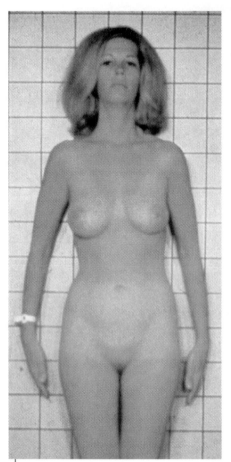

A person with androgenic insensitivity syndrome. Although she has male sex chromosomes, she developed a female body because of an insensitivity to the masculinizing effects of androgens.

Figure 11.12

At the start of this chapter, I said that you would encounter some remarkable things, and the diagnosis of Anne's case certainly qualifies as one of them. Anne's doctors concluded that her sex chromosomes were those of a man. No, this is not a misprint; they concluded that Anne, the attractive young housewife, had the genes of a genetic male. Three lines of evidence supported their diagnosis. First, analysis of cells scraped from the inside of Anne's mouth revealed that they were of the male XY type. Second, a tiny incision in Anne's abdomen, which enabled Anne's physicians to look inside, revealed a pair of internalized testes but no ovaries. Finally, hormone tests revealed that Anne's hormone levels were those of a male.

Anne suffers from **androgenic insensitivity syndrome**; all her symptoms stem from a mutation to the androgen receptor gene that rendered her androgen receptors defective (see Fink et al., 1999; Goldstein, 2000). During development, Anne's testes released normal amounts of androgens for a male, but her body could not respond to them, and her development thus proceeded as if no androgens had been released. Her external genitals, her brain, and her behavior developed along female lines, without the effects of androgens to override the female program, and her testes could not descend from her body cavity with no scrotum for them to descend into. Furthermore, Anne did not develop normal internal female reproductive ducts because, like other genetic males, her testes released Müllerian-inhibiting substance; that is why her vagina was short and her uterus undeveloped. At puberty, Anne's testes released enough estrogens to feminize her body in the absence of the counteracting effects of androgens; however, adrenal androstenedione was not able to stimulate the growth of pubic and axillary hair.

Money and Ehrhardt (1972) studied the psychosexual development of 10 androgen-insensitive patients. These researchers concluded that the placidity of their patients' childhood play and their goals, fantasies, sexual behavior, and maternal tendencies—several had adopted children—all conformed to the idealized stereotype of what constitutes femininity in North American culture. Apparently, genetic males who look like females, with no exposure to the masculinizing effects of androgens, come to act and think like normal females.

Androgenic insensitivity syndrome raises an interesting question of medical ethics. Many people believe that physicians should always disclose all relevant findings to their patients. If you were Anne's physician, would you tell her that she has the genes of a male? Would you tell her husband? Anne's vagina was surgically enlarged, she was counseled to consider adoption, and, as far as I know, she is still happily married and unaware of her genetic sex. On the other hand, I have heard from several women with androgenic insensitivity syndrome who recommend full disclosure: They had faced a variety of problems throughout their lives and learning the cause helped them.

The Case of the Girl Who Started to Develop a Man's Body

The patient—let's call her Elaine—sought treatment in 1972. Elaine was born with somewhat ambiguous external genitals, but she was raised by her parents as a girl without incident, until the onset of puberty, when she suddenly began to develop male secondary sex characteristics. This was extremely distressing. Her treatment had two aspects: surgical and hormonal. Surgical treatment was used to increase the size of her vagina and decrease the size of her clitoris; hormonal treatment was used to suppress androgen release so that her own estrogen could feminize her body. Following treatment, Elaine developed into an attractive young woman—narrow hips and a husky voice being the only signs of her brush with masculinity. Fifteen years later, she was married and enjoying a normal sex life (Money & Ehrhardt, 1972).

Elaine suffered from adrenogenital syndrome. **Adrenogenital syndrome** is a disorder of sexual development caused by a congenital deficiency in the release of the hormone *cortisol* from the adrenal cortex, which results in compensatory adrenal hyperactivity and the excessive release of adrenal androgens. This has little effect on the development of males, other than accelerating the onset of puberty, but it has major effects on the development of genetic females. Females who suffer from the adrenogenital syndrome are usually born with an enlarged clitoris and partially fused labia. Their gonads and internal ducts are usually normal because the adrenal androgens are released too late to stimulate the development of the Wolffian system.

Most female cases of adrenogenital syndrome are diagnosed at birth. In such cases, the abnormalities of the external genitals are immediately corrected, and cortisol is administered to reduce the levels of circulating adrenal androgens. Following early treatment, adrenogenital females grow up to be physically normal except that the onset of menstruation is likely to be later than normal. This makes them good subjects for studies of the effects of fetal androgen exposure on psychosexual development.

Adrenogenital teenage girls who have received early treatment typically display a high degree of tomboyishness and little interest in maternity (e.g., Hines, 2003). They prefer boys' clothes and toys, play mainly with boys, show little interest in handling babies, and tend to daydream about future careers rather than motherhood. It is important not to lose sight of the fact that many teenage girls display similar characteristics—and why not? Accordingly, the behavior of treated adrenogenital females, although perhaps tending toward the masculine, is well within the range considered normal in females by the current standards of our culture.

The most interesting questions about the development of females with adrenogenital syndrome concern their romantic and sexual preferences as adults. They seem to lag behind normal females in dating and marriage—perhaps because of the delayed onset of their menstrual cycle—but in other respects their sexual interests appear normal. Most are heterosexual, although it has been suggested that they have a slight tendency toward bisexuality. However, Zucker and others (1996) found that although females with adrenogenital syndrome had fewer heterosexual experiences and fantasies, they had no more homosexual experiences or fantasies.

Prior to the development of cortisol therapy in 1950, genetic females with adrenogenital syndrome were left untreated. Some were raised as boys and some as girls, but the direction of their pubertal development was unpredictable. In some cases, adrenal androgens predominated and masculinized their bodies; in others, ovarian estrogens predominated and feminized their bodies. Thus, some who were raised as boys were transformed at puberty into women, and some who were raised as girls were transformed into men, with devastating emotional consequences in both instances.

The Case of the Twin Who Lost His Penis

One of the most famous cases in the literature on sexual development is that of a male identical twin whose penis was accidentally destroyed during circumcision at the age of 7 months (see Figure 11.13 on page 351). Because there was no satisfactory way of surgically replacing the lost penis, a respected expert in such matters, John Money, recommended that the boy be castrated, that an artificial vagina be created, that the boy be raised as a

Clinical Implications

girl, and that estrogen be administered at puberty to feminize the body. After a great deal of consideration and anguish, the parents followed Money's advice.

Money's (1975) report of this case of *ablatio penis* has been influential. It has been seen by some as the ultimate test of the *nature–nurture controversy* (see Chapter 1) with respect to the development of sexual identity and behavior. It seemed to pit the masculinizing effects of male genes and male prenatal hormones against the effects of being reared as a female. And the availability of a genetically identical control subject, the twin brother, made the case all the more interesting.

According to Money, the outcome of this case strongly supports the *social-learning theory* of sexual identity. Money reported in 1975, when the patient was 12, that "she" had developed as a normal female, thus confirming his prediction that being gonadectomized, having the genitals surgically altered, and being raised as a girl would override the masculinizing effects of male genes and early androgens. Because it is such an interesting case, Money's description of it continues to be featured in some textbooks, each time carrying with it the message that the sexual identity and sexual behavior of men and women are largely a matter of upbringing.

However, a long-term follow-up study published by experts other than those who initially prescribed the treatment tells an entirely different story (Diamond & Sigmundson, 1997). Despite having female genitalia and being treated as a female, John/Joan developed along male lines. Apparently, the organ that determines the course of psychosocial development is the brain, not the genitals (Reiner, 1997). The following paraphrases from Diamond and Sigmundson's report give you a glimpse of John/Joan's life:

> From a very early age, Joan tended to act in a masculine way. She preferred boys' activities and games and displayed little interest in dolls, sewing, or other conventional female activities. When she was four, she was watching her father shave and her mother put on lipstick, and she began to put shaving cream on her face. When she was told to put makeup on like her mother, she said, "No, I don't want no makeup, I want to shave."
>
> "Things happened very early. As a child, I began to see that I felt different about a lot of things than I was supposed to. I suspected I was a boy from the second grade on."
>
> Despite the absence of a penis, Joan often tried to urinate while standing, and she would sometimes go to the boys' lavatory.
>
> Joan was attractive as a girl, but as soon as she moved or talked her masculinity became apparent. She was teased incessantly by the other girls, and she often retaliated violently, which resulted in her expulsion from school.
>
> Joan was put on an estrogen regimen at the age of 12 but rebelled against it. She did not want to feminize; she hated her developing breasts and refused to wear a bra.
>
> At 14, Joan decided to live as a male and switched to John. At that time, John's father tearfully revealed John's entire early history to him. "All of a sudden everything clicked. For the first time I understood who and what I was."
>
> John requested androgen treatment, a *mastectomy* (surgical removal of breasts), and *phaloplasty* (surgical creation of a penis). He became a handsome and popular young man. He married at the age of 25 and adopted his wife's children. He is strictly heterosexual.
>
> John's ability to ejaculate and experience orgasm returned following his androgen treatments. However, his early castration permanently eliminated his reproductive capacity.

John remained bitter about his early treatment and his inability to produce offspring. To save others from his experience, he cooperated in writing his biography, *As Nature Made Him* (Colapinto, 2000), and the world learned that his real name was David Reimer. But David never recovered from his emotional scars. On May 4, 2004, he committed suicide.

David's case suggests that the clinical practice of surgically modifying a person's sex at birth should be curtailed. Any such irrevocable treatments should await early puberty and the emergence of the patient's sexual identity and sexual attraction. Then, a compatible course of treatment can be selected.

Do These Exceptional Cases Prove the Rule?

Do current theories of hormones and sexual development pass the test imposed by the three preceding cases of exceptional sexual development? In my view, the answer is an emphatic yes. Although current theories do not supply all of the answers, especially when it comes to brain dimorphisms and behavior, they have contributed greatly to the understanding of exceptional sexual development.

David Reimer, the twin whose penis was accidentally destroyed.

Figure 11.13

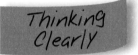

Thinking Clearly

For centuries, cases of abnormal sexual development have befuddled scholars, but now, armed with a basic understanding of the role of hormones in sexual development, they have been able to make sense of even the most puzzling of such cases. Moreover, the study of sexual development has pointed the way to effective treatments. Judge these contributions for yourself by comparing your current understanding of these three cases with the understanding that you would have had if you had encountered them before beginning this chapter.

Notice one more thing about the three cases: Each of the three subjects was male in some respects and female in others. Accordingly, each case is a serious challenge to the men-are-men-and-women-are-women assumption.

11.4

Effects of Gonadal Hormones on Adults

Once an individual reaches sexual maturity, gonadal hormones begin to play a role in activating reproductive behavior. These activational effects are the focus of the first two parts of this section, which has three parts. The first deals with the role of hormones in activating the reproduction-related behavior of men, and the second deals with the role of hormones in activating the reproduction-related behavior of women. The third part discusses the effects of anabolic steroid abuse.

Male Reproduction-Related Behavior and Testosterone

The important role played by gonadal hormones in the activation of male sexual behavior is clearly demonstrated by the asexualizing effects of orchidectomy. Bremer (1959) reviewed the cases of 157 orchidectomized Norwegians. Many had committed sex-related offenses and had agreed to castration to reduce the length of their prison terms.

Two important generalizations can be drawn from Bremer's study. The first is that orchidectomy leads to a reduction in sexual interest and behavior; the second is that the rate and degree of the loss is variable. About half the men became completely asexual within a few weeks of the operation; others quickly lost their ability to achieve an erection but continued to experience some sexual interest and pleasure; and a few continued to copulate successfully, although somewhat less enthusiastically, for the duration of the study. There were also body changes: a reduction of hair on the trunk, extremities, and face; the deposition of fat on the hips and chest; a softening of the skin; and a reduction in strength.

Of the 102 sex offenders in Bremer's study, only 3 were reconvicted of sex offenses. Accordingly, he recommended castration as an effective treatment of last resort for male sex offenders.

Why do some men remain sexually active for months after orchidectomy, despite the fact that testicular hormones are cleared from their bodies within days? It has been suggested that adrenal androgens may play some role in the maintenance of sexual activity in some castrated men, but there is no direct evidence for this hypothesis.

Orchidectomy, in one fell swoop—or, to put it more precisely, in two fell swoops—removes a pair of glands that release many hormones. Because testosterone is the major testicular hormone, the major symptoms of orchidectomy have been generally attributed to the loss of testosterone, rather than to the loss of some other testicular hormone or to some nonhormonal consequence of the surgery. The therapeutic effects of **replacement injections** of testosterone have confirmed this assumption.

The Case of the Man Who Lost and Regained His Manhood

Clinical Implications

The very first case report of the effects of testosterone replacement therapy concerned an unfortunate 38-year-old World War I veteran, who was castrated in 1918 at the age of 19 by a shell fragment that removed his testes but left his penis undamaged.

> His body was soft; it was as if he had almost no muscles at all; his hips had grown wider and his shoulders seemed narrower than when he was a soldier. He had very little drive. . . .
>
> Just the same this veteran had married, in 1924, and you' d wonder why, because the doctors had told him he would surely be **impotent** [unable to achieve an erection]. . . . he made some attempts at sexual intercourse "for his wife' s satisfaction" but he confessed that he had been unable to satisfy her at all. . . .
>
> Dr. Foss began injecting it [testosterone] into the feeble muscles of the castrated man. . . .
>
> After the fifth injection, erections were rapid and prolonged. . . . But that wasn' t all. During twelve weeks of treatment he had gained eighteen pounds, and all his clothes had become too small. Originally, he wore fourteen-and-a-half inch collars. Now fifteen-and-a-half were too tight. . . . testosterone had resurrected a broken man to a manhood he had lost forever. (de Kruif, 1945, pp. 97–100)

Since this first clinical trial, testosterone has revived the sexuality of many men. Testosterone does not, however, eliminate the *sterility* (inability to reproduce) of males who lack functional testes.

The fact that testosterone is necessary for male sexual behavior has led to two widespread assumptions: (1) that the level of a man's sexuality is a function of the amount of testosterone he has in his blood, and (2) that a man's sex drive can be increased by increasing his testosterone levels. Both assumptions are incorrect. Sex drive and testosterone levels are uncorrelated in healthy men, and testosterone injections do not increase their sex drive.

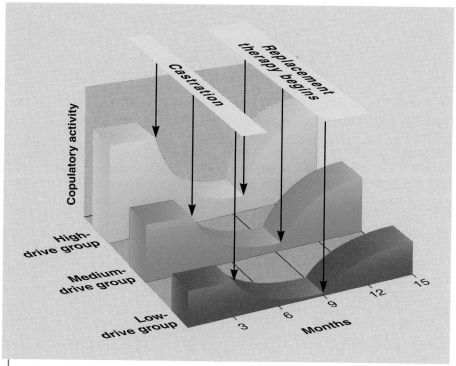

The sexual behavior of male guinea pigs with low, medium, and high sex drive. Sexual behavior was disrupted by castration and returned to its original level by very large replacement injections of testosterone.

(Adapted from Grunt & Young, 1952.)

Figure 11.14

It seems that each healthy male has far more testosterone than is required to activate the neural circuits that produce his sexual behavior and that having more than the minimum is of no advantage in this respect (Sherwin, 1988). A classic experiment by Grunt and Young (1952) clearly illustrates this point.

First, Grunt and Young rated the sexual behavior of each of the male guinea pigs in their experiment. Then, on the basis of the ratings, the researchers divided the male guinea pigs into three experimental groups: low, medium, and high sex drive. Following castration, the sexual behavior of all of the guinea pigs fell to negligible levels within a few weeks (see Figure 11.14), but it returned to presurgery levels after the initiation of a series of testosterone replacement injections. The important point is that although each subject received the same, very large replacement injections of testosterone, the injections simply returned each to its previous level of copulatory activity. The conclusion is clear: With respect to the effects of testosterone on sexual behavior, more is not necessarily better.

A brief comment about *Viagra* is relevant here. Many people believe that Viagra increases the sex drive of impotent men in the same way that testosterone does. It doesn't! Viagra acts selectively on the circulatory system to increase the ability of impotent men to achieve erections. It does not directly increase their motivation to engage in sexual activity.

Female Reproduction-Related Behavior and Gonadal Hormones

Sexually mature female rats and guinea pigs display 4-day cycles of gonadal hormone release. There is a gradual increase in the secretion of estrogens by the developing *follicle* (the capsule of cells surrounding the egg in the ovary) in the 2 days prior to ovulation, followed by a sudden surge in progesterone as the egg is released. These surges of estrogens and progesterone initiate **estrus**—a period of 12 to 18 hours during which the female is *fertile, receptive* (likely to assume the lordosis posture when mounted), *proceptive* (likely to engage in behaviors that serve to attract the male), and *sexually attractive* (smelling of chemicals that attract males).

The Evolutionary Perspective

The close relation between the cycle of hormone release and the **estrous cycle**—the cycle of sexual receptivity—in female rats and guinea pigs and in many other mammalian species suggests that female sexual behavior in these species is under hormonal control. The effects of ovariectomy confirm this conclusion; ovariectomy of female rats and guinea pigs produces a rapid decline of both proceptive and receptive behaviors. Furthermore, estrus can be induced in ovariectomized rats and guinea pigs by an injection of estradiol followed about a day and a half later by an injection of progesterone.

Women are different from female rats and guinea pigs when it comes to the hormonal control of their sexual behavior. Neither the sexual motivation nor the sexual behavior of women is inextricably linked with their menstrual cycles (see Sanders & Bancroft, 1982). Moreover, ovariectomy has surprisingly little direct effect on either their sexual motivation or their sexual behavior (e.g., Martin, Roberts, & Clayton, 1980). Other than sterility, the major consequence of ovariectomy in women is a decrease in vaginal lubrication.

Paradoxically, there is evidence that the sex drive of women is under the control of androgens, not estrogens (see Sherwin, 1988). Apparently, enough androgens are released from the human adrenal glands to maintain the sexual motivation of women even after their ovaries have been removed. Support for the theory that androgens control human female sexuality has come from three sources:

1. Experiments in nonhuman female primates: Replacement injections of testosterone, but not estradiol, increase the proceptivity of ovariectomized and adrenalectomized rhesus monkeys (see Everitt & Herbert, 1972; Everitt, Herbert, & Hamer, 1971).
2. Correlational studies in healthy women: Various measures of sexual motivation are correlated with testosterone levels but not with estradiol levels (see Bancroft et al., 1983; Morris et al., 1987).
3. Clinical studies of women following ovariectomy and adrenalectomy: Replacement injections of testosterone, but not of estradiol, rekindle their sexual motivation (see Sherwin, 1985; Sherwin, Gelfand, & Brender, 1985).

Clinical Implications

Although aspects of sexual motivation or behavior do not appear to be linked to menstrual cycles in women, other phenomena are. The most widely studied example is *premenstrual syndrome* (PMS). PMS refers to the cluster of physiological and behavioral disturbances that occur to many women in the days before their periods of postovulatory blood flow. The physiological disturbances commonly include breast swelling and tenderness, abdominal distension, water retention, fatigue, acne, headache, and joint pain. The behavioral disturbances commonly include depression, anger, insomnia, food cravings, and poor concentration. The direct cause of PMS is still unknown. Although PMS is clearly related to menstrual hormonal fluctuation, researchers have found no particular hormone level or pattern of hormonal levels that distinguishes between women who suffer from PMS and those who do not. Unfortunately, despite the fact that about 75% of women will experience PMS at some point in their lives, some physicians do not recognize it as a legitimate medical problem.

Anabolic Steroid Abuse

Anabolic steroids are steroids, such as testosterone, that have *anabolic* (growth-promoting) effects. Testosterone itself is not very useful as an anabolic drug because it is broken down soon after injection and because it has undesirable side effects. Chemists have managed to synthesize a number of potent anabolic steroids that are long-acting, but they have not managed to synthesize one that does not have side effects.

At first, anabolic steroids were used mainly by male competitive athletes and body-builders; then, during the 1990s, there was a marked increase in anabolic steroid use by female athletes and body-builders and by males interested solely in improving their physiques. In recent years, the use of steroids has reached troubling proportions. Studies indicate that over a million young Americans have used steroids (see Pope, Kouri, & Hudson, 2000). A recent survey by the National Institute on Drug Abuse indicated that 3.4% of 12th-grade males in the United States had used steroids.

Because steroids are illegal in most parts of the United States, it has been difficult to document their effects. Research is tightly regulated, and users are not usually forthcoming.

Effects of Anabolic Steroids on Athletic Performance. Do anabolic steroids really increase the muscularity and strength of the athletes who use them? Surprisingly, the scientific evidence is inconsistent (see Yesalis & Bahrke, 1995), even though many athletes and coaches believe that it is impossible to compete successfully at the highest levels of their sports without an anabolic steroid boost. The inconsistency of the scientific evidence likely results from two shortcomings of the experimental studies. First, the studies have tended to use doses of steroids smaller than those used by athletes and to administer the doses for shorter periods of time. Second, the studies have often been conducted on subjects who are not involved in intense anabolic training. However, despite the lack of consistent scientific evidence, it is difficult to ignore the muscular development of steroid users such as the man pictured in Figure 11.15.

An athlete who used anabolic steroids to augment his training program.

Figure 11.15

Physiological Effects of Anabolic Steroids. There is general agreement (see Yesalis & Bahrke, 1995) that people who take high doses of anabolic steroids risk several sex-related physiological side effects. In men, the negative feedback from high levels of anabolic steroids reduces gonadotropin release; this leads to a reduction in testicular activity, which can result in *testicular atrophy* (wasting away of the testes) and sterility. *Gynecomastia* (breast growth in men) can also occur, presumably as the result of the aromatization of anabolic steroids to estrogens. In women, anabolic steroids can produce *amenorrhea* (cessation of menstruation), sterility, *hirsutism* (excessive growth of body hair), growth of the clitoris, development of a masculine body shape, baldness, shrinking of the breasts, and deepening and coarsening of the voice. Unfortunately, many of the sex-related effects on women appear to be irreversible.

Both men and women who use anabolic steroids can suffer muscle spasms, muscle pains, blood in the urine, acne, general swelling from the retention of water, bleeding of the tongue, nausea, vomiting, and a variety of psychotic behaviors, including fits of depression and anger (Pope & Katz, 1987). Oral anabolic steroids produce cancerous liver tumors.

Behavioral Effects of Anabolic Steroids. Most of the research on the behavioral effects of anabolic steroids, aside from that focusing on athletic performance, has focused on aggression. There have been numerous anecdotal reports that steroid use increases aggression and irritability. However, these reports must be

Clinical Implications

Thinking Clearly

treated with caution for at least three reasons. First, because many people believe that testosterone is linked to aggression, reports of aggressive behavior in steroid users might be a consequence of expectation. Second, many individuals (e.g., professional fighters or football players) who use steroids are likely to have been aggressive before they started treatment. And third, aggressive behavior might be an indirect consequence of increased size and muscularity.

Despite the need for experimental assessment of the effects of anabolic steroids on aggression, few such experiments have been conducted. The best is one by Pope and colleagues (2000). They administered either testosterone or placebo injections in a double-blind study of 53 men. The subjects completed tests of aggression and kept daily aggression-related diaries; a "significant other" of each subject also kept a similar diary. Pope and colleagues found large increases in aggression in a few of the subjects.

There is no indication that the chronic use of high doses of steroids increases, improves, or redirects sexual motivation or sexual behavior. However, there are a few reports of disruptive effects in human steroid users, and some anabolic steroids have been shown to disrupt the copulatory behavior of both male and female rodents (see Clark & Henderson, 2003).

One last important point about the behavioral effects of anabolic steroids: So far, research on the effects of anabolic steroids in humans has focused on adults. The use of anabolic steroids in puberty, before developmental programs of sexual differentiation are complete, has the potential to produce lasting deleterious effects (see Farrell & McGinnis, 2003).

11.5
Neural Mechanisms of Sexual Behavior

Major differences among cultures in sexual practices and preferences indicate that the control of human sexual behavior involves the highest levels of the nervous system (e.g., association cortex), and the same point is made by controlled demonstrations of the major role played by experience in the sexual preferences and behaviors of nonhuman animals (see Woodson, 2002; Woodson & Balleine, 2002; Woodson, Balleine, & Gorski, 2002). Nevertheless, experimental research on the neural mechanisms of reproductive behavior has focused almost exclusively on hypothalamic circuits.

Why has research on the neural mechanisms of reproductive behavior focused almost exclusively on hypothalamic circuits? There are three obvious reasons. First, because of the difficulty of studying the neural mechanisms of complex human sexual behaviors, researchers have focused on the relatively simple, controllable copulatory behaviors, (e.g., lordosis, mounting, and ejaculation) of laboratory animals (see Agmo & Ellingsen, 2003), which tend to be controlled by the hypothalamus. Second, because the hypothalamus controls gonadotropin release, it was the obvious place to look for sexually dimorphic structures and circuits that might control copulation. And third, early studies confirmed that the hypothalamus does play a major role in sexual behavior, and this finding led subsequent neuroscientific research on sexual behavior to focus on that brain structure.

Structural Differences between the Male Hypothalamus and the Female Hypothalamus

You have already learned that the male hypothalamus and the female hypothalamus are functionally different in their control of anterior pituitary hormones (steady versus cyclic release, respectively). In the 1970s, structural differences between the male and female hypothalamus were discovered in rats (Raisman & Field, 1971). Most notably, Gorski and his colleagues (1978) discovered a nucleus in the **medial preoptic area** of the rat hypothalamus that was several times larger in males (see Figure 11.16). They called this nucleus the **sexually dimorphic nucleus**.

At birth, the sexually dimorphic nuclei of male and female rats are the same size. In the first few days after birth, the male sexually dimorphic nuclei grow at a high rate and the female sexually dimorphic nuclei do not. The growth of the male sexually dimorphic nuclei is triggered by estradiol, which has been aromatized from testosterone (see McEwen, 1987). Accordingly, castrating day-old (but not 4-day-old) male rats significantly reduces the size of their sexually dimorphic nuclei as adults, whereas injecting neonatal (newborn) female rats with testosterone significantly increases the size of theirs (Gorski, 1980). Although the overall size of the sexually dimorphic nucleus diminishes only slightly in male rats that are castrated in adulthood, specific areas of the nucleus do display significant degeneration (Bloch & Gorski, 1988).

The size of a male rat's sexually dimorphic nucleus is correlated with the rat's testosterone levels and aspects of its sexual activity (Anderson et al., 1986). However, bilateral lesions of the sexually dimorphic nucleus have only slight disruptive effects on male rat sexual behavior (e.g., De Jonge et al., 1989; Turkenburg et al., 1988), and the specific function of this nucleus is unclear.

Since the discovery of the sexually dimorphic nuclei in rats, many other sex differences in hypothalamic anatomy have been identified in rats and in other species (see Swaab & Hofman, 1995; Witelson, 1991). In humans, for example, there are nuclei in the preoptic (Swaab & Fliers, 1985), suprachiasmatic (Swaab et al., 1994), and anterior (Allen et al., 1989) regions of the hypothalamus that differ in men and women.

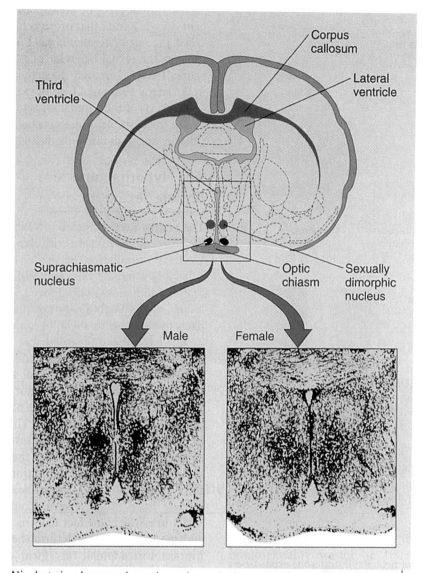

Nissl-stained coronal sections through the preoptic area of male and female rats. The sexually dimorphic nuclei are larger in male rats than in female rats.

(Adapted from Gorski et al., 1978.)

Figure 11.16

The Hypothalamus and Male Sexual Behavior

The medial preoptic area (which includes the sexually dimorphic nucleus) is one area of the hypothalamus that plays a key role in male sexual behavior. Destruction of the entire area abolishes sexual behavior in the males of all mammalian species that have been studied (see Hull et al., 1999). In contrast, medial preoptic area lesions do not eliminate the female sexual behaviors of females, but they do eliminate the male sexual behaviors (e.g., mounting) that are often observed in females (Singer, 1968). Thus, bilateral medial preoptic lesions appear to abolish male copulatory behavior in both sexes. On the other side of the coin, electrical stimulation of the medial preoptic area elicits copulatory behavior in male rats (Malsbury, 1971; Rodríguez-Manzo et al., 2000), and copulatory behavior can be reinstated in castrated male rats by medial preoptic implants of testosterone (Davidson, 1980).

It is not clear why males with medial preoptic lesions stop copulating. One possibility is that the lesions disrupt the ability of males to copulate; another is that the lesions reduce the motivation of the males to engage in sexual behavior. The evidence is mixed, but it favors the hypothesis that the medial preoptic area is involved in the motivational aspects of male sexual behavior (Paredes, 2003).

The medial preoptic area appears to control male sexual behavior via a tract that projects to an area of the midbrain called the *lateral tegmental field* (see Figure 11.17). Destruction of this tract disrupts the sexual behavior of male rats (Brackett & Edwards, 1984). Moreover, the activity of individual neurons in the lateral tegmental field of male rats is often correlated with aspects of the copulatory act (Shimura & Shimokochi, 1990).

Neuropharmacological approaches are being used to study the medial preoptic area's control of male sexual behavior. The following are three recent findings:

1. Extracellular levels of dopamine increase in the male medial preoptic area before and during copulation (Putnam, Sato, & Hull, 2003).
2. Copulatory activity reduces the number of androgen receptors in the male medial preoptic area (Fernández-Guasti, Swaab, & Rodríguez-Manzo, 2003), and blocking androgen receptors in this area prevents copulation (Harding & McGinnis, 2004).
3. Endogenous opioids appear to be released in the male medial preoptic area during copulation (Coolen et al., 2004).

The Hypothalamus and Female Sexual Behavior

The Evolutionary Perspective

The **ventromedial nucleus (VMN)** of the rat hypothalamus contains circuits that appear to be critical for female sexual behavior. Female rats with bilateral lesions of the VMN do not display lordosis, and they are likely to attack suitors who become too ardent.

You have already learned that an injection of progesterone brings into estrus an ovariectomized female rat that received an injection of estradiol about 36 hours before. Because the progesterone by itself does not induce estrus, the estradiol must in some way prime the nervous system so that the progesterone can exert its effect. This priming effect appears to be mediated by the large increase in the number of *progesterone receptors* that occurs in the VMN and surrounding area following an estradiol injection (Blaustein et al., 1988); the estradiol exerts this effect by entering VMN cells and influencing gene expression. Confirming the role of the VMN in estrus is the fact that microinjections of estradiol and progesterone directly into the VMN induce estrus in ovariectomized female rats (Pleim & Barfield, 1988).

The influence of the VMN on the sexual behavior of female rats appears to be mediated by a tract that descends to the *periaqueductal gray (PAG)* of the tegmentum (see Figure 11.17). Destruction of this tract eliminates female sexual behavior (Hennessey et al., 1990), as do lesions of the PAG itself (Sakuma & Pfaff, 1979).

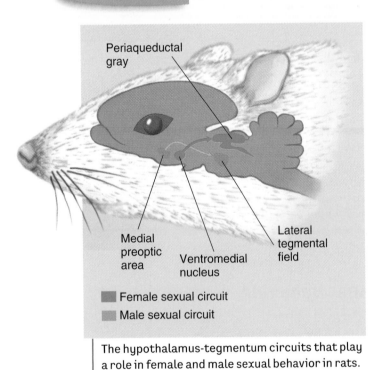

Periaqueductal gray

Medial preoptic area

Ventromedial nucleus

Lateral tegmental field

Female sexual circuit
Male sexual circuit

The hypothalamus-tegmentum circuits that play a role in female and male sexual behavior in rats.

Figure 11.17

In conclusion, although many parts of the brain play a role in sexual behavior, much of the research has focused on the role of the hypothalamus in the copulatory behavior of rats. Several areas of the hypothalamus influence this copulatory behavior, and several hypothalamic nuclei are sexually dimorphic in rats, but the medial preoptic area and the ventromedial nucleus are two of the most widely studied. Male rat sexual behavior is influenced by a tract that runs from the medial preoptic area to the lateral tegmental field, and female rat sexual behavior is influenced by a tract that runs from the ventromedial nucleus to the periaqueductal gray (see Figure 11.17).

11.6
Sexual Orientation, Hormones, and the Brain

So far, this chapter has not addressed the topic of sexual orientation. As you know, some people are **heterosexual** (sexually attracted to members of the other sex), some are **homosexual** (sexually attracted to members of the same sex), and some are **bisexual** (sexually attracted to members of both sexes). A discussion of research on sexual orientation is a fitting conclusion to this chapter because it brings together the chapter's exception-proves-the-rule and anti-"mamawawa" messages.

Sexual Orientation and Genes

Research has shown that differences in sexual orientation have a genetic basis. For example, Bailey and Pillard (1991) studied a group of male homosexuals who had twin brothers, and they found that 52% of the monozygotic twin brothers and 22% of the dizygotic twin brothers were homosexual. In a comparable study of female twins by the same group of researchers (Bailey et al., 1993), the concordance rates for homosexuality were 48% for monozygotic twins and 16% for dizygotic twins.

Sexual Orientation and Early Hormones

Many people mistakenly assume that homosexuals have lower levels of sex hormones. They don't: Heterosexuals and homosexuals do not differ in their levels of circulating hormones. Moreover, orchidectomy reduces the sexual behavior of both heterosexual and homosexual males, but it does not redirect it; and replacement injections simply reactivate the preferences that existed prior to surgery.

Many people also assume that sexual preference is a matter of choice. It isn't: People discover their sexual preferences; they don't choose them. Sexual preferences seem to develop very early, and a child's first indication of the direction of sexual attraction usually does not change as he or she matures. Could perinatal hormone exposure be the early event that shapes sexual orientation?

Efforts to determine whether perinatal hormone levels influence the development of sexual orientation have focused on nonhuman species. A consistent pattern of findings has emerged from this research (see Ellis & Ames, 1987). In rats, hamsters, ferrets, pigs, zebra finches, and dogs, perinatal castration of males and testosterone treatment of females have been shown to induce same-sex preferences (see Adkins-Regan, 1988; Baum et al., 1990; Hrabovszky & Hutson, 2002).

On the one hand, it's important to exercise prudence in applying the results of experiments on laboratory species to the development of sexual preferences in humans; it would be a mistake to ignore the profound cognitive and emotional components of human sexuality, which have no counterpart in laboratory animals. On

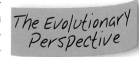

the other hand, it would also be a mistake to think that a pattern of results that runs so consistently through so many mammalian species has no relevance to humans.

Do perinatal hormone levels influence the sexual orientation of adult humans? Although directly relevant evidence is sparse, there are some indications that the answer is yes. The strongest support for this view comes from the quasiexperimental study of Ehrhardt and her colleagues (1985). They interviewed adult women whose mothers had been exposed to *diethylstilbestrol* (a synthetic estrogen) during pregnancy. The subjects' responses indicated that they were significantly more sexually attracted to women than was a group of matched control subjects. Ehrhardt and her colleagues concluded that perinatal estrogen exposure does encourage homosexuality and bisexuality in women but that its effect is relatively weak: The sexual behavior of all but 1 of the 30 subjects was still primarily heterosexual.

What Triggers the Development of Sexual Attraction?

The evidence indicates that most girls and boys living in Western countries experience their first feelings of sexual attraction at about 10 years of age, whether they are heterosexual or homosexual (see Quinsey, 2003). This finding is at odds with the usual assumption that sexual interest is triggered by puberty, which, as you have learned, currently tends to occur at 10.5 years of age in girls and at 11.5 years in boys.

McClintock and Herdt (1996) have suggested that the emergence of sexual attraction may be stimulated by adrenal cortex steroids. Unlike gonadal maturation, adrenal maturation occurs at about the age of 10.

Is There a Difference between the Brains of Homosexuals and Heterosexuals?

The brains of homosexuals and heterosexuals must differ in some way, but how? There have been several reports of neuroanatomical, neuropsychological, and hormonal response differences between homosexuals and heterosexuals (see Gladue, 1994). Most studies have compared male heterosexuals and homosexuals; studies of lesbians are scarce.

In the highly publicized study of LeVay (1991), the structure of one hypothalamic nucleus in male homosexuals was found to be intermediate between that in female heterosexuals and that in male heterosexuals. This study has not been consistently replicated, however. Indeed, no consistent difference between the brains of heterosexuals and homosexuals has yet been discovered.

Transsexualism

Transsexualism is a disorder of sexual identity in which the individual believes that he or she is trapped in a body of the other sex. To put it mildly, the transsexual faces a bizarre conflict: "I am a woman (or man) trapped in the body of a man (or woman). Help!"

It is important to appreciate the desperation of transsexuals; they do not merely think that life might be better if their gender were different. Although many transsexuals do seek *surgical sexual reassignment* (surgery to change their sex), the desperation of these people is better captured by the ways in which some of them dealt with their problem before surgical sexual reassignment was an option: Some biological males (psychological females) attempted self-castration, and others consumed copious quantities of estrogen-containing face creams in order to feminize their bodies.

Mianne Bagger, a transsexual who successfully completed sexual reassignment from male to female. An Australian golf champion, Mianne attracted plenty of media attention when she became the first known female transsexual to compete in a women's professional golf tournament in 2004.

Figure 11.18

What are the steps in sexual reassignment? I will describe the male-to-female procedure: The female-to-male procedure is much more complex (because a penis must be created) and far less satisfactory (for example, because a surgically created penis has no erectile potential), and male-to-female sexual reassignment is three times more prevalent.

The first step in male-to-female reassignment is thorough psychiatric assessment and counseling to establish that the individual is a true transsexual and to prepare "her" for what will follow. Second, a lifelong regimen of estrogen is initiated to feminize the body and maintain the changes. Third, the penis and testes are removed, and female external genitalia and vagina are surgically constructed. The vagina is lined with skin from the penis so that it will have sensory nerve endings that will respond to sexual stimulation. Finally, some patients have cosmetic surgery to feminize the face (e.g., to reduce the size of the Adam's apple). Generally, the adjustment of transsexuals after surgical sexual reassignment is good. Figure 11.18 shows a transsexual after successful sexual reassignment.

The causes of transsexualism are unknown. Transsexualism was once thought to be a product of social learning, that is, of inappropriate child-rearing practices (e.g., mothers dressing their little boys in dresses). The occasional case that is consistent with this view can be found but is likely just due to chance; in most cases, there is no obvious cause.

Clinical Implications

Independence of Sexual Orientation and Sexual Identity

To complete this chapter, I would like to remind you of two of its main messages and show you how useful they are in thinking about one of the puzzles of human sexuality. One of the two messages is that the exception proves the rule: that a powerful test of any theory is its ability to explain exceptional cases. The second message is that "mamawawa" thinking is seriously flawed.

Thinking Clearly

Here, I want to focus on the puzzling fact that sexual attraction, sexual identity, and body type are sometimes unrelated. For example, consider transsexuals: They, by definition, have the body type of one sex and the sexual identity of the other sex, but the orientation of their sexual attraction is an independent matter. Some transsexuals with a male body type are sexually attracted to females, others are sexually attracted to males, and others are sexually attracted to neither—and this is not changed by sexual reassignment (see Van Goozen et al., 2002).

Obviously, the mere existence of homosexuality and transsexualism is a challenge to the "mamawawa," the assumption that males and females belong to distinct and opposite categories. Many people tend to think of "femaleness" and "maleness" as being at opposite ends of a continuum, with a few abnormal cases somewhere between the two ideals. Perhaps this is how you tend to think. However, the fact that body type, sexual orientation, and sexual identity are often independent constitutes a serious attack on any assumption that femaleness and maleness lie at opposite ends of a single scale. Clearly, femaleness and maleness each combine several different attributes (e.g., body type, sexual orientation, and sexual identity), each of which can develop quite independently. This is a real puzzle for many people, including scientists, but one thing you learned in this chapter suggests a solution.

Until recently, it was assumed that the differentiation of the human brain into its female and male forms occurred through a single testosterone-based mechanism. However, a different notion has developed from recent evidence. Now, it is clear that male and female brains differ in many ways and that the differences develop at different times and by different mechanisms. If you keep this developmental principle in mind, you will have no difficulty understanding how one individual can be female in some ways and male in others.

This analysis exemplifies a point I make many times in this book: The study of biopsychology often has important personal and social implications. The search for the neural basis of a behavior frequently provides us with a greater understanding of that behavior. I hope that you now have a greater understanding of, and acceptance of, differences in human sexuality.

Key Terms

11.1 The Neuroendocrine System

Adrenal cortex (p. 335)
Androgens (p. 335)
Anterior pituitary (p. 336)
Amino acid derivative hormones (p. 335)
Copulation (p. 334)
Endocrine glands (p. 334)
Estradiol (p. 335)
Estrogens (p. 335)
Exocrine glands (p. 333)
Follicle-stimulating hormone (FSH) (p. 339)
Gonadotropin-releasing hormone (p. 339)
Gonadotropins (p. 336)
Gonads (p. 334)
Hormones (p. 334)
Hypothalamopituitary portal system (p. 337)
Luteinizing hormone (LH) (p. 339)
Menstrual cycle (p. 336)
Ovaries (p. 334)
Oxytocin (p. 337)
Paraventricular nuclei (p. 337)

Peptide hormones (p. 335)
Pituitary stalk (p. 336)
Posterior pituitary (p. 336)
Progesterone (p. 335)
Progestins (p. 335)
Protein hormones (p. 335)
Pulsatile hormone release (p. 339)
Releasing hormones (p. 338)
Sex chromosomes (p. 334)
Steroid hormones (p. 335)
Supraoptic nuclei (p. 337)
Testes (p. 334)
Testosterone (p. 335)
Thyrotropin (p. 338)
Thyrotropin-releasing hormone (p. 338)
Vasopressin (p. 337)
Zygote (p. 334)

11.2 Hormones and Sexual Development

Adrenocorticotropic hormone (p. 345)
Androstenedione (p. 346)
Aromatization (p. 343)
Defeminize (p. 344)
Demasculinize (p. 345)

Ejaculation (p. 345)
Feminize (p. 345)
Genitals (p. 342)
Gonadectomy (p. 341)
Growth hormone (p. 345)
H-Y antigen (p. 341)
Intromission (p. 345)
Lordosis (p. 345)
Masculinize (p. 344)
Müllerian-inhibiting substance (p. 341)
Müllerian system (p. 341)
Orchidectomy (p. 341)
Ovariectomy (p. 341)
Proceptive behaviors (p. 345)
Scrotum (p. 341)
Secondary sex characteristics (p. 345)
Wolffian system (p. 341)

11.3 Three Cases of Exceptional Human Sexual Development

Ablatio penis (p. 350)
Adrenogenital syndrome (p. 349)
Androgenic insensitivity syndrome (p. 348)

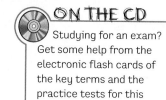

ON THE CD

Studying for an exam? Get some help from the electronic flash cards of the key terms and the practice tests for this chapter.

Hormones and Sex
What's Wrong With the Mamawawa?

This chapter opened by pointing out that sex hormones have two kinds of effects—developmental and activational—and by warning you against a common misconception: the belief that there are two kinds of hormones, male and female, which have parallel but opposite effects.

Regulation of gonadal hormones

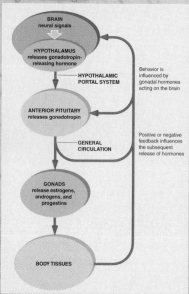

The Neuroendocrine System

The same sex hormones (androgens, estrogens, and progestins) are released by the ovaries and testes; sex differences in sex-hormone levels are merely a matter of degree. The release of sex hormones from the gonads is controlled by tropic hormones, which are released by the anterior pituitary under the control of hypothalamic releasing hormones.
(Pages 333–340)

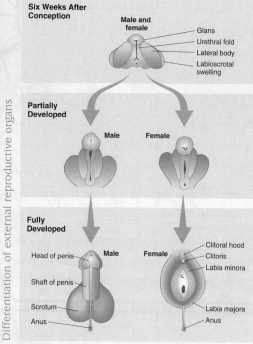

Differentiation of external reproductive organs

Six Weeks After Conception

Male and female — Glans, Urethral fold, Lateral body, Labioscrotal swelling

Partially Developed — Male / Female

Fully Developed — Male: Head of penis, Shaft of penis, Scrotum, Anus / Female: Clitoral hood, Clitoris, Labia minora, Labia majora, Anus

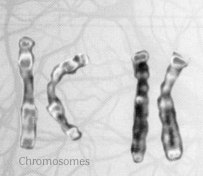

Chromosomes

Hormones and Sexual Development

Everybody develops ovaries except those with H-Y antigen, which is encoded on the Y chromosome. Subsequent sexual differentiation is controlled by testosterone: If it is not present, the female structure automatically develops; if it is present, the male structure develops. During puberty, estradiol feminizes the body, and testosterone masculinizes it.
(Pages 340–347)

Three Cases of Exceptional Human Sexual Development

David Reimer

Sometimes sexual differentiation of the body goes wrong, and some parts do not match the genetic sex. These exceptional cases test current theories of the developmental effects of sex hormones. They pass the test.
(Pages 347–351)

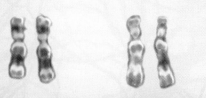

Visual Summary

Effects of Gonadal Hormones on Adults

In both men and women, testosterone is necessary for normal sexual motivation. Estradiol, in contrast, has no obvious motivational effects. (Pages 351–356)

Anabolic steriod use

Neural Mechanisms of Sexual Behavior

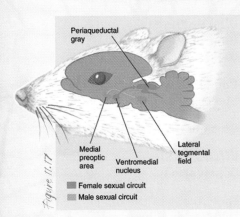

Periaqueductal gray

Medial preoptic area

Ventromedial nucleus

Lateral tegmental field

■ Female sexual circuit
■ Male sexual circuit

Figure 11.17

Most research on the brain mechanisms of sexual behavior has focused on the role of the hypothalamus in the copulatory behavior of laboratory rats. The ventromedial nucleus and the medial preoptic area have been found to be necessary for copulatory behavior of males and females, respectively. (Pages 356–359)

Sexual Orientation, Hormones, and the Brain

Some people are sexually attracted to members of the same sex; others believe that their true sex does not match the sex of their body. Interestingly, sexual orientation and sexual identity do not always go together. Why some people have a sexual identity or a pattern of sexual orientation inconsistent with their physical sex is unknown. (Pages 359–362)

Mianne Bagger after sexual reassignment

Themes Revisited

Three of the book's four major themes were repeatedly emphasized in this chapter. The evolutionary perspective was pervasive because most of the experimental studies of hormones and sex have been conducted in nonhuman species. The other major source of information about hormones and sex has been the study of human clinical cases, which is why the clinical implications theme was also prominent: in the cases of the woman who wasn't, the girl who started to develop a man's body, the twin who lost his penis, and the man who lost and regained his manhood.

The thinking-clearly-about-biopsychology theme was emphasized throughout the chapter because conventional ways of thinking about hormones and sex have often been at odds with the results of biopsychological research. If you are now better able to resist the seductive appeal of the men-are-men-and-women-are-women assumption, you are leaving this chapter a more broadminded and understanding person than when you began it. I hope you have gained an abiding appreciation of the fact that maleness and femaleness are multidimensional and, at times, ambiguous variations of each other.

Think about It

1. The onset of puberty in industrialized countries has changed from age 15 or 16 to age 10 or 11, but there has been no corresponding acceleration in psychological development. Precocious puberty is like a loaded gun in the hand of a child. Discuss.

2. Do you think adult sex-change operations should be permitted? Explain.

3. What should be done about the current epidemic of anabolic steroid abuse?

4. What treatment should be given to infants born with ambiguous external genitals? Why?

5. Sexual orientation, sexual identity, and body type are not always related. Discuss and provide evidence.

6. Heterosexuality cannot be understood without studying homosexuality. Discuss.

chapter 12

Sleep, Dreaming, and Circadian Rhythms
How Much Do You Need to Sleep?

Most of us have a fondness for eating and sex—the two highly esteemed motivated behaviors discussed in Chapters 10 and 11. But the amount of time devoted to these behaviors by even the most amorous gourmands pales in comparison to the amount of time spent sleeping: Most of us will sleep for well over 175,000 hours in our lifetimes.

This extraordinary commitment of time implies that sleep fulfills a critical biological function. But what is it? And what about dreaming: Why do we spend so much time dreaming? And why do we tend to get sleepy at about the same time every day? Answers to these questions await you in this chapter.

Almost every time I give a lecture about sleep, somebody asks "How much sleep do we need?" and each time, I provide the same unsatisfying answer. I explain that there are two fundamentally different answers to this question, but that neither has emerged a clear winner. One answer stresses the presumed health-promoting and recuperative powers of sleep and suggests that people need as much sleep as they can comfortably get. The other answer is that many of us sleep more than we need to and are consequently sleeping part of our lives away. Just think how your life could change if you slept 5 hours per night instead of 8. You would have an extra 21 waking hours each week, a mind-boggling 10,952 hours each decade.

As I prepared to write this chapter, I began to think of some of the personal implications of the idea that we get more sleep than we need. That is when I decided to do something a bit unconventional. While I write this chapter, I am going to be your subject in a sleep-reduction experiment. I am going to try to get no more than 5 hours of sleep per night—11:00 P.M. to 4:00 A.M.—until the first draft of this chapter is written. As I begin, I am excited by the prospect of having more time to write, but a little worried that this extra time might be obtained at a personal cost that is too dear.

It is now the next day—4:50 Saturday morning to be exact—and I am just beginning to write. There was a party last night, and I didn't make it to bed by 11:00; but considering that I slept for only 3 hours and 35 minutes, I feel quite good. I wonder what I will feel like later in the day. In any case, I will report my experiences to you at the end of the chapter.

The following case study challenges several common beliefs about sleep. Ponder its implications before proceeding into the body of the chapter.

The Case of the Woman Who Wouldn't Sleep

Miss M . . . is a busy lady who finds her ration of twenty-three hours of wakefulness still insufficient for her needs. Even though she is now retired she is still busy in the community, helping sick friends whenever requested. She is an active painter and . . . writer. Although she becomes tired physically, when she needs to sit down to rest her legs, she does not ever report feeling sleepy. During the night she sits on her bed . . . reading, writing, crocheting or painting. At about 2:00 A.M. she falls asleep without any preceding drowsiness often while still holding a book in her hands. When she wakes about an hour later, she feels as wide awake as ever. It would be wrong to say that she woke refreshed because she did not complain of tiredness in the first place.

To test her claim we invited her along to the laboratory. She came willingly but on the first evening we hit our first snag. She announced that she did not sleep at all if she had interesting things to do, and by her reckoning a visit to a university sleep laboratory counted as very interesting. Moreover, for the first time in years, she had someone to talk to for the whole of the night. So we talked.

In the morning we broke into shifts so that some could sleep while at least one person stayed with her and entertained her during the next day. The second night was a repeat performance of the first night. . . . Things had not gone according to plan. So far we were very impressed by her cheerful response to two nights of sleep deprivation, but we had very little by way of hard data to show others.

In the end we prevailed upon her to allow us to apply EEG electrodes and to leave her sitting comfortably on the bed in the bedroom. She had promised that she would co-operate by not resisting sleep although she claimed not to be especially tired. . . . At approximately 1:30 A.M., the EEG record showed the first signs of sleep even though . . . she was still sitting with the book in her hands. . . .

The only substantial difference between her sleep and what we might have expected from any other . . . lady was that it was of short duration. . . . [After 99 minutes], she had no further interest in sleep and asked to . . . join our company again.

(From *The Sleep Instinct*, pp. 42–44, by R. Meddis. Copyright © 1977, Routledge & Kegan Paul, London. Reprinted by permission of the Taylor & Francis Group.)

12.1
Physiological and Behavioral Events of Sleep

Many changes occur in the body during sleep. This section introduces you to the major ones.

Three Standard Psychophysiological Measures of Sleep

There are major changes in the human EEG during the course of a night's sleep (Loomis, Harvey, & Hobart, 1936). Although the EEG waves that accompany sleep are generally high-voltage and slow, there are periods throughout the night that are dominated by low-voltage, fast waves similar to those in nonsleeping subjects. In 1953, Aserinsky and Kleitman discovered that *rapid eye movements (REMs)* occur under the closed eyelids of sleeping subjects during these periods of low-voltage, fast EEG activity. And in 1962, Berger and Oswald discovered that there is also a loss of electromyographic activity in the neck muscles during these same sleep periods. Subsequently, the **electroencephalogram (EEG)**, the **electrooculogram (EOG)**, and the neck **electromyogram (EMG)** became the three standard psychophysiological bases for defining stages of sleep (Rechtschaffen & Kales, 1968).

Figure 12.1 is a photo of a subject participating in a sleep experiment. A subject's first night's sleep in a sleep laboratory is often fitful. That's why it is the usual practice to have each subject sleep several nights in the laboratory before commencing a study. The disturbance of sleep observed during the first night in a sleep laboratory is called the *first-night phenomenon*. It is well known to graders of introductory psychology examinations because of the creative definitions of it that are offered by students who forget that it is a sleep-related, rather than a sex-related, phenomenon.

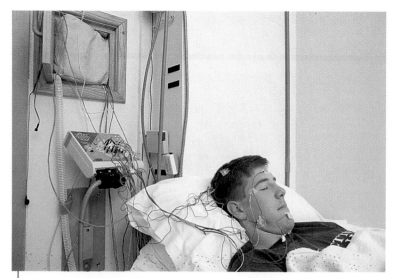

A subject participating in a sleep experiment.

Figure 12.1

Four Stages of Sleep EEG

There are four stages of sleep EEG: stage 1, stage 2, stage 3, and stage 4. Examples of these are presented in Figure 12.2.

After the eyes are shut and a person prepares to go to sleep, **alpha waves**—waxing and waning bursts of 8- to 12-Hz EEG waves—begin to punctuate the low-voltage, high-frequency waves of active wakefulness. Then, as the person falls asleep, there is a sudden transition to a period of stage 1 sleep EEG. The stage 1 sleep EEG is a low-voltage, high-frequency signal that is similar to, but slower than, that of active wakefulness.

There is a gradual increase in EEG voltage and a decrease in EEG frequency as the person progresses from stage 1 sleep through stages 2, 3, and 4. Accordingly, the stage 2 sleep EEG has a slightly higher amplitude and a lower frequency than the stage 1 EEG; in addition, it is punctuated by two characteristic wave forms: K complexes and sleep spindles. Each *K complex* is a single large negative wave (upward deflection) followed immediately by a single large positive wave (downward deflection). Each *sleep spindle* is a 1- to 2-second waxing and waning burst of 12- to 14-Hz waves. The stage 3 sleep EEG is defined by

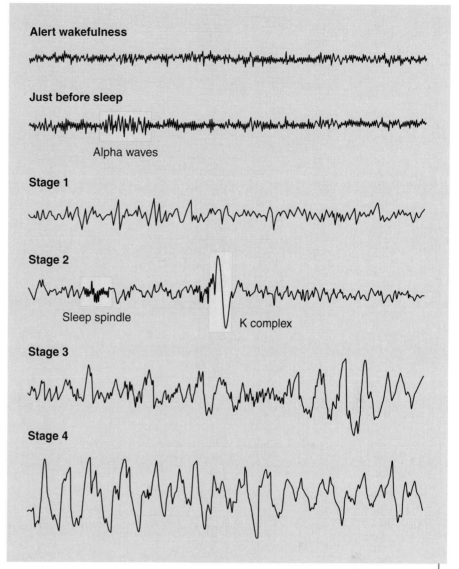

Alert wakefulness

Just before sleep

Alpha waves

Stage 1

Stage 2

Sleep spindle   K complex

Stage 3

Stage 4

The EEG of alert wakefulness, the EEG that precedes sleep onset, and the four stages of sleep EEG. Each trace is about 10 seconds long.

Figure 12.2

the occasional presence of **delta waves**—the largest and slowest EEG waves, with a frequency of 1 to 2 Hz—whereas the stage 4 sleep EEG is defined by a predominance of delta waves.

Once subjects reach stage 4 EEG sleep, they stay there for a time, and then they retreat back through the stages of sleep to stage 1. However, when they return to stage 1, things are not at all the same as they were the first time through. The first period of stage 1 EEG during a night's sleep (**initial stage 1 EEG**) is not marked by any striking electromyographic or electrooculographic changes, whereas subsequent periods of stage 1 sleep EEG (**emergent stage 1 EEG**) are accompanied by REMs and by a loss of tone in the muscles of the body core.

After the first cycle of sleep EEG—from initial stage 1 to stage 4 and back to emergent stage 1—the rest of the night is spent going back and forth through the stages. Figure 12.3 on page 370 illustrates the EEG cycles of a typical night's sleep and the close relation between emergent stage 1 sleep, REMs, and the loss of tone in core muscles. Notice that each cycle tends to be about 90 minutes long and that, as

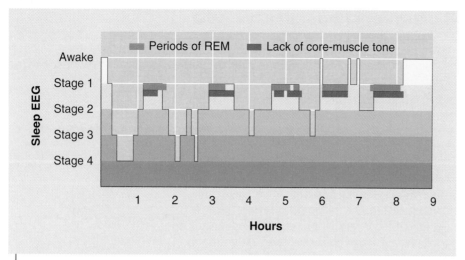

The course of EEG stages during a typical night's sleep and the relation of emergent stage 1 EEG to REMs and lack of tone in core muscles.

Figure 12.3

the night progresses, more and more time is spent in emergent stage 1 sleep, and less and less time is spent in the other stages, particularly stage 4. Notice also that there are brief periods during the night when the subject is awake; the person usually does not remember these periods of wakefulness in the morning.

Let's pause here to get some sleep-stage terms straight. The sleep associated with emergent stage 1 EEG is usually called **REM sleep** (pronounced "rehm"), after the associated rapid eye movements; whereas all other stages of sleep together are called *NREM sleep* (non-REM sleep). Stages 3 and 4 together are often referred to as **slow-wave sleep (SWS)**, after the delta waves that characterize them.

REMs, loss of core-muscle tone, and a low-amplitude, high-frequency EEG are not the only physiological correlates of REM sleep. Cerebral activity (e.g., oxygen consumption, blood flow, and neural firing) increases to waking levels in many brain structures, and there is a general increase in autonomic nervous system activity (e.g., in blood pressure, pulse, and respiration). Also, the muscles of the extremities occasionally twitch, and there is always some degree of clitoral or penile erection.

12.2
REM Sleep and Dreaming

Nathaniel Kleitman's laboratory was an exciting place in 1953. Kleitman's students had just discovered REM sleep, and they were driven by the fascinating implication of their discovery. With the exception of the loss of tone in the core muscles, all of the other measures suggested that REM sleep episodes were emotion-charged. Could REM sleep be the physiological correlate of dreaming? Could it provide researchers with a window into the subjective inner world of dreams? The researchers began by waking a few subjects in the middle of REM episodes and asking them if they had been dreaming. The results were remarkable:

> The vivid recall that could be elicited in the middle of the night when a subject was awakened while his eyes were moving rapidly was nothing short of miraculous. It [seemed to open] . . . an exciting new world to the subjects whose only previous dream memories had been the vague morning-after recall. Now, instead of perhaps some fleeting glimpse into the dream world each night, the subjects could be tuned into the middle of as many as ten or twelve dreams every night. (From *Some Must Watch While Some Must Sleep* by William C. Dement, Portable Stanford Books, Stanford Alumni Association, Stanford University, 1978, p. 37.)

Strong support for the theory that REM sleep is the physiological correlate of dreaming came from the observation that 80% of awakenings from REM sleep but only 7% of awakenings from NREM (non-REM) sleep led to dream recall. The dreams recalled from NREM sleep tended to be individual experiences (e.g., "I was falling"), unlike the stories associated with REM sleep. The phenomenon of dreaming, which for centuries had been the subject of wild speculation, was finally rendered accessible to scientific investigation.

Testing Common Beliefs about Dreaming

The high correlation between REM sleep and dream recall provided an opportunity to test some common beliefs about dreaming. The following are five such beliefs that have been subjected to empirical tests.

1. Many people believe that external stimuli can become incorporated into their dreams. Dement and Wolpert (1958) sprayed water on sleeping subjects after they had been in REM sleep for a few minutes, and a few seconds after the spray, each subject was awakened. In 14 of 33 cases, the water was incorporated into the dream report. The following narrative was reported by a subject who had been dreaming that he was acting in a play:

   > I was walking behind the leading lady when she suddenly collapsed and water was dripping on her. I ran over to her and water was dripping on my back and head. The roof was leaking. . . . I looked up and there was a hole in the roof. I dragged her over to the side of the stage and began pulling the curtains. Then I woke up. (p. 550)

2. Some people believe that dreams last only an instant, but research suggests that dreams run on "real time." In one study (Dement & Kleitman, 1957), subjects were awakened 5 or 15 minutes after the beginning of a REM episode and asked to decide on the basis of the duration of the events in their dreams whether they had been dreaming for 5 or 15 minutes. They were correct in 92 of 111 cases.

3. Some people claim that they do not dream. However, these people have just as much REM sleep as normal dreamers. Moreover, they report dreams if they are awakened during REM episodes (Goodenough et al., 1959), although they do so less frequently than do normal dreamers.

4. Penile erections are commonly assumed to be indicative of dreams with sexual content. However, erections are no more complete during dreams with frank sexual content than during those without it (Karacan et al., 1966). Even babies have REM-related penile erections.

5. Most people believe that sleeptalking and **somnambulism** (sleepwalking) occur during dreams. This is not so; sleeptalking and somnambulism occur least frequently during dreaming, when core muscles tend to be totally relaxed. They occur most frequently during stage 4 sleep.

Interpretation of Dreams

The idea that dreams are disguised messages has a long history. For example, the Bible describes how a dream of seven lean cattle following and devouring seven fat cattle warned that seven years of famine would follow seven years of plenty. It was Sigmund Freud's theory of dreams that refined this view of dreams and gave it legitimacy.

Freud believed that dreams are triggered by unacceptable repressed wishes, often of a sexual nature. He argued that because dreams represent unacceptable wishes, the dreams we experience (our *manifest dreams*) are merely disguised versions of our real dreams (our *latent dreams*): An unconscious censor disguises and subtracts information from our real dreams so that we can endure them. Freud thus concluded that one of the keys to understanding people and dealing with their psychological problems is to expose the meaning of their latent dreams through the interpretation of their manifest dreams.

There is no convincing evidence for the Freudian theory of dreams; indeed, the brain science of the 1890s, which served as its foundation, is now obsolete. Nevertheless, the Freudian theory of dreams has been the basis for many interesting stories; as a result, it continues to be widely disseminated to the general public through the entertainment and communication media as if it were fact.

The modern alternative to the Freudian theory of dreams is Hobson's (1989) activation-synthesis theory. It is based on the observation that, during REM sleep, many brain-stem circuits become active and bombard the cerebral cortex with neural signals. The essence of the **activation-synthesis theory** is that the information supplied to the cortex during REM sleep is largely random and that the resulting dream is the cortex's effort to make sense of these random signals.

Activation-synthesis theory does not deny that dreams have meaning, but it differs from Freudian theory in terms of where that meaning lies. Hobson's dreamers reveal themselves by what they add to the random jumble of brain-stem signals in order to create a coherent story, not by painful hidden messages contained in their dreams.

12.3
Why Do We Sleep, and Why Do We Sleep When We Do?

Now that you have been introduced to the properties of sleep and its various stages, the focus of this chapter shifts to a consideration of two fundamental questions about sleep: Why do we sleep? And why do we sleep when we do? The first question deals with the functions of sleep; the second deals with its timing and duration.

Two kinds of theories for sleep have been proposed: *recuperation theories* and *circadian theories*. The differences between these two theoretical approaches are revealed by the answers they offer to the two fundamental questions about sleep.

The essence of **recuperation theories of sleep** is that being awake disrupts the *homeostasis* (internal physiological stability) of the body in some way and sleep is required to restore it. Various recuperation theories differ in terms of the particular physiological disruption they propose as the trigger for sleep—for example, it is commonly believed that the function of sleep is to restore energy levels. However, regardless of the particular function postulated by restoration theories of sleep, they all imply that sleepiness is triggered by a deviation from homeostasis caused by wakefulness and that sleep is terminated by a return to homeostasis.

The essence of **circadian theories of sleep** is that sleep is not a reaction to the disruptive effects of being awake but the result of an internal timing mechanism—that is, we humans are all programmed to sleep at night regardless of what happens to us during the day. According to these theories, we have evolved to sleep at night because sleep protects us from accident and predation during the night. (Remember that humans evolved long before the advent of artificial lighting.)

The Evolutionary Perspective

Circadian theories of sleep focus more on when we sleep than on the function of sleep. However, one extreme version of a circadian theory proposes that sleep plays no role in the efficient physiological functioning of the body. According to this theory, early humans had enough time to get their eating, drinking, and reproducing out of the way during the daytime, and their strong motivation to sleep at night evolved to conserve their energy resources and to make them less susceptible to mishap (e.g., predation) in the dark. This theory suggests that sleep is like reproductive behavior in the sense that we are highly motivated to engage in it, but we don't need it to stay healthy.

Choosing between the recuperation and circadian approaches is the logical first step in the search for the physiological basis of sleep. Is the sleep system run by a biological clock that produces compelling urges to sleep at certain times of the day, perhaps to conserve energy and protect us from mishap; or is it a homeostatic system whose function is to correct some adverse consequence of staying awake? Or is it a combination of the two? Several lines of research that have a bearing on the answer to this question are discussed in the sections that follow.

Comparative Analysis of Sleep

The Evolutionary Perspective

All mammals and birds sleep, and their sleep is much like ours—characterized by high-amplitude, low-frequency EEG waves punctuated by periods of low-amplitude, high-frequency waves (see Winson, 1993). Even fish, reptiles, amphibians, and insects go through periods of inactivity and unresponsiveness that are similar to mammalian sleep (e.g., Shaw et al., 2000). Table 12.1 gives the average number of hours per day that various mammalian species spend sleeping.

The comparative investigation of sleep has led to several important conclusions. Let's consider four of these.

First, the fact that all mammals and birds sleep suggests that sleep serves some important physiological function, rather than merely protecting animals from mishap and conserving energy. The evidence is strongest in species that are at increased risk of predation when they sleep (e.g., antelopes) and in species that have evolved complex mechanisms that enable them to sleep. For example, some marine mammals, such as dolphins, sleep with only half of their brain at a time so that the other half can control resurfacing for air (see Rattenborg, Amlaner, & Lima, 2000). It is against the logic of natural selection for some animals to risk predation while sleeping and for others to have evolved complex mechanisms to permit them to sleep safely unless sleep itself serves some critical function (Rechtschaffen, 1998).

Second, the fact that all mammals and birds sleep suggests that the function of sleep is not some special, higher-order human function. For example, suggestions that sleep helps humans reprogram our complex brains or that it permits some kind of emotional release to maintain our mental health are incompatible with the comparative evidence.

Third, the large between-species differences in sleep time suggest that although sleep may be essential for survival, it is not necessarily needed in large quantities (refer to Table 12.1). Horses and many other animals get by quite nicely on 2 or 3 hours of sleep per day.

Fourth, many studies have tried to identify some characteristic that identifies various species as long sleepers or short sleepers. Why do cats tend to sleep about 14 hours a day and horses only about 2? Under the influence of recuperation theories, researchers have focused on energy-related factors in their efforts. However, there is no clear relationship between a species' sleep time and its level of activity, its body size, or its body temperature. The fact that giant sloths sleep 20 hours per day is a strong argument against the theory that sleep is a compensatory

Table 12.1

Average Number of Hours Slept per Day by Various Mammalian Species	
MAMMALIAN SPECIES	HOURS OF SLEEP PER DAY
Giant sloth	20
Opossum, brown bat	19
Giant armadillo	18
Owl monkey, nine-banded armadillo	17
Arctic ground squirrel	16
Tree shrew	15
Cat, golden hamster	14
Mouse, rat, gray wolf, ground squirrel	13
Arctic fox, chinchilla, gorilla, raccoon	12
Mountain beaver	11
Jaguar, vervet monkey, hedgehog	10
Rhesus monkey, chimpanzee, baboon, red fox	9
Human, rabbit, guinea pig, pig	8
Gray seal, gray hyrax, Brazilian tapir	6
Tree hyrax, rock hyrax	5
Cow, goat, elephant, donkey, sheep	3
Roe deer, horse	2

After gorging themselves on a kill, African lions often sleep almost continuously for 2 or 3 days. And where do they sleep? Anywhere they want!

Figure 12.4

reaction to energy expenditure. In contrast, circadian theories correctly predict that the daily sleep duration of each species is related to how vulnerable it is while it is asleep and how much time it must spend each day to feed itself and to take care of its other survival requirements. For example, zebras must graze almost continuously to get enough to eat and are extremely vulnerable to predatory attack when they are asleep—and they sleep only about 2 hours per day. In contrast, African lions often sleep more or less continuously for 2 or 3 days after they have gorged themselves on a kill. Figure 12.4 says it all.

12.5
Circadian Sleep Cycles

The world in which we live cycles from light to dark and back again once every 24 hours, and most surface-dwelling species have adapted to this regular change in their environment by developing a variety of so-called **circadian rhythms** (see Foster & Kreitzman, 2004). (*Circadian* means "lasting about 1 day.") For example, most species display a regular circadian sleep–wake cycle. Humans take advantage of the light of day to take care of their biological needs, and then they sleep for much of the night; *nocturnal animals*, such as rats, sleep for much of the day and stay awake at night.

Although the sleep–wake cycle is the most obvious circadian rhythm, it is virtually impossible to find a physiological, biochemical, or behavioral process in animals that does not display some measure of circadian rhythmicity. Each day, our bodies adjust themselves in a variety of ways to meet the demands of the two environments in which we live: light and dark.

Our circadian cycles are kept on their once-every-24-hours schedule by temporal cues in the environment. The most important of these cues for the regulation of mammalian circadian rhythms is the daily cycle of light and dark. Environmental cues, such as the light–dark cycle, that can *entrain* (control the timing of) circadian rhythms are called **zeitgebers** (pronounced "ZITE-gay-bers"), a German word that means "time givers."

In controlled laboratory environments, it is possible to lengthen or shorten circadian cycles by adjusting the duration of the light–dark cycle; for example, when exposed to alternating 10-hour periods of light and 10-hour periods of dark, subjects' circadian cycles begin to conform to a 20-hour day. In a world without 24-hour cycles of light and dark, other *zeitgebers* can entrain circadian cycles. For example, the circadian sleep–wake cycles of hamsters living in continuous darkness or in continuous light can be entrained by regular daily bouts of social interaction, hoarding, eating, or exercise (see Mistlberger, 1994; Mistlberger et al., 1996; Sinclair & Mistlberger, 1997). Hamsters display particularly clear circadian cycles and thus are frequent subjects of research on circadian rhythms.

Free-Running Circadian Sleep–Wake Cycles

The study of sleep in the absence of *zeitgebers* provides a powerful method for studying regulation of the temporal pattern of sleep. What happens to sleep–wake cycles

A free-running circadian sleep–wake cycle 25.3 hours in duration. Despite living in an unchanging environment with no time cues, the subject went to sleep each day approximately 1.3 hours later than he had the day before. (Adapted from Wever, 1979, p. 30.)

Figure 12.5

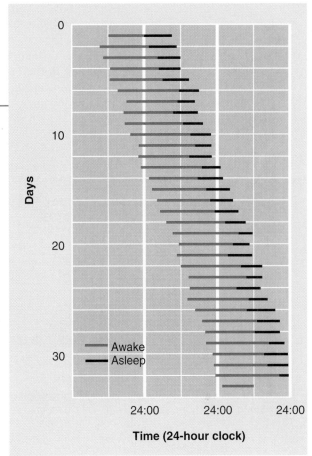

and other circadian rhythms in an environment that is devoid of *zeitgebers*? Remarkably, under conditions in which there are absolutely no temporal cues, humans and other animals maintain all of their circadian rhythms. Circadian rhythms in constant environments are said to be **free-running rhythms**, and their duration is called the **free-running period**. Free-running periods vary in length from subject to subject, are of relatively constant duration within a given subject, and are usually longer than 24 hours—about 25 hours in most humans (see Lavie, 2001). It seems that we all have an internal *biological clock* that habitually runs a little slow unless it is entrained by time-related cues in the environment. A typical free-running circadian sleep–wake cycle is illustrated in Figure 12.5. Notice its regularity. Without any external cues, this man fell asleep approximately every 25.3 hours for an entire month.

Perhaps the most remarkable characteristic of free-running circadian cycles is that they do not have to be learned. Even rats that are born and raised in an unchanging laboratory environment (in continuous light or in continuous darkness) display regular free-running sleep–wake cycles of about 25 hours (Richter, 1971).

So, what has research on circadian sleep–wake cycles taught us about the function of sleep? The fact that the regularity of the free-running period of such cycles is maintained despite day-to-day variations in physical and mental activity provides strong support for the dominance of circadian factors over recuperative factors in the regulation of sleep. Indeed, there have been several attempts to change the timing of sleep in both human and nonhuman subjects by having them engage in intensive physical or mental activity or by exposing them to infectious agents, but these attempts have had little, if any, effect on the subjects' subsequent sleep (see Rechtschaffen, 1998).

Jet Lag and Shift Work

People in modern industrialized societies are faced with two different disruptions of circadian rhythmicity: jet lag and shift work (see Figure 12.6). **Jet lag** occurs when the

The effects of shift work. Disruptions of a person's circadian rhythms, particularly when coupled with sleep loss, adversely affect performance. Would you want this physician to treat you while she is in this condition?

Figure 12.6

zeitgebers that control the phases of various circadian rhythms are accelerated during east-bound flights (*phase advances*) or decelerated during west-bound flights (*phase delays*). In *shift work*, the *zeitgebers* stay the same, but workers are forced to adjust their natural sleep–wake cycles in order to meet the demands of changing work schedules. Both of these disruptions produce sleep disturbances, fatigue, general malaise, and deficits on tests of physical and cognitive function. The disturbances can last for many days; for example, it typically takes about 10 days to completely adjust to a Tokyo-to-Boston flight—a phase advance of 10.5 hours.

It is a bit disturbing to consider that many difficult and dangerous jobs are routinely performed by people experiencing circadian disruptions: for example, pilots, emergency room personnel, and long-distance truck drivers. In fact, circadian disruptions have been implicated in several major human-made disasters: the *Challenger* space shuttle explosion, the Union Carbide chemical disaster in Bhopal, the *Exxon-Valdez* oil spill, and both the Three Mile Island and the Chernobyl reactor meltdowns.

What can be done to reduce the disruptive effects of jet lag and shift work? Two behavioral approaches have been proposed for the reduction of jet lag. One is gradually shifting one's sleep–wake cycle in the days prior to the flight. The other is administering treatments after the flight that promote the required shift in the circadian rhythm. For example, exposure to intense light early in the morning following an east-bound flight accelerates adaptation to the phase advance. Similarly, the results of a study of hamsters (Mrosovsky & Salmon, 1987) suggest that a good workout early in the morning of the first day after an east-bound flight might accelerate adaptation to the phase advance; hamsters that engaged in one 3-hour bout of wheel running 7 hours before their usual period of activity adapted quickly to an 8-hour advance in their light-dark cycle (see Figure 12.7).

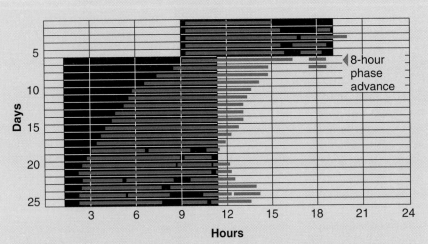

Hamsters were active each day during the 10-hour dark phase of their light-dark cycle (activity shown in red and darkness shown in black). Then, the light-dark cycle was advanced by 8 hours. The hamster circadian activity cycle gradually adapted to the phase advance over the ensuing 10 days.

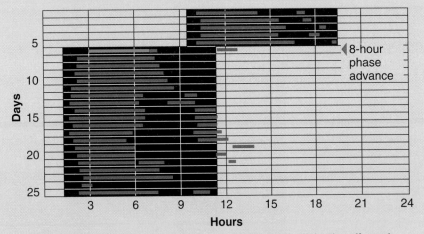

Hamsters that were forced to run in a running wheel on the day of the phase advance, 7 hours prior to their normal activity time (forced running shown in green), adapted to the phase advance in 1 day.

A period of forced exercise accelerates adaptation to an 8-hour phase advance in the circadian light–dark cycle. Daily activity is shown in red; periods of darkness are shown in black; and the period of forced exercise is shown in green. (Adapted from Mrosovsky & Salmon, 1987.)

Figure 12.7

Companies that employ shift workers have had great success in improving the productivity and job satisfaction of those workers by scheduling phase delays rather than phase advances; whenever possible, shift workers are transferred from their current schedule to one that begins later in the day. It is much more difficult to go to sleep 4 hours earlier and get up 4 hours earlier (a phase advance) than it is to go to sleep 4 hours later and get up 4 hours later (a phase delay). That is why east-bound flights tend to be more problematic for travelers than west-bound flights.

12.6
Effects of Sleep Deprivation

Recuperation theories of sleep make specific predictions about the effects of sleep deprivation. Because recuperation theories are based on the premise that sleep is a response to the accumulation of some debilitating effect of wakefulness, they predict (1) that long periods of wakefulness will produce physiological and behavioral disturbances, (2) that these disturbances will grow steadily worse as the sleep deprivation continues, and (3) that after a period of deprivation has ended, much of the missed sleep will be regained. Have these predictions been confirmed?

This section begins with a cautionary note about the personal experience of sleep deprivation. It next presents two classic sleep-deprivation case studies. Then, the major findings of sleep-deprivation studies in humans and laboratory animals are summarized.

Personal Experience of Sleep Deprivation: A Cautionary Note

I am sure that you have experienced the negative effects of sleep deprivation. When you sleep substantially less than you are used to, the next day you feel crabby and unable to function as well as you usually do. Although such experiences of sleep deprivation are compelling, you need to be cautious in interpreting your own experiences and the similar experiences of others. Let me illustrate this point by referring to a recurring news story.

Every few months, I see on the television news or read in the newspaper that most people need more sleep. To support this contention, an "expert" explains that many people in modern society work such long, irregular hours that they do not sleep enough and suffer all kinds of adverse effects as a result. To make this point, there are typically a few interviews with people such as long-distance truck drivers and shift workers who describe their sleep-related experiences. Two things never seem to occur to the news reporters or to the "expert." First, it never occurs to them that most people in our culture who sleep little or irregularly do so because they are under stress. Second, it never occurs to them that people who are forced to change their schedule of sleep also experience a major disruption of their circadian rhythms. Accordingly, stress and circadian disruptions might be responsible for, or at least contribute to, many of the adverse effects commonly attributed to loss of sleep (see Taub & Berger, 1973).

Compounding this problem of interpretation is the fact that people have proven to be poor judges of the impact of sleep deprivation on their performance. Both types of errors have been reported: In some cases, people claim that they cannot function after sleep loss but perform without decrement; in other cases, people claim that sleep loss has not adversely affected their performance when the data tell a different story.

Thinking Clearly

Consequently, your own experiences of sleep loss and the testimonials of others who have experienced sleep loss need to be interpreted cautiously. Determining the effects of sleep loss requires systematic research.

Two Classic Sleep-Deprivation Case Studies

Let's begin our consideration of the research on sleep deprivation by looking at two classic case studies. First is the case study of a group of sleep-deprived students, described by Kleitman (1963); second is the case of Randy Gardner, described by Dement (1978).

The Case of the Sleep-Deprived Students

While there were differences in the many subjective experiences of the sleep-evading persons, there were several features common to most. . . . [D]uring the first night the subject did not feel very tired or sleepy. He could read or study or do laboratory work, without much attention from the watcher, but usually felt an attack of drowsiness between 3 A.M. and 6 A.M. . . . Next morning the subject felt well, except for a slight malaise which always appeared on sitting down and resting for any length of time. However, if he occupied himself with his ordinary daily tasks, he was likely to forget having spent a sleepless night. During the second night . . . reading or study was next to impossible because sitting quietly was conducive to even greater sleepiness. As during the first night, there came a 2–3 hour period in the early hours of the morning when the desire for sleep was almost overpowering. . . . Later in the morning the sleepiness diminished once more, and the subject could perform routine laboratory work, as usual. It was not safe for him to sit down, however, without danger of falling asleep, particularly if he attended lectures. . . .

The third night resembled the second, and the fourth day was like the third. . . . At the end of that time the individual was as sleepy as he was likely to be. Those who continued to stay awake experienced the wavelike increase and decrease in sleepiness with the greatest drowsiness at about the same time every night. (Kleitman, 1963, pp. 220–221)

The Case of Randy Gardner

As part of a 1965 science fair project, Randy Gardner and two classmates, who were entrusted with keeping him awake, planned to break the then world record of 260 hours of consecutive wakefulness. Dement read about the project in the newspaper and, seeing an opportunity to collect some important data, joined the team, much to the comfort of Randy' s worried parents. Randy proved to be a friendly and cooperative subject, although he did complain vigorously when his team would not permit him to close his eyes for more than a few seconds at a time. However, in no sense could Randy' s behavior be considered abnormal or disturbed. Near the end of his vigil, Randy held a press conference attended by reporters and television crews from all over the United States, and he conducted himself impeccably. When asked how he had managed to stay awake for 11 days, he replied politely, "It' s just mind over matter." Randy went to sleep exactly 264 hours and 12 minutes after his alarm clock had awakened him 11 days before. And how long did he sleep? Only 14 hours the first night, and thereafter he returned to his usual 8-hour schedule. Although it may seem amazing that Randy did not have to sleep longer to "catch up" on his lost sleep, the lack of substantial recovery sleep is typical of such cases (Dement, 1978).

Mrs. Maureen Weston later supplanted Randy Gardner in the *Guinness Book of World Records*. During a rocking-chair marathon in 1977, Mrs. Weston kept rocking for 449 hours (18 days, 17 hours)—an impressive bit of "rocking around the clock." By the way, my own modest program of sleep reduction is now in its 10th day.

Experimental Studies of Sleep Deprivation in Humans

Investigations have assessed the effects on human subjects of sleep-deprivation schedules ranging from a slightly reduced amount of sleep during one night to total sleep deprivation for several nights, and they have assessed the effects of these schedules on dozens of different objective measures: measures of sleepiness, mood, cognition, motor performance, and physiological function.

Even moderate amounts of sleep deprivation—for example, 3 or 4 hours in one night—have been found to have three consistent effects. First, sleep-deprived subjects display an increase in sleepiness: They report being more sleepy, and they fall asleep more quickly if given the opportunity. Second, sleep-deprived subjects display disturbances on various written tests of mood. And third, they perform poorly on tests of vigilance, such as listening to a series of tones and responding when one differs slightly from the rest.

After 2 or 3 days of continuous sleep deprivation, subjects often experience microsleeps. **Microsleeps** are brief periods of sleep, typically about 2 or 3 seconds long, during which the eyelids droop and the subjects become less responsive to external stimuli, even though they can remain sitting or standing. Microsleeps disrupt performance on passive tests, such as tests of vigilance, but they are not necessary for such performance deficits to occur (Dinges et al., 1997; Ferrara, De Gennaro, & Bertini, 1999).

Remarkably, the effects of sleep deprivation on complex cognitive function, motor performance, and physiological function have been inconsistent. Deficits have been observed in some studies but not in others, even after lengthy periods of deprivation (e.g., Bonnet & Arand, 1996; Dinges et al., 1997; Gillberg et al., 1996; Harrison & Horne, 1997). For example, Martin (1986) concluded that adverse physiological changes following sleep deprivation have yet to be convincingly documented; Van-Helder and Radomski (1989) found that periods of sleep deprivation lasting up to 72 hours had no effect on physical strength or motor performance, except for reducing time to exhaustion; and active tests of complex cognitive ability (such as IQ tests) have proven to be largely immune to disruption by sleep deprivation (Binks, Waters, & Hurry, 1999; Percival, Horne, & Tilley, 1983). It should be pointed out, however, that although performance on intelligence tests is influenced little by sleep deprivation, Horne (1983) found that 32 hours of sleep deprivation greatly disrupted subjects' performance on several tests expressly designed to measure creativity.

To put sleep deprivation in perspective, I like to compare it to deprivation of the motivated behaviors discussed in Chapters 10 and 11. If subjects were deprived of the opportunity to eat or engage in sexual activity, the effects would be severe and unavoidable: In the first case, starvation and death would ensue; in the second, there would be a total loss of reproductive capacity. There have been no such dramatic effects reported in sleep-deprivation studies. Indeed, as you will soon learn, none of the three major predictions of the recuperation approach to understanding sleep has been confirmed.

Thinking Clearly

Sleep-Deprivation Studies with Laboratory Animals

The Evolutionary Perspective

Studies using a **carousel apparatus** (see Figure 12.8 on page 380) to deprive rats of sleep suggest that sleep deprivation may not be as inconsequential as the research

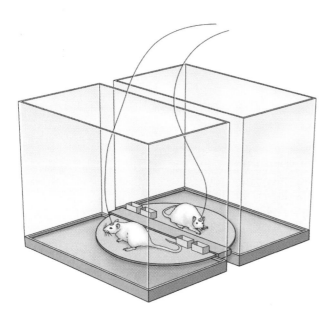

The carousel apparatus used to deprive an experimental rat of sleep while a yoked control rat is exposed to the same number and pattern of disk rotations. The disk on which both rats rest rotates every time the experimental rat has a sleep EEG. If the sleeping rat does not awaken immediately, it is deposited in the water.

(Adapted from Rechtschaffen et al., 1993.)

Figure 12.8

on human subjects suggests. The carousel apparatus is designed so that sleep-deprivation experiments can be conducted with a *yoked control* condition. Here is how it works. Two rats, an experimental rat and its *yoked control rat*, are placed in separate chambers of the apparatus. Each time the EEG activity of the experimental rat indicates that it is sleeping, the disk, which serves as the floor of half of both chambers, starts to slowly rotate. As a result, if the sleeping experimental rat does not awaken immediately, it gets shoved off the disk into a shallow pool of water. The yoked control is exposed to exactly the same pattern of disk rotations; but if it is not sleeping, it can easily avoid getting dunked by walking in the direction opposite to the direction of disk rotation. The experimental rats typically died after several days, while the yoked controls stayed reasonably healthy (see Rechtschaffen & Bergmann, 1995).

The fact that human subjects have been sleep-deprived for similar periods of time without dire consequences argues for caution in interpreting the results of the carousel sleep-deprivation experiments. It may be that repeatedly being awakened by the moving platform or, worse yet, being plunged into water while sleeping kills the experimental rats not because it keeps them from sleeping but because it is very stressful and physically damaging. This interpretation is consistent with the pathological symptoms that were revealed in the experimental rats by postmortem examination: for example, swollen adrenal glands, gastric ulcers, and internal bleeding. Indeed, it may not be possible to study the effects of sleep deprivation in nonhumans adequately because of the unavoidable confounding effects of extreme stress (see Benington & Heller, 1999; D'Almeida et al., 1997; Horne, 2000).

REM-Sleep Deprivation

Because of its association with dreaming, REM sleep has been the subject of intensive investigation. In an effort to reveal the particular functions of REM sleep, sleep researchers have specifically deprived sleeping subjects of REM sleep by waking them up each time a bout of REM sleep begins.

REM-sleep deprivation has been shown to have two consistent effects (see Figure 12.9). First, with each successive night of deprivation, there is a greater tendency for subjects to initiate REM sequences. Thus, as REM-sleep deprivation proceeds, subjects have to be awakened more and more frequently to keep them from accumulating significant amounts of REM sleep. For example, during the first night of REM-sleep deprivation in one experiment (Webb & Agnew, 1967), the subjects had to be awakened 17 times to keep them from having extended periods of REM sleep; but during the seventh night of deprivation, they had to be awakened 67 times. Second, following REM-sleep deprivation, subjects display a *REM rebound*; that is, they have more than their usual amount of REM sleep for the first two or three nights (Brunner et al., 1990).

The compensatory increase in REM sleep following a period of REM-sleep deprivation suggests that the amount of REM sleep is regulated separately from the amount of slow-wave sleep and that REM sleep serves a special function. Numerous theories of the functions of REM sleep have been proposed (see Webb, 1973; Winson, 1993). Most of them fall into one of three categories: (1) those that hypothesize that REM sleep is necessary for the maintenance of an individual's mental health, (2) those that hypothesize that REM sleep is necessary for the maintenance of normal levels of motivation, and (3) those that hypothesize that REM sleep is necessary for the processing of memories. None of these theories has emerged a clear winner. Reports that REM-sleep deprivation produces a variety of personality and motivational problems (e.g., Dement, 1960) have not proved replicable, and more recent reports that REM-sleep deprivation produces memory deficits for certain kinds of material learned the preceding day (see Hobson & Pace-Schott, 2002), while promising, are still controversial (see Maquet, 2001; Siegel, 2001).

One challenge faced by any theory of the function of REM sleep is to explain why **tricyclic antidepressant drugs** are not severely debilitating. Because tricyclic antidepressants selectively block REM sleep, patients who regularly take large doses (e.g., for depression) get little REM sleep for months at a time—and yet they experience no serious side effects from this REM-sleep loss. Another finding that is not addressed by most theories of REM sleep is that it is most prevalent in the weeks just before and after birth.

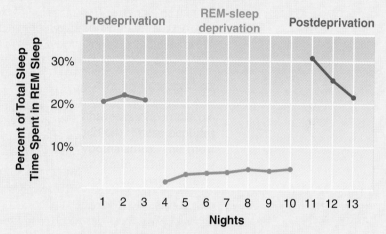

The number of awakenings required to deprive a subject of REM sleep increases as the period of deprivation ensues.

After a period of REM-sleep deprivation, subjects spend a greater than usual portion of their sleep time in REM sleep.

The two effects of REM-sleep deprivation.

Figure 12.9

One recent theory about REM sleep is based on the premise that this type of sleep serves no critical function: This is the *default theory of REM sleep* (Horne, 2000). According to this theory, it is difficult to stay continuously in NREM sleep, so the brain periodically switches to one of two other states. If there is any immediate bodily need to take care of (e.g., eating or drinking), the brain switches to wakefulness; if there are no immediate needs, it switches to the default state— REM sleep. According to the default theory, REM sleep and wakefulness are similar states, but REM sleep is more adaptive when there are no immediate bodily needs. Indirect support for this theory comes from the many similarities between REM sleep and wakefulness. For example, you have already learned about the high levels of neural activity, rapid heart rate, and high blood pressure that characterize REM sleep, and it has been found that subjects awaken easily and quickly from REM sleep (see Horne, 2000).

A study by Nycamp and colleagues (1998) provides more direct support for the default theory of REM sleep. These researchers awakened subjects every time they entered REM sleep, but instead of letting them go back to sleep immediately, the researchers substituted a 15-minute period of wakefulness for each lost REM period. Under these conditions, the subjects, unlike the controls, were not tired the next day, despite getting only 5 hours of sleep, and they displayed no REM rebound. In other words, there seemed to be no need for REM sleep if periods of wakefulness were substituted for it. This is consistent with the finding that as antidepressants reduce REM sleep, the number of nighttime awakenings increases (see Horne, 2000).

Sleep Deprivation Increases the Efficiency of Sleep

One of the most important findings of human sleep-deprivation research is that individuals who are deprived of sleep become more efficient sleepers. In particular, their sleep has a higher proportion of slow-wave sleep (stages 3 and 4), which seems to serve the main restorative function. Because this is such an important idea, let's take a look at six major pieces of evidence that support it.

ON THE CD

In the *Good Morning* module, the camera catches Pinel arriving at his office at 6:00 A.M. He discusses a common misconception about sleep.

First, although subjects regain only a small proportion of their total lost sleep after a period of sleep deprivation, they regain most of their lost stage 4 sleep (e.g., Borbély et al., 1981; De Gennaro, Ferrara, & Bertini, 2000; Lucidi et al., 1997). Second, after sleep deprivation, the slow-wave sleep EEG of humans is characterized by an even higher proportion than usual of slow waves (Borbély, 1981; Borbély et al., 1981). Third, short sleepers normally get as much slow-wave sleep as long sleepers do (e.g., Jones & Oswald, 1966; Webb & Agnew, 1970). Fourth, if subjects take an extra nap in the morning after a full night's sleep, their naptime EEG shows few slow waves, and the nap does not reduce the duration of the following night's sleep (e.g., Åkerstedt & Gillberg, 1981; Hume & Mills, 1977; Karacan et al., 1970). Fifth, subjects who gradually reduce their usual sleep time get less stage 1 and stage 2 sleep, but the duration of their slow-wave sleep remains about the same as before (Mullaney et al., 1977; Webb & Agnew, 1975). And sixth, repeatedly waking subjects up during REM sleep produces little, if any, increase in the sleepiness they experience the next day, whereas repeatedly waking subjects up during slow-wave sleep has major effects (Nykamp et al., 1998).

Thinking Clearly

The fact that sleep becomes more efficient in people who sleep less has an extremely important implication: It means that conventional sleep-deprivation studies are virtually useless for discovering how much humans need to sleep. The negative consequences of sleep loss in inefficient sleepers do not indicate whether the lost sleep was really needed; the true need for sleep can be assessed only by experiments in which sleep is regularly reduced for many weeks, to give the subjects an opportunity to adapt to less sleep by increasing their sleep to its maximal efficiency. Only when people are sleeping at their maximal efficiency is it possible to determine how much sleep they really need. Such sleep-reduction studies are discussed later in the chapter, but please pause here to think about this point; it is an extremely important one.

It is an appropriate time, here at the end of the section on sleep deprivation, for me to file a brief progress report. It has now been 2 weeks since I began my 5-hours-per-night sleep schedule. Generally, things are going well. My progress on this chapter has been faster than usual. I am not having any difficulty getting up on time or getting my work done, but I am finding that it takes a major effort to stay awake in the evening. If I try to read or watch a bit of television after 10:30, I experience microsleeps. Luckily for me, my so-called friends and loved ones delight in making sure that my transgressions last no more than a few seconds.

Scan your Brain

Before continuing with this chapter, scan your brain by completing the following exercise to make sure you understand the fundamentals of sleep. The correct answers are provided below. Before proceeding, review material related to your errors and omissions.

1. The three most commonly studied psychophysiological correlates of sleep are the EEG, EMG, and _____.

2. Stage 4 sleep EEG is characterized by a predominance of _____ waves.

3. _____ stage 1 EEG is accompanied by neither REM nor loss of core-muscle tone.

4. Dreaming occurs predominantly during _____ sleep.

5. The modern alternative to Freud's theory of dreaming is Hobson's _____ theory.

6. Environmental cues that can entrain circadian rhythms are called _____, or time givers.

7. In contrast to the prediction of the recuperation theories of sleep, when a subject stays awake longer than usual under free-running conditions, the following period of sleep tends to be _____.

8. The most convincing evidence that REM-sleep deprivation is not seriously debilitating comes from the study of patients taking _____.

9. After a lengthy period of sleep deprivation (e.g., several days), a subject's first night of sleep is only slightly longer than usual, but it contains a much higher proportion of _____ waves.

10. _____ sleep in particular, rather than sleep in general, appears to play the major recuperative role.

Scan Your Brain answers: (1) EOG, (2) delta, (3) Initial, (4) REM, (5) activation-synthesis, (6) zeitgebers, (7) shorter, (8) tricyclic antidepressants, (9) slow (or delta), (10) Slow-wave (or Stages 3 and 4).

12.7
Four Areas of the Brain Involved in Sleep

In this section, you will be introduced to four areas of the brain that are involved in sleep. You will learn more about some of them in the later section on sleep disorders.

Two Areas of the Hypothalamus Involved in Sleep

It is remarkable that two areas of the brain that are involved in the regulation of sleep were discovered early in the 20th century, long before the advent of modern behavioral neuroscience. The discovery was made by Baron Constantin von Economo, a Viennese neurologist.

The Case of Constantin von Economo, the Insightful Neurologist

During World War I, the world was swept by a serious viral infection of the brain: *encephalitis lethargica*. Many of its victims slept almost continuously. Baron Constantin von Economo discovered that the brains of

Clinical Implications

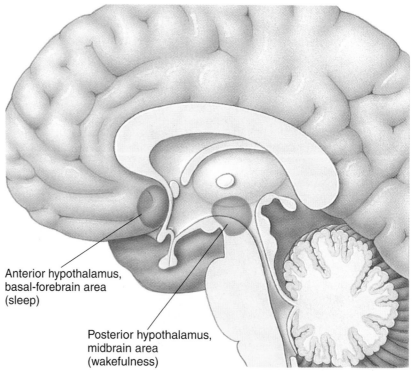

Anterior hypothalamus,
basal-forebrain area
(sleep)

Posterior hypothalamus,
midbrain area
(wakefulness)

Two regions of the brain involved in sleep. The anterior hypothalamus
and adjacent basal forebrain are thought to promote sleep; the
posterior hypothalamus and adjacent midbrain are thought to promote
wakefulness.

Figure 12.10

deceased victims who had problems with excessive sleep all had damage in
the *posterior hypothalamus* and adjacent parts of the midbrain. He then
turned his attention to the brains of a small group of victims of encephalitis lethargica who had had the opposite sleep-related problem: In contrast
to most victims, they had difficulty sleeping. He found that the brains of the
deceased victims in this minority always had damage in the *anterior hypothalamus* and adjacent parts of the basal forebrain. On the basis of these
clinical observations, von Economo concluded that the posterior hypothalamus promotes wakefulness, whereas the preoptic area promotes sleep.

Since von Economo's discovery of the involvement of the posterior hypothalamus
and the anterior hypothalamus in human wakefulness and sleep, respectively, that involvement has been confirmed by lesion studies in experimental animals (see Saper,
Chou, & Scammell, 2001). The locations of the posterior and anterior hypothalamus
are shown in Figure 12.10.

Reticular Activating System and Sleep

*The Evolutionary
Perspective*

Another area involved in sleep was discovered through the comparison of the effects of two different brain-stem transections in cats. First, in 1936, Bremer severed
the brain stems of cats between their *inferior colliculi* and *superior colliculi* in order
to disconnect their forebrains from ascending sensory input (see Figure 12.11). This
surgical preparation is called a **cerveau isolé preparation** (pronounced "ser-VOE
ees-o-LAY"—literally, "isolated forebrain").

Bremer found that the cortical EEG of the isolated cat forebrains was indicative
of almost continuous slow-wave sleep. Only when strong visual or olfactory stimuli
were presented (the cerveau isolé has intact visual and olfactory input) could the
continuous high-amplitude, slow-wave activity be changed to a **desynchronized**

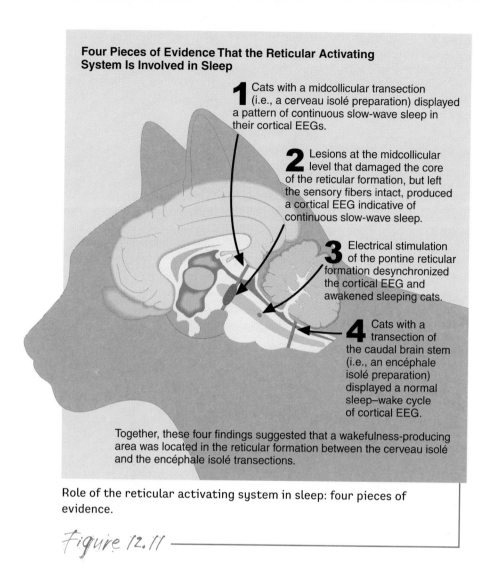

Four Pieces of Evidence That the Reticular Activating System Is Involved in Sleep

1 Cats with a midcollicular transection (i.e., a cerveau isolé preparation) displayed a pattern of continuous slow-wave sleep in their cortical EEGs.

2 Lesions at the midcollicular level that damaged the core of the reticular formation, but left the sensory fibers intact, produced a cortical EEG indicative of continuous slow-wave sleep.

3 Electrical stimulation of the pontine reticular formation desynchronized the cortical EEG and awakened sleeping cats.

4 Cats with a transection of the caudal brain stem (i.e., an encéphale isolé preparation) displayed a normal sleep–wake cycle of cortical EEG.

Together, these four findings suggested that a wakefulness-producing area was located in the reticular formation between the cerveau isolé and the encéphale isolé transections.

Role of the reticular activating system in sleep: four pieces of evidence.

Figure 12.11

EEG—a low-amplitude, high-frequency EEG. However, this arousing effect barely outlasted the stimuli.

Next, for comparison purposes, Bremer (1937) *transected* (cut through) the brain stems of a different group of cats. These transections were made in the caudal brain stem, and thus, they disconnected the brain from the rest of the nervous system (see Figure 12.11). This experimental preparation is called the **encéphale isolé preparation** (pronounced "on-say-FELL ees-o-LAY").

Although it cut most of the same sensory fibers as the cerveau isolé transection, the encéphale isolé transection did not disrupt the normal cycle of sleep EEG and wakefulness EEG. This suggested that a structure for maintaining wakefulness was located somewhere in the brain stem between the two transections.

Later, two important findings suggested that this wakefulness structure in the brain stem was the *reticular formation*. First, it was shown that partial transections at the cerveau isolé level disrupted normal sleep–wake on the cortical EEG (Lindsey, Bowden, & Magoun, 1949). Second, it was shown that electrical stimulation of the reticular formation of sleeping cats awakened them and produced a lengthy period of EEG desynchronization (Moruzzi & Magoun, 1949).

In 1949, Moruzzi and Magoun considered these four findings together: (1) the effects on cortical EEG of the cerveau isolé preparation, (2) the effects on cortical EEG of the encéphale isolé preparation, (3) the effects of reticular formation lesions, and (4) the effects on sleep of stimulation of the reticular formation. From these four key findings, Moruzzi and Magoun proposed that low levels of activity in the reticular formation produce sleep and that high levels produce wakefulness. Indeed, this theory is so widely accepted that the reticular formation is commonly referred to as the **reticular activating system**, even though maintaining wakefulness is only one of the functions of the many nuclei that it comprises.

Reticular REM-Sleep Nuclei

The fourth area of the brain that is involved in sleep controls REM sleep and is included in the brain area I have just described—it is part of the caudal reticular formation. It makes sense that an area of the brain involved in maintaining wakefulness would also be involved in the production of REM sleep because of the similarities between the two states. Indeed, REM sleep is controlled by a variety of nuclei scattered throughout the caudal reticular formation. Each site is responsible for controlling one of the major indices of REM sleep (Siegel, 1983; Vertes, 1983)— a site for the reduction of core-muscle tone, a site for EEG desynchronization, a site for rapid eye movements, and so on. The approximate location in the caudal brain stem of each of these REM-sleep nuclei is illustrated in Figure 12.12.

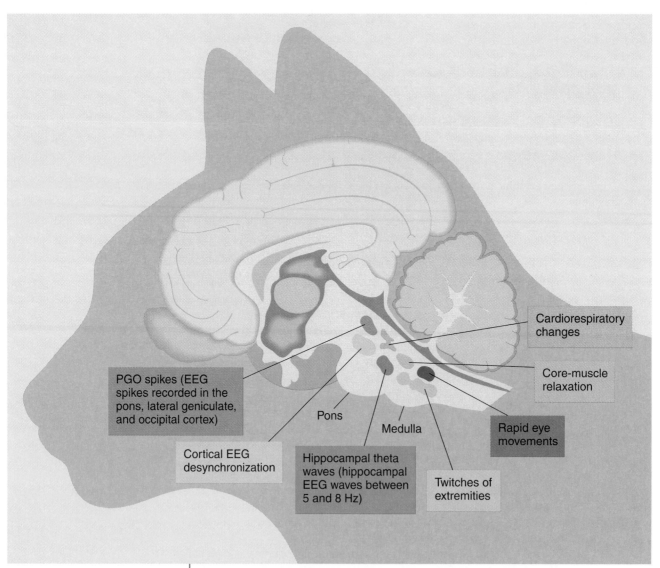

A sagittal section of the brain stem of the cat illustrating the areas that control the various physiological indexes of REM sleep. (Adapted from Vertes, 1983.)

Figure 12.12

Please think for a moment about the broad implications of these various REM-sleep nuclei. In thinking about the brain mechanisms of behavior, many people assume that if there is one name for a behavior, there is a single structure for it in the brain: In other words, they assume that evolutionary pressures have acted to shape the human brain according to our current language and theories. Here we see the weakness of this assumption: The brain is organized along different principles, and REM sleep occurs only when a network of independent structures becomes active together. Relevant to this is the fact that the physiological events that normally go together to define REM sleep sometimes break apart and occur separately—and the same is true of the changes that define slow-wave sleep. For example, during REM-sleep deprivation, penile erections, which normally occur during REM sleep, begin to occur during slow-wave sleep. And during total sleep deprivation, slow waves, which normally occur only during slow-wave sleep, begin to occur during wakefulness. This suggests that REM sleep, slow-wave sleep, and wakefulness are not each controlled by a single mechanism. Each state seems to result from the interaction of several mechanisms that are capable under certain conditions of operating independently of one another.

12.8

The Circadian Clock: Neural and Molecular Mechanisms

The fact that circadian sleep–wake cycles persist in the absence of temporal cues from the environment indicates that the physiological systems that regulate sleep are controlled by an internal timing mechanism—the **circadian clock**. The circadian clock has been the subject of such intensive investigation that it warrants its own section of this chapter.

Location of the Circadian Clock: The Suprachiasmatic Nuclei

The first breakthrough in the search for the circadian clock was Richter's 1967 discovery that large medial hypothalamic lesions disrupt circadian cycles of eating, drinking, and activity in rats. Next, specific lesions of the **suprachiasmatic nuclei (SCN)** of the medial hypothalamus were shown to disrupt various circadian cycles, including sleep–wake cycles. Although SCN lesions do not reduce the amount of time mammals spend sleeping, they do abolish its circadian periodicity. Further support for the conclusion that the suprachiasmatic nuclei contain a circadian timing mechanism comes from the observation that the nuclei display circadian cycles of electrical, metabolic, and biochemical activity that can be entrained by the light–dark cycle (see Buijs & Kalsbeek, 2001; Van Essevelt, Lehman, & Boer, 2000).

If there was any lingering doubt about the location of the circadian clock, it was eliminated by the brilliant experiment of Ralph and his colleagues (1990). They removed the SCN from the fetuses of a strain of mutant hamsters that had an abnormally short (20-hour) free-running sleep–wake cycle. Then, they transplanted the SCN into normal adult hamsters whose free-running sleep–wake cycles of 25 hours had been abolished by SCN lesions. These transplants restored free-running sleep–wake cycles in the recipients; but, remarkably, the cycles were about 20 hours long rather than the original 25 hours. Transplants in the other direction—that is, from normal hamster fetuses to SCN-lesioned adult mutants—had the complementary effect: They restored free-running sleep–wake cycles that were about 25 hours long rather than the original 20 hours.

Although the suprachiasmatic nuclei are unquestionably the major circadian clocks in mammals, they are not the only ones. Three lines of experiments, largely conducted in the 1980s and 1990s, pointed to the existence of other circadian timing mechanisms in the body. First, under certain conditions, bilateral SCN lesions have been shown to leave some circadian rhythms unaffected while abolishing others. Second, bilateral SCN lesions do not eliminate the ability of all environmental stimuli to entrain circadian rhythms; for example, SCN lesions can block entrainment by light but not by food or water availability. Third, just as suprachiasmatic neurons do, cells from other parts of the body display free-running circadian cycles of activity when maintained in tissue culture.

Mechanisms of Entrainment

How does the 24-hour light–dark cycle entrain the sleep–wake cycle and other circadian rhythms? To answer this question, researchers began at the obvious starting point: the eyes. They tried to identify and track the specific neurons that left the eyes and carried the information about light and dark that entrained the biological clock. Cutting the *optic nerves* before they reached the *optic chiasm* eliminated the ability of the light–dark cycle to entrain circadian rhythms; however, when the *optic tracts* were cut at the point where they left the optic chiasm, the ability of the light–dark cycle to entrain circadian rhythms was unaffected. As Figure 12.13 illustrates, these two findings indicated that visual axons critical for the entrainment of circadian rhythms branch off from the optic nerve in the vicinity of the optic chiasm. This finding led to the discovery of the *retinohypothalamic tracts*, which leave the optic chiasm and project to the adjacent suprachiasmatic nuclei.

Surprisingly, although the retinohypothalamic tracts mediate the ability of light to entrain photoreceptors, neither rods or cones are necessary for the entrainment. *Transgenic mice* lacking both rods and cones still show light-entrained circadian cycles (Freedman et al., 1999; Lucas et al., 1999). This finding suggested that the SCN must be getting information about light and dark from other receptors. These receptors were recently discovered, creating considerable excitement among neuroscientists.

Surprisingly, these mystery photoreceptors have proven to be neurons, a subtype of *retinal ganglion cells* with distinctive functional properties (see Berson, 2003; Hattar et al., 2002). During the course of evolution, these photoreceptors seem to have sacrificed the ability to respond quickly and briefly to rapid changes of neural activity in favor of the ability to respond consistently to slowly changing levels of background illumination. These photoreceptors also play a role in the adjustment of pupillary size in response to changes in background illumination (Lucas et al., 2003; Van Gelder et al., 2003).

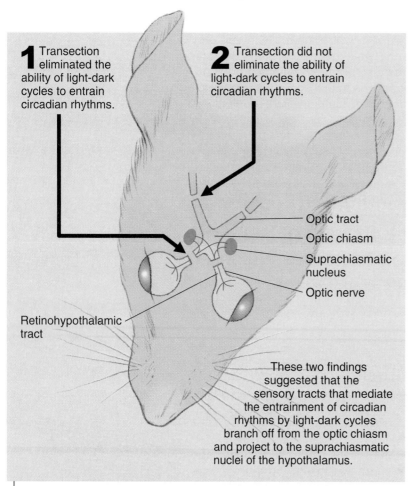

1 Transection eliminated the ability of light-dark cycles to entrain circadian rhythms.

2 Transection did not eliminate the ability of light-dark cycles to entrain circadian rhythms.

Optic tract
Optic chiasm
Suprachiasmatic nucleus
Optic nerve

Retinohypothalamic tract

These two findings suggested that the sensory tracts that mediate the entrainment of circadian rhythms by light-dark cycles branch off from the optic chiasm and project to the suprachiasmatic nuclei of the hypothalamus.

The discovery of the retinohypothalamic tracts. Neurons from each retina project to both suprachiasmatic nuclei.

Figure 12.13

The Evolutionary Perspective

Genetics of Circadian Rhythms

An important breakthrough in the study of the genetic basis of circadian rhythms came in 1988 when routine screening of a shipment of hamsters revealed that some of them had abnormally short 20-hour free-running circadian rhythms. Subsequent breeding experiments showed that the abnormality was the result of a genetic mutation, and the gene that was found was named *tau* (Ralph & Menaker, 1988).

The Evolutionary Perspective

Although tau was the first mammalian circadian gene to be identified, it was not the first to have its molecular structure characterized. This honor went to *clock*, a mammalian circadian gene discovered in mice. The structure of the clock gene was characterized in 1997, and that of the tau gene was characterized in 2000 (Lowrey et al., 2000). The molecular structures of several other mammalian circadian genes have now been characterized (see Morse & Sassone-Corsi, 2002).

The identification of circadian genes has led to two important discoveries. First, the same or similar circadian genes have been found in many species of different evolutionary ages (e.g., bacteria, flies, fish, frogs, mice, and humans). It seems that circadian rhythms evolved early in evolutionary history, and the same genes have been conserved in various descendant species (see Cermakian & Sassone-Corsi, 2002). Second, the identification of circadian genes provided a more direct method of exploring the circadian timing capacities of parts of the body other than the SCN. Although the existence of extra-SCN circadian timing mechanisms had been inferred from the results of research conducted in the 1980s and 1990s (as I have already described to you), direct evidence was lacking. Once researchers established that the circadian genes within SCN neurons transcribed their protein products on a circadian cycle, they began to examine the same genes in other cells of the body and were amazed by what they found: Circadian timing mechanisms similar to those in the SCN exist in most cells of the body (see Green & Menaker, 2003; Hastings, Reddy, & Maywood, 2003; Yamaguchi et al., 2003). Although most cells contain a genetic circadian clock, these cellular clocks are normally entrained by neural and hormonal signals from the SCN.

The Evolutionary Perspective

12.9
Drugs That Affect Sleep

Most drugs that influence sleep fall into two different classes: hypnotic and antihypnotic. **Hypnotic drugs** are drugs that increase sleep; **antihypnotic drugs** are drugs that reduce sleep. A third class of sleep-influencing drugs comprises those that influence its circadian rhythmicity; the main drug of this class is **melatonin**.

Clinical Implications

Hypnotic Drugs

The **benzodiazepines** (e.g., Valium and Librium) were developed and tested for the treatment of anxiety, yet they are the most commonly prescribed hypnotic medications. In the short term, they increase drowsiness, decrease the time it takes to fall asleep, reduce the number of awakenings during a night's sleep, and increase total sleep time. Thus, they can be effective in the treatment of occasional difficulties in sleeping.

Although benzodiazepines can be effective therapeutic hypnotic agents in the short term, their prescription for the treatment of chronic sleep difficulties is ill-advised. Still, they are commonly prescribed for this purpose—primarily by general practitioners. Four complications are associated with the chronic use of benzodiazepines as hypnotic agents: First, tolerance develops to the hypnotic effects of benzodiazepines; thus, patients must take larger and larger doses to maintain the drugs' efficacy. Second, cessation of benzodiazepine therapy after chronic use causes *insomnia* (sleeplessness), which can exacerbate the very problem that the benzodiazepines were intended to correct. Third, chronic benzodiazepine use is addictive. Fourth, benzodiazepines distort the normal pattern of sleep; they increase the duration of sleep by increasing the duration of stage 2 sleep, while actually decreasing the duration of stage 4 and REM sleep.

Antihypnotic Drugs

There are two main classes of antihypnotic drugs: *stimulants* (e.g., cocaine and amphetamine) and *tricyclic antidepressants*. Both stimulants and antidepressants increase the activity of catecholamines (norepinephrine, epinephrine, and dopamine) by either increasing their release or blocking their reuptake from the synapse, or both.

From the perspective of the treatment of sleep disorders, the most important property of antihypnotic drugs is that they act preferentially on REM sleep. They can totally suppress REM sleep even at doses that have little effect on total sleep time.

Using stimulant drugs to treat chronic excessive sleepiness is a risky proposition. Most stimulants are highly addictive, and they produce a variety of adverse side effects, such as loss of appetite. Moreover, unless these drugs are taken at just the right doses and at just the right times, there is a danger that they will interfere with normal sleep.

Melatonin

Melatonin is a hormone that is synthesized from the neurotransmitter serotonin in the **pineal gland** (see Moore, 1996). The pineal gland is an inconspicuous gland that René Descartes, whose dualistic philosophy was discussed in Chapter 1, once believed to be the seat of the soul. The pineal gland is located on the midline of the brain just ventral to the rear portion of the corpus callosum (see Figure 12.14).

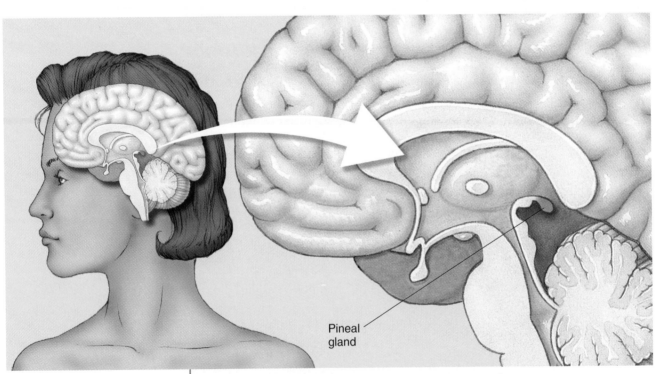

Pineal gland

The location of the pineal gland, the source of melatonin.

Figure 12.14

The pineal gland has important functions in birds, reptiles, amphibians, and fish (see Cassone, 1990). The pineal gland of these species has inherent timing properties and regulates circadian rhythms and seasonal changes in reproductive behavior through its release of melatonin. In humans and other mammals, however, the functions of the pineal gland and melatonin are not as apparent.

The Evolutionary Perspective

In humans and other mammals, circulating levels of melatonin display circadian rhythms under control of the suprachiasmatic nuclei (see Gillette & McArthur, 1996), with the highest levels being associated with darkness and sleep (see Foulkes et al., 1997). On the basis of this correlation, it has long been assumed that melatonin plays a role in promoting sleep or in regulating its timing in mammals.

In order to put the facts about melatonin in perspective, it is important to keep one significant point firmly in mind. In adult mammals, pinealectomy and the consequent elimination of melatonin have little effect. The pineal gland plays a role in the development of mammalian sexual maturity, but its functions after puberty are not at all obvious.

Does *exogenous* (externally produced) melatonin improve sleep, as widely believed? The evidence is mixed. Several studies have shown that large doses of melatonin during the day, when levels of *endogenous* (internally produced) melatonin are low, produce quicker and better sleep during subsequent nap tests (e.g., Haimov & Lavie, 1996). However, the effects of melatonin taken at bedtime have been inconsistent: A few studies have found subsequent sleep to be longer and more efficient (e.g., Attenburrow, Cowen, & Sharpely, 1996), but others have not (Baskett et al., 2003; Dawson & Encel, 1993).

In contrast to the controversy over the *soporific* (sleep-promoting) effects of exogenous melatonin in mammals, there is good evidence that it can influence mammalian circadian cycles (see Beaumont et al., 2004; Lewy, Ahmed, & Sack, 1996; Rajaratnam et al., 2003). Exposure to exogenous melatonin acts much like exposure to a period of darkness, which makes sense because high levels of endogenous melatonin are associated with darkness. Thus, a dose of melatonin before dusk may help jet-lagged travelers adapt to east-bound flights, whereas a dose after dawn can help with adaptation to west-bound flights. The shift in circadian rhythms is, however, typically slight—less than an hour.

Exogenous melatonin has been shown to have a therapeutic potential in the treatment of two types of sleep problems. Melatonin before bedtime has been shown to improve the sleep of those insomniacs who are melatonin-deficient (e.g., Haimov et al., 1995) and of blind patients who have sleep problems attributable to the lack of the synchronizing effects of the light–dark cycle (e.g., Sack & Lewy, 2001). Melatonin's effectiveness in the treatment of other sleep disorders remains controversial (see Almeida et al., 2003; Serfaty et al., 2002).

12.10

Sleep Disorders

Many sleep disorders fall into one of two complementary categories: insomnia and hypersomnia. **Insomnia** includes all disorders of initiating and maintaining sleep, whereas **hypersomnia** includes disorders of excessive sleep or sleepiness. A third major class of sleep disorders includes all those disorders that are specifically related to REM-sleep dysfunction.

Clinical Implications

In various surveys, approximately 30% of the respondents report significant sleep-related problems. However, it is important to recognize that complaints of sleep problems often come from people whose sleep appears normal in laboratory sleep tests. For example, many people who complain of insomnia actually sleep a reasonable amount (e.g., 6 hours or more a night), but they believe that they should sleep more. As a result, they spend more time in bed than they should and have difficulty getting to sleep. Often, the anxiety associated with their inability to sleep makes it even more difficult for them to sleep (see Espie, 2002). Such patients can often be helped if they can be convinced to go to bed only when they are very sleepy (see Anch et al., 1988). Others with disturbed sleep have more serious problems.

Insomnia

Many cases of insomnia are **iatrogenic** (physician-created). Paradoxically, sleeping pills (e.g., benzodiazepines) prescribed by well-intentioned physicians are a major cause of insomnia. At first, hypnotic drugs are effective in increasing sleep, but soon the patient is trapped in a rising spiral of drug use, as *tolerance* to the drug develops and progressively more of it is required to produce its original hypnotic effect. Soon, the patient cannot stop taking the drug without running the risk of experiencing *withdrawal symptoms*, which include insomnia. The case of Mr. B. illustrates this problem.

Mr. B., the Case of Iatrogenic Insomnia

Mr. B. was studying for a civil service exam, the outcome of which would affect his entire future. He was terribly worried about the test and found it difficult to get to sleep at night. Feeling that the sleep loss was affecting his ability to study, he consulted his physician for the express purpose of getting "something to make me sleep." His doctor prescribed a moderate dose of barbiturate at bedtime, and Mr. B. found that this medication was very effective . . . for the first several nights. After about a week, he began having trouble sleeping again and decided to take two sleeping pills each night. Twice more the cycle was repeated, until on the night before the exam he was taking four times as many pills as his doctor had prescribed. The next night, with the pressure off, Mr. B. took no medication. He had tremendous difficulty falling asleep, and when he did, his sleep was terribly disrupted. . . . Mr. B. now decided that he had a serious case of insomnia, and returned to his sleeping pill habit. By the time he consulted our clinic several years later, he was taking approximately 1,000 mg sodium amytal every night, and his sleep was more disturbed than ever. . . . Patients may go on for years and years—from one sleeping pill to another—never realizing that their troubles are caused by the pills.

(From *Some Must Watch While Some Must Sleep* by William C. Dement, Portable Stanford Books, Stanford Alumni Association, Stanford University, 1978, p. 80.)

Sleep apnea is another common cause of insomnia. In sleep apnea, the patient stops breathing many times each night. Each time, the patient awakens, begins to breathe again, and drifts back to sleep. Sleep apnea usually leads to a sense of having slept poorly and is thus often diagnosed as insomnia. However, some patients are totally unaware of their multiple awakenings and instead complain of excessive sleepiness during the day, which leads to a diagnosis of *hypersomnia* (Stepanski et al., 1984).

Sleep apnea disorders are thought to be of two types: (1) those resulting from obstruction of the respiratory passages by muscle spasms or *atonia* (lack of muscle tone), and (2) those resulting from the failure of the central nervous system to stimulate respiration. Sleep apnea is more common in males, in the overweight, and in the elderly.

Two other causes of insomnia—nocturnal myoclonus and restless legs—both involve the legs. **Nocturnal myoclonus** is a periodic twitching of the body, usually the legs, during sleep. Most patients suffering from this disorder complain of poor sleep and daytime sleepiness but are unaware of the nature of their problem. In contrast, people with **restless legs** are all too aware of their problem. They complain of a hard-to-describe tension or uneasiness in their legs that keeps them from falling asleep. Benzodiazepines are often prescribed in cases of nocturnal myoclonus and restless legs because of their hypnotic, *anxiolytic* (antianxiety), muscle-relaxant, and anticonvulsant properties; however, they are rarely effective.

In one study, insomniacs claimed to take an average of 1 hour to fall asleep and to sleep an average of only 4.5 hours per night; but when they were tested in a sleep laboratory, they were found to have an average *sleep latency* (time to fall asleep) of only 15 minutes and an average nightly sleep duration of 6.5 hours. It used to be common medical practice to assume that people who claimed to suffer from insomnia but slept more than 6.5 hours per night were neurotic. However, this practice stopped when some of those diagnosed as *neurotic pseudoinsomniacs* were subsequently found to be suffering from sleep apnea, nocturnal myoclonus, or other sleep-disturbing problems. Insomnia is not necessarily a problem of too little sleep; it is often a problem of too little undisturbed sleep (Stepanski et al., 1987).

Remarkably, one of the most effective treatments for insomnia is *sleep restriction therapy*. First, the amount of time that an insomniac is allowed to spend in bed is substantially reduced. Then, after a period of sleep restriction, the amount of time spent in bed is gradually increased in small increments, as long as sleep latency remains in the normal range. Even severe insomniacs benefit from this treatment (Morin, Kowatch, & O'Shanick, 1990; Spielman, Saskin, & Thorpy, 1987).

Hypersomnia

Narcolepsy is the most widely studied disorder in the hypersomnia category. It occurs in 1 out of 2000 individuals (Takahashi, 1999) and has two prominent symptoms (see Siegel, 2000). First, narcoleptics experience severe daytime sleepiness and repeated, brief (10- to 15-minute) daytime sleep episodes. Narcoleptics typically sleep only about an hour per day more than average; it is the inappropriateness of their sleep episodes that most clearly defines their condition. Most of us occasionally fall asleep on the beach, in front of the television, or in that most *soporific* (sleep-promoting) of all daytime sites—the large, stuffy, dimly lit lecture hall. But narcoleptics fall asleep in the middle of a conversation, while eating, while making love, or even while scuba diving.

The second prominent symptom of narcolepsy is cataplexy. **Cataplexy** is characterized by recurring losses of muscle tone during wakefulness, often triggered by an emotional experience. In its mild form, it may simply force the patient to sit down for a few seconds until it passes. In its extreme form, the patient drops to the ground as if shot and remains there for a minute or two, fully conscious.

In addition to the two prominent symptoms of narcolepsy (daytime sleep attacks and cataplexy), narcoleptics often experience two other symptoms: sleep paralysis and hypnagogic hallucinations. **Sleep paralysis** is the inability to move (paralysis) when falling asleep or waking up. **Hypnagogic hallucinations** are dreamlike experiences during wakefulness. Sleep paralysis and hypnagogic hallucinations are occasionally experienced by many people. Have you experienced them?

Three lines of evidence suggested that narcolepsy results from an abnormality in the mechanisms that trigger REM sleep. First, unlike normal people, narcoleptics often go directly into REM sleep when they fall asleep. Second and third, narcoleptics often experience dreamlike states and loss of muscle tone during wakefulness.

Some of the most exciting current research on the neural mechanisms of sleep in general and narcolepsy in particular began with the study of a strain of narcoleptic dogs. After 10 years of studying the genetics of these narcoleptic dogs, Lin and colleagues (1999) finally isolated the gene that causes the disorder. The gene encodes a receptor protein that binds to a neuropeptide called **orexin**, which exists in two forms: orexin-A and orexin-B (see Taheri, Zeitzer, & Mignot, 2002). In response to this discovery, Chemielli and colleagues (1999) bred *knockout mice* whose gene coding for the orexin-binding protein is dysfunctional. These mice display the symptoms of narcolepsy. This finding led other researchers to focus on the role of

The Evolutionary Perspective

orexin in human narcoleptics: Several studies have documented reduced levels in the cerebrospinal fluid of living narcoleptics and in the brains of deceased narcoleptics (see Mieda & Yanagisawa, 2002).

Where is orexin synthesized in the brain? As you might have anticipated from an earlier section of this chapter, orexin is synthesized by neurons in the region of the hypothalamus that has been linked to the promotion of wakefulness: the posterior hypothalamus (mainly its lateral regions). The orexin-producing neurons project diffusely throughout the brain, but they show many connections with neurons of the other wakefulness-promoting area of the brain: the reticular formation (see Pace-Schott & Hobson, 2002; Sucliffe & De Lecea, 2002).

When narcolepsy occurs in an identical twin, the probability that the other twin will be narcoleptic is only 25%. This finding suggests that environmental factors normally play a major role in the brain damage associated with narcolepsy. Perhaps exposure to a neurotoxin initiates an autoimmune reaction against some component of the orexin system in susceptible individuals.

REM-Sleep–Related Disorders

Several sleep disorders are specific to REM sleep; these are classified as *REM-sleep–related disorders*. Even narcolepsy, which is usually classified as a hypersomnic disorder, can reasonably be considered to be a REM-sleep–related disorder—for reasons you have just encountered.

Occasionally, patients are discovered who have little or no REM sleep. Although this disorder is rare, it is important because of its theoretical implications. Lavie and others (1984) described a patient who had suffered a brain injury that presumably involved damage to the REM-sleep controllers in the caudal reticular formation. The most important finding of this case study was that the patient did not appear to be adversely affected by his lack of REM sleep. After receiving his injury, he completed high school, college, and law school and established a thriving law practice.

Some patients experience REM sleep without core-muscle atonia. It has been suggested that the function of REM-sleep atonia is to prevent the acting out of dreams. This theory receives support from case studies of people who suffer from this disorder.

The Case of the Sleeper Who Ran Over Tackle

> I was a halfback playing football, and after the quarterback received the ball from the center he lateraled it sideways to me and I'm supposed to go around end and cut back over tackle and—this is very vivid—as I cut back over tackle there is this big 280-pound tackle waiting, so I, according to football rules, was to give him my shoulder and bounce him out of the way. . . . [W]hen I came to I was standing in front of our dresser and I had [gotten up out of bed and run and] knocked lamps, mirrors and everything off the dresser, hit my head against the wall and my knee against the dresser. (Schenck et al., 1986, p. 294)

Presumably, REM sleep without atonia is caused by damage to the nucleus magnocellularis or to an interruption of its output. The **nucleus magnocellularis** is the structure of the caudal reticular formation that controls muscle relaxation during REM sleep. In normal dogs, it is active only during REM sleep; in narcoleptic dogs, it is active during their narcoleptic attacks. Lesions of the caudal reticular formation often induce a similar REM-sleep–related disorder in cats.

The Evolutionary Perspective

> The cat, which is standing . . . may attack unknown enemies, play with an absent mouse, or display flight behavior. There are orienting movements of the head or eyes toward imaginary stimuli, although the animal does not respond to visual or auditory stimuli. (Jouvet, 1972, pp. 236–237)

The Effects of Long-Term Sleep Reduction

Y̶ou have already learned in this chapter that when people sleep less than they are used to sleeping, they do not feel or function well. I am sure that you have experienced these effects. But what do they mean? Most people—nonexperts and experts alike—believe that the adverse effects of sleep loss indicate that we need the sleep we typically get. However, there is an alternative interpretation, one that is consistent with the new awareness of the plasticity of the adult human brain. Perhaps the brain slowly adapts to the amount of sleep it usually gets—even though this amount may be far more than it needs—and is disturbed when there is a sudden reduction in the expected amount of sleep.

Fortunately, there is a way to determine which of these two interpretations of the effects of sleep loss is correct and to find out how much sleep people really need. The key is to study the effects of systematic programs of long-term sleep reduction. For example, if you reduced your regular amount of sleep from 8.5 hours per night to 6.5 hours per night, you would initially have some problems. But what if you regularly slept 6.5 hours per night for a couple of months—would you eventually become comfortable with sleeping 6.5 hours each night? The major point here is that if it is possible for you to adapt to a regular schedule of 6.5 hours of sleep per night without adverse consequences, then it is ludicrous to believe that you need 8.5 hours.

Let's see what has happened in studies of long-term sleep reduction. Because they are so time-consuming, few of these critical studies have been conducted; but there have been enough of them for a clear pattern of results to have emerged. I think you will by amazed by the results.

There have been two kinds of long-term sleep-reduction studies: studies in which the subjects sleep nightly and studies in which subjects sleep by napping. Following a brief discussion of these two kinds of studies and my own personal experience of long-term sleep reduction, the chapter concludes with an important, and somewhat disturbing, recent finding that is sure to challenge your thinking about sleep.

Long-Term Reduction of Nightly Sleep

There have been two studies in which healthy subjects have reduced their nightly sleep for several weeks or longer. In one (Webb & Agnew, 1974), a group of 16 subjects slept for only 5.5 hours per night for 60 days, with only one detectable deficit on an extensive battery of mood, medical, and performance tests: a slight deficit on a test of auditory vigilance.

In the other systematic study of long-term nightly sleep reduction (Friedman et al., 1977; Mullaney et al., 1977), 8 subjects reduced their nightly sleep by 30 minutes every 2 weeks until they reached 6.5 hours per night, then by 30 minutes every 3 weeks until they reached 5 hours, and then by 30 minutes every 4 weeks thereafter. After a subject indicated a lack of desire to reduce sleep further, the person slept for 1 month at the shortest duration of nightly sleep that was achieved, then for 2 months at the shortest duration plus 30 minutes. Finally, each subject slept each night for 1 year for however long the person preferred. The minimum duration of nightly sleep achieved during this experiment was 5.5 hours for 2 subjects, 5.0 hours for 4 subjects, and an impressive 4.5 hours for 2 subjects. In each of the subjects, a reduction in sleep time was associated with an increase in sleep efficiency: a decrease in the amount of time it took the subjects to fall asleep after going to bed, a decrease in the number of nighttime awakenings, and an increase in the proportion of stage 4 sleep. After the subjects had reduced their sleep to 6 hours per night, they began to experience daytime sleepiness, and this became a problem as sleep time was further reduced. Nevertheless, there were no deficits on any of the mood, medical, or performance tests given to the subjects throughout the experiment. The most encouraging result was that during a follow-up 1 year later, all subjects were sleeping less than they had previously—between 7 and 18 hours less each week—with no excessive sleepiness.

Long-Term Sleep Reduction by Napping

Most mammals and human infants display **polyphasic sleep cycles**; that is, they regularly sleep more than once per day. In contrast, most adult humans display **monophasic sleep cycles**; that is, they sleep once per day. Nevertheless, most adult humans do display polyphasic cycles of sleepiness, with periods of sleepiness occurring in late afternoon and late morning (Stampi, 1992a). Have you ever experienced them?

Do adult humans need to take sleep in one continuous period per day, or can they sleep effectively in several naps as human infants and other mammals do? Which of the two sleep patterns is more efficient? Research has shown that naps have recuperative powers out of proportion with their brevity (e.g., Gillberg et al., 1996; Horne & Reyner, 1996; Naitoh, 1992), suggesting that polyphasic sleep might be particularly efficient.

Interest in the value of polyphasic sleep was stimulated by the legend that Leonardo da Vinci managed to generate a steady stream of artistic and engineering accomplishments during his life by napping for 15 minutes every 4 hours, thereby limiting his sleep to 1.5 hours per day. As unbelievable as this may seem, it has been replicated in several experiments (see Stampi, 1992b). Here are the main findings of these truly mind-boggling experiments. First, the subjects required a long time, about 2 or 3 weeks, to adapt to a polyphasic sleep schedule. Second, once adapted to polyphasic sleep, the subjects were content and displayed no deficits on the performance tests that they received. Third, Leonardo's 4-hour schedule works quite well, but in unstructured working situations (e.g., as in around-the-world solo sailboat races; see Figure 12.15), subjects often vary the duration of the cycle without feeling negative consequences. Fourth, most subjects display a strong preference for particular sleep durations (e.g., 25 minutes) and refrain from sleeping too little, which leaves them unrefreshed, or too much, which leaves them groggy for several minutes when they awake—an effect called *sleep inertia*. Fifth, at first most of the sleep is slow-wave sleep, but eventually the subjects return to their usual relative proportions of REM and slow-wave sleep; however, REM and slow-wave sleep seldom occur during the same nap.

The following are the words of artist Giancarlo Sbragia, who adopted Leonardo's sleep schedule:

This schedule was difficult to follow at the beginning. . . . It took about 3 wk to get used to it. But I soon reached a point at which I felt a natural propensity for sleeping at this rate, and it turned out to be a thrilling and exciting experience.

. . . How beautiful my life became: I discovered dawns, I discovered silence, and concentration. I had more time for studying and reading—far more than I did before. I had more time for myself, for painting, and for developing my career. (Sbragia, 1992, p. 181)

Notice the sailor in the rigging; he is sailing the boat by himself. During long-distance solo sailboat races, sailors sleep for brief periods several times each day, and they seem to adapt well to this schedule of polyphasic sleep.

Figure 12.15

Long-Term Sleep Reduction: A Personal Case Study

I began this chapter 4 weeks ago with both zeal and trepidation. I was fascinated by the idea that I could wring 2 or 3 extra hours of living out of each day by sleeping less, and I hoped that adhering to a sleep-reduction program while writing about sleep would create an enthusiasm for the subject that would color my writing and be passed on to you. On the other hand, I was more than a little concerned about the negative effect that losing 3 hours of sleep per night might have on me.

The Case of the Author Who Reduced His Sleep

Rather than using the gradual stepwise reduction method of Friedman and his colleagues, I jumped directly into my 5-hours-per-night sleep schedule. This proved to be less difficult than you might think. I took advantage of a trip to the East Coast from my home on the West Coast to reset my circadian clock. While I was in the East, I got up at 7:00 A.M., which is 4:00 A.M. on the West Coast, and I just kept on the same schedule when I got home. I decided to add my extra waking hours to the beginning of my day rather than to the end so there would be no temptation for me to waste them; there are not too many distractions around this university at 5:00 A.M.

Figure 12.16 is a record of my sleep times for the 4-week period that it took me to write a first draft of this chapter. I didn't quite meet my goal of sleeping less than 5 hours every night, but I didn't miss by much: My overall mean was 5.05 hours per night. Notice that in the last week, there was a tendency for my circadian clock to run a bit slow; I began sleeping in until 4:30 A.M. and staying up until 11:30 P.M.

What were the positives and negatives of my experience? The main positive was the added time to do things: Having an extra 21 hours per week was wonderful. Furthermore, because my daily routine was out of synchrony with everybody else's, I spent little time sitting in rush-hour traffic.

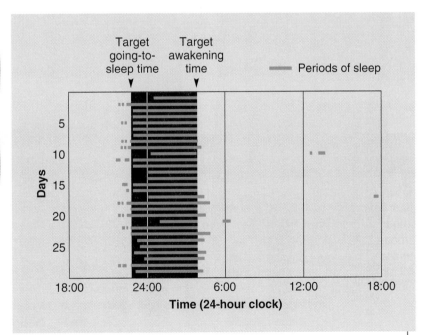

Record of Pinel's sleep during a 4-week sleep-reduction program.

Figure 12.16

> The only negative of the experience was sleepiness. It was no problem during the day, when I was active. However, staying awake during the last hour before I went to bed—an hour during which I usually engaged in sedentary activities, such as reading—was at times a problem. This is when I became personally familiar with the phenomenon of microsleeps, and it was then that I required some assistance in order to stay awake. Going to bed and falling asleep each night became a fleeting but satisfying experience.

I began this chapter with this question: How much sleep do we need? Then, I gave you my best professorial it-could-be-this, it-could-be-that answer. However, that was a month ago. Now, after experiencing sleep reduction firsthand, I am less inclined toward wishy-washiness on the topic of sleep. The fact that most committed subjects who are active during the day can reduce their sleep to about 5.5 hours per night without great difficulty or major adverse consequences suggested to me that the answer is about 5.5 hours of sleep. But that was before I reviewed the research on napping and polyphasic sleep schedules. Now, I must revise my estimate downward—substantially.

Thinking Clearly

Earlier, I said that this chapter would end with an important new finding about sleep that would challenge your thinking on this topic. Here it is. For decades, it has been reported that sleeping 8 or 9 hours or more per night is associated with health and longevity. Now a series of large-scale studies conducted in both the United States and Japan tell a different story (e.g., Ayas et al., 2003; Kripke et al., 2002; Patel et al., 2003; Tamakoshi & Ohno, 2004). Unlike older studies, these new studies did not include subjects who had been a major source of bias, for example, people who slept little because they were ill, depressed, or under stress. These new studies of sleep and health included only subjects who were healthy at the beginning of the study.

Clinical Implications

The results of the new studies are remarkably uniform (Kripke, 2004). For example, Figure 12.17 presents data from Tamakoshi and Ohno (2004), who followed 104,010 subjects for 10 years. You will immediately see that sleeping 8 or 9 hours per night is not the healthy ideal that we have assumed it to be: The fewest deaths occurred among people sleeping between 5 and 7 hours per night, far fewer than among those who slept 8 or 9 hours. How much do you sleep?

The mortality rates associated with different amounts of sleep, based on 104,010 subjects followed over 10 years. The mortality rate at 7 hours of sleep per night has been arbitrarily set at 100%, and the other mortality rates are presented in relation to it.

(Adapted from Tamakoshi & Ohno, 2004.)

Figure 12.17

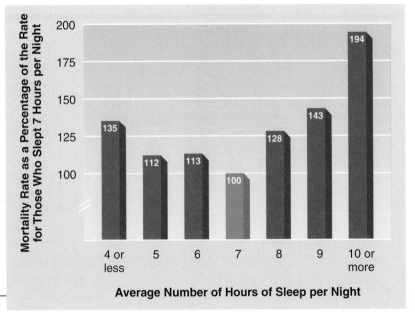

Key Terms

ON THE CD

Studying for an exam? Get some help from the electronic flash cards of the key terms and the practice tests for this chapter.

chapter 12

Sleep, Dreaming, and Circadian Rhythms
How Much Do You Need to Sleep?

Most people believe that everybody needs at least 8 hours of sleep per night: The case of Miss M. suggests otherwise.

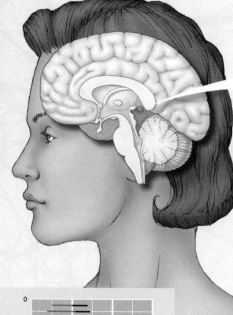

Physiological and Behavioral Events of Sleep: REM Sleep and Dreaming

EEG, EOG, EMG, and various measures of autonomic nervous system activity are typically recorded during sleep studies. Sleep of two types: (1) SWS, with slow EEG waves, few eye movements, muscle relaxation, and decreased autonomic nervous system activity, and (2) REM sleep, with fast EEG waves, rapid eye movements, total relaxation of core muscles, increased autonomic nervous system activity, and dreaming. (Pages 368–372)

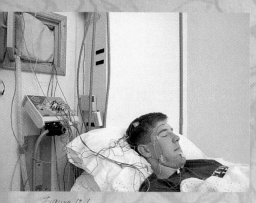

Figure 12.1

Stage 1

Stage 2

Stage 3

Stage 4

Figure 12.10

Why Do We Sleep?

Nobody knows why we sleep. The conventional view is that sleep is necessary to recuperate from the ill effects of being awake. A comparative analysis of sleep suggests that sleep does serve some critical function: All mammalian species sleep, even those at great risk of predation when they are sleeping. However, many species sleep only 2 or 3 hours per day. (Pages 372–374)

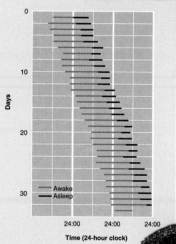

Circadian sleep-wake cycle

0

10

20

30

Days

Awake
Asleep

24:00   24:00   24:00
Time (24-hour clock)

Areas of the Brain Involved in Sleep and Its Circadian Regulation

The anterior hypothalamus promotes sleep, and the posterior hypothalamus suppresses sleep. A third area of the hypothalamus, the suprachiasmatic nuclei, contains a circadian timing mechanism that controls the timing of the sleep–wake cycle. Some reticular formation circuits promote wakefulness, and others play a role in REM sleep. (Pages 374–389)

Anterior hypothalamus, basal-forebrain area (sleep)

Posterior hypothalamus, midbrain area (wakefulness)

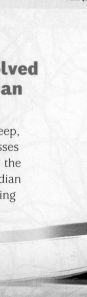

Visual Summary

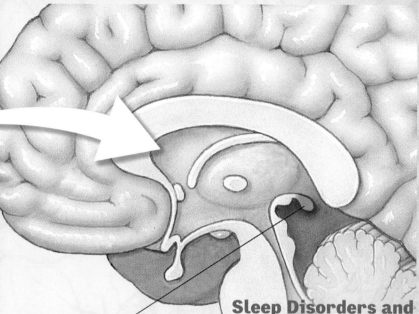

Pineal gland

Sleep Disorders and Drugs that Affect Sleep

There are three classes of drugs that affect sleep: those that promote sleep (hypnotic drugs), those that reduce sleep (antihypnotic drugs), and those that affect its circadian timing (e.g., melatonin). Sleep disorders are also divided into three classes: disorders of too little sleep (insomnia), disorders of too much sleep (hypersomnia), and disorders specifically related to REM sleep.

(Pages 389–394)

The Effects of Long-Term Sleep Reduction

When people gradually reduce their sleep, its efficiency increases, and they can sleep much less than the traditionally prescribed 8 hours with no apparent ill effects.

(Pages 395–398)

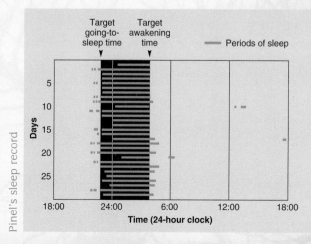

Pinel's sleep record

Themes Revisited

The evolutionary perspective theme played a prominent role in this chapter. You learned how thinking about the adaptive function of sleep and comparing sleep in different species have led to interesting insights. Also, you saw how research into the physiology and genetics of sleep has been conducted on nonhuman species.

The thinking-clearly-about-biopsychology theme pervaded the chapter—because its major purpose was to encourage you to reevaluate conventional ideas about sleep. Has this chapter changed your thinking about sleep? Writing it changed mine.

The clinical implications theme received emphasis in the section on sleep disorders. Perhaps most exciting and interesting were the recent research breakthroughs that have furthered our understanding of the genetics and physiology of narcolepsy. The clinical implications theme was also emphasized in discussion of the recent research on the relation between nightly sleep duration and longevity. Remarkably, in one major study, those who slept the recommended 8 or 9 hours per night tended to die sooner than those who slept between 5 and 7 hours.

Think about It

1. In what ways could your life be improved by changing when or how long you sleep each day? Discuss

2. Design a sleep-reduction program that is tailored to your own sleep pattern and lifestyle and is consistent with the research literature.

3. How has reading about sleep research changed your views about sleep? Give three specific examples.

4. Given that benzodiazepines contribute to insomnia, why are they so commonly prescribed for its treatment?

5. Your friend tells you that everybody needs 8 hours of sleep per night; she points out that every time she stays up late to study, she feels lousy the next day. Convince her that she is wrong.

Part 5

Biopsychology of Health

The preceding part of the book included chapters that dealt with three areas of research on motivation—hunger and eating, hormones and sex, and sleep. I hope that you enjoyed and benefited from those chapters. Did they lead you to re-evaluate your own behavior—or perhaps that of a friend or relative?

This final part of the book comprises three chapters that focus on health. Chapter 13 focuses on health psychology, examining the role of psychological factors, such as stress, in physical health. The first sections of this chapter, which discuss the adverse effects of addiction on health, should seem strangely familiar to you. You see, addiction is basically a problem of motivation, and thinking about addiction has undergone a dramatic change similar to those you encountered in the previous three chapters. You will learn that most addicts are not driven to take drugs by internal deviations from internal homeostasis, as was once believed; they are drawn to take drugs by the anticipated pleasurable effects of the drugs.

The final two chapters of the book focus on the neuroscience of two major classes of behavioral disorders. Chapter 14 deals with the brain pathology associated with disorders of language, which are largely disorders of the left hemisphere. In that chapter, you will learn the amazing story of people who have had their forebrains cut in half for the treatment of epilepsy. Chapter 15 deals with the brain pathology associated with psychiatric disorders. That chapter and the book end with the special case of S.B.; like you, he studied this book—and it changed his life.

chapter **13**

Health Psychology:
Addiction, Emotion, and Stress
Impact of Psychological Factors on Health

chapter **14**

Lateralization, Language, and
the Split Brain
The Left Brain and the Right Brain of Language

chapter **15**

Behavioral Neuroscience of
Psychiatric Disorders
The Brain Unhinged

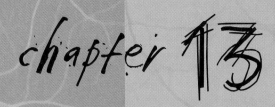

chapter 13

Health Psychology: Addiction, Emotion, and Stress
Impact of Psychological Factors on Health

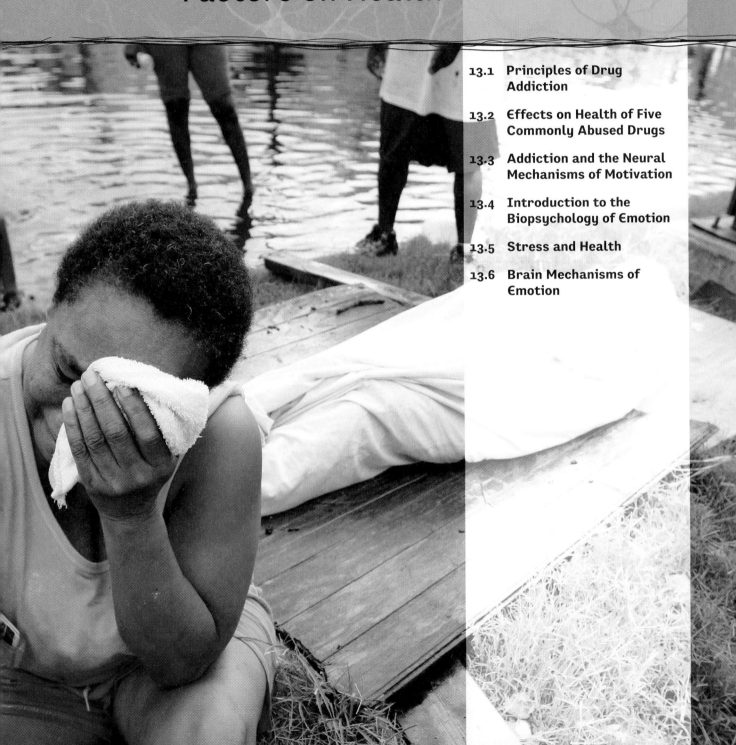

This chapter is about health psychology. **Health psychology** is an area of research that focuses on the effects of psychological factors on physical health. It is a multi-disciplinary research effort that combines major elements of behavioral neuroscience, clinical psychology, social psychology, and medicine.

This chapter deals with two major areas of health psychology. First, it deals with drug addiction, emphasizing the impact of addiction on physical health and longevity. Second, it deals with the biopsychology of emotion, emphasizing the negative impact on health of chronic stress.

Before you begin the sections of the chapter on drug addiction, I would like to make a request. You undoubtedly already have strong views about drugs and drug addiction. My request is that you try to set aside these views so that you can more easily form ones based on the evidence. In particular, I would like to warn you not to fall into the trap of assuming that a drug's legal status suggests anything about its safety. You will be less likely to assume that legal drugs are safe and illegal drugs are dangerous if you remember that most laws governing drug abuse in various parts of the world were enacted in the early part of the 20th century, long before there was any scientific research on the topic.

People's tendency to equate drug legality with drug safety was recently conveyed to me in a particularly ironic fashion, as the following narrative relates.

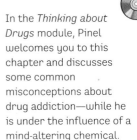

ON THE CD

In the *Thinking about Drugs* module, Pinel welcomes you to this chapter and discusses some common misconceptions about drug addiction—while he is under the influence of a mind-altering chemical.

The Ironic Case of the Drugged High School Teachers

I was invited to address a convention of high school teachers on the topic of drug abuse. When I arrived at the convention center to give my talk, I was escorted to a special suite, where I was encouraged to join the executive committee in a round of drug taking—the drug being a special high-proof single-malt whiskey. Later, the irony of the situation had its full impact. As I stepped to the podium under the influence of a psychoactive drug (the whiskey), I looked out through the haze of cigarette smoke at an audience of educators who had invited me to speak to them because they were concerned about the unhealthy impact of drugs on their students. The welcoming applause gradually gave way to the melodic tinkling of ice cubes in liquor glasses, and I began. They did not like what I had to say.

13.1
Principles of Drug Addiction

The repeated use of drugs often has two consequences: drug tolerance and physical dependence. This section focuses on these two phenomena and their relation to addiction.

Drug Tolerance

Drug tolerance is a state of decreased sensitivity to a drug that develops as a result of exposure to it. Drug tolerance can be demonstrated in two ways: by showing that a given dose of the drug has less effect than it had before drug exposure or by showing that it takes more of the drug to produce the same effect. In essence, what this means is that drug tolerance is a shift in the *dose-response curve* (a graph of the magnitude of the effect of different doses of the drug) to the right (see Figure 13.1 on page 406).

There are three important points to remember about the specificity of drug tolerance. The first is that exposure to one drug can produce tolerance to other drugs that act by the same mechanism; this is known as **cross tolerance**. The second is that drug tolerance often develops to some effects of a drug but not to

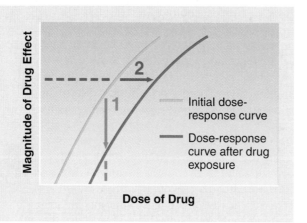

Drug tolerance is a shift in the dose-response curve to the right. Therefore,

1 In tolerant subjects, the same dose has less effect.

2 In tolerant subjects, a greater dose is required to produce the same effect.

Initial dose-response curve

Dose-response curve after drug exposure

Dose of Drug

Drug tolerance: A shift in the dose-response curve to the right as a result of exposure to the drug.

Figure 13.1

others. Failure to understand this second point can have tragic consequences for people who think that because they have become tolerant to some effects of a drug (e.g., to the nauseating effects of alcohol or tobacco), they are tolerant to all of them. In fact, tolerance may develop to some effects of a drug while sensitivity to other effects of the same drug increases—increases in the sensitivity to a drug is called **drug sensitization** (Robinson, 1991). The third important point about the specificity of drug tolerance is that it is not a unitary phenomenon; that is, there is no single mechanism that underlies all examples of it. When a drug is administered at active doses, many kinds of adaptive changes can occur to reduce its effects.

Two categories of changes underlie drug tolerance: metabolic and functional. Drug tolerance that results from changes that reduce the amount of the drug getting to its sites of action (e.g., by increasing the rate at which the drug is broken down by the liver) is called **metabolic tolerance**. Drug tolerance that results from changes that reduce the reactivity of the sites of action to the drug is called **functional tolerance**. Tolerance to **psychoactive drugs** (drugs that affect subjective experience and behavior by acting on the nervous system) is largely functional.

Drug Withdrawal Effects and Physical Dependence

After significant amounts of a drug have been in the body for a period of time (e.g., several days), its sudden elimination can trigger an adverse physiological reaction called a **withdrawal syndrome**. The effects of drug

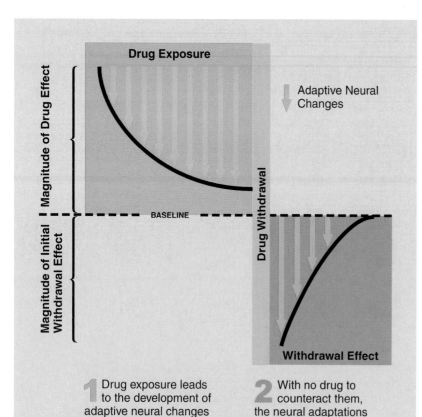

Drug Exposure

Magnitude of Drug Effect

Magnitude of Initial Withdrawal Effect

Adaptive Neural Changes

Drug Withdrawal

BASELINE

Withdrawal Effect

1 Drug exposure leads to the development of adaptive neural changes that produce tolerance by counteracting the drug effect.

2 With no drug to counteract them, the neural adaptations produce withdrawal effects opposite to the effects of the drug.

The relation between drug tolerance and withdrawal effects. The same adaptive neurophysiological changes that develop in response to drug exposure and produce drug tolerance manifest themselves as withdrawal effects once the drug is removed. As the neurophysiological changes develop, tolerance increases; as they subside, the severity of the withdrawal effects decreases.

Figure 13.2

withdrawal are virtually always opposite to the initial effects of the drug. For example, the withdrawal of anticonvulsant drugs often triggers convulsions, and the withdrawal of sleeping pills often produces insomnia. Individuals who suffer withdrawal reactions when they stop taking a drug are said to be **physically dependent** on that drug.

The fact that withdrawal effects are frequently opposite to the initial effects of the drug suggests that withdrawal effects may be produced by the same neural changes that produce drug tolerance (see Figure 13.2). According to this theory, exposure to a drug produces compensatory changes in the nervous system that offset the drug's effects and produce tolerance. Then, when the drug is eliminated from the body, these compensatory neural changes, without the drug to offset them, manifest themselves as withdrawal symptoms opposite to the initial effects of the drug.

Drug Tolerance and Conditioning

What do you think causes tolerance to a drug? The obvious answer is, "Drug exposure causes drug tolerance." As obvious as that answer is, it is not, strictly speaking, correct. You see, tolerance to psychoactive drugs has been shown by numerous experiments to be largely a product of *Pavlovian conditioning*.

In one demonstration that drug tolerance is conditioned (Crowell, Hinson, & Siegel, 1981), two groups of rats received 20 alcohol and 20 saline injections in an alternating sequence, 1 injection every other day. The only difference between the two groups was that the rats in one group received all 20 alcohol injections in a distinctive test room and the 20 saline injections in their colony room, while the rats in the other group received the alcohol in the colony room and the saline in the distinctive test room. At the end of the injection period, the tolerance of all rats to the *hypothermic* (temperature-reducing) effects of alcohol was assessed in both environments. As Figure 13.3 illustrates, tolerance was observed only when the rats were injected in the environment that had previously been paired with alcohol administration. There have been dozens of other demonstrations of the *situational specificity of drug tolerance*: The effect is large, reliable, and general.

Siegel views each incidence of drug administration as a Pavlovian conditioning trial in which various environmental stimuli that regularly predict the administration of the drug (e.g., pubs, washrooms, needles, other addicts) are conditional stimuli and the drug effects are unconditional stimuli (e.g., Siegel, 2004). The central assumption of the theory is that conditional stimuli that

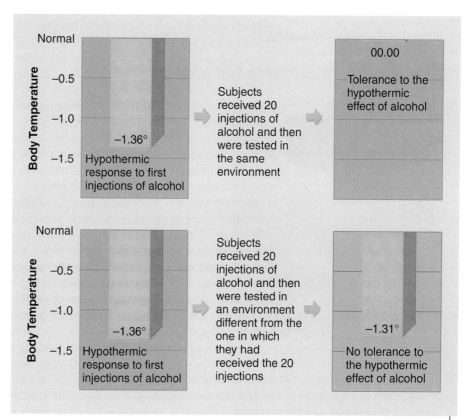

The situational specificity of tolerance to the hypothermic effects of alcohol. (Adapted from Crowell et al., 1981.)

Figure 13.3

predict drug administration come to elicit conditional responses opposite to the unconditional effects of the drug. Siegel has termed these hypothetical opposing conditional responses **conditioned compensatory responses**. The theory is that as the stimuli that repeatedly predict the effects of a drug come to elicit greater and greater conditioned compensatory responses, they increasingly counteract the unconditional effects of the drug and produce situationally specific tolerance. In other words, if an organism is in a situation in which it has previously experienced particular drug effects, that situation will trigger changes in the nervous system to counteract those drug effects.

Addiction: What Is It?

Addicts are habitual drug users, but not all habitual drug users are addicts. **Addicts** are those habitual drug users who continue to use a drug despite its adverse effects on their health and social life and despite their repeated efforts to stop using it (see Hyman & Malenka, 2001). The following case makes this point by describing one addict's interactions with two addictive drugs, one to which he became addicted and one to which he did not. The case is noteworthy in another respect: It shows that nobody, no matter how powerful their intellect, is immune to the addictive effects of drugs (see Figure 13.4).

The Case of Sigmund Freud

Clinical Implications

In 1883, a German army physician prescribed cocaine, which had recently been isolated, to Bavarian soldiers to help them deal with the demands of military maneuvers. When Freud read about this, he decided to procure some of the drug.

In addition to taking cocaine himself, Freud pressed it on his friends and associates, both for themselves and for their patients. He even sent some to his fiancée. In short, by today's standards, Freud was a public menace.

Freud's famous essay "Song of Praise" was about cocaine and was published in July 1884. Freud wrote in such glowing terms about his own personal experiences with cocaine that he created a wave of interest in the drug. But within a year, there was a critical reaction to Freud's premature advocacy of the drug. As evidence accumulated that cocaine was highly addictive and produced a psychosis-like state at high doses, so too did published criticisms of Freud.

Freud continued to praise cocaine until the summer of 1887, but soon thereafter he suddenly stopped all use of cocaine—both personally and professionally. Despite the fact that he had used cocaine for 3 years, he seems to have had no difficulty stopping.

Some 7 years later, in 1894, when Freud was 38, his physician and close friend ordered him to stop smoking because it was causing a heart arrhythmia. Freud was a heavy smoker; he smoked approximately 20 cigars per day.

Freud did stop smoking, but 7 weeks later he started again. On another occasion, Freud stopped for 14 months, but at the age of 58, he was still smoking 20 cigars a day—and still struggling against his addiction. He wrote to friends that smoking was adversely affecting his heart and making it difficult for him to work . . . yet he kept smoking.

In 1923, at the age of 67, Freud developed sores in his mouth. They were cancerous. When he was recovering from oral surgery, he wrote to a friend that smoking was the cause of his cancer . . . yet he kept smoking.

In addition to the cancer, Freud began to experience severe heart pains (tobacco angina) whenever he smoked . . . still he kept smoking.

Sigmund Freud.

Figure 13.4

At 73, Freud was hospitalized for his heart condition and stopped smoking. He made an immediate recovery. But 23 days later, he started to smoke again.

In 1936, at the age of 79, Freud was experiencing more heart trouble, and he had had 33 operations to deal with his recurring oral cancer. His jaw had been entirely removed and replaced by an artificial one. He was in constant pain, and he could swallow, chew, and talk only with difficulty . . . yet he kept smoking. Freud died of cancer in 1939.

Biological Theories of Addiction

Early attempts to explain the phenomenon of drug addiction attributed it to physical dependence. According to various **physical-dependence theories of addiction**, physical dependence traps addicts in a vicious circle of drug taking and withdrawal symptoms. The idea was that drug users whose intake has reached a level sufficient to induce physical dependence are driven by their withdrawal symptoms to self-administer the drug each time they attempt to curtail their intake. Accordingly, early drug addiction treatment programs were based on the physical-dependence perspective. These programs attempted to break the vicious circle of drug taking by gradually withdrawing drugs from addicts in a hospital environment. Unfortunately, once discharged, almost all **detoxified addicts** (addicts who have no drugs in their bodies and who are no longer experiencing withdrawal symptoms) return to their former drug-taking habits.

The failure of detoxification to cure addiction is one major piece of evidence against physical-dependence theories of addiction. A second is that some highly addictive drugs, such as cocaine and amphetamines, do not produce severe withdrawal distress (see Gawin, 1991). And a third is that the pattern of drug taking routinely displayed by many addicts involves an alternating cycle of binges and detoxification (Mello & Mendelson, 1972). There are a variety of reasons for this pattern of drug use. For example, some addicts adopt it because weekend binges are compatible with their work schedules, others adopt it because they do not have enough money to use drugs continuously, and others have it forced on them because their binges land them in jail periodically. However, whether detoxification is by choice or necessity, it does not stop addicts from renewing their drug-taking habits (see Leshner, 1997).

The failure of physical-dependence theories to account for some aspects of addiction has lent support to explanations that hold that most addicts take drugs not to escape from their daily lives or to avoid the unpleasant consequences of withdrawal or conditioned withdrawal, but rather primarily to obtain the drugs' positive effects. These **positive-incentive theories of addiction** hold that the primary factor in most cases of addiction is the craving for the positive-incentive (anticipated pleasure-producing) properties of the drugs. Consider the following statement of one addict:

> I'm just trying to get high as much as possible. . . . If I could get more money, I would spend it all on drugs. All I want is to get loaded. I just really like shooting dope. I don't have any use for sex; I'd rather shoot dope. I like to shoot dope better than anything else in the world.

One positive-incentive theory of addiction is based on the idea that the positive-incentive value of addictive drugs increases (i.e., becomes heightened) with drug use. Robinson and Berridge (2003) have suggested that the use of drugs sensitizes addiction-prone individuals to the drugs' positive-incentive value, thus rendering these users highly motivated to consume drugs and to seek drug-associated stimuli. A key point of Robinson and Berridge's **incentive-sensitization theory** deserves emphasis: They argue that it isn't the pleasure (liking) of drug taking per se that is the basis of addiction; it is the *anticipated* pleasure of drug taking (i.e., the drug's positive-incentive value). Initially, a drug's positive-incentive value is closely tied to its pleasurable effects; however, tolerance to those pleasurable effects often develops, whereas the addict's wanting of the drug becomes sensitized. Thus, in chronic addicts, the positive-incentive value of the drug is often out of proportion with the pleasure actually derived from it: Many addicts are miserable, their lives are in ruins, and the immediate drug effects are not that great anymore—but they crave the drug more than ever.

So which perspective on addiction is correct, the physical-dependence view or the positive-incentive view? Although there is no question that the alleviation of withdrawal symptoms is a factor in the drug use of many addicts, most evidence suggests that the positive-incentive value of addictive drugs is the primary factor in addiction (see Cardinal & Everitt, 2004; Everitt, Dickinson, & Robbins, 2001; Martin-Soelch et al., 2001).

I am sure that you will recognize from preceding chapters that the shift that has taken place in theories of the motivation to take drugs is similar to the shifts that have occurred in theories of the motivation to eat and sleep. In the 1950s and 1960s, motivation was thought of as a drive arising from inner physiological imbalances. A half-century of research has taught us that behavior is more often motivated by its anticipated pleasurable effects.

Causes of Relapse

Virtually all addicts have stopped taking the drug they abuse at some point, but they eventually *relapse* (start taking the drug again). Thus, understanding the causes of relapse is the key to understanding the effective treatment of addiction.

Three fundamentally different causes of relapse have been identified. The first is stress. Most therapists and patients point to stress as the major factor in relapse. The impact of stress on drug taking was illustrated in a dramatic fashion by the marked increases in cigarette and alcohol consumption that occurred among New Yorkers following the attacks of September 11, 2001. The second cause of relapse is *priming* (a single exposure to the formerly abused drug). Many addicts who have abstained for many weeks, and thus feel that they have their addiction under control, sample their formerly abused drug just once and are immediately plunged back into full-blown addiction. The third cause of relapse is exposure to environmental cues (e.g., people, times, places, or objects) that have previously been associated with drug taking, presumably by Pavlovian conditioning (see Di Ciano & Everitt, 2003; Kruzich, Congleton, & See, 2001). Such environmental cues have been shown to precipitate relapse. The fact that the many U.S. soldiers who became addicted to heroin while fighting in the Vietnam War easily shed their addiction when they returned home has been attributed to their removal from that drug-associated environment.

13.2
Effects on Health of Five Commonly Abused Drugs

This section discusses the health hazards associated with the chronic use of five commonly abused drugs: tobacco, alcohol, marijuana, cocaine, and the opiates. It focuses on the health hazards caused by the drugs themselves, not on the health hazards caused by the drugs' legal and social status.

To help you understand the importance of this distinction, think about what would happen to coffee fanatics if a law were passed against drinking or possessing coffee. Some would be able to stop drinking coffee, but many would continue to drink it; these users would be forced to purchase their drug from criminals and run the risk of arrest. As the price of coffee skyrocketed, many of the users would have to turn to crime and prostitution in order to pay for their habit, and they would run the risk of health problems caused by coffee *cut with* (increased in volume by the addition of) unknown substances. The point here is that many of these harmful effects that would come to be associated with coffee would be, in large part, a product of the law prohibiting it, not the coffee itself.

Tobacco

When a cigarette is smoked, *nicotine*—the major psychoactive ingredient of tobacco—and some 4,000 other chemicals, collectively referred to as *tar*, are absorbed through the lungs. Each year, tobacco is responsible for over 3 million deaths worldwide, 450,000 in the United States alone, and it contributes to about 20% of all deaths in Western countries (see Laviolette & Van der Kooy, 2004).

Tobacco

Because considerable tolerance develops to some of the immediate effects of tobacco, the effects of smoking a cigarette on nonsmokers and smokers can be quite different. Nonsmokers often respond to a few puffs of a cigarette with various combinations of nausea, vomiting, coughing, sweating, abdominal cramps, dizziness, flushing, and diarrhea. In contrast, smokers report that they are more relaxed, more alert, and less hungry after a cigarette.

There is no question that heavy smokers are drug addicts in every sense of the word (Jones, 1987). The compulsive drug craving, which is the major defining feature of addiction, is readily apparent in any habitual smoker who has run out of cigarettes or who is forced by circumstance to refrain from smoking for several hours. Furthermore, habitual smokers who stop smoking experience a variety of withdrawal effects, such as depression, anxiety, restlessness, irritability, constipation, and difficulties in sleeping and concentrating.

About 70% of all people who experiment with smoking become addicted—this figure compares unfavorably with 10% for alcohol and 30% for heroin. Moreover, only about 20% of all attempts to stop smoking are successful for 2 years or more (Schelling, 1992). Can you think of any other psychoactive drug that is self-administered almost continually—even while the addicts are walking along the street?

Twin studies (Lerman et al., 1999; True et al., 1999) indicate that nicotine addiction has a major genetic component. The heritability estimate is about 65%.

The consequences of long-term tobacco use are alarming. **Smoker's syndrome** is characterized by chest pain, labored breathing, wheezing, coughing, and a heightened susceptibility to infections of the respiratory tract. Chronic smokers are highly susceptible to a variety of potentially lethal lung disorders, including pneumonia, *bronchitis* (chronic inflammation of the bronchioles of the lungs), *emphysema* (loss of elasticity of the lung from chronic irritation), and lung cancer. Although the increased risk of lung cancer receives the greatest publicity, smoking also increases the risk of cancer of the larynx (voice box), mouth, esophagus, kidneys, pancreas, bladder, and stomach. Smokers also run a greater risk of developing a variety of cardiovascular diseases, which may culminate in heart attack or stroke.

Clinical Implications

Many smokers claim that they smoke despite the adverse effects because smoking reduces tension. However, smokers are actually more tense than nonsmokers: Their levels of tension are reasonably normal while they are smoking, but they increase markedly between cigarettes. Thus, the apparent relaxant effect of smoking merely reflects the increase in stress levels between cigarettes (see Parrott, 1999).

Sufferers from Buerger's disease provide a shocking illustration of the addictive power of nicotine. **Buerger's disease** is a condition in which the blood vessels, especially those supplying the legs, are constricted whenever nicotine enters the bloodstream:

> If a patient with this condition continues to smoke, gangrene may eventually set in. First a few toes may have to be amputated, then the foot at the ankle, then the leg at the knee,

and ultimately at the hip. Somewhere along this gruesome progression gangrene may also attack the other leg. Patients are strongly advised that if they will only stop smoking, it is virtually certain that the otherwise inexorable march of gangrene up the legs will be curbed. Yet surgeons report that it is not at all uncommon to find a patient with Buerger's disease vigorously puffing away in his hospital bed following a second or third amputation operation. (Brecher, 1972, pp. 215–216)

The adverse effects of tobacco smoke are unfortunately not restricted to those who smoke. There is now strong evidence that individuals who live or work with smokers are more likely to develop heart disease and cancer than those who don't. Even the unborn are vulnerable: Smoking during pregnancy increases the likelihood of miscarriage, stillbirth, and early death of the child. The levels of nicotine in the blood of breastfed infants are often as great as those in the blood of their smoking mothers.

Alcohol

Approximately 104 million Americans have consumed alcohol in the last month, 13 million of these are heavy users, and over 100,000 die each year from alcohol-related diseases and accidents. Alcohol is involved in roughly 3% of all deaths in the United States, including deaths from birth defects, ill health, accidents, and violence.

— Alcohol —

Because alcohol molecules are small and soluble in both fat and water, they invade all parts of the body. Alcohol is classified as a **depressant** because at moderate-to-high doses it depresses neural firing; however, at low doses it can stimulate neural firing and facilitate social interaction. Alcohol addiction has a major genetic component (McGue, 1999): Heritability estimates are about 55%.

With moderate doses, the alcohol drinker experiences various degrees of cognitive, perceptual, verbal, and motor impairment, as well as a loss of control that can lead to a variety of socially unacceptable actions. High doses result in unconsciousness; and if blood levels reach 0.5%, there is a risk of death from respiratory depression. The telltale red facial flush of alcohol intoxication is produced by the dilation of blood vessels in the skin; this dilation increases the amount of heat that is lost from the blood to the air and leads to a decrease in body temperature (*hypothermia*). Alcohol is also a *diuretic*; that is, it increases the production of urine by the kidneys.

Alcohol, like many addictive drugs, produces both tolerance and physical dependence. Alcohol withdrawal often produces a mild syndrome of headache, nausea, vomiting, and tremulousness, which is euphemistically referred to as a *hangover*.

A full-blown alcohol withdrawal syndrome comprises three phases (see De Witte et al., 2003). The first phase begins about 5 or 6 hours after the cessation of a long bout of heavy drinking and is characterized by severe tremors, agitation, headache, nausea, vomiting, abdominal cramps, profuse sweating, and sometimes hallucinations. The defining feature of the second phase, which typically occurs between 15 and 30 hours after cessation of drinking, is convulsive activity. The third phase, which usually begins a day or two after the cessation of drinking and lasts for 3 or 4 days, is called **delirium tremens (DTs)**. The DTs are characterized by disturbing hallucinations, bizarre delusions, agitation, confusion, *hyperthermia* (high temperature), and *tachycardia* (rapid heartbeat). The convulsions and the DTs produced by alcohol withdrawal can be lethal.

Alcohol attacks almost every tissue in the body (see Anderson et al., 1993). Chronic alcohol consumption is often associated with extensive brain damage (Hayakawa et al., 1992) and **Korsakoff's syndrome**—a neuropsychological disorder that is characterized by severe memory loss, sensory and motor dysfunction, and severe *dementia* (intellectual deterioration). Chronic alcohol consumption also

Clinical Implications

causes extensive scarring, or **cirrhosis**, of the liver, which is the major cause of death among heavy alcohol users. Because the liver plays a critical role in the distribution of energy and nutrients to the body, cirrhosis of the liver can have far-reaching effects—for example, liver damage in alcoholics disrupts thiamine (vitamin B_1) metabolism, and the resulting thiamine deficiency is a cause of much of the brain damage observed in alcoholics.

In addition to its effects on the brain and the liver, alcohol erodes the muscles of the heart and thus increases the risk of heart attack. It irritates the lining of the digestive tract and, in so doing, increases the risk of oral and liver cancer, stomach ulcers, *pancreatitis* (inflammation of the pancreas), and *gastritis* (inflammation of the stomach).

Not to be forgotten is the carnage that alcohol produces on our highways and in our homes. (The devastating effect of alcohol on the families of addicts was emphasized to me by a student who had grown up with an alcoholic parent; she asked me to stress the problem.)

Like nicotine, alcohol readily penetrates the placental membrane and affects the fetus. The result is that the offspring of mothers who consume substantial quantities of alcohol during pregnancy can develop **fetal alcohol syndrome (FAS)**. The FAS child suffers from some or all of the following symptoms (O'Leary, 2004): brain damage, mental retardation, poor coordination, poor muscle tone, low birth weight, retarded growth, and/or physical deformity. Because alcohol can disrupt brain development in so many ways (e.g., by disrupting neurotrophic support, by disrupting the production of cell-adhesion molecules, or by disrupting normal patterns of apoptosis), there is no time during pregnancy when alcohol consumption is safe (see Farber & Olney, 2003; Guerri, 2002). Moreover, there seems to be no safe amount. Although full-blown FAS is rarely seen in the babies of mothers who never had more than one drink a day during pregnancy, children of mothers who drank only moderately while pregnant are sometimes found to have a variety of cognitive problems, even though they are not diagnosed with FAS (see Korkman, Kettunen, & Autti-Ramo, 2003).

Marijuana

Marijuana is the name commonly given to the dried leaves and flowers of **Cannabis sativa**—the common hemp plant. Approximately 2 million Americans have used marijuana in the last month. The usual mode of consumption is to smoke these leaves in a *joint* (a cigarette of marijuana) or a pipe; but marijuana is also effective when ingested orally, if first baked into an oil-rich substrate, such as a chocolate brownie, to promote absorption from the gastrointestinal tract.

The psychoactive effects of marijuana are largely attributable to a constituent called **THC** (delta-9-tetrahydrocannabinol). However, marijuana contains over 80 *cannabinoids* (chemicals of the same chemical class as THC), which may also be psychoactive. Most of the cannabinoids are found in a sticky resin covering the leaves and flowers of the plant, which can be extracted and dried to form a dark corklike material called *hashish*. Hashish can be further processed into an extremely potent product called *hash oil*.

Marijuana

Written records of marijuana use go back 6,000 years in China, where its stems were used to make rope, its seeds were used as a grain, and its leaves and flowers were used for their psychoactive and medicinal effects. In the Middle Ages, cannabis cultivation spread from the Middle East into Western Europe; however, in Europe, the plant was grown primarily for the manufacture of rope, and its psychoactive properties were largely forgotten. During the period of European imperialism, rope was in high demand for sailing vessels. In 1611, the American colonies responded to this demand by growing cannabis as a cash crop—George Washington was one of the more notable cannabis growers.

The practice of smoking the leaves of *Cannabis sativa* and the word *marijuana* itself seem to have been introduced to the southern United States in the early part of the 20th century by Mexican immigrants; and the drug gradually became popular among certain subgroups, such as the poor in city ghettos and jazz musicians. In 1926, an article appeared in a New Orleans newspaper exposing the "menace of marijuana," and soon similar stories were appearing in newspapers all over the United States under titles such as "The Evil Weed," "The Killer Drug," and "Marijuana Madness." The population was told that marijuana turns normal people into violent, drug-crazed criminals who rapidly become addicted to heroin.

The result of the misrepresentation of the effects of marijuana by the U.S. news media was the enactment of many laws against the drug. In many states, marijuana was legally classified a **narcotic** (a legal term generally used to refer to opiates), and punishment for its use was dealt out accordingly. However, the structure of the active constituents of marijuana and their physiological and behavioral effects bear no resemblance to those of the other narcotics; thus, legally classifying marijuana as a narcotic was akin to passing a law that red is green.

The popularization of marijuana smoking among the middle and upper classes in the 1960s stimulated a massive program of research on marijuana; yet there is still considerable confusion about this drug among the general population. One of the difficulties in characterizing the effects of marijuana is that they are subtle, difficult to measure, and greatly influenced by the social situation:

> At low, usual "social" doses, the intoxicated individual may experience an increased sense of well-being: initial restlessness and hilarity followed by a dreamy, carefree state of relaxation; alteration of sensory perceptions including expansion of space and time; and a more vivid sense of touch, sight, smell, taste, and sound; a feeling of hunger, especially a craving for sweets; and subtle changes in thought formation and expression. To an unknowing observer, an individual in this state of consciousness would not appear noticeably different. (National Commission on Marijuana and Drug Abuse, 1972, p. 68)

Although the effects of typical social doses of marijuana are subtle, high doses do impair psychological functioning. Short-term memory is impaired, and the ability to carry out tasks involving multiple steps to reach a specific goal declines. Speech becomes slurred, and meaningful conversation becomes difficult. A sense of unreality, emotional intensification, sensory distortion, and motor impairment are also common. However, even after high doses, an unexpected knock at the door can often bring about the return of a reasonable semblance of normal behavior.

In the light of the documented effects of marijuana, the earlier claims that its use would trigger a wave of violent crimes seem absurd. It is difficult to imagine how anybody could believe that the red-eyed, gluttonous, sleepy, giggling products of common social doses of marijuana would be likely to commit violent criminal acts. In fact, marijuana seems to curb aggressive behavior (Tinklenberg, 1974).

The addiction potential of marijuana is low. Most people who use marijuana do so only occasionally, and most who use it as youths curtail their use in their 30s and 40s. Tolerance to marijuana develops during periods of sustained use; however, obvious withdrawal symptoms (e.g., nausea, diarrhea, sweating, chills, tremor, sleep disturbance) are rare, except in artificial laboratory situations in which massive oral doses are administered.

What are the health hazards of marijuana use? This is a difficult question to answer because there have been so many claims based on so little convincing evidence. However, most scientists who have carefully scrutinized the evidence have reached the same general conclusion: The occasional use of small amounts of marijuana, the pattern of use favored by most users, has few, if any, permanent adverse effects (Jacques et al., 2004). Even long-term heavy use of marijuana has effects that are far less severe than those of its legal cousins: nicotine and alcohol.

Two adverse effects of heavy marijuana use have been well documented. First, the minority of marijuana smokers who smoke it regularly tend to develop respiratory problems (see Zimmer & Morgan, 1997): cough, bronchitis, and asthma. Second, because marijuana produces *tachycardia* (elevated heart rate), single large

Clinical
Implications

doses can trigger heart attacks in susceptible individuals (e.g., elderly men who have previously suffered a heart attack).

Many people believe that marijuana use causes brain damage, in particular, damage to those areas of the brain involved in memory. Is this true? Rogers and Robbins (2001) reviewed the evidence. There is no convincing evidence that marijuana use causes brain damage, but the evidence pertaining to deficits in memory function is more complex. Some reviewers (e.g., Pope, Gruber, & Yurgelin-Todd, 1995) have concluded that there is no good evidence of neurocognitive deficits that outlast the period of marijuana exposure. However, two studies of particularly heavy long-term users found slight memory impairments—but the impairments did not seem to be permanent (Pope et al., 2001).

Some effects of marijuana have been shown to be of clinical benefit. It has been used, often illegally, to block the nausea of cancer patients undergoing chemotherapy and to stimulate the appetites of patients who have difficulty eating. Marijuana has also been shown to block seizures (Corcoran, McCaughran, & Wada, 1978), to dilate the bronchioles of asthmatics, to decrease the severity of *glaucoma* (a disorder characterized by an increase in the pressure of the fluid inside the eye), and to reduce some kinds of pain. Marijuana is legally used for medicinal purposes in some parts of the world (e.g., Canada).

Clinical Implications

Because THC is fat-soluble, it was initially assumed that it influenced the brain by inserting itself directly into neural membranes. However, we now know that THC binds to receptors that are particularly dense in the basal ganglia, hippocampus, cerebellum, and neocortex (Howlett et al., 1990), and presumably, it exerts most of its effects by binding to cannabinoid receptors (see Piomelli, 2003; Wilson & Nicoll, 2002). The cloning of the gene for the THC receptor (Matsuda et al., 1990) triggered a search for an endogenous THC-like chemical that binds to this receptor. Such a chemical has been isolated, its structure has been characterized (Devane et al., 1992) and named *anandamide* (which means "internal bliss"), but its function is still unknown (Di Marzo et al., 1998).

What might the function of anandamide be? One study has shown that it might protect the brain from excitotoxicity. Knockout mice with no type 1 cannabinoid receptors are more susceptible to seizures produced by *excitotoxins* (chemicals that kill neurons by overactivating them) (see Wilson & Nicoll, 2002).

The Evolutionary Perspective

I cannot end this discussion of marijuana (*Cannabis sativa*) without telling you the following story:

> You can imagine how surprised I was when my colleague went to his back door, opened it, and yelled, "Sativa, here Sativa, dinner time."
>
> "What was that you called your dog?" I asked as he returned to his beer.
>
> "Sativa," he said. "The kids picked it. I think they learned about it at school; a Greek goddess or something. Pretty, isn't it? And catchy too: Every kid on the street seems to remember her name."
>
> "Yes," I said. "Very pretty."

Cocaine and Other Stimulants

Stimulants are drugs whose primary effect is to produce general increases in neural and behavioral activity. Although stimulants all have a similar profile of effects, they differ greatly in their potency. Coca-Cola is a mild commercial stimulant preparation consumed by many people around the world. Today, its stimulant action is attributable to *caffeine*, but when it was first introduced, "the pause that refreshes" packed a real wallop in the form of small amounts of cocaine. Cocaine and its derivatives are the most commonly abused stimulants, and thus they are the focus of this discussion.

Cocaine is prepared from the leaves of the coca bush, which is found primarily in Peru and Bolivia. For centuries, a crude extract called *coca paste* has been made directly from the leaves and eaten.

Cocaine

Today, it is more common to treat the coca paste and extract *cocaine hydrochloride*, the nefarious white powder that is referred to simply as *cocaine* and typically consumed by snorting or by injection. Cocaine hydrochloride may be converted to its base form by boiling it in a solution of baking soda until the water has evaporated. The impure residue of this process is *crack*, which is a potent, cheap, smokable form of cocaine. Crack has rapidly become the preferred form of the drug for many cocaine users. However, because crack is impure, variable, and consumed by smoking, it is difficult to study, and most research on cocaine derivatives has thus focused on pure cocaine hydrochloride. Approximately 1.5 million Americans used cocaine or crack in the last month.

People eat, smoke, snort, or inject cocaine or its derivatives in order to experience its psychological effects. Users report being swept by a wave of well-being; they feel self-confident, alert, energetic, friendly, outgoing, fidgety, and talkative; and they have less than their usual desire for food and sleep.

Like alcohol, cocaine hydrochloride is frequently consumed in *binges* (see Gawin, 1991). Cocaine addicts tend to go on so-called *cocaine sprees*, binges in which extremely high levels of intake are maintained for periods of a day or two. During a cocaine spree, users become increasingly tolerant to the euphoria-producing effects of cocaine. Accordingly, larger and larger doses are often administered. The spree usually ends when the cocaine is gone or when it begins to have serious toxic effects.

Extremely high blood levels of cocaine are reached during cocaine sprees. The results commonly include sleeplessness, tremors, nausea, hyperthermia, and psychotic behavior. The syndrome of psychotic behavior observed during cocaine sprees is called **cocaine psychosis**. It is similar to, and has often been mistakenly diagnosed as, *paranoid schizophrenia*.

During cocaine sprees, there is a risk of loss of consciousness, seizures, respiratory arrest, heart attack, or stroke (Kokkinos & Levine, 1993). Although tolerance develops to most effects of cocaine (e.g., to the euphoria), repeated cocaine exposure sensitizes subjects (i.e., makes them even more responsive) to its motor and convulsive effects (see Robinson & Berridge, 1993).

Clinical Implications

Cocaine snorting can damage the nasal membranes, and cocaine smoking can damage the lungs; but both routes are safer than IV injection. Fatalities from cocaine overdose are most likely to follow IV injection.

Although cocaine is extremely addictive, the withdrawal effects triggered by abrupt termination of a cocaine spree are mild (Miller, Summers, & Gold, 1993). Common cocaine withdrawal symptoms include a negative mood swing and insomnia.

Cocaine facilitates catecholaminergic transmission. It does this by blocking the reuptake of *catecholamines* (dopamine, norepinephrine, and epinephrine) into presynaptic neurons. Its effects on dopaminergic transmission seem to play the major role in mediating its euphoria-inducing effects.

Cocaine and its various derivatives are not the only commonly abused stimulants. **Amphetamine** (speed) and its relatives also present major health problems. Amphetamine has been in wide illicit use since the 1960s—it is consumed orally in the potent form called *d-amphetamine* (dextroamphetamine). The effects of *d*-amphetamine are comparable to those of cocaine; for example, it produces a syndrome of psychosis called *amphetamine psychosis*.

In the 1990s, *d*-amphetamine was supplanted as the favored amphetaminelike drug by several more potent relatives. One is *methamphetamine* (see Cho, 1990). Methamphetamine (meth) is commonly used in its even more potent, smokable, crystalline form (ice or crystal). Another potent relative of amphetamine is *3,4-methylenedioxymethamphetamine* (MDMA, or ecstasy), which is taken orally.

The Evolutionary Perspective

Do stimulants have long-term adverse effects on the health of habitual users? Mounting evidence suggests that stimulants are neurotoxins (see Davidson et al., 2001). Recent research has focused on the effects of MDMA (ecstasy) because of its powerful effects and current prevalence (see Cole & Sumnall, 2003). The results of experiments on nonhuman animals are cause for concern: There is good evidence

from experiments on laboratory animals that MDMA can have toxic effects on both serotonergic and dopaminergic neurons (see Ricaurte et al., 2002).

Correlational studies in human users of MDMA support the hypothesis that it can cause brain damage. There are several reports that habitual users display abnormalities of serotonergic function and deficits in the performance of tests of memory, psychomotor function, and mood (e.g., McCardle et al., 2004). It has not yet been established that these effects in humans are caused specifically by the MDMA and are permanent, but considering the results of experiments in laboratory animals, there is clearly cause for concern. Women who use stimulants while they are pregnant tend to have children who score poorly on IQ tests (see Singer et al., 2002).

The Opiates: Heroin and Morphine

Opium—the sap that exudes from the seeds of the opium poppy—has several psychoactive ingredients. Most notable are **morphine** and *codeine*, its weaker relative. Morphine, codeine, and other drugs that have similar structures or effects are commonly referred to as the **opiates**. The opiates have a clear Jekyll-and-Hyde character. On their Dr. Jekyll side, the opiates are unmatched as **analgesics** (painkillers), and they are also extremely effective in the treatment of cough and diarrhea. But, unfortunately, the kindly Dr. Jekyll brings with him the evil Mr. Hyde—the risk of addiction.

Archeological evidence suggests that the practice of eating opium became popular in the Middle East sometime before 4000 B.C., and then it spread throughout Africa, Europe, and Asia (see Berridge & Edwards, 1981; Latimer & Goldberg, 1981). Three historic events fanned the flame of opiate addiction. First, in 1644, the Emperor of China banned tobacco smoking, and many Chinese tobacco smokers tried smoking opium and liked it (see Figure 13.5 on page 418). Because smoking opium has a greater effect on the brain than does eating it, many more people became addicted to opium as the practice of opium smoking slowly spread to other countries. Second, morphine, the most potent constituent of opium, was first isolated in 1803, and it became available commercially in the 1830s. Third, the hypodermic needle was invented in 1856, and soon injured soldiers (e.g., those of the American Civil War) were introduced to morphine through a needle; during this era, morphine addiction was known as *soldiers' disease*.

Opiates

Most people are surprised to learn that until the early part of the 20th century, opium was legally available in many parts of the world, including Europe and North America. Opium was available in cakes, candies, and wines, as well as in a variety of over-the-counter medicinal offerings. Opium potions such as *laudanum* (a very popular mixture of opium and alcohol), *Godfrey's Cordial*, and *Dalby's Carminative* were very popular. (The word *carminative* should win first prize for making a sow's ear at least sound like a silk purse: A carminative is a drug that expels gas from the digestive tract, thereby reducing stomach cramps and flatulence. *Flatulence* is the obvious pick for second prize.) There were even over-the-counter opium potions just for baby. Potions such as *Mrs. Winslow's Soothing Syrup* and the aptly labeled *Street's Infant Quietness* were popular in many households. Although pure morphine could not be purchased without a prescription at the time, it was so frequently prescribed by physicians for so many different maladies that morphine addiction was common among those who could afford doctors.

The **Harrison Narcotics Act**, passed in 1914, made it illegal to sell or use opium, morphine, or cocaine in the United States. However, the act did not include the semisynthetic opiate **heroin**. Heroin had been synthesized in 1870 by the addition of two acetyl groups to the morphine molecule, which greatly increased its ability to penetrate the blood–brain barrier. In 1898, heroin was marketed by the Bayer Drug Company; it was freely available without prescription and was widely advertised as a super aspirin. Tests showed that it was a more potent analgesic than morphine

An opium den. Opium dens became popular in China and spread to the west coast of North America.

Figure 13.5

and that it was less likely to induce nausea and vomiting. Moreover, the Bayer Drug Company claimed that heroin was not addictive; this is why it was not covered by the Harrison Narcotics Act.

The consequence of this omission was that opiate addicts in the United States, forbidden by law to use opium or morphine, turned to the readily available and much more potent heroin; and the flames of addiction were further fanned. In 1924, the U.S. Congress made it illegal for anybody to possess, sell, or use heroin. Unfortunately, the laws enacted to stamp out opiate addiction in the United States have been far from successful: An estimated 130,000 Americans currently use heroin, and organized crime flourishes on the proceeds.

The effect of opiates most valued by addicts is the *rush* that follows intravenous injection. The *heroin rush* is a wave of intense abdominal, orgasmic pleasure that evolves into a state of serene, drowsy euphoria. Many opiate users, drawn by these pleasurable effects, begin to use the drug more and more frequently. Then, tolerance and physical dependence develop and contribute to the problem.

Clinical Implications

Although opiates are highly addictive, the direct health hazards of chronic exposure are surprisingly minor. The main risks are constipation, pupil constriction, menstrual irregularity, and reduced libido (sex drive). Many opiate addicts have taken pure heroin or morphine for years with no serious ill effects. In fact, opiate addiction is more prevalent among doctors, nurses, and dentists than among other professionals (e.g., Brewster, 1986):

> An individual tolerant to and dependent upon an opiate who is socially or financially capable of obtaining an adequate supply of good quality drug, sterile syringes and needles, and other paraphernalia may maintain his or her proper social and occupational functions, remain in fairly good health, and suffer little serious incapacitation as a result of the dependence. (Julien, 1981, p. 117)

> One such individual was Dr. William Stewart Halsted, one of the founders of Johns Hopkins Medical School and one of the most brilliant surgeons of his day . . . known as "the father of modern surgery." And yet, during his career he was addicted to morphine, a fact that he was able to keep secret from all but his closest friends. In fact, the only time his habit caused him any trouble was when he was attempting to reduce his dosage. (McKim, 1986, p. 197)

The classic opiate withdrawal syndrome usually begins 6 to 12 hours after the last dose. The first withdrawal sign is typically an increase in restlessness; the addict begins to pace and fidget. Watering eyes, running nose, yawning, and sweating are also common during the early stages of opiate withdrawal. Then, the addict often falls into a fitful sleep, which typically lasts for several hours. After the sleep is over, the original symptoms may be joined in extreme cases by chills, shivering, profuse sweating, gooseflesh, nausea, vomiting, diarrhea, cramps, pains, dilated pupils, tremor, and muscle spasms. The gooseflesh skin and leg spasms of the opiate withdrawal syndrome are the basis for the expressions "going cold turkey" and "kicking the habit." The symptoms of opiate withdrawal are typically most severe in the second or third day after the last injection, and by the seventh day they have all but disappeared.

The symptoms of opiate withdrawal are not trivial, but their severity has been widely exaggerated. Opiate withdrawal is about as serious as a bad case of the flu—a far cry from the convulsions, delirium, and risk of death associated with alcohol withdrawal:

> Opiate withdrawal is probably one of the most misunderstood aspects of drug use. This is largely because of the image of withdrawal that has been portrayed in the movies and popular literature for many years. . . . Few addicts . . . take enough drug to cause the . . . severe withdrawal symptoms that are shown in the movies. Even in its most severe form, however, opiate withdrawal is not as dangerous or terrifying as withdrawal from barbiturates or alcohol. (McKim, 1986, p. 199)

Most risks of opiate addiction are indirect—that is, not attributable to the drug itself. Many are risks that arise out of the battle between the relentless addictive power of opiates and the attempts of governments to eradicate addiction by making drugs illegal. The opiate addicts who cannot give up their habit—treatment programs report success rates of only 10%—are caught in the middle. Because most opiate addicts must purchase their morphine and heroin from illicit dealers at greatly inflated prices, those who are not wealthy become trapped in a life of poverty and petty crime. They are poor, they are undernourished, they receive poor medical care, they are often driven to prostitution, and they run great risk of contracting AIDS and other infections (e.g., hepatitis, syphillis, gonorrhea) from unsafe sex and unsterile needles. Moreover, they never know for sure what they are injecting: Some street drugs are poorly processed, and virtually all have been *cut* (stretched by the addition of some similar-appearing substance) to some unknown degree.

Thinking Clearly

One particularly serious risk associated with heroin that is largely indirect is death from overdose. Overdose deaths are a risk any time addictive drugs are routinely administered via the intravenous route, but it is clear that the very laws designed to prevent heroin addiction are complicit in heroin-overdose deaths. The laws do not permit addicts to buy their drugs from reliable sources, and, as a result, waves of overdose deaths occur when shipments of contaminated drugs hit the street. Paradoxically, similar waves of deaths occur when shipments of particularly pure heroin hit the street—because addicts select doses on the basis of their previous experience with heroin that has been heavily cut.

The opiates, like marijuana, seem to exert their effects by binding to particular receptors whose normal function is to bind to endogenous chemicals. There are several classes of endogenous opiates (e.g., *endorphins*).

Comparison of the Health Hazards of Tobacco, Alcohol, Marijuana, Cocaine, and Heroin

One way of comparing the adverse effects of tobacco, alcohol, marijuana, cocaine, and heroin is to compare the prevalence of their use in a society as a whole. In terms of this criterion, it is clear that tobacco and alcohol have a far greater negative health impact on Americans than do marijuana, cocaine, and heroin (see Figure 13.6 on page 420). Another method of comparison is to look at death rates: Tobacco has been implicated in the deaths of approximately 450,000 Americans per year; alcohol, in approximately 100,000 per year; and all other drugs combined, in about 40,000 per year.

But what about the individual drug user? Who is taking greater health risks: the cigarette smoker, the alcohol drinker, the marijuana smoker, the cocaine user, or the heroin user? You now have the information to answer this question. Complete the following Check It Out demonstration, which will help you appreciate the positive impact that studying biopsychology is having on your understanding of important issues. Would you have ranked the health risks of these drugs in the same way before you began this chapter? Has your reaction to "The Ironic Case of the Drugged High School Teachers" changed?

Thinking Clearly

Prevalence of drug use in the United States. Figures are based on survey data from people 12 years of age and over who live in households and used the drug in question at least once in the last month.

Figure 13.6

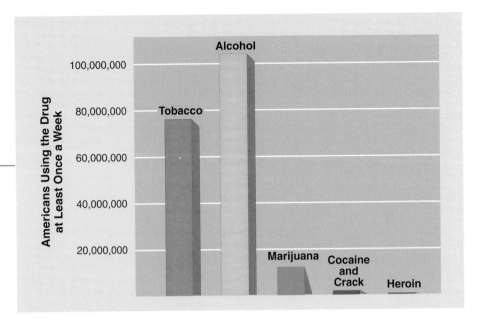

Check It Out
DRUGS THAT HARM: THE EVIDENCE

List the major direct health hazards of the following five drugs.
Omit the indirect hazards that result from the drugs' legal or social status.

Tobacco	Alcohol	Marijuana	Cocaine	Heroin
1. _____	1. _____	1. _____	1. _____	1. _____
2. _____	2. _____	2. _____	2. _____	2. _____
3. _____	3. _____	3. _____	3. _____	3. _____
4. _____	4. _____	4. _____	4. _____	4. _____
5. _____	5. _____	5. _____	5. _____	5. _____
6. _____	6. _____	6. _____	6. _____	6. _____

On the basis of comparisons among your lists, rank the five drugs in terms of their overall health risks.

Most Hazardous 1. _____
                 2. _____
                 3. _____
                 4. _____
Least Hazardous 5. _____

Addiction and the Neural Mechanisms of Motivation

With increasing appreciation by researchers that the positive-incentive value of drugs is the major factor in drug addiction, research on addiction has started to focus on the reinforcing effects of drugs. Most of this research has been conducted in nonhuman species.

The Evolutionary Perspective

Two Methods of Measuring Drug-Produced Reinforcement

Two methods have played important roles in the study of drug-produced reinforcement in nonhumans: the drug self-administration paradigm and the conditioned place preference paradigm. They are illustrated in Figure 13.7.

In the **drug self-administration paradigm**, laboratory rats or primates press a lever to inject drugs into themselves through implanted *cannulas* (thin tubes). They readily learn to self-administer intravenous injections of drugs to which humans become addicted. Furthermore, once they have learned to self-administer an addictive drug, their drug taking often mimics in major respects the drug taking of human addicts (Deroche-Gamonet, Belin, & Piazza, 2004; Robinson, 2004; Vanderschuren & Everitt, 2004). Studies in which microinjections have been self-administered directly into particular brain structures have proved particularly enlightening.

ON THE CD

Visit the *Drug Self-Administration Paradigm* module to see a rat taking cocaine.

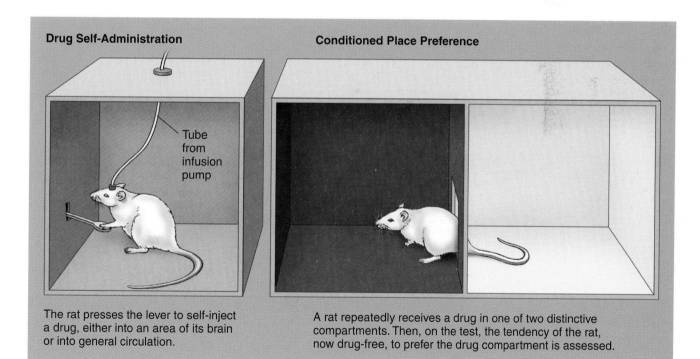

Drug Self-Administration

Tube from infusion pump

Conditioned Place Preference

The rat presses the lever to self-inject a drug, either into an area of its brain or into general circulation.

A rat repeatedly receives a drug in one of two distinctive compartments. Then, on the test, the tendency of the rat, now drug-free, to prefer the drug compartment is assessed.

Two behavioral paradigms that are used extensively in the study of the neural mechanisms of addiction: the drug self-administration paradigm and the conditioned place-preference paradigm.

Figure 13.7

In the **conditioned place-preference paradigm**, rats repeatedly receive a drug in one compartment (the *drug compartment*) of a two-compartment box. Then, during the test phase, the drug-free rat is placed in the box, and the proportion of time it spends in the drug compartment, as opposed to the equal-sized but distinctive *control compartment*, is measured. Rats usually prefer the drug compartment over the control compartment when the drug compartment has been associated with the effects of drugs to which humans become addicted. The main advantage of the conditioned place-preference paradigm is that the subjects are tested while they are drug-free, which means that the measure of the incentive value of a drug is not confounded by other effects the drug might have on behavior.

Early Evidence of the Involvement of Dopamine in Drug Addiction

In the 1970s, experiments began to implicate dopamine in the rewarding effects of natural reinforcers and of addictive drugs. For example, in rats, dopamine antagonists blocked the self-administration of, or conditioned place preference for, several different addictive drugs; and they reduced the reinforcing effects of food. These findings suggested that dopamine might signal something akin to reward or pleasure.

The Dopamine System

Evidence linking dopamine with addiction directed researchers to the dopamine system of the brain, which is illustrated in Figure 13.8. The neurons that compose the brain's dopamine system have their cell bodies in two midbrain nuclei: the *substantia nigra* and the **ventral tegmental area**.

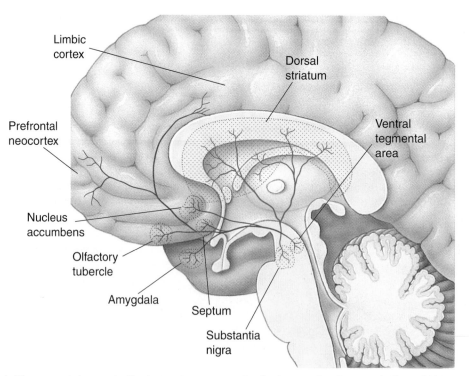

The mesotelencephalic dopamine system in the human brain, consisting of the nigrostriatal pathway (green) and the mesocorticolimbic pathway (red).
(Adapted from Klivington, 1992.)

Figure 13.8

Most of the axons of dopaminergic neurons that have their cell bodies in the substantia nigra project to the dorsal striatum; this component of the mesotelencephalic dopamine system is called the *nigrostriatal pathway*. It is degeneration in this pathway that is associated with Parkinson's disease.

Most of the axons of dopaminergic neurons that have their cell bodies in the ventral tegmental area project to various cortical and limbic sites. This component of the dopamine system is called the *mesocorticolimbic pathway*. The particular mesocorticolimbic neurons that project from the ventral tegmental area to the **nucleus accumbens** have been most frequently implicated in the reinforcing effects of addictive drugs.

Evidence Linking the Dopamine System and the Reinforcing Effects of Drugs

Four kinds of evidence from research on nonhuman animals have implicated the pathway from the ventral tegmental area to the nucleus accumbens in the reinforcing effects of addictive drugs. First, laboratory animals will press a lever to self-administer small quantities of addictive drugs directly into the nucleus accumbens. Second, laboratory animals develop conditioned place preferences for environments in which they have received microinjections of addictive drugs directly into the nucleus accumbens. Third, lesions to either the ventral tegmental area or the nucleus accumbens block both the self-administration of drugs into general circulation and the development of drug-induced conditioned place preferences. And fourth, the self-administration of addictive drugs is associated with increases in the release of dopamine in the nucleus accumbens (see Ikemoto & Panksepp, 1999; Spanagel & Weiss, 1999).

Some studies linking the nucleus accumbens to the effects of addictive drugs have been done in humans. Positron emission tomography (PET) has been used to measure dopamine levels in various parts of the human brain. There are two recurring findings. First, many addicts have reduced cerebral dopamine levels; second, dopamine levels in the nucleus accumbens and some of the other nuclei of the dopamine system increase markedly when addicts are exposed to their drug of choice (see Volkow et al., 2004).

Cognitive Neuroscience

The Dopamine System and Reward: The Current View

There is little doubt that the dopamine system is involved in the effects of addictive drugs; the evidence is strong. However, the exact functions of the nucleus accumbens and other parts of the dopamine system are still the focus of substantial debate (Wise, 2004).

The finding that natural reinforcers, such as food and sex, produce increases in dopamine release similar to those produced by addictive drugs suggested that the dopamine system might mediate the experience of reward or pleasure. However, the observation that neutral stimuli that signal the impending delivery of a reward themselves trigger dopamine release suggests that the dopamine system may be involved in the expectation of reward, rather than its experience (e.g., Fiorino, Coury, & Phillips, 1997; Weiss et al., 2000).

This *expectation-of-reward theory* has been supported by the study of single dopaminergic neurons in the ventral tegmental area of monkeys. Schultz (1997) found that these neurons responded to rewards only when the rewards were presented unpredictably—as in the early stages of a conditioning experiment. If a reward was expected—as in the late stages of a conditioning experiment—the reward itself did not increase the activity of dopaminergic neurons, but the conditional stimulus that predicted the reward did. In a subsequent study, Schultz and his colleagues (Fiorillo, Tobler, & Schultz, 2003) varied the certainty with which a conditional

Thinking Clearly

stimulus predicted reward, and the response of the dopaminergic neurons to that stimulus was greater when the reward was more certain to follow.

Supporters of the dopamine theory of addiction do not believe that it tells the entire story. Clearly, researchers are just starting to understand the neural mechanisms of addiction, and there is still a long way to go. Nevertheless, there has already been an attempt—albeit a premature one—to cure addiction with nucleus accumbens lesions. The lesions failed to block relapse in opiate addicts (Gao et al., 2003).

13.4
Introduction to the Biopsychology of Emotion

The remainder of the chapter deals with emotion. In particular, it focuses on the negative emotions and on the adverse health consequences associated with stress. Let's start with a brief introduction to the history of biopsychological research on emotion.

The Mind-Blowing Case of Phineas Gage

Clinical Implications

In 1848, Phineas Gage, a 25-year-old construction foreman for the Rutland and Burlington Railroad, was the victim of a tragic accident. In order to lay new tracks, the terrain had to be leveled, and Gage was in charge of the blasting. His task involved drilling holes in the rock, pouring some gun powder into each hole, covering it with sand, and tamping the material down with a large tamping iron before detonating it with a fuse. On the fateful day, the gunpowder exploded while Gage was tamping it, launching the 3-cm-thick, 90-cm-long tamping iron through his face, skull, and brain and out the other side.

Amazingly, Gage survived his accident, but he survived it a changed man. Before the accident, Gage had been a responsible, intelligent, socially well-adapted person, who was well liked by his friends and fellow workers. Once recovered, he appeared to be as able-bodied and intellectually capable as before, but his personality and emotional life had totally changed. Formerly a religious, respectful, reliable man, Gage became irreverent and impulsive. In particular, his abundant profanity offended many. He became so unreliable and undependable that he soon lost his job, and was never again able to hold a responsible position.

Gage became an itinerant, roaming the country for a dozen years until his death in San Francisco. His bizarre accident and apparently successful recovery made headlines around the world, but his death went largely unnoticed and unacknowledged.

Gage was buried next to the offending tamping iron. Five years later, neurologist John Harlow was granted permission from Gage's family to exhume the body and tamping iron to study them. Since then, Gage's skull and the tamping iron have been on display in the Warren Anatomical Medical Museum at Harvard University.

In 1994, Damasio and her colleagues brought the power of computerized reconstruction to bear on Gage's classic case. They began by taking an X-ray of the skull and measuring it precisely, paying particular attention to the position of the entry and exit holes. From these measurements, they reconstructed the accident and determined the likely region of Gage's brain damage (see Figure 13.9). It was appar-

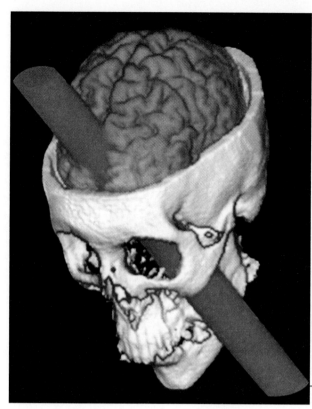

A reconstruction of the brain injury of Phineas Gage. The damage focused on the medial prefrontal lobes.
(Adapted from Damasio et al., 1994.)

Figure 13.9

ent that the damage to Gage's brain affected both *medial prefrontal lobes*, which we now know are involved in planning and emotion.

Darwin's Theory of the Evolution of Emotion

The first major event in the study of the biopsychology of emotion was the publication in 1872 of Darwin's book *The Expression of Emotions in Man and Animals*. In it, Darwin argued, largely on the basis of anecdotal evidence, that particular emotional responses, such as human facial expressions, tend to accompany the same emotional states in all members of a species.

Darwin believed that expressions of emotion, like other behaviors, are products of evolution; he therefore tried to understand them by comparing them in different species. From such interspecies comparisons, Darwin developed a theory of the evolution of emotional expression that was composed of three main ideas: (1) Expressions of emotion evolve from behaviors that indicate what an animal is likely to do next; (2) if the signals provided by such behaviors benefit the animal that displays them, they will evolve in ways that enhance their communicative function, and their original function may be lost; and (3) opposite messages are often signaled by opposite movements and postures (the *principle of antithesis*).

Consider how Darwin's theory accounts for the evolution of *threat displays*. Originally, facing one's enemies, rising up, and exposing one's weapons were the components of the early stages of combat. But once enemies began to recognize these behaviors as signals of impending aggression, a survival advantage accrued to attackers that could communicate their aggression most effectively and intimidate their victims without actually fighting. As a result, elaborate threat displays evolved, and actual combat declined.

To be most effective, signals of aggression and submission must be clearly distinguishable; thus, they tended to evolve in opposite directions. For example,

The Evolutionary Perspective

Aggression

Submission

Two woodcuts from Darwin's 1872 book *The Expression of Emotions in Man and Animals*, that he used to illustrate the principle of antithesis. The aggressive posture of dogs features ears forward, back up, hair up, and tail up; the submissive posture features ears back, back down, hair down, and tail down.

Figure 13.10

gulls signal aggression by pointing their beaks at one another and submission by pointing their beaks away from one another; primates signal aggression by staring and submission by averting their gaze. Figure 13.10 is a reproduction of the actual woodcuts that Darwin used in his 1872 book to illustrate this principle of antithesis in dogs.

James-Lange and Cannon-Bard Theories

The first physiological theory of emotion was proposed independently by James and Lange in 1884. According to the **James-Lange theory**, emotion-inducing sensory stimuli are received and interpreted by the cortex, which triggers changes in the visceral organs via the autonomic nervous system and in the skeletal muscles via the somatic nervous system. Then, the autonomic and somatic responses trigger the experience of emotion in the brain. In effect, what the James-Lange theory did was to reverse the usual common-sense way of thinking about the causal relation between the experience of emotion and its expression. James and Lange argued that the autonomic activity and behavior that are triggered by the emotional event (e.g., rapid heartbeat and running away) produce the feeling of emotion, not vice versa.

Around 1915, Cannon proposed an alternative to the James-Lange theory of emotion, and it was subsequently extended and promoted by Bard. According to the **Cannon-Bard theory**, emotional stimuli have two independent excitatory effects: They excite both the feeling of emotion in the brain and the expression of emotion in the autonomic and somatic nervous systems. That is, the Cannon-Bard theory, in contrast to the James-Lange theory, views emotional experience and emotional expression as parallel processes that have no direct causal relation.

The James-Lange and Cannon-Bard theories make different predictions about the role of feedback from autonomic and somatic nervous system activity in emotional experience. According to the James-Lange theory, emotional experience depends entirely on feedback from autonomic and somatic nervous system activity; according to the Cannon-Bard theory, emotional experience is totally independent of such feedback. Both extreme positions have proved to be incorrect. On the one hand, it seems that the autonomic and somatic feedback is not necessary for the experience of emotion: Human patients whose autonomic and somatic feedback has been largely eliminated by a broken neck are capable of a full range of emotional experiences (e.g., Lowe & Carroll, 1985). On the other hand, there have been numerous reports that autonomic and somatic responses to emotional stimuli can influence emotional experience.

Failure to find unqualified support for either the James-Lange or the Cannon-Bard theory led to a third theory. According to this theory, each of the three principal factors in an emotional response—the perception of the emotion-inducing stimulus, the autonomic and somatic responses to the stimulus, and the experience of the emotion—influences the other two (see Figure 13.11).

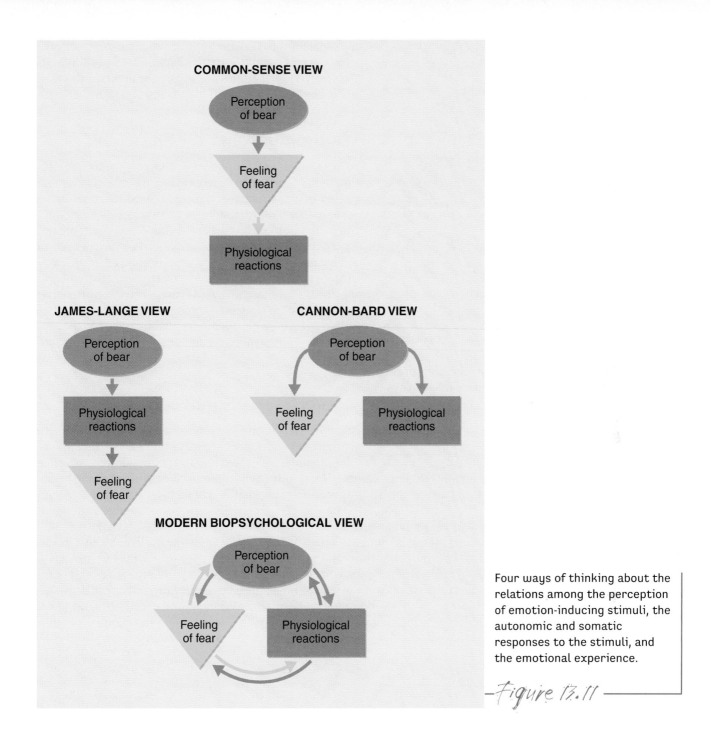

COMMON-SENSE VIEW

Perception of bear

Feeling of fear

Physiological reactions

JAMES-LANGE VIEW

Perception of bear

Physiological reactions

Feeling of fear

CANNON-BARD VIEW

Perception of bear

Feeling of fear

Physiological reactions

MODERN BIOPSYCHOLOGICAL VIEW

Perception of bear

Feeling of fear

Physiological reactions

Four ways of thinking about the relations among the perception of emotion-inducing stimuli, the autonomic and somatic responses to the stimuli, and the emotional experience.

—Figure 13.11

Sham Rage

In the late 1920s, Bard (1929) discovered that **decorticate** cats—cats whose cortex has been removed—respond aggressively to the slightest provocation: After a light touch, they arch their backs, erect their hair, growl, hiss, and expose their teeth.

The aggressive responses of decorticate animals are abnormal in two respects: They are inappropriately severe, and they are not directed at particular targets. Bard referred to the exaggerated, poorly directed aggressive responses of decorticate animals as **sham rage**.

Sham rage can be elicited in cats whose cerebral hemispheres have been removed down to, but not including, the hypothalamus; it cannot be elicited, however, if the

The Evolutionary Perspective

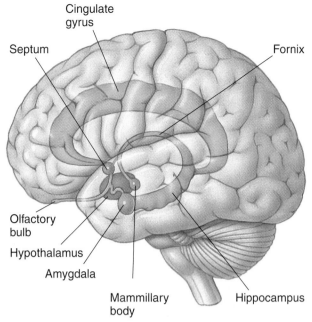

Cingulate gyrus

Septum

Fornix

Olfactory bulb

Hypothalamus

Amygdala

Mammillary body

Hippocampus

The location of the major limbic system structures. In general, they are arrayed near the midline in a ring around the thalamus. (See also Figure 2.27 on page 57.)

Figure 13.12

The Evolutionary Perspective

Clinical Implications

hypothalamus is also removed. On the basis of this observation, Bard concluded that the hypothalamus is critical for the expression of aggressive responses and that the function of the cortex is to inhibit and direct these responses.

Limbic System and Emotion

In 1937, Papez (pronounced "Payps") proposed that emotional expression is controlled by several interconnected neural structures that he referred to as the limbic system. The **limbic system** is a collection of nuclei and tracts that borders the thalamus (*limbic* means "border"). Figure 13.12 illustrates some of its key structures: the amygdala, mammillary body, hippocampus, fornix, cortex of the cingulate gyrus, septum, olfactory bulb, and hypothalamus (see Macchi, 1989). Papez proposed that emotional states are expressed through the action of the other limbic structures on the hypothalamus and that they are experienced through the action of the limbic structures on the cortex.

Kluver-Bucy Syndrome

In 1939, Kluver and Bucy observed a striking *syndrome* (pattern of behavior) in monkeys that had had their anterior temporal lobes removed. This syndrome, which is commonly referred to as the **Kluver-Bucy syndrome**, includes the following behaviors: the consumption of almost anything that is edible, increased sexual activity often directed at inappropriate objects, a tendency to repeatedly investigate familiar objects, a tendency to investigate objects with the mouth, and a lack of fear. Monkeys that could not be handled before surgery were transformed by bilateral anterior temporal lobectomy into tame subjects that showed no fear whatsoever—even in response to snakes, which terrify normal monkeys. In primates, most of the symptoms of the Kluver-Bucy syndrome appear to result from amygdala damage.

The Kluver-Bucy syndrome has been observed in several species. Following is a description of the syndrome in a human patient with a brain infection.

A Human Case of Kluver-Bucy Syndrome

He exhibited a flat affect, and although originally restless, ultimately became remarkably placid. He appeared indifferent to people or situations. He spent much time gazing at the television, but never learned to turn it on; when the set was off, he tended to watch reflections of others in the room on the glass screen. On occasion he became facetious, smiling inappropriately and mimicking the gestures and actions of others. Once initiating an imitative series, he would perseverate copying all movements made by another for extended periods of time. . . . He engaged in oral exploration of all objects within his grasp, appearing unable to gain information via tactile or visual means alone. All objects that he could lift were placed in his mouth and sucked or chewed. . . .

Although vigorously heterosexual prior to his illness, he was observed in hospital to make advances toward other male patients. . . . [H]e never made advances toward women, and, in fact, his apparent reversal of sexual polarity prompted his fiancée to sever their relationship. (Marlowe, Mancall, & Thomas, 1985, pp. 55–56)

The six early landmarks in the study of brain mechanisms of emotion just reviewed are listed in Table 13.1.

Table 13.1

Biopsychological Investigation of Emotion: Six Early Landmarks	
EVENT	DATE
Case of Phineas Gage	1848
Darwin's theory of the evolution of emotion	1872
James-Lange and Cannon-Bard theories	about 1900
Discovery of sham rage	1929
Limbic system theory of emotion	1937
Discovery of Kluver-Bucy syndrome	1939

13·5
Stress and Health

Clinical Implications

When the body is exposed to harm or threat, the result is a cluster of physiological changes that is generally referred to as *the stress response*—or just **stress**. All *stressors*, whether psychological (e.g., dismay at the loss of one's job) or physical (e.g., long-term exposure to cold), produce a similar core pattern of physiological changes; however, it is *chronic psychological stress* (e.g., in the form of chronic fear) that has been most frequently implicated in ill health (see Kiecolt-Glaser et al., 2002; Krantz & McCeney, 2002; Natelson, 2004).

The Stress Response

Hans Selye (pronounced "SELL-yay") first described the stress response in the 1950s, and he quickly recognized its dual nature. In the short term, it produces adaptive changes that help the animal respond to the stressor (e.g., mobilization of energy resources, inhibition of inflammation, and resistance to infection); in the long term, however, it produces changes that are maladaptive (e.g., enlarged adrenal glands).

Selye attributed the stress response to the activation of the *anterior-pituitary adrenal-cortex system*. He concluded that stressors acting on neural circuits stimulate the release of **adrenocorticotropic hormone (ACTH)** from the anterior pituitary, that the ACTH in turn triggers the release of **glucocorticoids** from the **adrenal cortex**, and that the glucocorticoids produce many of the effects of the stress response (see Erickson, Drevets, & Schulkin, 2003; Korte, 2001). The level of circulating glucocorticoids is the most commonly employed physiological measure of stress.

With his emphasis on the role of the anterior-pituitary adrenal-cortex system in stress, Selye largely ignored the contributions of the sympathetic nervous system. Stressors also activate the sympathetic nervous system, thereby increasing the amounts of epinephrine and norepinephrine released from the **adrenal medulla**. Most modern theories of stress (see Stanford & Salmon, 1993) acknowledge the major roles of both systems (see Figure 13.13).

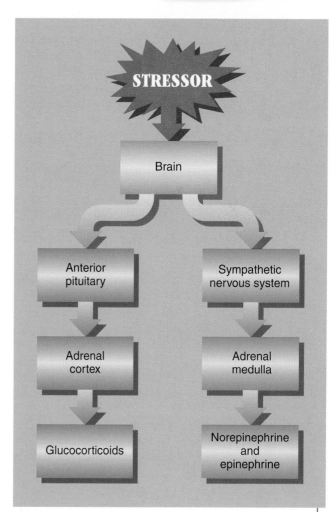

The two-system view of the stress response.

Figure 13.13

The magnitude of the stress response depends not only on the stressor and the individual; it also depends on the strategies the individual adopts to cope with the stress (McEwen, 1994). For example, in a study of women awaiting surgery for possible breast cancer, the levels of stress were lower in those who had convinced themselves to think about their problem in certain ways. Those who had convinced themselves that they could not possibly have cancer, that their prayers were certain to be answered, or that it was counterproductive to worry about it experienced less stress (Katz et al., 1970).

From the perspective of psychological science, the major contribution of Selye's theory was that it suggested a mechanism by which psychological factors can influence physical illness. Accordingly, Selye's theory provided the foundation for the subsequent development of the field of health psychology.

All kinds of common psychological stressors (e.g., losing a job, preparing for an examination, ending a relationship) are associated with high circulating levels of glucocorticoids, epinephrine, and norepinephrine; and these in turn have been implicated in many physical disorders (Salovey et al., 2000). For example, fear or stress prior to surgery has been associated with slower postsurgical recovery, including delays in wound healing (Kiecolt-Glaser et al., 1998).

The relation between chronic fear, stress, and ill health is readily apparent in animals undergoing subordination stress. Virtually all mammals—particularly males—experience threats from *conspecifics* (members of the same species) at certain points in their lives. When conspecific threat becomes an enduring feature of daily life, the result is **subordination stress**. Subordination stress is most readily studied in social species that form stable *dominance hierarchies* (pecking orders). What do you think happens to subordinate male rodents who are continually attacked by more dominant colony mates? Several studies (see Blanchard et al., 1993; Delville, Melloni, & Ferris, 1998) have reported that male rodents exposed to subordination stress are more likely to attack juveniles, to have testes that are reduced in size, to have shorter life spans, and to have lower levels of testosterone and higher levels of a particular glucocorticoid. The relevance of this finding to the problem of human bullying is all too apparent.

Stress and Gastric Ulcers

Stress has long been implicated in the development of gastric ulcers. **Gastric ulcers** are painful lesions to the lining of the stomach and duodenum, which in extreme cases can be life-threatening. In the United States alone, about 500,000 new cases are reported each year (see Livingston & Guth, 1992). Gastric ulcers occur more commonly in people living in stressful situations, and stressors (e.g., confinement to a restraint tube for a few hours) can produce these ulcers in laboratory animals.

For decades, gastric ulcers were regarded as the prototypical *psychosomatic disease* (physical disease with incontrovertible evidence of a psychological cause). However, this view seemed to change with the report that gastric ulcers are caused by bacteria. Indeed, it has been claimed that the ulcer-causing bacteria (*Helicobacter pylori*) are responsible for all cases of gastric ulcers except those caused by drugs such as aspirin (Blaser, 1996). This seemed to rule out stress as a causal factor in such ulcers, but a careful consideration of the evidence suggests otherwise (Overmier & Murison, 1997).

The facts do not deny that *H. pylori* damages the stomach wall or that antibiotic treatment of gastric ulcers helps many sufferers. The facts do, however, suggest that *H. pylori* infection alone is insufficient to produce the disorder in most people. Although it is true that most patients with gastric ulcers display signs of *H. pylori* infection, so too do 75% of healthy control subjects. Also, although it is true that antibiotics improve the condition of many patients with gastric ulcers, so do psychological treatments—and they do it without reducing signs of *H. pylori* infection. Apparently, there are other factors that increase the susceptibility of the stomach wall to damage from *H. pylori*, and one of these factors seems to be stress.

ON THE CD

A laboratory that specializes in stress and health is featured in the module *A Visit to a Special Clinical Psychology Laboratory*.

The Evolutionary Perspective

Clinical Implications

Psychoneuroimmunology: Stress, the Immune System, and the Brain

Clinical Implications

A major change in the study of stress and health came in the 1970s with the accumulation of reports that stress might reduce a person's resistance to infection. These reports had a great impact on the field of psychology, because they suggested that stress could play a role in infectious diseases, which up to that point had been regarded as "strictly physical."

The theoretical and clinical implications of the suggestion that stress can increase susceptibility to infection were so great that they led in the early 1980s to the emergence of a new field of biopsychological research. That field is **psychoneuroimmunology**—the study of interactions among psychological factors, the nervous system, and the immune system. What is the immune system?

Immune System. Microorganisms of every description revel in the warm, damp, nutritive climate of your body (see Ploegh, 1998). Your **immune system** keeps your body from being overwhelmed by these invaders. Before it can take any action against an invading microorganism, the immune system must have some way of distinguishing foreign cells from body cells. That is why **antigens**—protein molecules on the surface of a cell that identify it as native or foreign—play a major role in specific immune reactions (see Matzinger, 2002; Medzhitov & Janeway, 2002).

Immune system barriers to infection are often considered to be of two sorts (see Banchereau, 2002). First, there are nonspecific barriers, those that act generally and quickly against most invaders. These barriers include mucous membranes, which destroy many foreign microorganisms, and **phagocytosis**, the process by which foreign microorganisms and debris are consumed and destroyed by *phagocytes* (specialized body cells such as *microglia* that consume foreign microorganisms and debris)—see Figure 13.14.

Second, there are specific barriers, those that act specifically against particular strains of invaders. The specific barriers are of two types—cell-mediated and antibody-mediated—each defended by a different class of lymphocytes. **Lymphocytes** are specialized white blood cells that are produced in bone marrow and are stored in the lymphatic system. **Cell-mediated immunity** is directed by **T cells** (T lymphocytes); **antibody-mediated immunity** is directed by **B cells** (B lymphocytes).

The cell-mediated immune reaction begins when a **macrophage**—a type of large phagocyte—ingests a foreign microorganism (see Figure 13.15 on page 432). The macrophage then displays the microorganism's antigens on the surface of its cell membrane, and this attracts T cells. Each T cell has two kinds of receptors on its surface, one for molecules that are normally found on the surface of macrophages and other body cells, and one for a specific foreign antigen. There are millions of different receptors for foreign antigens on T cells, but there is only one kind on each T cell, and there are only a few T cells with each kind of receptor. After the microorganism has been ingested and its antigens have been displayed, a T cell with a receptor for the foreign antigen binds to the surface of the infected macrophage, which initiates a series of reactions (Grakoui et al., 1999; Malissen, 1999). Among these reactions is the multiplication of the bound T cell, creating more T cells with the specific receptor necessary to destroy all invaders that contain the target antigens and all body cells that have been infected by the invaders.

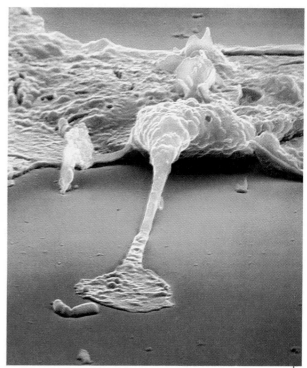

Phagocytosis: A macrophage hunts down and destroys a bacterium.

Figure 13.14

Cell-Mediated Immunity

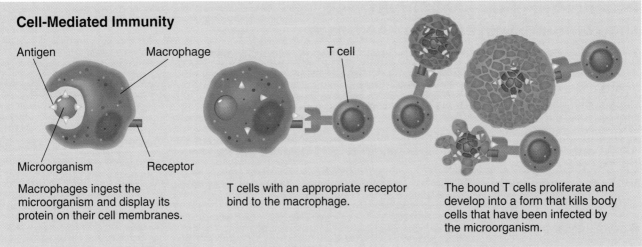

Antigen   Macrophage   T cell

Microorganism   Receptor

Macrophages ingest the microorganism and display its protein on their cell membranes.

T cells with an appropriate receptor bind to the macrophage.

The bound T cells proliferate and develop into a form that kills body cells that have been infected by the microorganism.

Antibody-Mediated Immunity

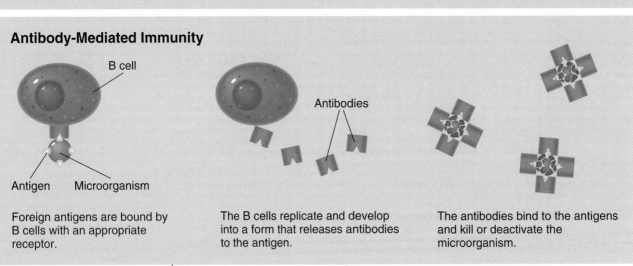

B cell

Antibodies

Antigen   Microorganism

Foreign antigens are bound by B cells with an appropriate receptor.

The B cells replicate and develop into a form that releases antibodies to the antigen.

The antibodies bind to the antigens and kill or deactivate the microorganism.

Specific barriers to infection: Cell-mediated immunity and antibody-mediated immunity. In cell-mediated immunity, microorganisms or body cells that they have invaded are killed by T cells; in antibody-mediated immunity, microorganisms are killed by antibodies produced by B cells.

Figure 13.15

The antibody-mediated immune reaction begins when a B cell binds to a foreign antigen for which it contains an appropriate receptor (see Figure 13.15). This causes the B cell to multiply and to synthesize a lethal form of its receptor molecules. These lethal receptor molecules, called **antibodies**, are released into the intracellular fluid, where they bind to the foreign antigens and destroy or deactivate the microorganisms that possess them. Memory B cells for the specific antigen are also produced during the process; these cells have a long life and accelerate antibody-mediated immunity if there is a subsequent infection by the same organism (see Ahmed & Gray, 1996).

Cell-mediated immunity and antibody-mediated immunity each take several days the first time a particular foreign antigen is recognized, but responses to subsequent invasions of microorganisms with the same antigen are much faster thanks to the memory T cells and B cells. This is why *vaccination* (the injection of small samples of an infective microorganism or its antigens into healthy individuals) is often an effective preventive measure against the effects of subsequent infection.

What Effect Does Stress Have on Immune Function?   It is widely believed that stress disrupts immune function. I am sure that you have heard this point made by family members, friends, and even by physicians. But is this true? By this point in the book, I am sure you appreciate that common beliefs are not necessarily true and that the ultimate criterion of truth is empirical evidence, not popular opinion.

Thinking Clearly

The following view of the relation between stress and immune function is based on a meta-analysis by Segerstrom and Miller (2004). What is a meta-analysis? A *meta-analysis* is a study that analyzes and combines the results of a group of previously published studies. For example, Segerstrom and Miller's meta-analysis is a combined analysis of the 300 or so empirical studies of the relationship between stress and immune function in humans that have been published since the advent of the field of psychoneuroimmunology. In short, the findings of Segerstrom and Miller are currently the ultimate word on this matter.

The Evolutionary Perspective

One of the most important contributions of Segerstrom and Miller's meta-analysis is that their results reconciled the seeming incompatibility of psychoneuroimmunological research findings and evolutionary psychology principles. Virtually every individual organism encounters many stressors during the course of its life, and it is difficult to see how a maladaptive response to stress, such as a disruption of immune function, could have evolved—or could have survived if it had been created by a genetic accident or as a nonadaptive by-product of an adaptive evolutionary change.

Segerstrom and Miller found that the effects of stress on immune function depended on the kind of stress. They found that acute (brief) stressors, such as public speaking, athletic competitions, or musical performances, actually led to improvements in immune function. Not surprisingly, the improvements in immune function following acute stress occurred mainly in nonspecific barriers, which can be marshaled quickly. In contrast, chronic (long-lasting) stressors, such as caring for a demented loved one, living with a handicap, or experiencing unemployment, adversely affected complex immune system processes.

How Does Stress Influence Immune Function? The mechanisms by which stress influences immune function have been difficult to specify because there are so many possibilities (see Dustin & Colman, 2002). Stress produces widespread changes in the body through its effects on the anterior-pituitary adrenal-cortex system and the sympathetic adrenal-medulla system, and there are innumerable mechanisms by which these systems could influence immune function. For example, both T cells and B cells have receptors for glucocorticoids; and lymphocytes have receptors for epinephrine, norepinephrine, and glucocorticoids.

It is important not to forget that there are also behavioral routes by which stress may affect immune function. For example, people under severe stress often display changed patterns of diet, exercise, sleep, and drug use, all of which could influence immune function.

Does Stress Affect Susceptibility to Infectious Disease? It has proven difficult to show unequivocally that stress causes increases in susceptibility to infectious diseases in human subjects. One reason for this difficulty is that only correlational studies are possible. Numerous studies have reported *positive* correlations between stress and ill health in human subjects; for example, students in one study reported more respiratory infections during final exams (Glaser et al., 1987). However, interpretation of such correlations is never straightforward: Subjects may report more illness during times of stress because they expect to be more ill, because their experience of illness during times of stress is more unpleasant, or because the stress caused changes in their behavior that in turn increased their susceptibility to infection.

Thinking Clearly

Another reason why it has proven difficult to show that stress causes increases in susceptibility to infectious diseases is that adverse effects of stress on immune function are not necessarily reflected in more illness. There are three reasons why particular decreases in immune function may not be reflected in increased infectious disease: (1) The immune system seems to have many redundant components; thus, disruption of one of them may have little or no effect on vulnerability to infection. (2) In young healthy individuals, the subjects of most psychoneuroimmunological investigations, stress-produced changes in immune function may be too short-lived to have substantial effects on the probability of infection. (3) Declines in some aspects of immune function may induce compensatory increases in others.

The Evolutionary Perspective

Despite the difficulties of proving a causal link between stress and infectious disease in humans, the evidence for such a link is strong, thanks to research involving controlled experiments conducted on laboratory animals. Several such experiments have convincingly demonstrated that chronic exposure to stressors can indeed disrupt immune function and increase susceptibility to infection (see Ben-Eliyahu et al., 2000; Quan et al., 2001). Accordingly, considered together, correlational studies on humans and experiments on laboratory animals have provided strong support for the basic tenets of psychoneuroimmunology.

Early Experience of Stress

Early exposure to severe stress can have a variety of adverse effects on subsequent development. Children subjected to maltreatment or other forms of severe stress display a variety of brain and endocrine system abnormalities (Teicher, 2002; Teicher et al., 2003). As you will learn in the next chapter, some psychiatric disorders are thought to result from an interaction between an inherited susceptibility to a disorder and early exposure to severe stress. Because early exposure to stress often increases the intensity of subsequent stress responses (e.g., increases the subsequent release of glucocorticoids in response to stressors), such exposure likely amplifies the adverse effects of subsequent stressors.

It is important to understand that the developmental window during which early stress can adversely affect neural and endocrine development begins before birth. Many experiments have demonstrated the adverse effects of prenatal stress in laboratory animals. In experiments on *prenatal stress*, pregnant females are exposed to stressors, and the adverse effects of that exposure on their offspring are subsequently assessed (see Avishai-Eliner et al., 2002; Kofman, 2002; Maccari et al., 2003).

The Evolutionary Perspective

One particularly interesting line of research on the role of early experience in the development of the stress response began with the observation that handling of rat pups by researchers for a few minutes per day during the first few weeks of their lives has a variety of salutary (health-promoting) effects (see Sapolsky, 1997). The majority of these effects seemed to result from a decrease in the magnitude of the handled pups' responses to stressful events. As adults, rats that were handled as pups displayed smaller increases in circulating glucocorticoids in response to stressors (see Francis & Meaney, 1999). It seemed remarkable that a few hours of handling early in life could have such a significant and lasting effect. In fact, evidence supports an alternative interpretation.

Liou and colleagues (1997) found that rat pups that are regularly handled are groomed (licked) more by their mothers, and they hypothesized that the salutary effects of early handling resulted from the extra grooming, rather than from the handling itself. They confirmed this hypothesis by showing that unhandled rat pups that received a lot of grooming from their mothers developed the same profile of increased glucocorticoid release that was observed in handled pups. This effect seems to have been produced by decreased negative feedback from greater numbers of glucocorticoid receptors in the hippocampus.

In general, early separation of rat pups from their mothers seems to have effects opposite to those of high levels of early grooming (see Cirulli, Berry, & Alleva, 2003; Pryce & Feldon, 2003; Rhees, Lephart, & Eliason, 2001). As adults, rats that were separated from their mothers in infancy display elevated behavioral and hormonal responses to stress.

Thinking Clearly

Those mother rats that are most reactive to stress provide the poorest maternal care to their offspring. This poor care has lasting adverse effects on the stress responses of the offspring (Meaney, 2001). Think about the significance of this sequence of events: It constitutes a nongenetic mechanism by which behavioral tendencies can be passed from generation to generation.

Stress and the Hippocampus

Many studies of the effects of stress on the brain suggest that the hippocampus is particularly susceptible to stress-induced effects. The reason for this susceptibility seems to be the particularly dense population of glucocorticoid receptors in the hippocampus (see McEwen, 2000b).

Two particular effects of stress on the structure of the hippocampus have been observed in several species of laboratory animals (McEwen, 2000a). Following exposure to a period of stress, the dendrites of *pyramidal cells* are shorter and show less branching, and the rate of adult neurogenesis of *granule cells* is reduced. Even a period of stress lasting only a few hours can induce structural changes in the hippocampus that last a month or more (Kim & Diamond, 2002).

13.6
Brain Mechanisms of Emotion

This concluding section of the chapter describes two important recent lines of research on the brain mechanisms of emotion: fear conditioning and the role of the amygdala in human emotion.

Fear Conditioning

Fear conditioning is the establishment of fear in response to a previously neutral stimulus (the *conditional stimulus*) by repeatedly presenting it before the delivery of an aversive stimulus (the *unconditional stimulus*). Fear conditioning plays an important role in health. We all encounter fear-inducing stimuli in our lives, but when fear becomes linked to frequently encountered neutral stimuli, levels of stress can become overwhelming and health can suffer.

Clinical Implications

In the typical fear-conditioning experiment, the subject, typically a rat, hears a tone (conditional stimulus) and then receives a mild electric shock to its feet (unconditional stimulus). After several pairings of the tone and the shock, the rat responds to the tone with a variety of defensive behaviors (e.g., freezing and increased susceptibility to startle) and sympathetic nervous system responses (e.g., increased heart rate and blood pressure). LeDoux and his colleagues have mapped the neural mechanism that mediates this form of auditory fear conditioning (see LeDoux, 2000a, 2000b).

LeDoux and his colleagues began their search for the neural mechanisms of auditory fear conditioning by making lesions in the auditory pathways of rats. They found that bilateral lesions to the *medial geniculate nucleus* (the auditory relay nucleus of the thalamus) blocked fear conditioning to a tone, but bilateral lesions to the auditory cortex did not. This finding indicated that for auditory fear conditioning to occur, it is necessary for signals elicited by the tone to reach the medial geniculate nucleus but not the auditory cortex. It also indicated that a pathway from the medial geniculate nucleus to a structure other than the auditory cortex plays a key role in fear conditioning. This pathway proved to be the pathway from the medial geniculate nucleus to the amygdala. Lesions of the amygdala, like lesions of the medial geniculate nucleus, blocked fear conditioning. The amygdala receives input from all sensory systems, and it is believed to be the structure in which the emotional significance of sensory signals is learned and retained.

Several pathways carry signals from the amygdala to brain-stem structures that control the various emotional responses. For example, a pathway to the periaqueductal gray of the midbrain elicits appropriate defensive responses (see Bandler &

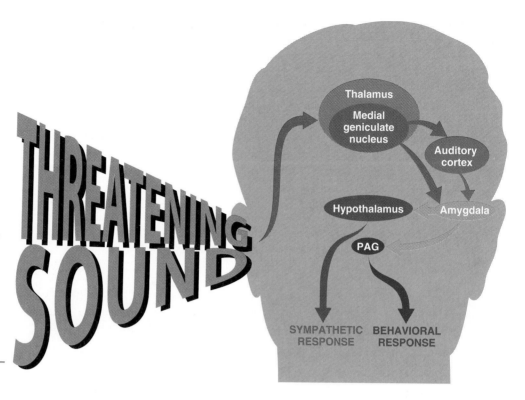

THREATENING SOUND

The structures that are thought to mediate the sympathetic and behavioral responses conditioned to an auditory conditional stimulus.

Figure 13.16 —

Shipley, 1994), whereas another pathway to the lateral hypothalamus elicits appropriate sympathetic responses.

The fact that auditory cortex lesions do not disrupt fear conditioning to simple tones does not mean that the auditory cortex is not involved in auditory fear conditioning. There are two pathways from the medial geniculate nucleus to the amygdala: the direct one, which you have already learned about, and an indirect one that projects via the auditory cortex (Romanski & LeDoux, 1992). Both routes are capable of mediating fear conditioning to simple sounds; if only one is destroyed, conditioning progresses normally. However, only the cortical route is capable of mediating fear conditioning to complex sounds (Jarrell et al., 1987).

Figure 13.16 illustrates the circuit of the brain that is thought to mediate fear conditioning to auditory conditional stimuli (see LeDoux, 1994). Sound signals from the medial geniculate nucleus of the thalamus reach the amygdala either directly or via the auditory cortex. The amygdala assesses the emotional significance of the sound on the basis of previous encounters with it and then activates the appropriate response circuits—for example, behavioral circuits in the periaqueductal gray and sympathetic circuits in the hypothalamus.

Role of the Amygdala in Human Emotion

The amygdala is the brain structure that has been most frequently implicated in human emotion—recall the Kluver-Bucy syndrome. Much of the evidence implicating the amygdala in human emotion has come from the study of neuropsychological patients with amygdalar damage. Many of them have difficulty recognizing facial expressions of fear. The case of S.P., which follows, is typical.

The Case of S.P., the Woman Who Couldn't Perceive Fear

At the age of 48, S.P. had her right amygdala and adjacent tissues removed for the treatment of epilepsy. Because her left amygdala had been damaged, she in effect had a bilateral amygdalar lesion.

Following her surgery, S.P. had an above-average I.Q., and her perceptual abilities were generally normal. Of particular relevance was the fact that she had no difficulty in identifying faces or extracting information from them (e.g., information about age or gender). However, S.P. did have a severe postsurgical deficit in recognizing facial expressions of fear and less striking deficits in recognizing facial expressions of disgust, sadness, and happiness.

In contrast, S.P. had no difficulty specifying which emotion would go with particular sentences. Also, she had no difficulty expressing various emotions using facial expressions on request (Anderson & Phelps, 2000).

This case is consistent with previous reports that the human amygdala is specifically involved in perceiving facial expressions of emotion, particularly of fear (e.g., Broks et al., 1998; Calder et al., 1996). S.P. had damage to structures other than her amygdala, and it was not possible to determine the extent to which that other damage contributed to the disruption in her perception of facial expressions other than fear.

The case of S.P. is similar to reported cases of Urbach-Wiethe disease (see Aggleton & Young, 2000). **Urbach-Wiethe disease** is a genetic disorder that often results in *calcification* (hardening by conversion to calcium carbonate, the main component of bone) of the amygdala and surrounding anterior medial temporal-lobe structures in both hemispheres. One Urbach-Wiethe patient with bilateral amygdalar damage was found to have lost the ability to recognize facial expressions of fear (Adolphs et al., 1994). Indeed, she could not describe fear-inducing situations or draw fearful expressions although she had no difficulty on tests involving other emotions.

Although recent research has focused on the role of the amygdala in the recognition of negative facial expressions, subjects with bilateral amygdalar damage also have difficulty recognizing a variety of other stimuli (e.g., patterns, landscapes), particularly those stimuli that the subjects report liking the least (Adolphs & Tranel, 1999). There is also evidence that the amygdala participates in positive emotions (see Hamann et al., 2002); several experiments on nonhuman animals suggest that the amygdala plays a role in learning about the beneficial value of stimuli and in the expression of positive emotions associated with such judgments (Baxter & Murray, 2002).

The Evolutionary Perspective

Unlike those parts of the brain that play major sensory and motor roles, the parts that play a role in emotion seem to vary substantially from person to person. This, of course, greatly complicates the search for the neural mechanisms of emotion. Consider the results of the following study. Adolphs and colleagues (1999) first tested the ability of nine neuropsychological patients with bilateral amygdalar damage to correctly identify facial expressions of emotion. As expected, the group of patients as a whole had difficulty identifying facial expressions of fear. However, there were substantial differences among the subjects: Some also had difficulty identifying other negative emotions, and two had no deficits whatsoever in identifying facial expressions. Remarkably, structural MRIs revealed that both of these two subjects had no surviving amygdalar tissue in either hemisphere.

Research on the role of the amygdala in human emotion provides a particularly good illustration of the difficulties of studying the neural mechanisms of emotion. You have just read about three of these difficulties. First, structures that participate in emotion seem to be involved in only some aspects of some emotions—for example, the amygdala seems to be specifically involved in the perception of the facial expression of fear. Second, the roles of one structure do not appear to be limited to a single emotion. And third, there seem to be substantial differences among individuals in the organization of their neural mechanisms of emotion.

The following case study ends the chapter by emphasizing the point that the brain mechanisms of emotion differ from person to person. Fortunately, the reactions of Charles Whitman to amygdalar damage are atypical.

The Case of Charles Whitman, the Texas Tower Sniper

After having lunch with his wife and his mother, Charles Whitman went home and typed a letter of farewell—perhaps as an explanation for what would soon happen.

He stated in his letter that he was having many compelling and bizarre ideas. Psychiatric care had been no help. He asked that his brain be autopsied after he was gone; he was sure that doctors would find the problem.

By all reports, Whitman had been a good person. An Eagle Scout at 12 and a high school graduate at 17, he then enlisted in the Marine Corps, where he established himself as expert marksman. After his discharge, he entered the University of Texas to study architectural engineering.

Nevertheless, in the evening of August 1, 1966, Whitman killed his wife and mother. He professed love for both of them, but he did not want them to face the aftermath of what was to follow.

The next morning, at about 11:30, Whitman went to the Tower of the University of Texas, carrying six guns, ammunition, several knives, food, and water. He clubbed the receptionist to death and shot four more people on his way to the observation deck. Once on the deck, he opened fire on people crossing the campus and on nearby streets. He was deadly, killing people as far as 300 meters away—people who assumed they were out of range.

At 1:24 that afternoon, the police fought their way to the platform and shot Whitman to death. All told, 17 people, including Whitman, had been killed, and another 31 had been wounded (Helmer, 1986).

An autopsy was conducted. Whitman was correct: They found a walnut-sized tumor in his right amygdala.

Key Terms

Health psychology (p. 405)

13.1 Principles of Drug Addiction

Addicts (p. 408)
Conditioned compensatory responses (p. 408)
Cross tolerance (p. 405)
Detoxified addicts (p. 409)
Drug sensitization (p. 406)
Drug tolerance (p. 405)
Functional tolerance (p. 406)
Incentive-sensitization theory (p. 409)
Metabolic tolerance (p. 406)
Physical-dependence theories of addiction (p. 409)
Physically dependent (p. 407)
Positive-incentive theories of addiction (p. 409)
Psychoactive drugs (p. 406)
Withdrawal syndrome (p. 406)

13.2 Effects on Health of Five Commonly Abused Drugs

Amphetamine (p. 416)
Analgesics (p. 417)
Buerger' s disease (p. 411)
Cannabis sativa (p. 413)
Cirrhosis (p. 413)
Cocaine (p. 415)
Cocaine psychosis (p. 416)
Delirium tremens (DTs) (p. 412)
Depressant (p. 412)
Fetal alcohol syndrome (FAS) (p. 413)
Harrison Narcotics Act (p. 418)
Heroin (p. 418)
Korsakoff' s syndrome (p. 412)
Morphine (p. 417)
Narcotic (p. 414)
Opiates (p. 417)
Smoker' s syndrome (p. 411)
Stimulants (p. 415)
THC (p. 413)

13.3 Addiction and the Neural Mechanisms of Motivation

Conditioned place-preference paradigm (p. 422)
Drug self-administration paradigm (p. 421)
Nucleus accumbens (p. 423)
Ventral tegmental area (p. 422)

13.4 Introduction to the Biopsychology of Emotion

Cannon-Bard theory (p. 426)
Decorticate (p. 427)
James-Lange theory (p. 426)
Kluver-Bucy syndrome (p. 428)
Limbic system (p. 428)
Sham rage (p. 427)

ON THE CD

Studying for an exam? Get some help from the electronic flash cards of the key terms and the practice tests for this chapter.

chapter 13

Health Psychology: Addiction, Emotion, and Stress
Impact of Psychological Factors on Health

Health psychology, the subject of this chapter, is a field of research that focuses on the role of psychological factors in physical health. Addiction, stress, and emotion are important subjects of health psychology research, and of this chapter.

Drug Addiction: Five Commonly Abused Drugs

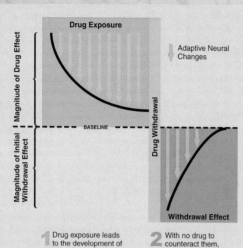

Drug tolerance and withdrawal

Magnitude of Drug Effect

Drug Exposure

Adaptive Neural Changes

Magnitude of Initial Withdrawal Effect

BASELINE

Drug Withdrawal

Withdrawal Effect

1 Drug exposure leads to the development of adaptive neural changes that produce tolerance by counteracting the drug effect.

2 With no drug to counteract them, the neural adaptations produce withdrawal effects opposite to the effects of the drug.

Addicts who display drug tolerance and withdrawal effiects are said to be physically dependent. Physical dependence was once thought to be the cause of drug addiction, but research suggests that the positive-incentive value of drugs is the main causal factor. Evidence suggests that two commonly used addictive drugs—alcohol and nicotine—pose the greatest threats to health in our society.
(Pages 405–420)

Tobacco

Alcohol

Marijuana

Cocaine

Addiction and the Neural Mechanisms of Motivation

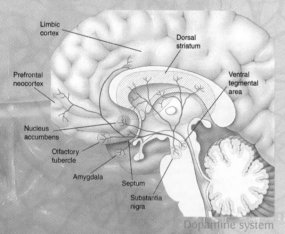

Limbic cortex

Dorsal striatum

Prefrontal neocortex

Ventral tegmental area

Nucleus accumbens

Olfactory tubercle

Amygdala

Septum

Substantia nigra

Dopamine system

Dopamine seems to play an important role in mediating the positive-incentive value of drugs. Many studies have implicated the dopamine pathway that runs from the ventral tegmental area to the nucleus accumbens. This dopamine pathway has also been implicated in the positive-incentive value of other reinforcers (e.g., food and sex).
(Pages 421–423)

Opiates

Visual Summary

Introduction to the Biopsychology of Emotion

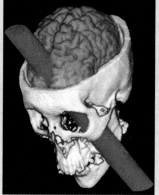

Phineas Gage

Research on emotion plays a role in health psychology because of the adverse effects of negative emotions. Influential in the early study of the biopsychology of emotion were Phineas Gage, Darwin's theory of emotion, the James-Lange and Cannon-Bard theories, sham rage, the limbic system, and the Kluver-Bucy syndrome. (Pages 424–429)

Stress and Health

Exposure to stressors leads to the release of glucocorticoids from the adrenal cortex and epinephrine and norepinephrine from the adrenal medulla. Chronic stress appears to increase vulnerability to a variety of disease processes. For example, chronic stress increases susceptibility to infection, an effect which is central to the field of psychoneuroimmunology. (Pages 429–435)

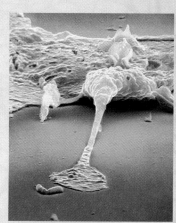

Phagocytosis

Brain Mechanisms of Emotion

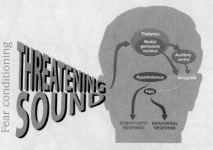

Fear conditioning

The neural mechanisms of emotion are complex. For example, it is now clear that a neural structure involved in one emotion might not be involved in others, and it might be involved in only some aspects of a particular emotion. Brain structures most frequently implicated in emotional phenomena are the prefrontal cortex and the amygdala. (Pages 435–438)

Themes Revisited

All four of the book's themes were reinforced in this chapter. The clinical implications theme appeared frequently because the chapter focused on health. You learned about the health problems created by addictive drugs and stress, and you learned that brain-damaged patients have taught us about the neural mechanisms of emotion. The evolutionary perspective theme also occurred frequently, because both comparative research and the consideration of evolutionary pressures have had a major impact on current thinking about the biopsychology of addiction, emotion, and the effects of stress on health.

The thinking-clearly-about-biopsychology theme was dominant throughout the section on drug addiction, because there are so many beliefs about addiction and addictive drugs that are incompatible with the evidence. It recurred where the text emphasized the importance of thinking clearly about the critical interpretation of reports of correlations between stress and ill health.

Finally, the cognitive neuroscience theme appeared once, in the discussion of the use of PET to study dopamine levels in addicts.

Think about It

1. There are many misconceptions about drug abuse. Describe three.
2. If you had an opportunity to redraft legislation related to drug abuse in the light of what you have learned in this chapter, what changes would you make? Explain.
3. Speculate: How might advances in the study of the mesotelencephalic dopamine system lead to effective treatments for drug addiction?
4. Genes are not the only means by which behavioral tendencies can be passed from generation to generation. Discuss, with reference to maternal care and susceptibility to stress.
5. Research on emotion has focused on fear. Why?

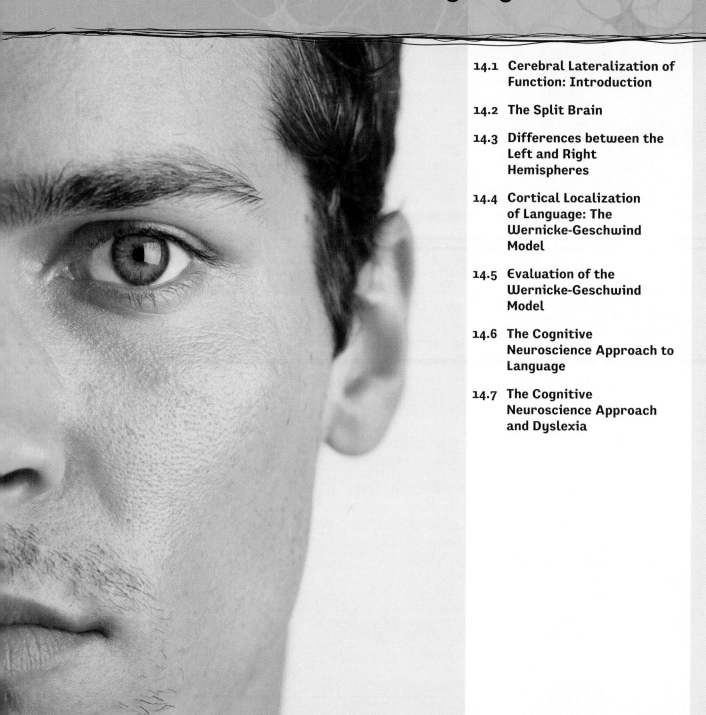

chapter 14

Lateralization, Language, and the Split Brain
The Left Brain and the Right Brain of Language

With the exception of a few midline orifices, we humans have two of almost everything—one on the left and one on the right. Even the brain, which most people view as the unitary and indivisible basis of self, reflects this general principle of bilateral duplication. In its upper reaches, the brain comprises two structures, the left and right cerebral hemispheres, which are entirely separate except for the **cerebral commissures** connecting them. The fundamental duality of the human forebrain and the locations of the cerebral commissures are illustrated in Figure 14.1.

Although the left and right hemispheres are similar in appearance, there are major differences between them in function. This chapter is about these differences, a topic commonly referred to as **lateralization of function**. The study of **split-brain patients**—patients whose left and right hemispheres have been separated by **commissurotomy**—is a major focus of discussion. Another focus is the cortical localization of language abilities in the left hemisphere; language abilities are the most highly lateralized of all cognitive abilities.

You will learn in this chapter that your left and right hemispheres have different abilities and that they have the capacity to function independently—to have different thoughts, memories, and emotions. Accordingly, this chapter will challenge the concept you have of yourself as a unitary being. I hope you both enjoy it.

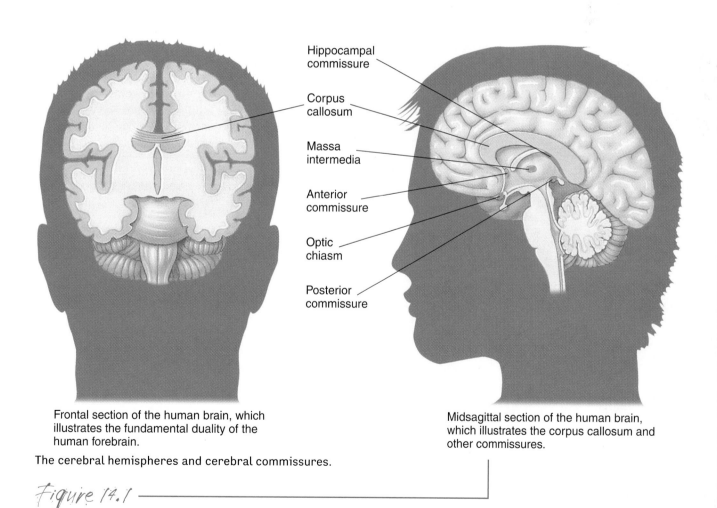

Hippocampal commissure

Corpus callosum

Massa intermedia

Anterior commissure

Optic chiasm

Posterior commissure

Frontal section of the human brain, which illustrates the fundamental duality of the human forebrain.

Midsagittal section of the human brain, which illustrates the corpus callosum and other commissures.

The cerebral hemispheres and cerebral commissures.

Figure 14.1

14.1

Cerebral Lateralization of Function: Introduction

I n 1836, Marc Dax, an unknown country doctor, presented a short report at a medical society meeting in France. It was his first and only scientific presentation. Dax was struck by the fact that of the 40 or so brain-damaged patients with speech problems whom he had seen during his career, not a single one had damage restricted to the right hemisphere. His report aroused little interest, and Dax died the following year unaware that he had anticipated one of the most important areas of modern neuropsychological research.

Clinical Implications

Aphasia, Apraxia, and Left-Hemisphere Damage

One reason Dax's paper had little impact was that most of his contemporaries believed that the brain acted as a whole and that specific functions could not be attributed to particular parts of it. This view began to change 25 years later, when Paul Broca reported his postmortem examination of two aphasic patients. **Aphasia** is a brain-damage–produced deficit in the ability to produce or comprehend language.

Both of Broca's patients had a left-hemisphere lesion that involved an area in the frontal cortex just in front of the face area of the primary motor cortex. Broca at first did not realize that there was a relation between aphasia and the side of the brain damage; he had not heard of Dax's report. However, by 1864, Broca had performed postmortem examinations on seven more aphasic patients, and he was struck by the fact that, like his first two, they all had damage to the *inferior prefrontal cortex* of the left hemisphere—which by then had become known as **Broca's area** (see Figure 14.2).

In the early 1900s, another example of *cerebral lateralization of function* was discovered. Hugo-Karl Liepmann found that **apraxia**, like aphasia, is almost always associated with left-hemisphere damage, despite the fact that its symptoms are *bilateral* (involving both sides of the body). Apraxic patients have difficulty performing movements when asked to perform them out of context, even though they often have no difficulty performing the same movements when they are not thinking about doing so.

The combined impact of the evidence that the left hemisphere plays a special role in both language and voluntary movement led to the concept of *cerebral dominance*. According to this concept, one hemisphere—usually the left—assumes the dominant role in the control of all complex behavioral and cognitive processes, and the other plays only a minor role. This concept led to the practice of referring to the left hemisphere as the *dominant hemisphere* and the right hemisphere as the *minor hemisphere*.

Clinical Implications

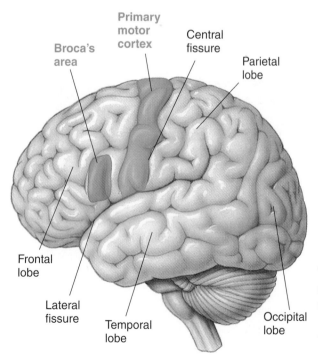

Broca's area

Primary motor cortex

Central fissure

Parietal lobe

Frontal lobe

Lateral fissure

Temporal lobe

Occipital lobe

The location of Broca's area: in the inferior left prefrontal cortex, just anterior to the face area of the left primary motor cortex.

Figure 14.2

Tests of Cerebral Lateralization

Early research on the cerebral lateralization of function compared the effects of left-hemisphere and right-hemisphere lesions. Now, however, other techniques are also used for this purpose. The sodium amytal test, the dichotic listening test, and functional brain imaging are three of them.

Sodium Amytal Test.   The **sodium amytal test** of language lateralization (Wada, 1949) is often given to patients prior to neurosurgery. The neurosurgeon uses the results of the test to plan the surgery; every effort is made to avoid damaging areas of the cortex that are likely to be involved in language. The sodium amytal test involves the injection of a small amount of sodium amytal into the carotid artery on one side of the neck. The injection anesthetizes the hemisphere on that side for a few minutes, thus allowing the capacities of the other hemisphere to be assessed. During the test, the patient is asked to recite well-known series (e.g., letters of the alphabet, days of the week, months of the year) and to name pictures of common objects. Then, an injection is administered to the other side, and the test is repeated. When the hemisphere that is dominant for speech, usually the left hemisphere, is anesthetized, the patient is rendered completely mute for a minute or two; then once the ability to talk returns, there are errors of serial order and naming. In contrast, when the minor speech hemisphere, usually the right, is anesthetized, mutism often does not occur at all, and errors are few.

Dichotic Listening Test.   Unlike the sodium amytal test, the **dichotic listening test** is noninvasive; thus, it can be administered to healthy subjects. In the standard dichotic listening test (Kimura, 1961), three pairs of spoken digits are presented through earphones; the digits of each pair are presented simultaneously, one to each ear. For example, a subject might hear the sequence 3, 9, 2 through one ear and at the same time 1, 6, 4 through the other. The subject is then asked to report all of the digits. Kimura found that most people report slightly more of the digits presented to the right ear than the left, which is indicative of left-hemisphere dominance for language. In contrast, Kimura found that all the patients who had been identified by the sodium amytal test as right-hemisphere dominant for language performed better with the left ear than the right.

   Why does the superior ear on the dichotic listening test indicate the dominance of the contralateral hemisphere? Kimura argued that although the sounds from each ear are projected to both hemispheres, the contralateral connections are stronger and take precedence when two different sounds are simultaneously competing for access to the same cortical auditory centers.

Functional Brain Imaging.   Lateralization of function has also been studied using functional brain-imaging techniques. While the subject engages in some activity, such as reading, the activity of the brain is monitored by positron emission tomography (PET) or functional magnetic resonance imaging (fMRI). On language tests, functional brain-imaging techniques typically reveal far greater activity in the left hemisphere than in the right hemisphere (see Martin, 2003).

Speech Laterality and Handedness

Two early lesion studies clarified the relation between the cerebral lateralization of speech and handedness. One study involved military personnel who suffered brain damage in World War II (Russell & Espir, 1961), and the other focused on neurological patients who underwent unilateral excisions for the treatment of neurological disorders (Penfield & Roberts, 1959). In both studies, approximately 60% of **dextrals** (right-handers) with left-hemisphere lesions and 2% of those with right-hemisphere lesions were diagnosed as aphasic; the comparable figures for **sinestrals** (left-handers) were about 30% and 24%, respectively. These results

Dextral   Sinestral

Most people, the dextrals, prefer to perform manual tasks with the right hand; others, the sinestrals, prefer to use the left hand.

Figure 14.3

indicate that the left hemisphere is dominant for language-related abilities in almost all dextrals and in the majority of sinestrals; they also indicate that sinestrals are more variable than dextrals with respect to language lateralization. (See Figure 14.3.)

Results of the sodium amytal test have confirmed the relation between handedness and language lateralization that was first observed in early lesion studies. For example, Milner (1974) found that almost all right-handed patients without brain damage were left-hemisphere dominant for speech (92%) and that most left-handed and ambidextrous patients without brain damage were also left-hemisphere dominant for speech (69%). Furthermore, she found that early left-hemisphere damage decreased left-hemisphere dominance for speech.

Sex Differences in Brain Lateralization

Interest in the possibility that the brains of females and males differ in their degree of lateralization was stimulated by McGlone's (1977, 1980) studies of unilateral stroke victims. McGlone found that male victims of unilateral strokes were three times more likely to suffer from aphasia than female victims. On the basis of this finding, McGlone concluded that the brains of males are more lateralized than the brains of females.

McGlone's hypothesis of a sex difference in brain lateralization has been widely embraced, and it has been used to explain almost every imaginable behavioral difference between the sexes. But support for McGlone's hypothesis has been mixed. Some researchers have failed to confirm her report of a sex difference in the effects of unilateral brain lesions (see Inglis & Lawson, 1982). However, several brain-imaging studies have confirmed that females, more than males, use both hemispheres in the performance of language-related tasks (e.g., Jaeger et al., 1998; Kansaku, Yamaura, & Kitazawa, 2000).

So far, you have learned about four methods of studying cerebral lateralization of function: comparing the effects of unilateral left- and right-hemisphere brain lesions, the sodium amytal test, the dichotic listening test, and functional brain imaging. The next section describes a fifth method.

In the early 1950s, the **corpus callosum**—the largest cerebral commissure—constituted a paradox of major proportions. Its size, an estimated 200 million axons, and its central position, right between the two cerebral hemispheres, implied that it performed an extremely important function; yet research in the 1930s and 1940s seemed to suggest that it did nothing at all. The corpus callosum had been cut in monkeys and in several other laboratory species, but the animals seemed no different after the surgery than they had been before. Similarly, human patients who were born without a corpus callosum seemed perfectly normal. In the early 1950s, Roger Sperry and his colleagues were intrigued by this paradox.

Groundbreaking Experiment of Myers and Sperry

The solution to the puzzle of the corpus callosum was provided in 1953 by an experiment on cats by Myers and Sperry. The experiment made two astounding theoretical points. First, it showed that one function of the corpus callosum is to transfer learned information from one hemisphere to the other. Second, it showed that when the corpus callosum is cut, each hemisphere can function independently; each split-brain cat appeared to have two brains. If you find the thought of a cat with two brains provocative, you will almost certainly be bowled over by similar observations about split-brain humans. But I am getting ahead of myself. Let's first consider the research on cats.

The Evolutionary Perspective

In their experiment, Myers and Sperry trained cats to perform a simple visual discrimination. On each trial, each cat was confronted by two panels, one with a circle on it and one with a square on it. The relative positions of the circle and square (right or left) were varied randomly from trial to trial, and the cats had to learn which symbol to press in order to get a food reward. Myers and Sperry correctly surmised that the key to split-brain research was to develop procedures for teaching and testing one hemisphere at a time. Figure 14.4 illustrates the method they used to isolate visual-discrimination

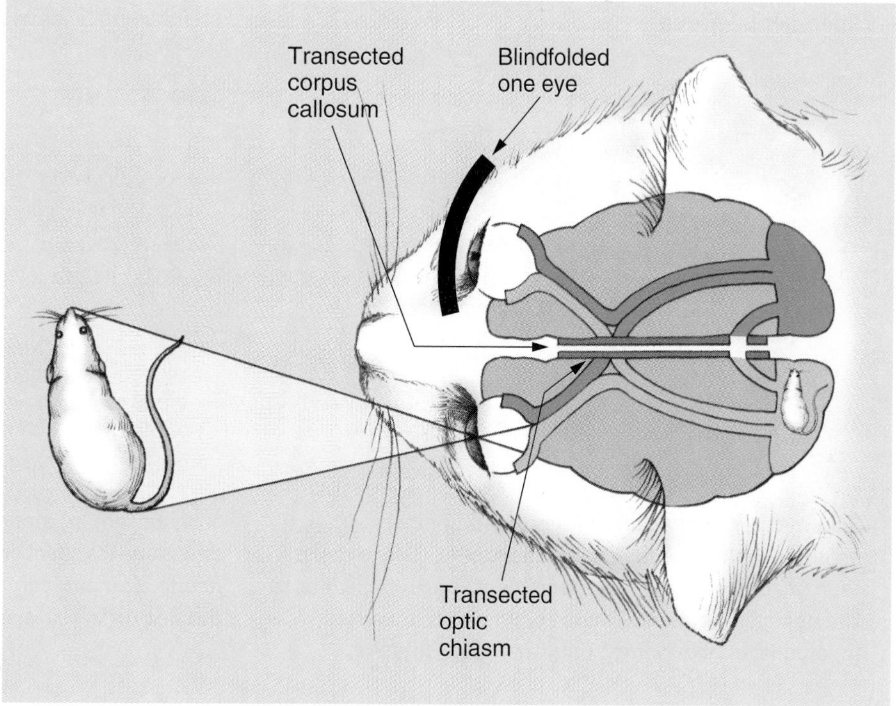

Restricting visual information to one hemisphere in cats. To restrict visual information to one hemisphere, Myers and Sperry (1) cut the corpus callosum, (2) cut the optic chiasm, and (3) blindfolded one eye. This restricted the visual information to the hemisphere ipsilateral to the uncovered eye.

Figure 14.4

Transected corpus callosum

Blindfolded one eye

Transected optic chiasm

learning in one hemisphere of the cats. There are two routes by which visual information can cross from one eye to the contralateral hemisphere: via the corpus callosum or via the optic chiasm. Accordingly, in their key experimental group, Myers and Sperry *transected* (cut completely through) both the optic chiasm and the corpus callosum of each cat and put a patch on one eye. This restricted all incoming visual information to the hemisphere ipsilateral to the uncovered eye.

The results of Myers and Sperry's experiment are illustrated in Figure 14.5. In the first phase of the study, all cats learned the task with a patch on one eye. The cats in the key experimental group (those with both the optic chiasm and the corpus callosum transected) learned the simple discrimination as rapidly as did unlesioned control cats or control cats with either the corpus callosum or the optic chiasm transected, despite the fact that cutting the optic chiasm produced a **scotoma**—an area of blindness—involving the entire medial half of each retina. This result suggested

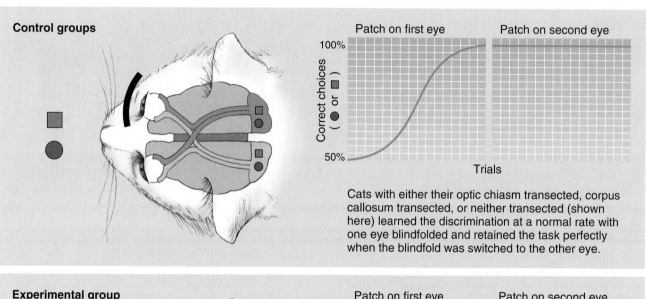

Control groups

Patch on first eye | Patch on second eye

Cats with either their optic chiasm transected, corpus callosum transected, or neither transected (shown here) learned the discrimination at a normal rate with one eye blindfolded and retained the task perfectly when the blindfold was switched to the other eye.

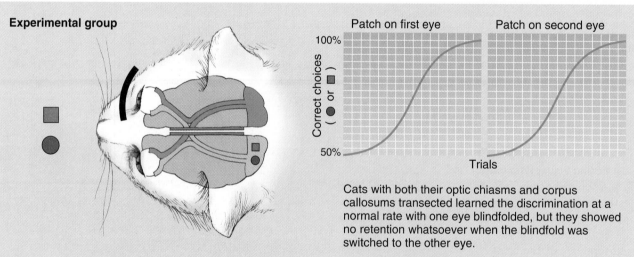

Experimental group

Patch on first eye | Patch on second eye

Cats with both their optic chiasms and corpus callosums transected learned the discrimination at a normal rate with one eye blindfolded, but they showed no retention whatsoever when the blindfold was switched to the other eye.

Schematic illustration of Myers and Sperry's (1953) groundbreaking split-brain experiment. There were four groups: (1) the key experimental group with both the optic chiasm and corpus callosum transected, (2) a control group with only the optic chiasm transected, (3) a control group with only the corpus callosum transected, and (4) an unlesioned control group. The performance of the three control groups did not differ, so they are illustrated here together.

Figure 14.5

that one hemisphere working alone can learn simple tasks as rapidly as two hemispheres working together.

More surprising were the results of the second phase of Myers and Sperry's experiment, during which the patch was transferred to each cat's other eye. The transfer of the patch had no effect on the performance of the intact control cats or of the control cats with either the optic chiasm or the corpus callosum transected; these subjects continued to perform the task with close to 100% accuracy. In contrast, transferring the eye patch had a devastating effect on the performance of the experimental cats. In effect, it blindfolded the hemisphere that had originally learned the task and tested the knowledge of the other hemisphere, which had been blindfolded during initial training. When the patch was transferred, the performance of the experimental cats dropped immediately to baseline (i.e., to 50% correct); and then the cats relearned the task with no savings whatsoever, as if they had never seen it before. Myers and Sperry concluded that the cat brain has the capacity to act as two separate brains and that the function of the corpus callosum is to transmit information between them.

Myers and Sperry's startling conclusions about the fundamental duality of the cat brain and the information-transfer function of the corpus callosum have been confirmed in a variety of species with a variety of test procedures. For example, split-brain monkeys cannot perform tasks requiring fine tactual discriminations (e.g., rough versus smooth) or fine motor responses (e.g., unlocking a puzzle) with one hand if they have learned the tasks with the other—provided that they are not allowed to watch their hands, which would allow the information to enter both hemispheres. There is no transfer of fine tactual and motor information in split-brain monkeys because the somatosensory and motor fibers involved in fine sensory and motor discriminations are all contralateral.

The Evolutionary Perspective

Commissurotomy in Human Epileptics

In the first half of the 20th century, when the normal function of the corpus callosum was still a mystery, it was known that epileptic discharges often spread from one hemisphere to the other through the corpus callosum. This fact and the fact that cutting the corpus callosum had proven in numerous studies to have no obvious effect on performance outside the contrived conditions of Sperry's laboratory led two neurosurgeons, Vogel and Bogen, to initiate a program of *commissurotomy* for the treatment of severe intractable cases of epilepsy.

The rationale underlying therapeutic commissurotomy—which typically involves transecting the corpus callosum and leaving the smaller commissures intact—was that the severity of the patient's convulsions might be reduced if the discharges could be limited to the hemisphere of their origin. The therapeutic benefits of commissurotomy turned out to be even greater than anticipated: Despite the fact that commissurotomy is performed in only the most severe cases, many commissurotomized patients do not experience another major convulsion.

Clinical Implications

Evaluation of the neuropsychological status of the split-brain patients was placed in the capable hands of Sperry and his associate Gazzaniga. They began by developing a battery of tests based on the same methodological strategy that had proved so informative in their studies of laboratory animals: delivering information to one hemisphere while keeping it out of the other.

They could not use the same visual-discrimination procedure that had been used in studies of split-brain laboratory animals (i.e., cutting the optic chiasm and blindfolding one eye) because cutting the optic chiasm produces a scotoma. Instead, they employed the procedure illustrated in Figure 14.6 on page 450. Each patient was asked to fixate on the center of a display screen; then, visual stimuli were flashed onto the left or right side of the screen for 0.1 second. The 0.1-second exposure time was long enough for the subjects to perceive the stimuli but short enough to preclude the confounding effects of eye movement. All stimuli thus presented in the left visual field were transmitted to the right visual cortex, and all stimuli thus

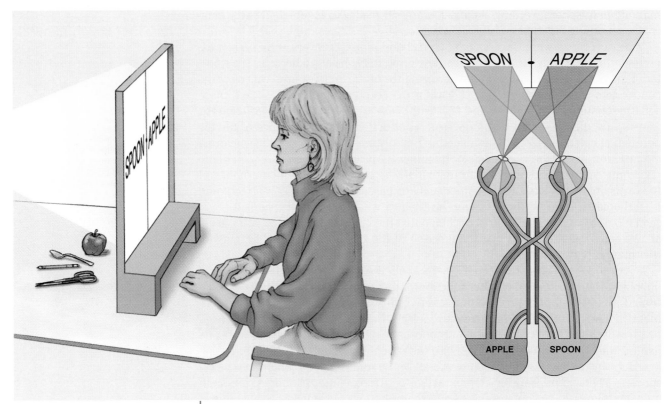

The testing procedure that was used to evaluate the neuropsychological status of split-brain patients. Visual input goes from each visual field to the contralateral hemisphere; fine tactile input goes from each hand to the contralateral hemisphere; and each hemisphere controls the fine motor movements of the contralateral hand.

Figure 14.6

presented in the right visual field were transmitted to the left visual cortex. Fine tactual and motor tasks were performed by each hand under a ledge. This procedure was used so that the nonperforming hemisphere, that is, the ipsilateral hemisphere, could not monitor the performance via the visual system.

The results of the tests on split-brain patients have confirmed the findings in split-brain laboratory animals in one major respect, but not in another. Like split-brain laboratory animals, human split-brain patients seem to have two independent brains, each with its own stream of consciousness, abilities, memories, and emotions (e.g., Gazzaniga, 1967; Gazzaniga & Sperry, 1967; Sperry, 1964). But unlike the hemispheres of split-brain laboratory animals, the hemispheres of split-brain patients are far from equal in their ability to perform certain tasks. Most notably, the left hemisphere of most split-brain patients is capable of speech, whereas the right hemisphere is not.

Before I recount some of the key results of the tests on split-brain humans, let me give you some advice. Some students become confused by the results of these tests because their tendency to think of the human brain as a single unitary organ is deeply engrained. If you become confused, think of each split-brain patient as two separate subjects: Ms. or Mr. Right Hemisphere, who understands a few simple instructions but cannot speak, who receives sensory information from the left visual field and left hand, and who controls the fine motor responses of the left hand; and Ms. or Mr. Left Hemisphere, who is verbally adept, who receives sensory information from the right visual field and right hand, and who controls the fine motor responses of the right hand. In everyday life, the behavior of most split-brain subjects is reasonably normal because their two brains go through life together and acquire much of the same information; however, in the neuropsychological laboratory, major discrepancies in what the two hemispheres learn can be created. As you are about to find out, this situation has some interesting consequences.

Evidence That the Hemispheres of Split-Brain Patients Function Independently

Here is how split-brain patients responded to Sperry's neuropsychological tests (see Figure 14.7). If a picture of an apple were flashed in the right visual field of a split-brain patient, the left hemisphere could do one of two things to indicate that it had received and stored the information. Because it is the hemisphere that speaks, the left hemisphere could simply tell the experimenter that it saw a picture of an apple. Or the patient could reach under the ledge with the right hand, feel the test objects that are there, and pick out the apple. Similarly, if the apple were presented to the left hemisphere by being placed in the patient's right hand, the left hemisphere could indicate to the experimenter that it was an apple either by saying so or by putting the apple down and picking out another apple with the right hand from the test objects under the ledge. If, however, the nonspeaking right hemisphere were asked to indicate the identity of an object that had previously been presented to the left hemisphere, it could not do so. Although objects that have been presented to the left hemisphere can be accurately identified with the right hand, performance is no better than chance with the left hand.

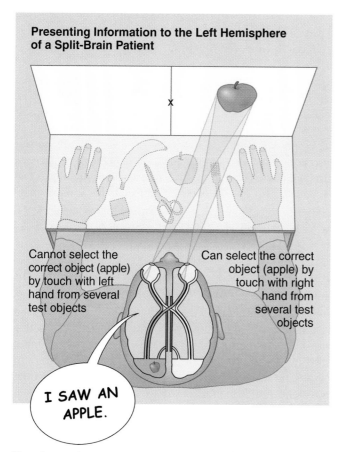

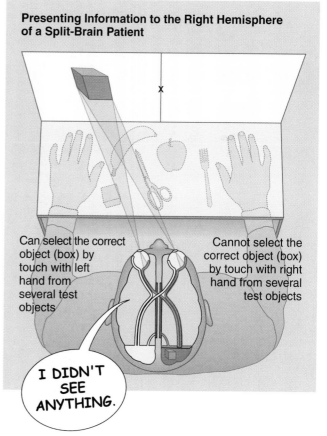

How Sperry's split-brain patients responded to one series of tests.

Figure 14.7

When test objects are presented to the right hemisphere either visually (in the left visual field) or tactually (in the left hand), the pattern of responses is entirely different. A split-brain patient asked to name an object flashed in the left visual field is likely to claim that nothing appeared on the screen. (Remember that it is the left hemisphere that is talking and the right hemisphere that has seen the stimulus.) A patient asked to name an object placed in the left hand is usually aware that something is there, presumably because of the crude tactual information carried by ipsilateral somatosensory fibers, but is unable to say what it is (see Fabri et al., 2001). Amazingly, all the while the patient is claiming (i.e., all the while that the left hemisphere is claiming) the inability to identify a test object presented in the left visual field or left hand, the left hand (i.e., the right hemisphere) can identify the correct object. Imagine how confused the patient must become when, in trial after trial, the left hand can feel an object and then fetch another just like it from a collection of test items under the ledge, while the left hemisphere is vehemently claiming that it does not know the identity of the test object.

Cross-Cuing

Although the two hemispheres of a split-brain subject have no means of direct neural communication, they sometimes communicate with each other indirectly by a process called **cross-cuing**. An example of cross-cuing occurred during a series of tests designed to determine whether the left hemisphere could respond to colors presented in the left visual field. To test this possibility, a red or a green stimulus was presented in the left visual field, and the split-brain subject was asked to verbally report the color: red or green. At first, the patient performed at a chance level on this task (50% correct); but after a time, performance improved appreciably, thus suggesting that the color information was somehow being transferred over neural pathways from the right hemisphere to the left. However, this proved not to be the case:

> We soon caught on to the strategy the patient used. If a red light was flashed and the patient by chance guessed red, he would stick with that answer. If the flashed light was red, and the patient by chance guessed green, he would frown, shake his head and then say, "Oh no, I meant red." What was happening was that the right hemisphere saw the red light and heard the left hemisphere make the guess "green." Knowing that the answer was wrong, the right hemisphere precipitated a frown and a shake of the head, which in turn cued in the left hemisphere to the fact that the answer was wrong and that it had better correct itself! . . . . The realization that the neurological patient has various strategies at his command emphasizes how difficult it is to obtain a clear neurological description of a human being with brain damage. (Gazzaniga, 1967, p. 27)

Learning Two Things at Once

In most of the classes I teach, there is a student who fits the following stereotype. He sits—or rather sprawls—near the back of the class; and despite good grades, he tries to create the impression that he is above it all by making sarcastic comments. I am sure you recognize him—and it is almost always a him. Such a student inadvertently triggered an interesting discussion in one of my classes. His comment went something like this: "If getting my brain cut in two could create two separate brains, perhaps I should get it done so that I could study for two different exams at the same time."

The question raised by this comment is a good one. If the two hemispheres of a split-brain patient are capable of total independence, then they should be able to learn two different things at the same time. Can they? Indeed they can. For example, in one test, two different visual stimuli appeared simultaneously on the test screen—let's say a pencil in the left visual field and an orange in the right visual field. Then, after a delay, the split-brain patient was asked to simultaneously reach into two bags—one with each hand—and grasp in each hand the object that had been on the screen. After grasping the objects, but before withdrawing them, the subject was asked to tell the experimenter what was in the two hands; the subject (i.e., the left hemisphere) replied, "Two oranges." Much to the bewilderment of the verbal left hemisphere, when the hands were withdrawn, there was an orange in the right hand and a pencil in the left. The two hemispheres of the split-brain subject had learned two different things at exactly the same time.

In another test in which two visual stimuli were presented simultaneously—again, let's say a pencil to the left visual field and an orange to the right—the split-brain subject was asked to pick up the presented object from an assortment of objects on a table, this time in full view. As the right hand reached out to pick up the orange under the direction of the left hemisphere, the right hemisphere saw what was happening and thought an error was being made (remember that the right hemisphere saw a pencil). On some trials, the right hemisphere dealt with this problem in the only way that it could: The left hand shot out, grabbed the right hand away from the orange, and redirected it to the pencil. This response is called the **helping-hand phenomenon**.

Yet another example of simultaneous learning in the two hemispheres involves the phenomenon of **visual completion**. As you may recall from Chapter 4, individuals with scotomas are often unaware of them because their brains have the capacity to fill them in (to complete them) by using information from the surrounding areas of the visual field. In a sense, each hemisphere of a split-brain patient is a subject with a scotoma covering the entire ipsilateral visual field.

The ability of each hemisphere of a split-brain patient to simultaneously and independently engage in completion has been demonstrated in studies using the **chimeric figures test**—named after *Chimera*, a mythical monster composed of the combined parts of different animals. Levy, Trevarthen, and Sperry (1972) flashed onto the center of a screen in front of their split-brain subjects photographs that had been created by fusing half faces of two different people. The subjects were then asked to describe what they saw or to indicate what they saw by pointing to it in a series of photographs of intact faces. Amazingly, each subject (i.e., each left hemisphere) reported seeing a complete, bilaterally symmetrical face, even when asked such leading questions as "Did you notice anything peculiar about what you just saw?" When the subjects were asked to describe what they saw, they usually described a completed version of the half that had been presented to the right visual field (i.e., the left hemisphere).

Dual Mental Functioning and Conflict in Split-Brain Patients

In most split-brain patients, the right hemisphere does not seem to have a strong will of its own; the left hemisphere seems to control most everyday activities. However, in a few patients, the right hemisphere takes a more active role in controlling behavior. In these latter cases, there can be serious conflicts between the left and right hemispheres. Patient 2C (let's call him Peter) was such a case.

The Case of Peter, the Split-Brain Patient Tormented by Conflict

At the age of 8, Peter began to suffer from complex partial seizures. Antiepileptic medication was ineffective, and at 20, he received a commissurotomy, which greatly improved his condition but did not completely block his seizures. A sodium amytal test administered prior to surgery showed that he was left-hemisphere dominant for language.

Following surgery, Peter, unlike most other split-brain patients, was not able to respond with the left side of his body to verbal input. When asked to

make whole-body movements (e.g., "Stand like a boxer") or movements of the left side of his body (e.g., "Touch your left ear with your left hand"), he could not respond correctly. Apparently, his left hemisphere could not, or would not, control the left side of his body via ipsilateral fibers. During such tests, Peter—or, more specifically, Peter's left hemisphere—often remarked that he hated the left side of his body.

The independent, obstinate, and sometimes mischievous behavior of Peter's right hemisphere often caused him (his left hemisphere) considerable frustration. He (his left hemisphere) complained that his left hand would turn off television shows that he was enjoying, that his left leg would not always walk in the intended direction, and that his left arm would sometimes perform embarrassing, socially unacceptable acts (e.g., striking a relative).

In the laboratory, he (his left hemisphere) sometimes became angry with his left hand, swearing at it, striking it, and trying to force it with his right hand to do what he (his left hemisphere) wanted. In these cases, his left hand usually resisted his right hand and kept performing as directed by his right hemisphere. In these instances, it was always clear that the right hemisphere was behaving with intent and understanding and that the left hemisphere had no clue why the despised left hand was doing what it was doing (Joseph, 1988).

14.3
Differences between the Left and Right Hemispheres

So far in this chapter, you have learned about five methods of studying cerebral lateralization of function: unilateral lesions, the sodium amytal test, the dichotic listening test, functional brain imaging, and studies of split-brain patients. This section takes a look at some of the major functional differences between the left and right cerebral hemispheres that have been discovered using these methods. Because the verbal and motor abilities of the left hemisphere are readily apparent (see Beeman & Chiarello, 1998; Reuter-Lorenz & Miller, 1998), most research on the lateralization of function has focused on uncovering the special abilities of the right hemisphere.

Slight Biases versus All-or-None Hemispheric Differences

Thinking Clearly

Before I introduce you to some of the differences between the left and right hemispheres, I need to clear up a common misconception: For many functions, there are no differences between the hemispheres; and when functional differences do exist, these tend to be slight biases in favor of one hemisphere or the other—not absolute differences (see Brown & Kosslyn, 1993). Disregarding these facts, the popular media inevitably portray left–right cerebral differences as absolute. As a result, it is widely believed that various abilities reside exclusively in one hemisphere or the other. For example, it is widely believed that the left hemisphere has exclusive control over language and the right hemisphere has exclusive control over emotion and creativity. The most disturbing thing about this misrepresentation is that educational programs are sometimes inspired by it.

Language-related abilities provide a particularly good illustration of the fact that lateralization of function is statistical rather than absolute. Language is the most lateralized of all cognitive abilities. Yet, even in this most extreme case, lateralization is far from total; there is substantial language-related activity in the right hemisphere. Following are three illustrations of this point: First, on the dichotic listening test, subjects who are left-hemisphere dominant for language tend to identify more digits with the right ear than the left ear, but this right-ear advantage is only slight, 55% to 45%. Second, in most split-brain patients, the left hemisphere is dominant for language, but the right hemisphere can understand many spoken or written words and simple sentences (see Baynes & Gazzaniga, 1997; Zaidel, 1987). And third, although there is considerable variability among split-brain patients in their right-hemisphere performance on tests of language comprehension (Gazzaniga, 1998), the language abilities of their right hemispheres tend to be comparable to those of a preschool child.

Some Examples of Lateralization of Function

Table 14.1 lists some of the abilities that have been shown to be lateralized. They are arranged in two columns: those that are controlled more by the left hemisphere and those that are controlled more by the right hemisphere. The study of lateralization of function has put the archaic notion of left-hemisphere dominance to rest. The right hemisphere has been shown to be functionally superior to the left in several respects. The three best-documented domains of right-hemisphere superiority are spatial ability, emotion, and musical ability. Also, the right hemisphere is superior in performing some memory tasks. Before discussing these four superiorities of the right hemisphere, let's take a look at an unexpected superiority of the left hemisphere.

Table 14.1

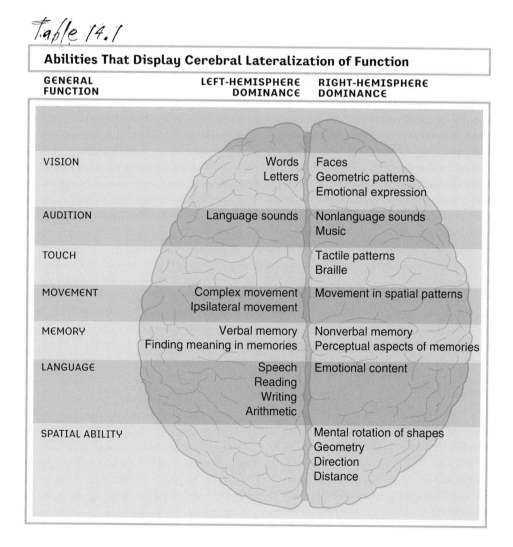

Abilities That Display Cerebral Lateralization of Function

GENERAL FUNCTION	LEFT-HEMISPHERE DOMINANCE	RIGHT-HEMISPHERE DOMINANCE
VISION	Words Letters	Faces Geometric patterns Emotional expression
AUDITION	Language sounds	Nonlanguage sounds Music
TOUCH		Tactile patterns Braille
MOVEMENT	Complex movement Ipsilateral movement	Movement in spatial patterns
MEMORY	Verbal memory Finding meaning in memories	Nonverbal memory Perceptual aspects of memories
LANGUAGE	Speech Reading Writing Arithmetic	Emotional content
SPATIAL ABILITY		Mental rotation of shapes Geometry Direction Distance

Superiority of the Left Hemisphere in Controlling Ipsilateral Movement.
One interesting and unexpected lateralized function was revealed by functional brain-imaging studies (see Haaland & Harrington, 1996). When complex, cognitively driven movements are made by one hand, most of the activity is observed in the *contralateral* hemisphere, as expected. However, some activation is also observed in the *ipsilateral* hemisphere, and these ipsilateral effects are substantially greater in the left hemisphere than in the right (Kim et al., 1993). Consistent with this observation is the fact that left-hemisphere lesions are more likely than right-hemisphere lesions to be associated with ipsilateral motor problems.

Superiority of the Right Hemisphere in Spatial Ability.
In a classic early study, Levy (1969) placed a three-dimensional block of a particular shape in either the right hand or the left hand of her split-brain subjects. Then, after they had thoroughly *palpated* (tactually investigated) it, she asked them to point to the two-dimensional test stimulus that best represented what the three-dimensional block would look like if it were made of cardboard and unfolded. She found a right-hemisphere superiority on this task, and she found that the two hemispheres seemed to go about the task in different ways. The performance of the left hand and right hemisphere was rapid and silent, whereas the performance of the right hand and left hemisphere was hesitant and often accompanied by a running verbal commentary that was difficult for the subjects to inhibit. Levy concluded that the right hemisphere is superior to the left at spatial tasks. This conclusion has been frequently confirmed (e.g., Funnell, Corballis, & Gazzaniga, 1999; Kaiser et al., 2000), and it is consistent with the finding that disorders of spatial perception (e.g., contralateral neglect—see Chapters 5 and 6) tend to be associated with right-hemisphere damage.

Superiority of the Right Hemisphere in Emotion.
According to the old idea of general left-hemisphere dominance, the right hemisphere was assumed to be uninvolved in emotion. This assumption has been proven false. Indeed, studies of the effects of unilateral brain lesions have found the right hemisphere to be superior to the left in some aspects of emotion: for example, in recognizing facial expressions of emotions (Bowers et al., 1985) and in the perception of others' moods (Tompkins & Mateer, 1985).

Sperry, Zaidel, and Zaidel (1979) assessed the behavioral reactions of the right hemispheres of split-brain patients to various emotion-charged images: photographs of relatives; of pets; of themselves; and of political, historical, and religious figures and emblems. The patients' behavioral reactions were appropriate, thus indicating that right hemispheres are capable of emotional expression. In addition, there was an unexpected finding: The emotional content of images presented to the right hemisphere was reflected in the patients' speech as well as in their nonverbal behavior. This suggested that emotional information was somehow being passed from the right to the verbal left hemisphere of the split-brain subjects. The ability of emotional reactions, but not visual information, to be passed from the right hemisphere to the left hemisphere created a bizarre situation. A subject's left hemisphere often reacted with the appropriate emotional verbal response to an image that had been presented to the right hemisphere, even though it did not know what the image was.

Consider the following remarkable exchange (paraphrased from Sperry, Zaidel, & Zaidel, 1979, pp. 161–162). The patient's right hemisphere was presented with an array of photos, and the patient was asked if one was familiar. He pointed to the photo of his aunt.

> *Experimenter*: "Is this a neutral, a thumbs-up, or a thumbs-down person?"
> *Patient*: With a smile, he made a thumbs-up sign and said, "This is a happy person."
> *Experimenter*: "Do you know him personally?"
> *Patient*: "Oh, it's not a him, it's a her."

Experimenter: "Is she an entertainment personality or an historical figure?"
Patient: "No, just . . ."
Experimenter: "Someone you know personally?"
Patient: He traced something with his left index finger on the back of his right hand, and then he exclaimed, "My aunt, my Aunt Edie."
Experimenter: "How do you know?"
Patient: "By the E on the back of my hand."

Pause and think about the experiences and thoughts of these two hemispheres as each struggled to perform the task.

Superiority of the Right Hemisphere in Musical Ability. Kimura (1964) compared the performance of 20 right-handers on the standard, digit version of the dichotic listening test with their performance on a version of the test involving the dichotic presentation of melodies. In the melody version of the test, Kimura simultaneously played two different melodies—one to each ear—and then asked the subjects to identify the two they had just heard from four that were subsequently played to them through both ears. The right ear (i.e., the left hemisphere) was superior in the perception of digits, whereas the left ear (i.e., the right hemisphere) was superior in the perception of melodies. This is consistent with the observation that right temporal lobe lesions are more likely to disrupt music discriminations than are left temporal lobe lesions.

Hemispheric Difference in Memory. Both the left and the right hemispheres have the ability to remember, but they seem to go about the task of remembering in different ways (see Gazzaniga, 1998). Although this hemispheric difference in memory style has been demonstrated in several ways, it is particularly well illustrated by the performance of split-brain patients on the following task, in which the left or right hemispheres of the patients are tested separately. The task is to guess which of two lights—top or bottom—will come on next, based on the hemisphere's memory of recent trials. The top light comes on 80% of the time in random sequence, but the subjects are not given this information. The fact that the top light comes on more than the bottom is quickly discovered by intact control subjects; however, because they try to figure out the nonexistent rule that predicts the exact sequence, they are correct only 68% of the time—even though they could score 80% if they always selected the top light.

The left hemispheres of split-brain subjects perform like intact controls: They attempt to find deeper meaning in their memories and as a result perform poorly on this task. In contrast, right hemispheres, like rats, do not try to interpret their memories and readily learn to maximize their correct responses by always selecting the top light. The left hemisphere attempts to place its experiences in a larger context, while the right hemisphere attends strictly to the perceptual aspects of the stimulus (see Metcalfe, Funnell, & Gazzaniga, 1995; Roser & Gazzaniga, 2004).

The two hemispheres also seem to differ somewhat with respect to what types of information they remember. In general, the left hemisphere plays the greater role in memory for verbal material, whereas the right hemisphere plays the greater role in memory for nonverbal material (e.g., Kelley et al., 2002).

What Is Lateralized—Broad Clusters of Abilities or Individual Cognitive Processes?

Take another look at Table 14.1, which summarizes major examples of cerebral lateralization of function. I have already alerted you to one way in which examples of cerebral lateralization are commonly misinterpreted: They reflect slight hemispheric biases, not all-or-none differences. Now that you have had the opportunity to digest the information in Table 14.1, I want to issue a second warning about it.

Thinking Clearly

You have undoubtedly encountered some of this information before: Is there a single educated person in this society who does not know that the left hemisphere is the logical language hemisphere and the right hemisphere is the emotional spatial hemisphere? Information like that in Table 14.1 summarizes the results of many studies and thus serves a useful function if it is not taken too literally. The problem is that such information is almost always taken too literally. Let me explain.

Early theories of cerebral laterality tended to ascribe complex clusters of mental abilities to one hemisphere or the other. The left hemisphere tended to perform better on language tests, so it was presumed to be dominant for language-related abilities; the right hemisphere tended to perform better on some spatial tests, so it was presumed to be dominant for space-related abilities; and so on. Perhaps this was a reasonable first step, but now the general view among researchers is that this approach is simplistic, illogical, and inconsistent with the evidence.

The problem is that categories such as language, emotion, musical ability, and spatial ability are each composed of dozens of different individual cognitive activities, and there is no reason to assume that all those activities associated with a general English label (e.g., spatial ability) will necessarily be lateralized in the same hemisphere. The inappropriateness of broad categories of cerebral lateralization has been confirmed. How is it possible to argue that all language-related abilities are lateralized in the left hemisphere, when the right hemisphere has proved superior in perceiving the intonation of speech and the identity of the speaker (Beeman & Chiarello, 1998)? Indeed, notable exceptions to all broad categories of cerebral lateralization have emerged (see Vogel, Bowers, & Vogel, 2003).

As a result of mounting evidence of the inappropriateness of broad categories of cerebral lateralization, many researchers are taking a different approach. They are basing their studies of cerebral lateralization on the work of cognitive psychologists, who have broken down complex cognitive tasks—such as reading, judging space, and remembering—into their *constituent cognitive processes*. Once the laterality of the individual cognitive elements has been determined, it should be possible to predict the laterality of cognitive tasks based on the specific cognitive elements that compose them.

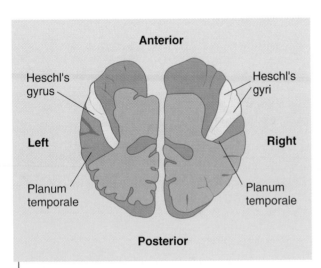

Two language areas of the cerebral cortex that display neuroanatomical asymmetry: the planum temporale (Wernicke' s area) and Heschl' s gyrus (primary auditory cortex).

Figure 14.8

Anatomical Asymmetries of the Brain

Casual inspection suggests that the left and right hemispheres are mirror images of one another, but they are not; many anatomical differences between them have been documented. Most of the research effort has been expended trying to document anatomical asymmetries in areas of cortex that are important for language. Three of these areas are the planum temporale, Heschl's gyrus, and the frontal operculum. The **planum temporale** is the area of temporal lobe cortex that lies in the posterior region of the lateral fissure; the left planum temporale is thought to play a role in the comprehension of language and is often referred to as *Wernicke's area*. **Heschl's gyrus** is located in the lateral fissure just anterior to the planum temporale in the temporal lobe; it is the location of primary auditory cortex. The **frontal operculum** is the area of frontal lobe cortex that lies just in front of the face area of the primary motor cortex; in the left hemisphere, it is the location of Broca's area.

Because the planum temporale, Heschl's gyrus, and the frontal operculum are all thought to be involved in language-related activities, one might expect that they would all be larger in the left hemisphere than in the right in most subjects; but they aren't. The left planum temporale does tend to be larger than the right, but in only 65% of human brains (Geschwind & Levitsky, 1968). In contrast, the cortex of Heschl's gyrus tends to be larger on the right, primarily because there are often two Heschl's gyri in the right hemisphere and only one in the left. (See Figure 14.8 for an illustration of these two anatomical asymmetries.) The laterality of the frontal operculum is less clear. The area of the frontal operculum that is visible on the surface of the brain tends to be larger on the right; but when the cortex buried within sulci of the frontal operculum is considered, there tends to be a greater volume of frontal operculum cortex on the left (Falzi, Perrone, & Vignolo, 1982).

A word of caution is in order. It is tempting to conclude that the tendency for the planum temporale to be larger in the left hemisphere predisposes the left hemisphere for language dominance. Indeed, the finding that the left planum temporale is larger than the right in fetal brains (Wada, Clarke, & Hamm, 1975) is consistent with this view. However, because most studies of neuroanatomical asymmetry are conducted at autopsy, there is no evidence that people with well-developed anatomical asymmetries tend to have more lateralized language functions. In fact, there is a substantial discrepancy between the proportion of the population that has been reported to have a larger left planum temporale (about 65%) and the proportion that is left-hemisphere dominant for language (over 90%).

Techniques for imaging the living human brain have made it easier to look for correlations between particular neuroanatomical asymmetries and particular performance measures. Such studies are important because they have the potential for revealing the functional advantages of cerebral lateralization. One such study is that of Schlaug and colleagues (1995). They used structural magnetic resonance imaging (MRI) to measure the asymmetry of the planum temporale and relate it to the presence of *perfect pitch* (the ability to identify the pitch of individual musical notes). The planum temporale was found to be more lateralized to the left hemisphere in musicians with perfect pitch than in nonmusicians or in musicians without perfect pitch (see Figure 14.9).

Most studies of anatomical asymmetries of the brain have measured differences in gross neuroanatomy, comparing the sizes of particular gross structures in the left and right hemispheres. Recently, however, anatomists have started to study differences in cellular structure between corresponding areas of the two hemispheres that have been found to differ in function (see Gazzaniga, 2000; Hutsler & Galuske, 2003). For example, the hand area in the hemisphere contralateral to a person's preferred hand, in addition to being larger, has more lateral connections (see Hammond, 2002).

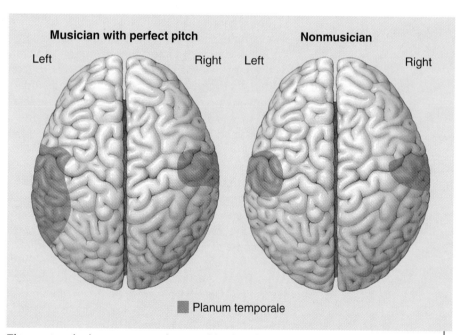

Planum temporale

The anatomical asymmetry detected in the planum temporale of musicians by magnetic resonance imaging. In most people, the planum temporale is larger in the left hemisphere than in the right; this difference was found to be greater in musicians with perfect pitch than in either musicians without perfect pitch or control subjects. (Adapted from Schlaug et al., 1995.)

Figure 14.9

Theories of Cerebral Asymmetry

Several theories have been proposed to explain why cerebral asymmetry evolved. All of them are based on the same general premise: that it is advantageous for areas of the brain that perform similar functions to be located in the same hemisphere. However, each theory of cerebral asymmetry postulates a different fundamental distinction between left and right hemisphere function. The following are three prominent theories of cerebral asymmetry.

Analytic–Synthetic Theory. One theory of cerebral asymmetry is the analytic–synthetic theory. The *analytic–synthetic theory of cerebral asymmetry* holds that there are two basic modes of thinking, an analytic mode and a synthetic mode, which have become segregated during the course of evolution in the left and right hemispheres, respectively. According to this theory,

> . . . the left hemisphere operates in a more logical, analytical, computerlike fashion, analyzing stimulus information input sequentially and abstracting the relevant details, to which it attaches verbal labels; the right hemisphere is primarily a synthesizer, more concerned with the overall stimulus configuration, and organizes and processes information in terms of gestalts, or wholes. (Harris, 1978, p. 463)

Although the analytic–synthetic theory has been the darling of pop psychology, its vagueness is a problem. Because it is not possible to specify the degree to which any task requires either analytic or synthetic processing, it has been difficult to subject the analytic–synthetic theory to empirical tests.

Motor Theory. A second theory of cerebral asymmetry is the motor theory (see Kimura, 1979). According to the *motor theory of cerebral asymmetry*, the left hemisphere is specialized not for the control of speech per se but for the control of fine movements, of which speech is only one category. Support for this theory comes from reports that lesions that produce aphasia also produce other motor deficits. For example, Kimura (1987) found a correlation between the disruption of language abilities by lesions and the disruption of voluntary nonspeech oral movements by the same lesions; Kimura and Watson (1989) found that left frontal lesions produced deficits in the ability to make both individual speech sounds and individual facial movements, whereas left temporal and parietal lesions produced deficits in the ability to make sequences of speech sounds and sequences of facial movements; and Wolff and others (1990) found that subjects with reading disabilities also had difficulty performing a finger-tapping test.

Linguistic Theory. A third theory of cerebral asymmetry is the linguistic theory. The *linguistic theory of cerebral asymmetry* posits that the primary role of the left hemisphere is language—in contrast to the analytic–synthetic and motor theories, which view language as a secondary specialization residing in the left hemisphere because of its primary specialization for analytic thought and skilled motor activity, respectively.

The linguistic theory of cerebral asymmetry is based to a large degree on the study of deaf people who use *American Sign Language* (a sign language with a structure similar to that of spoken language) and who then suffer unilateral brain damage (see Hickok, Bellugi, & Klima, 2001). W.L. was such a case.

The Case of W.L., the Man Who Experienced Aphasia for Sign Language

Clinical Implications

W.L. is a congenitally deaf, right-handed male. He has two deaf, signing brothers and grew up using American Sign Language. Until his stroke, he had relied on sign language as his primary means of communication with his spouse, relatives, and friends.

W.L. has a history of cardiovascular disease; and 7 months prior to testing, he was admitted to hospital complaining of right-side weakness and motor problems. A CT scan revealed a large lesion in the left frontotemporoparietal cortex (the same general area in which damage often produces aphasia). At that time, W.L.'s wife noticed that he was making many uncharacteristic errors in signing and was having difficulty understanding the signs of others.

Fortunately, W.L.'s neuropsychologists managed to obtain a 2-hour videotape of an interview with him recorded 10 months before his stroke, which served as a valuable source of prestroke performance measures. Formal poststroke neuropsychological testing confirmed that W.L. had suffered a specific loss in his ability to use and understand sign language. The fact that he could produce and understand complex pantomime gestures suggested that his sign-language aphasia was not the result of motor or sensory deficits, and the results of cognitive tests suggested that it was not the result of general cognitive deficits (Corina et al., 1992).

Case studies like that of W.L. are particularly important because they illustrate a striking dissociation between two kinds of communicative gestures: linguistic (sign) gestures and nonlinguistic (pantomime) gestures. The fact that left-hemisphere damage can disrupt the use of sign language but not pantomime gestures suggests that the fundamental specialization of the left hemisphere is language.

Evolution of Cerebral Lateralization of Function

The Evolutionary Perspective

Cerebral lateralization is often assumed to be an exclusive feature of the human brain. One theory of the evolution of cerebral asymmetry is based on the motor theory of cerebral asymmetry: Left-hemisphere dominance for motor control is thought to have evolved in early hominids in response to their use of tools, and then the propensity for vocal language is thought to have subsequently evolved in the left hemisphere because of its greater motor dexterity. This theory of the evolution of cerebral lateralization of function is challenged by reports of handedness in nonhuman primates.

The first studies of hand preference in nonhuman primates found that some individual monkeys tended to use one hand more than the other but that there was no general tendency for the right to be preferred over the left (Colell, Segarra, & Sabater-Pi, 1995). However, more recently, there have been several reports that the nonhuman primates most closely related to humans display a right-hand preference for certain tasks (see Hopkins, 1996). For example, Hopkins (1995) found that chimpanzees tend to use their right hands to extract peanut butter from a transparent tube. Subsequently, Hopkins and Pilcher (2001) found the hand area to be larger in the left primary motor cortex than in the right primary motor cortex in a mixed sample of apes (e.g., gorillas, orangutans, and chimpanzees). Evidence of handedness in nonhuman primates rules out the possibility that tool use by early hominids was the major factor in the evolution of cerebral lateralization of function.

Hand preference is not the only evidence of cerebral lateralization of function in nonhuman primates. In some nonhuman primate species, the left hemispheres have been found to be dominant for the production (see Owren, 1990) and discrimination (Heffner & Heffner, 1984) of communicative vocalizations, and the cortical area homologous to Wernicke's area has been found to be larger in the left hemisphere (Gannon et al., 1998). Moreover, in some nonhuman primate species, the right hemisphere has proven to be superior in the discrimination of facial identity and expression (Vermeire, Hamilton, & Erdmann, 1998). All these findings suggest that the evolution of cerebral laterality preceded the evolution of humans. But by how much?

There is now strong evidence that cerebral lateralization of function is not of recent evolutionary origin. Lateralization of function has been demonstrated in many species of mammals, birds, amphibians, reptiles, and fish; that is, many species display a tendency to perform a particular response with, or toward, a particular side (left or right) of the body. Moreover, systematic asymmetries in nervous system anatomy have been described in many of these species. However, I am unaware of any research that has managed to link the degree of a particular nervous system asymmetry with the incidence of a particular behavioral asymmetry.

14.4

Cortical Localization of Language: The Wernicke-Geschwind Model

So far, this chapter has focused on the functional asymmetry of the brain, with an emphasis on the lateralization of language-related functions. At this point, the focus shifts from language lateralization to language localization. In contrast to language lateralization, which refers to the relative control of language-related functions by the left and right hemispheres, *language localization* refers to the location within the hemispheres of the circuits that participate in language-related activities.

Like most introductions to language localization, the following discussion begins with the *Wernicke-Geschwind model*, the predominant theory of language localization. Because most of the research on the localization of language has been conducted and interpreted within the context of this model, reading about the localization of language without a basic understanding of the Wernicke-Geschwind model would be like watching a game of chess without knowing the rules—not a very fulfilling experience.

ON THE CD

See the *Wernicke-Geschwind Model of Language* module for a clear and vivid explanation of the model.

Historical Antecedents of the Wernicke-Geschwind Model

The history of the localization of language and the history of the lateralization of function began at the same point, with Broca's assertion that a small area in the inferior portion of the left prefrontal cortex (Broca's area) is the center for speech production. Broca hypothesized that programs of articulation are stored within this area and that speech is produced when these programs activate the adjacent area of the precentral gyrus, which controls the muscles of the face and oral cavity. According to Broca, damage restricted to Broca's area should disrupt speech production without producing deficits in language comprehension.

The next major event in the study of the cerebral localization of language occurred in 1874, when Carl Wernicke (pronounced "VER-ni-key") concluded on the basis of 10 clinical cases that there is a language area in the left temporal lobe just posterior to the primary auditory cortex (i.e., in the left planum temporale). This second language area, which Wernicke argued was the cortical area of language comprehension, subsequently became known as **Wernicke's area**.

Clinical Implications

Wernicke suggested that selective lesions of Broca's area produce a syndrome of aphasia whose symptoms are primarily **expressive**—characterized by normal comprehension of both written and spoken language and by speech that retains its meaningfulness despite being slow, labored, disjointed, and poorly articulated. This hypothetical form of aphasia became known as **Broca's aphasia**. In contrast, Wernicke suggested that selective lesions of Wernicke's area produce a syndrome of aphasia whose deficits are primarily **receptive**—characterized by poor comprehension of both written and spoken language and speech that is meaningless but still retains the superficial structure, rhythm, and intonation of normal speech. This hypothetical form of aphasia became known as **Wernicke's aphasia**, and the normal-sounding but nonsensical speech of Wernicke's aphasia became known as **word salad**.

The following are examples of the kinds of speech that are presumed to be associated with selective damage to Broca's and Wernicke's areas (Geschwind, 1979, p. 183):

Broca's aphasia: A patient who was asked about a dental appointment replied haltingly and indistinctly: "Yes. . . . Monday. . . . Dad and Dick. . . . Wednesday nine o'clock. . . . 10 o'clock. . . . doctors. . . . and. . . . teeth."

Wernicke's aphasia: A patient who was asked to describe a picture that showed two boys stealing cookies reported smoothly: "Mother is away here working her work to get her better, but when she's looking the two boys looking in the other part. She's working another time."

Wernicke reasoned that damage to the pathway connecting Broca's and Wernicke's areas—the **arcuate fasciculus**—would produce a third type of aphasia, one he called **conduction aphasia**. He contended that comprehension and spontaneous speech would be largely intact in patients with damage to the arcuate fasciculus but that they would have difficulty repeating words that they had just heard.

The left **angular gyrus**—the area of left temporal and parietal cortex just posterior to Wernicke's area—is another cortical area that has been implicated in language. Its role in language was recognized in 1892 by Dejerine on the basis of the postmortem examination of one special patient. The patient suffered from **alexia** (the inability to read) and **agraphia** (the inability to write). What made this case special was that the alexia and agraphia were exceptionally pure: Although the patient could not read or write, he had no difficulty speaking or understanding speech. Dejerine's postmortem examination revealed damage in the pathways connecting the visual cortex with the left angular gyrus. He concluded that the left angular gyrus is responsible for comprehending language-related visual input, which is received directly from the adjacent left visual cortex and indirectly from the right visual cortex via the corpus callosum.

During the era of Broca, Wernicke, and Dejerine, many influential scholars (e.g., Freud, Head, and Marie) opposed their attempts to localize various language-related abilities to specific neocortical areas. In fact, advocates of the holistic approach to brain function gradually gained the upper hand, and interest in the cerebral localization of language waned. However, in the mid-1960s, Norman Geschwind (1970) revived the old localizationist ideas of Broca, Wernicke, and Dejerine, added some new data and insightful interpretation, and melded the mix into a powerful theory: the Wernicke-Geschwind model.

The Wernicke-Geschwind Model

The following are the seven components of the **Wernicke-Geschwind model**: primary visual cortex, angular gyrus, primary auditory cortex, Wernicke's area, arcuate fasciculus, Broca's area, and primary motor cortex. All of these are in the left hemisphere and are shown in Figure 14.10.

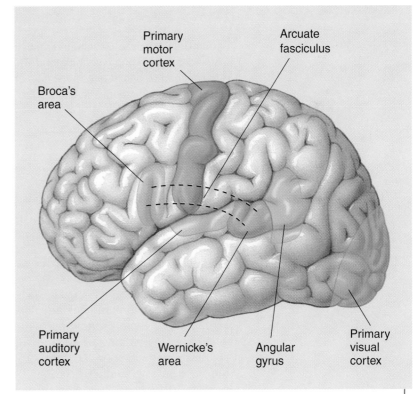

Primary motor cortex

Arcuate fasciculus

Broca's area

Primary auditory cortex

Wernicke's area

Angular gyrus

Primary visual cortex

The seven components of the Wernicke-Geschwind model.

Figure 14.10

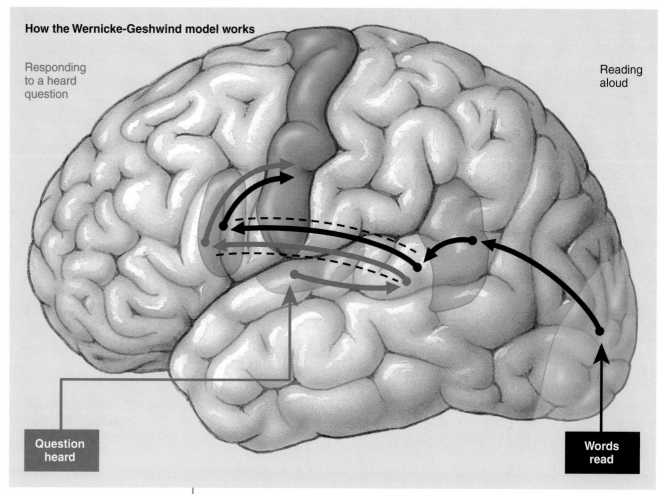

How the Wernicke-Geshwind model works

Responding to a heard question

Reading aloud

Question heard

Words read

How the Wernicke-Geschwind model works in a person who is responding to a heard question and reading aloud. The hypothetical circuit that allows the person to respond to heard questions is in green; the hypothetical circuit that allows the person to read aloud is in black.

Figure 14.11

The following two examples illustrate how the Wernicke-Geschwind model is presumed to work (see Figure 14.11). First, when you are having a conversation, the auditory signals triggered by the speech of the other person are received by your primary auditory cortex and conducted to Wernicke's area, where they are comprehended. If a response is in order, Wernicke's area generates the neural representation of the thought underlying the reply, and it is transmitted to Broca's area via the left arcuate fasciculus. In Broca's area, this signal activates the appropriate program of articulation that drives the appropriate neurons of your primary motor cortex and ultimately your muscles of articulation. Second, when you are reading aloud, the signal received by your primary visual cortex is transmitted to your left angular gyrus, which translates the visual form of the word into its auditory code and transmits it to Wernicke's area for comprehension. Wernicke's area then triggers the appropriate responses in your arcuate fasciculus, Broca's area, and motor cortex, respectively, to elicit the appropriate speech sounds.

Before proceeding to the following evaluation of the Wernicke-Geschwind model, scan your brain to confirm that you understand the model's fundamentals. The correct answers are provided below. Review material related to your errors and omissions before proceeding.

According to the Wernicke-Geschwind model, the following seven areas of the left cerebral cortex play a role in language-related activities:

1. The _____ gyrus translates the visual form of a read word into an auditory code.
2. The _____ cortex controls the muscles of articulation.
3. The _____ cortex perceives the written word.
4. _____ area is the center for language comprehension.

5. The _____ cortex perceives the spoken word.
6. _____ area contains the programs of articulation.
7. The left _____ carries signals from Wernicke's area to Broca's area.

Scan Your Brain answers: (1) angular, (2) primary motor, (3) primary visual, (4) Wernicke's, (5) primary auditory, (6) Broca's, (7) arcuate fasciculus

14·5

Evaluation of the Wernicke-Geschwind Model

Unless you are reading this text from back to front, you should have read the preceding description of the Wernicke-Geschwind model with some degree of skepticism. By this point in the text, you will almost certainly recognize that any model of a complex cognitive process that involves a few localized neocortical centers joined in a serial fashion by a few arrows is sure to have major shortcomings, and you will appreciate that the neocortex is not divided into neat compartments whose cognitive functions conform to vague concepts such as language comprehension, speech motor programs, and conversion of written language to auditory language. Initial skepticism aside, the ultimate test of a theory's validity is the degree to which its predictions are consistent with the empirical evidence.

Before we examine this evidence, I want to emphasize one point. The Wernicke-Geschwind model was initially based on case studies of aphasic patients with strokes, tumors, and penetrating brain injuries. Damage in such cases is almost always diffuse, and it inevitably encroaches on subcortical fibers coursing through the lesion site to other areas of the brain (see Bogen & Bogen, 1976). For example, illustrated in Figure 14.12 on page 466 is the extent of the cortical damage in one of Broca's two original cases (see Mohr, 1976).

Thinking Clearly

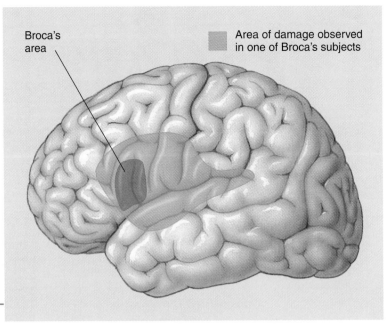

Broca's area

Area of damage observed in one of Broca's subjects

The extent of brain damage in one of Broca's two original patients. Like this patient, most aphasic patients have diffuse brain damage. It is thus difficult to determine from studying them the precise location of particular cortical language areas.

(Adapted from Mohr, 1976.)

Figure 14.12

Effects of Damage to Various Areas of Cortex on Language-Related Abilities

In view of the fact that the Wernicke-Geschwind model grew out of the study of patients with cortical damage, it is appropriate to begin evaluating it by assessing its ability to predict the language-related deficits produced by damage to various parts of the cortex.

Surgical Removal of Cortical Tissue. The study of patients in whom discrete areas of cortex have been surgically removed has proved particularly informative with regard to understanding the cortical localization of language. This is because the location and extent of these patients' lesions can be derived with reasonable accuracy from the surgeon's report. The study of neurosurgical patients has not confirmed the predictions of the Wernicke-Geschwind model by any stretch of the imagination. See the six cases summarized in Figure 14.13.

Surgery that destroys all of Broca's area but little surrounding tissue typically has no lasting effects on speech (Penfield & Roberts, 1959; Rasmussen & Milner, 1975; Zangwill, 1975). Some speech problems were observed after the removal of Broca's area, but their temporal course suggested that they were products of postsurgical *edema* (swelling) in the surrounding neural tissue rather than of the *excision* (cutting out) of Broca's area per se. Prior to the use of effective anti-inflammatory drugs, patients with excisions of Broca's area often regained consciousness with their language abilities fully intact only to have serious language-related problems develop over the next few hours and then subside in the following weeks. Similarly, permanent speech difficulties were not produced by discrete surgical lesions to the arcuate fasciculus, and permanent alexia and agraphia were not produced by surgical lesions restricted to the cortex of the angular gyrus (Rasmussen & Milner, 1975).

The consequences of surgical removal of Wernicke's area are less well documented; surgeons have been hesitant to remove it in light of Wernicke's dire predictions. Nevertheless, in some cases, a good portion of Wernicke's area has been removed without lasting language-related deficits (e.g., Ojemann, 1979; Penfield & Roberts, 1959).

Supporters of the Wernicke-Geschwind model argue that, despite the precision of surgical excision, negative evidence obtained from the study of the effects of brain

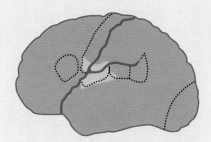

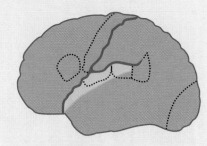

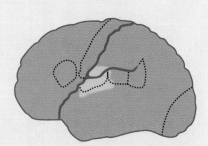

Case J.M. No speech difficulties for 2 days after his surgery, but by Day 3 he was almost totally aphasic; 18 days after his operation he had no difficulty in spontaneous speech, naming, or reading, but his spelling and writing were poor.

Case H.N. After his operation, he had a slight difficulty in spontaneous speech, but 4 days later he was unable to speak; 23 days after surgery, there were minor deficits in spontaneous speech, naming, and reading aloud, and a marked difficulty in oral calculation.

Case J.C. There were no immediate speech problems; 18 hours after his operation he became completely aphasic, but 21 days after surgery, only mild aphasia remained.

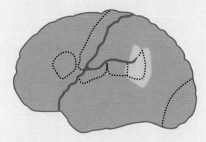

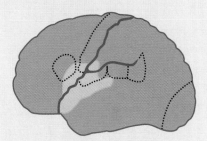

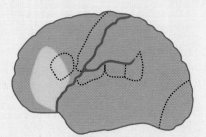

Case P.R. He had no immediate speech difficulties; 2 days after his operation, he had some language-related problems, but they cleared up.

Case D.H. This operation was done in two stages; following completion of the second stage, no speech-related problems were reported.

Case A.D. He had no language-related problems after his operation, except for a slight deficit in silent reading and writing.

The lack of permanent disruption of language-related abilities after surgical excision of the classic Wernicke-Geschwind language areas.

(Adapted from Penfield & Roberts, 1959.)

Figure 14.13

surgery should be discounted. They argue that the brain pathology that warranted the surgery may have reorganized the control of language by the brain.

Accidental or Disease-Related Brain Damage. Hécaen and Angelergues (1964) rated the articulation, fluency, comprehension, naming ability, ability to repeat spoken sentences, reading, and writing of 214 right-handed patients with small, medium, or large accidental or disease-related lesions to the left hemisphere. The extent and location of the damage in each case were determined by either postmortem histological examination or visual inspection during subsequent surgery. Figure 14.14 on page 468 summarizes the deficits found by Hécaen and Angelergues in patients with relatively localized damage to one of five different regions of left cerebral cortex.

Hécaen and Angelergues found that small lesions to Broca's area seldom produced lasting language deficits and that those restricted to Wernicke's area sometimes did not produce such deficits. Medium-sized lesions did produce some deficits; but in contrast to the predictions of the Wernicke-Geschwind model, problems of articulation were just as likely to occur following medium-sized parietal or temporal lesions as

Clinical Implications

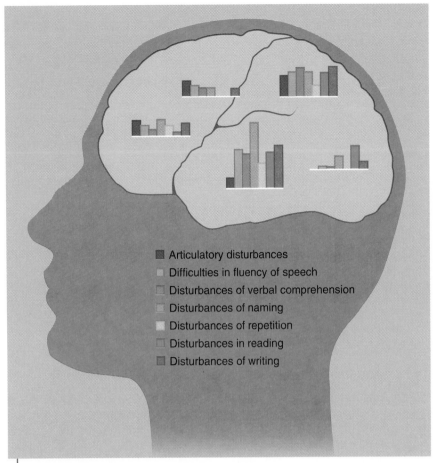

- ■ Articulatory disturbances
- □ Difficulties in fluency of speech
- □ Disturbances of verbal comprehension
- □ Disturbances of naming
- □ Disturbances of repetition
- ■ Disturbances in reading
- ■ Disturbances of writing

The relative effects on language-related abilities of damage to one of five general areas of left-hemisphere cortex.

(Adapted from Hécaen & Angelergues, 1964.)

Figure 14.14

Clinical Implications

they were following comparable lesions in the vicinity of Broca's area. All other symptoms that were produced by medium-sized lesions were more likely to appear following parietal or temporal lesions than following frontal damage.

Consistent with the Wernicke-Geschwind model, large lesions (those involving three lobes) in the anterior areas of the brain were more likely to be associated with articulation problems than were large lesions in the posterior areas of the brain. It is noteworthy that none of the 214 subjects displayed syndromes of aphasia that were either totally expressive (Broca's aphasia) or totally receptive (Wernicke's aphasia).

CT and Structural MRI Scans of Aphasic Patients. Since the development of computed tomography (CT) and structural magnetic resonance imaging (MRI), it has been possible to visualize the brain damage of living aphasic patients (see Damasio, 1989). In early CT studies by Mazzocchi and Vignolo (1979) and Naeser and colleagues (1981), none of the aphasic patients had cortical damage restricted to Broca's and Wernicke's areas, and all had extensive damage to subcortical white matter. Consistent with the Wernicke-Geschwind model, large anterior lesions of the left hemisphere were more likely to produce deficits in language expression than were large posterior lesions, and large posterior lesions were more likely to produce deficits in language comprehension than were large anterior lesions. Also, in both studies, **global aphasia**—a severe disruption of all language-related abilities—was associated with very large left-hemisphere lesions that involved both anterior and posterior cortex as well as substantial portions of subcortical white matter.

The findings of Damasio's (1989) structural MRI study were similar to those of the aforementioned CT studies, with one important addition. Damasio found a few aphasic patients whose damage was restricted to the medial frontal lobes (to the supplementary motor area and the anterior cingulate cortex), an area not included in the Wernicke-Geschwind model. Similarly, several CT and MRI studies have found cases of aphasia resulting from damage to subcortical structures (see Alexander, 1989)—for example, to the left subcortical white matter, the left basal ganglia, or the left thalamus (e.g., Naeser et al., 1982).

Electrical Stimulation of the Cortex and Localization of Language

The first large-scale electrical brain-stimulation studies of humans were conducted by Penfield and his colleagues in the 1940s at the Montreal Neurological Institute (see Feindel, 1986). One purpose of the studies was to map the language areas of each patient's brain so that tissue involved in language could be avoided during the surgery. The mapping was done by assessing the responses of conscious patients who were under local anesthetic to stimulation applied to various points on the cortical surface. The description of the effects of each stimulation were dictated to a stenographer—this was before the days of tape recorders—and then a tiny numbered card was dropped on the stimulation site for subsequent photography.

Figure 14.15 illustrates the responses to stimulation of a 37-year-old right-handed epileptic patient. He had started to have seizures about 3 months after receiving a blow to the head; at the time of his operation, in 1948, he had been suffering from seizures for 6 years, despite efforts to control them with medication. In considering his responses, remember that the cortex just posterior to the central fissure is

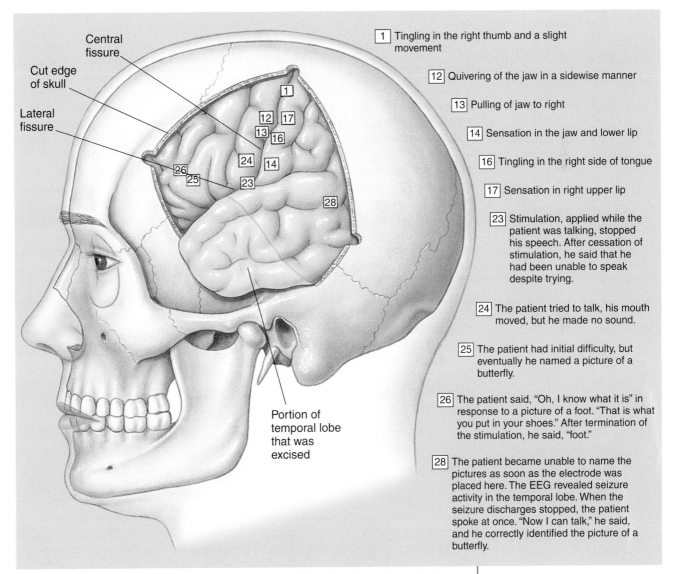

The responses of the left hemisphere of a 37-year-old epileptic to electrical stimulation. Numbered cards were placed on the brain during surgery to mark the sites where brain stimulation had been applied.

(Adapted from Penfield & Roberts, 1959.)

Figure 14.15

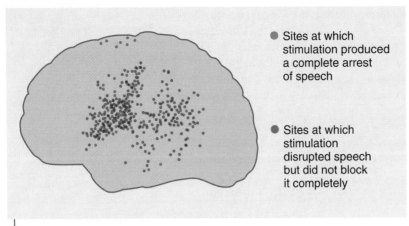

- Sites at which stimulation produced a complete arrest of speech
- Sites at which stimulation disrupted speech but did not block it completely

The wide distribution of left hemisphere sites where cortical stimulation either blocked speech or disrupted it.

(Adapted from Penfield & Roberts, 1959.)

Figure 14.16

primary somatosensory cortex and that the cortex just anterior to the central fissure is primary motor cortex.

Because electrical stimulation of the cortex is much more localized than a brain lesion, it has been a useful method for testing predictions of the Wernicke-Geschwind model. Penfield and Roberts (1959) published the first large-scale study of the effects of cortical stimulation on speech. They found that sites at which stimulation blocked or disrupted speech in conscious neurosurgical patients were scattered throughout a large expanse of frontal, temporal, and parietal cortex, rather than being restricted to the Wernicke-Geschwind language areas (see Figure 14.16). They also found no tendency for particular kinds of speech disturbances to be elicited from particular areas of the cortex: Sites at which stimulation produced disturbances of pronunciation, confusion of counting, inability to name objects, or misnaming of objects were pretty much intermingled. Right-hemisphere stimulation almost never disrupted speech.

In a more recent series of cortical stimulation studies, Ojemann and his colleagues (see Ojemann, 1983) assessed naming, reading of simple sentences, short-term verbal memory, ability to mimic movements of the face and mouth, and ability to recognize **phonemes**—individual speech sounds—during cortical stimulation. They found (1) that the areas of cortex at which stimulation could disrupt language extended far beyond the boundaries of the Wernicke-Geschwind language areas, (2) that each of the language tests was disrupted by stimulation at widely scattered sites, and (3) that there were major differences among the subjects in the organization of language abilities.

Because the disruptive effects of stimulation at a particular site were frequently quite specific (i.e., disrupting only a single test), Ojemann suggested that the language cortex is organized like a mosaic, with the discrete columns of tissue that perform a particular function widely distributed throughout the language areas of cortex.

Current Status of the Wernicke-Geschwind Model

Empirical evidence has supported the Wernicke-Geschwind model in two general respects. First, the evidence has confirmed that important roles are played in language by Broca's and Wernicke's areas; many aphasics have diffuse cortical damage that involves one or both of these areas. Second, there is a tendency for aphasias associated with anterior damage to involve deficits that are more expressive and those associated with posterior damage to involve deficits that are more receptive.

However, the evidence has not been supportive of the specific predictions of the Wernicke-Geschwind model. First, damage restricted to the boundaries of the Wernicke-Geschwind cortical areas often has little lasting effect on the use of language. Second, brain damage that does not include any of the Wernicke-Geschwind areas can produce aphasia. Third, Broca's and Wernicke's aphasias rarely exist in the pure forms implied by the Wernicke-Geschwind model; aphasia virtually always involves both expressive and receptive symptoms (see Benson, 1985). Fourth, there seem to be major differences in the localization of cortical language areas in different individuals.

Despite these problems, the Wernicke-Geschwind model has been an extremely important theory. It guided the study and clinical diagnosis of aphasia for more than four decades. Indeed, clinical neuropsychologists still use *Broca's aphasia* and *Wernicke's aphasia* as diagnostic categories, but with an understanding that the syndromes are much less selective and the precipitating damage much more diffuse and variable than implied by the model (Alexander, 1997).

Because of the lack of empirical support for its major predictions, the Wernicke-Geschwind model has been largely abandoned by researchers, but it is still prominent in the classroom and clinic. The last two sections of this chapter focus on an alternative to the Wernicke-Geschwind perspective on the neural mechanisms of language: the *cognitive neuroscience approach*.

14.6
The Cognitive Neuroscience Approach to Language

Cognitive Neuroscience

The cognitive neuroscience approach is currently dominating research on language and its disorders. What is this approach, and how does it differ from the traditional perspective? The following are three related ideas that define the cognitive neuroscience approach to language. Although these ideas were originally premises, or assumptions, that directed cognitive neuroscience research on language, each one has been supported by a substantial amount of evidence (see Patterson & Ralph, 1999; Saffran, 1997).

Premise 1: Language-related behaviors are mediated by activity in those particular areas of the brain that are involved in the specific cognitive processes required for the behaviors. The Wernicke-Geschwind model theorized that particular areas of the brain involved in language were each dedicated to a specific, but complex, activity such as speech, comprehension, or reading. But cognitive neuroscience research has found that each of these activities can itself be broken down into *constituent cognitive processes*, which may be organized in different parts of the brain (Neville & Bavelier, 1998). Accordingly, these constituent cognitive processes, not the general Wernicke-Geschwind activities, appear to be the appropriate level at which to conduct analysis. Cognitive neuroscientists typically divide the cognitive processes involved in language into three categories of activity: **phonological analysis** (analysis of the sound of language), **grammatical analysis** (analysis of the structure of language), and **semantic analysis** (analysis of the meaning of language).

Premise 2: The areas of the brain involved in language are not dedicated solely to that purpose (Nobre & Plunkett, 1997). In the Wernicke-Geschwind model, large areas of left cerebral cortex were thought to be dedicated solely to language, whereas the cognitive neuroscience approach assumes that many of the constituent cognitive processes involved in language also play roles in other behaviors (see Bischoff-Grethe et al., 2000). For example, some of the areas of the brain that participate in short-term memory and visual pattern recognition are clearly involved in reading as well.

Premise 3: Because many of the areas of the brain that perform specific language functions are also parts of other functional systems, these areas are likely to be small, widely distributed, and specialized (Neville & Bavelier, 1998). In contrast, the language areas of the Wernicke-Geschwind model are assumed to be large, circumscribed, and homogeneous.

In addition to these three premises, the cognitive neuroscience approach to language is distinguished from the traditional approach by its methodology. The

Wernicke-Geschwind model rested heavily on the analysis of brain-damaged patients, whereas researchers using the cognitive neuroscience approach also have at their disposal an increasing array of techniques—most notably, functional brain imaging—for studying the localization of language in healthy subjects.

Functional Brain Imaging and Language

Functional brain-imaging techniques have revolutionized the study of the localization of language. In the last decade, there have been numerous PET and fMRI studies of subjects engaging in various language-related activities (see Bookheimer, 2002; Gernsbacher & Kaschak, 2003; Martin, 2003). I have selected two to describe to you. As you are about to learn, I selected them because they are of high quality, have interesting findings, and feature two different approaches. The first is the fMRI study of silent reading by Bavelier and colleagues (1997); the second is the PET study of object naming by Damasio and colleagues (1996).

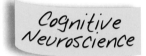

Bavelier's fMRI Study of Reading. Bavelier and colleagues used fMRI to measure the brain activity of healthy subjects while they read silently. The researchers' general purpose was not to break down reading into its constituent cognitive processes or elements but to get a sense of the extent of cortical involvement in reading.

The methodology of Bavelier and colleagues was noteworthy in two respects. First, they used a particularly sensitive fMRI machine that allowed them to identify areas of activity with more accuracy than in most previous studies and without having to average the scores of several subjects. Second, they recorded activity during the reading of sentences—rather than during the simpler, controllable, and unnatural activities most often used in functional brain-imaging studies of language (e.g., listening to individual words).

The subjects in Bavelier and colleagues' study viewed sentences displayed on a screen. Interposed between periods of silent reading were control periods, during which the subjects were presented with strings of consonants. The differences in activity during the reading and control periods served as the basis for calculating the areas of cortical activity associated with reading. Because of the computing power required for the detailed analyses, only the lateral cortical surfaces were monitored.

Let's begin by considering the findings observed in individual subjects on individual trials, before any averaging took place. Three important points emerged from this analysis. First, the areas of activity were patchy; that is, they were tiny areas of activity separated by areas of inactivity. Second, the patches of activity were variable; that is, the areas of activity differed from subject to subject and even from trial to trial in the same subject. Third, although some activity was observed in the classic Wernicke-Geschwind areas, it was widespread over the lateral surfaces of the brain. The widespread, spotty activity over the left cortex is consistent with the basic premises of the cognitive neuroscience approach and with previous research—in particular, with brain stimulation studies of language.

Figure 14.17 illustrates the reading-related increases of activity averaged over all the trials and subjects in the study by Bavelier and colleagues—as they are typically reported. The averaging creates the false impression that large, homogeneous expanses of tissue were active during reading, whereas the patches of activity induced on any given trial comprised only between 5% and 10% of the illustrated areas. Still, two points are clear: First, although there was significant activity in the right hemisphere, there was far more activity in the left hemisphere; second, the activity extended far beyond those areas predicted by the Wernicke-Geschwind model to be involved in silent reading (e.g., activity in Broca's area and motor cortex would not have been predicted).

Damasio's PET Study of Naming. In contrast to the purpose of the study by Bavelier and colleagues, which was to assess the extent of activity associated with

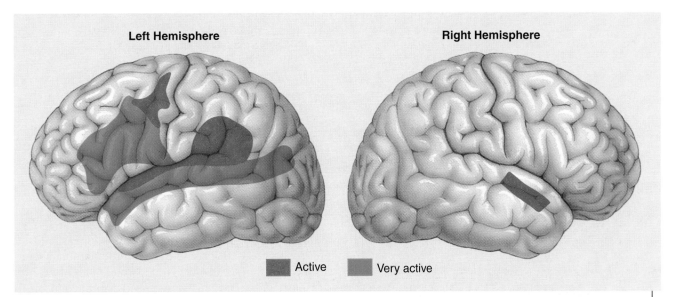

Left Hemisphere

Right Hemisphere

■ Active ■ Very active

The areas in which reading-associated increases in activity were observed in the fMRI study of Bavelier and colleagues (1997). These maps were derived by averaging the scores of all subjects, each of whom displayed patchy increases of activity in 5–10% of the indicated areas on any particular trial.

Figure 14.17

silent reading, the objective of Damasio and colleagues (1996) was to look selectively at the temporal-lobe activity involved in naming objects within particular categories. Damasio and colleagues recorded the PET activity in the left temporal lobes of healthy subjects while they named images presented on a screen. The images were of three different types: famous faces, animals, and tools. To get a specific measure of the temporal-lobe activity involved in naming, they subtracted from the activity recorded during this task the activity recorded while the subjects judged the orientation of the images. The researchers focused on the left temporal lobes of the subjects to permit a more fine-grained PET analysis.

Naming objects activated the left temporal lobe outside the classic Wernicke's language area. Remarkably, the precise area that was activated by the naming depended on the category: Famous faces, animals, and tools each activated a slightly different area. In general, the areas for naming famous faces, animals, and tools are arrayed from anterior to posterior along the middle portions of the left temporal lobe.

Damasio and colleagues have not been the only ones to report category-specific naming-related activity in the left temporal lobes (see Gerlach, Law, & Paulson, 2002; Löw et al., 2003; Martin et al., 1996; Nobre & Plunkett, 1997). Moreover, the existence of category-specific lexical areas in the left temporal lobes has been supported by the analysis of aphasic patients with damage in that area. Some patients have naming difficulties that are specific to particular categories (see Kurbat & Farah, 1998), and specific deficits in naming famous faces, animals, and tools have been shown to correspond to the three areas of the left temporal lobe that were identified by the PET study (Damasio et al., 1996).

One last point about the cognitive neuroscience approach to language: There has been so much enthusiasm for the use of new functional brain-imaging technology to study language that there has been a tendency for knowledge gained from the study of brain lesions to be ignored. But this is not how science works best: Science works best when new data are added to past data rather than supplanting them. For example, significant right-hemisphere activity is virtually always recorded by functional brain imaging during language-related activities, suggesting that the right hemisphere

Cognitive Neuroscience

Thinking Clearly

plays a significant role in language; yet lesions of the right hemisphere rarely disrupt the same activities, suggesting that its role is not critical. Clearly, a consideration of both types of research is needed to solve this puzzle (see Price et al., 1999).

This, the final section of the chapter, looks further at the cognitive neuroscience approach introduced in the preceding section. It focuses on dyslexia, one of the major subjects of cognitive neuroscience research.

Clinical Implications

Dyslexia is a pathological difficulty in reading, one that does not appear to result from general visual, motor, or intellectual deficits. There are two fundamentally different types of dyslexias: *developmental dyslexias*, which become apparent when a child is learning to read; and *acquired dyslexias*, which are caused by brain damage in individuals who were already capable of reading. Developmental dyslexia is a widespread problem; for example, approximately 15% of English-speaking males and 5% of English-speaking females fail to learn to read despite relatively normal visual, motor, and intellectual abilities (Nicolson, Fawcett, & Dean, 2001; Shaywitz, 1996).

Although the causes of acquired dyslexia are usually apparent, the causes of developmental dyslexia are not. The problem in discovering the causes of developmental dyslexia is not that no abnormalities have been discovered in the brains of individuals suffering from the disorder. Many differences between the brains of dyslexics and normal readers have been reported (see Farmer & Klein, 1995). For example, dyslexics often do not display the usual left-larger-than-right asymmetry in the size of the planum temporale, and they often have cerebellar abnormalities.

Although many structural abnormalities have been identified in the brains of patients suffering from developmental dyslexia, three problems have impeded the discovery of the neural basis of this disorder. First, none of the reported structural abnormalities seem to play a critical role in the disorder. Second, there are several types of developmental dyslexia, and these are likely to have different causes. Third, it is difficult to rule out the possibility that particular brain "abnormalities" observed in developmental dyslexics are the result, rather than the cause, of the disorder; perhaps the lack of reading experience causes the brains of dyslexics to develop differently than those of normal readers.

Although developmental dyslexia was once thought to be a specific disorder of reading, it is now apparent that patients with developmental dyslexias often display a variety of subtle visual, auditory, and motor deficits (Nicolson, Fawcett, & Dean, 2001; Wilmer et al., 2004). A debate regarding these deficits is ongoing (see Ramus, 2003). Some experts believe that the sensory and motor deficits are primary and that developmental dyslexia results from them (McCandliss & Noble, 2003; Renvall & Hari, 2002). Others believe that the sensory and motor deficits are too slight to account for the reading difficulties and that the primary deficit in developmental dyslexia is language-related (Ramus, 2003).

There is a genetic component to developmental dyslexia; it has a heritability estimate of about 50% (Fisher & DeFries, 2002). It has been suggested that the disorder may be caused by the early exposure of genetically susceptible individuals to a virus or a toxin, but there is no strong evidence for this notion.

Developmental Dyslexia: Cultural Diversity and Biological Unity

Although it is established that developmental dyslexia is influenced by genetic factors and is associated with abnormalities of brain function, it has long been considered by many to be a psychological rather than a neural disorder. Why? Because developmental dyslexia is influenced by culture.

For many years, those whose thinking was warped by the physiology-or-psychology dichotomy (see Chapter 1) assumed that because developmental dyslexia is influenced by culture, it could not possibly be a brain disorder. Paulesu and colleagues (2001) recently used the cognitive neuroscience approach to drive the final nail into the coffin of this misguided way of thinking about dyslexia.

The work of Paulesu and colleagues is based on the remarkable finding that about twice as many English speakers as Italian speakers are diagnosed as dyslexic. This fact has to do with the complexity of the respective languages. English consists of 40 phonemes (individual speech sounds), which can be spelled, by one count, in 1,120 different ways. In contrast, Italian is composed of 25 phonemes, which can be spelled in 33 different ways. As a result, Italian-speaking children learn to read much more quickly than English-speaking children and are less likely to develop reading disorders.

Paulesu and colleagues (2000) began by comparing PET activity in the brains of normal English-speaking and Italian-speaking adults. These researchers hypothesized that since the cognitive demands of reading aloud are different for Italian- and English-speaking subjects, they should use different parts of their brains while reading. That is exactly what the researchers found. Although the same general areas were active during reading in both groups, Italian readers displayed more activity in the left superior temporal lobe, whereas English readers displayed more activity in the left inferior temporal and frontal lobes.

Next, Paulesu and colleagues (2001) turned their attention to developmental dyslexia. They recorded PET scans of the brains of normal and dyslexic British, French, and Italian university students while the subjects read individual words in their own language. (University students were used to rule out lack of access to education as a possible confounding factor.) Despite the fact that the Italian dyslexics had less severe reading problems, all three groups of dyslexics displayed the same pattern of abnormal PET activity when reading: less than normal reading-related activity in the posterior region of the temporal lobe, near its boundary with the occipital lobe. Thus, although dyslexia can manifest itself differently in people who speak different languages, the underlying neural pathology appears to be the same.

Cognitive Neuroscience Analysis of Reading Aloud: Deep and Surface Dyslexia

Cognitive psychologists have long recognized that reading aloud can be accomplished in two entirely different ways. One is by a **lexical procedure**, which is based on specific stored information that has been acquired about written words: The reader simply looks at the word, recognizes it, and says it. The other way reading can be accomplished is by a **phonetic procedure**: The reader looks at the word, recognizes the letters, sounds them out, and says the word. The lexical procedure dominates in the reading of familiar words; the phonetic procedure dominates in the reading of unfamiliar words.

This simple cognitive analysis of reading aloud has proven useful in understanding the symptoms of two different kinds of dyslexia resulting from brain damage. These two different classes of acquired dyslexia are *surface dyslexia* and *deep dyslexia*. Similar syndromes are observed for developmental dyslexia, but they tend to be less severe.

In cases of **surface dyslexia**, patients have lost their ability to pronounce words based on their specific memories of the words (i.e., they have lost the *lexical procedure*), but they can still apply rules of pronunciation in their reading (i.e., they can still use the *phonetic procedure*). Accordingly, they retain their ability to pronounce words whose pronunciation is consistent with common rules (e.g., *fish, river*, or *glass*) and their ability to pronounce nonwords according to common rules of pronunciation (e.g., *spleemer* or *twipple*); but they have great difficulty pronouncing words that do not follow common rules of pronunciation (e.g., *have, lose,* or *steak*). The errors they make often involve the misapplication of common rules of pronunciation; for example, *have, lose,* and *steak* are typically pronounced as if they rhyme with *cave, hose,* and *beak.*

In cases of **deep dyslexia**, patients have lost their ability to apply rules of pronunciation in their reading (i.e., they have lost the *phonetic procedure*), but they can still pronounce familiar concrete words based on their specific memories of them (i.e., they can still use the *lexical procedure*). Accordingly, they are completely incapable of pronouncing nonwords and have difficulty pronouncing uncommon words and words whose meaning is abstract. In attempting to pronounce words, patients with deep dyslexia try to react to them by using various lexical strategies, such as responding to the overall look of the word, the meaning of the word, or the derivation of the word. This leads to a characteristic pattern of errors. A patient with deep dyslexia might say "quill" for *quail* (responding to the overall look of the word), "hen" for *chicken* (responding to the meaning of the word), or "wise" for *wisdom* (responding to the derivation of the word).

I used to have difficulty keeping these two syndromes straight. Now I remember which is which by reminding myself that surface dyslexics have difficulty reacting to the overall shape of the word, which is metaphorically more superficial (less deep) than a problem in applying rules of pronunciation, which is experienced by deep dyslexics.

Where are the lexical and phonetic procedures performed in the brain? Much of the research attempting to answer this question has focused on the study of deep dyslexia. Deep dyslexics most often have extensive damage to the left-hemisphere language areas, suggesting that the disrupted phonetic procedure is widely distributed in the frontal and temporal areas of the left hemisphere. But which part of the brain maintains the lexical procedure in deep dyslexics? There have been two theories, both of which have received some support.

One theory is that the surviving lexical abilities of deep dyslexics are mediated by activity in surviving parts of the left-hemisphere language areas. Evidence for this theory comes from the observation of such activity while deep dyslexics are reading (Laine et al., 2000; Price et al., 1998). The other theory is that the surviving lexical abilities of deep dyslexics are mediated by activity in the right hemisphere. Support for this view comes from the following remarkable case study.

Cognitive Neuroscience

The Case of N.I., the Woman Who Read with Her Right Hemisphere

Clinical Implications

Prior to the onset of her illness, N.I. was a healthy girl. At the age of 13, she began to experience periods of aphasia, and several weeks later, she suffered a generalized convulsion. She subsequently had many convulsions, and her speech and motor abilities deteriorated badly. CT scans indicated ischemic brain damage to the left hemisphere.

Two years after the onset of her disorder, N.I. was experiencing continual seizures and blindness in her right visual field, and there was no meaningful movement or perception in her right limbs. In an attempt to relieve these symptoms, a total left **hemispherectomy** was performed; that is, her left hemisphere was totally removed. Her seizures were totally arrested by this surgery.

The reading performance of N.I. is poor, but she displays a pattern of retained abilities strikingly similar to those displayed by deep dyslexics or split-brain patients reading with their right hemispheres. For example, she recognizes letters but is totally incapable of translating them into sounds; she can read concrete familiar words; she cannot pronounce even simple nonsense words (e.g., *neg*); and her reading errors indicate that she is reading on the basis of the meaning and appearance of words rather than by translating letters into sounds (e.g., when presented with the word *fruit,* she responded, "Juice. . . . it' s apples and pears and . . fruit"). In other words, she suffers from a severe case of deep dyslexia (Patterson, Vargha-Khadem, & Polkey, 1989).

The case of N.I. completes the circle: The chapter began with a discussion of language and lateralization of function, and the case of N.I. concludes it on the same note.

Key Terms

Cerebral commissures (p. 443)
Commissurotomy (p. 443)
Lateralization of function (p. 443)
Split-brain patients (p. 443)

14.1 Cerebral Lateralization of Function: Introduction

Aphasia (p. 444)
Apraxia (p. 444)
Broca' s area (p. 444)
Dextrals (p. 445)
Dichotic listening test (p. 445)
Sinestrals (p. 445)
Sodium amytal test (p. 445)

14.2 The Split Brain

Chimeric figures test (p. 453)
Corpus callosum (p. 447)
Cross-cuing (p. 452)
Helping-hand phenomenon (p. 453)
Scotoma (p. 448)
Visual completion (p. 453)

14.3 Differences between the Left and Right Hemispheres

Frontal operculum (p. 458)
Heschl' s gyrus (p. 458)
Planum temporale (p. 458)

14.4 Cortical Localization of Language: The Wernicke-Geschwind Model

Agraphia (p. 463)
Alexia (p. 463)
Angular gyrus (p. 463)
Arcuate fasciculus (p. 463)
Broca' s aphasia (p. 462)
Conduction aphasia (p. 463)
Expressive (p. 462)
Receptive (p. 462)
Wernicke' s aphasia (p. 462)
Wernicke' s area (p. 462)
Wernicke-Geschwind model (p. 463)
Word salad (p. 462)

14.5 Evaluation of the Wernicke-Geschwind Model

Global aphasia (p. 468)
Phonemes (p. 470)

14.6 The Cognitive Neuroscience Approach to Language

Grammatical analysis (p. 471)
Phonological analysis (p. 471)
Semantic analysis (p. 471)

14.7 The Cognitive Neuroscience Approach and Dyslexia

Deep dyslexia (p. 476)
Dyslexia (p. 474)
Hemispherectomy (p. 476)
Lexical procedure (p. 475)
Phonetic procedure (p. 475)
Surface dyslexia (p. 475)

ON THE CD

Studying for an exam? Get some help from the electronic flash cards of the key terms and the practice tests for this chapter.

Lateralization, Language and the Split Brain
The Left Brain and Right Brain of Language

This chapter discussed three related topics (brain mechanisms of language, lateralization of function, and the split brain). €ach led to the same conclusion: that the left and right hemispheres make different contributions to behavior.

Dextral

Cerebral Lateralization of Function

The first documented examples of lateralization of function were the discoveries that aphasia and apraxia tend to result from left-hemisphere damage. These discoveries led to the view that the left hemisphere is generally dominant to the right, but we now know that the right hemisphere is dominant to the left in a number of respects.

(Pages 444–446)

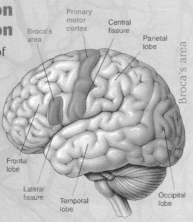

Broca's area
Primary motor cortex
Central fissure
Parietal lobe
Broca's area
Frontal lobe
Lateral fissure
Temporal lobe
Occipital lobe

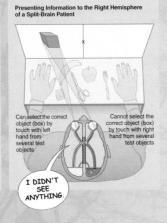

Presenting Information to the Left Hemisphere of a Split-Brain Patient

Cannot select the correct object (apple) by touch with left hand from several test objects

Can select the correct object (apple) by touch with right hand from several test objects

I SAW AN APPLE.

Figure 14.7

Presenting Information to the Right Hemisphere of a Split-Brain Patient

Can select the correct object (box) by touch with right hand from several test objects

Cannot select the correct object (box) by touch with right hand from several test objects

I DIDN'T SEE ANYTHING.

The Split Brain

Split-brains are produced by commissurotomy (cutting the cerebral commissures). In controlled laboratory situations, the two hemispheres of split-brain patients can be tested independently. Such tests have shown that split-brain patients have two independent streams of consciousness, and that the two hemispheres have different abilities.

(Pages 447–454)

Experience and brain laterality

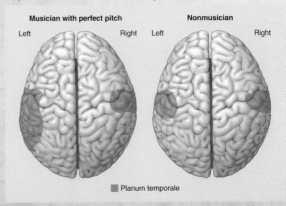

Musician with perfect pitch
Left
Right

Nonmusician
Left
Right

■ Planum temporale

Differences between the Left and Right Hemispheres

There are many functional differences between the human cerebral hemispheres. These differences tend to to take the form of slight biases in favor of one hemisphere or the other. The most lateralized functions tend to be language-related abilities; in most people, the left hemisphere plays a much greater role than the right in the production and comprehension of language. The right hemisphere tends to be superior to the left in some spatial, emotional, and musical abilities.

(Pages 454–462)

Visual Summary

Sinestral

The Wernicke-Geschwind Model and Its Evaluation

Which areas of the left hemisphere play a role in language, and what is each area's function? The Wernicke-Geschwind model of the cortical localization of language has been the dominant view. However, its predictions have not been confirmed. The neural circuits controlling language are diffuse, and their location varies from subject to subject.

(Pages 462–471)

Wernicke-Geschwind model

The Cognitive Neuroscience Approach to Language: Dyslexia

Most cognitive neuroscientific research on language has focused on dyslexia (a specific pathological deficit in reading ability). There are two fundamentally different types of dyslexia: developmental dyslexia, which becomes apparent when a child normally learns to read, and acquired dyslexia, which is produced by brain trauma.

(Pages 471–477)

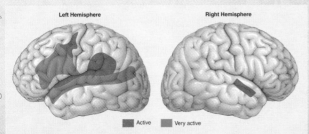

Reading-related activity

Themes Revisited

The clinical implications theme is the most prevalent, because much of what we know about the lateralization of function and the localization of language in the brain comes from the study of neuropsychological patients. However, the cognitive neuroscience approach is now playing a particularly prominent role in the study of the localization of language, which is why the cognitive neuroscience theme was also prevalent, particularly in the second half of the chapter.

Because lateralization of function and language localization are topics that are often covered by the popular media, many widely held ideas about these subjects are overly simplistic. In this chapter, the thinking-clearly-about-biopsychology tags mark aspects of laterality and language about which it is particularly important that you think clearly.

Evolutionary analysis has not played a major role in the study of the localization of language, largely because humans are the only species with well-developed language. However, it has played a key role in efforts to understand why cerebral lateralization of function evolved in the first place. Indeed, the major breakthrough in understanding the split-brain phenomenon came from comparative research.

Think about It

1. The decision to perform commissurotomies on epileptic patients turned out to be a good one. Other, similar, decisions have not proven so successful (e.g., the decision to perform prefrontal lobotomies on the mentally ill). Was this just the luck of the draw? Discuss.

2. Design an fMRI study to identify the areas of the brain involved in comprehending speech.

3. Why do you think cerebral lateralization of function evolved?

4. Evaluate the Wernicke-Geschwind model of language.

5. Compare the Wernicke-Geschwind approach with the modern cognitive neuroscience approach to the cerebral localization of language.

chapter 15

Behavioral Neuroscience of Psychiatric Disorders
The Brain Unhinged

This chapter is about the behavioral neuroscience of *psychiatric disorders*. Before we begin, let's consider the answers to two fundamental questions: What are psychiatric disorders? How do they differ from neuropsychological disorders, which you learned about in Chapter 8?

Defining psychiatric disorders is fairly straightforward: A **psychiatric disorder** (or psychological disorder) is a disorder of psychological function sufficiently severe to warrant treatment by a psychiatrist or clinical psychologist. Explaining how psychiatric disorders differ from neuropsychological disorders is more difficult because there really are no clear-cut differences between the two types of disorders.

The convention of viewing psychological disorders as being of two fundamentally different types—psychiatric or neuropsychological—is the product of the archaic mind–brain (psychology–biology) dichotomy, discussed in Chapter 1. Neuropsychological disorders are those that were assumed to be products of dysfunctional brains; psychiatric disorders are those that were assumed to be products of dysfunctional minds in the absence of brain pathology. As you will learn in this chapter, there is now plenty of evidence that psychiatric disorders are disorders of dysfunctional brains, and thus the main basis for distinguishing between psychiatric and neuropsychological disorders no longer exists (see Hyman, 2000).

Thinking Clearly

Still, the conventional categories of neuropsychological and psychiatric disorders persist, and there tend to be some differences between them. For example, psychiatric disorders tend to be influenced more by experiential factors (e.g., stress), tend to be the product of more subtle forms of brain pathology, and tend to be less well understood.

This chapter begins by discussing research on four psychiatric disorders: schizophrenia, affective (emotional) disorders, anxiety disorders, and Tourette syndrome. In each case, you will learn how advances in understanding the neural mechanisms of the disorder have gone hand in hand with the development of therapeutic drugs. For each of the four disorders, the initial breakthrough was the fortuitous discovery of an effective drug; then, study of the drug's mechanisms led to theories of the disorder's neural mechanisms and the development of drugs that are even more effective. The chapter ends with a discussion of the steps involved in establishing the efficacy of new *psychotherapeutic* drugs.

15.1
Schizophrenia

The term *schizophrenia* means the splitting of psychic functions. The term was coined in the early years of the 20th century to describe what was assumed at that time to be the primary symptom of the disorder: the breakdown of integration among emotion, thought, and action.

Schizophrenia is the disease that is most commonly associated with the concept of madness. It attacks about 1% of individuals of all races and cultural groups, typically beginning in adolescence or early adulthood. Schizophrenia occurs in many forms, but the case of Lena introduces you to some of its common features.

The Case of Lena, the Catatonic Schizophrenic

Clinical Implications

Lena's mother was hospitalized with schizophrenia when Lena was 2. She died in the hospital under peculiar circumstances, a suspected suicide. As a child, Lena displayed periods of hyperactivity; as an adolescent, she was viewed by others as odd. Although she enjoyed her classes and got good grades, she seldom established relationships with her fellow students. Lena rarely dated. However, she married her husband only a few months after meeting him. He was a quiet man who tried to avoid fuss or stress at all costs and who was attracted to Lena because she was quiet and withdrawn.

Shortly after their marriage, Lena's husband noticed that Lena was becoming even more withdrawn. She would sit for hours barely moving a muscle. He also found her having lengthy discussions with nonexistent persons.

About 2 years after he first noticed her odd behavior, Lena's husband found her sitting on the floor in an odd posture staring into space. She was totally unresponsive. When he tried to move her, Lena displayed *waxy flexibility*—that is, she reacted like a mannequin, not resisting movement but holding her new position until she was moved again. At that point, he took her to the hospital, where her disorder was immediately diagnosed as *stuporous catatonic schizophrenia* (schizophrenia characterized by long periods of immobility and waxy flexibility).

In the hospital, Lena displayed a speech pattern that is displayed by many schizophrenics; *echolalia* (a speech pattern characterized by repetition of some or all of what has just been heard).

Doctor: How are you feeling today?
Lena: I am feeling today, feeling the feelings today.
Doctor: Are you still hearing the voices?
Lena: Am I still hearing the voices, voices?

(Meyer & Salmon, 1988)

What Is Schizophrenia?

Clinical Implications

One major difficulty in studying and treating schizophrenia is the lack of a clear understanding of what it is (Andreasen, 2000; Peralta & Cuesta, 2000). Its symptoms are complex and diverse; they overlap greatly with those of other psychiatric disorders, and they frequently change during the progression of the disorder. As a result, there have been many attempts to break schizophrenia down into several disorders, but none of these attempts has proved successful.

The following are common symptoms of schizophrenia, but none of them appears in all cases. Indeed, the recurrence of only one of these symptoms for 8 months is grounds for the diagnosis of schizophrenia:

Bizarre delusions. Delusions of being controlled (e.g., "Martians are making me think evil thoughts"), delusions of persecution (e.g., "My mother is trying to poison me"), delusions of grandeur (e.g., "Shaq admires my sneakers").

Inappropriate affect. Failure to react with an appropriate level of emotionality to positive or negative events (Keltner, Kring, & Bonanno, 1999; Kring, 1999).

Hallucinations. Imaginary voices telling the person what to do or commenting negatively on the person's behavior.

Incoherent thought. Illogical thinking, peculiar associations among ideas, or belief in supernatural forces.

Odd behavior. Long periods with no movement (*catatonia*), a lack of personal hygiene, talking in rhymes, avoiding social interaction, echolalia.

482 **PART FIVE** Biopsychology of Health

Causal Factors in Schizophrenia

In the first half of the 20th century, the cloak of mysticism began to be removed from mental illness by a series of studies that established schizophrenia's genetic basis. First, it was discovered that although only 1% of the population develops schizophrenia, the probability of schizophrenia's occurring in a close biological relative (i.e., in a parent, child, or sibling) of a schizophrenic is about 10%, even if the relative was adopted shortly after birth by a healthy family (e.g., Kendler & Gruenberg, 1984; Rosenthal et al., 1980). Then, it was discovered that the concordance rates for schizophrenia are higher in identical twins (45%) than in fraternal twins (10%)—see Holzman and Matthyse (1990) and Kallman (1946). Finally, adoption studies have shown that the risk of schizophrenia is increased by the presence of the disorder in biological parents but not by its presence in adoptive parents (Gottesman & Shields, 1982).

The fact that the concordance rate for schizophrenia in identical twins is substantially less than 100% suggests that differences in experience contribute significantly to differences among people in the development of schizophrenia. The current view is that some people inherit a potential for schizophrenia, which may or may not be activated by experience. Supporting this view is a recent comparison of the offspring of a large sample of identical twins who were themselves discordant for schizophrenia (i.e., one had the disorder and one did not): The incidence of schizophrenia was as great in the offspring of the nonschizophrenic twins as in the offspring of the schizophrenic twins (Gottesman & Bertelsen, 1989).

It is clear that schizophrenia has multiple causes. Regions on several different chromosomes have been implicated in the vulnerability to schizophrenia (see Cowan, Kopnisky, & Hyman, 2002; Kennedy et al., 2003; Torrey & Yoken, 2000). Also, a variety of early experiential factors have been implicated in the development of schizophrenia—for example, early infections, autoimmune reactions, toxins, traumatic injury, and stress. These early experiences are thought to alter the normal course of neurodevelopment, leading to schizophrenia in individuals with a genetic susceptibility (see Conklin & Iacono, 2002; Lewis & Levitt, 2002).

Discovery of the First Antischizophrenic Drugs

The first major breakthrough in the study of the biochemistry of schizophrenia was the accidental discovery in the early 1950s of the first antischizophrenic drug, **chlorpromazine**. Chlorpromazine was developed by a French drug company as an antihistamine. Then, in 1950, a French surgeon noticed that chlorpromazine given prior to surgery to counteract swelling had a calming effect on some of his patients, and he suggested that it might have a calming effect on difficult-to-handle psychotic patients. His suggestion proved to be incorrect, but the research it triggered led to the discovery that chlorpromazine alleviates schizophrenic symptoms: Agitated schizophrenics were calmed by chlorpromazine, and emotionally blunted schizophrenics were activated by it. Don't get the idea that chlorpromazine cures schizophrenia. It doesn't. But in many cases it reduces the severity of schizophrenic symptoms enough to allow institutionalized patients to be discharged.

Clinical Implications

Shortly after the antischizophrenic action of chlorpromazine was first documented, an American psychiatrist became interested in reports that the snakeroot plant had long been used in India for the treatment of mental illness. He gave **reserpine**—the active ingredient of the snakeroot plant—to his schizophrenic patients and confirmed its antischizophrenic action. Reserpine is no longer used in the treatment of schizophrenia because it produces a dangerous decline in blood pressure at the doses needed for the treatment.

Although the chemical structures of chlorpromazine and reserpine are dissimilar, their antischizophrenic effects are similar in two major respects. First, the antischizophrenic effect of both drugs is manifested only after a patient has been medicated for 2 or 3 weeks. Second, the onset of the antischizophrenic effect of the medication is usually associated with motor effects similar to the symptoms of Parkinson's disease: tremors at rest, muscular rigidity, and a general decrease in voluntary movement. These similarities suggested to researchers that chlorpromazine and reserpine were acting through the same mechanism, one that was related to Parkinson's disease.

Dopamine Theory of Schizophrenia

Clinical Implications

Paradoxically, the next major breakthrough in the study of schizophrenia came from research on Parkinson's disease. In 1960, it was reported that the *striatums* of persons who had died of Parkinson's disease had been depleted of dopamine (Ehringer & Hornykiewicz, 1960). This finding suggested that a disruption of dopaminergic transmission might produce Parkinson's disease and, because of the relation between Parkinson's disease and the antischizophrenic effects of chlorpromazine and reserpine, also suggested that antischizophrenic drug effects might be produced in the same way. Thus was born the *dopamine theory of schizophrenia*—the theory that schizophrenia is caused by too much dopamine and, conversely, that antischizophrenic drugs exert their effects by decreasing dopamine levels.

Lending instant support to the dopamine theory of schizophrenia were two already well-established facts. First, the antischizophrenic drug reserpine was known to deplete the brain of dopamine and other monoamines by breaking down the synaptic vesicles in which they were stored and which protected them from degrading enzymes. Second, drugs such as amphetamine and cocaine, which can trigger schizophrenic episodes in normal subjects, were known to increase the extracellular levels of dopamine and other monoamines in the brain.

An important step in the evolution of the dopamine theory of schizophrenia came in 1963, when Carlsson and Lindqvist assessed the effects of chlorpromazine on extracellular levels of dopamine and its *metabolites* (molecules that are created when another molecule is broken down). Although they expected to find that chlorpromazine, like reserpine, depletes the brain of dopamine, they didn't. The extracellular levels of dopamine were unchanged by chlorpromazine, and the extracellular levels of its metabolites were increased. The researchers concluded that both chlorpromazine and reserpine antagonize transmission at dopamine synapses but that they do it in different ways—reserpine by depleting the brain of dopamine and chlorpromazine by binding to dopamine receptors. Carlsson and Lindqvist argued that chlorpromazine is a *receptor blocker* at dopamine synapses—that is, that it binds to dopamine receptors without activating them and, in so doing, keeps dopamine from activating them (see Figure 15.1). We now know that many psychoactive drugs are receptor blockers, but chlorpromazine was the first to be identified as such.

Carlsson and Lindqvist further postulated that the lack of activity at postsynaptic dopamine receptors sent a feedback signal to the presynaptic cells that increased their release of dopamine, which was broken down in the synapses. This explained why dopaminergic activity was reduced while extracellular levels of dopamine stayed about the same and extracellular levels of its metabolites were increased. Carlsson and Lindqvist's findings led to an important revision of the dopamine theory of schizophrenia: Rather than high dopamine levels per se, the main factor in schizophrenia was presumed to be high levels of activity at dopamine receptors.

In the mid-1970s, Snyder and his colleagues (Creese, Burt, & Snyder, 1976) assessed the degree to which the various antischizophrenic drugs that had been developed by that time bind to dopamine receptors. First, they added radioactively labeled dopamine to samples of dopamine-receptor-rich neural membrane obtained from calf striatums. Then, they rinsed away the unbound dopamine molecules from the samples and measured the amount of radioactivity left in them to obtain a measure of the number of dopamine receptors. Next, in other samples, they measured each drug's ability to block the binding of radioactive dopamine to the sample, the assumption being that the drugs with a high affinity for dopamine receptors would leave fewer sites available for the dopamine. In general, they found that chlorpromazine and the other effective antischizophrenic drugs had a high affinity for dopamine receptors, whereas ineffective antischizophrenic drugs had a low affinity. There were, however, several major exceptions, one of them being haloperidol. Although **haloperidol** was one of the most potent antischizophrenic drugs of its day, it had a relatively low affinity for dopamine receptors.

A solution to the haloperidol puzzle came with the discovery that dopamine binds to more than one receptor subtype—five have been identified (Hartmann & Civelli, 1997). It turns out that chlorpromazine and the other antischizophrenic drugs in the same chemical class (the **phenothiazines**) all bind effectively to both D_1 and D_2 receptors, whereas haloperidol and the other antischizophrenic drugs in its chemical class (the **butyrophenones**) all bind effectively to D_2 receptors but not to D_1 receptors.

This discovery of the selective binding of butyrophenones to D_2 receptors led to another important revision in the dopamine theory of schizophrenia. It suggested that schizophrenia is caused by hyperactivity specifically at D_2 receptors, rather than at dopamine receptors in general. Snyder and his colleagues (see Snyder, 1978) subsequently confirmed that the degree to which **neuroleptics**—antischizophrenic drugs—bind to D_2 receptors is highly correlated with their effectiveness in suppressing schizophrenic symptoms (see Figure 15.2). For example, the butyrophenone *spiroperidol* had the greatest affinity for D_2 receptors and the most potent antischizophrenic effect.

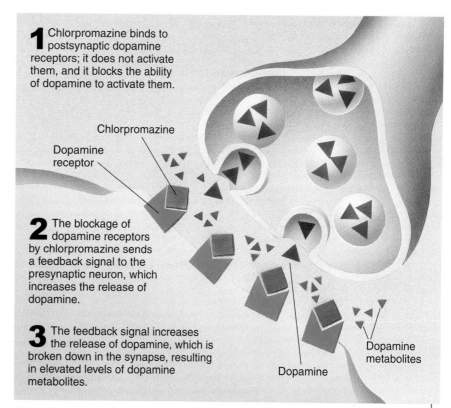

1 Chlorpromazine binds to postsynaptic dopamine receptors; it does not activate them, and it blocks the ability of dopamine to activate them.

Chlorpromazine

Dopamine receptor

2 The blockage of dopamine receptors by chlorpromazine sends a feedback signal to the presynaptic neuron, which increases the release of dopamine.

3 The feedback signal increases the release of dopamine, which is broken down in the synapse, resulting in elevated levels of dopamine metabolites.

Dopamine metabolites

Dopamine

Chlorpromazine is a receptor blocker at dopamine synapses. Chlorpromazine was the first receptor blocker to be identified, and its discovery changed psychopharmacology.

Figure 15.1

ON THE CD

The *Dopamine Theory* module illustrates the main support for this theory by showing how typical neuroleptics block activity at D_2 receptors.

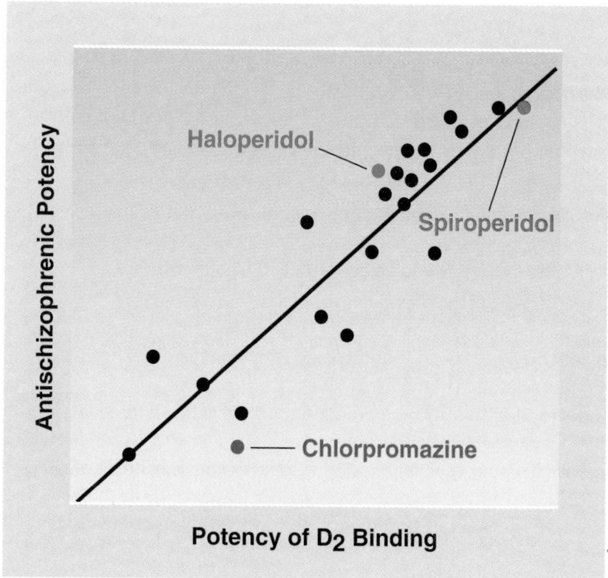

Haloperidol

Spiroperidol

Chlorpromazine

Antischizophrenic Potency

Potency of D₂ Binding

The positive correlation between the ability of various neuroleptics to bind to D_2 receptors and their clinical potency.

(Adapted from Snyder, 1978.)

Figure 15.2

Current Research on the Neural Basis of Schizophrenia

Although the evidence implicating D_2 receptors in schizophrenia is strong, it has become apparent that the D_2 version of the dopamine theory of schizophrenia cannot explain several key findings. Appreciation of these limitations has led to the current version of the theory. This version holds that excessive activity at D_2 receptors is involved in the disorder but that there are other, as yet unidentified, causal factors. The major events in the development of the dopamine theory are summarized in Table 15.1.

The following are four key discoveries about schizophrenia that cannot be resolved by a strict interpretation of the D_2 version of the dopamine theory. These four discoveries are key to the current view that although overactivity at D_2 receptors plays a major role in schizophrenia, other factors are yet to be identified.

Receptors Other Than D_2 Receptors Are Involved in Schizophrenia. Recent research has implicated neurotransmitters other than dopamine in schizophrenia (see Tallman, 2000). These include glutamate (Javitt & Coyle, 2004; Konradi & Heckers, 2003; Moghaddam, 2003), GABA (Benes & Berretta, 2001), and serotonin (Sawa & Snyder, 2002). The most compelling evidence that D_2 receptors are not the sole mechanism underlying schizophrenia came from the development of *atypical neuroleptics* (antischizophrenic drugs that are not primarily D_2 receptor blockers). For example, **clozapine**, an effective atypical neuroleptic, has an affinity for D_1 receptors, D_4 receptors, and several serotonin receptors, but only a slight affinity for D_2 receptors.

Clozapine has some promising therapeutic properties. It is often effective in treating schizophrenics who have not responded to typical neuroleptics, and it does not produce Parkinsonian side effects. Unfortunately, the therapeutic utility of clozapine is limited because it produces a severe blood disorder in about 1% of patients who use it (see Wong & Van Tol, 2003).

The discovery of atypical neuroleptics led to qualification of the D_2 theory of schizophrenia rather than its abandonment, for two reasons. First, all of the atypical neuroleptics have been found to bind weakly to D_2 receptors. Second, evidence of the involvement of D_2 receptors in schizophrenia does not rest entirely on the relation between the therapeutic efficacy of drugs and the strength with which they bind to those receptors. For example, recently diagnosed schizophrenics who have not been exposed to neuroleptics have more D_2 receptors and more extracellular dopamine than do nonschizophrenics (Abi-Dargham et al., 2000).

Table 15.1

The Key Events That Led to the Development and Refinement of the Dopamine Theory of Schizophrenia

Early 1950s	The antischizophrenic effects of both chlorpromazine and reserpine were documented and related to their Parkinsonian side effects.
Late 1950s	The brains of recently deceased Parkinson's patients were found to be depleted of dopamine.
Early 1960s	It was hypothesized that schizophrenia was associated with excessive activity at dopaminergic synapses.
1960s and early 1970s	Chlorpromazine and other clinically effective neuroleptics were found to act as receptor blockers at dopamine synapses.
Mid-1970s	The affinity of neuroleptics for dopamine receptors was found to be only roughly correlated with their antischizophrenic potency.
Late 1970s	The binding of existing antischizophrenic drugs to D_2 receptors was found to be highly correlated with their antischizophrenic potency.
1980s and 1990s	It became clear that a strict interpretation of the D_2 version of the dopamine theory of schizophrenia cannot account for all of the research findings.

It Takes Several Weeks of Neuroleptic Therapy to Alleviate Schizophrenic Symptoms. As you have already learned, it takes several weeks of neuroleptic therapy to alleviate schizophrenic symptoms. However, neuroleptics effectively block activity at D_2 receptors within hours. This time lag indicates that the blockage of D_2 receptors is not the specific mechanism of the neuroleptics' therapeutic effect. It appears that blocking D_2 receptors triggers some slow-developing compensatory change in the brain that is the key factor in the therapeutic effect.

Schizophrenia Is Associated with Widespread Brain Damage. Brain-imaging studies of schizophrenic patients typically reveal widespread abnormalities, including an abnormally small cerebral cortex and abnormally large cerebral ventricles (see Frith & Dolan, 1998—as shown in Figure 15.3.) However, although the brain damage is widespread, it is not evenly distributed. For example, cortical damage is most prevalent in prefrontal, cingulate, and medial temporal areas of the cortex. Two things about the pattern of brain damage observed in many schizophrenics are problematic for the dopamine theory: One is that there is little evidence of structural damage to dopaminergic circuits (see Egan & Weinberger, 1997; Nopoulis et al., 2001); the other is that the dopamine theory provides no rationale for the diffuse pattern of brain damage that is often observed.

One major question about the brain pathology of schizophrenics is whether or not it is developmental: Do the brains of schizophrenics develop abnormally, or do they develop normally and then suffer some type of damage? One important finding suggests that schizophrenia is a result of disordered early brain development: The

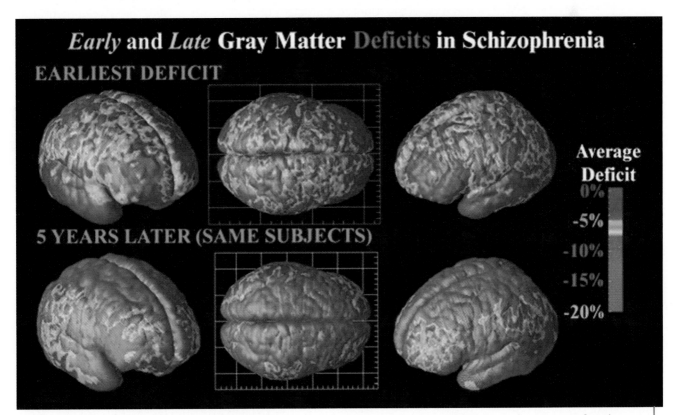

The progressive development of cortical loss as assessed by high-resolution MRI in early-onset schizophrenia. Normally, schizophrenia is not diagnosed until adulthood, at which point the brain damage seems to be fully developed. Here we see the progression of cortical damage in a group of patients with the rare early-onset form of schizophrenia. The tissue loss began in the posterior parietal cortex and then spread into temporal and frontal areas, until it involved much of the cortex. (From Thompson et al., 2001.)

Figure 15.3 ——————

brain pathology associated with schizophrenia tends to be extensive when the disorder is first diagnosed, and there is little evidence of subsequent damage (see Wong, Buckle, & Van Tol, 2000).

Several reports have suggested that normal brain laterality does not develop in the brains of schizophrenics (Rockstroh et al., 1998, 2001; Shapleske et al., 2001). Again, the dopamine theory provides no explanation for this effect.

Neuroleptics Help Only Some Schizophrenics. Typical neuroleptics (i.e., D_2 receptor blockers) do not help all schizophrenics (see Wong & Van Tol, 2003): About 30% are not helped at all, and the remainder usually gain relief from only some of the symptoms. Neuroleptics tend to be more effective in treating *positive schizophrenic symptoms* (such as incoherence, hallucinations, and delusions), which are assumed to be caused by increased neural activity, than they are in treating *negative schizophrenic symptoms* (such as lack of affect, cognitive deficits, and poverty of speech), which are assumed to be caused by brain damage. Many patients who are initially helped by neuroleptics soon develop tolerance to their therapeutic effects and relapse.

The point is that if schizophrenia results from excessive activity at D_2 receptors, then blockers of those receptors should alleviate all symptoms in all schizophrenics. The fact that these drugs do not do so is a challenge to a strict interpretation of the D_2 version of the dopamine theory of schizophrenia.

The fact that neuroleptics help only some patients suggests that the diagnosis of schizophrenia currently encompasses a variety of patients with different disorders. Indeed, many researchers in the field prefer to use "the schizophrenias" to acknowledge that the current diagnostic category undoubtedly includes several related disorders. Until this problem of diagnosis is solved, the development of a better theory and more effective treatments for those diagnosed with schizophrenia will be difficult.

Thinking Clearly

15.2
Affective Disorders: Depression and Mania

All of us have experienced depression. Depression is a normal reaction to grievous loss such as the loss of a loved one, the loss of self-esteem, the loss of personal possessions, or the loss of health. However, there are people whose tendency toward depression is out of proportion. These people repeatedly fall into the depths of despair and lose the capacity to experience pleasure, often for no apparent reason; and their depression can be so extreme that it is almost impossible for them to meet the essential requirements of their daily lives—to keep a job, to maintain social contacts, or even to maintain an acceptable level of personal hygiene. It is these people who are said to be suffering from clinical **depression**. The case of P.S. introduces you to some of the main features of clinical depression.

The Case of P.S., the Weeping Widow

Clinical Implications

P.S. was a 57-year-old widow and mother of four. She was generally cheerful and friendly and known for her meticulous care of her home and children. She took great pride in having reared her children by herself following the death of her husband 14 years earlier.

For no apparent reason, her life began to change. She suddenly appeared more fatigued, less cheerful, and more lackadaisical about her housework. Over the ensuing weeks, she stopped going to church and cancelled all of her regular social engagements, including the weekly family dinner, which she routinely hosted. She started to spend all her time sleeping or rocking back and forth and sobbing in her favorite chair. She wasn't eating, bathing, or changing her clothes. And her house was rapidly becoming a garbage dump. She woke up every morning at about 3:00 A.M. and was unable to get back to sleep.

Things got so bad that her two children who were still living with her called her oldest son for advice. He drove from the nearby town where he lived. What he found reminded him of an episode about 10 years earlier, when his mother had attempted suicide by slitting her wrists.

At the hospital, P.S. answered few questions. She cried throughout the admission interview and sat rocking in her chair wringing her hands and rolling her head up towards the ceiling. When asked to explain what was bothering her, she just shook her head no.

She was placed on a regimen of antidepressant medication. Several weeks later, she was discharged, much improved (Spitzer et al., 1983).

Major Categories of Affective Disorders

Depression is not the only *affective disorder* (psychotic disorder of emotion). The other major type is **mania**, which is in many respects the opposite of depression. Mania is an affective disorder characterized by overconfidence, impulsivity, distractibility, and high energy.

During periods of mild mania, people are talkative, energetic, impulsive, positive, and very confident. In this state, they can be very effective at certain jobs and can be great fun to be with. But when mania becomes extreme, it is a serious clinical problem. The florid manic often awakens in a state of unbridled enthusiasm, with an outflow of incessant chatter that careens nonstop from topic to topic. No task is too difficult. No goal is unattainable. This confidence and grandiosity, coupled with high energy, distractibility, and a leap-before-you-look impulsiveness, result in a continual series of disasters. Mania often leaves behind it a trail of unfinished projects, unpaid bills, and broken relationships.

Many depressive patients experience periods of mania. Those who do are said to suffer from **bipolar affective disorder**. Those depressives who do not experience periods of mania are said to suffer from **unipolar affective disorder**.

Depression is often divided into two categories. Depression triggered by a negative experience (e.g., the death of a friend, the loss of a job) is called **reactive depression**; depression with no apparent cause is called **endogenous depression**.

The high incidence of affective disorders in industrialized Western societies has been well documented. About 6% of people suffer from unipolar affective disorder at some point in their lives, and about 1% suffer from bipolar affective disorder. Unipolar affective disorder tends to be twice as prevalent in women as in men, but there is no sex difference in the incidence of bipolar affective disorder. About 10% of those suffering from affective disorders commit suicide (see Culbertson, 1997; Weissman & Olfson, 1995).

Causal Factors in Affective Disorders

Genetic factors contribute to differences among people in the development of affective disorders (see MacKinnon, Jamison, & DePaulo, 1997). Twin studies of affective disorders suggest a concordance rate of about 60% for identical twins and 15% for fraternal twins, whether they are reared together or apart. Although there

ON THE CD

The module called *Recognizing Mood Disorders (Affective Disorders)* includes a general overview of affective disorders and a 45-second audio clip of a patient describing one such disorder.

Clinical Implications

are many exceptions, there is a tendency for affected twins to suffer from the same type of disorder, unipolar or bipolar; and the concordance rates for bipolar disorders tend to be higher than those for unipolar disorders.

Most of the research on the causal role of experience in affective disorders has focused on the role of stress in the etiology of depression. Several studies have shown that stressful experiences can trigger attacks of depression in already depressed individuals. For example, Brown (1993) found that over 84% of patients seeking treatment for depression had experienced severe stress in the preceding year, in comparison to 32% of control subjects. However, it has been more difficult to confirm the hypothesis that early exposure to stress increases the likelihood of developing depression in adulthood (Kessler, 1997).

Discovery of Antidepressant Drugs

Four major classes of drugs are used in the treatment of affective disorders: monoamine oxidase inhibitors, tricyclic antidepressants, lithium, and selective monoamine-reuptake inhibitors.

Monoamine Oxidase Inhibitors. **Iproniazid**, the first antidepressant drug, was originally developed for the treatment of tuberculosis, for which it proved to be a dismal flop. However, interest in the antidepressant potential of the drug was kindled by the observation that it left patients with tuberculosis less depressed about their disorder. As a result, iproniazid was tested on a mixed group of psychiatric patients and was found to be effective against depression. It was first marketed as an antidepressant drug in 1957.

Iproniazid is a monoamine agonist; it increases the levels of monoamines (e.g., norepinephrine and serotonin) by inhibiting the activity of *monoamine oxidase (MAO)*, the enzyme that breaks down monoamine neurotransmitters in the cytoplasm of the neuron. **MAO inhibitors** have several side effects; the most dangerous is known as the **cheese effect**. Foods such as cheese, wine, and pickles contain an amine called *tyramine*, which is a potent elevator of blood pressure. Normally, these foods have little effect on blood pressure, because tyramine is rapidly broken down in the liver by MAO. However, people who take MAO inhibitors and consume tyramine-rich foods run the risk of strokes caused by surges in blood pressure.

Tricyclic Antidepressants. The **tricyclic antidepressants** are so named because of their antidepressant action and because their chemical structures include three rings of atoms. **Imipramine**, the first tricyclic antidepressant, was initially thought to be an antischizophrenic drug. However, when its effects on a mixed sample of psychiatric patients were assessed, its antidepressant effect was immediately obvious. Tricyclic antidepressants block the reuptake of both serotonin and norepinephrine, thus increasing their levels in the brain. They are a safer alternative to MAO inhibitors.

Lithium. The discovery of the ability of **lithium**—a simple metallic ion—to block mania is yet another important pharmacological breakthrough that was made by accident. John Cade, an Australian psychiatrist, mixed the urine of manic patients with lithium to form a soluble salt; then he injected the salt into a group of guinea pigs to see if it would induce mania. As a control, he injected lithium into another group. Instead of inducing mania, the urine solution seemed to calm the guinea pigs; and because the lithium control injections had the same effect, Cade concluded that lithium, not uric acid, was the calming agent. In retrospect, Cade's conclusion was incredibly foolish. We now know that at the doses he used, lithium salts produce extreme nausea. To Cade's untrained eye, his subjects' inactivity may have looked like calmness. But the subjects weren't calm; they were sick. In any case, flushed with what he thought was the success of his guinea pig experiments, in 1954 Cade tried lithium on a group of 10 manic patients, and it proved remarkably effective.

There was little immediate reaction to Cade's report. Few scientists were impressed by Cade's scientific credentials, and few drug companies were interested in spending millions of dollars to evaluate the therapeutic potential of a metallic ion that could not be protected by a patent. Accordingly, the therapeutic potential of lithium was not fully appreciated until the late 1960s, when it was it was discovered that the ion—in addition to acting against mania—reduced the depression of a few bipolar patients.

Lithium is considered to be a **mood stabilizer**, a drug that blocks the rapid transition between depression and mania rather than treating depression. Until recently, lithium was the treatment of choice for bipolar affective disorder, but it has largely been supplanted by mood stabilizers that are also effective against depression. Interestingly, most mood stabilizers also have anti-epileptic effects.

Selective Monoamine-Reuptake Inhibitors. In the late 1980s, a new class of drugs—the selective serotonin-reuptake inhibitors (SSRIs)—was introduced for treating depression. Selective serotonin-reuptake inhibitors exert agonistic effects on serotonergic transmission by blocking the reuptake of serotonin from synapses—see Figure 15.4.

Fluoxetine, which is marketed as **Prozac**, was the first SSRI to be developed. Now there are many more (e.g., Paxil, Zoloft, Luvox, Remeron). Prozac's structure is a slight variation of that of imipramine and other tricyclic antidepressants; in fact, Prozac is no more effective than imipramine in treating depression. Nevertheless, it was immediately embraced by the psychiatric community and has been prescribed in many millions of cases.

The remarkable popularity of Prozac and other SSRIs is attributable to two things: First, they were initially reported to have few side effects; second, they can be

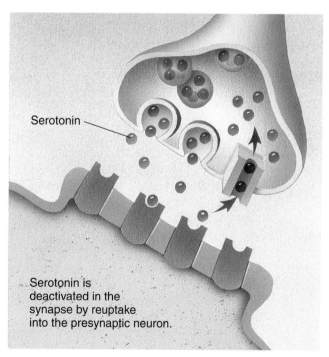

Serotonin

Serotonin is deactivated in the synapse by reuptake into the presynaptic neuron.

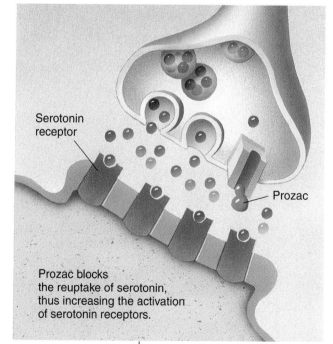

Serotonin receptor

Prozac

Prozac blocks the reuptake of serotonin, thus increasing the activation of serotonin receptors.

Blocking of serotonin reuptake by fluoxetine (Prozac).

Figure 15.4

effective against a wide range of psychological disorders in addition to depression. Because SSRIs are so effective against disorders that were once considered to be the exclusive province of psychotherapy (e.g., lack of self-esteem, fear of failure, excessive sensitivity to criticism, and inability to experience pleasure), they have had a major impact on psychiatry and clinical psychology.

The success of the SSRIs spawned the introduction of a similar class of drugs, the *selective norepinephrine-reuptake inhibitors (SNRIs)*. These (e.g., Reboxetine) have proven to be as effective as the SSRIs in the treatment of depression. Also effective against depression are drugs (e.g., Wellbutrin, Effexor) that block the reuptake of more than one monoamine neurotransmitter.

Effectiveness of Drugs in the Treatment of Depression. Hollon, Thase, and Markowitz (2002) compared the efficacies of the various pharmacological treatments for depression. The results were about the same for MAO inhibitors, tricyclic antidepressants, and selective monoamine-reuptake inhibitors: About 50% of depressed subjects improved, compared to 25% of the placebo controls. Although all three categories of drugs benefit some patients experiencing attacks of depression, they are of little use in preventing recurrence of attacks.

It is important to stress that the initial claims about the safety of monoamine-reuptake inhibitors are being seriously challenged. There is now some evidence for the following side effects: increased suicide risk, addiction, sexual dysfunction, motor problems, gastrointestinal problems, obesity, and anxiety. These findings are under intensive investigation, and I expect that some clear answers about the hazards of monoamine-reuptake inhibitors and how to minimize them will soon be forthcoming.

Theories of Depression

The search for the neural mechanisms of affective disorders has focused on depression. However, the fact that depression and mania often occur in the same patients—that is, in those with bipolar affective disorder—suggests that the mechanisms of the two are closely related.

Clinical Implications

Monoamine Theory of Depression. The most widely accepted theory of depression is the *monoamine theory*. The monoamine theory of depression holds that depression is associated with underactivity at serotonergic and noradrenergic synapses. It is based on the fact that monoamine oxidase inhibitors, tricyclic antidepressants, selective serotonin-reuptake inhibitors, and selective norepinephrine-reuptake inhibitors are all agonists of serotonin, norepinephrine, or both.

The monoamine theory of depression has been supported by the results of some autopsy studies (see Nemeroff, 1998). Certain subtypes of norepinephrine and serotonin receptors have been found to be more numerous in depressed individuals who have not received pharmacological treatment. This implicates a deficit in monoamine release: When an insufficient amount of a neurotransmitter is released at a synapse, there are usually compensatory increases in the number of receptors for that neurotransmitter. This process of compensatory proliferation of receptors is called **up-regulation**.

Overall, support for the monoamine theory of depression is weak. The main problem is that it is largely based on the fact that monoamine agonists are used to treat depressed patients, but this evidence is not so convincing when one considers that only about 25% of patients are actually helped by these treatments.

Diathesis–Stress Model of Depression. A second theory of depression is the *diathesis–stress model*. According to this theory (see Nemeroff, 1998), some people inherit a **diathesis** (genetic susceptibility), which is incapable of initiating the disorder by itself. The central idea of the diathesis–stress model is that if susceptible individuals are exposed to stress early in life, their systems become permanently sensitized, and they overreact to mild stressors for the rest of their lives.

Support for the diathesis–stress model of depression is largely indirect: It is based on the finding that depressed people tend to release more stress hormones (see Brown, Rush, & McEwen, 1999; Holsboer, 2000; Young et al., 2000). Depressed individuals synthesize more hypothalamic *corticotropin-releasing hormone*, release more *adrenocorticotropic hormone* from the anterior pituitary, and release more *glucocorticoids* from the adrenal cortex. Moreover, injections of *dexamethasone*, a synthetic glucocorticoid, do not reduce the release of glucocorticoids through negative feedback in many depressed patients, though they do in normal subjects.

Antidepressant Effect of Sleep Deprivation

I would be remiss if I did not point out one of the most puzzling findings about the treatment of depression: More than 50% of depressed patients display dramatic improvements after one night of sleep deprivation (Demet et al., 1999). The antidepressant action of sleep deprivation cannot be explained by current theories of depression. Also, the finding is of little therapeutic relevance because the depression returns once the patients return to their normal sleep pattern. However, studying how sleep deprivation reduces depression may lead to a better understanding of the neural mechanism of depression and to the development of new antidepressant drugs.

Brain Pathology and Affective Disorders

The discovery—made possible by brain-imaging technology—of changes in the brains of patients with unipolar affective disorder is changing the way that people are thinking of the disorder (see Drevets, 2001). It has long been assumed that affective disorders are entirely psychological (see Chapter 1); however, as evidence of abnormalities in the brains of depressed patients has accumulated, this view has become difficult to defend. Figure 15.5 illustrates the pathology in the brain of one depressed patient.

Individuals diagnosed with depression display damage to many parts of their brains (see Kaufman et al., 2001); however, damage is most frequently observed in three areas (see Drevets, 2001). Two of these three areas are the amygdala and the prefrontal cortex, which, as you learned in Chapter 14, play roles in the perception and experience of emotion. The third area comprises several of the terminal sites of the mesotelencephalic dopamine system, which, as you learned in Chapter 13, may be involved in the experience of pleasure. Because depressed patients often suffer from **anhedonia**, the inability to experience pleasure, it is not surprising that they would display abnormalities in the striatal and limbic structures of the mesotelencephalic dopamine system.

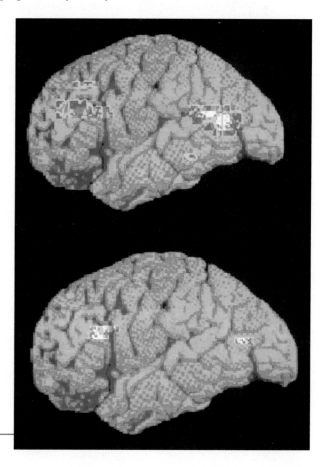

PET scans of the brains of a depressed patient (top) and a recovered patient (bottom). Red and yellow indicate areas of abnormally low blood flow.

Anxiety—chronic fear that persists in the absence of any direct threat—is a common psychological correlate of stress. Anxiety is adaptive if it motivates effective coping behaviors; however, when it becomes so severe that it disrupts normal functioning, it is referred to as an **anxiety disorder**. All anxiety disorders are associated with feelings of anxiety (e.g., fear, worry, despondency) and with a variety of physiological stress reactions—for example, *tachycardia* (rapid heartbeat), *hypertension* (high blood pressure), nausea, breathing difficulty, sleep disturbances, and high glucocorticoid levels.

Anxiety disorders are the most prevalent of all psychiatric disorders; in Great Britain, for example, 1 in 5 women and 1 in 10 men take antianxiety medication each year (Dunbar, Perera, & Jenner, 1989). An estimated 25% of people suffer from an anxiety disorder at some point in their lives.

The case of M.R., a woman who was afraid to leave her home, serves to introduce anxiety.

The Case of M.R., the Woman Who Was Afraid to Go Out

M.R. was a 35-year-old woman who developed a pathological fear of leaving home. The onset of her problem was sudden. Following an argument with her husband, she went out to mail a letter and cool off, but before she could accomplish her task, she was overwhelmed by dizziness and fear. She immediately struggled back to her house and rarely left it again, for about 2 years. Then, she gradually started to improve.

Her recovery was abruptly curtailed, however, by the death of her sister and another argument with her husband. Following the argument, she tried to go shopping, panicked, and had to be escorted home by a stranger. Following that episode, she was not able to leave her house by herself without experiencing an anxiety attack. Shortly after leaving home by herself, she would feel dizzy and sweaty, and her heart would start to pound; at that point, she would flee home to avoid a full-blown panic attack.

Although M.R. could manage to go out if she was escorted by her husband or one of her children, she felt anxious the entire time. Even with an escort, she was terrified of crowds—crowded stores, restaurants, or movie theaters were out of the question.

Five Classes of Anxiety Disorders

There are five major classes of anxiety disorders: generalized anxiety disorders, phobic anxiety disorders, panic disorders, obsessive-compulsive disorders, and posttraumatic stress disorder.

Generalized anxiety disorders are characterized by stress responses and extreme feelings of anxiety that occur in the absence of any obvious precipitating stimulus. **Phobic anxiety disorders** are similar to generalized anxiety disorders except that they are triggered by exposure to particular objects (e.g., birds, spiders) or situations (e.g., crowds, darkness). **Panic disorders** are characterized by rapid-onset attacks of extreme fear and severe symptoms of stress (e.g., choking, heart palpitations, shortness of breath); they are often components of generalized anxiety and phobic disorders, but they also occur as separate disorders. **Obsessive-compulsive disorders** are characterized by frequently recurring, uncontrollable, anxiety-producing thoughts (obsessions) and impulses (compulsions). Responding to them—for example, by repeated compulsive hand washing—is a means of dissipating the anxiety associated with them. **Posttraumatic stress disorder** is a persistent pattern of psychological distress following exposure to extreme stress (McNally, 2003; McNally, Bryant, & Ehlers, 2003; Newport & Nemeroff, 2000).

M.R., the woman who was afraid to go out, suffered from a common phobic anxiety disorder: agoraphobia. **Agoraphobia** is the pathological fear of public places and open spaces.

Etiology of Anxiety Disorders

Because anxiety disorders are often triggered by identifiable stressful events and because the anxiety is often focused on particular objects or situations, the role of experience in shaping the disorder is often readily apparent (see Anagnostaras, Craske, & Fanselow, 1999). For example, in addition to having agoraphobia, M.R. was obsessed by her health—particularly by high blood pressure, although hers was in the normal range. The fact that both her grandfather and father suffered from high blood pressure and died of heart attacks clearly shaped this component of her disorder.

Like other psychiatric disorders, anxiety disorders have a significant genetic component. The concordance rates for various anxiety disorders are substantially higher for identical twins than for fraternal twins. Still, although identical twins have the same genetic susceptibility to anxiety disorders, the timing and focus of their attacks often reflect their individual experiences (see Gross & Hen, 2004).

Pharmacological Treatment of Anxiety Disorders

Two major classes of drugs are effective against anxiety disorders: benzodiazepines and serotonin agonists.

Benzodiazepines. Benzodiazepines such as *chlordiazepoxide* (Librium) and *diazepam* (Valium) are widely prescribed for the treatment of anxiety disorders. They are also prescribed as hypnotics (sleep-inducing drugs), anticonvulsants, and muscle relaxants. Indeed, benzodiazepines are the most widely prescribed psychoactive drugs; approximately 10% of adult North Americans are currently taking them. The benzodiazepines have several adverse side effects: sedation, ataxia (disruption of motor activity), tremor, nausea, and a withdrawal reaction that includes rebound anxiety. Another serious problem with benzodiazepines is that they are highly addictive. Consequently, they should be prescribed only for short-term use (see Gray & McNaughton, 2000).

The behavioral effects of benzodiazepines are thought to be mediated by their agonistic action on $GABA_A$ receptors. Benzodiazepines bind to a $GABA_A$ receptor at a different site than the one at which GABA molecules bind and, in so doing, increase the binding of GABA molecules to the receptor. $GABA_A$ receptors are distributed widely throughout the brain.

Serotonin Agonists. Serotonin agonists are also widely used in the treatment of anxiety disorders. For example, *buspirone*, which is often prescribed for the treatment of anxiety, has selective agonist effects at one subtype of serotonin receptor, the $5\text{-}HT_{1A}$ receptor. The main advantage of buspirone over the benzodiazepines is its specificity: It produces *anxiolytic* (antianxiety) effects without producing ataxia, muscle relaxation, and sedation, the common side effects of the benzodiazepines. Buspirone does, however, have other side effects (e.g., dizziness, nausea, headache, and insomnia).

The serotonin agonists that are used to treat depression (i.e., monoamine oxidase inhibitors, tricyclic antidepressants, and selective serotonin-reuptake inhibitors) also tend to have anxiolytic effects. Indeed, SSRIs are also commonly used in the treatment of anxiety disorders.

Animal Models of Anxiety

Animal models have played an important role in the study of anxiety and in the assessment of the anxiolytic potential of new drugs (see Gray & McNaughton, 2000; Green, 1991; Treit, 1985). These models typically involve animal defensive behaviors, the implicit assumption being that defensive behaviors are motivated by fear and that fear and anxiety are similar states. Three animal behaviors that model anxiety are elevated-plus-maze performance, defensive burying, and risk assessment (see Figure 15.6).

In the *elevated-plus-maze test*, rats are placed on a four-armed plus-sign–shaped maze that is 50 centimeters above the floor. Two arms have sides and two arms have no sides, and the measure of anxiety is the proportion of time the rats spend in the enclosed arms, rather than venturing onto the exposed arms (see Pellow et al., 1985).

In the *defensive-burying test*, rats are shocked by a wire-wrapped wooden dowel mounted on the wall of a familiar test chamber. The measure of anxiety is the amount of time the rats spend spraying bedding material from the floor of the chamber at the source of the shock with forward thrusting movements of their head and forepaws (see Treit et al., 1993).

In the *risk-assessment test*, after a single brief exposure to a cat on the surface of a laboratory burrow system, rats flee to their burrows and freeze. Then, they engage in a variety of risk-assessment behaviors (e.g., scanning the surface from the mouth

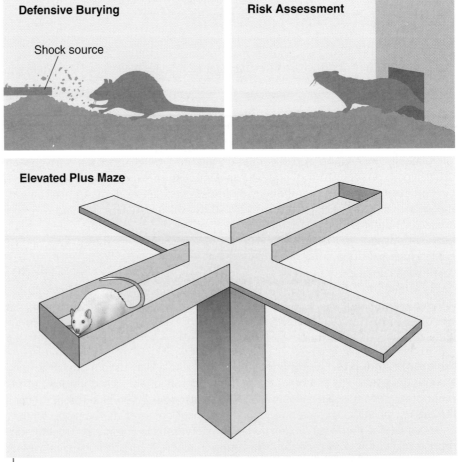

Three tests of rodent anxiety: defensive burying, risk assessment, and performance in an elevated plus maze. In each panel, a rat is shown engaging in an anxiety-related behavior.

Figure 15.6

of the burrow or exploring the surface in a cautious stretched posture) before their behavior returns to normal (see Blanchard, Blanchard, & Rodgers, 1991; Blanchard et al., 1990). The measures of anxiety are the amounts of time that the rats spend in freezing and in risk assessment.

The elevated-plus-maze, defensive-burying, and risk-assessment tests of anxiety have all been validated by demonstrations that benzodiazepines reduce the various indexes of anxiety used in the tests, whereas nonanxiolytic drugs usually do not. There is a potential problem with this line of evidence, however. The potential problem stems from the fact that many cases of anxiety do not respond well to benzodiazepine therapy. Accordingly, existing animal models of anxiety may be models of benzodiazepine-sensitive anxiety rather than of anxiety in general, and thus the models may not be sensitive to anxiolytic drugs that act by a different (i.e., a non-GABAergic) mechanism. For example, the serotonin agonist *buspirone* does not have a reliable anxiolytic effect in the elevated-plus-maze test.

Thinking Clearly

Neural Bases of Anxiety Disorders

Like current theories of the neural bases of schizophrenia and depression, current theories of the neural bases of anxiety disorders rest heavily on the analysis of therapeutic drug effects. The fact that many anxiolytic drugs are agonists at either $GABA_A$ receptors (e.g., the benzodiazepines) or serotonin receptors (e.g., buspirone and Prozac) has focused attention on the possible role in anxiety disorders of deficits in both GABAergic and serotonergic transmission.

Speculations about the brain structures involved in anxiety disorders have focused on the amygdala because of the central role it plays in fear and defensive behavior (see LeDoux, 1995). In support of the involvement of the amygdala in anxiety disorders are the following findings: The amygdala has a high concentration of $GABA_A$ receptors; and in animal models, local infusion of benzodiazepines into the amygdala produces anxiolytic effects, and local injections of GABA antagonists into the amygdala can block the anxiolytic effects of *systemic* (into general circulation) injections of benzodiazepines (see Davis, Rainie, & Cassell, 1994).

Brain-imaging studies of patients suffering from anxiety have not revealed obvious structural pathology in the amygdala or any other brain structure. In contrast, many functional brain changes have been reported, but so far none has been consistently replicated. The likely problem is that anxiety is such a broad diagnostic category that brain images that are obtained by averaging observations from several subjects are inevitably clouded by variability among subjects (Reiman et al., 2000).

15.4
Tourette Syndrome

ourette syndrome is the last of the four psychiatric disorders discussed in this chapter. It differs from the first three (schizophrenia, affective disorders, and anxiety) in the specificity of its effects. And they are as interesting as they are specific. The case of R.G. introduces you to Tourette syndrome.

The Case of R.G.—Barking Mad

When R.G. was 15, he developed *tics* (involuntary, repetitive, stereotyped movements or vocalizations). For the first week, his tics took the form of involuntary blinking, but after that they started to involve other parts of the body, particularly his arms and legs.

R.G. and his family were religious, so it was particularly distressing when his tics became verbal. He began to curse repeatedly and involuntarily. Involuntary cursing is a common symptom of Tourette syndrome and of several other psychiatric and neurological disorders (Van Lancker & Cummings, 1999). R.G. also started to bark like a dog. Finally, he developed echolalia: When his mother said, "Dinner is ready," he responded, "Is ready, is ready."

Prior to the onset of R.G.'s symptoms, he was an A student, apparently happy and with an outgoing, engaging personality. Once his symptoms developed, he was jeered at, imitated, and ridiculed by his schoolmates. He responded by becoming anxious, depressed, and withdrawn. His grades plummeted.

Once R.G. was taken to a psychiatrist by his parents, his condition was readily diagnosed—the symptoms of Tourette syndrome are unmistakable. Medication eliminated 99% of his symptoms, and once his disorder was explained to him and he realized he was not mad, he resumed his former outgoing manner (Spitzer et al., 1983).

Many people with Tourette syndrome experience no symptoms other than tics. Accordingly, if their friends, family members, and colleagues are understanding and supportive, these people can live happy, productive lives—for example, Tim Howard (shown in the photo on page 497) is goalkeeper for Manchester United, one of the top soccer teams in the world.

What Is Tourette Syndrome?

Tourette syndrome is a disorder of **tics** (involuntary, repetitive, stereotyped movements or vocalizations) (Jankovic, 2001; Leckman et al., 2001). It typically begins in childhood with simple motor tics, such as eye blinking or head movements, but the symptoms develop over time, becoming more complex and severe. Common complex motor tics include making lewd gestures, hitting, touching objects, squatting, hopping, and twirling. Common verbal tics include inarticulate sounds (e.g., barking, coughing, grunting), *coprolalia* (uttering obscenities), *echolalia* (repetition of another's words), and *palilalia* (repetition of one's own words).

Tourette syndrome develops in approximately 0.7% of children and is three times more frequent in males than in females. There is a major genetic component: Concordance rates are 55% for identical twins and 8% for fraternal twins (see Pauls, 2001).

Some patients with Tourette syndrome also display signs of *attention-deficit/ hyperactivity disorder*, obsessive-compulsive disorder, or both (Sheppard et al., 1999). For example, R.G. was obsessed by odd numbers and refused to sit in even-numbered seats.

Although the tics of Tourette syndrome are involuntary, they can be suppressed for brief periods of time with great concentration and effort from the patient. However, if they are suppressed, a discomfort or tension builds up in the body, which is eventually released in the form of a bout of particularly frequent and intense tics.

Imagine how difficult it would be to get on with your life if you suffered from an extreme form of Tourette syndrome—for example if you frequently grabbed your genitals and started barking like a dog. No matter how intelligent, capable, and kind you were inside, not many people would be willing to socialize with or employ you (see Kushner, 1999).

Impediments to the Study of the Neuropathology of Tourette Syndrome

Little is known about the neural mechanisms of Tourette syndrome, in part because of several major impediments that make studying them difficult (see Swerdlow & Young, 2001). The following are three of these: First, there are no animal models of Tourette syndrome; as a result, controlled experiments are difficult, and studies that involve direct manipulation of the brain are impossible. Second, no particular genes have yet been implicated in the development of the disorder, and thus a potentially important source of clues about its neurochemical basis is absent. Third, because of the involuntary movements that characterize the disorder, brain imaging is difficult and must be restricted to brief periods during which patients are capable of controlling their tics.

Brain Mechanisms of Tourette Syndrome

Little information can be gleaned about Tourette syndrome from published postmortem neuropathological investigations. Remarkably, this literature describes only seven cases, and all of these are complicated by ambiguities of diagnosis and the coexistence of other disorders, such as epilepsy (see Swerdlow & Young, 2001).

This shortage of postmortem studies of the brains of Tourette patients is not a chance situation. Tourette patients typically receive most of their medical care in childhood, when they first display signs of the disorder and the symptoms are most severe. Thus, when they die, they are usually no longer in contact with the specialists who treated them as children, and thus their brains are rarely examined for links to Tourette syndrome. Consequently, the few brains that have been subjected to postmortem study have been brains of atypical Tourette patients who were receiving neurological care just prior to their death.

Many abnormalities have been reported in functional brain images of Tourette patients who are actively suppressing their tics. However, only two of these reported abnormalities have been consistently observed (Peterson, 2001). First, abnormalities are almost always observed in the basal ganglia. Second, abnormalities are commonly observed in areas of limbic and association cortex. You may recall that the basal ganglia are part of a major feedback circuit: They receive input from many areas of the cortex, and much of their output goes to the thalamus, which in turn projects back to many areas of the cortex. The results of functional brain-imaging studies suggest that the neuropathology of Tourette syndrome lies in this circuit.

Treatment of Tourette Syndrome

Although tics are the defining feature of Tourette syndrome, treatment typically begins by focusing on other aspects of the disorder. First, the patient, family members, friends, and teachers are educated about the nature of the syndrome. Second, the treatment focuses on the ancillary emotional problems (e.g., anxiety and depression). Once these first two steps have been taken, attention turns to treating the symptoms.

The tics of Tourette syndrome are usually treated with *neuroleptics* (the D_2 receptor blockers that are used in the treatment of schizophrenia). However, there have been few controlled studies demonstrating the effectiveness of these drugs against Tourette syndrome (Lang, 2001; Riddle & Carlson, 2001).

The apparent success of D_2 receptor blockers in the treatment of Tourette syndrome is consistent with the hypothesis that the disorder is related to an abnormality of the basal ganglia–thalamus–cortex feedback circuit. In particular, the efficacy of these drugs implicates the *striatum*, which is the target of many of the dopaminergic projections into the basal ganglia. The current hypothesis is that Tourette syndrome is a neurodevelopmental disorder that results from excessive dopaminergic innervation of the striatum and the associated limbic cortex (see Jankovic, 2001).

The Case of P.H., the Neuroscientist with Tourette Syndrome

Tourette syndrome has been P.H.'s problem for more than three decades (Hollenbeck, 2001). Taking advantage of his position as a medical school faculty member, he regularly offers a series of lectures on the topic. Along with students, many other Tourette patients and their families are attracted to his lectures.

Encounters with Tourette patients of his own generation taught P.H. a real lesson. He was astounded to learn that most of them did not have his thick skin. About half of them were still receiving treatment for psychological wounds inflicted during childhood.

For the most part, these patients' deep-rooted pain and anxiety did not result from the tics themselves. They derived from being ridiculed and tormented by others and from the self-righteous advice repeatedly offered by well-meaning "clods." The malfunction may be in the basal ganglia, but in reality this is more a disorder of the onlooker than of the patient.

> There is no character, howsoever good and fine, but it can be destroyed by ridicule, howsoever poor and witless.
>
> MARK TWAIN

Scan your Brain

You have just learned about four psychiatric disorders, and you are about to find out about the current requirements for the development of new psychotherapeutic drugs. This is therefore an appropriate point for you to assess your knowledge of the first sections of this chapter. Complete each of the following sentences with the correct term. The answers are below.

1. Waxy flexibility is a symptom of catatonic _____.

2. Chlorpromazine was initially developed as an _____.

3. _____ is the main active ingredient of the snakeroot plant.

4. _____ is an atypical neuroleptic.

5. _____ receptors are believed to play a major role in schizophrenia.

6. _____ depression has no apparent environmental trigger.

7. Imipramine is a _____ antidepressant.

8. Iproniazid, the first antidepressant drug, was originally developed for the treatment of _____.

9. _____ are drugs that produce the cheese effect.

10. The diathesis–stress model is a theory of _____.

11. The pathological fear of public places and open spaces characterizes an anxiety disorder called _____.

12. Valium and Librium are _____, which are used in the treatment of anxiety disorders.

13. The elevated-plus-maze test is an animal model of _____.

14. Tourette syndrome is a disorder of _____.

15. The _____ is the subcortical structure most frequently implicated in Tourette syndrome.

16. Tourette syndrome is often treated with a _____.

Scan Your Brain answers: (1) schizophrenia, (2) antihistamine, (3) Reserpine, (4) Clozapine, (5) D₂, (6) Endogenous, (7) tricyclic, (8) tuberculosis, (9) MAO inhibitors, (10) depression, (11) agoraphobia, (12) benzodiazepines, (13) anxiety, (14) tics, (15) striatum, (16) neuroleptic.

15.5

Clinical Trials: Development of New Psychotherapeutic Drugs

Almost daily, there are news reports of exciting discoveries that appear to be pointing to effective new therapeutic drugs or treatments. But most often, the promise does not materialize. For example, half a century after the revolution in molecular biology began, not a single form of gene therapy is yet in use. The reason is that the journey from promising basic research to useful drug or other medical treatment is excruciatingly complex, time-consuming, and expensive.

The difficulties of developing psychotherapeutic drugs are not apparent in the preceding sections of this chapter because, so far, the chapter has focused on early drug discoveries and their role in the development of theories of psychiatric dysfunction. In the early years, the development of psychotherapeutic drugs was largely a hit-or-miss process. New drugs were tested on patient populations with little justification and then quickly marketed to an unsuspecting public, often before it was discovered that they were ineffective for their original purpose.

Things have changed. The testing of experimental drugs on human subjects and the subsequent release of the drugs for sale are now strictly regulated by government agencies.

The process of gaining permission from the government to market a new psychotherapeutic drug begins with the synthesis of the drug, the development of procedures for synthesizing it economically, and the collection of evidence from nonhuman subjects showing that the drug is likely safe for human consumption and has potential therapeutic benefits. These initial steps take a long time—at least 5 years—and only if the evidence is sufficiently promising is permission granted to proceed to clinical trials. **Clinical trials** are studies conducted on human subjects to assess the therapeutic efficacy of an untested drug or other treatment. This entire process is summarized in Table 15.2.

Thinking Clearly

Table 15.2

Phases of Drug Development

TIME	BASIC RESEARCH	COST
At least 5 years	Discovery of the drug, development of efficient methods of synthesis, and testing with animal models	
About 1 year	**Application to begin clinical trials and the review of basic research by government agency**	
	HUMAN CLINICAL TRIALS	COST
About 1.5 years	**Phase I** Screening for safety and finding the maximum safe dose	About $10 million
About 2 years	**Phase II** Establishing most effective doses and schedules of treatment	About $20 million
About 3.5 years	**Phase III** Clear demonstrations that the drug is therapeutic	About $45 million
About 1.5 years	**Application to begin marketing and reviews of results of clinical trials by government agency**	
	SELLING TO THE PUBLIC	
Ongoing	Recovering development costs and continuing to monitor the safety of the drug	

Source: Adapted from Zivin (2000).

This final section of the chapter focuses on clinical trials. But before we begin, I want to emphasize the critical role played by research on nonhuman subjects in the development of effective therapeutic drugs for human patients. Without a solid foundation of comparative research, it is extremely difficult to gain governmental permission to begin clinical trials.

Clinical Trials: The Three Phases

Once approval has been obtained from the appropriate government agencies, clinical trials of a new drug with therapeutic potential can commence. Clinical trials are conducted in three separate phases: (1) screening for safety, (2) establishing the testing protocol, and (3) the final tests (see Zivin, 2000).

Screening for Safety.   The purpose of the first phase of a clinical trial is to determine whether the drug is safe for human use and, if it is, to determine how much of the drug can be tolerated. Administering the drug to humans for the first time is always a risky process because there is no way of knowing for certain how they will respond. The subjects in phase 1 are typically healthy paid volunteers. Phase 1 clinical trials always begin with tiny doses, which are gradually increased as the tests proceed. The reactions of the subjects are meticulously monitored, and if strong adverse reactions are observed, phase 1 is curtailed. It usually requires about 1.5 years and about $10 million to complete phase 1.

Establishing the Testing Protocol.   The purpose of the second phase of a clinical trial is to establish the *protocol* (the conditions) under which the final tests are likely to provide a clear result. For example, in phase 2, researchers hope to discover which doses are likely to be therapeutically effective, how frequently they should be administered, how long they need to be administered to have a therapeutic effect, what benefits are likely to occur, and which patients are likely to be helped. Phase 2 tests are conducted on patients suffering from the target disorder; the tests usually include *placebo-control groups* (groups of subjects who receive a control substance rather than the drug), and their designs are *double-blind*—that is, the tests are conducted so that neither the patients nor the physicians interacting with them know which treatment (drug or placebo) each patient has received. It typically requires about 2 years and about $20 million to complete phase 2.

The Final Tests.   Phase 3 of a clinical trial is typically a double-blind, placebo-control study on large numbers—often, many thousands—of patients suffering from the target disorder. The design of the phase 3 tests is based on the results of phase 2 so that the final tests are likely to demonstrate positive therapeutic effects, if these exist. The first test of the final phase is often not conclusive, but if it is promising, a second test based on a redesigned protocol may be conducted. In most cases, two independent successful tests are required to convince government regulatory agencies. A successful test is one in which the beneficial effects are substantially greater than the adverse side effects. The typical length of the final test phase is about 3.5 years, and the typical cost is about $45 million.

Controversial Aspects of Clinical Trials

The clinical trial process is not without controversy. The following are the major focuses of criticism and debate (Zivin, 2000).

Requirement for Double-Blind Design and Placebo Controls.   In most clinical trials, patients are assigned to drug or placebo groups randomly. Patients are always fully informed of this before they volunteer, but they do not know for sure which treatment they will be receiving (see Woods et al., 2001). Accordingly, some patients whose only hope for recovery may be the latest experimental treatment will, without knowing it, receive the placebo. Drug companies and government agencies concede that this is true, but they argue that there can be no convincing evidence that the experimental treatment is effective until a double-blind, placebo-control trial is complete.

The Need for Active Placebos. The double-blind, placebo-control procedure seems perfect for clinical testing, but it isn't (see Salamone, 2000). At therapeutic doses, many drugs have side effects that are obvious to people taking them, and thus the subjects in double-blind, placebo-control studies who receive the drug can be certain that they are in the drug group. This knowledge may greatly contribute to the positive effects of the drug, independent of any real therapeutic effect. Accordingly, it is now widely recognized that an active placebo is better than an inert placebo as the control drug. **Active placebos** are control drugs that have no therapeutic effect but produce side effects similar to those produced by the drug under evaluation.

Length of Time Required. Patients desperately seeking new treatments are frustrated by the amount of time needed for clinical trials. Accordingly, researchers, drug companies, and government agencies are striving to speed up the evaluation process, but without sacrificing the quality of the procedures designed to protect patients from ineffective treatments.

Financial Issues. The drug companies pay the scientists, physicians, technicians, assistants, and patients involved in drug trials. Considering the millions they spend and the fact that only 20% of the candidate drugs entering phase 1 testing ever gain final approval (Zivin, 2000), it should come as no surprise that drug companies are anxious to recoup their costs. In view of this pressure, many have questioned the impartiality of those conducting the trials. The scientists themselves have often complained that drug companies make them sign agreements that prohibit them from publishing or discussing negative findings without the consent of the sponsoring company.

Another financial issue is the fact that drug companies seldom develop drugs to treat rare disorders because such treatments will not be profitable. Drugs for which the market is too small for them to be profitable are called *orphan drugs*. Governments in Europe and North America have enacted legislation to promote the development of orphan drugs (see Maeder, 2003).

Effectiveness of Clinical Trials

Despite the controversy that surrounds the clinical trial process, there is no question that it works.

> A long, dismal history tells of charlatans who make unfounded promises and take advantage of people at the time when they are least able to care for themselves. The clinical trial process is the most objective method ever devised to assess the efficacy of a treatment. It is expensive and slow, and in need of constant refinements and oversight, but the process is trustworthy. (Zivin, 2000, p. 75)

Certainly, the clinical trial process is far from perfect. For example, concerns about the ethics of randomized double-blind, placebo-control studies are often warranted. Still, the vast majority of those in the medical and research professions accept that these studies are the essential critical test of any new therapy. This is particularly true of psychotherapeutic drugs because psychiatric disorders often respond to placebo treatments and because assessment of their severity is subjective and can be greatly influenced by the expectations of the therapist. Everybody agrees that clinical trials are too expensive and take too long. But one expert responds to this concern in the following way: Clinical trials can be trustworthy, fast,

Thinking Clearly

or cheap; but in any one trial, only two of the three are possible (Zivin, 2000). Think about it.

Conclusion

The chapter, and indeed the book, ends with the case of S.B., who suffers from bipolar affective disorder. S.B.'s case is appropriate here because S.B. benefited greatly from the clinical trial process and because S.B.'s case demonstrates the value of a biopsychological education that stresses clear thinking and the importance of taking responsibility for one's own health. You see, S.B. took a course similar to the one that you are currently taking, and the things that he learned in the course enabled him to steer his own treatment to a positive outcome.

The Case of S.B., the Biopsychology Student Who Took Control

I met S.B. when he was a third-year undergraduate. That year, he was a student in my biopsychology course, and he also volunteered to work in my laboratory. S.B. is a quiet, pleasant, shy person; he has an unassuming manner, but he is kind, knowledgeable, and intelligent, with broad interests. For example, I was surprised to learn that he was a skilled artist, interested in medical illustration, so we chatted at length about the illustrations in this book.

I was delighted to discover that S.B.'s grades confirmed my positive impression of him. He had the highest grades in the program. In addition, it soon became apparent that he had a real "touch" for research, so I invited him to become my graduate student. He accepted and has been truly exceptional. As you can tell, I am very proud of him.

S.B. is now going to describe his case to you in his own words. I wanted to tell you about him myself so that you would have a clear picture of his situation. As you are about to discover, S.B.'s view of himself, sometimes obscured by a black cloud of depression, often bears little relation to reality.

As an undergraduate student, I suffered from depression. Although my medication improved things somewhat, I still felt stupid, disliked, and persecuted. There were some positives in my undergraduate years. Dr. Pinel was very good to me, and I liked his course. He always emphasized that the most important part of his course was learning to be an independent thinker, and I was impressed by how he had been able to diagnose his own brain tumor. I did not appreciate at the time just how important these lessons would be.

A few months after beginning graduate school, my depression became so severe that I could not function. My psychiatrist advised me to take a leave of absence, which I did. I returned a few months later, filled with antipsychotics and antidepressants, barely capable of keeping things together.

You can appreciate how pleased I was 2 years later, when I started to snap out of it. It occurred to me that I was feeling better than I had ever felt. My productivity and creativity increased. I read, wrote, and drew, and new ideas for experiments flooded into my head. Things were going so well that I found that I was sleeping only 2 or 3 hours a night, and my brain was so energized that my friends sometimes begged me to talk more slowly so that they could follow what I was saying.

But my euphoria soon came to an abrupt end. I was still energetic and creative, but the content of my ideas changed. My consciousness was again dominated by feelings of inferiority, stupidity, and persecution. Thoughts of suicide were a constant companion.

As a last resort, I called my psychiatrist, and when she saw me, she immediately had me committed. My diagnosis was bipolar affective disorder with a *mixed episode*. As she explained, mixed episodes are transition states between mania and depression and are associated with particularly high suicide rates.

Heavily sedated, I slept for much of the first week. When I came out of my stupor, two resident psychiatrists informed me that I would be placed on a mood stabilizer and would likely have to take it for the rest of my life. Two things made me feel uncomfortable about this. First, many patients in the ward were taking this drug, and they seemed like bloated zombies; second, my physicians seemed to know less about this drug and its mechanisms than I did. So I requested that they give me access to the hospital library so I could learn about my disorder and drug. In effect, I was pulling a "Pinel."

I was amazed by what I found. The drug favored by the residents had been shown several months before to be no more effective in the treatment of bipolar affective disorder than an active placebo. Moreover, a new drug that had recently cleared clinical trials was proving very effective with few side effects.

When I confronted my psychiatrists with this evidence, they were astounded and agreed to prescribe the new drug. As I write these words, I am feeling well and am enjoying graduate school. I still find it difficult to believe that I had enough nerve to question my physicians and prescribe for myself. I never imagined that the lessons learned from this book would have such a positive impact on my life. I am glad that I could tell you my story, and I hope that you benefit from it.

(Used by permission of Steven Barnes.)

Key Terms

Psychiatric disorder (p. 481)

15.1 Schizophrenia

Butyrophenones (p. 485)
Chlorpromazine (p. 483)
Clozapine (p. 486)
Haloperidol (p. 485)
Neuroleptics (p. 485)
Phenothiazines (p. 485)
Reserpine (p. 483)

15.2 Affective Disorders: Depression and Mania

Anhedonia (p. 493)
Bipolar affective disorder (p. 489)
Cheese effect (p. 490)
Depression (p. 488)
Diathesis (p. 492)
Endogenous depression (p. 489)
Imipramine (p. 490)
Iproniazid (p. 490)
Lithium (p. 490)

Mania (p. 489)
MAO inhibitors (p. 490)
Mood stabilizer (p. 491)
Prozac (p. 491)
Reactive depression (p. 489)
Tricyclic antidepressants (p. 490)
Unipolar affective disorder (p. 489)
Up-regulation (p. 492)

15.3 Anxiety Disorders

Agoraphobia (p. 495)
Anxiety (p. 494)
Anxiety disorder (p. 494)
Benzodiazepines (p. 495)
Generalized anxiety disorders (p. 494)
Obsessive-compulsive disorders (p. 494)
Panic disorders (p. 494)
Phobic anxiety disorders (p. 494)
Posttraumatic stress disorder (p. 495)

15.4 Tourette Syndrome

Tics (p. 498)

15.5 Clinical Trials: Development of New Psychotherapeutic Drugs

Active placebos (p. 503)
Clinical trials (p. 501)

ON THE CD

Studying for an exam? Get some help from the electronic flash cards of the key terms and the practice tests for this chapter.

Behavioral Neuroscience of Psychiatric Disorders
The Brain Unhinged

This chapter focused on the neural mechanisms of four classes of psychiatric disorders: schizophrenia, affective disorders, anxiety disorders, and Tourette syndrome. It concluded with a description and discussion of the development of psychotherapeutic drugs.

Schizophrenia

The fact that most antischizophrenic drugs block activity at D_2 receptors is support for the dopamine theory of schizophrenia. However, other evidence suggests that D_2 receptors cannot be the entire story. For example, atypical antischizophrenic drugs have little effect on D_2 receptors, and many schizophrenics have widespread brain damage with little damage to the dopamine circuits.
(Pages 481–488)

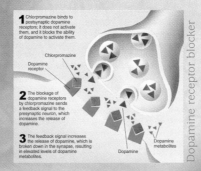

1 Chlorpromazine binds to postsynaptic dopamine receptors; it does not activate them, and it blocks the ability of dopamine to activate them.

Chlorpromazine

Dopamine receptor

2 The blockage of dopamine receptors by chlorpromazine sends a feedback signal to the presynaptic neuron, which increases the release of dopamine.

3 The feedback signal increases the release of dopamine, which is broken down in the synapse, resulting in elevated levels of dopamine metabolites.

Dopamine

Dopamine metabolites

Dopamine receptor blocker

Affective Disorders

Many depressed patients experience periods of mania. Those who do suffer from bipolar affective disorder; those who do not suffer from unipolar affective disorder. Monoamine oxidase inhibitors, tricyclic antidepressants, and monoamine-reuptake inhibitors are used in the treatment of affective disorders. Because all of these drugs are monoamine agonists, the monoamine theory is the major theory of depression.
(Pages 488–493)

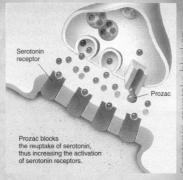

Serotonin receptor

Prozac

Prozac blocks the reuptake of serotonin, thus increasing the activation of serotonin receptors.

Serotonin reuptake blocker

Anxiety Disorders

Anxiety is adaptive when it motivates effective coping behaviors; when it becomes so severe and pervasive that it disrupts normal functioning, it is referred to as an anxiety disorder. Because drugs that are effective in the treatment of anxiety disorders tend to be GABAA receptor agonists or serotonin agonists, research on the basis for anxiety disorders has focused on reduced activity at GABAA and serotonin receptors.
(Pages 494–497)

Defensive Burying

Shock source

Risk Assessment

Elevated Plus Maze

Tests of rodent anxiety

Tourette Syndrome

Tourette syndrome is a disorder of tics. It starts in childhood with simple tics such as blinking or head nodding, but the tics grow more complex over time. Complex tics often observed in those with the fully developed disorder include touching objects, making lewd gestures, hopping, barking, grunting, and swearing. Tourette syndrome is thought to be a disorder of the basal ganglia.
(Pages 497–500)

Tim Howard, Tourette patient

Clinical Trials: Development of New Psychotherapeutic Drugs

The process of gaining permission to market a new psychotherapeutic drug begins with synthesis of the drug, development of protocols for producing large amounts of it economically, and collection of evidence from nonhuman subjects showing that the drug is likely to produce therapeutic benefits in human patients and be safe for them to take. Once these criteria are met, permission is granted to begin clinical trials (tests in humans). Clinical trials occur in three phases: screening for safety, establishing the testing protocol, and the final double-blind test. The clinical trials alone cost about $75 million.
(Pages 500–504)

TIME	BASIC RESEARCH	
At least 5 years	Discovery of the drug, development of efficient methods of synthesis, and testing with animal models	
About 1 year	Application to begin clinical trials and the review of basic research by government agency	
	HUMAN CLINICAL TRIALS	COST
About 1.5 years	**Phase I** Screening for safety and finding the maximum safe dose	About $10 million
About 2 years	**Phase II** Establishing most effective doses and schedules of treatment	About $20 million
About 3.5 years	**Phase III** Clear demonstrations that the drug is therapeutic	About $45 million
About 1.5 years	Application to begin marketing and reviews of results of clinical trials by government agency	
	SELLING TO THE PUBLIC	
Ongoing	Recovering development costs and continuing to monitor the safety of the drug	

Themes Revisited

This chapter focused on the biopsychology of psychiatric disorders, so not surprisingly the clinical implications theme was predominant. Nevertheless, the other three major themes of this book also received substantial coverage.

The thinking-clearly-about-biopsychology theme arose during the discussions of the differences between psychiatric and neuropsychological disorders, the diagnosis of schizophrenia, the interpretation of animal-model and brain-imaging studies of anxiety, and the reasons why postmortem studies of typical Tourette patients are rare and at several points during the discussion of clinical trials.

The cognitive neuroscience theme was apparent in the discussion of functional brain-imaging studies of affective disorders, anxiety disorders, and Tourette syndrome. Functional brain-imaging techniques have been particularly important in the study of these particular psychiatric disorders because they do not appear to be associated with any obvious structural damage to the brain.

The evolutionary perspective theme came up twice: in the section on animal models of anxiety and in the discussion of the important role played by research on nonhuman subjects in gaining official clearance to commence human clinical trials.

Think about It

1. Blunders often play an important role in scientific progress. Discuss with respect to the development of psychotherapeutic drugs.

2. The mechanism by which a disorder is alleviated is not necessarily opposite to the mechanism by which it was caused. Discuss.

3. Judge people by what they do, not by what they say. Discuss with respect to Tourette syndrome.

4. Tourette syndrome is a disorder of onlookers. Explain and discuss.

5. Clinical trials are no more than government bureaucracy. The prescription of drugs should be left entirely to the discretion of physicians. Discuss.

6. The failure to require active placebos in the evaluation of new psychotherapeutic drugs is a serious problem. Explain and discuss.

Epilogue

You must feel relieved to be finishing this book. Still, I hope that you feel a tiny bit of regret that our time together is over.

Like good friends, we have shared good times and bad. We have shared the fun and wonder of Rhonda, the dexterous cashier; the Nads basketball team; people who rarely sleep; the "mamawawa"; split brains; and brain transplantation. But we have also been touched by many personal tragedies: for example, the victims of Alzheimer's disease and MPTP poisoning; the lost mariner; H.M.; and Professor P., the biopsychologist who experienced brain surgery from the other side of the knife. Thank you for allowing me to share *Basics of Biopsychology* with you. I hope you have found it to be a worthwhile experience.

Our mutual experiences have transcended space and time. Right now, it is Tuesday morning, April 4, 2006, and I am sitting at my desk feeling pleased to be finally writing this last paragraph. I can see the Pacific Ocean through my rapidly greening garden, and the birds are singing—life is good. Where and when are you?

Appendixes

Appendix I

The Autonomic Nervous System

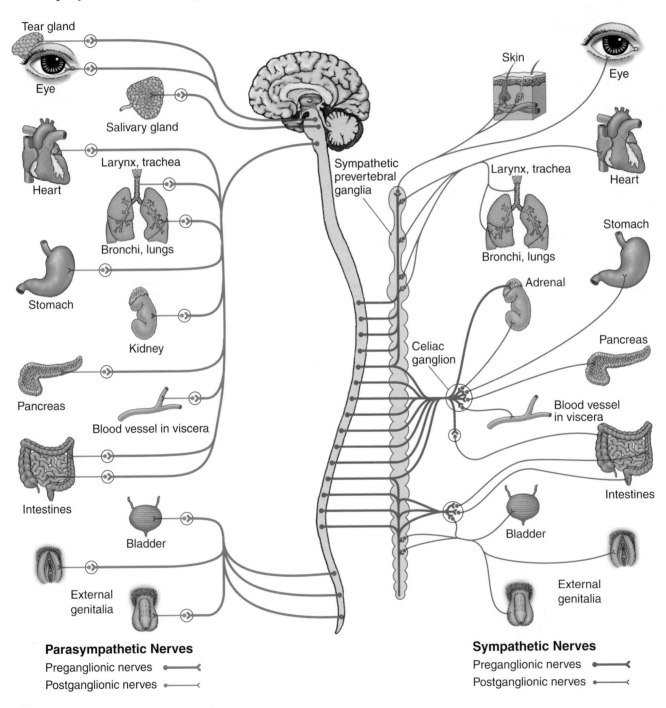

Parasympathetic Pathways

Tear gland

Eye

Salivary gland

Heart

Larynx, trachea

Bronchi, lungs

Stomach

Kidney

Pancreas

Blood vessel in viscera

Intestines

Bladder

External genitalia

Sympathetic prevertebral ganglia

Celiac ganglion

Sympathetic Pathways

Skin

Eye

Heart

Larynx, trachea

Bronchi, lungs

Stomach

Adrenal

Pancreas

Blood vessel in viscera

Intestines

Bladder

External genitalia

Parasympathetic Nerves

Preganglionic nerves

Postganglionic nerves

Sympathetic Nerves

Preganglionic nerves

Postganglionic nerves

Appendix II

Some Functions of Sympathetic and Parasympathetic Activation

ORGAN	SYMPATHETIC EFFECT	PARASYMPATHETIC EFFECT
Salivary gland	Decreases secretion	Increases secretion
Heart	Increases heart rate	Decreases heart rate
Blood vessels	Constricts blood vessels in most organs	Dilates blood vessels in a few organs
Penis	Ejaculation	Erection
Iris radial muscles	Dilates pupils	No effect
Iris sphincter muscles	No effect	Constricts pupils
Tear gland	No effect	Stimulates secretion
Sweat gland	Stimulates secretion	No effect
Stomach and intestine	No effect	Stimulates secretion
Lungs	Dilates bronchioles; inhibits mucous secretion	Constricts bronchioles; stimulates mucous secretion
Arrector pili muscles	Erects hair and creates gooseflesh	No effect

Appendix III

The Cranial Nerves

It is common to group cranial nerves by their major functions: primarily motor, primarily sensory, or a blend of major sensory and motor functions. This appendix illustrates that system of organization. Be aware, however, that all cranial nerves that are primarily motor contain some sensory neurons (see Appendix IV).

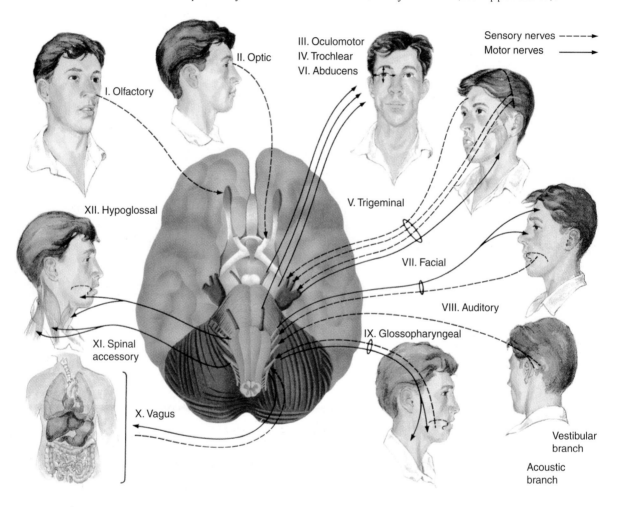

Appendix IV

Functions of the Cranial Nerves

NUMBER	NAME	GENERAL FUNCTION	SPECIFIC FUNCTIONS
I	Olfactory	Sensory	Smell
II	Optic	Sensory	Vision
III	Oculomotor	Motor	Eye movement and pupillary constriction
		Sensory	Sensory signals from certain eye muscles
IV	Trochlear	Motor	Eye movement
		Sensory	Sensory signals from certain eye muscles
V	Trigeminal	Sensory	Facial sensations
		Motor	Chewing
VI	Abducens	Motor	Eye movement
		Sensory	Sensory signals from certain eye muscles
VII	Facial	Sensory	Taste from anterior two-thirds of tongue
		Motor	Facial expression, secretion of tears, salivation, cranial blood vessel dilation
VIII	Auditory-Vestibular	Sensory	Audition; sensory signals from the organs of balance in the inner ear
IX	Glossopharyngeal	Sensory	Taste from posterior third of tongue
		Motor	Salivation, swallowing
X	Vagus	Sensory	Sensations from abdominal and thoracic organs
		Motor	Control over abdominal and thoracic organs and muscles of the throat
XI	Spinal Accessory	Motor	Movement of neck, shoulders, and head
		Sensory	Sensory signals from muscles of the neck
XII	Hypoglossal	Motor	Tongue movements
		Sensory	Sensory signals from tongue muscles

Appendix V
Nuclei of the Thalamus

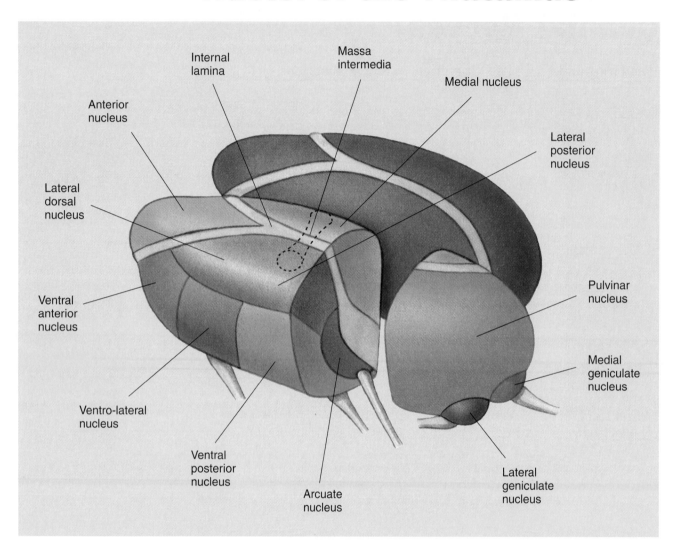

Appendix VI

Nuclei of the Hypothalamus

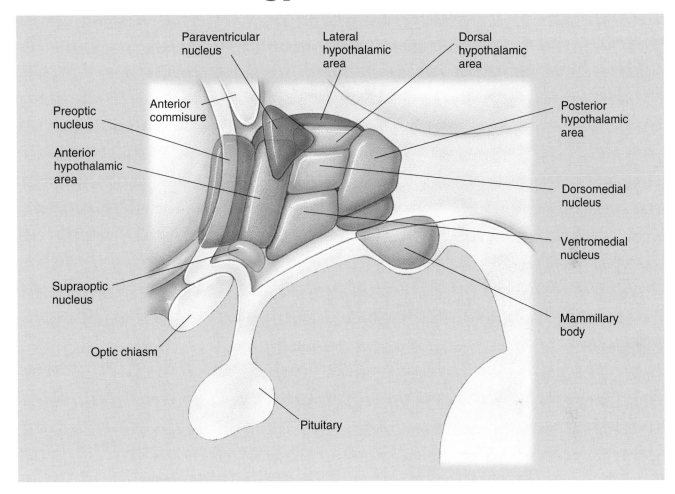

Paraventricular nucleus

Lateral hypothalamic area

Dorsal hypothalamic area

Preoptic nucleus

Anterior commisure

Posterior hypothalamic area

Anterior hypothalamic area

Dorsomedial nucleus

Ventromedial nucleus

Supraoptic nucleus

Mammillary body

Optic chiasm

Pituitary

Ablatio penis. Accidental destruction of the penis.

Absolute refractory period. A brief period (typically 1 to 2 milliseconds) after the initiation of an action potential during which it is impossible to elicit another action potential in the same neuron.

Absorption spectrum. A graph of the ability of a substance to absorb light of different wavelengths.

Absorptive phase. The metabolic phase during which the body is operating on the energy from a recently consumed meal and is storing the excess as body fat, glycogen, and proteins.

Accommodation. The process of adjusting the configuration of the lenses to bring images into focus on the retina.

Acetylcholine. A small-molecule neurotransmitter at neuromuscular junctions and at many synapses in both the CNS and the PNS.

Acetylcholinesterase. The enzyme that breaks down the neurotransmitter acetylcholine.

Action potential (AP). A massive momentary reversal of a neuron's membrane potential from about −70 mV to about +50 mV.

Activation-synthesis theory. The theory that dream content reflects the cerebral cortex's inherent tendency to make sense of, and give form to, the random signals it receives from the brain stem during REM sleep.

Active placebos. Control drugs that have no therapeutic effect but produce side effects similar to those produced by the drug under evaluation in a clinical trial.

Acuity. The ability to see the details of objects.

Addicts. Habitual drug users who continue to use a drug despite its adverse effects on their health and social life and despite their repeated efforts to stop using it.

Adipsia. Complete cessation of drinking.

Adrenal cortex. The outer layer of the adrenal glands, which releases glucocorticoids in response to stressors as well as steroid hormones in small amounts.

Adrenal medulla. The core of each adrenal gland, which releases epinephrine and norepinephrine in response to stressors.

Adrenocorticotropic hormone (ACTH). The anterior pituitary hormone that triggers the release of gonadal and adrenal hormones from the adrenal cortices.

Adrenogenital syndrome. A sexual developmental disorder in which high levels of adrenal androgens, resulting from congenital adrenal hyperplasia, masculinize the bodies of genetic females.

Afferent nerves. Nerves that carry sensory signals to the central nervous system; sensory nerves.

Ageusia. The inability to taste.

Aggregation. The alignment of cells within different areas of the embryo during development to form various structures.

Agnosia. An inability to consciously recognize sensory stimuli of a particular class that is not attributable to a sensory deficit or to verbal or intellectual impairment.

Agonists. Drugs that facilitate the effects of a particular neurotransmitter.

Agoraphobia. Pathological fear of public places and open spaces.

Agraphia. A specific inability to write; one that does not result from general visual, motor, or intellectual deficits.

Alexia. A specific inability to read; one that does not result from general visual, motor, or intellectual deficits.

Alleles. The two genes that control the same trait.

All-or-none responses. Responses that are not graded, that either occur to their full extent or not at all.

Alpha waves. Regular, 8- to 12-per-second, high-amplitude EEG waves that typically occur during relaxed wakefulness and just before falling asleep.

Alzheimer's disease. The major cause of dementia in old age, characterized by neurofibrillary tangles, amyloid plaques, and neuron loss.

Amacrine cells. A type of retinal neuron whose specialized function is lateral communication.

Amino acid derivative hormones. Hormones that are synthesized in a few simple steps from amino acids.

Amino acids. The building blocks and breakdown products of proteins.

Amphetamine. A stimulant drug whose effects are similar to those of cocaine.

Amphibians. Species that spend their larval phase in water and their adult phase on land.

Amygdala. A structure of the medial temporal lobe that plays a role in the memory for the emotional significance of experiences.

Amyloid. A protein that is normally present in small amounts in the human brain but is a major constituent of the numerous plaques in the brains of Alzheimer's patients.

Anabolic steroids. Steroid drugs that are similar to testosterone and have powerful anabolic (growth-promoting) effects.

Analgesics. Drugs that reduce pain.

Analogous. Having a similar structure because of convergent evolution (e.g., a bird's wing and a bee's wing are analogous).

Androgenic insensitivity syndrome. The developmental disorder of genetic males in which a mutation to the androgen receptor gene renders the androgen receptors defective and causes the development of a female body.

Androgens. The class of steroid hormones that includes testosterone.

Androstenedione. The adrenal androgen that triggers the growth of pubic and axillary hair in human females.

Aneurysm. A pathological balloonlike dilation that forms in the wall of a blood vessel at a point where the elasticity of the vessel wall is defective.

Angular gyrus. The gyrus of the posterior cortex at the boundary between the temporal and parietal lobes, which in the left hemisphere is thought to play a role in reading.

Anhedonia. The inability to experience pleasure.

Animal model. A condition that occurs or is induced in a nonhuman animal and is similar in some respects to a human disease.

Anorexia nervosa. An eating disorder that is characterized by a pathological fear of obesity and that results in health-threatening weight loss.

Anosmia. The inability to smell.

Anosognosia. The common failure of neuropsychological patients to recognize their own symptoms.

Antagonistic muscles. Pairs of muscles that act in opposition.

Antagonists. Drugs that inhibit the effects of a particular neurotransmitter.

Anterior. Toward the nose end of a vertebrate.

Anterior cingulate cortex. The cortex of the anterior cingulate gyrus, which is involved in the emotional reaction to painful stimulation.

Anterior pituitary. The part of the pituitary gland that releases tropic hormones.

Anterograde amnesia. Loss of memory for events occurring after the amnesia-inducing brain injury.

Anterograde degeneration. The degeneration of the distal segment of a cut axon.

Anterolateral system. The division of the somatosensory system that ascends in the anterolateral portion of spinal white matter and carries signals related to pain and temperature.

Antibodies. Proteins that bind specifically to antigens on the surface of invading micro-organisms and in so doing promote the destruction of the micro-organisms.

Antibody-mediated immunity. The immune reaction by which B cells destroy invading micro-organisms.

Antigens. Proteins on the surface of cells that identify them as native or foreign.

Antihypnotic drugs. Sleep-reducing drugs.

Anxiety. Chronic fear that persists in the absence of any direct threat.

Anxiety disorder. Anxiety that is so extreme and so pervasive that it disrupts normal functioning.

Aphagia. Complete cessation of eating.

Aphasia. A brain-damage–produced deficit in the ability to use or comprehend language.

Apoptosis. Cell death that is actively induced by genetic programs; programmed cell death.

Appetizer effect. The increase in hunger that is produced by the consumption of small amounts of palatable food.

Apraxia. A disorder in which patients have great difficulty performing movements when asked to do so out of context but can readily perform them spontaneously in natural situations.

Arcuate fasciculus. The major neural pathway between Broca's area and Wernicke's area.

Aromatization. The chemical process by which testosterone is converted to estradiol.

Arteriosclerosis. A condition in which blood vessels are blocked by the accumulation of fat deposits on their walls.

Asomatognosia. A deficiency in the awareness of parts of one's own body that is typically produced by damage to the parietal lobe.

Aspartate. An amino acid neurotransmitter.

Aspiration lesion. An area of brain damage produced by drawing away tissue with suction through the tip of a glass pipette.

Association cortex. Any area of the cortex that receives input from more than one sensory system.

Astereognosia. An inability to recognize objects by touch that is not attributable to a simple sensory deficit or to general intellectual impairment.

Astrocytes. Large, star-shaped glial cells that play a role in the passage of chemicals from the blood into CNS neurons and perform several other important functions that are not yet well understood.

Ataxia. Loss of motor coordination.

Auditory nerve. The branch of cranial nerve VIII that carries auditory signals from the hair cells in the basilar membrane.

Autism. A neurodevelopmental disorder characterized by (1) a reduced ability to interpret the emotions and intentions of others, (2) a reduced capacity for social interaction and communication, and (3) a preoccupation with a single subject or activity.

Autonomic nervous system (ANS). The part of the peripheral nervous system that participates in the regulation of the body's internal environment.

Autoreceptors. A type of metabotropic receptor located on the presynaptic membrane and sensitive to a neuron's own neurotransmitter.

Axon hillock. The conical structure at the junction between the axon and cell body.

B cells. B lymphocytes; lymphocytes that manufacture antibodies against antigens they encounter.

Basal forebrain. A midline area of the forebrain, which is located just in front of and above the hypothalamus and is the brain's main source of acetylcholine.

Basal ganglia. A group of subcortical telencephalon nuclei that are important components of the motor system.

Basal metabolic rate. The rate at which an individual utilizes energy to maintain bodily processes.

Basilar membrane. The membrane of the organ of Corti in which the hair cell receptors are embedded.

Benign tumors. Tumors that are surgically removable with little risk of further growth in the body.

Benzodiazepines. A class of GABA agonists with anxiolytic, sedative, and anticonvulsant properties; drugs such as chlordiazepoxide (Librium) and diazepam (Valium).

Betz cells. Large pyramidal neurons of the primary motor cortex that synapse directly on motor neurons in the lower regions of the spinal cord.

Bilateral medial temporal lobectomy. The removal of the medial portions of both temporal lobes, including the hippocampus, the amygdala, and the adjacent cortex.

Binocular. Involving both eyes.

Binocular disparity. The difference in the position of the retinal image of the same object on the two retinas.

Biopsychology. The scientific study of the biology of behavior.

Bipolar affective disorder. A disorder of emotion in which the patient experiences periods of mania interspersed with periods of depression.

Bipolar cells. Bipolar neurons that form the middle layer of the retina.

Bipolar neuron. A neuron with two processes extending from its cell body.

Bisexual. Sexually attracted to members of both sexes.

Blind spot. The area on the retina where the bundle of axons of the retinal ganglion cells penetrates the receptor layer and leaves the eye as the optic nerve.

Blindsight. The ability of some patients who are blind as a consequence of cortical damage to unconsciously see some aspects of their visual environments.

Blobs. Peglike, cytochrome oxidase–rich, dual-opponent color columns.

Blood–brain barrier. The mechanism that keeps certain toxic substances in the blood from passing into brain tissue.

Botox. A neurotoxin that is produced by a bacterium and that blocks the release of acetylcholine at neuromuscular junctions.

Brain stem. The part of the brain on which the cerebral hemispheres rest; in general, it regulates reflex activities that are critical for survival (e.g., heart rate and respiration).

Bregma. The point on the surface of the skull where two of the major sutures intersect, commonly used as a reference point in stereotaxic surgery on rodents.

Broca's aphasia. A hypothetical disorder of speech production with no associated deficits in language comprehension.

Broca's area. The area of the inferior prefrontal cortex of the left hemisphere hypothesized by Broca to be the center of speech production.

Buerger's disease. A condition in which the blood vessels, especially those supplying the legs, are constricted whenever nicotine enters the bloodstream, the ultimate result being gangrene and amputation.

Bulimia nervosa. An eating disorder that is characterized by recurring cycles of fasting, bingeing, and purging without dangerous weight loss.

Butyrophenones. A class of antischizophrenic drugs that bind primarily to D_2 receptors.

CA1 subfield. The region of the hippocampus that is commonly damaged by cerebral ischemia.

Cafeteria diet. A diet offered to experimental animals that is composed of a wide variety of palatable foods.

Cannabis sativa. The common hemp plant, which is the source of marijuana.

Cannon-Bard theory. The theory that emotional experience and emotional expression are parallel processes that have no direct causal relation.

Carousel apparatus. An apparatus used to study the effects of sleep deprivation in laboratory rats.

Cartesian dualism. The philosophical position of René Descartes, who argued that the universe is composed of two elements: physical matter and the human mind.

Cataplexy. A disorder that is characterized by recurring losses of muscle tone during wakefulness and is often seen in cases of narcolepsy.

Catecholamines. A group of small-molecule neurotransmitters (dopamine, norepinephrine, and epinephrine).

Caudate. One of the basal ganglia; part of the striatum.

Cell-adhesion molecules (CAMs). Molecules on the surface of cells that have the ability to recognize specific molecules on the surface of other cells and bind to them.

Cell-mediated immunity. The immune reaction by which T cells destroy invading micro-organisms.

Central canal. The small CSF-filled channel that runs the length of the spinal cord.

Central fissure. A major furrow in the surface of the human neocortex between the frontal and parietal lobes.

Central nervous system (CNS). The portion of the nervous system within the skull and spine.

Central sensorimotor programs. Patterns of activity that are programmed into the sensorimotor system.

Cephalic phase. The metabolic phase during which the body prepares for food that is about to be absorbed.

Cerebellum. The metencephalic structure that has been shown to mediate the retention of Pavlovian eyeblink conditioning.

Cerebral angiography. A contrast X-ray technique for visualizing the cerebral circulatory system by infusing a radio-translucent dye into a cerebral artery.

Cerebral aqueduct. The narrow channel that connects the third and fourth ventricles.

Cerebral cannula. A fine, hollow tube usually implanted with its tip located in a particular brain structure for the purpose of introducing or extracting substances.

Cerebral commissures. Tracts that connect the left and right cerebral hemispheres.

Cerebral cortex. The layer of neural tissue covering the cerebral hemispheres of humans and other mammals.

Cerebral hemorrhage. Bleeding in the brain.

Cerebral ischemia. An interruption of the blood supply to an area of the brain; a common cause of medial temporal lobe amnesia.

Cerebral ventricles. The four CSF-filled internal chambers of the brain: the two lateral ventricles, the third ventricle, and the fourth ventricle.

Cerebrospinal fluid (CSF). The colorless fluid that fills the subarachnoid space, the central canal, and the cerebral ventricles.

Cerebrum. The portion of the brain that sits on the brain stem; in general, it plays a role in complex adaptive processes (e.g., learning, perception, and motivation).

Cerveau isolé preparation. An experimental preparation in which the forebrain is disconnected from the rest of the brain by a midcollicular transection.

Change blindness. The difficulty perceiving major changes to unattended-to parts of a visual image when the changes are introduced during brief interruptions in the presentation of the image.

Cheese effect. The surges in blood pressure that occur when individuals taking MAO inhibitors consume tyramine-rich foods, such as cheese.

Chemoaffinity hypothesis. The hypothesis that growing axons are attracted to the correct targets by different chemicals released by the target sites.

Chemoattractants. Chemicals that are released by glial cells and guide migrating neurons by attracting them.

Chemorepellants. Chemicals that are released by glial cells and guide migrating neurons by repelling them.

Chimeric figures test. A test of visual completion in split-brain subjects that uses pictures composed of the left and right halves of two different faces.

Chlorpromazine. The first antischizophrenic drug.

Cholecystokinin (CCK). A peptide that is released by the gastrointestinal tract and is thought to function as a satiety signal.

Chordates. Animals with dorsal nerve cords.

Chromosomes. Threadlike structures in the cell nucleus that contain the genes; each chromosome is a DNA molecule.

Ciliary muscles. The eye muscles that control the shape of the lenses.

Cingulate cortex. The limbic cortex of the cingulate gyrus.

Cingulate gyrus. A gyrus on the midline surface of the human cortex, buried within the longitudinal fissure.

Cingulate motor areas. Two small areas of secondary motor cortex located in the cortex of the cingulate gyrus of each hemisphere.

Circadian clock. An internal timing mechanism that is capable of maintaining daily cycles of physiological functions, even when there are no temporal cues from the environment.

Circadian rhythms. Diurnal (daily) cycles of body functions.

Circadian theories of sleep. Theories based on the premise that sleep is controlled by an internal timing mechanism and is not a reaction to the adverse effects of wakefulness.

Cirrhosis. Scarring, typically of the liver.

Clinical. Pertaining to illness or treatment.

Clinical trials. Studies conducted on human subjects to assess the therapeutic efficacy of an untested drug or other treatment.

Clozapine. An atypical neuroleptic that is used to treat schizophrenia, does not produce Parkinsonian side effects, and does not have a high affinity for D_2 receptors.

Cocaine. A potent catecholamine agonist and stimulant that is highly addictive.

Cocaine psychosis. Psychotic behavior observed during a cocaine spree, similar in many respects to paranoid schizophrenia.

Cochlea. The long, coiled tube in the inner ear that is filled with fluid and contains the organ of Corti and its auditory receptors.

Cocktail-party phenomenon. The ability to unconsciously monitor the contents of one conversation while consciously focusing on another.

Cocontraction. The simultaneous contraction of antagonistic muscles.

Codon. A group of three consecutive nucleotide bases on a DNA or messenger RNA strand; each codon specifies the particular amino acid that is to be added to an amino acid chain during protein synthesis.

Coexistence. The presence of more than one neurotransmitter in the same neuron.

Cognitive map theory. The theory that the main function of the hippocampus is to store memories of spatial location.

Cognitive neuroscience. A division of biopsychology that focuses on the use of functional brain imaging to study the neural bases of human cognition (complex mental processes such as thought, memory, attention, and perception).

Collateral sprouting. The growth of axon branches from mature neurons, usually to postsynaptic sites abandoned by adjacent axons that have degenerated.

Color constancy. The tendency of an object to appear the same color even when the wavelengths of light that it reflects change.

Commissurotomy. Surgical severing of the cerebral commissures.

Comparative approach. The study of biological processes by comparing different species—usually from the evolutionary perspective.

Complementary colors. Pairs of colors that produce white or gray when combined in equal measure; every color has a complementary color.

Completion. The visual system's automatic use of information obtained from receptors around the blind spot, or scotoma, to create a perception of the missing portion of the retinal image.

Complex cells. Neurons in the visual cortex that respond optimally to straight-edge stimuli in a certain orientation in any part of their receptive field.

Complex partial seizures. Seizures that are characterized by various complex psychological phenomena and are thought to result from temporal lobe discharges.

Component theory. The theory that the relative amount of activity produced in three different classes of cones by light determines its perceived color (also called *trichromatic theory*).

Computed tomography (CT). A computer-assisted X-ray procedure that can be used to visualize the brain and other internal structures of the living body.

Concussion. Disturbance of consciousness following a blow to the head with no cerebral bleeding or obvious structural damage.

Conditioned compensatory responses. Physiological responses opposite to the effects of a drug that are thought to be elicited by stimuli that are regularly associated with experiencing the drug effects.

Conditioned place-preference paradigm. A test that assesses a laboratory animal's preference for environments in which it has previously experienced drug effects.

Conditioned taste aversion. An avoidance response developed by animals to the taste of food whose consumption has been followed by illness.

Conduction aphasia. Aphasia that is thought to result from damage to the neural pathway between Broca's area and Wernicke's area.

Cones. The visual receptors in the retina that mediate high-acuity color vision in good lighting.

Congenital. Present at birth.

Conspecifics. Members of the same species.

Contralateral. Projecting from one side of the body to the other.

Contralateral neglect. A disturbance of the patient's ability to respond to visual, auditory, and somatosensory stimuli on the side of the body opposite to a site of brain damage, usually the left side of the body following damage to the right parietal lobe.

Contrast enhancement. The intensification of the perception of edges.

Contrast X-ray techniques. X-ray techniques that involve the injection into one compartment of the body a substance that absorbs X-rays either less than or more than the surrounding tissue.

Contrecoup injuries. Contusions that occur on the side of the brain opposite to the side of a blow.

"Control of behavior" versus "conscious perception" theory. The theory that the dorsal stream mediates behavioral interactions with objects in the absence of conscious awareness and the ventral stream mediates conscious perception of objects.

Contusions. Closed-head injuries that involve damage to the cerebral circulatory system, which produces internal hemorrhaging.

Convergent evolution. The evolution in unrelated species of similar solutions to the same environmental demands.

Convolutions. Folds on the surface of the cerebral hemispheres.

Convulsions. Motor seizures.

Copulation. Sexual intercourse.

Corpus callosum. The largest cerebral commissure.

Cranial nerves. The 12 pairs of nerves extending from the brain (e.g., the optic nerves, the olfactory nerves, and the vagus nerves).

Cross-cuing. Nonneural communication between hemispheres that have been separated by commissurotomy.

Cross section. Section cut at a right angle to any long, narrow structure of the CNS.

Cross tolerance. Tolerance to the effects of one drug that develops as the result of exposure to another drug that acts by the same mechanism.

Curare. A receptor blocker of cholinergic synapses that acts at nicotinic receptors and produces paralysis by blocking transmission at neuromuscular junctions.

Cytochrome oxidase. An enzyme present in particularly high concentrations in the mitochondria of dual-opponent color cells of the visual cortex.

Decorticate. Lacking a cortex.

Decussate. To cross over to the other side of the brain.

Deep dyslexia. A reading disorder in which the phonetic procedure is disrupted while the lexical procedure is not.

Defeminize. To suppress or disrupt female characteristics.

Delayed nonmatching-to-sample test. A test in which the subject is presented with an unfamiliar sample object and then, after a delay, is presented with a choice between the sample object and an unfamiliar object, where the correct choice is the unfamiliar object.

Delirium tremens (DTs). The phase of alcohol withdrawal syndrome characterized by hallucinations, delusions, agitation, confusion, hyperthermia, and tachycardia.

Delta waves. The largest and slowest EEG waves.

Demasculinize. To suppress or disrupt male characteristics.

Dementia. General intellectual deterioration.

Dendritic spines. Tiny nodules of various shapes that are located on the surfaces of many dendrites and are the sites of most excitatory synapses in the mature mammalian brain.

2-Deoxyglucose (2-DG). A substance similar to glucose that is taken up by active neurons in the brain and accumulates in them because, unlike glucose, it cannot be metabolized.

Deoxyribonucleic acid (DNA). The double-stranded, coiled molecule of genetic material; a chromosome.

Depolarize. To decrease the resting membrane potential.

Deprenyl. A monoamine agonist that has been shown to retard the development of Parkinson's disease.

Depressant. A drug that depresses neural activity.

Depression. A normal reaction to grievous loss; when depression is excessive, disruptive, and recurring, it is classified as a psychiatric disorder.

Dermatome. An area of the body that is innervated by the left and right dorsal roots of one segment of the spinal cord.

Desynchronized EEG. Low-amplitude, high-frequency EEG.

Detoxified addicts. Addicts who have none of the drug to which they are addicted in their body and who are no longer experiencing withdrawal symptoms.

Dextrals. Right-handers.

Diathesis. A genetic susceptibility to a disorder, as in the diathesis–stress model of depression.

Dichotic listening test. A test of language lateralization in which two different sequences of three spoken digits are presented simultaneously, one to each ear, and the subject is asked to report all of the digits heard.

Dichotomous traits. Traits that occur in one form or the other, never in combination.

Diencephalon. A major division of the mammalian brain, composed of the thalamus and the hypothalamus.

Diet-induced thermogenesis. The homeostasis-defending increases in body temperature that are associated with increases in body fat.

Digestion. The process by which food is broken down and absorbed through the lining of the gastrointestinal tract.

Digit span. The longest sequence of random digits that can be repeated correctly 50% of the time—most people have a digit span of 7.

Directed synapses. Synapses at which the site of neurotransmitter release and the site of neurotransmitter reception are in close proximity.

Distal segment. The segment of a cut axon between the cut and the axon terminals.

DNA-binding proteins. Proteins that bind to DNA molecules and in so doing either induce or block gene expression.

Dominant trait. The trait of a dichotomous pair that is expressed in the phenotypes of heterozygous individuals.

L-Dopa. The chemical precursor of dopamine, which is used in the treatment of Parkinson's disease.

Dopamine. One of the catecholamine neurotransmitters, which has been implicated in reward, Parkinson's disease, and schizophrenia.

Dorsal. Toward the surface of the back of a vertebrate or toward the top of the head.

Dorsal-column medial-lemniscus system. The division of the somatosensory system that ascends in the dorsal portion of the spinal white matter and carries signals related to touch and proprioception.

Dorsal columns. The somatosensory tracts that ascend in the dorsal portion of the spinal cord white matter.

Dorsal horns. The two dorsal arms of the spinal gray matter.

Dorsal stream. The group of visual pathways that flows from the primary visual cortex to the dorsal prestriate cortex to the posterior parietal cortex; according to one theory, its function is the control of visually guided behavior.

Dorsolateral corticorubrospinal tract. The descending motor tract that synapses in the red nucleus of the midbrain, decussates, and descends in the dorsolateral spinal white matter.

Dorsolateral corticospinal tract. The motor tract that leaves the primary motor cortex, descends to the medullary pyramids, decussates, and then descends in the contralateral dorsolateral spinal white matter.

Dorsolateral prefrontal association cortex. The area of the prefrontal association cortex that plays a role in the evaluation of external stimuli and the initiation of complex voluntary motor responses.

Down syndrome. A disorder associated with the presence of an extra chromosome 21, resulting in disfigurement and mental retardation.

Drug self-administration paradigm. A test of the addictive potential of drugs in which laboratory animals can inject drugs into themselves by pressing a lever.

Drug sensitization. An increase in the sensitivity to a drug effect that develops as the result of exposure to the drug.

Drug tolerance. A state of decreased sensitivity to a drug that develops as a result of exposure to the drug.

Dual-opponent color cells. Neurons that respond to the differences in the wavelengths of light stimulating adjacent areas of their receptive field.

Duodenum. The upper portion of the intestine through which most of the glucose and amino acids are absorbed into the bloodstream.

Duplexity theory. The theory that cones and rods mediate photopic and scotopic vision, respectively.

Dynamic contraction. Contraction of a muscle that causes the muscle to shorten.

Dynamic phase. The first phase of the VMH syndrome, characterized by grossly excessive eating and rapid weight gain.

Dyslexia. A pathological difficulty in reading, one that does not result from general visual, motor, or intellectual deficits.

EEG recording. A technique for recording moment-to-moment variations in the electrical potential between two areas in the brain via electrodes placed on the scalp.

Efferent nerves. Nerves that carry motor signals from the central nervous system to the skeletal muscles or internal organs.

Ejaculation. Ejection of sperm.

Electroconvulsive shock (ECS). An intense, brief, diffuse, seizure-inducing current administered to the brain via large electrodes attached to the scalp.

Electroencephalogram (EEG). A measure of the gross electrical activity of the brain, commonly recorded through scalp electrodes.

Electrolytic lesion. A lesion (an area of damage) created by passing an electric current through the tip of an electrode positioned in the brain.

Electromyogram (EMG). A measure of the electrical activity of muscles.

Electron microscopy. A neuroanatomical technique used to study the fine details of cellular structure.

Electrooculogram (EOG). A measure of eye movement.

Embolism. The blockage of blood flow in a smaller blood vessel by a plug that was formed in a larger blood vessel and carried by the bloodstream to the smaller one.

Emergent stage 1 EEG. All periods of stage 1 sleep EEG except initial stage 1; each is associated with REMs.

Encapsulated tumors. Tumors that grow within their own membrane.

Encéphale isolé preparation. An experimental preparation in which the brain is separated from the rest of the nervous system by a transection of the caudal brain stem.

Encephalitis. The inflammation associated with brain infection.

Endocrine glands. Ductless glands that release chemicals called hormones directly into the circulatory system.

Endogenous depression. Depression that occurs with no apparent cause.

Endorphins. Endogenous (internally produced) opiate analgesics.

Engram. A change in the brain that stores a memory.

Enzymatic degradation. The breakdown of chemicals by enzymes—one of the two mechanisms for deactivating released neurotransmitters.

Enzymes. Proteins that stimulate or inhibit biochemical reactions without being affected by them.

Epidemiology. The study of the factors that influence the distribution of a disease in the general population.

Epilepsy. A neurological disorder characterized by spontaneously recurring seizures.

Epileptic auras. Psychological symptoms that precede the onset of a convulsion.

Epinephrine. One of the catecholamine neurotransmitters.

Episodic memories. Explicit memories for the particular events and experiences of one's life.

Estradiol. The most common estrogen.

Estrogens. The class of steroid hormones that are released in large amounts by the ovaries; an example is estradiol.

Estrous cycle. The cycle of sexual receptivity displayed by many female mammals.

Estrus. The portion of the estrous cycle characterized by proceptivity, sexual receptivity, and fertility (*estrus* is a noun and *estrous* an adjective).

Ethology. The study of the behavior of animals in their natural environments.

Evolutionary perspective. The approach that focuses on the environmental pressures that likely led to the evolution of the characteristics (e.g., of brain and behavior) of current species.

Evolve. To undergo gradual orderly change.

Excitatory postsynaptic potentials (EPSPs). Graded postsynaptic depolarizations, which increase the likelihood that an action potential will be generated.

Exocrine glands. Glands that release chemicals into ducts that carry them to targets, mostly on the surface of the body.

Exocytosis. The process of releasing a neurotransmitter.

Explicit memories. Conscious memories.

Expressive. Pertaining to the generation of language; that is, pertaining to writing or talking.

Extensors. Muscles that act to straighten or extend a joint.

Fasciculation. The tendency of developing axons to grow along the paths established by preceding axons.

Fasting phase. The metabolic phase that begins when energy from the preceding meal is no longer sufficient to meet the immediate needs of the body and during which energy is extracted from fat and glycogen stores.

Fear conditioning. Establishing fear of a previously neutral conditional stimulus by pairing it with an aversive unconditional stimulus.

Feminize. To enhance or produce female characteristics.

Fetal alcohol syndrome (FAS). A syndrome produced by prenatal exposure to alcohol and characterized by brain damage, mental retardation, poor coordination, poor muscle tone, low birth weight, retarded growth, and/or physical deformity.

Fissures. The large furrows between gyri on the cortical surface.

Fitness. According to Darwin, the ability of an organism to survive and contribute its genes to the next generation.

Flavor. The combined impression of taste and smell.

Flexors. Muscles that act to bend or flex a joint.

Follicle-stimulating hormone (FSH). The gonadotropic hormone that stimulates development of ovarian follicles.

Fornix. The major tract of the limbic system; it runs from the hippocampus to the septum.

Fovea. The central indentation of the retina, which is specialized for high-acuity vision.

Fraternal twins. Twins that develop from different zygotes and thus are no more similar than any pair of siblings; dizygotic twins.

Free fatty acids. The main source of the body's energy during the fasting phase; released from adipose tissue in response to high levels of glucagon.

Free nerve endings. Neuron endings that lack specialized structures on them and that detect cutaneous pain and changes in temperature.

Free-running period. The duration of one cycle of a free-running rhythm.

Free-running rhythms. Circadian rhythms that do not depend on environmental cues to keep them on a regular schedule.

Frontal lobe. The large lobe at the front of each cerebral hemisphere.

Frontal operculum. The area of prefrontal cortex that in the left hemisphere is the location of Broca's area.

Frontal sections. Any slices of brain tissue cut in a plane that is parallel to the face; also termed *coronal sections*.

Functional MRI (fMRI). A magnetic resonance imaging technique for inferring brain activity by measuring increased oxygen flow into particular areas.

Functional segregation. Organization into different areas, each of which performs a different function; for example, in sensory systems, different areas of secondary and association cortex analyze different aspects of the same sensory stimulus.

Functional tolerance. Tolerance resulting from a reduction in the reactivity of the nervous system (or other sites of action) to a drug.

Gametes. Egg cells and sperm cells.

Gamma-aminobutyric acid (GABA). An amino acid neurotransmitter; the most prevalent inhibitory neurotransmitter in the mammalian brain.

Ganglia. Clusters of neuronal cell bodies in the peripheral nervous system (singular *ganglion*).

Gastric ulcers. Painful lesions to the lining of the stomach or duodenum.

Gate-control theory. The theory that signals descending from the brain can activate neural gating circuits in the spinal cord to block incoming pain signals.

Gene. A unit of inheritance; for example, the section of a chromosome that controls the synthesis of one protein.

Gene expression. The production of the protein specified by a particular gene.

Gene knockout techniques. Procedures for creating organisms that lack a particular gene.

Gene replacement techniques. Procedures for creating organisms in which a particular gene has been replaced with another.

General paresis. The insanity and intellectual deterioration resulting from syphilitic infection.

Generalized anxiety disorders. Anxiety disorders that are not precipitated by any obvious event.

Generalized seizures. Seizures that involve the entire brain.

Genitals. The external reproductive organs.

Genotype. The traits that an organism can pass on to its offspring through its genetic material.

Glia-mediated migration. One of two major modes of neural migration during development, by which immature neurons move out from the central canal along radial glial cells.

Glial cells. Several classes of nonneural cells of the nervous system, whose important contributions to nervous system function are just starting to be understood.

Global aphasia. Severe disruption of all language-related abilities.

Globus pallidus. One of the basal ganglia.

Glucagon. A pancreatic hormone that promotes the release of free fatty acids from adipose tissue, their conversion to ketones, and the use of both as sources of energy.

Glucocorticoids. Steroid hormones that are released from the adrenal cortex in response to stressors.

Gluconeogenesis. The process by which protein is converted to glucose.

Glucose. A simple sugar that is the breakdown product of complex carbohydrates; it is the body's primary, directly utilizable source of energy.

Glucostatic theory. The theory that eating is controlled by deviations from a hypothetical blood glucose set point.

Glutamate. The brain's most prevalent excitatory neurotransmitter, whose excessive release causes much of the brain damage resulting from cerebral ischemia.

Glycine. One of the amino acid neurotransmitters.

Golgi complex. Structures in the cell bodies and terminal buttons of neurons that package neurotransmitters and other molecules in vesicles.

Golgi stain. A neural stain that completely darkens a few of the neurons in each slice of tissue, thereby revealing their silhouettes.

Golgi tendon organs. Receptors that are embedded in tendons and are sensitive to the amount of tension in the skeletal muscles to which their tendons are attached.

Gonadectomy. The surgical removal of the gonads (testes or ovaries); castration.

Gonadotropin. The pituitary tropic hormone that stimulates the release of hormones from the gonads.

Gonadotropin-releasing hormone. The hypothalamic releasing hormone that controls the release of the two gonadotropic hormones from the anterior pituitary.

Gonads. The testes and the ovaries.

Graded responses. Responses whose magnitude is indicative of the magnitude of the stimuli that induce them.

Grammatical analysis. Analysis of the structure of language.

Grand mal seizure. A seizure whose symptoms are loss of consciousness, loss of equilibrium, and a violent tonic-clonic convulsion.

Growth cone. Amoebalike structure at the tip of each growing axon or dendrite that guides growth to the appropriate target.

Growth hormone. The anterior pituitary hormone that acts directly on bone and muscle tissue to produce the pubertal growth spurt.

Gyri. Ridges between the fissures on the cortical surface.

Hair cells. The receptors of the auditory system.

Haloperidol. A butyrophenone that was used as an antischizophrenic drug.

Harrison Narcotics Act. The act, passed in 1914, that made it illegal to sell or use opium, morphine, or cocaine in the United States.

Health psychology. An area of research that focuses on the effects of psychological factors on physical health.

Helping-hand phenomenon. The redirection of one hand of a split-brain patient by the other hand.

Hematoma. A bruise.

Hemianopsic. Having a scotoma that covers half of the visual field.

Hemispherectomy. The removal of one cerebral hemisphere.

Heritability estimate. A numerical estimate of the proportion of variability in a particular trait that occurred in a particular study and that resulted from the genetic variation among the subjects in that study.

Heroin. A powerful semisynthetic opiate.

Heschl's gyrus. The temporal lobe gyrus that is the location of primary auditory cortex.

Heterosexual. Sexually attracted to members of the other sex.

Heterozygous. Possessing two different genes for a particular trait.

Hierarchical organization. Organization into a series of levels that can be ranked with respect to one another; for example, primary cortex, secondary cortex, and association cortex perform progressively more detailed analyses.

Hippocampus. A structure of the medial temporal lobes that plays a role in memory for spatial location.

Homeostasis. The stability of an organism's constant internal environment.

Hominids. The family of primates that includes *Homo sapiens* (humans), *Homo erectus*, and *Australopithecus*.

Homologous. Having a similar structure because of a common evolutionary origin (e.g., a human's arm and a bird's wing are homologous).

Homosexual. Sexually attracted to members of the same sex.

Homozygous. Possessing two identical genes for a particular trait.

Horizontal cells. Type of retinal neurons whose specialized function is lateral communication.

Horizontal sections. Any slices of brain tissue cut in a plane that is parallel to the top of the brain.

Hormones. Chemicals released by the endocrine system directly into the circulatory system.

Human genome project. The international research effort to construct a detailed map of the human chromosomes.

Huntington's disease. A progressive terminal disorder of motor and intellectual function that is produced in adulthood by a dominant gene.

H-Y antigen. The protein that stimulates the cells of the medullary portion of the primordial gonads to proliferate and develop into testes.

Hyperphagia. Excessive eating.

Hyperpolarize. To increase the resting membrane potential.

Hypersomnia. Disorders characterized by excessive sleep or sleepiness.

Hypnagogic hallucinations. Dreamlike experiences that occur during wakefulness.

Hypnotic drugs. Sleep-promoting drugs.

Hypothalamopituitary portal system. The vascular network that carries hormones from the hypothalamus to the anterior pituitary.

Hypothalamus. A diencephalic structure of the limbic system; it controls the pituitary gland and plays a major role in motivated behavior.

Hypoxia. Shortage of oxygen supply to tissue—for example, to the brain.

Iatrogenic. Physician-created.

Identical twins. Twins that develop from the same zygote and are thus genetically identical; monozygotic twins.

Imipramine. The first tricyclic antidepressant drug.

Immune system. The system that protects the body against infectious micro-organisms.

Implicit memories. Memories that are expressed by improved performance without conscious recall or recognition.

Impotent. Unable to achieve a penile erection.

Incentive-sensitization theory. Theory that addictions develop when drug use sensitizes the neural circuits mediating wanting of the drug—not necessarily liking for the drug.

Incomplete-pictures test. A test of memory measuring the improved ability to identify fragmented figures that have been previously observed.

Indolamines. A subclass of monoamines that includes only one neurotransmitter, serotonin.

Inferior. Toward the bottom of the primate head or brain.

Inferior colliculi. The structures of the tectum that receive auditory input from the superior olives.

Inferotemporal cortex. The cortex of the inferior temporal lobe, in which is located an area of secondary visual cortex that is involved in object recognition.

Infiltrating tumors. Tumors that grow diffusely through surrounding tissue.

Inhibitory postsynaptic potentials (IPSPs). Graded postsynaptic hyperpolarizations, which decrease the likelihood that an action potential will be generated.

Initial stage 1 EEG. The period of the stage 1 EEG that occurs at the onset of sleep; it is not associated with REM.

Inside-out pattern. The pattern of cortical development in which orderly waves of tangential migrations progress systematically from deeper to more superficial layers.

Insomnia. Disorders of initiating and maintaining sleep.

Instinctive behaviors. Behaviors that occur in all like members of a species, even when there seems to have been no opportunity for them to have been learned.

Insulin. A pancreatic hormone that facilitates the entry of glucose into cells and the conversion of bloodborne fuels to forms that can be stored.

Interneurons. Neurons with short axons or no axons at all, whose function is to integrate neural activity within a single brain structure.

Intrafusal motor neuron. A motor neuron that innervates an intrafusal muscle.

Intrafusal muscle. A threadlike muscle that adjusts the tension on a muscle spindle.

Intromission. Insertion of the penis into the vagina.

Ion channels. Pores in neural membranes through which specific ions pass.

Ionotropic receptors. Receptors that are associated with ligand-activated ion channels.

Ions. Positively or negatively charged particles.

Iproniazid. The first antidepressant drug; a monoamine oxidase inhibitor.

Ipsilateral. On the same side of the body.

Isometric contraction. Contraction of a muscle that increases the force of its pull but does not shorten the muscle.

James-Lange theory. The theory that emotional experience results from the brain's perception of the pattern of autonomic and somatic nervous system responses elicited by emotion-inducing sensory stimuli.

Jet lag. The adverse effects on body function of the acceleration of zeitgebers during east-bound flights or their deceleration during west-bound flights.

Ketones. Breakdown products of free fatty acids that are used by muscles as a source of energy during the fasting phase.

Kluver-Bucy syndrome. The syndrome of behavioral changes (e.g., lack of fear and hypersexuality) that is induced in primates by bilateral damage to the anterior temporal lobes.

Korsakoff's syndrome. A neuropsychological disorder that is common in alcoholics and whose primary symptom is severe memory loss.

Lateral. Away from the midline of the body of a vertebrate, toward the body's lateral surfaces.

Lateral fissure. The major fissure, or furrow, of the lateral surface of the human cortex; it is the superior boundary of the temporal lobe.

Lateral geniculate nuclei. The six-layered thalamic structures that receive input from the retinas and transmit their output to the primary visual cortex.

Lateral hypothalamus (LH). The area of the hypothalamus once thought to be the feeding center.

Lateral inhibition. Inhibition of adjacent neurons or receptors in a topographic array.

Lateralization of function. The unequal representation of various psychological functions in the two hemispheres of the brain.

Leaky-barrel model. A settling-point model of body-fat regulation.

Learning. The brain's ability to change in response to experience.

Leptin. A protein normally synthesized in fat cells; it is thought to act as a negative feedback fat signal, reducing consumption.

Lesion methods. Methods of studying brain function by destroying specific brain structures and assessing the effects of the damage; brain lesions can be made by electric current, by aspiration (suction), or by knife cuts.

Lexical procedure. A procedure for reading aloud that is based on specific stored information acquired about written words.

Ligand. A molecule that binds to another molecule; neurotransmitters are ligands of their receptors.

Limbic system. A collection of interconnected nuclei and tracts that borders the thalamus and is widely assumed to play a role in emotion.

Lipids. Fats.

Lipogenesis. The production of body fat.

Lipolysis. The breakdown of body fat.

Lipostatic theory. The theory that eating is controlled by deviations from a hypothetical body-fat set point.

Lithium. A metallic ion that is used in the treatment of bipolar affective disorder.

Lobectomy. An operation in which a lobe, or a major part of one, is removed from the brain.

Lobotomy. An operation in which a lobe, or a major part of one, is separated from the rest of the brain by a large cut but is not removed.

Longitudinal fissure. The large fissure, or furrow, that separates the left and right hemispheres.

Long-term memories. The type of memories that are lasting, that persist even after the person stops thinking about them.

Long-term potentiation (LTP). The enduring facilitation of synaptic transmission that occurs following activation of synapses by high-intensity, high-frequency stimulation of the presynaptic neurons.

Lordosis. The arched-back, rump-up, tail-to-the-side posture of female rodent sexual receptivity, which serves to facilitate intromission.

Luteinizing hormone (LH). The gonadotropic hormone that causes the developing ovum to be released from its follicle.

Lymphocytes. Specialized white blood cells that are produced in bone marrow and play important roles in the body's immune reactions.

Macrophage. A large phagocyte that plays a role in cell-mediated immunity.

Magnetic resonance imaging (MRI). A procedure in which high-resolution images of the structures of the living brain are constructed from the measurement of waves that hydrogen atoms emit when they are activated by radio-frequency waves in a magnetic field.

Magnocellular layers. The layers of the lateral geniculate nuclei that are composed of neurons with large cell bodies; the bottom two layers (also called *M layers*).

Malignant tumors. Tumors that may continue to grow in the body even after attempted surgical removal.

Mammals. Species whose young are fed from mammary glands.

Mammillary bodies. Two bumps visible on the inferior surface of the mammalian forebrain, just behind the hypothalamus; they are components of the limbic system.

Mania. An affective disorder in which the patient is overconfident, impulsive, distractible, and highly energetic.

MAO inhibitors. Antidepressant drugs that increase the level of monoamine neurotransmitters by inhibiting the action of monoamine oxidase.

Masculinize. To enhance or produce male characteristics.

Massa intermedia. The structure that is located in the third ventricle and connects the two lobes of the thalamus.

Medial. Toward the midline of the body of a vertebrate.

Medial diencephalic amnesia. Amnesia that is associated with damage to the medial diencephalon (e.g., Korsakoff's amnesia).

Medial dorsal nuclei. The thalamic relay nuclei of the olfactory system.

Medial geniculate nuclei. The auditory thalamic nuclei that receive input from the inferior colliculi and project to primary auditory cortex.

Medial lemniscus. The somatosensory pathway between the dorsal column nuclei and the ventral posterior nucleus of the thalamus.

Medial preoptic area. The area of the hypothalamus that includes the sexually dimorphic nuclei and that plays a key role in the control of male sexual behavior.

Medial temporal lobe amnesia. Amnesia associated with bilateral damage to the medial temporal lobes; its major feature is anterograde amnesia for explicit memories in combination with preserved intellectual functioning.

Mediodorsal nuclei. A pair of medial diencephalic nuclei in the thalamus, damage to which is thought to be responsible for many of the memory deficits associated with Korsakoff's syndrome.

Meiosis. The process of cell division that produces cells (e.g., egg cells and sperm cells) with half the chromosomes of the parent cell.

Melatonin. A hormone that is synthesized from serotonin in the pineal gland and influences the circadian rhythm of sleep.

Membrane potential. The difference in electrical charge between the inside and the outside of a cell.

Memory. The brain's ability to store and access the learned effects of experiences.

Memory consolidation. The transfer of short-term memories to long-term storage.

Meninges. The three protective membranes that cover the brain and spinal cord (singular *meninx*).

Meningiomas. Tumors that grow between the meninges.

Meningitis. Inflammation of the meninges, usually caused by bacterial infection.

Menstrual cycle. The hormone-regulated cycle in women of follicle growth, egg release, buildup of the uterus lining, and menstruation.

Mesencephalon. The midbrain.

Messenger RNA. A strand of RNA that is transcribed from DNA and carries the genetic code out of the cell nucleus to direct the synthesis of a protein.

Metabolic tolerance. Tolerance that results from a reduction in the amount of a drug getting to its sites of action.

Metabotropic receptors. Receptors that are associated with signal proteins and G proteins.

Metastatic tumors. Tumors that originate in one organ and spread to another.

Metencephalon. The division of the brain that includes the cerebellum and the pons.

Microelectrodes. Extremely fine recording electrodes, which are used for intracellular recording.

Microglia. Glial cells that respond to injury or disease by engulfing cellular debris and triggering inflammatory responses.

Microsleeps. Brief periods of sleep that occur in sleep-deprived subjects while they remain sitting or standing.

Migration. The movement of cells from their site of creation in the ventricular zone of the neural tube to their ultimate location in the mature nervous system.

Mitosis. The process of cell division that produces cells with the same number of chromosomes as the parent cell.

Monoamines. Small-molecule neurotransmitters that are synthesized from a single amino acid; they are of two types, catecholamines and indolamines.

Monocular. Involving only one eye.

Monophasic sleep cycles. Sleep cycles that regularly involve only one period of sleep per day, typically at night.

Mood stabilizer. A drug that blocks the rapid transition between depression and mania.

Morphine. The major psychoactive ingredient in opium.

Morris water maze test. A widely used test of spatial memory in which rats must learn to swim directly to a platform hidden just beneath the surface of a circular pool of murky water.

Motor end-plate. The receptive area on a muscle fiber at a neuromuscular junction.

Motor equivalence. The ability of the sensorimotor system to carry out the same basic movement in different ways that involve different muscles.

Motor homunculus. The somatotopic map of the human primary motor cortex.

Motor pool. All of the motor neurons that innervate the fibers of a given muscle.

Motor unit. A single motor neuron and all of the skeletal muscle fibers that are innervated by it.

MPTP. A neurotoxin that produces a disorder in primates that is similar to Parkinson's disease.

Müllerian-inhibiting substance. The testicular hormone that causes the precursor of the female reproductive ducts (the Müllerian system) to degenerate and the testes to descend.

Müllerian system. The embryonic precursor of the female reproductive ducts.

Multiple sclerosis (MS). A progressive disease that attacks the myelin of axons in the CNS.

Multipolar neuron. A neuron with more than two processes extending from its cell body.

Multipotent. Capable of developing into a limited number of types of mature body cell.

Mumby box. An apparatus that is used in a rat version of the delayed nonmatching-to-sample test.

Muscle spindles. Receptors that are embedded in skeletal muscle tissue and are sensitive to changes in muscle length.

Mutations. Accidental alterations in individual genes that arise during chromosome duplication.

Myelencephalon (medulla). The major division of the brain adjacent to the spinal cord.

Narcolepsy. A disorder in the hypersomnia category that is characterized by repeated, brief daytime sleep attacks and cataplexy.

Narcotic. A legal category of drugs, mostly opiates.

Nasal hemiretina. The half of each retina next to the nose.

Natural selection. The idea that heritable traits that are associated with high rates of survival and reproduction are preferentially passed on to future generations.

Nature–nurture issue. The debate about the relative contributions of nature (genes) and nurture (experience) to the behavioral capacities of individuals.

Necrosis. Passive cell death, which is characterized by inflammation.

Negative feedback mechanisms. Systems in which feedback from changes in one direction elicit compensatory effects in the opposite direction.

Neocortex. Six-layered cortex of recent evolutionary origin; most human cortex is neocortex.

Nerve growth factor (NGF). A neurotrophin that attracts the growing axons of the sympathetic nervous system and promotes their survival.

Nerves. Bundles of axons in the peripheral nervous system.

Neural plate. A small patch of ectodermal tissue on the dorsal surface of the vertebrate embryo, from which the neural groove, the neural tube, and, ultimately, the mature nervous system develop.

Neural proliferation. The rapid increase in the number of neurons that follows the formation of the neural tube.

Neural regeneration. The regrowth of damaged neurons.

Neural tube. The tube that is formed in the vertebrate embryo when the edges of the neural groove fuse and that develops into the central nervous system.

Neuroanatomy. The study of the structure of the nervous system.

Neurochemistry. The study of the chemical bases of neural activity.

Neuroendocrinology. The study of the interactions between the nervous system and the endocrine system.

Neurogenesis. The growth of new neurons.

Neuroleptics. Drugs that alleviate schizophrenic symptoms.

Neuromuscular junctions. The synapses of a motor neuron on a muscle.

Neurons. Cells of the nervous system that are specialized for receiving and transmitting electrochemical signals.

Neuropathology. The study of nervous system disorders.

Neuropeptides. Large-molecule neurotransmitters that are composed of chains of amino acids.

Neuropharmacology. The study of the effects of drugs on neural activity.

Neurophysiology. The study of the functions and activities of the nervous system.

Neuroscience. The scientific study of the nervous system.

Neurotoxins. Neural poisons.

Neurotrophins. Chemicals that are supplied to developing neurons by their targets and that promote their survival.

Nigrostriatal pathway. The pathway along which axons from the substantia nigra project to the striatum.

Nissl stain. A neural stain that has an affinity for structures in neuron cell bodies.

Nitric oxide. A soluble-gas neurotransmitter that is thought to serve as a signal from postsynaptic neurons to presynaptic neurons in the maintenance of LTP.

NMDA (N-methyl-D-aspartate) receptors. Glutamate receptors that play key roles in the development of stroke-induced brain damage and long-term potentiation at glutaminergic synapses.

Nocturnal myoclonus. Periodic sleep-disrupting twitching of body, usually the legs, during sleep.

Nodes of Ranvier. The gaps between adjacent myelin segments on an axon.

Nondirected synapses. Synapses at which the site of neurotransmitter release and the site of neurotransmitter reception are not close together.

Norepinephrine. One of the catecholamine neurotransmitters; it is released by noradrenergic neurons.

Nuclei. The DNA-containing structures of cells; also, clusters of neuronal cell bodies in the central nervous system (singular *nucleus*).

Nucleotide bases. A class of chemical substances that includes adenine, thymine, guanine, and cytosine—the constituents of the genetic code.

Nucleus accumbens. Nucleus of the ventral striatum and a major terminal of the mesocorticolimbic dopamine pathway.

Nucleus magnocellularis. The nucleus of the caudal reticular formation that promotes relaxation of the core muscles during REM sleep and during cataplectic attacks.

Nutritive density. Calories per unit volume of a food.

Ob/ob mice. Mice that are homozygous for the mutant ob gene; their body fat produces no leptin, and they become very obese.

Obsessive-compulsive disorders. Anxiety disorders characterized by recurring uncontrollable, anxiety-producing thoughts and impulses.

Occipital lobe. The lobe at the back of the cerebral hemispheres; in humans, its functions are entirely visual.

Off-center cells. Visual neurons that respond to lights shone in the center of their receptive fields with "off" firing and to lights shone in the periphery of their fields with "on" firing.

Olfactory bulbs. The first cranial nerves, whose output goes primarily to the amygdala and piriform cortex.

Olfactory mucosa. The mucous membrane that lines the upper nasal passages and contains the olfactory receptor cells.

Oligodendrocytes. Glial cells that myelinate axons of the central nervous system; also known as *oligodendroglia*.

Ommatidia. The visual receptors of the horseshoe crab.

On-center cells. Visual neurons that respond to lights shone in the center of their receptive fields with "on" firing and to lights shone in the periphery of their fields with "off" firing.

Operator genes. Short segments of DNA that determine whether or not messenger RNA will be transcribed from associated structural genes.

Opiates. Morphine, codeine, heroin, and other chemicals with similar structures or effects.

Opponent-process theory. The theory that a visual receptor or a neuron signals one color when it responds in one way (e.g., by increasing its firing rate) and signals its complementary color when it responds in the opposite way (e.g., by decreasing its firing rate).

Optic chiasm. The X-shaped structure on the inferior surface of the cerebral hemispheres; it is the decussation of the optic nerves.

Optic tectum. The main destination of retinal ganglion cells in lower vertebrates.

Orbitofrontal cortex. The cortex of the inferior frontal lobes, which receives olfactory input from the thalamus.

Orchidectomy. The removal of the testes.

Orexin. A neuropeptide that has been implicated in narcolepsy in dogs and in knockout mice.

Organ of Corti. The auditory receptor organ, comprising the basilar membrane, the hair cells, and the tectorial membrane.

Ossicles. The three small bones of the middle ear: the malleus, the incus, and the stapes.

Oval window. The membrane that transfers vibrations from the ossicles to the fluid of the cochlea.

Ovariectomy. The removal of the ovaries.

Ovaries. The female gonads.

Oxytocin. One of the two major peptide hormones of the posterior pituitary, which in females stimulates contractions of the uterus during labor and the ejection of milk during suckling.

Pacinian corpuscles. The largest and most deeply positioned cutaneous receptors, which are sensitive to sudden displacements of the skin.

Panic disorders. Anxiety disorders characterized by recurring rapid-onset attacks of extreme fear and severe symptoms of stress (choking, heart palpitations, and shortness of breath).

Parallel processing. The simultaneous analysis of a signal in different ways by the multiple parallel pathways of a neural network.

Parasympathetic nerves. Those motor nerves of the autonomic nervous system that project from the brain (as components of cranial nerves) or from the sacral region of the spinal cord.

Paraventricular nuclei. Hypothalamic nuclei that play a role in eating and synthesize hormones released by the posterior pituitary.

Parietal lobe. The lobe on the dorsal surface of each cerebral hemisphere; it is located between the lateral, central, and longitudinal fissures.

Parkinson's disease. A movement disorder that is associated with degeneration of dopaminergic neurons in the nigrostriatal pathway.

Partial seizures. Seizures that do not involve the entire brain.

Parvocellular layers. The layers of the lateral geniculate nuclei that are composed of neurons with small cell bodies; the top four layers (also called *P layers*).

Peptide hormones. Hormones that are short chains of amino acids.

Peptides. Short chains of amino acids, some of which function as neurotransmitters.

Perception. The higher-order process of integrating, recognizing, and interpreting complex patterns of sensations.

Periaqueductal gray (PAG). The gray matter around the cerebral aqueduct, which contains opiate receptors and activates a descending analgesia circuit.

Perimetry test. The procedure used to map scotomas.

Peripheral nervous system (PNS). The portion of the nervous system outside the skull and spine.

Perseveration. The tendency to continue making a formerly correct response that is currently incorrect.

Petit mal seizure. A generalized seizure that is characterized by a disruption of consciousness and a 3-per-second spike-and-wave EEG discharge.

Phagocytosis. The consumption and destruction of dead tissue and foreign micro-organisms by specialized body cells (phagocytes).

Phantom limb. The vivid perception that an amputated limb still exists.

Pharmacological. Involving drugs; pharmacological methods of studying the brain involve administering drugs that either increase or decrease the effects of particular neurotransmitters.

Phenothiazines. A class of antischizophrenic drugs that bind effectively to both D_1 and D_2 receptors.

Phenotype. An organism's observable traits.

Pheromones. Chemicals that are released by an animal and elicit through their odor specific patterns of behavior in its conspecifics.

Phobic anxiety disorders. Anxiety disorders characterized by extreme, largely irrational fears of specific objects or situations.

Phonemes. Individual speech sounds.

Phonetic procedure. A procedure for reading aloud that involves the recognition of letters and the application of a language's rules of pronunciation.

Phonological analysis. Analysis of the sound of language.

Photopic spectral sensitivity curve. The graph of the sensitivity of cone-mediated vision to different wavelengths of light.

Photopic vision. Cone-mediated vision, which predominates when lighting is good.

Physical-dependence theories of addiction. Theories holding that the main factor that motivates drug addicts to keep taking drugs is the prevention or termination of withdrawal symptoms.

Physically dependent. Being in a state in which the discontinuation of drug taking will induce withdrawal reactions.

Pineal gland. The endocrine gland that is the human body's sole source of melatonin.

Pioneer growth cones. The first growth cones to travel along a particular route in the developing nervous system.

Piriform cortex. An area of medial temporal cortex that is adjacent to the amygdala and that receives direct olfactory input.

Pituitary gland. The gland that is suspended from the hypothalamus.

Pituitary stalk. The structure connecting the hypothalamus and the pituitary gland.

Place cells. Neurons that develop place fields—that is, that respond only when the subject is in a particular place in a familiar test environment.

Planum temporale. An area of temporal lobe cortex that lies in the posterior region of the lateral fissure and, in the left hemisphere, roughly corresponds to Wernicke's area.

Polyphasic sleep cycles. Sleep cycles that regularly involve more than one period of sleep per day.

Pons. The bulge on the ventral surface of the metencephalon.

Positive-incentive theory. The idea that behaviors (e.g., eating and drinking) are motivated by their anticipated pleasurable effects.

Positive-incentive theories of addiction. Theories holding that the primary factor in most cases of addiction is a craving for the pleasure-producing properties of drugs.

Positive-incentive value. The anticipated pleasure involved in the performance of a particular behavior, such as eating a particular food or drinking a particular beverage.

Positron emission tomography (PET). A technique for visualizing brain activity, usually by measuring the accumulation of radioactive 2-deoxyglucose (2-DG) or radioactive water in the various areas of the brain.

Postcentral gyri. The gyri located just behind the central fissures.

Posterior. Toward the tail end of a vertebrate or toward the back of the head.

Posterior parietal (association) cortex. An area of association cortex that receives input from the visual, auditory, and somatosensory systems and is involved in the perception of spatial location and guidance of voluntary behavior.

Posterior pituitary. The part of the pituitary gland that contains the terminals of hypothalamic neurons.

Posttraumatic amnesia (PTA). Amnesia produced by a nonpenetrating head injury (a blow to the head that does not penetrate the skull).

Posttraumatic stress disorder. An anxiety disorder exhibited as a persistent pattern of psychological distress that follows a period of exposure to extreme stress.

Precentral gyri. The gyri located just in front of the central fissures.

Prefrontal cortex. The portion of the frontal cortex in front of the motor cortex; the last part of the human brain to reach maturity.

Premotor cortex. The area of secondary motor cortex that lies between the supplementary motor area and the lateral fissure.

Prestriate cortex. The band of tissue in the occipital lobe that surrounds the primary visual cortex and contains areas of secondary visual cortex.

Primary motor cortex. The cortex of the precentral gyrus, which is the major point of departure for motor signals descending from the cerebral cortex into lower levels of the sensorimotor system.

Primary sensory cortex. An area of sensory cortex that receives most of its input directly from the thalamic relay nuclei of one sensory system.

Primary visual cortex. The area of the cortex that receives direct input from the lateral geniculate nuclei (also called *striate cortex*).

Primates. One of 14 different orders of mammals; there are five families of primates: prosimians, New-World monkeys, Old-World monkeys, apes, and hominids.

Proceptive behaviors. Behaviors that solicit the sexual advances of members of the other sex.

Progesterone. A progestin that prepares the uterus and breasts for pregnancy.

Progestins. The class of steroid hormones that includes progesterone.

Prosopagnosia. Visual agnosia for faces.

Protein hormones. Hormones that are long chains of amino acids.

Proteins. Long chains of amino acids.

Proximal segment. The segment of a cut axon between the cut and the cell body.

Prozac. The trade name of fluoxetine, the first selective serotonin-reuptake inhibitor developed for treating depression.

Psychiatric disorder. A disorder of psychological function sufficiently severe to require treatment by a psychiatrist or clinical psychologist.

Psychoactive drugs. Drugs that influence subjective experience and behavior by acting on the nervous system.

Psychoneuroimmunology. The study of interactions among psychological factors, the nervous system, and the immune system.

Pulsatile hormone release. The typical pattern of hormone release, which occurs in large surges several times a day.

Punch-drunk syndrome. The dementia and cerebral scarring that result from repeated concussions.

Purkinje effect. In intense light, red and yellow wavelengths look brighter than blue or green wavelengths of equal intensity; in dim light, blue and green wavelengths look brighter than red and yellow wavelengths of equal intensity.

Putamen. One of the basal ganglia; a part of the striatum.

Pyramidal cell layer. The major layer of cell bodies in the hippocampus.

Pyramidal cells. Large multipolar cortical neurons with a pyramid-shaped cell body, an apical dendrite, and a very long axon.

Radial arm maze test. A widely used test of rats' spatial ability in which the same arms of a maze are baited on each trial, and the rats must learn to visit only the baited arms only one time on each trial.

Radial glial cells. Glial cells that exist in the neural tube only during the period of neural migration and that form a network along which radial migration occurs.

Radial migration. Movement of cells in the developing neural tube from the ventricular zone in a straight line outward toward the tube's outer wall.

Reactive depression. Depression that is triggered by a negative experience.

Receptive. Pertaining to the comprehension of language and speech.

Receptive field. The area of the visual field within which it is possible for the appropriate stimulus to influence the firing of a visual neuron.

Receptor blockers. Antagonistic drugs that bind to postsynaptic receptors without activating them and block the access of the usual neurotransmitter.

Receptor subtypes. The different types of receptors to which a particular neurotransmitter can bind.

Receptors. Cells that are specialized to receive chemical, mechanical, or radiant signals from the environment; also proteins that contain binding sites for particular neurotransmitters.

Recessive trait. The trait of a dichotomous pair that is not expressed in the phenotype of heterozygous individuals.

Reciprocal innervation. The principle of spinal cord circuitry that causes a muscle to automatically relax when a muscle that is antagonistic to it contracts.

Recuperation theories of sleep. Theories based on the premise that being awake disturbs the body's homeostasis and the function of sleep is to restore it.

Recurrent collateral inhibition. The inhibition of a neuron that is produced by its own activity via a collateral branch of its axon and an inhibitory interneuron.

Red nucleus. A motor nucleus of the mesencephalon.

Reference memory. Memory for the general principles and skills that are required to perform a task.

Relative refractory period. A period after the absolute refractory period during which a higher-than-normal amount of stimulation is necessary to make a neuron fire.

Releasing hormones. Hypothalamic hormones that stimulate the release of hormones from the anterior pituitary.

REM sleep. The stage of sleep characterized by rapid eye movements, loss of core muscle tone, and emergent stage 1 EEG.

Repetition priming tests. Tests of implicit memory; in one example, a list of words is presented, then fragments of the original words are presented and the subject is asked to complete them.

Replacement injections. Injections of a hormone whose natural release has been curtailed by the removal of the gland that normally releases it.

Replication. The process by which the DNA molecule duplicates itself.

Reserpine. The first monoamine antagonist to be used in the treatment of schizophrenia; the active ingredient of the snakeroot plant.

Response-chunking hypothesis. The idea that practice combines the central sensorimotor programs that control individual responses into programs that control sequences of responses (chunks of behavior).

Resting potential. The steady membrane potential of a neuron at rest, usually about −70 mV.

Restless legs. Tension or uneasiness in the legs that keeps people from falling asleep.

Reticular activating system. The hypothetical arousal system in the reticular formation.

Reticular formation. A complex network of nuclei in the core of the brain stem that contains, among other things, motor programs that regulate complex species-common movements such as walking and swimming.

Retina-geniculate-striate pathway. The major visual pathway from each retina to the striate cortex (primary visual cortex) via the lateral geniculate nuclei of the thalamus.

Retinal ganglion cells. Retinal neurons whose axons leave the eyeball and form the optic nerve.

Retinex theory. Land's theory that the color of an object is determined by its reflectance, which the visual system calculates by comparing the ability of adjacent surfaces to reflect short, medium, and long wavelengths.

Retinotopic. Organized, like the primary visual cortex, according to a map of the retina.

Retrograde amnesia. Loss of memory for events or information learned before the amnesia-inducing brain injury.

Retrograde degeneration. Degeneration of the proximal segment of a cut axon.

Reuptake. The drawing back into the terminal button of neurotransmitter molecules after their release into the synapse; the more common of the two mechanisms for deactivating a released neurotransmitter.

Rhinal cortex. An area of medial temporal cortex adjacent to the amygdala and hippocampus.

Rhodopsin. The photopigment of rods.

Ribonucleic acid (RNA). A molecule that is similar to DNA except that it has the nucleotide base uracil and a phosphate and ribose backbone.

Ribosome. A structure in the cell's cytoplasm that translates the genetic code from strands of messenger RNA.

Rods. The visual receptors in the retina that mediate achromatic, low-acuity vision under dim light.

Saccades. The rapid movements of the eyes between fixations.

Sagittal sections. Any slices of brain tissue cut in a plane that is parallel to the side of the brain.

Saltatory conduction. Conduction of an action potential from one node of Ranvier to the next along a myelinated axon.

Satiety. The motivational state that terminates a meal when there is food remaining.

Savants. Intellectually handicapped individuals who nevertheless display amazing and specific cognitive or artistic abilities; savant abilities are sometimes associated with autism.

Schwann cells. The glial cells that compose the myelin sheaths of PNS axons and promote their regeneration.

Scotoma. An area of blindness produced by damage to, or disruption of, an area of the visual system.

Scotopic spectral sensitivity curve. The graph of the sensitivity of rod-mediated vision to different wavelengths of light.

Scotopic vision. Rod-mediated vision, which predominates in dim light.

Scrotum. The sac that holds the male testes outside the body cavity.

Second messenger. A chemical synthesized in a neuron in response to the binding of a neurotransmitter to a metabotropic receptor in its cell membrane.

Secondary motor cortex. Areas of the cerebral cortex that receive much of their input from association cortex and send much of their output to primary motor cortex.

Secondary sensory cortex. Areas of sensory cortex that receive most of their input from the primary sensory cortex of one sensory system or from other areas of secondary cortex of the same system.

Secondary sex characteristics. Body features, other than the reproductive organs, that distinguish men from women.

Secondary visual cortex. Areas of prestriate and inferotemporal cortex that receive most of their input from primary visual cortex.

Selective attention. The ability to focus on a small subset of the multitude of stimuli that are being received at any one time.

Semantic analysis. Analysis of the meaning of language.

Semantic memories. Explicit memories for general facts and knowledge.

Semicircular canals. The receptive organs of the vestibular system.

Sensation. The process of detecting the presence of stimuli.

Sensitive period. The period during the development of a particular trait, usually early in life, when a particular experience is likely to change the course of that development.

Sensitivity. In vision, the ability to detect the presence of dimly lit objects.

Sensory feedback. Sensory signals that are produced by a response and are often used to guide the continuation of the response.

Sensory-specific satiety. The fact that the consumption of a particular food produces increased satiety for foods of the same taste than for other foods.

Septum. A limbic nucleus that is located at the anterior tip of the cingulate cortex.

Serotonin. The indolamine neurotransmitter.

Set point. The value of a physiological parameter that is maintained constantly by physiological or behavioral mechanisms; for example, the body's energy resources are often assumed to be maintained at a constant optimal level by compensatory changes in hunger.

Set-point assumption. The assumption that hunger is typically triggered by the decline of the body's energy reserves below their set point.

Settling point. The point at which various factors that influence the level of some regulated function (such as body weight) achieve an equilibrium.

Sex chromosomes. The pair of chromosomes that determine an individual's sex: XX for a female and XY for a male.

Sex-linked traits. Traits that are influenced by genes on the sex chromosomes.

Sexually dimorphic nucleus. The nucleus in the medial preoptic area of rats that is larger in males than in females.

Sham eating. The experimental protocol in which an animal chews and swallows food, which immediately exits its body through a tube implanted in its esophagus.

Sham rage. The exaggerated, poorly directed aggressive responses of decorticate animals.

Short-term memories. The type of memories that are fleeting, that last only as long as the person thinks about them.

Simple cells. Neurons in the visual cortex that respond maximally to straight-edge stimuli in a certain position and orientation.

Simple partial seizures. Partial seizures in which the symptoms are primarily sensory or motor or both.

Simultanagnosia. A disorder characterized by the inability to attend to more than one thing at a time.

Sinestrals. Left-handers.

Skeletal muscle (extrafusal muscle). Striated muscle that is attached to the skeleton and is usually under voluntary control.

Sleep apnea. A condition in which sleep is repeatedly disturbed by momentary interruptions in breathing.

Sleep paralysis. A sleep disorder characterized by the inability to move (paralysis) just as a person is falling asleep or waking up.

Slow-wave sleep (SWS). Stages 3 and 4 of sleep, which are characterized by the largest and slowest EEG waves.

Smoker's syndrome. The chest pain, labored breathing, wheezing, coughing, and heightened susceptibility to infections of the respiratory tract commonly observed in tobacco smokers.

Sodium amytal test. A test involving the anesthetization of first one cerebral hemisphere and then the other to determine which hemisphere plays the dominant role in language.

Sodium–potassium pumps. Active transport mechanisms that pump Na^+ ions out of neurons and K^+ ions in.

Solitary nucleus. The medullary relay nucleus of the gustatory system.

Soluble gases. A class of small-molecule neurotransmitters (e.g., nitric oxide).

Somal translocation. One of two major modes of neural migration, in which an extension grows out from the undeveloped neuron and draws the cell body up into it.

Somatic nervous system (SNS). The part of the peripheral nervous system that interacts with the external environment.

Somatosensory homunculus. The somatotopic map that corresponds to the primary somatosensory cortex.

Somatotopic. Organized, like the primary somatosensory cortex, according to a map of the surface of the body.

Somnambulism. Sleepwalking.

Spatial summation. The integration of signals that occur at different sites on the neuron's membrane.

Species. A group of organisms that is reproductively isolated from other organisms; the members of one species cannot produce fertile offspring by mating with members of other species.

Spindle afferent neurons. Neurons that carry signals from muscle spindles into the spinal cord via the dorsal root.

Split-brain patients. Commissurotomized patients.

Static phase. The second phase of the VMH syndrome, during which the grossly obese animal maintains a stable level of obesity.

Stem cells. Developing cells that have the capacity for self-renewal and the potential to develop into various types of mature cells.

Stereognosis. The process of identifying objects by touch.

Stereotaxic instrument. A device for performing stereotaxic surgery, composed of two parts: a head holder and an electrode holder.

Stereotaxic surgery. A surgical procedure used to position experimental devices precisely inside the brain.

Steroid hormones. Hormones that are synthesized from cholesterol.

Stimulants. Drugs that produce general increases in neural and behavioral activity.

Stimulation methods. Methods of studying brain function by passing an electric current through an electrode permanently implanted in the brain in order to activate specific neurons and assess the behavioral effects of the stimulation.

Stress. The physiological response to physical or psychological threat.

Stretch reflex. A reflexive counteracting reaction to an unanticipated external stretching force on a muscle.

Striatum. A structure of the basal ganglia that is the terminal of the dopaminergic nigrostriatal pathway and is damaged in Parkinson's patients; it seems to play a role in memory for consistent relationships between stimuli and responses in multiple-trial tasks.

Strokes. Sudden-onset cerebrovascular disorders that cause brain damage.

Structural genes. Genes that contain the information required for the synthesis of a particular protein.

Subordination stress. Stress experienced by animals, typically males, that are continually attacked by higher-ranking conspecifics.

Substantia nigra. The midbrain nucleus whose neurons project via the nigrostriatal pathway to the striatum of the basal ganglia; it is part of the mesotelencephalic dopamine system and degenerates in cases of Parkinson's disease.

Superior. Toward the top of the primate head.

Superior colliculi. A pair of structures on the dorsal surface of the midbrain; their function is largely visual.

Superior olives. Medullary nuclei that play a role in sound localization.

Superior temporal gyri. The most dorsal gyri of the lateral surface of the temporal lobes.

Supplementary motor area. The area of secondary motor cortex that is within and adjacent to the longitudinal fissure.

Suprachiasmatic nuclei (SCN). Nuclei of the medial hypothalamus that control the circadian cycles of various body functions.

Supraoptic nuclei. Hypothalamic nuclei in which the hormones of the posterior pituitary are synthesized.

Surface dyslexia. A reading disorder in which the lexical procedure is disrupted while the phonetic procedure is not.

Sympathetic nerves. Those motor nerves of the autonomic nervous system that project from the CNS in the lumbar and thoracic areas of the spinal cord.

Synaptic vesicles. Small spherical membranes that store neurotransmitter molecules and release them into the synaptic cleft.

Synaptogenesis. The formation of new synapses.

Synergistic muscles. Pairs of muscles whose contraction produces a movement in the same direction.

T cells. T lymphocytes; lymphocytes that bind to foreign micro-organisms and cells that contain them and, in so doing, destroy them.

Tangential migration. Movement of cells in the developing neural tube in a direction parallel to the tube's walls.

Taste buds. Clusters of taste receptors found on the tongue and in parts of the oral cavity.

Tectorial membrane. The cochlear membrane that rests on the hair cells.

Tectum. The division of the midbrain that comprises the superior and inferior colliculi and receives auditory and visual information about spatial location.

Tegmentum. The ventral division of the midbrain.

Telencephalon. The most anterior division of the brain; the cerebral hemispheres.

Temporal hemiretina. The half of each retina next to the temple.

Temporal lobe. The most ventral lobe of the cerebral hemispheres.

Temporal summation. The integration of neural signals that occur at different times at the same synapse.

Testes. The male gonads.

Testosterone. The most common androgen.

Thalamus. The diencephalic structure that is located at the anterior end of the brain stem; it contains many sensory relay nuclei.

THC. Delta-9-tetrahydrocannabinol, the main psychoactive constituent of marijuana.

3-per-second spike-and-wave discharge. The characteristic EEG pattern of the petit mal seizure.

Threshold of excitation. The level of depolarization necessary to generate an action potential, usually about -65 mV.

Thrombosis. The blockage of blood flow by a plug (a thrombus) at the site of its formation.

Thyrotropin. The anterior pituitary hormone that stimulates the release of hormones from the thyroid gland.

Thyrotropin-releasing hormone. The hypothalamic hormone that stimulates the release of thyrotropin from the anterior pituitary.

Tics. Involuntary, repetitive, stereotyped movements or vocalizations; the defining feature of Tourette syndrome.

Tonotopic. Organized, like the primary auditory cortex, according to the frequency of sound.

Topographic gradient hypothesis. The hypothesis that axonal growth is guided by the relative position of the cell bodies on intersecting gradients, rather than by point-to-point coding of neural connections.

Totipotent. Capable of developing into any type of mature body cell.

Toxic psychosis. A chronic psychiatric disorder produced by exposure to a neurotoxin.

Tracts. Bundles of axons in the central nervous system.

Transcription. The first phase of gene expression, in which the DNA base-sequence code is converted to an RNA base-sequence code.

Transduction. The conversion of one form of energy to another.

Transfer RNA. Molecules of RNA that carry amino acids to ribosomes during protein synthesis; each kind of amino acid is carried by a different kind of transfer RNA molecule.

Transgenic mice. Mice into which the genetic material of another species has been introduced.

Translation. The second phase of gene expression, in which the RNA base-sequence code gives rise to a sequence of amino acids.

Transneuronal degeneration. Degeneration of a neuron caused by damage to another neuron to which it is linked by a synapse.

Transsexualism. A disorder of sexual identity in which the individual believes that he or she is trapped in a body of the other sex.

Tricyclic antidepressant drugs (or tricyclic antidepressants). Drugs with an antidepressant action and a three-ring molecular structure; they selectively suppress REM sleep.

True-breeding lines. Breeding lines in which interbred members always produce offspring with the same trait, generation after generation.

Tumor (neoplasm). A mass of cells that grows independently of the rest of the body.

Tympanic membrane. The eardrum.

Unipolar affective disorder. A disorder of emotion in which a patient experiences depression but no periods of mania.

Unipolar neuron. A neuron with one process extending from its cell body.

Unit recording. A technique for recording the activity of individual neurons in the brain.

Up-regulation. An increase in the number of receptors for a neurotransmitter in response to decreased release of that neurotransmitter.

Urbach-Wiethe disease. A genetic disorder that often results in the calcification of the amygdala and surrounding brain structures.

Vasopressin. One of the two major peptide hormones of the posterior pituitary; it facilitates reabsorption of water by kidneys and is thus also called *antidiuretic hormone.*

Ventral. Toward the chest surface of a vertebrate or toward the bottom of the head.

Ventral horns. The two ventral arms of the spinal gray matter.

Ventral posterior nucleus. A thalamic relay nucleus in both the somatosensory and gustatory systems.

Ventral stream. The group of visual pathways that flows from the primary visual cortex to the ventral pre-striate cortex to the inferotemporal cortex; according to one theory, its function is conscious visual perception.

Ventral tegmental area. The midbrain nucleus of the mesotelencephalic dopamine system that is a major source of the mesocorticolimbic pathway.

Ventricular zone. The region adjacent to the ventricle in the developing neural tube; the zone where neural proliferation occurs.

Ventromedial cortico-brainstem-spinal tract. The indirect ventromedial motor pathway, which descends bilaterally from the primary motor cortex to several interconnected brain stem motor structures and then descends in the ventromedial portions of the spinal cord.

Ventromedial corticospinal tract. The direct ventromedial motor pathway, which descends ipsilaterally from the primary motor cortex directly into the ventromedial areas of the spinal white matter.

Ventromedial hypothalamus (VMH). The area of the hypothalamus that was once thought to contain the satiety center.

Ventromedial nucleus (VMN). A hypothalamic nucleus that is thought to be involved in female sexual behavior.

Vertebrates. Chordates that possess spinal bones.

Vestibular nucleus. The brain stem nucleus that receives information about balance from receptors in the semicircular canals.

Vestibular system. The sensory system that detects changes in the direction and intensity of head movements and that contributes to the maintenance of balance through its output to the motor system.

Visual agnosia. A failure to recognize visual stimuli that is not attributable to sensory, verbal, or intellectual impairment.

Visual association cortex. Areas of visual cortex that receive input from areas of secondary visual cortex and from the secondary areas of other sensory systems.

Visual completion. The completion or filling in of a scotoma by the brain.

Voltage-activated ion channels. Ion channels that open and close in response to changes in the level of the membrane potential.

Wernicke-Geschwind model. An influential model of cortical language localization in the left hemisphere.

Wernicke's aphasia. A hypothetical disorder of language comprehension with no associated deficits in speech production.

Wernicke's area. The area of the left temporal cortex hypothesized by Wernicke to be the center of language comprehension.

"Where" versus "what" theory. The theory that the dorsal stream mediates the perception of where things are and the ventral stream mediates the perception of what things are.

Williams syndrome. A neurodevelopmental disorder characterized by severe mental retardation, accompanied by preserved language and social skills.

Withdrawal reflex. The reflexive withdrawal of a limb when it comes in contact with a painful stimulus.

Withdrawal syndrome. The illness brought on by the elimination from the body of a drug on which the person is physically dependent.

Wolffian system. The embryonic precursor of the male reproductive ducts.

Word salad. Speech that has the overall sound and flow of normal speech but is totally incomprehensible.

Working memory. Temporary memory necessary for the successful performance of a task on which one is currently working.

Zeitgebers. Environmental cues, such as the light–dark cycle, that entrain circadian rhythms.

Zygote. The cell formed from the amalgamation of a sperm cell and an ovum.

Abi-Dargham, A., Rodenhiser, J., Printz, D., Zea-Ponce, Y., Gil, R., Kegeles, L. S., et al. (2000). Increased baseline occupancy of D2 receptors by dopamine in schizophrenia. *Pro-ceedings of the National Academy of Sciences, U.S.A., 97,* 8104–8109.

Adkins-Regan, E. (1988). Sex hormones and sexual orientation in animals. *Psychobiology, 16,* 335–347.

Adolphs, R., Sears, L., & Piven, J. (2001). Abnormal processing of social information from faces in autism. *Journal of Cognitive Neuroscience, 13,* 232–240.

Adolphs, R., & Tranel, D. (1999). Preferences for visual stimuli following amygdala damage. *Journal of Cognitive Neuroscience, 11,* 610–616.

Adolphs, R., Tranel, D., Damasio, H., & Damasio, A. (1994). Impaired recognition of emotion in facial expressions following bilateral damage to the human amygdala. *Nature, 372,* 669–672.

Adolphs, R., Tranel, D., Hamann, S., Young, A. W., Calder, A. J., Phelps, E. A., et al. (1999). Recognition of facial emotion in nine individuals with bilateral amygdala damage. *Neuro-psychologia, 37,* 1111–1117.

Aggleton, J. P., & Young, A. W. (2000). The enigma of the amygdala: On its contribution to human emotion. In R. D. Lane & L. Nadel (Eds.), *Cognitive neuroscience of emotion* (pp. 106–128). New York: Oxford University Press.

Aglioti, S., Smania, N., & Peru, A. (1999). Frames of reference for mapping tactile stimuli in brain-damaged patients. *Journal of Cognitive Neuroscience, 11,* 67–79.

Agmo, A., & Ellingsen, E. (2003). Relevance of non-human animal studies to the understanding of human sexuality. *Scandinavian Journal of Psychology, 44,* 293–301.

Agnew, N., & Demas, M. (1998, September). Preserving the Laetoli footprints. *Scientific American, 279,* 46–55.

Ahima, R. S., & Osei, S. Y. (2004). Leptin signaling. *Physiology & Behavior, 81,* 223–241.

Ahmed, R., & Gray, D. (1996). Immunological memory and protective immunity: Understanding their relation. *Science, 272,* 54–60.

Åkerstedt, R., & Gillberg, M. (1981). The circadian variation of experimentally displaced sleep. *Sleep, 4,* 159–169.

Albright, T. D., Kandel, E. R., & Posner, M. I. (2000). Cognitive neuroscience. *Current Opinion in Neurobiology, 10,* 612–624.

Alexander, M. P. (1989). Clinical-anatomical correlations of aphasia following predominantly subcortical lesions. In H. Goodglass (Ed.), *Handbook of neuropsychology* (Vol. II, Pt. 2, pp. 47–66). New York: Elsevier.

Alexander, M. P. (1997). Aphasia: Clinical and anatomic aspects. In T. E. Feinberg & M. J. Farah, (Eds.), *Behavioral neurology and neuropsychology* (pp. 133–149). New York: McGraw-Hill.

Allen, L. S., Hines, M., Shryne, J. E., & Gorski, R. A. (1989). Two sexually dimorphic cell groups in the human brain. *Journal of Neuroscience, 9,* 497–506.

Allsop, T. E., & Fazakerley, J. K. (2000). Altruistic cell suicide and the specialized case of the virus-infected nervous system. *Trends in Neurosciences, 23,* 284–290.

Almeida, M. L. G., Ontiveros, U. M. P., Cortes, S. J., & Heinze, M. G. (2003). Treatment of primary insomnia with melatonin: A double-blind, placebo-controlled, crossover study. *Journal of Psychiatry & Neuroscience, 28,* 191–196.

Ambrose, S. H. (2001). Paleolithic technology and human evolution. *Science, 291,* 1748–1753.

Anagnostaras, S. G., Craske, M. G., & Fanselow, M. S. (1999). Anxiety: At the intersection of genes and experience. *Nature Reviews Neuroscience, 2,* 780–782.

Anand, B. K., & Brobeck, J. R. (1951). Localization of a "feeding center" in the hypothalamus of the rat. *Proceedings of the Society for Experimental Biology and Medicine, 77,* 323–324.

Anch, A. M., Browman, C. P., Mitler, M. M., & Walsh, J. K. (1988). *Sleep: A scientific perspective.* Englewood Cliffs, NJ: Prentice Hall.

Andersen, R. A., & Buneo, C. A. (2003). Sensorimotor integration in posterior parietal cortex. *Advances in Neurology, 93,* 159–177.

Anderson, A. K., & Phelps, E. A. (2000). Expression without recognition: Contributions of the human amygdala to emotional communication. *Psychological Science, 11,* 106–111.

Anderson, P., Cremona, A., Paton, A., Turner, C., & Wallace, P. (1993). The risk of alcohol. *Addiction, 88,* 1493–1508.

Anderson, R. H., Fleming, D. E., Rhees, R. W., & Kinghorn, E. (1986). Relationships between sexual activity, plasma testosterone, and the volume of the sexually dimorphic nucleus of the preoptic area in prenatally stressed and non-stressed rats. *Brain Research, 370,* 1–10.

Andreasen, N. C. (2000). Schizophrenia: The fundamental questions. *Brain Research Reviews, 31,* 106–112.

Antonini, A., & Stryker, M. P. (1993). Rapid remodeling of axonal arbors in the visual cortex. *Science, 260,* 1819–1821.

Apkarian, A. V. (1995). Functional imaging of pain: New insights regarding the role of the cerebral cortex in human pain perception. *Seminars in the Neurosciences, 7,* 279–293.

Araújo, S. J., & Tear, G. (2003). Axon guidance mechanisms and molecules: Lessons from invertebrates. *Nature Reviews Neuroscience, 4,* 910–922.

Arieli, A., Sterkin, A., Grinvald, A., & Aertsen, A. (1996). Dynamics of ongoing activity: Explanation of the large variability in evoked cortical responses. *Science, 273,* 1868–1870.

Aserinsky, E., & Kleitman, N. (1953). Regularly occurring periods of eye motility and concomitant phenomena, during sleep. *Science, 118,* 273–274.

Assad, J. A. (2003). Neural coding of behavioral relevance in parietal cortex. *Current Opinion in Neurobiology, 13,* 194–197.

Assanand, S., Pinel, J. P. J., & Lehman, D. R. (1998a). Personal theories of hunger and eating. *Journal of Applied Social Psychology, 28,* 998–1015.

Assanand, S., Pinel, J. P. J., & Lehman, D. R. (1998b). Teaching theories of hunger and eating: Overcoming students' misconceptions. *Teaching Psychology, 25,* 44–46.

Attenburrow, M. E. J., Cowen, P. J., & Sharpely, A. L. (1996). Low dose melatonin improves sleep in healthy middle-aged subjects. *Psychopharmacology, 126,* 179–181.

Auld, V. J. (2001). Why didn't the glia cross the road? *Trends in Neurosciences, 24,* 309–311.

Avishai-Eliner, S., Kristen, L. B., Sandman, C. A., & Baram, T. Z. (2002). Stressed-out, or in (utero)? *Trends in Neurosciences, 25,* 518–524.

Ayas, N. T., White, D. P., Manson, J. E., Stampfer, M. J., Speizer, F. E., Malhotra, A., & Hu, F. B. (2003). A prospective study of sleep duration and coronary heart disease in women. *Archives of Internal Medicine, 163,* 205–209.

Baddeley, A., Vargha-Khadem, F., & Mishkin, M. (2002). Preserved recognition in a case of developmental amnesia: Implications for the acquisition of semantic memory? *Journal of Cognitive Neuroscience, 13*, 357–369.

Bailey, J. M., Pillard, R. C., Neale, M. C., & Agyei, Y. (1993). Heritable factors influence sexual orientation in women. *Archives of General Psychiatry, 50*, 217–223.

Bailey, M. J., & Pillard, R. C. (1991). A genetic study of male sexual orientation. *Archives of General Psychiatry, 48*, 1089–1096.

Baker, B. J., & Booth, D. A. (1989). Preference conditioning by concurrent diets with delayed proportional reinforcement. *Physiology & Behavior, 46*, 585–590.

Balthazart, J., & Ball, G. F. (1998). New insights into the regulation and function of brain estrogen synthase (aromatase). *Trends in Neurosciences, 21*, 243–249.

Banchereau, J. (2002, November). The long arm of the immune system. *Scientific American, 287*, 52–59.

Bancroft, J., Sanders, D., Davidson, D., & Warner, P. (1983). Mood, sexuality, hormones and the menstrual cycle: III. Sexuality and the role of androgens. *Psychosomatic Medicine, 45*, 509–516.

Bandler, R., & Shipley, M. T. (1994). Columnar organization in the midbrain periaqueductal gray: Modules for emotional expression? *Trends in Neurosciences, 17*, 379–389.

Bankiewicz, K. S., Plunkett, R. J., Jaconowitz, D. M., Porrino, L., di Porzio, U., London, W. T., et al. (1990). The effect of fetal mesencephalon implants on primate MPTP-induced Parkinsonism: Histochemical and behavioral studies. *Journal of Neuroscience, 72*, 231–244.

Barash, S. (2003). Paradoxical activities: Insight into the relationship of parietal and prefrontal cortices. *Trends in Neurosciences, 26*, 582–589.

Bard, P. (1929). The central representation of the sympathetic system. *Archives of Neurology and Psychiatry, 22*, 230–246.

Bar-Gad, I., & Bergman, H. (2001). Stepping out of the box: Information processing in the neural networks of the basal ganglia. *Current Opinion in Neurobiology, 11*, 689–695.

Baron, J. C. (1989). Depression of energy metabolism in distant brain structures: Studies with positron emission tomography in stroke patients. *Seminars in Neurology, 9*, 281–285.

Barres, B. A., & Smith, S. J. (2001). Cholesterol—making or breaking the synapse. *Science, 294*, 1296–1297.

Bartholmeo, P., & Chokron, S. (2002). Orienting of attention in left unilateral neglect. *Neuroscience and Biobehavioural Reviews, 26*, 217–234.

Basbaum, A. I., & Fields, H. L. (1978). Endogenous pain control mechanisms: Review and hypothesis. *Annals of Neurology, 4*, 451–462.

Bashir, Z. I., & Collingridge, G. L. (1992). Synaptic plasticity: Long-term potentiation in the hippocampus. *Current Opinion in Neurobiology, 2*, 328–335.

Baskett, J. J., Broad, J. B., Wood, P. C., Duncan, J. R., Pledger, M. J., English, J., & Arendt, J. (2003). Does melatonin improve sleep in older people? A randomized crossover trial. *Age and Ageing, 32*, 164–170.

Baum, M. J., Erskine, M. S., Kornberg, E., & Weaver, C. E. (1990). Prenatal and neonatal testosterone exposure interact to affect differentiation of sexual behavior and partner preference in female ferrets. *Behavioral Neuroscience, 104*, 183–198.

Bavelier, D., Corina, D., Jessard, P., Padmanabhan, S., Clark, V. P., Karni, A., et al. (1997). Sentence reading: A functional MRI study at 4 tesla. *Journal of Cognitive Neuroscience, 9*, 664–686.

Baxter, M. G., & Chiba, A. A. (1999). Cognitive functions of the basal forebrain. *Current Opinion in Neurobiology, 9*, 178–183.

Baxter, M. G., & Murray, E. A. (2002). The amygdala and reward. *Nature Reviews Neuroscience, 3*, 563–573.

Baynes, K., & Gazzaniga, M. S. (1997). Callosal disconnection. In T. E. Feinberg & M. J. Farah (Eds.), *Behavioral neurology and neuropsychology* (pp. 419–425). New York: McGraw-Hill.

Beaumont, M., Batejat, D., Pierard, C., Van Beers, P., Denis, J., Coste, O., et al. (2004). Caffeine or melatonin effects on sleep and sleepiness after rapid eastward transmeridian travel. *Journal of Applied Physiology, 96*, 50–58.

Bechara, A., Tranel, D., Damasio, H., Adolphs, R., Rockland, C., & Damasio, A. R. (1995). Double dissociation of conditioning and declarative knowledge relative to the amygdala and hippocampus in humans. *Science, 269*, 1115–1118.

Beck, B. (2001). KO's and organization of peptidergic feeding behavior mechanisms. *Neuroscience and Biobehavioural Reviews, 25*, 143–158.

Beeman, M. J., & Chiarello, C. (1998). Complementary right- and left-hemisphere language comprehension. *Current Directions in Psychological Science, 7*, 2–8.

Behl, C. (2002). Oestrogen as a neuroprotective hormone. *Nature Reviews Neuroscience, 3*, 433–442.

Bellugi, U., Lichtenberger, L., Mills, D., Galaburda, A., & Korenberg, J. R. (1999). Bridging cognition, the brain and molecular genetics: Evidence from Williams syndrome. *Trends in Neurosciences, 22*, 197–207.

Ben-Eliyahu, S., Shakhar, G., Page, G. G., Stefanski, V., & Shakhar, K. (2000). Suppression of NK cell activity and of resistance to metastasis by stress: A role for adrenal catecholamines and beta-adrenoceptors. *Neuroimmunomodula-tion, 8*, 154–164.

Benes, F. M., & Berretta, S. (2001). GABAergic interneurons: Implications for understanding schizophrenia and bipolar disorder. *Neuropsychopharmacology, 25*, 1–27.

Benington, J. H., & Heller, H. C. (1999). Implications of sleep deprivation experiments for our understanding of sleep homeostasis. *Sleep, 22*, 1033–1043.

Benson, D. F. (1985). Aphasia. In K. M., Heilman & E. Valenstein (Eds.), *Clinical neuropsychology* (pp. 17–47). New York: Oxford University Press.

Benson, D. L., Colman, D. R., & Huntley, G. W. (2001). Molecules, maps and synapse specificity. *Nature Reviews Neuroscience, 2*, 899–908.

Berger, R. J., & Oswald, I. (1962). Effects of sleep deprivation on behaviour, subsequent sleep, and dreaming. *Journal of Mental Science, 106*, 457–465.

Bergman, T. J., Beehner, J. C., Cheney, D. L., & Seyfarth, R. M. (2003). Hierarchical classification by rank and kinship in baboons. *Science, 302*, 1234–1236.

Bernstein, L. J., & Robertson, L. C. (1998). Illusory conjunctions of color and motion with shape following bilateral parietal lesions. *Psychological Science, 9*, 167–175.

Berridge, K. C. (2004). Motivation concepts in behavioral neuroscience. *Physiology & Behavior, 81*, 179–209.

Berridge, V., & Edwards, G. (1981). *Opium and the people: Opiate use in nineteenth-century England*. New York: St. Martin's Press.

Berridge, K. C., & Robinson, T. E. (2003). Parsing reward. *Trends in Neurosciences, 26*, 507–513.

Berson, D. M. (2003). Strange vision: Ganglion cells as circadian photoreceptors. *Trends in Neurosciences, 26*, 314–320.

Berthoud, H.-R. (2002). Multiple neural systems controlling food intake and body weight. *Neuroscience and Biobehavioural Reviews, 26*, 393–428.

Best, P. J., White, A. M., & Minai, A. (2001). Spatial processing in the brain: The activity of hippocampal place cells. *Annual Review of Neuroscience, 24*, 459–486.

Bezard, E., Brotchie, J. M., & Gross, C. E. (2001). Pathophysiology of levodopa-induced dyskinesia: Potential for new therapies. *Nature Reviews Neuroscience, 2*, 577–588.

Bi, G.-Q., & Poo, M.-M. (2001). Synaptic modification by correlated activity: Hebb's postulate revisited. *Annual Review of Neuroscience, 24*, 139–166.

Binks, P. G., Waters, W. F., & Hurry, M. (1999). Short-term total sleep deprivation does not selectively impair higher cortical functioning. *Sleep, 22*, 328–334.

Bischoff-Grethe, A., Proper, S. M., Mao, H., Daniels, K. A., & Berns, G. S. (2000). Conscious and unconscious processing of nonverbal predictability in Wernicke's area. *Journal of Neuroscience, 20*, 1975–1981.

Bishop, D. V. M. (1999). An innate basis for language? *Science, 286*, 2283–2355.

Björklund, A., & Lindvall, O. (2000). Cell replacement therapies for central nervous system disorders. *Nature, 3*, 537–544.

Blackburn, G. L. (2001). Pasteur's quadrant and malnutrition. *Nature, 409*, 397–401.

Blakely, R. D. (2001). Dopamine's reversal of fortune. *Science, 293*, 2408–2409.

Blanchard, D. C., Blanchard, R. J., & Rodgers, R. J. (1991). Risk assessment and animal models of anxiety. In J. Olivier, J. Mos, & J. L. Slangen (Eds.), *Animal models in psychopharmacology* (pp. 117–134). Basel, Switzerland: Birkhauser Verlag.

Blanchard, D. C., Blanchard, R. J., Tom, P., & Rodgers, R. J. (1990). Diazepam changes risk assessment in an anxiety/defense test battery. *Psychopharmacology, 101*, 511–518.

Blanchard, D. C., Sakai, R. R., McEwen, B., Weiss, S. M., & Blanchard, R. J. (1993). Subordination stress: Behavioral, brain, and neuroendocrine correlates. *Behavioural Brain Research, 58*, 113–121.

Blaser, M. J. (1996, February). The bacteria behind ulcers. *Scientific American, 275*, 104–107.

Blaustein, J. D., King, J. C., Toft, D. O., & Turcotte, J. (1988). Immunocytochemical localization of estrogen-induced pro-gestin receptors in guinea pig brain. *Brain Research, 474*, 1–15.

Blessing, W. W. (1997). Inadequate frameworks for understanding bodily homeostasis. *Trends in Neurosciences, 20*, 235–239.

Bliss, T., & Schoepfer, R. (2004). Controlling the ups and downs of synaptic strength. *Science, 304*, 973–974.

Bliss, T. V. P., & Lømø, T. (1973). Long-lasting potentiation of synaptic transmission in the dentate area of the anaesthetized rabbit following stimulation of the perforant path. *Journal of Physiology, 232*, 331–356.

Bloch, G. J., & Gorski, R. A. (1988). Cytoarchitectonic analysis of the SDN-POA of the intact and gonadectomized rat. *Journal of Comparative Neurology, 275*, 604–612.

Bloch, G. J., & Mills, R. (1995). Prepubertal testosterone treatment of neonatally gonadectomized male rats: Defeminization and masculinization of behavioral and endocrine function in adulthood. *Neuroscience and Behavioural Reviews, 19*, 187–200.

Bloch, G. J., Mills, R., & Gale, S. (1995). Prepubertal testosterone treatment of female rats: Defeminization of behavioral and endocrine function in adulthood. *Neuroscience and Biobehavioural Reviews, 19*, 177–186.

Blundell, J. E., & Finlayson, G. (2004). Is susceptibility to weight gain characterized by homeostatic or hedonic risk factors for overconsumption? *Physiology & Behavior, 82*, 21–25.

Blundell, J. E., & Halford, J. C. G. (1998). Serotonin and appetite regulation. *CNS Drugs, 9*, 473–495.

Boehning, D., & Snyder, S. H. (2003). Novel neural modulators. *Annual Review of Neuroscience, 26*, 105–131.

Bogen, J. G., & Bogen, G. M. (1976). Wernicke's region—where is it? *Annals of the New York Academy of Sciences, 280*, 834–843.

Bolles, R. C. (1980). Some functionalistic thought about regulation. In F. M. Toates & T. R. Halliday (Eds.), *Analysis of motivational processes* (pp. 63–75). London: Academic Press.

Bonnel, A., Mottron, L., Peretz, I., Trudel, M., Gallun, E., & Bonnel, A. M. (2003). Enhanced pitch sensitivity in individuals with autism: A signal detection analysis. *Journal of Cognitive Neuroscience, 15*, 226–235.

Bonnet, M. H., & Arand, D. L. (1996). Insomnia—nocturnal sleep disruption—daytime fatigue: The consequences of a week of insomnia. *Sleep, 19*, 453–461.

Bookheimer, S. (2002). Functional MRI of language: New approaches to understanding the cortical organization of semantic processing. *Annual Review of Neuroscience, 25*, 151–188.

Booth, D. A. (1981). The physiology of appetite. *British Medical Bulletin, 37*, 135–140.

Booth, D. A., Fuller, J., & Lewis, V. (1981). Human control of body weight: Cognitive or physiological? Some energy-related perceptions and misperceptions. In L. A. Cioffi (Ed.), *The body weight regulatory system: Normal and disturbed systems* (pp. 305–314). New York: Raven Press.

Borbély, A. A. (1981). The sleep process: Circadian and homeostatic aspects. *Advances in Physiological Sciences, 18*, 85–91.

Borbély, A. A., Baumann, F., Brandeis, D., Strauch, I., & Lehmann, D. (1981). Sleep deprivation: Effect on sleep stages and EEG power density in man. *Electroencephalography and Clinical Neurophysiology, 51*, 483–493.

Borszcz, G. S. (1999). Differential contributions of medullary, thalamic, and amygdaloid serotonin to the antinociceptive action of morphine administered into the periaqueductal gray: A model of morphine analgesia. *Behavioural Neuroscience, 113*, 612–631.

Bouchard, T. J., Jr. (1998). Genetic and environmental influences on adult intelligence and special mental abilities. *Human Biology, 70*, 257–279.

Bouchard, T. J., Jr., & Pedersen, N. (1998). Twins reared apart: Nature's double experiment. In E. L. Grigorenko & S. Scarr (Eds.), *On the way to individuality: Current methodological issues in behavioral genetics*. Commack, NY: Nova Science Publishers.

Bowers, D., Bauer, R. M., Coslett, H. B., & Heilman, K. M. (1985). Processing of face by patients with unilateral hemisphere lesions. I. Dissociations between judgements of facial affect and facial identity. *Brain and Cognition, 4*, 258–272.

Brackett, N. L., & Edwards, D. A. (1984). Medial preoptic connections with the midbrain tegmentum are essential for male sexual behavior. *Physiology & Behavior, 32*, 79–84.

Braun, C., Schweizer, R., Elbert, T., Birbaumer, N., & Taub, E. (2000). Differential activation in somatosensory cortex for different discrimination tasks. *Journal of Neuroscience, 20*, 446–450.

Brecher, E. M. (1972). *Licit and illicit drugs*. Boston: Little, Brown & Co.

Breitner, J. C. S. (1990). Life table methods and assessment of familial risk in Alzheimer's disease. *Archives of General Psychiatry, 47*, 395–396.

Bremer, F. (1936). Nouvelles recherches sur le mécanisme du sommeil. *Comptes rendus de la Société de Biologie, 22*, 460–464.

Bremer, F. L. (1937). L'activité cérébrale au cours du sommeil et de la narcose. Contribution à l'étude du mécanisme du sommeil. *Bulletin de l'Académie Royale de Belgique, 4*, 68–86.

Bremer, J. (1959). *Asexualization*. New York: Macmillan.

Brewster, J. M. (1986). Prevalence of alcohol and other drug problems among physicians. *Journal of the American Medical Association, 255*, 1913–1920.

Brivanlou, A. H., Gage, F. H., Jaenisch, R., Jessell, T., Melton, D., & Rossant, J. (2003). Setting standards for human embryonic stem cells. *Science, 300*, 913–916.

Broberg, D. J., & Bernstein, I. L. (1989). Cephalic insulin release in anorexic women. *Physiology & Behavior, 45*, 871–875.

Broks, P., Young, A. W., Maratos, E. J., Coffey, P. J., Calder, A. J., Isaac, C. L., et al. (1998). Face processing impairments after encephalitis: Amygdala damage and recognition of fear. *Neuropsychologia, 36*, 59–70.

Brooks, M. J., & Melnik, G. (1995). The refeeding syndrome: An approach to understanding its complications and preventing its occurrence. *Pharmacotherapy, 15*, 713–726.

Brooks, V. B. (1986). *The neural basis of motor control.* New York: Oxford University Press.

Brown, E. S., Rush, A. J., & McEwen, B. S. (1999). Hippocampal remodeling and damage by corticosteroids: Implications for mood disorders. *Neuropsychopharmacology, 21*, 474–484.

Brown, G. W. (1993). The role of life events in the aetiology of depressive and anxiety disorders. In S. C. Stanford & S. Salmon (Eds.) *Stress: From synapse to syndrome* (pp. 23–50). San Diego: Academic Press.

Brown, H. D., & Kosslyn, S. M. (1993). Cerebral lateralization. *Current Opinion in Neurobiology, 3*, 183–186.

Brown, M. W., & Aggleton, J. P. (2001). Recognition memory: What are the roles of the perirhinal cortex and hippocampus? *Nature Reviews Neuroscience, 2*, 51–61.

Brown, R. E. (1994). *An introduction to neuroendocrinology.* Cambridge, England: Cambridge University Press.

Brown, R. E., & Milner, P. M. (2003). The legacy of Donald Hebb: More than the Hebb Synapse. *Nature Reviews Neuroscience, 4*, 1013–1019.

Brownell, K. D., & Rodin, J. (1994). The dieting maelstrom: Is it possible and advisable to lose weight? *American Psychologist, 49*, 781–791.

Brun, V. H., Otnaes, M. K., Molden, S., Steffenach, H.-A., Witter, M. P., Moser, M.-B., & Moser, E. I. (2002). Place cells and place recognition maintained by direct entorhinal-hippocampal circuitry. *Science, 296*, 2243–2246.

Brunner, D. P., Dijk, D.-J., Tobler, I., & Borbély, A. A. (1990). Effect of partial sleep deprivation on sleep stages and EEG power spectra: Evidence for non-REM and REM sleep homeostasis. *Electroencephalography and Clinical Neurophysiology, 75*, 492–499.

Bucci, T. J. (1992). Dietary restriction: Why all the interest? An overview. *Laboratory Animal, 21*, 29–34.

Buckley, M. J., & Gaffan, D. (1998). Perirhinal cortex ablation impairs visual object identification. *Journal of Neuroscience, 18*(6), 2268–2275.

Buijs, R. M., & Kalsbeek, A. (2001). Hypothalamic integration of central and peripheral clocks. *Nature Reviews Neuroscience, 2*, 521–526.

Bunin, M. A., & Wightman, R. M. (1999). Paracrine neurotransmission in the CNS: Involvement of 5-HT. *Trends in Neurosciences, 22*, 377–382.

Buonomano, D. V., & Merzenich, M. M. (1998). Cortical plasticity: From synapses to maps. *Annual Reviews of Neuroscience, 21*, 149–186.

Bussey, T. J., Warburton, E. C., Aggleton, J. P., & Muir, J. L. (1998). Fornix lesions can facilitate acquisition of the transverse patterning task: A challenge for "configural" theories of hippocampal function. *Journal of Neuroscience, 18*(4), 1622–1631.

Butters, N., & Delis, D. C. (1995). Clinical assessment of memory disorders in amnesia and dementia. *Annual Review of Psychology, 46*, 493–523.

Cabanac, M. (1971). Physiological role of pleasure. *Science, 173*, 1103–1107.

Cabeza, R., & Nyberg, L. (1997). Imaging cognition: An empirical review of PET studies with normal subjects. *Journal of Cognitive Neuroscience, 9*(1), 1–26.

Cabeza, R., & Nyberg, L. (2000). Imaging cognition II: An empirical review of 275 PET and fMRI studies. *Journal of Cognitive Neuroscience, 12*(1), 1–47.

Cain, D. P. (1997). LTP, NMDA, genes and learning. *Current Opinion in Neurobiology, 7*, 235–242.

Calder, A. J., Young, A. W., Rowland, D., Perrett, D. I., Hodges, J. R., & Etcoff, N. L. (1996). Facial emotion recognition after bilateral amygdala damage: Differentially severe impairment of fear. *Cognitive Neuropsychology, 13*, 699–745.

Calles-Escandon, J., & Horton, E. S. (1992). The thermogenic role of exercise in the treatment of morbid obesity: A critical evaluation. *American Journal of Clinical Nutrition, 55*, 533S–537S.

Calne, S., Schoenberg, B., Martin, W., Uitti, J., Spencer, P., & Calne, D. B. (1987). Familial Parkinson's disease: Possible role of environmental factors. *Canadian Journal of Neurological Sciences, 14*, 303–305.

Cameron, H. A., Woolley, C. S., McEwen, B. S., & Gould, E. (1993). Differentiation of newly born neurons and glia in the dentate gyrus of the adult rat. *Neuroscience, 56*, 337–344.

Campbell, K., & Gotz, M. (2002). Radial glia: Multi-purpose cells for vertebrate brain development. *Trends in Neurosciences, 25*, 235–238.

Campfield, L. A., & Smith, F. J. (1990). Transient declines in blood glucose signal meal initiation. *International Journal of Obesity, 14*(Suppl. 3), 15–33.

Campfield, L. A., Smith, F. J., Gulsez, Y., Devos, R., & Burn, P. (1995). Mouse Ob protein: Evidence for a peripheral signal linking adiposity and central neural networks. *Science, 269*, 546–550.

Cannon, W. B., & Washburn, A. L. (1912). An explanation of hunger. *American Journal of Physiology, 29*, 441–454.

Capaday, C. (2002). The special nature of human walking and its neural control. *Trends in Neurosciences, 25*, 370–376.

Cardinal, R. N., & Everitt, B. J. (2004). Neural and psychological mechanisms underlying appetitive learning: Links to drug addiction. *Current Opinion in Neurobiology, 14*, 156–162.

Carlsson, A., & Lindqvist, M. (1963). Effect of chlorpromazine or haloperidol on formation of 3-methoxytyramine and normetanephrine in mouse brains. *Acta Pharmacologica et Toxicologica, 20*, 140–144.

Carlsson, K., Petrovic, P., Skare, S., Petersson, K. M., & Ingvar, M. (2000). Tickling expectations: Neural processing in anticipation of a sensory stimulus. *Journal of Cognitive Neuroscience, 12*, 691–703.

Carothers, A. D., Castilla, E. E., Dutra, M. G., & Hook, E. B. (2001). Search for ethnic, geographic, and other factors in the epidemiology of Down syndrome in South America: Analysis of data from the ECLAMC project, 1967–1997. *American Journal of Medical Genetics, 103*, 149–156.

Caselli, R. J. (1997). Tactile agnosia and disorders of tactile perception. In T. E. Feinberg & M. J. Farah (Eds.), *Behavioral neurology and neuropsychology* (pp. 277–288). New York: McGraw-Hill.

Cassone, V. M. (1990). Effects of melatonin on vertebrate circadian systems. *Trends in Neurosciences, 13*(11), 457–467.

Cenci, M. A., Whishaw, I. Q., & Schallert, T. (2002). Animal models of neurological deficits: How relevant is the rat? *Nature Reviews Neuroscience, 3*, 574–579.

Cermakian, N., & Sassone-Corsi, P. (2002). Environmental stimulus perception and control of circadian clocks. *Current Opinion in Neurobiology, 12*, 359–365.

Chatterjee, S., & Callaway, E. M. (2003). Parallel colour-opponent pathways to primary visual cortex. *Nature, 426*, 668–671.

Chemielli, R. M., Willie, J. T., Sinton, C. M., Elmquist, J. K., Scammell, T., Lee, C., et al. (1999). Narcolepsy in orexin knockout mice: Molecular genetics of sleep regulation. *Cell, 98*, 427–451.

Cheng, J., Cao, Y., & Olson, L. (1996). Spinal cord repair in adult paraplegic rats: Partial restoration of hind limb function. *Science, 273*, 510–513.

Cho, A. K. (1990). Ice: A new dosage form of an old drug. *Science, 249,* 631–634.

Chorover, S. L., & Schiller, P. H. (1965). Short-term retrograde amnesia in rats. *Journal of Comparative and Physiological Psychology, 59,* 73–78.

Christie, B. R., Kerr, D. S., & Abraham, W. C. (1994). Flip side of synaptic plasticity: Long-term depression mechanisms in the hippocampus. *Hippocampus, 4,* 127–135.

Christoff, K., & Gabrieli, J. D. E. (2000). The frontopolar cortex and human cognition: Evidence for a rostrocaudal hierarchical organization within the human prefrontal cortex. *Psychobiology, 28,* 168–186.

Chun, M. M., & Marois, R. (2002). The dark side of visual attention. *Current Opinion in Neurobiology, 12,* 184–189.

Cirulli, F., Berry, A., & Alleva, E. (2003). Early disruption of the mother–infant relationship: Effects on brain plasticity and implications for psychopathology. *Neuroscience and Biobehavioural Reviews, 27,* 73–82.

Clark, A. S., & Henderson, L. P. (2003). Behavioral and physiological responses to anabolic-androgenic steroids. *Neuroscience and Biobehavioural Reviews, 27,* 413–436.

Claverie, J. M. (2001). What if there are only 30,000 human genes? *Science, 291,* 1255–1257.

Clayton, N. S. (2001). Hippocampal growth and maintenance depend on food-caching experience in juvenile mountain chickadees (*Poecile gambeli*). *Behavioral Neuroscience, 115,* 614–625.

Clements, J. D., Lester, R. A. J., Tong, G., Jahr, C. E., & Westbrook, G. L. (1992). The time course of glutamate in the synaptic cleft. *Science, 258,* 1498–1501.

Clifton, P. G. (2000). Meal patterning in rodents: Psychopharmacological and neuroanatomical studies. *Neuroscience and Biobehavioural Reviews, 24,* 213–222.

Cohen, I., Navarro, V., Clemenceau, S., Baulac, M., & Miles, R. (2002). On the origin of interictal activity in human temporal lobe epilepsy *in vitro. Science, 298,* 1418–1421.

Cohen, Y. E., & Andersen, R. A. (2002). A common reference name for movement plans in the posterior parietal cortex. *Nature Reviews Neuroscience, 3,* 553–562.

Cohen, Y. E., & Knudsen, E. I. (1999). Maps versus clusters: Different representations of auditory space in the midbrain and forebrain. *Trends in Neurosciences, 22,* 128–135.

Colapinto, J. (2000). *As nature made him: The boy who was raised as a girl.* New York: HarperCollins.

Cole, J. C., & Sumnall, H. R. (2003). The pre-clinical behavioral pharmacology of 3,4-methylenedioxymethamphetamine (MDMA). *Neuroscience and Biobehavioural Reviews, 27,* 199–217.

Colell, M., Segarra, M. D., & Sabater-Pi, J. (1995). Manual laterality in chimpanzees (*Pan troglodytes*) in complex tasks. *Journal of Comparative Psychology, 109,* 298–307.

Coleman, D. L. (1979). Obesity genes: Beneficial effects in heterozygous mice. *Science, 203,* 663–665.

Coleman, M. P., & Perry, V. H. (2002). Axon pathology in neurological disease: A neglected therapeutic target. *Trends in Neurosciences, 25,* 532–537.

Collette, F., & Van der Linden, M. (2002). Brain imaging of the central executive component of working memory. *Neuroscience and Biobehavioural Reviews, 26,* 105–125.

Collie, A., & Maruff, P. (2000). The neuropsychology of preclinical Alzheimer's disease and mild cognitive impairment. *Neuroscience and Biobehavioural Reviews, 24,* 365–374.

Collier, G. (1986). The dialogue between the house economist and the resident physiologist. *Nutrition and Behavior, 3,* 9–26.

Collier, G. H. (1980). An ecological analysis of motivation. In F. M. Toates & T. R. Halliday (Eds.), *Analysis of motivational processes* (pp. 125–151). London: Academic Press.

Colombo, M., & Broadbent, N. (2000). Is the avian hippocampus a functional homologue of the mammalian hippocampus? *Neuroscience and Biobehavioural Reviews, 24,* 465–484.

Colvin, M. K., Dunbar, K., & Grafman, J. (2001). The effects of frontal lobe lesions on goal achievement in the water jug task. *Journal of Cognitive Neuroscience, 13,* 1129–1147.

Conklin, H. M., & Iacono, W. G. (2002). Schizophrenia: A neurodevelopmental perspective. *Current Directions in Psychological Science, 11,* 33–37.

Connolly, J. D., Andersen, R. A., & Goodale, M. A. (2003). fMRI evidence for a "parietal reach region" in the human brain. *Experimental Brain Research, 153,* 140–145.

Cook, M. N., Bolivar, V. J., McFadyen, M. P., & Flaherty, L. (2002). Behavioral differences among 129 substrains: Implications for knockout and transgenic mice. *Behavioral Neuroscience, 116,* 600–611.

Coolen, L. M., Fitzgerald, M. E., Yu, L., & Lehman, M. N. (2004). Activation of mu opioid receptors in the medial preoptic area following copulation in male rats. *Neuroscience, 124,* 11–21.

Corbetta, M., Miezin, F. M., Dobmeyer, S., Shulman, G. L., & Petersen, S. E. (1990). Attentional modulation of neural processing of shape, color, and velocity in humans. *Science, 248,* 1556–1559.

Corcoran, M., McCaughran, J. A., Jr., & Wada, J. A. (1978). Antiepileptic and prophylactic effects of tetrahydrocannabinols in amygdaloid kindled rats. *Epilepsia, 19,* 47–55.

Corina, D. P., Poizner, H., Bellugi, U., Feinberg, T., Dowd, D., & O'Grady-Batch, L. (1992). Dissociation between linguistic and nonlinguistic gestural systems: A case for compositionality. *Brain and Language, 43,* 414–447.

Corkin, S. (1968). Acquisition of motor skill after bilateral medial temporal-lobe excision. *Neuropsychologia, 6,* 255–265.

Corkin, S. (2002). What's new with the amnesic patient H.M.? *Nature Reviews Neuroscience, 3,* 153–160.

Corkin, S., Milner, B., & Rasmussen, R. (1970). Somatosensory thresholds. *Archives of Neurology, 23,* 41–59.

Corwin, J. T., & Warchol, M. E. (1991). Auditory hair cells. *Annual Review of Neuroscience, 14,* 301–333.

Cottman, C. W., & Berchtold, N. C. (2002). Exercise: A behavioral intervention to enhance brain health and plasticity. *Trends in Neurosciences, 25,* 295–301.

Courtney, S. M., & Ungerleider, L. G. (1997). What fMRI has taught us about human vision. *Current Opinion in Neurobiology, 7,* 554–561.

Cowan, W. M. (1979, September). The development of the brain. *Scientific American, 241,* 113–133.

Cowan, W. M., Kopnisky, K. L., & Hyman, S. E. (2002). The human genome project and its impact on psychiatry. *Annual Review of Neuroscience, 25,* 1–50.

Crabbe, J. C., Wahlsten, D., & Dudek, B. C. (1999). Genetics of mouse behavior: Interactions with laboratory environment. *Science, 284,* 1670–1672.

Craelius, W. (2002). The bionic man: Restoring mobility. *Science, 295,* 1018–1019.

Craig, A. D. (2002). How do you feel? Interoception: The sense of the physiological condition of the body. *Nature Reviews Neuroscience, 3,* 655–666.

Craig, A. D. (2003). Pain mechanisms: Labeled lines versus convergence in central processing. *Annual Review of Neuroscience, 26,* 1–30.

Craig, A. D., Reiman, E. M., Evans, A., & Bushnell, M. C. (1996). Functional imaging of an illusion of pain. *Nature, 384,* 258–260.

Creese, I., Burt, D. R., & Snyder, S. H. (1976). Dopamine receptor binding predicts clinical and pharmacological potencies of antischizophrenic drugs. *Science, 192,* 481–483.

Crisp, A. H. (1983). Some aspects of the psychopathology of anorexia nervosa. In P. L. Darby, P. E. Garfinkel, D. M. Garner, & D. V. Coscina (Eds.), *Anorexia nervosa: Recent developments in research* (pp. 15–28). New York: Alan R. Liss.

Crowell, C. R., Hinson, R. E., & Siegel, S. (1981). The role of conditional drug responses in tolerance to the hypothermic effects of ethanol. *Psychopharmacology, 73*, 51–54.

Crunelli, V., & Leresche, N. (2002). Childhood absence epilepsy: Genes, channels, neurons and networks. *Nature Reviews Neuroscience, 3*, 371–382.

Culbertson, F. M. (1997). Depression and gender. *American Psychologist, 52*, 25–31.

Culham, J. C., & Kanwisher, N. G. (2001). Neuroimaging of cognitive functions in human parietal cortex. *Current Opinion in Neurobiology, 11*, 157–163.

Curtiss, S. (1977). *Genie: A psycholinguistic study of a modern-day "wild child."* New York: Academic Press.

D'Almeida, V., Hipólide, D. C., Azzalis, L. A., Lobo, L. L., Junqueira, V. B. C., & Tufik, S. (1997). Absence of oxidative stress following paradoxical sleep deprivation in rats. *Neu-roscience Letters, 235*, 25–28.

Daly, M., & Wilson, M. (1983). *Sex, evolution, and behavior.* Boston: Allard Grant Press.

Damasio, H. (1989). Neuroimaging contributions to the understanding of aphasia. In F. Boller & J. Grafman (Eds.), *Handbook of neuropsychology* (Vol. 2, pp. 3–46). New York: Elsevier.

Damasio, H., Grabowski, T., Frank, R., Galaburda, A. M., & Damasio, A. R. (1994). The return of Phineas Gage: Clues about the brain from the skull of a famous patient. *Science, 264*, 1102–1105.

Damasio, H., Grabowski, T. J., Tranel, D., Hichwa, R. D., & Damasio, A. R. (1996). A neural basis for lexical retrieval. *Nature, 380*, 499–505.

Darian-Smith, I., Burman, K., & Darian-Smith, C. (1999). Parallel pathways mediating manual dexterity in the macaque. *Experimental Brain Research, 128*, 101–108.

Darlison, M. G., & Richter, D. (1999). Multiple genes for neuropeptides and their receptors: Co-evolution and physiology. *Trends in Neurosciences, 22*, 81–88.

Darnell, J. E., Jr. (1997). STATS and gene regulation. *Science, 277*, 1630–1635.

Davidson, C., Gow, A. J., Lee, T. H., & Ellinwood, E. H. (2001). Methamphetamine neurotoxicity: Necrotic and apoptotic mechanisms and relevance to human abuse and treatment. *Brain Research Reviews, 36*, 1–22.

Davidson, J. M. (1980). Hormones and sexual behavior in the male. In D. T. Krieger & J. C. Hughes (Eds.), *Neuroendocrinol-ogy* (pp. 232–238). Sunderland, MA: Sinauer Associates.

Davis, M., Rainie, D., & Cassell, M. (1994). Neurotransmission in the rat amygdala related to fear and anxiety. *Trends in Neurosciences, 17*, 208–214.

Dawson, D., & Encel, N. (1993). Melatonin and sleep in humans. *Journal of Pineal Research, 15*, 1–2.

Dawson, T. M., & Dawson, V. L. (2003). Molecular pathways of neurodegenerations in Parkinson's disease. *Science, 302*, 819–822.

Dayer, A. G., Cleaaver, K. M., Abouantoun, T., & Cameron, H. A. (2005). New GABAergic interneurons in the adult neocortex and striatum are generated from different precursors. *Journal of Cell Biology, 168*, 415–427.

Debski, E. A., & Cline, H. T. (2002). Activity-dependent mapping in the retinotectal projection. *Current Opinion in Neurobiology, 12*, 93–99.

de Castro, J. M., & Plunkett, S. (2002). A general model of intake regulation. *Neuroscience and Biobehavioural Reviews, 26*, 581–595.

DeCatanzaro, D., Muir, C., Spironello, E., Binger, T., & Thomas, J. (2000). Intense arousal of novel male mice in proximity to previously inseminated females: Inactivation of males via chlorpromazine does not diminish the capacity to disrupt pregnancy. *Psychobiology, 28*, 110–114.

de Gelder, B. (2000). Neuroscience. More to seeing than meets the eye. *Science, 289*, 1148–1208.

De Gennaro, L., Ferrara, M., & Bertini, M. (2000). Muscle twitch activity during REM sleep: Effect of sleep deprivation and relation with rapid eye movement activity. *Psychobiology, 28*, 432–436.

Dehaene, S. (2002). Single-neuron arithmetic. *Science, 297*, 1652–1653.

De Jonge, F. H., Louwerse, A. L., Ooms, M. P., Evers, P., Endert, E., & van de Poll, N. E. (1989). Lesions of the SDN-POA inhibit sexual behavior of male Wistar rats. *Brain Research Bulletin, 23*, 483–492.

de Kruif, P. (1945). *The male hormone.* New York: Harcourt, Brace.

Delville, Y., Melloni, R. H., Jr., & Ferris, C. F. (1998). Behavioral and neurobiological consequences of social subjugation during puberty in golden hamsters. *Journal of Neuroscience, 18*, 2667–2672.

Dement, W. C. (1960). The effect of dream deprivation. *Sci-ence, 131*, 1705–1707.

Dement, W. C. (1978). *Some must watch while some must sleep.* New York: W. W. Norton.

Dement, W. C., & Kleitman, N. (1957). The relation of eye movement during sleep to dream activity: An objective method for the study of dreaming. *Journal of Experimental Psychology, 53*, 339–553.

Dement, W. C., & Wolpert, E. A. (1958). The relation of eye movements, body motility and external stimuli to dream content. *Journal of Experimental Psychology, 55*, 543–553.

Demet, E. M., Chicz-Demet, A., Fallon, J. H., & Sokolski, K. N. (1999). Sleep deprivation therapy in depressive illness and Parkinson's disease. *Progressive Neuro-Psychopharmacology & Biological Psychiatry, 23*, 753–784.

Denham, T. P., Haberle, S. G., Lentfer, C., Fullagar, R., Field, J., Therin, M., et al. (2003). Origins of agriculture at Kuk Swamp in the highlands of New Guinea. *Science, 301*, 189–193.

De Renzi, E. (1997). Visuospatial and constructional disorders. In T. E. Feinberg & M. J. Farah (Eds.), *Behavioral neurology and neuropsychology* (pp. 297–308). New York: McGraw-Hill.

Deroche-Gamonet, V., Belin, D., & Piazza, P. V. (2004). Evidence for addiction-like behavior in the rat. *Science, 305*, 1014–1017.

Deutch, A. Y., & Roth, R. H. (1999). Neurotransmitters. In M. J. Zigmond, F. E. Bloom, S. C. Landis, J. L. Roberts, & L. R. Squire (Eds.), *Fundamental neuroscience* (pp. 193–234). New York: Academic Press.

De Valois, R. L., Cottaris, N. P., Elfar, S. D., Mahon, L. E., & Wilson, J. A. (2000). Some transformations of color information from lateral geniculate nucleus to striate cortex. *Proceedings of the National Academy of Sciences, U.S.A., 97*, 4997–5002.

Devane, W. A., Hanus, L., Breuer, A., Pertwee, R. G., Stevenson, L. A., Griffin, G., et al. (1992). Isolation and structure of a brain constituent that binds to the cannabinoid receptor. *Science, 258*, 1946–1949.

De Vry, J., & Schreiber, R. (2000). Effects of selected serotonin 5-HT1 and 5-HT2 receptoragonists on feeding behavior: Possible mechanisms of action. *Neuroscience and Biobehavioural Reviews, 24*, 341–353.

de Waal, F. B. M. (1999, December). The end of nature versus nurture. *Scientific American, 281*, 94–99.

De Witte, P., Pinto, E., Ansseau, M., & Verbanck, P. (2003). Alcohol and withdrawal: From animal research to clinical issues. *Neuroscience and Biobehavioural Reviews, 27*, 189–197.

Dewsbury, D. A. (1991). Psychobiology. *American Psychologist, 46*, 198–205.

Diamond, A. (1985). Development of the ability to use recall to guide action, as indicated by infants' performance on AB. *Child Development, 56*, 868–883.

Diamond, A. (1991). Neuropsychological insights into the meaning of object concept development. In S. Carey & R. Gelman (Eds.), *The epigenesis of mind: Essays on biology and cognition* (pp. 67–110). Hillsdale, NJ: Lawrence Erlbaum.

Diamond, M., & Sigmundson, H. K. (1997). Sex reassignment at birth: Long-term review and clinical implications. *Archives of Pediatric and Adolescent Medicine, 151*, 298–304.

Diamond, M. C. (1986). I want a girl just like the girl. . . . *Discover, 7*, 65–68.

DiCarlo, J. J., & Johnson, K. O. (2000). Spatial and temporal structure of receptive fields in primate somatosensory area 3b: Effects of stimulus scanning direction and orientation. *Journal of Neuroscience, 20*, 495–510.

DiCarlo, J. J., Johnson, K. O., & Hsaio, S. S. (1998). Structure of receptive fields in area 3b of primary somatosensory cortex in the alert monkey. *Journal of Neuroscience, 18*, 2626–2645.

Di Ciano, P., & Everitt, B. J. (2003). Differential control over drug-seeking behavior by drug-associated conditioned reinforcers and discriminative stimuli predictive of drug availability. *Behavioral Neuroscience, 117*, 952–960.

Dietz, V. (2002a). Do human bipeds use quadrupedal coordination? *Trends in Neurosciences, 25*, 462–467.

Dietz, V. (2002b). Proprioception and locomotor disorders. *Nature Reviews Neuroscience, 3*, 781–790.

DiFiglia, M., Sapp, E., Chase, K. O., Davies, S. W., Bates, G. P., Vonsattel, J. P., & Aronin, N. (1997). Aggregation of Huntington in neuronal intranuclear inclusions and dystrophic neurites in brain. *Science, 277*, 1990–1993.

Di Marzo, V., Melck, D., Bisogno, T., & De Petrocellis, L. (1998). Endocannabinoids: Endogenous cannabinoid receptor ligands with neuromodulatory action. *Trends in Neurosciences, 21*, 521–528.

Dinges, D. F., Pack, F., Williams, K., Gillen, K. A., Powell, J. W., Ott, G. E., et al. (1997). Cumulative sleepiness, mood disturbance, and psychomotor vigilance performance decrements during a week of sleep restricted to 4–5 hours per night. *Sleep, 20*, 267–277.

Dirnagl, U., Iadecola, C., & Moskowitz, M. A. (1999). Pathobiology of ischaemic stroke: An integrated view. *Trends in Neurosciences, 22*, 391–397.

Dirnagl, U., Simon, R. P., & Hallenbeck, J. M. (2003). Ischemic tolerance and endogenous neuroprotection. *Trends in Neurosciences, 24*, 248–254.

Dixon, M. J., Bub, D. N., & Arguin, M. (1998). Semantic and visual determinants of face recognition in a prosopagnosic patient. *Journal of Cognitive Neuroscience, 10*, 362–376.

Dobelle, W. H., Mladejovsky, M. G., & Girvin, J. P. (1974). Artificial vision for the blind: Electrical stimulation of visual cortex offers hope for a functional prosthesis. *Science, 183*, 440–444.

Döbrössy, M., & Dunnett, S. B. (2001). The influence of environment and experience on neural grafts. *Nature Reviews Neuroscience, 2*, 871–909.

Donoghue, J. P. (1995). Plasticity of adult sensorimotor representations. *Current Opinion in Neurobiology, 5*, 749–754.

Doty, R. L. (2001). Olfaction. *Annual Review of Psychology, 52*, 423–452.

Doupe, A. J., & Heisenberg, M. (2000). Neurobiology of behaviour. Old principles and new approaches. *Current Opinion in Neurobiology, 10*, 755–756.

Doya, K. (2000). Complementary roles of basal ganglia and cerebellum in learning and motor control. *Current Opinion in Neurobiology, 10*, 732–739.

Drevets, W. C. (2001). Neuroimaging and neuropathological studies of depression: Implications for the cognitive-emotional features of mood disorders. *Current Opinion in Neurobiology, 11*, 240–249.

Drew, T., Jiang, W., & Widajewicz, W. (2002). Contributions of the motor cortex to the control of the hindlimbs during locomotion in the cat. *Brain Research Reviews, 40*, 178–191.

Drewnowski, A., Halmi, K. A., Pierce, B., Gibbs, J., & Smith, G. P. (1987). Taste and eating disorders. *American Journal of Clinical Nutrition, 46*, 442–450.

Drummey, A. B., & Newcombe, N. (1995). Remembering versus knowing the past: Children's explicit and implicit memories for pictures. *Journal of Experimental Child Psychology, 59*, 540–565.

Duffy, S. N., Craddock, K. J., Abel, T., & Nguyen, P. V. (2001). Environmental enrichment modifies the PKA-dependence of hippocampal LTP and improves hippocampus-dependent memory. *Learning and Memory, 8*, 26–34.

Dunbar, G. C., Perera, M. H., & Jenner, F. A. (1989). Patterns of benzodiazepine use in Great Britain as measured by a general population survey. *British Journal of Psychiatry, 155*, 836–841.

Dunbar, R. (2003). Evolution of the social brain. *Science, 302*, 1160–1161.

Dunnett, S. B., Björklund, A., & Lindvall, O. (2001). Cell therapy in Parkinson's disease—stop or go? *Nature Reviews Neuroscience, 2*, 365–368.

Dustin, M. L., & Colman, D. R. (2002). Neural and immunological synaptic relations. *Science, 298*, 785–789.

Duva, C. A., Kornecook, T. J., & Pinel, J. P. J. (2000). Animal models of medial temporal lobe amnesia: The myth of the hippocampus. In M. Haug & R. E. Whalen (Eds.), *Animal models of human emotion and cognition* (pp. 197–214). Washington, DC: American Psychological Association.

Eagleman, D. M. (2001). Visual illusions and neurobiology. *Nature Reviews Neuroscience, 2*, 920–926.

Egan, M. F., & Weinberger, D. R. (1997). Neurobiology of schizophrenia. *Current Opinion in Neurobiology, 7*, 701–707.

Ehrhardt, A. A., Meyer-Bahlburg, H. F. L., Rosen, L. R., Feldman, J. F., Veridiano, N. P., Zimmerman, I., & McEwen, B. S. (1985). Sexual orientation after prenatal exposure to exogenous estrogen. *Archives of Sexual Behavior, 14*, 57–77.

Ehringer, H., & Hornykiewicz, O. (1960). Verteilung von Noradrenalin und Dopamin (3-Hydroxytyramin) im gehirn des Menschen und ihr Verhalten bei Erkrankungen des Extrapyramidalen Systems. *Klinische Wochenschrift, 38*, 1236–1239.

Eichenbaum, H. (1996). Learning from LTP: A comment on recent attempts to identify cellular and molecular mechanisms of memory. *Learning & Memory, 3*, 61–73.

Eichenbaum, H. (1999). Conscious awareness, memory and the hippocampus. *Nature, 2*, 775–776.

Eigsti, I. M., & Shapiro, T. (2004). A systems neuroscience approach to autism: Biological, cognitive, and clinical perspectives. *Mental Retardation and Developmental Disabilities Research Reviews, 9*, 205–215.

Eitan, S., Solomon, A., Lavie, V., Yoles, E., Hirschberg, D. L., Belkin, M., & Schwartz, M. (1994). Recovery of visual response of injured adult rat optic nerves treated with trans-glutaminase. *Science, 264*, 1764–1768.

Elbert, T., Pantev, C., Wienbruch, C., Rockstroh, B., & Taub, E. (1995). Increased cortical representation of the fingers of the left hand in string players. *Science, 270*, 305–307.

Elbert, T., & Rockstroh, B. (2004). Reorganization of human cerebral cortex: The range of changes following use and injury. *The Neuroscientist, 10*, 129–141.

Ellis, L., & Ames, M. A. (1987). Neurohormonal functioning and sexual orientation: A theory of homosexuality-heterosexuality. *Psychological Bulletin, 101*, 233–258.

Engel, A. K., Fries, P., & Singer, W. (2001). Dynamic predictions: Oscillations and synchrony in top-down processing. *Nature Reviews Neuroscience, 2*, 704–716.

Engel, S. A. (1999). Using neuroimaging to measure mental representations: Finding color-opponent neurons in visual cortex. *Current Directions in Psychological Science, 8*, 23–27.

Erickson, K., Drevets, W., & Schulkin, J. (2003). Glucocorticoid regulation of diverse cognitive functions in normal and pathological emotional states. *Neuroscience and Biobehavioural Reviews, 27*, 233–246.

Erikkson, P. S., Perfilieva, E., Björk-Eriksson, T., Alborn, A., Nordberg, C., Peterson, D. A., & Gage, F. H. (1998). Neurogenesis in the adult human hippocampus. *Nature Medicine, 4*, 1313–1317.

Errington, M. L., Galley, P. T., & Bliss, T. V. P. (2003). Long-term potentiation in the dentate gyrus of the anaesthetized rat is accompanied by an increase in extracellular glutamate: Real-time measurements using a novel dialysis electrode. *Philosophical Transactions of the Royal Society of London, 358*, 675–687.

Espie, C. A. (2002). Insomnia: Conceptual issues in the development, persistence, and treatment of sleep disorder in adults. *Annual Review of Neuroscience, 53*, 215–243.

Everitt, B. J., Dickinson, A., & Robbins, T. W. (2001). The neuropsychological basis of addictive behaviour. *Brain Research Reviews, 36*, 129–138.

Everitt, B. J., & Herbert, J. (1972). Hormonal correlates of sexual behavior in sub-human primates. *Danish Medical Bulletin, 19*, 246–258.

Everitt, B. J., Herbert, J., & Hamer, J. D. (1971). Sexual receptivity of bilaterally adrenalectomized female rhesus monkeys. *Physiology & Behavior, 8*, 409–415.

Everitt, B. J., & Robbins, T. W. (1997). Central cholinergic systems and cognition. *Annual Review of Psychology, 48*, 649–684.

Fabbro, F., Tavano, A., Corti, S., Bresolin, N., De Fabrtiis, P., & Borgatti, R. (2004). Long-term neuropsychological deficits after cerebellar infarctions in two young adult twins. *Neuropsychologia, 42*, 536–545.

Fabri, M., Polonara, G., Del Pesce, M., Quattrini, A., Salvolini, U., & Manzoni, T. (2001). Posterior corpus callosum and interhemispheric transfer of somatosensory information: An fMRI and neuropsychological study of a partially callosot-omized patient. *Journal of Cognitive Neuroscience, 13*, 1071–1079.

Falkenburger, B. H., Barstow, K. L., & Mintz, I. M. (2001). Dendro-dendritic inhibition through reversal of dopamine transport. *Science, 293*, 2465–2470.

Falzi, G., Perrone, P., & Vignolo, L. A. (1982). Right-left asymmetry in anterior speech region. *Archives of Neurology, 39*, 239–240.

Farah, M. J. (1990). *Visual agnosia: Disorders of object recognition and what they tell us about normal vision.* Cambridge, MA: MIT Press.

Farber, N. B., & Olney, J. W. (2003). Drugs of abuse that cause developing neurons to commit suicide. *Developmental Brain Research, 147*, 37–45.

Farmer, J., Zhao, X., Van Praag, H., Wodke, K., Gage, F. H., & Christie, B. R. (2004). Effects of voluntary exercise on synaptic plasticity and gene expression in the dentate gyrus of adult male Sprague-Dawley rats *in vivo. Neuroscience, 124*, 71–79.

Farmer, M. E., & Klein, R. M. (1995). The evidence for a temporal processing deficit linked to dyslexia: A review. *Psychonomic Bulletin and Review, 2*, 460–493.

Farooqi, I. S., Jebb, S. A., Langmack, G., Lawrence, E., Cheetham, C. H., Prentice, A. M., et al. (1999). Effects of recombinant leptin therapy in a child with congenital leptin deficiency. *New England Journal of Medicine, 341*, 879–884.

Farrell, S. F., & McGinnis, M. Y. (2003). Effects of pubertal anabolic-androgenic steroid (AAS) administration on reproductive and aggressive behaviors in male rats. *Behavioral Neuroscience, 117*, 904–911.

Fazio, F., Perani, D., Gilardi, M. C., Colombo, F., Cappa, S. F., Vallar, G., et al. (1992). Metabolic impairment in human amnesia: A PET study of memory networks. *Journal of Cerebral Blood Flow and Metabolism, 12*, 353–358.

Feindel, W. (1986). Electrical stimulation of the brain during surgery for epilepsy—historical highlights. In G. P. Varkey (Ed.), *Anesthetic considerations for craniotomy in awake patients* (pp. 75–87). Boston: Little, Brown.

Feng, A. S., & Ratnam, R. (2000). Neural basis of hearing in real-world situations. *Annual Review of Psychology, 51*, 699–725.

Fentress, J. C. (1973). Development of grooming in mice with amputated forelimbs. *Science, 179*, 704–705.

Fernald, R. D. (2000). Evolution of eyes. *Current Opinion in Neurobiology, 10*, 444–450.

Fernández-Guasti, A., Swaab, D., & Rodríguez-Manzo, G. (2003). Sexual behavior reduces hypothalamic androgen receptor immunoreactivity. *Psychoneuroendocrinology, 28*, 501–512.

Ferrara, M., De Gennaro, L., & Bertini, M. (1999). The effects of slow-wave sleep (SWS) deprivation and time of night on behavioral performance upon awakening. *Physiology & Behavior, 68*, 55–61.

Fields, R. D. (2004, April). The other half of the brain. *Scientific American, 290*, 55–61.

Fields, R. D., & Stevens-Graham, B. (2002). New insights into neuron-glia communication. *Science, 298*, 556–562.

Filbin, M. T. (2003). Myelin-associated inhibitors of axonal regeneration in the adult mammalian CNS. *Nature Reviews Neuroscience, 4*, 703–712.

Fillion, T. J., & Blass, E. M. (1986). Infantile experience with suckling odors determines adult sexual behavior in male rats. *Science, 231*, 729–731.

Fink, G., Sumner, B., Rosie, R., Wilson, H., & McQueen, J. (1999). Androgen actions on central serotonin neurotransmission: Relevance for mood, mental state and memory. *Behavioural Brain Research, 105*, 53–68.

Finlay, B. L., & Darlington, R. B. (1995). Linked regularities in the development and evolution of mammalian brains. *Science, 268*, 1578–1584.

Fiorillo, C. D., Tobler, P. N., & Schultz, W. (2003). Discrete coding of reward probability and uncertainty by dopamine neurons. *Science, 299*, 1898–1902.

Fiorino, D. F., Coury, A., & Phillips, A. G. (1997). Dynamic changes in nucleus accumbens dopamine efflux during the Coolidge effect in male rats. *Journal of Neuroscience, 17*, 4849–4855.

Fisher, S. E., & DeFries, J. C. (2002). Developmental dyslexia: Genetic dissection of a complex cognitive trait. *Nature Reviews Neuroscience, 3*, 767–780.

Foster, R. G., & Kreitzman, L. (2004). *Rhythms of life.* London: Profiles.

Foulkes, N. S., Borjigin, J., Snyder, S. H., & Sassone-Corsi, P. (1997). Rhythmic transcription: The molecular basis of circadian melatonin synthesis. *Trends in Neurosciences, 20*, 487–492.

Fournier, A. E., & Strittmatter, S. M. (2001). Repulsive factors and axon regeneration in the CNS. *Current Opinion in Neurobiology, 11,* 89–94.

Francis, D. D., & Meaney, M. J. (1999). Maternal care and the development of stress responses. *Current Opinion in Neurobiology, 9,* 128–134.

Freedman, M. S., Lucas, R. J., Soni, B., von Schantz, M., Muñoz, M., David-Gray, Z., & Foster, R. (1999). Regulation of mammalian circadian behavior by non-rod, non-cone, ocular photoreceptors. *Science, 284,* 502–504.

Freund, H. J. (2003). Somatosensory and motor disturbances in patients with parietal lobe lesions. *Advances in Neurology, 93,* 179–193.

Friedman, J., Globus, G., Huntley, A., Mullaney, D., Naitoh, P., & Johnson, L. (1977). Performance and mood during and after gradual sleep reduction. *Psychophysiology, 14,* 245–250.

Friedman-Hill, S. R., Robertson, L. C., & Treisman, A. (1995). Parietal contributions to visual feature binding: Evidence from a patient with bilateral lesions. *Science, 269,* 853–855.

Fries, P., Fernández, G., & Jensen, O. (2003). When neurons form memories. *Trends in Neurosciences, 26,* 123–124.

Frith, C., & Dolan, R. J. (1998). Images of psychopathology. *Current Opinion in Neurobiology, 8,* 259–262.

Funnell, M. G., Corballis, P. M., & Gazzaniga, M. S. (1999). A deficit in perceptual matching in the left hemisphere of a callostomy patient. *Neuropsychologia, 37,* 1143–1154.

Fuster, J. M. (2000). The prefrontal cortex of the primate: A synopsis. *Psychobiology, 28,* 125–131.

Gabrieli, J. D. E., Corkin, S., Mickel, S. F., & Growdon, J. H. (1993). Intact acquisition and long-term retention of mirror-tracing skill in Alzheimer's disease and in global amnesia. *Behavioral Neuroscience, 107,* 899–910.

Gaffan, D. (1974). Recognition impaired and association intact in the memory of monkeys after transection of the fornix. *Journal of Comparative and Physiological Psychology, 86,* 1100–1109.

Gage, F. H. (2000). Mammalian neural stem cells. *Science, 287,* 1433–1438.

Gaiarsa, J.-L., Caillard, O., & Ben-Ari, Y. (2002). Long-term plasticity at GABAergic and glycenergic synapses: Mechanisms and functional significance. *Trends in Neurosciences, 25,* 564–570.

Galef, B. G. (1989). Laboratory studies of naturally-occurring feeding behaviors: Pitfalls, progress and problems in ethoexperimental analysis. In R. J. Blanchard, P. F. Brain, D. C. Blanchard, & S. Parmigiani (Eds.), *Ethoexperimental approaches to the study of behavior* (pp. 51–77). Dordrecht, The Netherlands: Kluwer Academ-ic Publishers.

Galef, B. G. (1995). Food selection: Problems in understanding how we choose foods to eat. *Neuroscience and Biobehavioural Reviews, 20,* 67–73.

Galef, B. G. (1996). Social enhancement of food preferences in Norway rats: A brief review. In C. M. Heyes & B. G. Galef, Jr. (Eds.), *Social learning in animals: The roots of culture* (pp. 49–64). New York: Academic Press.

Galef, B. G., & Wright, T. J. (1995). Groups of naive rats learn to select nutritionally adequate foods faster than do isolated naive rats. *Animal Behavior, 49,* 403–409.

Gannon, P. J., Holloway, R. L., Broadfield, D. C., & Braun, A. R. (1998). Asymmetry of chimpanzee planum temporale: Humanlike pattern of Wernicke's brain language area homolog. *Science, 279,* 220–222.

Gao, E., & Suga, N. (2000). Experience-dependent plasticity in the auditory cortex and the inferior colliculus of bats: Role of the corticofugal system. *Proceedings of the National Academy of Sciences U.S.A., 97,* 8081–8086.

Gao, G., Wang, X., He, S., Li, W., Wang, Q., Liang, Q., et al. (2003). Clinical study for alleviating opiate drug psychological dependence by a method of ablating the nucleus accumbens with stereotactic surgery. *Stereotactic and Functional Neurosurgery, 81,* 96–104.

Garwicz, M. (2002). Spinal reflexes provide motor error signals to cerebellar modules—relevance for motor coordination. *Brain Research Reviews, 40,* 152–165.

Gauthier, I., Behrmann, M., & Tarr, M. J. (1999). Can face recognition really be dissociated from object recognition? *Journal of Cognitive Neuroscience, 11,* 349–370.

Gawin, F. H. (1991). Cocaine addiction: Psychology and neurophysiology. *Science, 251,* 1580–1586.

Gazzaniga, M. S. (1967, August). The split brain in man. *Scientific American, 217,* 24–29.

Gazzaniga, M. S. (1998, July). The split brain revisited. *Scientific American, 278,* 51–55.

Gazzaniga, M. S. (2000). Regional differences in cortical organization. *Science, 289,* 1887–1888.

Gazzaniga, M. S., & Sperry, R. W. (1967). Language after section of the cerebral commissure. *Brain, 90,* 131–148.

Gegenfurtner, K. R., & Kiper, D. C. (2003). Color vision. *Annual Review of Neuroscience, 26,* 181–206.

Geng, J. J., & Behrmann, M. (2002). Probability cuing of target location facilitates visual search implicitly in normal participants and patients with hemispatial neglect. *Psychological Science, 13,* 520–525.

Georgopoulos, A. P. (1991). Higher order motor control. *Annual Review of Neuroscience, 14,* 361–377.

Georgopoulos, A. P. (1995). Current issues in directional motor control. *Trends in Neurosciences, 18,* 506–510.

Gerlach, C., Law, I., & Paulson, O. B. (2002). When action turns into words. Activation of motor-based knowledge during categorization of manipulable objects. *Journal of Cognitive Neuroscience, 14,* 1230–1239.

Gernsbacher, M. A., & Kaschak, M. P. (2003). Neuroimaging studies of language production and comprehension. *Annual Review of Psychology, 54,* 91–114.

Geschwind, N. (1970). The organization of language and the brain. *Science, 170,* 940–944.

Geschwind, N. (1979, September). Specializations of the human brain. *Scientific American, 241,* 180–199.

Geschwind, N., & Levitsky, W. (1968). Human brain: Left-right asymmetries in temporal speech region. *Science, 161,* 186–187.

Gibbs, J., Young, R. C., & Smith, G. P. (1973). Cholecystokinin decreases food intake in rats. *Journal of Comparative and Physiological Psychology, 84,* 488–495.

Gibson, A. D., & Garbers, D. L. (2000). Guanylyl cyclases as a family of putative odorant receptors. *Annual Review of Neuroscience, 23,* 417–439.

Gilbert, C. D., & Wiesel, T. N. (1992). Receptive field dynamics in adult primary visual cortex. *Nature, 356,* 150–152.

Gilbertson, T., Damak, S., & Margolskee, R. F. (2000). The molecular physiology of taste transduction. *Current Opinion in Neurobiology, 10,* 519–527.

Gillberg, M., Kecklund, G., Axelsson, J., & Åkerstedt, T. (1996). The effects of a short daytime nap after restricted night sleep. *Sleep, 19,* 570–575.

Gillette, M. U., & McArthur, A. J. (1996). Circadian actions of melatonin at the suprachiasmatic nucleus. *Behavioural Brain Research, 73,* 135–139.

Gilliam, T. C., Gusella, J. F., & Lehrach, H. (1987). Molecular genetic strategies to investigate Huntington's disease. *Advances in Neurology, 48,* 17–29.

Gingrich, J. R., & Roder, J. (1998). Inducible gene expression in the nervous system of transgenic mice. *Annual Review of Neuroscience, 21*, 377–405.

Gladue, B. A. (1994). The biopsychology of sexual orientation. *Current Directions in Psychological Science, 3*, 150–154.

Glaser, R., Rice, J., Sheridan, J., Fertel, R., Stout, J., Speicher, C., et al. (1987). Stress-related immune suppression: Health implications. *Brain, Behavior, and Immunity, 1*, 7–20.

Glickstein, M. (2000). How are visual areas of the brain connected to motor areas for the sensory guidance of movement? *Trends in Neurosciences, 23*, 613–617.

Goedert, M. (1993). Tau protein and the neurofibrillary pathology of Alzheimer's disease. *Trends in Neurosciences, 16*, 460–465.

Gold, R. M., Jones, A. P., Sawchenko, P. E., & Kapatos, G. (1977). Paraventricular area: Critical focus of a longitudinal neurocircuitry mediating food intake. *Physiology & Behavior, 18*, 1111–1119.

Goldberg, J. L., & Barres, B. A. (2000). The relationship between neuronal survival and regeneration. *Annual Review of Neuroscience, 23*, 576–612.

Goldman, S. A., & Nottebohm, F. (1983). Neuronal production, migration, and differentiation in a vocal control nucleus of the adult female canary brain. *Proceedings of the National Academy of Sciences, U.S.A., 80*, 2390–2394.

Goldowitz, D., & Hamre, K. (1998). The cells and molecules that make a cerebellum. *Trends in Neurosciences, 21*, 375–382.

Goldstein, I. (2000, August). Male sexual circuitry. *Scientific American, 283*, 70–75.

Gollin, E. S. (1960). Developmental studies of visual recognition of incomplete objects. *Perceptual Motor Skills, 11*, 289–298.

Goodale, M. A. (1993). Visual pathways supporting perception and action in the primate cerebral cortex. *Current Opinion in Neurobiology, 3*, 578–585.

Goodale, M. A., & Milner, A. D. (1992). Separate visual pathways for perception and action. *Trends in Neurosciences, 15*, 20–25.

Goodale, M. A., Milner, A. D., Jakobson, L. S., & Carey, D. P. (1991). A neurological dissociation between perceiving objects and grasping them. *Nature, 349*, 154–156.

Goodenough, D. R., Shapiro, A., Holden, M., & Steinschriber, L. (1959). A comparison of "dreamers" and "nondreamers": Eye movements, electroencephalograms, and the recall of dreams. *Journal of Abnormal and Social Psychology, 59*, 295–303.

Gorski, R. A. (1980). Sexual differentiation in the brain. In D. T. Krieger & J. C. Hughes (Eds.). *Neuroendocrinology* (pp. 215–222). Sunderland, MA: Sinauer.

Gorski, R. A., Gordom, J. H., Shryne, J. E., & Southam, A. M. (1978). Evidence for a morphological sex difference within the medial preoptic area of the rat brain. *Brain Research, 148*, 333–346.

Gottesman, I. I., & Bertelsen, A. (1989). Confirming unexpressed genotypes for schizophrenia. *Archives of General Psychiatry, 46*, 867–872.

Gottesman, I. I., & Shields, J. (1982). *Schizophrenia: The epigenetic puzzle*. Cambridge, England: Cambridge University Press.

Gould, E., Reeves, A. J., Graziano, M. S. A., & Gross, C. G. (1999). Neurogenesis in the neocortex of adult primates. *Science, 286*, 548–552.

Goy, R. W., & McEwen, B. S. (1980). *Sexual differentiation of the brain*. Cambridge, MA: MIT Press.

Grady, K. L., Phoenix, C. H., & Young, W. C. (1965). Role of the developing rat testis in differentiation of the neural tissues mediating mating behavior. *Journal of Comparative and Physiological Psychology, 59*, 176–182.

Graff-Radford, N., Damasio, H., Yamada, T., Eslinger, P. J., & Damasio, A. R. (1985). Nonhaemorrhagic thalamic infarction. *Brain, 108*, 485–516.

Grakoui, A., Bromley, S. K., Sumen, C., Davis, M. M., Shaw, A. S., Allen, P. M., & Dustin, M. L. (1999). The immunological synapse: A molecular machine controlling T cell activation. *Science, 285*, 221–227.

Grant, P. R. (1991, October). Natural selection and Darwin's finches. *Scientific American, 265*, 82–87.

Gray, J. A., & McNaughton, N. (2000). *The neuropsychology of anxiety*. London: Oxford University Press.

Graziano, M. S. A., & Gross, C. G. (1998). Spatial maps for the control of movement. *Current Opinion in Neurobiology, 8*, 195–201.

Green, C. B., & Menaker, M. (2003). Clock on the brain. *Science, 301*, 319–320.

Green, S. (1991). Benzodiazepines, putative anxiolytics and animal models of anxiety. *Trends in Neurosciences, 14*, 101–103.

Greenamyre, J. T., & Hastings, T. G. (2004). Parkinson's—divergent causes, convergent mechanisms. *Science, 304*, 1120–1122.

Greene, P. E., Fahn, S., Tsai, W. Y., Winfield, H., Dillon, S., Kao, R., et al. (1999). Double-blind controlled trial of human embryonic dopaminergic tissue transplants in advanced Parkinson's disease: Long-term unblinded follow-up phase. *Neurology, 52*(Suppl. 2).

Greengard, P. (2001). The neurobiology of slow synaptic transmission. *Science, 294*, 1024–1030.

Grillner, S. (1985). Neurobiological bases of rhythmic motor acts in vertebrates. *Science, 228*, 143–149.

Grillner, S., & Dickinson, M. (2002). Motor systems. *Current Opinion in Neurobiology, 12*, 629–632.

Grimson, W. E. L., Kikinis, R., Jolesz, F. A., & Black, P. M. (1999, June). Virtual-reality technology. *Scientific American, 280*, 63–69.

Groenewegen, H. J. (2003). The basal ganglia and motor control. *Neural Plasticity, 10*, 107–120.

Gross, C., & Hen, R. (2004). The developmental origins of anxiety. *Nature Reviews Neuroscience, 5*, 545–552.

Gross, C. G., Moore, T., & Rodman, H. R. (2004). Visually guided behavior after V1 lesions in young and adult monkeys and its relation to blindsight in humans. *Progress in Brain Research, 144*, 279–294.

Grossman, E., Donnelly, M., Price, R., Pickens, D., Morgan, V., Neighbor, G., & Blake, R. (2000). Brain areas involved in perception of biological motion. *Journal of Cognitive Neuroscience, 12*, 711–720.

Grove, E. A., & Fukuchi-Shimogori, T. (2003). Generating the cerebral cortical area map. *Annual Review of Neuroscience, 26*, 355–380.

Grumbach, M. M. (2002). The neuroendocrinology of human puberty revisited. *Hormone Research, 57*, S2–S14.

Grunt, J. A., & Young, W. C. (1952). Differential reactivity of individuals and the response of the male guinea pig to testosterone propionate. *Endocrinology, 51*, 237–248.

Guan, K.-L., & Rao, Y. (2003). Signalling mechanisms mediating neuronal responses to guidance cues. *Nature Reviews Neuroscience, 4*, 941–956.

Guerri, C. (2002). Mechanisms involved in central nervous system dysfunctions induced by prenatal ethanol exposure. *Neurotoxicity Research, 4*, 327–335.

Guo, Y., & Udin, S. B. (2000). The development of abnormal axon trajectories after rotation of one eye in *Xenopus*. *Journal of Neuroscience, 20*, 4189–4197.

Gutfreund, Y., Zheng, W., & Knudsen, E. I. (2002). Gated visual input to the central auditory system. *Science, 297*, 1556–1559.

Haaland, K. Y., & Harrington, D. L. (1996). Hemispheric asymmetry of movement. *Current Opinion in Neurobiology, 6*, 796–800.

Haffenden, A. M., & Goodale, M. A. (1998). The effect of pictorial illusion on prehension and perception. *Journal of Cognitive Neuroscience, 10*, 122–136.

Haimov, I., & Lavie, P. (1996). Melatonin—a soporific hormone. *Current Directions in Psychological Science, 5*(4), 106–111.

Haimov, I., Lavie, P., Laudon, M., Herer, P., & Zisapel, N. (1995). Melatonin replacement therapy of elderly insomniacs. *Sleep, 18*, 598–603.

Haist, F., Bowden, G. J., & Mao, H. (2001). Consolidation of human memory over decades revealed by functional magnetic resonance imaging. *Nature Reviews Neuroscience, 4*, 1057–1058.

Halford, J. C. G., & Blundell, J. E. (2000a). Pharmacology of appetite suppression. In E. Jucker (Ed.). *Progress in drug research* (Vol. 54, 25–58). Basel: Birkhäuser, Verlag.

Halford, J. C. G., & Blundell, J. E. (2000b). Separate systems for serotonin and leptin in appetite control. *Annals of Medicine, 32*, 222–232.

Hallett, M. (2001). Plasticity of the human motor cortex and recovery from stroke. *Brain Research Review, 36*, 169–174.

Hamann, S. B., Ely, T. D., Hoffman, J. M., & Kilts, C. D. (2002). Ecstasy and agony: Activation of the human amygdala in positive and negative emotion. *Psychological Science, 13*, 135–141.

Hammond, G. (2002). Correlates of human handedness in primary motor cortex: A review and hypothesis. *Neuroscience and Biobehavioural Reviews, 26*, 285–292.

Hanashima, C., Li, S. C., Shen, L., Lai, E., & Fishell, G. (2004). *Foxg 1* suppresses early cortical cell fate. *Science, 303*, 56–59.

Hanson, G. R., Bunsey, M. D., & Riccio, D. C. (2002). The effects of pretraining and reminder treatments on retrograde amnesia in rats: Comparison of lesions to the fornix or perirhinal and entorhinal cortices. *Neurobiology Learning & Memory, 78*, 365–378.

Happé, F., & Frith, U. (1996). The neuropsychology of autism. *Brain, 119*, 1377–1400.

Haqq, C. M., King, C.-Y., Ukiyama, E., Falsafi, S., Haqq, T. N., Donahoe, P. K., & Weiss, M. A. (1994). Molecular basis of mammalian sexual determination: Activation of Müllerian inhibiting substance gene expression by SRY. *Science, 266*, 1494–1500.

Harata, N., Pyle, J. L., Aravanis, A. M., Mozhayeva, M., Kavalali, E. T., & Tsien, R. W. (2001). Limited numbers of recycling vesicles in small CNS nerve terminals: Implications for neural signaling and vesicular cycling. *Trends in Neurosciences, 24*, 637–643.

Harding, S. M., & McGinnis, M. Y. (2004). Androgen receptor blockade in the MPOA or VMN: Effects on male sociosexual behaviors. *Physiology & Behavior, 81*, 671–680.

Hardy, J., & Selkoe, D. J. (2002). The amyloid hypothesis of Alzheimer's disease: Progress and problems on the road to therapeutics. *Science, 297*, 353–356.

Harris, G. W. (1955). *Neural control of the pituitary gland.* London: Edward Arnold.

Harris, G. W., & Levine, S. (1965). Sexual differentiation of the brain and its experimental control. *Journal of Physiology, 181*, 379–400.

Harris, K. M. (1995). How multiple-synapse boutons could preserve input specificity during an interneuronal spread of LTP. *Trends in Neurosciences, 18*, 365–369.

Harris, K. M., Fiala, J. C., & Ostroff, L. (2003). Structural changes at dendritic spine synapses during long-term potentiation. *Philosophical Transactions of the Royal Society of London, 358*, 745–748.

Harris, K. M., & Kater, S. B. (1994). Dendritic spines: Cellular specializations imparting both stability and flexibility to synaptic function. *Annual Review of Neuroscience, 17*, 341–371.

Harris, L. J. (1978). Sex differences in spatial ability: Possible environmental, genetic, and neurological factors. In M. Kinsbourne (Ed.), *Asymmetrical function of the brain* (p. 463). Cambridge, England: Cambridge University Press.

Harris, L. J., Clay, J., Hargreaves, F. J., & Ward, A. (1933). Appetite and choice of diet: The ability of the vitamin B deficient rat to discriminate between diets containing and lacking the vitamin. *Proceedings of the Royal Society of London (B), 113*, 161–190.

Harrison, Y., & Horne, J. A. (1997). Sleep deprivation affects speech. *Sleep, 20*, 871–877.

Hartmann, D. S., & Civelli, O. (1997). Dopamine receptor diversity: Molecular and pharmacological perspectives. *Progressive Drug Research, 48*, 173–194.

Harvey, P. H., & Krebs, J. R. (1990). Comparing brains. *Science, 249*, 140–145.

Hastings, M. H., Reddy, A. B., & Maywood, E. S. (2003). A clockwork web: Circadian timing in brain and periphery, in health and disease. *Nature Reviews Neuroscience, 4*, 649–661.

Hata, Y., & Stryker, M. P. (1994). Control of thalamocortical afferent rearrangement by postsynaptic activity in developing visual cortex. *Science, 265*, 1732–1735.

Hattar, S., Liao, H.-W., Takao, M., Berson, D. M., & Yau, K.-W. (2002). Melanopsin-containing retinal ganglion cells: Architecture, projections, and intrinsic photosensitivity. *Science, 295*, 1065–1070.

Hatten, M. E. (2002). New directions in neural migration. *Science, 297*, 1660–1665.

Hauser, M. D. (1999). Perseveration, inhibition and the prefrontal cortex: A new look. *Current Opinion in Neurobiology, 9*, 214–222.

Hayakawa, K., Kumagai, H., Suzuki, Y., Furusawa, N., Haga, T., Hoshi, T., et al. (1992). MRI imaging of chronic alcoholism. *Acta Radiologica, 33*, 201–206.

Haydon, P. G. (2001). Glia: Listening and talking to the synapse. *Nature Reviews Neuroscience, 2*, 185–193.

Heap, L. C., Pratt, O. E., Ward, R. J., Waller, S., Thomson, A. D., Shaw, G. K., & Peters, T. J. (2002). Individual susceptibility to Wernicke-Korsakoff syndrome and alcoholism-induced cognitive deficit: Impaired thiamine utilitzation found in alcoholics and alcohol abusers. *Psychiatric Genetics, 12*, 217–224.

Hebb, D. O. (1949). *The organization of behavior.* New York: John Wiley & Sons.

Hécaen, H., & Angelergues, R. (1964). Localization of symptoms in aphasia. In A. V. S. de Reuck & M. O'Connor (Eds.), *CIBA foundation symposium on the disorders of language* (pp. 222–256). London: Churchill Press.

Heffner, H. E., & Heffner, R. S. (1984). Temporal lobe lesions and perception of species-specific vocalizations by macaques. *Science, 226*, 75–76.

Heffner, H. E., & Masterton, R. B. (1990). Sound localization in mammals: Brainstem mechanisms. In M. Berkley & W. Stebbins (Eds.), *Comparative perception, Vol. I: Discrimination.* New York: John Wiley & Sons.

Heilman, K. M., Watson, R. T., & Rothi, L. J. G. (1997). Disorders of skilled movements: Limb apraxia. In T. E. Feinberg & M. J. Farah (Eds.), *Behavioral neurology and neuropsychology* (pp. 227–236). New York: McGraw-Hill.

Heilman, K. M., Watson, R. T., & Valenstein, E. (1997). Neglect: Clinical and anatomic aspects. In T. E. Feinberg & M. J. Farah (Eds.), *Behavioral neurology and neuropsychology.* (pp. 309–317). New York: McGraw-Hill.

Helmer, W. J. (1986, February). The madman in the tower. *Texas Monthly.*

Hemmer, B., Archelos, J. J., & Hartung, H.-P. (2002). New concepts in the immunopathogenesis of multiple sclerosis. *Nature Reviews Neuroscience, 3*, 291–301.

Hendry, S. H. C., & Calkins, D. J. (1998). Neuronal chemistry and functional organization in the primate visual system. *Trends in Neurosciences, 21*(8), 344–349.

Henke, K., Kroll, N. E. A., Behniea, H., Amaral, D. G., Miller, M. B., Rafal, R., & Gazzaniga, M. S. (1999). Memory lost and regained following bilateral hippocampal damage. *Journal of Cognitive Neuroscience, 11*, 682–697.

Hennessey, A. C., Camak, L., Gordon, F., & Edwards, D. A. (1990). Connections between the pontine central gray and the ventromedial hypothalamus are essential for lordosis in female rats. *Behavioral Neuroscience, 104*, 477–488.

Hetherington, A. W., & Ranson, S. W. (1940). Hypothalamic lesions and adiposity in the rat. *Anatomical Record, 78*, 149–172.

Heuser, J. E., Reese, T. S., Dennis, M. J., Jan, Y., Jan, L., & Evans, L. (1979). Synaptic vesicle exocytosis captured by quick freezing and correlated with quantal transmitter release. *Journal of Cell Biology, 81*, 275–300.

Heuss, C., & Gerber, U. (2000). G-protein–independent signaling by G-protein–coupled receptors. *Trends in Neurosciences, 23*, 469–474.

Heymsfield, S. N., Greenberg, A. S., Fujioka, K., Dixon, R. M., Kushner, R., Hunt, T., et al. (1999). Recombinant leptin for weight loss in obese and lean adults. *Journal of the American Medical Association, 282*, 1568–1575.

Hickok, G., Bellugi, U., & Klima, E. S. (2001, June). Sign language in the brain: How does the human brain process language? New studies of deaf signers hint at an answer. *Scientific American, 284*, 58–65.

Hines, M. (2003). Sex steroids and human behavior: Prenatal androgen exposure and sex-typical play behavior in children. *Annals of the New York Academy of Sciences, 1007*, 272–282.

Hobson, J. A. (1989). *Sleep.* New York: Scientific American Library.

Hobson, J. A., & Pace-Schott, E. F. (2002). The cognitive neuroscience of sleep: Neuronal systems, consciousness and learning. *Nature Reviews Neuroscience, 3*, 679–693.

Hockfield, S., & Kalb, R. G. (1993). Activity-dependent structural changes during neuronal development. *Current Opinion in Neurobiology, 3*, 87–92.

Hollenbeck, P. J. (2001). Insight and hindsight into Tourette syndrome. In D. J. Cohen, C. G. Goetz, & J. Jankovic (Eds.) *Tourette syndrome* (pp. 363–367). Philadelphia: Lippincott Williams & Wilkins.

Hollon, S. D., Thase, M. E., & Markowitz, J. C. (2002). Treatment and prevention of depression. *Psychological Science in the Public Interest, 3*, 39–77.

Holmberg, J., & Frisén, J. (2002). Ephrins are not only unattractive. *Trends in Neurosciences, 25*, 239–243.

Holmes, M. M., Galea, L. A. M., Mistlberger, R. E., & Kempermann, G. (2004). Adult hippocampal neurogenesis and voluntary running activity: Circadian and dose-dependent effects. *Journal of Neuroscience Research, 76*(2), 216–222.

Holsboer, F. (2000). The corticosteroid receptor hypothesis of depression. *Neuropsychopharmacology, 23*, 477–501.

Holzman, P. S., & Matthyse, S. (1990). The genetics of schizophrenia: A review. *Current Directions in Psychological Science, 1*, 279–286.

Hopkins, W. D. (1995). Chimpanzee handedness revisited: 55 years since Finch (1941). *Psychonomic Bulletin & Review, 3*, 449–457.

Hopkins, W. D. (1996). Hand preferences for a coordinated bimanual task in 110 chimpanzees (*Pan troglodytes*): Cross-sectional analysis. *Journal of Comparative Psychology, 109*(3), 291–297.

Hopkins, W. D., & Pilcher, D. L. (2001). Neuroanatomical localization of the motor hand area with magnetic resonance imaging: The left hemisphere is larger in great apes. *Behavioral Neuroscience, 115*, 1159–1164.

Horne, J. A. (1983). Sleep loss and "divergent" thinking ability. *Sleep, 11*, 528–536.

Horne, J. A. (2000). REM sleep—by default? *Neuroscience and Biobehavioural Reviews, 24*, 777–797.

Horne, J. A., & Reyner, L. A. (1996). Counteracting driver sleepiness: Effects of napping, caffeine, and placebo. *Psychophysiology, 33*, 306–309.

Howe, M. L. (2003). Memories from the cradle. *Current Directions in Psychological Science, 12*, 62–65.

Howlett, A. C., Bidaut-Russell, M., Devane, W. A., Melvin, L. S., Johnson, M. R., & Herkenham, M. (1990). The cannabinoid receptor: Biochemical, anatomical and behavioral characterization. *Trends in Neurosciences, 13*, 420–423.

Hrabovszky, Z., & Hutson, J. M. (2002). Androgen imprinting of the brain in animal models and humans with intersex disorders: Review and recommendations. *The Journal of Urology, 168*, 2142–2148.

Huang, E. J., & Reichardt, L. F. (2001). Neurotrophins: Roles in neuronal development and function. *Annual Review of Neuroscience, 24*, 677–736.

Hubel, D. H., & Wiesel, T. N. (1979, September). Brain mechanisms of vision. *Scientific American, 241*, 150–162.

Hubel, D. H., Wiesel, T. N., & LeVay, S. (1977). Plasticity of ocular dominance columns in the monkey striate cortex. *Philosophical Transactions of the Royal Society of London, 278*, 377–409.

Hubel, D. H., Wiesel, T. N., & Stryker, M. P. (1977). Orientation columns in macaque monkey visual cortex demonstrated by the 2-deoxyglucose autoradiographic technique. *Nature, 269*, 328–330.

Hugdahl, K. (1996). Cognitive influences on human autonomic nervous system function. *Current Opinion in Neurobiology, 6*, 252–258.

Huguenard, J. R. (2000). Reliability of axonal propagation: The spike doesn't stop here. *Proceedings of the National Academy of Sciences, U.S.A., 97*, 9349–9350.

Hull, E. M., Lorrain, D. S., Du, J., Matuszewich, L., Lumley, L. A., Putnam, S. K., & Moses, J. (1999). Hormone-neurotransmitter interaction in the control of sexual behavior. *Behavioural Brain Research, 105*, 105–116.

Hume, K. I., & Mills, J. N. (1977). Rhythms of REM and slow wave sleep in subjects living on abnormal time schedules. *Waking and Sleeping, 1*, 291–296.

Hurlbert, A. (2003). Colour vision: Primary visual cortex shows its influence. *Current Biology, 13*, 270–272.

Hurlbert, A., & Wolf, K. (2004). Color contrast: A contributory mechanism to color constancy. *Progress in Brain Research, 144*, 147–160.

Hustvedt, B. E., & Løvø, A. (1972). Correlation between hyperinsulinemia and hyperphagia in rats with ventromedial hypothalamic lesions. *Acta Physiologica Scandinavica, 84*, 29–33.

Hutsler, J., & Galuske, R. A. W. (2003). Hemispheric asymmetries in cerebral cortical networks. *Trends in Neurosciences, 26*, 429–435.

Huttenlocher, P. R. (1994). Synaptogenesis, synapse elimination, and neural plasticity in human cerebral cortex. In C. A. Nelson (Ed.), *Threats to optimal development: The Minnesota symposium on child psychology* (Vol. 27, 35–54). Hillsdale, NJ: Lawrence Erlbaum.

Hyman, S. (2000). Mental illness: Genetically complex disorders of neural circuitry and neural communication. *Neuron, 28*, 321–323.

Hyman, S. E., & Malenka, R. C. (2001). Addiction and the brain: The neurobiology of compulsion and its persistence. *Nature Reviews Neuroscience, 2*, 695–703.

Ikeda, H., Heinke, B., Ruscheweyh, R., & Sandkuhler, J. (2003). Synaptic plasticity in spinal lamina I projection neurons that mediate hyperalgesia. *Science, 299*, 1237–1240.

Ikemoto, S., & Panksepp, J. (1999). The role of nucleus accumbens dopamine in motivated behavior: A unifying interpretation with special reference to reward-seeking. *Brain Research Reviews, 31*, 6–41.

Illert, M., & Kümmel, H. (1999). Reflex pathways from large muscle spindle afferents and recurrent axon collaterals to motoneurones of wrist and digit muscles: A comparison in cats, monkeys and humans. *Experimental Brain Research, 128*, 13–19.

Inatani, M., Irie, F., Plump, A. S., Tessier-Lavigne, M., & Yamaguchi, Y. (2003). Mammalian brain morphogenesis and midline axon guidance require heparin sulfate. *Science, 302*, 1044–1046.

Inglis, J., & Lawson, J. S. (1982). A meta-analysis of sex differences in the effects of unilateral brain damage on intelligence test results. *Canadian Journal of Psychology, 36*, 670–683.

Institute of Laboratory Animal Resources: Commission on Life Sciences (1996). *Guide for the care and use of laboratory animals.* Washington: National Academy Press.

Intriligator, J. M., Xie, R., & Barton, J. J. S. (2002). Blindsight modulation of motion perception. *Journal of Cognitive Neuroscience, 14*, 1174–1183.

Inui, A. (2001). Ghrelin: An orexigenic and somatotrophic signal from the stomach. *Nature Reviews Neuroscience, 2*, 551–560.

Irwin, D. E. (1996). Integrating information across saccadic eye movements. *Current Directions in Psychological Science, 5*, 94–100.

Iwamura, Y. (1998). Hierarchical somatosensory processing. *Current Opinion in Neurobiology, 8*, 522–528.

Iwaniuk, A. N., & Whishaw, I. Q. (2000). On the origin of skilled forelimb movements. *Trends in Neurosciences, 23*, 372–376.

Jacques, J. P., Zombek, S., Guillain, C., & Duez, P. (2004). Cannabis: Experts agree more than they admit. *Revue medicale de Bruxelles, 25*, 87–92.

Jaeger, J. J., Lockwood, A. H., Van Valin, R. D., Kemmerer, D. L., Murphy, B. W., & Wack, D. S. (1998). Sex differences in brain regions activated by grammatical and reading tasks. *NeuroReport, 9*, 2803–2807.

Jakel, R. J., & Maragos, W. F. (2000). Neuronal cell death in Huntington's disease: A potential role for dopamine. *Trends in Neurosciences, 23*, 239–245.

James, L. E., & MacKay, D. G. (2001). H.M., word knowledge, and aging: Support for a new theory of long-term retrograde amnesia. *Current Directions in Psychological Science, 12*, 485–492.

Jameson, K. A., Highnote, S. M., & Wasserman, L. M. (2001). Richer color experience in observers with multiple photopigment opsin genes. *Psychonomic Bulletin & Review, 8*(2), 244–261.

Janardhan, V., & Qureshi, A. I. (2004). Mechanisms of ischemic brain injury. *Current Cardiology Reports, 6*, 117–123.

Jankovic, J. (2001). Tourette's syndrome. *New England Journal of Medicine, 345*, 1184–1192.

Jarrell, T. W., Gentile, C. G., Romanski, L. M., McCabe, P. M., & Schneiderman, N. (1987). Involvement of cortical and thalamic auditory regions in retention of differential bradycardia conditioning to acoustic conditioned stimuli in rabbits. *Brain Research, 412*, 285–294.

Javitt, D. C., & Coyle, J. T. (2004, January). Decoding schizophrenia. A fuller understanding of signaling in the brain of people with this disorder offers new hope for improved therapy. *Scientific American, 290*, 48–55.

Jeannerod, M., Arbib, M. A., Rizzolatti, G., & Sakarta, H. (1995). Grasping objects: The cortical mechanisms of visuo-motor transformation. *Trends in Neurosciences, 18*(7), 314–327.

Jeannerod, M., & Farne, A. (2003). The visuomotor functions of posterior parietal areas. *Advances in Neurology, 93*, 205–217.

Jegalian, K., & Lahn, B. T. (2001, February). Why the Y is so weird. *Scientific American, 284*, 56–61.

Jenkins, I. H., Brooks, D. J., Bixon, P. D., Frackowiak, R. S. J., & Passingham, R. E. (1994). Motor sequence learning: A study with positron emission tomography. *Journal of Neuroscience, 14*(6), 3775–3790.

Jessell, T. M., & Sanes, J. R. (2000). Development. The decade of the developing brain. *Current Opinion in Neurobiology, 10*, 599–611.

Johnson, K. O. (2001). The roles and functions of cutaneous mechanoreceptors. *Current Opinion in Neurobiology, 11*, 455–461.

Johnson, M. H. (2001). Functional brain development in humans. *Nature Reviews Neuroscience, 2*, 475–483.

Johnston, T. D. (1987). The persistence of dichotomies in the study of behavioral development. *Developmental Review, 7*, 149–182.

Jones, E. G. (2000). Cortical and subcortical contributions to activity-dependent plasticity in primate somatosensory cortex. *Annual Review of Neuroscience, 23*, 1–37.

Jones, H. S., & Oswald, I. (1966). Two cases of healthy insomnia. *Electroencephalography and Clinical Neurophysiology, 24*, 378–380.

Jones, H. W., & Park, I. J. (1971). A classification of special problems in sex differentiation. In D. Bergsma (Ed.), *The clinical delineation of birth defects. Part X: The endo-crine system* (pp. 113–121). Baltimore: Williams and Wilkins.

Jones, R. T. (1987). Tobacco dependence. In H. Y. Meltzer (Ed.), *Psychopharmacology: The third generation of progress* (pp. 1589–1596). New York: Raven Press.

Jordan, H., Reis, J. E., Hoffman, J. E., & Landau, B. (2002). Intact perception of biological motion in the face of profound spatial deficits: Williams syndrome. *Psychological Science, 13*, 162–167.

Joseph, R. (1988). Dual mental functioning in a split-brain patient. *Journal of Clinical Psychology, 44*, 771–779.

Jost, A. (1972). A new look at the mechanisms controlling sex differentiation in mammals. *Johns Hopkins Medical Journal, 130*, 38–53.

Jouvet, M. (1972). The role of monoamines and acetylcholine-containing neurons in the regulation of the sleep-waking cycle. *Ergebnisse der Physiologie, 64*, 166–307.

Julien, R. M. (1981). *A primer of drug action.* San Francisco: W. H. Freeman.

Juusola, M., French, A. S., Uusitalo, R. O., & Weckström, M. (1996). Information processing by graded-potential transmission through tonically active synapses. *Trends in Neurosciences, 19*, 292–297.

Kaas, J. H., & Collins, C. E. (2001). The organization of sensory cortex. *Current Opinion in Neurobiology, 11*, 498–504.

Kaas, J. H., Krubtzer, L. A., Chino, Y. M., Langston, A. L., Polley, E. H., & Blair, N. (1990). Reorganization of retinotopic cortical maps in adult mammals after lesions of the retina. *Science, 248*, 229–231.

Kaas, J. H., Nelson, R. J., Sur, M., & Merzenich, M. M. (1981). Organization of somatosensory cortex in primates. In F. O. Schmitt, F. G. Worden, G. Adelman, & S. G. Dennis (Eds.), *The organization of the cerebral cortex* (pp. 237–261). Cambridge, MA: MIT Press.

Kagawa, Y. (1978). Impact of Westernization on the nutrition of Japanese: Changes in physique, cancer, longevity, and centenarians. *Preventive Medicine, 7*, 205–217.

Kaiser, J., Lutzenberger, W., Preissl, H., Ackermann, H., & Birbaumer, N. (2000). Right-hemisphere dominance for the processing of sound-source lateralization. *Journal of Neuroscience, 20*, 6631–6639.

Kalaria, R. N. (2001). Advances in molecular genetics and pathology of cerebrovascular disorders. *Trends in Neurosciences, 24*, 392–400.

Kalil, R. E. (1989, December). Synapse formation in the developing brain. *Scientific American, 261*, 76–85.

Kallman, F. J. (1946). The genetic theory of schizophrenia: An analysis of 691 schizophrenic twin index families. *American Journal of Psychiatry, 103*, 309–322.

Kandel, E. R. (2001). The molecular biology of memory storage: A dialogue between genes and synapses. *Science, 294*, 1030–1038.

Kandel, E. R., & Squire, L. R. (2000). Neuroscience: Breaking down barriers to the study of brain and mind. *Science, 290*, 1113–1120.

Kansaku, K., Yamaura, A., & Kitazawa, S. (2000). Sex differences in lateralization revealed in the posterior language areas. *Cerebral Cortex, 10*, 866–872.

Kapur, N. (1997). *Injured brains of medical minds*. Oxford, England: Oxford University Press.

Karacan, I., Goodenough, D. R., Shapiro, A., & Starker, S. (1966). Erection cycle during sleep in relation to dream anxiety. *Archives of General Psychiatry, 15*, 183–189.

Karacan, I., Williams, R. L., Finley, W. W., & Hursch, C. J. (1970). The effects of naps on nocturnal sleep: Influence on the need for stage-1 REM and stage-4 sleep. *Biological Psychiatry, 2*, 391–399.

Karsch, F. J. (1987). Central actions of ovarian steroids in the feedback regulation of pulsatile secretion of luteinizing hormone. *Annual Review of Physiology, 49*, 365–382.

Kastner, S., De Weerd, P., Desimone, R., & Ungerleider, L. G. (1998). Mechanisms of directed attention in the human extrastriate cortex as revealed by functional MRI. *Science, 282*, 108–112.

Katz, J. L., Ackman, P., Rothwax, Y., Sachar, E. J., Weiner, H., Hellman, L., & Gallagher, T. F. (1970). Psychoendocrine aspects of cancer of the breast. *Psychosomatic Medicine, 32*, 1–18.

Katz, L. C., & Crowley, J. C. (2002). Development of cortical circuits: Lessons from ocular dominance columns. *Nature Reviews Neuroscience, 3*, 34–42.

Katz, L. C., & Shatz, C. J. (1996). Synaptic activity and the construction of cortical circuits. *Science, 274*, 1133–1138.

Kaufman, J., Martin, A., King, R. A., & Charney, D. (2001). Are child-, adolescent-, and adult-onset depression one and the same disorder? *Biological Psychiatry, 49*, 980–1001.

Kaut, K. P., & Bunsey, M. D. (2001). The effects of lesions to the rat hippocampus or rhinal cortex on olfactory and spatial memory: Retrograde and anterograde findings. *Cognitive, Affective, & Behavioral Neuroscience, 1*, 270–286.

Kavanagh, G. L., & Kelly, J. B. (1988). Hearing in the ferret (*Mustela putorius*): Effects of primary auditory cortical lesions on thresholds for pure tone detection. *Journal of Neurophysiology, 60*, 879–888.

Kelley, W. M., Ojemann, J. G., Wetzel, R. D., Derdeyn, C. P., Moran, C. J., Cross, D. T., et al. (2002). Wada testing reveals frontal lateralization for the memorization of words and faces. *Journal of Cognitive Neuroscience, 14*, 116–125.

Keltner, D., Kring, A. M., & Bonanno, G. A. (1999). Fleeting signs of the course of life: Facial expression and personal adjustment. *Current Directions in Psychological Science, 8*, 18–22.

Kempermann, G., & Gage, F. H. (1999, May). New nerve cells for the adult brain. *Scientific American, 282*, 48–53.

Kendler, K. S., & Gruenberg, A. M. (1984). An independent analysis of the Danish adoption study of schizophrenia: VI. The relationship between psychiatric disorders as defined by DSM-III in the relatives and adoptees. *Archives of General Psychiatry, 41*, 555–564.

Kennedy, J. L., Farrer, L. A., Andreasen, N. C., Mayeux, R., & St. George-Hyslop, P. (2003). The genetics of adult-onset neuropsychiatric disease: Complexities and conundra? *Science, 302*, 822–826.

Kentridge, R. W., Heywood, C. A., & Weiskrantz, L. (1997). Residual vision in multiple retinal locations within a scotoma: Implications for blindsight. *Journal of Cognitive Neuroscience, 9*, 191–202.

Kerkoff, G. (2001). Spatial hemineglect in humans. *Progress in Neurobiology, 63*, 1–27.

Kessels, R. P. C., De Haan, E. H. F., Kappelle, L. J., & Postma, A. (2001). Varieties of human spatial memory: A meta-analysis on the effects of hippocampal lesions. *Brain Research Reviews, 35*, 295–303.

Kessler, R. C. (1997). The effects of stressful life events on depression. *Annual Review of Psychology, 48*, 191–214.

Keys, A., Broz, J., Henschel, A., Mickelsen, O., & Taylor H. L. (1950). *The biology of human starvation*. Minneapolis: The University of Minnesota Press.

Kiecolt-Glaser, J. K., McGuire, L., Robles, T. F., & Glaser, R. (2002). Emotions, morbidity, and mortality: New perspectives from psychoneuroimmunology. *Annual Review of Psychology, 53*, 83–107.

Kiecolt-Glaser, J. K., Page, G. G., Marucha, P. T., MacCallum, R. C., & Glaser, R. (1998). Psychological influences on surgical recovery. *American Psychologist, 53*, 1209–1218.

Kiehl, K. A., Liddle, P. F., Smith, A. M., Mendrek, A., Forster, B. B., & Hare, R. D. (1999). Neural pathways involved in the processing of concrete and abstract words. *Human Brain Mapping, 7*, 225–233.

Killacky, H. P. (1995). Evolution of the human brain: A neuroanatomical perspective. In M. S. Gazzaniga (Ed.), *The cognitive neurosciences*. Cambridge, MA: MIT Press.

Kim, J. J., & Diamond, D. M. (2002). The stressed hippocampus, synaptic plasticity and lost memories. *Nature Reviews Neuroscience, 3*, 453–462.

Kim, S.-G., Ashe, J., Hendrich, K., Ellermann, J. M., Merkle, H., Ugurbil, K., & Georgopoulos, A. P. (1993). Functional magnetic resonance imaging of motor cortex: Hemispheric asymmetry and handedness. *Science, 261*, 615–617.

Kimberg, D. Y., D'Esposito, M., & Farah, M. J. (1998). Cognitive functions in the prefrontal cortex—working memory and executive control. *Current Directions in Psychological Science, 6*, 185–192.

Kimura, D. (1961). Some effects of temporal-lobe damage on auditory perception. *Canadian Journal of Psychology, 15*, 156–165.

Kimura, D. (1964). Left-right differences in the perception of melodies. *Quarterly Journal of Experimental Psychology, 16*, 355–358.

Kimura, D. (1979). Neuromotor mechanisms in the evolution of human communication. In H. E. Steklis & M. J. Raleigh (Eds.), *Neurobiology of social communication in primates* (pp. 197–219). New York: Academic Press.

Kimura, D. (1987). Sex differences, human brain organization. In G. Adelman (Ed.), *Encyclopedia of neuroscience* (Vol. II, pp. 1084–1085). Boston: Birkhäuser.

Kimura, D., & Watson, N. (1989). The relation between oral movement control and speech. *Brain and Language, 37*, 565–590.

Kind, P. C., & Neumann, P. E. (2001). Plasticity: Downstream of glumate. *Trends in Neurosciences, 24*, 553–555.

King, A. J., Schnupp, J. W. H., & Thompson, I. D. (1998). Signals from the superficial layers of the superior colliculus enable the development of the auditory space map in the deeper layers. *Journal of Neuroscience, 18*, 9394–9408.

Klawans, H. L. (1990). *Newton's madness: Further tales of clinical neurology*. New York: Harper & Row.

Klein, D. A., & Walsh, T. B. (2004). Eating disorders: Clinical features and pathophysiology. *Physiology & Behavior, 81*, 359–374.

Kleinman, A., & Cohen, A. (1997, March). Psychiatry's global challenge: An evolving crisis in the developing world signals the need for a better understanding of the links between culture and mental disorders. *Scientific American, 276*, 86–89.

Kleitman, N. (1963). *Sleep and wakefulness*. Chicago: University of Chicago Press.

Klivington, K. A. (Ed.). (1992). *Gehirn und Geist*. Heidelberg, Germany: Spektrum Akademischer Verlag.

Kluver, H., & Bucy, P. C. (1939). Preliminary analysis of the temporal lobes in monkeys. *Archives of Neurology and Psychiatry, 42*, 979–1000.

Knowlton, B. J., Mangels, J. A., & Squire, L. R. (1996). A neo-striatal habit learning system in humans. *Science, 273*, 1399–1402.

Knudsen, E. I., & Brainard, M. S. (1991). Visual instruction of the neural map of auditory space in the developing optic tectum. *Science, 253*, 85–87.

Koechlin, E., Ody, C., & Kouneiher, F. (2003). The architecture of cognitive control in the human prefrontal cortex. *Science, 302*, 1181–1185.

Koekkoek, S. K. E., Hulscher, H. C., Dortland, B. R., Hensbroek, R. A., Elgersma, Y., Ruigrok, T. J. H., & De Zeeuw, C. I. (2003). Cerebellar LTD and learning-dependent timing of conditioned eyelid responses. *Science, 301*, 1736–1739.

Kofman, O. (2002). The role of prenatal stress in the etiology of developmental behavioural disorders. *Neuroscience and Biobehavioural Reviews, 26*, 457–470.

Köhling, R. (2002). GABA becomes exciting. *Science, 298*, 1350–1351.

Kokaia, Z., & Lindvall, O. (2003). Neurogenesis after ischaemic brain insults. *Current Opinion in Neurobiology, 13*, 127–132.

Koketsu, D., Mikami, A., Miyamoto, Y., & Hisatsune, T. (2003). Nonrenewal of neurons in the cerebral neocortex of adult macaque monkeys. *Journal of Neuroscience, 23*, 937–942.

Kokkinos, J., & Levine, S. R. (1993). Stroke. *Neurologic Complications of Drug and Alcohol Abuse, 11*, 577–590.

Kolb, B., Gibb, R., & Robinson, T. E. (2003). Brain plasticity and behavior. *Current Directions in Psychological Science, 12*, 1–5.

Kollias, S. S., Alkadhi, H., Jaermann, T., Crelier, G., & Hepp-Reymond, M.-C. (2001). Identification of multiple nonprimary motor cortical areas with simple movements. *Brain Research Reviews, 36*, 185–195.

König, P., & Verschure, P. F. M. J. (2002). Neurons in action. *Science, 296*, 1817–1818.

Konishi, M. (2003). Coding of auditory space. *Annual Review of Neuroscience, 26*, 31–35.

Konradi, C., & Heckers, S. (2003). Molecular aspects of glutamate dysregulation: Implications for schizophrenia and its treatment. *Pharmacology and Therapeutics, 97*, 153–179.

Koolhaas, J. M., Schuurman, T., & Wierpkema, P. R. (1980). The organization of intraspecific agonistic behaviour in the rat. *Progress in Neurobiology, 15*, 247–268.

Koopmans, H. S. (1981). The role of the gastrointestinal tract in the satiation of hunger. In L. A. Cioffi, W. B. T. James, & T. B. Van Italie (Eds.), *The body weight regulatory system: Normal and disturbed mechanisms* (pp. 45–55). New York: Raven Press.

Kopelman, P. G. (2000). Obesity as a medical problem. *Nature, 404*, 635–648.

Korkman, M., Kettunen, S., & Autti-Ramo, I. (2003). Neurocognitive impairment in early adolescence following prenatal alcohol exposure of varying duration. *Neuropsychology, Development, and Cognition. Section C, Child Neuropsychology, 9*, 117–128.

Kornack, D. R., & Rakic, P. (1999). Continuation of neurogenesis in the hippocampus of the adult macaque monkey. *Proceedings of the National Academy of Sciences, U.S.A., 96*, 5768–5773.

Kornack, D. R., & Rakic, P. (2001). Cell proliferation without neurogenesis in adult primate neocortex. *Science, 294*, 2127–2129.

Korte, S. M. (2001). Corticosteroids in relation to fear, anxiety and psychopathology. *Neuroscience and Biobehavioural Reviews, 25*, 117–142.

Kosslyn, S. M., Ganis, G., & Thompson, W. L. (2001). Neural foundations of imagery. *Nature Reviews Neuroscience, 2*, 635–642.

Kourtzi, Z., & Kanwisher, N. (2000). Activation in human MT/MST by static images with implied motion. *Journal of Cognitive Neuroscience 12*, 48–55.

Koutalos, Y., & Yau, K.-W. (1993). A rich complexity emerges in phototransduction. *Current Opinion in Neurobiology, 3*, 513–519.

Kozloski, J., Hamzei-Sichani, F., & Yuste, R. (2001). Stereotyped position of local synaptic targets in neocortex. *Science, 293*, 868–870.

Krantz, D. S., & McCeney, M. K. (2002). Effects of psychological and social factors on organic disease: A critical assessment of research on coronary heart disease. *Annual Review of Psychology, 53*, 341–369.

Krieglstein, J. (1997). Mechanisms of neuroprotective drug actions. *Clinical Neuroscience, 4*, 184–193.

Kring, A. M. (1999). Emotion in schizophrenia: Old mystery, new understanding. *Current Directions in Psychological Science, 8*, 160–163.

Kripke, D. F. (2004). Do we sleep too much? *Sleep, 27*, 13–14.

Kripke, D. F., Garfinkel, L., Wingard, D. L., Klauber, M. R., & Marler, M. R. (2002). Mortality associated with sleep duration and insomnia. *Archives of General Psychiatry, 59*, 131–136.

Kruzich, P. J., Congleton, K. M., & See, R. E. (2001). Conditioned reinstatement of drug-seeking behavior with a discrete compound stimulus classically conditioned with intravenous cocaine. *Behavioral Neuroscience, 115*, 1086–1092.

Kuczmarski, R. J. (1992). Prevalence of overweight and weight gain in the United States. *American Journal of Clinical Nutrition, 55*, 495S–502S.

Kurbat, M. A., & Farah, M. J. (1998). Is the category-specific deficit for living things spurious? *Journal of Cognitive Neuroscience, 10*, 355–361.

Kushner, H. I. (1999). *A cursing brain? The histories of Tourette syndrome*. Cambridge, MA: Harvard University Press.

Laeng, B., & Caviness, V. S. (2001). Prosopagnosia as a deficit in encoding curved surface. *Journal of Cognitive Neuroscience, 13*, 556–576.

Laine, M., Salmelin, R., Helenius, P., & Marttila, R. (2000). Brain activation during reading in deep dyslexia: An MEG study. *Journal of Cognitive Neuroscience, 12*, 622–634.

Land, E. H. (1977, April). The retinex theory of color vision. *Scientific American, 237*, 108–128.

Lang, A. E. (2001). Update on the treatment of tics. *Advances in Neurology, 85*, 355–362.

Langston, J. W. (1985). MPTP and Parkinson's disease. *Trends in Neurosciences, 8*, 79–83.

Langston, J. W. (1986). MPTP-induced Parkinsonism: How good a model is it? In S. Fahn, C. P. Marsden, P. Jenner, & P. Teychenne (Eds.), *Recent developments in Parkinson's disease* (pp. 119–126). New York: Raven Press.

Lashley, K. S. (1941). Patterns of cerebral integration indicated by the scotomas of migraine. *Archives of Neurology and Psychiatry, 46,* 331–339.

Lashley, K. S. (1950). In search of the engram. *Symposia of the Society for Experimental Biology, 4,* 454–482.

Latimer, D., & Goldberg, J. (1981). *Flowers in the blood.* New York: Franklin Watts.

Lavie, P., Pratt, H., Scharf, B., Peled, R., & Brown, J. (1984). Localized pontine lesion: Nearly total absence of REM sleep. *Neurology, 34,* 1118–1120.

Lavie, P. (2001). Sleep–wake as a biological rhythm. *Annual Review of Neuroscience, 52,* 277–303.

Laviolette, S. R., & Van der Kooy, D. (2004). The neurobiology of nicotine addiction: Bridging the gap from molecules to behaviour. *Nature Reviews Neuroscience, 5,* 55–65.

Lawrence, D. G., & Kuypers, H. G. J. M. (1968a). The functional organization of the motor system in the monkey: I. The effects of bilateral pyramidal lesions. *Brain, 91,* 1–14.

Lawrence, D. G., & Kuypers, H. G. J. M. (1968b). The functional organization of the motor system in the monkey: II. The effects of lesions of the descending brain-stem pathways. *Brain, 91,* 15–36.

Le, W., & Appel, S. H. (2004). Mutant genes responsible for Parkinson's disease. *Current Opinion in Pharmacology, 4,* 79–84.

Leckman, J. F., Peterson, B. S., King, R. A., Scahill, L., & Cohen, D. J. (2001). Phenomenology of tics and natural history of tic disorders. In D. J. Cohen, C. G. Goetz, & J. Jankovic (Eds.), *Tourette syndrome* (pp. 1–14). Philadelphia: Lippincott Williams & Wilkins.

Lederhendler, I., & Schulkin, J. (2000). Behavioral neuroscience: Challenges for the era of molecular biology. *Trends in Neurosciences, 23,* 451–453.

LeDoux, J. E. (1994, June). Emotion, memory and the brain. *Scientific American, 270,* 50–57.

LeDoux, J. E. (1995). Emotion: Clues from the brain. *Annual Review of Psychology, 46,* 209–235.

LeDoux, J. E. (2000a). Cognitive-emotional interactions: Listen to the brain. In R. D. Lane & L. Nadel (Eds.), *Cognitive neuroscience of emotion* (pp. 129–155). New York: Oxford University Press.

LeDoux, J. E. (2000b). Emotion circuits in the brain. *Annual Review of Neuroscience, 23,* 155–184.

Lee, S. H., & Sheng, M. (2000). Development of neuron–neuron synapse. *Current Opinion in Neurobiology, 10,* 125–131.

Lee, V. M. (2001). Tauists and βaptists united—well almost! *Science, 293,* 1446–1495.

Leibowitz, S. F., Hammer, N. J., & Chang, K. (1981). Hypothalamic paraventricular nucleus lesions produce overeating and obesity in the rat. *Physiology & Behavior, 27,* 1031–1040.

Leker, R. R., & Shohami, E. (2002). Cerebral ischemia and trauma—different etiologies yet similar mechanisms: Neuroprotective opportunities. *Brain Research Reviews, 39,* 55–73.

Lemke, G. (2001). Glial control of neuronal development. *Annual Review of Neuroscience, 24,* 87–105.

Lennoff, H. M., Wang, P. P., Greenberg, F., & Bellugi, U. (1997, December). Williams syndrome and the brain. *Scientific American, 279,* 68–73.

Lennox, W. G. (1960). *Epilepsy and related disorders.* Boston: Little, Brown.

Leon, M., & Johnson, B. A. (2003). Olfactory coding in the mammalian olfactory bulb. *Brain Research Reviews, 42,* 23–32.

Lerman, C., Caporaso, N. E., Audrain, J., Main, D., Bowman, E. D., Lockshin, B., et al. (1999). Evidence suggesting the role of specific genetic factors in cigarette smoking. *Health Psychology, 18,* 14–20.

Leshner, A. I. (1997). Addiction is a brain disease, and it matters. *Science, 278,* 45–46.

LeVay, S. (1991). A difference in hypothalamic structure between heterosexual and homosexual men. *Science, 253,* 1034–1037.

LeVay, S., Hubel, D. H., & Wiesel, T. N. (1975). The pattern of ocular dominance columns in macaque visual cortex revealed by a reduced silver stain. *Journal of Comparative Neurology, 159,* 559–576.

Levi-Montalcini, R. (1952). Effects of mouse motor transplantation on the nervous system. *Annals of the New York Academy of Sciences, U.S.A., 55,* 330–344.

Levi-Montalcini, R. (1975). NGF: An uncharted route. In F. G. Worden, J. P. Swazey, & G. Adelman (Eds.), *The neurosciences: Paths of discovery* (pp. 245–265). Cambridge, MA: MIT Press.

Levin, H. S. (1989). Memory deficit after closed-head injury. *Journal of Clinical and Experimental Neuropsychology, 12,* 129–153.

Levin, H. S., Papanicolaou, A., & Eisenberg, H. M. (1984). Observations on amnesia after non-missile head injury. In L. R. Squire & N. Butters (Eds.), *Neuropsychology of memory* (pp. 247–257). New York: Guilford Press.

Levine, J. A., Eberhardt, N. L., & Jensen, M. D. (1999). Role of nonexercise activity thermogenesis in resistance to fat gain in humans. *Science, 283,* 212–214.

Levitt, J. B. (2001). Function following form. *Science, 292,* 232–234.

Levitt, P. (2004). Sealing cortical cell fate. *Science, 303,* 48–49.

Levy, J. (1969). Possible basis for the evolution of lateral specialization of the human brain. *Nature, 224,* 614–615.

Levy, J., Trevarthen, C., & Sperry, R. W. (1972). Perception of bilateral chimeric figures following hemispheric deconnection. *Brain, 95,* 61–78.

Lewcock, J. W., & Reed, R. R. (2003). ORs rule the roost in the olfactory system. *Science, 302,* 2078–2079.

Lewis, D. A., & Levitt, P. (2002). Schizophrenia as a disorder of neurodevelopment. *Annual Review of Neuroscience, 25,* 409–432.

Lewy, A. J., Ahmed, S., & Sack, R. L. (1996). Phase shifting the human circadian clock using melatonin. *Behavioural Brain Research, 73,* 131–134.

Li, M. O., Sarkisian, M. R., Mehal, W. Z., Rakic, P., & Flavell, R. A. (2003). Phosphatidylserine receptor is required for clearance of apoptotic cells. *Science, 302,* 1560–1562.

Li, Y., Field, P. M., & Raisman, G. (1998). Regeneration of adult rat corticospinal axons induced by transplanted olfactory ensheathing cells. *Journal of Neuroscience, 18,* 10514–10524.

Libby, P. (2002, May). Atherosclerosis: The new view. *Scientific American, 286,* 5, 47–55.

Lin, L., Faraco, J., Li, R., Kadotani, H., Rogers, W., Lin, X., et al. (1999). The sleep disorder canine narcolepsy is caused by a mutation in the hypocretin (orexin) receptor 2 gene. *Cell, 98,* 365–376.

Linden, D. J. (2003). From molecules to memory in the cerebellum. *Science, 301,* 1682–1683.

Lindsay, P. H., & Norman, D. A. (1977). *Human information processing* (2nd ed.). New York: Academic Press.

Lindsey, D. B., Bowden, J., & Magoun, H. W. (1949). Effect upon the EEG of acute injury to the brain stem activating system. *Electroencephalography and Clinical Neurophysiology, 1,* 475–486.

Liou, J. D., Ma, Y. Y., Gibson, L. H., Su, H., Charest, N., Lau, Y. F., & Yang-Feng, T. L. (1997). Cytogenetic and molecular studies of a familial paracentric inversion of Y chromosome present in a patient with ambiguous genitalia. *American Journal of Medical Genetics, 16*(70), 134–137.

Lipert, J., Bauder, H., Miltner, W. H. R., Taub, E., & Weiller, C. (2000). Treatment-induced cortical reorganization after stroke in humans. *Stroke, 31*, 1210–1216.

Lisman, J. (2003). Long-term potentiation: Outstanding questions and attempted synthesis. *Philosophical Transactions of the Royal Society of London, 358*, 829–842.

Lisman, J., Lichtman, J. W., & Sanes, J. R. (2003). LTP: Perils and progress. *Nature Reviews Neuroscience, 4*, 926–929.

Liu, L., Wong, T. P., Pozza, M. F., Lingenhoehl, K., Wang, Y., Sheng, M., et al. (2004). Role of NMDA receptor subtypes in governing the direction of hippocampal synaptic plasticity. *Science, 304*, 1021–1024.

Livingston, E. H., & Guth, P. H. (1992). Peptic ulcer disease: Wounds in the walls of the stomach develop only after elaborate cellular and molecular defensive mechanisms are breached. *American Scientist, 80*, 592–598.

Livingstone, M. S., & Hubel, D. H. (1984). Anatomy and physiology of a color system in the primate visual cortex. *Journal of Neuroscience, 4*, 309–356.

Livingstone, M. S., & Hubel, D. S. (1988). Segregation of form, color, movement, and depth: Anatomy, physiology, and perception. *Science, 240*, 740–749.

Livingstone, M. S., & Tsao, D. Y. (1999). Receptive fields of disparity-selective neurons in macaque striate cortex. *Nature Reviews Neuroscience, 2*, 825–832.

Lo, E. H., Dalkara, T., & Moskowitz, M. A. (2003). Mechanisms, challenges and opportunities in stroke. *Nature Reviews Neuroscience, 4*, 399–415.

Lo, Y.-J., & Poo, M.-M. (1991). Activity-dependent synaptic competition in vitro: Heterosynaptic suppression of developing synapses. *Science, 254*, 1019–1022.

Logothetis, N. (1998). Object vision and visual awareness. *Current Opinion in Neurobiology, 8*, 536–544.

Logothetis, N. K., & Sheinberg, D. L. (1996). Visual object recognition. *Annual Review of Neuroscience, 19*, 577–621.

Loomis, A. L., Harvey, E. N., & Hobart, G. (1936). Electrical potentials of the human brain. *Journal of Experimental Psychology, 19*, 249–279.

Losick, R., & Shapiro, L. (1998). Bringing the mountain to Mohammed. *Science, 282*, 1430–1431.

Lotze, M., Montoya, P., Erb, M., Hülsmann, E., Flor, H., Klose, U., et al. (1999). Activation of cortical and cerebellar motor areas during executed and imagined hand movements: An fMRI study. *Journal of Cognitive Neuroscience, 11*, 491–501.

Löw, A., Bentin, S., Rockstroh, B., Silberman, Y., Gomolla, A., Cohen, R., & Elbert, T. (2003). Semantic categorization in the human brain: Spatiotemporal dynamics revealed by magnetoencephalography. *Psychological Science, 14*, 367–372.

Lowe, J., & Carroll, D. (1985). The effects of spinal injury on the intensity of emotional experience. *The British Journal of Clinical Psychology, 24*, 135–136.

Lowe, M. R. (1993). The effects of dieting on eating behavior: A three-factor model. *Psychological Bulletin, 114*, 100–121.

Lowrey, P. L., Shimomura, K., Antoch, M. P., Yamazaki, S., Zemenides, P. D., Ralph, M. R., et al. (2000). Positional syntenic cloning and functional characterization of the mammalian circadian mutation tau. *Science, 288*, 483–491.

Lucas, R. J., Freedman, M. S., Muñoz, M., Garcia-Fernández, J. M., & Foster, R. G. (1999). Regulation of the mammalian pineal by non-rod, non-cone, ocular photoreceptors. *Science, 284*, 505–507.

Lucas, R. J., Hattar, S., Takao, M., Berson, D. M., Foster, R. G., & Yau, K.-W. (2003). Diminished pupillary light reflex at high irradiances in melanopsin-knockout mice. *Science, 299*, 245–247.

Lucidi, F., Devoto, A., Violani, C., Mastracci, P., & Bertini, M. (1997). Effects of different sleep duration on delta sleep in recovery nights. *Psychophysiology, 34*, 227–233.

Ludwig, M., & Pittman, Q. J. (2003). Talking back: Dendritic neurotransmitter release. *Trends in Neurosciences, 26*, 255–261.

Luo, M., Fee, M. S., & Katz, L. C. (2003). Encoding pheromonal signals in the accessory olfactory bulb of behaving mice. *Science, 299*, 1196–1201.

Lüscher, C., & Frerking, M. (2001). Restless AMPA receptors: Implications for synaptic transmission and plasticity. *Trends in Neurosciences, 24*, 665–670.

Lynch, M. A. (2004). Long-term potentiation and memory. *Physiological Review, 84*, 87–136.

Macaluso, E., Driver, J., & Frith, C. D. (2003). Multimodal spatial representations engaged in human parietal cortex during both saccadic and manual spatial orienting. *Current Biology, 13*, 990–999.

Maccaferri, G., & Lacaille, J. C. (2003). Hippocampal interneuron classifications—making things as simple as possible, not simpler. *Trends in Neurosciences, 26*(10), 564–571.

Maccari, S., Darnaudery, M., Morley-Fletcher, S., Zuena, A. R., Cinque, C., & Van Reeth, O. (2003). Prenatal stress and long-term consequences: Implications of glucocorticoid hormones. *Neuroscience and Biobehavioural Reviews, 27*, 119–127.

Macchi, G. (1989). Anatomical substrate of emotional reactions. In F. Boller & J. Grafman (Eds.), *Handbook of neuropsychology* (Vol. 3, pp. 283–304). New York: Elsevier.

Machado, M. G., Oliveira, H. A., Cipolotti, R., Santos, C. A., Oliveira, E. F., Donald, R. M., & Krauss, M. P. (2003). Anatomical and functional abnormalities of central nervous system in autistic disorder: A MRI and SPECT study. *Archives of Neurology, 61*, 957–961.

MacKinnon, D. F., Jamison, K. R., & DePaulo, J. R. (1997). Genetics of manic depressive illness. *Annual Review of Neuroscience, 20*, 355–373.

Maeder, T. (2003, May). The orphan drug backlash. *Scientific American, 288*, 81–87.

Maguire, A. A., Burgess, N., Donnett, J. G., Frackowiak, R. S. J., Frith, C. D., & O'Keefe, J. (2000). Knowing where and getting there: A human navigation network. *Science, 280*, 921–924.

Maguire, E. A., Frith, C. D., Burgess, N., Donnett, J. G., & O'Keefe, J. (1998). Knowing where things are: Parahippocampal involvement in encoding object locations in virtual large-scale space. *Journal of Cognitive Neuroscience, 19*, 61–76.

Malenka, R. C. (2003). The long-term potential of LTP. *Nature Reviews Neuroscience, 4*, 923–926.

Malissen, B. (1999). Dancing the immunological two-step. *Science, 285*, 207–208.

Malsbury, C. W. (1971). Facilitation of male rat copulatory behavior by electrical stimulation of the medial preoptic area. *Physiology & Behavior, 7*, 797–805.

Manson, J. E., Willett, W. C., Stampfer, M. J., Colditz, G. A., Hunter, D. J., Hankinson, S. E., et al. (1995). Body weight and mortality among women. *New England Journal of Medicine, 333*, 677–685.

Maquet, P. (2001). The role of sleep in learning and memory. *Science, 294*, 1048–1052.

Maries, E., Dass, B., Collier, T. J., Kordower, J. H., & Steece-Collier, K. (2003). The role of α-synuclein in Parkinson's disease: Insights from animal models. *Nature Reviews Neuroscience, 4*, 727–738.

Marin, O., & Rubenstein, J. L. R. (2001). A long, remarkable journey: Tangential migration in the telencephalon. *Nature Reviews Neuroscience, 2*, 780–790.

Marin, O., & Rubenstein, J. L. R. (2003). Cell migration in the forebrain. *Annual Review of Neuroscience, 26,* 441–483.

Marin, O., Yaron, A., Bagri, A., Tessier-Lavigne, M., & Rubenstein, J. L. R. (2001). Sorting of striatal and cortical interneurons regulated by semaphoring-neuropilin interactions. *Science, 293,* 872–875.

Mark, V. H., Ervin, F. R., & Yakolev, P. I. (1962). The treatment of pain by stereotaxic methods. First International Symposium on Stereoencephalotomy (Philadelphia, 1961). *Confina Neurologica, 22,* 238–245.

Markus, A., Patel, T. D., & Snider, W. (2002). Neurotrophic factors and axonal growth. *Current Opinion in Neurobiology, 12,* 523–531.

Marlowe, W. B., Mancall, E. L., & Thomas, J. J. (1985). Complete Kluver-Bucy syndrome in man. *Cortex, 11,* 53–59.

Martin, A., Wiggs, C. L., Ungerleider, L. G., & Haxby, J. V. (1996). Neural correlates of category-specific knowledge. *Nature, 379,* 649–652.

Martin, J. B. (1986). Sleep deprivation and exercise. In K. B. Pandolf (Ed.), *Exercise and sport sciences reviews* (pp. 213–229). New York: Macmillan.

Martin, J. B. (1987). Molecular genetics: Applications to the clinical neurosciences. *Science, 238,* 765–772.

Martin, R. C. (2003). Language processing: Functional organization and neuroanatomical basis. *Annual Review of Psychology, 54,* 55–89.

Martin, R. J., White, B. D., & Hulsey, M. G. (1991). The regulation of body weight. *American Scientist, 79,* 528–541.

Martin, R. L., Roberts, W. V., & Clayton, P. J. (1980). Psychiatric status after a one-year prospective follow-up. *Journal of the American Medical Association, 244,* 350–353.

Martinez, L. M., & Alonso, J.-M. (2003). Complex receptive fields in primary visual cortex. *The Neuroscientist, 9,* 317–331.

Martin-Soelch, C., Leenders, K. L., Chevalley, A.-F., Missimer, J., Künig, G., Magyar, S., et al. (2001). Reward mechanisms in the brain and their role in dependence: Evidence from neurophysiological and neuroimaging studies. *Brain Research Reviews, 36,* 139–149.

Masland, R. H. (2001). Neuronal diversity in the retina. *Current Opinion in Neurobiology, 11,* 431–436.

Masoro, E. J. (1988). Food restriction in rodents: An evaluation of its role in the study of aging [Minireview]. *Journal of Gerontology, 43,* 59–64.

Masterton, R. B. (1992). Role of the central auditory system in hearing: The new direction. *Trends in Neurosciences, 15,* 280–285.

Matsuda, L. A., Lolait, S. J., Brownstein, M. J., Young, A. C., & Bonner, T. I. (1990). Structure of a cannabinoid receptor and functional expression of the cloned DNA. *Nature, 346,* 561–564.

Matzinger, P. (2002). The danger model: A renewed sense of self. *Science, 296,* 301–305.

Mayr, E. (2000, July). Darwin's influence on modern thought. *Scientific American, 283,* 70–83.

Mazzocchi, F., & Vignolo, L. A. (1979). Localisation of lesions in aphasia: Clinical–CT scan correlations in stroke patients. *Cortex. 15,* 627–654.

McCandliss, B. D., & Noble, K. G. (2003). The development of reading impairment: A cognitive neuroscience model. *Mental Retardation and Developmental Disabilities Research Reviews, 9,* 196–204.

McCann, T. S. (1981). Aggression and sexual activity of male southern elephant seals, *Mirounga leonina. Journal of Zoology, 195,* 295–310.

McCardle, K., Luebbers, S., Carter, J. D., Croft, R. J., & Stough, C. (2004). Chronic MDMA (Ecstasy) use, cognition and mood. *Psychopharmacology, 173,* 434–439.

McCarthy, M. M., Auger, A. P., & Perrot-Sinal, T. S. (2002). Getting excited about GABA and sex differences in the brain. *Trends in Neurosciences, 25,* 307–313.

McClintock, M. K., & Herdt, G. (1996). Rethinking puberty: The development of sexual attraction. *Current Directions in Psychological Sciences, 5,* 178–183.

McCormick, D. A. (1999). Membrane potential and action potential. In M. J. Zigmond, F. E. Bloom, S. C. Landis, J. L. Roberts, & L. R. Squire (Eds.), *Fundamental neuroscience* (pp. 129–154). New York: Academic Press.

McCrory, P. R., & Berkovic, S. F. (1998). Second impact syndrome. *Neurology, 50,* 677–683.

McDonald, J. W., Liu, X.-Z., Qu, Y., Liu, S., Mickey, S. K., Turetsky, D., et al. (1999). Transplanted embryonic stem cells survive, differentiate and promote recovery in injured rat spinal cord. *Nature Medicine, 5,* 1410–1412.

McDonald, R. J., & White, N. M. (1993). Triple dissociation of memory systems: Hippocampus, amygdala, and dorsal striatum. *Behavioral and Neural Biology, 59,* 107–119.

McEwen, B. (1994). Introduction: Stress and the nervous system. *Seminars in the Neurosciences, 6,* 195–196.

McEwen, B. S. (1983). Gonadal steroid influences on brain development and sexual differentiation. In R. O. Greep (Ed.), *Reproductive physiology IV.* Baltimore: University Park Press.

McEwen, B. S. (1987). Sexual differentiation. In G. Adelman (Ed.), *Encyclopedia of neuroscience* (Vol. II, pp. 1086–1088). Boston: Birkhäuser.

McEwen, B. S. (2000a). Effects of adverse experiences for brain structure and function. *Biological Psychiatry, 48,* 721–731.

McEwen, B. S. (2000b). The neurobiology of stress: From serendipity to clinical relevance. *Brain Research, 886,* 172–189.

McGaugh, J. L. (2002). Memory consolidation and the amygdala: A systems perspective. *Trends in Neurosciences, 25,* 456–461.

McGlone, J. (1977). Sex differences in the cerebral organization of verbal functions in patients with unilateral brain lesions. *Brain, 100,* 775–793.

McGlone, J. (1980). Sex differences in human brain asymmetry: A critical survey. *Behavioral and Brain Sciences, 3,* 215–263.

McGue, M. (1999). The behavioral genetics of alcoholism. *Current Directions in Psychological Science, 8,* 109–115.

McKim, W. A. (1986). *Drugs and behavior: An introduction to behavioral pharmacology.* Englewood Cliffs, NJ: Prentice-Hall.

McLaughlin, T., Hindges, R., & O'Leary, D. D. M. (2003). Regulation of axial patterning of the retina and its topographic mapping in the brain. *Current Opinion in Neurobiology, 13,* 57–69.

McMurray, C. T. (2001). Huntington's disease: New hope for therapeutics. *Trends in Neurosciences, 24,* S32–S38.

McNally, G. P. (1999). Pain facilitatory circuits in the mammalian central nervous system: Their behavioral significance and role in morphine analgesic tolerance. *Neuroscience and Biobehavioural Reviews, 23,* 1059–1078.

McNally, R. J. (2003). Progress and controversy in the study of posttraumatic stress disorder. *Annual Review of Psychology, 54,* 229–252.

McNally, R. J., Bryant, R. A., & Ehlers, A. (2003). Does early psychological intervention promote recovery from posttraumatic stress? *Psychological Science in the Public Interest, 4,* 45–79.

Meaney, M. J. (2001). Maternal care, gene expression, and the transmission of individual differences in stress reactivity across generations. *Annual Review of Neuroscience, 24,* 1161–1192.

Meddis, R. (1977). *The sleep instinct.* London: Routledge & Kegan Paul.

Medina, J. F., Nores, W. L., Ohyama, T., & Mauk, M. D. (2000). Mechanisms of cerebellar learning suggested by eyelid conditioning. *Current Opinion in Neurobiology, 10,* 717–724.

Medina, J. F., Repa, J. C., Mauk, M. D., & LeDoux, J. E. (2002). Parallels between cerebellum- and amygdala-dependent conditioning. *Nature Reviews Neuroscience, 3*, 122–131.

Medzhitov, R., & Janeway, C. A., Jr., (2002). Decoding the patterns of self and nonself by the innate immune system. *Science, 296*, 298–301.

Mello, N. K., & Mendelson, J. H. (1972). Drinking patterns during work-contingent and noncontingent alcohol acquisition. *Psychosomatic Medicine, 34*, 139–165.

Melzack, R. (1992, April). Phantom limbs. *Scientific American, 266*, 120–126.

Melzack, R., & Wall, P. D. (1965). Pain mechanisms: A new theory. *Science, 150*, 971–979.

Melzack, R., & Wall, P. D. (1982). *The challenge of pain*. London: Penguin Books.

Mercer, J. G., & Speakman, J. R. (2001). Hypothalamic neuropeptide mechanisms for regulating energy balance: From rodent models to human obesity. *Neuroscience and Biobehavioural Reviews, 25*, 101–116.

Metcalfe, J., Funnell, M., & Gazzaniga, M. S. (1995). Right hemisphere memory veridicality: Studies of a split-brain patient. *Psychological Science, 6*, 157–165.

Meunier, M., Murray, E. A., Bachevalier, J., & Mishkin, M. (1990). Effects of perirhinal cortical lesions on visual recognition memory in rhesus monkeys. *Society for Neuroscience Abstracts, 17*, 337.

Meyer, R. G., & Salmon, P. (1988). *Abnormal psychology* (2nd ed.). Boston: Allyn & Bacon.

Mieda, M., & Yanagisawa, M. (2002). Sleep, feeding, and neuropeptides: Roles of orexins and orexin receptors. *Current Opinion in Neurobiology, 12*, 339–345.

Miller, G. L., & Knudsen, E. I. (1999). Early visual experience shapes the representation of auditory space in the forebrain gaze fields of the barn owl. *Journal of Neuroscience, 19*, 2326–2336.

Miller, N. S., Summers, G. L., & Gold, M. S. (1993). Cocaine dependence: Alcohol and other drug dependence and withdrawal characteristics. *Journal of Addictive Diseases, 12*, 25–35.

Milner, B. (1965). Memory disturbances after bilateral hippocampal lesions. In P. Milner & S. Glickman (Eds.), *Cognitive processes and the brain* (pp. 104–105). Princeton, NJ: D. Van Nostrand.

Milner, B. (1974). Hemispheric specialization: Scope and limits. In F. O. Schmitt & F. G. Worden (Eds.), *The neurosciences: Third study program* (pp. 75–89). Cambridge, MA: MIT Press.

Milner, B., Corkin, S., & Teuber, H. L. (1968). Further analysis of the hippocampal amnesic syndrome: 14-year follow-up study of H.M. *Neuropsychologia, 6*, 317–338.

Milner, D., & Goodale, M. A. (1993). Visual pathways to perception and action. *Progress in Brain Research, 95*, 317–337.

Milner, P. M. (1993, January). The mind and Donald O. Hebb. *Scientific American, 268*, 124–129.

Milner, P. M., & White, N. M. (1987). What is physiological psychology? *Psychobiology, 15*, 2–6.

Mishkin, M., & Appenzeller, T. (1987, June). The anatomy of memory. *Scientific American, 256*, 80–89.

Mishkin, M., & Delacour, J. (1975). An analysis of short-term visual memory in the monkey. *Journal of Experimental Psychology: Animal Behavior Processes, 1*, 326–334.

Mistlberger, R. E. (1994). Circadian food-anticipatory activity: Formal models and physiological mechanisms. *Neuroscience and Biobehavioural Reviews, 18*, 171–195.

Mistlberger, R. E., de Groot, M. H. M., Bossert, J. M., & Marchant, E. G. (1996). Discrimination of circadian phase in intact and suprachiasmatic nuclei-ablated rats. *Brain Research, 739*, 12–18.

Moghaddam, B. (2003). Bringing order to the glutamate chaos in schizophrenia. *Neuron, 40*, 881–884.

Mogil, J. S., Yu, L., & Basbaum, A. I. (2000). Pain genes? Natural variation and transgenic mutants. *Annual Review of Neuroscience, 23*, 777–811.

Mohr, J. P. (1976). Broca's area and Broca's aphasia. In H. Whitaker & H. A. Whitaker (Eds.), *Studies in neurolinguistics* (Vol. 1, pp. 201–235). New York: Academic Press.

Molday, R. S., & Hsu, Y.-T. (1995). The cGMP-gated channel of photoreceptor cells: Its structural properties and role in phototransduction. *Behavioral and Brain Sciences, 18*, 441–451.

Momma, S., Johansson, C. B., & Frisén, J. (2000). Get to know your stem cells. *Current Opinion in Neurobiology, 10*, 45–49.

Money, J. (1975). Ablatio penis: Normal male infant sex-reassigned as a girl. *Archives of Sexual Behavior, 4*(1), 65–71.

Money, J., & Ehrhardt, A. A. (1972). *Man & woman, boy & girl*. Baltimore: Johns Hopkins University Press.

Montmayeur, J. P., & Matsunami, H. (2002). Receptors for bitter and sweet taste. *Current Opinion in Neurobiology, 12*, 366–371.

Moore, R. Y. (1996). Neural control of the pineal gland. *Behavioural Brain Research, 73*, 125–130.

Moran, J., & Desimone, R. (1985). Selective attention gates visual processing in the extrastriate cortex. *Science, 229*, 782–784.

Moran, M. H. (2004). Gut peptides in the control of food intake: 30 years of ideas. *Physiology & Behavior, 82*, 175–180.

Morin, C. M., Kowatch, R. A., & O'Shanick, G. (1990). Sleep restriction for the inpatient treatment of insomnia. *Sleep, 13*, 183–186.

Morris, M. K., Bowers, D., Chatterjee, A., & Heilman, K. M. (1992). Amnesia following a discrete basal forebrain lesion. *Brain, 115*, 1827–1847.

Morris, N. M., Udry, J. R., Khan-Dawood, F., & Dawood, M. Y. (1987). Marital sex frequency and midcycle female testosterone. *Archives of Sexual Behavior, 16*, 27–37.

Morris, R. G. M., Moser, E. I., Riedel, G., Martin, S. J., Sandin, J., Day, M., & O'Carroll, C. O. (2003). Elements of a neurobiological theory of the hippocampus: The role of activity-dependent synaptic plasticity in memory. *Philosophical Transactions of the Royal Society of London, 358*, 773–786.

Morse, D., & Sassone-Corsi, P. (2002). Time after time: Inputs to and outputs from the mammalian circadian oscillators. *Trends in Neurosciences, 25*, 632–637.

Morshead, C. M., & van der Kooy, D. (2001). A new "spin" on neural stem cells? *Current Opinion in Neurobiology, 11*, 59–65.

Mort, D. J., Malhotra, P., Mannan, S. K., Rorden, C., Pambakian, A., Kennard, C., & Husain, M. (2003). The anatomy of visual neglect. *Brain, 126*, 1986–1997.

Moruzzi, G., & Magoun, H. W. (1949). Brain stem reticular formation and activation of the EEG. *Electroencephalography and Clinical Neurophysiology, 1*, 455–473.

Moser, E. I., & Paulsen, O. (2001). New excitement in cognitive space: Between place cells and spatial memory. *Current Opinion in Neurobiology, 11*, 745–751.

Mott, D. D., & Dingledine, R. (2003). Interneuron research—challenges and strategies. *Trends in Neurosciences, 26*(9), 484–488.

Mountcastle, V. B., & Powell, T. P. S. (1959). Neural mechanisms subserving cutaneous sensibility with special references to the role of afferent inhibition in sensory perception and discrimination. *Bulletin of Johns Hopkins Hospital, 105*, 201–232.

Mrosovsky, N., & Salmon, P. A. (1987). A behavioral method for accelerating re-entrainment of rhythms to new light-dark cycles. *Nature, 330*, 372–373.

Mudher, A., & Lovestone, S. (2002). Alzheimer's disease—do tauists and baptists finally shake hands? *Trends in Neurosciences, 25*, 22–26.

Mühlnickel, W., Elbert, T., Taub, E., & Flor, H. (1998). Reorganization of auditory cortex in tinnitus. *Proceedings of the National Academy of Sciences, U.S.A., 95*, 10340–10343.

Mullaney, D. J., Johnson, L. C., Naitoh, P., Friedman, J. K., & Globus, G. G. (1977). Sleep during and after gradual sleep reduction. *Psychophysiology, 14*, 237–244.

Müller, N. G., Machado, L., & Knight, R. T. (2002). Contributions of subregions of the prefrontal cortex to working memory: Evidence from brain lesions in humans. *Journal of Cognitive Neuroscience, 14*, 673–686.

Müller, R.-A., Kleinhans, N., Kemmotsu, N., Pierce, K., & Courchesne, E. (2003). Abnormal variability and distribution of functional maps in autism: An fMRI study of visuomotor learning. *The American Journal of Psychiatry, 160*, 1847–1862.

Müller, R.-A., Pierce, K., Ambrose, J. B., Allen, G., & Cour-chesne, E. (2001). Atypical patterns of cerebral motor activation in autism: A functional magnetic resonance study. *Biological Psychiatry, 49*, 665–676.

Mumby, D. G. (2001). Perspectives on object-recognition memory following hippocampal damage: Lessons from studies in rats. *Behavioural Brain Research, 14*, 159–181.

Mumby, D. G., Cameli, L., & Glenn, M. J. (1999). Impaired allocentric spatial working memory and intact retrograde memory after thalamic damage caused by thiamine deficiency in rats. *Behavioral Neuroscience, 113*, 42–50.

Mumby, D. G., & Pinel, J. P. J. (1994). Rhinal cortex lesions impair object recognition in rats. *Behavioral Neuroscience, 108*, 11–18.

Mumby, D. G., Pinel, J. P. J., & Wood, E. R. (1989). Nonrecurring items delayed nonmatching-to-sample in rats: A new paradigm for testing nonspatial working memory. *Psy-chobiology, 18*, 321–326.

Mumby, D. G., Wood, E. R., Duva, C. A., Kornecook, T. J., Pinel, J. P. J., & Phillips, A. G. (1996). Ischemia-induced object-recognition deficits in rats are attenuated by hippocampal ablation before or soon after ischemia. *Behavioral Neuroscience, 110*(2), 266–281.

Mumby, D. G., Wood, E. R., & Pinel, J. P. J. (1992). Object-recognition memory is only mildly impaired in rats with lesions of the hippocampus and amygdala. *Psychobiology, 20*, 18–27.

Münte, T. F., Altenmüller, E., & Jänke, L. (2002). The musician's brain as a model of neuroplasticity. *Nature Reviews Neuroscience, 3*, 473–478.

Murphy, M. R., & Schneider, G. E. (1970). Olfactory bulb removal eliminates mating behavior in the male golden hamster. *Science, 157*, 302–304.

Murray, E. A. (1996). What have ablation studies told us about the neural substrates of stimulus memory? *Seminars in the Neurosciences, 8*, 13–22.

Murray, E. A., & Richmond, B. J. (2001). Role of perirhinal cortex in object perception, memory, and associations. *Current Opinion in Neurobiology, 11*, 188–193.

Myers, R. E., & Sperry, R. W. (1953). Interocular transfer of a visual form discrimination habit in cats after section of the optic chiasma and corpus callosum. In *Abstracts of Papers from Platform* (p. 351), American Association of Anatomists.

Nadarajah, B., & Parnavelas, J. G. (2002). Modes of neuronal migration in the developing cerebral cortex. *Nature Reviews Neuroscience, 3*, 423–432.

Nadel, L., & Moscovitch, M. (1997). Memory consolidation, retrograde amnesia and the hippocampal complex. *Current Opinion in Neurobiology, 7*, 217–227.

Naeser, M. A., Alexander M. P., Helm-Estabrooks, N., Levine, H. L., Laughlin, S. A., & Geschwind, N. (1982). Aphasia with predominantly subcortical lesion sites. *Archives of Neurolinguistics, 39*, 2–14.

Naeser, M. A., Hayward, R. W., Laughlin, S. A., & Zatz, L. M. (1981). Quantitative CT scan studies in aphasia. *Brain and Language, 12*, 140–164.

Naitoh, P. (1992). Minimal sleep to maintain performance: The search for sleep quantum in sustained operations. In C. Stampi (Ed.), *Why we nap: Evolution, chronobiology, and functions of polyphasic and ultrashort sleep*. Boston: Birkhaüser.

Nakahara, K., Hayashi, T., Konishi, S., & Miyashita, Y. (2002). Functional MRI of macaque monkeys performing a cognitive set-shifting task. *Science, 295*, 1532–1536.

Natelson, B. H. (2004). Stress, hormones and disease. *Physiology & Behavior, 82*, 139–143.

National Commission on Marijuana and Drug Abuse. (1972). *Marijuana: A signal of misunderstanding*. New York: New American Library.

Nau, R., & Brück, W. (2002). Neuronal injury in bacterial meningitis: Mechanisms and implications for therapy. *Trends in Neurosciences, 25*, 38–45.

Naya, Y., Yoshida, M., & Miyashita, Y. (2001). Backward spreading of memory-retrieval signal in the primate temporal cortex. *Science, 291*, 661–664.

Nemeroff, C. B. (1998, June). The neurobiology of depression. *Scientific American, 278*, 42–49.

Nestle, M. (2003). The ironic politics of obesity. *Science, 299*, 781.

Netter, F. H. (1962). *The CIBA collection of medical illustrations. Vol. 1, The nervous system*. New York: CIBA.

Neves, S. R., Ram, P. T., & Iyengar, R. (2002). G protein pathways. *Science, 296*, 1636–1639.

Neville, H., & Bavelier, D. (1998). Neural organization and plasticity of language. *Current Opinion in Neurobiology, 8*, 254–258.

Newcombe, N., & Fox, N. (1994). Infantile amnesia: Through a glass darkly. *Child Development, 65*, 31–40.

Newcombe, N. S. (2002). The nativist-empiricist controversy in the context of recent research on spatial and quantitative development. *Psychological Science, 13*(5), 395–400.

Newcombe, N. S., Drummey, A. B., Fox, N. A., Lie, E., & Ottinger-Alberts, W. (2000). Remembering early childhood: How much, how, and why (or why not). *Current Directions in Psychological Science, 9*, 55–58.

Newport, D. J., & Nemeroff, C. B. (2000). Neurobiology of post-traumatic stress disorder. *Current Opinion in Neurobiology, 10*, 211–218.

Newsom-Davis, J., & Vincent, A. (1991). Antibody-mediated neurological disease. *Current Opinion in Neurobiology, 1*, 430–435.

Nicolesis, M. A. L., & Chapin, J. K. (October, 2002). People with nerve or limb injuries may one day be able to command wheelchairs, prosthetics and even paralyzed arms and legs by "thinking them through" the motions. *Scientific American, 287*, 47–53.

Nicolson, I. R., Fawcett, A. J., & Dean, P. (2001). Developmental dyslexia: The cerebellar deficit hypothesis. *Trends in Neurosciences, 24*, 508–516.

Nieder, A., Freedman, D. J., & Miller, E. K. (2002). Representation of the quantity of visual items in the primate prefrontal cortex. *Science, 297*, 1708–1711.

Nielsen, J. B. (2002). Motoneuronal drive during human walking. *Brain Research Reviews, 40*, 192–201.

Nijhawan, D., Honarpour, N., & Wang, X. (2000). Apoptosis in neural development and disease. *Annual Review of Neuroscience, 23*, 73–89.

Nobre, A. C., & Plunkett, K. (1997). The neural system of language: Structure and development. *Current Opinion in Neurobiology, 7*, 262–268.

Noebels, J. L. (2003). The biology of epilepsy genes. *Annual Review of Neuroscience, 26*, 599–625.

Nopoulis, P. C., Ceilley, J. W., Gailis, E. A., & Andreasen, N. C. (2001). An MRI study of midbrain morphology in patients with schizophrenia: Relationship to psychosis, neuroleptics, and cerebellar neural circuitry. *Biological Psychiatry, 49,* 13–19.

Northcutt, R. G., & Kaas, J. H. (1995). The emergence and evolution of mammalian neocortex. *Trends in Neurosciences, 18*(9), 373–418.

Noselli, S., & Perrimon, N. (2000). Are there close encounters between signaling pathways? *Science, 290,* 68–69.

Nudo, R. J., Jenkins, W. M., & Merzenich, M. M. (1996). Repetitive microstimulation alters the cortical representation of movements in adult rats. *Somatosensory Motor Research, 7,* 463–483.

Nyberg, L., Habib, R., McIntosh, A. R., & Tulving, E. (2000). Reactivation of encoding-related brain activity during memory retrieval. *Proceedings of the National Academy of Sciences, U.S.A., 97,* 11120–11124.

Nykamp, K., Rosenthal, L., Folkerts, M., Roehrs, T., Guido, P., & Roth, T. (1998). The effects of REM sleep deprivation on the level of sleepiness/alertness. *Sleep, 21,* 609–614.

Ohbayashi, M., Ohki, K., & Miyashita, Y. (2003). Conversion of working memory to motor sequence in the monkey premotor cortex. *Science, 301,* 233–236.

Ohtaki, H., Mori, S., Nakamachi, T., Dohi, K., Yin, L., Endo, S., et al. (2003). Evaluation of neuronal cell death after a new global ischemia model in infant mice. *Acta Neurochirurgica Suppl., 86,* 97–100.

Ohyama, T., Nores, W. L., Murphy, M., & Mauk, M. D. (2003). What the cerebellum computes. *Trends in Neurosciences, 26,* 222–227.

Ohzawa, I. (1998). Mechanisms of stereoscopic vision: The disparity energy model. *Current Opinion in Neurobiology, 8,* 509–515.

Ojemann, G. A. (1979). Individual variability in cortical localization of language. *Journal of Neurosurgery, 50,* 164–169.

Ojemann, G. A. (1983). Brain organization for language from the perspective of electrical stimulation mapping. *Behavioral and Brain Sciences, 2,* 189–230.

O'Keefe, J. (1993). Hippocampus, theta, and spatial memory. *Current Opinion in Neurobiology, 3,* 917–924.

O'Keefe, J., & Dostrovsky, T. (1971). The hippocampus as a spatial map: Preliminary evidence from unit activity in the freely moving rat. *Brain Research, 34,* 171–175.

O'Keefe, J., & Nadel, L. (1978). *The hippocampus as a cognitive map.* Oxford, England: Clarendon Press.

O'Keefe, J., & Speakman, A. (1987). Single unit activity in the rat hippocampus during a spatial memory task. *Experimental Brain Research, 68,* 1–27.

Olds, J., & Milner, P. (1954). Positive reinforcement produced by electrical stimulation of septal area and other regions of rat brain. *Journal of Comparative and Physiological Psychology, 47,* 419–427.

O'Leary, C. M. (2004). Fetal alcohol syndrome: Diagnosis, epidemiology, and developmental outcomes. *Journal of Paediatrics and Child Health, 40,* 2–7.

O'Leary, D. D. M., Ruff, N. L., & Dyck, R. H. (1994). Development, critical period plasticity, and adult reorganization of mammalian somatosensory systems. *Current Opinion in Neurobiology, 4,* 535–544.

Olson, C. R. (2003). Brain representations of object-centered space in monkeys and humans. *Annual Review of Neuroscience, 26,* 331–354.

O'Neill, L., Murphy, M., & Gallager, R. B. (1994). What are we? Where did we come from? Where are we going? *Science, 263,* 181–184.

Ormerod, B. K., & Galea, L. A. M. (2001). Mechanism and function of adult neurogenesis. In C. A. Shaw & J. C. McEachern

(Eds.), *Towards a theory of neuroplasticity* (pp. 85–100). Philadelphia: Taylor & Francis.

Overmier, J. B., & Murison, R. (1997). Animal models reveal the "psych" in the psychosomatics of peptic ulcers. *Current Directions in Psychological Science, 6,* 180–184.

Owens, D. F., & Kriegstein, A. R. (2002). Is there more to GABA than synaptic inhibition? *Nature Reviews Neuroscience, 3,* 715–727.

Owren, M. J. (1990). Acoustic classification of alarm calls by vervet monkeys (*Cercopithecus aethiops*) and humans (*Homo sapiens*): II. Synthetic calls. *Journal of Comparative Psychology, 104,* 29–40.

Pääbo, S. (1995). The Y chromosome and the origin of all of us (men). *Science, 268,* 1141–1142.

Pace-Schott, E. F., & Hobson, J. A. (2002). The neurobiology of sleep: Genetics, cellular physiology and subcortical networks. *Nature Reviews Neuroscience, 3,* 591–605.

Packard, M. G., & Knowlton, B. J. (2002). Learning and memory functions of the basal ganglia. *Annual Review of Neuroscience, 25,* 563–593.

Pallas, S. P. (2001). Intrinsic and extrinsic factors that shape neocortical specification. *Trends in Neurosciences, 24,* 417–423.

Palovskaya, M., Ring, H., Groswasser, Z., & Hochstein, S. (2002). Searching with unilateral neglect. *Journal of Cognitive Neuroscience, 14,* 745–756.

Panksepp, J. (2003). Feeling the pain of social loss. *Science, 302,* 237–239.

Papez, J. W. (1937). A proposed mechanism of emotion. *Archives of Neurology and Psychiatry, 38,* 725–743.

Paredes, R. G. (2003). Medial preoptic area/anterior hypothalamus and sexual motivation. *Scandinavian Journal of Psychology, 44,* 203–212.

Parnas, H., Segel, L., Dudel, J., & Parnas, I. (2000). Autoreceptors, membrane potential and the regulation of transmitter release. *Trends in Neurosciences, 23,* 60–68.

Parrott, A. C. (1999). Does cigarette smoking *cause* stress? *American Psychologist, 54,* 817–820.

Parsons, L. M., Fox, P. T., Downs, J. H., Glass, T., Hirsch, T. B., Martin, C. C., et al. (1995). Use of implicit motor imagery for visual shape discrimination as revealed by PET. *Nature, 375,* 54–58.

Patel, S. R., Ayas, N. T., White, D. P., Speizer, F. E., Stampfer, M. J., & Hu, F. B. (2003). A prospective study of sleep duration and mortality risk in women. *Sleep, 26,* A184.

Paterson, S. J., Brown, J. H., Gsödl, M. K., Johnson, M. H., & Karmiloff-Smith, A. (1999). Cognitive modularity and genetic disorders. *Science, 286,* 2355–2358.

Patterson, K., & Ralph, M. A. L. (1999). Selective disorders of reading? *Current Opinion in Neurobiology, 9,* 235–239.

Patterson, K., Vargha-Khadem, F., & Polkey, C. E. (1989). Reading with one hemisphere. *Brain, 112,* 39–63.

Patton, G. C. (1988). The spectrum of eating disorders in adolescence. *Journal of Psychosomatic Research, 32,* 579–584.

Paulesu, E., Démonet, J.-F., Fazio, F., McCrory, E., Chanoine, V., Brunswick, N., et al. (2001). Dyslexia: Cultural diversity and biological unity. *Science, 291,* 2165–2167.

Paulesu, E., McCrory, E., Fazio, F., Menoncello, L., Brunswick, N., Cappa, S. F., et al. (2000). A cultural effect on brain function. *Nature Reiews Neuroscience, 3,* 91–96.

Pauls, D. L. (2001). Update on the genetics of Tourette syndrome. In D. J. Cohen, C. G. Goetz, & J. Jankovic (Eds.) *Tourette syndrome* (pp. 281–293). Philadelphia: Lippincott Williams & Wilkins.

Payne, B. R., & Lomber, S. G. (2001). Reconstructing functional systems after lesions of cerebral cortex. *Nature Reviews Neuroscience, 2,* 911–919.

Pellow, S., Chopin, P., File, S. E., & Briley, M. (1985). Validation of open:closed arm entries in an elevated plus-maze as a measure of anxiety in the rat. *Journal of Neuroscience Methods, 14,* 149–167.

Penfield, W., & Boldrey, E. (1937). Somatic motor and sensory representations in cerebral cortex of man as studied by electrical stimulation. *Brain, 60,* 389–443.

Penfield, W., & Evans, J. (1935). The frontal lobe in man: A clinical study of maximum removals. *Brain, 58,* 115–133.

Penfield, W., & Rasmussen, T. (1950). *The cerebral cortex of man: A clinical study of the localization of function.* New York: Macmillan.

Penfield, W., & Roberts, L. (1959). *Speech and brain mechanisms.* Princeton, NJ: Princeton University Press.

Peralta, V., & Cuesta, M. J. (2000). Clinical models of schizophrenia: A critical approach to competing conceptions. *Psychopathology, 33,* 252–258.

Percival, J. E., Horne, J. A., & Tilley, A. J. (1983). Effects of sleep deprivation on tests of higher cerebral functioning. In *Sleep 1982* (pp. 390–391). Sixth European Congress on Sleep Research, Zurich. Basel, Switzerland: Karger.

Perkel, D. J., & Farries, M. A. (2000). Complementary "bottom-up" and "top-down" approaches to basal ganglia function. *Current Opinion in Neurobiology, 10,* 725–731.

Peterson, A. T., Soberón, J., & Sánchez-Cordero, V. (1999). Conservatism of ecological niches in evolutionary time. *Science, 285,* 1265–1267.

Peterson, B. S. (2001). Neuroimaging studies of Tourette syndrome: A decade of progress. In D. J. Cohen, C. G. Goetz, & J. Jankovic (Eds.), *Tourette syndrome* (pp. 179–196). Philadelphia: Lippincott Williams & Wilkins.

Petrides, M. (1996). Lateral frontal cortical contribution to memory. *Seminars in the Neurosciences, 8,* 57–63.

Petrides, M. (2000). Dissociable roles of mid-dorsolateral prefrontal and anterior inferotemporal cortex in visual working memory. *Journal of Neuroscience, 20,* 7496–7503.

Pfeiffer, C. A. (1936). Sexual differences of the hypophyses and their determination by the gonads. *American Journal of Anatomy, 58,* 195–225.

Phelps, M. E., & Mazziotta, J. (1985). Positron tomography: Human brain function and biochemistry. *Science, 228,* 804.

Phillips, T., & Belknap, J. K. (2002). Complex-trait genetics: Emergence of multivariate strategies. *Nature Reviews Neuroscience, 3,* 478–485.

Phoenix, C. H., Goy, R. W., Gerall, A. A., & Young, W. C. (1959). Organizing action of prenatally administered testosterone proprionate on the tissues mediating mating behavior in the female guinea pig. *Endocrinology, 65,* 369–382.

Picard, N., & Strick, P. L. (2001). Imaging the premotor areas. *Current Opinion in Neurobiology, 11,* 663–672.

Pierce, K., & Courchesne, E. (2001). Evidence for a cerebellar role in reduced exploration and stereotyped behavior in autism. *Biological Psychiatry, 49,* 655–664.

Pietrobon, D., & Striessnig, J. (2003). Neurobiology of migraine. *Nature Reviews Neuroscience, 4,* 386–398.

Pinel, J. P. J. (1969). A short gradient of ECS-produced amnesia in a one-trial appetitive learning situation. *Journal of Comparative and Physiological Psychology, 68,* 650–655.

Pinel, J. P. J., Assanand, S., & Lehman, D. R. (2000). Hunger, eating, and ill health. *American Psychologist, 55,* 1105–1116.

Piomelli, D. (2003). The molecular logic of endocannabinoid signaling. *Nature Reviews Neuroscience, 4,* 873–884.

Pleim, E. T., & Barfield, R. J. (1988). Progesterone versus estrogen facilitation of female sexual behavior by intracranial administration to female rats. *Hormones and Behavior, 22,* 150–159.

Ploegh, H. L. (1998). Viral strategies of immune evasion. *Science, 280,* 248–252.

Plomin, R., & DeFries, J. C. (1998, May). The genetics of cognitive abilities and disabilities. *Scientific American, 278,* 62–69.

Polivy, J., & Herman, P. C. (2002). Causes of eating disorders. *Annual Review of Neuroscience, 53,* 187–213.

Pons, T. P., Garraghty, P. E., Ommaya, A. K., Kaas, J. H., Taub, E., & Mishkin, M. (1991). Massive cortical reorganization after sensory deafferentation in adult macaques. *Science, 252,* 1857–1860.

Pope, H. G., Gruber, A. J., Hudson, J. I., Huestis, M. A., & Yurgelun-Todd, D. (2001). Neuropsychological performance in long-term cannabis users. *Archives of General Psychiatry, 58,* 909–915.

Pope, H. G., Gruber, A. J., & Yurgelun-Todd, D. (1995). The residual neuropsychological effects of cannabis: The current status of research. *Drug and Alcohol Dependence, 38,* 25–34.

Pope, H. G., & Katz, D. L. (1987). Bodybuilder's psychosis. *Lancet, 1*(8537), 863.

Pope, H. G., Jr., Kouri, E. M., & Hudson, J. I. (2000). Effects of supraphysiologic doses of testosterone on mood and aggression in normal men. *Archives of General Psychiatry, 57,* 133–140.

Poppele, R., & Bosco, G. (2003). Sophisticated spinal contributions to motor control. *Trends in Neurosciences, 26,* 269–276.

Porter, R., & Lemon, R. N. (1993). Corticospinal function and voluntary movement. *Monographs of the Physiological Society, No. 45.* Oxford University Press.

Postle, B. R., Corkin, S., & Growdon, J. H. (1996). Intact implicit memory for novel patterns in Alzheimer's disease. *Learning & Memory, 3,* 305–312.

Pouget, A., & Driver, J. (2000). Relating unilateral neglect to the neural coding of space. *Current Opinion in Neurobiology, 10,* 242–249.

Powley, T. L., Opsahl, C. A., Cox, J. E., & Weingarten, H. P. (1980). The role of the hypothalamus in energy homeostasis. In P. J. Morgane & J. Panksepp (Eds.), *Handbook of the hypothalamus, 3A: Behavioral studies of the hypothalamus* (pp. 211–298). New York: Marcel Dekker.

Price, C. J., Howard, D., Patterson, K., Warburton, E. A., Friston, K. J., & Frackowiak, R. S. J. (1998). A functional neuroimaging description of two deep dyslexic patients. *Journal of Cognitive Neuroscience, 10,* 303–315.

Price, C. J., Mummery, C. J., Moore, C. J., Frackowiak, R. S. J., & Friston, K. J. (1999). Delineating necessary and sufficient neural systems with functional imaging studies of neuropsychological patients. *Journal of Cognitive Neuroscience, 11,* 371–382.

Price, D. D. (2000). Psychological and neural mechanisms of the affective dimension of pain. *Science, 288,* 1769–1772.

Price, J., & Williams, B. P. (2001). Neural stem cells. *Current Opinion in Neurobiology, 11,* 564–567.

Price, R. A., & Gottesman, I. I. (1991). Body fat in identical twins reared apart: Roles for genes and environment. *Behavioral Genetics, 21,* 1–7.

Primakoff, P., & Myles, D. G. (2002). Penetration, adhesion, and fusion in mammalian sperm-egg interaction. *Science, 296,* 2183–2185.

Pryce, C. R., & Feldon, J. (2003). Long-term neurobehavioural impact of the postnatal environment in rats: Manipulations, effects, and mediating mechanisms. *Neuroscience and Biobehavioural Reviews, 27,* 57–71.

Putnam, S. K., Sato, S., & Hull, E. M. (2003). Effects of testosterone metabolites on copulation and medial preoptic dopamine release in castrated male rats. *Hormones and Behavior, 44,* 419–426.

Qi, Y., Stapp, D., & Qiu, M. (2002). Origin and molecular specification of oligodendrocytes in the telencephalon. *Trends in Neurosciences, 25,* 223–225.

Quan, N., Avitsur, R., Stark, J. L., He, L., Shah, M., & Caligiuri, M. (2001). Social stress increases the susceptibility to endotoxic shock. *Journal of Neuroimmunology, 115*, 36–45.

Quinsey, V. L. (2003). The etiology of anomalous sexual preferences in men. *Annals of the New York Academy of Sciences, 989*, 105–117.

Raff, M. C., Whitmore, A. V., & Finn, J. T. (2002). Axonal self-destruction and neurodegeneration. *Science, 296*, 868–871.

Rainville, P. (2002). Brain mechanisms of pain affect and pain modulation. *Current Opinion in Neurobiology, 12*, 195–204.

Raisman, G. (1997). An urge to explain the incomprehensible: Geoffrey Harris and the discovery of the neural control of the pituitary gland. *Annual Review of Neuroscience, 20*, 533–566.

Raisman, G., & Field, P. M. (1971). Sexual dimorphism in the neuropil of the preoptic area of the rat and its dependence on neonatal androgens. *Brain Research, 54*, 1–29.

Rajaratnam, S. M., Dijk, D. J., Middleton, B., Stone, B. M., & Arendt, J. (2003). Melatonin phase-shifts human circadian rhythms with no evidence of changes in the duration of endogenous melatonin secretion or the 24-hour production of reproductive hormones. *The Journal of Clinical Endocrinology and Metabolism, 88*, 4303–4309.

Ralph, M. R., Foster, T. G., Davis, F. C., & Menaker, M. (1990). Transplanted suprachiasmatic nucleus determines circadian period. *Science, 247*, 975–978.

Ralph, M. R., & Menaker, M. (1988). A mutation of the circadian system in golden hamsters. *Science, 241*, 1225–1227.

Rämä, P., Sala, J. B., Gillen, J. S., Pekar, J. J., & Courtney, S. M. (2001). Dissociation of the neural systems for working memory maintenance of verbal and nonspatial visual information. *Cognitive, Affective, & Behavioral Neuroscience, 1*, 161–171.

Ramachandran, V. S. (1992, May). Blind spots. *Scientific American, 260*, 86–91.

Ramachandran, V. S., & Blakeslee, S. (1998). *Phantoms in the brain.* New York: William Morrow.

Ramachandran, V. S., & Rogers-Ramachandran, D. (2000). Phantom limbs and neuronal plasticity. *Archives of Neurology, 57*, 317–320.

Ramnani, N., & Passingham, R. E. (2001). Changes in the human brain during rhythm learning. *Journal of Cognitive Neuroscience, 13*, 952–966.

Ramus, F. (2003). Developmental dyslexia: Specific phonological deficit or general sensorimotor dysfunction? *Current Opinion in Neurobiology, 13*, 212–218.

Rao, S. C., Rainer, G., & Miller, E. K. (1997). Integration of what and where in the primate prefrontal cortex. *Science, 276*, 821–824.

Rasmussen, T., & Milner, B. (1975). Clinical and surgical studies of the cerebral speech areas in man. In K. J. Zulch, O. Creutzfeldt, & G. C. Galbraith (Eds.), *Cerebral localization* (pp. 238–257). New York: Springer-Verlag.

Ratliff, F. (1972, June). Contour and contrast. *Scientific American, 226*, 90–101.

Rattenborg, N. C., Amlaner, C. J., & Lima, S. L. (2000). Behavioral, neurophysiological and evolutionary perspectives on unihemispheric sleep. *Neuroscience and Biobehavioural Reviews, 24*, 817–842.

Rauschecker, J. P., Tian, B., & Hauser, M. (1995). Processing of complex sounds in the macaque nonprimary auditory cortex. *Science, 268*, 111–114.

Ravizza, S. M., & Ivry, R. B. (2001). Comparison of the basal ganglia and cerebellum in shifting attention. *Journal of Cognitive Neuroscience, 13*, 285–297.

Ravussin, E., & Danforth, E., Jr. (1999). Beyond sloth—physical activity and weight gain. *Science, 283*, 184–185.

Raynor, H. A., & Epstein, L. H. (2001). Dietary variety, energy regulation, and obesity. *Psychological Bulletin, 127*, 325–341.

Reame, N., Sauder, S. E., Kelch, R. P., & Marshall, J. C. (1984). Pulsatile gonadotropin secretion during the human menstrual cycle: Evidence for altered frequency of gonadotropin releasing hormone secretion. *Journal of Clinical Endocrinology and Metabolism, 59*, 328.

Reber, P. J., Knowlton, B. J., & Squire, L. R. (1996). Dissociable properties of memory system: Differences in the flexibility of declarative and nondeclarative knowledge. *Behavioral Neuroscience, 110*(5), 861–871.

Rechtschaffen, A. (1998). Current perspectives on the function of sleep. *Perspectives in Biology and Medicine, 41*(3), 359–390.

Rechtschaffen, A., & Bergmann, B. M. (1995). Sleep deprivation in the rat by the disk-over-water method. *Behavioural Brain Research, 69*, 55–63.

Rechtschaffen, A., Gilliland, M. A., Bergmann, B. M., & Winter, J. B. (1993). Physiological correlates of prolonged sleep deprivation in rats. *Science, 221*, 182–184.

Rechtschaffen, A., & Kales, A. (1968). *A manual of standardized terminology, techniques and scoring systems for sleep stages of human subjects.* Washington, DC: U.S. Government Printing Office.

Redd, M., & de Castro, J. M. (1992). Social facilitation of eating: Effects of social instruction on food intake. *Physiology & Behavior, 52*, 749–754.

Rees, G., Kreiman, G., & Koch, C. (2002). Neural correlates of consciousness in humans. *Nature Reviews Neuroscience, 3*, 261–270.

Rees, G., Russell, C., Frith, C. D., & Driver, J. (1999). Inattentional blindness versus inattentional amnesia for fixated but ignored words. *Science, 286*, 2504–2507.

Reid, R. C., & Alonso, J.-M. (1996). The processing and encoding of information in the visual cortex. *Current Opinion in Neurobiology, 6*, 475–480.

Reiman, E. M., Lane, R. D., Ahern, G. L., Schwartz, G. E., & Davidson, R. J. (2000). Positron emission tomography in the study of emotion, anxiety, and anxiety disorders. In R. D. Lane & L. Nadel (Eds.), *Cognitive neuroscience of emotion* (pp. 389–406). New York: Oxford University Press.

Reiner, W. (1997). To be male or female—that is the question. *Archives of Pediatrics and Adolescent Medicine, 151*, 224–225.

Remple, M. S., Bruneau, R. M., VandenBerg, P. M., Goertzen, C., & Kleim, J. A. (2001). Sensitivity of cortical movement representations to motor experience: Evidence that skill learning but not strength training induces cortical reorganization. *Behavioural Brain Research, 123*, 133–141.

Rensink, R. A. (2002). Change detection. *Annual Review of Psychology, 53*, 245–277.

Renvall, R., & Hari, R. (2002). Auditory cortical responses to speech-like stimuli in dyslexic adults. *Journal of Cognitive Neuroscience, 14*, 757–768.

Rettig, J., & Neher, E. (2002). Emerging roles of presynaptic proteins in calcium-triggered exocytosis. *Science, 298*, 781–785.

Reuter-Lorenz, P. A., & Miller, A. C. (1998). The cognitive neuroscience of human laterality: Lessons from the bisected brain. *Current Directions in Psychological Science, 7*, 15–20.

Reynolds, D. V. (1969). Surgery in the rat during electrical analgesia induced by focal brain stimulation. *Science, 164*, 444–445.

Rhees, R. W., Lephart, E. D., & Eliason, D. (2001). Effects of maternal separation during early postnatal development on male sexual behavior and female reproductive function. *Behavioural Brain Research, 123*, 1–10.

Rhodes, J. S., Van Praag, H., Jeffrey, S., Girard, I., Mitchell, G. S., Garland, T., Jr., & Gage, F. H. (2002). Exercise increases hippocampal neurogenesis to high levels but does not improve spatial learning in mice bred for increased voluntary wheel running. *Behavioral Neuroscience, 117*, 1006–1016.

Ricaurte, G. A., Yuan, J., Hatzidimitriou, G., Cord, B. J., & McCann, U. D. (2002). Severe dopaminergic neurotoxicity in primates after a common recreational dose regimen of MDMA ("Ecstasy"). *Science, 297*, 2260–2263.

Riccio, D. C., Millin, P. M., & Gisquet-Verrier, P. (2003). Retrograde amnesia: Forgetting back. *Current Directions in Psychological Science, 12*, 41–44.

Richards, W. (1971, May). The fortification illusions of migraines. *Scientific American, 224*, 89–97.

Richter, C. P. (1967). Sleep and activity: Their relation to the 24-hour clock. *Proceedings of the Association for Research on Nervous and Mental Disorders, 45*, 8–27.

Richter, C. P. (1971). Inborn nature of the rat's 24-hour clock. *Journal of Comparative and Physiological Psychology, 75*, 1–14.

Riddle, M. A., & Carlson, J. (2001). Clinical psychopharmacology for Tourette syndrome and associated disorders. In D. J. Cohen, C. G. Goetz, & J. Jancovic (Eds), *Tourette syndrome*. Philadelphia: Lippincott Williams & Wilkins.

Ridley, A. J., Schwartz, M. A., Burridge, K., Firtel, R. A., Ginsberg, M. H., Borisy, G., et al. (2003). Cell migration: Integrating signals from front to back. *Science, 302*, 1704–1711.

Rijntjes, M., Dettmers, C., Büchel, C., Kiebel, S., Frackowiak, R. S. J., & Weiller, C. (1999). A blueprint for movement: Functional and anatomical representations in the human motor system. *Journal of Neuroscience, 19*, 8043–8048.

Ritter, R. C. (2004). Gastrointestinal mechanisms of satiation for food. *Physiology & Behavior, 81*, 249–273.

Rizzolatti, G., Fogassi, L., & Gallese, V. (2002). Motor and cognitive functions of the ventral premotor cortex. *Current Opinion in Neurobiology, 12*, 149–154.

Robinson, T. E. (1991). Persistent sensitizing effects of drugs on brain dopamine systems and behavior: Implications for addiction and relapse. In J. Barchas & S. Korenman (Eds.), *The biological basis of substance abuse and its therapy*. New York: Oxford University Press.

Robinson, T. E. (2004). Addicted rats. *Science, 305*, 951–953.

Robinson, T. E., & Berridge, K. C. (1993). The neural basis of drug craving: An incentive-sensitization theory of addiction. *Brain Research Reviews, 18*, 247–291.

Rockstroh, B., Clementz, B. A., Pantev, C., Blumenfeld, L. D., Sterr, A., & Elbert, T. (1998). Failure of dominant left-hemispheric activation to right-ear stimulation in schizophrenia. *Neuroreport, 9*, 3819–3822.

Rockstroh, B., Kissler, J., Mohr, B., Eulitz, C., Lommen, U., Wienbruch, C., et al. (2001). Altered hemispheric asymmetry of auditory magnetic fields to tones and syllables in schizophrenia. *Biological Psychiatry, 49*, 694–703.

Rodgers, R. J., Halford, J. C. G., Nunes de Souza, R. L., Canto de Souza, A. L., Piper, D. C., Arch, J. R. S., et al. (2001). SB-334867, a selective orexin-1 receptor antagonist, enhances behavioural satiety and blocks the hyperphagic effect of orexin-A in rats. *European Journal of Neuroscience, 13*, 1444–1452.

Rodier, P. M. (2000, February). The early origins of autism. *Scientific American, 284*, 56–63.

Rodin, J. (1985). Insulin levels, hunger, and food intake: An example of feedback loops in body weight regulation. *Health Psychology, 4*, 1–24.

Rodríguez-Manzo, G., Pellicer, F., Larsson, K., & Fernández-Guasti, A. (2000). Stimulation of the medial preoptic area facilitates sexual behavior but does not reverse sexual satiation. *Behavioral Neuroscience, 114*, 553–560.

Roe, A. W., Pallas, S. L., Hahm, J.-O., & Sur, M. (1990). A map of visual space induced in primary auditory cortex. *Science, 250*, 818–820.

Rogers, P. J., & Blundell, J. E. (1980). Investigation of food selection and meal parameters during the development of dietary induced obesity. *Appetite, 1*, 85–88.

Rogers, R. D., & Robbins, T. W. (2001). Investigating the neurocognitive deficits associated with chronic drug misuse. *Current Opinion in Neurobiology, 11*, 250–257.

Rolls, B. J. (1986). Sensory-specific satiety. *Nutrition Reviews, 44*, 93–101.

Rolls, B. J. (1990). The role of sensory-specific satiety in food intake and food selection. In E. D. Capaldi & T. L. Powley (Eds.), *Taste, experience, and feeding* (pp. 28–42). Washington, DC: American Psychological Association.

Rolls, B. J., Rolls, E. T., Rowe, E. A., & Sweeney, K. (1981). Sensory specific satiety in man. *Physiology & Behavior, 27*, 137–142.

Rolls, E. T. (1981). Central nervous mechanisms related to feeding and appetite. *British Medical Bulletin, 37*, 131–134.

Rolls, E. T., Robertson, R. G., & Georges-François, P. (1995). The representation of space in the primate hippocampus. *Society for Neuroscience Abstracts, 21*, 1492.

Romanski, L. M., & LeDoux, J. E. (1992). Equipotentiality of thalamo-cortico-amygdala projections as auditory conditioned stimulus pathways. *Journal of Neuroscience, 12*, 4501–4509.

Rosa, M. G. P., Tweedale, R., & Elston, G. N. (2000). Visual responses of neurons in the middle temporal area of New World monkeys after lesions of striate cortex. *Journal of Neuroscience, 20*, 5552–5563.

Rosenthal, D., Wender, P. H., Kety, S. S., Welner, J., & Schulsinger, F. (1980). The adopted-away offspring of schizophrenics. *American Journal of Psychiatry, 128*, 87–91.

Roser, M., & Gazzaniga, M. S. (2004). Automatic brains—interpretive minds. *Current Directions in Psychological Science, 13*, 56–59.

Rossignol, S. (2000). Locomotion and its recovery after spinal injury. *Current Opinion in Neurobiology, 10*, 708–716.

Rossion, B., Schiltz, C., Robaye, L., Pirenne, D., & Crommelinck, M. (2001). How does the brain discriminate familiar and unfamiliar faces? A PET study of face categorical perception. *Journal of Cognitive Neuroscience, 13*, 1019–1034.

Rothwell, J. C., Traub, M. M., Day, B. L., Obeso, J. A., Thomas, P. K., & Marsden, C. D. (1982). Manual motor performance in a deafferented man. *Brain, 105*, 515–542.

Rothwell, N. J., & Stock, M. J. (1982). Energy expenditure derived from measurements of oxygen consumption and energy balance in hyperphagic, "cafeteria"-fed rats. *Journal of Physiology, 324*, 59–60.

Rourke, B. P., Ahmad, S. A., Collins, D. W., Hayman-Abello, B. A., Hayman-Abello, S. E., & Warriner, E. M. (2002). Child clinical/pediatric neuropsychology: Some recent advances. *Annual Review of Psychology, 53*, 309–339.

Rowe, J. B., Toni, I., Josephs, O., Frackowiak, R. S., & Pasingham, R. E. (2000). The prefrontal cortex: Response selection or maintenance within working memory? *Science, 288*, 1656–1660.

Rowland, N. (1981). Glucoregulatory feeding in cats. *Physiology & Behavior, 26*, 901–903.

Rowland, N. E. (1990). Sodium appetite. In E. D. Capaldi & T. L. Powley (Eds.), *Taste, experience, and feeding* (pp. 94–104). Washington, DC: American Psychological Association.

Rozin, P., Dow, S., Moscovitch, M., & Rajaram, S. (1998). What causes humans to begin and end a meal? A role for memory for what has been eaten, as evidenced by a study of multiple meal eating in amnesic patients. *Psychological Science, 9*, 392–396.

Rozin, P. N., & Schulkin, J. (1990). Food selection. In E. M. Stricker (Ed.), *Handbook of behavioral neurobiology* (pp. 297–328). New York: Plenum Press.

Rudy, J. W., & Sutherland, R. J. (1992). Configural and elemental associations and the memory coherence problem. *Journal of Cognitive Neuroscience, 4*, 208–216.

Rushworth, M. F., Johansen-Berg, H., Gobel, S. M., & Devlin, J. T. (2003). The left parietal and premotor cortices: Motor attention and selection. *Neuroimage, 20*, 89–100.

Rushworth, M. F. S. (2000). Anatomical and functional subdivision within the primate lateral prefrontal cortex. *Psychobiology, 28*, 187–196.

Russell, W. R., & Espir, M. I. E. (1961). *Traumatic aphasia—a study of aphasia in war wounds of the brain.* London: Oxford University Press.

Rutter, M., & Silberg, J. (2002). Gene-environment interplay in relation to emotional and behavioral disturbance. *Annual Review of Psychology, 53*, 463–490.

Rutter, M. L. (1997). Nature-nurture integration: The example of antisocial behavior. *American Psychologist, 52*, 390–398.

Rymer, R. (1993). *Genie.* New York: HarperCollins.

Sack, R. L., & Lewy, A. J. (2001). Circadian rhythm sleep disorders: Lessons from the blind. *Sleep Medicine Reviews, 5*, 189–206.

Sacks, O. (1985). *The man who mistook his wife for a hat and other clinical tales.* New York: Summit Books.

Saffran, E. M. (1997). Aphasia: Cognitive neuropsychological aspects. In T. E. Feinberg & M. J. Farah (Eds.), *Behavioral neurology and neuropsychology* (pp. 151–166). New York: McGraw-Hill.

Sakuma, Y., & Pfaff, D. W. (1979). Mesencephalic mechanisms for the integration of female reproductive behavior in the rat. *American Journal of Physiology, 237*, 285–290.

Salamone, J. D. (2000). A critique of recent studies on placebo effects of antidepressants: Importance of research on active placebos. *Psychopharmacology, 152*, 1–6.

Salovey, P., Rothman, A. J., Detweiler, J. B., & Steward, W. T. (2000). Emotional states and physical health. *American Psychologist, 55*, 110–121.

Salzer, J. L. (2002). Nodes of Ranvier come of age. *Trends in Neurosciences, 25*(1), 2–5.

Sanders, D., & Bancroft, J. (1982). Hormones and the sexuality of women—the menstrual cycle. *Clinics in Endocrinology and Metabolism, 11*, 639–659.

Sanes, J. N. (2003). Neocortical mechanisms in motor learning. *Current Opinion in Neurobiology, 13*, 225–231.

Sanes, J. N., & Donoghue, J. P. (2000). Plasticity and primary motor cortex. *Annual Review of Neuroscience*, 393–415.

Sanes, J. N., Donoghue, J. P., Thangaraj, V., Edelman, R. R., & Warach, S. (1995). Shared neural substrates controlling hand movements in human motor cortex. *Science, 268*, 1775–1777.

Sanes, J. N., Suner, S., & Donoghue, J. P. (1990). Dynamic organization of primary motor cortex output to target muscles in adult rats. I. Long-term patterns of reorganization following motor or mixed peripheral nerve lesions. *Experimental Brain Research, 79*, 479–491.

Saper, C. B., Chou, T. C., & Scammell, T. E. (2001). The sleep switch: Hypothalamic control of sleep and wakefulness. *Trends in Neurosciences, 24*, 726–731.

Sapolsky, R. M. (1997). The importance of a well-groomed child. *Science, 277*, 1620–1622.

Savic, I. (2002). Imaging of brain activation by odorants in humans. *Current Opinion in Neurobiology, 12*, 455–461.

Savill, J., Gregory, C., & Haslett, C. (2003). Eat me or die. *Science, 302*, 1516–1517.

Sawa, A., & Snyder, S. H. (2002). Schizophrenia: Diverse approaches to a complex disease. *Science, 296*, 692–695.

Sawada, H., & Shimohama, S. (2000). Neuroprotective effects of estradiol in mesencephalic dopaminergic neurons. *Neuroscience and Biobehavioural Reviews, 24*, 143–147.

Sawle, G. V., & Myers, R. (1993). The role of positron emission tomography in the assessment of human neurotransplantation. *Trends in Neurosciences, 16*, 172–176.

Sbragia, G. (1992). Leonardo da Vinci and ultrashort sleep: Personal experience of an eclectic artist. In C. Stampi (Ed.), *Why we nap: Evolution, chronobiology, and functions of polyphasic and ultrashort sleep.* Boston: Birkhaüser.

Schally, A. V., Kastin, A. J., & Arimura, A. (1971). Hypothalamic follicle-stimulating hormone (FSH) and luteinizing hormone (LH)–regulating hormone: Structure, physiology, and clinical studies. *Fertility and Sterility, 22*, 703–721.

Schärli, H., Harman, A. M., & Hogben, J. H. (1999a). Blindsight in subjects with homonymous visual field defects. *Journal of Cognitive Neuroscience, 11*, 52–66.

Schärli, H., Harman, A. M., & Hogben, J. H. (1999b). Residual vision in a subject with damaged visual cortex. *Journal of Cognitive Neuroscience, 11*, 502–510.

Scheiffele, P. (2003). Cell–cell signaling during synapse formation in the CNS. *Annual Review of Neuroscience, 26*, 485–508.

Schelling, T. C. (1992). Addictive drugs: The cigarette experience. *Science, 255*, 430–433.

Schenck, C. H., Bundlie, S. R., Ettinger, M. G., & Mahowald, M. W. (1986). Chronic behavioral disorders of human REM sleep: A new category of parasomnia. *Sleep, 9*, 293–308.

Schieber, M. H. (1999). Somatotopic gradients in the distributed organization of the human primary motor cortex hand area: Evidence from small infarcts. *Experimental Brain Research, 128*, 139–148.

Schieber, M. H., & Hibbard, L. S. (1993). How somatotopic is the motor cortex hand area? *Science, 261*, 489–492.

Schieber, M. H., & Poliakov, A. V. (1998). Partial inactivation of the primary motor cortex hand area: Effects on individuated finger movements. *Journal of Neuroscience, 18*, 9038–9054.

Schiffman, S. S., & Erickson, R. P. (1980). The issue of primary tastes versus a taste continuum. *Neuroscience and Biobehavioural Reviews, 4*, 109–117.

Schlaug, G., Jäncke, L., Huang, Y., & Steinmetz, H. (1995). *In vivo* evidence of structural brain asymmetry in musicians. *Science, 267*, 699–701.

Schreiner, C. E. (1992). Functional organization of the auditory cortex: Maps and mechanisms. *Current Opinion in Neurobiology, 2*, 516–521.

Schreiner, C. E., Read, H. L., & Sutter, M. L. (2000). Modular organization of frequency integration in primary auditory cortex. *Annual Review of Neuroscience, 23*, 501–529.

Schultz, W. (1997). Dopamine neurons and their role in reward mechanisms. *Current Opinion in Neurobiology, 7*, 191–197.

Schultz, W., Tremblay, L., & Hollerman, J. R. (2003). Changes in behavior-related neuronal activity in the striatum during learning. *Trends in Neurosciences, 26*, 321–328.

Schwartz, G. J., & Azzara, A. V. (2004). Sensory neurobiological analysis of neuropeptide modulation of meal size. *Physiology & Behavior, 82*, 81–87.

Schwartz, M. W., Peskind, E., Raskind, M., Nicolson, M., Moore, J., Morawiecki, A., et al. (1996a). Cerebrospinal fluid leptin levels: Relationship to plasma levels and to adiposity in humans. *Nature Medicine, 2*, 589–593.

Schwartz, M. W., Seeley, R. J., Campfield, L. A., Burn, P., & Baskin, D. G. (1996b). Identification of hypothalamic targets of leptin action. *Journal of Clinical Investigation, 98*, 1101–1106.

Sclafani, A. (1990). Nutritionally based learned flavor preferences in rats. In E. D. Capaldi & T. L. Powley (Eds.), *Taste, experience, and feeding* (pp. 139–156). Washington, DC: American Psychological Association.

Scoville, W. B., & Milner, B. (1957). Loss of recent memory after bilateral hippocampal lesions. *Journal of Neurology, Neurosurgery and Psychiatry, 20*, 11–21.

Seaberg, R. M., & van der Kooy, D. (2003). Stem and progenitor cells: The premature desertion of rigorous definitions. *Trends in Neurosciences, 26*, 125–131.

Searle, J. R. (2000). Consciousness. *Annual Review of Neuroscience, 23*, 557–578.

Seeley, R. J., & Schwartz, M. W. (1997). The regulation of energy balance: Peripheral hormonal signals and hypothalamic neuropeptides. *Current Directions in Psychological Science, 6*, 39–44.

Segerstrom, S. C., & Miller, G. E. (2004). Psychological stress and the human immune system: A meta-analytic study of 30 years of inquiry. *Psychological Bulletin, 130*, 601–630.

Seitz, R. J., Roland, P. E., Bohm, C., Greitz, T., & Stone-Elanders, S. (1990). Motor learning in man: A positron emission tomographic study. *NeuroReport, 1*, 17–20.

Selkoe, D. J. (1991, November). Amyloid protein and Alzheimer's. *Scientific American, 265*, 68–78.

Selkoe, D. J. (2002). Alzheimer's disease is a synaptic failure. *Science, 298*, 789–791.

Semple, M. N., & Scott, B. H. (2003). Cortical mechanisms in hearing. *Current Opinion in Neurobiology, 13*, 167–173.

Serfaty, M., Kennell-Webb, S., Warner, J., Blizard, R., & Raven, P. (2002). Double blind randomized placebo controlled trial of low dose melatonin for sleep disorders in dementia. *International Journal of Geriatric Psychiatry, 17*, 1120–1127.

Serizawa, S., Miyamichi, K., Nakatani, H., Suzuki, M., Saito, M., Yoshihara, Y., & Sakano, H. (2003). Negative feedback regulation ensures the one receptor—one olfactory neuron rule in mouse. *Science, 302*, 2088–2094.

Servos, P., Engel, S. A., Gati, J., & Menon, R. (1999). fMRI evidence for an inverted face representation in human somatosensory cortex. *Neuroreport, 10*(7), 1393–1395.

Sewards, T. V., & Sewards, M. A. (2001). Cortical association areas in the gustatory system. *Neuroscience and Biobehavioural Reviews, 25*, 395–407.

Shapely, R., & Hawken, M. (2002). Neural mechanisms for color perception in the primary visual cortex. *Current Opinion in Neurobiology, 12*, 426–432.

Shapiro, B. H., Levine, D. C., & Adler, N. T. (1980). The testicular feminized rat: A naturally occurring model of androgen independent brain masculinization. *Science, 209*, 418–420.

Shapleske, J., Rossell, S. L., Simmons, A., David, A. S., & Woodruff, P. W. R. (2001). Are auditory hallucinations the consequence of abnormal cerebral lateralization? A morphometric MRI study of the sylvian fissure and planum temporale. *Biological Psychiatry, 49*, 685–693.

Shaw, P. J., Cirelli, C., Greenspan, R. J., & Tononi, G. (2000). Correlates of sleep and waking in *Drosophila melanogaster. Science, 287*, 1834–1837.

Shaywitz, S. E. (1996, November). Dyslexia. *Scientific American, 275*, 98–104.

Sheng, M., & Kim, M. J. (2002). Postsynaptic signaling and plasticity mechanisms. *Science, 298*, 776–780.

Shepherd, G. M., & Erulkar, S. D. (1997). Centenary of the synapse: From Sherrington to the molecular biology of the synapse and beyond. *Trends in Neurosciences, 20*, 385–392.

Sheppard, D. M., Bradshaw, J. L., Purcell, R., & Pantelis, C. (1999). Tourette's and comorbid syndromes: Obsessive compulsive and attention deficit hyperactivity disorder. A common etiology? *Clinical Psychology Review, 19*, 531–552.

Sherry, D. F., & Vaccarino, A. L. (1989). Hippocampus and memory for food caches in black-capped chickadees. *Behavioral Neuroscience, 103*, 308–318.

Sherwin, B. B. (1985). Changes in sexual behavior as a function of plasma sex steroid levels in post-menopausal women. *Maturitas, 7*, 225–233.

Sherwin, B. B. (1988). A comparative analysis of the role of androgen in human male and female sexual behavior: Behavioral specificity, critical thresholds, and sensitivity. *Psychobiology, 16*, 416–425.

Sherwin, B. B., Gelfand, M. M., & Brender, W. (1985). Androgen enhances sexual motivation in females: A prospective cross-over study of sex steroid administration in the surgical menopause. *Psychosomatic Medicine, 47*, 339–351.

Shimura, T., & Shimokochi, M. (1990). Involvement of the lateral mesencephalic tegmentum in copulatory behavior of male rats: Neuron activity in freely moving animals. *Neuroscience Research, 9*, 173–183.

Shin, J. C., & Ivry, R. B. (2003). Spatial and temporal sequence learning in patients with Parkinson's disease or cerebellar lesions. *Journal of Cognitive Neuroscience, 15*, 1232–1243.

Siegel, J. M. (1983). A behavioral approach to the analysis of reticular formation unit activity. In T. E. Robinson (Ed.), *Behavioral approaches to brain research* (pp. 94–116). New York: Oxford University Press.

Siegel, J. M. (2000, January). Narcolepsy. *Scientific American, 282*, 77–81.

Siegel, J. M. (2001). The REM sleep-memory consolidation hypothesis. *Science, 294*, 1058–1063.

Siegel, S. (2004). Intra-administration associations and withdrawal symptoms: Morphine-elicited morphine withdrawal. *Experimental and Clinical Psychopharmacology, 10*, 162–183.

Silberberg, G., Gupta, A., & Markram, H. (2002). Stereotypy in neocortical microcircuits. *Trends in Neurosciences, 25*(5), 227–230.

Silk, J. B., Alberts, S. C., & Altmann, J. (2003). Social bonds of female baboons enhance infant survival. *Science, 302*, 1231–1233.

Simerly, R. B. (2002). Wired for reproduction: Organization and development of sexually dimorphic circuits in the mammalian forebrain. *Annual Review of Neuroscience, 25*, 507–536.

Sinclair, S. V., & Mistlberger, R. E. (1997). Scheduled activity reorganizes circadian phase of Syrian hamsters under full and skeleton photoperiods. *Behavioural Brain Research, 87*, 127–137.

Singer, J. (1968). Hypothalamic control of male and female sexual behavior. *Journal of Comparative and Physiological Psychology, 66*, 738–742.

Singer, L. T., Arendt, R., Minnes, S., Farkas, K., Salvator, A., Kirchner, K. L., & Kliegman, R. (2002). Cognitive and motor outcomes of cocaine-exposed infants. *Journal of the American Medical Association, 287*, 1952–1960.

Sirigu, A., & Duhamel, J. R. (2001). Motor and visual imagery as two complementary but neurally dissociable mental processes. *Journal of Cognitive Neuroscience, 13*, 910–919.

Sladek, J. R., Jr., Redmond, D. E., Jr., Collier, T. J., Haber, S. N., Elsworth, J. D., Deutch, A. Y., & Roth, R. H. (1987). Transplantation of fetal dopamine neurons in primate brain reverses MPTP induced Parkinsonism. In F. J. Seil, E. Herbert, & B. M. Carlson (Eds.), *Progress in brain research* (Vol. 71, pp. 309–323). New York: Elsevier.

Slezak, M., & Pfrieger, F. W. (2003). New roles for astrocytes: Regulation of CNS synaptogenesis. *Trends in Neurosciences, 26*, 531–535.

Sluder, G., & McCollum, D. (2000). The mad ways of meiosis. *Science, 289*, 254–255.

Smith, D. V., & Margolskee, R. F. (March, 2001). Making sense of taste. *Scientific American, 284,* 32–39.

Smith, E. E. (2000). Neural bases of human working memory. *Current Directions in Psychological Science, 9,* 45–49.

Snyder, S. H. (1978). Neuroleptic drugs and neurotransmitter receptors. *Journal of Clinical and Experimental Psychiatry, 133,* 21–31.

Sofroniew, M. V., Howe, C. L., & Mobley, W. C. (2001). Nerve growth factor signaling, neuroprotection, and neural repair. *Annual Review of Neuroscience, 24,* 1217–1281.

Soloman, S. M., & Kirby, D. F. (1990). The refeeding syndrome: A review. *Journal of Parenteral and Enteral Nutrition, 14,* 90–97.

Spanagel, R., & Weiss, F. (1999). The dopamine hypothesis of reward: Past and current status. *Trends in Neurosciences, 22,* 521–527.

Spear, L. P. (2000). Neurobehavioral changes in adolescence. *Current Directions in Psychological Science, 9,* 111–114.

Spencer, R. M. C., Zelaznik, H. N., Diedrichsen, J., & Ivry, R. B. (2003). Disrupted timing of discontinuous but not continuous movements by cerebellar lesions. *Science, 300,* 1437–1440.

Sperry, R. W. (1963). Chemoaffinity in the orderly growth of nerve fiber patterns and connections. *Proceedings of the National Academy of Sciences, U.S.A., 50,* 703–710.

Sperry, R. W. (1964, January). The great cerebral commissure. *Scientific American, 210,* 42–52.

Sperry, R. W., Zaidel, E., & Zaidel, D. (1979). Self recognition and social awareness in the deconnected minor hemisphere. *Neuropsychologia, 17,* 153–166.

Spielman, A. J., Saskin, P., & Thorpy, M. J. (1987). Treatment of chronic insomnia by restriction of time in bed. *Sleep, 10,* 45–56.

Spillman, L., & Werner, J. S. (1996). Long-range interactions in visual perception. *Trends in Neurosciences, 19,* 428–434.

Spitzer, R. L., Skodol, A. E., Gibbon, M., & Williams, J. B. W. (1983). *Psychopathology: A case book.* New York: McGraw-Hill.

Squire, L. R. (1987). *Memory and brain.* New York: Oxford University Press.

Squire, L. R., Amaral, D. G., Zola-Morgan, S., Kritchevsky, M., & Press, G. (1989). Description of brain injury in the amnesic patient N.A. based on magnetic resonance imaging. *Experimental Neurology, 105,* 23–35.

Squire, L. R., Clark, R. E., & Knowlton, B. J. (2001). Retrograde amnesia. *Hippocampus, 11,* 50–55.

Squire, L. R., Slater, P. C., & Chace, P. M. (1975). Retrograde amnesia: Temporal gradient in very long term memory following electroconvulsive therapy. *Science, 187,* 77–79.

Squire, L. R., & Spanis, C. W. (1984). Long gradient of retrograde amnesia in mice: Continuity with the findings in humans. *Behavioral Neuroscience, 98,* 345–348.

Squire, L. R., & Zola-Morgan, S. (1985). The neuropsychology of memory: New links between humans and experimental animals. *Annals of the New York Academy of Sciences, 444,* 137–149.

Squire, L. R., & Zola-Morgan, S. (1991). The medial temporal lobe memory system. *Science, 253,* 1380–1386.

St. George-Hyslop, P. H. (2000, December). Piecing together Alzheimer's. *Scientific American, 283,* 76–83.

Stampi, C. (1992a). Evolution, chronobiology, and functions of polyphasic and ultrashort sleep: Main issues. In C. Stampi (Ed.), *Why we nap: Evolution, chronobiology, and functions of polyphasic and ultrashort sleep.* Boston: Birkhaüser.

Stampi, C. (Ed.). (1992b). *Why we nap: Evolution, chronobiology, and functions of polyphasic and ultrashort sleep.* Boston: Birkhaüser.

Stanford, S. C., & Salmon, P. (1993). *Stress: From synapse to syndrome.* London: Academic Press.

Stefano, G. B., Goumon, Y., Casares, F., Cadet, P., Fricchione, G. L., Rialas, C., et al. (2000). Endogenous morphine. *Trends in Neurosciences, 23,* 436–442.

Stein, D. G. (2001). Brain damage, sex hormones and recovery: A new role for progesterone and estrogen? *Trends in Neurosciences, 24,* 386–391.

Steinman, L., Martin, R., Bernard, C., Conlon, P., & Oksenberg, J. R. (2002). Multiple sclerosis: Deeper understanding of its pathogenesis reveals new targets for therapy. *Annual Review of Neuroscience, 25,* 491–505.

Stepanski, E., Lamphere, J., Badia, P., Zorick, F., & Roth, T. (1984). Sleep fragmentation and daytime sleepiness. *Sleep, 7,* 18–26.

Stepanski, E., Lamphere, J., Roehrs, T., Zorick, F., & Roth, T. (1987). Experimental sleep fragmentation in normal subjects. *International Journal of Neuroscience, 33,* 207–214.

Stone, T. W. (1996). *CNS neurotransmitters and neuromodulators. Neuroactive steroids.* Boca Raton, FL: CRC Press.

Strickland, D., & Bertoni, J. M. (2004). Parkinson's prevalence estimated by a state registry. *Movement Disorders, 19,* 318–323.

Strömland, K., Nordin, V., Miller, M., Åkerström, B., & Gillberg, C. (1994). Autism in thalidomide embryopathy: A population study. *Developmental Medicine and Child Neurology, 36,* 351–356.

Strubbe, J. H., & Steffens, A. B. (1977). Blood glucose levels in portal and peripheral circulation and their relation to food intake in the rat. *Physiology & Behavior, 19,* 303–307.

Strubbe, J. H., & Van Dijk, G. (2002). The temporal organization of ingestive behaviour and its interaction with regulation of energy balance. *Neuroscience and Biobehavioural Reviews, 26,* 485–498.

Sucliffe, J. G., & De Lecea, L. (2002). The hypocretins: Setting the arousal threshold. *Nature Reviews Neuroscience, 3,* 339–349.

Sullivan, E. V., & Marsh, L. (2003). Hippocampal volume deficits in alcoholic Korsakoff's syndrome. *Neurology, 61,* 1716–1719.

Sunday, S. R., & Halmi, K. A. (1990). Taste perceptions and hedonicas in eating disorders. *Physiology & Behavior, 48,* 587–594.

Suzuki, W. A., & Clayton, N. S. (2000). The hippocampus and memory: A comparative and ethological perspective. *Current Opinion in Neurobiology, 10,* 768–773.

Swaab, D. F., & Fliers, E. (1985). A sexually dimorphic nucleus in the human brain. *Science, 188,* 1112–1115.

Swaab, D. F., & Hofman, M. A. (1995). Sexual differentiation of the human hypothalamus in relation to gender and sexual orientation. *Trends in Neurosciences, 18,* 264–270.

Swaab, D. F., Zhou, J. N., Ehlhart, T., & Hofman, M. A. (1994). Development of vasoactive intestinal polypeptide neurons in the human suprachiasmatic nucleus in relation to birth and sex. *Developmental Brain Research, 79,* 249–259.

Swanson, L. W. (2000). What is the brain? *Trends in Neurosciences, 23,* 519–527.

Swanson, L. W., & Petrovich, G. D. (1998). What is the amygdala? *Trends in Neurosciences, 21,* 323–331.

Sweeney, M. E., Hill, P. A., Baney, R., & DiGirolamo, M. (1993). Severe vs. moderate energy restriction with and without exercise in the treatment of obesity: Efficiency of weight loss. *American Journal of Clinical Nutrition, 57,* 127–134.

Swerdlow, N. R., & Young, A. B. (2001). Neuropathology in Tourette syndrome: An update. In D. J. Cohen, C. G. Goetz, & J. Jankovic (Eds.), *Tourette syndrome* (pp. 151–161). Philadelphia: Lippincott Williams & Wilkins.

Swinnen, S. P. (2002). Intermanual coordination: From behavioral principles to neural-network interactions. *Nature Reviews Neuroscience, 3,* 350–361.

Szameitat, A. J., Schubert, T., Muller, K., & Von Cramon, D. Y. (2002). Localization of executive functions in dual-task performance with fMRI. *Journal of Cognitive Neuroscience, 14,* 1184–1199.

Taheri, S., Zeitzer, J. M., & Mignot, E. (2002). The role of hypocretins (orexins) in sleep regulation and narcolepsy. *Annual Review of Neuroscience, 25*, 283–313.

Takahashi, J. S. (1999). Narcolepsy genes wake up the sleep field. *Science, 285*, 2076–2077.

Takemura, N. U. (2005). Evidence for neurogenesis within the white matter beneath the temporal neocortex of the adult rat brain. *Neuroscience, 134*, 121–131.

Tallman, J. F. (2000). Development of novel antipsychotic drugs. *Brain Research Interactive, 31*, 385–390.

Tamakoshi, A., & Ohno, Y. (2004). Self-reported sleep duration as a predictor of all-cause mortality: Results from the JACC study, Japan. *Sleep, 27*, 51–54.

Tanji, J., & Hoshi, E. (2001). Behavioral planning in the prefrontal cortex. *Current Opinion in Neurobiology, 11*, 164–170.

Tank, D. W., Sugimori, M., Connor, J. A., & Llinás, R. R. (1988). Spatially resolved calcium dynamics of mammalian Purkinje cells in cerebellar slice. *Science, 242*, 773–777.

Tattersall, I., & Matternes, J. H. (2000, January). Once we were not alone. *Scientific American, 282*, 56–62.

Taub, E., Uswatte, G., & Elbert, T. (2002). New treatments in neurorehabilitation founded on basic research. *Nature Reviews Neuroscience, 3*, 228–236.

Taub, J. M., & Berger, R. J. (1973). Performance and mood following variations in the length and timing of sleep. *Psychophysiology, 10*, 559–570.

Taylor, D. M., Tillery, S. I. H., & Schwartz, A. B. (2002). Direct cortical control of 3D neuroprosthetic devices. *Science, 296*, 1829–1832.

Taylor, J. R., Elsworth, J. D., Roth, J. R., Sladek, J. R., Jr., & Redmond, D. E., Jr. (1990). Cognitive and motor deficits in the acquisition of an object retrieval/detour task in MPTP-treated monkeys. *Brain, 113*, 617–637.

Teicher, M. H. (2002, March). Scars that won't heal: The neurobiology of child abuse. *Scientific American, 286*, 68–75.

Teicher, M. H., Andersen, S. L., Polcari, A., Anderson, C. M., Navalta, C. P., & Kim, D. M. (2003). The neuro-biological consequences of early stress and childhood maltreatment. *Neuroscience and Biobehavioural Reviews, 27*, 33–44.

Teitelbaum, P. (1961). Disturbances in feeding and drinking behavior after hypothalamic lesions. In M. R. Jones (Ed.), *Nebraska Symposium on Motivation* (pp. 39–69). Lincoln: University of Nebraska Press.

Teitelbaum, P., & Epstein, A. N. (1962). The lateral hypothalamic syndrome: Recovery of feeding and drinking after lateral hypothalamic lesions. *Psychological Review, 69*, 74–90.

Tetrud, J. W., & Langston, J. W. (1989). The effect of deprenyl (Selegiline) on the natural history of Parkinson's disease. *Science, 245*, 519–522.

Teuber, H.-L. (1975). Recovery of function after brain injury in man. In *Outcomes of severe damage to the nervous system. Ciba Foundation Symposium 34*. Amsterdam: Elsevier North-Holland.

Teuber, H.-L., Battersby, W. S., & Bender, M. B. (1960). Recovery of function after brain injury in man. In *Outcome of severe damage to the nervous system. Ciba Foundation Symposium 34*. Amsterdam: Elsevier North-Holland.

Teuber, H.-L., Milner, B., & Vaughan, H. G., Jr. (1968). Persistent anterograde amnesia after stab wound of the basal brain. *Neuropsychologia, 6*, 267–282.

Thach, W. T., & Bastian, A. J. (2004). Role of the cerebellum in the control and adaptation of gait in health and disease. *Progress in Brain Research, 143*, 353–366.

Thompson, P. M., Vidal, C., Giedd, J. N., Gochman, P., Blumenthal, J., Nicolson, R., Toga, A. W., & Rapoport, J. L. (2001). Mapping adolescent brain change reveals dynamic wave of accelerated gray matter loss in very early-onset schizophrenia.

Proceedings of the National Academy of Sciences (USA), 98, 11650–11655.

Thomson, A. D. (2000). Mechanisms of vitamin deficiency in chronic alcohol misusers and the development of the Wernicke-Korsakoff syndrome. *Alcoholism and Alcoholism Supplement, 35*, 2–7.

Tinklenberg, J. R. (1974). Marijuana and human aggression. In L. L. Miller (Ed.), *Marijuana, effects on human behavior* (pp. 339–358). New York: Academic Press.

Toates, F. M. (1981). The control of ingestive behaviour by internal and external stimuli—a theoretical review. *Appetite, 2*, 35–50.

Tompkins, C. A., & Mateer, C. A. (1985). Right hemisphere appreciation of intonational and linguistic indications of affect. *Brain and Language, 24*, 185–203.

Tong, F. (2003). Primary visual cortex and visual awareness. *Nature Reviews Neuroscience, 4*, 219–229.

Tonge, D. A., & Golding, J. P. (1993). Regeneration and repair of the peripheral nervous system. *Seminars in the Neurosciences, 5*, 385–390.

Tootell, R. B. H., Dale, A. M., Sereno, M. I., & Malach, R. (1996). New images from human visual cortex. *Trends in Neurosciences, 19*, 481–489.

Torrey, E. F., & Yoken, R. H. (2000). Familial and genetic mechanisms in schizophrenia. *Brain Research Interactive, 31*, 113–117.

Townsend, J., Courchesne, E., Covington, J., Westerfield, M., Singer Harris, N., Lyden, P., et al. (1999). Spatial attention deficits in patients with acquired or developmental cerebellar abnormality. *Journal of Neuroscience, 19*, 5632–5643.

Tranel, D., & Damasio, A. R. (1985). Knowledge without awareness: An autonomic index of facial recognition by prosopagnosics. *Science, 228*, 1453–1454.

Treffert, D. A., & Wallace, G. L. (2002, June). Islands of genius. *Scientific American, 286*, 76–85.

Treit, D. (1985). Animal models for the study of anti-anxiety agents: A review. *Neuroscience and Biobehavioural Reviews, 9*, 203–222.

Treit, D., Robinson, A., Rotzinger, S., & Pesold, C. (1993). Anxiolytic effects of serotonergic interventions in the shock-probe burying test and the elevated plus-maze test. *Behavioural Brain Research, 54*, 23–34.

Tresch, M. C., Saltiel, P., d'Avella, A., & Bizzi, E. (2002). Coordination and localization in spinal motor systems. *Brain Research Reviews, 40*, 66–79.

Treue, S. (2003). Visual attention: The where, what, how and why of saliency. *Current Opinion in Neurobiology, 13*, 428–432.

Trottier, G., Srivastava, L., & Walker, C. D. (1999). Etiology of infantile autism: A review of recent advances in genetic and neurobiological research. *Journal of Psychiatry and Neuroscience, 24*, 103–115.

True, W. R., Xian, H., Scherrer, J. F., Madden, P. A. F., Bucholz, K. K., Heath, A. C., et al. (1999). Common genetic vulnerability for nicotine and alcohol dependence in men. *Archives of General Psychiatry, 56*, 655–661.

Tsien, J. Z. (2000, April). Building a brainier mouse. *Scientific American, 282*, 62–68.

Tsodyks, M., Kenet, T., Grinvald, A., & Arieli, A. (1999). Link-ing spontaneous activity of single cortical neurons and the underlying functional architecture. *Science, 286*, 1943–1946.

Tulving, E. (2002). Episodic memory: From mind to brain. *Annual Review of Neuroscience, 53*, 1–25.

Turkenburg, J. L., Swaab, D. F., Endert, E., Louwerse, A. L., & van de Poll, N. E. (1988). Effects of lesions of the sexually dimorphic nucleus on sexual behavior of testosterone-treated female Wistar rats. *Brain Research Bulletin, 329*, 195–203.

Turkheimer, E. (2000). Three laws of behavior genetics and what they mean. *Current Directions in Psychological Science, 9*(5), 160–164.

Ulrich, R. E. (1991). Commentary: Animal rights, animal wrongs and the question of balance. *Psychological Science, 2*, 197–201.

Ungerleider, L. G., & Haxby, J. V. (1994). "What" and "where" in the human brain. *Current Opinion in Neurobiology, 4*, 157–165.

Ungerleider, L. G., & Mishkin, M. (1982). Two cortical visual systems. In D. J. Ingle, M. A. Goodale, & R. J. W. Mansfield (Eds.), *Analysis of visual behavior* (pp. 549–586). Cambridge, MA: MIT Press.

Vanderschuren, L. J. M. J., & Everitt, B. J. (2004). Drug seeking becomes compulsive after prolonged cocaine self-administration. *Science, 305*, 1017–1019.

Van Essen, D. C., Anderson, C. H., & Felleman, D. J. (1992). Information processing in the primate visual system: An integrated systems perspective. *Science, 255*, 419–423.

Van Essevelt, L. E., Lehman, M. N., & Boer, G. J. (2000). The suprachiasmatic nucleus and the circadian time-keeping system revisited. *Brain Research Review, 33*, 34–77.

Van Gelder, R. N., Wee, R., Lee, J. A., & Tu, D. C. (2003). Reduced pupillary light responses in mice lacking cryptochromes. *Science, 299*, 222.

Van Goozen, S. H. M., Slabbekoorn, D., Gooren, L. J. G., Sanders, G., & Cohen-Kettenis, P. T. (2002). Organizing and activating effects of sex hormones in homosexual transsexuals. *Behavioral Neuroscience, 116*, 982–988.

VanHelder, T., & Radomski, M. W. (1989). Sleep deprivation and the effect on exercise performance. *Sports Medicine, 7*, 235–247.

Van Lancker, D., & Cummings, J. L. (1999). Expletives: Neurolinguistic and neurobehavioral perspectives on swearing. *Brain Research Reviews, 31*, 83–104.

Vann, S. D., & Aggleton, J. P. (2004). The mammillary bodies: Two memory systems in one? *Nature Reviews Neuroscience, 5*, 35–43.

Van Praag, H., Christie, B. R., Sejnowski, T. J., & Gage, F. H. (1999). Running enhances neurogenesis, learning, and long-term potentiation in mice. *Proceedings of the National Academy of Sciences, U.S.A., 19*, 13427–13431.

Van Praag, H., Schinder, A. F., Christie, B. R., Toni, N., Palmer, T. D., & Gage, F. H. (2002). Functional neurogenesis in the adult hippocampus. *Nature, 415*, 1030–1034.

Vargha-Khadem, F., Gadian, D. G., Watkins, K. E., Connelly, A., van Paesschen, W., & Mishkin, M. (1997). Differential effects of early hippocampal pathology on episodic and semantic memory. *Science, 277*, 376–380.

Vekua, A., Lordkipanidze, D., Rightmire, G. P., Agusti, J., Ferring, R., Maisuradze, G., et al. (2002). A new skull of early *Homo* from Dmanisi, Georgia. *Science, 297*, 85–89.

Vermeij, G. J. (1996). Animal origins. *Science, 274*, 525–526.

Vermeire, B. A., Hamilton, C. R., & Erdmann, A. L. (1998). Right-hemisphere superiority in split-brain monkeys for learning and remembering facial discriminations. *Behavioral Neuroscience, 112*, 1048–1061.

Vertes, R. P. (1983). Brainstem control of the events of REM sleep. *Progress in Neurobiology, 22*, 241–288.

Vicario-Abejón, C., Owens, D., McKay, R., & Segal, M. (2002). Role of neurotrophins in central synapse formation and stabilization. *Nature Reviews Neuroscience, 3*, 965–974.

Vila, M., Wu, D. C., & Przedborski, S. (2001). Engineered modeling and the secrets of Parkinson's disease. *Trends in Neurosciences, 24*, S49–S55.

Vogel, J. J., Bowers, C. A., & Vogel, D. S. (2003). Cerebral lateralization of spatial abilities: A meta-analysis. *Brain and Cognition, 52*, 197–204.

Volkow, N. D., Fowler, J. S., Wang, G. J., & Swanson, J. M. (2004). Dopamine in drug abuse and addiction: Results from imaging studies and treatment implications. *Molecular Psychiatry, 9*, 557–569.

Voogd, J., & Glickstein, M. (1998). The anatomy of the cerebellum. *Trends in Neurosciences, 21*, 370–374.

Vuilleumier, P., Schwartz, S., Clarke, K., Husain, M., & Driver, J. (2002). Testing memory for unseen visual stimuli in patients with extinction and spatial neglect. *Journal of Cognitive Neuroscience, 14*, 875–886.

Wada, J. A. (1949). A new method for the determination of the side of cerebral speech dominance. *Igaku to Seibutsugaku, 14*, 221–222.

Wada, J. A., Clarke, R., & Hamm, A. (1975). Cerebral hemispheric asymmetry in humans. *Archives of Neurology, 32*, 239–246.

Wahlgren, N. G., & Ahmed, N. (2004). Neuroprotection in cerebral ischaemia: Facts and fancies—the need for new approaches. *Cerebrovascular Diseases, 17*, 153–166.

Wakayama, T., Tabar, V., Rodriguez, I., Perry, A. C. F., Studer, L., & Mombaerts, P. (2001). Differentiation of embryonic stem cell lines generated from adult somatic cells by nuclear transfer. *Science, 292*, 740–743.

Wald, G. (1964). The receptors of human color vision. *Science, 145*, 1007–1016.

Walford, R. L., & Walford, L. (1994). *The anti-aging plan*. New York: Four Walls Eight Windows.

Wall, J. T., Xu, J., & Wang, X. (2002). Human brain plasticity: An emerging view of the multiple substrates and mechanisms that cause cortical changes and related sensory dysfunctions after injuries of sensory inputs from the body. *Brain Research Review, 39*, 181–215.

Wan, H., Aggleton, J. P., & Brown, M. W. (1999). Different contributions of the hippocampus and perirhinal cortex to recognition memory. *Journal of Neuroscience, 19*, 1142–1148.

Wang, W., Meadows, L. R., den Haan, J. M. M., Sherman, N. E., Chen, Y., Blokland, E., et al. (1995). Human H-Y: A male-specific histocompatibility antigen derived from the SMCY protein. *Science, 269*, 1588–1590.

Wang, X., Wu, Y.-C., Fadok, V. A., Lee, M.-C., Gengyo-Ando, K., Cheng, L.-C., et al. (2003). Cell corpse engulfment mediated by *C. elegans* phosphatidylserine receptor through CED-5 and CED-12. *Science, 302*, 1563–1566.

Watson, J. B. (1930). *Behaviorism*. New York: W. W. Norton.

Waxham, M. N. (1999). Neurotransmitter receptors. In M. J. Zigmond, F. E. Bloom, S. C. Landis, J. L. Roberts, & L. R. Squire (Eds.), *Fundamental neuroscience* (pp. 235–268). New York: Academic Press.

Webb, W. B. (1973). Selective and partial deprivation of sleep. In W. P. Koella & P. Levin (Eds.), *Sleep: Physiology, biochemistry, psychology, pharmacology, clinical implications* (pp. 176–204). Basel, Switzerland: Karger.

Webb, W. B., & Agnew, H. W. (1967). Sleep cycling within the twenty-four hour period. *Journal of Experimental Psychology, 74*, 167–169.

Webb, W. B., & Agnew, H. W. (1970). Sleep stage characteristics of long and short sleepers. *Science, 163*, 146–147.

Webb, W. B., & Agnew, H. W. (1974). The effects of a chronic limitation of sleep length. *Psychophysiology, 11*, 265–274.

Webb, W. B., & Agnew, H. W. (1975). The effects on subsequent sleep of an acute restriction of sleep length. *Psychophysiology, 12*, 367–370.

Webber, K. M., Casadesus, G., Marlatt, M. W., Perry, G., Hamlin, C. R., Atwood, C. S., Bowen, R. L., & Smith, M. A. (2005). Estrogen bows to a new master: The role of gonadotropins in Alzheimer pathogenesis. *Annals of the New York Academy of Sciences, 1052*, 201–209.

Wechsler-Reya, R., & Scott, M. P. (2001). The developmental biology of brain tumors. *Annual Review of Neuroscience, 24,* 385–428.

Weiller, C., & Rijntjes, M. (1999). Learning, plasticity, and recovery in the central nervous system. *Experimental Brain Research, 128,* 134–138.

Weindruch, R. (1996, January). Caloric restriction and aging. *Scientific American, 274,* 46–52.

Weindruch, R., & Walford, R. L. (1988). *The retardation of aging and disease by dietary restriction.* Springfield, IL: Charles C. Thomas.

Weindruch, R., Walford, R. L., Fligiel, S., & Guthrie, D. (1986). The retardation of aging in mice by dietary restriction: Longevity, cancer, immunity, and lifetime energy intake. *Journal of Nutrition, 116,* 641–654.

Weingarten, H. P. (1983). Conditioned cues elicit feeding in sated rats: A role for learning in meal initiation. *Science, 220,* 431–433.

Weingarten, H. P. (1984). Meal initiation controlled by learned cues: Basic behavioral properties. *Appetite, 5,* 147–158.

Weingarten, H. P. (1985). Stimulus control of eating: Implications for a two-factor theory of hunger. *Appetite, 6,* 387–401.

Weingarten, H. P. (1990). Learning, homeostasis, and the control of feeding behavior. In E. D. Capaldi & T. L. Powley (Eds.), *Taste, experience, and feeding* (pp. 14–27). Washington, DC: American Psychological Association.

Weingarten, H. P., & Kulikovsky, O. T. (1989). Taste-to-postingestive consequence conditioning: Is the rise in sham feeding with repeated experience a learning phenomenon? *Physiology & Behavior, 45,* 471–476.

Weiskrantz, L. (2002). Prime-sight and blindsight. *Conscious-ness and Cognition, 11,* 568–581.

Weiskrantz, L. (2004). Roots of blindsight. *Progress in Brain Research, 144,* 229–241.

Weiskrantz, L., Warrington, E. K., Sanders, M. D., & Marshall, J. (1974). Visual capacity in the hemianopic field following a restricted occipital ablation. *Brain, 97,* 709–728.

Weiss, F., Maldonado-Vlaar, C. S., Parsons, L. H., Kerr, T. M., Smith, D. L., & Ben-Shahar, O. (2000). Control of cocaine-seeking behavior by drug-associated stimuli in rats: Effects on recovery of extinguished operant-responding and extracellular dopamine levels in amygdala and nucleus accumbens. *Proceedings of the National Academy of Sciences U.S.A., 97,* 4321–4326.

Weissman, M. M., & Olfson, M. (1995). Depression in women: Implications for health care research. *Science, 269,* 799–801.

Weliky, M., & Katz, C. (1997). Disruption of orientation tuning in visual cortex by artificially correlated neuronal activity. *Nature, 386,* 680–685.

Wenning, A. (1999). Sensing effectors make sense. *Trends in Neurosciences, 22,* 550–555.

Wessinger, C. M., VanMeter, J., Tian, B., Van Lare, J., Pekar, J., & Rauschecker, J. P. (2001). Hierarchical organization of the human auditory cortex revealed by functional magnetic resonance imaging. *Journal of Cognitive Neuroscience, 13,* 1–7.

West, M. J., Slomianka, L., & Gunderson, H. J. G. (1991). Unbiased stereological estimation of the total number of neurons in the subdivisions of the rat hippocampus using the optical fractionator. *Anatomical Record, 231,* 482–497.

Wever, R. A. (1979). *The circadian system of man.* Seewiesen-Andechs, Germany: Max-Planck-Institut für Verhaltensphysiologie.

Wheeler, M. E., Petersen, S. E., & Buckner, R. L. (2000). Memory's echo: Vivid remembering reactivates sensory-specific cortex. *Proceedings of the National Academy of Sciences, U.S.A., 97,* 11125–11129.

White, N. M. (1997). Mnemonic functions of the basal ganglia. *Current Opinion in Neurobiology, 7,* 164–169.

Wickelgren, W. A. (1968). Sparing of short-term memory in an amnesic patient: Implications for strength theory of memory. *Neuropsychologia, 6,* 31–45.

Willett, W. C. (1994). Diet and health: What should we eat? *Science, 264,* 532–537.

Willett, W. C., Skerrett, P. J., & Giovannucci, E. L. (2001). *Eat, drink, and be healthy: The Harvard Medical School guide to healthy eating.* New York: Simon & Schuster.

Willett, W. C., & Stampfer, M. J. (2003, January). Rebuild the food pyramid. *Scientific American, 288,* 65–71.

Williams, G., Cai, X. J., Elliot, J. C., & Harrold, J. A. (2004). Anabolic neuropeptides. *Physiology & Behavior, 81,* 211–222.

Williams, J. H. G., Whiten, A., Suddendorf, T., & Perret, D. I. (2001). Imitation, mirror neurons and autism. *Neuroscience and Biobehavioural Reviews, 25,* 287–295.

Williams, M. (1970). *Brain damage and the mind.* Baltimore: Penguin Books.

Willingham, D. B. (1999). The neural basis of motor-skill learning. *Current Directions in Psychological Science, 8,* 178–182.

Wilmer, J. B., Richardson, A. J., Chen, Y., & Stein, J. F. (2004). Two visual motion processing deficits in developmental dyslexia associated with different reading skills deficits. *Journal of Cognitive Neuroscience, 16,* 528–540.

Wilson, B. A. (1998). Recovery of cognitive functions following nonprogressive brain injury. *Current Opinion in Neurobiology, 8,* 281–287.

Wilson, G. T., Heffernan, K., & Black, C. M. D. (1996). Eating disorders. In E. J. Mash & R. A. Barkley (Eds.), *Child psychopathology* (pp. 541–571). New York: Guilford Press.

Wilson, M. A., & McNaughton, B. L. (1993). Dynamics of the hippocampal ensemble code for space. *Science, 261,* 1055–1058.

Wilson, R. I., & Nicoll, R. A. (2002). Endocannabinoid signaling in the brain. *Science, 296,* 678–682.

Wiltstein, S. (1995, October 26). Quarry KO'd by dementia. *The Vancouver Sun,* 135.

Winocur, G., Oxbury, S., Roberts, R., Agnetti, V., & Davis, C. (1984). Amnesia in a patient with bilateral lesions to the thalamus. *Neuropsychologia, 22,* 123–143.

Winson, J. (1993). The biology and function of rapid eye movement sleep. *Current Opinion in Neurobiology, 3,* 243–248.

Wirtshafter, D., & Davis, J. D. (1977). Set points, settling points, and the control of body weight. *Physiology & Behavior, 19,* 75–78.

Wise, P. M., Dubal, D. B., Wilson, M. E., Shane, W. R., Böttner, M., & Rosewell, K. L. (2001). Estradiol is a protective factor in the adult and aging brain: Understanding of mechanisms derived from *in vivo* and *in vitro* studies. *Brain Research Review, 37,* 313–319.

Wise, R. A. (2004). Dopamine, learning and motivation. *Nature Reviews Neuroscience, 5,* 483–493.

Witelson, S. F. (1991). Neural sexual mosaicism: Sexual differentiation of the human temporo-parietal region for functional asymmetry. *Psychoneuroendocrinology, 16,* 133–153.

Wolff, P. H., Michel, G. F., Ovrut, M., & Drake, C. (1990). Rate and timing precision of motor coordination in developmental dyslexia. *Developmental Psychology, 26,* 349–359.

Wolpaw, J. R., & Tennissen, A. (2001). Activity-dependent spinal cord plasticity in health and disease. *Annual Review of Neuroscience, 24,* 807–843.

Wong, A. H., Buckle, C. E., & Van Tol, H. H. (2000). Dopamine receptor gene transfer into rat striatum using a recombinant adenoviral vector: Rotational behaviour. *Neuroscience Letters, 291,* 135–138.

Wong, A. H. C., & Van Tol, H. H. M. (2003). Schizophrenia: From phenomenology to neurobiology. *Neuroscience and Biobehavioural Reviews, 27,* 269–306.

Wood, B., & Collard, M. (1999). The human genus. *Science, 284,* 65–71.

Wood, E. R., Mumby, D. G., Pinel, J. P. J., & Phillips, A. G. (1993). Impaired object recognition memory in rats following ischemia-induced damage to the hippocampus. *Behavioral Neuroscience, 107,* 51–62.

Woodruff-Pak, D. S. (1993). Eyeblink classical conditioning in H.M.: Delay and trace paradigms. *Behavioral Neuroscience, 107,* 911–925.

Woods, S. C. (1991). The eating paradox: How we tolerate food. *Psychological Review, 98,* 488–505.

Woods, S. C., & Ramsay, D. S. (2000). Pavlovian influences over food and drug intake. *Behavioural Brain Research, 110,* 175–182.

Woods, S. C., Schwartz, M. W., Baskin, D. G., & Seeley, R. J. (2000). Food intake and the regulation of body weight. *Annual Review of Neuroscience, 51,* 255–277.

Woods, S. C., & Strubbe, J. H. (1994). The psychology of meals. *Psychonomic Bulletin & Review, 1,* 141–155.

Woods, S. W., Stolar, M., Sernyak, M. J., & Charney, D. S. (2001). Consistency of atypical antipsychotic superiority to placebo in recent clinical trials. *Biological Psychiatry, 49,* 64–70.

Woodson, J. C. (2002). Including "learned sexuality" in the organization of sexual behavior. *Neuroscience and Biobehavioural Reviews, 26,* 69–80.

Woodson, J. C., & Balleine, B. W. (2002). An assessment of factors contributing to instrumental performance for sexual reward in the rat. *The Quarterly Journal of Experimental Psychology, 55(B),* 75–88.

Woodson, J. C., Balleine, B. W., & Gorski, R. A. (2002). Sexual experience interacts with steroid exposure to shape the partner preferences of rats. *Hormones and Behavior, 42,* 148–157.

Woodson, J. C., & Gorski, R. A. (2000). Structural sex differences in the mammalian brain: Reconsidering the male/female dichotomy. In A. Matsumoto (Ed.), *Sexual differentiation of the brain* (pp. 229–255). Boca Raton, FL: CRC Press.

Wooten, G. F., Currie, L. J., Bovbjerg, V. E., Lee, J. K., & Patrie, J. (2004). Are men at greater risk for Parkinson's disease than women? *Journal of Neurology, Neurosurgery, and Psychiatry, 75,* 637–639.

Wüst, S., Kasten, E., & Sabel, A. (2002). Blindsight after optic nerve injury indicates functionality of spared fibers. *Journal of Cognitive Neuroscience, 14,* 243–253.

Xu, D., Bureau, Y., McIntyre, D. C., Nicholson, D. W., Liston, P., Zhu, Y., et al. (1999). Attenuation of ischemia-induced cellular and behavioral deficits by X chromosome–linked inhibitor of apoptosis protein overexpression in the rat hippocampus. *Journal of Neuroscience, 19,* 5026–5033.

Yabuta, N. H., Sawatari, A., & Callaway, E. M. (2001). Two functional channels from primary visual cortex to dorsal visual cortical areas. *Science, 292,* 297–301.

Yamaguchi, S., Isejima, H., Matsuo, T., Okura, R., Yagita, K., Kobayashi, M., & Okamura, H. (2003). Synchronization of cellular clocks in the suprachiasmatic nucleus. *Science, 302,* 1408–1412.

Yesalis, C. E., & Bahrke, M. S. (1995). Anabolic-androgenic steroids: Current issues. *Sports Medicine, 19,* 326–340.

Young, E. A., Lopez, J. F., Murphy-Weinberg, V., Watson, S. J., &

Akil, H. (2000). Hormonal evidence for altered responsiveness to social stress in major depression. *Neuropsy-chopharmacology, 23,* 411–418.

Yuste, R., & Bonhoeffer, T. (2001). Morphological changes in dendritic spines associated with long-term synaptic plasticity. *Annual Review of Neuroscience, 24,* 1071–1089.

Yuste, R., & Bonhoeffer, T. (2004). Genesis of dendritic spines: Insights from ultrastructural and imaging studies. *Nature Reviews Neuroscience, 5,* 24–34.

Zaidel, E. (1987). Language in the disconnected right hemisphere. In G. Adelman (Ed.), *Encyclopedia of neuroscience* (pp. 563–564). Cambridge, MA: Birkhäuser.

Zangwill, O. L. (1975). Excision of Broca's area without persis-tent aphasia. In K. J. Zulch, O. Creutzfeldt, & G. C. Galbraith (Eds.), *Cerebral localization* (pp. 258–263). New York: Springer-Verlag.

Zeki, S. M. (1993a). *A vision of the brain.* Oxford: Blackwell Scientific.

Zeki, S. M. (1993b). The visual association cortex. *Current Opinion in Neurobiology, 3,* 155–159.

Zhang, Y., Proenca, R., Maffie, M., Barone, M., Leopold, L., & Friedman, J. M. (1994). Positional cloning of the mouse obese gene and its human homologue. *Nature, 372,* 425–432.

Zimitat, C., Kril, J., Harper, C. G., & Nixon, P. F. (1990). Progression of neurological disease in thiamine deficient rats is enhanced by ethanol. *Alcohol, 7,* 493–501.

Zimmer, L., & Morgan, J. P. (1997). *Marijuana myths, marijuana facts: A review of the scientific evidence.* New York: Lindesmith Center.

Zivin, J. A. (2000, April). Understanding clinical trials. *Scientific American, 282,* 69–75.

Zoghbi, H. Y. (2003). Postnatal neurodevelopmental disorders: Meeting at the synapse? *Science, 302,* 826–830.

Zola-Morgan, S., Squire, L. R., & Amaral, D. G. (1986). Human amnesia and the medial temporal region: Enduring memory impairment following a bilateral lesion limited to field CA1 of the hippocampus. *Journal of Neuroscience, 6,* 2950–2967.

Zola-Morgan, S. M., Squire, L. R., Amaral, D. G., & Suzuki, W. A. (1989). Lesions of perirhinal and parahippocampal cortex that spare the amygdala and hippocampal formation produce severe memory impairment. *Journal of Neuroscience, 9,* 4355–4370.

Zola-Morgan, S., Squire, L. R., & Mishkin, M. (1982). The neuroanatomy of amnesia: Amygdala-hippocampus versus temporal stem. *Science, 218,* 1337–1339.

Zola-Morgan, S., Squire, L. R., Rempel, N. L., Clower, R. P., & Amaral, D. G. (1992). Enduring memory impairment in monkeys after ischemic damage to the hippocampus. *Journal of Neuroscience, 12,* 2582–2596.

Zucker, K. J., Bradley, S. J., Oliver, G., Blake, J., Fleming, S., & Hood, J. (1996). Psychosexual development of women with congenital adrenal hyperplasia. *Hormones and Behavior, 30,* 300–318.

Zucker, R. S., Kullman, D. M., & Bennett, M. (1999). Release of neurotransmitters. In M. J. Zigmond, F. E. Bloom, S. C. Landis, J. L. Roberts, & L. R. Squire (Eds.), *Fundamental neuroscience* (pp. 155–192). New York: Academic Press.

Zur, D., & Ullman, S. (2003). Filling-in of retinal scotomas. *Vision Research, 43,* 971–982.

Credits

Photo Credits

Part 1 **3T** © Scott Markewitz/Getty Images/Photographer's Choice; **3M** © age fotostock/SuperStock; **3B** © Kay Chernush/Getty Images/The Image Bank

Chapter 1 **4** © Scott Markewitz/Getty Images/Photographer's Choice; **5, 34** © Med. Ills. SBHA/Getty Images/Stone; **11** © Dale and Marion Zimmerman/Animals, Animals; **13TL, 34** © Kevin Shafer/Peter Arnold, Inc.; **13TR, 34** © Thinkstock/Alamy; **13BL, 34** © Erwin & Peggy Bauer/Bruce Coleman, Inc.; **13BM, 34** © Erwin & Peggy Bauer/Bruce Coleman, Inc.; **13BR, 34** © A. Comoost/Peter Arnold, Inc.; **14T** © Ken Fisher/Getty Images/Stone; **14B** © John Reader/Photo Researchers, Inc.; **21** © David Phillips/Photo Researchers, Inc.; **32, 35** © K. Wanstall/The Image Works

Chapter 2 **36** © age fotostock/SuperStock; **45T** Courtesy of T. Chan-Ling; **46T** © Ed Reschke/Peter Arnold, Inc.; **46M, 46B** Courtesy of my good friends Carl Ernst and Brian Christie, Department of Psychology, University of British Columbia; **47, 62, 63** Courtesy of Jerold J. M. Chun, M.D., Ph.D.; **59** Courtesy of Miles Herkenham, Unit of Functional Neuroanatomy, N.I.M.H. Bethesda, MD; **60** © Manfred Kage/Peter Arnold, Inc.

Chapter 3 **64** © Kay Chernush/Getty Images/The Image Bank; **76** J. E. Heuser et al., *Journal of Cell Biology,* 1979, 81, 275–300 by copyright permission of The Rockefeller University Press; **80** Courtesy of Floyd E. Bloom, M.D., The Scripps Research Institute, La Jolla, California; **89** © Science Photo Library/Photo Researchers, Inc.; **91L, 97** © Scott Camazine/Photo Researchers, Inc.; **91R, 97** Courtesy of Bruce Foster and Robert Hare, University of British Columbia; **92** From "Positron Tomography: Human Brain Function and Biochemistry" by Michael E. Phelps and John C. Mazziotta, *Science,* 228 [9701], May 17, 1985, p. 804. Courtesy of Drs. Michael E. Phelps and John Mazziotta, UCLA School of Medicine; **93** Courtesy of Kent Kiehl and Peter Liddle, Department of Psychiatry, University of British Columbia

Part 2 **99T** © Digital Vision/Getty Images; **99M** © Ariel Skelley/CORBIS; **99B** © Kennan Ward/CORBIS

Chapter 4 **100** © Digital Vision/Getty Images; **103, 138, 139** © Digital Archive Japan/Alamy; **105TL** © JORGEN SCHYTTE/Peter Arnold, Inc.; **105TM** © Michael Fairchild/Peter Arnold, Inc.; **105TR** © John Cancalosi/Peter Arnold, Inc.; **105BL** © Gerhard Jaegle/Das Fotoarchiv/Peter Arnold, Inc.; **105BM** Cyril Laubscher ©Dorling Kindersley; **105BR** © Colin Varndell/Nature

Picture Library; **108R, 138, 139** © Ralph C. Eagle/Photo Researchers, Inc.; **108L** © Science Photo Library/Photo Researchers, Inc.; **123T** From "Brain Mechanism of Vision" by D. H. Hubel and T. N. Wiesel. Reprinted by permission of *Scientific American,* vol. 241, p 151. © 1979 by Scientific American, Inc.; **123B** From "Orientation Columns in Macaque Monkey Visual Cortex Demonstrated by the 2-Deoxyglucose Autoradiographic Technique" by D. H. Hubel, T. N. Wiesel, and M. P. Stryker. Reprinted by permission from *Nature,* vol. 269, p. 329. Copyright 1977 by Macmillan Magazines Ltd.

Chapter 5 **140** © Ariel Skelley/CORBIS; **158** © Roman Soumar/CORBIS; **161, 169** © Omikron/Photo Researchers, Inc.; **164, 169** Photographs prepared by James Enns, Department of Psychology, University of British Columbia

Chapter 6 **170** © Kennan Ward/CORBIS; **188** © Science Photo Library/Photo Researchers, Inc.

Part 3 **203T** © David Grossman/The Image Works; **203M** © Roger Ressmeyer/CORBIS; **203B** © Marc Grimberg/Getty Images/The Image Bank

Chapter 7 **204** © David Grossman/The Image Works; **209, 228** Courtesy of Naweed I. Syed, Ph.D., Departments of Anatomy and Medical Physiology, The University of Calgary; **220, 229** Courtesy of my friends Carl Ernst and Brian Christie, Department of Psychology, University of British Columbia; **224** AP/Wide World Photos; **226, 229** Courtesy of the Williams Syndrome Association, Inc.

Chapter 8 **231** © Roger Ressmeyer/CORBIS; **232** Courtesy of Kenneth Berry, Head of Neuropathology, Vancouver General Hospital; **233T** © CMSP/Custom Medical Stock; **233B, 262** Courtesy of Dr. Pinel; **234** © Volker Steger/Peter Arnold, Inc.; **236T** © 1996 Scott Camazine; **236B, 262** © Bettmann/CORBIS; **239** Courtesy of Kenneth E. Salyer, Director, International Craniofacial Institute; **240** © Dr. David Rosenbaum/Phototake; **245, 262** © James Stevens/Science Photo Library/Photo Researchers, Inc.; **246** © Cecil Fox/Photo Researchers, Inc.; **255, 263** These beautiful images are courtesy of my good friends Carl Ernst and Brian Christie, Department of Psychology, University of British Columbia; **259** © Pete Saloutos/CORBIS

Chapter 9 **264** © Marc Grimberg/Getty Images/The Image Bank; **273** © Kevin R. Morris/CORBIS; **291** Courtesy of Tank et al., 1988

Part 4 **299T** © Stewart Cohen/Getty Images/Taxi; **299M** © Juan Silva/Getty

Images/The Image Bank; **299B** © Robert Daly/Getty Images/Stone

Chapter 10 **300** © Stewart Cohen/Getty Images/Taxi; **303, 331** © Richard Reinauer/Color-Pic, Inc.; **307** © Eric Futran/Getty Images/FoodPix; **308** © Viviane Moos/CORBIS; **323, 332** © A. Ramey/PhotoEdit, Inc.; **325, 331** The Jackson Lab, Bar Harbor, ME; **327, 332** © Topham/The Image Works

Chapter 11 **332** © Juan Silva/Getty Images/The Image Bank; **334, 364, 365** © CNRI/Photo Researchers, Inc.; **335TL** © Addenbrookes Hospital/SPL/Photo Researchers, Inc.; **335TR** © Addenbrookes Hospital/Photo Researchers, Inc.; **348** Howard W. Jones, Jr., M.D.; **351, 364** CP/Winnipeg Free Press; **355, 365** © Gabo/Focus/Trivel/Woodfin Camp & Associates; **357** Adapted from Gorski et al., 1978; **361, 365** © WILL BURGESS/Reuters/CORBIS

Chapter 12 **366** © Robert Daly/Getty Images/Stone; **368, 400** © Hank Morgan/Photo Researchers, Inc.; **374** © Animals, Animals; **375, 400** © Sean Justice/Getty Images/The Image Bank; **396** © Will & Deni McIntyre/CORBIS

Part 5 **403T** AP/Wide World Photos; **403M** Stockbyte; **403B** © Pierre Perrin/CORBIS/Sygma

Chapter 13 **404** AP/Wide World Photos; **408** © Hulton Archive/Getty Images; **411, 440** © Skjold Photographs/The Image Works; **412, 440** © Royalty-Free/CORBIS; **413, 440** © Jeffrey L. Rotman/CORBIS; **415, 440** © The Cover Story/CORBIS; **417, 440** © Mark Peterson/CORBIS; **418** © Michael S. Yamashita/CORBIS; **420, 440** Courtesy of Maggie Edwards; **425, 441** From: Damasio H, Grabowski T, Frank R, Galaburda AM, Damasio AR: The return of Phineas Gage: Clues about the brain from a famous patient. *Science,* 264:1102-1105, 1994. Department of Neurology and Image Analysis Facility, University of Iowa; **431, 441** Lennert Nillson/Bonnierforlagen AB

Chapter 14 **442** Stockbyte; **446L, 478** © RAY STUBBLEBINE/Reuters/CORBIS; **446R, 479** © Reuters/CORBIS

Chapter 15 **480, 506** © Pierre Perrin/CORBIS/Sygma; **481, 506** © Sven Schrader/Getty Images/Stone; **487** Dr. Paul Thompson, Laboratory of Neuro Imaging at UCLA; **488, 506** © Hans Neleman/Getty Images/Iconica; **493** © WDCN/Univ. College London/Photo Researchers, Inc.; **494, 506** © David Hanover/Getty Images/Stone; **497, 507** © Vladimir Rys/Bongarts/Getty Images

Illustration Credits

Figures 1.2, 1.12–1.16, 2.4, 2.14, 2.23, 2.27, 2.28, 3.1, 3.7, 3.9, 3.10, 3.14–3.18, 4.29–4.31, 5.3, 5.7, 5.13, 5.17, 5.21, 6.2–6.5, 6.10–6.18, 7.2, 7.3, 7.7, 7.8, 7.12, 8.25, 8.26, 9.2, 9.3, 9.7–9.9, 9.12, 9.16–9.19, 10.14, 11.10, 12.8, 12.10, 12.13, 13.7, 13.8, 14.1, 14.4, 14.5–14.7, 14.11, 15.6, Appendix I: Frank Forney

Figures 1.8, 2.2, 2.3, 2.5, 2.20, 3.3, 3.4, 4.12, 4.13, 5.10, 5.11, 11.1, 13.15: Frank Forney/Schneck-DePippo Graphics

Figures 1.9, 1.10, 2.7, 3.2, 3.6, 3.12, 4.14, 4.15, 4.17, 4.18, 5.16, 6.7, 6.8, 6.15, 7.6, 8.15, 8.16, 8.21, 8.22, 9.4, 9.10, 9.13, 9.14, 10.2–10.4, 10.7, 10.11, 10.15, 11.9, 11.16, 12.2, 12.7, 12.9, 12.11, 12.12, 13.2, 13.3, 13.10, 13.13, 14.9, 14.13, 14.15, 14.16, 15.2: Schneck-DePippo Graphics

Figures 1.17, 2.29, 3.13: Modern Graphics, Inc./Omegatype Typography, Inc.

Figures 2.6, 2.9, 3.8, 8.5, 15.1, 15.4: Mark Leftowitz

Figure 2.8: Frank Forney/Mark Leftowitz

Figure 2.10: Modern Graphics, Inc./Mark Leftowitz

Figures 2.15, 2.17, 3.5, 4.16, 4.19, 9.6, 9.15, 10.8, 10.9, 10.18, 12.16, 13.1, 13.2, 13.11: Modern Graphics, Inc./Schneck-DePippo Graphics

Figures 2.16, 2.18, 2.24, 4.26, 5.12, 5.14, 5.19, 6.6, 13.12, 14.2, 14.10, 14.12: William C. Ober and Claire W. Garrison

Figures 2.21, 2.22, 2.25, 2.26, 11.4: Frank Forney/William C. Ober and Claire W. Garrison

Figures 4.1, 11.7: Frank Forney/Omegatype Typography, Inc.

Figures 4.5, 4.10: Frank Forney/Celadon Digital Studios

Figures 4.6, 10.16: Modern Graphics, Inc.

Figures 4.8, 4.11, 4.22, 4.23: Celadon Digital Studios

Figure 4.24: Modern Graphics, Inc./Celadon Digital Studios

Figures 4.28, 8.20, 10.10, 10.12, 10.13: Academy Artworks

Figures 5.1, 5.2: Leo Harrington

Figures 5.4, 5.6, 5.18, 7.9, 8.19, 9.1, 9.5, 11.8, 11.18, 12.3, 12.5, 12.14, 14.8: Illustrious Interactive

Figures 5.5, 5.8, 11.5: Adrienne Lehmann

Figures 5.9, 7.1, 7.5, 8.17, 13.16: Frank Forney/Illustrious Interactive

Figure 6.1: Modern Graphics, Inc./Leo Harrington

Figure 8.18: Modern Graphics, Inc./Illustrious Interactive

Figure 10.1: Gale Mueller

Figure 11.6: Frank Forney/Adrienne Lehmann

Figure 11.12: Frank Forney/Gale Mueller

Figure 12.17: Omegatype Typography, Inc.

Athletic performance, anabolic steroids and, 355
Atonia, 392, 394
Attention, 163–166
Attention-deficit/hyperactivity disorder, 498
Atypical neuroleptics, 486
Auditory canal, 145
Auditory cortex, 149, 175, 219, 436
Auditory nerves, 145, 146, 147, 149, A-4, A-5
Auditory system, 144–149
Auditory-vestibular nerve, 145, 231, A-5
Auras, epileptic, 240
Australopithecus, 14–15
Autism, 222–225
Autoimmune disorder, 245
Autoimmune reaction, 394
Automatisms, 241
Autonomic nervous system (ANS), 37, A-2
Autoradiograph, 123
Autoreceptors, 78
Autotransplantation, of adrenal medulla, 258
Aversions, conditioned taste, 159, 308–309, 317, 328, 329
Axoaxonic synapse, 74
Axodendritic synapse, 74
Axon(s), 41
  myelination of, 73, 214, 215
  of retinal ganglion cells, 107, 108, 114
Axon growth, 209–211
Axon guidance molecules, 212
Axon hillock, 41, 69
Axonal conduction, 72–73
Axosomatic synapse, 74
Axotomy, 249, 250

B cells, 431, 432, 433
Bacterial infections, of brain, 237
Balance, 231
Ballistic movements, 172
Barn owl, sound location by, 148–149, 219
Basal forebrain, 272, 384
Basal ganglia, 56–58, 182–183, 415
  contralateral, 198
  and Tourette syndrome, 499
Basal metabolic rate, 320, 324
Basilar membrane, 145, 146
Bayer Drug Company, 417, 418
Behavior(s)
  aggressive, 345, 355–356, 414, 425–426, 427–428
  anabolic steroids and, 355–356
  biology of, 9, 27–33
  copulatory, 344–345, 356, 357–358
  evolution and, 11–12

female reproduction-related, 353–354
instinctive, 29
male-reproduction-related, 351–353
perinatal hormones and, 344–345
proceptive, 345
sexual, 353, 354, 356–359
Behavioral biology, 7. See also Biopsychology
Behavioral neuroscience, 5, 7. See also Biopsychology
Behavioral therapy, and autism, 225
Behaviorism, 29
Benign tumors, 232
Benzodiazepines, 389–390, 392, 393, 495, 497
Betz cells, 184
Biceps, 188, 189
Bilateral anterior temporal lobectomy, 428
Bilateral medial temporal lobectomy, 276
  amnesic effects of, 265–270
  in monkeys, 278
  object-recognition deficits and, 280–283
Bimodal neurons, 179–180
Binding problem, 143
Binge eating, 326–327
Binges, cocaine, 416
Binocular, 120–121
Binocular disparity, 105–106
Biological clock, 375
Biopsychology, 5, 7–8, 18–19
Bipolar affective disorder, 489, 491, 504–505
Bipolar cells, 106, 109
Bipolar neuron, 43
Bipotential precursor, 342
Birds, 16
  neurogenesis in, 220
  spatial memory of, 285
Bisexual, 359
Blind spot, 107, 109
Blindness, color, 23
Blindsight, 130
Blobs, 127
Blood-brain barrier, 40, 65
Blood glucose levels, 313
Blood pressure, MAO inhibitors and, 490
Body fat, 320, 321
Body weight. See also Obesity
  brain weight and, 17
  changes in energy utilization efficiency and, 319–320
  positive-incentive perspective on, 307–309
  regulation of, 318–322
  set-point theories of, 305–307
Botox, 88

Bottom-up neural mechanisms, 164
Botulinium toxin, 88
Brain, 37. See also Lateralization of function
  asymmetry of, 458–459, 460–461
  bacterial infections of, 237
  dopamine systems of, 422–424
  and dyslexia, 474
  evolution of, 16–18
  five divisions of, 50–51
  and language, 462–464
  major structures of, 51–60
  mechanisms of emotions in, 435–438
  methods for studying, 82–89
  postnatal growth and development of, 213–216
  sex differences in, 343–344
  sexual orientation and, 360
  sleep and, 383–387
  tumors in, 231–233
Brain damage, 141. See also specific types of damage
  accidental or disease-related, 467–468
  acquired dyslexia and, 474
  aphasia and, 444
  in auditory cortex, 149
  and autism, 223
  causes of, 232–239
  to cerebellum, 182
  cerebrovascular disorders as, 233–235
  chemical senses and, 162–163
  chronic alcohol consumption and, 412, 413
  closed-head injuries and, 235–236
  depression and, 493
  genetic factors in, 238–239
  in hippocampus, 270
  infections of brain and, 237
  ischemia-induced, 234–235
  language-related abilities and, 466–468
  marijuana and, 415
  MDMA use and, 417
  narcolepsy and, 394
  neuroplastic responses to, 249–255
  neurotoxins in, 237–238
  of Phineas Gage, 424–425
  to posterior parietal cortex, 175
  to prefrontal cortex, 287
  to primary motor cortex, 181–182
  to primary somatosensory cortex, 155
  in primary visual cortex, 128–129
  programmed cell death and, 239

recovery of function after, 253–255
  reducing, 256–261
  rehabilitative training and, 258–261
  in schizophrenia, 487–488
Brain imaging, 7, 89–92, 446. See also Computed tomography; Functional brain imaging; Functional MRI; Magnetic resonance imaging; Positron emission tomography
  and affective disorders, 493
  and anxiety, 497
  and schizophrenia, 487
Brain stem, 51
  and autism, 224–225
  evolution of, 17
  sleep and, 384–386
Brain stem motor nuclei, 174
Bregma, 83
Brightness, 103, 110
Broca's aphasia, 462, 463, 471
Broca's area, 444, 458, 462, 463, 464, 466
  language and, 470
  lesions to, 467, 468
  removal of, 466
Buerger's disease, 411–412
Bulimia nervosa, 327
Buspirone, 495, 497
Buttons, terminal, 41, 72, 74, 75
Butyrophenones, 485

CA1 subfield, 270, 271, 281
CA2 subfield, 271
CA3 subfield, 271
CA4 subfield, 271
Cafeteria diet, 312
Caffeine, 415
Calcium ions, 75, 234, 235, 291, 292
Calorie-restriction experiments, 319
CAMs. See Cell-adhesion molecules
Cancer, 213
  brain tumor as, 232–233
  lung, 232, 411
  pain of, 152
Cannabinoids, 413
Cannabis sativa, 413, 414
Cannon-Bard theory, of emotion, 426, 427
Cannula, 89
Carbohydrates, 303
Carbon monoxide, 80
Cardiovascular diseases, smoking and, 411
Carminative, 417
Carotid artery, 91, 234
Carousel apparatus, 379–380
Cartesian dualism, 27

Concussion, 236, 273–276
Conditional stimulus, 407, 423, 435
Conditioned compensatory response, 408
Conditioned place-preference paradigm, 421, 422
Conditioned taste aversion, 159, 317, 328, 329
Conditioning, 423
  drug tolerance and, 407–408
  of fear, 435–436
  Pavlovian, 268, 288, 310, 407, 410
Conduction
  of action potential, 71–73
  saltatory, 73
Conduction aphasia, 463
Conductive deafness, 149
Cones, 108, 109, 124, 125, 388
Configural association theory, 285–286
Congenital, 233
Consolidation, of memory, 268, 274–276
Conspecifics, 12
  pheromones and, 159
  stress and, 430
Constituent cognitive processes, 458, 471
Constraint-induced therapy, 259
Contraction, isometric, 189
Contralateral, 54
Contralateral basal ganglia, 198
Contralateral neglect, 156, 175–176, 177
Contralateral premotor cortex, 198
Contralateral primary motor cortex, 198
Contralateral somatosensory cortex, 198
Contrast enhancement, 116–118
Contrast X-ray techniques, 89
Contrecoup injuries, 236
Control compartment, 422
"Control of behavior" versus "conscious perception" theory, 133–134
Contusions, 236
Convergence, 105, 109–110
Convergent evolution, 15
Convolutions, 17, 54
Convulsions, 240
Coprolalia, 498
Copulation, 334
  anabolic steroids and, 356
  medial preoptic lesions and, 357–358
  perinatal hormones and, 344–345
  social dominance and, 11
Coronal sections, 48
Corpus callosum, 55, 58, 443, 447, 448, 449

Cortex. See also Cerebral cortex
  adrenal, 335, 349, 360, 429, 493
  anterior cingulate, 157
  association, 130–131, 141–142, 174–178
  auditory, 149, 175, 219, 436
  entorhinal, 246
  of primordial gonad, 341
  removal of, 427, 466–467
Cortical reorganization, 252
Corticotropin-releasing hormone, 493
Cortisol, 349
Courtship display, 11–12
Covert attention, 166
Crack, 416
Crackpot, 237
Cranial nerves, 38–39, 145, 162, 163, 186, 231, A-4
Cresyl violet, 47
Cribriform plate, 160, 272
Critical thinking, 6
Cross-cuing, 452
Cross-modal rewiring experiments, 218
Cross section, 48
Cross tolerance, 405
CSF. See Cerebrospinal fluid
CT. See Computed tomography
Cultural factors, developmental dyslexia and, 474–475
Curare, 87–88
Cut drugs, 419
Cutaneous receptors, 150
Cyanosis, 242
Cytochrome oxidase, 127
Cytoplasm, 24, 25, 42
Cytoplasmic extensions, 209
Cytosine, 23

D_2 receptor blockers, 488, 499
D_2 receptors, 485, 486, 487
Dalby's Carminative, 417
Daughter cells, 21
Deafness, 149
  linguistic theory of cerebral asymmetry and, 460
Decorticate, 427
Decussate, 54, 151
Deep dyslexia, 475, 476
Default theory of REM sleep, 381–382
Defeminize, 344
Defensive-burying test, 496, 497
Delayed nonmatching-to-sample test
  with monkeys, 278–279
  with rats, 279–283
Delirium tremens (DTs), 412
Delta waves, 369, 370
Delusions, bizarre, 482
Demasculinize, 345
Dementia, 236, 245, 272, 412. *See also* Alzheimer's disease

Dendrites, 41, 214, 215
Dendritic spines, 59, 74, 293
Dendrodendritic synapse, 74
Dentate gyrus, 220, 255, 271, 289
2-Deoxyglucose (2-DG), 91, 122, 161
Deoxyribonucleic acid (DNA), 23, 24
Deoxyribose, 23, 24
Depolarize, 68
Deprenyl, 248, 249
Depressant, 412
Depression, 488
  drug treatment for, 492
  magnetic resonance imaging and, 493
  theories of, 492–493
Depth of focus, 104
Depth perception, 121
Dermatomes, 150–151
Descending analgesic circuit, 158–159
Descending motor pathways, 184–188
Desynchronized EEG, 384–385, 386
Detoxified addicts, 409
Developmental dyslexias, 474–475
Dexamethasone, 493
Dexfenfluramine, 317
Dextrals, 445, 446
Dextroamphetamine, 416
2-DG. See 2-Deoxyglucose
Diathesis, 492
Diathesis–stress model of depression, 492–493
Dichotic listening test, 445
Dichotomous traits, 19, 20
Diencephalon, 50, 51, 53–54
Diet, cafeteria, 312
Diet-induced thermogenesis, 320, 324
Dietary deficiencies, 309
Diethylstilbestrol, 344, 360
Dieting. *See also* Weight-loss programs
  anorexia and, 327
Differential permeability, 66
Differentiation, of cells, 206
Digestion, 302–303
Digestive tracts, 413
Digit span, 266
Directed synapses, 74
Directional coordinates, in vertebrate nervous system, 47–48
Disparity, binocular, 105–106
Distal, 48
Distal segment, 249
Diversity, genetic, 22
Dizygotic twins, 31. *See also* Twin studies
DNA. *See* Deoxyribonucleic acid

DNA-binding proteins, 24, 239
Dogs, narcolepsy in, 393, 394
Dominance hierarchies, 430
Dominant gene, in Huntington's disease, 243
Dominant hemisphere, 444
Dominant trait, 20
L-Dopa, 65, 80, 81, 243
Dopamine, 249, 390, 416
  cocaine as agonist of, 86–87
  copulation and, 358
  and drug addiction, 422–424
  metabolites of, 484
  as neurotransmitter, 79–80, 81
  and Parkinson's disease, 65, 243
Dopamine receptors, 484–485
Dopamine synapses, 485
Dopamine system, 422–424
Dopamine theory of schizophrenia, 484–485, 486
Dopaminergic circuits, 487
Dorsal, 48
Dorsal-column medial-lemniscus system, 151
Dorsal column nuclei, 151
Dorsal columns, 151
Dorsal horns, 49
Dorsal nerve cords, 12
Dorsal root, 150, 190
  of spinal cord, 49, 50
Dorsal root ganglion, 49, 50
Dorsal stream, 132–134, 166
Dorsal striatum, 423
Dorsolateral corticorubrospinal tract, 184, 185
Dorsolateral corticospinal tract, 184, 185
Dorsolateral motor pathways, 187–188
Dorsolateral prefrontal association cortex, 175, 176–178, 198
Dose-response curve, 405, 406
Double-blind design, 502–503
Down syndrome, 23, 162, 238–239
Dreaming, 370–372
Drinking, cessation of, 314
Drug abuse, 412–419
  of anabolic steroids, 354–356
Drug addiction
  biological theories of, 409–410
  conditioning in, 407–408
  dopamine and, 422–424
  drug tolerance and, 405–406
  drug withdrawal and physical dependence and, 406–407
  neural mechanisms of motivation and, 421–424
  physical-dependence theories of, 409
  relapse and, 410
Drug compartment, 422

Fetal alcohol syndrome (FAS), 413

Fetal hormones, reproductive organ development and, 340–343

Fetal tissue, transplanting of, 257–258

Fetus, smoking and, 413

First messengers, 77

First-night phenomenon, 368

Fissure(s), 54
central, 55, 58, 180, 444
lateral, 55, 58, 147, 148, 162, 444
longitudinal, 55, 58, 128, 147

Fitness, 10

Flavor, 159, 307

Flexors, 188, 189

Fluoxetine, 317, 491

fMRI. *See* Functional MRI

Follicle, 354

Follicle-stimulating hormone (FSH), 330

Food-caching birds, hippocampal size in, 285

Forebrain, 50, 51, 147, 207
basal, 272, 384

Fornix, 56, 57, 58

Fortification illusions, 101–102, 123–124

Fossil records, 10

Fourier analysis, 145

Fovea, 107, 108, 110, 115, 119

Fraternal twins, 31. *See also* Twin studies

Free fatty acids, 304

Free nerve endings, 150

Free-running circadian sleep-wake cycles, 374–375, 387

Free-running period, 375

Free-running rhythms, 375

Frequency, 144, 145

Freudian theory of dreams, 372

Frogs, axon regeneration in, 209–210, 211

Frontal lobe, 55, 58, 444

Frontal operculum, 458, 459

Frontal sections, 48

Functional brain imaging, 178, 179, 287, 445, 456. *See also* Functional MRI
and language, 472–474
and sensorimotor learning, 197–199
and Tourette syndrome, 499

Functional columns, 147

Functional MRI (fMRI), 91–92, 93, 196, 445
and auditory cortex, 148, 219
and human dual-opponent color cells, 128
and lateralization, 445
and motor homunculus, 181
and reading, 472
and vision, 166

Functional segregation, 143, 172, 173–174

Functional tolerance, 406

Functionally homogeneous, 143

Fusiform face area, 134

G proteins. *See* Guanosine-triphosphate-sensitive proteins

GABA. *See* Gamma-aminobutyric acid

GABA$_A$ receptors, 495, 497

Gametes, 21

Gamma-aminobutyric acid (GABA), 79, 81, 495

Ganglia, 44
basal, 56–58, 182–183, 198, 415, 499
dorsal root, 49, 50

Gases, soluble, 80–81, 293

Gastric operations, to treat obesity, 325

Gastric ulcers, stress and, 430

Gastritis, 413

Gastrointestinal tract, 302–303
and satiety, 315–316

Gate-control theory, of pain, 157

Gene(s), 9, 21
clock, 389
dominant, 243
Hoxa 1, 225
for narcolepsy, 393
ob/ob, 325, 326
operator, 24
recessive, 238
structural, 24, 26
tau, 389

Gene expression, 24–25, 78
estradiol and, 358
long-term maintenance of memory and, 293
steroid hormones and, 335

Gene knockout techniques, 92

Gene mutations, and Parkinson's disease, 243

Gene replacement techniques, 92–93

General paresis, 237

Generalized anxiety disorders, 494

Generalized epilepsy, 240

Generalized seizures, 241–242

Genetic code, 23, 24–25

Genetic diversity, meiosis and, 22

Genetic engineering, 92–94

Genetics
of affective disorders, 489–490
of alcohol addiction, 412
and Alzheimer's disease, 246
of anxiety disorders, 495
and autism, 223
and brain damage, 238–239
of circadian rhythms, 389
of human obesity, 323
Mendelian, 19–21

and multiple sclerosis, 245
of nicotine addiction, 411
of schizophrenia, 483
of sexual orientation, 359
of Tourette syndrome, 498

Genitals, 342

Genotype, 21

Gland(s), 333–334, A-3
adrenal, 335
endocrine, 334
exocrine, 333–334
mammary, 12
pineal, 390–391
pituitary, 54, 56, 336, 337, 338, 339, 345, 356, 429, 493

Glaucoma, marijuana and, 415

Glia, 210

Glia-mediated migration, 208

Glial cells, 44–45, 212

Glial stem cells, 207

Global aphasia, 468

Globus pallidus, 57, 58

Glossopharyngeal cranial nerve, 162, A-4, A-5

Glucagon, 304

Glucocorticoid receptors, 435

Glucocorticoids, 429, 430, 433, 493

Gluconeogenesis, 304

Glucose, 303
blood levels of, 313

Glucostatic theory, 306, 313

Glutamate, 79, 81, 113, 291, 293
in cerebral ischemia, 234, 235
in schizophrenia, 486

Glutamate antagonist, 235

Glutamate receptors, 234

Glutaminergic synapses, 291

Glycine, 25, 79, 81

Glycogen, 303

Godfrey's Cordial, 417

Golgi complex, 42, 74, 75

Golgi stain, 46, 59

Golgi tendon organs, 189

Gonadal hormones, 336
effects on adults of, 351–356
summary model of, 339–340

Gonadectomy, 341

Gonadotropic hormone, 345

Gonadotropin, 336, 340, 343

Gonadotropin-releasing hormone, 339

Gonads, 334–335, 340–341. *See also* Ovaries; Testes

G-protein–linked receptor, 113

Graded responses, 68

Grammatical analysis, 471

Grand mal seizure, 242

Granule cell, 435

Granule cell layer, 289, 290

Gray matter, 49

Growth cone, 209

Growth hormone, 345

Guanine, 23

Guanosine-triphosphate-sensitive proteins (G proteins), 77, 113

Guidance molecules, 210, 212

Guinea pigs
estrous cycle of, 354
ovariectomy in, 354
sexual behavior in, 344–345, 353, 354

Guinness Book of World Records, 379

Gustation. *See* Taste

Gustatory system, 161–162

Gynecomastia, 355

Gyrus, 54
angular, 463, 464, 466
cingulate, 56, 58, 157
dentate, 220, 255, 271, 289
Heschl's, 458, 459
postcentral, 55, 58, 154
precentral, 55, 58, 180

Habit formation, 288

Hair cells, 145, 146

Hallucinations, 393, 412, 482

Haloperidol, 485

Hammer, 145

Hamsters
pheromones and, 159
sleep-wake cycle of, 376, 387, 388

Hand preference, of nonhuman primates, 461

Handedness, language lateralization and, 445–446

Hangover, 412

Harrison Narcotics Act, 417–418

Hash oil, 413

Hashish, 413

Head holder, 83

Headaches, migraine, 101, 102, 129

Health, stress and, 429–435

Health psychology, definition of, 405

Hearing. *See* Auditory system

Hearing loss, age-related, 149

Heart attack, 411, 413, 415

Hebb's postulate for learning, 290

Hebb's theory, of memory consolidation, 274

Heliobacter pylori, 430

Helping-hand phenomenon, 453

Hematoma, 236

Hemianopsic, 129

Hemispherectomized patients, 157

Hemispherectomy, 476

Hemispheres. *See* Lateralization of function

Heritability, of individual differences, 30–33

Heritability estimate, 33, 411, 412, 474

Mesotelencephalic dopamine system, 422, 493
Messenger RNA, 24, 25
Meta-analysis, 433
Metabolic rate, basal, 320, 324
Metabolic tolerance, 406
Metabolism, energy, 303–304, 314, 319–320
Metabolites, of dopamine, 484
Metabotropic receptor, 77
Metastatic tumors, 232, 233
Metencephalon, 50, 51, 52–53, 58
Methamphetamine, 416
3,4-Methylenedioxymethamphetamine (MDMA), 416–417
1-Methyl-4-phenyl-1,2,3,6-tetrahydropyridine (MPTP), 248–249
Mice
    knockout, 92, 225, 393, 415
    mutant obese, 325–326
    narcolepsy in, 393
    transgenic, 93, 388
Microelectrode, 66, 118
Microglia, 45, 431
Microscopy, electron, 47
Microsleeps, 379, 398
Microtubules, 42, 74, 75
Midbrain, 50, 51, 52, 147, 207. See also Mesencephalon
Midsagittal section, 48
Migraine headaches, 101, 102, 129
Migration, of developing neurons, 207–209
Mind-brain issue, 27–29
Minerals, in diet, 309
Minnesota Study of Twins Reared Apart, 31
Minor hemisphere, 444
Mirror-drawing test, 267
Mitochondria, 42, 74
Mitosis, 21, 22
Mixed episode, 504
Mnemonic processes, 268
Mondrians, 126, 127
Monkeys, 13, 14
    attention and, 164–165
    binocular cells of, 120, 121
    expectation of reward theory and, 423–424
    hand preference in, 461
    Kluver-Bucy syndrome in, 428
    object-recognition deficits in, 278–279, 280
    perseveration error by, 216
    primary auditory cortex of, 148
    primary motor cortex of, 181
    primary visual cortex of, 123, 127
    rehabilitative hand training of, 258–259
    secondary motor cortex of, 178

sensorimotor system of, 187
    split brain in, 449
    transplanting fetal tissue in, 257
    visual cortex of, 131
    visual memories in, 286
Monoamine oxidase (MAO), 490
Monoamine oxidase inhibitors, 490, 492
Monoamine theory of depression, 492
Monoamines, 79–80, 81
Monocular, 119
Monocular deprivation, 217, 218
Monophasic sleep cycles, 396
Monozygotic twins, 31. See also Twin studies
    autism and, 223
    sexual orientation and, 359
Mood stabilizer, 491
Morphine, 417–418
Morris water maze test, 283–284, 290
Motion, perception of, 130
Motivation
    limbic system and, 56
    male sexual behavior and, 358
    neural mechanisms of, 421–424
    REM sleep and, 381
Motor cortex, 178
Motor disorders, basal ganglion and, 57
Motor end-plate, 188
Motor equivalence, 195–196
Motor homunculus, 180
Motor learning, 182
Motor neurons, 73
Motor nuclei, of cranial nerves, 186
Motor output, sensory input and, 172–173
Motor pathways, descending, 184–188
Motor pool, 188
Motor theory of cerebral asymmetry, 460, 461
Motor units, 188
Mountain chickadees, hippocampal size in, 285
Movement
    ballistic, 172
    ipsilateral, 456
    limb, 188
    voluntary, 184, 187, 444
Movement agnosia, 134
MPTP. See 1-Methyl-4-phenyl-1,2,3,6-tetrahydropyridine
MPTP model of Parkinson's disease, 248–249
Mrs. Winslow's Soothing Syrup, 417
MS. See Multiple sclerosis
Müllerian-inhibiting substance, 341, 348
Müllerian system, 341

Multiple sclerosis (MS), 162, 245
Multiple-unit recording, 85, 86
Multipolar motor neuron, 50
Multipolar neuron, 43
Multipotent, 206, 258
Mumby box, 280, 281
Mumps, 237
Muscle length, 189
Muscle-spindle feedback, 189, 190, 192
Muscle spindle receptor, 190
Muscle spindles, 189
Muscle tension, 189
Muscles, 188–189
    ciliary, 104
    receptors of, 189–190
Music training, organization of auditory cortex and, 219, 221
Musical ability, 455, 457
Mutant obese mice, 325–326
Mutations, 23, 243
Myelencephalon, 50, 51–52, 58
Myelin, 41, 44, 73
    in multiple sclerosis, 245
Myelin sheaths, 251
Myelination, 73, 214, 215

Naming, PET study of, 472–474
Napping, 382, 396
Narcolepsy, 393, 394
Narcotic, 414
Nasal hemiretina, 110, 114
National Institute on Drug Abuse, 355
Natural selection, 10, 116
Nature-nurture issue, 29–30, 350
NEAT. See Nonexercise activity thermogenesis
Necrosis, 212, 239
Negative feedback mechanisms, 305
Neocortex, 55, 58, 415
Neonates, 218
Neoplasm, 232
Nerve deafness, 149
Nerve growth factor (NGF), 212, 256
Nerves, 44
    afferent, 37
    cranial, 38–39, 145, 162, 163, 186, 231
    efferent, 37
    parasympathetic, 37–38, A-2
    spinal, 49–50
    sympathetic, 37–38, A-2
Nervous system, 9. See also Autonomic nervous system; Central nervous system; Peripheral nervous system
    cells of, 40–45
    directional coordinates in, 47–48
    divisions of, 37–39
    layout of, 37–40

meninges, ventricles, and cerebrospinal fluid of, 39
Neural crest, 206
Neural degeneration, 249–250
Neural groove, 207
Neural plate, induction of, 206–207
Neural proliferation, 207
Neural regeneration, 209, 250–252
Neural reorganization, 252–255
Neural stem cells, 207
Neural tube, 206, 207, 208
Neuroanatomical techniques, 45–47, 59, 277–283
Neuroanatomy, 8
Neurochemistry, 8
Neurodegeneration, blocking, 256
Neurodegenerative disease, 213
Neurodevelopment, 205
    disorders of, 221–226
    effect of experience on, 217–219
    phases of, 206–213
Neuroendocrine system, 333–340
Neuroendocrinology, 8
Neurofibrillary tangles, 246, 247
Neurogenesis
    in adult mammals, 219–221
    in hippocampus, 255
Neuroleptics, 485, 488
    atypical, 486
    Tourette syndrome and, 499
    treatment with, 486, 487, 488
Neuroma, acoustic, 233
Neuromuscular junction, 81, 88, 188
Neuron(s), 5
    anatomy of, 40–44
    bimodal, 179–180
    bipolar, 43
    cholinergic, 81
    classes of, 43–44
    death of, 212–213
    inter-, 43–44, 73
    intrafusal motor, 189, 190, 191
    motor, 50, 73
    multipolar, 43
    postsynaptic, 234, 289–290, 291–293
    postsynaptic potentials of, 68–71
    presynaptic, 288, 292–293
    rate of firing of, 72
    resting membrane potential of, 66–67
    retinal, 106–108
    sensory, 50
    study of, 45–47, 118
    unipolar, 43
    without axons, 73
Neuropathology, 8
Neuropeptide Y, 317

Neuropeptides, 79, 81, 393. *See also* Peptide neurotransmitters

Neuropharmacology, 8

Neurophysiological diseases, multiple sclerosis as, 245

Neurophysiology, 8

Neuroplasticity
in adults, 219–221
in response to nervous system damage, 249–255
treatment of nervous system damage and, 256–261

Neuropsychological diseases
Alzheimer's disease as, 245–247
animal models of, 247–249
epilepsy as, 240–242
Huntington's disease as, 243–244
Parkinson's disease as, 242–243

Neuroscience, 5, 7–8

Neurotic pseudoinsomniacs, 393

Neurotoxins, 89, 237–238

Neurotransmitters, 42, 68
acetylcholine, 81
activation of receptors by, 76–78
amino acid, 79, 81, 242
excitatory, 79
inhibitory, 79
monoamine, 79–80, 81
peptide, 75, 78
release of, 75–76
reuptake of, 491
small-molecule, 75, 78
soluble-gas, 80, 81, 293
steps in action of, 87
in synaptic transmission, 73–79
synthesis and transport of, 74–75
termination of effect of, 78–79

Neurotransplantation, 257–258

Neurotrophic factors, 251

Neurotrophins, 212

New-World monkeys, 13

NGF. *See* Nerve growth factor

Nicotine, 411. *See also* Tobacco

Nicotinic acetylcholine receptors, 88

Nigrostriatal pathway, 243, 423

Nissl stain, 46–47, 59, 357

Nitric oxide, 80, 81, 293

NMDA (N-methyl-D-aspartate) receptors, 234, 290–292, 293

Nociceptive stimuli, 150. *See also* Pain

Nocturnal animals, 374

Nocturnal myoclonus, 392, 393

Nodes of Ranvier, 41, 73

Nonanxiolytic drugs, 497

Nondirected neurotransmitter release, 75

Nondirected synapse, 74

Nonexercise activity thermogenesis (NEAT), 324

Nonhumans, as experimental subjects, 18

Noradrenaline, 80

Noradrenergic, 80

Norepinephrine, 390
cocaine as agonist of, 86–87, 416
depression and, 490
as neurotransmitter, 79–80, 81
stress and, 429, 430

NREM sleep, 370, 381

Nuclei, 44
brain stem motor, 174
cochlear, 147
dorsal column, 151
hypothalamic, A-7
intralaminar, 151, 152–153
ipsilateral cochlear, 147
lateral geniculate, 53, 58, 114, 128, 141, 218
medial dorsal, 160, 161
medial geniculate, 147, 435
mediodorsal, 271, 272
motor, 186
parafascicular, 151, 152
paraventricular, 315, 337
reticular REM-sleep, 386–387
sensory relay, 53
suprachiasmatic, 387–388, 391
supraoptic, 337
thalamic, 153, A-6
thalamic relay, 141
visual relay, 128

Nucleotide bases, 23

Nucleus
of cell, 21, 42
red, 52, 53, 58, 184

Nucleus accumbens, 423

Nucleus magnocellularis, 394

Nurture. *See* Nature-nurture issue

Nutritive density, 310

Obesity, 301. *See also* Body weight
in humans, 323–326
serotonergic drugs and, 326
VMH syndrome and, 314

Object agnosia, 134

Object-based contralateral neglect, 176

Object-recognition memory, 277–283

Objective tests, 225

Ob/ob mice, 325

Obsessive-compulsive disorders, 494, 498

Occipital cortex, 226

Occipital lobe, 55, 58, 128, 444

Ocular dominance, 121

Ocular dominance columns, 121, 217

Oculomotor cranial nerve, A-4, A-5

Odors, human, 159

Off-center cells, 119

6-OHDA, 89

Okinawans, calorie consumption by, 318–319

Old-World monkeys, 13, 14

Olfaction, 159

Olfactory bulbs, 160
neurogenesis in, 220

Olfactory ensheathing cells, 257

Olfactory mucosa, 160

Olfactory nerves, 39, A-4, A-5

Olfactory system, 160–161

Olfactory tracts, 160

Oligodendrocytes, 44

Oligodendroglia, 251

Ommatida, 116

On-center cells, 119

On the Origin of Species (Darwin), 9

One-olfactory-receptor-one-neuron rule, 160

Operator genes, 24

Operculum, frontal, 458, 459

Opiates, 81, 158, 417–419

Opponent-process theory, of color vision, 124–125

Optic chiasm, 54, 58, 388, 443, 448

Optic nerves, 39, 388, A-4, A-5

Optic tectum, 209, 211

Optic tracts, 388

Optical imaging techniques, 291

Orbitofrontal cortex, 160, 161

Orbits, 161

Orchidectomy, 341, 351, 352

Orexin, 393, 394

Organ of Corti, 145, 146

Organization of Behavior, The (Hebb), 7

Orphan drugs, 503

Ossicles, 145, 149

Oval window, 145, 146

Ovariectomy, 341, 354

Ovaries, 256, 334, 335, 340, 341

Overdose, of heroin, 419

Overt attention, 166

Ovum, 206, 334

Owl, barn, sound location by, 148–149, 219

Oxytocin, 337, 338

P channel, 115

Pacinian corpuscles, 150

PAG. *See* Periaqueductal gray

Pain, 150
adaptiveness of, 156–157
chronic, 152
descending control of, 157–159
emotional reaction to, 157
gate-control theory of, 157
marijuana and, 415

paradoxes of, 156–157
phantom limb, 259–261
trigeminal nerve and, 151–152

Painkillers, 417

Palilalia, 498

Pancreatitis, 413

Panic disorders, 494

Papillae, 161

Parafascicular nuclei, 151, 152

Parallel hierarchical system, 172, 173–174

Parallel processing, 143

Paranoid schizophrenia, 416

Parasympathetic activation, A-3

Parasympathetic nerves, 37–38, A-2

Paraventricular nuclei, 315, 337

Parietal cortex, 18, 226

Parietal lobe, 28, 55, 58, 444

Parkinson's disease, 57, 65, 242–243, 288
MPTP model of, 248–249
neurotransplantation and, 257–258
nigrostriatal pathway damage in, 423
olfactory deficit with, 162
symptoms of, 484

Partial epilepsy, 240

Partial seizures, 240–241

Parvocellular layers, 115

Pavlovian conditioning, 407, 410
of eyeblink, 268, 288
of hunger, 310

Pecking order, 430

Penicillin, 237

Penile erection, 371

Penis, 342

Peptide hormones, 335, 336

Peptide neurotransmitters, 75, 78

Peptides, 75, 330
hunger and satiety, 317

Perception, 143
attention in, 164
of brightness, 110
of color, 103
edge, 116–124
of motion, 130

Perfect pitch, 225, 459

Perforant path, 288

Periaqueductal gray (PAG), 52, 53, 58, 157, 358, 359, 435

Perimetry test, 128

Perinatal hormones
behavioral development and, 344–345
sexual orientation and, 359–360

Peripheral nervous system (PNS), 37, 44
regeneration in, 250–251

Perseveration, 215, 216

Perseveration error, 215, 216

PET. *See* Positron emission tomography